The Lexington Introduction to Literature

D1224500

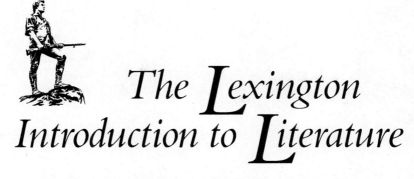

The Lexington Introduction to Literature

Reading and Responding to Texts

Gary Waller
Carnegie Mellon University

Kathleen McCormick
Carnegie Mellon University

Lois Josephs Fowler
Carnegie Mellon University

D. C. HEATH AND COMPANY
Lexington, Massachusetts   Toronto

ACQUISITIONS EDITOR: *Paul Smith*

DEVELOPMENTAL, PRODUCTION EDITOR: *Judith Leet*

DESIGNER: *Cia Boynton*

PRODUCTION COORDINATOR: *Michael O'Dea*

PERMISSIONS: *Margaret Roll*

COVER: *Kozanji* by Kenzo Okado. The National Trust for Historic Preservation, Nelson A. Rockefeller Collection. Photograph by Lee Boltin.

Acknowledgments are found on page 1259.

Copyright © 1987 by D. C. Heath and Company.

All rights reserved. No part of this publication may be reproduced or transmitted in any form or by any means, electronic or mechanical, including photocopy, recording, or any information storage or retrieval system, without permission in writing from the publisher.

Published simultaneously in Canada.

Printed in the United States of America.

International Standard Book Number: 0-669-09556-7

Library of Congress Catalog Card Number: 86-81356

Preface for Teachers

Creating the *Lexington Introduction to Literature* has been an exciting experience—and we hope the excitement will spread to students and teachers alike. Among our aims, we have attempted to make it both highly stimulating for students and practical for teachers and classroom use. But its most distinctive feature is that it pioneers a fundamental shift in the way we teach introductory literature courses and reflects some of the most useful insights, concepts, and tools of recent theory and criticism. For a decade or more, major changes in the ways we *read* and *respond* to literature have been exciting scholars and critics. Now, we believe, it is time that teachers and undergraduates share in the excitement.

Our approach, in brief, combines two major strands of recent literary theory. The first is *reader-centered* or *reader-response criticism,* which focuses less on finding meanings "in" texts and more on the *process* by which meaning is created by the interaction of text and reader. The second is *cultural criticism,* in which both readers and texts alike are studied within the complex cultural dynamics of their time and are thus not regarded as isolated entities.

The *Lexington Introduction to Literature* has developed out of the theoretical interests and the classroom experiences of its editors. We emphasize both theoretical awareness and practical pedagogy since we believe that one of the most *useful* strategies a teacher can have is a powerful sense of theory —an awareness of what his or her goals are and what strategies can best effect them. What has most excited us, however, is the way our students have responded to the development of the course from which the *Lexington Introduction to Literature* has emerged. In many ways the heroes of the whole process have been our students. We hope that other students, elsewhere, also will enjoy becoming part of an ongoing process of reading and writing with cultural awareness, stimulated by the *Lexington Introduction to Literature.*

Throughout the anthology, we speak—and with much enthusiasm—of a major change in the ways readers can understand literature. Yet in many respects the selections in this anthology are deliberately conservative. Most of the works we have selected—fiction, poetry, drama, and essays—are familiar and frequently taught in introductory courses. Some of the less familiar texts (especially those written in the last decade or so) are a reflection of the editors' teaching experiences and also of their hopes that today's students will find them lively and thought-provoking.

Because of the unusual approach to reading presented here, we suggest that students be urged to pay careful attention to the introductions preceding each genre. The general introduction, "On Becoming a Strong Reader" (pages 1–24), provides an account of our overall approach to reading, with an emphasis on its practical application, especially to writing. Because the study of reading is rooted in historical and cultural factors, the tendencies to pure subjectivism, characteristic of some kinds of reader-response criticism, are avoided.

What are the essentials of our approach? Primarily we want students to become strong and self-aware readers, conscious of the goals and strategies they have as readers of and writers about literature. We want students to become aware that reading literature is enjoyable, but more—that it has powerful cognitive and cultural dimensions, the exploration of which can make them more powerful readers. We see "reading" in the broadest sense not just as focused on reading and interpreting texts, but as fundamental to interpreting our lives and our broader culture: the strategies of reading literature connect intimately and significantly with the ways we read our culture and interpret our history.

We introduce a number of powerful concepts to students. To give them a range of strategies by which they can become strong readers, we explain how both text and reader bring distinctive **repertoires,** both **literary** and **general,** to bear on the reading situation, and how these in turn are derived from the **literary** and **general ideology** of their culture. Thus reading consists of a **matching of repertoires,** to which *both* reader and text contribute. These concepts are thoroughly explained and exemplified in the introductions to the four genres, in relation to both traditional and contemporary literary texts. (Key terms used throughout the text are set in boldface and defined in the Glossary.)

Our advocacy of the **response statement** as a major mode of student writing is another key aspect by which students avoid the tediousness of mere *summarizing,* the simplistic subjectivity of *free association,* and the pretended objectivity of traditional *interpretation.* We believe the response statement, in which students become increasingly aware of the larger cognitive and cultural dimensions of reading, is an enormously exciting pedagogical practice. It involves students in analyzing their own reading practices; it directs them to explore the broader implications of their reading and writing processes.

Although the *Lexington Introduction to Literature* does not hesitate to introduce students to some current theoretical concepts, we nevertheless want to stress that throughout the anthology they are rooted in concrete examples. In the introductions to the four genres, we have provided detailed suggestions for implementing our approach to reading both canonical and experimental kinds of literature. Most important, the "Reading and Responding" sections for each genre contain directed questions, response-statement assignments, and drafts of response statements written by our students. We generally include two or more revisions of each response statement to demonstrate ways in which students can become more self-aware about their reading strategies, become stronger readers of the text, and write more formal essays.

Such detailed attention to the interaction of reading and writing reflects one of our major concerns: to make this anthology, which translates recent literary theory into practice, work in the classroom, that is, to help students understand and enjoy the complex and vital process of reading literature. We hope that your students find the *Lexington Introduction to Literature* as exciting as ours found its development.

Acknowledgments

In planning and preparing this anthology, we wish to thank many people. From the start, Paul Smith has been an enthusiastic and perceptive editor. As the manuscript took shape, Judith Leet has been extremely patient and helpful. To them and others at D. C. Heath, we are very grateful. At Carnegie Mellon, we particularly want to thank our colleagues, students, and the heroically patient efforts of our research assistants and typists, most especially Jacqueline Hall and Laurie Walz.

Gary Waller wishes to thank, from a previous life, Ed Jewinski (who helped with the Canadian selections here), Michael Moore, and Susan Rudy Dorscht. He also wants to thank his two collaborators who added practical experience and theoretical rigor to his massive but only partly focused enthusiasm for the project. Kathleen McCormick wishes to thank William E. Sheidley, William and Mary Curtin, Lee Jacobus, Margaret Higonnet, Jack Davis, and Hap Fairbanks for their many years of stimulating and heated discussions of literary theory and pedagogy. Lois Fowler wishes to thank her husband David Fowler and his sharp eye, the students in her class "Reading Texts," and indeed all her students who teach while they learn. In fact, all three of us thank our students who not only (they said) enjoyed our courses but willingly gave their time (and, frequently, their writing for us to use).

We would like to thank those who offered valuable guidance and suggestions on the manuscript: Douglas Atkins, University of Kansas; Stephen Cohan, Syracuse University; Eric Gould, University of Denver; Donald Gray, Indiana University; David Kann, California Polytechnic Institute; James Kinney, Virginia Commonwealth University; Susan Meisenhelder, California State College-San Bernardino; Jasper Neel, Northern Illinois University; Michael Shugrue, CUNY-Staten Island; Elaine Supowitz, Community College of Allegheny County; and Ed White, California State University-San Bernardino.

GARY WALLER
KATHLEEN MCCORMICK
LOIS JOSEPHS FOWLER

Topical Contents

Contents

POETRY   373

Introducing Poetry   375

Reading and Responding to Poetry   396

Anthology of Poetry   423

DRAMA   621

Introducing Drama   623

Reading and Responding to Drama   638

ESSAY   1095

Introducing the Essay   1097

Reading and Responding to Essays   1115

Anthology of Essays   1158

The Lexington Introduction to Literature

Introduction: Becoming a Strong Reader

One Text, Many Readings

A group of college students is reading Donald Justice's poem, "Counting the Mad." One student reads it aloud.

This one was put in a jacket,
This one was sent home,
This one was given bread and meat
But would eat none,
And this one cried No No No No   5
All day long

This one looked at the window
As though it were a wall,
This one saw things that were not there,
This one things that were,   10
And this one cried No No No No
All day long

This one thought himself a bird
This one a dog,
And this one thought himself a man,   15
An ordinary man,
And cried and cried No No No No
All day long.

What do the students make of this poem by a contemporary American poet? What meanings do they find in it? Some recognize immediately that it recalls the nursery rhyme "This Little Piggy Went to Market" and immediately dismiss it as trivial, arguing that nothing written like a nursery rhyme should be taken seriously. Other students, in fact, think the poem makes fun of mad people. Others find themselves quite disturbed that such a serious subject as madness is addressed in a nursery rhyme.

Still other readers see the poem differently. They read it ironically, arguing that the tone of the poem is sarcastic and that if anyone is being made fun of it is the "ordinary" people in the world who think that madness is something that happens to other people, to misfits in institutions, to people who think they are birds. Another reader suggests that "ordinary" people wish their lives *were* like a nursery rhyme, and that this poem is meant to satirize them.

Then there are those students who don't see the connection with "This Little Piggy" at all. Their reading concentrates on showing how the poem is very sad, a reminder of how tragic insanity can be. This, they say, is what the poet "intended."

How do we choose among these various readings? Which is correct? Are some better than others? When students learn of other readings quite different from and perhaps contradictory to their own, do they change theirs? When many readers are looking at the same poem, they come up with very different readings. Why should this be? Is it because some people are better readers than others? Or is it because different readers bring different personal perspectives to their interpretations?

Such questions raise issues relevant to the nature of reading and interpretation, and to our understanding of what "literature" is. When *you* were reading the poem, did you have some of the reactions we have recorded? Go back to the poem now and make a few notes on your personal response to it, trying to locate your views among those we have suggested. Jot down answers to the following questions:

- What did the author intend this poem to do? How do you find that out?
- If you knew what the author intended, would that make a difference to your reading?
- Would you then know there was a "correct" meaning?
- How do your own views of the poem's issues—madness, nursery rhymes, and so forth—affect you as you read it?
- Does it matter if different readers have different views about madness? Does it mean that they will emerge with different readings of the poem? And how can you tell which will be better?
- If the poem were read in a different society with *different* views of madness—where mental illness is treated by psychiatrists and therapists rather than by institutionalization—would that make a difference to the reading?

The Approach of This Anthology

This anthology of literary texts—stories, poems, plays, essays—focuses on the interaction between texts and readers. In this book we will regard "meaning" as something that readers *create with* a text rather than as something they *find in* texts. This book gives priority to *your* reactions to texts rather than to the reactions of others. We hope that in using this anthology you will both enjoy reading literature and also come to some understanding of the richness of the reading process. Our emphasis on what the reader brings to a literary text in the act of reading—and then in writing about reading—constitutes a relatively new approach to literary studies. This approach is part of a wider realization in many fields of knowledge that "reality" is the product of interpretation and perception: it is not stable and fixed, or detached from our own experiences of it. Einstein and other scientists have helped us to understand that the nature of reality is "relative," that it is determined by the viewpoint of the interpreter, and by his or her place within complex social and historical contexts.

To begin, we ask a few simple questions. When reading a "text," where does the meaning we find—and perhaps talk or write about—come *from*? One basic principle in the approach of this anthology is that a text's meaning is not fixed or stable. It is not, in a simple sense, "in" the text. Meaning doesn't just sit there, waiting to be extracted. We believe, along with many contemporary literary critics, that if meaning is *in* anything, it is *in* readers' *experiences* of the text, both personal and collective.

A more traditional view saw the text as a set of neutral facts waiting to be described, with its meanings "inside" the text, and needing an expert to explain it correctly. Our more contemporary view argues that reading is much more *interactive*. Every time readers describe their experiences they inevitably bring their own personal perspective to bear upon that experience. We frame questions about a given experience based on our needs and desires, and we interpret the situation accordingly. We don't ever see "reality" directly; we frame a *model* of it. Reality, therefore, is inseparable from the questions people pose about it and from the way they describe it.

As we describe these principles in more detail, we want you to apply some of them to the reading of literature in this anthology. First of all, every reading is an interpretation. No work of literature contains meanings in itself apart from interpretation, that is, apart from the understanding (and questions) that a reader brings to it. Its meanings are constructed—or as we sometimes put it in this anthology, "produced"—partly from what the text gives you, partly from what you bring to the text. You read, interpret, and eventually write your responses to your readings based on your own questions, assumptions, and expectations. You may, however, change your initial assumptions, especially when you discuss your ideas and responses with others. In that case the meanings you produce from your reading experiences may also change and evolve.

If the meanings that readers find in texts are subject to change, does that mean that there are no unchanging, correct, objective meanings to the literature we read? Yes, it does. We judge the adequacy of what other readers say and write about texts not by whether the meanings they produce are "objective" or true. We judge them rather by whether they are coherent, stimulating, illuminating, interesting, or persuasive—and perhaps also by whether they help other people produce their own meanings. Readers can describe the *process* of their interaction with the text but should not assume that they have direct access to what the author put "in" the work.

This model of interpretation suggests that reading is a continuing *dialogue* between reader and text—or if many readers are involved, a kind of "polylogue." In this model, both the text and the reader play active parts. Sometimes one is more powerful than the other, just as in a conversation one person will sometimes dominate the other; at other times both participate more or less equally. As in an invigorating conversation, the most dynamic reading occurs between a powerful reader and a powerful text. Powerful or what we will call "strong" readers are those who have learned about reading and can bring the most relevant experiences of their lives to bear on that reading. A powerful text is one that raises important and stimulating questions and raises them provocatively. One aim of this anthology is to give readers powerful and absorbing literary texts to read in order to encourage powerful readers, who will become in turn powerful writers.

The Place of Theory

Every discipline has a theory underlying it: a *theory* is the set of fundamental questions that a particular discipline asks. We learn, for example, theories of physics and theories of psychology, but as experts change their ideas over time and acquire new information, so these theories often undergo change. In addition, at any one time, several competing theories may exist to try to explain the same phenomenon. But even though certain approaches to a discipline change, a fundamental set of issues with which everyone in the discipline tries to deal remains fairly stable.

Students of physics, psychology, engineering, or biology are used to talking and even arguing about the theories of their discipline. Students who have studied such subjects may have been introduced to the term **paradigm,** the theoretical framework of a discipline. The contemporary historian of science Thomas G. Kuhn has coined the term **paradigm shift** to define the situation in which the framework of knowledge about a particular subject changes, often quite rapidly as the old theory becomes outdated and no longer answers new questions adequately. In the early seventeenth century, a dramatic paradigm shift occurred when humans changed their notion of the earth's position in the solar system from one in which the earth was the center to one in which the sun is the center. The famous Italian Renaissance scientist Galileo Galilei contributed to this paradigm shift when he said that the earth revolved around the sun rather than the sun around the earth. Another example occurred in the nineteenth century when geologists and biologists changed from a creationist to an evolutionary, Darwinian model of life.

In a similar transformation, literary theory has shifted from assuming that meaning exists objectively in texts to assuming that meaning is *relative,* not fixed or absolute, and that meaning arises as the result of a complex interaction between the reader and the text—and the cultures from which both emerge. Our approach in this anthology acknowledges not only that this shift has occurred in literary studies but that it is starting to affect the way literature is taught in undergraduate classes—as well as being widely discussed among literary critics, professors, and graduate students.

The Reading Situation

We will be introducing some important terms in the course of this anthology. (These occur in boldface in the text and are defined in the glossary.) You will want to study them carefully. We employ them as convenient ways of explaining the relationship between a text and a reader, and what happens in the act of reading a text.

Reading is never just an individual, personal, subjective experience. It is always done within a larger context. Interpretations are the product of a very large number of factors that work in different combinations to produce different readings.

First, what does the text bring to the reading situation? When a text is written, it incorporates both explicit and implicit ideas and values derived from its society. The term *ideology* refers to the deep-seated beliefs, assumptions, customs, and practices of a society. Some of these beliefs relate to literature—like which literary genres the society prefers (Shakespeare's society preferred drama), whether the author is seen as a unique genius or as a spokesperson for the society, or whether women's writing is valued as much as men's. In the nineteenth century, for instance, women authors like Charlotte Brontë thought their books would be better received if published under male names. We refer to such matters as *literary ideology.* We will refer to all other *non-literary* beliefs of the society as its *general ideology*—its culture, institutions, social customs, and so forth.

Any individual text is written out of its society's general and literary ideology. The **repertoire** of a text refers to the particular combination of ideas, experiences, habits, norms, conventions, and assumptions that allows that text to be written. We further divide the repertoire of the text into two kinds. Because we are interested in literary analysis, we can distinguish that part of the repertoire that refers to literary matters as the **literary repertoire.** This would include such matters as literary form, plot, characterization, metrical pattern, and so forth. The non-literary repertoire we term the text's **general repertoire.** This includes such matters as moral ideas, values, religious beliefs, and so forth.

In the same way, individual readers absorb many—often contradictory —values, ideas, beliefs, and practices from the literary and general ideologies of their society. Thus every individual reader, like every text, has a particular literary repertoire and general repertoire. In the interface of reader and text, what we will call the *reading situation,* a **matching of repertoires** between text and reader occurs, as represented on page 7.

Ideology and the Reading Situation

And now we turn to look in more detail at the important concept *ideology.* Since readers exist in cultural and historical contexts that exert tremendous influence on them, both readers and texts are products of their own places in history, their societies, social classes, religious and political viewpoints. Thus you can see both readers and texts are produced by the ideology of their culture.

Although very important, ideology is a tricky concept that can be easily misunderstood or used too vaguely. We use *ideology* here to mean the deeply ingrained—sometimes only partly conscious—habits, beliefs, and lifestyles of a particular society. **Ideology** includes all those practices and beliefs that most members of a society take for granted as "natural" or "universal" and assume to be true, even if they are neither natural nor universal but rather are *specific* to that culture. Ideology encompasses everything from a society's sense of appropriate table manners to its dominant view of the death penalty. It includes beliefs about religion, family, education, the value of an individual, and ways of organizing politics—all of the *assumptions* we have about the way we live or should live.

Whereas any society contains a great variety of beliefs and social practices, some are always identified with the majority of the members of that society, or believed by and enforced by its most powerful members. These beliefs are sometimes referred to as the *dominant* ideology. All societies are held together by ideology, which functions like a kind of glue that binds their members. Ideology is therefore neither a good nor a bad thing: it is an inevitable part of what it is to be a society— the one "universal" or "natural" thing there is in all societies. Ideology is always characterized by the acceptance by the member of a society of certain ways of living as appropriate or natural—and the rejection of, sometimes even the incomprehensibility of—alternatives.

Literary ideology refers to the particular assumptions each society has about literature and focuses on such questions as these:
- Is the writing of literature believed to be an important part of the society's life?
- Is poetry believed to be the expression of the thoughts of the poet, or does it rather set out the society's common beliefs?
- Is literature controlled by political forces?
- Is the reading or writing of literature seen as entertainment?
- Is literature seen as "reflecting" reality?

These are not just academic questions or matters of personal taste. Different societies give different answers to them. Taken together, the answers

Model of Reader-Text Interface.

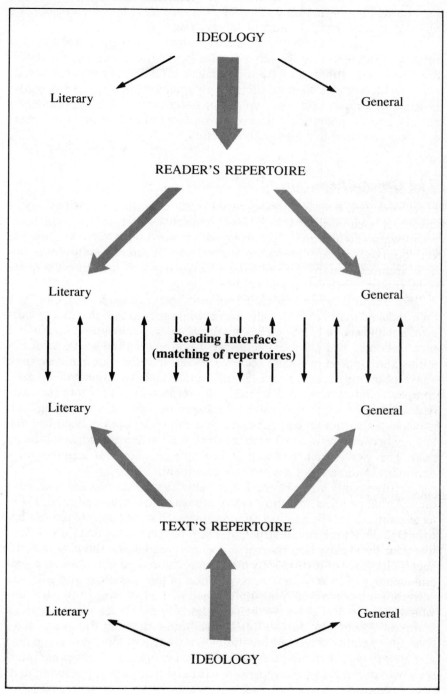

will reflect the distinctive assumptions of a particular society about the writing and reading of literature. They show us the ways by which a society's ideology is articulated through its literary practices.

General ideology and literary ideology—both yours and the text's—are important influences on the way you read (and write about) texts. They all don't have to be discussed fully and exhaustively whenever you do a "reading" of a literary text. That would certainly spoil the fun of, say, lying on the beach with a novel. But when you want to understand the importance of reading and the potential impact of literature upon readers and upon society, then you need to consider such factors.

The General Repertoire of the Text

Every time you read a work—especially one from the distant past—you encounter assumptions, beliefs, and perspectives that are different from your own and which make up that work's **general repertoire**. As a reader, you too have a *general repertoire,* that is, a set of values, assumptions, beliefs, and expectations derived from your society that influence the questions you put to the texts you read.

For example, when you read Sophocles' play *Antigone,* you may be a little shocked to discover that the bodies of traitors to the state are, by custom, not allowed to be buried but are displayed in public until they rot and turn to bones. You can become aware, from reading the scenes with Polonius and Ophelia in Shakespeare's *Hamlet,* that the dominant views in Shakespeare's age seem to have taken for granted that a father had virtually complete control over his daughter's life—especially over whom she married. Such a view is reprehensible to most of us today. Encountering such issues in texts from an earlier period, you can recognize the historical distancing between the original time the work was written and when it is being read. The views about personal choice by a woman that were counter-dominant in these two texts are now dominant.

Yet frequently you will encounter views that contradict the dominant ones. Antigone rejects her brother Creon's orthodox views on burial. *Hamlet* also introduces the counter-dominant view that the control Polonius has over Ophelia is cruel and destructive. The repertoire of the text (just, in fact, like your own) can often be complex and contradictory, showing how the general ideology of texts reflects the contradictions and changes in the general ideology of society. In the essay section of this anthology you will read extracts from Raymond Williams's *Keywords,* which will show you how words always reflect changing social values. You may talk about love with a common vocabulary, but you often mean quite different things and have assumptions quite different from those of other generations. When you read any literary text, therefore, the ways in which your general repertoire intersects with the text's general repertoire will determine how you respond to it.

The Literary Repertoire of the Text

Included in the literary repertoire of the text are its formal strategies: point of view, plot, rhyme scheme, metaphor, and so forth. Stories are told from particular points of view; poems have certain rhyme schemes; plays are divided into acts; essays follow a certain rhetorical structure. Earlier paradigms for reading literature often emphasized the study of these formal text features to the exclusion of all else. We suggest that while your reading of a text may be enhanced by paying attention to the fact that it is, say, a sonnet written in iambic pentameter, the major focus of your attention should be on your reactions and responses to a text. When you investigate your responses, you may find that certain text strategies have had strong influences on you. For example, if a story is told from the point of view of a twenty year old, you may automatically identify with the character more than you would if it were told from the perspective of someone older. Other text strategies, however, may be less important to you. We do not expect you ever to pay attention to all the strategies of a text, or to pay attention to any of them purely for the sake of noting their existence. What is important is how text strategies influence the way you read and respond to the text.

Another characteristic of texts is what are called **blanks** or **gaps**—absences of connections—that readers must fill in order to make sense of the text. One obvious gap occurs between the end of one chapter and the beginning of the next in a novel where a reader must use his or her imagination to decide what comes next or what comes in between. A more subtle gap is what is often called the *theme* of a story, which is never explicitly stated. Characters are described and situations occur, but "what it's all about" is a gap that the reader must fill in.

The lack of exact directions to actors in a play also constitutes a gap. In Shakespeare's *Hamlet,* which you will read in the drama section, Hamlet tries to trick King Claudius into revealing his guilt by having a group of actors perform a mime and a play, both of which are fairly obvious in their meaning to an audience. The text, however, does not specify what the King is doing while Hamlet's two little plays are being acted. Does the King get the point right away? Does he understand it? Why does he wait for the second play? The director and actors must fill in these gaps and decide what Claudius's facial expressions will be, how he will move, and where he will sit. And as most of you probably know, no two directors will fill in these gaps in exactly the same way. The gaps in any text allow readers much interpretive freedom.

Texts also contain **indeterminacies** or "ambiguities"—words, phrases, idioms which are seemingly "universal" in their application and which, as we read through a poem, we automatically fill out with our own personal meanings. When you read Robert Burns's line "My love is like a red, red rose," what is "my love"? Or, more particularly, as *you* read that line, who is *your* love? Is she black, white, blonde, excitable, stable, witty, flirtatious? Is he strong, carefree, sensitive, benign, bad-tempered? That is, as readers read "my love," they bring their own meaning to that *indeterminate* phrase. Each reader gives it precise meaning.

Another kind of indeterminacy is the description of a character or a setting: once again, the text gives us cetain details but not all. Note the description of the character in Bruce Springsteen's song, "Darkness on the Edge of Town," printed on page 618 in the poetry section:

> Some folks are born into a good life,
> Other folks get it anyway, anyhow,
> I lost my money and I lost my wife,
> Them things don't seem to matter much to me now.

The reader (or listener) must fill out the details: the exact nature of the speaker's sadness—its causes, its consequences—is all left to the reader's active involvement. The ways in which we choose to fill in these gaps and indeterminacies will depend on many factors: our knowledge of literary and social conventions, our personal beliefs and experiences, the cultural influences acting upon us, in short, on *our* ideology.

The General Repertoire of the Reader

Why do readers read texts differently? In part because each reader brings to a text a different set of experiences, concerns, knowledge, and expectations about such matters as religion, politics, gender roles, and general lifestyle. Whenever you read, your repertoire intersects with that of the text. Much of this matching of repertoires is highly conscious, but some may happen unconsciously. In fact, reading seems to be a "natural" process that people perform unself-consciously—until they encounter a text repertoire that differs from their own. For example, you may sympathize with the narrator in Gilman's story "The Yellow Wallpaper" because you believe that people with psychological problems should be treated with dignity and respect and not with condescension, as her husband appears to treat her. On the other hand, you might find yourself annoyed with the narrator's strangely unpredictable behavior if you believe that people's psychological difficulties could be avoided if they simply disciplined and controlled themselves better. Both readings are possible—but neither is objectively "in" the text. And neither reading is dependent wholly on the information given about the narrator in the story. You may at first think that your sympathies toward the woman are given in the text, but when you discover that other readers respond differently to her, you then recognize the role of your own **general repertoire** —in this case, your beliefs about the nature and treatment of mental illness—in helping to produce your response.

These different interpretations of "The Yellow Wallpaper" seem plausible because our culture tolerates different views about mental illness and hence different interpretive options. But some interpretations will seem less plausible. The dominant ideology of a particular period minimizes the likelihood of or even excludes certain interpretive possibilities, and so they would rarely be found in readers' repertoires. For example, none of you probably interpreted the narrator in "The Yellow Wallpaper" as speaking either in the voice of god or the voice of the devil, although these interpretations of mental instability would have been quite possible in an earlier historical period.

With texts written in a distant historical period or in a very different society, you come to realize that the matching of repertoires is an awkward one. It is as if you and the text are not speaking the same language. In such cases, you may consult reference books or dictionaries in order to enlarge your repertoire—that is, broaden your knowledge about ideas, beliefs, or feelings that differ from your own. Reading a poem by Shakespeare or a Guy de Maupassant story, for instance, most readers become aware of a need to consider social and cultural forces that are often very unlike their own. But in enlarging your repertoire in this way, of course you don't take yourself out of your own world and move back in time to an earlier period. Rather, you find that your present general repertoire starts to include more possibilities.

It's obvious that many of the texts you will read in a literature course were written in other times and places, with different ideological presuppositions. And despite all the research you may do on an earlier text in order to enlarge your repertoire, you still bring a repertoire of presuppositions to bear on your readings that is derived from your own cultural setting, not the setting of the text. After all, you live in the late twentieth century, not in Shakespeare's England or nineteenth-century France. You read a text in your own period of history, not in the time it was written. Likewise, you read it with questions, anxieties, and interests that come into existence because of your particular place in history. In the Middle Ages, people worried about the spread of the plague; today we worry about the threat of nuclear war. And today we are more conscious of the equality of men and women and of different races; in earlier periods most people assumed that men were superior to women and that certain races were "naturally" superior. Thus each reader approaches a text with a set of dominant ideological assumptions. The text offers you clues by which you may put meanings together; it offers you particular perspectives. But it is always you, the reader, not the author, who decides what perspective to adopt.

A good writer will try to lay down as many directions as possible to attract your curiosity, interest, and involvement, and in that way influence you—and all other readers. But *you* create the meanings of the texts you read on the basis of what your repertoire contains. You bring your own associations to help make meanings from the text, and your readings may therefore often be quite different from the writer's. You may be a woman, a man, Hispanic, American Indian, Chinese, black, white, middle-aged, or young, and such factors help form your readings. You bring many gender-specific questions to your reading. You often respond immediately (positively or negatively) to certain reading experiences you feel strongly about. And, of course, you may well change your readings of texts very drastically if your life experiences change. Everyone at some time has the experience of re-reading a novel or a poem, and interpreting it quite differently because of what has happened to him or her in the meantime.

Our fundamental point is that the beliefs you have as people affect you as readers: reading is not something isolated from the rest of your life. And indeed it's often said that the role of great literature is to activate as much as possible of readers' experience as human beings—to make readers look at themselves, their society, their history in fresh and stimulating and sometimes disturbing ways.

The Literary Repertoire of the Reader

General repertoire refers to assumptions about life; **literary repertoire** refers specifically to characteristic assumptions about literature. Readers' *literary repertoires* consist of their knowledge and assumptions about what literature "is" or "should be," based on their own previous reading experiences. Most readers, for instance, have read poems before they come to read the poems here. They are aware that a story has certain conventions, such as clear characterizations, some description, some degree of conflict that will eventually be resolved, and a good plot. Readers expect these conventions to be in a story because the majority of stories they have read have them, and they are often the aspects of a story discussed in English classes. If you expect all stories to be realistic, you will probably find yourself puzzled by Kafka's "Metamorphosis" or Sukenick's "The Birds." They may even seem senseless if you try to read them as realistic stories. One way to try to understand them is to enlarge your literary repertoire to include conventions other than realism. Familiarizing yourself with experimental fiction may not help you *like* such stories, but it will broaden your ability to categorize and read various kinds of stories.

Your **reading strategies** (your methods and styles of reading) and **reading goals** (your purposes for reading) contribute greatly to your responses to texts. One reading strategy that you might find yourself adopting is to skim a text on a first reading and then reread more carefully for a particular purpose, such as comparing your cultural background with that of the text, creating an overall theme for the text, or discovering your own position on the subject matter presented in the text. Some readers try to resolve or at least minimize ambiguities in a text, whereas other readers play as much as possible with the texts they read and try to multiply or create ambiguities or **gaps** in the text. Some readers employ a strategy of reading literally; others read symbolically.

Clearly readers adopt different reading strategies because they have different *goals* for reading. Some readers, particularly those who do not reread, often have as their primary reading goal to do the minimum and do it quickly—but they often miss many of the rich, if less obvious, text strategies. Readers who downplay ambiguities often have as their goal to demonstrate authoritatively that a text means only one thing. Readers who play with multiple meanings frequently report that their goal is to enjoy the expansive connotative power of language. We suggest you adopt as one of your self-conscious reading goals various ways in which you can create diverse and often contradictory readings of texts—as a means of exploring your own repertoire in relationship to the text's repertoire.

Some readers, for example, will feel fascinated and challenged by a complex and ambiguous story such as Barth's "Lost in the Funhouse." They will read and reread it slowly and carefully trying to make sense of it. Other readers will choose to ignore its ambiguities by paying attention only to those parts that make sense to them immediately. Still other readers will try to understand the story by placing it in a larger context of other similar texts they have read. How you approach a story, the goals you have for reading, and the reading strategies that you use play an influential role in your experience of a text.

It should be clear by now that any reading you do is produced by multiple influences. Consequently, remember that *the text alone does not dictate the reading you produce,* that *you* bring to the text a vital part of the meanings you discover, and that in turn your repertoire has been made available to you from the ideology of your society.

Strong Readings

Some texts try to provide their readers with very explicit directions on how they wish to be read. You can resist them, fight back, as it were, but often your best enjoyment comes, initially at least, from following the direction in which the text wants to take you. Some texts have a highly powerful literary repertoire: they may have a very concentrated argument or use powerfully accumulated metaphors. Such strategies may be designed to guide or limit your readings—to give you definite "boundary conditions" by which your reading is, to an extent, controlled. You may be content to adapt your repertoire to that of the text.

On the other hand—and this is increasingly true as texts raise disturbing or moving questions for you—you may want to acknowledge that your repertoire does not exactly match the text's, and you may choose to explore those differences.

A **strong reading** of a text is a clearly articulated reading that self-consciously goes "against the grain" of a text. It is not simply a perverse or imperceptive reading—or a misreading. It can only develop if a reader is aware of the dominant text strategies and the conventions for interpreting them, and then chooses for various reasons—be they specifically literary or more general—to read the text differently. You can, in other words, recognize that a text may be trying to force you to read and respond in a given manner, but you may choose to use your historical perspective and cultural awareness to resist that prescribed way of reading. You become thereby a *strong reader*. Strong reading is something we wish very much to encourage—where you define a particular perspective on a text, develop it persuasively, and articulate its implications, especially in writing.

Such an approach to reading requires you to become very self-aware of what you are doing. You become like an interrogator or a detective. This text has designs on me, you might say. Then you ask yourself: What are these designs? How did the text get to become as it is? Do I agree with what it wants me to do? Can I argue with it? Are the issues it raises ones I share? Are the assumptions *behind* those issues ones that I share?

Readers can and should choose to construct strong readings in various ways. First, you may discover that your repertoire of literary knowledge or part of your general repertoire is at such odds with the text that you cannot accept the text's position, and you feel you must then read it "against the grain." Second, you may see significances when you are reading a text, particularly an older one, that you know were not in its writer's repertoire, such as seeing in William Blake's poem "The Tyger" a force akin to nuclear energy. Third, you may deliberately try to read the text from perspectives other than your own usual one, for example reading from a feminist, a socialist, or a fundamentalist perspective.

Becoming a strong reader does not imply giving bizarre or subjective or improbable readings of poems for their own sake. For example, we are not advocating an approach in which readers arbitrarily decide that all poems they read are about baseball just because they are baseball fans! Different readings, because they go against the grain of the text and because they may also go against the readings of many of your classmates, must be closely reasoned and justified by a clear analysis of how your own interests, beliefs, and preoccupations inform—and for you, perhaps demand—your different interpretation. To learn to produce strong readings often involves hard work. You must look at your assumptions closely, and you may have to do research and discuss your position in detail, but the more you do these things, the more your readings become powerful—and yours.

At this point we might pose a familiar question: What limits are there to interpretation? Can, in fact, one say *anything* about a text? How can you tell a good from a bad interpretation? There is a very serious sense in which no interpretation of a poem can be ruled out so long as it is interestingly argued, well developed and supported, and engaging to hear or read. Readers cannot be "faithful to what the text says": what the text says depends in part on what readers want it to say. We approach the question of "legitimate" versus "illegitimate" or "valid" versus "invalid" readings by acknowledging straight off that there are no pure or objective readings, and we only ask that a reading try, as explicitly as possible, to make its perspective clear. But in practice some readings will certainly seem more bizarre or less acceptable. This is so not because they are necessarily less "correct" but because they are less plausible in our society. Thus if you choose to give a text a distinctive strong reading, you must be prepared to justify it. And who knows? Your strange or unusual or marginal reading might eventually become the dominant reading among your classmates.

In specific terms, how does all this affect your reading? When you read, you should ask questions and raise issues—often with some very strong feelings or ideas—about the text that affirm or challenge your most cherished assumptions. For example, you, as Americans of assorted backgrounds, might construct questions that raise issues about varied ethnic experiences. Women's rights is another ideologically sensitive issue. Men and women tend to ask different questions and to bring gender-specific interests to bear on their readings. When reading Milan Kundera's "Hitchhiking Game," you may ask to what extent relationships between men and women are guided by their different views of social games and conventions. We want to emphasize that this is highly appropriate—and in classroom discussion may make for some of the most interesting exchanges. Similarly you might consider the nature of the girl's development in Lynne Barrett's "Inventory": Does she learn to survive in a male-dominated world by adopting a masculine role? What is a "masculine" or a "feminine" role? Or you might ask why Johnson in Ann Petry's "Like a Winding Sheet" can vent his frustration at society only by beating his wife. Or as you will see in the poetry section, your personal views of women may be quite different from those assumed in Lovelace's or Wyatt's or (to take a modern example) Adrienne Rich's poems. In all of these cases—and indeed whenever you read—you will be encouraged to analyze both the assumptions you bring to your readings and the assumptions you discover in the text. In this way, we hope that you will become *strong* readers, that your readings will be those you want because you are committed to them and understand more fully how you have developed them.

Preparing to Write a Response Statement

The kind of writing we especially recommend is the **response statement.** To write a response statement, ask yourself the following:

- How did you respond to the text?
- How did the text and you, as the reader, affect that response?
- What does your response tell you about yourself and your society?

Response statements discuss the *experience* of reading: they stress not the meaning of the text but the effect of reading the text, and they try to account for the factors that produce such an effect.

Response statements have developed in the past fifteen years, largely under the influence of critics David Bleich and Norman N. Holland. Often response statements can simply become "subjective" statements of the effects of reading, accounts of how particular texts match up with the personalities of particular readers. We think response statements can be used in a variety of significant ways, not just for "subjective" associations but rather as ways of focusing attention on the experience of reading. Response statements can help you explore whether and how your literary and general repertoires match the text's. They can help to focus class discussion on conflicting ideologies—the conflict between the general repertoire of a text and your general repertoire—or on conflicts among various readers' general repertoires. They can also serve as informal preparations for writing longer, more formal papers that interpret literary or other kinds of texts.

In a response statement, a reader is asked to pay very close attention not just to the text but to the experience of reading the text. Paying close attention to the reading process is a critical skill to cultivate. Watch, for instance, your *initial* reaction. What was the immediate effect of reading a text on you? Was it confusion? Suspense? Boredom? Amusement? Did you "identify" with the characters? Did you find the situation incredible? Frightening? Perplexing? Hilarious? At this first level, developing a good response statement means focusing on your predominant initial response, which will often change as you read and reread, and trying to describe the process by which you are affected.

The next level of analysis—a more important level—is to try to explain what influenced your response. In accord with the model for reading described above, readers should focus on both the *nature of the text* and the *nature of the reader.*

What does the text bring to your reading? As a reader, you might ask yourself about the following:

- subject matter
- language
- structure and organization
- the use of familiar (or unfamiliar) conventions
- social norms
- characters
- themes
- gaps and blanks in the structure of the text that the reader has to fill in

All of these can be seen as formal features of the text, but it is insufficient to simply note that they are there. What needs to be focused on is how they contribute to the effect of the text and thus on the reading produced.

And how does a reader's repertoire affect his or her written response statement? Here you as a reader need to focus on the prior knowledge, expectations, and assumptions you bring to your reading—and as far as possible on the underlying ideological bases of your reading.

To help you prepare a strong reading, ask yourself about the following:

- What was your prior knowledge or expectations of the text before reading it?
- What are your reading strategies?
- How much do you know about the text's literary or social conventions?
- How deep is your knowledge of the historical period in which the text was written—and the differences between an audience's expectations then and today?
- What are your values and assumptions about the social conventions and actions described in the text?

Finally, as you develop your response statement, ask yourself: What does your response and your analysis of what produced it tell you about yourself and your society? This is not simply a question about your personality, your likes and dislikes, your unhappy (or happy) childhood, or whether you used to refuse to eat your broccoli and beans. Rather, this question asks you to address more substantial social and cultural matters, your style of reading, values, code of behavior, notions of what is "normal," "conventional," "universal," "true," and what parts of your ideology influence (and are implied by) your reading.

The above guidelines are generally applicable to all response statements. We follow various selections in this anthology with specific response-statement questions to help students analyze the many influences—cultural, social, moral, historical, psychological—on their reactions to specific texts. In each of the other introductions—to fiction, poetry, essay, and drama—we provide specific suggestions and also some examples of response statements from our own students.

Writing a Response Statement from Annotations

As with all reading, *annotations*—including the notes readers make in the margins, underlining, queries, longer notes made in journals—are an essential part of the process. Most serious readers believe that they cannot *read* without simultaneously using a means to *write*—a pencil, pen, perhaps a word processor. Annotations should be used to record impressions and reactions; they register puzzlement, agreement or disagreement, key words or phrases. A tape recorder can also be used to register ongoing verbal reactions to the reading experience. From such rough beginnings, readers can learn to become increasingly conscious of their reading process and their developing interpretations—and thus learn gradually what assumptions they bring to their readings.

As an example of the way annotations can be built up into a response statement and (if appropriate) become the basis for a more formal paper, consider these annotations:

WILLIAM BUTLER YEATS (1865–1939)

Crazy Jane Talks with the Bishop

I met the Bishop on the road   *religious expectations*
And much said he and I.   *confrontation?*
"Those breasts are flat and fallen now, *"I" a woman*
Those veins must soon be dry;
Live in a heavenly mansion,   *Advice from*   5
Not in some foul sty."   *dualism*   *the godly!*
                        (mansion, sty)

"Fair and foul are near of kin,   *reader's religious*
And fair needs foul," I cried.   *(and sexual) views*
"My friends are gone, but that's a truth
Nor grave nor bed denied,   10
Learned in bodily lowliness
And in the heart's pride.

"A woman can be proud and stiff   *wonderful pun*
When on love intent;   *What do I think of*
But Love has pitched his mansion in   *the conjunction of*   15
The place of excrement;   *sex + religion?*
For nothing can be sole or whole
That has not been rent."   *Maybe looking back*
                                       she's not so crazy

As this reader moved through the poem jotting down her responses, certain reactions were triggered, and the gradual process of building a consistent meaning began. You can see some of her marginal notes. Who is the "I" in the poem? Presumably a woman, the Crazy Jane of the title. When "the Bishop" is introduced in the opening line, then the promise of the title (Crazy Jane *talks* with the Bishop) is fulfilled, though "much" in line 2 suggests a confrontation. The Bishop's message is harsh, and a reader may find his or her own views on religious and sexual matters immediately called upon. A dissimilarity of repertoires—yours and the text's—on ideas about religion may greatly affect the interpretation. Is "heavenly mansion" versus "foul sty" a fair comparison? Do you as a reader read it negatively or positively?

In this reader's view, the argument unfolds with a distinct concentration on the general human problem of how our religious and sexual natures confront each other. The "dualism" noted alongside lines 5–6 can be the starting point for a strong reading of the poem's philosophical contradictions, or the tragic consequences of having a dualistic view of the human being, or the influence of traditional religion in the world.

In her response statement, the same student wrote as follows:

I feel that the meeting of these two characters represents the tension in human life between those who are accepted and those who are not. Crazy Jane shows what the society would be like if people could do what they liked. She is "crazy." She represents the part of human nature that is unruly and that needs the discipline of the church. The other character, the Bishop, is treated unfairly by the poet, I think. We all need the security and authority of something outside ourselves.

If you decide to use response statements in the way we suggest, then *even as you read the poem,* you will question the process by which you produce a reading, such as:

- What expectations did you have upon reading the poem's title?
- How were these fulfilled as you read?
- Whose side are you on in Crazy Jane's argument with the Bishop?
- What individual and intellectual positions lie behind each side of the argument?
- Do you find yourself engaged because of your own assumptions about the issues they discuss?

A different student wrote:

The presence of a Bishop in the poem suggests authority, power, and tradition. The Bishop's words are curt and dismissive. They assume that the world is disgusting (only heaven is worthwhile) and that the body is inferior to the soul. Crazy Jane's argument is that things are more complex than that, and that "whole"ness (or "sole"ness) is produced by struggle. I found myself torn between the authority figure and the crazed sincerity of the mad woman. Maybe her views are crazy, but the fact that she has to "cry" them and be so extreme in her examples shows how desperate she is. I felt by the poem's end caught between a need for some traditional guidance and my own instincts, which are closer to hers and yet seemingly lack authority. Maybe it's because I'm a woman and, like Crazy Jane, resist the male authority of the Bishop.

To develop this initial response statement further, the student might take the last remark and work out a particularly powerful reading of the poem along the lines of male authority and female resistance. Do women readers approach the poem with different assumptions from men? Do religious believers for whom a Bishop might be a term connoting authoritarianism or intolerance take a more favorable view of Crazy Jane? Do pious churchgoers, or those with a "need for guidance," take a more favorable view of the Bishop? Such questions focus on the assumptions readers bring to texts and therefore on some of the factors that help produce their eventual readings.

Outside of class, when you are reading a poem, a story, or anything else, you are not necessarily going to be doing so with a specific response statement assignment. Yet *whenever you read,* you do in fact bring certain assumptions and expectations with you. By learning to ask yourself focused questions, and by tracing your responses and their sources, you become much more self-aware and powerful readers.

Discussing Texts in Class

Response statements not only are important writing exercises but also are a means by which readers can share or "negotiate" their readings. Most students are used to class discussion, but we urge that discussions be used not to iron out differences among different readings—and so arrive at some kind of consensus—but rather to explore the assumptions behind and the implications of different readings. Hearing other readers, you may want to change your own reading, but that should not be the primary aim of class discussion.

In developing any interpretation of a literary text, readers necessarily select certain information and either fail to notice or deliberately ignore other information. Class discussion therefore becomes an important way for you to expand or at least become conscious of the limitations or strengths of your own specific interpretations. Your reading experience can be enhanced and your interpretive possibilities enlarged if you try to adopt what Wolfgang Iser calls a **wandering viewpoint,** that is, if you allow yourself to modify your perspective continually as you move through the text toward closure. In other words, allow yourself to revise your ideas about what the text is "about" and what it means to you as you read through the text and gain new information. So try to be as open to the text as possible. Reading in this way can be a kind of substitute for or preview of class discussion in which you try to be attuned to as many textual details as possible. But even with a wandering viewpoint, readers are still constrained by the information to which they respond.

Class discussion is important in helping you determine how your own particular repertoires (and ultimately your culture's ideology) all influence your reading strategies and interpretations and in helping you understand where those beliefs come from in the first place. In class you will discover that students with different orientations will respond to different textual details, and you can explore how they combine those details to form interpretations that may differ markedly from your own. But it is not enough just to recognize that people have opinions and ideas that differ from your own. You should individually—and as a class—try to explore where those ideas come from. This will necessarily involve you in discussions of your society and your particular place in it that determine the values you have.

For example, we find in studying "The Hitchhiking Game" by Milan Kundera that many of our students are disturbed by the narrator's referring to the woman in the story as "the girl" while the man is never referred to as "the boy." A number of students, men and women, in our classes are also upset by the man's "worshipping" rather than loving the woman. They see both the narrator and the man as assuming that women are powerless in the face of men, that they are objects for men to place on (and remove from) pedestals whimsically. Clearly these students have been influenced by the women's movement in this country: they expect women and men to be treated and referred to equally. Other students in our classes, however, do not even notice or are at least not offended by "girl" and "worshipped." Some readers may be offended by the explicit sexual nature of the story; still others will delight in the game element of the story and will willingly join in, becoming self-conscious about how their opinions of the man and woman (like those of the man and woman in the story) are in continual flux. None of these interpretations is more or less correct or incorrect; they are different—the products of different ideological factors and reading strategies.

How readers take up these different attitudes depends on such factors as their education, personal experiences, family life, religion—the cultural attitudes about which they are most aware. One of the most important points to note from class discussion is that while readers are part of the same culture, their opinions often diverge because each has been influenced differently by the culture as a result of varied socioeconomic, religious, and familial backgrounds. You are, in short, influenced by different factors, any number of which are operating simultaneously in society.

In searching for the cultural determinants underlying a particular interpretation, you will increase your awareness of the various discourses operating within society, and you will gain a sense of which ones are particularly dominant within your class. Such an awareness can help you understand one another's positions and also enable you to expand your own position. Although your opinions are personal, they are not subjective. They originate from your family, your culture, and your history. To explore these influences is one of the most exciting literary endeavors in which any of us can engage.

Rereading

Now go back to the poem "Counting the Mad" on page 1. There we presented a common scene, the classroom, in which a literary work is read. Now that you have been introduced to some of the issues of reading and interpretation, go back to the poem and try to explain how and why you had the responses to it that you did. Can you explain what the text brought and what you brought to your reading and how the two interacted? Do you think you produced a strong reading?

The repertoire of the text tries to separate the mad from the sane by categorizing and limiting the attributes of the mad. But these distinctions break down at the end when the voice who cried "No No No No" is revealed to think of himself as "an ordinary man." So the repertoire of this text attempts to undermine the conventional distinction between the sane and the mad.

What about the text strategies? The dominant strategy is the use of the strong beat and some of the words of the nursery rhyme "This Little Piggy." Whenever one text makes either implicit or explicit reference to another, and particularly when the interpretive possibilities of one can be enhanced by a knowledge of the other, we have an example of **intertextuality.** How does the intertextual relationship between the nursery rhyme and the poem influence you? We can say that the nature of this relationship—whether it is one of irony, triviality, or something else entirely—is a **gap** in the poem that you as a reader with your own repertoire (assumptions about madness, ordinary people, nursery rhymes, and poetry) will have to fill in. The more you integrate your analysis of the text's repertoire and strategies with your own values and assumptions, the stronger your reading will be.

One of our students found a way to integrate his assumptions about nursery rhymes, madness, and society into a strong reading that focused on the distinction between insiders and outsiders. Here is an extract from his response, with parenthetical teacher comments that explain why his reading is a strong one:

I believe that all of society's interactions rest on a distinction between inside and outside. People like to feel that they "belong," and one of the ways they do this is to exclude others like, for example, the insane. I really liked "Counting the Mad" because it suggests, at least to me, that these distinctions don't hold up. I agree completely.	(Awareness of his general ideology about society.) (Awareness of his response to the poem and beginning to explain the ideological causes for it.)
A nursery rhyme is something that is on the inside of society. It's nice, rhythmic, generally comforting, and not threatening to anyone. Nursery rhymes don't, as far as I know, deal with serious subjects. Serious subjects are "outside" nursery rhymes. That's why this poem is disturbing. It puts a serious subject inside a nursery rhyme. But it's not just any serious subject, it's madness, which is a taboo for most people. People who read nursery rhymes would be shocked to read this poem because they, like myself, don't expect to find a discussion of madness in a nursery rhyme.	(Analysis of his repertoire of knowledge on nursery rhymes.) (Effect of the strategy of intertextuality on him as a reader; generalizing this effect based on his knowledge of conventional expectations of nursery rhymes.)

Not only will readers who want to establish clear inside/outside distinctions be shocked that madness got inside a nursery rhyme, but also they'll be shocked that madness may be inside them. All through the poem, the descriptions of the insane make them seem outside normal society: one of them thinks that a window is a wall, another sees things that aren't there, others think they're animals. All this would let the reader who wants to establish inside/outside distinctions do so quite comfortably--"these people act weird and not like me." But these comfortable distinctions don't work at the end: the craziest, or at least the noisiest, man thinks he's ordinary--just like everybody else, just like all the ordinary people who might read this poem. I couldn't help identifying with that man at the end. Even when you're supposedly sane and "normal," crazy things can happen to you, and you know if someone saw you in one of those particularly bad times, they'd probably say, "He's out of his mind." So insanity isn't outside at all. It's potentially in every one of us, and the poem makes you feel that by its surprise ending. Just when you thought it was safe, the outside, the strange, is within.

(Provocative thesis that begins to analyze the effects of the poem based on this reader's own assumptions about madness and normalcy and the implications of these assumptions—goes well beyond what the text "says" and indicates a potentially strong reading.)

(Analysis of a certain type of response to the poem based on specific assumptions, though not his own.)

(Strong emotional response.)

(Analysis and generalization of response.)

While this student acknowledges that some people will have other responses than his, he implies that his response is "better" not because it is closer to any supposedly "real" meaning of the poem, but because it is enlightened, more sensitive to society's outcasts. What do you think?

It should be clear by now that readings and interpretations are neither *right* nor *wrong*. Works of literature are not like that. They serve to open up meanings, not close or limit them. They provide opportunities for readers to construct their own readings—what we have termed "strong" readings —not to try to find an author's "intention" or one objective interpretation of the text.

Moreover, you should by now realize that the issues raised by the process of reading—the assumptions you bring to reading and the implications your readings point to—are at least as important as any "interpretation" or meaning you come up with. Men and women are interpreting beings: we are all thrown into a world we did not create and in which we struggle continually to find meanings. We do so among texts, codes, and languages that always have been read and interpreted by many others before us. We join with others—friends, classmates, teachers—to interpret the texts of literature and the other texts we find in the world. What we have traditionally privileged as literature offers us concentrated and moving opportunities to make discoveries about ourselves, as we struggle to find meaning amid the codes of our culture. The more self-conscious we become about the forces —textual, psychological, social, cultural—that influence our readings, the stronger readers we shall become, both of literary texts and of the texts of the wider world that literature enables us to read and reread.

 *Fiction*

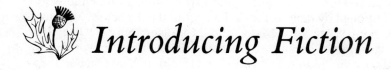 *Introducing Fiction*

Fiction in Our Lives

Fiction is the easiest type of literature for many readers to read. Even in the age of cable television, short stories and novels are the kinds of literature we turn to most frequently for relaxation, entertainment, and a simple desire to "escape" from the world. Fiction—more than poetry or drama—seems to be directly related to people's lives. The language of fiction often appears to be *transparent,* that is, it frequently sounds like "everyday speech," and it often tells a story without overtly calling attention to itself as literature. The language seems natural and, as is commonly said, acts like a "mirror" reflecting reality.

When asked what you do when you read fiction, you might initially respond that with many stories you do almost nothing; you just read and "get into" the story, discovering the meaning as you go along. Yet "meanings" are often deep or mysterious things that seem to be imposed by English teachers. Ordinary readers of fiction expect to read for the "story." They turn the pages, and the meaning comes to them almost effortlessly. Hence the term "page turners" is sometimes applied to the kind of novel you pick up in airport bookstores and can't put down until the last page.

The Interaction of Fiction and Readers

Let us start by systematizing the factors that influence the reader's reading experiences—what the *reader* brings to any piece of fiction. (For a diagram and a fuller discussion of what the reader brings and what the text brings to the reading situation, see the general introduction, pages 5–13.)

1. Reading experiences are influenced by the **readers' general repertoire,** that is, their knowledge, beliefs, and expectations of how the world operates, conditioned by their historical and cultural perspective. You may, for instance, sympathize with Major and Mrs. Monarch in "The Real Thing" by Henry James because you believe that the modern world sadly lacks any real sense of "old world dignity" and tradition. If your general repertoire includes such beliefs, you may find the artist's reluctance to use them as models rather heartless. Or you may find yourself especially struck by Pauline's dilemma in "SeeMotherMotherIsVeryNice" because of your own racial background or work experiences. Such reactions are dependent on your own general repertoire—your experiences of and beliefs about human values, lifestyles, or the demands and possibilities of different societies. Keep in mind that your general repertoire is the product of the particular ideology of the society in which you live. You probably do not interpret Aurelie's lack of children in Kate Chopin's "Regret" as the punishment of god, though such an interpretation might once have seemed plausible. Your views may be in line with those dominant in your society or contrary to them, but either way they are inevitably influenced by your place in a particular society with a particular history.

2. Reading experiences are also influenced by the **readers' literary repertoire,** their specific knowledge and assumptions about what literature (or for our purposes here, what fiction) is or should be, and about the strategies they should use to read it. Most readers, for example, assume that a story should have certain *conventions* such as clear characterizations, some degree of tension or conflict that will eventually be resolved, and a good plot. Readers expect these conventions to be in a story because the majority of stories have them and because they are often discussed in English classes. Some readers have a narrow literary repertoire, based on a combination of their past reading experiences and their personal taste: they may think that "fiction" means science fiction or detective fiction because these are the only kinds of stories they read. As you will see in this fiction section, it is possible to enlarge your literary repertoire by exposing yourself to new types of stories that differ from those you usually read. But how you respond to any story—familiar or unfamiliar—will always depend on the **assumptions** about fiction that you bring to it.

Readers' assumptions about fiction influence the other part of their literary repertoire, their **reading strategies**—such as their tolerance for ambiguity, their willingness to reread, their degree of curiosity, their impulse to synthesize material. The strategy of creating meaning from a story that initially seems strange is called **naturalization.** One possible reading strategy you might use to naturalize Donald Barthelme's "Porcupines at the University" would be to draw on a repertoire of narrative modes—cartoons, dreams, films—that use deliberately incongruous scenes for dramatic effect in order to build linkages and significances where none apparently exist "in" the text. The background with which you approach a story, the goals you have for reading, and the reading strategies that you use play a large role in your experience of the text.

On the other side, various factors in the *text* influence your reading experience.

1. The **text's general repertoire** is produced ultimately by the ideological position of the author. Any text incorporates within it, either implicitly or explicitly, some of its society's *ideology*—references to the values and styles of the time when it was written, even if it is critical of those values. For example, the general repertoire of Faulkner's "A Rose for Emily" (p. 253) is drawn from the American South during the early part of the twentieth century. The text's repertoire encompasses values about the status of blacks in relation to whites, women in relation to men, and the South in relation to the North. Because much of the repertoire of a story is not explicitly spelled out, the more knowledge readers have of the American South, the more their repertoires will *intersect* with that of the story. This intersection enables readers to develop well-informed and useful responses. For example, although you read from a perspective formed in the late twentieth century, you can still gain knowledge of earlier periods that will help you analyze how responses to a story may have changed over time. Your attitudes towards women, for instance, are probably very different from the attitudes expressed in the story, yet part of your general repertoire incorporates an understanding of prejudice, discrimination, and gossip. Consequently you have an identifiable basis on which to respond to this story.

2. By the text's **literary repertoire** we mean its use of literary **conventions** and various **text strategies**. Among these are the **point of view** from which a story is told, the chronology or order in which it is told, the **setting** and **mood,** the way the **characters** are described and developed—all of which influence the way readers respond to stories. For example, when you read Hawthorne's "Young Goodman Brown" (p. 142), you will probably decide that the characters' names are a kind of index to their individual natures: the use of names like "Goodman" and "Faith" is a convention that indicates that the characters are meant to represent larger concepts. You will also note that the dark and strange mood of the forest is a *text strategy* that makes it difficult for you to tell whether the events are really happening or are just part of Goodman Brown's imagination (either waking or dreaming). Because of its ambiguous nature, this setting helps to make the story much more intriguing.

One particularly interesting type of text strategy is its **gaps**—missing connections in the text that must be supplied by the reader. When you read Sukenick's "The Birds" (p. 126), you will notice many physical gaps—actual spaces on the page—that you will need to connect with larger contexts. But you will also notice many other missing connections and seemingly unrelated bits of text, such as the message on the fortune cookie, "You will soon plan another oriental meal," which does not seem to "mean" anything. You will find comments by the narrator supposedly telling you what the story is about, as well as a poem, questions and answers, and even an exam. And it is up to you to decide whether and how to connect all these disparate segments—to fill in the gaps, the missing connections, between them. Contemporary stories have more obvious gaps than more traditional realistic stories, but all stories have gaps. You can never be sure why Goodman Brown went into the forest. You don't know whether John in "The Yellow Wallpaper" meant to be so cruel and insensitive to his wife. You don't know when Emily's gray lock of hair in "A Rose for Emily" fell onto the pillow next to Homer's corpse. Gaps, therefore, are often what make a story most interesting for its readers. They encourage you to use your imagination to fill out the story according to your own expectations and assumptions.

When you read, you will pay more attention to some text strategies than others because of your literary repertoire (or literary background). We will highlight certain text strategies in this introduction, and your teacher will perhaps ask you to focus on others when you read particular stories. But bear in mind that reading is always an *interactive* process so that while the text's literary repertoire is influencing you, your literary repertoire helps to determine what text strategies you decide are important.

We want to emphasize that reading is an *interactive* process to which both reader and text contribute. Using Edgar Allan Poe's "The Cask of Amontillado" and Gertrude Stein's "As a Wife Has a Cow," we can apply some of these terms to a specific reading experience. These two stories are probably as different as any two stories can be in terms of use of language, plot, character, setting—that is, their overall literary repertoire. They demand very different types of reading strategies from their readers. How you respond to them will depend in large part on your own literary repertoire (on the assumptions you have acquired about short stories and on your familiarity with the types of text strategies they employ).

As you read these stories, try to examine your own literary repertoire. To do so, briefly list some of the assumptions you have about short stories in general, that is, what you expect to find before you begin *any* short story. You may develop a clearer sense of your expectations about fiction *after* you have finished reading these two stories and have discovered how they challenge or conform to your general assumptions about fiction. After reading these stories, ask yourself the following questions.

1. Which story did you like better?
2. Which one do you feel more comfortable with—and why?
3. Which requires you to take a more active role?
4. Which one did you learn more from?
5. Which was more interesting to you—and why?

In posing such questions, you are starting to analyze your literary repertoire. You are starting to develop a response that is not merely on a subjective level but one that is produced out of your social and cultural situation.

EDGAR ALLAN POE (1809–1849)

The Cask of Amontillado

The thousand injuries of Fortunato I had borne as I best could; but when he ventured upon insult, I vowed revenge. You, who so well know the nature of my soul, will not suppose, however, that I gave utterance to a threat. *At length* I would be avenged; this was a point definitely settled—but the very definititiveness with which it was resolved precluded the idea of risk. I must not only punish, but punish with impunity. A wrong is unredressed when retribution overtakes its redresser. It is equally unredressed when the avenger fails to make himself felt as such to him who has done the wrong.

It must be understood, that neither by word nor deed had I given Fortunato cause to doubt my good-will. I continued, as was my wont, to smile in his face, and he did not perceive that my smile *now* was at the thought of his immolation.

He had a weak point—this Fortunato—although in other regards he was a man to be respected and even feared. He prided himself on his connoisseurship in wine. Few Italians have the true virtuoso spirit. For the most part their enthusiasm is adopted to suit the time and opportunity—to practise imposture upon the British and Austrian *millionnaires.* In painting and gemmary Fortunato, like his countrymen, was a quack—but in the matter of old wines he was sincere. In this respect I did not differ from him materially: I was skilful in the Italian vintages myself, and bought largely whenever I could.

It was about dusk, one evening during the supreme madness of the carnival season, that I encountered my friend. He accosted me with excessive warmth, for he had been drinking much. The man wore motley. He had on a tight-fitting parti-striped dress, and his head was surmounted by the conical cap and bells. I was so pleased to see him, that I thought I should never have done wringing his hand.

I said to him: "My dear Fortunato, you are luckily met. How remarkably well you are looking to-day! But I have received a pipe[1] of what passes for Amontillado, and I have my doubts."

"How?" said he. "Amontillado? A pipe? Impossible! And in the middle of the carnival!"

"I have my doubts," I replied; "and I was silly enough to pay the full Amontillado price without consulting you in the matter. You were not to be found, and I was fearful of losing a bargain."

"Amontillado!"

"I have my doubts."

"Amontillado!"

"And I must satisfy them."

"Amontillado!"

"As you are engaged, I am on my way to Luchesi. If any one has a critical turn, it is he. He will tell me——"

---

[1] a large vat.

"Luchesi cannot tell Amontillado from Sherry."

"And yet some fools will have it that his taste is a match for your own."

"Come, let us go."

"Whither?"

"To your vaults."

"My friend, no; I will not impose upon your good nature. I perceive you have an engagement. Luchesi——"

"I have no engagement;—come."

"My friend, no. It is not the engagement, but the severe cold with which I perceive you are afflicted. The vaults are insufferably damp. They are encrusted with nitre."

"Let us go, nevertheless. The cold is merely nothing. Amontillado! You have been imposed upon. And as for Luchesi, he cannot distinguish Sherry from Amontillado."

Thus speaking, Fortunato possessed himself of my arm. Putting on a mask of black silk, and drawing a *roquelaire*[2] closely about my person, I suffered him to hurry me to my palazzo.

There were no attendants at home; they had absconded to make merry in honor of the time. I had told them that I should not return until the morning, and had given them explicit orders not to stir from the house. These orders were sufficient, I well knew, to insure their immediate disappearance, one and all, as soon as my back was turned.

I took from their sconces two flambeaux, and giving one to Fortunato, bowed him through several suites of rooms to the archway that led into the vaults. I passed down a long and winding staircase, requesting him to be cautious as he followed. We came at length to the foot of the descent, and stood together on the damp ground of the catacombs of the Montresors.

The gait of my friend was unsteady, and the bells upon his cap jingled as he strode.

"The pipe?" said he.

"It is farther on," said I; "but observe the white web-work which gleams from these cavern walls."

He turned toward me, and looked into my eyes with two filmy orbs that distilled the rheum of intoxication.

"Nitre?" he asked, at length.

"Nitre," I replied. "How long have you had that cough?"

"Ugh! ugh! ugh!—ugh! ugh! ugh!—ugh! ugh! ugh!—ugh! ugh! ugh!—ugh! ugh! ugh!"

My poor friend found it impossible to reply for many minutes.

"It is nothing," he said, at last.

"Come," I said, with decision, "we will go back; your health is precious. You are rich, respected, admired, beloved; you are happy, as once I was. You are a man to be

---

[2] a short cape.

missed. For me it is no matter. We will go back; you will be ill, and I cannot be responsible. Besides, there is Luchesi——"

"Enough," he said; "the cough is a mere nothing; it will not kill me. I shall not die of a cough."

"True—true," I replied; "and, indeed, I had no intention of alarming you unnecessarily; but you should use all proper caution. A draught of this Medoc will defend us from the damps."

Here I knocked off the neck of a bottle which I drew from a long row of its fellows that lay upon the mould.

"Drink," I said, presenting him the wine.

He raised it to his lips with a leer. He paused and nodded to me familiarly, while his bells jingled.

"I drink," he said, "to the buried that repose around us."

"And I to your long life."

He again took my arm, and we proceeded.

"These vaults," he said, "are extensive."

"The Montresors," I replied, "were a great and numerous family."

"I forget your arms."

"A huge human foot d'or,[3] in a field azure; the foot crushes a serpent rampant whose fangs are imbedded in the heel."

"And the motto?"

"*Nemo me impune lacessit.*"[4]

"Good!" he said.

The wine sparkled in his eyes and the bells jingled. My own fancy grew warm with the Medoc. We had passed through walls of piled bones, with casks and puncheons intermingling, into the inmost recesses of the catacombs. I paused again, and this time I made bold to seize Fortunato by an arm above the elbow.

"The nitre!" I said; "see, it increases. It hangs like moss upon the vaults. We are below the river's bed. The drops of moisture trickle among the bones. Come, we will go back ere it is too late. Your cough——"

"It is nothing," he said; "let us go on. But first, another draught of the Medoc."

I broke and reached him a flagon of De Grâve.[5] He emptied it at a breath. His eyes flashed with a fierce light. He laughed and threw the bottle upward with a gesticulation I did not understand.

I looked at him in surprise. He repeated the movement—a grotesque one.

"You do not comprehend?" he said.

"Not I," I replied.

"Then you are not of the brotherhood."

"How?"

"You are not of the masons."

"Yes, yes," I said; "yes, yes."

---

[3] of gold.
[4] "No one wounds me with impunity"—Scottish royal motto.
[5] kind of red wine.

"You? Impossible! A mason?"

"A mason," I replied.

"A sign," he said.

"It is this," I answered, producing a trowel from beneath the folds of my *roque-laire*.

"You jest," he exclaimed, recoiling a few paces. "But let us proceed to the Amontillado."

"Be it so," I said, replacing the tool beneath the cloak, and again offering him my arm. He leaned upon it heavily. We continued our route in search of the Amontillado. We passed through a range of low arches, descended, passed on, and descending again, arrived at a deep crypt, in which the foulness of the air caused our flambeaux rather to glow than flame.

At the most remote end of the crypt there appeared another less spacious. Its walls had been lined with human remains, piled to the vault overhead, in the fashion of the great catacombs of Paris. Three sides of this interior crypt were still ornamented in this manner. From the fourth the bones had been thrown down, and lay promiscuously upon the earth, forming at one point a mound of some size. Within the wall thus exposed by the displacing of the bones, we perceived a still interior recess, in depth about four feet, in width three, in height six or seven. It seemed to have been constructed for no especial use within itself, but formed merely the interval between two of the colossal supports of the roof of the catacombs, and was backed by one of their circumscribing walls of solid granite.

It was in vain that Fortunato, uplifting his dull torch, endeavored to pry into the depth of the recess. Its termination the feeble light did not enable us to see.

"Proceed," I said; "herein is the Amontillado. As for Luchesi——"

"He is an ignoramus," interrupted my friend, as he stepped unsteadily forward, while I followed immediately at his heels. In an instant he had reached the extremity of the niche, and finding his progress arrested by the rock, stood stupidly bewildered. A moment more and I had fettered him to the granite. In its surface were two iron staples, distant from each other about two feet, horizontally. From one of these depended a short chain, from the other a padlock. Throwing the links about his waist, it was but the work of a few seconds to secure it. He was too much astounded to resist. Withdrawing the key I stepped back from the recess.

"Pass your hand," I said, "over the wall; you cannot help feeling the nitre. Indeed it is *very* damp. Once more let me *implore* you to return. No? Then I must positively leave you. But I must first render you all the little attentions in my power."

"The Amontillado!" ejaculated my friend, not yet recovered from his astonishment.

"True," I replied; "the Amontillado."

As I said these words I busied myself among the pile of bones of which I have before spoken. Throwing them aside, I soon uncovered a quantity of building stone and mortar. With these materials and with the aid of my trowel, I began vigorously to wall up the entrance of the niche.

I had scarcely laid the first tier of the masonry when I discovered that the intoxication of Fortunato had in a great measure worn off. The earliest indication I had of this was a low moaning cry from the depth of the recess. It was *not* the cry of a drunken man. There was then a long and obstinate silence. I laid the second tier, and the third, and the fourth; and then I heard the furious vibrations of the chain. The noise lasted for several minutes, during which, that I might hearken to it with the more satisfaction, I ceased my labors and sat down upon the bones. When at last the clanking subsided, I resumed the trowel, and finished without interruption the fifth, the sixth, and the seventh tier. The wall was now nearly upon a level with my breast. I again paused, and holding the flambeaux over the masonwork, threw a few feeble rays upon the figure within.

A succession of loud and shrill screams, bursting suddenly from the throat of the chained form, seemed to thrust me violently back. For a brief moment I hesitated—I trembled. Unsheathing my rapier, I began to grope with it about the recess; but the thought of an instant reassured me. I placed my hand upon the solid fabric of the catacombs, and felt satisfied. I reapproached the wall. I replied to the yells of him who clamored. I re-echoed—I aided—I surpassed them in volume and in strength. I did this, and the clamorer grew still.

It was now midnight, and my task was drawing to a close. I had completed the eighth, the ninth, and the tenth tier. I had finished a portion of the last and the eleventh; there remained but a single stone to be fitted and plastered in. I struggled with its weight; I placed it partially in its destined position. But now there came from out the niche a low laugh that erected the hairs upon my head. It was succeeded by a sad voice, which I had difficulty in recognizing as that of the noble Fortunato. The voice said—

"Ha! ha! ha!—he! he!—a very good joke indeed—an excellent jest. We will have many a rich laugh about it at the palazzo— he! he! he!—over our wine—he! he! he!"

"The Amontillado!" I said.

"He! he! he!—he! he! he!—yes, the Amontillado. But is it not getting late? Will not they be awaiting us at the palazzo, the Lady Fortunato and the rest? Let us be gone."

"Yes," I said, "let us be gone."

"For the love of God, Montresor!"

"Yes," I said, "for the love of God!"

But to these words I hearkened in vain for a reply. I grew impatient. I called aloud:

"Fortunato!"

No answer. I called again:

"Fortunato!"

No answer still. I thrust a torch through the remaining aperture and let it fall within. There came forth in return only a jingling of the bells. My heart grew sick—on account of the dampness of the catacombs. I hastened to make an end of my labor. I forced the last stone into its position; I plastered it up. Against the new masonry I re-erected the old rampart of bones. For the half of a century no mortal has disturbed them. *In pace requiescat!*[6]

---

[6] Rest in peace!

A Strong Reading of Edgar Allan Poe's "The Cask of Amontillado"

We asked our students the same questions we gave you on p. 30; from a number of them we received strong reactions. Let us look at an extract from one of their **response statements,** both to consider the issues it raises about the nature of fiction and to discover ways in which the informal response can be developed into a formal paper.

> I expect a story to have some unity and some ambiguous points. I don't want stories I read to be so blatant and straightforward as to be comprehensible by a third grader because part of the fun of reading a story is to have some unclear sections so you can add your own imaginative ideas to it. But the story must also have something to hold it together.
>
> "The Cask of Amontillado" was a perfect kind of story for me. I've read other stories by Poe and knew before I even began that I'd probably like it— and I did. I knew that Fortunato was going to get killed, and I spent most of the story trying to figure out how it would happen. But I got tricked near the end and thought Montresor wasn't going to do it after all. That's Poe all over —lots of suspense that holds your interest (I read the story very fast). Because it seems like it's actually happening, this is a story I could really get into.

This student clearly knows what he thinks of this story. And we think he wrote a useful, straightforward response statement. He has specific opinions—we might say literary theories—in his literary repertoire about the ways stories should be written. His opinions are his own, but they certainly cannot be said to be "subjective" because they are informed by many influences—by other stories he has read, by his schooling, and by his familiarity with Poe's other writings—that constitute part of the literary ideology of his culture. In the following discussion, we will suggest how this student could, with more probing of his assumptions, with class discussion of other students' responses, and with some research, develop a formal paper in which he could more clearly articulate the reasons underlying his responses to the story.

Are Plots Realistic?

Let us investigate a well-known text strategy found in much fiction, past and present—*plot.* One point implied, but not clearly stated, in the student response statement above was that Poe's story had a good plot and therefore appeared realistic. Let us consider this story and how our student could revise his response statement to develop a more formal paper by focusing on his assumptions about plot and its relationship to realism.

When most readers read a story like "The Cask of Amontillado," they pay little attention to such seemingly abstract matters as their own reading strategies or the text's strategies simply because they find Poe's story relatively straightforward to read. But why is this story relatively easy to read? In a number of ways, it conforms to many expectations most readers have about fiction in their literary repertoire. First of all, it has what many would call "a good plot," a series of actions that develop in a clear sequence or unfold *chronologically,* leading to a clear *climax.* Most readers expect a story to have a plot and a climax, and so their presence seems "natural" rather than a literary convention to them. In his paper, our student explicitly developed some of his longstanding assumptions about plot and "reality."

Readers like our student often say that plots make stories seem lifelike. If, however, you met a friend whom you had not seen in a long time, you would most likely not ask her if her life had been following a good plot. You know that plots are not something that you attribute to people's lives even though you may talk about their—or your own—lives as having many exciting events that proceed chronologically and that have a series of climaxes. You do not say that people's lives follow a plot because the events that occur in their lives are often fragmented, unrelated, and unresolved. People's lives, in short, are too complicated to be confined to plots. As the twentieth-century Italian dramatist Pirandello writes in *Six Characters in Search of an Author,* "Life is full of infinite absurdities, which strangely enough, do not even need to appear plausible, since they are true." When you think about it, you might begin to realize that there is something contrived about the notion of a plot having a neat beginning, middle, and end. Life does not present itself to us in such well-defined sequences. Yet often the highest praise given to a story is that its plot is *realistic.*

This statement is not as paradoxical as it first might seem when you realize that the assumptions of your literary repertoire can be very distinct from those of your general repertoire. The notion of what is realistic in a story derives from a reader's exposure to certain conventions of storytelling—not from actual parallels between a story and the experiences of everyday life. Readers who are accustomed to reading stories expect certain things like plot to be there. In the twentieth century, authors like Gertrude Stein have attempted to write texts without the convention of plot.

Is Point of View Natural or Contrived?

Similar points can be made about **point of view,** another seemingly "natural" part of fiction that one might easily take for granted. In addition to having a plot, "The Cask of Amontillado" is told from a point of view with which readers are familiar, the **first person.** From the first line of the story, the "I" of first-person narrator is easily recognizable ("The thousand injuries of Fortunato I had borne as I best could . . ."), and Montresor's point of view is the perspective from which the entire story is told.

Although **third-person omniscient,** another common point of view, provides insight into all the characters' thoughts, many readers prefer first person because of the sense of immediacy it gives them when reading. Although our student did not write about point of view, when asked in class why he reported feeling as if the story were "actually happening," he responded without hesitation that the "I" of the story seemed to be talking to him personally. Developing this point in his formal paper, he talked explicitly about the impact of a story written from the first person.

A *consistent* point of view, like a specific plot, is something most readers expect of a story. Both are part of most readers' literary repertoires, not because this is the way stories *must* be written but because this is the way stories have been written until very recently. The consistency of a particular point of view probably strikes the reader as "natural" rather than conventional. When reading a story, readers generally do not even stop to consider that it might have been told from other perspectives. Yet, as with plot, point of view in a story is not natural but highly conventional. If you watch "Nightline" or one of the networks' evening news programs, or just listen to two friends recount an argument they have had, you already know that no "true" story—in the sense of complete or unified—can ever be told. In your day-to-day living, you generally are at least aware of the possibility of *multiple perspectives*. Hence the cliché, "there are two sides to every story." There are, of course, many more than two. Yet in their reading experiences, readers readily accept a story told from a single perspective or single point of view mainly because their assumptions about fiction convince them that unified stories are more "realistic" than stories that are told from multiple perspectives—or that have no discernible perspective at all. Readers' common notions about fiction include not only a "willing suspension of disbelief" but a **naturalization** of this suspension of disbelief, so a single point of view seems "normal" rather than conventional. Thus a unified story told from a single point of view is the kind of story that readers, like the student who wrote the earlier response statement, are most familiar with; hence it is the kind most easily read.

How Do Expectations about Genre Influence Reading Strategies?

Two of the text strategies of "The Cask of Amontillado," *plot* and *point of view,* probably seem so natural that they go unnoticed by most readers, or even if noticed, seem appropriate to make the reading of "The Cask of Amontillado" comfortable. Two other text strategies, *setting* and *mood,* also draw the reader into this story. Whether or not you have read Poe's stories before, the cryptic opening and the mysterious, dark setting quickly inform you that this is a *type* of story that you have probably read before—a *suspense* story. If you have prior knowledge of suspense stories in your literary repertoire, you can classify this piece of fiction. Recall that in his response statement, our student noted that he had read stories by Poe before and responded to a new one with enthusiasm. Knowing the kinds of stories that Poe wrote obviously made it easier for this student to read this story; he suggests that he already knew how to read it, and that this knowledge made him interact more fully with the story, allowing him to guess how Fortunato would be killed. He has classified a certain **genre** (or *category*) of fiction, the horror or suspense story, which evoked in him certain kinds of reading strategies. For his formal paper, we asked him to develop these points further by explaining the clues he had found in the story that let him know how to classify it and the reading strategies he had then adopted. A reader also learns to recognize and classify other genres—science fiction tales or fairy tales, for instance.

If you have already read a number of Poe's macabre horror tales, you suspect immediately from the tone that this story will also be frightening and chilling. When your initial assumptions are fulfilled, the Poe text conforms to and reinforces your literary repertoire. Again note how readers' literary repertoires can differ from their general repertoires: a reader may like reading horror stories or seeing scary movies but would not like to experience terror firsthand. Life experiences can, however, sometimes enhance the experience of reading a story. If you have ever been really terrified—or perhaps just frightened by a sudden noise in a dark cellar—your experience of terror upon reading this story may be greater than it is for a person who has never had such experiences. Once again, all readers bring their own repertoires—literary and general—to bear upon all their readings.

Strategies That Readers Use to Make Meaning: Gertrude Stein's "As a Wife Has a Cow"

The recognition that "The Cask of Amontillado" is a suspense story influences subsequent reading strategies; for example, once the story is seen as a suspense story, most readers will probably look for clues as to how the tale of horror will unfold. When these clues are found, this initial reading strategy is reinforced. A reader may perhaps find **irony** in the exchange between Montresor and Fortunato when Fortunato states, "I shall not die of a cough," and Montresor replies, "True—true." If you perceive the irony in these lines, it is because *you expect*—based on your previous experience with horror stories—that Fortunato will die of something. Thus your expectations, though reinforced by the text you are reading, are only *in part* determined by this text. Your expectations are, to a large extent, determined by the texts you already have in your literary repertoire from which you have learned not only the conventions of tales of suspense but also how to recognize irony.

Reading strategies also help to determine whether or not a reader enjoys the story. Some readers, like our student, argue that they read "The Cask of Amontillado" in a very *active* way—consciously searching for clues, actively trying to figure out how the story will develop and end, consciously attempting to fill in the gaps about Montresor's motivation for killing Fortunato and about how exactly he will go about carrying out his plans. For some readers, this sense of active participation in the story contributes to the enjoyment of it.

Other readers argue that they read the story in a more *passive* way; they wait for clues to be set out explicitly and try not to anticipate how the story will develop or end. These readers like the sense of being "taken in" or carried along by the tale. Still others may find the story too macabre or too predictable—or they may simply just not like suspense stories. Readers' reactions to a story are a result of the intersection of their literary repertoire with that of the text's.

Now look at Stein's "As a Wife Has a Cow" and compare it to Poe's story, keeping in mind the questions that we gave you on page 30.

GERTRUDE STEIN (1874–1946)

As a Wife Has a Cow
A Love Story

Nearly all of it to be as a wife has a cow, a love story. All of it to be as a wife has a cow, all of it to be as a wife has a cow, a love story.

As to be all of it as to be a wife as a wife has a cow, a love story, all of it as to be all of it as a wife all of it as to be as a wife has a cow a love story, all of it as a wife has a cow as a wife has a cow a love story.

Has made, as it has made as it has made, has made has to be as a wife has a cow, a love story. Has made as to be as a wife has a cow a love story. As a wife has a cow, as a wife has a cow, a love story. Has to be as a wife has a cow a love story. Has made as to be as a wife has a cow a love story.

When he can, and for that when he can, for that. When he can and for that when he can. For that. When he can. For that when he can. For that. And when he can and for that. Or that, and when he can. For that and when he can.

And to in six and another. And to and in and six and another. And to and in and six and another. And to in six and and to and in and six and another. And to and in and six and another. And to and six and in and another and and to and six and another and and to and in and six and and to and six and in and another.

In came in there, came in there come out of there. In came in come out of there. Come out there in came in there. Come out of there and in and come out of there. Came in there, come out of there.

Feeling or for it, as feeling or for it, came in or come in, or come out of there or feeling as feeling or feeling as for it.

As a wife has a cow.

Came in and come out.

As a wife has a cow a love story.

As a love story, as a wife has a cow, a love story.

Not and now, now and not, not and now, by and by not and now, as not, as soon as not not and now, now as soon now now as soon, now as soon as soon as now. Just as soon just now just now just as soon just as soon as now. Just as soon as now.

And in that, as and in that, in that and and in that, so that, so that and in that, and in that and so that and as for that and as for that and that. In that. In that and and for that as for that and in that. Just as soon and in that. In that as that and just as soon. Just as soon as that.

Even now, now and even now and now and even now. Not as even now, therefor, even now and therefor, therefor and even now and even now and therefor even now. So not to and moreover and even now and therefor and moreover and even now and so and even now and therefor even now.

Do they as they do so. And do they do so.

We feel we feel. We feel or if we feel if we feel or if we feel. We feel or if we feel. As it is made made a day made a day or two made a day, as it is made a day or two, as it is made a day. Made a day. Made a day. Not away a day. By day. As it is made a day.

On the fifteenth of October as they say, said anyway, what is it as they expect, as they expect it or as they expected it, as they expect it and as they expected it, expect it or for it, expected it and it is expected of it. As they say said anyway. What is it as they expect for it, what is it and it is as they expect of it. What is it. What is the fifteenth of October as they say as they expect or as they expected as they expect for it. What is it as they say the fifteenth of October as they say and as expected of it, the fifteenth of October as they say, what is it as expected of it. What is it and the fifteenth of October as they say and expected of it.

And prepare and prepare so prepare to prepare and prepare to prepare and prepare so as to prepare, so to prepare and prepare to prepare to prepare for and to prepare for it to prepare, to prepare for it, in preparation, as preparation in preparation by preparation. They will be too busy afterwards to prepare. As preparation prepare, to prepare, as to preparation and to prepare. Out there.

Have it as having having it as happening, happening to have it as having, having to have it as happening. Happening and have it as happening and having it happen as happening and having to have it happen as happening, and my wife has a cow as now, my wife having a cow as now, my wife having a cow as now and having a cow as now and having a cow and having a cow now, my wife has a cow and now. My wife has a cow.

Developing New Reading Strategies in Response to New Text Strategies

When our student turned to "As a Wife Has a Cow," he found very different problems related to the process of reading fiction:

> If I must be honest, I severely disliked Stein's "As a Wife Has a Cow." Her story (if you can call it that) conflicts with practically everything I know, believe, or have been taught about writing. As I said earlier about Poe, I expect a literary piece to be somewhat understandable. From the start, Stein's piece is so unclear that it never even gave me a chance to form a basis to build upon. I

know that if I had been asked to write a short story as a homework assignment and I turned in a paper with writing like Stein's, any teacher would have given me a grade of about zero; yet Stein is critically acclaimed for daring to write with a style that contradicts every existing technique. Stein completely ignores any sense of reality at all, and she defies all grammatical and syntactic guidelines. I could develop more sensible and coherent sentences by drawing words and phrases from a hat and arranging them in a random fashion.

A story like "As a Wife," which most readers find difficult to read, calls attention to those reading strategies that we have in our literary repertoires and that make Poe's "Cask of Amontillado" easier to read. Whereas Poe's story usually confirms a reader's assumptions about fiction because its text strategies—plot, character, point of view, setting—are very similar to the stories most readers have in their repertoires, Stein's "As a Wife Has a Cow" completely challenges most assumptions about fiction. Our student commented that its text strategies struck him as highly eccentric and baffling. What types of reading strategies should be used to process such a text?

Stein's story lacks a clearly definable plot; it doesn't have well-developed characters, and in fact it doesn't tell a story at all. Our student asked whether one could rightly call it a story. "As a Wife Has a Cow" has many gaps, and part of a reader's responses to it will be determined by the extent to which these gaps either *challenge* or *threaten* the reader's learned expectations for fiction. Students will feel less threatened by these gaps if they already have some strategies to fill them in. Those students who enjoy reading the text feel that it allows them great freedom of association. Sometimes such readers have prior or special knowledge that they can apply to their reading. For example, one student reported that she enjoyed the story not for what it said but for how it sounded. She used her music repertoire to develop nontraditional strategies for reading the story:

> When reading a story, I usually prefer that the plot be obvious and clear, as it is in Poe's "Cask of Amontillado." For this reason, I was surprised that I liked Gertrude Stein's "As a Wife Has a Cow." After I looked it over for a time and reread it, I found that I didn't have to read it for plot or character development, but that I could read it for something else—for the way it sounded. It is musical and I enjoyed the sensation of saying it aloud. I liked, to my surprise, the feeling of saying words without thought. The repetition and variations on certain word patterns remind me of the repetition of certain themes in music. A composer often takes a rather simple pattern and elaborates on it almost endlessly, modifying it, yet staying within certain bounds. When I listen to those variations in, say, a symphony, I am moved; I *feel something,* but it's not really that I'm thinking. I felt the same way with "As a Wife Has a Cow": I was repeating various word patterns and their variations, listening to and feeling the sounds of the words without really thinking about their meanings.

This student, unlike the student who preferred Poe, had certain knowledge in her repertoire that enabled her to develop strategies for enjoying "As a

Wife Has a Cow." Although she had never encountered this kind of writing style before, she chose not to reject it immediately just because it was un-conventional. This does not mean that her response statement is better thought out than the student's quoted above—only that it is different. This difference comes in large part from their different repertoires of knowledge, but also from more subtle differences in their *cognitive styles,* the general ways in which they take in, process, and react to what they perceive. Some readers may simply have a higher tolerance for ambiguity than others.

Other students have read Gertrude Stein's work before this assignment and, therefore, have in their literary repertoire some knowledge of her text strategies and some experience developing reading strategies to negotiate Stein's texts. They know that in the early 1900s she was interested in Picasso and the radically new cubist movement in painting. *Cubism* was a move-ment in modern abstract art that often depicted natural forms in terms of simple geometric shapes, portraying the form from a number of points of view simultaneously. Cubism also depicted intersecting shapes and sharp angles without immediate reference to natural objects. As a technique in writing, it makes use of the abstract structural relationships of words, lead-ing to strange associations of imagery and often to the simultaneous bring-ing together of multiple perspectives on a subject.

Students familiar with cubism have a repertoire of knowledge that is able to *match* the repertoire of the Stein text, and they can match it much more closely than the two students discussed above. This matching of reper-toires does not insure that students will respond deeply to the story, only that they will have a greater understanding of the strategies Stein uses and a more informed perspective from which to evaluate whether or not Stein was successful in her goals. Here are extracts from two very different responses, both of which are informed by a knowledge of cubism.

> I feel that Gertrude Stein's use of language as an object is similar to cubist painters' expressive use of abstract form and color. Picasso and others frac-tured the subjects they painted so that the viewer is much more conscious of the form and style of their paintings than of the content. It's the same with Stein's work: the reader is more aware of the words as words than as carriers of meanings. But with cubism, as opposed to purely abstract art, there is still some content. I remember learning in my art class last year that Picasso's paintings are disturbing to many people because they create a tension between form and content. When you look at one of his guitars, you still want to know it is a guitar, even if it's fractured. "As a Wife Has a Cow" has that same kind of tension. Though it would be hard (or impossible) to say what it's about, I kept thinking that, if I reread it, I'd discover its content—which of course I didn't. I was "teased" by Stein's story, and I liked that.

This student likes "As a Wife" not only because she is familiar with its con-ventions but because it elicits the same response, "the tension between form and content," that she has enjoyed with other cubist forms of art. Part of her repertoire—formed by her training in art class and her previous reading of

Stein—has prepared her to read "As a Wife Has a Cow" in a more receptive fashion.

Another student with a similar repertoire responds quite differently:

> I can appreciate what Stein is trying to do. I know she was active in the cubist movement—good friends with Picasso and interested in the new experiments in painting—but to get the effect of cubism you have to see the distortion all at once. This works well in painting, but it doesn't translate into language. We have to read this story sequentially—one word at a time. We can't get the whole picture at once, and that is necessary to appreciate the form. A Picasso painting can make a strong impression because it's so powerful and unfamiliar—even strangely beautiful. All Stein does is give me a headache.

This student, using different criteria, argues that the effect of Picasso's cubist painting is very different from the effect of Stein's cubist writing. Therefore, he does not respond favorably to Stein's experimental work, especially its repetitive qualities and ambiguities.

These varied responses occurred among members of the same class, and the class discussion was heated and partisan. Students for whom Stein's work was strange and disconcerting were at first completely baffled that anyone could possibly understand or like "As a Wife." The class seemed to divide itself naturally into groups—with one group demanding explicit analyses of the assumptions and repertoires of the other groups. The goals of this lively class discussion were to examine how readers' literary repertoires, their prior assumptions about fiction, knowledge (or lack of knowledge) of cubism, training and background, and general tolerance for ambiguity influenced their reading experiences. There was, understandably, more disagreement about "As a Wife" than about "The Cask of Amontillado" because readers' repertoires differed far more widely in relation to the Stein story.

Moving from a Response Statement to a Formal Paper

From class discussion, students discovered that no reading of or response to a text is prescribed or dictated by that text. Consequently, in order to defend a particular reading, each student had to analyze carefully the literary repertoires of both reader and text that gave rise to it. Further, class discussion allowed students to enlarge their repertoires by sharing knowledge, and while this class discussion by no means demanded that they change their own opinions of the stories, it allowed them to explain more persuasively why they had the reactions they did.

For example, the student quoted on page 41 discovered that if he were going to argue convincingly in his formal paper that Poe's writing is "realistic" and that Stein's writing "ignores any sense of reality," he needed to be much more explicit about what he feels the conventions of **realism** are in fiction writing. Further, he needed to acknowledge that "As a Wife" does have strategies, those of cubism, and that he could not in fact create a more coherent story by "drawing words and phrases from a hat," as he had asserted. Nonetheless, he should learn to probe the reasons why he had made such an assertion. Rather than simply arguing that Stein's story "contradicts every existing technique," he can expand his literary repertoire by reading more about Stein and the cubist movement. He can then explain both the technique Stein uses and also why he thinks that technique is ineffective as a story-telling device.

Further, he needs to explore the larger implications of his rejection of Stein's techniques. In rejecting Stein, is he rejecting all experimental or avant-garde movements in art, literature, and theater? If so, what does this indicate about his **cognitive style**, his openness to different experiences, or changing tradition in any art form? Is he rejecting Stein just because she is different from what he understands as the mainstream, or is he learning to articulate his own critical or aesthetic position? Does he believe that his position is subject to change?

In moving from a response statement to a formal paper, we do not advocate that you change your response to the stories (although that sometimes happens), but rather that you probe your own repertoire to explore your underlying assumptions about fiction and your strategies for reading texts.

What about your reactions to these stories? Whether you dismiss "As a Wife Has a Cow" as nonsense or revel in its play of language and have fun with it depends in large part on the ways in which your literary repertoire intersects with the story's. Reading a text like "As a Wife Has a Cow" can, by challenging your expectations, make you more conscious of your reading strategies and assumptions about fiction and may cause you to expand some traditional expectations about short stories. By reading such a text you can see the interactive nature of the reading process and come to recognize how all reading is affected by factors of which you aren't always conscious.

The Reader's Interpretive Strategies: Cultural Influences

To gain further perspective on how readers and texts interact, we want now to focus on the reader's interpretive strategies. We want to examine how a reader's earlier educational experiences and previous knowledge of literary conventions can affect his or her response to the next two stories. "The Canary Prince" and "The Metamorphosis" both describe a *metamorphosis* or a transformation. The prince in "The Canary Prince" changes into a canary, and Gregor Samsa in "The Metamorphosis" changes into a bug. The ways that readers react to these metamorphoses will differ, however, depending on their literary repertoires, that is, their familiarity with stories like these, their opinions (favorable or not) about the conventions the stories employ, and their strategies for reading them.

When reading the story "The Canary Prince," below, ask yourself the following questions, questions upon which you can build your response statement:

1. What *kind* of story is it?
2. Are its text strategies and conventions familiar to you? If so, where have you encountered stories like this before?
3. After you have read a page or two, how do you expect the story will develop and end?
4. Are your expectations confirmed or not?

As you read "The Metamorphosis," which you will find on page 221, ask yourself these questions:

1. Can you classify this story in the same way you classified "The Canary Prince"? Why or why not?
2. Are its text strategies and conventions familiar to you? If so, from what contexts?
3. What kinds of expectations do you have, midway through your reading, about how the story will end? Are they confirmed or not?
4. What text strategies and what reader strategies (your own expectations and assumptions) influence the ways you respond to the story?

ITALO CALVINO (1923–1985)

The Canary Prince

There was a king who had a daughter. Her mother was dead, and the stepmother was jealous of the girl and always spoke badly of her to the king. The maiden defended herself as best she could, but the stepmother was so contrary and insistent that the king, though he loved his daughter, finally gave in. He told the queen to send the girl away, but to some place where she would be comfortable, for he would never allow her to be mistreated. "Have no fear of that," said the stepmother, who then had the girl shut up in a castle in the heart of the forest. To keep her company, the queen selected a group of ladies-in-waiting, ordering them never to let the girl go out of the house or even to look out the windows. Naturally they received a salary worthy of a royal household. The girl was given a beautiful room and all she wanted to eat and drink. The only thing she couldn't do was go outdoors. But the ladies, enjoying so much leisure time and money, thought only of themselves and paid no attention to her.

Every now and then the king would ask his wife, "And how is our daughter? What is she doing with herself these days?" To prove that she did take an interest in the girl, the queen called on her. The minute she stepped from her carriage, the ladies-in-waiting all rushed out and told her not to worry, the girl was well and happy. The queen went up to the girl's room for a moment. "So you're comfortable, are you? You need nothing, do you? You're looking well, I see; the country air is doing you good. Stay happy, now. Bye-bye, dear!" And off she went. She informed the king she had never seen his daughter so content.

On the contrary, always alone in that room, with ladies-in-waiting who didn't so much as look at her, the princess spent her days wistfully at the window. She sat there leaning on the windowsill, and had she not thought to put a pillow under them, she would have got calluses on her elbows. The window looked out on the forest, and all day long the princess saw nothing but treetops, clouds and, down below, the hunters' trail. Over that trail one day came the son of a king in pursuit of a wild boar. Nearing the castle known to have been unoccupied for no telling how many years, he was amazed to see washing spread out on the battlements, smoke rising from the chimneys, and open casements. As he looked about him, he noticed a beautiful maiden at one of the upper windows and smiled at her. The maiden saw the prince too, dressed in yellow, with hunter's leggings and gun, and smiling at her, so she smiled back at him. For a whole hour, they smiled, bowed, and curtsied, being too far apart to communicate in any other way.

The next day, under the pretext of going hunting, the king's son returned, dressed in yellow, and they stared at each other this time for two hours; in addition to smiles, bows, and curtsies, they put a hand over their hearts and waved handkerchiefs at great length. The third day the prince stopped for three hours, and they blew each other kisses. The fourth day he was there as usual, then from behind a tree a witch peeped and began to guffaw: "Ho, ho, ho, ho!"

"Who are you? What's so funny?" snapped the prince.

"What's so funny? Two lovers silly enough to stay so far apart!"

"Would you know how to get any closer to her, ninny?" asked the prince.

"I like you both," said the witch, "and I'll help you."

She knocked at the door and handed the ladies-in-waiting a big old book with yellow, smudgy pages, saying it was a gift to the princess so the young lady could pass the time reading. The ladies took it to the girl, who opened it at once and read: "This is a magic book. Turn the pages forward, and the man becomes a bird; turn them back, and the bird becomes a man once more."

The girl ran to the window, placed the book on the sill, and turned the pages in great haste while watching the youth in yellow standing in the path. Moving his arms, he was soon flapping wings and changed into a canary, dressed in yellow as he was. Up he soared above the treetops and headed straight for the window, coming to rest on the cushioned sill. The princess couldn't resist picking up the beautiful canary and kissing him; then remembering he was a young man, she blushed. But on second thought she wasn't ashamed at all and made haste to turn him back into a youth. She picked up the book and thumbed backward through it; the canary ruffled his yellow feathers, flapped his wings, then moved arms and was once more the youth dressed in yellow with the hunter's leggings who knelt before her, declaring, "I love you!"

By the time they finished confessing all their love for one another, it was evening. Slowly, the princess leafed through the book. Looking into her eyes the youth turned back into a canary, perched on the windowsill, then on the eaves, then trusting to the wind, flew down in wide arcs, lighting on the lower limb of a tree. At that, she turned the pages back in the book and the canary was a prince once more who jumped down, whistled for his dogs, threw a kiss toward the window, and continued along the trail out of sight.

So every day the pages were turned forward to bring the prince flying up to the window at the top of the tower, then turned backward to restore his human form, then forward again to enable him to fly away, and finally backward for him to get home. Never in their whole life had the two young people known such happiness.

One day the queen called on her stepdaughter. She walked about the room, saying, "You're all right, aren't you? I see you're a trifle slimmer, but that's certainly no cause for concern, is it? It's true, isn't it, you've never felt better?" As she talked, she checked to see that everything was in place. She opened the window and peered out. Here came the prince in yellow along the trail with his dogs. "If this silly girl thinks she is going to flirt at the window," said the stepmother to herself, "she has another thought coming to her." She sent the girl for a glass of water and some sugar, then hurriedly removed five or six hairpins from her own hair and concealed them in the pillow with the sharp points sticking straight up. "That will teach her to lean on the window!" The girl returned with the water and sugar, but the queen said, "Oh, I'm no longer thirsty; you drink it, my dear! I must be getting back to your father. You don't need anything, do you? Well, goodbye." And she was off.

As soon as the queen's carriage was out of sight, the girl hurriedly flipped over the pages of the book, the prince turned into a canary, flew to the window, and struck the pillow like an arrow. He instantly let out a shrill cry of pain. The yellow feathers were stained with blood; the canary had driven the pins into his breast. He rose with a convulsive flapping, trusted himself to the wind, descended in irregular arcs, and lit on the ground with outstretched wings. The frightened princess, not yet fully aware of what had happened, quickly turned the pages back in the hope there would be no wounds when he regained his human form. Alas, the prince reappeared dripping blood from the deep stabs that had rent the yellow garment on his chest, and lay back surrounded by his dogs.

At the howling of the dogs, the other hunters came to his aid and carried him off on a stretcher of branches, but he didn't so much as glance up at the window of his beloved, who was still overwhelmed with grief and fright.

Back at his palace, the prince showed no promise of recovery, nor did the doctors know what to do for him. The wounds refused to heal over, and constantly hurt. His father the king posted proclamations on every street corner promising a fortune to anyone who could cure him, but not a soul turned up to try.

The princess meanwhile was consumed with longing for her lover. She cut her sheets into thin strips which she tied one to the other in a long, long rope. Then one night she let herself down from the high tower and set on the hunters' trail. But because of the thick darkness and the howls of the wolves, she decided to wait for daylight. Finding an old oak with a hollow trunk, she nestled inside and, in her exhaustion, fell asleep at once. She woke up while it was still pitch-dark, under the impression she had heard a whistle. Listening closely, she heard another whistle, then a third and a fourth, after which she saw four candle flames advancing. They were four witches coming from the four corners of the earth to their appointed meeting under that tree. Through a crack in the trunk the princess, unseen by them, spied on the four crones carrying candles and sneering a welcome to one another: "Ah, ah, ah!"

They lit a bonfire under the tree and sat down to warm themselves and roast a couple of bats for dinner. When they had eaten their fill, they began asking one another what they had seen of interest out in the world.

"I saw the sultan of Turkey, who bought himself twenty new wives."

"I saw the emperor of China, who has let his pigtail grow three yards long."

"I saw the king of the cannibals, who ate his chamberlain by mistake."

"I saw the king of this region, who has the sick son nobody can cure, since I alone know the remedy."

"And what is it?" asked the other witches.

"In the floor of his room is a loose tile. All one need do is lift the tile, and there underneath is a phial containing an ointment that would heal every one of his wounds."

It was all the princess inside the tree could do not to scream for joy. By this time the witches had told one another all they had to say, so each went her own way. The princess jumped from the tree and set out in the dawn for the city. At the first secondhand dealer's she came to, she bought an old doctor's gown and a pair of spectacles, and knocked at the royal palace. Seeing the little doctor with such scant paraphernalia, the servants weren't going to let him in, but the king said, "What harm could he do my son who can't be any worse off than he is now? Let him see what he can do." The sham doctor asked to be left alone with the sick man, and the request was granted.

Finding her lover groaning and unconscious in his sickbed, the princess felt like weeping and smothering him with kisses. But she restrained herself because of the urgency of carrying out the witch's directions. She paced up and down the room until she stepped on a loose tile, which she raised and discovered a phial of ointment. With it she rubbed the prince's wounds, and no sooner had she touched each one with ointment than the wound disappeared completely. Overjoyed she called the king, who came in and saw his son sleeping peacefully, with the color back in his cheeks, and no trace of any of the wounds.

"Ask for whatever you like, doctor," said the king. "All the wealth in the kingdom is yours."

"I wish no money," replied the doctor, "Just give me the prince's shield bearing the family coat-of-arms, his standard, and his yellow vest that was rent and bloodied." Upon receiving the three items, she took her leave.

Three days later, the king's son was again out hunting. He passed the castle in the heart of the forest, but didn't deign to look up at the princess's window. She immediately picked up the book, leafed through it, and the prince had no choice but change into a canary. He flew into the room, and the princess turned him back into a man.

"Let me go," he said. "Isn't it enough to have pierced me with those pins of yours and caused me so much agony?" The prince, in truth, no longer loved the girl, blaming her for his misfortune.

On the verge of fainting, she exclaimed, "But I saved your life! I am the one who cured you!"

"That's not so," said the prince. "My life was saved by a foreign doctor who asked for no recompense except my coat-of-arms, my standard, and my bloodied vest!"

"Here are your coat-of-arms, your standard, and your vest! The doctor was none other than myself! The pins were the cruel doing of my stepmother!"

The prince gazed into her eyes, dumbfounded. Never had she looked so beautiful. He fell at her feet asking her forgiveness and declaring his deep gratitude and love.

That very evening he informed his father he was going to marry the maiden in the castle in the forest.

"You may marry only the daughter of a king or an emperor," replied his father.

"I shall marry the woman who saved my life."

So they made preparations for the wedding, inviting all the kings and queens in the vicinity. Also present was the princess's royal father, who had been informed of nothing. When the bride came out, he looked at her and exclaimed "My daughter!"

"What!" said the royal host. "My son's bride is your daughter? Why did she not tell us?"

"Because," explained the bride, "I no longer consider myself the daughter of a man who let my stepmother imprison me." And she pointed at the queen.

Learning of all his daughter's misfortune, the father was filled with pity for the girl and with loathing for his wicked wife. Nor did he wait until he was back home to have the woman seized. Thus the marriage was celebrated to the satisfaction and joy of all, with the exception of that wretch.

The Reader's Strategy of Naturalizing in Calvino's "The Canary Prince"

What kind of story is "The Canary Prince"? Most readers would fairly quickly recognize its type (or *genre*) as a fairy story. Once they are aware of the type, readers can see how their prior knowledge of literary conventions (that is, their literary repertoire) helps determine how they develop their initial responses to individual texts. For example, many gaps occur in "The Canary Prince," but once the story is recognized as a fairy tale, readers will probably not be troubled by these gaps, as they might well have been by those in "As a Wife Has a Cow." Filling in certain gaps in "The Canary Prince" will seem unnecessary or inappropriate—whether the prince and princess are really compatible, or how a book can magically turn a man into a canary—because most readers *expect* these kinds of unexplained situations in a fairy tale.

Some of our students have suggested that they do not ask probing questions, such as these, of "The Canary Prince" because they were introduced to fairy tales early in their lives, at a time when the distinction between imagination and reality was blurred. Further, because fairy tales are not frequently taught in English classes, most readers probably don't change the reading strategies from those they had as children, when they simply **naturalized** strange events by attributing them to magic. This is the way fairy stories *are,* adult readers say, without thinking of the well-established reading conventions. To **naturalize** a story is to find ways of normalizing or "making natural" strange or disturbing events. When readers naturalize a text, they find ways to explain away its stranger aspects, either by attributing them to a world of fantasy (as with fairy tales) or by seeing them as signs or symbols for something that is more readily understandable or more common in their experience.

There is, however, no "natural" reason for readers to accept unquestioningly the events that occur in fairy stories. They could, for example, read to analyze the *symbolism* of fairy tales. The stepmother seems always to stand for the intrusion of evil into a family. The prince, in contrast, seems always to stand for the reestablishment of order, justice, and love. Such a symbolic analysis can lead a reader to investigate the cultural norms and attitudes, particularly the gender definitions, of the times in which fairy tales were written.

You could read "The Canary Prince" from, say, a feminist perspective: the princess, after all, is the resourceful character of the story. Rather than being rescued by the handsome prince, she herself successfully escapes imprisonment on her own and goes on to save the prince.

We call this kind of reading a *strong reading,* a reading deliberately made according to a distinctive reader viewpoint, a viewpoint that is explicit and consistent throughout. Such strong readings of "The Canary Prince"—from a symbolic or feminist perspective—may appear to go "against the grain" or against the seemingly natural way of reading a fairy tale, which some readers might argue should just be read and enjoyed, not analyzed. But such readings do not go against the grain of the text itself as much as they go against the common notions of how a fairy tale should be read. It is the reader, whose literary repertoire has been developed by the social and educational contexts in which he or she previously read fairy stories, who determines how fairy stories (or any other kind of story) should be read. It is not the text itself but the *reader,* classifying texts into genres and responding to literary conventions, who determines how a text is read and what questions should be asked of a text.

One of our students, for example, told us an interesting story about his inability to naturalize film cartoons after learning to be conscious about his repertoire. During finals week, he and some of his friends decided to go to a cartoon festival for "a complete break from thinking." But much to his surprise, instead of sitting back and mindlessly enjoying the cartoons, this student found himself shocked by, and highly critical of, the sexism and racism of the cartoons. "How could I have missed all that before?" he asked. He had missed the racism and sexism before because he did not have the interpretive strategies to read the film "against the grain," to read in a more critical and informed way. He has become a strong reader because he can now question the dominant cultural ways of reading—even of reading cartoons—that were formerly part of his repertoire.

Calling Upon the Reader's Literary Repertoire: Kafka's "The Metamorphosis"[1]

Now, by contrast, let us consider a seemingly more "realistic" story. When readers encounter Kafka's "The Metamorphosis," their responses to Gregor Samsa's metamorphosis are usually very different from their responses to the Canary Prince's. Readers try to explain this difference by pointing to the realistic tone of the story; however, it also results from the different literary repertoires readers usually bring to Kafka's story. Gregor's metamorphosis can be seen as just as strange and magical as the Canary Prince's, but because the tone and setting of "The Metamorphosis" give the illusion of realism, many of our students report that they are unable to categorize this story into a conventional genre or type, such as a fairy tale or a science fiction story. In other words, they have nothing in their literary repertoires that uses the same conventions as Kafka's story. Had they been able to classify "The Metamorphosis," students might have naturalized Gregor's metamorphosis in the same way that they naturalized the Canary Prince's.

In fact, many readers find that "The Metamorphosis" challenges their general repertoire much as Stein's "As a Wife Has a Cow" challenges their literary repertoire. Everyone knows from experience that people do not (normally) turn into bugs. But "The Metamorphosis" is, after all, a piece of fiction, not a factual report in a newspaper. The aesthetic problem is not that readers need to believe that people can actually turn into bugs but rather that they need to figure out a way of explaining how Gregor did. Most readers probably don't have this problem with "The Canary Prince" because they easily accept that his metamorphosis was caused by magic. And one expects to find magic in fairy stories. No cause or causal agent, however, is suggested in Kafka's story. This absence of a causal agent is the most obvious *gap* in the text, and it helps to account for the large number of interpretations of it. In some ways, neither "The Metamorphosis" nor "As a Wife Has a Cow" "makes sense," but most readers probably have more strategies in their repertoires for making sense of "The Metamorphosis" than they have for making sense of "As a Wife Has a Cow." "The Metamorphosis" at least has as text strategies a plot, well-developed characters, and a clearly defined setting. And although most students cannot classify it as a

---

[1] See text of Kafka's "The Metamorphosis" on page 221.

certain type of story, the problems it raises are more familiar than those raised by "As a Wife Has a Cow."

You have no doubt been taught in English classes to assume that if a text does not make *literal* sense, it might make sense *symbolically* or *metaphorically* (see p. 383). As one of our students commented: "Kafka's story is more like something taught in English classes where you're expected to find deep meaning: it sounds realistic, but because it doesn't literally make sense, I feel I must read it metaphorically." If you choose to read Gregor's metamorphosis metaphorically, it becomes possible to develop a number of different interpretations of it. Readers can draw on their knowledge of the literary convention of symbolism and decide that Gregor's turning into a bug must *stand for* something. Or they may use their knowledge of psychology and hypothesize that perhaps Gregor is suffering from a delusion and only *thinks* he is a bug because everyone treats him so poorly. Or in another kind of psychological reading, they may use *personal experiences* of rejection to identify with Gregor because, although most readers have never thought they were a bug, most have at some time felt left out or misunderstood. With this sort of figurative rather than literal interpretation, ways can be found to explain the realistic tone of the story by arguing that Gregor thought and felt he was a bug.

Why do readers use such different strategies to interpret these two stories? Although knowledge of symbolism, psychology, and personal experiences of rejection might well be in your repertoires as you read "The Canary Prince," they would probably be activated only when you read "The Metamorphosis," mainly because the Prince's metamorphosis in the fairy tale can be naturalized without an elaborate symbolic analysis. After developing a psychological analysis of "The Metamorphosis" and comparing it to "The Canary Prince," one student wrote:

> Such a psychological analysis as this can be applied to a work that is *perceived to contain* a possible psychological interpretation. To attempt such an analysis on a fairy tale like "The Canary Prince" would be sheer folly. It may seem like a contradiction to say, on the one hand, that readers can choose to read a text as they want while, on the other hand, forbidding them to analyze a fairy tale psychologically. This paradox is cleared up when I recognized "The Canary Prince" as a fairy tale. I did not expect to find symbolism or deep psychological meaning in it, hence I did not find it. If the work in question could be perceived as something other than a fairy tale, however, then a new set of expectations might conceivably warrant a psychological analysis.

Thus the way these two metamorphoses are read and interpreted depends in large part on how the readers' cultural and educational experiences—at home and in English classes, and also those provided by the wider culture—have influenced their reading strategies. If a reader is unfamiliar with fairy tales and magic, he or she might also have constructed an elaborate psychological analysis of "The Canary Prince," because people, after all, don't turn into birds any more than they turn into bugs.

The Reader's General Repertoire

In the general introduction we introduced the notion of **ideology** (p. 6) as a very large determining force behind the repertoires readers bring to their reading. Just as fiction writers define themselves against society's dominant patterns of belief and values, so all readers are influenced by their ideological positions.

Ideological interpretation is therefore extremely useful if readers are to understand both the production of a work by its author and the production of their own readings of that work. It is often very difficult for readers to articulate their own repertoire—the ideas and attitudes they take for granted about religion, politics, lifestyles, the value of the individual, and the like. Yet this is exactly where the ideology of the society surfaces in the individual. Such underlying attitudes of readers, developed from their general repertoires, powerfully influence their readings of texts. Now we want to point out how your general repertoire influences your responses to the two following literary works.

As you read "A & P" (p. 55) by John Updike, ask yourself the following questions:

1. What attitudes—implicit as well as explicit—do you find expressed about relations between men and women?
2. With such a familiar setting as a supermarket, how can significant issues about sexual roles and gender-related behavior be addressed?
3. What degree of sympathy do you have for the narrator? For the young girls?
4. What role do you think your gender and race play in the way you respond to this story?

As you read "SeeMotherMotherIsVeryNice" (p. 62) by Toni Morrison, ask yourself:

1. What attitudes do you find about the relations between black men and women and between black and white society?
2. How does your gender and race affect the way you respond to this story?

Then ask yourself what cultural attitudes in your general repertoire these stories confirm or challenge.

1. Are your notions about the nature of sex roles and sexual display in public places confirmed or challenged by "A & P"?
2. Are your notions about success in our society confirmed by "See MotherMotherIsVeryNice"?

The titles of both these stories make them sound as if they should be pleasant, ordinary, and enjoyable stories: Updike's story promises to be about that very ordinary institution, the supermarket; Morrison's promises to be about a "very nice" mother. The strange title of Morrison's story, an unusual text strategy, may make you curious about or suspicious of the story before you begin reading it. What does the absence of spaces between the words signify to you? Do you sense energy in the line? Frenzy? A chantlike quality? Do you find these stories pleasant and enjoyable to read? Why or why not? With such questions in mind, we suggest you first read the Updike text.

JOHN UPDIKE (b. 1932)

A & P

In walks these three girls in nothing but bathing suits. I'm in the third checkout slot, with my back to the door, so I don't see them until they're over by the bread. The one that caught my eye first was the one in the plaid green two-piece. She was a chunky kid, with a good tan and a sweet broad soft-looking can with those two crescents of white just under it, where the sun never seems to hit, at the top of the backs of her legs. I stood there with my hand on a box of HiHo crackers trying to remember if I rang it up or not. I ring it up again and the customer starts giving me hell. She's one of those cash-register-watchers, a witch about fifty with rouge on her cheekbones and no eyebrows, and I know it made her day to trip me up. She'd been watching cash registers for fifty years and probably never seen a mistake before.

By the time I got her feathers smoothed and her goodies into a bag—she gives me a little snort in passing, if she'd been born at the right time they would have burned her over in Salem—by the time I get her on her way the girls had circled around the bread and were coming back, without a pushcart, back my way along the counters, in the aisle between the checkouts and the Special bins. They didn't even have shoes on. There was this chunky one, with the two-piece—it was bright green and the seams on the bra were still sharp and her belly was still pretty pale so I guessed she just got it (the suit)—there was this one, with one of those chubby berry-faces, the lips all bunched together under her nose, this one, and a tall one, with black hair that hadn't quite frizzed right, and one of these sunburns right across under the eyes, and a chin that was too long—you know, the kind of girl other girls think is very "striking" and "attractive" but never quite makes it, as they very well know, which is why they like her so much—and then the third one, that wasn't quite so tall. She was the queen. She kind of led them, the other two peeking around and making their shoulders round. She didn't look around, not this queen, she just walked straight on slowly, on these long white primadonna legs. She came down a little hard on her heels, as if she didn't walk in bare feet that much, putting down her heels and then letting the weight move along to her toes as if she was testing the floor with every step, putting a little deliberate extra action into it. You never know for sure how girls' minds work (do you really think it's a mind in there or just a little buzz like a bee in a glass jar?) but you got the idea she had talked the other two into coming in here with her, and now she was showing them how to do it, walk slow and hold yourself straight.

She had on a kind of dirty-pink—beige maybe, I don't know—bathing suit with a little nubble all over it and, what got me, the straps were down. They were off her shoulders looped loose around the cool tops of her arms, and I guess as a result the suit had slipped a little on her, so all around the top of the cloth there was this shining rim. If it hadn't been there you wouldn't have known there could have been anything whiter than those shoulders. With the straps pushed off, there was nothing between the top of the suit and the top of her head except just *her,* this clean bare plane of the top of her chest down from the shoulder bones like a dented sheet of metal tilted in the light. I mean, it was more than pretty.

She had a sort of oaky hair that sun and salt had bleached, done up in a bun that was unravelling, and a kind of prim face. Walking into the A & P with your straps down, I suppose it's the only kind of face you *can* have. She held her head so high her neck, coming up out of those white shoulders, looked kind of stretched, but I didn't mind. The longer her neck was, the more of her there was.

She must have felt in the corner of her eye me and over my shoulder Stokesie in the second slot watching, but she didn't tip. Not this queen. She kept her eyes moving across the racks, and stopped, and turned so slow it made my stomach rub the inside of my apron, and buzzed to the other two, who kind of huddled against her for relief, and then they all three of them went up the cat-and-dog-food-breakfast-cereal-macaroni-rice-raisins-seasonings-spreads-spaghetti-soft-drinks-crackers-and-cookies aisle. From the third slot I look straight up this aisle to the meat counter, and I watched them all the way. The fat one with the tan sort of fumbled with the cookies, but on second thought she put the package back. The sheep pushing their carts down the aisle—the girls were walking against the usual traffic (not that we have one-way signs or anything)—were pretty hilarious. You could see them, when Queenie's white shoulders dawned on them, kind of jerk, or hop, or hiccup, but their eyes snapped back to their own baskets and on they pushed. I bet you could set off dynamite in an A & P and the people would by and large keep reaching and checking oatmeal off their lists and muttering "Let me see, there was a third thing, began with A, asparagus, no, ah, yes, applesauce!" or whatever it is they do mutter. But there was no doubt, this jiggled them. A few house-slaves in pin curlers even looked around after pushing their carts past to make sure what they had seen was correct.

You know, it's one thing to have a girl in a bathing suit down on the beach, where what with the glare nobody can look at each other much anyway, and another thing in the cool of the A & P, under the fluorescent lights, against all those stacked packages, with her feet paddling along naked over our checker-board green-and-cream rubber-tile floor.

"Oh Daddy," Stokesie said beside me. "I feel so faint."

"Darling," I said. "Hold me tight." Stokesie's married, with two babies chalked up on his fuselage already, but as far as I can tell that's the only difference. He's twenty-two, and I was nineteen this April.

"Is it done?" he asks, the responsible married man finding his voice. I forgot to say he thinks he's going to be manager some sunny day, maybe in 1990 when it's called the Great Alexandrov and Petrooshki Tea Company or something.

What he meant was, our town is five miles from a beach, with a big summer colony out on the Point, but we're right in the middle of town, and the women generally put on a shirt or shorts or something before they get out of the car into the street. And anyway these are usually women with six children and varicose veins mapping their legs and nobody, including them, could care less. As I say, we're right in the middle of town, and if you stand at our front doors you can see two banks and the Congregational church and the newspaper store and three real-estate offices and about twenty-seven old freeloaders tearing up Central Street because the sewer broke again. It's not as if we're on the Cape; we're north of Boston and there's people in this town haven't seen the ocean for twenty years.

The girls had reached the meat counter and were asking McMahon something. He pointed, they pointed, and they shuffled out of sight behind a pyramid of Diet Delight peaches. All that was left for us to see was old McMahon patting his mouth and looking after them sizing up their joints. Poor kids, I began to feel sorry for them, they couldn't help it.

Now here comes the sad part of the story, at least my family says it's sad, but I don't think it's so sad myself. The store's pretty empty, it being Thursday afternoon, so there was nothing much to do except lean on the register and wait for the girls to show up again. The whole store was like a pinball machine and I didn't know which tunnel they'd come out of. After a while they come around out of the far aisle, around the light bulbs, records at discount of the Caribbean Six or Tony Martin Sings or some such gunk you wonder they waste the wax on, six-packs of candy bars, and plastic toys done up in cellophane that fall apart when a kid looks at them anyway. Around they come, Queenie still leading the way, and holding a little gray jar in her hand. Slots Three through Seven are unmanned and I could see her wondering between Stokes and me, but Stokesie with his usual luck draws an old party in baggy gray pants who stumbles up with four giant cans of pineapple juice (what do these bums *do* with all that pineapple juice? I've often asked myself) so the girls come to me. Queenie puts down the jar and I take it into my fingers icy cold. Kingfish Fancy Herring Snacks in Pure Sour Cream: 49¢. Now her hands are empty, not a ring or a bracelet, bare as God made them, and I wonder where the money's coming from. Still with that prim look she lifts a folded dollar bill out of the hollow at the center of her nubbled pink top. The jar went heavy in my hand. Really, I thought that was so cute.

Then everybody's luck begins to run out. Lengel comes in from haggling with a truck full of cabbages on the lot and is about to scuttle into that door marked MAN-AGER behind which he hides all day when the girls touch his eye. Lengel's pretty dreary, teaches Sunday school and the rest, but he doesn't miss much. He comes over and says, "Girls, this isn't the beach."

Queenie blushes, though maybe it's just a brush of sunburn I was noticing for the first time, now that she was so close. "My mother asked me to pick up a jar of herring snacks." Her voice kind of startled me, the way voices do when you see the people first, coming out so flat and dumb yet kind of tony, too, the way it ticked over "pick up" and "snacks." All of a sudden I slid right down her voice into her living room. Her father and the other men were standing around in ice-cream coats and bow ties and the women were in sandals picking up herring snacks on toothpicks off a big glass plate and they were all holding drinks the color of water with olives and sprigs of mint in them. When my parents have somebody over they get lemonade and if it's a real racy affair Schlitz in tall glasses with "They'll Do It Every Time" cartoons stencilled on.

"That's all right," Lengel said. "But this isn't the beach." His repeating this struck me as funny, as if it had just occurred to him, and he had been thinking all these years the A & P was a great big dune and he was the head lifeguard. He didn't like my smiling—as I say he doesn't miss much—but he concentrates on giving the girls that sad Sunday-school-superintendent stare.

Queenie's blush is no sunburn now, and the plump one in plaid, that I liked better from the back—a really sweet can—pipes up, "We weren't doing any shopping. We just came in for the one thing."

"That makes no difference," Lengel tells her, and I could see from the way his eyes went that he hadn't noticed she was wearing a two-piece before. "We want you decently dressed when you come here."

"We *are* decent," Queenie says suddenly, her lower lip pushing, getting sore now that she remembers her place, a place from which the crowd that runs the A & P must look pretty crummy. Fancy Herring Snacks flashed in her very blue eyes.

"Girls, I don't want to argue with you. After this come in here with your shoulders covered. It's our policy." He turns his back. That's policy for you. Policy is what the kingpins want. What the others want is juvenile delinquency.

All this while, the customers had been showing up with their carts but, you know, sheep, seeing a scene, they had all bunched up on Stokesie, who shook open a paper bag as gently as peeling a peach, not wanting to miss a word. I could feel in the silence everybody getting nervous, most of all Lengel, who asks me, "Sammy, have you rung up their purchase?"

I thought and said "No" but it wasn't about that I was thinking. I go through the punches, 4, 9, GROC, TOT—it's more complicated than you think, and after you do it often enough, it begins to make a little song, that you hear words to, in my case "Hello *(bing)* there, you *(gung)* hap-py *pee*-pul *(splat)*!"—the *splat* being the drawer flying out. I uncrease the bill, tenderly as you may imagine, it just having come from between the two smoothest scoops of vanilla I had ever known there were, and pass a half and a penny into her narrow pink palm, and nestle the herrings in a bag and twist its neck and hand it over, all the time thinking.

The girls, and who'd blame them, are in a hurry to get out, so I say "I quit" to Lengel quick enough for them to hear, hoping they'll stop and watch me, their unsuspected hero. They keep right on going, into the electric eye; the door flies open and they flicker across the lot to their car, Queenie and Plaid and Big Tall Goony-Goony (not that as raw material she was so bad), leaving me with Lengel and a kink in his eyebrow.

"Did you say something, Sammy?"

"I said I quit."

"I thought you did."

"You didn't have to embarrass them."

"It was they who were embarrassing us."

I started to say something that came out "Fiddle-de-do." It's a saying of my grandmother's, and I know she would have been pleased.

"I don't think you know what you're saying," Lengel said.

"I know you don't," I said. "But I do." I pull the bow at the back of my apron and start shrugging it off my shoulders. A couple of customers that had been heading for my slot begin to knock against each other, like scared pigs in a chute.

Lengel sighs and begins to look very patient and old and gray. He's been a friend of my parents for years. "Sammy, you don't want to do this to your Mom and Dad," he tells me. It's true, I don't. But it seems to me that once you begin a gesture it's fatal not to go through with it. I fold the apron, "Sammy" stitched in red on the pocket, and put it on the counter, and drop the bow tie on top of it. The bow tie is theirs, if you've ever wondered. "You'll feel this for the rest of your life," Lengel says, and I know that's true, too, but remembering how he made that pretty girl blush makes me so scrunchy inside I punch the No Sale tab and the machine whirs "pee-pul" and the drawer splats out. One advantage to this scene taking place in summer, I can follow this up with a clean exit, there's no fumbling around getting your coat and galoshes, I just saunter into the electric eye in my white shirt that my mother ironed the night before, and the door heaves itself open, and outside the sunshine is skating around on the asphalt.

I look around for my girls, but they're gone, of course. There wasn't anybody but some young married screaming with children about some candy they didn't get by the door of a powder-blue Falcon station wagon. Looking back in the big windows, over the bags of peat moss and aluminum lawn furniture stacked on the pavement, I could see Lengel in my place in the slot, checking the sheep through. His face was dark gray and his back stiff, as if he's just had an injection of iron, and my stomach kind of fell as I felt how hard the world was going to be to me hereafter.

Creating Themes: The Divided Self in Updike's "A & P"

One of the usual ways to naturalize texts is to create what are conventionally called "themes." A *theme* is, by convention, said to be an idea or set of ideas that a reader or critic perceives a story to be about, such as appearance and reality, rebirth, a quest, good and evil, or the dark night of the soul. In practice, most themes are, in fact, produced as much by the reader as by the text. Readers' general repertoires of values and beliefs help to determine what they decide a story is "about" thematically. In short, the themes you supposedly discover in "A & P" will depend, in large part, on your general repertoire of assumptions about the events it deals with. These assumptions will, for instance, influence the particular information you pick up about the narrator, the people with whom he works, and the girls who come to the store. Whether you like the story or not may depend in large part on how its repertoire matches your own. For example, as you were reading "A & P," did you find yourself becoming indignant about or uncomfortable with the actions that occur? If so, why? What values do you have that lead you to react negatively or positively?

This story, you might argue, suggests that the seemingly serene surface of life is very fragile and that relations between the sexes always have the potential to evoke primitive reactions. You might argue that Sammy seems to be both lascivious and chivalrous. He shares some of the sexist attitudes of his superiors in the store; when the girls first come in, he sees them as inviting sensual objects: "this chunky one . . . this one . . . a tall one" and "the queen . . . on these long white prima-donna legs." By deprecating how girls' minds work ("do you really think it's a mind in there or just a little buzz like a bee in a glass jar?"), he shares in male sexist stereotypes. Yet later he impulsively sides with the girls against the older women and the store manager. If you focus on these two aspects of Sammy's behavior, you may argue as one of our students did:

> The story suggests that no person is a single self but rather that some people—and in particular Sammy whose thoughts we have access to—are composed of many contradictory selves. While one of these selves may be dominant in one situation, other sides can unexpectedly surface with a change in perspective—in this story, with the realization that one must make serious choices, even in a supermarket.

The inability to distinguish between different moral views or aspects of the self is a common concern of much contemporary fiction. Sammy, the narrator, undergoes great changes in the incident in the A & P. You know that on some level you act one way with your parents, another way in class, and still other ways with your friends. If you saw yourself in these three different contexts, could you say which one is the "real" you? Which is the "real" Sammy—the one contemplating the "scoops of vanilla" or the one who quits his job? Probably your initial response would be that they are both a part of him. Yet despite understanding that you can be different people in different contexts, the commonsensical notion of a *unified self* still prevails because it is a powerful part of the way our culture and language define people.

You will therefore notice the two sides of Sammy's behavior only if your general repertoire allows you to admit that people are not always unified and consistent. A number of our students, for example, do not see Sammy as contradictory but rather pay attention to only one side of his behavior. As one female student commented, "I hated Sammy. He's sexist. All he does is find ways to degrade women. I was glad he got fired. What a creep!" Nowhere in her response statement did this student acknowledge that Sammy got fired because he defended the girls. When asked what she thought was the theme of "A & P," this student responded: " 'A & P' presents us with the universal theme that men are sexist (which we all know), but there's a twist here because in this story Sammy gets punished in the end." One of the men in our class commented, "Poor Sammy. He's the kind of guy you can really feel sorry for. He tried to be nice to those girls and what happens? He loses his job, and those stuck-up girls don't even know he exists. He was somewhat stupid, though, to even bother trying to defend them." This student, in contrast to the woman quoted above, doesn't seem to believe that Sammy has any sexist attitudes. He states the theme of the story from a male position: "Attractive and aloof girls can often be big trouble. They can cause a guy to make a fool out of himself."

We have suggested now three possible themes for "A & P"—that all people are contradictory, that all men are sexist, and that attractive women can turn men into fools. Although these themes are very different from one another, how can we say that any one of them is more "correct" than any other? Although readers generally think of themes as something *in* stories, these three student responses indicate that readers *produce* themes as their general repertoires interact with the general repertoire of the text.

How do you react to Sammy's behavior? Whether you are disturbed by it or not, whether you feel that either the girls' or Lengel's attitudes are reprehensible, depends on your beliefs about the nature of sex roles, love relationships, and the self. Even if you have never thought deeply about any of these subjects, you still have ideas about them formed by the culture of which you are a part. When Sammy thinks that the girl has "the two smoothest scoops of vanilla I had ever known," are you offended or amused? Or do you somehow feel *both* reactions, showing that you too can be ambivalent or divided within yourself?

When you write your own responses to this story, ask yourself not only what your ideas are on these subjects but also where these ideas come from. While some of them are formed by the literature you read, most are formed in larger cultural contexts. Would you wear a bathing suit into a grocery store? Why or why not? Reading and responding to this story should affect you in at least two ways. You should realize, first, that your general repertoire influences the ways in which you respond to any text. And you should realize, second, that reading texts that force you to analyze your general repertoire can help you become much more self-conscious about your values, beliefs, and attitudes. Once you are aware of your belief system, you can consider maintaining or altering it.

Now we will examine how readers' and texts' repertoires interact with other kinds of current issues—the issues of race relations, poverty, and success in "SeeMotherMotherIsVeryNice."

TONI MORRISON (b. 1931)

SeeMotherMotherIsVeryNice

The easiest thing to do would be to build a case out of her foot. That is what she herself did. But to find out the truth about how dreams die, one should never take the word of the dreamer. The end of her lovely beginning was probably the cavity in one of her front teeth. She preferred, however, to think always of her foot. Although she was the ninth of eleven children and lived on a ridge of red Alabama clay seven miles from the nearest road, the complete indifference with which a rusty nail was met when it punched clear through her foot during her second year of life saved Pauline Williams from total anonymity. The wound left her with a crooked, archless foot that flopped when she walked—not a limp that would have eventually twisted her spine, but a way of lifting the bad foot as though she were extracting it from little whirlpools that threatened to pull it under. Slight as it was, this deformity explained for her many things that would have been otherwise incomprehensible: why she alone of all the children had no nickname; why there were no funny jokes and anecdotes about funny things she had done; why no one ever remarked on her food preferences—no saving of the wing or neck for her—no cooking of the peas in a separate pot without rice because she did not like rice; why nobody teased her; why she never felt at home anywhere, or that she belonged anyplace. Her general feeling of separateness and unworthiness she blamed on her foot. Restricted, as a child, to this cocoon of her family's spinning, she cultivated quiet and private pleasures. She liked, most of all, to arrange things. To line things up in rows—jars on shelves at canning, peach pits on the step, sticks, stones, leaves—and the members of her family let these arrangements be. When by some accident somebody scattered her rows, they always stopped to retrieve them for her, and she was never angry, for it gave her a chance to rearrange them again. Whatever portable plurality she found, she organized into neat lines, according to their size, shape, or gradations of color. Just as she would never align a pine needle with the leaf of a cottonwood tree, she would never put the jars of tomatoes next to the green beans. During all of her four years of going to school, she was enchanted by numbers and depressed by words. She missed— without knowing what she missed—paints and crayons.

Near the beginning of World War I, the Williamses discovered, from returning neighbors and kin, the possibility of living better in another place. In shifts, lots, batches, mixed in with other families, they migrated, in six months and four journeys, to Kentucky, where there were mines and millwork.

"When all us left from down home and was waiting down by the depot for the truck, it was nighttime. June bugs was shooting everywhere. They lighted up a tree leaf, and I seen a streak of green every now and again. That was the last time I seen real june bugs. These things up here ain't june bugs. They's something else. Folks here call them fireflies. Down home they was different. But I recollect that streak of green. I recollect it well."

In Kentucky they lived in a real town, ten to fifteen houses on a single street, with water piped right into the kitchen. Ada and Fowler Williams found a five-room frame house for their family. The yard was bounded by a once-white fence against which Pauline's mother planted flowers and within which they kept a few chickens. Some of her brothers joined the Army, one sister died, and two got married, increasing the living space and giving the entire Kentucky venture a feel of luxury. The relocation was especially comfortable to Pauline, who was old enough to leave school. Mrs. Williams got a job cleaning and cooking for a white minister on the other side of town, and Pauline, now the oldest girl at home, took over the care of the house. She kept the fence in repair, pulling the pointed stakes erect, securing them with bits of wire, collected eggs, swept, cooked, washed, and minded the two younger children—a pair of twins called Chicken and Pie, who were still in school. She was not only good at housekeeping, she enjoyed it. After her parents left for work and the other children were at school or in mines, the house was quiet. The stillness and isolation both calmed and energized her. She could arrange and clean without interruption until two o'clock, when Chicken and Pie came home.

When the war ended and the twins were ten years old, they too left school to work. Pauline was fifteen, still keeping house, but with less enthusiasm. Fantasies about men and love and touching were drawing her mind and hands away from her work. Changes in weather began to affect her, as did certain sights and sounds. These feelings translated themselves to her in extreme melancholy. She thought of the death of newborn things, lonely roads, and strangers who appear out of nowhere simply to hold one's hand, woods in which the sun was always setting. In church especially did these dreams grow. The songs caressed her, and while she tried to hold her mind on the wages of sin, her body trembled for redemption, salvation, a mysterious rebirth that would simply happen, with no effort on her part. In none of her fantasies was she ever aggressive; she was usually idling by the riverbank, or gathering berries in a field when a someone appeared, with gentle and penetrating eyes, who—with no exchange of words—understood; and before whose glance her foot straightened and her eyes dropped. The someone had no face, no form, no voice, no odor. He was a simple Presence, an all-embracing tenderness with strength and a promise of rest. It did not matter that she had no idea of what to do or say to the Presence—after the wordless knowing and the soundless touching, her dreams disintegrated. But the Presence would know what to do. She had only to lay her head on his chest and he would lead her away to the sea, to the city, to the woods . . . forever.

There was a woman named Ivy who seemed to hold in her mouth all of the sounds of Pauline's soul. Standing a little apart from the choir, Ivy sang the dark sweetness that Pauline could not name; she sang the death-defying death that Pauline yearned for; she sang of the Stranger who *knew* . . .

Precious Lord take my hand
Lead me on, let me stand
I am tired, I am weak, I am worn.
Through the storms, through the night

Lead me on to the light
Take my hand, precious Lord, lead me on.

When my way grows drear
Precious Lord linger near,
When my life is almost gone
Hear my cry hear my call
Hold my hand lest I fall
Take my hand, precious Lord, lead me on.

Thus it was that when the Stranger, the someone, did appear out of nowhere, Pauline was grateful but not surprised.

He came, strutting right out of a Kentucky sun on the hottest day of the year. He came big, he came strong, he came with yellow eyes, flaring nostrils, and he came with his own music.

Pauline was leaning idly on the fence, her arms resting on the crossrail between the pickets. She had just put down some biscuit dough and was cleaning the flour from under her nails. Behind her at some distance she heard whistling. One of these rapid, high-note riffs that black boys make up as they go while sweeping, shoveling, or just walking along. A kind of city-street music where laughter belies anxiety, and joy is as short and straight as the blade of a pocketknife. She listened carefully to the music and let it pull her lips into a smile. The whistling got louder, and still she did not turn around, for she wanted it to last. While smiling to herself and holding fast to the break in somber thoughts, she felt something tickling her foot. She laughed aloud and turned to see. The whistler was bending down tickling her broken foot and kissing her leg. She could not stop her laughter—not until he looked up at her and she saw the Kentucky sun drenching the yellow, heavy-lidded eyes of Cholly Breedlove.

"When I first seed Cholly, I want you to know it was like all the bits of color from that time down home when all us chil'ren went berry picking after a funeral and I put some in the pocket of my Sunday dress, and they mashed up and stained my hips. My whole dress was messed with purple, and it never did wash out. Not the dress nor me. I could feel that purple deep inside me. And that lemonade Mama used to make when Pap came in out the fields. It be cool and yellowish, with seeds floating near the bottom. And that streak of green them june bugs made on the trees the night we left from down home. All of them colors was in me. Just sitting there. So when Cholly come up and tickled my foot, it was like them berries, that lemonade, them streaks of green the june bugs made, all come together. Cholly was thin then, with real light eyes. He used to whistle, and when I heerd him, shivers come on my skin."

Pauline and Cholly loved each other. He seemed to relish her company and even to enjoy her country ways and lack of knowledge about city things. He talked with her about her foot and asked, when they walked through the town or in the fields, if she were tired. Instead of ignoring her infirmity, pretending it was not there, he made it seem like something special and endearing. For the first time Pauline felt that her bad foot was an asset.

And he did touch her, firmly but gently, just as she had dreamed. But minus the gloom of setting suns and lonely riverbanks. She was secure and grateful; he was kind and lively. She had not known there was so much laughter in the world.

They agreed to marry and go 'way up north, where Cholly said steel mills were begging for workers. Young, loving, and full of energy, they came to Lorain, Ohio. Cholly found work in the steel mills right away, and Pauline started keeping house.

And then she lost her front tooth. But there must have been a speck, a brown speck easily mistaken for food but which did not leave, which sat on the enamel for months, and grew, until it cut into the surface and then to the brown putty underneath, finally eating away to the root, but avoiding the nerves, so its presence was not noticeable or uncomfortable. Then the weakened roots, having grown accustomed to the poison, responded one day to severe pressure, and the tooth fell free, leaving a ragged stump behind. But even before the little brown speck, there must have been the conditions, the setting that would allow it to exist in the first place.

In that young and growing Ohio town whose side streets, even, were paved with concrete, which sat on the edge of a calm blue lake, which boasted an affinity with Oberlin, the underground railroad station, just thirteen miles away, this melting pot on the lip of America facing the cold but receptive Canada—What could go wrong?

"Me and Cholly was getting along good then. We come up north; supposed to be more jobs and all. We moved into two rooms up over a furniture store, and I set about housekeeping. Cholly was working at the steel plant, and everything was looking good. I don't know what all happened. Everything changed. It was hard to get to know folks up here, and I missed my people. I weren't used to so much white folks. The ones I seed before was something hateful, but they didn't come around too much. I mean, we didn't have too much truck with them. Just now and then in the fields, or at the commissary. But they wa'nt all over us. Up north they was everywhere—next door, downstairs, all over the streets—and colored folks few and far between. Northern colored folk was different too. Dicty-like. No better than whites for meanness. They could make you feel just as no-count, 'cept I didn't expect it from them. That was the lonesomest time of my life. I 'member looking out them front windows just waiting for Cholly to come home at three o'clock. I didn't even have a cat to talk to."

In her loneliness, she turned to her husband for reassurance, entertainment, for things to fill the vacant places. Housework was not enough; there were only two rooms, and no yard to keep or move about in. The women in the town wore high-heeled shoes, and when Pauline tried to wear them, they aggravated her shuffle into a pronounced limp. Cholly was kindness still, but began to resist her total dependence on him. They were beginning to have less and less to say to each other. He had no problem finding other people and other things to occupy him—men were always climbing the stairs asking for him, and he was happy to accompany them, leaving her alone.

Pauline felt uncomfortable with the few black women she met. They were amused by her because she did not straighten her hair. When she tried to make up her face as they did, it came off rather badly. Their goading glances and private

snickers at her way of talking (saying "chil'ren") and dressing developed in her a desire for new clothes. When Cholly began to quarrel about the money she wanted, she
decided to go to work. Taking jobs as a dayworker helped with the clothes, and even
a few things for the apartment, but it did not help with Cholly. He was not pleased
with her purchases and began to tell her so. Their marriage was shredded with quar-
rels. She was still no more than a girl, and still waiting for that plateau of happiness,
that hand of a precious Lord who, when her way grew drear, would always linger
near. Only, now she had a clearer idea of what drear meant. Money became the
focus of all their discussions, hers for clothes, his for drink. The sad thing was that
Pauline did not really care for clothes and makeup. She merely wanted other women
to cast favorable glances her way.

After several months of doing daywork, she took a steady job in the home of a
family of slender means and nervous, pretentious ways.

*"Cholly commenced to getting meaner and meaner and wanted to fight me all of
the time. I give him as good as I got. Had to. Look like working for that woman and
fighting Cholly was all I did. Tiresome. But I holt on to my jobs, even though working
for that woman was more than a notion. It wasn't so much her meanness as just sim-
pleminded. Her whole family was. Couldn't get along with one another worth nothing. You'd think with a pretty house like that and all the money they could holt on to,
they would enjoy one another. She haul off and cry over the leastest thing. If one of
her friends cut her short on the telephone, she'd go to crying. She should of been glad
she had a telephone. I ain't got one yet. I recollect oncet how her baby brother who she
put through dentistry school didn't invite them to some big party he throwed. They
was a big to-do about that. Everybody stayed on the telephone for days. Fussing and
carrying on. She asked me 'Pauline, what would you do if your own brother had a
party and didn't invite you?' I said ifn I really wanted to go to that party, I reckoned
I'd go anyhow. Never mind what he want. She just sucked her teeth a little and made
out like what I said was dumb. All the while I was thinking how dumb she was. Whoever told her that her brother was her friend? Folks can't like folks just 'cause they has
the same mama. I tried to like that woman myself. She was good about giving me
stuff, but I just couldn't like her. Soon as I worked up a good feeling on her account,
she'd do something ignorant and start in to telling me how to clean and do. If I left her
on her own, she'd drown in dirt. I didn't have to pick up after Chicken and Pie the
way I had to pick up after them. None of them knew so much as how to wipe their
behinds. I know, 'cause I did the washing. And couldn't pee proper to save their lives.
Her husband ain't hit the bowl yet. Nasty white folks is about the nastiest things they
is. But I would have stayed on 'cepting for Cholly come over by where I was working
and cut up so. He come there drunk wanting some money. When that white woman
see him, she turned red. She tried to act strong-like, but she was scared bad. Anyway,
she told Cholly to get out or she would call the police. He cussed her and started pulling on me. I would of gone upside his head, but I don't want no dealings with the
police. So I taken my things and left. I tried to get back, but she didn't want me no
more if I was going to stay with Cholly. She said she would let me stay if I left him. I*

thought about that. But later on it didn't seem none too bright for a black woman to leave a black man for a white woman. She didn't never give me the eleven dollars she owed me, neither. That hurt bad. The gas man had cut the gas off, and I couldn't cook none. I really begged that woman for my money. I went to see her. She was mad as a wet hen. Kept on telling me I owed her for uniforms and some old broken-down bed she give me. I didn't know if I owed her or not, but I needed my money. She wouldn't let up none, neither, even when I give her my word Cholly wouldn't come back there no more. Then I got so desperate I asked her if she would loan it to me. She was quiet for a spell, and then she told me I shouldn't let a man take advantage over me. That I should have more respect, and it was my husband's duty to pay the bills, and if he couldn't, I should leave and get alimony. All such simple stuff. What was he gone give me alimony on? I seen she didn't understand that all I needed from her was my eleven dollars to pay the gas man so I could cook. She couldn't get that one thing through her thick head. 'Are you going to leave him, Pauline?' she kept on saying. I thought she'd give me my money if I said I would, so I said 'Yes, ma'am.' 'All right,' she said. 'You leave him, and then come back to work, and we'll let bygones be bygones.' 'Can I have my money today?' I said. 'No' she said. 'Only when you leave him. I'm only thinking of you and your future. What good is he, Pauline, what good is he to you?' How you going to answer a woman like that, who don't know what good a man is, and say out of one side of her mouth she's thinking of your future but won't give you your own money so you can buy something besides baloney to eat? So I said, 'No good, ma'am. He ain't no good to me. But just the same, I think I'd best stay on.' She got up, and I left. When I got outside, I felt pains in my crotch, I had held my legs together so tight trying to make that woman understand. But I reckon now she couldn't understand. She married a man with a slash in his face instead of a mouth. So how could she understand?"

One winter, Pauline discovered she was pregnant. When she told Cholly, he surprised her by being pleased. He began to drink less and come home more often. They eased back into a relationship more like the early days of their marriage, when he asked if she was tired or wanted him to bring her something from the store. In this state of ease, Pauline stopped doing daywork and returned to her own housekeeping. But the loneliness in those two rooms had not gone away. When the winter sun hit the peeling green paint of the kitchen chairs, when the smoked hocks were boiling in the pot, when all she could hear was the truck delivering furniture downstairs, she thought about back home, about how she had been all alone most of the time then too, but that this lonesomeness was different. Then she stopped staring at the green chairs, at the delivery truck; she went to the movies instead. There in the dark her memory was refreshed, and she succumbed to her earlier dreams. Along with the idea of romantic love, she was introduced to another—physical beauty. Probably the most destructive ideas in the history of human thought. Both originated in envy, thrived in insecurity, and ended in disillusion. In equating physical beauty with virtue, she stripped her mind, bound it, and collected self-contempt by the heap. She forgot lust and simple caring for. She regarded love as possessive mating, and romance as the goal of the spirit. It would be for her a wellspring from which she would draw the most destructive emotions, deceiving the lover and seeking to imprison the beloved, curtailing freedom in every way.

She was never able, after her education in the movies, to look at a face and not assign it some category in the scale of absolute beauty, and the scale was one she absorbed in full from the silver screen. There at last were the darkened woods, the lonely roads, the riverbanks, the gentle, knowing eyes. There the flawed became whole, the blind sighted, and the lame and halt threw away their crutches. There death was dead, and people made every gesture in a cloud of music. There the black-and-white images came together, making a magnificent whole—all projected through the ray of light from above and behind.

It was really a simple pleasure, but she learned all there was to love and all there was to hate.

"The onliest time I be happy seem like was when I was in the picture show. Every time I got, I went. I'd go early, before the show started. They'd cut off the lights, and everything be black. Then the screen would light up, and I'd move right on in them pictures. White men taking such good care of they women, and they all dressed up in big clean houses with the bathtubs right in the same room with the toilet. Them pictures gave me a lot of pleasure, but it made coming home hard, and looking at Cholly hard. I don't know. I 'member one time I went to see Clark Gable and Jean Harlow. I fixed my hair up like I'd seen hers on a magazine. A part on the side, with one little curl on my forehead. It looked just like her. Well, almost just like. Anyway, I sat in that show with my hair done up that way and had a good time. I thought I'd see it through to the end again, and I got up to get me some candy. I was sitting back in my seat, and I taken a big bite of that candy, and it pulled a tooth right out of my mouth. I could of cried. I had good teeth, not a rotten one in my head. I don't believe I ever did get over that. There I was, five months pregnant, trying to look like Jean Harlow, and a front tooth gone. Everything went then. Look like I just didn't care no more after that. I let my hair go back, plaited it up, and settled down to just being ugly. I still went to the pictures, though, but the meanness got worse. I wanted my tooth back. Cholly poked fun at me, and we started fighting again. I tried to kill him. He didn't hit me too hard, 'cause I were pregnant I guess, but the fights, once they got started up again, kept up. He begin to make me madder than anything I knowed, and I couldn't keep my hands off him. Well, I had that baby—a boy—and after that got pregnant again with another one. But it weren't like I thought it was gone be. I loved them and all, I guess, but maybe it was having no money, or maybe it was Cholly, but they sure worried the life out of me. Sometimes I'd catch myself hollering at them and beating them, and I'd feel sorry for them, but I couldn't seem to stop. When I had the second one, a girl, I 'member I said I'd love it no matter what it looked like. She looked like a black ball of hair. I don't recollect trying to get pregnant that first time. But that second time, I actually tried to get pregnant. Maybe 'cause I'd had one already and wasn't scairt to do it. Anyway, I felt good, and wasn't thinking on the carrying, just the baby itself. I used to talk to it whilst it be still in the womb. Like good friends we was. You know. I be hanging wash and I knowed lifting weren't good for it, I'd say to

it holt on now I gone hang up these few rags, don't get froggy; it be over soon. It wouldn't leap or nothing. Or I be mixing something in a bowl for the other chile and I'd talk to it then too. You know, just friendly talk. On up til the end I felted good about that baby. I went to the hospital when my time come. So I could be easeful. I didn't want to have it at home like I done with the boy. They put me in a big room with a whole mess of women. The pains was coming, but not too bad. A little old doctor come to examine me. He had all sorts of stuff. He gloved his hand and put some kind of jelly on it and rammed it up between my legs. When he left off, some more doctors come. One old one and some young ones. The old one was learning the young ones about babies. Showing them how to do. When he got to me he said now these here women you don't have any trouble with. They deliver right away and with no pain. Just like horses. The young ones smiled a little. They looked at my stomach and between my legs. They never said nothing to me. Only one looked at me. Looked at my face, I mean. I looked right back at him. He dropped his eyes and turned red. He knowed, I reckon, that maybe I weren't no horse foaling. But them others. They didn't know. They went on. I seed them talking to them white women: 'How you feel? Gonna have twins?' Just shucking them, of course, but nice talk. Nice friendly talk. I got edgy, and when them pains got harder, I was glad. Glad to have something else to think about. I moaned something awful. The pains wasn't as bad as I let on, but I had to let them people know having a baby was more than a bowel movement. I hurt just like them white women. Just 'cause I wasn't hooping and hollering before didn't mean I wasn't feeling pain. What'd they think? That just 'cause I knowed how to have a baby with no fuss that my behind wasn't pulling and aching like theirs? Besides, that doctor don't know what he talking about. He must never seed no mare foal. Who say they don't have no pain? Just 'cause she don't cry? 'Cause she can't say it, they think it ain't there? If they looks in her eyes and see them eyeballs lolling back, see the sorrowful look, they'd know. Anyways, the baby come. Big old healthy thing. She looked different from what I thought. Reckon I talked to it so much before I conjured up a mind's eye view of it. So when I seed it, it was like looking at a picture of your mama when she was a girl. You knows who she is, but she don't look the same. They give her to me for a nursing, and she liked to pull my nipple off right away. She caught on fast. Not like Sammy, he was the hardest child to feed. But Pecola look like she knowed right off what to do. A right smart baby she was. I used to like to watch her. You know they makes them greedy sounds. Eyes all soft and wet. A cross between a puppy and a dying man. But I knowed she was ugly. Head full of pretty hair, but Lord she was ugly."

When Sammy and Pecola were still young, Pauline had to go back to work. She was older now, with no time for dreams and movies. It was time to put all of the pieces together, make coherence where before there had been none. The children gave her this need; she herself was no longer a child. So she became, and her process of becoming was like most of ours: she developed a hatred for things that mystified or obstructed her; acquired virtues that were easy to maintain; assigned herself a role in the scheme of things; and harked back to simpler times for gratification.

She took on the full responsibility and recognition of breadwinner and returned to church. First, however, she moved out of the two rooms into a spacious first floor of a building that had been built as a store. She came into her own with the women who had despised her, by being more moral than they; she avenged herself on Cholly by forcing him to indulge in the weaknesses she despised. She joined a church where shouting was frowned upon, served on Stewardess Board No. 3, and became a member of Ladies Circle No. 1. At prayer meeting she moaned and sighed over Cholly's ways, and hoped God would help her keep the children from the sins of the father. She stopped saying "chil'ren" and said "childring" instead. She let another tooth fall, and was outraged by painted ladies who thought only of clothes and men. Holding Cholly as a model of sin and failure, she bore him like a crown of thorns, and her children like a cross.

It was her good fortune to find a permanent job in the home of a well-to-do family whose members were affectionate, appreciative, and generous. She looked at their houses, smelled their linen, touched their silk draperies, and loved all of it. The child's pink nightie, the stacks of white pillow slips edged with embroidery, the sheets with top hems picked out with blue cornflowers. She became what is known as an ideal servant, for such a role filled practically all her needs. When she bathed the little Fisher girl, it was in a porcelain tub with silvery taps running infinite quantities of hot, clear water. She dried her in fluffy white towels and put her in cuddly night clothes. Then she brushed the yellow hair, enjoying the roll and slip of it between her fingers. No zinc tub, no buckets of stove-heated water, no flaky, stiff, grayish towels washed in a kitchen sink, dried in a dusty backyard, no tangled black puffs of rough wool to comb. Soon she stopped trying to keep her own house. The things she could afford to buy did not last, had no beauty or style, and were absorbed by the dingy storefront. More and more she neglected her house, her children, her man—they were like the afterthoughts one has just before sleep, the early-morning and late-evening edges of her day, the dark edges that made the daily life with the Fishers lighter, more delicate, more lovely. Here she could arrange things, clean things, line things up in neat rows. Here her foot flopped around on deep pile carpets, and there was no uneven sound. Here she found beauty, order, cleanliness, and praise. Mr. Fisher said, "I would rather sell her blueberry cobblers than real estate." She reigned over cupboards stacked high with food that would not be eaten for weeks, even months; she was queen of canned vegetables bought by the case, special fondants and ribbon candy curled up in tiny silver dishes. The creditors and service people who humiliated her when she went to them on her own behalf respected her, were even intimidated by her, when she spoke for the Fishers. She refused beef slightly dark or with edges not properly trimmed. The slightly reeking fish that she accepted for her own family she would all but throw in the fishman's face if he sent it to the Fisher house. Power, praise, and luxury were hers in this household. They even gave her what she had never had—a nickname—Polly. It was her pleasure to stand in her kitchen at the end of a day and survey her handiwork. Knowing there were soap bars by the dozen, bacon by the rasher, and reveling in her shiny pots and pans and polished floors. Hearing, "We'll never let her go. We could never find anybody like Polly. She will *not* leave the kitchen until everything is in order. Really, she is the ideal servant."

Pauline kept this order, this beauty, for herself, a private world, and never introduced it into her storefront, or to her children. Them she bent toward respectability, and in so doing taught them fear: fear of being clumsy, fear of being like their father, fear of not being loved by God, fear of madness like Cholly's mother's. Into her son she beat a loud desire to run away, and into her daughter she beat a fear of growing up, fear of other people, fear of life.

All the meaningfulness of her life was in her work. For her virtues were intact. She was an active church woman, did not drink, smoke, or carouse, defended herself mightily against Cholly, rose above him in every way, and felt she was fulfilling a mother's role conscientiously when she pointed out their father's faults to keep them from having them, or punished them when they showed any slovenliness, no matter how slight, when she worked twelve to sixteen hours a day to support them. And the world itself agreed with her.

It was only sometimes, sometimes, and then rarely, that she thought about the old days, or what her life had turned to. They were musings, idle thoughts, full sometimes of the old dreaminess, but not the kind of thing she cared to dwell on.

"I started to leave him once, but something came up. Once, after he tried to set the house on fire, I was all set in my mind to go. I can't even 'member now what held me. He sure ain't give me much of a life. But it wasn't all bad. Sometimes things wasn't all bad. He used to come easing into bed sometimes, not too drunk. I make out like I'm asleep, 'cause it's late, and he taken three dollars out of my pocketbook that morning or something. I hear him breathing, but I don't look around. I can see in my mind's eye his black arms thrown back behind his head, the muscles like great big peach stones sanded down, with veins running like little swollen rivers down his arms. Without touching him I be feeling those ridges on the tips of my fingers. I sees the palms of his hands calloused to granite, and the long fingers curled up and still. I think about the thick, knotty hair on his chest, and the two big swells his breast muscles make. I want to rub my face hard in his chest and feel the hair cut my skin. I know just where the hair growth slacks out—just above his navel—and how it picks up again and spreads out. Maybe he'll shift a little, and his leg will touch me, or I feel his flank just graze my behind. I don't move even yet. Then he lift his head, turn over, and put his hand on my waist. If I don't move, he'll move his hand over to pull and knead my stomach. Soft and slow-like. I still don't move, because I don't want him to stop. I want to pretend sleep and have him keep on rubbing my stomach. Then he will lean his head down and bite my tit. Then I don't want him to rub my stomach anymore. I want him to put his hand between my legs. I pretend to wake up, and turn to him, but not opening my legs. I want him to open them for me. He does, and I be soft and wet where his fingers are strong and hard. I be softer than I ever been before. All my strength in his hand. My brain curls up like wilted leaves. A funny, empty feeling is in my hands. I want to grab holt of something, so I hold his head. His mouth is under my chin. Then I don't want his hand between my legs no more, because I think I am softening away. I stretch my legs open, and he is on top of me. Too heavy to hold, and too light not to. He puts his thing in me. In me. In me. I wrap my feet around his back so he can't get away. His face is next to mine. The bed springs sounds like them

crickets used to back home. He puts his fingers in mine, and we stretches our arms outwise like Jesus on the cross. I hold on tight. My fingers and my feet hold on tight, because everything else is going, going. I know he wants me to come first. But I can't. Not until he does. Not until I feel him loving me. Just me. Sinking into me. Not until I know that my flesh is all that be on his mind. That he couldn't stop if he had to. That he would die rather than take his thing out of me. Of me. Not until he has let go of all he has, and give it to me. To me. To me. When he does, I feel a power. I be strong, I be pretty, I be young. And then I wait. He shivers and tosses his head. Now I be strong enough, pretty enough, and young enough to let him make me come. I take my fingers out of his and put my hands on his behind. My legs drop back onto the bed. I don't make no noise, because the chil'ren might hear. I begin to feel those little bits of color floating up into me—deep in me. That streak of green from the june-bug light, the purple from the berries trickling along my thighs, Mama's lemonade yellow runs sweet in me. Then I feel like I'm laughing between my legs, and the laughing gets all mixed up with the colors, and I'm afraid I'll come, and afraid I won't. But I know I will. And I do. And it be rainbow all inside. And it lasts and lasts and lasts. I want to thank him, but don't know how, so I pat him like you do a baby. He asks me if I'm all right. I say yes. He gets off me and lies down to sleep. I want to say something, but I don't. I don't want to take my mind offen the rainbow. I should get up and go to the toilet, but I don't. Besides, Cholly is asleep with his leg throwed over me. I can't move and don't want to.

"But it ain't like that anymore. Most times he's thrashing away inside me before I'm woke, and through when I am. The rest of the time I can't even be next to his stinking drunk self. But I don't care 'bout it no more. My Maker will take care of me. I know He will. I know He will. Besides, it don't make no difference about this old earth. There is sure to be a glory. Only thing I miss sometimes is that rainbow. But like I say, I don't recollect it much anymore."

The Reader's Repertoire and the General Ideology: Morrison's "SeeMotherMotherIsVeryNice"

The role that our general repertoire plays when we interpret texts can be clearly seen in those stories that deal with minority groups—groups by definition on the margins of society's dominant system of thought and belief. Toni Morrison's "SeeMotherMotherIsVeryNice" traces the passage of a young black woman into adulthood and suggests that while this woman's dreams of money, success, and happiness may be just like anyone else's in this country—black or white, lower or middle class—her potential for realizing those dreams is drastically limited because of her color and socioeconomic status.

Regardless of gender, color, or socioeconomic status, most readers follow with interest Pauline's many experiences. At the age of fifteen, she feels like an outcast—alone and set apart from her family and neighbors. She dreams of falling in love. After she moves to Ohio with Cholly, she experiences a new kind of loneliness, the loneliness that comes from living in a new place and having no friends. She alters her old behavior patterns and feigns an interest in clothes and makeup, just to fit in with the people around her. She goes to the movies and imagines herself in the role of the heroine. Most readers have experienced some, if not all, of the feelings and emotions of love, rejection, and dissatisfaction that Pauline experiences, and it is likely that they will, on some level, identify with her emotionally. To insure reader sympathy, the narrator even says at one point that "her process of becoming was like most of ours." One of our students, for example, commented: "Gender and race seem to make no difference to me when I read this story. I'm a nineteen-year-old white male and sometimes I'm afraid that, in pursuing success, I could end up stifling my own desires in an attempt to do what society says good white males should be doing—being doctors, or lawyers, or engineers. I think I could be a lot more miserable in a nine-to-five white-collar job than Polly is as a cleaning woman."

You might want to ask two questions about Pauline: Does *she* feel she has attained success? Do *you* feel that she has? In many respects, she does take control of her own life. When Cholly stops supporting the family, Pauline takes action: "she took on the full responsibility and recognition of breadwinner and returned to the church." Polly begins to act in ways that society approves of, and she becomes increasingly dependent on that social approbation. It might seem to some readers, however, that she becomes strongly divided from herself. They might argue that, although she loves Cholly and her children, she distances herself from them emotionally: "holding Cholly as a model of sin and failure, she bore him like a chain of thorns, and her children like a cross." Although she loses interest in her own physical appearance and "was outraged by painted ladies who thought of only clothes and men," Pauline does not lose her desire to be associated in some way with the attractive, well-to-do elements of her society. Realizing that she cannot hope to have a porcelain bathtub, fluffy white towels, and shiny pots and pans of her own, she decides to experience these luxuries vicariously—by becoming an "ideal servant." She begins to live two lives: one of poverty, degradation, and "slightly reeking fish"; the other of beauty, elegance, and "properly trimmed" beef. Working in the household of the Fishers, "power, praise, and luxury were hers."

This story presents many readers with a dilemma. On the one hand, some readers may respond deeply to Pauline's arguing that her emotions and problems are almost "universal." On the other hand, other readers, influenced by many of the dominant cultural assumptions about success in our society, may try to achieve some distance from Pauline—even to feel superior to her. One of our students wrote: "I feel some sympathy for Polly. I think she could have made a lot more of herself. I don't identify with her, though, because I've always been told that you have to set your sights high in order to succeed, and that's what I'm going to do."

You may not want to believe that Pauline's fate could well be yours. In other words, the general repertoire of this story may be one that you—whether black, white, oriental, Hispanic, female or male, poor or wealthy—want to reject, perhaps because it challenges your belief that all people can succeed in this country if they want to.

Polly finds a way to feel successful in society. But many readers may feel that her role ironically perpetuates her and her family's inability to attain a higher stature in the community, one that might threaten a predominantly white society. One student asked: "She was so competent. Why didn't she put all that energy into her own family instead of into somebody else's?" By becoming a servant, Polly fails to free herself from the role of black as slave to whites. Her children too seem destined to continue this role: "Into her son she beat a loud desire to run away, and into her daughter she beat a fear of growing up, fear of other people, fear of life."

But what other choice, the reader may ask, is open to Polly? Like most Americans, she wants power and luxury, but while society gives her these dreams, it fails to provide her the means to attain them for herself. Satisfied with the vicarious experiences of power and luxury, Pauline ironically reinforces her marginal position in society. But we are told "the world itself" agreed with Polly's choices.

This story raises many questions that can be developed in your response statements or in class discussion. Inevitably your own assumptions and beliefs—even fears and hopes—regarding success, motherhood, racial relations, poverty, and wealth will surface and help determine your own reading. If, for example, you find this story disturbing, you are probably confronting more than your literary repertoire. You are confronting your broader general repertoire on issues that may be quite sensitive, issues that you may not have seriously explored before you read this story. A story like "SeeMotherMotherIsVeryNice" is therefore especially useful for highlighting important reasons why readers read literature at all—to help formulate ideas and feelings, to take a stance towards events and issues in the world, and to share these views with others. When you read the play *Raisin in the Sun,* you will again confront issues similar to those in Morrison's story.

Another social question that the story may raise for you is the amount of freedom individuals have in our society. But note that the story itself does not resolve this question. Some of you may feel that Polly makes the best she can of a bad situation, that she is strong and resourceful, and that she has strength of character you admire. Others may focus not so much on Polly as on the American Dream itself. You may find yourselves appalled that the dreams our society encourages—dreams similar to those of Willy Loman in *Death of a Salesman* (p. 901)—can be so unrealistic that people are forced to demean themselves in order to experience the myth of success on any level. But whatever reaction you have to this text, it will necessarily involve your ideas and beliefs about social and political equality. Even if you perceive your reaction as having no relevance or implications beyond the bounds of the story, that perception itself has political implications. Whether you find that this story confirms or challenges your general repertoire, it will at least have made you more conscious of what your beliefs are —and perhaps will cause you to examine the underlying sources of those beliefs.

Producing Your Strong Readings of Fiction

As you become more proficient or expert readers, you will become more knowledgeable about ways in which the prevailing ideology helps to form your literary and general repertoires and those of various texts. Even more important, you will become more aware that you have to *produce* your own readings of texts and become responsible for them. When you turn from reading the text to producing your own responses to it—whether they take the form of response statements, class discussion, or more formal papers— you are using the text as a starting point to construct your own readings. You probe your own responses, examine your assumptions, and then create an interpretation, a "text" that is yours. Your readings, finally, are your own. But while readers do choose their own readings, all readers are the products of their society, of their cultural and ideological position, and of strong emotional and unconscious forces. Reading involves developing diverse and compelling strategies to make your chosen perspective intelligible to others. The work of criticism is to produce meanings that grow out of your active, ongoing dialogue with the text. By actively producing and becoming responsible for your readings of texts, you will enjoy, and understand more deeply, the fiction you read. Moreover, you will understand more of the insightful process of reading and interpreting—and their relation to your knowledge of the world.

Reading and Responding to Fiction

Read this story and the discussion that follows on page 86.

LYNNE BARRETT (b. 1950)

Inventory

"What do you think?" said the Appliances manager. "Cotton?"

"Nylon," said the other man. "The skinny ones wear little nylon bikinis. Maybe with 'Tuesday' embroidered on them."

They stood right below me looking up through the iron mesh deck of the Appliances stockroom. I had my thighs clenched. I relaxed; I kept counting transistor radios.

"This one's a kid though. What are you honey, seventeen? A baby. White cotton spankies."

I mouthed, "twennytwotwennythreetwennyfour," and marked 24 on the line for SKU 37079 in the book. They really couldn't see much looking up through the grid. And I decided long ago that looking doesn't count. I closed my big notebook and backed down the steps, my sandals going clink clonk clink, while the men watched.

"What are you, Patty?" the Appliances manager said, "seventeen?"

"Eighteen in September." I reached the floor. I glanced over at the other man, a delivery guy, a greaser.

"And anyway," I said, walking away, "anyway they're pink cotton stretch lace. You can see all of them you want over in Lingerie, you know?"

The Appliances manager laughed his laugh like a snore.

That's what they like, when you talk back. If I told them at home, my father would holler, my mother would cry. But you just can't bother to get upset; I learned that the first week when Mrs. Grissing taught me the job. "The store makes you wear skirts and climb all over God's little acres to count the crap they haven't sold," Mrs.

Grissing said. "And when you've got your fanny up in the air crawling into those bins, of course they'll peek. Big deal." Mrs. Grissing had worked for S. Kotch nineteen years. Every day her bra cut a deeper crevice into the fat of her back.

As I walked out through Appliances, all the color t.v.'s announced "Jeopardy. Jeopardy. Jeopardy." The clock radios agreed on 10:30. I'd quit Appliances early.

I crossed the main aisle into Paints, but Eddie wasn't there. No one in Paints or Hardware. In Automotive I found Eddie cutting a key for a customer. The manager of Hardware and Automotive drank, so Eddie pretty much had to cover. Eddie was supposed to be his assistant in charge of Paints, but, as Eddie said, no one bought paint at S. Kotch. People just aren't cheap about paint. Eddie was sixteen, still in high school in Singac, a tall kid with bad skin, but he was the only halfway cool person in the store as far as I was concerned.

Another customer lined up holding spark plugs. Eddie shrugged. So I decided to take off and tour the store. Over on the Softgoods side I could look at the Fall clothes just in, though I really didn't want to go off to college in clothes from S. Kotch.

As I passed Giftware, I said hello to Mrs. Sabatez, who was dusting. Mrs. Sabatez, a thin Cuban woman, dusted all day.

"I think somebody looked for you," she said.

"Oh? Who?"

"A pretty girl," said Mrs. Sabatez. "The girl was pretty." She nodded at her lambswool duster.

Maybe Eddie was right. He said that Mrs. Sabatez did downers. I smiled at her and moved on.

The hardest part of the job was killing time. Mrs. Grissing and her sidekick Mrs. Main were union reps and they landed themselves the easiest job in the store. Every three weeks we were supposed to count all the Hardgoods, floor and stockroom. At the start of the summer I counted as fast as I could until Mrs. Grissing took me aside: "Babes, you'll hurt yourself, climbing those shelves like an orangoutang. Three weeks is what it takes so take three weeks."

Not that Mrs. Grissing ever climbed anything. She and Mrs. Main might estimate, might guess, might never look at all. If the count last time in the book was 12 they just put 6 and three weeks later 0. Once it was 0 it was always 0. They never seemed to grasp that our boss, Cherrybeth, and her boss, Mr. Wold, ordered from the books. Like the fishhooks. Cherrybeth sent me to Sporting Goods my first day counting on my own, and the book began with fishhooks. Every SKU showed 0 on the floor/0 in stock, 0/0, 0/0, 0/0 for pages. I found hundreds of fishhooks tangled on the shelves and cartons of thousands jamming Sporting Goods storage. And you should have seen the lures.

Anyway, after she got a load of my counts in Sporting Goods, Cherrybeth explained that, as union reps, Mrs. Grissing and Mrs. Main would be difficult to fire. She relied on me. Now the two old bags mostly used their Basic Books as lap trays for games of Go Fish in the Paperbacks and Records stockroom. I did inventory, which still meant slowing to stretch the books over three weeks. Usually I worked all morning and then hung out with Eddie in Paints mixing weird colors on the mixing machine.

Or, like now, I shopped. I'd crossed Jewelry and Accessories to the center of Soft-goods, Juniors A Go Go, where all day tapes played and a sort of mini-lightshow cast pink and purple amoeba shapes onto the clothes. In June I bought three psychedelic nylon dresses with front zippers here on my discount, to wear to work. They were cheap, and at the end of the summer, as my mother said, I could just throw them out.

Suede minis had come in, not bad if they were real. I touched them "hunn-twothreefurfi—" This job got me counting everything. Even reading, I would find myself turning the pages, just counting them. Numbers blurred through my mouth "leven twel thirdeen furdeen fideen." I counted in my sleep. I dreamed "furdyse-venfurdyeightfurdyniiiiine fiddy" till I woke myself and lay restless and ready to cry.

I used to be the only one in my family who didn't talk in my sleep. If I woke at night the house was full of noises. My older sister Maureen, before she ran away, would sing, my mother would cough and mutter, my father was always swearing, always angry, "Bastards all you bastards get you bastards!" But I slept quietly, until now, barely moving.

"Finished Appliances already, babes?" asked Mrs. Grissing.

I jumped. She stood under the slide projector, shifting back and forth to the music. I tried to think of a good reason to be over here, but she went on, "Well, great, because Mr. Wold wants to see you before lunchbreak."

She moved away from Juniors A Go Go and I followed. "Mr. Wold? What for?"

"Cherrybeth didn't come in today."

"I know. I thought she was sick." Cherrybeth hadn't come in today or Monday, but I knew she'd gone to the shore for the weekend, and Cherrybeth usually got a one or two day sunburn when she went to the shore.

"She's sick all right," Mrs. Grissing said. "She got married."

"Really? Which guy? The VW or the Mustang?"

"I didn't know you and Miss S. Kotch were so close." Last year Cherrybeth was Miss S. Kotch of New Jersey; Mrs. Grissing thought it was funny to call her that. Mrs. Grissing, as she put it, "didn't care for Cherrybeth."

Now, in the main aisle, I realized Mrs. Grissing was wearing a different dress than she started out with. This time I was sure. Mrs. Grissing was gradually trading her wardrobe for clothes from the store. We had to check our coats and purses at the Employees' Desk so we couldn't sneak things out, but the system didn't prevent out-right exchanges. Mrs. Grissing had on some blue thing that morning—I'd guessed it was a housecoat—and now she wore a new check dress.

We passed Mrs. Sabatez, dusting.

"Keep up the good work, Senora," Mrs. Grissing told her.

"Anyway," I said, "so she got married, huh?"

Mrs. Grissing led the way up the interior staircase next to Cameras.

"So why does Mr. Wold want to see me?"

She put on her all-informed look and said, "I'll let him tell you, babes."

She led the way past Complaints, past Credit, to the Hardgoods office. Our office, Basic Books, was near the time clock and Personnel, but Mr. Wold was with all the big deals. Mrs. Grissing took the Appliances book, tapped on Mrs. Wold's door, stuck her head in and said, "Here she is, Jeff."

I knew Mr. Wold by sight well enough to try and look busy when he walked by. Now he jiggled a chair close to the side of his desk for me.

He was thirtyish, with the kind of dip and roll to his light hair that was popular when I was a kid, like Troy Donahue. There was a combined baseball coach-and-math teacher in my high school who looked like him and some girls had crushes on him but I didn't. And Mr. Wold's nose was too little.

"Patty, as you know," he said, "Miss Jennings has resigned her position as manager of Basic Books."

I tried to look like I knew.

"I'm going to miss her—very much." He looked at me hard, then away. He started unbuttoning the cuffs of his long sleeve blue shirt and rolling them up. He said, "I'm offering you a promotion to that managerial position."

"You are?" I'd worked there two months. I said, "I'm not very experienced."

"Cherrybeth—" He paused. I thought, there *can't* have been anything going on with him and Cherrybeth. "Cherrybeth recommended you. She praised your initiative. This will be a real boost to your career in merchandising."

"Oh yes." My career in merchandising was the line I used to get the job. No one wanted to hire for the summer so I stopped saying I was going to college, figuring I could just quit in September. I still could. It didn't look like Cherrybeth gave all that much notice.

"It's going to be tough," he said, "to replace you in inventory and I may ask you to help out with the counts for a while. This is our light season in Hardgoods, so I'll be able to break you in gradually with the order forms. Cherrybeth—" By now he had his sleeves rolled and he compared to see that they were exactly even. "She said you had done some forms for her?"

"Yes."

"So that's fine," he said. "If you'll stop in at Personnel they'll give you your manager's badge."

I started to stand up and saw that he expected to shake hands, so I did—his hand was warm and small—and kept standing. He said, "I'll be looking forward to working with you Patty." I pulled my hand away.

"Oh my eye," he said, "my eye! I have something in my eye." He winked his right eye shut open shut and held it. "Patty, I've got something in my eye." I stepped over. His eye was squinched up so tight a fan of wrinkles ran up across his nose. "Ow," he said. "Will you look and see? Get it out. Ow!"

I tried to see. I smelled coffee. "Open your eye," I said, "and roll it around."

He took his hand away and opened his eye wide.

It was bloodshot near the corner, but I couldn't see anything in it. His irises were light light blue.

"Ow," he said, "don't you see it?"

As I leaned over, his right hand waved around and came to rest on my shoulder as if for balance. He rolled his eye and whenever my finger got close he shut it.

"I don't see anything in there," I said.

"I *feel* it. Must be an eyelash. Look close, I'll hold still." He opened his eye and looked way to the left, into his nose. And his hand wandered down to my breast. I thought it must be accidental, but as I tried to shift away he found my nipple and pulled at it.

I said, "Oh, I see it," and jabbed my finger sharp into the corner of his eye.

"Ouchouch*shit!*" Mr. Wold clapped both hands to his head.

"Got it," I said, looking at my fingertip which had nothing on it. I shook it over the trash basket and backed around the desk. Mr. Wold had his hands over his face. I suspected he was laughing.

"I better get over to Personnel," I said, and closed the office door behind me.

Only as I wrote for the fifth time, Tierney, Partricia K., on the Withdrawal From Union Form SK-A-47, did I see: I had to be the one they promoted, because neither Mrs. Grissing nor Mrs. Main would quit being union rep to become a manager. I heard myself telling Mr. Wold, "I'm not very experienced." Stupid, stupid. "So stupid," I said.

Neither secretary appeared to hear me. The younger one was trying to get green tape to feed straight through her letter gun so she could punch out my name for my badge. The older one, opposite, was putting my forms into files as I finished them.

"Do I get my union membership fee back?" I asked the younger. "I only joined in June."

The older one looked up. "The grace period for withdrawal from union is two weeks."

"But it was $35."

"I'm sorry. But you won't have dues taken from your paycheck anymore; that's just like a raise."

"It doesn't seem fair," said the younger. She clicked the gun a few times, then broke the tape off.

"Don't I get a raise when I become a manager?" I asked.

"You'll be eligible for a raise at the end of the first six month employment period. That's the union schedule."

"But she's not in the union anymore," said the younger.

"Right, which means she isn't really entitled to their protection. They could make her wait a year. But the store honors the union schedule anyway. And meanwhile," the elder said to me, "you don't have to pay union dues anymore, which is just like a raise."

"I see," I said.

The younger one said, "EA or IE?"

I spelled, "T I E R N E Y," as she twisted the dial for each letter. She lifted the tape delicately between long white fingernails and attached it to the badge.

"Here you go," she said.

I took the badge and started to pin it on, but I got a weird feeling when I touched my chest, so I switched and put the badge higher up, near my shoulder, hoping they hadn't seen.

The older secretary read, "Miss Tierney MANAGER Basic Books. Very good," she said to the younger, "congratulations," to me.

"Congratulations," said the younger, giving me a look.

When I left Personnel I punched out for lunch and from the refrigerator behind the Employees' Desk the guard handed me my paper bag. I bought a Wink from the machine and took lunch into Cherrybeth's office. Mrs. Grissing had left the Appliances book on the desk. Then I saw that Cherrybeth's Puerto Rico and Bermuda posters were gone. The office looked bare and new. Of course, the store was new; S. Kotch moved the branch here in March. Cherrybeth told me how, last summer at the old Newark store during the riots, all the men took hunting guns from Sporting Goods and held the store until the National Guard came to convoy them out. I pictured Mr. Wold holding a shotgun, his sleeves rolled up.

I unwrapped my tuna sandwich and found it had been mushed. Mayonnaise saturated the white bread. I couldn't eat it. I threw it out. I sipped my Wink and sat at the desk. My desk. I started opening drawers. Order forms, carbon paper, blank pages to replace full pages in the inventory books. In the bottom drawer I found a cardigan sweater Cherrybeth must have left, and under it a pair of pantyhose with nail polish daubed around a hole in the heel attempting but failing to stop a run. Also a sample size can of White Rain hairspray and a roll of butterscotch lifesavers with only three left and they'd crystallized. I threw out the hairspray, candy, pantyhose, and a broken comb I found in the center drawer. There was a hairbrush, too, and I started to pull Cherrybeth's yellow hair from it, then threw the whole thing out.

Then I got up, locked the door, turned out the light, huddled up in the desk chair. They always turned the air conditioning in the store so high the offices were freezing. I shivered and shivered, so I put Cherrybeth's cardigan around me. I could smell in it the old grapefruit smell of her sweat.

Then, testing, I touched my breast, to see if I'd feel weird again, and when I brushed lightly I did. Then I grabbed myself hard and it went away. No big deal, I told myself. Lots of guys had touched me. Mr. Wold was just the oldest. It would have mattered when I was fourteen, but not now. It seemed to me my life had been a progression of abandoned defenses, giving myself up in stages, kissing, frenchkissing, touching through clothes, touching under clothes, and when I went steady with Nick, everything. Which I'd thought was a big deal, but now that we were broken up, was it really? Just like kissing. When I was twelve I thought it was the greatest thing in the world that Barry Super kissed me, that he'd always be important. Well, kissing didn't mean much after a while, you could be kissed by just about anyone and take it. There were the slobbering kissers, the teeth on teeth ones, the guys who dug their tongues into the root of yours so it hurt, the nibblers, the lickers, the guys who started to talk and drooled down your throat; oh, I knew all about kissing. And how many guys had squeezed my breast? One two three . . . seven, and two weeks ago at that party Kerry Sterling, who hadn't called since, and Mr. Wold. Nine. What did it matter.

The thing is, if you're a girl, people touch you and think they've gotten something. Taken something away.

Certainly that's what my father went so nuts over, when Maureen took off. He took it out on me, wouldn't let me have the car, waited up. Just the other night after that party he grabbed my arms as I came in the front door. I thought he was going to check for needle marks—since he went to the police lecture on runaways he learned ten signs of drug addiction he always checked me for—but instead he hollered, "Do they touch you? Do you let the little bastards get their hands on you?"

The thing about Maureen was, she never dated. She was a groupie from the word go. Even early on, she would rather go into New York to greet groups at the airport than go out with an ordinary boy. So my father thought she was safe. And then she went to a Hollies concert and never came back. She sent a postcard from L.A. saying she was the girlfriend of one of the guys who *really* played the Monkees music and then she went to San Francisco and last time she wrote she said she was changing her name to Tenth Cloud. Which drove my father even crazier. But he always blamed some long-haired demon who had taken her while it was clear to me that she'd done it herself.

One time I went with Maureen to a monster concert in the Village: fourteen groups. It went on for hours with long waits for set-ups. Maureen flirted with musicians during sound checks and then while they played she danced in front of them, touching her hair, biting her lips. One singer with a platinum ponytail got her frantic: she bit and bit so close I thought she'd bite his crotch and I saw he was the pursued, the girl. In the months before she ran away, Maureen would come home from sneaking into discotheques and we'd sit on her bed while she told me that she'd kissed one or rubbed two's arm and look, here was three's sleeve, four's roach, she'd boast and boast, fisicksevunateniiine.

God it was cold. So cold I was hugging myself, shivering. I got up and opened the office and punched back in: exactly thirty minutes. I could always tell now when lunch was over. I took the Hardware and Automotive book downstairs and went back to Juniors A Go Go, where I'd been when Mrs. Grissing interrupted. It was chilly here, too. Maybe it was true that they lowered the thermostat when Fall clothes came in.

In Juniors A Go Go I picked out one of the suede minis and a vest to match, together $26, and then a yellow crinkly gauze blouse, $12, which came to $38, with my store discount minus $3.80: $34.20, pretty close to my union membership fee. So I didn't feel too bad.

I took them into the dressing room and went to the far end, past the garment racks of layaways, and found a corner. I changed into my new outfit. The skirt was shorter than my usual, but heavy so it wouldn't ride up. It had its own chain belt, too; it was pretty nice for S. Kotch. I transferred my manager's badge to my new blouse, then pulled all the tags off and rolled them up with my old dress and Cherrybeth's sweater and stuffed them in a waste bin. I wondered where Mrs. Grissing got rid of her old outfits; I should ask her.

Instead of going back out I went through to the dock where Softgoods were unloaded. This was the core of the store, where all the stuff came into the departments. There were some guys down at one end eating sandwiches and listening to a transistor; they waved to me as I picked my way across. I climbed onto the Appliances dock on the Hardgoods side and went through the stockroom. My heart was slamming so hard I could see it lift and drop my badge, but no one would catch me.

When I came out onto Appliances carrying my book, I could have been just finishing the count there, as I had in the morning, as if nothing had happened. When I looked at my reflection in the silver top of a stove I looked okay. It was a tough outfit, and my hair was finally getting long.

The clock radios said 2:00. The color t.v.'s showed nothing going on, just newsmen talking.

When I crossed the main aisle, I looked down through the departments. Only Mrs. Sabatez, way down in Clocks dusting, moved. No one else among the displays of Hardware, Houseware, Giftware, Cameras; all the inventory spread out waiting, cheap and unbought. The store was dead.

I crossed into Automotive. I didn't see Eddie so I sat in the Test Your Reaction Time display. It was a set-up like we had in Driver Ed. with red and green lights and a timer to measure how fast you moved your foot from the gas to the brake pedal at the signal. But here they'd installed it in a mock front seat, with a dial on the dash to read out your reaction time and a chart that told you what that was in car lengths at different speeds. They'd fitted it with S. Kotch car decor items: foot pedals shaped like bare feet, leopard terry slipcovers, a leatherette wrap for the steering wheel. Kids liked to sit in it and pretend to drive while their parents shopped, though they were disappointed it didn't move like those kiddie cars they have in front of supermarkets, that jiggle a while for a nickel.

I plugged in the cord to start the timer and tested myself. I was always very fast. But then it's easy when you know a signal's coming.

After a while Eddie came out of Paints stockroom and noticed me. He said hi and came over and started playing with the am/fm car radios on their display. "What do you want to hear?" he asked. "Do you know I found a teensy little country and western station from up in Mahwah the other day?"

"Piss," I said. I'd gotten distracted and missed the signal. If I'd been going 40 m.p.h. my stopping distance would have been fourteen car lengths. I said, "Country and western in New Jersey?"

He started turning the display. The sample car radios were hung on a tall rack that had wiring down the middle of it so that they could be plugged in. Eddie was forever trying to catch some shy station with a 10 watt signal or pull in soul from Detroit, which meant he would move the display around Automotive, dragging the extension cords along.

"Where's your boss?" I asked.

"He's still out to yesterday's lunch."

Eddie was getting the Temptations. He started tuning all the radios in the same way. I looked at him: A tall kid with bad skin—or rather it was obvious that he had bad skin in winter. Eddie always went out at lunchbreak and stood against the concrete wall of the store and took the sun in his face, so now he was tan to the collar of his shirt and the scars only showed at his temples. He'd brought some barbells from Sporting Goods to "build up his pecs" as he said, but he was still just as skinny as in

June, in the white button-down shirt and khaki pants they made him wear to work.

It occurred to me that this was how I always looked at Eddie, and yet he was the only halfway cool person in the store. Early in the summer I'd suspected he liked me; he'd mentioned movies, but I'd kept it an on-the-job friendship. How silly, when I'd go off to a party and make out with Kerry Sterling, who never called. I thought, if I were a man and Eddie a girl, I'd look at him differently. The Appliances manager was turned on identifying underwear; Mr. Wold put on his act to fool me, just to feel me up; they'd think a kid of sixteen was meant to peek at. I tried peeking at Eddie. If I looked as he lifted I could see the damp shadow of his underarm. Was he wearing an undershirt? No. There was the line of his spine, clear through his shirt. He had a flat little ass. And when he turned I could tell his cock lay to the left. Oh, you could do it to anyone, I thought. Why not Eddie?

Eddie said, "You'd probably rather listen to Cream or something."

I said, "Jefferson Airplane."

He smiled. "Maybe Grace Slick is one of your sister's friends by now."

I'd told Eddie about Maureen. He thought the name Tenth Cloud was great; he suggested cloud names for my whole family, Storm Cloud for my father and Rain Cloud for Mom and I should be Fog or Mist or Haze because I was all over the store.

"Oh, hey," I said, remembering, "I got promoted. I'm manager of Basic Books." I showed him my badge.

He asked what happened.

"Cherrybeth got married and quit."

"She was here this morning," he said. "Did she find you?"

"Cherrybeth?"

"Yeah, she came in when we were busy. She asked if you were counting Hardware."

"Mrs. Sabatez said someone was looking for me. I wonder what she would have said."

Eddie went to the counter. "Wait," he said, "she asked me—" He looked around the register and then went into Paints. "I was busy so—yeah, here. Good thing you reminded me."

He brought over an S. Kotch bag, the smallest size. Cherrybeth had written on it:

Dear Patty,

Chuck and I are getting married this Sat, but I told them I already was so they couldn't hassel me. He's the one I told you about remember? So now you'll be the only one in the store who can do fractions. You're one in a zillion, kiddo. Take no shit.

Cherrybeth Russo (to be)

P.S. Don't run for Miss S. Kotch it's fixed.

I showed the note to Eddie. I felt better thinking she had tried to see me. Maybe she would have warned me about Mr. Wold. Sometimes she called him "Mr. Mold" I remembered. I wondered if he'd fixed the contest for her.

I said to Eddie, "Don't you think we should celebrate?"

"Your promotion?"

"Yes, my promotion. How often does a seventeen-year-old get to manage Basic Books or anything, huh?"

"Okay," he said. "Let's have a drink."

"Sure, a drink," I said. "But what can we drink?" I got out of the display car and started hunting around. "Quaker oil? Anti-freeze? Does Mr. Ellicott get into the anti-freeze much?"

"No," he said, "but he's got—come on." He led me over into Paints, into the storeroom, into the far back. "Did you forget these?" he said. "Mr. Ellicott's rock-n-rye."

We had found them a month or so before, a set of four pint bottles hidden behind a row of S. Kotch Interior Enamel. Mr. Ellicott had filled them with rye and put in rock candy crystals. Eddie said he knew other people who made it, it was a liqueur. We figured Mr. Ellicott had put them there in better days, then forgotten them.

So we sat where we always sat, on the bench by the mixing machine, and Eddie opened a bottle and we drank. It was rough and sweet and mixed with the smell of Paints stockroom, like the smell of everybody's basement on a rainy day, the smell of glue sniffing when I was twelve, before they took the high out of glue. We took turns swigging the rock-n-rye and toasting:

"To Basic Books."

"To Miss Tierney, Manager of Basic Books."

"To Cherrybeth Jennings Russo-to-be."

We toasted Mrs. Grissing, Mrs. Main, Mr. Ellicott, S. Kotch, Mrs. Sabatez. I had it in my head to toast Mr. Wold but couldn't quite say it. Eddie got up and put a gallon can on the mixing machine, just so we could watch it shake. He took a pair of paint mixing sticks and started drumming on cans of paint with the mixer as back beat. He played around the stockroom, rapping on my head as he passed by. Once Eddie and I talked about what would be the best song to have played at your funeral and he said he wanted "Knock on Wood" or "Grapevine," something with such a beat that no one would be able to keep from moving, including, maybe, him. Now he finished with a wipe-out solo on some primer and flopped down beside me on the bench and opened the next bottle of rock-n-rye. I found myself studying his khaki thigh.

"To Eddie DeSantis," I said. "To your career in merchandizing."

"My career," Eddie said, and drank. "Hey," he said, "maybe they'll fire Ellicott and make me head of Hardware and Automotive. I'm sixteen, after all."

"Maybe they'll fire all the old guys and put kids in charge."

"To the first teenage-run discount department store."

"We can take over—"

"—have splash parties in the Children's wading pools—"

"—rock concerts in Juniors A Go Go—"

"When I'm Branch Manager," Eddie began his campaign speech.

"Let me tell your fortune," I said, and took his hand. He jerked in surprise, and as I held his palm and concentrated, I could feel a quiver in his knuckles, though he held still. I tried to recall, of all the guys I dated, whether I had ever touched one first. I had, when attracted, talked to them, waited near them, willed them towards me, but that first touch, crossing the distance, had never been mine.

"Well," I said, "what a nice long lifeline you have here."

"Oh good," said Eddie.

"And," I twisted his hand and looked at the side, "two marriages."

"Two?"

"One short and unhappy, one long and unhappy."

"Great," said Eddie.

"Well, maybe those are the lines for children, I'm not sure, I only studied this for a while when I was thirteen or so."

"So maybe it's two children, one short and unhappy, one long and unhappy?"

Eddie is cool, I thought. "It's not just the lines, either," I said. "It's the mounds."

"The mounds?"

"All the fleshy parts." I rubbed his hand, which was thin and calloused and had some light green paint on it. "There are ones for scientific and mathematic and artistic, but I don't remember which is which. But this," I squeezed the outer part of his hand, "is the mound of the moon. That's imagination."

"Do I have imagination?"

"You're very imaginative. And this is the mound of Aphrodite. Venus." I touched the flesh below his thumb. His hand was sweating lightly. Oh, this was fun. "It shows sensuality." I brushed his wrist.

"Patty?" he said. "Do you want to go out after work?"

"Oh," I said, "no. Let's not go out after work. Let's not date, no phoning or not phoning, let's just do stuff the way, you know, you hear music, you move, you don't have to think about it."

"Patty?" he said. "Are you okay? Are you going to get sick on that stuff?"

"No, no, I'm fine," I said, running my hand along his spine, each vertebra, through cloth, distinct enough to number, reaching down to where his shirt would end and I'd find skin.

Response Statement Assignment

After rereading the general guidelines for writing response statements (p. 15), write a response statement on the following topic: To what extent do your views of appropriate behavior by girls of Patty's age and position affect your reading of "Inventory"? Does the story confirm or challenge your views?

Sample Student Response Statement

As a female reader myself, I think I would have more understanding of Patty's behavior in ''Inventory'' than a male reader. Most girls of her age have been in Patty's position--

harassed by a superior at work. Even if it's fairly harmless, she wonders if she's been debased by it. That's one of the inevitable problems about growing up as a female in our society, and Lynne Barrett's story captures the feeling of being young and female today.

What to me is especially relevant and recognizable is the way Patty appears so cool, so self-aware about what's going on. It's not that she's less innocent but more self-conscious. She knows if she told her parents about answering the men back, there would be a bad reaction: ''If I told them at home, my father would holler, my mother would cry.'' Although she is very conscious of what Mr. Wold is after, she seems very much in control of the situation.

But what I found most revealing is her attitude to Eddie. Here is where I'm sure it helps to be the same gender as Patty. Many men and boys think that all women are innocent of such tactics--that women don't like to be aggressive in the ''battle of the sexes.'' But most do. Gone are the days when girls were all sugar and spice. Yet the boys still think the girls are, or ought to be, passive. It's the same kind of double standard that is referred to in the ''Miss S. Kotch of New Jersey'' contest where the most attractive and wholesome girl is supposed to be chosen as Miss S. Kotch. But in fact, the contest is ''fixed''--and probably required a few favors on the side. It's useful to ask ourselves how many men still think women are or ought to be ashamed of such things in this day and age.

Unless he knows himself as a male exceptionally well, a male reader might not relate easily to Patty's worldliness. He might well see her as a ''slut'' and find her threatening as well as immoral. She might appear to be just too much in control. But most women know that a woman's motives are as mixed as any man's.

Discussion

Here we find a potentially interesting, self-conscious analysis, revealing a particularly close matching of repertoires between reader and text. This response statement shows how a reading arises from a specific general repertoire. If you are a woman, do you agree with the writer that male readers are likely to react differently? Do you find this reader's views perhaps too extreme in its narrow type of feminism? If you are a male, do you agree that most men would disapprove of Patty's behavior? Or as another of our women students wrote, "They would laugh at Patty, but they probably wouldn't take her out. Or if they did, they wouldn't want to marry her."

What does such a response tell you about gender-specific characteristics in our society? Or about the conservatism of our dominant ideology about gender roles?

In order to deepen an initial response to a story, readers should not just think about the story itself or their own reactions to it, but also they should look for material outside the story—yet relevant to it—that can be brought into the discussion. In suggesting to our student how to revise this initial response statement into a more developed, more persuasive paper, we asked her to expand on two issues that would deepen the analysis. The first related to the opening paragraph in which the writer used the phrase "growing up as a female in our society." She was asked to go into more detail, using her knowledge of the ideological influences to which young women today are subject to show how they influenced her response to the story.

We suggested that she do some research and reading on the contemporary women's movement, of which she seemed only vaguely aware. In class discussion, some of the men spoke of the women's movement as a "sixties and seventies issue" and seemed to think it had achieved its goals and should not be carried to extremes. Some of the women students disagreed strongly, saying that there were still many barriers to women's true equality —not so much in laws and regulations but in subtle attitudes and assumptions that many men (and some women) still had. We pointed out that they were discussing the relationship between a society's **ideology** and the particular **general repertoires** of individual men and women.

We then directed our student writer's attention to the notion that people are "written" by different discourses, that their lives are the product of their society's different and often contradictory ideological practices. We asked her to consider how that applied to what she termed "the inevitable problems about growing up as a female in our society."

The second point we asked our student to expand on was a related question that came up apparently incidentally in her discussion of the Miss S. Kotch competition—whether women should be aggressive in the "battle of the sexes." Although the phrase is a cliché, we wanted our student to expand on it in her revision in order to explore various cultural and historical forces that helped her form her opinion.

Response Statement: First Revision

The resulting revision produced a new paragraph to follow the original first paragraph:

```
History shows that every society makes its own special
demands on its members. Throughout the past, women seem to have
had ideal standards imposed on them. They have been required to
be pure, innocent, and above all the property of the men in
their lives--first their fathers and then their husbands. Today
```

we like to think that all this has changed: women have voting and other civil rights, as well as jobs and their own salaries (even if not equal to male salaries). Yet psychologically not very much is different. You can still see this in the typical way men behave in relation to women. Even women are "conditioned" to think of themselves as having to be on a pedestal and as not being aggressive toward males. That's the "dominant" way of thinking in our society's ideology still. This story shows an ordinary young girl trying to do something about the situation, just as all of us (male and female alike) should rethink how men and women should treat one another.

This second paragraph is gradually turning the initial response into a strong reading. Do you see how the student has intensified her initial reaction by writing about the ideas and feelings that lie behind it? What was a strong but undeveloped assertion in the original response statement is becoming a much more sustained argument. Our student is able to develop this strong reading by examining the assumptions underlying her own reaction—by considering how that part of her repertoire relating to "growing up as a female in our society" matches with the story's.

The second change, which also intensified the original response, came in the rewriting of paragraph 3 of the original response statement. She turned that paragraph into several new ones as follows:

But what I found most revealing is her attitude to Eddie. Here is where I'm sure it helps to be the same gender as Patty. Many men think that all women are innocent about such tactics-- that women don't like to be aggressive in the "battle of the sexes." *[Here is student's new addition:]* When a girl is attracted to someone, she is supposed to wait around, to be passive, even though she may be anxious to see him. Her role is to be asked, to be up on a pedestal. Any kind of open display of feelings, like those Patty shows to Eddie, are definitely "inappropriate."

By "battle of the sexes," I mean the ways men try to keep the upper hand, the power. Gone are the days when girls were all sugar and spice, yet the males think they are or should be. Why is this? Because that would help them stay in control. If women are allowed to express themselves, things could get out of hand for the men.

It is significant to see what Patty does. In a way she is doing to Eddie (who after all is younger than she is) what Mr. Wold was trying to do to her. In some respects her behavior seems exploitive, but as a female reader myself, I can see her as taking a little well-deserved revenge on the whole male sex for the way women have been treated in the past.

You can see how she's torn: on the one hand she just wants to be Eddie's friend; on the other hand she has genuine curiosity about what it would be like to be a woman with that kind of power.

The lesson is that women, like men, are complicated. They are what is called ''written by contradictory discourses.'' It's the same kind of double standard referred to in the ''Miss S. Kotch of New Jersey'' contest, where presumably the most attractive and wholesome girl is chosen as Miss S. Kotch, but where, in fact, it is ''fixed''--and probably required a few favors on the side. It's surprising to think how many men still think women are or ought to be ashamed of such things in this day and age.

Again, this expansion—part rereading of the story, part deepening of the original response—has turned the initial response statement into a much stronger reading, one in which our student becomes much more self-conscious and informed about the feminist position she has adopted. Of course her sense of feminism as "revenge" isn't the most positive kind of feminism. But she does state what her assumptions are about relations between the sexes; she articulates some of the cultural forces that helped her develop these assumptions and that influenced her response to Patty; and she has begun to explore some of the implications of these assumptions for a young woman in our society.

Additional Response Assignments

1. The title of this story suggests a list or stocktaking. Did you change your expectations or definitions of the word *inventory* as you read the story? Trace your process of reading the story, noting key points in which you altered or developed your sense of how the story would progress.
2. What in your general and literary repertoire influenced the ways in which you developed and revised expectations for and interpretations of this story?
3. The story is told in a very conversational tone, close to ordinary speech. Do you think such a style is appropriate to "literature"? What does your answer to this question tell you about your assumptions about "literature"?
4. The conclusion of the story is very open-ended. What do you imagine might happen next? What is the effect of the story stopping where it does?

CHARLOTTE PERKINS GILMAN (1860–1935)
The Yellow Wall-Paper

It is very seldom that mere ordinary people like John and myself secure ancestral halls for the summer.

A colonial mansion, a hereditary estate. I would say a haunted house, and reach the height of romantic felicity—but that would be asking too much of fate!

Still I will proudly declare that there is something queer about it.

Else, why should it be let so cheaply? And why have stood so long untenanted?

John laughs at me, of course, but one expects that in marriage.

John is practical in the extreme. He has no patience with faith, an intense horror of superstition, and he scoffs openly at any talk of things not to be felt and seen and put down in figures.

John is a physician, and *perhaps*—(I would not say it to a living soul, of course, but this is dead paper and a great relief to my mind—) *perhaps* that is one reason I do not get well faster.

You see he does not believe I am sick!

And what can one do?

If a physician of high standing, and one's own husband, assures friends and relatives that there is really nothing the matter with one but temporary nervous depression—a slight hysterical tendency—what is one to do?

My brother is also a physician, and also of high standing, and he says the same thing.

So I take phosphates or phosphites—whichever it is, and tonics, and journeys, and air, and exercise, and am absolutely forbidden to "work" until I am well again.

Personally, I disagree with their ideas.

Personally, I believe that congenial work, with excitement and change, would do me good.

But what is one to do?

I did write for a while in spite of them; but it *does* exhaust me a good deal—having to be so sly about it, or else meet with heavy opposition.

I sometimes fancy that in my condition if I had less opposition and more society and stimulus—but John says the very worst thing I can do is to think about my condition, and I confess it always makes me feel bad.

So I will let it alone and talk about the house.

The most beautiful place! It is quite alone, standing well back from the road, quite three miles from the village. It makes me think of English places that you read about, for there are hedges and walls and gates that lock, and lots of separate little houses for the gardeners and people.

There is a *delicious* garden! I never saw such a garden—large and shady, full of box-bordered paths, and lined with long grape-covered arbors with seats under them.

There were greenhouses, too, but they are all broken now.

There was some legal trouble, I believe, something about the heirs and co-heirs; anyhow, the place has been empty for years.

That spoils my ghostliness, I am afraid, but I don't care—there is something strange about the house—I can feel it.

I even said so to John one moonlight evening, but he said what I felt was a *draught,* and shut the window.

I get unreasonably angry with John sometimes. I'm sure I never used to be so sensitive. I think it is due to this nervous condition.

But John says if I feel so, I shall neglect proper self-control; so I take pains to control myself—before him, at least, and that makes me very tired.

I don't like our room a bit. I wanted one downstairs that opened on the piazza and had roses all over the window, and such pretty old-fashioned chintz hangings! but John would not hear of it.

He said there was only one window and not room for two beds, and no near room for him if he took another.

He is very careful and loving, and hardly lets me stir without special direction.

I have a schedule prescription for each hour in the day; he takes all care from me, and so I feel basely ungrateful not to value it more.

He said we came here solely on my account, that I was to have perfect rest and all the air I could get. "Your exercise depends on your strength, my dear," said he, "and your food somewhat on your appetite; but air you can absorb all the time." So we took the nursery at the top of the house.

It is a big, airy room, the whole floor nearly, with windows that look all ways, and air and sunshine galore. It was nursery first and then playroom and gymnasium, I should judge; for the windows are barred for little children, and there are rings and things in the walls.

The paint and paper look as if a boys' school had used it. It is stripped off—the paper—in great patches all around the head of my bed, about as far as I can reach, and in a great place on the other side of the room low down. I never saw a worse paper in my life.

One of those sprawling flamboyant patterns committing every artistic sin.

It is dull enough to confuse the eye in following, pronounced enough to constantly irritate and provoke study, and when you follow the lame uncertain curves for a little distance they suddenly commit suicide—plunge off at outrageous angles, destroy themselves in unheard of contradictions.

The color is repellent, almost revolting; a smouldering unclean yellow, strangely faded by the slow-turning sunlight.

It is a dull yet lurid orange in some places, a sickly sulphur tint in others.

No wonder the children hated it! I should hate it myself if I had to live in this room long.

There comes John, and I must put this away,—he hates to have me write a word.

* * *

We have been here two weeks, and I haven't felt like writing before, since that first day.

I am sitting by the window now, up in this atrocious nursery, and there is nothing to hinder my writing as much as I please, save lack of strength.

John is away all day, and even some nights when his cases are serious.

I am glad my case is not serious!

But these nervous troubles are dreadfully depressing.

John does not know how much I really suffer. He knows there is no *reason* to suffer, and that satisfies him.

Of course it is only nervousness. It does weigh on me so not to do my duty in any way!

I meant to be such a help to John, such a real rest and comfort, and here I am a comparative burden already!

Nobody would believe what an effort it is to do what little I am able—to dress and entertain, and order things.

It is fortunate Mary is so good with the baby. Such a dear baby!

And yet I *cannot* be with him, it makes me so nervous.

I suppose John never was nervous in his life. He laughs at me so about this wall-paper!

At first he meant to repaper the room, but afterwards he said that I was letting it get the better of me, and that nothing was worse for a nervous patient than to give way to such fancies.

He said that after the wall-paper was changed it would be the heavy bedstead, and then the barred windows, and then that gate at the head of the stairs, and so on.

"You know the place is doing you good," he said, "and really, dear, I don't care to renovate the house just for a three months' rental."

"Then do let us go downstairs," I said, "there are such pretty rooms there."

Then he took me in his arms and called me a blessed little goose, and said he would go down cellar, if I wished, and have it whitewashed into the bargain.

But he is right enough about the beds and windows and things.

It is as airy and comfortable a room as any one need wish, and, of course, I would not be so silly as to make him uncomfortable just for a whim.

I'm really getting quite fond of the big room, all but that horrid paper.

Out of one window I can see the garden, those mysterious deep-shaded arbors, the riotous old-fashioned flowers, and bushes and gnarly trees.

Out of another I get a lovely view of the bay and a little private wharf belonging to the estate. There is a beautiful shaded lane that runs down there from the house. I always fancy I see people walking in these numerous paths and arbors, but John has cautioned me not to give way to fancy in the least. He says that with my imaginative power and habit of storymaking, a nervous weakness like mine is sure to lead to all manner of excited fancies, and that I ought to use my will and good sense to check the tendency. So I try.

I think sometimes that if I were only well enough to write a little it would relieve the press of ideas and rest me.

But I find I get pretty tired when I try.

It is so discouraging not to have any advice and companionship about my work. When I get really well, John says we will ask Cousin Henry and Julia down for a long visit; but he says he would as soon put fireworks in my pillow-case as to let me have those stimulating people about now.

I wish I could get well faster.

But I must not think about that. This paper looks to me as if it *knew* what a vicious influence it had!

There is a recurrent spot where the pattern lolls like a broken neck and two bulbous eyes stare at you upside down.

I get positively angry with the impertinence of it and the everlastingness. Up and down and sideways they crawl, and those absurd, unblinking eyes are everywhere. There is one place where two breadths didn't match, and the eyes go all up and down the line, one a little higher than the other.

I never saw so much expression in an inanimate thing before, and we all know how much expression they have! I used to lie awake as a child and get more entertainment and terror out of blank walls and plain furniture than most children could find in a toy-store.

I remember what a kindly wink the knobs of our big, old bureau used to have, and there was one chair that always seemed like a strong friend.

I used to feel that if any of the other things looked too fierce I could always hop into that chair and be safe.

The furniture in this room is no worse than inharmonious, however, for we had to bring it all from downstairs. I suppose when this was used as a playroom they had to take the nursery things out, and no wonder! I never saw such ravages as the children have made here.

The wall-paper, as I said before, is torn off in spots, and it sticketh closer than a brother—they must have had perseverance as well as hatred.

Then the floor is scratched and gouged and splintered, the plaster itself is dug out here and there, and this great heavy bed which is all we found in the room, looks as if it had been through the wars.

But I don't mind it a bit—only the paper.

There comes John's sister. Such a dear girl as she is, and so careful of me! I must not let her find me writing.

She is a perfect and enthusiastic housekeeper, and hopes for no better profession. I verily believe she thinks it is the writing which made me sick!

But I can write when she is out, and see her a long way off from these windows.

There is one that commands the road, a lovely shaded winding road, and one that just looks off over the country. A lovely country, too, full of great elms and velvet meadows.

This wall-paper has a kind of sub-pattern in a different shade, a particularly irritating one, for you can only see it in certain lights, and not clearly then.

But in the places where it isn't faded and where the sun is just so—I can see a strange, provoking, formless sort of figure, that seems to skulk about behind that silly and conspicuous front design.

There's sister on the stairs!

* * *

Well, the Fourth of July is over! The people are all gone and I am tired out. John thought it might do me good to see a little company, so we just had mother and Nellie and the children down for a week.

Of course I didn't do a thing. Jennie sees to everything now.

But it tired me all the same.

John says if I don't pick up faster he shall send me to Weir Mitchell* in the fall.

But I don't want to go there at all. I had a friend who was in his hands once, and she says he is just like John and my brother, only more so!

Besides, it is such an undertaking to go so far.

I don't feel as if it was worth while to turn my hand over for anything, and I'm getting dreadfully fretful and querulous.

I cry at nothing, and cry most of the time.

Of course I don't when John is here, or anybody else, but when I am alone.

And I am alone a good deal just now. John is kept in town very often by serious cases, and Jennie is good and lets me alone when I want her to.

So I walk a little in the garden or down that lovely lane, sit on the porch under the roses, and lie down up here a good deal.

I'm getting really fond of the room in spite of the wall-paper. Perhaps *because* of the wall-paper.

It dwells in my mind so!

I lie here on this great immovable bed—it is nailed down, I believe—and follow that pattern about by the hour. It is as good as gymnastics, I assure you. I start, we'll say, at the bottom, down in the corner over there where it has not been touched, and I determine for the thousandth time that I *will* follow that pointless pattern to some sort of a conclusion.

I know a little of the principle of design, and I know this thing was not arranged on any laws of radiation, or alternation, or repetition, or symmetry, or anything else that I ever heard of.

It is repeated, of course, by the breadths, but not otherwise.

Looked at in one way each breadth stands alone, the bloated curves and flourishes—a kind of "debased Romanesque" with *delirium tremens*[2] go waddling up and down in isolated columns of fatuity.

But, on the other hand, they connect diagonally, and the sprawling outlines run off in great slanting waves of optic horror, like a lot of wallowing seaweeds in full chase.

The whole thing goes horizontally, too, at least it seems so, and I exhaust myself in trying to distinguish the order of its going in that direction.

They have used a horizontal breadth for a frieze, and that adds wonderfully to the confusion.

There is one end of the room where it is almost intact, and there, when the crosslights fade and the low sun shines directly upon it, I can almost fancy radiation after all,—the interminable grotesques seem to form around a common centre and rush off in headlong plunges of equal distraction.

It makes me tired to follow it. I will take a nap I guess.

* * *

I don't know why I should write this.

---

[1] Weir Mitchell: Silas Weir Mitchell (1829–1914), American doctor and author of works on psychology and writing.
[2] drunken ravings.

I don't want to.

I don't feel able.

And I know John would think it absurd. But I *must* say what I feel and think in some way—it is such a relief!

But the effort is getting to be greater than the relief.

Half the time now I am awfully lazy, and lie down ever so much.

John says I mustn't lose my strength, and has me take cod liver oil and lots of tonics and things, to say nothing of ale and wine and rare meat.

Dear John! He loves me very dearly, and hates to have me sick. I tried to have a real earnest reasonable talk with him the other day, and tell him how I wish he would let me go and make a visit to Cousin Henry and Julia.

But he said I wasn't able to go, nor able to stand it after I got there; and I did not make out a very good case for myself, for I was crying before I had finished.

It is getting to be a great effort for me to think straight. Just this nervous weakness I suppose.

And dear John gathered me up in his arms, and just carried me upstairs and laid me on the bed, and sat by me and read to me till it tired my head.

He said I was his darling and his comfort and all he had, and that I must take care of myself for his sake, and keep well.

He says no one but myself can help me out of it, that I must use my will and self-control and not let any silly fancies run away with me.

There's one comfort, the baby is well and happy, and does not have to occupy this nursery with the horrid wall-paper.

If we had not used it, the blessed child would have! What a fortunate escape! Why, I wouldn't have a child of mine, an impressionable little thing, live in such a room for worlds.

I never thought of it before, but it is lucky that John kept me here after all, I can stand it so much easier than a baby, you see.

Of course I never mention it to them any more—I am too wise,—but I keep watch of it all the same.

There are things in that paper that nobody knows but me, or ever will.

Behind that outside pattern the dim shapes get clearer every day.

It is always the same shape, only very numerous.

And it is like a woman stooping down and creeping about behind that pattern. I don't like it a bit. I wonder—I begin to think—I wish John would take me away from here!

* * *

It is so hard to talk with John about my case, because he is so wise, and because he loves me so.

But I tried it last night.

It was moonlight. The moon shines in all around just as the sun does.

I hate to see it sometimes, it creeps so slowly, and always comes in by one window or another.

John was asleep and I hated to waken him, so I kept still and watched the moonlight on that undulating wall-paper till I felt creepy.

The faint figure behind seemed to shake the pattern, just as if she wanted to get out.

I got up softly and went to feel and see if the paper *did* move, and when I came back John was awake.

"What is it, little girl?" he said. "Don't go walking about like that—you'll get cold."

I thought it was a good time to talk, so I told him that I really was not gaining here, and I wished he would take me away.

"Why, darling!" he said, "our lease will be up in three weeks, and I can't see how to leave before.

"The repairs are not done at home, and I cannot possibly leave town just now. Of course if you were in any danger, I could and would, but you really are better, dear, whether you can see it or not. I am a doctor, dear, and I know. You are gaining flesh and color, your appetite is better, I feel really much easier about you."

"I don't weigh a bit more," said I, "nor as much; and my appetite may be better in the evening when you are here, but it is worse in the morning when you are away!"

"Bless her little heart!" said he with a big hug, "she shall be as sick as she pleases! But now let's improve the shining hours by going to sleep, and talk about it in the morning!"

"And you won't go away?" I asked gloomily.

"Why, how can I, dear? It is only three weeks more and then we will take a nice little trip of a few days while Jennie is getting the house ready. Really dear you are better!"

"Better in body perhaps—" I began, and stopped short, for he sat up straight and looked at me with such a stern, reproachful look that I could not say another word.

"My darling," said he, "I beg of you, for my sake and for our child's sake, as well as for your own, that you will never for one instant let that idea enter your mind! There is nothing so dangerous, so fascinating, to a temperament like yours. It is a false and foolish fancy. Can you not trust me as a physician when I tell you so?"

So of course I said no more on that score, and we went to sleep before long. He thought I was asleep first, but I wasn't, and lay there for hours trying to decide whether that front pattern and the back pattern really did move together or separately.

* * *

On a pattern like this, by daylight, there is a lack of sequence, a defiance of law, that is a constant irritant to a normal mind.

The color is hideous enough, and unreliable enough, and infuriating enough, but the pattern is torturing.

You think you have mastered it, but just as you get well underway in following, it turns a back-somersault and there you are. It slaps you in the face, knocks you down, and tramples upon you. It is like a bad dream.

The outside pattern is a florid arabesque, reminding one of a fungus. If you can imagine a toadstool in joints, an interminable string of toadstools, budding and sprouting in endless convolutions—why, that is something like it.

That is, sometimes!

There is one marked peculiarity about this paper, a thing nobody seems to notice but myself, and that is that it changes as the light changes.

When the sun shoots in through the east window—I always watch for that first long, straight ray—it changes so quickly that I never can quite believe it.

That is why I watch it always.

By moonlight—the moon shines in all night when there is a moon—I wouldn't know it was the same paper.

At night in any kind of light, in twilight, candlelight, lamplight, and worst of all by moonlight, it becomes bars! The outside pattern I mean, and the woman behind it is as plain as can be.

I didn't realize for a long time what the thing was that showed behind, that dim sub-pattern, but now I am quite sure it is a woman.

By daylight she is subdued, quiet. I fancy it is the pattern that keeps her so still. It is so puzzling. It keeps me quiet by the hour.

I lie down ever so much now. John says it is good for me, and to sleep all I can.

Indeed he started the habit by making me lie down for an hour after each meal.

It is a very bad habit I am convinced, for you see I don't sleep.

And that cultivates deceit, for I don't tell them I'm awake—O no!

The fact is I am getting a little afraid of John.

He seems very queer sometimes, and even Jennie has an inexplicable look.

It strikes me occasionally, just as a scientific hypothesis,—that perhaps it is the paper!

I have watched John when he did not know I was looking, and come into the room suddenly on the most innocent excuses, and I've caught him several times *looking at the paper!* And Jennie too. I caught Jennie with her hand on it once.

She didn't know I was in the room, and when I asked her in a quiet, a very quiet voice, with the most restrained manner possible, what she was doing with the paper —she turned around as if she had been caught stealing, and looked quite angry— asked me why I should frighten her so!

Then she said that the paper stained everything it touched, that she had found yellow smooches on all my clothes and John's, and she wished we would be more careful!

Did not that sound innocent? But I know she was studying that pattern, and I am determined that nobody shall find it out but myself!

* * *

Life is very much more exciting now than it used to be. You see I have something more to expect, to look forward to, to watch. I really do eat better, and am more quiet than I was.

John is so pleased to see me improve! He laughed a little the other day, and said I seemed to be flourishing in spite of my wall-paper.

I turned it off with a laugh. I had no intention of telling him it was *because* of the wall-paper—he would make fun of me. He might even want to take me away.

I don't want to leave now until I have found it out. There is a week more, and I think that will be enough.

* * *

I'm feeling ever so much better! I don't sleep much at night, for it is so interesting to watch developments; but I sleep a good deal in the daytime.

In the daytime it is tiresome and perplexing.

There are always new shoots on the fungus, and new shades of yellow all over it. I cannot keep count of them, though I have tried conscientiously.

It is the strangest yellow, that wall-paper! It makes me think of all the yellow things I ever saw—not beautiful ones like buttercups, but old foul, bad yellow things.

But there is something else about that paper—the smell! I noticed it the moment we came into the room, but with so much air and sun it was not bad. Now we have had a week of fog and rain, and whether the windows are open or not, the smell is here.

It creeps all over the house.

I find it hovering in the dining-room, skulking in the parlor, hiding in the hall, lying in wait for me on the stairs.

It gets into my hair.

Even when I go to ride, if I turn my head suddenly and surprise it—there is that smell!

Such a peculiar odor, too! I have spent hours in trying to analyze it, to find what it smelled like.

It is not bad—at first, and very gentle, but quite the subtlest, most enduring odor I ever met.

In this damp weather it is awful. I wake up in the night and find it hanging over me.

It used to disturb me at first. I thought seriously of burning the house—to reach the smell.

But now I am used to it. The only thing I can think of that it is like is the *color* of the paper! A yellow smell.

There is a very funny mark on this wall, low down, near the mopboard. A streak that runs around the room. It goes behind every piece of furniture, except the bed, a long, straight, even *smooch,* as if it had been rubbed over and over.

I wonder how it was done and who did it, and what they did it for. Round and round and round—round and round and round!—it makes me dizzy!

* * *

I really have discovered something at last.

Through watching so much at night, when it changes so, I have finally found out. The front pattern *does* move—and no wonder! The woman behind shakes it!

Sometimes I think there are a great many women behind, and sometimes only one, and she crawls around fast, and her crawling shakes it all over.

Then in the very bright spots she keeps still, and in the very shady spots she just takes hold of the bars and shakes them hard.

And she is all the time trying to climb through. But nobody could climb through that pattern—it strangles so; I think that is why it has so many heads.

They get through, and then the pattern strangles them off and turns them upside down, and makes their eyes white!

If those heads were covered or taken off it would not be half so bad.

* * *

I think that woman gets out in the daytime!

And I'll tell you why—privately—I've seen her!

I can see her out of every one of my windows!

It is the same woman, I know, for she is always creeping, and most women do not creep by daylight.

I see her in that long shaded lane, creeping up and down. I see her in those dark grape arbors, creeping all around the garden.

I see her on that long road under the trees, creeping along, and when a carriage comes she hides under the blackberry vines.

I don't blame her a bit. It must be very humiliating to be caught creeping by daylight!

I always lock the door when I creep by daylight. I can't do it at night, for I know John would suspect something at once.

And John is so queer now, that I don't want to irritate him. I wish he would take another room! Besides, I don't want anybody to get that woman out at night but myself.

I often wonder if I could see her out of all the windows at once.

But, turn as fast as I can, I can only see out of one at one time.

And though I always see her, she *may* be able to creep faster than I can turn!

I have watched her sometimes away off in the open country, creeping as fast as a cloud shadow in a high wind.

* * *

If only that top pattern could be gotten off from the under one! I mean to try it, little by little.

I have found out another funny thing, but I shan't tell it this time! It does not do to trust people too much.

There are only two more days to get this paper off, and I believe John is beginning to notice. I don't like the look in his eyes.

And I heard him ask Jennie a lot of professional questions about me. She had a very good report to give.

She said I slept a good deal in the daytime.

John knows I don't sleep very well at night, for all I'm so quiet!

He asked me all sorts of questions, too, and pretended to be very loving and kind.

As if I couldn't see through him!

Still, I don't wonder he acts so, sleeping under this paper for three months.

It only interests me, but I feel sure John and Jennie are secretly affected by it.

* * *

Hurrah! This is the last day, but it is enough. John is to stay in town over night, and won't be out until this evening.

Jennie wanted to sleep with me—the sly thing! but I told her I should undoubtedly rest better for a night all alone.

That was clever, for really I wasn't alone a bit! As soon as it was moonlight and that poor thing began to crawl and shake the pattern, I got up and ran to help her.

I pulled and she shook, I shook and she pulled, and before morning we had peeled off yards of that paper.

A strip about as high as my head and half around the room.

And then when the sun came and that awful pattern began to laugh at me, I declared I would finish it to-day!

We go away to-morrow, and they are moving all my furniture down again to leave things as they were before.

Jennie looked at the wall in amazement, but I told her merrily that I did it out of pure spite at the vicious thing.

She laughed and said she wouldn't mind doing it herself, but I must not get tired. How she betrayed herself that time!

But I am here, and no person touches this paper but me,—not *alive!*

She tried to get me out of the room—it was too patent! But I said it was so quiet and empty and clean now that I believed I would lie down again and sleep all I could; and not to wake me even for dinner—I would call when I woke.

So now she is gone, and the servants are gone, and the things are gone, and there is nothing left but that great bedstead nailed down, with the canvas mattress we found on it.

We shall sleep downstairs to-night, and take the boat home to-morrow.

I quite enjoy the room, now it is bare again.

How those children did tear about here!

This bedstead is fairly gnawed!

But I must get to work.

I have locked the door and thrown the key down into the front path.

I don't want to go out, and I don't want to have anybody come in, till John comes.

I want to astonish him.

I've got a rope up here that even Jennie did not find. If that woman does get out, and tries to get away, I can tie her!

But I forgot I could not reach far without anything to stand on!

This bed will *not* move!

I tried to lift and push it until I was lame, and then I got so angry I bit off a little piece at one corner—but it hurt my teeth.

Then I peeled off all the paper I could reach standing on the floor. It sticks horribly and the pattern just enjoys it! All those strangled heads and bulbous eyes and waddling fungus growths just shriek with derision!

I am getting angry enough to do something desperate. To jump out of the window would be admirable exercise, but the bars are too strong even to try.

Besides I wouldn't do it. Of course not. I know well enough that a step like that is improper and might be misconstrued.

I don't like to *look* out of the windows even—there are so many of those creeping women, and they creep so fast.

I wonder if they all come out of that wall-paper as I did?

But I am securely fastened now by my well-hidden rope—you don't get *me* out in the road there!

I suppose I shall have to get back behind the pattern when it comes night, and that is hard!

It is so pleasant to be out in this great room and creep around as I please!

I don't want to go outside. I won't, even if Jennie asks me to.

For outside you have to creep on the ground, and everything is green instead of yellow.

But here I can creep smoothly on the floor, and my shoulder just fits in that long smooch around the wall, so I cannot lose my way.

Why there's John at the door!

It is no use, young man, you can't open it!

How he does call and pound!

Now he's crying for an axe.

It would be a shame to break down that beautiful door!

"John dear!" said I in the gentlest voice, "the key is down by the front steps, under a plaintain leaf!"

That silenced him for a few moments.

Then he said—very quietly indeed, "Open the door, my darling!"

"I can't," said I. "The key is down by the front door under a plaintain leaf!"

And then I said it again, several times, very gently and slowly, and said it so often that he had to go and see, and he got it of course, and came in. He stopped short by the door.

"What is the matter?" he cried. "For God's sake, what are you doing!"

I kept on creeping just the same, but I looked at him over my shoulder.

"I've got out at last," said I, "in spite of you and Jane. And I've pulled off most of the paper, so you can't put me back!"

Now why should that man have fainted? But he did, and right across my path by the wall, so that I had to creep over him every time!

Response Statement Assignments

1. The narrator of this story is usually perceived as an *unreliable* narrator. How is your response to the story influenced by this kind of narrator?
2. What other stories have you read with unreliable narrators? In what ways do they influence the **strategies** that you use to read and interpret this story?
3. How do your **assumptions** about madness influence the way you respond to the characters in the story? Do you sympathize with the narrator? Her husband? Neither? Both?
4. Explore what you feel is our society's dominant **ideology** about madness. How specifically has this ideology influenced your **repertoire,** and how does it influence the ways in which you respond to the story?

D. H. LAWRENCE (1885–1930)

The Rocking Horse Winner

There was a woman who was beautiful, who started with all the advantages, yet she had no luck. She married for love, and the love turned to dust. She had bonny children, yet she felt they had been thrust upon her, and she could not love them. They looked at her coldly, as if they were finding fault with her. And hurriedly she felt she must cover up some fault in herself. Yet what it was that she must cover up she never knew. Nevertheless, when her children were present, she always felt the centre of her heart go hard. This troubled her, and in her manner she was all the more gentle and anxious for her children, as if she loved them very much. Only she herself knew that at the centre of her heart was a hard little place that could not feel love, no, not for anybody. Everybody else said of her: "She is such a good mother. She adores her children." Only she herself, and her children themselves, knew it was not so. They read it in each other's eyes.

There were a boy and two little girls. They lived in a pleasant house, with a garden, and they had discreet servants, and felt themselves superior to anyone in the neighbourhood.

Although they lived in style, they felt always an anxiety in the house. There was never enough money. The mother had a small income, and the father had a small income, but not nearly enough for the social position which they had to keep up. The father went in to town to some office. But though he had good prospects, these prospects never materialized. There was always the grinding sense of the shortage of money, though the style was always kept up.

At last the mother said: "I will see if *I* can't make something." But she did not know where to begin. She racked her brains, and tried this thing and the other, but could not find anything successful. The failure made deep lines come into her face. Her children were growing up, they would have to go to school. There must be more money, there must be more money. The father, who was always very handsome and expensive in his tastes, seemed as if he never *would* be able to do anything worth doing. And the mother, who had a great belief in herself, did not succeed any better, and her tastes were just as expensive.

And so the house came to be haunted by the unspoken phrase: *There must be more money! There must be more money!* The children could hear it all the time, though nobody said it aloud. They heard it at Christmas, when the expensive and splendid toys filled the nursery. Behind the shining modern rocking-horse, behind the smart doll's-house, a voice would start whispering: "There *must* be more money! There *must* be more money!" And the children would stop playing, to listen for a moment. They would look into each other's eyes, to see if they had all heard. And each one saw in the eyes of the other two that they too had heard. "There *must* be more money! There *must* be more money!"

It came whispering from the springs of the still-swaying rocking-horse, and even the horse, bending his wooden, champing head, heard it. The big doll, sitting so pink and smirking in her new pram, could hear it quite plainly, and seemed to be smirking all the more self-consciously because of it. The foolish puppy, too, that took the place of the teddy-bear, he was looking so extraordinarily foolish for no other reason but that he heard the secret whisper all over the house: "There *must* be more money!"

Yet nobody ever said it aloud. The whisper was everywhere, and therefore no one spoke it. Just as no one ever says: "We are breathing!" in spite of the fact that breath is coming and going all the time.

"Mother," said the boy Paul one day, "why don't we keep a car of our own? Why do we always use uncle's, or else a taxi?"

"Because we're the poor members of the family," said the mother.

"But why *are* we, mother?"

"Well—I suppose," she said slowly and bitterly, "it's because your father has no luck."

The boy was silent for some time.

"Is luck money, mother?" he asked rather timidly.

"No, Paul. Not quite. It's what causes you to have money."

"Oh!" said Paul vaguely. "I thought when Uncle Oscar said *filthy lucker,* it meant money."

"*Filthy lucre* does mean money," said the mother. "But it's lucre, not luck."

"Oh!" said the boy. "Then what *is* luck, mother?"

"It's what causes you to have money. If you're lucky you have money. That's why it's better to be born lucky than rich. If you're rich, you may lose your money. But if you're lucky, you will always get more money."

"Oh! Will you? And is father not lucky?"

"Very unlucky, I should say," she said bitterly.

The boy watched her with unsure eyes.

"Why?" he asked.

"I don't know. Nobody ever knows why one person is lucky and another unlucky."

"Don't they? Nobody at all? Does *nobody* know?"

"Perhaps God. But He never tells."

"He ought to, then. And aren't you lucky either, mother?"

"I can't be, if I married an unlucky husband."

"But by yourself, aren't you?"

"I used to think I was, before I married. Now I think I am very unlucky indeed."

"Why?"

"Well—never mind! Perhaps I'm not really," she said.

The child looked at her, to see if she meant it. But he saw, by the lines of her mouth, that she was only trying to hide something from him.

"Well, anyhow," he said stoutly, "I'm a lucky person."

"Why?" said his mother, with a sudden laugh.

He stared at her. He didn't even know why he had said it.

"God told me," he asserted, brazening it out.

"I hope He did, dear!" she said, again with a laugh, but rather bitter.

"He did, mother!"

"Excellent!" said the mother, using one of her husband's exclamations.

The boy saw she did not believe him; or, rather, that she paid no attention to his assertion. This angered him somewhat, and made him want to compel her attention.

He went off by himself, vaguely, in a childish way, seeking for the clue to "luck." Absorbed, taking no heed of other people, he went about with a sort of stealth, seeking inwardly for luck. He wanted luck, he wanted it, he wanted it. When the two girls were playing dolls in the nursery, he would sit on his big rocking-horse, charging madly into space, with a frenzy that made the little girls peer at him uneasily. Wildly the horse careered, the waving dark hair of the boy tossed, his eyes had a strange glare in them. The little girls dared not speak to him.

When he had ridden to the end of his mad little journey, he climbed down and stood in front of his rocking-horse, staring fixedly into its lowered face. Its red mouth was slightly open, its big eye was wide and glassy-bright.

"Now!" he would silently command the snorting steed. "Now, take me to where there is luck! Now take me!"

And he would slash the horse on the neck with the little whip he had asked Uncle Oscar for. He *knew* the horse could take him to where there was luck, if only he forced it. So he would mount again, and start on his furious ride, hoping at last to get there. He knew he could get there.

"You'll break your horse, Paul!" said the nurse.

"He's always riding like that! I wish he'd leave off!" said his elder sister Joan.

But he only glared down on them in silence. Nurse gave him up. She could make nothing of him. Anyhow he was growing beyond her.

One day his mother and his Uncle Oscar came in when he was on one of his furious rides. He did not speak to them.

"Hallo, you young jockey! Riding a winner?" said his uncle.

"Aren't you growing too big for a rocking-horse? You're not a very little boy any longer, you know," said his mother.

But Paul only gave a blue glare from his big, rather close-set eyes. He would speak to nobody when he was in full tilt. His mother watched him with an anxious expression on her face.

At last he suddenly stopped forcing his horse into the mechanical gallop, and slid down.

"Well, I got there!" he announced fiercely, his blue eyes still flaring, and his sturdy long legs straddling apart.

"Where did you get to?" asked his mother.

"Where I wanted to go," he flared back at her.

"That's right, son!" said Uncle Oscar. "Don't you stop till you get there. What's the horse's name?"

"He doesn't have a name," said the boy.

"Gets on without all right?" asked the uncle.

"Well, he has different names. He was called Sansovino last week."

"Sansovino, eh? Won the Ascot. How did you know his name?"

"He always talks about horse-races with Bassett," said Joan.

The uncle was delighted to find that his small nephew was posted with all the racing news. Bassett, the young gardener, who had been wounded in the left foot in the war and had got his present job through Oscar Cresswell, whose batman he had been, was a perfect blade of the "turf." He lived in the racing events, and the small boy lived with him.

Oscar Cresswell got it all from Bassett.

"Master Paul comes and asks me, so I can't do more than tell him, sir," said Bassett, his face terribly serious, as if he were speaking of religious matters.

"And does he ever put anything on a horse he fancies?"

"Well—I don't want to give him away—he's a young sport, a fine sport, sir. Would you mind asking him himself? He sort of takes a pleasure in it, and perhaps he'd feel I was giving him away, sir, if you don't mind."

Bassett was serious as a church.

The uncle went back to his nephew and took him off for a ride in the car.

"Say, Paul, old man, do you ever put anything on a horse?" the uncle asked.

The boy watched the handsome man closely.

"Why, do you think I oughtn't to?" he parried.

"Not a bit of it! I thought perhaps you might give me a tip for the Lincoln."

The car sped on into the country, going down to Uncle Oscar's place in Hampshire.

"Honour bright?" said the nephew.

"Honour bright, son!" said the uncle.

"Well, then, Daffodil."

"Daffodil! I doubt it, sonny. What about Mirza?"

"I only know the winner," said the boy. "That's Daffodil."

"Daffodil, eh?"

There was a pause. Daffodil was an obscure horse comparatively.

"Uncle!"

"Yes, son?"

"You won't let it go any further, will you? I promised Bassett."

"Bassett be damned, old man! What's he got to do with it?"

"We're partners. We've been partners from the first. Uncle, he lent me my first five shillings, which I lost. I promised him, honour bright, it was only between me and him; only you gave me that ten-shilling note I started winning with, so I thought you were lucky. You won't let it go any further, will you?"

The boy gazed at his uncle from those big, hot, blue eyes, set rather close together. The uncle stirred and laughed uneasily.

"Right you are, son! I'll keep your tip private. Daffodil, eh? How much are you putting on him?"

"All except twenty pounds," said the boy. "I keep that in reserve."

The uncle thought it a good joke.

"You keep twenty pounds in reserve, do you, you young romancer? What are you betting, then?"

"I'm betting three hundred," said the boy, gravely. "But it's between you and me, Uncle Oscar! Honour bright?"

The uncle burst into a roar of laughter.

"It's between you and me all right, you young Nat Gould," he said, laughing. "But where's your three hundred?"

"Bassett keeps it for me. We're partners."

"He won't go quite as high as I do, I expect. Perhaps he'll go a hundred and fifty."

"What, pennies?" laughed the uncle.

"Pounds," said the child, with a surprised look at his uncle. "Bassett keeps a bigger reserve than I do."

Between wonder and amusement Uncle Oscar was silent. He pursued the matter no further, but he determined to take his nephew with him to the Lincoln races.

"Now, son," he said, "I'm putting twenty on Mirza, and I'll put five for you on any horse you fancy. What's your pick?"

"Daffodil, uncle."

"No, not the fiver on Daffodil!"

"I should if it was my own fiver," said the child.

"Good! Good! Right you are! A fiver for me and a fiver for you on Daffodil."

The child had never been to a race-meeting before, and his eyes were blue fire. He pursed his mouth tight, and watched. A Frenchman just in front had put his money on Lancelot. Wild with excitement, he flayed his arms up and down, yelling *"Lancelot! Lancelot!"* in his French accent.

Daffodil came in first, Lancelot second, Mirza third. The child, flushed and with eyes blazing, was curiously serene. His uncle brought him four five-pound notes, four to one.

"What am I to do with these?" he cried, waving them before the boy's eyes.

"I suppose we'll talk to Bassett," said the boy. "I expect I have fifteen hundred now; and twenty in reserve; and this twenty."

His uncle studied him for some moments.

"Look here, son!" he said. "You're not serious about Bassett and that fifteen hundred, are you?"

"Yes, I am. But it's between you and me, uncle. Honour bright!"

"Honour bright all right, son! But I must talk to Bassett."

"If you'd like to be a partner, uncle, with Bassett and me, we could all be partners. Only, you'd have to promise, honour bright, uncle, not to let it go beyond us three. Bassett and I are lucky, and you must be lucky, because it was your ten shillings I started winning with. . . ."

Uncle Oscar took both Bassett and Paul into Richmond Park for an afternoon, and there they talked.

"It's like this, you see, sir," Bassett said. "Master Paul would get me talking about racing events, spinning yarns, you know, sir. And he was always keen on knowing if I'd made or if I'd lost. It's about a year since, now, that I put five shillings on Blush of Dawn for him—and we lost. Then the luck turned, with that ten shillings he had from you, that we put on Singhalese. And since that time, it's been pretty steady, all things considering. What do you say, Master Paul?"

"We're all right when we're sure," said Paul. "It's when we're not quite sure that we go down."

"Oh, but we're careful then," said Bassett.

"But when are you *sure?*" smiled Uncle Oscar.

"It's Master Paul, sir," said Bassett, in a secret, religious voice. "It's as if he had it from heaven. Like Daffodil, now, for the Lincoln. That was as sure as eggs."

"Did you put anything on Daffodil?" asked Oscar Cresswell.

"Yes, sir. I made my bit."

"And my nephew?"

Bassett was obstinately silent, looking at Paul.

"I made twelve hundred, didn't I Bassett? I told uncle I was putting three hundred on Daffodil."

"That's right," said Bassett, nodding.

"But where's the money?" asked the uncle.

"I keep it safe locked up, sir. Master Paul he can have it any minute he likes to ask for it."

"What, fifteen hundred pounds?"

"And twenty! And *forty,* that is, with the twenty he made on the course."

"It's amazing!" said the uncle.

"If Master Paul offers you to be partners, sir, I would, if I were you; if you'll excuse me," said Bassett.

Oscar Cresswell thought about it.

"I'll see the money," he said.

They drove home again, and sure enough, Bassett came round to the garden-house with fifteen hundred pounds in notes. The twenty pounds reserve was left with Joe Glee, in the Turf Commission deposit.

"You see, it's all right, uncle, when I'm *sure!* Then we go strong, for all we're worth. Don't we, Bassett?"

"We do that, Master Paul."

"And when are you sure?" said the uncle, laughing.

"Oh, well, sometimes I'm *absolutely* sure, like about Daffodil," said the boy; "and sometimes I have an idea; and sometimes I haven't even an idea, have I, Bassett? Then we're careful, because we mostly go down."

"You do, do you! And when you're sure, like about Daffodil, what makes you sure, sonny?"

"Oh, well, I don't know," said the boy uneasily. "I'm sure, you know, uncle; that's all."

"It's as if he had it from heaven, sir," Bassett reiterated.

"I should say so!" said the uncle.

But he became a partner. And when the Leger was coming on, Paul was "sure" about Lively Spark, which was a quite inconsiderable horse. The boy insisted on putting a thousand on the horse, Bassett went for five hundred, and Oscar Cressell two hundred. Lively Spark came in first, and the betting had been ten to one against him. Paul had made ten thousand.

"You see," he said, "I was absolutely sure of him."

Even Oscar Cresswell had cleared two thousand.

"Look here, son," he said, "this sort of thing makes me nervous."

"It needn't, uncle! Perhaps I shan't be sure again for a long time."

"But what are you going to do with your money?" asked the uncle.

"Of course," said the boy, "I started it for mother. She said she had no luck, because father is unlucky, so I thought if *I* was lucky, it might stop whispering."

"What might stop whispering?"

"Our house. I *hate* our house for whispering."

"What does it whisper?"

"Why—why"—the boy fidgeted—"why, I don't know. But it's always short of money, you know, uncle."

"I know it, son, I know it."

"You know people send mother writs, don't you, uncle?"

"I'm afraid I do," said the uncle.

"And then the house whispers, like people laughing at you behind your back. It's awful, that is! I thought if I was lucky . . ."

"You might stop it," added the uncle.

The boy watched him with big blue eyes, that had an uncanny cold fire in them, and he said never a word.

"Well, then!" said the uncle. "What are we doing?"

"I shouldn't like mother to know I was lucky," said the boy.

"Why not, son?"

"She'd stop me."

"I don't think she would."

"Oh!"—and the boy writhed in an odd way—"I *don't* want her to know, uncle."

"All right, son! We'll manage it without her knowing."

They managed it very easily. Paul, at the other's suggestion, handed over five thousand pounds to his uncle, who deposited it with the family lawyer, who was then to inform Paul's mother that a relative had put five thousand pounds into his hands, which sum was to be paid out a thousand pounds at a time, on the mother's birthday, for the next five years.

"So she'll have a birthday present of a thousand pounds for five successive years," said Uncle Oscar. "I hope it won't make it all the harder for her later."

Paul's mother had her birthday in November. The house had been "whispering" worse than ever lately, and, even in spite of his luck, Paul could not bear up against it. He was very anxious to see the effect of the birthday letter, telling his mother about the thousand pounds.

When there were no visitors, Paul now took his meals with his parents, as he was beyond the nursery control. His mother went into town nearly every day. She had discovered that she had an odd knack of sketching furs and dress materials, so she worked secretly in the studio of a friend who was the chief "artist" for the leading drapers. She drew the figures of ladies in furs and ladies in silk and sequins for the newspaper advertisements. This young woman artist earned several thousand pounds a year, but Paul's mother only made several hundreds, and she was again dissatisfied. She so wanted to be first in something, and she did not succeed, even in making sketches for drapery advertisements.

She was down to breakfast on the morning of her birthday. Paul watched her face as she read her letters. He knew the lawyer's letter. As his mother read it, her face hardened and became more expressionless. Then a cold, determined look came on her mouth. She hid the letter under the pile of others, and said not a word about it.

"Didn't you have anything nice in the post on your birthday, mother?" said Paul.

"Quite moderately nice," she said, her voice cold and absent.

She went away to town without saying more.

But in the afternoon Uncle Oscar appeared. He said Paul's mother had had a long interview with the lawyer, asking if the whole five thousand could not be advanced at once, as she was in debt.

"What do you think, uncle?" said the boy.

"I leave it to you, son."

"Oh, let her have it, then! We can get some more with the other," said the boy.

"A bird in the hand is worth two in the bush, laddie!" said Uncle Oscar.

"But I'm sure to *know* for the Grand National; or the Lincolnshire; or else the Derby. I'm sure to know for *one* of them," said Paul.

So Uncle Oscar signed the agreement, and Paul's mother touched the whole five thousand. Then something very curious happened. The voices in the house suddenly went mad, like a chorus of frogs on a spring evening. There were certain new furnishings, and Paul had a tutor. He was *really* going to Eton, his father's school, in the following autumn. There were flowers in the winter, and a blossoming of the luxury Paul's mother had been used to. And yet the voices in the house, behind the sprays of mimosa and almond blossom, and from under the piles of iridescent cushions, simply trilled and screamed in a sort of ecstasy: "There *must* be more money! Oh-h-h; there *must* be more money. Oh, now, now-w! Now-w-w—there *must* be more money!—more than ever! More than ever!"

It frightened Paul terribly. He studied away at his Latin and Greek with his tutors. But his intense hours were spent with Bassett. The Grand National had gone by: he had not "known," and had lost a hundred pounds. Summer was at hand. He was in agony for the Lincoln. But even for the Lincoln he didn't "know," and he lost fifty pounds. He became wild-eyed and strange, as if something were going to explode in him.

"Let it alone, son! Don't you bother about it!" urged Uncle Oscar. But it was as if the boy couldn't really hear what his uncle was saying.

"I've got to know for the Derby! I've got to know for the Derby!" the child reiterated, his big blue eyes blazing with a sort of madness.

His mother noticed how overwrought he was.

"You'd better go to the seaside. Wouldn't you like to go now to the seaside, instead of waiting? I think you'd better," she said, looking down at him anxiously, her heart curiously heavy because of him.

But the child lifted his uncanny blue eyes.

"I couldn't possibly go before the Derby, mother!" he said. "I couldn't possibly!"

"Why not?" she said, her voice becoming heavy when she was opposed. "Why not? You can still go from the seaside to see the Derby with your Uncle Oscar, if that's what you wish. No need for you to wait here. Besides, I think you care too much about these races. It's a bad sign. My family has been a gambling family, and you won't know till you grow up how much damage it has done. But it has done damage. I shall have to send Bassett away, and ask Uncle Oscar not to talk racing to you, unless you promise to be reasonable about it; go away to the seaside and forget it. You're all nerves!"

"I'll do what you like, mother, so long as you don't send me away till after the Derby," the boy said.

"Send you away from where? Just from this house?"

"Yes," he said, gazing at her.

"Why, you curious child, what makes you care about this house so much, suddenly? I never knew you loved it."

He gazed at her without speaking. He had a secret within a secret, something he had not divulged, even to Bassett or to his Uncle Oscar.

But his mother, after standing undecided and a little bit sullen for some moments, said:

"Very well, then! Don't go the seaside till after the Derby if you don't wish it. But promise me you won't let your nerves go to pieces. Promise you won't think so much about horse-racing and events, as you call them!"

"Oh, no," said the boy casually. "I won't think much about them, mother. You needn't worry. I wouldn't worry, mother, if I were you."

"If you were me and I were you," said his mother, "I wonder what we *should* do!"

"But you know you needn't worry, mother, don't you?" the boy repeated.

"I should be awfully glad to know it," she said wearily.

"Oh, well, you *can,* you know. I mean, you *ought* to know you needn't worry," he insisted.

"Ought I? Then I'll see about it," she said.

Paul's secret of secrets was his wooden horse, that which had no name. Since he was emancipated from a nurse and a nursery-governess, he had had his rocking-horse removed to his own bedroom at the top of the house.

"Surely, you're too big for a rocking-horse!" his mother had remonstrated.

"Well, you see, mother, till I can have a *real* horse, I like to have *some* sort of animal about," had been his quaint answer.

"Do you feel he keeps you company?" she laughed.

"Oh, yes! He's very good, he always keeps me company, when I'm there," said Paul.

So the horse, rather shabby, stood in an arrested prance in the boy's bedroom.

The Derby was drawing near, and the boy grew more and more tense. He hardly heard what was spoken to him, he was very frail, and his eyes were really uncanny. His mother had sudden strange seizures of uneasiness about him. Sometimes, for half-an-hour, she would feel a sudden anxiety about him that was almost anguish. She wanted to rush to him at once, and know he was safe.

Two nights before the Derby, she was at a big party in town, when one of her rushes of anxiety about her boy, her first-born, gripped her heart till she could hardly speak. She fought with the feeling, might and main, for she believed in commonsense. But it was too strong. She had to leave the dance and go downstairs to telephone to the country. The children's nursery-governess was terribly surprised and startled at being rung up in the night.

"Are the children all right, Miss Wilmot?"

"Oh, yes, they are quite all right."

"Master Paul? Is he all right?"

"He went to bed as right as a trivet. Shall I run up and look at him?"

"No," said Paul's mother reluctantly. "No! Don't trouble. It's all right. Don't sit up. We shall be home fairly soon." She did not want her son's privacy intruded upon.

"Very good," said the governess.

It was about one o'clock when Paul's mother and father drove up to their house. All was still. Paul's mother went to her room and slipped off her white fur cloak. She had told her maid not to wait up for her. She heard her husband downstairs, mixing a whisky-and-soda.

And then, because of the strange anxiety at her heart, she stole upstairs to her son's room. Noiselessly she went along the upper corridor. Was there a faint noise? What was it?

She stood, with arrested muscles, outside his door, listening. There was a strange, heavy, and yet not loud noise. Her heart stood still. It was a soundless noise, yet rushing and powerful. Something huge, in violent, hushed motion. What was it? What in God's name was it? She ought to know. She felt that she knew the noise. She knew what it was.

Yet she could not place it. She couldn't say what it was. And on and on it went, like a madness.

Softly, frozen with anxiety and fear, she turned the door-handle.

The room was dark. Yet in the space near the window, she heard and saw something plunging to and fro. She gazed in fear and amazement.

Then suddenly she switched on the light, and saw her son, in his green pyjamas, madly surging on the rocking-horse. The blaze of light suddenly lit him up, as he urged the wooden horse, and lit her up, as she stood, blonde, in her dress of pale green and crystal, in the doorway.

"Paul!" she cried. "Whatever are you doing?"

"It's Malabar!" he screamed, in a powerful, strange voice. "It's Malabar!"

His eyes blazed at her for one strange and senseless second, as he ceased urging his wooden horse. Then he fell with a crash to the ground, and she, all her tormented motherhood flooding upon her, rushed to gather him up.

But he was unconscious, and unconscious he remained, with some brainfever. He talked and tossed, and his mother sat stonily by his side.

"Malabar! It's Malabar! Bassett, Bassett, I *know*! It's Malabar!"

So the child cried, trying to get up and urge the rocking-horse that gave him his inspiration.

"What does he mean by Malabar?" asked the heart-broken mother.

"I don't know," said the father stonily.

"What does he mean by Malabar?" she asked her brother Oscar.

"It's one of the horses running for the Derby," was the answer.

And, in spite of himself, Oscar Cresswell spoke to Bassett, and himself put a thousand on Malabar: at fourteen to one.

The third day of the illness was critical: they were waiting for a change. The boy, with his rather long, curly hair, was tossing ceaselessly on the pillow. He neither slept nor regained consciousness, and his eyes were like blue stones. His mother sat, feeling her heart had gone, turned actually into a stone.

In the evening, Oscar Cresswell did not come, but Bassett sent a message, saying could he come up for one moment, just one moment? Paul's mother was very angry at the intrusion, but on second thought she agreed. The boy was the same. Perhaps Bassett might bright him to consciousness.

The gardener, a shortish fellow with a little brown moustache, and sharp little brown eyes, tip-toed into the room, touched his imaginary cap to Paul's mother, and stole to the bedside, staring with glittering, smallish eyes, at the tossing, dying child.

"Master Paul!" he whispered. "Master Paul! Malabar came in first all right, a clean win. I did as you told me. You've made over seventy thousand pounds, you have; you've got over eighty thousand. Malabar came in all right, Master Paul."

"Malabar! Malabar! Did I say Malabar, mother? Did I say Malabar? Do you think I'm lucky, mother? I knew Malabar, didn't I? Over eighty thousand pounds! I call that lucky, don't you, mother? Over eighty thousand pounds! I knew, didn't I know I knew! Malabar came in all right. If I ride my horse till I'm sure, then I tell you, Bassett, you can go as high as you like. Did you go for all you were worth, Bassett?"

"I went a thousand on it, Master Paul."

"I never told you, mother, that if I can ride my horse, and, *get there,* then I'm absolutely sure—oh absolutely! Mother, did I ever tell you? I *am* lucky!"

"No, you never did," said the mother.

But the boy died in the night.

And even as he lay dead, his mother heard her brother's voice saying to her: "My God, Hester, you're eighty-odd thousand to the good, and a poor devil of a son to the bad. But, poor devil, he's best gone out of a life where he rides his rocking-horse to find a winner."

Response Statement Assignments

1. To what extent did you find this story "realistic"?
2. When you read about the house talking, did you find that believable? What reading strategies helped you **naturalize** the notion of the house talking?
3. How did you interpret the boy's insight into winners?
4. What other fiction have you read that helped you interpret this story?
5. Do you think the story is trying to convey moral insights? What moral issues do you find raised by the story? How, for instance, is your perception of the issues raised in the story influenced by prevalent attitudes toward love, money, and family relationships in our society?
6. Do you think you would take a different perspective on those issues if you shared a social background similar to the characters in the story? In explaining this, compare and contrast relevant aspects of your **repertoire** with that of the text.

MILAN KUNDERA (b. 1929)

The Hitchhiking Game

1

The needle on the gas gauge suddenly dipped toward empty and the young driver of the sports car declared that it was maddening how much gas the car ate up. "See that we don't run out of gas again," protested the girl (about twenty-two), and reminded the driver of several places where this had already happened to them. The young man replied that he wasn't worried, because whatever he went through with her had the charm of adventure for him. The girl objected; whenever they had run out of gas on the highway it had, she said, always been an adventure only for her. The young man had hidden and she had had to make ill use of her charms by thumbing a ride and letting herself be driven to the nearest gas station, then thumbing a ride back with a can of gas. The young man asked the girl whether the drivers who had given her a ride had been unpleasant, since she spoke as if her task had been a hardship. She replied (with awkward flirtatiousness) that sometimes they had been *very* pleasant but that it hadn't done her any good as she had been burdened with the can and had had to leave them before she could get anything going. "Pig," said the young man. The girl protested that she wasn't a pig, but that he really was. God knows how many girls stopped him on the highway, when he was driving the car alone! Still driving, the young man put his arm around the girl's shoulders and kissed her gently on the forehead. He knew that she loved him and that she was jealous. Jealousy isn't a pleasant quality, but if it isn't overdone (and if it's combined with modesty), apart from its inconvenience there's even something touching about it. At least that's what the young man thought. Because he was only twenty-eight, it seemed to him that he was old and knew everything that a man could know about women. In the girl sitting beside him he valued precisely what, until now, he had met with least in women: purity.

The needle was already on empty, when to the right the young man caught sight of a sign, announcing that the station was a quarter of a mile ahead. The girl hardly had time to say how relieved she was before the young man was signaling left and driving into a space in front of the pumps. However, he had to stop a little way off, because beside the pumps was a huge gasoline truck with a large metal tank and a bulky hose, which was refilling the pumps. "We'll have to wait," said the young man to the girl and got out of the car. "How long will it take?" he shouted to the man in overalls. "Only a moment," replied the attendant, and the young man said: "I've heard that one before." He wanted to go back and sit in the car, but he saw that the girl had gotten out the other side. "I'll take a little walk in the meantime," she said. "Where to?" the young man asked on purpose, wanting to see the girl's embarrassment. He had known her for a year now but she would still get shy in front of him. He enjoyed her moments of shyness, partly because they distinguished her from the women he'd met before, partly because he was aware of the law of universal transience, which made even his girl's shyness a precious thing to him.

2

The girl really didn't like it when during the trip (the young man would drive for several hours without stopping) she had to ask him to stop for a moment somewhere near a clump of trees. She always got angry when, with feigned surprise, he asked her why he should stop. She knew that her shyness was ridiculous and old-fashioned. Many times at work she had noticed that they laughed at her on account of it and deliberately provoked her. She always got shy in advance at the thought of how she was going to get shy. She often longed to feel free and easy about her body, the way most of the women around her did. She had even invented a special course in self-persuasion: she would repeat to herself that at birth every human being received one out of the millions of available bodies, as one would receive an allotted room out of the millions of rooms in an enormous hotel. Consequently, the body was fortuitous and impersonal, it was only a ready-made, borrowed thing. She would repeat this to herself in different ways, but she could never manage to feel it. This mind-body dualism was alien to her. She was too much one with her body; that is why she always felt such anxiety about it.

She experienced this same anxiety even in her relations with the young man, whom she had known for a year and with whom she was happy, perhaps because he never separated her body from her soul and she could live with him *wholly*. In this unity there was happiness, but right behind the happiness lurked suspicion, and the girl was full of that. For instance, it often occurred to her that the other women (those who weren't anxious) were more attractive and more seductive and that the young man, who did not conceal the fact that he knew this kind of woman well, would someday leave her for a woman like that. (True, the young man declared that he'd had enough of them to last his whole life, but she knew that he was still much younger than he thought.) She wanted him to be completely hers and she to be completely his, but it often seemed to her that the more she tried to give him everything, the more she denied him something: the very thing that a light and superficial love or a flirtation gives to a person. It worried her that she was not able to combine seriousness with lightheartedness.

But now she wasn't worrying and any such thoughts were far from her mind. She felt good. It was the first day of their vacation (of their two-week vacation, about which she had been dreaming for a whole year), the sky was blue (the whole year she had been worrying about whether the sky would really be blue), and he was beside her. At his, "Where to?" she blushed, and left the car without a word. She walked around the gas station, which was situated beside the highway in total isolation, surrounded by fields. About a hundred yards away (in the direction in which they were traveling), a wood began. She set off for it, vanished behind a little bush, and gave herself up to her good mood. (In solitude it was possible for her to get the greatest enjoyment from the presence of the man she loved. If his presence had been continuous, it would have kept on disappearing. Only when alone was she able to *hold on* to it.)

When she came out of the wood onto the highway, the gas station was visible. The large gasoline truck was already pulling out and the sports car moved forward toward the red turret of the pump. The girl walked on along the highway and only at times looked back to see if the sports car was coming. At last she caught sight of it. She stopped and began to wave at it like a hitchhiker waving at a stranger's car. The sports car slowed down and stopped close to the girl. The young man leaned toward the window, rolled it down, smiled, and asked, "Where are you headed, miss?" "Are you going to Bystritsa?" asked the girl, smiling flirtatiously at him. "Yes, please get in," said the young man, opening the door. The girl got in and the car took off.

3

The young man was always glad when his girl friend was gay. This didn't happen too often; she had a quite tiresome job in an unpleasant environment, many hours of overtime without compensatory leisure and, at home, a sick mother. So she often felt tired. She didn't have either particularly good nerves or self-confidence and easily fell into a state of anxiety and fear. For this reason he welcomed every manifestation of her gaiety with the tender solicitude of a foster parent. He smiled at her and said: "I'm lucky today. I've been driving for five years, but I've never given a ride to such a pretty hitchhiker."

The girl was grateful to the young man for every bit of flattery; she wanted to linger for a moment in its warmth and so she said, "You're very good at lying."

"Do I look like a liar?"

"You look like you enjoy lying to women," said the girl, and into her words there crept unawares a touch of the old anxiety, because she really did believe that her young man enjoyed lying to women.

The girl's jealousy often irritated the young man, but this time he could easily overlook it for, after all, her words didn't apply to him but to the unknown driver. And so he just casually inquired, "Does it bother you?"

"If I were going with you, then it would bother me," said the girl and her words contained a subtle, instructive message for the young man; but the end of her sentence applied only to the unknown driver, "but I don't know you, so it doesn't bother me."

"Things about her own man always bother a woman more than things about a stranger" (this was now the young man's subtle, instructive message to the girl), "so seeing that we are strangers, we could get on well together."

The girl purposely didn't want to understand the implied meaning of his message, and so she now addressed the unknown driver exclusively:

"What does it matter, since we'll part company in a little while?"

"Why?" asked the young man.

"Well, I'm getting out at Bystritsa."

"And what if I get out with you?"

At these words the girl looked up at him and found that he looked exactly as she imagined him in her most agonizing hours of jealousy. She was alarmed at how he was flattering her and flirting with her (an unknown hitchhiker), and *how becoming it was to him.* Therefore she responded with defiant provocativeness, "What would *you* do with me, I wonder?"

"I wouldn't have to think too hard about what to do with such a beautiful woman," said the young man gallantly and at this moment he was once again speaking far more to his own girl than to the figure of the hitchhiker.

But this flattering sentence made the girl feel as if she had caught him at something, as if she had wheedled a confession out of him with a fraudulent trick. She felt toward him of brief flash of intense hatred and said, "Aren't you rather too sure of yourself?"

The young man looked at the girl. Her defiant face appeared to him to be completely convulsed. He felt sorry for her and longed for her usual, familiar expression (which he used to call childish and simple). He leaned toward her, put his arm around her shoulders, and softly spoke the name with which he usually addressed her and with which he now wanted to stop the game.

But the girl released herself and said: "You're going a bit too fast!"

At this rebuff the young man said: "Excuse me, miss," and looked silently in front of him at the highway.

4

The girl's pitiful jealousy, however, left her as quickly as it had come over her. After all, she was sensible and knew perfectly well that all this was merely a game. Now it even struck her as a little ridiculous that she had repulsed her man out of jealous rage. It wouldn't be pleasant for her if he found out why she had done it. Fortunately women have the miraculous ability to change the meaning of their actions after the event. Using this ability, she decided that she had repulsed him not out of anger but so that she could go on with the game, which, with its whimsicality, so well suited the first day of their vacation.

So again she was the hitchhiker, who had just repulsed the overenterprising driver, but only so as to slow down his conquest and make it more exciting. She half turned toward the young man and said caressingly:

"I didn't mean to offend you, mister!"

"Excuse me, I won't touch you again," said the young man.

He was furious with the girl for not listening to him and refusing to be herself when that was what he wanted. And since the girl insisted on continuing in her role, he transferred his anger to the unknown hitchhiker whom she was portraying. And all at once he discovered the character of his own part: he stopped making the gallant remarks with which he had wanted to flatter his girl in a roundabout way, and began to play the tough guy who treats woman to the coarser aspects of his masculinity: willfulness, sarcasm, self-assurance.

This role was a complete contradiction of the young man's habitually solicitous approach to the girl. True, before he had met her, he had in fact behaved roughly rather than gently toward women. But he had never resembled a heartless tough guy, because he had never demonstrated either a particularly strong will or ruthlessness. However, if he did not resemble such a man, nonetheless he had *longed* to at one time. Of course it was a quite naive desire, but there it was. Childish desires withstand all the snares of the adult mind and often survive into ripe old age. And this childish desire quickly took advantage of the opportunity to embody itself in the proffered role.

The young man's sarcastic reserve suited the girl very well—it freed her from herself. For she herself was, above all, the epitome of jealousy. The moment she stopped seeing the gallantly seductive young man beside her and saw only his inaccessible face, her jealousy subsided. The girl could forget herself and give herself up to her role.

Her role? What was her role? It was a role out of trashy literature. The hitchhiker stopped the car not to get a ride, but to seduce the man who was driving the car. She was an artful seductress, cleverly knowing how to use her charms. The girl slipped into this silly, romantic part with an ease that astonished her and held her spellbound.

5

There was nothing the young man missed in his life more than lightheartedness. The main road of his life was drawn with implacable precision. His job didn't use up merely eight hours a day, it also infiltrated the remaining time with the compulsory boredom of meetings and home study, and, by means of the attentiveness of his countless male and female colleagues, it infiltrated the wretchedly little time he had left for his private life as well. This private life never remained secret and sometimes even became the subject of gossip and public discussion. Even two weeks' vacation didn't give him a feeling of liberation and adventure; the gray shadow of precise planning lay even here. The scarcity of summer accommodations in our country compelled him to book a room in the Tatras six months in advance, and since for that he needed a recommendation from his office, its omnipresent brain thus did not cease knowing about him even for an instant.

He had become reconciled to all this, yet all the same from time to time the terrible thought of the straight road would overcome him—a road along which he was being pursued, where he was visible to everyone, and from which he could not turn aside. At this moment that thought returned to him. Through an odd and brief conjunction of ideas the figurative road became identified with the real highway along which he was driving—and this led him suddenly to do a crazy thing.

"Where did you say you wanted to go?" he asked the girl.

"To Banska Bystritsa," she replied.

"And what are you going to do there?"

"I have a date there."

"Who with?"

"With a certain gentleman."

The car was just coming to a large crossroads. The driver slowed down so he could read the road signs, then turned off to the right.

"What will happen if you don't arrive for that date?"

"It would be your fault and you would have to take care of me."

"You obviously didn't notice that I turned off in the direction of Nove Zamky."

"Is that true? You've gone crazy!"

"Don't be afraid. I'll take care of you," said the young man.

So they drove and chatted thus—the driver and the hitchhiker who did not know each other.

The game all at once went into a higher gear. The sports car was moving away not only from the imaginary goal of Banska Bystritsa, but also from the real goal, toward which it had been heading in the morning: the Tatras and the room that had been booked. Fiction was suddenly making an assault upon real life. The young man was moving away from himself and from the implacable straight road, from which he had never strayed until now.

"But you said you were going to the Low Tatras!" The girl was surprised.

"I am going, miss, wherever I feel like going. I'm a free man and I do what I want and what it pleases me to do."

6

When they drove into Nove Zamky it was already getting dark.

The young man had never been here before and it took him a while to orient himself. Several times he stopped the car and asked the passersby directions to the hotel. Several streets had been dug up, so that the drive to the hotel, even though it was quite close by (as all those who had been asked asserted), necessitated so many detours and roundabout routes that it was almost a quarter of an hour before they finally stopped in front of it. The hotel looked unprepossessing, but it was the only one in town and the young man didn't feel like driving on. So he said to the girl, "Wait here," and got out of the car.

Out of the car he was, of course, himself again. And it was upsetting for him to find himself in the evening somewhere completely different from his intended destination—the more so because no one had forced him to do it and as a matter of fact he hadn't even really wanted to. He blamed himself for this piece of folly, but then became reconciled to it. The room in the Tatras could wait until tomorrow and it wouldn't do any harm if they celebrated the first day of their vacation with something unexpected.

He walked through the restaurant—smoky, noisy, and crowded—and asked for the reception desk. They sent him to the back of the lobby near the staircase, where behind a glass panel a superannuated blonde was sitting beneath a board full of keys. With difficulty, he obtained the key to the only room left.

The girl, when she found herself alone, also threw off her role. She didn't feel ill-humored, though, at finding herself in an unexpected town. She was so devoted to the young man that she never had doubts about anything he did, and confidently entrusted every moment of her life to him. On the other hand the idea once again popped into her mind that perhaps—just as she was now doing—other women had waited for her man in his car, those women whom he met on business trips. But surprisingly enough this idea didn't upset her at all now. In fact, she smiled at the thought of how nice it was that today she was this other woman, this irresponsible, indecent other woman, one of those women of whom she was so jealous. It seemed to her that she was cutting them all out, that she had learned how to use their weapons; how to give the young man what until now she had not known how to give him: lightheartedness, shamelessness, and dissoluteness. A curious feeling of satisfaction filled her, because she alone had the ability to be all women and in this way (she alone) could completely captivate her lover and hold his interest.

The young man opened the car door and led the girl into the restaurant. Amid the din, the dirt, and the smoke he found a single, unoccupied table in a corner.

7

"So how are you going to take care of me now?" asked the girl provocatively.

"What would you like for an aperitif?"

The girl wasn't too fond of alcohol, still she drank a little wine and liked vermouth fairly well. Now, however, she purposely said: "Vodka."

"Fine," said the young man. "I hope you won't get drunk on me."

"And if I do?" said the girl.

The young man did not reply but called over a waiter and ordered two vodkas and two steak dinners. In a moment the waiter brought a tray with two small glasses and placed it in front of them.

The man raised his glass, "To you!"

"Can't you think of a wittier toast?"

Something was beginning to irritate him about the girl's game. Now sitting face to face with her, he realized that it wasn't just the *words* which were turning her into a stranger, but that her *whole persona* had changed, the movements of her body and her facial expression, and that she unpalatably and faithfully resembled that type of woman whom he knew so well and for whom he felt some aversion.

And so (holding his glass in his raised hand), he corrected his toast: "O.K., then I won't drink to you, but to your kind, in which are combined so successfully the better qualities of the animal and the worse aspects of the human being."

"By 'kind' do you mean all women?" asked the girl.

"No, I mean only those who are like you."

"Anyway it doesn't seem very witty to me to compare a woman with an animal."

"O.K.," the young man was still holding his glass aloft, "then I won't drink to your kind, but to your soul. Agreed? To your soul, which lights up when it descends from your head into your belly, and which goes out when it rises back up to your head."

The girl raised her glass. "O.K., to my soul, which descends into my belly."

"I'll correct myself once more," said the young man. "To your belly, into which your soul descends."

"To my belly," said the girl, and her belly (now that they had named it specifically), as it were, responded to the call; she felt every inch of it.

Then the waiter brought their steaks and the young man ordered them another vodka and some soda water (this time they drank to the girl's breasts), and the conversation continued in this peculiar, frivolous tone. It irritated the young man more and more how *well able* the girl was to become the lascivious miss. If she was able to do it so well, he thought, it meant that she really *was* like that. After all, no alien soul had entered into her from somewhere in space. What she was acting now was she herself; perhaps it was that part of her being which had formerly been locked up and which the pretext of the game had let out of its cage. Perhaps the girl supposed that by means of the game she was *disowning* herself, but wasn't it the other way around? Wasn't she becoming herself only through the game? Wasn't she freeing herself through the game? No, opposite him was not sitting a strange woman in his girl's body; it was his girl, herself, no one else. He looked at her and felt growing aversion toward her.

However, it was not only aversion. The more the girl withdrew from him *psychically,* the more he longed for her *physically.* The alien quality of her soul drew attention to her body, yes, as a matter of fact it turned her body into a body for *him* as if until now it had existed for the young man hidden within clouds of compassion, tenderness, concern, love, and emotion, as if it had been lost in these clouds (yes, as if this body had been lost!). It seemed to the young man that today he was seeing his girl's body for the first time.

After her third vodka and soda the girl got up and said flirtatiously, "Excuse me."

The young man said, "May I ask you where you are going, miss?"

"To piss, if you'll permit me," said the girl and walked off between the tables back toward the plush screen.

8

She was pleased with the way she had astounded the young man with this word, which—in spite of all its innocence—he had never heard from her. Nothing seemed to her truer to the character of the woman she was playing than this flirtatious emphasis placed on the word in question. Yes, she was pleased, she was in the best of moods. The game captivated her. It allowed her to feel what she had not felt till now: a *feeling* of *happy-go-lucky irresponsibility.*

She, who was always uneasy in advance about her every next step, suddenly felt completely relaxed. The alien life in which she had become involved was a life without shame, without biographical specifications, without past or future, without obligations. It was a life that was extraordinarily free. The girl, as a hitchhiker, could do anything, *everything was permitted her.* She could say, do, and feel whatever she liked.

She walked through the room and was aware that people were watching her from all the tables. It was a new sensation, one she didn't recognize: *indecent joy caused by her body.* Until now she had never been able to get rid of the fourteen-year-old girl within herself who was ashamed of her breasts and had the disagreeable feeling that she was indecent, because they stuck out from her body and were visible. Even though she was proud of being pretty and having a good figure, this feeling of pride was always immediately curtailed by shame. She rightly suspected that feminine beauty functioned above all as sexual provocation and she found this distasteful. She longed for her body to relate only to the man she loved. When men stared at her breasts in the street it seemed to her that they were invading a piece of her most secret privacy which should belong only to herself and her lover. But now she was the hitchhiker, the woman without a destiny. In this role she was relieved of the tender bonds of her love and began to be intensely aware of her body. And her body became more aroused the more alien the eyes watching it.

She was walking past the last table when an intoxicated man, wanting to show off his worldliness, addressed her in French: *"Combien, mademoiselle?"*

The girl understood. She thrust out her breasts and fully experienced every movement of her hips, then disappeared behind the screen.

9

It was a curious game. This curiousness was evidenced, for example, in the fact that the young man, even though he himself was playing the unknown driver remarkably well, did not for a moment stop seeing his girl in the hitchhiker. And it was precisely this that was tormenting. He saw his girl seducing a strange man, and had the bitter privilege of being present, of seeing at close quarters how she looked and of hearing what she said when she was cheating on him (when she had cheated on him, when she would cheat on him). He had the paradoxical honor of being himself the pretext for her unfaithfulness.

This was all the worse because he worshipped rather than loved her. It had always seemed to him that her inward nature was *real* only within the bounds of fidelity and purity, and that beyond these bounds it simply didn't exist. Beyond these bounds she would cease to be herself, as water ceases to be water beyond the boiling point. When he now saw her crossing this horrifying boundary with nonchalant elegance, he was filled with anger.

The girl came back from the rest room and complained: "A guy over there asked me: *Combien, mademoiselle?*"

"You shouldn't be surprised," said the young man, "after all, you look like a whore."

"Do you know that it doesn't bother me in the least?"

"Then you should go with the gentleman!"

"But I have you."

"You can go with him after me. Go and work out something with him."

"I don't find him attractive."

"But in principle you have nothing against it, having several men in one night."

"Why not, if they're good-looking."

"Do you prefer them one after the other or at the same time?"

"Either way," said the girl.

The conversation was proceeding to still greater extremes of rudeness; it shocked the girl slightly but she couldn't protest. Even in a game there lurks a lack of freedom; even a game is a trap for the players. If this had not been a game and they had really been two strangers, the hitchhiker could long ago have taken offense and left. But there's no escape from a game. A team cannot flee from the playing field before the end of the match, chess pieces cannot desert the chessboard: the boundaries of the playing field are fixed. The girl knew that she had to accept whatever form the game might take, just because it was a game. She knew that the more extreme the game became, the more it would be a game and the more obediently she would have to play it. And it was futile to evoke good sense and warn her dazed soul that she must keep her distance from the game and not take it seriously. Just because it was only a game her soul was not afraid, did not oppose the game, and narcotically sank deeper into it.

The young man called the waiter and paid. Then he got up and said to the girl, "We're going."

"Where to?" The girl feigned surprise.

"Don't ask, just come on," said the young man.

"What sort of way is that to talk to me?"

"The way I talk to whores," said the young man.

10

They went up the badly lit staircase. On the landing below the second floor a group of intoxicated men was standing near the rest room. The young man caught hold of the girl from behind so that he was holding her breast with his hand. The men by the rest room saw this and began to call out. The girl wanted to break away, but the young man yelled at her: "Keep still!" The men greeted this with general ribaldry and addressed several dirty remarks to the girl. The young man and the girl reached the second floor. He opened the door of their room and switched on the light.

It was a narrow room with two beds, a small table, a chair, and a washbasin. The young man locked the door and turned to the girl. She was standing facing him in a defiant pose with insolent sensuality in her eyes. He looked at her and tried to discover behind her lascivious expression the familiar features which he loved tenderly. It was as if he were looking at two images through the same lens, at two images superimposed one upon the other with the one showing through the other. These two images showing through each other were telling him that *everything* was in the girl, that her soul was terrifyingly amorphous, that it held faithfulness and unfaithfulness, treachery and innocence, flirtatiousness and chastity. This disorderly jumble seemed disgusting to him, like the variety to be found in a pile of garbage. Both images continued to show through each other and the young man understood that the girl differed only on the surface from other women, but deep down was the same as they: full of all possible thoughts, feelings, and vices, which justified all his secret misgivings and fits of jealousy. The impression that certain outlines delineated her as an individual was only a delusion to which the other person, the one who was looking, was subject—namely himself. It seemed to him that the girl he loved was a creation of his desire, his thoughts, and his faith and that the *real* girl now standing in front of him was hopelessly alien, hopelessly *ambiguous.* He hated her.

"What are you waiting for? Strip," he said.

The girl flirtatiously bent her head and said, "Is it necessary?"

The tone in which she said this seemed to him very familiar; it seemed to him that once long ago some other woman had said this to him, only he no longer knew which one. He longed to humiliate her. Not the hitchhiker, but his own girl. The game merged with life. The game of humiliating the hitchhiker became only a pretext for humiliating his girl. The young man had forgotten that he was playing a game. He simply hated the woman standing in front of him. He stared at her and took a fifty-crown bill from his wallet. He offered it to the girl. "Is that enough?"

The girl took the fifty crowns and said: "You don't think I'm worth much."

The young man said: "You aren't worth more."

The girl nestled up against the young man. "You can't get around me like that! You must try a different approach, you must work a little!"

She put her arms around him and moved her mouth toward his. He put his fingers on her mouth and gently pushed her away. He said: "I only kiss women I love."

"And you don't love me?"

"No."

"Whom do you love?"

"What's that got to do with you? Strip!"

11

She had never undressed like this before. The shyness, the feeling of inner panic, the dizziness, all that she had always felt when undressing in front of the young man (and she couldn't hide in the darkness), all this was gone. She was standing in front of him self-confident, insolent, bathed in light, and astonished at where she had all of a sudden discovered the gestures, heretofore unknown to her, of a slow, provocative striptease. She took in his glances, slipping off each piece of clothing with a caressing movement and enjoying each individual stage of this exposure.

But then suddenly she was standing in front of him completely naked and at this moment it flashed through her head that now the whole game would end, that, since she had stripped off her clothes, she had also stripped away her dissimulation, and that being naked meant that she was now herself and the young man ought to come up to her now and make a gesture with which he would wipe out everything and after which would follow only their most intimate lovemaking. So she stood naked in front of the young man and at this moment stopped playing the game. She felt embarrassed and on her face appeared the smile, which really belonged to her—a shy and confused smile.

But the young man didn't come to her and didn't end the game. He didn't notice the familiar smile. He saw before him only the beautiful, alien body of his own girl, whom he hated. Hatred cleansed his sensuality of any sentimental coating. She wanted to come to him, but he said: "Stay where you are, I want to have a good look at you." Now he longed only to treat her as a whore. But the young man had never had a whore and the ideas he had about them came from literature and hearsay. So he turned to these ideas and the first thing he recalled was the image of a woman in black underwear (and black stockings) dancing on the shiny top of a piano. In the little hotel room there was no piano, there was only a small table covered with a linen cloth leaning against the wall. He ordered the girl to climb up on it. The girl made a pleading gesture, but the young man said, "You've been paid."

When she saw the look of unshakable obsession in the young man's eyes, she tried to go on with the game, even though she no longer could and no longer knew how. With tears in her eyes she climbed onto the table. The top was scarcely three feet square and one leg was a little bit shorter than the others so that standing on it the girl felt unsteady.

But the young man was pleased with the naked figure, now towering above him, and the girl's shy insecurity merely inflamed his imperiousness. He wanted to see her body in all positions and from all sides, as he imagined other men had seen it and would see it. He was vulgar and lascivious. He used words that she had never heard from him in her life. She wanted to refuse, she wanted to be released from the game. She called him by his first name, but he immediately yelled at her that she had no right to address him so intimately. And so eventually in confusion and on the verge of tears, she obeyed, she bent forward and squatted according to the young man's wishes, saluted, and then wiggled her hips as she did the Twist for him. During a slightly more violent movement, when the cloth slipped beneath her feet and she nearly fell, the young man caught her and dragged her to the bed.

He had intercourse with her. She was glad that at least now finally the unfortunate game would end and they would again be the two people they had been before and would love each other. She wanted to press her mouth against his. But the young man pushed her head away and repeated that he only kissed women he loved. She burst into loud sobs. But she wasn't even allowed to cry, because the young man's furious passion gradually won over her body, which then silenced the complaint of her soul. On the bed there were soon two bodies in perfect harmony, two sensual bodies, alien to each other. This was exactly what the girl had most dreaded all her life and had scrupulously avoided till now: love-making without emotion or love. She knew that she had crossed the forbidden boundary, but she proceeded across it without objections and as a full participant—only somewhere, far off in a corner of her consciousness, did she feel horror at the thought that she had never known such pleasure, never so much pleasure as at this moment—beyond that boundary.

12

Then it was all over. The young man got up off the girl and, reaching out for the long cord hanging over the bed, switched off the light. He didn't want to see the girl's face. He knew that the game was over, but didn't feel like returning to their customary relationship. He feared this return. He lay beside the girl in the dark in such a way that their bodies would not touch.

After a moment he heard her sobbing quietly. The girl's hand diffidently, childishly touched his. It touched, withdrew, then touched again, and then a pleading, sobbing voice broke the silence, calling him by his name and saying, "I am me, I am me . . ."

The young man was silent, he didn't move, and he was aware of the sad emptiness of the girl's assertion, in which the unknown was defined in terms of the same unknown quantity.

And the girl soon passed from sobbing to loud crying and went on endlessly repeating this pitiful tautology: "I am me, I am me, I am me . . ."

The young man began to call compassion to his aid (he had to call it from afar, because it was nowhere near at hand), so as to be able to calm the girl. There were still thirteen days' vacation before them.

Response Statement Assignments

1. Do you feel that the events in this story could actually happen, or do they seem too contrived—possible only in the world of fiction? On what basis can you make *fact* versus *fiction* distinctions?
2. Can you identify with either the man or the woman? Do you feel that one or the other of them is "right"?
3. What role do you think your gender plays in the way you respond to this story?
4. What **reading strategies** did you use to go about interpreting the story? What, for example, would you say it is *about?*
5. What are the assumptions of this story (a) about the nature of the relations between men and women, (b) about the individual, (c) about language, (d) about the nature of a short story? Do the attitudes of the story confirm or challenge your own assumptions?

RONALD SUKENICK (b. 1932)

The Birds

The the the

        Nuthatch walks up the tree a Prussian soldier pivots walks back down

        birds

   the

        Nuthatch slick arctic acrobat seal bullets through blank air silence of page the stream carries mainly on its glassy surface rippled clouds inventing themselves from minute to minute toss in a stone

The the I want to tell you the story about "ear-tree." It was on Icelandic that eighteen-hour flight from Luxemburg where your feet swell up. We cruised among fantastic shapes, formations piling shifting flowing, distortions of distortions of distortions at all altitudes. The plane skimmed across a kind of ocean of streaming transformations, the wings clipped white cumuli, and on the actual ocean waves were ripples were wrinkles, viscid metal crawling across the earth, the land itself a slower lava, somewhat thicker, especially that of Iceland, where that was what it was. I was looking out over the wing as I watched a wisp of white blew back from the engine, then another, another, and after a pause, a band of grey I looked up the aisle for the stewardess when I looked back the smoke was roiling from the engine a greasy black plume with suddenly red at its root . . .

Wings pulled in it allowed itself to fall, a stroke of scarlet from green to green.

It began in '62 a Chinese restaurant naturally midtown I remember very well because that was the phase when I had a thing with fortune cookies I am always interested in any overt confrontation

with chance though if you stop to think about it every moment is such a confrontation for each of us as likely to provide the cue for something tasty an

adventure something other than sex a coincidence in any case one was tired of sex I mean of thinking about it preferably a

coincidence such things renew my faith in the unknown however the fortune merely said, "You will soon plan another oriental meal" but that wasn't the interesting thing.

Corrosive chatter. Starlings are a bore despite iridescences. They're too precocious, and have no intelligence. "We put the snake live into the freezer it was at least two feet long and when we took it out it was frozen into this really interesting shape stiff as a board but then we hung it up and it began to smell. What ever happened to Phillip Morris? And mockies? There always used to be a lot of mockies. I had an aunt who always used to smoke Phillip Morris. She got lung cancer though. She was a mockie. She's dead now. I guess that's what happens to them."

The Yellow-shafted Flicker appears around April. The male has a black "mustache." Its strange laugh haunts the woods but seems to be a courtship cry. Lovemaking involves reciprocal undulations of the long necks like oriental dancers. The underwing is an astonishing pink-gold. Note the pure white rump in flight.

The dress was made of clinging white nylon jersey of a thinness that in certain angles of light would outline the thighs or reveal the curve of a breast and which, when taut against the skin, assumed something of the warm flesh tone. The loose ankle-length curtain of skirt was slit at the side to the top of the thigh. The backless halter scooped down to the point at which the swell and division of the buttocks become apparent, and was slashed to the waist in front, baring both the inner and outer curves of the breasts, leaving the nipples free to poke and bob through the material.

"A pattern was seen in the use of females to bite and kick the policemen" *New York Times* 5/7/68.

Its drumming, distinct from other peckers, resembles the sound of a muffled machine gun, a soft, hollow automatic weapon.

He came stumbling up in Tompkins square with his red scabby face and clapped a hand on my shoulder: "Say buddy I'm a junkie no I mean not a junkie a wino." That was how I met Sparrow. Oh nobody knew what his name really was we called him Sparrow. After the saying, "Hot as a Sparrow." He used to say things to me like, "The salient fact about American culture is that we all have to get back to nipples and start over again. Whole cockamanie country." He's also the one who said "I wuz-a fuck 'is-a wife." When he talked like that we used to call him "the Cardinal" because he seemed so intellectual. Like a Cardinal I mean, if you really look at one.

With one stroke rose half an arc then wings pulled in allowed itself to fall like diving over a wave.

I want to write a story that does a lot of infolding and outfolding. Majestic infolding and outfolding. No petty invective and venom. No comic bits, no noodgy satire like Shawanga Lodge casino. Calm, slow exfoliations. The life cycle of Whistling Swans. Inexorable curves of passion. Rise and fall of continents. Concrete. Innocent. Beautiful. No meaning.

    30 million Americans living in poverty
    it says in I. F. Stone
    in the richest country in the world
    people eat clay to still the pains of an empty belly
    children come to school too hungry to learn
    and the infants of the poor suffer
    irreversible brain damage from protein deprivation
    the 42.7% of our farmers
    with incomes of less than $2,500 a year
    received only 4.5% of total farm subsidies
    while the top 10%
    many of them farm corporations or vertical trusts
    received 64.5%
    with a budget allocated 80% to the Pentagon
    and 10% to health education and welfare

This is what I call pure poetry. This is the New American Poetry, the poetry of pure fact. This is the purity that has been missing from our poems.

Red-winged Blackbirds floating in like Piper Cubs, suns on shoulders. Phoebe brooding on her egg. Towhee, Picasso camouflage, comic butler in tails. Catbird chat. Brown Thrasher variations. Oriole riff. Pheasants waltz across the road. In the field a Crow barks. A Hawk hangs in the air, absolutely still. Grouse explode in the underbrush. Doves at their vespers. Invisible, huge in the night sky, a train of Canada Geese goes honking and gabbling full five minutes from engine to caboose.

There was an item on the menu and the Chinese was translated as "Ear-tree." It was right between Shar Ding Op (chickens, Chinese frankfurter, water chestnut) and Hong Hong Duk (lobster tails, pig flesh, Chinese vegetable). Myself I was all for getting the "Ten Ingredient." I felt expansive and experimental. But Phoebe, who was a big girl, tended toward "Mile High Rice," with maybe an order of "Stopped Duck," or "Blistered Beef," whatever that was. So then we asked ourselves, well, what would "the Sparrow" do? Our eyes met for an instant. There was no doubt about it: "Ear-tree." We didn't even have to speak.

"Seen as how I'm a nice guy, I'll give you a tip. We like to stop guys with long hair, especially in old cars. They look like students. You're a teacher. Teach and be taught."

I put the ticket in my pocket. "Yeah. Well I didn't know driving with studded snow tires was illegal in this state after May first as of ten days ago." I opened my car door.

"Hey. Come 'ere."

I walked back to the patrol car.

"It's not illegal."

"No?"

"No, it's unlawful."

"Oh."

I walked back to my car and opened the door.

"Hey. Come 'ere."

I walked back to the patrol car.

"Ya know what illegal is?"

"No, what?"

"It's a sick bird. Hah hah hah."

Q. When does a bird break the law?

A. When it's a Robin.

Q. What characteristic distinguishes the Bald Eagle?

A. Its balls.

Q. When is a bird not a bird?

A. When it's a horse.

        poor Americans are four times as likely to die
        before the age of 35 as the average citizen
        Negro women in Mississippi die
        six times as often in childbirth as white women
        in some urban ghettos of the North
        one child in ten dies in infancy
        the health gap between rich and poor is growing
        in 1940 the infant mortality rate for non-whites
        was 70% higher than that for whites
        in 1962 the rate was 90% greater
        the life expectancy of an American Negro is 61 years
        that of a white American
        is 68
        it says
        in the *Sunday*
        Times

The Downy Woodpecker, in his prison outfit, is easily confused with the Hairy, which in fact is almost identical. However the Downy is smaller than the Hairy, and its call, *pik,* is softer than Hairy's. The Black-capped Chickadee is the friendliest of acrobats. The Bobwhite is a gallinaceous bird, very henny in other words, and acts it. But let us ascend from the ridiculous to the majestic. The Whistling Swan is common. It has a wingspan of over seven feet. Like other swans, it has a deep, ponderous flight, neck extended. When swimming neck is stiff and straight; secondaries are not raised.

Q. What bird would you be glad to see if you were out of gas?
A. The Petrel.
Q. What birds can't fly straight?
A. Terns.
Q. What birds are often run over by trains?
A. Rails.
Q. What bird's ass would you not want to sit on?
A. The Pintail's.
Q. Which-a bird is not-a yours-a?
A. Myna.
Q. When does a bird make a sacrifice?
A. When it's a Bunting.
Q. What bird blows his whistle?
Q. Old Dickcissel, old Dickcissel.

                              birds

        the

                         what do they say
through the empty air
                         keep-back keep-back
peter-peter-peter
                         tea-cher tea-cher
o-say mari-a
                         hurry worry flurry blurry
drink-your-tea drink-your-tea
                         old sam peabodypeabodypeabody
ticket-ticket-ticket-ticket

```
                        wide-a-wake
rounde-lay rounde-lay
                        trees trees if you please
witchery-witchery-witchery
                        whip-three-beers
chicky-tucky-tuck
                        chicky-tucky-tuck
```

We are all, of course, familiar with that kind of anthropomorphic slop. What do the birds really say when you listen hard and understand what they are saying? They say k-a-a-a. They say kwrrk. They say

```
                        kow-kow-kow
keeur                                                   kleep
                        kzrrt
prrrp                                                   bzee
                        plick
rronk                                                   tlu-tlu
                        krr-oww
zrurrr                                                  wheet
                        peent
tsweep                                                  cuh-cuh
                        churree
che-bunk                                                kraaa
                        che-bek
jeet                                                    hooah
                        tschizzik
kirrik                                                  ssllick
                        karr-reek
kwuririp                                                kek-kek-kek
                        kee-oo
auw                                                     churweeoo
                ooah-ooo-oo-oo
pchip ee pcheewee                                       breep
```

But then again, what does it matter what they say? What matters is that they carve shapes from nothingness, decorate the silence, make melodious distinctions to distinguish one moment finely from the next.

I call waiter. What thisee here, I say, He says, That is "ear-tree," a delicious Oriental specialty. But Phoebe no likee. What is? she ask. She little girl, no muchee eatee. "Ear-tree" is a popular and delicious Cantonese dish, say waiter. He Chinee fella. It is highly recommended, he say. But what is? I say. Waiter shrug and stare to other sidee room with inscrutable Chinee face. No likee, Phoebe say. You got Chicken Chow Mein. Waiter nod. I order Chop Suey. Then other customer come. They order "ear-tree." Waiter go in Kitchen, we hear yellee to cook: Two spaghettis! I callee waiter. What this "ear-tree," I say. I pointee at menu. You say is Canton dish. Then waiter answer: It doesn't matter what you say. What matters is to hurl the words at the silence of the page like hand grenades. With feeling. Look out! someone screamed. He's got a gun!

"But why 'ear-tree'?" asked Phoebe, wide-eyed. She was a slim, light-haired pale face on summer vacation from Bryn Mawr College, but with very big boobs.

"Ah, these ees the ow-you-say question my young chérie," answered Sparrow. She was at the same time flattered and offended by his insistence that she use his first name, for it implied both a compliment and an impropriety. Why, she wondered, as she stared out the porthole and watched the clouds transform themselves from moment to moment, feeling the touch of his sharkskin on her bare microskirted thigh, did her parents allow a trip to Europe in the company of this strange, dark, manly business acquaintance of her father's, with his profile, his greying sideburns, and his carriage and skin texture that reminded her so much of an erect cock? She quivered a bit in her seat, and fastened her safety belt. He was mainly Latin in descent, from a Franco-Italian Spanish family with an intermixture of Greco-Moorish blood, that settled on the island of Malta some centuries ago in the wake of the conquest of Jerusalem. Sparrow. Spiro? Ero? She wondered if it was his real name. He was the kind of person that might be incognito. The jetliner shuddered through a cumulonimbus. She pulled a lever easing her seat into a reclining position that thrust her long full firm young thighs up and forward from the pelvis where the thin stuff of her microgarb caught and bunched under her seatbelt.

"But why 'ear-tree'?" asked Phoebe.

"My charming eediot," rejoined his vibrant basso, "if we knew these . . ." His middle and index fingers grazed her thigh confidentially, and came to rest near the hem of her skirt. She pretended not to notice, since she didn't know what else to do, and turned to look through the porthole where she saw a sheep running across the wing, no not a sheep a puff of smoke, another, another then after a pause a band of grey a plume of roiling black with suddenly red at its root . . .

"Built entirely without design precedent or orderly planning, created bit by bit on sheer impulse, a natural artist's instinct, and the fantasy of the moment": Simone Rodia's Watts Towers. Connections proliferate, meanings drop away.

Sparrow left England traveling as a young Greek sailor named George and Nick. I found him easily before the ship had cleared harbor leaning against the starboard rail in tight white pants and striped blue shirt. The day was blue with white clouds, whitecaps, gulls dove and hung above the churning stern. The gulls of Dover scream like Harpies and fly on wings of rusty iron. Sparrow was traveling as a young Greek sailor named George and Nick, but he spoke with a thick Italian accent. " 'owza da boy?" he greeted me. His theory was that from his Italian accent he would be taken for a notorious Neapolitan intellectual known as "the Cardinal" who was inclined to proletarian dress and argot as a disguise. If however he were recognized as the Greek sailor boy George and Nick masquerading as the Cardinal in proletdrag, he would still be ahead of the game. This was the evasive measure known as bifurcation. While the authorities are interrogating George and Nick, Sparrow slips out between the two of them. Or if they settle on George, Nick sidles off and meantime George subdivides into Sparrow-Spiro-Ero. The principle here is progressive fission as in certain microorganisms. They never catch up with you, whoever you are. But this, ironically, is the hang-up of the method, since some agents have been left stranded in a maze of sloughed identities nursing a king-size identity problem. Often you will see an old hand slap a green agent on the back, wink, and growl avuncularly, "Say kid, what you say we go fission?" This is the process referred to, so beware.

Sparrow pointed toward a couple standing on the bridge next to the skipper, and slipped a homing pigeon out of his attaché case. The man was tall and slender, sun-tanned, and of a distinguished allure in the French sense. The woman was tall and slender, suntanned, and also of a distinguished allure, etc. At this distance it was a little difficult to tell them apart, though they were both quite distinct from the skipper, who was pale and squat and emanated banality. The bird ruffled and fluttered, happy to escape its confinement. Sparrow set it on his wrist, raised it high in the air, and whispered "Dai! Dai!" The pigeon flapped off while Sparrow began reciting the Paolo and Francesca episode from the fifth canto of the *Commedia.* We watched as the bird hovered over the woman's head for a moment, then perched on her shoulder. We watched as she reached up and removed the message from the bird's leg, still looking straight ahead. We watched as she swallowed the note, took the pigeon, twisted its neck, and let it flop to the deck. Then the suntanned man was standing alone on the bridge, near the squat skipper, still looking straight ahead. Sparrow pointed to the man and shrugged. "I wuz-a fuck 'iz-a wife," he said in explanation. Just then said lady appeared at the rail near us and stood there looking straight ahead. "Beh!" said Sparrow. Was he as surprised as I was to recognize Phoebe? There was probably no telling. She looked straight ahead, her eyes on the horizon. The gulls dipped and hung in our wake. Sparrow cleared his throat. "Eartree," he said. Phoebe turned to him, her charcoal eyes smoldering in her olive face: "Millions of people are starving. A sixth of the population lives in poverty. In the richest nation in the world, in the history of the world. Abroad we practice mass murder, at home slow genocide. How long can we continue to regard as democratic a nation run like a company town for corporate profit, built-in poverty, endemic racism? Starving children suffer irreversible brain damage while Senators get rich. Soldiers die while profits soar. Democracy by tear gas, Mace, and political assassination. What are we going to do?"

"We like to stop guys with long hair and old cars," he said. "First of all old cars are a drug on the market like. I mean seen as how you got an old car it means you ain't got a new car right. And if all you was to pay is a few bucks on an old car you ain't puttin much back into the system are yiz? And that breaks the law of the market which is free enterprise.

"Now we ain't got nothin against long hair see. But what about all these guys that set up shop as barbers, they gotta make their profit, right? That breaks the law of supply and demand.

"Now another thing is long hair ain't neat like. And if it ain't neat it's unruly. And if it's unruly it's unlawful in this state according to a law on the books as of ten days ago by which appearance can be considered an extension of overt behavior during periods of national emergency such as for example now.

"Now seen as how guys with long hair and old cars don't fit in a system for guys with old hair and long cars, what that means is you're a troublemaker which is an offense by the new law that considers mental attitude an extension of overt behavior during times of national emergency 063589 state penal code and authorizes the arresting officer to put certain questions to the accused according to the mental stop-and-search provision on grounds of reasonable suspicion like long hair and old cars. Wrong answers are considered grounds for perjury.

Part I *Short Answer* (10 points)
1. How would you define "illegal"?
2. What characteristic distinguishes the Bald Eagle?
3. When does a bird break the law?
4. What birds can't fly straight?
5. What bird's ass would you not want to sit on?

Part II *Essay* (90 points)
Choose *one* of the following:

       a) This story is "entirely without design precedent or orderly planning, created bit by bit on sheer impulse, a natural artist's instinct, and the fantasy of the moment." Why do you think the police don't like that? Discuss.

       b) What is "ear-tree"? Give examples.

In Part II, I answered b). This was my answer: "Connections proliferate, meanings disperse. The painter studies his nude, his landscape."

IN SPIRIT OF JOY AND REVOLUTIONARY EXULTATION, THOUSANDS OF STUDENTS OCCUPIED THE SORBONNE TODAY.

THE STUDENTS STARTED MOVING INTO THE UNIVERSITY LATE LAST NIGHT, AFTER COMPLETING THEIR JOINT PROTEST MARCH WITH THE WORKERS OF PARIS AND SPENDING THE EVENING DANCING ON THE COBBLED STREETS OF THE LATIN QUARTER.

IN THE GRANDIOSE COBBLED COURTYARD OF THE MAIN BUILDING A SMALL JAZZ BAND PLAYED ALL THROUGH THE NIGHT.

AFTER 10 DAYS OF BLOODY CLASHES WITH THE POLICE, NOT A SINGLE POLICEMAN WAS IN SIGHT. STUDENTS IN WHITE HELMETS DIRECTED TRAFFIC. THE GOVERNMENT HAD SURRENDERED THIS PART OF THE CITY TO THE STUDENTS.

HUNDREDS OF THOUSANDS OF STUDENTS TOOK TO THE STREETS NOT ONLY IN PARIS BUT IN MOST PROVINCIAL CITIES.

MANY HAD A FEAR THAT GOVERNMENTAL POWER HAD BROKEN DOWN.

THE STUDENTS THEMSELVES DELIBERATELY HARKED BACK TO THE BATTLE CRIES THAT HAD SERVED EARLIER FRENCH REVOLUTIONARIES.

TWO THOUSAND WORKERS, IMITATING THE REBELLIOUS STU-

DENTS OF THE SORBONNE, HAVE OCCUPIED THE AIRCRAFT CON-
STRUCTION PLANT OF SUD-AVIATION AT NANTES, ON THE ATLANTIC
COAST, AND ARE HOLDING THE PLANT MANAGER AND HIS PRINCI-
PAL AIDES PRISONERS.

THE WORKERS, WHO WERE ALREADY ON STRIKE, MOVED INTO
THE PLANT EARLY LAST NIGHT AND WELDED THE MAIN GATE
CLOSED. THEY THREW UP BARRICADES ON THE ROADS LEADING TO
THE PLANT. THEY CLOSED DOWN THE NANTES AIRPORT, WHICH IS
ADJACENT TO THE FACTORY.

FRANCE'S SOCIAL REVOLT SPREAD AND CHANGED IN NATURE
TODAY AS AN ESTIMATED 100,000 STRIKERS OCCUPIED DOZENS OF
FACTORIES IN ALL PARTS OF THE COUNTRY.

THE STRIKE MOVEMENT SPREAD SO SWIFTLY THAT, WITHIN HALF
AN HOUR EARLY THIS EVENING, REPORTS REACHED PARIS THAT
SEVEN MAJOR INDUSTRIAL PLANTS AND SHIPYARDS HAD BEEN
TAKEN OVER IN LE HAVRE ALONE.

PRODUCERS AND DIRECTORS OF THE GOVERNMENT'S TELEVI-
SION AND RADIO SYSTEM WENT ON STRIKE AND THE SYSTEM'S
NEWSMEN VOTED TO REFUSE TO ACCEPT ANY FURTHER DIRECTIVES
FROM THE INFORMATION MINISTRY OR OTHER GOVERNMENT
AGENCIES ON THEIR NEWS REPORTS.

WORKERS SEIZED THE GOLD-DOMED OPERA AND THE OPERA CO-
MIQUE.

THE SPEECHES AT THE NATIONAL ASSEMBLY SEEMED STRANGELY
IRRELEVANT. FRANCOIS MITTERAND, THE OPPOSITION LEADER, AND
WALDECK ROCHET, THE HEAD OF THE COMMUNIST PARTY, WERE AS
HOPELESSLY OUT OF TOUCH AS PREMIER GEORGES POMPIDOU.
THEY WERE ALL PART OF THE "ESTABLISHMENT."

ONE OF THE STUDENT LEADERS, DANIEL COHN-BENDIT, CALLED
THE COMMUNISTS "STALINIST CREEPS." MR. COHN-BENDIT, CALLED
DANNY THE RED, APPEARS TO HOLD VIEWS CLOSE TO ANARCHISM.

THE BLACK FLAG OF THE ANARCHISTS MADE ITS APPEARANCE
DURING THE MASSIVE PARADE OF STUDENTS AND WORKERS YES-
TERDAY.

THE RED FLAG WAS HOISTED OVER SEVERAL PLANTS.

THE RED AND THE BLACK FLAGS APPEARED TOGETHER, AN AB-
NORMAL SITUATION BECAUSE THE COMMUNISTS AND ANARCHISTS
HAVE LONG BEEN ENEMIES. THE JOINT APPEARANCE WAS ONE OF THE
MANY SIGNS THAT SOMETHING NEW HAD HAPPENED.

IF THE MOVEMENT IS AN UNCONTROLLED REVOLUTIONARY UP-
SURGE, THE COUNTRY MAY BE PLUNGED INTO ANARCHY.

THE DECISION OF THE WORKERS APPEARS TO HAVE BEEN A SPON-
TANEOUS MOVE BY THE RANK-AND-FILE STRIKERS, WHO ACTED
WITHOUT ORDERS FROM POLITICAL PARTIES OR LABOR UNIONS.

THE STUDENT REVOLT WAS SIMILARLY UNOFFICIAL IN ITS ORIGIN.

IT IS THIS POPULAR AND REVOLUTIONARY CHARACTER OF THE MOVEMENT THAT LEADS MANY OBSERVERS TO FEEL THAT THE STUDENTS MAY HAVE UNLEASHED FORCES THAT CANNOT BE HARNESSED OR TAMED BY CONVENTIONAL MEANS, EITHER BY THE GOVERNMENT OR THE TRADITIONAL OPPOSITION PARTIES. INCLUDING THE COMMUNISTS.

JUST WHAT CAUSED THE STUDENTS' AND WORKERS' REVOLT TO ASSUME SUCH EXPLOSIVE DIMENSIONS IS STILL A MYSTERY TO MOT OBSERVER HERE.

MANY HAVE LINKED THE DISILLUSION OF THE FRENCH STUDENT TO A GLOBAL STUDENT MALAISE.

THE GAULLIST ADMINISTRATION, LIKE MANY PRIVATE CITIZENS, IS CONVINCED THAT A TRULY REVOLUTIONARY SITUATION EXISTS AND THAT THE DEMOCRATIC INSTITUTIONS OF FRANCE ARE THREATENED.

THE PRINCIPAL THREAT LIES IN THE SPONTANEOUS, POPULAR AND UTTERLY UNCONTROLLED NATURE OF THE MOVEMENT.

THE REVOLT, BY ITS SPONTANEOUS, TOTALLY UNCONTROLLED AND UNCONTROLLABLE NATURE HAD BECOME A TRULY REVOLUTIONARY EVENT.

IF THE COMMUNIST PARTY HAS MANAGED TO TAKE OVER THE MOVEMENT, THEN, IRONICALLY, THE INSTITUTIONS ARE SAFE AND THE POLITICAL CONTEST IS LIKELY TO MOVE BACK INTO THE NATIONAL ASSEMBLY, WITH VOTES OF CONFIDENCE AND VOTES OF CENSURE AND TRADITIONAL SPEECHES—AND SOONER OR LATER A NEW ELECTION.

SOMETHING HAS BEEN CREATED THAT IS IRREVERSIBLE. THERE WILL BE NO GOING BACK TO THE STATUS QUO.
The police want an end to this disorder and that depends on one question and one question only: What is "ear-tree"? This in turn leads us to the matter of the identity of the man called "Ero." Destroy this as you read. It is printed in a soluble ink which you can lick off the page sentence by sentence. The ink has various flavors depending on the parts of speech to make this easier to understand and swallow.

To get to the point, the police suspect a plot, yet all they see is disorder. They suspect that disorder is part of the plot, if not the point of it. They imagine that they merely have to figure out the plot to put an end to the disorder. But they don't understand the plot and believe the explanation lies with the meaning of the word "ear-tree." In turn they believe that this meaning will lead them to a man called Ero. In real life Ero is an eminent ornithologist, but the police believe that he is the leader of an international liberation conspiracy, and that only in his mind are all the connections coherently held together, the whole matter fully understood. To make matters worse, they aren't even sure whether Ero is dead or alive, or for that matter whether that is his right name.

I first met Ero in Tompkins Square Park. He was disguised as a bum. Although he was given to a kind of banal chattering—he sometimes compared himself to a Starling—I soon realized that this was a mere verbal subterfuge, so to speak, which could not prevent the escape of sudden flashes of the profoundest insight. For example he once remarked, almost as a nonsequitur, that the whole country had to get back to nipples. It was not long before I was captivated by his brilliance and charisma. At about that point I met another of his admirers, an English "bird" named Phoebe. Though she attended an American college, she was married, however, she had an ambiguous relation with her husband, and while she traveled with him a good deal, she spent much of the time in the protection of her parents. Ero once indicated to me quite clearly that there had been something between them, but then, she was beautiful and he—he was Ero.

To continue, at that time Phoebe and I used to frequent Chinese restaurants. That was because it used to be Ero's way to plant his messages in fortune cookies and leave strictly to chance whether you received them or not—Ero favored chance because he said we must remain open to the unknown. They say that he still does this, and that you might for all you know receive a message from him yourself in your very next fortune cookie—a message that might change your life. Anyway we were sitting in this Cantonese place in midtown, speaking Pigeon English to put the natives at ease and to confuse the police. The waiter recommended "ear-tree"—could he have been Ero?—but when he ordered it for someone else called it "spaghetti."

At first I thought that "ear-tree" had something to do with birds—a kind of tree that birds liked to sing in, or to. Ero was of course filled with bird lore. Birds were something special for him. He said that bird songs constituted a kind of code which, when correctly deciphered, turned out to have absolutely no meaning. On the other hand he had a whole system of private symbolism worked out on the basis of what the various species meant to him, and would often express himself in its terms. This was a code the police never cracked, though God knows they tried. For example, he once sent me a message composed completely of bird images. These involved the Red-winged Blackbird, the Phoebe, the Rufous sided Towhee, the Catbird, the Brown Thrasher, the Oriole (Orchard), the Pheasant, the Crow, the Hawk, the Grouse, the Dove, the Canada Goose, in that order. Knowing his system based on his emotional response to different birds, I worked the symbols out as follows:

> Red-winged Blackbird = calm dash
> Phoebe = domestic
> Rufous-sided Towhee = human comedy
> Catbird = eccentric relativism
> Brown Thrasher = rich
> Oriole (Orchard) = hot butter
> Pheasant = beautiful fortune, pathetic sacrifice
> Crow = wisdom floats intensely
> Hawk = kill with grace
> Grouse = explosion

Dove = dumb animals
Canada Goose = away, away

Decoded and allowing for variation in the given images in which the birds appeared, this means, roughly: "The *calm dash* of our once *domestic* culture has faded along with our old *human comedy.* In its place we have an *eccentric relativism* that is as *rich* as experience itself, yet as slippery as *hot butter.* Today's tragic hero is a man of *beautiful fortune, pathetic sacrifice*—his role as rich as the flux itself, and his denouement as meaningless. But in this streaming chaos *wisdom floats intensely* could one but be deadly enough with the fine net of intelligence. For wisdom and art mean precisely to kill the quick of our experience as it races past, but to *kill with grace* so that the victim may be preserved, as if alive, from oblivion. The universe is a long, an infinite *explosion* in which we are driven for an instant like *dumb animals* as it rushes *away, away.*"

Unfortunately, when I showed this interpretation to Ero, he got very angry and tore it up. When I asked what his system of bird symbolism meant to him he replied: "Nothing. A feather here and there, a color, a squawk, disconnected, opaque, totally self-contained, ending in a triumph of birdness, song and soar, itself opaque and without equivalent, but the feeling ordered and defined—like that of a bird's song, or of its flight."

That was my last encounter with Ero, as such. Immediately after that he assumed the guise of Spiro the spy, then of the Cardinal, then of George and Nick, and then literally disappeared in a welter of dividing and subdividing identities—Orson, Chet Nexus, the Beach Boy, Madame Lafayette, the Light-fingered Trio—to name just a few. Originally intended as an evasive measure against an assassination plot, this frenzy of transformations, some believe, may have made him a victim of terminal identity fission, a malignant psychological disorder which progressively rarefies the ego so that it ultimately loses consciousness of itself and in effect ceases to exist. Some say that he was seized and murdered in one of his ephemeral metamorphoses —thrown overboard by the squat skipper and the pimply homosexual second mate as George and Nick, on board a plane that crashed in mysterious circumstances off Iceland, shot dead in a Chinese restaurant by a Cuban exile who ordered "ear-tree" and got spaghetti. No one really knows.

What we do now know definitely, or at least what I know and you will in thirty seconds, is the meaning of "ear-tree." Shhh. It was on Icelandic that eighteen-hour flight from Luxemburg where your feet swell up when the insight came to me. Three A.M. and I couldn't sleep. We had been traveling maybe nine, ten hours. Nothing could have been further from my mind than that old riddle. I leaned back against my pillow and thought *oreiller,* French for pillow. I had been in France. Then I thought *pommier,* apple tree, *cerisier,* cherry tree, *pêcher,* peach tree, *oranger,* orange tree. Then I thought *oreille,* ear. Then I thought voila! *oreiller,* "ear-tree." But why "ear-tree" on a Chinese menu? Of course! Spaghetti. In Chinese restaurants in France, *lo-mein,* which as we know was brought from China to Italy as *spaghetti,* is often called *pilaf* or *pilaw,* from the Arabic, because it is used as a pillow for some kind of ragout or sauce. So some Chinese who knew neither French nor English nor

Arabic very well, translated *lo-mein* to *pilaw, pilaw* to *oreiller,* and *oreiller* from French to English as "ear-tree." I immediately dropped off into a profound slumber from which I awoke next morning completely refreshed.

When I arrived in New York, I went back to that same Chinese restaurant and ordered a large "ear-tree." It was of excellent quality, at least three stars, and I polished it off with tremendous satisfaction. The message in my fortune cookie read: "Connections proliferate, meanings are dispelled. The traveler studies out his map."

"Je suis réellement désolé I'm really sorry to have waited so long before answering you but I am totally caught up in the events that have taken place in May and in June in France. You've undoubtedly had some echoes but it's difficult to imagine the extraordinary enthusiasm that sustained the young people during the month of May."

"To form a perfect conception of the beauty and elegance of these Swans, you must observe them when they are not aware of your proximity . . . the neck, which at other times is held stiffly upright, moves in graceful curves . . . with a sudden effort a flood of water is thrown over the back and wings, when it is seen rolling off in sparkling globules, like so many large pearls. The bird then shakes its wings, beats the water, and as if giddy with delight shoots away, gliding . . . with surprising agility and grace. Imagine, reader, that a flock of fifty Swans are thus sporting before you, as they have more than once in my sight, and you will feel, as I have felt, more happy and void of care than I can describe."

The dress was made of clinging white nylon jersey of a thinness that in certain angles of light outline the thighs or reveal the curve of a breast and which, when taut against the skin, assumed something of the warm flesh tone. Slashed to the waist, it left the nipples free to poke and bob through the material.

in the richest country in the world/ people eat clay to still the pains of an empty belly/ children come to school too hungry to learn/ and the infants of the poor suffer/ irreversible brain damage from protein deprivation

JUST WHAT CAUSED THE STUDENTS' AND WORKERS' REVOLT TO ASSUME SUCH EXPLOSIVE DIMENSIONS IS STILL A MYSTERY TO MOT OBSERVER HERE MANY HAVE LINKED THE DISILLUSION OF THE FRENCH STUDENT TO A GLOBAL STUDENT MALAISE

Ero is an eminent ornithologist, but the police believe that he is the leader of an international liberation conspiracy, and that only in his mind are all the connections coherently held together

"A pattern was seen in the use of females to bite and kick the policemen" *New York Times* 5/7/68. Its drumming, distinct from other peckers, resembles the sound of a muffled machine gun, a soft, hollow automatic weapon.

"Les manifestations sur les barricades the demonstrations on the barricades were only one aspect, perhaps secondary, of this surprising movement, much more astonishing was the climate in the streets. We organized every day and during the month of May all-day meetings each of which gathered up to a hundred people sometimes until two in the morning."

THE REVOLT BY ITS SPONTANEOUS TOTALLY

Ronald Sukenick   139

UNCONTROLLED AND UNCONTROLLABLE NATURE HAD BECOME A
TRULY REVOLUTIONARY EVENT

"Spontanément spontaneously, the people
raised the real problems, confusedly felt and it was this, exactly that was extraordinary—it was not a question of the usual political theories struggling but of notions as
vague as human dignity, the responsibility of each man, the infinite resources of the
emotion of enthusiasm facing efficiency, the power of technology—"

IF THE
MOVEMENT IS AN UNCONTROLLED REVOLUTIONARY UPSURGE THE
COUNTRY MAY BE PLUNGED INTO ANARCHY

"entirely without design
precedent or orderly planning, created bit by bit on sheer impulse"

coincidence such
things renew my faith in the unknown I am always interested in any overt confrontation with chance though if you stop to think about it every moment is such a confrontation for each of us Ero favored chance because he said we must remain open
to the unknown

the stream carries mainly on its glassy surface rippled clouds inventing themselves from minute to minute, fantastic shapes, formations piling
shifting flowing, distortions of distortions of distortions

"Nous attendons we await
November, December but also the movements that cannot fail to appear in Italy,
Germany perhaps the United States . . ."

in the richest country in the world

an inter-
national liberation conspiracy

the children of the poor

caused the revolt to assume
such explosive spontaneous totally uncontrolled and uncontrollable

a soft hollow
automatic weapon

left the nipples free to poke and bob

much more astonishing was
the climate in the streets

a small jazz band played all through the night

the infinite
resources of the emotion of enthusiasm

created bit by bit on sheer impulse

we await
November December

formations piling shifting flowing

we must remain open to the
unknown

the bird then shakes its wings beats the water and shoots away gliding like
other Swans it has a deep ponderous flight the underwing is an astonishing pink-gold
stroke of scarlet from green to green Nuthatch bullets through blank air Red-winged

Blackbirds floating in in the field a Crow barks
   Pheasants waltz across the road
   Grouse explode in the underbrush
   a Hawk

     hangs
     in the air

        birds

Response Statement Assignments

1. Despite its unconventional nature, how might you go about making sense of this story? What new or infrequently used **reading strategies** might you use to read it?
2. Can you adapt any strategies that you use to read other kinds of texts, such as art or music, to make sense of this story?
3. The writer Donald Barthelme has said that *collage* is one of our century's major art forms. (A collage is a collection of various materials brought together to form a work of art.) Does his remark help you comprehend this story? In what other aspects of your **repertoire** are you familiar with collage?
4. Remember that reading is a learned, conventional process; therefore, there is no one "correct" way to read or write a story. Nonetheless, because its style is not the norm, "The Birds" might seem to you strange and difficult to comprehend. What assumptions in your **general** and **literary repertoires** contribute to your difficulty in reading the story? What assumptions of yours about the nature of short fiction does this story violate?

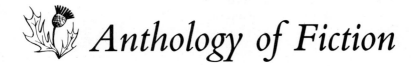 *Anthology of Fiction*

NATHANIEL HAWTHORNE (1804–1864)

Young Goodman Brown

Young Goodman Brown came forth at sunset into the street at Salem village; but put his head back, after crossing the threshold, to exchange a parting kiss with his young wife. And Faith, as the wife was aptly named, thrust her own pretty head into the street, letting the wind play with the pink ribbons of her cap while she called to Goodman Brown.

"Dearest heart," whispered she, softly and rather sadly, when her lips were close to his ear, "prithee put off your journey until sunrise and sleep in your own bed to-night. A lone woman is troubled with such dreams and such thoughts that she's afeared of herself sometimes. Pray tarry with me this night, dear husband, of all nights in the year."

"My love and my Faith," replied young Goodman Brown, "of all nights in the year, this one night must I tarry away from thee. My journey, as thou callest it, forth and back again, must needs be done 'twixt now and sunrise. What, my sweet, pretty wife, dost thou doubt me already, and we but three months married?"

"Then God bless you!" said Faith, with the pink ribbons; "and may you find all well when you come back."

"Amen!" cried Goodman Brown. "Say thy prayers, dear Faith, and go to bed at dusk, and no harm will come to thee."

So they parted; and the young man pursued his way until, being about to turn the corner by the meeting-house, he looked back and saw the head of Faith still peeping after him with a melancholy air, in spite of her pink ribbons.

"Poor little Faith!" thought he, for his heart smote him. "What a wretch am I to leave her on such an errand! She talks of dreams, too. Methought as she spoke there was trouble in her face, as if a dream had warned her what work is to be done to-night. But no, no; 't would kill her to think it. Well, she's a blessed angel on earth; and after this one night I'll cling to her skirts and follow her to heaven."

With this excellent resolve for the future, Goodman Brown felt himself justified in making more haste on his present evil purpose. He had taken a dreary road, darkened by all the gloomiest trees of the forest, which barely stood aside to let the narrow path creep through, and closed immediately behind. It was all as lonely as could be; and there is this peculiarity in such a solitude, that the traveller knows not who may be concealed by the innumerable trunks and the thick boughs overhead; so that with lonely footsteps he may yet be passing through an unseen multitude.

"There may be a devilish Indian behind every tree," said Goodman Brown to himself; and he glanced fearfully behind him as he added, "What if the devil himself should be at my very elbow!"

His head being turned back, he passed a crook of the road, and, looking forward again, beheld the figure of a man, in grave and decent attire, seated at the foot of an old tree. He arose at Goodman Brown's approach and walked onward side by side with him.

"You are late, Goodman Brown," said he. "The clock of the Old South was striking as I came through Boston, and that is full fifteen minutes agone."

"Faith kept me back a while," replied the young man, with a tremor in his voice, caused by the sudden appearance of his companion, though not wholly unexpected.

It was now deep dusk in the forest, and deepest in that part of it where these two were journeying. As nearly as could be discerned, the second traveller was about fifty years old, apparently in the same rank of life as Goodman Brown, and bearing a considerable resemblance to him, though perhaps more in expression than features. Still they might have been taken for father and son. And yet, though the elder person was as simply clad as the younger, and as simple in manner too, he had an indescribable air of one who knew the world, and who would not have felt abashed at the governor's dinner table or in King William's court, were it possible that his affairs should call him thither. But the only thing about him that could be fixed upon as remarkable was his staff, which bore the likeness of a great black snake, so curiously wrought that it might almost be seen to twist and wriggle itself like a living serpent. This, of course, must have been an ocular deception, assisted by the uncertain light.

"Come, Goodman Brown," cried his fellow-traveller, "this is a dull pace for the beginning of a journey. Take my staff, if you are so soon weary."

"Friend," said the other, exchanging his slow pace for a full stop, "having kept covenant by meeting thee here, it is my purpose now to return whence I came. I have scruples touching the matter thou wot'st of."

"Sayest thou so?" replied he of the serpent, smiling apart. "Let us walk on, nevertheless, reasoning as we go; and if I convince thee not thou shalt turn back. We are but a little way in the forest yet."

"Too far! too far!" exclaimed the goodman, unconsciously resuming his walk. "My father never went into the woods on such an errand, nor his father before him.

We have been a race of honest men and good Christians since the days of the martyrs; and shall I be the first of the name of Brown that ever took this path and kept"—

"Such company, thou wouldst say," observed the elder person, interpreting his pause. "Well said, Goodman Brown! I have been as well acquainted with your family as with ever a one among the Puritans; and that's no trifle to say. I helped your grandfather, the constable, when he lashed the Quaker woman so smartly through the streets of Salem; and it was I that brought your father a pitch-pine knot, kindled at my own hearth, to set fire to an Indian village, in King Philip's war. They were my good friends, both; and many a pleasant walk have we had along this path, and returned merrily after midnight. I would fain be friends with you for their sake."

"If it be as thou sayest," replied Goodman Brown, "I marvel they never spoke of these matters; or, verily, I marvel not, seeing that the least rumor of the sort would have driven them from New England. We are a people of prayer, and good works to boot, and abide no such wickedness."

"Wickedness or not," said the traveller with the twisted staff, "I have a very general acquaintance here in New England. The deacons of many a church have drunk the communion wine with me; the selectmen of divers towns make me their chairman; and a majority of the Great and General Court are firm supporters of my interest. The governor and I, too— But these are state secrets."

"Can this be so?" cried Goodman Brown, with a stare of amazement at his undisturbed companion. "Howbeit, I have nothing to do with the governor and council; they have their own ways, and are no rule for a simple husbandman like me. But, were I to go on with thee, how should I meet the eye of that good old man, our minister, at Salem village? Oh, his voice would make me tremble both Sabbath day and lecture day."

Thus far the elder traveller had listened with due gravity; but now burst into a fit of irrepressible mirth, shaking himself so violently that his snake-like staff actually seemed to wriggle in sympathy.

"Ha! ha! ha!" shouted he again and again; then composing himself, "Well, go on, Goodman Brown, go on; but, prithee, don't kill me with laughing."

"Well, then, to end the matter at once," said Goodman Brown, considerably nettled, "there is my wife, Faith. It would break her dear little heart; and I'd rather break my own."

"Nay, if that be the case," answered the other, "e'en go thy ways, Goodman Brown. I would not for twenty old women like the one hobbling before us that Faith should come to any harm."

As he spoke he pointed his staff at a female figure on the path, in whom Goodman Brown recognized a very pious and exemplary dame, who had taught him his catechism in youth, and was still his moral and spiritual adviser, jointly with the minister and Deacon Gookin.

"A marvel, truly that Goody Cloyse should be so far in the wilderness at nightfall," said he. "But with your leave, friend, I shall take a cut through the woods until we have left this Christian woman behind. Being a stranger to you, she might ask whom I was consorting with and whither I was going."

"Be it so," said his fellow-traveller. "Betake you to the woods, and let me keep the path."

Accordingly the young man turned aside, but took care to watch his companion, who advanced softly along the road until he had come within a staff's length of the old dame. She, meanwhile, was making the best of her way, with singular speed for so aged a woman, and mumbling some indistinct words—a prayer, doubtless—as she went. The traveller put forth his staff and touched her withered neck with what seemed the serpent's tail.

"The devil!" screamed the pious old lady.

"Then Goody Cloyse knows her old friend?" observed the traveller, confronting her and leaning on his writhing stick.

"Ah, forsooth, and is it your worship indeed?" cried the good dame. "Yea, truly is it, and in the very image of my old gossip, Goodman Brown, the grandfather of the silly fellow that now is. But—would your worship believe it?—my broomstick hath strangely disappeared, stolen, as I suspect, by that unhanged witch, Goody Cory, and that, too, when I was all anointed with the juice of smallage, and cinquefoil, and wolf's bane"—

"Mingled with fine wheat and the fat of a new-born babe," said the shape of old Goodman Brown.

"Ah, your worship knows the recipe," cried the old lady, cackling aloud. "So, as I was saying, being all ready for the meeting, and no horse to ride on, I made up my mind to foot it; for they tell me there is a nice young man to be taken into communion to-night. But now your good worship will lend me your arm, and we shall be there in a twinkling."

"That can hardly be," answered her friend. "I may not spare you my arm, Goody Cloyse; but here is my staff, if you will."

So saying, he threw it down at her feet, where, perhaps, it assumed life, being one of the rods which its owner had formerly lent to the Egyptian magi. Of this fact, however, Goodman Brown could not take cognizance. He had cast up his eyes in astonishment, and, looking down again, beheld neither Goody Cloyse nor the serpentine staff, but his fellow-traveller alone, who waited for him as calmly as if nothing had happened.

"That old woman taught me my catechism," said the young man; and there was a world of meaning in this simple comment.

They continued to walk onward, while the elder traveller exhorted his companion to make good speed and persevere in the path, discoursing so aptly that his arguments seemed rather to spring up in the bosom of his auditor than to be suggested by himself. As they went, he plucked a branch of maple to serve for a walking stick, and began to strip it of the twigs and little boughs, which were wet with evening dew. The moment his fingers touched them they became strangely withered and dried up as with a week's sunshine. Thus the pair proceeded, at a good free pace, until suddenly, in a gloomy hollow of the road, Goodman Brown sat himself down on the stump of a tree and refused to go any farther.

"Friend," he said, stubbornly, "my mind is made up. Not another step will I budge on this errand. What if a wretched old woman do choose to go to the devil when I thought she was going to heaven: is that any reason why I should quit my dear Faith and go after her?"

"You will think better of this by and by," said his acquaintance, composedly. "Sit here and rest yourself a while; and when you feel like moving again, there is my staff to help you along."

Without more words, he threw his companion the maple stick, and was as speedily out of sight as if he had vanished into the deepening gloom. The young man sat a few moments by the roadside, applauding himself greatly, and thinking with how clear a conscience he should meet the minister in his morning walk, nor shrink from the eye of good old Deacon Gookin. And what calm sleep would be his that very night, which was to have been spent so wickedly, but so purely and sweetly now, in the arms of Faith! Amidst these pleasant and praiseworthy meditations, Goodman Brown heard the tramp of horses along the road, and deemed it advisable to conceal himself within the verge of the forest, conscious of the guilty purpose that had brought him thither, though now so happily turned from it.

On came the hoof tramps and the voices of the riders, two grave old voices, conversing soberly as they drew near. These mingled sounds appeared to pass along the road, within a few yards of the young man's hiding-place; but, owing doubtless to the depth of the gloom at that particular spot, neither the travellers nor their steeds were visible. Though their figures brushed the small boughs by the wayside, it could not be seen that they intercepted, even for a moment, the faint gleam from the strip of bright sky athwart which they must have passed. Goodman Brown alternately crouched and stood on tiptoe, pulling aside the branches and thrusting forth his head as far as he durst without discerning so much as a shadow. It vexed him the more, because he could have sworn, were such a thing possible, that he recognized the voices of the minister and Deacon Gookin, jogging along quietly, as they were wont to do, when bound to some ordination or ecclesiastical council. While yet within hearing, one of the riders stopped to pluck a switch.

"Of the two, reverend sir," said the voice like the deacon's, "I had rather miss an ordination dinner than to-night's meeting. They tell me that some of our community are to be here from Falmouth and beyond, and others from Connecticut and Rhode Island, besides several of the Indian powwows, who, after their fashion, know almost as much deviltry as the best of us. Moreover, there is a goodly young woman to be taken into communion."

"Mighty well, Deacon Gookin!" replied the solemn old tones of the minister. "Spur up, or we shall be late. Nothing can be done, you know, until I get on the ground."

The hoofs clattered again; and the voices, talking so strangely in the empty air, passed on through the forest, where no church had ever been gathered or solitary Christian prayed. Whither, then, could these holy men be journeying so deep into the heathen wilderness? Young Goodman Brown caught hold of a tree for support, being ready to sink down on the ground, faint and overburdened with the heavy sickness of his heart. He looked up to the sky, doubting whether there really was a heaven above him. Yet there was the blue arch, and the stars brightening in it.

"With heaven above and Faith below, I will yet stand firm against the devil!" cried Goodman Brown.

While he still gazed upward into the deep arch of the firmament and had lifted his hands to pray, a cloud, though no wind was stirring, hurried across the zenith and hid the brightening stars. The blue sky was still visible, except directly overhead, where this black mass of cloud was sweeping swiftly northward. Aloft in the air, as if from the depths of the cloud, came a confused and doubtful sound of voices. Once the listener fancied that he could distinguish the accents of towns-people of his own, men and women, both pious and ungodly, many of whom he had met at the communion table, and had seen others rioting at the tavern. The next moment, so indistinct were the sounds, he doubted whether he had heard aught but the murmur of the old forest, whispering without a wind. Then came a stronger swell of those familiar tones, heard daily in the sunshine at Salem village, but never until now from a cloud of night. There was one voice, of a young woman, uttering lamentations, yet with an uncertain sorrow, and entreating for some favor, which, perhaps, it would grieve her to obtain; and all the unseen multitude, both saints and sinners, seemed to encourage her onward.

"Faith!" shouted Goodman Brown, in a voice of agony and desperation; and the echoes of the forest mocked him, crying, "Faith! Faith!" as if bewildered wretches were seeking her all through the wilderness.

The cry of grief, rage, and terror was yet piercing the night, when the unhappy husband held his breath for a response. There was a scream, drowned immediately in a louder murmur of voices, fading into far-off laughter, as the dark cloud swept away, leaving the clear and silent sky above Goodman Brown. But something fluttered lightly down through the air and caught on the branch of a tree. The young man seized it, and beheld a pink ribbon.

"My Faith is gone!" cried he after one stupefied moment. "There is no good on earth; and sin is but a name. Come, devil; for to thee is this world given."

And, maddened with despair, so that he laughed loud and long, did Goodman Brown grasp his staff and set forth again, at such a rate that he seemed to fly along the forest path rather than to walk or run. The road grew wilder and drearier and more faintly traced, and vanished at length, leaving him in the heart of the dark wilderness, still rushing onward with the instinct that guides mortal man to evil. The whole forest was peopled with frightful sounds—the creaking of the trees, the howling of wild beasts, and the yell of Indians; while sometimes the wind tolled like a distant church bell, and sometimes gave a broad roar around the traveller, as if all Nature were laughing him to scorn. But he was himself the chief horror of the scene, and shrank not from its other horrors.

"Ha! ha! ha!" roared Goodman Brown when the wind laughed at him. "Let us hear which will laugh loudest. Think not to frighten me with your deviltry. Come witch, come wizard, come Indian powwow, come devil himself, and here comes Goodman Brown. You may as well fear him as he fear you."

In truth, all through the haunted forest there could be nothing more frightful than the figure of Goodman Brown. On he flew among the black pines, brandishing his staff with frenzied gestures, now giving vent to an inspiration of horrid blasphemy, and now shouting forth such laughter as set all the echoes of the forest laughing like demons around him. The fiend in his own shape is less hideous than when he rages in the breast of man. Thus sped the demoniac on his course, until, quivering among the trees, he saw a red light before him, as when the felled trunks and branches of a clearing have been set on fire, and throw up their lurid blaze against the sky, at the hour of midnight. He paused, in a lull of the tempest that had driven him onward, and heard the swell of what seemed a hymn, rolling solemnly from a distance with the weight of many voices. He knew the tune; it was a familiar one in the choir of the village meeting-house. The verse died heavily away, and was lengthened by a chorus, not of human voices, but of all the sounds of the benighted wilderness pealing in awful harmony together. Goodman Brown cried out, and his cry was lost to his own ear by its unison with the cry of the desert.

In the interval of silence he stole forward until the light glared full upon his eyes. At one extremity of an open space, hemmed in by the dark wall of the forest, arose a rock, bearing some rude, natural resemblance either to an altar or a pulpit, and surrounded by four blazing pines, their tops aflame, their stems untouched, like candles at an evening meeting. The mass of foliage that had overgrown the summit of the rock was all on fire, blazing high into the night and fitfully illuminating the whole field. Each pendent twig and leafy festoon was in a blaze. As the red light arose and fell, a numerous congregation alternately shone forth, then disappeared in shadow, and again grew, as it were, out of the darkness, peopling the heart of the solitary woods at once.

"A grave and dark-clad company," quoth Goodman Brown.

In truth they were such. Among them, quivering to and fro between gloom and splendor, appeared faces that would be seen next day at the council board of the province, and others which, Sabbath after Sabbath, looked devoutly heavenward, and benignantly over the crowded pews, from the holiest pulpits in the land. Some affirm that the lady of the governor was there. At least there were high dames well known to her, and wives of honored husbands, and widows, a great multitude, and ancient maidens, all of excellent repute, and fair young girls, who trembled lest their mothers should espy them. Either the sudden gleams of light flashing over the obscure field bedazzled Goodman Brown, or he recognized a score of the church members of Salem village famous for their especial sanctity. Good old Deacon Gookin had arrived, and waited at the skirts of that venerable saint, his revered pastor. But, irreverently consorting with these grave, reputable, and pious people, these elders of the church, these chaste dames and dewy virgins, there were men of dissolute lives and women of spotted fame, wretches given over to all mean and filthy vice, and suspected even of horrid crimes. It was strange to see that the good shrank not from the wicked, nor were the sinners abashed by the saints. Scattered also among their pale-faced enemies were the Indian priests, or powwows, who had often scared their native forest with more hideous incantations than any known to English witchcraft.

"But where is Faith?" thought Goodman Brown; and, as hope came into his heart, he trembled.

Another verse of the hymn arose, a slow and mournful strain, such as the pious love, but joined to words which expressed all that our nature can conceive of sin, and darkly hinted at far more. Unfathomable to mere mortals is the lore of fiends. Verse after verse was sung; and still the chorus of the desert swelled between like the deepest tone of a mighty organ; and with the final peal of that dreadful anthem there came a sound, as if the roaring wind, the rushing streams, the howling beasts, and every other voice of the unconcerted wilderness were mingling and according with the voice of guilty man in homage to the prince of all. The four blazing pines threw up a loftier flame, and obscurely discovered shapes and visages of horror on the smoke wreaths above the impious assembly. At the same moment the fire on the rock shot redly forth and formed a glowing arch above its base, where now appeared a figure. With reverence be it spoken, the figure bore no slight similitude, both in garb and manner, to some grave divine of the New England churches.

"Bring forth the converts!" cried a voice that echoed through the field and rolled into the forest.

At the word, Goodman Brown stepped forth from the shadow of the trees and approached the congregation, with whom he felt a loathful brotherhood by the sympathy of all that was wicked in his heart. He could have well-nigh sworn that the shape of his own dead father beckoned him to advance, looking downward from a smoke wreath, while a woman, with dim features of despair, threw out her hand to warn him back. Was it his mother? But he had no power to retreat one step, nor to resist, even in thought, when the minister and good old Deacon Gookin seized his arms and led him to the blazing rock. Thither came also the slender form of a veiled female, led between Goody Cloyse, that pious teacher of the catechism, and Martha Carrier, who had received the devil's promise to be queen of hell. A rampant hag was she. And there stood the proselytes beneath the canopy of fire.

"Welcome, my children," said the dark figure, "to the communion of your race. Ye have found thus young your nature and your destiny. My children, look behind you!"

They turned; and flashing forth, as it were, in a sheet of flame, the fiend worshippers were seen; the smile of welcome gleamed darkly on every visage.

"There," resumed the sable form, "are all whom ye have reverenced from youth. Ye deemed them holier than yourselves and shrank from your own sin, contrasting it with their lives of righteousness and prayerful aspirations heavenward. Yet here are they all in my worshipping assembly. This night it shall be granted you to know their secret deeds: how hoary-bearded elders of the church have whispered wanton words to the young maids of their households; how many a woman, eager for widows' weeds, has given her husband a drink at bedtime and let him sleep his last sleep in her bosom; how beardless youths have made haste to inherit their fathers' wealth; and how fair damsels—blush not, sweet ones—have dug little graves in the garden, and bidden me, the sole guest, to an infant's funeral. By the sympathy of your human hearts for sin ye shall scent out all the places—whether in church, bedchamber, street, field, or forest—where crime has been committed, and shall exult to behold the whole earth one stain of guilt, one mighty blood spot. Far more than this. It shall be yours to penetrate, in every bosom, the deep mystery of sin, the fountain of all wicked arts, and which inexhaustibly supplies more evil impulses than human power—than my power at its utmost—can make manifest in deeds. And now, my children, look upon each other."

They did so; and, by the blaze of the hell-kindled torches, the wretched man beheld his Faith, and the wife her husband, trembling before that unhallowed altar.

"Lo, there ye stand, my children," said the figure, in a deep and solemn tone, almost sad with its despairing awfulness, as if his once angelic nature could yet mourn for our miserable race. "Depending upon one another's hearts, ye had still hoped that virtue were not all a dream. Now are ye undeceived. Evil is the nature of mankind. Evil must be your only happiness. Welcome again, my children, to the communion of your race."

"Welcome," repeated the fiend worshippers in one cry of despair and triumph.

And there they stood, the only pair, as it seemed, who were yet hesitating on the verge of wickedness in this dark world. A basin was hollowed, naturally, in the rock. Did it contain water, reddened by the lurid light? or was it blood? or, perchance, a liquid flame? Herein did the shape of evil dip his hand and prepare to lay the mark of baptism upon their foreheads, that they might be partakers of the mystery of sin, more conscious of the secret guilt of others, both in deed and thought, than they could now be of their own. The husband cast one look at his pale wife, and Faith at him. What polluted wretches would the next glance show them to each other, shuddering alike at what they disclosed and what they saw!

"Faith! Faith!" cried the husband, "look up to heaven, and resist the wicked one."

Whether Faith obeyed he knew not. Hardly had he spoken when he found himself amid calm night and solitude, listening to a roar of the wind which died heavily away through the forest. He staggered against the rock, and felt it chill and damp; while a hanging twig, that had been all on fire, besprinkled his cheek with the coldest dew.

The next morning young Goodman Brown came slowly into the street of Salem village, staring around him like a bewildered man. The good old minister was taking a walk along the graveyard to get an appetite for breakfast and meditate his sermon, and bestowed a blessing, as he passed, on Goodman Brown. He shrank from the venerable saint as if to avoid an anathema. Old Deacon Gookin was at domestic worship, and the holy words of his prayer were heard through the open window. "What God doth the wizard pray to?" quoth Goodman Brown. Goody Cloyse, that excellent old Christian, stood in the early sunshine at her own lattice, catechizing a little girl who had brought her a pint of morning's milk. Goodman Brown snatched away the child as from the grasp of the fiend himself. Turning the corner by the meeting-house, he spied the head of Faith, with the pink ribbons, gazing anxiously forth, and bursting into such joy at sight of him that she skipped along the street and almost kissed her husband before the whole village. But Goodman Brown looked sternly and sadly into her face, and passed on without a greeting.

Had Goodman Brown fallen asleep in the forest and only dreamed a wild dream of a witch-meeting?

Be it so if you will; but, alas! it was a dream of evil omen for young Goodman Brown. A stern, a sad, a darkly meditative, a distrustful, if not a desperate man did he become from the night of that fearful dream. On the Sabbath day, when the congregation were singing a holy psalm, he could not listen because an anthem of sin rushed loudly upon his ear and drowned all the blessed strain. When the minister spoke from the pulpit with power and fervid eloquence, and, with his hand on the open Bible, of the sacred truths of our religion, and of saint-like lives and triumphant deaths, and of future bliss or misery unutterable, then did Goodman Brown turn pale, dreading lest the roof should thunder down upon the gray blasphemer and his hearers. Often, awaking suddenly at midnight, he shrank from the bosom of Faith; and at morning or eventide, when the family knelt down at prayer, he scowled and muttered to himself, and gazed sternly at his wife, and turned away. And when he had lived long, and was borne to his grave a hoary corpse, followed by Faith, an aged woman, and children and grandchildren, a goodly procession, besides neighbors not a few, they carved no hopeful verse upon his tombstone, for his dying hour was gloom.

HENRY JAMES (1843–1916)
The Real Thing

1

When the porter's wife, who used to answer the house-bell, announced "A gentleman and a lady, sir," I had, as I often had in those days—the wish being father to the thought—an immediate vision of sitters. Sitters my visitors in this case proved to be; but not in the sense I should have preferred. There was nothing at first however to indicate that they mightn't have come for a portrait. The gentleman, a man of fifty, very high and very straight, with a moustache slightly grizzled and a dark grey walking-coat admirably fitted, both of which I noted professionally—I don't mean as a barber or yet as a tailor—would have struck me as a celebrity if celebrities often were striking. It was a truth of which I had for some time been conscious that a figure with a good deal of frontage was, as one might say, almost never a public institution. A glance at the lady helped to remind me of this paradoxical law: she also looked too distinguished to be a "personality." Moreover one would scarcely come across two variations together.

Neither of the pair immediately spoke—they only prolonged the preliminary gaze suggesting that each wished to give the other a chance. They were visibly shy; they stood there letting me take them in—which, as I afterwards perceived, was the most practical thing they could have done. In this way their embarrassment served their cause. I had seen people painfully reluctant to mention that they desired anything so gross as to be presented on canvas; but the scruples of my new friends appeared almost insurmountable. Yet the gentleman might have said "I should like a portrait of my wife," and the lady might have said "I should like a portrait of my husband." Perhaps they weren't husband and wife—this naturally would make the matter more delicate. Perhaps they wished to be done together—in which case they ought to have brought a third person to break the news.

"We come from Mr. Rivet," the lady finally said with a dim smile that had the effect of a moist sponge passed over a "sunk" piece of painting, as well as of a vague allusion to vanished beauty. She was as tall and straight, in her degree, as her companion, and with ten years less to carry. She looked as sad as a woman could look whose face was not charged with expression; that is her tinted oval mask showed waste as an exposed surface shows friction. The hand of time had played over her freely, but to an effect of elimination. She was slim and stiff, and so well-dressed, in dark blue cloth, with lappets and pockets and buttons, that it was clear she employed the same tailor as her husband. The couple had an indefinable air of prosperous thrift—they evidently got a good deal of luxury for their money. If I was to be one of their luxuries it would behoove me to consider my terms.

"Ah Claude Rivet recommended me?" I echoed; and I added that it was very kind of him, though I could reflect that, as he only painted landscape, this wasn't a sacrifice.

The lady looked very hard at the gentleman, and the gentleman looked around the room. Then staring at the floor a moment and stroking his moustache, he rested his pleasant eyes on me with the remark: "He said you were the right one."

"I try to be, when people want to sit."

"Yes, we should like to," said the lady anxiously.

"Do you mean together?"

My visitors exchanged a glance. "If you could do anything with *me* I suppose it would be double," the gentleman stammered.

"Oh yes, there's naturally a higher charge for two figures than for one."

"We should like to make it pay," the husband confessed.

"That's very good of you," I returned, appreciating so unwonted a sympathy—for I supposed he meant pay the artist.

A sense of strangeness seemed to dawn on the lady. "We mean for the illustrations—Mr. Rivet said you might put one in."

"Put in—an illustration?" I was equally confused.

"Sketch her off, you know," said the gentleman, colouring.

It was only then that I understood the service Claude Rivet had rendered me; he had told them how I worked in black-and-white, for magazines, for storybooks, for sketches of contemporary life, and consequently had copious employment for models. These things were true, but it was not less true—I may confess it now; whether because the aspiration was to lead to everything or to nothing I leave the reader to guess—that I couldn't get the honours, to say nothing of the emoluments, of a great painter of portraits out of my head. My "illustrations" were my potboilers; I looked to a different branch of art—far and away the most interesting it had always seemed to me—to perpetuate my fame. There was no shame in looking to it also to make my fortune; but that fortune was by so much further from being made from the moment my visitors wished to be "done" for nothing. I was disappointed; for in the pictorial sense I had immediately *seen* them. I had seized their type—I had already settled what I would do with it. Something that wouldn't absolutely have pleased them, I afterwards reflected.

"Ah you're—you're—a?" I began as soon as I had mastered my surprise. I couldn't bring out the dingy word "models": it seemed so little to fit the case.

"We haven't had much practice," said the lady.

"We've go to *do* something, and we've thought that an artist in your line might perhaps make something of us," her husband threw off. He further mentioned that they didn't know many artists and that they had gone first, on the off-chance—he painted views of course, but sometimes put in figures; perhaps I remembered—to Mr. Rivet, whom they had met a few years before at a place in Norfolk where he was sketching.

"We used to sketch a little ourselves," the lady hinted.

"It's very awkward, but we absolutely *must* do something," her husband went on.

"Of course we're not so *very* young," she admitted with a wan smile.

With the remark that I might as well know something more about them the husband had handed me a card extracted from a neat new pocket-book—their appurtenances were all of the freshest—and inscribed with the words "Major Monarch." Impressive as these words were they didn't carry my knowledge much further; but my visitor presently added: "I've left the army and we've had the misfortune to lose our money. In fact our means are dreadfully small."

"It's awfully trying—a regular strain," said Mrs. Monarch.

They evidently wished to be discreet—to take care not to swagger because they were gentlefolk. I felt them willing to recognise this as something of a drawback, at the same time that I guessed at an underlying sense—their consolation in adversity —that they *had* their points. They certainly had; but these advantages struck me as preponderantly social; such for instance as would help to make a drawing-room look well. However, a drawing-room was always, or ought to be, a picture.

In consequence of his wife's allusion to their age Major Monarch observed: "Naturally it's more for the figure that we thought of going in. We can still hold ourselves up." On the instant I saw that the figure was indeed their strong point. His "naturally" didn't sound vain, but it lighted up the question. "*She* has the best one," he continued, nodding at his wife with a pleasant after-dinner absence of circumlocution. I could only reply, as if we were in fact sitting over our wine, that this didn't prevent his own from being very good; which led him in turn to make answer: "We thought that if you ever have to do people like us we might be something like it. *She* particularly—for a lady in a book, you know."

I was so amused by them that, to get more of it, I did my best to take their point of view; and though it was an embarrassment to find myself appraising physically, as if they were animals on hire or useful blacks, a pair whom I should have expected to meet only in one of the relations in which criticism is tacit, I looked at Mrs. Monarch judicially enough to be able to exclaim after a moment with conviction: "Oh yes, a lady in a book!" She was singularly like a bad illustration.

"We'll stand up, if you like," said the Major; and he raised himself before me with a really grand air.

I could take his measure at a glance—he was six feet two and a perfect gentleman. It would have paid any club in process of formation and in want of a stamp to engage him at a salary to stand in the principal window. What struck me at once was that in coming to me they had rather missed their vocation; they could surely have been turned to better account for advertising purposes. I couldn't of course see the thing in detail, but I could see them make somebody's fortune—I don't mean their own.

There was something in them for a waistcoat-maker, a hotel-keeper or a soap-vendor. I could imagine "We always use it" pinned on their bosoms with the greatest effect; I had a vision of the brilliancy with which they would launch a table d'hôte.

Mrs. Monarch sat still, not from pride but from shyness, and presently her husband said to her: "Get up, my dear, and show how smart you are." She obeyed, but she had no need to get up to show it. She walked to the end of the studio and then came back blushing, her fluttered eyes on the partner of her appeal. I was reminded of an incident I had accidentally had a glimpse of in Paris—being with a friend there, a dramatist about to produce a play, when an actress came to him to ask to be entrusted with a part. She went through her paces before him, walked up and down as Mrs. Monarch was doing. Mrs. Monarch did it quite as well, but I abstained from applauding. It was very odd to see such people apply for such poor pay. She looked as if she had ten thousand a year. Her husband had used the word that described her: she was in the London current jargon essentially and typically "smart." Her figure was, in the same order of ideas, conspicuously and irreproachably "good." For a woman of her age her waist was surprisingly small; her elbow moreover had the orthodox crook. She held her head at the conventional angle, but why did she come to *me?* She ought to have tried on jackets at a big shop. I feared my visitors were not only destitute but "artistic"—which would be a great complication. When she sat down again I thanked her, observing that what a draughtsman most valued in his model was the faculty of keeping quiet.

"Oh *she* can keep quiet," said Major Monarch. Then he added jocosely: "I've always kept her quiet."

"I'm not a nasty fidget, am I?" It was going to wring tears from me, I felt, the way she hid her head, ostrich-like, in the other broad bosom.

The owner of this expanse addressed his answer to me. "Perhaps it isn't out of place to mention—because we ought to be quite business-like, oughtn't we?—that when I married her she was known as the Beautiful Statue."

"Oh dear!" said Mrs. Monarch ruefully.

"Of course I should want a certain amount of expression," I rejoined.

"Of *course!*"—and I had never heard such unanimity.

"And then I suppose you know that you'll get awfully tired."

"Oh we *never* get tired!" they eagerly cried.

"Have you had any kind of practice?"

They hesitated—they looked at each other. "We've been photographed—*immensely*," said Mrs. Monarch.

"She means the fellows have asked us themselves," added the Major.

"I see—because you're so good-looking."

"I don't know what they thought, but they were always after us."

"We always got our photographs for nothing," smiled Mrs. Monarch.

"We might have brought some, my dear," her husband remarked.

"I'm not sure we have any left. We've given quantities away," she explained to me.

"With our autographs and that sort of thing," said the Major.

"Are they to be got in the shops?" I enquired as a harmless pleasantry.

"Oh yes, *hers*—they used to be."

"Not now," said Mrs. Monarch with her eyes on the floor.

2

I could fancy the "sort of thing" they put on the presentation copies of their photographs, and I was sure they wrote a beautiful hand. It was odd how quickly I was sure of everything that concerned them. If they were now so poor as to have to earn shillings and pence they could never have had much of a margin. Their good looks had been their capital, and they had good-humouredly made the most of the career that this resource marked out for them. It was in their faces, the blankness, the deep intellectual repose of the twenty years of country-house visiting that had given them pleasant intonations. I could see the sunny drawing-rooms, sprinkled with periodicals she didn't read, in which Mrs. Monarch had continuously sat; I could see the wet shrubberies in which she had walked, equipped to admiration for either exercise. I could see the rich covers the Major had helped to shoot and the wonderful garments in which, late at night, he repaired to the smoking-room to talk about them. I could imagine their leggings and waterproofs, their knowing tweeds and rugs, their rolls of sticks and cases of tackle and neat umbrellas; and I could evoke the exact appearance of their servants and the compact variety of their luggage on the platforms of country stations.

They gave small tips, but they were liked; they didn't do anything themselves, but they were welcome. They looked so well everywhere; they gratified the general relish for stature, complexion and "form." They knew it without fatuity or vulgarity, and they respected themselves in consequence. They weren't superficial; they were thorough and kept themselves up—it had been their line. People with such a taste for activity had to have some line. I could feel how even in a dull house they could have been counted on for the joy of life. At present something had happened—it didn't matter what, their little income had grown less, it had grown least—and they had to do something for pocket-money. Their friends could like them, I made out, without liking to support them. There was something about them that represented credit—their clothes, their manners, their type; but if credit is a large empty pocket in which an occasional chink reverberates, the chink at least must be audible. What they wanted of me was to help to make it so. Fortunately they had no children—I soon divined that. They would also perhaps wish our relations to be kept secret: this was why it was "for the figure"—the reproduction of the face would betray them.

I liked them—I felt, quite as their friends must have done—they were so simple; and I had no objection to them if they would suit. But somehow with all their perfections I didn't easily believe in them. After all they were amateurs, and the ruling passion of my life was the detestation of the amateur. Combined with this was another perversity—an innate preference for the represented subject over the real one: the defect of the real one was so apt to be a lack of representation. I liked things that appeared; then one was sure. Whether they *were* or not was a subordinate and almost always a profitless question. There were other considerations, the first of which was that I already had two or three recruits in use, notably a young person with big feet, in alpaca, from Kilburn, who for a couple of years had come to me regularly for my illustrations and with whom I was still—perhaps ignobly—satisfied. I frankly explained to my visitors how the case stood, but they had taken more precautions than I supposed. They had reasoned out their opportunity, for Claude Rivet had told them of the projected *édition de luxe* of one of the writers of our day—the rarest of the novelists—who, long neglected by the multitudinous vulgar and dearly prized by the attentive (need I mention Philip Vincent?) had had the happy fortune of seeing, late in life, the dawn and then the full light of a higher criticism; an estimate in which on the part of the public there was something really of expiation. The edition preparing, planned by a publisher of taste, was practically an act of high reparation; the wood-cuts with which it was to be enriched were the homage of English art to one of the most independent representatives in English letters. Major and Mrs. Monarch confessed to me they had hoped I might be able to work *them* into my branch of the enterprise. They knew I was to do the first of the books, "Rutland Ramsay," but I had to make clear to them that my participation in the rest of the affair—this first book was to be a test—must depend on the satisfaction I should give. If this should be limited my employers would drop me with scarce common forms. It was therefore a crisis for me, and naturally I was making special preparations, looking about for new people, should they be necessary, and securing the best types. I admitted however that I should like to settle down to two or three good models who would do for everything.

"Should we have often to—a—put on special clothes?" Mrs. Monarch timidly demanded.

"Dear yes—that's half the business."

"And should we be expected to supply our own costumes?"

"Oh no; I've got a lot of things. A painter's models put on—or put off—anything he likes."

"And you mean—a—the same?"

"The same?"

Mrs. Monarch looked at her husband again.

"Oh she was just wondering," he explained, "if the costumes are in *general* use." I had to confess that they were, and I mentioned further that some of them—I had a lot of genuine greasy last-century things—had served their time, a hundred years ago, on living world-stained men and women; on figures not perhaps so far removed, in the vanished world, from *their* type, the Monarchs', *quoi!* of a breeched and bewigged age. "We'll put on anything that *fits*," said the Major.

"Oh I arrange that—they fit in the pictures."

"I'm afraid I should do better for the modern books. I'd come as you like," said Mrs. Monarch.

"She has got a lot of clothes at home: they might do for contemporary life," her husband continued.

"Oh I can fancy scenes in which you'd be quite natural." And indeed I could see the slipshod rearrangements of stale properties—the stories I tried to produce pictures for without the exasperation of reading them—whose sandy tracts the good lady might help to people. But I had to return to the fact that for this sort of work—

the daily mechanical grind—I was already equipped: the people I was working with were fully adequate.

"We only thought we might be more like *some* characters," said Mrs. Monarch mildly, getting up.

Her husband also rose; he stood looking at me with a dim wistfulness that was touching in so fine a man. "Wouldn't it be rather a pull sometimes to have—a—to have—?" He hung fire; he wanted me to help him by phrasing what he meant. But I couldn't—I didn't know. So he brought it out awkwardly: "The *real* thing; a gentleman, you know, or a lady." I was quite ready to give a general assent—I admitted that there was a great deal in that. This encouraged Major Monarch to say, following up his appeal with an unacted gulp: "It's awfully hard—we've tried everything." The gulp was communicative; it proved too much for his wife. Before I knew it Mrs. Monarch had dropped again upon a divan and burst into tears. Her husband sat down beside her, holding one of her hands; whereupon she quickly dried her eyes with the other, while I felt embarrassed as she looked up at me. "There isn't a confounded job I haven't applied for—waited for—prayed for. You can fancy we'd be pretty bad first. Secretaryships and that sort of thing? You might as well ask for a peerage. I'd be *anything*—I'm strong; a messenger or a coalheaver. I'd put on a gold-laced cap and open carriage-doors in front of the haberdasher's; I'd hang about a station to carry portmanteaux; I'd be a postman. But they won't *look* at you; there are thousands as good as yourself already on the ground. *Gentlemen,* poor beggars, who've drunk their wine, who've kept their hunters!"

I was as reassuring as I knew how to be, and my visitors were presently on their feet again while, for the experiment, we agreed on an hour. We were discussing it when the door opened and Miss Churm came in with a wet umbrella. Miss Churm had to take the omnibus to Maida Vale and then walk half a mile. She looked a trifle blowsy and slightly splashed. I scarcely ever saw her come in without thinking afresh how odd it was that, being so little in herself, she should yet be so much in others. She was a meagre little Miss Churm, but was such an ample heroine of romance. She was only a freckled cockney, but she could represent everything, from a fine lady to a shepherdess; she had the faculty as she might have had a fine voice or long hair. She couldn't spell and she loved beer, but she had two or three "points," and practice, and a knack, and mother-wit, and a whimsical sensibility, and a love of the theatre, and seven sisters, and not an ounce of respect, especially for the *h*. The first thing my visitors saw was that her umbrella was wet, and in their spotless perfection they visibly winced at it. The rain had come on since their arrival.

"I'm all in a soak; there *was* a mess of people in the 'bus. I wish you lived near a stytion," said Miss Churm. I requested her to get ready as quickly as possible, and she passed into the room in which she always changed her dress. But before going out she asked me what she was to get into this time.

"It's the Russian princess, don't you know?" I answered; "the one with the 'golden eyes,' in black velvet, for the long thing in the *Cheapside*."

"Golden eyes? I *say!*" cried Miss Churm, while my companions watched her with intensity as she withdrew. She always arranged herself, when she was late, before I could turn round; and I kept my visitors a little on purpose, so that they might get an idea, from seeing her, what would be expected of themselves. I mentioned that she was quite my notion of an excellent model—she was really very clever.

"Do you think she looks like a Russian princess?" Major Monarch asked with lurking alarm.

"When I make her, yes."

"Oh if you have to *make* her—!" he reasoned, not without point.

"That's the most you can ask. There are so many who are not makeable."

"Well now, *here's* a lady"—and with a persuasive smile he passed his arm into his wife's—"who's already made!"

"Oh I'm not a Russian princess," Mrs. Monarch protested a little coldly. I could see she had known some and didn't like them. There at once was a complication of a kind I never had to fear with Miss Churm.

This young lady came back in black velvet—the gown was rather rusty and very low on her lean shoulders—and with a Japanese fan in her red hands. I reminded her that in the scene I was doing she was to look over some one's head. "I forget whose it is; but it doesn't matter. Just look over a head."

"I'd rather look over a stove," said Miss Churm; and she took her station near the fire. She fell into position, settled herself into a tall attitude, gave a certain backward inclination to her head and a certain forward droop to her fan, and looked, at least to my prejudiced sense, distinguished and charming, foreign and dangerous. We left her looking so while I went downstairs with Major and Mrs. Monarch.

"I believe I could come about as near it as that," said Mrs. Monarch.

"Oh you think she's shabby, but you must allow for the alchemy of art."

However, they went off with an evident increase of comfort founded on their de- monstrable advantage in being the real thing. I could fancy them shuddering over Miss Churm. She was very droll about them when I went back, for I told her what they wanted.

"Well, if *she* can sit I'll tyke to book-keeping," said my model.

"She's very ladylike," I replied as an innocent form of aggravation.

"So much the worse for *you*. That means she can't turn round."

"She'll do for the fashionable novels."

"Oh yes, she'll *do* for them!" my model humorously declared. "Ain't they bad enough without her?" I had often sociably denounced them to Miss Churm.

3

It was for the elucidation of a mystery in one of these works that I first tried Mrs. Monarch. Her husband came with her, to be useful if necessary—it was sufficiently clear that as a general thing he would prefer to come with her. At first I wondered if this were for "propriety's" sake—if he were going to be jealous and meddling. The idea was too tiresome, and if it had been confirmed it would speedily have brought our acquaintance to a close. But I soon saw there was nothing in it and that if he accompanied Mrs. Monarch it was—in addition to the chance of being wanted— simply because he had nothing else to do. When they were separate his occupation was gone and they never *had* been separate. I judged rightly that in their awkward situation their close union was their main comfort and that this union had no weak spot. It was a real marriage, an encouragement to the hesitating, a nut for pessimists to crack. Their address was humble—I remember afterwards thinking it had been the only thing about them that was really professional—and I could fancy the lamentable lodgings in which the Major would have been left alone. He could sit there more or less grimly with his wife—he couldn't sit there anyhow without her.

He had too much tact to try and make himself agreeable when he couldn't be useful; so when I was too absorbed in my work to talk he simply sat and waited. But I liked to hear him talk—it made my work, when not interrupting it, less mechanical, less special. To listen to him was to combine the excitement of going out with the economy of staying at home. There was only one hindrance—that I seemed not to know any of the people this brilliant couple had known. I think he wondered extremely, during the term of our intercourse, whom the deuce I *did* know. He hadn't a stray sixpence of an idea to fumble for, so we didn't spin it very fine; we confined ourselves to questions of leather and even of liquor—saddlers and breeches-makers and how to get excellent claret cheap—and matters like "good trains" and the habits of small game. His lore on these last subjects was astonishing—he managed to interweave the station-master with the ornithologist. When he couldn't talk about greater things he could talk cheerfully about smaller, and since I couldn't accompany him into reminiscences of the fashionable world he could lower the conversation without a visible effort to my level.

So earnest a desire to please was touching in a man who could so easily have knocked one down. He looked after the fire and had an opinion on the draught of the stove without my asking him, and I could see that he thought many of my arrangements not half knowing. I remember telling him that if I were only rich I'd offer him a salary to come and teach me how to live. Sometimes he gave a random sigh of which the essence might have been: "Give me even such a bare old barrack as *this,* and I'd do something with it!" When I wanted to use him he came alone; which was an illustration of the superior courage of women. His wife could bear her solitary second floor, and she was in general more discreet; showing by various small reserves that she was alive to the propriety of keeping our relations markedly professional—not letting them slide into sociability. She wished it to remain clear that she and the Major were employed, not cultivated, and if she approved of me as a superior, who could be kept in his place, she never thought me quite good enough for an equal.

She sat with great intensity, giving the whole of her mind to it, and was capable of remaining for an hour almost as motionless as before a photographer's lens. I could see she had been photographed often, but somehow the very habit that made her good for that purpose unfitted her for mine. At first I was extremely pleased with her ladylike air, and it was a satisfaction, on coming to follow her lines, to see how good they were and how far they could lead the pencil. But after a little skirmishing I began to find her too insurmountably stiff; do what I would with it my drawing looked like a photograph or a copy of a photograph. Her figure had no variety of expression—she herself had no sense of variety. You may say that this was my business and was only a question of placing her. Yet I placed her in every conceivable position and she managed to obliterate their differences. She was always a lady certainly, and into the bargain was always the same lady. She was the real thing, but always the same thing. There were moments when I rather writhed under the serenity of her confidence that she *was* the real thing. All her dealings with me and all her husband's were an implication that this was lucky for *me*. Meanwhile I found myself trying to invent types that approached her own, instead of making her own transform itself—in the clever way that was not impossible for instance to poor Miss Churm. Arrange as I would and take the precautions I would, she always came out, in my pictures, too tall—landing me in the dilemma of having represented a fascinating woman as seven feet high, which (out of respect perhaps to my own very much scantier inches) was far from my idea of such a personage.

The case was worse with the Major—nothing I could do would keep *him* down, so that he became useful only for the representation of brawny giants. I adored variety and range, I cherished human accidents, the illustrative note; I wanted to characterise closely, and the thing in the world I most hated was the danger of being ridden by a type. I had quarrelled with some of my friends about it; I had parted company with them for maintaining that one *had* to be, and that if the type was beautiful— witness Raphael and Leonardo—the servitude was only a gain. I was neither Leonardo nor Raphael—I might only be a presumptuous young modern searcher; but I held that everything was to be sacrificed sooner than character. When they claimed that the obsessional form could easily *be* character I retorted, perhaps superficially, "Whose?" It couldn't be everybody's—it might end in being nobody's.

After I had drawn Mrs. Monarch a dozen times I felt surer even than before that the value of such a model as Miss Churm resided precisely in the fact that she had no positive stamp, combined of course with the other fact that what she did have was a curious and inexplicable talent for imitation. Her usual appearance was like a curtain which she could draw up at request for a capital performance. This performance was simply suggestive; but it was a word to the wise—it was vivid and pretty. Sometimes even I thought it, though she was plain herself, too insipidly pretty; I made it a reproach to her that the figures drawn from her were monotonously (*bêtement,* as we used to say) graceful. Nothing made her more angry; it was so much her pride to feel she could sit for characters that had nothing in common with each other. She would accuse me at such moments of taking away her "reputytion."

It suffered a certain shrinkage, this queer quantity, from the repeated visits of my new friends. Miss Churm was greatly in demand, never in want of employment, so I had no scruple in putting her off occasionally, to try them more at my ease. It was certainly amusing at first to do the real thing—it was amusing to do Major Monarch's trousers. They *were* the real thing, even if he did come out colossal. It was amusing to do his wife's back hair—it was so mathematically neat—and the particular "smart" tension of her tight stays. She lent herself especially to positions in which the face was somewhat averted or blurred; she abounded in ladylike back views and *profils perdus.* When she stood erect she took naturally one of the attitudes in which court-painters represent queens and princesses; so that I found myself wondering whether, to draw out this accomplishment, I couldn't get the editor of the *Cheapside* to publish a really royal romance, "A Tale of Buckingham Palace." Sometimes however the real thing and the make-believe came into contact; by which I mean that Miss Churm, keeping an appointment or coming to make one on days when I had much work in hand, encountered her invidious rivals. The encounter was not on their part, for they noticed her no more than if she had been the housemaid; not from intentional loftiness, but simply because as yet, professionally, they didn't know how to fraternise, as I could imagine they would have liked—or at least that the Major would. They couldn't talk about the omnibus—they always walked; and they didn't know what else to try—she wasn't interested in good trains or cheap claret. Besides, they must have felt—in the air—that she was amused at them, secretly derisive of their ever knowing how. She wasn't a person to conceal the limits of her faith if she had had a chance to show them. On the other hand Mrs. Monarch didn't think her tidy; for why else did she take pains to say to me—it was going out of the way, for Mrs. Monarch—that she didn't like dirty women?

One day when my young lady happened to be present with my other sitters—she even dropped in, when it was convenient, for a chat—I asked her to be so good as to lend a hand in getting tea, a service with which she was familiar and which was one of a class that, living as I did in a small way, with slender domestic resources, I often appealed to my models to render. They liked to lay hands on my property, to break the sitting, and sometimes the china—it made them feel Bohemian. The next time I saw Miss Churm after this incident she surprised me greatly by making a scene about it—she accused me of having wished to humiliate her. She hadn't resented the outrage at the time, but had seemed obliging and amused, enjoying the comedy of asking Mrs. Monarch, who sat vague and silent, whether she would have cream and sugar, and putting an exaggerated simper into the question. She had tried intonations—as if she too wished to pass for the real thing—till I was afraid my other visitors would take offence.

Oh they were determined not to do this, and their touching patience was the measure of their great need. They would sit by the hour, uncomplaining, till I was ready to use them; they would come back on the chance of being wanted and would walk away cheerfully if it failed. I used to go to the door with them to see in what magnificent order they retreated. I tried to find other employment for them—I introduced them to several artists. But they didn't "take," for reasons I could appreciate, and I became rather anxiously aware that after such disappointments they fell back upon me with a heavier weight. They did me the honour to think me most *their* form. They weren't romantic enough for the painters, and in those days there were few serious workers in black-and-white. Besides, they had an eye to the great job I had mentioned to them—they had secretly set their hearts on supplying the right essence for my pictorial vindication of our fine novelist. They knew that for this undertaking I should want no costume-effects, none of the frippery of past ages—that it was a case in which everything would be contemporary and satirical and presumably genteel. If I could work them into it their future would be assured, for the labour would of course be long and the occupation steady.

One day Mrs. Monarch came without her husband—she explained his absence by his having had to go to the City. While she sat there in her usual relaxed majesty there came at the door a knock which I immediately recognised as the subdued appeal of a model out of work. It was followed by the entrance of a young man whom I at once saw to be a foreigner and who proved in fact an Italian acquainted with no English word but my name, which he uttered in a way that made it seem to include all others. I hadn't then visited his country, nor was I proficient in his tongue; but as he was not so meanly constituted—what Italian is?—as to depend only on that member for expression he conveyed to me, in familiar but graceful mimicry, that he was in search of exactly the employment in which the lady before me was engaged. I was not struck with him at first, and while I continued to draw I dropped few signs of interest or encouragement. He stood his ground however—not importunately, but with a dumb dog-like fidelity in his eyes that amounted to innocent impudence, the manner of a devoted servant—he might have been in the house for years—unjustly suspected. Suddenly it struck me that this very attitude and expression made a picture; whereupon I told him to sit down and wait till I should be free. There was another picture in the way he obeyed me, and I observed as I worked that there were others still in the way he looked wonderingly, with his head thrown back, about the high studio. He might have been crossing himself in Saint Peter's. Before I finished I said to myself "The fellow's a bankrupt orange-monger, but a treasure."

When Mrs. Monarch withdrew he passed across the room like a flash to open the door for her, standing there with the rapt pure gaze of the young Dante spellbound by the young Beatrice. As I never insisted, in such situations, on the blankness of the British domestic, I reflected that he had the making of a servant—and I needed one, but couldn't pay him to be only that—as well as of a model: in short I resolved to adopt my bright adventurer if he would agree to officiate in the double capacity. He jumped at my offer, and in the event my rashness—for I had really known nothing about him—wasn't brought home to me. He proved a sympathetic though a desultory ministrant, and had in a wonderful degree the *sentiment de la pose.* It was uncultivated, instinctive, a part of the happy instinct that had guided him to my door and helped him to spell out my name on the card nailed to it. He had had no other introduction to me than a guess, from the shape of my high north window, seen outside, that my place was a studio and that as a studio it would contain an artist. He had wandered to England in search of fortune, like other itinerants, and had embarked, with a partner and a small green hand-cart, on the sale of penny ices. The ices had melted away and the partner had dissolved in their train. My young man wore tight yellow trousers with reddish stripes and his name was Oronte. He was sallow but fair, and when I put him into some old clothes of my own he looked like an Englishman. He was as good as Miss Churm, who could look, when requested, like an Italian.

4

I thought Mrs. Monarch's face slightly convulsed when, on her coming back with her husband, she found Oronte installed. It was strange to have to recognise in a scrap of a lazzarone a competitor to her magnificent Major. It was she who scented danger first, for the Major was anecdotically unconscious. But Oronte gave us tea, with a hundred eager confusions—he had never been concerned in so queer a process—and I think she thought better of me for having at last an "establishment." They saw a couple of drawings that I had made of the establishment, and Mrs. Monarch hinted that it never would have struck her he had sat for them. "Now the drawings you make from *us,* they look exactly like us," she reminded me, smiling in triumph; and I recognised that this was indeed just their defect. When I drew the Monarchs I couldn't anyhow get away from them—get into the character I wanted to represent; and I hadn't the least desire my model should be discoverable in my picture. Miss Churm never was, and Mrs. Monarch thought I hid her, very properly, because she was vulgar; whereas if she was lost it was only as the dead who go to heaven are lost—in the gain of an angel the more.

By this time I had got a certain start with "Rutland Ramsay," the first novel in the great projected series; that is I had produced a dozen drawings, several with the help of the Major and his wife, and I had sent them in for approval. My understanding with the publishers, as I have already hinted, had been that I was to be left to do my work, in this particular case, as I liked, with the whole book committed to me; but my connexion with the rest of the series was only contingent. There were moments when, frankly, it *was* a comfort to have the real thing under one's hand; for there were characters in "Rutland Ramsay" that were very much like it. There were people presumably as erect as the Major and women of as good a fashion as Mrs. Monarch. There was a great deal of country-house life—treated, it is true, in a fine fanciful ironical generalised way—and there was a considerable implication of knickerbockers and kilts. There were certain things I had to settle at the outset; such things for instance as the exact appearance of the hero and the particular bloom and figure of the heroine. The author of course gave me a lead, but there was a margin for interpretation. I took the Monarchs into my confidence, I told them frankly what I was about, I mentioned my embarrassments and alternatives. "Oh take *him!*" Mrs. Monarch murmured sweetly, looking at her husband; and "What could you want better than my wife?" the Major enquired with the comfortable candour that now prevailed between us.

I wasn't obliged to answer these remarks—I was only obliged to place my sitters. I wasn't easy in mind, and I postponed a little timidly perhaps the solving of my question. The book was a large canvas, the other figures were numerous, and I worked off at first some of the episodes in which the hero and the heroine were not concerned. When once I had set *them* up I should have to stick to them—I couldn't make my young man seven feet high in one place and five feet nine in another. I inclined on the whole to the latter measurement, though the Major more than once reminded me that *he* looked about as young as any one. It was indeed quite possible to arrange him, for the figure, so that it would have been difficult to detect his age. After the spontaneous Oronte had been with me a month, and after I had given him to understand several times over that his native exuberance would presently constitute an insurmountable barrier to our further intercourse, I waked to a sense of his heroic capacity. He was only five feet seven, but the remaining inches were latent. I tried him almost secretly at first, for I was really rather afraid of the judgement my other models would pass on such a choice. If they regarded Miss Churm as little better than a snare what would they think of the representation by a person so little the real thing as an Italian street-vendour of a protagonist formed by a public school?

If I went a little in fear of them it wasn't because they bullied me, because they had got an oppressive foothold, but because in their really pathetic decorum and mysteriously permanent newness they counted on me so intensely. I was therefore very glad when Jack Hawley came home: he was always of such good counsel. He painted badly himself, but there was no one like him for putting his finger on the place. He had been absent from England for a year; he had been somewhere—I don't remember where—to get a fresh eye. I was in a good deal of dread of any such organ, but we were old friends; he had been away for months and a sense of emptiness was creeping into my life. I hadn't dodged a missile for a year.

He came back with a fresh eye, but with the same old black velvet blouse, and the first evening he spent in my studio we smoked cigarettes till the small hours. He had done no work himself, he had only got the eye; so the field was clear for the production of my little things. He wanted to see what I had produced for the *Cheapside,* but he was disappointed in the exhibition. That at least seemed the meaning of two or three comprehensive groans which, as he lounged on my big divan, his leg folded under him, looking at my latest drawings, issued from his lips with the smoke of the cigarette.

"What's the matter with you?" I asked.

"What's the matter with *you?*"

"Nothing save that I'm mystified."

"You are indeed. You're quite off the hinge. What's the meaning of this new fad?" And he tossed me, with visible irreverence, a drawing in which I happened to have depicted both my elegant models. I asked if he didn't think it good, and he replied that it struck him as execrable, given the sort of thing I had always represented myself to him as wishing to arrive at; but I let that pass—I was so anxious to see exactly what he meant. The two figures in the picture looked colossal, but I supposed this was *not* what he meant, inasmuch as, for aught he knew to the contrary, I might have been trying for some such effect. I maintained that I was working exactly in the same way as when he last had done me the honour to tell me I might do something some day. "Well, there's a screw loose somewhere," he answered; "wait a bit and I'll discover it." I depended upon him to do so: where else was the fresh eye? But he produced at last nothing more luminous than "I don't know—I don't like your types." This was lame for a critic who had never consented to discuss with me anything but the question of execution, the direction of strokes and the mystery of values.

"In the drawings you've been looking at I think my types are very handsome."

"Oh they won't do!"

"I've been working with new models."

"I see you have. *They* won't do."

"Are you very sure of that?"

"Absolutely—they're stupid."

"You mean *I* am—for I ought to get round that."

"You *can't*—with such people. Who are they?"

I told him, so far as was necessary, and he concluded heartlessly: "Ce sont des gens qu'il faut mettre à la porte."

"You've never seen them; they're awfully good"—I flew to their defence.

"Not seen them? Why all this recent work of yours drops to pieces with them. It's all I want to see of them."

"No one else has said anything against it—the *Cheapside* people are pleased."

"Every one else is an ass, and the *Cheapside* people the biggest asses of all. Come, don't pretend at this time of day to have pretty illusions about the public, especially about publishers and editors. It's not for *such* animals you work—it's for those who know, *coloro che sanno;* so keep straight for *me* if you can't keep straight for yourself. There was a certain sort of thing you used to try for—and a very good thing it was. But this twaddle isn't *in* it." When I talked with Hawley later about "Rutland Ramsay" and its possible successors he declared that I must get back into my boat again or I should go to the bottom. His voice in short was the voice of warning.

I noted the warning, but I didn't turn my friends out of doors. They bored me a good deal; but the very fact that they bored me admonished me not to sacrifice them—if there was anything to be done with them—simply to irritation. As I look back at this phase they seem to me to have pervaded my life not a little. I have a vision of them as most of the time in my studio, seated against the wall on an old velvet bench to be out of the way, and resembling the while a pair of patient courtiers in a royal antechamber. I'm convinced that during the coldest weeks of the winter they held their ground because it saved them fire. Their newness was losing its gloss, and it was impossible not to feel them objects of charity. Whenever Miss Churm arrived they went away, and after I was fairly launched in "Rutland Ramsay" Miss Churm arrived pretty often. They managed to express to me tacitly that they supposed I wanted her for the low life of the book, and I let them suppose it, since they had attempted to study the work—it was lying about the studio—without discovering that it dealt only with the highest circles. They had dipped into the most brilliant of our novelists without deciphering many passages. I still took an hour from them, now and again, in spite of Jack Hawley's warning: it would be time enough to dismiss them, if dismissal should be necessary, when the rigour of the season was over. Hawley had made their acquaintance—he had met them at my fireside—and thought them a ridiculous pair. Learning that he was a painter they tried to approach him, to show him too that they were the real thing; but he looked at them, across the big room, as if they were miles away: they were a compendium of everything he most objected to in the social system of his country. Such people as that, all convention and patent-leather, with ejaculations that stopped conversation, had no business in a studio. A studio was a place to learn to see, and how could you see through a pair of feather-beds?

The main inconvenience I suffered at their hands was that at first I was shy of letting it break upon them that my artful little servant had begun to sit to me for "Rutland Ramsay." They knew I had been odd enough—they were prepared by this time to allow oddity to artists—to pick a foreign vagabond out of the streets when I might have had a person with whiskers and credentials; but it was some time before they learned how high I rated his accomplishments. They found him in an attitude more than once, but they never doubted I was doing him as an organ-grinder. There were several things they never guessed, and one of them was that for a striking scene in the novel, in which a footman briefly figured, it occurred to me to make use of Major Monarch as the menial. I kept putting this off, I didn't like to ask him to don the livery—besides the difficulty of finding a livery to fit him. At last, one day late in the winter, when I was at work on the despised Oronte, who caught one's idea on the wing, and was in the glow of feeling myself go very straight, they came in, the Major and his wife, with their society laugh about nothing (there was less and less to laugh at); came in like country-callers—they always reminded me of that—who have walked across the park after church and are presently persuaded to stay to luncheon. Luncheon was over, but they could stay to tea—I knew they wanted it. The fit was on me, however, and I couldn't let my ardour cool and my work wait, with the fading daylight, while my model prepared it. So I asked Mrs. Monarch if she would mind laying it out—a request which for an instant brought all the blood to her face. Her eyes were on her husband's for a second, and some mute telegraphy passed between them. Their folly was over the next instant; his cheerful shrewdness put an end to it. So far from pitying their wounded pride, I must add, I was moved to give it as complete a lesson as I could. They bustled about together and got out the cups and saucers and made the kettle boil. I know they felt as if they were waiting on my servant, and when the tea was prepared I said: "He'll have a cup, please—he's tired." Mrs. Monarch brought him one where he stood, and he took it from her as if he had been a gentleman at a party squeezing a crush-hat with an elbow.

Then it came over me that she had made a great effort for me—made it with a kind of nobleness—and that I owed her a compensation. Each time I saw her after this I wondered what the compensation could be. I couldn't go on doing the wrong thing to oblige them. Oh it *was* the wrong thing, the stamp of the work for which they sat—Hawley was not the only person to say it now. I sent in a large number of the drawings I had made for "Rutland Ramsay," and I received a warning that was more to the point than Hawley's. The artistic adviser of the house for which I was working was of opinion that many of my illustrations were not what had been looked for. Most of these illustrations were the subjects in which the Monarchs had figured. Without going into the question of what *had* been looked for, I had to face the fact that at this rate I shouldn't get the other books to do. I hurled myself in despair on Miss Churm—I put her through all her paces. I not only adopted Oronte publicly as my hero, but one morning when the Major looked in to see if I didn't require him to finish a *Cheapside* figure for which he had begun to sit the week before, I told him I had changed my mind—I'd do the drawing from my man. At this my visitor turned pale and stood looking at me. "Is *he* your idea of an English gentleman?" he asked.

I was disappointed, I was nervous, I wanted to get on with my work; so I replied with irritation: "Oh my dear Major—I can't be ruined for *you!*"

It was a horrid speech, but he stood another moment—after which, without a word, he quitted the studio. I drew a long breath, for I said to myself that I shouldn't see him again. I hadn't told him definitely that I was in danger of having my work rejected, but I was vexed at his not having felt the catastrophe in the air, read with me the moral of our fruitless collaboration, the lesson that in the deceptive atmosphere of art even the highest respectability may fail of being plastic.

I didn't owe my friends money, but I did see them again. They reappeared together three days later, and, given all the other facts, there was something tragic in that one. It was a clear proof they could find nothing else in life to do. They had threshed the matter out in a dismal conference—they had digested the bad news that they were not in for the series. If they weren't useful to me even for the *Cheapside* their function seemed difficult to determine, and I could only judge at first that they had come, forgivingly, decorously, to take a last leave. This made me rejoice in secret that I had little leisure for a scene; for I had placed both my other models in position together and I was pegging away at a drawing from which I hoped to derive glory. It had been suggested by the passage in which Rutland Ramsay, drawing up a chair to Artemisia's piano-stool, says extraordinary things to her while she ostensibly fingers out a difficult piece of music. I had done Miss Churm at the piano before—it was an attitude in which she knew how to take on an absolutely poetic grace. I wished the two figures to "compose" together with intensity, and my little Italian had entered perfectly into my conception. The pair were vividly before me, the piano had been pulled out; it was a charming show of blended youth and murmured love, which I had only to catch and keep. My visitors stood and looked at it, and I was friendly to them over my shoulder.

They made no response, but I was used to silent company and went on with my work, only a little disconcerted—even though exhilarated by the sense that *this* was at least the ideal thing—at not having got rid of them after all. Presently I heard Mrs. Monarch's sweet voice beside or rather above me: "I wish her hair were a little better done." I looked up and she was staring with a strange fixedness at Miss Churm, whose back was turned to her. "Do you mind my just touching it?" she went on—a question which made me spring up for an instant as with the instinctive fear that she might do the young lady a harm. But she quieted me with a glance I shall never forget—I confess I should like to have been able to paint *that*—and went for a moment to my model. She spoke to her softly, laying a hand on her shoulder and bending over her; and as the girl, understanding, gratefully assented, she disposed her rough curls, with a few quick passes, in such a way as to make Miss Churm's head twice as charming. It was one of the most heroic personal services I've ever seen rendered. Then Mrs. Monarch turned away with a low sigh and, looking about her as if for something to do, stooped to the floor with a noble humility and picked up a dirty rag that had dropped out of my paint-box.

The Major meanwhile had also been looking for something to do, and, wandering to the other end of the studio, saw before him my breakfast-things neglected, unremoved. "I say, can't I be useful *here*?" he called out to me with an irrepressible quaver. I assented with a laugh that I fear was awkward, and for the next ten minutes, while I worked, I heard the light clatter of china and the tinkle of spoons and glass. Mrs. Monarch assisted her husband—they washed up my crockery, they put it away. They wandered off into my little scullery, and I afterwards found that they had cleaned my knives and that my slender stock of plate had an unprecedented surface.

When it came over me, the latent eloquence of what they were doing, I confess that my drawing was blurred for a moment—the picture swam. They had accepted their failure, but they couldn't accept their fate. They had bowed their heads in bewilderment to the perverse and cruel law in virtue of which the real thing could be so much less precious than the unreal; but they didn't want to starve. If my servants were my models, then my models might be my servants. They would reverse the parts—the others would sit for the ladies and gentlemen and *they* would do the work. They would still be in the studio—it was an intense dumb appeal to me not to turn them out. "Take us on," they wanted to say—"we'll do *anything*."

My pencil dropped from my hand; my sitting was spoiled and I got rid of my sitters, who were also evidently rather mystified and awestruck. Then, alone with the Major and his wife I had a most uncomfortable moment. He put their prayer into a single sentence: "I say, you know—just let *us* do for you, can't you?" I couldn't—it was dreadful to see them emptying my slops; but I pretended I could, to oblige them, for about a week. Then I gave them a sum of money to go away, and I never saw them again. I obtained the remaining books, but my friend Hawley repeats that Major and Mrs. Monarch did me a permanent harm, got me into false ways. If it be true I'm content to have paid the price—for the memory.

GUY DE MAUPASSANT (1850–1893)

Miss Harriet

Translated by Ernest Boyd

There were seven of us in the drag, four women, and three men, one of whom was on the box-seat beside the coachman. We were following, at a walking pace, the winding coast road up the hill.

Having set out from Étretat at daybreak to visit the ruins of Tancarville, we were still half asleep, benumbed by the fresh air of the morning. The women, especially, who were little accustomed to early rising, let their eyelids fall every moment, nodding their heads or yawning, quite insensible to the glory of the dawn.

It was autumn. On both sides of the road the bare fields stretched out, yellowed by the stubble of oats and wheat which covered the soil like a badly shaved beard. The misty earth looked as if it were steaming. Larks were singing in the air, while other birds piped in the bushes.

At length the sun rose in front of us, a bright red on the edge of the horizon; and as it ascended, growing clearer from minute to minute, the country seemed to awake, to smile, to stretch itself, to slip off its night-gown of white mist, like a young girl leaving her bed. The Comte d'Étraille, who was seated on the box, cried:

"Look! look! a hare!" and he stretched out his arm to the left, pointing to a patch of clover. The animal scurried along, almost concealed by the field, only its large ears visible. Then it swerved across a deep furrow, stopped, started off again at top speed, changed its course, stopped anew, uneasy, spying out every danger, and undecided as to the route it should take. Suddenly it began to run, with great bounds of its hind legs, disappearing finally in a large patch of beet root. All the men had wakened up to watch the animal's movements.

René Lemanoir then exclaimed:

"We are not at all gallant this morning," and looking at his neighbor, the little Baroness de Sérennes, who was struggling with drowsiness, he said to her in a subdued voice: "You are thinking of your husband, Baroness. Reassure yourself; he will not return before Saturday, so you still have four days."

She replied, with a sleepy smile:

"How silly you are." Then, shaking off her torpor, she added: "Now, let somebody say something that will make us all laugh. You, Monsieur Chenal, who have the reputation of having more successes than the Duc de Richelieu, tell us a love-story in which you have been involved, anything you like."

Léon Chenal, an old painter, who had once been very handsome, very strong, very proud of his physique, and very popular, took his long white beard in his hand and smiled; then, after a few moments' reflection, he became suddenly grave.

"Ladies, it will not be an amusing tale; for I am going to relate to you the most lamentable love-affair of my life, and I sincerely hope that none of my friends may ever inspire a similar passion."

1

"At that time I was twenty-five years old, and I was daubing along the coast of Normandy. I mean by 'daubing' wandering about, with a knapsack on one's back, from inn to inn, under the pretext of making studies and sketches from nature. I know nothing more enjoyable than that happy-go-lucky wandering life, in which you are perfectly free, without shackles of any kind, without a care, without a single preoccupation, without even a thought of tomorrow. You go in any direction you please, without any guide save your fancy, without any counsellor save what pleases your eyes. You pull up, because a running brook seduces you, or because you are attracted, in front of an inn, by the smell of fried potatoes. Sometimes it is the perfume of clematis which decides you in your choice, or the glance of the servant at an inn. Do not despise these rustic affections. These girls have souls as well as bodies, firm cheeks and fresh lips; their vigorous kisses are strong and fragrant, like wild fruits. Love is always worth while, come whence it may. A heart that beats when you make your appearance, an eye that weeps when you go away, these are things so rare, so sweet, so precious, that they must never be despised.

"I have had rendezvous in ditches full of primroses, behind the stable in which the cattle slept, and among the straw in garrets still warm from the heat of the day. I have memories of coarse grey linen on supple, strong bodies, and of hearty, fresh, free kisses, more delicate, in their sincere brutality, than the subtle joys accorded by charming and distinguished women.

"But what one chiefly loves in these pilgrimages of adventure is the country, the woods, the sunrises, the twilights, the light of the moon. For the painter these are honeymoon trips with Nature. You are alone with her in a long, quiet rendezvous.

You go to bed in the fields amid marguerites and wild poppies, and, with eyes wide open, under the bright sunlight, you regard far away some little village, with pointed clock-tower which sounds the hour of noon.

"You sit down by the side of a spring which gushes out from the foot of an oak, amid a covering of tall, fragile weeds, glistening with life. You go down on your knees, bend forward, and drink the cold and pellucid water, wetting your moustache and nose; you drink it with a physical pleasure, as though you were kissing the spring, lip to lip. Sometimes, when you find a deep hole along the course of these tiny brooks, you plunge into it, quite naked, and on your skin, from head to foot, like an icy and delicious caress, you feel the swift and gentle quivering of the current.

"You are gay on the hills, melancholy on the shores of the lagoons, exalted when the sun is drowned in an ocean of blood-red clouds and wakes red reflections in the rivers. And at night, under the moon, as she passes across the roof of heaven, you think of things, singular things, which would never have occurred to your mind under the brilliant light of day.

"So, in wandering through this same country where we are this year, I came one day to the little village of Bénouville, on the rocky coast between Yport and Étretat. I came from Fécamp, following the cliff, the tall cliff, perpendicular as a wall, with its bastions of chalk falling sheer down into the sea. I had walked since morning on the close-clipped grass, as smooth and yielding as a carpet, which grows along the edge of the cliff, fanned by the salt breezes of the ocean. Singing lustily, I walked with long strides, looking sometimes at the slow, curving flight of a gull, with its sweep of white wings sailing over the blue heavens, sometimes at the green sea, or at the brown sails of a fishing bark. In short, I had passed a happy day, a day of liberty and freedom from care.

"I was told there was a little farmhouse where travellers were put up, a kind of inn kept by a peasant, which stood in a Normandy courtyard, surrounded by a double row of beeches.

"Leaving the cliff, I reached the hamlet, which was shut in by great trees, and I presented myself at the house of Mother Lecacheur.

"She was an old country woman, wrinkled and austere, who always seemed to receive customers reluctantly, with a kind of contempt.

"It was the month of May: the flowering apple-trees covered the court with a roof of perfumed flowers, with a whirling shower of pink blossoms which rained unceasingly upon the people and upon the grass.

"I said:

"'Well, Madame Lecacheur, have you a room for me?'

"Astonished to find that I knew her name, she answered:

"'That depends; everything is let; but all the same, there will be no harm in looking.'

"In five minutes we had come to an agreement, and I deposited my bag upon the earthen floor of a rustic room, furnished with a bed, two chairs, a table, and a wash-stand. The room opened into the large, smoky kitchen, where the lodgers took their meals with the people of the farm and with the woman herself, who was a widow.

"I washed my hands, after which I went out. The old woman was making a chicken fricassee for dinner in a large fireplace, in which hung the stew-pot, black with smoke.

" 'You have visitors, then, at the present time?' I said to her.

"She answered in an offended tone of voice:

" 'I have a lady, an English lady, of a certain age. She is occupying the other room.'

"For an extra five sous a day, I obtained the privilege of dining out in the court when the weather was fine.

"My place was accordingly set in front of the door, and I began to champ the lean limbs of the Normandy chicken, to drink the clear cider, and to munch the hunk of white bread, which, though four days old, was excellent.

"Suddenly the wooden gate which opened on to the highway was opened, and a strange person walked toward the house. She was very thin, very tall, enveloped in a Scotch shawl with red cheeks. You would have believed that she had no arms, if you had not seen a long hand appear just above the hips, holding a white tourist's umbrella. The face of a mummy, surrounded with sausage-rolls of plaited grey hair, which shook at every step she took, made me think, I know not why, of a pickled herring adorned with curling-papers. Lowering her eyes, she passed quickly in front of me, and entered the house.

"This singular apparition amused me. She undoubtedly was my neighbor, the 'English lady of a certain age' of whom our hostess had spoken.

"I did not see her again that day. The next day, when I had begun to paint at the end of the beautiful valley which you know, which extends as far as Étretat, lifting my eyes suddenly, I perceived something singularly attired standing on the crest of the declivity; it looked like a pole decked out with flags. It was she. On seeing me, she disappeared.

"I returned to the house at midday for lunch, and took my seat at the common table, so as to make the acquaintance of this eccentric old creature. But she did not respond to my polite advances, was insensible even to my little attentions. I perseveringly poured water out for her, I passed her the dishes with an air. A slight, almost imperceptible movement of the head, and an English word, murmured so low that I did not understand it, were her only acknowledgments.

"I ceased taking any notice of her, although she had disturbed my thoughts. At the end of three days, I knew as much about her as Madame Lecacheur did herself.

"She was called Miss Harriet. Seeking a secluded village in which to pass the summer, she had stopped at Bénouville, some six weeks before, and did not seem disposed to leave it. She never spoke at table, ate rapidly, reading all the while a small book of Protestant propaganda. She gave a copy of this book to everybody. The curé himself had received no less than four copies, at the hands of an urchin to whom she had paid two sous' commission. She said sometimes to our hostess, abruptly, without the slightest preliminary leading up to this declaration:

" 'I love the Savior above all; I worship Him in all creation; I adore Him in all nature; I carry Him always in my heart.'

"And she would immediately present the old woman with one of her brochures destined to convert the universe.

"In the village she was not liked. In fact, the schoolmaster had declared that she was an atheist, and a kind of stigma attached to her. The curé, who had been consulted by Madame Lecacheur, responded:

" 'She is a heretic, but God does not wish the death of the sinner, and I believe her to be a person of pure morals.'

"These words, 'atheist,' 'heretic,' words which no one could precisely define, threw doubts into some minds. It was asserted further, that this Englishwoman was rich, and that she had passed her life in travelling through every country in the world, because her family had thrown her off. Why had her family thrown her off? Because of her impiety, of course.

"She was, in reality, one of those people of exalted principles, one of those obstinate puritans of whom England produces so many, one of those good and insupportable old women who haunt the tables d'hôte of every hotel in Europe, who spoil Italy, poison Switzerland, render the charming cities of the Mediterranean uninhabitable, carry everywhere their fantastic manias, their petrified vestal morals, their indescribable toilettes, and a certain odor of india-rubber, which makes one believe that at night they slip themselves into a case of that material. When I met one of these people in a hotel, I used to flee like the birds when they see a scarecrow in a field.

"This woman, however, appeared so singular that she did not displease me.

"Madame Lecacheur, hostile by instinct to everything that was not peasant, felt in her narrow soul a kind of hatred for the ecstatic extravagances of the old maid. She had found a phrase by which to describe her, a phrase assuredly contemptuous, which had sprung to her lips I know not how, invented probably by some confused and mysterious travail of soul. She said: 'That woman is a demoniac.' This phrase, applied to the austere and sentimental creature, seemed to me irresistibly comic. I, myself, never called her now anything else but 'the demoniac,' feeling a singular pleasure in pronouncing this word aloud on seeing her.

"I would ask Mother Lecacheur: 'Well, what is our demoniac doing today?' To which the peasant would respond with a scandalized air:

" 'What do you think, sir? She picked up a toad with a crushed paw, carried it to her room, put it in her wash-stand, and dressed its wound as if it were a human. If that is not profanation, I should like to know what is!'

"On another occasion, when walking along the shore, she had bought a large fish which had just been caught, simply to throw it back into the sea again. The sailor, from whom she had bought it, though paid handsomely, was greatly provoked at this act—more exasperated, indeed, than if she had put her hand into his pocket and taken his money. For a whole month he could not speak of the circumstance without getting into a fury and denouncing it as an outrage. Oh yes! She was indeed a demoniac, this Miss Harriet, and Mother Lecacheur must have had an inspiration of genius in thus christening her.

"The stable-boy, who was called Sapeur, because he had served in Africa in his youth, entertained other opinions. He said, with a knowing air: 'She is an old hag who has had her day.' If the poor woman had but known.

"Céleste, the little servant, did not like waiting on her, but I was never able to understand why. Probably her only reason was that she was a stranger, of another race, of a different tongue, and of another religion. She was a demoniac, in brief!

"She passed her time wandering about the country, adoring and searching for God in nature. I found her one evening on her knees in a cluster of bushes. Having discovered something red through the leaves, I brushed aside the branches, and Miss Harriet at once rose to her feet, confused at having been found thus, looking at me with eyes as frightened as those of an owl surprised in open day.

"Sometimes, when I was working among the rocks, I would suddenly see her on the edge of the cliff, standing like a semaphore signal. She gazed passionately at the vast sea, glittering in the sunlight, and the boundless sky empurpled with fire. Sometimes I would distinguish her at the bottom of a valley, walking quickly, with her elastic English step; and I would go toward her, mysteriously attracted, simply to see her visionary expression, her dried-up, ineffable features, full of an inward and profound happiness.

"Often I would encounter her in the corner of a field sitting on the grass, under the shadow of an apple-tree, with her little Bible lying open on her knee, while she looked meditatively into the distance.

"I could no longer tear myself away from that quiet country neighborhood, bound to it as I was by a thousand links of love for its soft and sweeping landscapes. I was happy at this farm, which was out of the world, far removed from everything, but in close proximity to the soil, the good, healthy, beautiful green soil, which we ourselves shall fertilize with our bodies some day. And, I must confess, there was perhaps a certain amount of curiosity which kept me at Mother Lecacheur's. I wished to become acquainted a little with this strange Miss Harriet, and to learn what passes in the solitary souls of those wandering old English dames."

2

"We became acquainted in a rather singular manner. I had just finished a study which I thought good, and so it was. It was sold for ten thousand francs, fifteen years later. It was as simple as twice two make four, and had nothing to do with academic rules. The whole of the right side of my canvas represented a rock, an enormous jagged rock, covered with seawrack, brown, yellow, and red, across which the sun poured like a stream of oil. The light fell upon the stone, and gilded it as if with fire, but the sun itself was behind me and could not be seen. That was all. A foreground dazzling with light, blazing, superb.

"On the left was the sea, not the blue sea, the slate-colored sea, but a sea of jade, greenish, milky, and hard under the deep sky.

"I was so pleased with my work that I danced as I carried it back to the inn. I wished that the whole world could have seen it at one and the same moment. I can remember that I showed it to a cow which was browsing by the wayside, exclaiming, at the same time: 'Look at that, my old beauty; you will not often see its like again.'

"When I had reached the front of the house, I immediately called out to Mother Lecacheur, bawling with all my might:

" 'Look at this! You won't see anything like it in a hurry.'

"The woman came and looked at my work with stupid eyes, which distinguished nothing, and did not even recognize whether the picture represented an ox or a house.

"Miss Harriet was coming into the house, and she passed behind me just at the moment when, holding out my canvas at arm's length, I was exhibiting it to the old innkeeper. The 'demoniac' could not help but see it, for I took care to exhibit the thing in such a way that it could not escape her notice. She stopped abruptly and stood motionless, stupefied. It was her rock which was depicted, the one which she usually climbed to dream away her time undisturbed.

"She uttered a British 'Oh,' which was at once so accentuated and so flattering, that I turned round to her, smiling, and said:

" 'This is my latest study, Mademoiselle.'

"She murmured ecstatically, comically, and tenderly:

" 'Oh! Monsieur, you understand nature in a most thrilling way!'

"I colored up, indeed I did, and was more excited by that compliment than if it had come from a queen. I was seduced, conquered, vanquished. I could have embraced her—upon my honor.

"I took my seat at the table beside her, as I had always done. For the first time, she spoke, following out her thought aloud:

" 'Oh! I love nature so much.'

"I offered her bread, water, wine. She now accepted these with a slight, dry smile. I then began to converse with her about the scenery.

"After the meal, we rose from the table together and walked leisurely across the court; then, attracted by the fiery glow which the setting sun cast over the surface of the sea, I opened the outside gate which faced in the direction of the cliff, and we walked on side by side, happy as two persons are who have just learned to understand and penetrate each other's motives and feelings.

"It was a misty, relaxing evening, one of those enjoyable evenings which impart happiness to mind and body alike. All is joy, all is charm. The luscious and balmy air, loaded with the perfume of grass, with the tang of seaweed, with the odor of the wild flowers, caresses the nostrils with its wild perfume, the palate with its salty savor, the soul with a penetrating sweetness. We were walking as on the brink of the abyss which overlooked the vast sea, which rolled its little waves a hundred yards below our feet.

"We drank, with open mouth and expanded chest, that fresh breeze from the ocean which glides slowly over the skin, salted by long contact with the waves.

"Wrapped in her plaid shawl, with a look of inspiration as she faced the breeze, the Englishwoman gazed fixedly at the great sun ball as it descended toward the horizon. Far off in the distance a three-master in full sail was outlined on the blood-red sky and a steamship, somewhat nearer, passed along, leaving behind it a trail of smoke on the horizon. The red sun-globe sank slowly lower and lower and presently touched the water just behind the motionless vessel, which, in its dazzling effulgence, looked as though framed in a flame of fire. We saw it plunge, grow smaller and disappear, swallowed up by the ocean.

"Miss Harriet gazed in rapture at the last gleams of the dying day. She seemed longing passionately to embrace the sky, the sea, the whole landscape.

"She murmured: 'Ah! I love—I love—' I saw a tear in her eye. She went on: 'I wish I were a little bird, so that I could mount up into the firmament.'

"She remained standing as I had often before seen her, perched on the cliff, her face as red as her shawl. I should have liked to have sketched her in my album. It would have been a caricature of ecstasy.

"I turned away so as not to laugh.

"I then spoke to her of painting as I would have done to a fellow-artist, using the technical terms common among the devotees of the profession. She listened attentively, eagerly seeking to divine the meaning of the terms, so as to understand my thoughts. From time to time she would exclaim: 'Oh! I understand, I understand. It is very interesting.'

"We returned home.

"The next day, on seeing me, she approached me, cordially holding out her hand; and we at once became firm friends.

"She was a good creature who had a kind of soul on springs, which became enthusiastic at a bound. She lacked equilibrium, like all women who are spinsters at the age of fifty. She seemed to be preserved in vinegary innocence, but her heart still retained something of youth and of girlish effervescence. She loved both nature and animals with a fervent ardor, a love like old wine, mellow through age, a sensual love that she had never bestowed on men.

"One thing is certain: a bitch feeding her pups, a mare roaming in a meadow with a foal at its side, a bird's nest full of young ones, squeaking, with their open mouths and enormous heads, and no feathers, made her quiver with the most violent emotion.

"Poor solitary beings! Sad wanderers from table d'hôte to table d'hôte, poor beings, ridiculous and lamentable, I love you ever since I became acquainted with Miss Harriet!

"I soon discovered that she had something she would like to tell me, but dared not, and I was amused at her timidity. When I started out in the morning with my box on my back, she would accompany me to the end of the village, silent, but evidently struggling inwardly to find words with which to begin a conversation. Then she would leave me abruptly, and walk away quickly with her jaunty step.

"One day, however, she plucked up courage:

" 'I would like to see how you paint pictures. Will you show me? I have been very curious.'

"And she colored up as though she had given utterance to words of extreme audacity.

"I conducted her to the bottom of the Petit-Val, where I had commenced a large picture.

"She remained standing near me, following all my gestures with concentrated attention. Then, suddenly, fearing, perhaps, that she was disturbing me, she said to me: 'Thank you,' and walked away.

"But in a short time she became more familiar, and accompanied me every day, with visible pleasure. She carried her folding-stool under her arm, would not consent to my carrying it, and she sat by my side. She would remain there for hours immovable and mute, following with her eye the point of my brush in its every movement. When I would obtain, by a large splotch of color spread on with a knife, a striking and unexpected effect, she would, in spite of herself, give vent to a half-suppressed 'Oh!' of astonishment, of joy, of admiration. She had the most tender respect for my canvases, an almost religious respect for that human reproduction of a part of Nature's divine work. My studies appeared to her as a species of holy pictures, and sometimes she spoke to me of God, with the idea of converting me.

"Oh! He was a queer creature, this God of hers. He was a sort of village philosopher without any great resources, and without great power; for she always pictured him to herself as being in despair over injustices committed under his eyes, as if he were helpless to prevent them.

"She was, however, on excellent terms with him, affecting even to be the confidante of his secrets and of his whims. She said: 'God wills,' or 'God does not will,' just like a sergeant announcing to a recruit: 'The colonel has commanded.'

"At the bottom of her heart she deplored my ignorance of the intentions of the Eternal, which she strove to impart to me.

"Every day I found in my pockets, in my hat when I lifted it from the ground, in my box of colors, in my polished shoes, standing in the mornings in front of my door, those little pious brochures, which she, no doubt, received directly from Paradise.

"I treated her as one would an old friend, with unaffected cordiality. But I soon perceived that she had changed somewhat in her manner, though, for a while, I paid little attention to it.

"When I was painting, whether in my valley or in some country lane, I would see her suddenly appear with her rapid, springy walk. She would then sit down abruptly, out of breath, as though she had been running or were overcome by some profound emotion. Her face would be red, that English red which is denied to the people of all other countries; then, without any reason, she would turn ashy pale and seem about to faint away. Gradually, however, her natural color would return and she would begin to speak.

"Then, without warning, she would break off in the middle of a sentence, spring up from her seat and walk away so rapidly and so strangely that I was at my wits' ends to discover whether I had done or said anything to displease or wound her.

"I finally came to the conclusion that those were her normal manners, somewhat modified no doubt in my honor during the first days of our acquaintance.

"When she returned to the farm, after walking for hours on the windy coast, her long curls often hung straight down, as if their springs had been broken. This had hitherto seldom given her any concern, and she would come to dinner without embarrassment, all dishevelled by her sister, the breeze.

"But now she would go up to her room in order to adjust what I called her lamp-glasses. When I would say to her, with familiar gallantry, which, however, always offended her: 'You are as beautiful as a star today, Miss Harriet,' a little blood would immediately mount into her cheeks, the blood of a young maiden, the blood of sweet fifteen.

"Then she became very shy, and ceased coming to watch me paint. I thought:

" 'This is only a fit of temper. It will pass.'

"But it did not pass away. When I spoke to her now, she would answer me, either with an air of affected indifference, or in a sullen anger; and she became by turns rude, impatient, and nervous. I never saw her except at meals, and we spoke but little. I concluded, at length, that I must have offended her in something: and, accordingly, I said to her one evening:

" 'Miss Harriet, why have you changed towards me? What have I done to displease you? You are causing me much pain!'

"She responded in an angry tone, which was very funny: 'I have not changed towards you. It is not true, not true,' and she ran upstairs and shut herself up in her room.

"At times she would look upon me with strange eyes. Since that time I have often said to myself that those condemned to death must look thus when informed that their last day has come. In her eye there lurked a species of madness, an insanity at once mystical and violent—something more, a fever, an exasperated desire, impatient and impotent, for the unrealized and unrealizable!

"It seemed to me that there was also going on within her a combat, in which her heart struggled against an unknown force that she wished to overcome—perhaps, even, something else. But what could I know? What could I know?"

3

"It was indeed a singular revelation.

"For some time I had been working as soon as it got light on a picture the subject of which was as follows:

"A deep ravine, enclosed, surmounted by two thickets of rushes and trees, extended into the distance and was lost, submerged in that milky vapor, in that cloud-like cotton-down that sometimes floats over valleys at daybreak. And at the extreme end of that heavy, transparent fog one saw, or rather guessed, two human figures, a youth and a maiden, their arms interlaced, embracing, she with her head raised towards him, he bending over her, their lips joined.

"A first ray of the sun, glistening through the branches, pierced that fog of the dawn, illuminated it with a rosy reflection just behind the rustic lovers, framing their vague shadows in a silvery background. It was good; really good.

"I was working on the declivity which led to the valley of Étretat. On this particular morning I had, by chance, the sort of floating vapor which I needed.

"Suddenly something rose up in front of me like a phantom; it was Miss Harriet. On seeing me she was about to flee. But I called after her, saying: 'Come here, come here, Mademoiselle. I have a nice little picture for you.'

"She came forward, though with seeming reluctance. I handed her my sketch. She said nothing, but stood for a long time motionless, looking at it. Suddenly she burst into tears. She wept spasmodically, like men who have been struggling hard against shedding tears, but who can do so no longer, and abandon themselves to grief, resisting still. I got up, trembling, moved myself by the sight of a sorrow I did not understand, and I took her by the hand with a gesture of brusque affection, a real French impulse, in which action outruns thought.

"She let her hands rest in mine for a few seconds, and I felt them quiver, as if her whole nervous system were on the rack. Then she withdrew her hands abruptly, or, rather, tore them out of mine.

"I recognized that shiver as soon as I had felt it; I knew it perfectly. Ah! the love-thrill of a woman, whether she is fifteen or fifty years of age, whether she is of the people or in society, goes so straight to my heart that I never have any difficulty in understanding it!

"Her whole frail being trembled, vibrated, swooned. I knew it. She walked away before I had time to say a word, leaving me as surprised as if I had witnessed a miracle, and as troubled as if I had committed a crime.

"I did not go in to breakfast. I took a walk on the edge of the cliff, feeling that I could just as soon weep as laugh, looking on the adventure as both comic and deplorable, and my position as ridiculous, believing her unhappy enough to go mad.

"I asked myself what I ought to do. I decided that my only course was to leave the place, and at once made up my mind to do so.

"Somewhat sad and perplexed, I wandered about until dinner-time, and entered the farmhouse just when the soup had been served.

"I sat down at the table as usual. Miss Harriet was there, eating away solemnly, without speaking to anyone, without even lifting her eyes. Her manner and expression were the same as usual.

"I waited patiently till the meal had been finished, then, turning toward the landlady, I said: 'Well, Madame Lecacheur, it will not be long now before I shall have to take my leave of you.'

"The good woman, surprised and troubled, replied in her drawling voice: 'My dear sir, what's this? You are going to leave us after I have become so accustomed to you?'

"I glanced at Miss Harriet out of the corner of my eye. Her countenance did not change in the least. But Céleste, the little servant, looked up at me. She was a fat girl of about eighteen, rosy, fresh, as strong as a horse, and possessing the rare attribute of cleanliness. I had kissed her at odd times in out-of-the-way corners, after the manner of travellers—nothing more.

"The dinner being at length over, I went to smoke my pipe under the apple-trees, walking up and down from one end of the enclosure to the other. All the reflections which I had made during the day, the strange discovery of the morning, that passionate and grotesque attachment for me, the recollections which that revelation had suddenly called up, recollections at once charming and perplexing, perhaps also that look which the servant had cast on me at the announcement of my departure—all these things, mixed up and combined, put me now in a reckless humor, gave me a tickling sensation of kisses on the lips, and in my veins a something which urged me on to commit some folly.

"Night was coming on, casting its dark shadows under the trees, when I descried Céleste, who had gone to fasten up the poultry-yard at the other end of the enclosure. I darted towards her, running so noiselessly that she heard nothing, and as she got up from closing the small trap-door by which the chickens got in and out, I clasped her in my arms and rained on her coarse, fat face a shower of kisses. She struggled, laughing all the same, as she was accustomed to do in such circumstances. Why did I suddenly loose my grip of her? Why did I at once experience a shock? What was it that I heard behind me?

"It was Miss Harriet, who had come upon us, who had seen us and who stood in front of us motionless as a specter. Then she disappeared in the darkness.

"I was ashamed, embarrassed, more sorry at having been thus surprised by her than if she had caught me committing some criminal act.

"I slept badly that night. I was completely unnerved and haunted by sad thoughts. I seemed to hear loud weeping, but in this I was no doubt deceived. Moreover, I thought several times that I heard someone walking up and down in the house and opening the hall-door.

"Toward morning I was overcome by fatigue and fell asleep. I got up late and did not go downstairs until the late breakfast, being still in a bewildered state, not knowing what kind of expression to put on.

"No one had seen Miss Harriet. We waited for her at table, but she did not appear. At length, Mother Lecacheur went to her room. The Englishwoman had gone out. She must have set out at break of day, as she often did to see the sun rise.

"Nobody seemed surprised at this and we began to eat in silence.

"The weather was hot, very hot, one of those still, sultry days when not a leaf stirs. The table had been placed out of doors, under an apple-tree, and we drank so much that Sapeur had to go constantly to the cellar to replenish the cider-jug. Céleste brought the dishes from the kitchen, a ragout of mutton with potatoes, a cold rabbit, and a salad. Afterwards she placed before us a dish of cherries, the first of the season.

"As I wanted to wash and freshen these, I begged the servant to go and bring a pitcher of cold water.

"In about five minutes she returned, declaring that the well was dry. She had lowered the pitcher to the full extent of the cord, and had touched the bottom, but on drawing the pitcher up again, it was empty. Mother Lecacheur, anxious to examine the thing for herself, went and looked down the hole. She returned announcing that there must be something in the well, something altogether unusual. Doubtless a neighbor had thrown some bundles of straw down, out of spite.

"I wanted to look down the well, too, thinking I could better make out what it was. I leaned over the brink. I perceived, indistinctly, a white object. What could it be? I then conceived the idea of lowering a lantern at the end of a cord. The yellow flame danced on the stone walls, and gradually sank deeper. All four of us were leaning over the opening, Sapeur and Céleste having now joined us. The lantern rested on a black and white, indistinct mass, singular, incomprehensible. Sapeur exclaimed:

" 'It is a horse. I see the hoofs. It must have escaped from the meadow during the night, and fallen in.'

"But suddenly a cold shiver attacked my spine, I first recognized a foot, then a leg which protruded; the whole body and the other leg were submerged.

"I groaned and trembled so violently that the light of the lamp danced hither and thither over the object.

" 'It is a woman, who—who—is down there! It is Miss Harriet.'

"Sapeur alone did not flinch. He had witnessed worse things in Africa.

"Mother Lecacheur and Céleste began to scream piercingly, and ran away.

"But the corpse had to be recovered. I attached the boy securely by the loins, then I lowered him slowly, by means of the pulley, and watched him disappear in the darkness. In his hands he had a lantern, and another rope. Soon his voice, seeming to come from the center of the earth, cried:

" 'Stop.'

"I then saw him fish something out of the water. It was the other leg. He bound the two feet together and shouted anew:

" 'Haul up.'

"I commenced to wind him up, but I felt as if my arms were broken, my muscles relaxed, and I was in terror lest I should let the boy fall to the bottom. When his head appeared over the brink, I asked:

" 'Well,' as if I expected he had a message from the woman lying at the bottom.

"We both got on to the stone slab at the edge of the well, and, face to face, leaning over the aperture, hoisted the body.

"Mother Lecacheur and Céleste watched us from a distance, hidden behind the wall of the house. When they saw the black slippers and white stockings of the corpse emerge from the hole, they disappeared.

"Sapeur seized the ankles, and we pulled up that poor, chaste woman in the most immodest posture. The head was in a shocking state, bruised and black; and the long, grey hair, hanging down, out of curl for ever, was muddy and dripping with water.

" 'Good Lord, how thin she is!' exclaimed Sapeur, in a contemptuous tone.

"We carried her into the room, and as the women did not put in an appearance, I, with the assistance of the lad, dressed the corpse for burial.

"I washed her sad, disfigured face. By the touch of my hand an eye was slightly opened; it fixed me with that pale stare, with that cold, that terrible look which corpses have, a look which seems to come from the beyond. I plaited up, as well as I could, her dishevelled hair, and I arranged on her forehead a novel and singular coiffure. Then I took off her dripping wet garments, baring, not without a feeling of shame, as though I had been guilty of some profanation, her shoulders and her chest, and her long arms, slim as the twigs of branches.

"Then I went to fetch some flowers, poppies, corn-flowers, marguerites, and fresh, sweet-smelling grass, with which to strew her funeral couch.

"Being the only person near her, it was necessary for me to fulfil the usual formalities. In a letter found in her pocket written at the last moment, she asked that her body be buried in the village in which she had passed the last days of her life. A frightful thought then oppressed my heart. Was it not on my account that she wished to be laid at rest in this place?

"Toward evening, all the female gossips of the locality came to view the remains of the deceased; but I would not allow a single person to enter, I wanted to be alone; and I watched by the corpse the whole night.

"By the light of the candles, I looked at the body of this miserable woman, wholly unknown, who had died so lamentably and so far away from home. Had she left no friends, no relatives behind her? What had her infancy been? What had been her life? Whence had she come, all alone, a wanderer, like a dog driven from home? What secrets of suffering and of despair were sealed up in that uncouth body, like a shameful defect, concealed all her life beneath that ridiculous exterior, which had driven away from her all affection and all love?

"What unhappy beings there are! I felt that upon that human creature weighed the eternal injustice of implacable nature! Life was over with her, without her ever having experienced, perhaps, that which sustains the most miserable of us all—the hope of being once loved! Otherwise, why should she thus have concealed herself, have fled from others? Why did she love everything so tenderly and so passionately, everything living that was not a man?

"I understood, also, why she believed in a God, and hoped for compensation from him for the miseries she had endured. She had now begun to decompose, and to become, in turn, a plant. She would blossom in the sun, and be eaten up by the cattle, carried away in seed by the birds, and as flesh by the beasts, again to become human flesh. But that which is called the soul had been extinguished at the bottom of the dark well. She suffered no longer. She had changed her life for that of others yet to be born.

"Hours passed away in this silent and sinister communion with the dead. A pale light announced the dawn of a new day, and a bright ray glistened on the bed, casting a line of fire on the bed-clothes and on her hands. This was the hour she had so much loved, when the waking birds began to sing in the trees.

"I opened the window wide, I drew back the curtains, so that the whole heavens might look in upon us. Then bending toward the glassy corpse, I took in my hands the mutilated head, and slowly, without terror or disgust, imprinted a long, long kiss upon those lips, which had never before received the salute of love."

Léon Chenal was silent. The women wept. We heard the Comte d'Étraille on the box-seat blow his nose several times in succession. Only the coachman nodded. The horses, no longer feeling the sting of the whip, had slackened their pace and were dragging us slowly along. And the brake hardly moved at all, having become suddenly heavy, as if laden with sorrow.

KATE CHOPIN (1851–1904)

Regret

Mamzelle Aurélie possessed a good strong figure, ruddy cheeks, hair that was changing from brown to gray, and a determined eye. She wore a man's hat about the farm, and an old blue army overcoat when it was cold, and sometimes topboots.

Mamzelle Aurélie had never thought of marrying. She had never been in love. At the age of twenty she had received a proposal, which she had promptly declined, and at the age of fifty she had not yet lived to regret it.

So she was quite alone in the world, except for her dog Ponto, and the negroes who lived in her cabins and worked her crops, and the fowls, a few cows, a couple of mules, her gun (with which she shot chicken-hawks), and her religion.

One morning Mamzelle Aurélie stood upon her gallery, contemplating, with arms akimbo, a small band of very small children who, to all intents and purposes, might have fallen from the clouds, so unexpected and bewildering was their coming, and so unwelcome. They were the children of her nearest neighbor, Odile, who was not such a near neighbor, after all.

The young woman had appeared but five minutes before, accompanied by these four children. In her arms she carried little Elodie; she dragged Ti Nomme by an unwilling hand; and Marcéline and Marcélette followed with irresolute steps.

Her face was red and disfigured from tears and excitement. She had been summoned to a neighboring parish by the dangerous illness of her mother; her husband was away in Texas—it seemed to her a million miles away; and Valsin was waiting with the mule-cart to drive her to the station.

"It's no question, Mamzelle Aurélie; you jus' got to keep those youngsters fo' me tell I come back. Dieu sait,[1] I would n' botha you with 'em if it was any otha way to do! Make 'em mine you, Mamzelle Aurélie; don' spare 'em. Me, there, I'm half crazy between the chil'ren, an' Léon not home, an' maybe not even to fine po' maman alive encore!"—a harrowing possibility which drove Odile to take a final hasty and convulsive leave of her disconsolate family.

She left them crowded into the narrow strip of shade on the porch of the long, low house; the white sunlight was beating in on the white old boards; some chickens were scratching in the grass at the foot of the steps, and one had boldly mounted, and was stepping heavily, solemnly, and aimlessly across the gallery. There was a pleasant odor of pinks in the air, and the sound of negroes' laughter was coming across the flowering cotton-field.

Mamzelle Aurélie stood contemplating the children. She looked with a critical eye upon Marcéline, who had been left staggering beneath the weight of the chubby Elodie. She surveyed with the same calculating air Marcélette mingling her silent tears with the audible grief and rebellion of Ti Nomme. During those few contemplative moments she was collecting herself, determining upon a line of action which should be identical with a line of duty. She began by feeding them.

---

[1] "God knows."

If Mamzelle Aurélie's responsibilities might have begun and ended there, they could easily have been dismissed; for her larder was amply provided against an emergency of this nature. But little children are not little pigs; they require and demand attentions which were wholly unexpected by Mamzelle Aurélie, and which she was ill prepared to give.

She was, indeed, very inapt in her management of Odile's children during the first few days. How could she know that Marcélette always wept when spoken to in a loud and commanding tone of voice? It was a peculiarity of Marcélette's. She became acquainted with Ti Nomme's passion for flowers only when he had plucked all the choicest gardenias and pinks for the apparent purpose of critically studying their botanical construction.

" 'Tain't enough to tell 'im, Mamzelle Aurélie," Marcéline instructed her; "you got to tie 'im in a chair. It's w'at maman all time do w'en he's bad: she tie 'im in a chair." The chair in which Mamzelle Aurélie tied Ti Nomme was roomy and comfortable, and he seized the opportunity to take a nap in it, the afternoon being warm.

At night, when she ordered them one and all to bed as she would have shooed the chickens into the hen-house, they stayed uncomprehending before her. What about the little white nightgowns that had to be taken from the pillow-slip in which they were brought over, and shaken by some strong hand till they snapped like ox-whips? What about the tub of water which had to be brought and set in the middle of the floor, in which the little tired, dusty, sunbrowned feet had every one to be washed sweet and clean? And it made Marcéline and Marcélette laugh merrily—the idea that Mamzelle Aurélie should for a moment have believed that Ti Nomme could fall asleep without being told the story of *Croque-mitaine*[2] or *Loupgarou*,[3] or both; or that Elodie could fall asleep at all without being rocked and sung to.

"I tell you, Aunt Ruby," Mamzelle Aurélie informed her cook in confidence, "me, I'd rather manage a dozen plantation' than fo' chil'ren. It's terrassent! Bonté! Don't talk to me about chil'ren!"

" 'Tain' ispected sich as you would know airy thing 'bout 'em, Mamzelle Aurélie. I see dat plainly yistiddy w'en I spy dat li'le chile playin' wid yo' baskit o' keys. You don' know dat makes chillun grow up hard-headed, to play wid keys? Des like it make 'em teeth hard to look in a looking-glass. Them's the things you got to know in the raisin' an' manigement o' chillun."

Mamzelle Aurélie certainly did not pretend or aspire to such subtle and far-reaching knowledge on the subject as Aunt Ruby possessed, who had "raised five an' bared (buried) six" in her day. She was glad enough to learn a few little mother-tricks to serve the moment's need.

Ti Nomme's sticky fingers compelled her to unearth white aprons that she had not worn for years, and she had to accustom herself to his moist kisses—the expressions of an affectionate and exuberant nature. She got down her sewing-basket, which she seldom used, from the top shelf of the armoire, and placed it within the ready and easy reach which torn slips and buttonless waists demanded. It took her

---

[2] the bogey-man.
[3] the werewolf.

some days to become accustomed to the laughing, the crying, the chattering that echoed through the house and around it all day long. And it was not the first or the second night that she could sleep comfortably with little Elodie's hot, plump body pressed close against her, and the little one's warm breath beating her cheek like the fanning of a bird's wing.

But at the end of two weeks Mamzelle Aurélie had grown quite used to these things, and she no longer complained.

It was also at the end of two weeks that Mamzelle Aurélie, one evening, looking away toward the crib where the cattle were being fed, saw Valsin's blue cart turning the bend of the road. Odile sat beside the mulatto, upright and alert. As they drew near, the young woman's beaming face indicated that her homecoming was a happy one.

But this coming, unannounced and unexpected, threw Mamzelle Aurélie into a flutter that was almost agitation. The children had to be gathered. Where was Ti Nomme? Yonder in the shed, putting an edge on his knife at the grindstone. And Marcéline and Marcélette? Cutting and fashioning doll-rags in the corner of the gallery. As for Elodie, she was safe enough in Mamzelle Aurélie's arms; and she had screamed with delight at the sight of the familiar blue cart which was bringing her mother back to her.

The excitement was all over, and they were gone. How still it was when they were gone! Mamzelle Aurélie stood upon the gallery, looking and listening. She could no longer see the cart; the red sunset and the blue-gray twilight had together flung a purple mist across the fields and road that hid it from her view. She could no longer hear the wheezing and creaking of its wheels. But she could still faintly hear the shrill, glad voices of the children.

She turned into the house. There was much work awaiting her, for the children had left a sad disorder behind them; but she did not at once set about the task of righting it. Mamzelle Aurélie seated herself beside the table. She gave one slow glance through the room, into which the evening shadows were creeping and deepening around her solitary figure. She let her head fall upon her bended arm, and began to cry. Oh, but she cried! Not softly, as women often do. She cried like a man, with sobs that seemed to tear her very soul. She did not notice Ponto licking her hand.

STEPHEN CRANE (1871–1900)

The Bride Comes to Yellow Sky

1

The great Pullman was whirling onward with such dignity of motion that a glance from the window seemed simply to prove that the plains of Texas were pouring eastward. Vast flats of green grass, dull-hued spaces of mesquit and cactus, little groups of frame houses, woods of light and tender trees, all were sweeping into the east, sweeping over the horizon, a precipice.

A newly married pair had boarded this coach at San Antonio. The man's face was reddened from many days in the wind and sun, and a direct result of his new black clothes was that his brick-colored hands were constantly performing in a most conscious fashion. From time to time he looked down respectfully at his attire. He sat with a hand on each knee, like a man waiting in a barber's shop. The glances he devoted to other passengers were furtive and shy.

The bride was not pretty, nor was she very young. She wore a dress of blue cashmere, with small reservations of velvet here and there, and with steel buttons abounding. She continually twisted her head to regard her puff sleeves, very stiff, straight, and high. They embarrassed her. It was quite apparent that she had cooked, and that she expected to cook, dutifully. The blushes caused by the careless scrutiny of some passengers as she had entered the car were strange to see upon this plain, under-class countenance, which was drawn in placid, almost emotionless lines.

They were evidently very happy. "Ever been in a parlor-car before?" he asked, smiling with delight.

"No," she answered; "I never was. It's fine, ain't it?"

"Great! And then after a while we'll go forward to the diner, and get a big lay-out. Finest meal in the world. Charge a dollar."

"Oh, do they?" cried the bride. "Charge a dollar? Why, that's too much—for us —ain't it, Jack?"

"Not this trip, anyhow," he answered bravely. "We're going to go the whole thing."

Later he explained to her about the trains. "You see, it's a thousand miles from one end of Texas to the other; and this train runs right across it, and never stops but four times." He had the pride of an owner. He pointed out to her the dazzling fittings of the coach; and in truth her eyes opened wider as she contemplated the sea-green figured velvet, the shining brass, silver, and glass, the wood that gleamed as darkly brilliant as the surface of a pool of oil. At one end a bronze figure sturdily held a support for a separated chamber, and at convenient places on the ceiling were frescos in olive and silver.

To the minds of the pair, their surroundings reflected the glory of their marriage that morning in San Antonio; this was the environment of their new estate; and the man's face in particular beamed with an elation that made him appear ridiculous to the negro porter. This individual at times surveyed them from afar with an amused and superior grin. On other occasions he bullied them with skill in ways that did not make it exactly plain to them that they were being bullied. He subtly used all the manners of the most unconquerable kind of snobbery. He oppressed them; but of this oppression they had small knowledge, and they speedily forgot that infrequently a number of travellers covered them with stares of derisive enjoyment. Historically there was supposed to be something infinitely humorous in their situation.

"We are due in Yellow Sky at 3:42," he said, looking tenderly into her eyes.

"Oh, are we?" she said, as if she had not been aware of it. To evince surprise at her husband's statement was part of her wifely amiability. She took from a pocket a little silver watch; and as she held it before her, and stared at it with a frown of attention, the new husband's face shone.

"I bought it in San Anton' from a friend of mine," he told her gleefully.

"It's seventeen minutes past twelve," she said, looking up at him with a kind of shy and clumsy coquetry. A passenger, noting this play, grew excessively sardonic, and winked at himself in one of the numerous mirrors.

At last they went to the dining-car. Two rows of negro waiters, in glowing white suits, surveyed their entrance with the interest, and also the equanimity, of men who had been forewarned. The pair fell to the lot of a waiter who happened to feel pleasure in steering them through their meal. He viewed them with the manner of a fatherly pilot, his countenance radiant with benevolence. The patronage, entwined with the ordinary deference, was not plain to them. And yet, as they returned to their coach, they showed in their faces a sense of escape.

To the left, miles down a long purple slope, was a little ribbon of mist where moved the keening Rio Grande. The train was approaching it at an angle, and the apex was Yellow Sky. Presently it was apparent that, as the distance from Yellow Sky grew shorter, the husband became commensurately restless. His brick-red hands were more insistent in their prominence. Occasionally he was even rather absent-minded and far-away when the bride leaned forward and addressed him.

As a matter of truth, Jack Potter was beginning to find the shadow of a deed weigh upon him like a leaden slab. He, the town marshal of Yellow Sky, a man known, liked, and feared in his corner, a prominent person, had gone to San Antonio to meet a girl he believed he loved, and there, after the usual prayers, had actually induced her to marry him, without consulting Yellow Sky for any part of the transaction. He was now bringing his bride before an innocent and unsuspecting community.

Of course people in Yellow Sky married as it pleased them in accordance with a general custom; but such was Potter's thought of his duty to his friends, or of their idea of his duty, or of an unspoken form which does not control men in these matters, that he felt he was heinous. He had committed an extraordinary crime. Face to face with this girl in San Antonio, and spurred by his sharp impulse, he had gone headlong over all the social hedges. At San Antonio he was like a man hidden in the dark. A knife to sever any friendly duty, any form, was easy to his hand in that remote city. But the hour of Yellow Sky—the hour of daylight—was approaching.

He knew full well that his marriage was an important thing to his town. It could only be exceeded by the burning of the new hotel. His friends could not forgive him. Frequently he had reflected on the advisability of telling them by telegraph, but a new cowardice had been upon him. He feared to do it. And now the train was hurrying him toward a scene of amazement, glee, and reproach. He glanced out of the window at the line of haze swinging slowly in toward the train.

Yellow Sky had a kind of brass band, which played painfully, to the delight of the populace. He laughed without heart as he thought of it. If the citizens could dream of his prospective arrival with his bride, they would parade the band at the station and escort them, amid cheers and laughing congratulations, to his adobe home.

He resolved that he would use all the devices of speed and plainscraft in making the journey from the station to his house. Once within that safe citadel, he could issue some sort of vocal bulletin, and then not go among the citizens until they had time to wear off a little of their enthusiasm.

The bride looked anxiously at him. "What's worrying you, Jack?"

He laughed again. "I'm not worrying, girl; I'm only thinking of Yellow Sky."

She flushed in comprehension.

A sense of mutual guilt invaded their minds and developed a finer tenderness. They looked at each other with eyes softly aglow. But Potter often laughed the same nervous laugh; the flush upon the bride's face seemed quite permanent.

The traitor to the feelings of Yellow Sky narrowly watched the speeding landscape. "We're nearly there," he said.

Presently the porter came and announced the proximity of Potter's home. He held a brush in his hand, and, with all his airy superiority gone, he brushed Potter's new clothes as the latter slowly turned this way and that way. Potter fumbled out a coin and gave it to the porter, as he had seen others do. It was a heavy and muscle-bound business, as that of a man shoeing his first horse.

The porter took their bag, and as the train began to slow they moved forward to the hooded platform of the car. Presently the two engines and their long string of coaches rushed into the station of Yellow Sky.

"They have to take water here," said Potter, from a constricted throat and in mournful cadence, as one announcing death. Before the train stopped his eye had swept the length of the platform, and he was glad and astonished to see there was none upon it but the station-agent, who, with a slightly hurried and anxious air, was walking toward the water-tanks. When the train had halted, the porter alighted first, and placed in position a little temporary step.

"Come on, girl," said Potter, hoarsely. As he helped her down they each laughed on a false note. He took the bag from the negro, and bade his wife cling to his arm. As they slunk rapidly away, his hang-dog glance perceived that they were unloading the two trunks, and also that the station-agent, far ahead near the baggage-car, had turned and was running toward him, making gestures. He laughed, and groaned as he laughed, when he noted the first effect of his marital bliss upon Yellow Sky. He gripped his wife's arm firmly to his side, and they fled. Behind them the porter stood, chuckling fatuously.

2

The California express on the Southern Railway was due at Yellow Sky in twenty-one minutes. There were six men at the bar of the Weary Gentleman saloon. One was a drummer who talked a great deal and rapidly; three were Texans who did not care to talk at that time; and two were Mexican sheep-herders, who did not talk as a general practice in the Weary Gentleman saloon. The barkeeper's dog lay on the board walk that crossed in front of the door. His head was on his paws, and he glanced drowsily here and there with the constant vigilance of a dog that is kicked on occasion. Across the sandy street were some vivid green grass-plots, so wonderful in appearance, amid the sands that burned near them in a blazing sun, that they caused a doubt in the mind. They exactly resembled the grass mats used to represent lawns on the stage. At the cooler end of the railway station, a man without a coat sat in a tilted chair and smoked his pipe. The fresh-cut bank of the Rio Grande circled near the town, and there could be seen beyond it a great plum-colored plain of mesquit.

Save for the busy drummer and his companions in the saloon, Yellow Sky was dozing. The new-comer leaned gracefully upon the bar, and recited many tales with the confidence of a bard who has come upon a new field.

"—and at the moment that the old man fell downstairs with the bureau in his arms, the old woman was coming up with two scuttles of coal, and of course—"

The drummer's tale was interrupted by a young man who suddenly appeared in the open door. He cried: "Scratchy Wilson's drunk, and has turned loose with both hands." The two Mexicans at once set down their glasses and faded out of the rear entrance of the saloon.

The drummer, innocent and jocular, answered: "All right, old man. S'pose he has? Come in and have a drink, anyhow."

But the information had made such an obvious cleft in every skull in the room that the drummer was obliged to see its importance. All had become instantly solemn. "Say," said he, mystified, "what is this?" His three companions made the introductory gesture of eloquent speech; but the young man at the door forestalled them.

"It means, my friend," he answered, as he came into the saloon, "that for the next two hours this town won't be a health resort."

The barkeeper went to the door, and locked and barred it; reaching out of the window, he pulled in heavy wooden shutters, and barred them. Immediately a solemn, chapel-like gloom was upon the place. The drummer was looking from one to another.

"But, say," he cried, "what is this, anyhow? You don't mean there is going to be a gun-fight?"

"Don't know whether there'll be a fight or not," answered one man, grimly; "but there'll be some shootin'—some good shootin'."

The young man who had warned them waved his hand. "Oh, there'll be a fight fast enough, if any one wants it. Anybody can get a fight out there in the street. There's a fight just waiting."

The drummer seemed to be swayed between the interest of a foreigner and a perception of personal danger.

"What did you say his name was?" he asked.

"Scratchy Wilson," they answered in chorus.

"And will he kill anybody? What are you going to do? Does this happen often? Does he rampage around like this once a week or so? Can he break in that door?"

"No; he can't break down that door," replied the barkeeper. "He's tried it three times. But when he comes you'd better lay down on the floor, stranger. He's dead sure to shoot at it, and a bullet may come through."

Thereafter the drummer kept a strict eye upon the door. The time had not yet called for him to hug the floor, but, as a minor precaution, he sidled near the wall. "Will he kill anybody?" he said again.

The men laughed low and scornfully at the question.

"He's out to shoot, and he's out for trouble. Don't see any good in experimentin' with him."

"But what do you do in a case like this? What do you do?"

A man responded: "Why, he and Jack Potter—"

"But," in chorus the other men interrupted, "Jack Potter's in San Anton'."

"Well, who is he? What's he got to do with it?"

"Oh, he's the town marshal. He goes out and fights Scratchy when he gets on one of these tears."

"Wow!" said the drummer, mopping his brow. "Nice job he's got."

The voices had toned away to mere whisperings. The drummer wished to ask further questions, which were born of an increasing anxiety and bewilderment; but when he attempted them, the men merely looked at him in irritation and motioned him to remain silent. A tense waiting hush was upon them. In the deep shadows of the room their eyes shone as they listened for sounds from the street. One man made three gestures at the barkeeper; and the latter, moving like a ghost, handed him a glass and a bottle. The man poured a full glass of whisky, and set down the bottle noiselessly. He gulped the whisky in a swallow, and turned again toward the door in immovable silence. The drummer saw that the barkeeper, without a sound, had taken a Winchester from beneath the bar. Later he saw this individual beckoning him, so he tiptoed across the room.

"You better come with me back of the bar."

"No, thanks," said the drummer, perspiring; "I'd rather be where I can make a break for the back door."

Whereupon the man of bottles made a kindly but peremptory gesture. The drummer obeyed it, and, finding himself seated on a box with his head below the level of the bar, balm was laid upon his soul at sight of various zinc and copper fittings that bore a resemblance to armor-plate. The barkeeper took a seat comfortably upon an adjacent box.

"You see," he whispered, "this here Scratchy Wilson is a wonder with a gun—a perfect wonder; and when he goes on the war-trail, we hunt our holes—naturally. He's about the last one of the old gang that used to hang out along the river here. He's a terror when he's drunk. When he's sober he's all right—kind of simple—wouldn't hurt a fly—nicest fellow in town. But when he's drunk—whoo!"

There were periods of stillness. "I wish Jack Potter was back from San Anton'," said the barkeeper. "He shot Wilson up once—in the leg—and he would sail in and pull out the kinks in this thing."

Presently they heard from a distance the sound of a shot, followed by three wild yowls. It instantly removed a bond from the men in the darkened saloon. There was a shuffling of feet. They looked at each other. "Here he comes," they said.

3

A man in a maroon-colored flannel shirt, which had been purchased for purposes of decoration, and made principally by some Jewish women on the East Side of New York, rounded a corner and walked into the middle of the main street of Yellow Sky. In either hand the man held a long, heavy, blue-black revolver. Often he yelled, and these cries rang through a semblance of a deserted village, shrilly flying over the roofs in a volume that seemed to have no relation to the ordinary vocal strength of a man. It was as if the surrounding stillness formed the arch of a tomb over him. These cries of ferocious challenge rang against walls of silence. And his boots had red tops with gilded imprints, of the kind beloved in winter by little sledding boys on the hillsides of New England.

The man's face flamed in a rage begot of whisky. His eyes, rolling, and yet keen for ambush, hunted the still doorways and windows. He walked with the creeping movement of the midnight cat. As it occurred to him, he roared menacing information. The long revolvers in his hands were as easy as straws; they were removed with an electric swiftness. The little fingers of each hand played sometimes in a musician's way. Plain from the low collar of the shirt, the cords of his neck straightened and sank, straightened and sank, as passion moved him. The only sounds were his terrible invitations. The calm adobes preserved their demeanor at the passing of this small thing in the middle of the street.

There was no offer of fight—no offer of fight. The man called to the sky. There were no attractions. He bellowed and fumed and swayed his revolvers here and everywhere.

The dog of the barkeeper of the Weary Gentleman saloon had not appreciated the advance of events. He yet lay dozing in front of his master's door. At sight of the dog, the man paused and raised his revolver humorously. At sight of the man, the dog sprang up and walked diagonally away, with a sullen head, and growling. The man yelled, and the dog broke into a gallop. As it was about to enter the alley, there was a loud noise, a whistling, and something spat the ground directly before it. The dog screamed, and, wheeling in terror, galloped headlong in a new direction. Again there was a noise, a whistling, and sand was kicked viciously before it. Fear-stricken, the dog turned and flurried like an animal in a pen. The man stood laughing, his weapons at his hips.

Ultimately the man was attracted by the closed door of the Weary Gentleman saloon. He went to it and, hammering with a revolver, demanded drink.

The door remaining imperturbable, he picked a bit of paper from the walk, and nailed it to the framework with a knife. He then turned his back contemptuously upon this popular resort and, walking to the opposite side of the street and spinning there on his heel quickly and lithely, fired at the bit of paper. He missed it by a half inch. He swore at himself, and went away. Later he comfortably fusilladed the windows of his most intimate friend. The man was playing with this town; it was a toy for him.

But still there was no offer of fight. The name of Jack Potter, his ancient antagonist, entered his mind, and he concluded that it would be a glad thing if he should go to Potter's house, and by bombardment induce him to come out and fight. He moved in the direction of his desire, chanting Apache scalp-music.

When he arrived at it, Potter's house presented the same still front as had the other adobes. Taking up a strategic position, the man howled a challenge. But this house regarded him as might a great stone god. It gave no sign. After a decent wait, the man howled further challenges, mingling with them wonderful epithets.

Presently there came the spectacle of a man churning himself into deepest rage over the immobility of a house. He fumed at it as the winter wind attacks a prairie cabin in the North. To the distance there should have gone the sound of a tumult like the fighting of two hundred Mexicans. As necessity bade him, he paused for breath or to reload his revolvers.

4

Potter and his bride walked sheepishly and with speed. Sometimes they laughed together shamefacedly and low.

"Next corner, dear," he said finally.

They put forth the efforts of a pair walking bowed against a strong wind. Potter was about to raise a finger to point the first appearance of the new home when, as they circled the corner, they came face to face with a man in a maroon-colored shirt, who was feverishly pushing cartridges into a large revolver. Upon the instant the man dropped his revolver to the ground and, like lightning, whipped another from its holster. The second weapon was aimed at the bridegroom's chest.

There was a silence. Potter's mouth seemed to be merely a grave for his tongue. He exhibited an instinct to at once loosen his arm from the woman's grip, and he dropped the bag to the sand. As for the bride, her face had gone as yellow as old cloth. She was a slave to hideous rites, gazing at the apparitional snake.

The two men faced each other at a distance of three paces. He of the revolver smiled with a new and quiet ferocity.

"Tried to sneak up on me," he said. "Tried to sneak up on me!" His eyes grew more baleful. As Potter made a slight movement, the man thrust his revolver venomously forward. "No; don't you do it, Jack Potter. Don't you move a finger toward a gun just yet. Don't you move an eyelash. The time has come for me to settle with you and I'm goin' to do it my own way, and loaf along with no interferin'. So if you don't want a gun bent on you, just mind what I tell you."

Potter looked at his enemy. "I ain't got a gun on me Scratchy," he said. "Honest, I ain't." He was stiffening and steadying, but yet somewhere at the back of his mind a vision of the Pullman floated: the sea-green figured velvet, the shining brass, silver, and glass, the wood that gleamed as darkly brilliant as the surface of a pool of oil— all the glory of marriage, the environment of the new estate. "You know I fight when it comes to fighting, Scratchy Wilson; but I ain't got a gun on me. You'll have to do all the shootin' yourself."

His enemy's face went livid. He stepped forward, and lashed his weapon to and fro before Potter's chest. "Don't you tell me you ain't got no gun on you, you whelp. Don't tell me no lie like that. There ain't a man in Texas ever seen you without no gun. Don't take me for no kid." His eyes blazed with light, and his throat worked like a pump.

"I ain't takin' you for no kid," answered Potter. His heels had not moved an inch backward. "I'm takin' you for a damn fool. I tell you I ain't got a gun, and I ain't. If you're goin' to shoot me up, you better begin now; you'll never get a chance like this again."

So much enforced reasoning had told on Wilson's rage; he was calmer. "If you ain't got a gun, why ain't you got a gun?" he sneered. "Been to Sunday-school?"

"I ain't got a gun because I've just come from San Anton' with my wife. I'm married," said Potter. "And if I'd thought there was going to be any galoots like you prowling around when I brought my wife home, I'd had a gun, and don't you forget it."

"Married!" said Scratchy, not at all comprehending.

"Yes, married. I'm married," said Potter, distinctly.

"Married?" said Scratchy. Seemingly for the first time, he saw the drooping, drowning woman at the other man's side. "No!" he said. He was like a creature allowed a glimpse of another world. He moved a pace backward, and his arm, with the revolver, dropped to his side. "Is this the lady?" he asked.

"Yes; this is the lady," answered Potter.

There was another period of silence.

"Well," said Wilson at last, slowly, "I s'pose it's all off now."

"It's all off if you say so, Scratchy. You know I didn't make the trouble." Potter lifted his valise.

"Well, I 'low it's off, Jack," said Wilson. He was looking at the ground. "Married!" He was not a student of chivalry; it was merely that in the presence of this foreign condition he was a simple child of the earlier plains. He picked up his starboard revolver, and, placing both weapons in their holsters, he went away. His feet made funnel-shaped tracks in the heavy sand.

JAMES JOYCE (1882–1941)

The Dead

Lily, the caretaker's daughter, was literally run off her feet. Hardly had she brought one gentleman into the little pantry behind the office on the ground floor and helped him off with his overcoat than the wheezy hall-door bell clanged again and she had to scamper along the bare hallway to let in another guest. It was well for her she had not to attend to the ladies also. But Miss Kate and Miss Julia had thought of that and had converted the bathroom upstairs into a ladies' dressing-room. Miss Kate and Miss Julia were there, gossiping and laughing and fussing, walking after each other to the head of the stairs, peering down over the banisters and calling down to Lily to ask her who had come.

It was always a great affair, the Misses Morkan's annual dance. Everybody who knew them came to it, members of the family, old friends of the family, the members of Julia's choir, any of Kate's pupils that were grown up enough and even some of Mary Jane's pupils too. Never once had it fallen flat. For years and years it had gone off in splendid style as long as anyone could remember; ever since Kate and Julia, after the death of their brother Pat, had left the house in Stoney Batter and taken Mary Jane, their only niece, to live with them in the dark gaunt house on Usher's Island, the upper part of which they had rented from Mr Fulham, the corn-factor on the ground floor. That was a good thirty years ago if it was a day. Mary Jane, who was then a little girl in short clothes, was now the main prop of the household for she had the organ in Haddington Road. She had been through the Academy and gave a pupils' concert every year in the upper room of the Antient Concert Rooms. Many of her pupils belonged to better-class families on the Kingstown and Dalkey line. Old as they were, her aunts also did their share. Julia, though she was quite grey, was still the leading soprano in Adam and Eve's, and Kate, being too feeble to go about much, gave music lessons to beginners on the old square piano in the back room. Lily, the caretaker's daughter, did house-maid's work for them. Though their life was modest they believed in eating well; the best of everything: diamond-bone sir-loins, three-shilling tea and the best bottled stout. But Lily seldom made a mistake in the orders so that she got on well with her three mistresses. They were fussy, that was all. But the only thing they would not stand was back answers.

Of course they had good reason to be fussy on such a night. And then it was long after ten o'clock and yet there was no sign of Gabriel and his wife. Besides they were dreadfully afraid that Freddy Malins might turn up screwed. They would not wish for worlds that any of Mary Jane's pupils should see him under the influence; and when he was like that it was sometimes very hard to manage him. Freddy Malins always came late but they wondered what could be keeping Gabriel: and that was what brought them every two minutes to the banisters to ask Lily had Gabriel or Freddy come.

—O, Mr Conroy, said Lily to Gabriel when she opened the door for him, Miss Kate and Miss Julia thought you were never coming. Good-night, Mrs Conroy.

—I'll engage they did, said Gabriel, but they forget that my wife here takes three mortal hours to dress herself.

He stood on the mat, scraping the snow from his goloshes, while Lily led his wife to the foot of the stairs and called out:

—Miss Kate, here's Mrs Conroy.

Kate and Julia came toddling down the dark stairs at once. Both of them kissed Gabriel's wife, said she must be perished alive and asked was Gabriel with her.

—Here I am as right as the mail, Aunt Kate! Go on up. I'll follow, called out Gabriel from the dark.

He continued scraping his feet vigorously while the three women went upstairs, laughing, to the ladies' dressing-room. A light fringe of snow lay like a cape on the shoulders of his overcoat and like toecaps on the toes of his goloshes; and, as the buttons of his overcoat slipped with a squeaking noise through the snow-stiffened frieze, a cold fragrant air from out-of-doors escaped from crevices and folds.

—Is it snowing again, Mr. Conroy? asked Lily.

She had preceded him into the pantry to help him off with his overcoat. Gabriel smiled at the three syllables she had given his surname and glanced at her. She was a slim, growing girl, pale in complexion and with hay-coloured hair. The gas in the pantry made her look still paler. Gabriel had known her when she was a child and used to sit on the lowest step nursing a rag doll.

—Yes, Lily, he answered, and I think we're in for a night of it.

He looked up at the pantry ceiling, which was shaking with the stamping and shuffling of feet on the floor above, listened for a moment to the piano and then glanced at the girl, who was folding his overcoat carefully at the end of a shelf.

—Tell me, Lily, he said in a friendly tone, do you still go to school?

—O no, sir, she answered. I'm done schooling this year and more.

—O, then, said Gabriel gaily, I suppose we'll be going to your wedding one of these fine days with your young man, eh?

The girl glanced back at him over her shoulder and said with great bitterness:

—The men that is now is only all palaver and what they can get out of you.

Gabriel coloured as if he felt he had made a mistake and, without looking at her, kicked off his goloshes and flicked actively with his muffler at his patent-leather shoes.

He was a stout tallish young man. The high colour of his cheeks pushed upwards even to his forehead where it scattered itself in a few formless patches of pale red; and on his hairless face there scintillated restlessly the polished lenses and the bright gilt rims of the glasses which screened his delicate and restless eyes. His glossy black hair was parted in the middle and brushed in a long curve behind his ears where it curled slightly beneath the groove left by his hat.

When he had flicked lustre into his shoes he stood up and pulled his waistcoat down more tightly on his plump body. Then he took a coin rapidly from his pocket.

—O Lily, he said, thrusting it into her hands, it's Christmas-time, isn't it? Just . . . here's a little. . . .

He walked rapidly towards the door.

—O no, sir! cried the girl, following him. Really, sir, I wouldn't take it.

—Christmas-time! Christmas-time! said Gabriel, almost trotting to the stairs and waving his hand to her in deprecation.

The girl, seeing that he had gained the stairs, called out after him:

—Well, thank you, sir.

He waited outside the drawing-room door until the waltz should finish, listening to the skirts that swept against it and to the shuffling of feet. He was still discomposed by the girl's bitter and sudden retort. It had cast a gloom over him which he tried to dispel by arranging his cuffs and the bows of his tie. Then he took from his waistcoat pocket a little paper and glanced at the headings he had made for his speech. He was undecided about the lines from Robert Browning for he feared they would be above the heads of his hearers. Some quotation that they could recognise from Shakespeare or from the Melodies would be better. The indelicate clacking of the men's heels and the shuffling of their soles reminded him that their grade of culture differed from his. He would only make himself ridiculous by quoting poetry to them which they could not understand. They would think that he was airing his superior education. He would fail with them just as he had failed with the girl in the pantry. He had taken up a wrong tone. His whole speech was a mistake from first to last, an utter failure.

Just then his aunts and his wife came out of the ladies' dressing-room. His aunts were two small plainly dressed old women. Aunt Julia was an inch or so the taller. Her hair, drawn low over the tops of her ears, was grey; and grey also, with darker shadows, was her large flaccid face. Though she was stout in build and stood erect her slow eyes and parted lips gave her the appearance of a woman who did not know where she was or where she was going. Aunt Kate was more vivacious. Her face, healthier than her sister's, was all puckers and creases, like a shrivelled red apple, and her hair, braided in the same old-fashioned way, had not lost its ripe nut colour.

They both kissed Gabriel frankly. He was their favourite nephew, the son of their dead elder sister, Ellen, who had married T. J. Conroy of the Port and Docks.

—Gretta tells me you're not going to take a cab back to Monkstown to-night, Gabriel, said Aunt Kate.

—No, said Gabriel, turning to his wife, we had quite enough of that last year, hadn't we? Don't you remember, Aunt Kate, what a cold Gretta got out of it? Cab windows rattling all the way, and the east wind blowing in after we passed Merrion. Very jolly it was. Gretta caught a dreadful cold.

Aunt Kate frowned severely and nodded her head at every word.

—Quite right, Gabriel, quite right, she said. You can't be too careful.

—But as for Gretta there, said Gabriel, she'd walk home in the snow if she were let.

Mrs Conroy laughed.

—Don't mind him, Aunt Kate, she said. He's really an awful bother, what with green shades for Tom's eyes at night and making him do the dumb-bells, and forcing Eva to eat the stirabout. The poor child! And she simply hates the sight of it! . . . O, but you'll never guess what he makes me wear now!

She broke out into a peal of laughter and glanced at her husband, whose admiring and happy eyes had been wandering from her dress to her face and hair. The two aunts laughed heartily too, for Gabriel's solicitude was a standing joke with them.

—Goloshes! said Mrs Conroy. That's the latest. Whenever it's wet underfoot I must put on my goloshes. To-night even he wanted me to put them on, but I wouldn't. The next thing he'll buy me will be a diving suit.

Gabriel laughed nervously and patted his tie reassuringly while Aunt Kate nearly doubled herself, so heartily did she enjoy the joke. The smile soon faded from Aunt Julia's face and her mirthless eyes were directed towards her nephew's face. After a pause she asked:

—And what are goloshes, Gabriel?

—Goloshes, Julia! exclaimed her sister. Goodness me, don't you know what goloshes are? You wear them over your . . . over your boots, Gretta, isn't it?

—Yes, said Mrs Conroy. Guttapercha things. We both have a pair now. Gabriel says everyone wears them on the continent.

—O, on the continent, murmured Aunt Julia, nodding her head slowly.

Gabriel knitted his brows and said, as if he were slightly angered:

—It's nothing very wonderful but Gretta thinks it very funny because she says the word reminds her of Christy Minstrels.

—But tell me, Gabriel, said Aunt Kate, with brisk tact. Of course, you've seen about the room. Gretta was saying . . .

—O, the room is all right, replied Gabriel. I've taken one in the Gresham.

—To be sure, said Aunt Kate, by far the best thing to do. And the children, Gretta, you're not anxious about them?

—O, for one night, said Mrs Conroy. Besides, Bessie will look after them.

—To be sure, said Aunt Kate again. What a comfort it is to have a girl like that, one you can depend on! There's that Lily, I'm sure I don't know what has come over her lately. She's not the girl she was at all.

Gabriel was about to ask his aunt some questions on this point but she broke off suddenly to gaze after her sister who had wandered down the stairs and was craning her neck over the banisters.

—Now, I ask you, she said, almost testily, where is Julia going? Julia! Julia! Where are you going?

Julia, who had gone halfway down one flight, came back and announced blandly:

—Here's Freddy.

At the same moment a clapping of hands and a final flourish of the pianist told that the waltz had ended. The drawing-room door was opened from within and some couples came out. Aunt Kate drew Gabriel aside hurriedly and whispered into his ear:

—Slip down, Gabriel, like a good fellow and see if he's all right, and don't let him up if he's screwed. I'm sure he's screwed. I'm sure he is.

Gabriel went to the stairs and listened over the banisters. He could hear two persons talking in the pantry. Then he recognised Freddy Malins' laugh. He went down the stairs noisily.

—It's such a relief, said Aunt Kate to Mrs Conroy, that Gabriel is here. I always feel easier in my mind when he's here. . . . Julia, there's Miss Daly and Miss Power will take some refreshment. Thanks for your beautiful waltz, Miss Daly. It made lovely time.

A tall wizen-faced man, with a stiff grizzled moustache and swarthy skin, who was passing out with his partner said:

—And may we have some refreshment, too, Miss Morkan?

—Julia, said Aunt Kate summarily, and here's Mr Browne and Miss Furlong. Take them in, Julia, with Miss Daly and Miss Power.

—I'm the man for the ladies, said Mr Browne, pursing his lips until his moustache bristled and smiling in all his wrinkles. You know, Miss Morkan, the reason they are so fond of me is—

He did not finish his sentence, but, seeing that Aunt Kate was out of earshot, at once led the three young ladies into the back room. The middle of the room was occupied by two square tables placed end to end, and on these Aunt Julia and the caretaker were straightening and smoothing a large cloth. On the sideboard were arrayed dishes and plates, and glasses and bundles of knives and forks and spoons. The top of the closed square piano served also as a sideboard for viands and sweets. At a smaller sideboard in one corner two young men were standing, drinking hop-bitters.

Mr Browne led his charges thither and invited them all, in jest, to some ladies' punch, hot, strong and sweet. As they said they never took anything strong he opened three bottles of lemonade for them. Then he asked one of the young men to move aside, and, taking hold of the decanter, filled out for himself a goodly measure of whisky. The young men eyed him respectfully while he took a trial sip.

—God help me, he said, smiling, it's the doctor's orders.

His wizened face broke into a broader smile, and the three young ladies laughed in musical echo to his pleasantry, swaying their bodies to and fro, with nervous jerks of their shoulders. The boldest said:

—O, now, Mr Browne, I'm sure the doctor never ordered anything of the kind.

Mr Browne took another sip of his whisky and said, with sidling mimicry:

—Well, you see, I'm like the famous Mrs Cassidy, who is reported to have said: *Now, Mary Grimes, if I don't take it, make me take it, for I feel I want it.*

His hot face had leaned forward a little too confidentially and he had assumed a very low Dublin accent so that the young ladies, with one instinct, received his speech in silence. Miss Furlong, who was one of Mary Jane's pupils, asked Miss Daly what was the name of the pretty waltz she had played; and Mr Browne, seeing that he was ignored, turned promptly to the two young men who were more appreciative.

A red-faced young woman, dressed in pansy, came into the room, excitedly clapping her hands and crying:

—Quadrilles! Quadrilles!

Close on her heels came Aunt Kate, crying:

—Two gentlemen and three ladies, Mary Jane!

—O, here's Mr Bergin and Mr Kerrigan, said Mary Jane. Mr Kerrigan, will you take Miss Power? Miss Furlong, may I get you a partner, Mr Bergin. O, that'll just do now.

—Three ladies, Mary Jane, said Aunt Kate.

The two young gentlemen asked the ladies if they might have the pleasure, and Mary Jane turned to Miss Daly.

—O, Miss Daly, you're really awfully good, after playing for the last two dances, but really we're so short of ladies to-night.

—I don't mind in the least, Miss Morkan.

—But I've a nice partner for you, Mr Bartell D'Arcy, the tenor. I'll get him to sing later on. All Dublin is raving about him.

—Lovely voice, lovely voice! said Aunt Kate.

As the piano had twice begun the prelude to the first figure Mary Jane led her recruits quickly from the room. They had hardly gone when Aunt Julia wandered slowly into the room, looking behind her at something.

—What is the matter, Julia? asked Aunt Kate anxiously. Who is it?

Julia, who was carrying in a column of table-napkins, turned to her sister and said, simply, as if the question had surprised her:

—It's only Freddy, Kate, and Gabriel with him.

In fact right behind her Gabriel could be seen piloting Freddy Malins across the landing. The latter, a young man of about forty, was of Gabriel's size and build, with very round shoulders. His face was fleshy and pallid, touched with colour only at the thick hanging lobes of his ears and at the wide wings of his nose. He had coarse features, a blunt nose, a convex and receding brow, tumid and protruded lips. His heavy-lidded eyes and the disorder of his scanty hair made him look sleepy. He was laughing heartily in a high key at a story which he had been telling Gabriel on the stairs and at the same time rubbing the knuckles of his left fist backwards and forwards into his left eye.

—Good-evening, Freddy, said Aunt Julia.

Freddy Malins bade the Misses Morkan good-evening in what seemed an off-hand fashion by reason of the habitual catch in his voice and then, seeing that Mr Browne was grinning at him from the sideboard, crossed the room on rather shaky legs and began to repeat in an undertone the story he had just told to Gabriel.

—He's not so bad, is he? said Aunt Kate to Gabriel.

Gabriel's brows were dark but he raised them quickly and answered:

—O no, hardly noticeable.

—Now, isn't he a terrible fellow! she said. And his poor mother made him take the pledge on New Year's Eve. But come on, Gabriel, into the drawing-room.

Before leaving the room with Gabriel she signalled to Mr Browne by frowning and shaking her forefinger in warning to and fro. Mr Browne nodded in answer and, when she had gone, said to Freddy Malins:

—Now, then, Teddy, I'm going to fill you out a good glass of lemonade just to buck you up.

Freddy Malins, who was nearing the climax of his story, waved the offer aside impatiently but Mr Browne, having first called Freddy Malins' attention to a disarray in his dress, filled out and handed him a full glass of lemonade. Freddy Malins' left hand accepted the glass mechanically, his right hand being engaged in the mechanical readjustment of his dress. Mr Browne, whose face was once more wrinkling with mirth, poured out for himself a glass of whisky while Freddy Malins exploded, before he had well reached the climax of his story, in a kink of high-pitched bronchitic laughter and, setting down his untasted and overflowing glass, began to rub the knuckles of his left fist backwards and forwards into his left eye, repeating words of his last phrase as well as his fit of laughter would allow him.

Gabriel could not listen while Mary Jane was playing her Academy piece, full of runs and difficult passages, to the hushed drawing-room. He liked music but the piece she was playing had no melody for him and he doubted whether it had any melody for the other listeners, though they had begged Mary Jane to play something. Four young men, who had come from the refreshment-room to stand in the doorway at the sound of the piano, had gone away quietly in couples after a few minutes. The only persons who seemed to follow the music were Mary Jane herself, her hands racing along the key-board or lifted from it at the pauses like those of a priestess in momentary imprecation, and Aunt Kate standing at her elbow to turn the page.

Gabriel's eyes, irritated by the floor, which glittered with beeswax under the heavy chandelier, wandered to the wall above the piano. A picture of the balcony scene in *Romeo and Juliet* hung there and beside it was a picture of the two murdered princes in the Tower which Aunt Julia had worked in red, blue and brown wools when she was a girl. Probably in the school they had gone to as girls that kind of work had been taught, for one year his mother had worked for him as a birthday present a waistcoat of purple tabinet, with little foxes' heads upon it, lined with brown satin and having round mulberry buttons. It was strange that his mother had had no musical talent though Aunt Kate used to call her the brains carrier of the Morkan family. Both she and Julia had always seemed a little proud of their serious and matronly sister. Her photograph stood before the pierglass. She held an open book on her knees and was pointing out something in it to Constantine who, dressed in a man-o'-war suit, lay at her feet. It was she who had chosen the names for her sons for she was very sensible of the dignity of family life. Thanks to her, Constantine was now senior curate in Balbriggan and, thanks to her, Gabriel himself had taken his degree in the Royal University. A shadow passed over his face as he remembered her sullen opposition to his marriage. Some slighting phrases she had used still rankled in his memory; she had once spoken of Gretta as being country cute and that was not true of Gretta at all. It was Gretta who had nursed her during all her last long illness in their house at Monkstown.

He knew that Mary Jane must be near the end of her piece for she was playing again the opening melody with runs of scales after every bar and while he waited for the end the resentment died down in his heart. The piece ended with a trill of octaves in the treble and a final deep octave in the bass. Great applause greeted Mary Jane as, blushing and rolling up her music nervously, she escaped from the room. The most vigorous clapping came from the four young men in the doorway who had gone away to the refreshment-room at the beginning of the piece but had come back when the piano had stopped.

Lancers were arranged. Gabriel found himself partnered with Miss Ivors. She was a frank-mannered talkative young lady, with a freckled face and prominent brown eyes. She did not wear a low-cut bodice and the large brooch which was fixed in the front of her collar bore on it an Irish device.

When they had taken their places she said abruptly:

—I have a crow to pluck with you.

—With me? said Gabriel.

She nodded her head gravely.

—What is it? asked Gabriel, smiling at her solemn manner.

—Who is G. C.? answered Miss Ivors, turning her eyes upon him.

Gabriel coloured and was about to knit his brows, as if he did not understand, when she said bluntly:

—O, innocent Amy! I have found out that you write for *The Daily Express.* Now, aren't you ashamed of yourself?

—Why should I be ashamed of myself? asked Gabriel, blinking his eyes and trying to smile.

—Well, I'm ashamed of you, said Miss Ivors frankly. To say you'd write for a rag like that. I didn't think you were a West Briton.

A look of perplexity appeared on Gabriel's face. It was true that he wrote a literary column every Wednesday in *The Daily Express,* for which he was paid fifteen shillings. But that did not make him a West Briton surely. The books he received for review were almost more welcome than the paltry cheque. He loved to feel the covers and turn over the pages of newly printed books. Nearly every day when his teaching in the college was ended he used to wander down the quays to the second-hand booksellers, to Hickey's on Bachelor's Walk, to Webb's or Massey's on Aston's Quay, or to O'Clohissey's in the by-street. He did not know how to meet her charge. He wanted to say that literature was above politics. But they were friends of many years' standing and their careers had been parallel, first at the University and then as teachers: he could not risk a grandiose phrase with her. He continued blinking his eyes and trying to smile and murmured lamely that he saw nothing political in writing reviews of books.

When their turn to cross had come he was still perplexed and inattentive. Miss Ivors promptly took his hand in a warm grasp and said in a soft friendly tone:

—Of course, I was only joking. Come, we cross now.

When they were together again she spoke of the University question and Gabriel felt more at ease. A friend of hers had shown her his review of Browning's poems. That was how she had found out the secret: but she liked the review immensely. Then she said suddenly:

—O, Mr Conroy, will you come for an excursion to the Aran Isles this summer? We're going to stay there a whole month. It will be splendid out in the Atlantic. You ought to come. Mr Clancy is coming, and Mr Kilkelly and Kathleeen Kearney. It would be splendid for Gretta too if she'd come. She's from Connacht, isn't she?

—Her people are, said Gabriel shortly.

—But you will come, won't you? said Miss Ivors, laying her warm hand eagerly on his arm.

—The fact is, said Gabriel, I have already arranged to go—

—Go where? asked Miss Ivors.

—Well, you know, every year I go for a cycling tour with some fellows and so—

—But where? asked Miss Ivors.

—Well, we usually go to France or Belgium or perhaps Germany, said Gabriel awkwardly.

—And why do you go to France and Belgium, said Miss Ivors, instead of visiting your own land?

—Well, said Gabriel, it's partly to keep in touch with the languages and partly for a change.

—And haven't you your own language to keep in touch with—Irish? asked Miss Ivors.

—Well, said Gabriel, if it comes to that, you know, Irish is not my language.

Their neighbours had turned to listen to the cross-examination. Gabriel glanced right and left nervously and tried to keep his good humour under the ordeal which was making a blush invade his forehead.

—And haven't you your own land to visit, continued Miss Ivors, that you know nothing of, your own people, and your own country?

—O, to tell you the truth, retorted Gabriel suddenly, I'm sick of my own country, sick of it!

—Why? asked Miss Ivors.

Gabriel did not answer for his retort had heated him.

—Why? repeated Miss Ivors.

They had to go visiting together and, as he had not answered her, Miss Ivors said warmly:

—Of course, you've no answer.

Gabriel tried to cover his agitation by taking part in the dance with great energy. He avoided her eyes for he had seen a sour expression on her face. But when they met in the long chain he was surprised to feel his hand firmly pressed. She looked at him from under her brows for a moment quizzically until he smiled. Then, just as the chain was about to start again, she stood on tiptoe and whispered into his ear:

—West Briton!

When the lancers were over Gabriel went away to a remote corner of the room where Freddy Malins' mother was sitting. She was a stout feeble old woman with white hair. Her voice had a catch in it like her son's and she stuttered slightly. She had been told that Freddy had come and that he was nearly all right. Gabriel asked her whether she had had a good crossing. She lived with her married daughter in Glasgow and came to Dublin on a visit once a year. She answered placidly that she had had a beautiful crossing and that the captain had been most attentive to her. She spoke also of the beautiful house her daughter kept in Glasgow, and of all the nice friends they had there. While her tongue rambled on Gabriel tried to banish from his mind all memory of the unpleasant incident with Miss Ivors. Of course the girl or woman, or whatever she was, was an enthusiast but there was a time for all things. Perhaps he ought not to have answered her like that. But she had no right to call him a West Briton before people, even in joke. She had tried to make him ridiculous before people, heckling him and staring at him with her rabbit's eyes.

He saw his wife making her way towards him through the waltzing couples. When she reached him she said into his ear:

—Gabriel, Aunt Kate wants to know won't you carve the goose as usual. Miss Daly will carve the ham and I'll do the pudding.

—All right, said Gabriel.

—She's sending in the younger ones first as soon as this waltz is over so that we'll have the tables to ourselves.

—Were you dancing? asked Gabriel.

—Of course I was. Didn't you see me? What words had you with Molly Ivors?

—No words. Why? Did she say so?

—Something like that. I'm trying to get that Mr D'Arcy to sing. He's full of conceit, I think.

—There were no words, said Gabriel moodily, only she wanted me to go for a trip to the west of Ireland and I said I wouldn't.

His wife clasped her hands excitedly and gave a little jump.

—O, do go, Gabriel, she cried. I'd love to see Galway again.

—You can go if you like, said Gabriel coldly.

She looked at him for a moment, then turned to Mrs Malins and said:

—There's a nice husband for you, Mrs Malins.

While she was threading her way back across the room Mrs Malins, without adverting to the interruption, went on to tell Gabriel what beautiful places there were in Scotland and beautiful scenery. Her son-in-law brought them every year to the lakes and they used to go fishing. Her son-in-law was a splendid fisher. One day he caught a fish, a beautiful big big fish, and the man in the hotel boiled it for their dinner.

Gabriel hardly heard what she said. Now that supper was coming near he began to think again about his speech and about the quotation. When he saw Freddy Malins coming across the room to visit his mother Gabriel left the chair free for him and retired into the embrasure of the window. The room had already cleared and from the back room came the clatter of plates and knives. Those who still remained in the drawing-room seemed tired of dancing and were conversing quietly in little groups. Gabriel's warm trembling fingers tapped the cold pane of the window. How cool it must be outside! How pleasant it would be to walk out alone, first along by the river and then through the park! The snow would be lying on the branches of the trees and forming a bright cap on the top of the Wellington Monument. How much more pleasant it would be there than at the supper-table!

He ran over the headings of his speech: Irish hospitality, sad memories, the Three Graces, Paris, the quotation from Browning. He repeated to himself a phrase he had written in his review: *One feels that one is listening to a thought-tormented music.* Miss Ivors had praised the review. Was she sincere? Had she really any life of her own behind all her propagandism? There had never been any ill-feeling between them until that night. It unnerved him to think that she would be at the supper-table, looking up at him while he spoke with her critical quizzing eyes. Perhaps she would not be sorry to see him fail in his speech. An idea came into his mind and gave him courage. He would say, alluding to Aunt Kate and Aunt Julia: *Ladies and Gentlemen, the generation which is now on the wane among us may have had its faults but for my part I think it had certain qualities of hospitality, of humour, of humanity, which the new and very serious and hypereducated generation that is growing up around us seems to me to lack.* Very good: that was one for Miss Ivors. What did he care that his aunts were only two ignorant old women?

A murmur in the room attracted his attention. Mr Browne was advancing from the door, gallantly escorting Aunt Julia, who leaned upon his arm, smiling and hanging her head. An irregular musketry of applause escorted her also as far as the piano and then, as Mary Jane seated herself on the stool, and Aunt Julia, no longer smiling, half turned so as to pitch her voice fairly into the room, gradually ceased. Gabriel recognised the prelude. It was that of an old song of Aunt Julia's—*Arrayed for the Bridal.* Her voice, strong and clear in tone, attacked with great spirit the runs which embellish the air and though she sang very rapidly she did not miss even the smallest of the grace notes. To follow the voice, without looking at the singer's face, was to feel and share the excitement of swift and secure flight. Gabriel applauded loudly with all the others at the close of the song and loud applause was borne in from the invisible supper-table. It sounded so genuine that a little colour struggled into Aunt Julia's face as she bent to replace in the music stand the old leather-bound song-book that had her initials on the cover. Freddy Malins, who had listened with his head perched sideways to hear her better, was still applauding when everyone else had ceased and talking animatedly to his mother who nodded her head gravely and slowly in acquiescence. At last, when he could clap no more, he stood up suddenly and hurried across the room to Aunt Julia whose hand he seized and held in both his hands, shaking it when words failed him or the catch in his voice proved too much for him.

—I was just telling my mother, he said, I never heard you sing so well, never. No, I never heard your voice so good as it is to-night. Now! Would you believe that now? That's the truth. Upon my word and honour that's the truth. I never heard your voice sound so fresh and so . . . so clear and fresh, never.

Aunt Julia smiled broadly and murmured something about compliments as she released her hand from his grasp. Mr Browne extended his open hand towards her and said to those who were near him in the manner of a showman introducing a prodigy to an audience:

—Miss Julia Morkan, my latest discovery!

He was laughing very heartily at this himself when Freddy Malins turned to him and said:

—Well, Browne, if you're serious you might make a worse discovery. All I can say is I never heard her sing half so well as long as I am coming here. And that's the honest truth.

—Neither did I, said Mr Browne. I think her voice has greatly improved.

Aunt Julia shrugged her shoulders and said with meek pride:

—Thirty years ago I hadn't a bad voice as voices go.

—I often told Julia, said Aunt Kate emphatically, that she was simply thrown away in that choir. But she never would be said by me.

She turned as if to appeal to the good sense of the others against a refractory child while Aunt Julia gazed in front of her, a vague smile of reminiscence playing on her face.

—No, continued Aunt Kate, she wouldn't be said or led by anyone, slaving there in that choir night and day, night and day. Six o'clock on Christmas morning! And all for what?

—Well, isn't it for the honour of God, Aunt Kate? asked Mary Jane, twisting round on the piano-stool and smiling.

Aunt Kate turned fiercely on her niece and said:

—I know all about the honour of God, Mary Jane, but I think it's not at all honourable for the pope to turn out the women out of the choirs that have slaved there all their lives and put little whipper-snappers of boys over their heads. I suppose it is for the good of the Church if the pope does it. But it's not just, Mary Jane, and it's not right.

She had worked herself into a passion and would have continued in defence of her sister for it was a sore subject with her but Mary Jane, seeing that all the dancers had come back, intervened pacifically:

—Now, Aunt Kate, you're giving scandal to Mr Browne who is of the other persuasion.

Aunt Kate turned to Mr Browne, who was grinning at this allusion to his religion, and said hastily:

—O, I don't question the pope's being right. I'm only a stupid old woman and I wouldn't presume to do such a thing. But there's such a thing as common everyday politeness and gratitude. And if I were in Julia's place I'd tell that Father Healy straight up to his face. . . .

—And besides, Aunt Kate, said Mary Jane, we really are all hungry and when we are hungry we are all very quarrelsome.

—And when we are thirsty we are also quarrelsome, added Mr Browne.

—So that we had better go to supper, said Mary Jane, and finish the discussion afterwards.

On the landing outside the drawing-room Gabriel found his wife and Mary Jane trying to persuade Miss Ivors to stay for supper. But Miss Ivors, who had put on her hat and was buttoning her cloak, would not stay. She did not feel in the least hungry and she had already overstayed her time.

—But only for ten minutes, Molly, said Mrs Conroy. That won't delay you.

—To take a pick itself, said Mary Jane, after all your dancing.

—I really couldn't, said Miss Ivors.

—I am afraid you didn't enjoy yourself at all, said Mary Jane hopelessly.

—Ever so much, I assure you, said Miss Ivors, but you really must let me run off now.

—But how can you get home? asked Mrs Conroy.

—O, it's only two steps up the quay.

Gabriel hesitated a moment and said:

—If you will allow me, Miss Ivors, I'll see you home if you really are obliged to go.

But Miss Ivors broke away from them.

—I won't hear of it, she cried. For goodness sake go in to your suppers and don't mind me. I'm quite well able to take care of myself.

—Well, you're the comical girl, Molly, said Mrs Conroy frankly.

—*Beannacht libh,*[1] cried Miss Ivors, with a laugh, as she ran down the staircase.

Mary Jane gazed after her, a moody puzzled expression on her face, while Mrs Conroy leaned over the banisters to listen for the hall-door. Gabriel asked himself was he the cause of her abrupt departure. But she did not seem to be in ill humour: she had gone away laughing. He stared blankly down the staircase.

At that moment Aunt Kate came toddling out of the supper-room, almost wringing her hands in despair.

—Where is Gabriel? she cried. Where on earth is Gabriel? There's everyone waiting in there, stage to let, and nobody to carve the goose!

—Here I am, Aunt Kate! cried Gabriel, with sudden animation, ready to carve a flock of geese, if necessary.

A fat brown goose lay at one end of the table and at the other end, on a bed of creased paper strewn with sprigs of parsley, lay a great ham, stripped of its outer skin and peppered over with crust crumbs, a neat paper frill round its shin and beside this was a round of spiced beef. Between these rival ends ran parallel lines of side-dishes: two little minsters of jelly, red and yellow; a shallow dish full of blocks of blancmange and red jam, a large green leaf-shaped dish with a stalk-shaped handle, on which lay bunches of purple raisins and peeled almonds, a companion dish on which lay a solid rectangle of Smyrna figs, a dish of custard topped with grated nutmeg, a small bowl full of chocolates and sweets wrapped in gold and silver papers and a glass vase in which stood some tall celery stalks. In the centre of the table there stood, as sentries to a fruit-stand which upheld a pyramid of oranges and American apples, two squat old-fashioned decanters of cut glass, one containing port and the other dark sherry. On the closed square piano a pudding in a huge yellow dish lay in waiting and behind it were three squads of bottles of stout and ale and minerals, drawn up according to the colours of their uniforms, the first two black, with brown and red labels, the third and smallest squad white, with transverse green sashes.

Gabriel took his seat boldly at the head of the table and, having looked to the edge of the carver, plunged his fork firmly into the goose. He felt quite at ease now for he was an expert carver and liked nothing better than to find himself at the head of a well-laden table.

—Miss Furlong, what shall I send you? he asked. A wing or a slice of the breast?

—Just a small slice of the breast.

—Miss Higgins, what for you?

—O, anything at all, Mr Conroy.

While Gabriel and Miss Daly exchanged plates of goose and plates of ham and spiced beef Lily went from guest to guest with a dish of hot floury potatoes wrapped in a white napkin. This was Mary Jane's idea and she had also suggested apple sauce for the goose but Aunt Kate had said that plain roast goose without apple sauce had always been good enough for her and she hoped she might never eat worse. Mary Jane waited on her pupils and saw that they got the best slices and Aunt Kate and Aunt Julia opened and carried across from the piano bottles of stout and ale for the

---

[1] "A blessing on you"—an Irish farewell.

gentlemen and bottles of minerals for the ladies. There was a great deal of confusion and laughter and noise, the noise of orders and counter-orders, of knives and forks, of corks and glass-stoppers. Gabriel began to carve second helpings as soon as he had finished the first round without serving himself. Everyone protested loudly so that he compromised by taking a long draught of stout for he had found the carving hot work. Mary Jane settled down quietly to her supper but Aunt Kate and Aunt Julia were still toddling round the table, walking on each other's heels, getting in each other's way and giving each other unheeded orders. Mr Browne begged of them to sit down and eat their suppers and so did Gabriel but they said there was time enough so that, at last, Freddy Malins stood up and, capturing Aunt Kate, plumped her down on her chair amid general laughter.

When everyone had been well served Gabriel said, smiling:

—Now, if anyone wants a little more of what vulgar people call stuffing let him or her speak.

A chorus of voices invited him to begin his own supper and Lily came forward with three potatoes which she had reserved for him.

—Very well, said Gabriel amiably, as he took another preparatory draught, kindly forget my existence, ladies and gentlemen, for a few minutes.

He set to his supper and took no part in the conversation with which the table covered Lily's removal of the plates. The subject of talk was the opera company which was then at the Theatre Royal. Mr Bartell D'Arcy, the tenor, a dark-complexioned young man with a smart moustache, praised very highly the leading contralto of the company but Miss Furlong thought she had a rather vulgar style of production. Freddy Malins said there was a negro chieftain singing in the second part of the Gaiety pantomime who had one of the finest tenor voices he had ever heard.

—Have you heard him? he asked Mr Bartell D'Arcy across the table.

—No, answered Mr Bartell D'Arcy carelessly.

—Because, Freddy Malins explained, now I'd be curious to hear your opinion of him. I think he has a grand voice.

—It takes Teddy to find out the really good things, said Mr Browne familiarly to the table.

—And why couldn't he have a voice too? asked Freddy Malins sharply. Is it because he's only a black?

Nobody answered this question and Mary Jane led the table back to the legitimate opera. One of her pupils had given her a pass for *Mignon*. Of course it was very fine, she said, but it made her think of poor Georgina Burns. Mr Browne could go back farther still, to the old Italian companies that used to come to Dublin—Tietjens, Ilma de Murzka, Campanini, the great Trebelli, Giuglini, Ravelli, Aramburo. Those were the days, he said, when there was something like singing to be heard in Dublin. He told too of how the top gallery of the old Royal used to be packed night after night, of how one night an Italian tenor had sung five encores to *Let Me Like a Soldier Fall,* introducing a high C every time, and of how the gallery boys would sometimes in their enthusiasm unyoke the horses from the carriage of some great *prima donna* and pull her themselves through the streets to her hotel. Why did they never play the grand old operas now, he asked, *Dinorah, Lucrezia Borgia?* Because they could not get the voices to sing them: that was why.

—O, well, said Mr Bartell D'Arcy, I presume there are as good singers to-day as there were then.

—Where are they? asked Mr Browne defiantly.

—In London, Paris, Milan, said Mr Bartell D'Arcy warmly. I suppose Caruso, for example, is quite as good, if not better than any of the men you have mentioned.

—Maybe so, said Mr Browne. But I may tell you I doubt it strongly.

—O, I'd give anything to hear Caruso sing, said Mary Jane.

—For me, said Aunt Kate, who had been picking a bone, there was only one tenor. To please me, I mean. But I suppose none of you ever heard of him.

—Who was he, Miss Morkan? asked Mr Bartell D'Arcy politely.

—His name, said Aunt Kate, was Parkinson. I heard him when he was in his prime and I think he had then the purest tenor voice that was ever put into a man's throat.

—Strange, said Mr Bartell D'Arcy. I never even heard of him.

—Yes, yes, Miss Morkan is right, said Mr Browne. I remember hearing of old Parkinson but he's too far back for me.

—A beautiful pure sweet mellow English tenor, said Aunt Kate with enthusiasm.

Gabriel having finished, the huge pudding was transferred to the table. The clatter of forks and spoons began again. Gabriel's wife served out spoonfuls of the pudding and passed the plates down the table. Midway down they were held up by Mary Jane, who replenished them with raspberry or orange jelly or with blancmange and jam. The pudding was of Aunt Julia's making and she received praises for it from all quarters. She herself said that it was not quite brown enough.

—Well, I hope, Miss Morkan, said Mr Browne, that I'm brown enough for you because, you know, I'm all brown.

All the gentlemen, except Gabriel, ate some of the pudding out of compliment to Aunt Julia. As Gabriel never ate sweets the celery had been left for him. Freddy Malins also took a stalk of celery and ate it with his pudding. He had been told that celery was a capital thing for the blood and he was just then under the doctor's care. Mrs Malins, who had been silent all through the supper, said that her son was going down to Mount Melleray in a week or so. The table then spoke of Mount Melleray, how bracing the air was down there, how hospitable the monks were and how they never asked for a penny-piece from their guests.

—And do you mean to say, asked Mr Browne incredulously, that a chap can go down there and put up there as if it were a hotel and live on the fat of the land and then come away without paying a farthing?

—O, most people give some donation to the monastery when they leave, said Mary Jane.

—I wish we had an institution like that in our Church, said Mr Browne candidly.

He was astonished to hear that the monks never spoke, got up at two in the morning and slept in their coffins. He asked what they did it for.

—That's the rule of the order, said Aunt Kate firmly.

—Yes, but why? asked Mr Browne.

Aunt Kate repeated that it was the rule, that was all. Mr Browne still seemed not to understand. Freddy Malins explained to him, as best he could, that the monks were trying to make up for the sins committed by all the sinners in the outside world.

The explanation was not very clear for Mr Browne grinned and said:

—I like that idea very much but wouldn't a comfortable spring bed do them as well as a coffin?

—The coffin, said Mary Jane, is to remind them of their last end.

As the subject had grown lugubrious it was buried in a silence of the table during which Mrs Malins could be heard saying to her neighbour in an indistinct undertone:

—They are very good men, the monks, very pious men.

The raisins and almonds and figs and apples and oranges and chocolates and sweets were now passed about the table and Aunt Julia invited all the guests to have either port or sherry. At first Mr Bartell D'Arcy refused to take either but one of his neighbours nudged him and whispered something to him upon which he allowed his glass to be filled. Gradually as the last glasses were being filled the conversation ceased. A pause followed, broken only by the noise of the wine and by unsettlings of chairs. The Misses Morkan, all three, looked down at the tablecloth. Someone coughed once or twice and then a few gentlemen patted the table gently as a signal for silence. The silence came and Gabriel pushed back his chair and stood up.

The patting at once grew louder in encouragement and then ceased altogether. Gabriel leaned his ten trembling fingers on the tablecloth and smiled nervously at the company. Meeting a row of upturned faces he raised his eyes to the chandelier. The piano was playing a waltz tune and he could hear the skirts sweeping against the drawing-room door. People, perhaps, were standing in the snow on the quay outside, gazing up at the lighted windows and listening to the waltz music. The air was pure there. In the distance lay the park where the trees were weighted with snow. The Wellington Monument wore a gleaming cap of snow that flashed westward over the white field of Fifteen Acres.

He began:

—Ladies and Gentlemen.

—It has fallen to my lot this evening, as in years past, to perform a very pleasing task but a task for which I am afraid my poor powers as a speaker are all too inadequate.

—No, no! said Mr Browne.

—But, however that may be, I can only ask you to-night to take the will for the deed and to lend me your attention for a few moments while I endeavour to express to you in words what my feelings are on this occasion.

—Ladies and Gentlemen. It is not the first time that we have gathered together under this hospitable roof, around this hospitable board. It is not the first time that we have been the recipients—or perhaps, I had better say, the victims—of the hospitality of certain good ladies.

He made a circle in the air with his arm and paused. Everyone laughed or smiled at Aunt Kate and Aunt Julia and Mary Jane who all turned crimson with pleasure. Gabriel went on more boldly:

—I feel more strongly with every recurring year that our country has no tradition which does it so much honour and which it should guard so jealously as that of its hospitality. It is a tradition that is unique as far as my experience goes (and I have visited not a few places abroad) among the modern nations. Some would say, perhaps, that with us it is rather a failing than anything to be boasted of. But granted even that, it is, to my mind, a princely failing, and one that I trust will long be cultivated among us. Of one thing, at least, I am sure. As long as this one roof shelters the good ladies aforesaid—and I wish from my heart it may do so for many and many a long year to come—the tradition of genuine warm-hearted courteous Irish hospitality, which our forefathers have handed down to us and which we in turn must hand down to our descendants, is still alive among us.

A hearty murmur of assent ran round the table. It shot through Gabriel's mind that Miss Ivors was not there and that she had gone away discourteously: and he said with confidence in himself:

—Ladies and Gentlemen.

—A new generation is growing up in our midst, a generation actuated by new ideas and new principles. It is serious and enthusiastic for these new ideas and its enthusiasm, even when it is misdirected, is, I believe, in the main sincere. But we are living in a sceptical and, if I may use the phrase, a thought-tormented age: and sometimes I fear that this new generation, educated or hypereducated as it is, will lack those qualities of humanity, of hospitality, of kindly humour which belonged to an older day. Listening tonight to the names of all those great singers of the past it seemed to me, I must confess, that we were living in a less spacious age. Those days might, without exaggeration, be called spacious days: and if they are gone beyond recall let us hope, at least, that in gatherings such as this we shall still speak of them with pride and affection, still cherish in our hearts the memory of those dead and gone great ones whose fame the world will not willingly let die.

—Hear, hear! said Mr Browne loudly.

—But yet, continued Gabriel, his voice falling into a softer inflection, there are always in gatherings such as this sadder thoughts that will recur to our minds: thoughts of the past, of youth, of changes, of absent faces that we miss here to-night. Our path through life is strewn with many such sad memories: and were we to brood upon them always we could not find the heart to go on bravely with our work among the living. We have all of us living duties and living affections which claim, and rightly claim, our strenuous endeavours.

—Therefore, I will not linger on the past. I will not let any gloomy moralising intrude upon us here to-night. Here we are gathered together for a brief moment from the bustle and rush of our everyday routine. We are met here as friends, in the spirit of good-fellowship, as colleagues, also to a certain extent, in the true spirit of *camaraderie,* and as the guests of—what shall I call them?—the Three Graces of the Dublin musical world.

The table burst into applause and laughter at this sally. Aunt Julia vainly asked each of her neighbours in turn to tell her what Gabriel had said.

—He says we are the Three Graces, Aunt Julia, said Mary Jane.

Aunt Julia did not understand but she looked up, smiling, at Gabriel, who continued in the same vein:

—Ladies and Gentlemen.

—I will not attempt to play to-night the part that Paris played on another occasion. I will not attempt to choose between them. The task would be an invidious one and one beyond my poor powers. For when I view them in turn, whether it be our chief hostess herself, whose good heart, whose too good heart, has become a byword with all who know her, or her sister, who seems to be gifted with perennial youth and whose singing must have been a surprise and a revelation to us all to-night, or, last but not least, when I consider our youngest hostess, talented, cheerful, hard-working and the best of nieces, I confess, Ladies and Gentlemen, that I do not know to which of them I should award the prize.

Gabriel glanced down at his aunts and, seeing the large smile on Aunt Julia's face and the tears which had risen to Aunt Kate's eyes, hastened to close. He raised his glass of port gallantly, while every member of the company fingered a glass expectantly, and said loudly:

—Let us toast them all three together. Let us drink to their health, wealth, long life, happiness and prosperity and may they long continue to hold the proud and self-won position which they hold in their profession and the position of honour and affection which they hold in our hearts.

All the guests stood up, glass in hand, and, turning towards the three seated ladies, sang in unison, with Mr Browne as leader:

For they are jolly gay fellows,
For they are jolly gay fellows,
For they are jolly gay fellows,
Which nobody can deny.

Aunt Kate was making frank use of her handkerchief and even Aunt Julia seemed moved. Freddy Malins beat time with his pudding-fork and the singers turned towards one another, as if in melodious conference, while they sang, with emphasis:

Unless he tells a lie,
Unless he tells a lie.

Then, turning once more towards their hostesses, they sang:

For they are jolly gay fellows,
For they are jolly gay fellows,
For they are jolly gay fellows,
Which nobody can deny.

The acclamation which followed was taken up beyond the door of the supper-room by many of the other guests and renewed time after time, Freddy Malins acting as officer with his fork on high.

The piercing morning air came into the hall where they were standing so that Aunt Kate said:

—Close the door, somebody. Mrs Malins will get her death of cold.

—Browne is out there, Aunt Kate, said Mary Jane.

—Browne is everywhere, said Aunt Kate, lowering her voice.

Mary Jane laughed at her tone.

—Really, she said archly, he is very attentive.

—He has been laid on here like the gas, said Aunt Kate in the same tone, all during the Christmas.

She laughed herself this time good-humouredly and then added quickly:

—But tell him to come in, Mary Jane, and close the door. I hope to goodness he didn't hear me.

At that moment the hall-door was opened and Mr Browne came in from the doorstep, laughing as if his heart would break. He was dressed in a long green overcoat with mock astrakhan cuffs and collar and wore on his head an oval fur cap. He pointed down the snow-covered quay from where the sound of shrill prolonged whistling was borne in.

—Teddy will have all the cabs in Dublin out, he said.

Gabriel advanced from the little pantry behind the office, struggling into his overcoat and, looking round the hall, said:

—Gretta not down yet?

—She's getting on her things, Gabriel, said Aunt Kate.

—Who's playing up there? asked Gabriel.

—Nobody. They're all gone.

—O no, Aunt Kate, said Mary Jane. Bartell D'Arcy and Miss O'Callaghan aren't gone yet.

—Someone is strumming at the piano, anyhow, said Gabriel.

Mary Jane glanced at Gabriel and Mr Browne and said with a shiver:

—It makes me feel cold to look at you two gentlemen muffled up like that. I wouldn't like to face your journey home at this hour.

—I'd like nothing better this minute, said Mr Browne stoutly, than a rattling fine walk in the country or a fast drive with a good spanking goer between the shafts.

—We used to have a very good horse and trap at home, said Aunt Julia sadly.

—The never-to-be-forgotten Johnny, said Mary Jane, laughing.

Aunt Kate and Gabriel laughed too.

—Why, what was wonderful about Johnny? asked Mr Browne.

—The late lamented Patrick Morkan, our grandfather, that is, explained Gabriel, commonly known in his later years as the old gentleman, was a glue-boiler.

—O, now, Gabriel, said Aunt Kate, laughing, he had a starch mill.

—Well, glue or starch, said Gabriel, the old gentleman had a horse by the name of Johnny. And Johnny used to work in the old gentleman's mill, walking round and round in order to drive the mill. That was all very well; but now comes the tragic part about Johnny. One fine day the old gentleman thought he'd like to drive out with the quality to a military review in the park.

—The Lord have mercy on his soul, said Aunt Kate compassionately.

—Amen, said Gabriel. So the old gentleman, as I said, harnessed Johnny and put on his very best tall hat and his very best stock collar and drove out in grand style from his ancestral mansion somewhere near Back Lane, I think.

Everyone laughed, even Mrs Malins, at Gabriel's manner and Aunt Kate said:

—O now, Gabriel, he didn't live in Back Lane, really. Only the mill was there.

—Out from the mansion of his forefathers, continued Gabriel, he drove with Johnny. And everything went on beautifully until Johnny came in sight of King

Billy's statue: and whether he fell in love with the horse King Billy sits on or whether he thought he was back again in the mill, anyhow he began to walk round the statue.

Gabriel paced in a circle around the hall in his goloshes amid the laughter of the others.

—Round and round he went, said Gabriel, and the old gentleman, who was a very pompous old gentleman, was highly indignant. *Go on, sir! What do you mean, sir? Johnny! Johnny! Most extraordinary conduct! Can't understand the horse!*

The peals of laughter which followed Gabriel's imitation of the incident were interrupted by a resounding knock at the hall-door. Mary Jane ran to open it and let in Freddy Malins. Freddy Malins, with his hat well back on his head and his shoulders humped with cold, was puffing and steaming after his exertions.

—I could only get one cab, he said.

—O, we'll find another along the quay, said Gabriel.

—Yes, said Aunt Kate. Better not keep Mrs Malins standing in the draught.

Mrs Malins was helped down the front steps by her son and Mr Browne and, after many manœuvres, hoisted into the cab. Freddy Malins clambered in after her and spent a long time settling her on the seat, Mr Browne helping him with advice. At last she was settled comfortably and Freddy Malins invited Mr Browne into the cab. There was a good deal of confused talk, and then Mr Browne got into the cab. The cabman settled his rug over his knees, and bent down for the address. The confusion grew greater and the cabman was directed differently by Freddy Malins and Mr Browne, each of whom had his head out through a window of the cab. The difficulty was to know where to drop Mr Browne along the route and Aunt Kate, Aunt Julia and Mary Jane helped the discussion from the doorstep with cross-directions and contradictions and abundance of laughter. As for Freddy Malins he was speechless with laughter. He popped his head in and out of the window every moment, to the great danger of his hat, and told his mother how the discussion was progressing till at last Mr Browne shouted to the bewildered cabman above the din of everybody's laughter:

—Do you know Trinity College?

—Yes, sir, said the cabman.

—Well, drive bang up against Trinity College gates, said Mr Browne, and then we'll tell you where to go. You understand now?

—Yes, sir, said the cabman.

—Make like a bird for Trinity College.

—Right, sir, cried the cabman.

The horse was whipped up and the cab rattled off along the quay amid a chorus of laughter and adieus.

Gabriel had not gone to the door with the others. He was in a dark part of the hall gazing up the staircase. A woman was standing near the top of the first flight, in the shadow also. He could not see her face but he could see the terracotta and salmon-pink panels of her skirt which the shadow made appear black and white. It was his wife. She was leaning on the banisters, listening to something. Gabriel was surprised at her stillness and strained his ear to listen also. But he could hear little save the noise of laughter and dispute on the front steps, a few chords struck on the piano and a few notes of a man's voice singing.

He stood still in the gloom of the hall, trying to catch the air that the voice was singing and gazing up at his wife. There was grace and mystery in her attitude as if she were a symbol of something. He asked himself what is a woman standing on the stairs in the shadow, listening to distant music, a symbol of. If he were a painter he would paint her in that attitude. Her blue felt hat would show off the bronze of her hair against the darkness and the dark panels of her skirt would show off the light ones. *Distant Music* he would call the picture if he were a painter.

The hall-door closed; and Aunt Kate, Aunt Julia and Mary Jane came down the hall, still laughing.

—Well, isn't Freddy terrible? said Mary Jane. He's really terrible.

Gabriel said nothing but pointed up the stairs towards where his wife was standing. Now that the hall-door was closed the voice and the piano could be heard more clearly. Gabriel held up his hand for them to be silent. The song seemed to be in the old Irish tonality and the singer seemed uncertain both of his words and of his voice. The voice, made plaintive by distance and by the singer's hoarseness, faintly illuminated the cadence of the air with words expressing grief:

> *O, the rain falls on my heavy locks*
> *And the dew wets my skin,*
> *My babe lies cold . . .*

—O, exclaimed Mary Jane. It's Bartell D'Arcy singing and he wouldn't sing all the night. O, I'll get him to sing a song before he goes.

—O do, Mary Jane, said Aunt Kate.

Mary Jane brushed past the others and ran to the staircase but before she reached it the singing stopped and the piano was closed abruptly.

—O, what a pity! she cried. Is he coming down, Gretta?

Gabriel heard his wife answer yes and saw her come down towards them. A few steps behind her were Mr Bartell D'Arcy and Miss O'Callaghan.

—O, Mr D'Arcy, cried Mary Jane, it's downright mean of you to break off like that when we were all in raptures listening to you.

—I have been at him all the evening, said Miss O'Callaghan, and Mrs Conroy too and he told us he had a dreadful cold and couldn't sing.

—O, Mr D'Arcy, said Aunt Kate, now that was a great fib to tell.

—Can't you see that I'm as hoarse as a crow? said Mr D'Arcy roughly.

He went into the pantry hastily and put on his overcoat. The others, taken aback by his rude speech, could find nothing to say. Aunt Kate wrinkled her brows and made signs to the others to drop the subject. Mr D'Arcy stood swathing his neck carefully and frowning.

—It's the weather, said Aunt Julia, after a pause.

—Yes, everybody has colds, said Aunt Kate readily, everybody.

—They say, said Mary Jane, we haven't had snow like it for thirty years; and I read this morning in the newspapers that the snow is general all over Ireland.

—I love the look of snow, said Aunt Julia sadly.

—So do I, said Miss O'Callaghan. I think Christmas is never really Christmas unless we have the snow on the ground.

—But poor Mr D'Arcy doesn't like the snow, said Aunt Kate, smiling.

Mr D'Arcy came from the pantry, fully swathed and buttoned, and in a repentant tone told them the history of the cold. Everyone gave him advice and said it was a great pity and urged him to be very careful of his throat in the night air. Gabriel watched his wife who did not join in the conversation. She was standing right under the dusty fanlight and the flame of the gas lit up the rich bronze of her hair which he had seen her drying at the fire a few days before. She was in the same attitude and seemed unaware of the talk about her. At last she turned towards them and Gabriel saw that there was colour on her cheeks and that her eyes were shining. A sudden tide of joy went leaping out of his heart.

—Mr D'Arcy, she said, what is the name of that song you were singing?

—It's called *The Lass of Aughrim,* said Mr D'Arcy, but I couldn't remember it properly. Why? Do you know it?

—*The Lass of Aughrim,* she repeated. I couldn't think of the name.

—It's a very nice air, said Mary Jane. I'm sorry you were not in voice to-night.

—Now, Mary Jane, said Aunt Kate, don't annoy Mr D'Arcy. I won't have him annoyed.

Seeing that all were ready to start she shepherded them to the door where good-night was said:

—Well, good-night, Aunt Kate, and thanks for the pleasant evening.

—Good-night, Gabriel. Good-night, Gretta!

—Good-night, Aunt Kate, and thanks ever so much. Good-night, Aunt Julia.

—O, good-night, Gretta, I didn't see you.

—Good-night, Mr D'Arcy. Good-night, Miss O'Callaghan.

—Good-night, Miss Morkan.

—Good-night, again.

—Good-night, all. Safe home.

—Good-night. Good-night.

The morning was still dark. A dull yellow light brooded over the houses and the river; and the sky seemed to be descending. It was slushy underfoot; and only streaks and patches of snow lay on the roofs, on the parapets of the quay and on the area railings. The lamps were still burning redly in the murky air and, across the river, the palace of the Four Courts stood out menacingly against the heavy sky.

She was walking on before him with Mr Bartell D'Arcy, her shoes in a brown parcel tucked under one arm and her hands holding her skirt up from the slush. She had no longer any grace of attitude but Gabriel's eyes were still bright with happiness. The blood went bounding along his veins; and the thoughts were rioting through his brain, proud, joyful, tender, valorous.

She was walking on before him so lightly and so erect that he longed to run after her noiselessly, catch her by the shoulders and say something foolish and affectionate into her ear. She seemed to him so frail that he longed to defend her against something and then to be alone with her. Moments of their secret life together burst like stars upon his memory. A heliotrope envelope was lying beside his breakfast-cup and he was caressing it with his hand. Birds were twittering in the ivy and the sunny web of the curtain was shimmering along the floor: he could not eat for happiness. They were standing on the crowded platform and he was placing a ticket inside the warm palm of her glove. He was standing with her in the cold, looking in through a grated window at a man making bottles in a roaring furnace. It was very cold. Her face, fragrant in the cold air, was quite close to his; and suddenly she called out to the man at the furnace.

—Is the fire hot, sir?

But the man could not hear her with the noise of the furnace. It was just as well. He might have answered rudely.

A wave of yet more tender joy escaped from his heart and went coursing in warm flood along his arteries. Like the tender fires of stars moments of their life together, that no one knew of or would ever know of, broke upon and illumined his memory. He longed to recall to her those moments, to make her forget the years of their dull existence together and remember only their moments of ecstasy. For the years, he felt, had not quenched his soul or hers. Their children, his writing, her household cares had not quenched all their souls' tender fire. In one letter that he had written to her then he had said: *Why is it that words like these seem to me so dull and cold? Is it because there is no word tender enough to be your name?*

Like distant music these words that he had written years before were borne towards him from the past. He longed to be alone with her. When the others had gone away, when he and she were in their room in the hotel, then they would be alone together. He could call her softly:

—Gretta!

Perhaps she would not hear at once: she would be undressing. Then something in his voice would strike her. She would turn and look at him. . . .

At the corner of Winetavern Street they met a cab. He was glad of its rattling noise as it saved him from conversation. She was looking out of the window and seemed tired. The others spoke only a few words, pointing out some building or street. The horse galloped along wearily under the murky morning sky, dragging his old rattling box after his heels, and Gabriel was again in a cab with her, galloping to catch the boat, galloping to their honeymoon.

As the cab drove across O'Connell Bridge Miss O'Callaghan said:

—They say you never cross O'Connell Bridge without seeing a white horse.

—I see a white man this time, said Gabriel.

—Where? asked Mr Bartell D'Arcy.

Gabriel pointed to the statue, on which lay patches of snow. Then he nodded familiarly to it and waved his hand.

—Good-night, Dan, he said gaily.

When the cab drew up before the hotel Gabriel jumped out and, in spite of Mr Bartell D'Arcy's protest, paid the driver. He gave the man a shilling over his fare. The man saluted and said:

—A prosperous New Year to you, sir.

—The same to you, said Gabriel cordially.

She leaned for a moment on his arm in getting out of the cab and while standing at the curbstone, bidding the others good-night. She leaned lightly on his arm, as lightly as when she had danced with him a few hours before. He had felt proud and happy then, happy that she was his, proud of her grace and wifely carriage. But now, after the kindling again of so many memories, the first touch of her body, musical and strange and perfumed, sent through him a keen pang of lust. Under cover of her silence he pressed her arm closely to his side; and, as they stood at the hotel door, he felt that they had escaped from their lives and duties, escaped from home and friends and run away together with wild and radiant hearts to a new adventure.

An old man was dozing in a great hooded chair in the hall. He lit a candle in the office and went before them to the stairs. They followed him in silence, their feet falling in soft thuds on the thickly carpeted stairs. She mounted the stairs behind the porter, her head bowed in the ascent, her frail shoulders curved as with a burden, her skirt girt tightly about her. He could have flung his arms about her hips and held her still for his arms were trembling with desire to seize her and only the stress of his nails against the palms of his hands held the wild impulse of his body in check. The porter halted on the stairs to settle his guttering candle. They halted too on the steps below him. In the silence Gabriel could hear the falling of the molten wax into the tray and the thumping of his own heart against his ribs.

The porter led them along a corridor and opened a door. Then he set his unstable candle down on a toilet-table and asked at what hour they were to be called in the morning.

—Eight, said Gabriel.

The porter pointed to the tap of the electric-light and began a muttered apology but Gabriel cut him short.

—We don't want any light. We have enough light from the street. And I say, he added, pointing to the candle, you might remove that handsome article, like a good man.

The porter took up his candle again, but slowly for he was surprised by such a novel idea. Then he mumbled good-night and went out. Gabriel shot the lock to.

A ghostly light from the street lamp lay in a long shaft from one window to the door. Gabriel threw his overcoat and hat on a couch and crossed the room towards the window. He looked down into the street in order that his emotion might calm a little. Then he turned and leaned against a chest of drawers with his back to the light. She had taken off her hat and cloak and was standing before a large swinging mirror, unhooking her waist. Gabriel paused for a few moments, watching her, and then said:

—Gretta!

She turned away from the mirror slowly and walked along the shaft of light towards him. Her face looked so serious and weary that the words would not pass Gabriel's lips. No, it was not the moment yet.

—You look tired, he said.

—I am a little, she answered.

—You don't feel ill or weak?

—No, tired: that's all.

She went on to the window and stood there, looking out. Gabriel waited again and then, fearing that diffidence was about to conquer him, he said abruptly:

—By the way, Gretta!

—What is it?

—You know that poor fellow Malins? he said quickly.

—Yes. What about him?

—Well, poor fellow, he's a decent sort of chap after all, continued Gabriel in a false voice. He gave me back that sovereign I lent him and I didn't expect it really. It's a pity he wouldn't keep away from that Browne, because he's not a bad fellow at heart.

He was trembling now with annoyance. Why did she seem so abstracted? He did not know how he could begin. Was she annoyed, too, about something? If she would only turn to him or come to him of her own accord! To take her as she was would be brutal. No, he must see some ardour in her eyes first. He longed to be master of her strange mood.

—When did you lend him the pound? she asked, after a pause.

Gabriel strove to restrain himself from breaking out into brutal language about the sottish Malins and his pound. He longed to cry to her from his soul, to crush her body against his, to overmaster her. But he said:

—O, at Christmas, when he opened that little Christmas-card shop in Henry Street.

He was in such a fever of rage and desire that he did not hear her come from the window. She stood before him for an instant, looking at him strangely. Then, suddenly raising herself on tiptoe and resting her hands lightly on his shoulders, she kissed him.

—You are a very generous person, Gabriel, she said.

Gabriel, trembling with delight at her sudden kiss and at the quaintness of her phrase, put his hands on her hair and began smoothing it back, scarcely touching it with his fingers. The washing had made it fine and brilliant. His heart was brimming over with happiness. Just when he was wishing for it she had come to him of her own accord. Perhaps her thoughts had been running with his. Perhaps she had felt the impetuous desire that was in him and then the yielding mood had come upon her. Now that she had fallen to him so easily he wondered why he had been so diffident.

He stood, holding her head between his hands. Then, slipping one arm swiftly about her body and drawing her towards him, he said softly:

—Gretta dear, what are you thinking about?

She did not answer nor yield wholly to his arm. He said again, softly:

—Tell me what it is, Gretta. I think I know what is the matter. Do I know?

She did not answer at once. Then she said in an outburst of tears:

—O, I am thinking about that song, *The Lass of Aughrim.*

She broke loose from him and ran to the bed and, throwing her arms across the bed-rail, hid her face. Gabriel stood stock-still for a moment in astonishment and then followed her. As he passed in the way of the cheval glass he caught sight of himself in full length, his broad, well-filled shirt-front, the face whose expression always puzzled him when he saw it in a mirror and his glimmering gilt-rimmed eyeglasses. He halted a few paces from her and said:

—What about the song? Why does that make you cry?

She raised her head from her arms and dried her eyes with the back of her hand like a child. A kinder note than he had intended went into his voice.

—Why, Gretta? he asked.

—I am thinking about a person long ago who used to sing that song.

—And who was the person long ago? asked Gabriel, smiling.

—It was a person I used to know in Galway when I was living with my grand-mother, she said.

The smile passed away from Gabriel's face. A dull anger began to gather again at the back of his mind and the dull fires of his lust began to glow angrily in his veins.

—Someone you were in love with? he asked ironically.

—It was a young boy I used to know, she answered, named Michael Furey. He used to sing that song, *The Lass of Aughrim*. He was very delicate.

Gabriel was silent. He did not wish her to think that he was interested in this delicate boy.

—I can see him so plainly, she said after a moment. Such eyes as he had: big dark eyes! And such an expression in them—an expression!

—O then, you were in love with him? said Gabriel.

—I used to go out walking with him, she said, when I was in Galway.

A thought flew across Gabriel's mind.

—Perhaps that was why you wanted to go to Galway with that Ivors girl? he said coldly.

She looked at him and asked in surprise:

—What for?

Her eyes made Gabriel feel awkward. He shrugged his shoulders and said:

—How do I know. To see him perhaps.

She looked away from him along the shaft of light towards the window in silence.

—He is dead, she said at length. He died when he was only seventeen. Isn't that a terrible thing to die so young as that?

—What was he? asked Gabriel, still ironically.

—He was in the gasworks, she said.

Gabriel felt humiliated by the failure of his irony and by the evocation of this figure from the dead, a boy in the gasworks. While he had been full of memories of their secret life together, full of tenderness and joy and desire, she had been comparing him in her mind with another. A shameful consciousness of his own person assailed him. He saw himself as a ludicrous figure, acting as a pennyboy for his aunts, a nervous well-meaning sentimentalist, orating to vulgarians and idealising his own clownish lusts, the pitiable fatuous fellow he had caught a glimpse of in the mirror. Instinctively he turned his back more to the light lest she might see the shame that burned upon his forehead.

He tried to keep his tone of cold interrogation but his voice when he spoke was humble and indifferent.

—I suppose you were in love with this Michael Furey, Gretta, he said.

—I was great with him at that time, she said.

Her voice was veiled and sad. Gabriel, feeling now how vain it would be to try to lead her whither he had purposed, caressed one of her hands and said, also sadly:

—And what did he die of so young, Gretta? Consumption, was it?

—I think he died for me, she answered.

A vague terror seized Gabriel at this answer as if, at that hour when he had hoped to triumph, some impalpable and vindictive being was coming against him, gathering forces against him in its vague world. But he shook himself free of it with an effort of reason and continued to caress her hand. He did not question her again for he felt that she would tell him of herself. Her hand was warm and moist: it did not respond to his touch but he continued to caress it just as he had caressed her first letter to him that spring morning.

—It was in the winter, she said, about the beginning of the winter when I was going to leave my grandmother's and come up here to the convent. And he was ill at the time in his lodgings in Galway and wouldn't be let out and his people in Oughterard were written to. He was in decline, they said, or something like that. I never knew rightly.

She paused for a moment and sighed.

—Poor fellow, she said. He was very fond of me and he was such a gentle boy. We used to go out together, walking, you know, Gabriel, like the way they do in the country. He was going to study singing only for his health. He had a very good voice, poor Michael Furey.

—Well; and then? asked Gabriel.

—And then when it came to the time for me to leave Galway and come up to the convent he was much worse and I wouldn't be let see him so I wrote a letter saying I was going up to Dublin and would be back in the summer and hoping he would be better then.

She paused for a moment to get her voice under control and went on:

—Then the night before I left I was in my grandmother's house in Nuns' Island, packing up, and I heard gravel thrown up against the window. The window was so wet I couldn't see so I ran downstairs as I was and slipped out the back into the garden and there was the poor fellow at the end of the garden, shivering.

—And did you not tell him to go back? asked Gabriel.

—I implored of him to go home at once and told him he would get his death in the rain. But he said he did not want to live. I can see his eyes as well as well! He was standing at the end of the wall where there was a tree.

—And did he go home? asked Gabriel.

—Yes, he went home. And when I was only a week in the convent he died and he was buried in Oughterard where his people came from. O, the day I heard that, that he was dead!

She stopped, choking with sobs, and, overcome by emotion, flung herself face downward on the bed, sobbing in the quilt. Gabriel held her hand for a moment longer, irresolutely, and then, shy of intruding on her grief, let it fall gently and walked quietly to the window.

She was fast asleep.

Gabriel, leaning on his elbow, looked for a few moments unresentfully on her tangled hair and half-open mouth, listening to her deep-drawn breath. So she had had that romance in her life: a man had died for her sake. It hardly pained him now to think how poor a part he, her husband, had played in her life. He watched her while she slept as though he and she had never lived together as man and wife. His curious eyes rested long upon her face and on her hair: and, as he thought of what she must have been then, in that time of her first girlish beauty, a strange friendly pity for her entered his soul. He did not like to say even to himself that her face was no longer beautiful but he knew that it was no longer the face for which Michael Furey had braved death.

Perhaps she had not told him all the story. His eyes moved to the chair over which she had thrown some of her clothes. A petticoat string dangled to the floor. One boot stood upright, its limp upper fallen down: the fellow of it lay upon its side. He wondered at his riot of emotions of an hour before. From what had it proceeded? From his aunt's supper, from his own foolish speech, from the wine and dancing, the merry-making when saying good-night in the hall, the pleasure of the walk along the river in the snow. Poor Aunt Julia! She, too, would soon be a shade with the shade of Patrick Morkan and his horse. He had caught that haggard look upon her face for a moment when she was singing *Arrayed for the Bridal*. Soon, perhaps, he would be sitting in that same drawing-room, dressed in black, his silk hat on his knees. The blinds would be drawn down and Aunt Kate would be sitting beside him, crying and blowing her nose and telling him how Julia had died. He would cast about his mind for some words that might console her, and would find only lame and useless ones. Yes, yes: that would happen very soon.

The air of the room chilled his shoulders. He stretched himself cautiously along under the sheets and lay down beside his wife. One by one they were all becoming shades. Better pass boldly into that other world, in the full glory of some passion, than fade and wither dismally with age. He thought of how she who lay beside him had locked in her heart for so many years that image of her lover's eyes when he had told her that he did not wish to live.

Generous tears filled Gabriel's eyes. He had never felt like that himself towards any woman but he knew that such a feeling must be love. The tears gathered more thickly in his eyes and in the partial darkness he imagined he saw the form of a young man standing under a dripping tree. Other forms were near. His soul had approached that region where dwell the vast hosts of the dead. He was conscious of, but could not apprehend, their wayward and flickering existence. His own identity was fading out into a grey impalpable world: the solid world itself which these dead had one time reared and lived in was dissolving and dwindling.

A few light taps upon the pane made him turn to the window. It had begun to snow again. He watched sleepily the flakes, silver and dark, falling obliquely against the lamplight. The time had come for him to set out on his journey westward. Yes, the newspapers were right: snow was general all over Ireland. It was falling on every part of the dark central plain, on the treeless hills, falling softly upon the Bog of Allen and, farther westward, softly falling into the dark mutinous Shannon waves. It was falling, too, upon every part of the lonely churchyard on the hill where Michael Furey lay buried. It lay thickly drifted on the crooked crosses and headstones, on the spears of the little gate, on the barren thorns. His soul swooned slowly as he heard the snow falling faintly through the universe and faintly falling, like the descent of their last end, upon all the living and the dead.

FRANZ KAFKA (1883–1924)

The Metamorphosis

Translated by Willa and Edwin Muir

1

As Gregor Samsa awoke one morning from uneasy dreams he found himself transformed in his bed into a gigantic insect. He was lying on his hard, as it were armor-plated, back and when he lifted his head a little he could see his dome-like brown belly divided into stiff arched segments on top of which the bed quilt could hardly keep in position and was about to slide off completely. His numerous legs, which were pitifully thin compared to the rest of his bulk, waved helplessly before his eyes.

What has happened to me? he thought. It was no dream. His room, a regular human bedroom, only rather too small, lay quiet between the four familiar walls. Above the table on which a collection of cloth samples was unpacked and spread out—Samsa was a commercial traveler—hung the picture which he had recently cut out of an illustrated magazine and put into a pretty gilt frame. It showed a lady, with a fur cap on and a fur stole, sitting upright and holding out to the spectator a huge fur muff into which the whole of her forearm had vanished!

Gregor's eyes turned next to the window, and the overcast sky—one could hear rain drops beating on the window gutter—made him quite melancholy. What about sleeping a little longer and forgetting all this nonsense, he thought, but it could not be done, for he was accustomed to sleep on his right side and in his present condition he could not turn himself over. However violently he forced himself towards his right side he always rolled on to his back again. He tried it at least a hundred times, shutting his eyes to keep from seeing his struggling legs, and only desisted when he began to feel in his side a faint dull ache he had never experienced before.

Oh God, he thought, what an exhausting job I've picked on! Traveling about day in, day out. It's much more irritating work than doing the actual business in the office, and on top of that there's the trouble of constant traveling, of worrying about train connections, the bed and irregular meals, casual acquaintances that are always new and never become intimate friends. The devil take it all! He felt a slight itching up on his belly; slowly pushed himself on his back nearer to the top of the bed so that he could lift his head more easily, identified the itching place which was surrounded by many small white spots the nature of which he could not understand and made to touch it with a leg, but drew the leg back immediately, for the contact made a cold shiver run through him.

He slid down again into his former position. This getting up early, he thought, makes one quite stupid. A man needs his sleep. Other commercials live like harem women. For instance, when I come back to the hotel of a morning to write up the orders I've got, these others are only sitting down to breakfast. Let me just try that with my chief; I'd be sacked on the spot. Anyhow, that might be quite a good thing for me, who can tell? If I didn't have to hold my hand because of my parents I'd have given notice long ago, I'd have gone to the chief and told him exactly what I think of him. That would knock him endways from his desk! It's a queer way of doing, too, this sitting on high at a desk and talking down to employees, especially when they have to come quite near because the chief is hard of hearing. Well, there's still hope; once I've saved enough money to pay back my parents' debts to him—that should take another five or six years—I'll do it without fail. I'll cut myself completely loose then. For the moment, though, I'd better get up, since my train goes at five.

He looked at the alarm clock ticking on the chest. Heavenly Father! he thought. It was half-past six o'clock and the hands were quietly moving on, it was even past the half-hour, it was getting on toward a quarter to seven. Had the alarm clock not gone off? From the bed one could see that it had been properly set for four o'clock; of course it must have gone off. Yes, but was it possible to sleep quietly through that ear-splitting noise? Well, he had not slept quietly, yet apparently all the more soundly for that. But what was he to do now? The next train went at seven o'clock; to catch that he would need to hurry like mad and his samples weren't even packed up, and he himself wasn't feeling particularly fresh and active. And even if he did catch the train he wouldn't avoid a row with the chief, since the firm's porter would have been waiting for the five o'clock train and would have long since reported his failure to turn up. The porter was a creature of the chief's, spineless and stupid. Well, supposing he were to say he was sick? But that would be most unpleasant and would look suspicious, since during his five years' employment he had not been ill once. The chief himself would be sure to come with the sick-insurance doctor, would reproach his parents with their son's laziness and would cut all excuses short by referring to the insurance doctor, who of course regarded all mankind as perfectly healthy malingerers. And would he be so far wrong on this occasion? Gregor really felt quite well, apart from a drowsiness that was utterly superfluous after such a long sleep, and he was even unusually hungry.

As all this was running through his mind at top speed without his being able to decide to leave his bed—the alarm clock had just struck a quarter to seven—there came a cautious tap at the door behind the head of his bed. "Gregor," said a voice—it was his mother's—"it's a quarter to seven. Hadn't you a train to catch?" That gentle voice! Gregor had a shock as he heard his own voice answering hers, unmistakably his own voice, it was true, but with a persistent horrible twittering squeak behind it like an undertone, that left the words in their clear shape only for the first moment and then rose up reverberating round them to destroy their sense, so that one could not be sure one had heard them rightly. Gregor wanted to answer at length and explain everything, but in the circumstances he confined himself to saying: "Yes, yes, thank you, Mother, I'm getting up now." The wooden door between them must have kept the change in his voice from being noticeable outside, for his mother contented herself with this statement and shuffled away. Yet this brief exchange of words had made the other members of the family aware that Gregor was still in the house, as they had not expected, and at one of the side doors his father was already knocking, gently, yet with his fist. "Gregor, Gregor," he called, "what's the matter with you?" And after a little while he called again in a deeper voice: "Gregor! Gregor!" At the other side door his sister was saying in a low, plaintive tone: "Gregor? Aren't you well? Are you needing anything?" He answered them both at once: "I'm just ready," and did his best to make his voice sound as normal as possible by enunciating the words very clearly and leaving long pauses between them. So his father went back to his breakfast, but his sister whispered: "Gregor, open the door, do." However, he was not thinking of opening the door, and felt thankful for the prudent habit he had acquired in traveling of locking all doors during the night, even at home.

His immediate intention was to get up quietly without being disturbed, to put on his clothes and above all eat his breakfast, and only then to consider what else was to be done, since in bed, he was well aware, his meditations would come to no sensible conclusion. He remembered that often enough in bed he had felt small aches and pains, probably caused by awkward postures, which had proved purely imaginary once he got up, and he looked forward eagerly to seeing this morning's delusions gradually fall away. That the change in his voice was nothing but the precursor of a severe chill, a standing ailment of commercial travelers, he had not the least possible doubt.

To get rid of the quilt was quite easy; he had only to inflate himself a little and it fell off by itself. But the next move was difficult, especially because he was so uncommonly broad. He would have needed arms and hands to hoist himself up; instead he had only the numerous little legs which never stopped waving in all directions and which he could not control in the least. When he tried to bend one of them it was the first to stretch itself straight; and did he succeed at last in making it do what he wanted, all the other legs meanwhile waved the more wildly in a high degree of unpleasant agitation. "But what's the use of lying idle in bed," said Gregor to himself.

He thought that he might get out of bed with the lower part of his body first, but this lower part, which he had not yet seen and of which he could form no clear conception, proved too difficult to move; it shifted so slowly; and when finally, almost wild with annoyance, he gathered his forces together and thrust out recklessly, he had miscalculated the direction and bumped heavily against the lower end of the bed, and the stinging pain he felt informed him that precisely this lower part of his body was at the moment probably the most sensitive.

So he tried to get the top part of himself out first, and cautiously moved his head towards the edge of the bed. That proved easy enough, and despite its breadth and mass the bulk of his body at last slowly followed the movement of his head. Still, when he finally got his head free over the edge of the bed he felt too scared to go on advancing, for after all if he let himself fall in this way it would take a miracle to keep his head from being injured. And at all costs he must not lose consciousness now, precisely now; he would rather stay in bed.

But when after a repetition of the same efforts he lay in his former position again, sighing, and watched his little legs struggling against each other more wildly than ever, if that were possible, and saw no way of bringing any order into this arbitrary confusion, he told himself again that it was impossible to stay in bed and that the most sensible course was to risk everything for the smallest hope of getting away from it. At the same time he did not forget meanwhile to remind himself that cool reflection, the coolest possible, was much better than desperate resolves. In such moments he focused his eyes as sharply as possible on the window, but, unfortunately, the prospect of the morning fog, which muffled even the other side of the narrow street, brought him little encouragement and comfort. "Seven o'clock already," he said to himself when the alarm clock chimed again, "seven o'clock already and still such a thick fog." And for a little while he lay quiet, breathing lightly, as if perhaps expecting such complete repose to restore all things to their real and normal condition.

But then he said to himself: "Before it strikes a quarter past seven I must be quite out of this bed, without fail. Anyhow, by that time someone will have come from the office to ask for me, since it opens before seven." And he set himself to rocking his whole body at once in a regular rhythm, with the idea of swinging it out of the bed. If he tipped himself out in that way he could keep his head from injury by lifting it at an acute angle when he fell. His back seemed to be hard and was not likely to suffer from a fall on the carpet. His biggest worry was the loud crash he would not be able to help making, which would probably cause anxiety, if not terror, behind all the doors. Still, he must take the risk.

When he was already half out of the bed—the new method was more a game than an effort, for he needed only to hitch himself across by rocking to and fro—it struck him how simple it would be if he could get help. Two strong people—he thought of his father and the servant girl—would be amply sufficient; they would only have to thrust their arms under his convex back, lever him out of the bed, bend down with their burden and then be patient enough to let him turn himself right over on to the floor, where it was to be hoped his legs would then find their proper function. Well, ignoring the fact that the doors were all locked, ought he really to call for help? In spite of his misery he could not suppress a smile at the very idea of it.

He had got so far that he could barely keep his equilibrium when he rocked himself strongly, and he would have to nerve himself very soon for the final decision since in five minutes' time it would be a quarter past seven—when the front doorbell rang. "That's someone from the office," he said to himself, and grew almost rigid, while his little legs only jigged about all the faster. For a moment everything stayed quiet. "They're not going to open the door," said Gregor to himself, catching at some kind of irrational hope. But then of course the servant girl went as usual to the door with her heavy tread and opened it. Gregor needed only to hear the first good morning of the visitor to know immediately who it was—the chief clerk himself. What a fate, to be condemned to work for a firm where the smallest omission at once gave rise to the gravest suspicion! Were all employees in a body nothing but scoundrels, was there not among them one single loyal devoted man who, had he wasted only an hour or so of the firm's time in a morning, was so tormented by conscience as to be driven out of his mind and actually incapable of leaving his bed? Wouldn't it really have been sufficient to send an apprentice to inquire—if any inquiry were necessary at all—did the chief clerk himself have to come and thus indicate to the entire family, an innocent family, that this suspicious circumstance could be investigated by no one less versed in affairs than himself? And more through the agitation caused by these reflections than through any act of will Gregor swung himself out of bed with all his strength. There was a loud thump, but it was not really a crash. His fall was broken to some extent by the carpet, his back, too, was less stiff than he thought, and so there was merely a dull thud, not so very startling. Only he had not lifted his head carefully enough and had hit it; he turned it and rubbed it on the carpet in pain and irritation.

"That was something falling down in there," said the chief clerk in the next room to the left. Gregor tried to suppose to himself that something like what had happened to him today might some day happen to the chief clerk; one really could not deny that it was possible. But as if in brusque reply to this supposition the chief clerk took a couple of firm steps in the next-door room and his patent leather boots creaked. From the right-hand room his sister was whispering to inform him of the situation: "Gregor, the chief clerk's here." "I know," muttered Gregor to himself; but he didn't dare to make his voice loud enough for his sister to hear it.

"Gregor," said his father now from the left-hand room, "the chief clerk has come and wants to know why you didn't catch the early train. We don't know what to say to him. Besides, he wants to talk to you in person. So open the door, please. He will be good enough to excuse the untidiness of your room." "Good morning, Mr. Samsa," the chief clerk was calling amiably meanwhile. "He's not well," said his mother to the visitor, while his father was still speaking through the door, "he's not well, sir, believe me. What else would make him miss a train! The boy thinks about nothing but his work. It makes me almost cross the way he never goes out in the evenings; he's been here the last eight days and has stayed at home every single evening. He just sits there quietly at the table reading a newspaper or looking through railway timetables. The only amusement he gets is doing fretwork. For instance, he spent two or three evenings cutting out a little picture frame; you would be surprised to see how pretty it is; it's hanging in his room; you'll see it in a minute when Gregor opens the door. I must say I'm glad you've come, sir; we should never have got him to unlock the door by ourselves; he's so obstinate; and I'm sure he's unwell, though he wouldn't have it to be so this morning." "I'm just coming," said Gregor slowly and carefully, not moving an inch for fear of losing one word of the conversation. "I can't think of any other explanation, madam," said the chief clerk, "I hope it's nothing serious. Although on the other hand I must say that we men of business— fortunately or unfortunately—very often simply have to ignore any slight indisposition, since business must be attended to." "Well, can the chief clerk come in now?" asked Gregor's father impatiently, again knocking on the door. "No," said Gregor. In the left-hand room a painful silence followed this refusal, in the right-hand room his sister began to sob.

Why didn't his sister join the others? She was probably newly out of bed and hadn't even begun to put on her clothes yet. Well, why was she crying? Because he wouldn't get up and let the chief clerk in, because he was in danger of losing his job, and because the chief would begin dunning his parents again for the old debts? Surely these were things one didn't need to worry about for the present. Gregor was still at home and not in the least thinking of deserting the family. At the moment, true, he was lying on the carpet and no one who knew the condition he was in could seriously expect him to admit the chief clerk. But for such a small discourtesy, which could plausibly be explained away somehow later on, Gregor could hardly be dismissed on the spot. And it seemed to Gregor that it would be much more sensible to leave him in peace for the present than to trouble him with tears and entreaties. Still, of course, their uncertainty bewildered them all and excused their behavior.

"Mr. Samsa," the chief clerk called now in a louder voice, "what's the matter with you? Here you are, barricading yourself in your room, giving only 'yes' and 'no' for answers, causing your parents a lot of unnecessary trouble and neglecting—I mention this only in passing—neglecting your business duties in an incredible fashion. I am speaking here in the name of your parents and of your chief, and I beg you quite seriously to give me an immediate and precise explanation. You amaze me, you amaze me. I thought you were a quiet, dependable person, and now all at once you seem bent on making a disgraceful exhibition of yourself. The chief did hint to me early this morning a possible explanation for your disappearance—with reference to the cash payments that were entrusted to you recently—but I almost pledged my solemn word of honor that this could not be so. But now that I see how incredibly obstinate you are, I no longer have the slightest desire to take your part at all. And your position in the firm is not so unassailable. I came with the intention of telling you all this in private, but since you are wasting my time so needlessly I don't see why your parents shouldn't hear it too. For some time past your work has been most unsatisfactory; this is not the season of the year for a business boom, of course, we admit that, but a season of the year for doing no business at all, that does not exist, Mr. Samsa, must not exist."

"But, sir," cried Gregor, beside himself and in his agitation forgetting everything else, "I'm just going to open the door this very minute. A slight illness, an attack of giddiness, has kept me from getting up. I'm still lying in bed. But I feel all right again. I'm getting out of bed now. Just give me a moment or two longer! I'm not quite so well as I thought. But I'm all right, really. How a thing like that can suddenly strike one down! Only last night I was quite well, my parents can tell you, or rather I did have a slight presentiment. I must have showed some sign of it. Why didn't I report it at the office! But one always thinks that an indisposition can be got over without staying in the house. Oh sir, do spare my parents! All that you're reproaching me with now has no foundation; no one has ever said a word to me about it. Perhaps you haven't looked at the last orders I sent in. Anyhow, I can still catch the eight o'clock train, I'm much the better for my few hours' rest. Don't let me detain you here, sir; I'll be attending to business very soon, and do be good enough to tell the chief so and to make my excuses to him!"

And while all this was tumbling out pell-mell and Gregor hardly knew what he was saying, he had reached the chest quite easily, perhaps because of the practice he had had in bed, and was now trying to lever himself upright by means of it. He meant actually to open the door, actually to show himself and speak to the chief clerk; he was eager to find out what the others, after all their insistence, would say at the sight of him. If they were horrified then the responsibility was no longer his and he could stay quiet. But if they took it calmly, then he had no reason either to be upset, and could really get to the station for the eight o'clock train if he hurried. At first he slipped down a few times from the polished surface of the chest, but at length with a last heave he stood upright; he paid no more attention to the pains in the lower part of his body, however they smarted. Then he let himself fall against the back of a near-by chair, and clung with his little legs to the edges of it. That brought him into control of himself again and he stopped speaking, for now he could listen to what the chief clerk was saying.

"Did you understand a word of it?" the chief clerk was asking; "surely he can't be trying to make fools of us?" "Oh dear," cried his mother, in tears, "perhaps he's terribly ill and we're tormenting him. Grete! Grete!" she called out then. "Yes Mother?" called his sister from the other side. They were calling to each other across Gregor's room. "You must go this minute for the doctor. Gregor is ill. Go for the doctor, quick. Did you hear how he was speaking?" "That was no human voice," said the chief clerk in a voice noticeably low beside the shrillness of the mother's. "Anna! Anna!" his father was calling through the hall to the kitchen, clapping his hands, "get a locksmith at once!" And the two girls were already running through the hall with a swish of skirts—how could his sister have got dressed so quickly?—and were tearing the front door open. There was no sound of its closing again; they had evidently left it open, as one does in houses where some great misfortune has happened.

But Gregor was now much calmer. The words he uttered were no longer understandable, apparently, although they seemed clear enough to him, even clearer than before, perhaps because his ear had grown accustomed to the sound of them. Yet at any rate people now believed that something was wrong with him, and were ready to help him. The positive certainty with which these first measures had been taken comforted him. He felt himself drawn once more into the human circle and hoped for great and remarkable results from both the doctor and the locksmith, without really distinguishing precisely between them. To make his voice as clear as possible for the decisive conversation that was now imminent he coughed a little, as quietly as he could, of course, since this noise too might not sound like a human cough for all he was able to judge. In the next room meanwhile there was complete silence. Perhaps his parents were sitting at the table with the chief clerk, whispering, perhaps they were all leaning against the door and listening.

Slowly Gregor pushed the chair towards the door, then let go of it, caught hold of the door for support—the soles at the end of his little legs were somewhat sticky—and rested against it for a moment after his efforts. Then he set himself to turning the key in the lock with his mouth. It seemed, unhappily, that he hadn't really any teeth —what could he grip the key with?—but on the other hand his jaws were certainly very strong; with their help he did manage to set the key in motion, heedless of the fact that he was undoubtedly damaging them somewhere, since a brown fluid issued from his mouth, flowed over the key and dripped on the floor. "Just listen to that," said the chief clerk next door; "he's turning the key." That was a great encouragement to Gregor; but they should all have shouted encouragement to him, his father and mother too: "Go on, Gregor," they should have called out, "keep going, hold on to that key!" And in the belief that they were all following his efforts intently, he clenched his jaws recklessly on the key with all the force at his command. As the turning of the key progressed he circled round the lock, holding on now only with his mouth, pushing on the key, as required, or pulling it down again with all the weight of his body. The louder click of the finally yielding lock literally quickened Gregor. With a deep breath of relief he said to himself: "So I didn't need the lock-smith," and laid his head on the handle to open the door wide.

Since he had to pull the door towards him, he was still invisible when it was really wide open. He had to edge himself slowly round the near half of the double door, and to do it very carefully if he was not to fall plump upon his back just on the threshold. He was still carrying out this difficult manoeuvre, with no time to observe anything else, when he heard the chief clerk utter a loud "Oh!"—it sounded like a gust of wind—and now he could see the man, standing as he was nearest to the door, clapping one hand before his open mouth and slowly backing away as if driven by some invisible steady pressure. His mother—in spite of the chief clerk's being there her hair was still undone and sticking up in all directions—first clasped her hands and looked at his father, then took two steps towards Gregor and fell on the floor among her outspread skirts, her face hidden on her breast. His father knotted his fist with a fierce expression on his face as if he meant to knock Gregor back into his room, then looked uncertainly round the living room, covered his eyes with his hands and wept till his great chest heaved.

Gregor did not go now into the living room, but leaned against the inside of the firmly shut wing of the door, so that only half his body was visible and his head above it bending sideways to look at the others. The light had meanwhile strength-ened; on the other side of the street one could see clearly a section of the endlessly long, dark gray building opposite—it was a hospital—abruptly punctuated by its row of regular windows; the rain was still falling, but only in large singly discernible and literally singly splashing drops. The breakfast dishes were set out on the table lavishly, for breakfast was the most important meal of the day to Gregor's father, who lingered it out for hours over various newspapers. Right opposite Gregor on the wall hung a photograph of himself on military service, as a lieutenant, hand on sword, a carefree smile on his face, inviting one to respect his uniform and military bearing. The door leading to the hall was open, and one could see that the front door stood open too, showing the landing beyond and the beginning of the stairs going down.

"Well," said Gregor, knowing perfectly that he was the only one who had re-tained any composure, "I'll put my clothes on at once, pack up my samples and start off. Will you only let me go? You see, sir, I'm not obstinate, and I'm willing to work; traveling is a hard life, but I couldn't live without it. Where are you going, sir? To the office? Yes? Will you give a true account of all this? One can be temporarily inca-pacitated, but that's just the moment for remembering former services and bearing in mind that later on, when the incapacity has been got over, one will certainly work with all the more industry and concentration. I'm loyally bound to serve the chief, you know that very well. Besides, I have to provide for my parents and my sister. I'm in great difficulties, but I'll get out of them again. Don't make things any worse for me than they are. Stand up for me in the firm. Travelers are not popular there, I know. People think they earn sacks of money and just have a good time. A prejudice there's no particular reason for revising. But you, sir, have a more comprehensive view of affairs than the rest of the staff, yes, let me tell you in confidence, a more comprehensive view than the chief himself, who, being the owner, lets his judgment easily be swayed against one of his employees. And you know very well that the traveler, who is never seen in the office almost the whole year round, can so easily fall a victim to gossip and ill luck and unfounded complaints, which he mostly knows nothing about, except when he comes back exhausted from his rounds, and only then suffers in person from their evil consequences, which he can no longer trace back to the original causes. Sir, sir, don't go away without a word to me to show that you think me in the right at least to some extent!"

But at Gregor's very first words the chief clerk had already backed away and only stared at him with parted lips over one twitching shoulder. And while Gregor was speaking he did not stand still one moment but stole away towards the door, without taking his eyes off Gregor, yet only an inch at a time, as if obeying some secret injunction to leave the room. He was already at the hall, and the suddenness with which he took his last step out of the living room would have made one believe he had burned the sole of his foot. Once in the hall he stretched his right arm before him towards the staircase, as if some supernatural power were waiting there to deliver him.

Gregor perceived that the chief clerk must on no account be allowed to go away in this frame of mind if his position in the firm were not to be endangered to the utmost. His parents did not understand this so well; they had convinced themselves in the course of years that Gregor was settled for life in this firm, and besides they were so occupied with their immediate troubles that all foresight had forsaken them. Yet Gregor had this foresight. The chief clerk must be detained, soothed, persuaded and finally won over; the whole future of Gregor and his family depended on it! If only his sister had been there! She was intelligent; she had begun to cry while Gregor was still lying quietly on his back. And no doubt the chief clerk, so partial to ladies, would have been guided by her; she could have shut the door of the flat and in the hall talked him out of his horror. But she was not there, and Gregor would have to handle the situation himself. And without remembering that he was still unaware what powers of movement he possessed, without even remembering that his words in all possibility, indeed in all likelihood, would again be unintelligible, he let go the wing of the door, pushed himself through the opening, started to walk towards the chief clerk, who was already ridiculously clinging with both hands to the railing on the landing; but immediately, as he was feeling for a support, he fell down with a little cry upon all his numerous legs. Hardly was he down when he experienced for the first time this morning a sense of physical comfort; his legs had firm ground under them; they were completely obedient, as he noted with joy; they even strove to carry him forward in whatever direction he chose; and he was inclined to believe that a final relief from all his sufferings was at hand. But in the same moment as he found himself on the floor, rocking with suppressed eagerness to move, not far from his mother, indeed just in front of her, she, who had seemed so completely crushed, sprang all at once to her feet, her arms and fingers outspread, cried: "Help, for God's sake, help!" bent her head down as if to see Gregor better, yet on the contrary kept backing senselessly away; had quite forgotten that the laden table stood behind her;

sat upon it hastily, as if in absence of mind, when she bumped into it; and seemed altogether unaware that the big coffee pot beside her was upset and pouring coffee in a flood over the carpet.

"Mother, Mother," said Gregor in a low voice, and looked up at her. The chief clerk, for the moment, had quite slipped from his mind; instead, he could not resist snapping his jaws together at the sight of the streaming coffee. That made his mother scream again, she fled from the table and fell into the arms of his father, who hastened to catch her. But Gregor had now no time to spare for his parents; the chief clerk was already on the stairs; with his chin on the banisters he was taking one last backward look. Gregor made a spring, to be as sure as possible of overtaking him; the chief clerk must have divined his intention, for he leaped down several steps and vanished; he was still yelling "Ugh!" and it echoed through the whole staircase.

Unfortunately, the flight of the chief clerk seemed completely to upset Gregor's father, who had remained relatively calm until now, for instead of running after the man himself, or at least not hindering Gregor in his pursuit, he seized in his right hand the walking stick which the chief clerk had left behind on a chair, together with a hat and greatcoat, snatched in his left hand a large newspaper from the table and began stamping his feet and flourishing the stick and the newspaper to drive Gregor back into his room. No entreaty of Gregor's availed, indeed no entreaty was even understood, however humbly he bent his head his father only stamped on the floor the more loudly. Behind his father his mother had torn open a window, despite the cold weather, and was leaning far out of it with her face in her hands. A strong draught set in from the street to the staircase, the window curtains blew in, the newspapers on the table fluttered, stray pages whisked over the floor. Pitilessly Gregor's father drove him back, hissing and crying "Shoo!" like a savage. But Gregor was quite unpracticed in walking backwards, it really was a slow business. If he only had a chance to turn round he could get back to his room at once, but he was afraid of exasperating his father by the slowness of such a rotation and at any moment the stick in his father's hand might hit him a fatal blow on the back or on the head. In the end, however, nothing else was left for him to do since to his horror he observed that in moving backwards he could not even control the direction he took; and so, keeping an anxious eye on his father all the time over his shoulder, he began to turn round as quickly as he could, which was in reality very slowly. Perhaps his father noted his good intentions, for he did not interfere except every now and then to help him in the manoeuvre from a distance with the point of the stick. If only he would have stopped making that unbearable hissing noise! It made Gregor quite lose his head. He had turned almost completely round when the hissing noise so distracted him that he even turned a little the wrong way again. But when at last his head was fortunately right in front of the doorway, it appeared that his body was too broad simply to get through the opening. His father, of course, in his present mood was far from thinking of such a thing as opening the other half of the door, to let Gregor have enough space. He had merely the fixed idea of driving Gregor back into his room as quickly as possible. He would never have suffered Gregor to make the circumstantial preparations for standing up on end and perhaps slipping his way through the door. Maybe he was now making more noise than ever to urge Gregor forward, as if no obstacle impeded him; to Gregor, anyhow, the noise in his rear sounded no longer like the voice of one single father; this was really no joke, and Gregor thrust himself—come what might—into the doorway. One side of his body rose up, he was tilted at an angle in the doorway, his flank was quite bruised, horrid blotches stained the white door, soon he was stuck fast and, left to himself, could not have moved at all, his legs on one side fluttered trembling to the air, those on the other were crushed painfully to the floor— when from behind his father gave him a strong push which was literally a deliverance and he flew far into the room, bleeding freely. The door was slammed behind him with the stick, and then at last there was silence.

2

Not until it was twilight did Gregor awake out of a deep sleep, more like a swoon than a sleep. He would certainly have waked up of his own accord not much later, for he felt himself sufficiently rested and well-slept, but it seemed to him as if a fleeting step and a cautious shutting of the door leading into the hall had aroused him. The electric lights in the street cast a pale sheen here and there on the ceiling and the upper surfaces of the furniture, but down below, where he lay, it was dark. Slowly, awkwardly trying out his feelers, which he now first learned to appreciate, he pushed his way to the door to see what had been happening there. His left side felt like one single long, unpleasant tense scar, and he had actually to limp on his two rows of legs. One little leg, moreover, had been severely damaged in the course of that morning's events—it was almost a miracle that only one had been damaged—and trailed uselessly behind him.

He had reached the door before he discovered what had really drawn him to it: the smell of food. For there stood a basin filled with fresh milk in which floated little sops of white bread. He could almost have laughed with joy, since he was now still hungrier than in the morning, and he dipped his head almost over the eyes straight into the milk. But soon in disappointment he withdrew it again; not only did he find it difficult to feed because of his tender left side—and he could only feed with the palpitating collaboration of his whole body—he did not like the milk either, although milk had been his favorite drink and that was certainly why his sister had set it there for him, indeed it was almost with repulsion that he turned away from the basin and crawled back to the middle of the room.

He could see through the crack of the door that the gas was turned on in the living room, but while usually at this time his father made a habit of reading the afternoon newspaper in a loud voice to his mother and occasionally to his sister as well, not a sound was now to be heard. Well, perhaps his father had recently given up this habit of reading aloud, which his sister had mentioned so often in conversation and in her letters. But there was the same silence all around, although the flat was certainly not empty of occupants. "What a quiet life our family has been leading," said Gregor to himself, and as he sat there motionless staring into the darkness he felt great pride in the fact that he had been able to provide such a life for his parents and sister in such a fine flat. But what if all the quiet, the comfort, the contentment were now to end in horror? To keep himself from being lost in such thoughts Gregor took refuge in movement and crawled up and down the room.

Once during the long evening one of the side doors was opened a little and quickly shut again, later the other side door too; someone had apparently wanted to come in and then thought better of it. Gregor now stationed himself immediately before the living room door, determined to persuade any hesitating visitor to come in or at least to discover who it might be; but the door was not opened again and he waited in vain. In the early morning, when the doors were locked, they had all wanted to come in, now that he had opened one door and the other had apparently been opened during the day, no one came in and even the keys were on the other side of the doors.

It was late at night before the gas went out in the living room, and Gregor could easily tell that his parents and his sister had all stayed awake until then, for he could clearly hear the three of them stealing away on tiptoe. No one was likely to visit him, not until the morning, that was certain; so he had plenty of time to meditate at his leisure on how he was to arrange his life afresh. But the lofty, empty room in which he had to lie flat on the floor filled him with an apprehension he could not account for, since it had been his very own room for the past five years—and with a half-unconscious action, not without a slight feeling of shame, he scuttled under the sofa, where he felt comfortable at once, although his back was a little cramped and he could not lift his head up, and his only regret was that his body was too broad to get the whole of it under the sofa.

He stayed there all night, spending the time partly in a light slumber, from which his hunger kept waking him up with a start, and partly in worrying and sketching vague hopes, which all led to the same conclusion, that he must lie low for the present and, by exercising patience, and the utmost consideration, help the family to bear the inconvenience he was bound to cause them in his present condition.

Very early in the morning, it was still almost night, Gregor had the chance to test the strength of his new resolutions, for his sister, nearly fully dressed, opened the door from the hall and peered in. She did not see him at once, yet when she caught sight of him under the sofa—well, he had to be somewhere, he couldn't have flown away, could he?—she was so startled that without being able to help it she slammed the door shut again. But as if regretting her behavior she opened the door again immediately and came in on tiptoe, as if she were visiting an invalid or even a stranger. Gregor had pushed his head forward to the very edge of the sofa and watched her. Would she notice that he had left the milk standing, and not for lack of hunger, and would she bring in some other kind of food more to his taste? If she did not do it of her own accord, he would rather starve than draw her attention to the fact, although he felt a wild impulse to dart out from under the sofa, throw himself at her feet and beg her for something to eat. But his sister at once noticed, with surprise, that the basin was still full, except for a little milk that had been spilt all around it, she lifted it immediately, not with her bare hands, true, but with a cloth and carried it away. Gregor was wildly curious to know what she would bring instead, and made various speculations about it. Yet what she actually did next, in the goodness of her heart, he could never have guessed at. To find out what he liked she brought him a whole selection of food, all set out on an old newspaper. There were old, half-decayed vegetables, bones from last night's supper covered with a white sauce that had thickened; some raisins and almonds; a piece of cheese that Gregor would have called uneatable two days ago; a dry roll of bread, a buttered roll, and a roll both buttered and salted. Besides all that, she set down again the same basin, into which she had poured some water, and which was apparently to be reserved for his exclusive use. And with fine tact, knowing that Gregor would not eat in her presence, she withdrew quickly and even turned the key, to let him understand that he could take his ease as much as he liked. Gregor's legs all whizzed towards the food. His wounds must have healed completely, moreover, for he felt no disability, which amazed him and made him reflect how more than a month ago he had cut one finger a little with a knife and had still suffered pain from the wound only the day before yesterday. Am I less sensitive now? he thought, and sucked greedily at the cheese, which above all the other edibles attracted him at once and strongly. One after another and with tears of satisfaction in his eyes he quickly devoured the cheese, the vegetables and the sauce; the fresh food, on the other hand, had no charms for him, he could not even stand the smell of it and actually dragged away to some little distance the things he could eat. He had long finished his meal and was only lying lazily on the same spot when his sister turned the key slowly as a sign for him to retreat. That roused him at once, although he was nearly asleep, and he hurried under the sofa again. But it took considerable self-control for him to stay under the sofa, even for the short time his sister was in the room, since the large meal had swollen his body somewhat and he was so cramped he could hardly breathe. Slight attacks of breathlessness afflicted him and his eyes were starting a little out of his head as he watched his unsuspecting sister sweeping together with a broom not only the remains of what he had eaten but even the things he had not touched, as if these were now of no use to anyone, and hastily shoveling it all into a bucket, which she covered with a wooden lid and carried away. Hardly had she turned her back when Gregor came from under the sofa and stretched and puffed himself out.

In this manner Gregor was fed, once in the early morning while his parents and the servant girl were still asleep, and a second time after they had all had their midday dinner, for then his parents took a short nap and the servant girl could be sent out on some errand or other by his sister. Not that they would have wanted him to starve, of course, but perhaps they could not have borne to know more about his feeding than from hearsay, perhaps too his sister wanted to spare them such little anxieties wherever possible, since they had quite enough to bear as it was.

Under what pretext the doctor and the locksmith had been got rid of on that first morning Gregor could not discover, for since what he had said was not understood by the others it never struck any of them, not even his sister, that he could understand what they said, and so whenever his sister came into his room he had to content himself with hearing her utter only a sigh now and then and an occasional appeal to the saints. Later on, when she had got a little used to the situation—of course she could never get completely used to it—she sometimes threw out a remark which was kindly meant or could be so interpreted. "Well, he liked his dinner today," she would say when Gregor had made a good clearance of his food; and when he had not eaten, which gradually happened more and more often, she would say almost sadly: "Everything's been left standing again."

But although Gregor could get no news directly, he overheard a lot from the neighboring rooms, and as soon as voices were audible, he would run to the door of the room concerned and press his whole body against it. In the first few days especially there was no conversation that did not refer to him somehow, even if only indirectly. For two whole days there were family consultations at every mealtime about what should be done; but also between meals the same subject was discussed, for there were always at least two members of the family at home, since no one wanted to be alone in the flat and to leave it quite empty was unthinkable. And on the very first of these days the household cook—it was not quite clear what and how much she knew of the situation—went down on her knees to his mother and begged leave to go, and when she departed, a quarter of an hour later, gave thanks for her dismissal with tears in her eyes as if for the greatest benefit that could have been conferred on her, and without any prompting swore a solemn oath that she would never say a single word to anyone about what had happened.

Now Gregor's sister had to cook too, helping her mother; true, the cooking did not amount to much, for they ate scarcely anything. Gregor was always hearing one of the family vainly urging another to eat and getting no answer but: "Thanks, I've had all I want," or something similar. Perhaps they drank nothing either. Time and again his sister kept asking his father if he wouldn't like some beer and offered kindly to go and fetch it herself, and when he made no answer suggested that she could ask the concierge to fetch it, so that he need feel no sense of obligation, but then a round "No" came from his father and no more was said about it.

In the course of that very first day Gregor's father explained the family's financial position and prospects to both his mother and his sister. Now and then he rose from the table to get some voucher or memorandum out of the small safe he had rescued from the collapse of his business five years earlier. One could hear him opening the complicated lock and rustling papers out and shutting it again. This statement made by his father was the first cheerful information Gregor had heard since his imprisonment. He had been of the opinion that nothing at all was left over from his father's business, at least his father had never said anything to the contrary, and of course he had not asked him directly. At the time Gregor's sole desire was to do his utmost to help the family to forget as soon as possible the catastrophe which had overwhelmed the business and thrown them all into a state of complete despair. And so he had set to work with unusual ardor and almost overnight had become a commercial traveler instead of a little clerk, with of course much greater chances of earning money, and his success was immediately translated into good round coin which he could lay on the table for his amazed and happy family. These had been fine times, and they had never recurred, at least not with the same sense of glory, although later on Gregor had earned so much money that he was able to meet the expenses of the whole household and did so. They had simply got used to it, both the family and Gregor; the money was gratefully accepted and gladly given, but there was no special uprush of warm feeling. With his sister alone had he remained intimate, and it was a secret plan of his that she, who loved music, unlike himself, and could play movingly on the violin, should be sent next year to study at the Conservatorium, despite the great expense that would entail, which must be made up in some other way. During his brief visits home the Conservatorium was often mentioned in the talks he had with his sister, but always merely as a beautiful dream which could never come true, and his parents discouraged even these innocent references to it; yet Gregor had made up his mind firmly about it and meant to announce the fact with due solemnity on Christmas Day.

Such were the thoughts, completely futile in his present condition, that went through his head as he stood clinging upright to the door and listening. Sometimes out of sheer weariness he had to give up listening and let his head fall negligently against the door, but he always had to pull himself together again at once, for even the slight sound his head made was audible next door and brought all conversation to a stop. "What can he be doing now?" his father would say after a while, obviously turning towards the door, and only then would the interrupted conversation gradually be set going again.

Gregor was now informed as amply as he could wish—for his father tended to repeat himself in his explanations, partly because it was a long time since he had handled such matters and partly because his mother could not always grasp things at once—that a certain amount of investments, a very small amount it was true, had survived the wreck of their fortunes and had even increased a little because the dividends had not been touched meanwhile. And besides that, the money Gregor brought home every month—he had kept only a few dollars for himself—had never been quite used up and now amounted to a small capital sum. Behind the door Gregor nodded his head eagerly, rejoiced at this evidence of unexpected thrift and foresight. True, he could really have paid off some more of his father's debts to the chief with his extra money, and so brought much nearer the day on which he could quit his job, but doubtless it was better the way his father had arranged it.

Yet this capital was by no means sufficient to let the family live on the interest of it; for one year, perhaps, or at the most two, they could live on the principal, that was all. It was simply a sum that ought not to be touched and should be kept for a rainy day; money for living expenses would have to be earned. Now his father was still hale enough but an old man, and he had done no work for the past five years and could not be expected to do much; during these five years, the first years of leisure in his laborious though unsuccessful life, he had grown rather fat and become sluggish. And Gregor's old mother, how was she to earn a living with her asthma, which troubled her even when she walked through the flat and kept her lying on a sofa every other day panting for breath beside an open window? And was his sister to earn her bread, she who was still a child of seventeen and whose life hitherto had been so pleasant, consisting as it did in dressing herself nicely, sleeping long, helping in the housekeeping, going out to a few modest entertainments and above all playing the violin? At first whenever the need for earning money was mentioned Gregor let go his hold on the door and threw himself down on the cool leather sofa beside it, he felt so hot with shame and grief.

Often he just lay there the long nights through without sleeping at all, scrabbling for hours on the leather. Or he nerved himself to the great effort of pushing an armchair to the window, then crawled up over the window sill and, braced against the chair, leaned against the window panes, obviously in some recollection of the sense of freedom that looking out of a window always used to give him. For in reality day by day things that were even a little way off were growing dimmer to his sight; the hospital across the street, which he used to execrate for being all too often before his eyes, was now quite beyond his range of vision, and if he had not known that he lived in Charlotte Street, a quiet street but still a city street, he might have believed that his window gave on a desert waste where gray sky and gray land blended indistinguishably into each other. His quick-witted sister only needed to observe twice that the armchair stood by the window; after that whenever she had tidied the room she always pushed the chair back to the same place at the window and even left the inner casements open.

If he could have spoken to her and thanked her for all she had to do for him, he could have borne her ministrations better; as it was, they oppressed him. She certainly tried to make as light as possible of whatever was disagreeable in her task, and as time went on she succeeded, of course, more and more, but time brought more enlightenment to Gregor too. The very way she came in distressed him. Hardly was she in the room when she rushed to the window, without even taking time to shut the door, careful as she was usually to shield the sight of Gregor's room from the others, and as if she were almost suffocating tore the casements open with hasty fingers, standing then in the open draught for a while even in the bitterest cold and drawing deep breaths. This noisy scurry of hers upset Gregor twice a day; he would crouch trembling under the sofa all the time, knowing quite well that she would certainly have spared him such a disturbance had she found it at all possible to stay in his presence without opening a window.

On one occasion, about a month after Gregor's metamorphosis, when there was surely no reason for her to be still startled at his appearance, she came a little earlier than usual and found him gazing out of the window, quite motionless, and thus well placed to look like a bogey. Gregor would not have been surprised had she not come in at all, for she could not immediately open the window while he was there, but not only did she retreat, she jumped back as if in alarm and banged the door shut; a stranger might well have thought that he had been lying in wait for her there meaning to bite her. Of course he hid himself under the sofa at once, but he had to wait until midday before she came again, and she seemed more ill at ease than usual. This made him realize how repulsive the sight of him still was to her, and that it was bound to go on being repulsive, and what an effort it must cost her not to run away even from the sight of the small portion of his body that stuck out from under the sofa. In order to spare her that, therefore, one day he carried a sheet on his back to the sofa—it cost him four hours' labor—and arranged it there in such a way as to hide him completely, so that even if she were to bend down she could not see him. Had she considered the sheet unnecessary, she would certainly have stripped it off the sofa again, for it was clear enough that this curtaining and confining of himself was not likely to conduce Gregor's comfort, but she left it where it was, and Gregor even fancied that he caught a thankful glance from her eye when he lifted the sheet carefully a very little with his head to see how she was taking the new arrangement.

For the first fortnight his parents could not bring themselves to the point of entering his room, and he often heard them expressing their appreciation of his sister's activities, whereas formerly they had frequently scolded her for being as they thought a somewhat useless daughter. But now, both of them often waited outside the door, his father and his mother, while his sister tidied his room, and as soon as she came out she had to tell them exactly how things were in the room, what Gregor had eaten, how he had conducted himself this time and whether there was not perhaps some slight improvement in his condition. His mother, moreover, began relatively soon to want to visit him, but his father and sister dissuaded her at first with arguments which Gregor listened to very attentively and altogether approved. Later, however, she had to be held back by main force, and when she cried out: "Do let me in to Gregor, he is my unfortunate son! Can't you understand that I must go to him?" Gregor thought that it might be well to have her come in, not every day, of course, but perhaps once a week; she understood things, after all, much better than his sister, who was only a child despite the efforts she was making and had perhaps taken on so difficult a task merely out of childish thoughtlessness.

Gregor's desire to see his mother was soon fulfilled. During the daytime he did not want to show himself at the window, out of consideration for his parents, but he could not crawl very far around the few square yards of floor space he had, nor could he bear lying quietly at rest all during the night, while he was fast losing any interest he had ever taken in food, so that for mere recreation he had formed the habit of crawling crisscross over the walls and ceiling. He especially enjoyed hanging suspended from the ceiling; it was much better than lying on the floor; one could breathe more freely; one's body swung and rocked lightly; and in the almost blissful absorption induced by this suspension it could happen to his own surprise that he let go and fell plump on the floor. Yet he now had his body much better under control than formerly, and even such a big fall did him no harm. His sister at once remarked the new distraction Gregor had found for himself—he left traces behind him of the sticky stuff on his soles wherever he crawled—and she got the idea in her head of giving him as wide a field as possible to crawl in and of removing the pieces of furniture that hindered him, above all the chest of drawers and the writing desk. But that was more than she could manage all by herself; she did not dare ask her father to help her; and as for the servant girl, a young creature of sixteen who had had the courage to stay on after the cook's departure, she could not be asked to help, for she had begged as an especial favor that she might keep the kitchen door locked and open it only on a definite summons; so there was nothing left but to apply to her mother at an hour when her father was out. And the old lady did come, with exclamations of joyful eagerness, which, however, died away at the door of Gregor's room. Gregor's sister, of course, went in first, to see that everything was in order before letting his mother enter. In great haste Gregor pulled the sheet lower and rucked it more in folds so that it really looked as if it had been thrown accidentally over the sofa. And this time he did not peer out from under it; he renounced the pleasure of seeing his mother on this occasion and was only glad that she had come at all. "Come in, he's out of sight," said his sister, obviously leading her mother in by the hand. Gregor could now hear the two women struggling to shift the heavy old chest from its place, and his sister claiming the greater part of the labor for herself, without listening to the admonitions of her mother who feared she might overstrain herself. It took a long time. After at least a quarter of an hour's tugging his mother objected that the chest had better be left where it was, for in the first place it was too heavy and could never be got out before his father came home, and standing in the middle of the room like that it would only hamper Gregor's movements, while in the second place it was not at all certain that removing the furniture would be doing a service to Gregor. She was inclined to think to the contrary; the sight of the naked walls made her own heart heavy, and why shouldn't Gregor have the same feeling, considering that he had been used to his furniture for so long and might feel forlorn without it. "And doesn't it look," she concluded in a low voice—in fact she had been almost whispering all the time as if to avoid letting Gregor, whose exact whereabouts she did not know, hear even the tones of her voice, for she was convinced that he could not understand her words—"doesn't it look as if we were showing him, by taking away his furniture, that we have given up hope of his ever getting better and are just leaving him coldly to himself? I think it would be best to keep his room exactly as it has always been, so that when he comes back to us he will find everything unchanged and be able all the more easily to forget what has happened in between."

On hearing these words from his mother Gregor realized that the lack of all direct human speech for the past two months together with the monotony of family life must have confused his mind, otherwise he could not account for the fact that he had quite earnestly looked forward to having his room emptied of furnishing. Did he really want his warm room, so comfortably fitted with old family furniture, to be turned into a naked den in which he would certainly be able to crawl unhampered in all directions but at the price of shedding simultaneously all recollection of his human background? He had indeed been so near the brink of forgetfulness that only the voice of his mother, which he had not heard for so long, had drawn him back from it. Nothing should be taken out of his room; everything must stay as it was; he could not dispense with the good influence of the furniture on his state of mind; and even if the furniture did hamper him in his senseless crawling round and round, that was no drawback but a great advantage.

Unfortunately his sister was of the contrary opinion; she had grown accustomed, and not without reason, to consider herself an expert in Gregor's affairs as against her parents, and so her mother's advice was now enough to make her determined on the removal not only of the chest and the writing desk, which had been her first intention, but of all the furniture except the indispensable sofa. This determination was not, of course, merely the outcome of childish recalcitrance and of the self-confidence she had recently developed so unexpectedly and at such cost; she had in fact perceived that Gregor needed a lot of space to crawl about in, while on the other hand he never used the furniture at all, so far as could be seen. Another factor might have been also the enthusiastic temperament of an adolescent girl, which seeks to indulge itself on every opportunity and which now tempted Grete to exaggerate the horror of her brother's circumstances in order that she might do all the more for him. In a room where Gregor lorded it all alone over empty walls no one save herself was likely ever to set foot.

And so she was not to be moved from her resolve by her mother who seemed moreover to be ill at ease in Gregor's room and therefore unsure of herself, was soon reduced to silence and helped her daughter as best she could to push the chest outside. Now, Gregor could do without the chest, if need be, but the writing desk he must retain. As soon as the two women had got the chest out of his room, groaning as they pushed it, Gregor stuck his head out from under the sofa to see how he might intervene as kindly and cautiously as possible. But as bad luck would have it, his mother was the first to return, leaving Grete clasping the chest in the room next door where she was trying to shift it all by herself, without of course moving it from the spot. His mother however was not accustomed to the sight of him, it might sicken her and so in alarm Gregor backed quickly to the other end of the sofa, yet could not prevent the sheet from swaying a little in front. That was enough to put her on the alert. She paused, stood still for a moment and then went back to Grete.

Although Gregor kept reassuring himself that nothing out of the way was happening, but only a few bits of furniture were being changed round, he soon had to admit that all this trotting to and fro of the two women, their little ejaculations and the scraping of furniture along the floor affected him like a vast disturbance coming from all sides at once, and however much he tucked in his head and legs and cowered to the very floor he was bound to confess that he would not be able to stand it for long. They were clearing his room out; taking away everything he loved; the chest in which he kept his fret saw and other tools was already dragged off; they were now loosening the writing desk which had almost sunk into the floor, the desk at which he had done all his homework when he was at the commercial academy, at the grammar school before that, and, yes, even at the primary school—he had no more time to waste in weighing the good intentions of the two women, whose existence he had by now almost forgotten, for they were so exhausted that they were laboring in silence and nothing could be heard but the heavy scuffling of their feet.

And so he rushed out—the women were just leaning against the writing desk in the next room to give themselves a breather—and four times changed his direction, since he really did not know what to rescue first, then on the wall opposite, which was already otherwise cleared, he was struck by the picture of the lady muffled in so much fur and quickly crawled up to it and pressed himself to the glass, which was a good surface to hold on to and comforted his hot belly. This picture at least, which was entirely hidden beneath him, was going to be removed by nobody. He turned his head towards the door of the living room so as to observe the women when they came back.

They had not allowed themselves much of a rest and were already coming; Grete had twined her arm round her mother and was almost supporting her. "Well, what shall we take now?" said Grete, looking round. Her eyes met Gregor's from the wall. She kept her composure, presumably because of her mother, bent her head down to her mother, to keep her from looking up, and said, although in a fluttering, unpremeditated voice: "Come, hadn't we better go back to the living room for a moment?" Her intentions were clear enough to Gregor, she wanted to bestow her mother in safety and then chase him down from the wall. Well, just let her try it! He clung to his picture and would not give it up. He would rather fly in Grete's face.

But Grete's words had succeeded in disquieting her mother, who took a step to one side, caught sight of the huge brown mass on the flowered wallpaper, and before she was really conscious that what she saw was Gregor screamed in a loud, hoarse voice: "Oh God, oh God!" fell with outspread arms over the sofa as if giving up and did not move. "Gregor!" cried his sister, shaking her fist and glaring at him. This was the first time she had directly addressed him since his metamorphosis. She ran into the next room for some aromatic essence with which to rouse her mother from her fainting fit. Gregor wanted to help too—there was still time to rescue the picture—but he was stuck fast to the glass and had to tear himself loose; he then ran after his sister into the next room as if he could advise her, as he used to do; but then had to stand helplessly behind her; she meanwhile searched among various small bottles and when she turned round started in alarm at the sight of him; one bottle fell on the floor and broke; a splinter of glass cut Gregor's face and some kind of corrosive medicine splashed him; without pausing a moment longer Grete gathered up all the bottles she could carry and ran to her mother with them; she banged the door shut with her foot. Gregor was now cut off from his mother, who was perhaps nearly dying because of him; he dared not open the door for fear of frightening away his sister, who had to stay with her mother; there was nothing he could do but wait; and harassed by self-reproach and worry he began now to crawl to and fro, over everything, walls, furniture and ceiling, and finally in his despair, when the whole room seemed to be reeling round him, fell down on to the middle of the big table.

A little while elapsed, Gregor was still lying there feebly and all around was quiet, perhaps that was a good omen. Then the doorbell rang. The servant girl was of course locked in her kitchen, and Grete would have to open the door. It was his father. "What's been happening?" were his first words; Grete's face must have told him everything. Grete answered in a muffled voice, apparently hiding her head on his breast: "Mother has been fainting, but she's better now. Gregor's broken loose." "Just what I expected," said his father, "just what I've been telling you, but you women would never listen." It was clear to Gregor that his father had taken the worst interpretation of Grete's all too brief statement and was assuming that Gregor had been guilty of some violent act. Therefore Gregor must now try to propitiate his father, since he had neither time nor means for an explanation. And so he fled to the door of his own room and crouched against it, to let his father see as soon as he came in from the hall that his son had the good intention of getting back into his room immediately and that it was not necessary to drive him there, but that if only the door were opened he would disappear at once.

Yet his father was not in the mood to perceive such fine distinctions. "Ah!" he cried as soon as he appeared, in a tone which sounded at once angry and exultant. Gregor drew his head back from the door and lifted it to look at his father. Truly, this was not the father he had imagined to himself; admittedly he had been too absorbed of late in his new recreation of crawling over the ceiling to take the same interest as before in what was happening elsewhere in the flat, and he ought really to be prepared for some changes. And yet, and yet, could that be his father? The man who used to lie wearily sunk in bed whenever Gregor set out on a business journey; who welcomed him back of an evening lying in a long chair in a dressing gown; who could not really rise to his feet but only lifted his arms in greeting, and on the rare occasions when he did go out with his family, on one or two Sundays a year and on high holidays, walked between Gregor and his mother, who were slow walkers anyhow, even more slowly than they did, muffled in his old greatcoat, shuffling laboriously forward with the help of his crook-handled stick which he set down most cautiously at every step and, whenever he wanted to say anything, nearly always came to a full stop and gathered his escort around him? Now he was standing there in fine shape; dressed in a smart blue uniform with gold buttons, such as bank messengers wear; his strong double chin bulged over the stiff high collar of his jacket; from under his bushy eyebrows his black eyes darted fresh and penetrating glances; his onetime tangled white hair had been combed flat on either side of a shining and carefully exact parting. He pitched his cap, which bore a gold monogram, probably the badge of some bank, in a wide sweep across the whole room on to a sofa and with the tail-ends of his jacket thrown back, his hands in his trouser pockets, advanced with a grim visage towards Gregor. Likely enough he did not himself know what he meant to do; at any rate he lifted his feet uncommonly high, and Gregor was dumbfounded at the enormous size of his shoe soles. But Gregor could not risk standing up to him, aware as he had been from the very first day of his new life that his father believed only the severest measures suitable for dealing with him. And so he ran before his father, stopping when he stopped and scuttling forward again when his father made any kind of move. In this way they circled the room several times without anything decisive happening; indeed the whole operation did not even look like a pursuit because it was carried out so slowly. And so Gregor did not leave the floor, for he feared that his father might take as a piece of peculiar wickedness any excursion of his over the walls or the ceiling. All the same, he could not stay this course much longer, for while his father took one step he had to carry out a whole series of movements. He was already beginning to feel breathless, just as in his former life his lungs had not been very dependable. As he was staggering along, trying to concentrate his energy on running, hardly keeping his eyes open; in his dazed state never even thinking of any other escape than simply going forward; and having almost forgotten that the walls were free to him, which in this room were well provided with finely carved pieces of furniture full of knobs and crevices—suddenly something lightly flung landed close behind him and rolled before him. It was an apple; a second apple followed immediately; Gregor came to a stop in alarm; there was no point in running on, for his father was determined to bombard him. He had filled his pockets with fruit from the dish on the sideboard and now shying apple after apple, without taking particularly good aim for the moment. The small red apples rolled about the floor as if magnetized and cannoned into each other. An apple thrown without much force grazed Gregor's back and glanced off harmlessly. But another following immediately landed right on his back and sank in; Gregor wanted to drag himself forward, as if this startling, incredible pain could be left behind him: but he felt as if nailed to the spot and flattened himself out in a complete derangement of all his senses. With his last conscious look he saw the door of his room being torn open and his mother rushing out ahead of his screaming sister, in her underbodice, for her daughter had loosened her clothing to let her breathe more freely and recover from her swoon, he saw his mother rushing towards his father, leaving one after another behind her on the floor her loosened petticoats, stumbling over her petticoats straight to his father and embracing him, in complete union with him—but here Gregor's sight began to fail—with her hands clasped round his father's neck as she begged for her son's life.

3

The serious injury done to Gregor, which disabled him for more than a month—the apple went on sticking in his body as a visible reminder, since no one ventured to remove it—seemed to have made even his father recollect that Gregor was a member of the family, despite his present unfortunate and repulsive shape, and ought not to be treated as an enemy, that, on the contrary, family duty required the suppression of disgust and the exercise of patience, nothing but patience.

And although his injury had impaired, probably for ever, his power of movement, and for the time being it took him long, long minutes to creep across his room like an old invalid—there was no question now of crawling up the wall—yet in his own opinion he was sufficiently compensated for this worsening of his condition by the fact that towards evening the living-room door, which he used to watch intently for an hour or two beforehand, was always thrown open, so that lying in the darkness of his room, invisible to the family, he could see them all at the lamp-lit table and listen to their talk, by general consent as it were, very different from his earlier eavesdropping.

True, their intercourse lacked the lively character of former times, which he had always called to mind with a certain wistfulness in the small hotel bedrooms where he had been wont to throw himself down, tired out, on damp bedding. They were now mostly very silent. Soon after supper his father would fall asleep in his armchair; his mother and sister would admonish each other to be silent; his mother, bending low over the lamp, stitched at fine sewing for an underwear firm; his sister, who had taken a job as a salesgirl, was learning shorthand and French in the evenings on the chance of bettering herself. Sometimes his father woke up, and as if quite unaware that he had been sleeping said to his mother: "What a lot of sewing you're doing today!" and at once fell asleep again, while the two women exchanged a tired smile.

With a kind of mulishness his father persisted in keeping his uniform on even in the house; his dressing gown hung uselessly on its peg and he slept fully dressed where he sat, as if he were ready for service at any moment and even here only at the beck and call of his superior. As a result, his uniform, which was not brand-new to start with, began to look dirty, despite all the loving care of the mother and sister to keep it clean, and Gregor often spent whole evenings gazing at the many greasy spots on the garment, gleaming with gold buttons always in a high state of polish, in which the old man sat sleeping in extreme discomfort and yet quite peacefully.

As soon as the clock struck ten his mother tried to rouse his father with gentle words and to persuade him after that to get into bed, for sitting there he could not have a proper sleep and that was what he needed most since he had to go to duty at six. But with the mulishness that had obsessed him since he became a bank messenger he always insisted on staying longer at the table, although he regularly fell asleep again and in the end only with the greatest trouble could be got out of his armchair and into his bed. However insistently Gregor's mother and sister kept urging him with gentle reminders, he would go on slowly shaking his head for a quarter of an hour keeping his eyes shut, and refuse to get to his feet. The mother plucked at his sleeve, whispering endearments in his ear, the sister left her lessons to come to her mother's help, but Gregor's father was not to be caught. He would only sink down deeper in his chair. Not until the two women hoisted him up by the armpits did he open his eyes and look at them both, one after the other, usually with the remark: "This is a life. This is the peace and quiet of my old age." And leaning on the two of them he would heave himself up, with difficulty, as if he were a great burden to himself, suffer them to lead him as far as the door and then wave them off and go on alone while the mother abandoned her needlework and the sister her pen in order to run after him and help him farther.

Who could find time, in this overworked and tired-out family, to bother about Gregor more than was absolutely needful? The household was reduced more and more; the servant girl was turned off; a gigantic bony charwoman with white hair flying round her head came in morning and evening to do the rough work; everything else was done by Gregor's mother, as well as great piles of sewing. Even various family ornaments, which his mother and sister used to wear with pride at parties and celebrations, had to be sold, as Gregor discovered of an evening from hearing them all discuss the prices obtained. But what they lamented most was the fact that they could not leave the flat which was much too big for their present circumstances, because they could not think of any way to shift Gregor. Yet Gregor saw well enough that consideration for him was not the main difficulty preventing the removal, for they could have easily shifted him in some suitable box with a few air holes in it; what really kept them from moving into another flat was rather their own complete hopelessness and the belief that they had been singled out for a misfortune such as had never happened to any of their relations or acquaintances. They fulfilled to the uttermost all that the world demands of poor people, the father fetched breakfast for the small clerks in the bank, the mother devoted her energy to making underwear for strangers, the sister trotted to and fro behind the counter at the behest of customers, but more than this they had not the strength to do. And the wound in Gregor's back began to nag at him afresh when his mother and sister, after getting his father into bed, came back again, left their work lying, drew close to each other and sat cheek by cheek; when his mother, pointing towards his room, said: "Shut that door now, Grete," and he was left again in darkness, while next door the women mingled their tears or perhaps sat dry-eyed staring at the table.

Gregor hardly slept at all by night or by day. He was often haunted by the idea that next time the door opened he would take the family's affairs in hand again just as he used to do; once more, after this long interval, there appeared in his thoughts the figures of the chief and the chief clerk, the commercial travelers and the apprentices, the porter who was so dull-witted, two or three friends in other firms, a chambermaid in one of the rural hotels, a sweet and fleeting memory, a cashier in a milliner's shop, whom he had wooed earnestly but too slowly—they all appeared, together with strangers or people he had quite forgotten, but instead of helping him and his family they were one and all unapproachable and he was glad when they vanished. At other times he would not be in the mood to bother about his family, he was only filled with rage at the way they were neglecting him, and although he had no clear idea of what he might care to eat he would make plans for getting into the larder to take the food that was after all his due, even if he were not hungry. His sister no longer took thought to bring him what might especially please him, but in the morning and at noon before she went to business hurriedly pushed into his room with her foot any food that was available, and in the evening cleared it out again with one sweep of the broom, heedless of whether it had been merely tasted, or—as most frequently happened—left untouched. The cleaning of his room, which she now did always in the evenings, could not have been more hastily done. Streaks of dirt stretched along the walls, here and there lay balls of dust and filth. At first Gregor used to station himself in some particularly filthy corner when his sister arrived, in order to reproach her with it, so to speak. But he could have sat there for weeks without getting her to make any improvements; she could see the dirt as well as he did, but she had simply made up her mind to leave it alone. And yet, with a touchiness that was new to her, which seemed anyhow to have infected the whole family, she jealously guarded her claim to be the sole caretaker of Gregor's room. His mother once subjected his room to a thorough cleaning, which was achieved only by means of several buckets of water—all this dampness of course upset Gregor too and he lay widespread, sulky and motionless on the sofa—but she was well punished for it. Hardly had his sister noticed the changed aspect of his room than she rushed in high dudgeon into the living room and, despite the imploringly raised hands of her mother, burst into a storm of weeping, while her parents—her father had of course been startled out of his chair—looked on at first in helpless amazement; then they too began to go into action; the father reproached the mother on his right for not having left the cleaning of Gregor's room to his sister; shrieked at the sister on his left that never again was she to be allowed to clean Gregor's room; while the mother tried to pull the father into his bedroom, since he was beyond himself with agitation; the sister, shaken with sobs, then beat upon the table with her small fists; and Gregor hissed loudly with rage because not one of them thought of shutting the door to spare him such a spectacle and so much noise.

Still, even if the sister, exhausted by her daily work, had grown tired of looking after Gregor as she did formerly, there was no need for his mother's intervention or for Gregor's being neglected at all. The charwoman was there. This old widow, whose strong bony frame had enabled her to survive the worst a long life could offer, by no means recoiled from Gregor. Without being in the least curious she had once by chance opened the door of his room and at the sight of Gregor, who, taken by surprise, began to rush to and fro although no one was chasing him, merely stood there with her arms folded. From that time she never failed to open his door a little for a moment, morning and evening, to have a look at him. At first she even used to call him to her, with words which apparently she took to be friendly, such as: "Come along, then, you old dung beetle!" or "Look at the old dung beetle, then!" To such allocutions Gregor made no answer, but stayed motionless where he was, as if the door had never been opened. Instead of being allowed to disturb him so senselessly whenever the whim took her, she should rather have been ordered to clean out his room daily, that charwoman! Once, early in the morning—heavy rain was lashing on the windowpanes, perhaps a sign that spring was on the way—Gregor was so exasperated when she began addressing him again that he ran at her, as if to attack her, although slowly and feebly enough. But the charwoman instead of showing fright merely lifted high a chair that happened to be beside the door, and as she stood there with her mouth wide open it was clear that she meant to shut it only when she brought the chair down on Gregor's back. "So you're not coming any nearer?" she asked, as Gregor turned away again, and quietly put the chair back into the corner.

Gregor was now eating hardly anything. Only when he happened to pass the food laid out for him did he take a bit of something in his mouth as a pastime, kept it there for an hour at a time and usually spat it out again. At first he thought it was chagrin over the state of his room that prevented him from eating, yet he soon got used to the various changes in his room. It had become a habit in the family to push into his room things there was no room for elsewhere, and there were plenty of these now, since one of the rooms had been let to three lodgers. These serious gentlemen —all three of them with full beards, as Gregor once observed through a crack in the door—had a passion for order, not only in their own room but, since they were now members of the household, in all its arrangements, especially in the kitchen. Superfluous, not to say dirty, objects they could not bear. Besides, they had brought with them most of the furnishings they needed. For this reason many things could be dispensed with that it was no use trying to sell but that should not be thrown away either. All of them found their way into Gregor's room. The ash can likewise and the kitchen garbage can. Anything that was not needed for the moment was simply flung into Gregor's room by the charwoman, who did everything in a hurry; fortunately Gregor usually saw only the object, whatever it was, and the hand that held it. Perhaps she intended to take the things away again as time and opportunity offered, or to collect them until she could throw them all out in a heap, but in fact they just lay wherever she happened to throw them, except when Gregor pushed his way through the junk heap and shifted it somewhat, at first out of necessity, because he had not room enough to crawl, but later with increasing enjoyment, although after such excursions, being sad and weary to death, he would lie motionless for hours. And since the lodgers often ate their supper at home in the common living room, the living-room door stayed shut many an evening, yet Gregor reconciled himself quite easily to the shutting of the door, for often enough on evenings when it was opened he had disregarded it entirely and lain in the darkest corner of his room, quite unnoticed by the family. But on one occasion the charwoman left the door open a little and it stayed ajar even when the lodgers came in for supper and the lamp was lit. They set themselves at the top end of the table where formerly Gregor and his father and mother had eaten their meals, unfolded their napkins and took knife and fork in hand. At once his mother appeared in the other doorway with a dish of meat and close behind her his sister with a dish of potatoes piled high. The food steamed with a thick vapor. The lodgers bent over the food set before them as if to scrutinize it before eating, in fact the man in the middle, who seemed to pass for an authority with the other two, cut a piece of meat as it lay on the dish, obviously to discover if it were tender or should be sent back to the kitchen. He showed satisfaction, and Gregor's mother and sister, who had been watching anxiously, breathed freely and began to smile.

The family itself took its meals in the kitchen. Nonetheless, Gregor's father came into the living room before going into the kitchen and with one prolonged bow, cap in hand, made a round of the table. The lodgers all stood up and murmured something in their beards. When they were alone again they ate their food in almost complete silence. It seemed remarkable to Gregor that among the various noises coming from the table he could always distinguish the sound of their masticating teeth, as if this were a sign to Gregor that one needed teeth in order to eat, and that with toothless jaws even of the finest make one could do nothing. "I'm hungry enough," said Gregor sadly to himself, "But not for that kind of food. How these lodgers are stuffing themselves, and here am I dying of starvation!"

On that very evening—during the whole of his time there Gregor could not remember ever having heard the violin—the sound of violin-playing came from the kitchen. The lodgers had already finished their supper, the one in the middle had brought out a newspaper and given the other two a page apiece, and now they were leaning back at ease reading and smoking. When the violin began to play they pricked up their ears, got to their feet, and went on tiptoe to the hall door where they stood huddled together. Their movements must have been heard in the kitchen, for Gregor's father called out: "Is the violin-playing disturbing you, gentlemen? It can be stopped at once." "On the contrary," said the middle lodger, "could not Fräulein Samsa come and play in this room, beside us, where it is much more convenient and comfortable?" "Oh certainly," cried Gregor's father, as if he were the violin-player. The lodgers came back into the living room and waited. Presently Gregor's father arrived with the music stand, his mother carrying the music and his sister with the violin. His sister quietly made everything ready to start playing; his parents, who had never let rooms before and so had an exaggerated idea of the courtesy due to lodgers, did not venture to sit down on their own chairs; his father leaned against the door, the right hand thrust between two buttons of his livery coat, which was formally buttoned up; but his mother was offered a chair by one of the lodgers and, since she left the chair just where he had happened to put it, sat down in a corner to one side.

Gregor's sister began to play; the father and mother, from either side, intently watched the movements of her hands. Gregor, attracted by the playing, ventured to move forward a little until his head was actually inside the living room. He felt hardly any surprise at his growing lack of consideration for the others; there had been a time when he prided himself on being considerate. And yet just on this occasion he had more reason than ever to hide himself, since owing to the amount of dust which lay thick in his room and rose into the air at the slightest movement, he too was covered with dust; fluff and hair and remnants of food trailed with him, caught on his back and along his sides; his indifference to everything was much too great for him to turn on his back and scrape himself clean on the carpet, as once he had done several times a day. And in spite of his condition, no shame deterred him from advancing a little over the spotless floor of the living room.

To be sure, no one was aware of him. The family was entirely absorbed in the violin-playing; the lodgers, however, who first of all had stationed themselves, hands in pockets, much too close behind the music stand so that they could all have read the music, which must have bothered his sister, had soon retreated to the window, half-whispering with downbent heads, and stayed there while his father turned an anxious eye on them. Indeed, they were making it more than obvious that they had been disappointed in their expectation of hearing good or enjoyable violin-playing, that they had had more than enough of the performance and only out of courtesy suffered a continued disturbance of their peace. From the way they all kept blowing the smoke of their cigars high in the air through nose and mouth one could divine their irritation. And yet Gregor's sister was playing so beautifully. Her face leaned sideways, intently and sadly her eyes followed the notes of music. Gregor crawled a little farther forward and lowered his head to the ground so that it might be possible for his eyes to meet hers. Was he an animal, that music had such an effect upon him? He felt as if the way were opening before him to the unknown nourishment he craved. He was determined to push forward till he reached his sister, to pull at her skirt and so let her know that she was to come into his room with her violin, for no one here appreciated her playing as he would appreciate it. He would never let her out of his room, at least, not so long as he lived; his frightful appearance would become, for the first time, useful to him; he would watch all the doors of his room at once and spit at intruders; but his sister should need no constraint, she should stay with him of her own free will; she should sit beside him on the sofa, bend down her ear to him and hear him confide that he had had the firm intention of sending her to the Conservatorium, and that, but for his mishap, last Christmas—surely Christmas was long past?—he would have announced it to everybody without allowing a single objection. After this confession his sister would be so touched that she would burst into tears, and Gregor would then raise himself to her shoulder and kiss her on the neck, which, now that she went to business, she kept free of any ribbon or collar.

"Mr. Samsa!" cried the middle lodger, to Gregor's father, and pointed, without wasting any more words, at Gregor, now working himself slowly forwards. The violin fell silent, the middle lodger first smiled to his friends with a shake of the head and then looked at Gregor again. Instead of driving Gregor out, his father seemed to think it more needful to begin by soothing down the lodgers, although they were not at all agitated and apparently found Gregor more entertaining than the violin-playing. He hurried toward them and, spreading out his arms, tried to urge them back into their own room and at the same time to block their view of Gregor. They now began to be really a little angry, one could not tell whether because of the old man's behavior or because it had just dawned on them that all unwittingly they had such a neighbor as Gregor next door. They demanded explanations of his father, they waved their arms like him, tugged uneasily at their beards, and only with reluctance backed towards their room. Meanwhile Gregor's sister, who stood there as if lost when her playing was so abruptly broken off, came to life again, pulled herself together all at once after standing for a while holding violin and bow in nervelessly hanging hands and staring at her music, pushed her violin into the lap of her mother, who was still sitting in her chair fighting asthmatically for breath, and ran into the lodgers' room to which they were now being shepherded by her father rather more quickly than before. One could see the pillows and blankets on the beds flying under her accustomed fingers and being laid in order. Before the lodgers had actually reached their room she had finished making the beds and slipped out.

The old man seemed once more to be so possessed by his mulish self-assertiveness that he was forgetting all the respect he should show to his lodgers. He kept driving them on and driving them on until in the very door of the bedroom the middle lodger stamped his foot loudly on the floor and so brought him to a halt. "I beg to announce," said the lodger, lifting one hand and looking also at Gregor's mother and sister, "that because of the disgusting conditions prevailing in this household and family"—here he spat on the floor with emphatic brevity—"I give you notice on the spot. Naturally I won't pay you a penny for the days I have lived here, on the contrary I shall consider bringing an action for damages against you, based on claims—believe me—that will be easily susceptible of proof." He ceased and stared straight in front of him, as if he expected something. In fact his two friends at once rushed into the breach with these words: "And we too give notice on the spot." On that he seized the door-handle and shut the door with a slam.

Gregor's father, groping with his hands, staggered forward and fell into his chair; it looked as if he were stretching himself there for his ordinary evening nap, but the marked jerking of his head, which was as if uncontrollable, showed that he was far from asleep. Gregor had simply stayed quietly all the time on the spot where the lodgers had espied him. Disappointment at the failure of his plan, perhaps also the weakness arising from extreme hunger, made it impossible for him to move. He feared, with a fair degree of certainty, that at any moment the general tension would discharge itself in a combined attack upon him, and he lay waiting. He did not react even to the noise made by the violin as it fell off his mother's lap from under her trembling fingers and gave out a resonant note.

"My dear parents," said his sister, slapping her hand on the table by way of introduction, "things can't go on like this. Perhaps you don't realize that, but I do. I won't utter my brother's name in the presence of this creature, and so all I say is: we must try to get rid of it. We've tried to look after it and to put up with it as far as is humanly possible, and I don't think anyone could reproach us in the slightest."

"She is more than right," said Gregor's father to himself. His mother, who was still choking for lack of breath, began to cough hollowly into her hand with a wild look in her eyes.

His sister rushed over to her and held her forehead. His father's thoughts seemed to have lost their vagueness at Grete's words, he sat more upright, fingering his service cap that lay among the plates still lying on the table from the lodgers' supper, and from time to time looked at the still form of Gregor.

"We must try to get rid of it," his sister now said explicitly to her father, since her mother was coughing too much to hear a word, "it will be the death of both of you, I can see that coming. When one has to work as hard as we do, all of us, one can't stand this continual torment at home on top of it. At least I can't stand it any longer." And she burst into such a passion of sobbing that her tears dropped on her mother's face, where she wiped them off mechanically.

"My dear," said the old man sympathetically, and with evident understanding, "but what can we do?"

Gregor's sister merely shrugged her shoulders to indicate the feeling of helplessness that had now overmastered her during her weeping fit, in contrast to her former confidence.

"If he could understand us," said her father, half questioningly; Grete, still sobbing, vehemently waved a hand to show how unthinkable that was.

"If he could understand us," repeated the old man, shutting his eyes to consider his daughter's conviction that understanding was impossible, "then perhaps we might come to some agreement with him. But as it is—"

"He must go," cried Gregor's sister, "That's the only solution, Father. You must just try to get rid of the idea that this is Gregor. The fact that we've believed it for so long is the root of all our trouble. But how can it be Gregor? If this were Gregor, he would have realized long ago that human beings can't live with such a creature, and he'd have gone away on his own accord. Then we wouldn't have any brother, but we'd be able to go on living and keep his memory in honor. As it is, this creature persecutes us, drives away our lodgers, obviously wants the whole apartment to himself and would have us all sleep in the gutter. Just look, Father," she shrieked all at once, "he's at it again!" And in an access of panic that was quite incomprehensible to Gregor she even quitted her mother, literally thrusting the chair from her as if she would rather sacrifice her mother than stay so near to Gregor, and rushed behind her father, who also rose up, being simply upset by her agitation, and half-spread his arms out as if to protect her.

Yet Gregor had not the slightest intention of frightening anyone, far less his sister. He had only begun to turn round in order to crawl back to his room, but it was certainly a startling operation to watch, since because of his disabled condition he could not execute the difficult turning movements except by lifting his head and then bracing it against the floor over and over again. He paused and looked round. His good intentions seemed to have been recognized; the alarm had only been momentary. Now they were all watching him in melancholy silence. His mother lay in her chair, her legs stiffly outstretched and pressed together, her eyes almost closing for sheer weariness; his father and his sister were sitting beside each other, his sister's arm around the old man's neck.

Perhaps I can go on turning round now, thought Gregor, and began his labors again. He could not stop himself from panting with the effort, and had to pause now and then to take breath. Nor did anyone harass him, he was left entirely to himself. When he had completed the turn-round he began at once to crawl straight back. He was amazed at the distance separating him from his room and could not understand how in his weak state he had managed to accomplish the same journey so recently, almost without remarking it. Intent on crawling as fast as possible, he barely noticed that not a single word, not an ejaculation from his family, interfered with his progress. Only when he was already in the doorway did he turn his head round, not completely, for his neck muscles were getting stiff, but enough to see that nothing had changed behind him except that his sister had risen to her feet. His last glance fell on his mother, who was not quite overcome by sleep.

Hardly was he well inside his room when the door was hastily pushed shut, bolted and locked. The sudden noise in his rear startled him so much that his little legs gave beneath him. It was his sister who had shown such haste. She had been standing ready waiting and had made a light spring forward, Gregor had not even heard her coming, and she cried "At last!" to her parents as she turned the key in the lock.

"And what now?" said Gregor to himself, looking round in the darkness. Soon he made the discovery that he was now unable to stir a limb. This did not surprise him, rather it seemed unnatural that he should ever actually have been able to move on these feeble little legs. Otherwise he felt relatively comfortable. True, his whole body was aching, but it seemed that the pain was gradually growing less and would finally pass away. The rotting apple in his back and the inflamed area around it, all covered with soft dust, already hardly troubled him. He thought of his family with tenderness and love. The decision that he must disappear was one that he held to even more strongly than his sister, if that were possible. In this state of vacant and peaceful meditation he remained until the tower clock struck three in the morning. The first broadening of light in the world outside the window entered his consciousness once more. Then his head sank to the floor of its own accord and from his nostrils came the last faint flicker of his breath.

When the charwoman arrived early in the morning—what between her strength and her impatience she slammed all the doors so loudly, never mind how often she had been begged not to do so, that no one in the whole apartment could enjoy any quiet sleep after her arrival—she noticed nothing unusual as she took her customary peep into Gregor's room. She thought he was lying motionless on purpose, pretending to be in the sulks; she credited him with every kind of intelligence. Since she happened to have the long-handled broom in her hand she tried to tickle him up with it from the doorway. When that too produced no reaction she felt provoked and poked at him a little harder, and only when she had pushed him along the floor without meeting any resistance was her attention aroused. It did not take her long to establish the truth of the matter, and her eyes widened, she let out a whistle, yet did not waste much time over it but tore open the door of the Samsas' bedroom and yelled into the darkness at the top of her voice: "Just look at this, it's dead; it's lying here dead and done for!"

Mr. and Mrs. Samsa started up in their double bed and before they realized the nature of the charwoman's announcement had some difficulty in overcoming the shock of it. But then they got out of bed quickly, one on either side, Mr. Samsa throwing a blanket over his shoulders, Mrs. Samsa in nothing but her nightgown; in this array they entered Gregor's room. Meanwhile the door of the living room opened, too, where Grete had been sleeping since the advent of the lodgers; she was completely dressed as if she had not been to bed, which seemed to be confirmed also by the paleness of her face. "Dead?" said Mrs. Samsa, looking questioningly at the-charwoman, although she could have investigated for herself, and the fact was obvious enough without investigation. "I should say so," said the charwoman, proving her words by pushing Gregor's corpse a long way to one side with her broomstick. Mrs. Samsa made a movement as if to stop her, but checked it. "Well," said Mr. Samsa, "now thanks be to God." He crossed himself, and the three women followed his example. Grete, whose eyes never left the corpse, said: "Just see how thin he was.

It's such a long time since he's eaten anything. The food came out again just as it went in." Indeed, Gregor's body was completely flat and dry, as could only now be seen when it was no longer supported by the legs and nothing prevented one from looking closely at it.

"Come in beside us, Grete, for a little while," said Mrs. Samsa with a tremulous smile, and Grete, not without looking back at the corpse, followed her parents into their bedroom. The charwoman shut the door and opened the window wide. Although it was so early in the morning a certain softness was perceptible in the fresh air. After all, it was already the end of March.

The three lodgers emerged from their room and were surprised to see no breakfast; they had been forgotten. "Where's our breakfast?" said the middle lodger peevishly to the charwoman. But she put her finger to her lips and hastily, without a word, indicated by gestures that they should go into Gregor's room. They did so and stood, their hands in the pockets of their somewhat shabby coats, around Gregor's corpse in the room where it was now fully light.

At that the door of the Samsas' bedroom opened and Mr. Samsa appeared in his uniform, his wife on one arm, his daughter on the other. They all looked a little as if they had been crying; from time to time Grete hid her face on her father's arm.

"Leave my house at once!" said Mr. Samsa, and pointed to the door without disengaging himself from the women. "What do you mean by that?" said the middle lodger, taken somewhat aback, with a feeble smile. The two others put their hands behind them and kept rubbing them together, as if in gleeful expectation of a fine set-to in which they were bound to come off the winners. "I mean just what I say," answered Mr. Samsa, and advanced in a straight line with his two companions towards the lodger. He stood his ground at first quietly, looking at the floor as if his thoughts were taking a new pattern in his head. "Then let us go, by all means," he said, and looked up at Mr. Samsa as if in a sudden access of humility he were expecting some renewed sanction for this decision. Mr. Samsa merely nodded briefly once or twice with meaning eyes. Upon that the lodger really did go with long strides into the hall, his two friends had been listening and had quite stopped rubbing their hands for some moments and now went scuttling after him as if afraid that Mr. Samsa might get into the hall before them and cut them off from their leader. In the hall they all three took their hats from the rack, their sticks from the umbrella stand, bowed in silence and quitted the apartment. With a suspiciousness which proved quite unfounded Mr. Samsa and the two women followed them out to the landing; leaning over the banister they watched the three figures slowly but surely going down the long stairs, vanishing from sight at a certain turn of the staircase on every floor and coming into view again after a moment or so; the more they dwindled, the more the Samsa family's interest in them dwindled, and when a butcher's boy met them and passed them on the stairs coming up proudly with a tray on his head, Mr. Samsa and the two women soon left the landing and as if a burden had been lifted from them went back into their apartment.

They decided to spend this day in resting and going for a stroll; they had not only deserved such a respite from work, but absolutely needed it. And so they sat down at the table and wrote three notes of excuse, Mr. Samsa to his board of management, Mrs. Samsa to her employer and Grete to the head of her firm. While they were writing, the charwoman came in to say that she was going now, since her morning's work was finished. At first they only nodded without looking up, but as she kept hovering there they eyed her irritably. "Well?" said Mr. Samsa. The charwoman stood grinning in the doorway as if she had good news to impart to the family but meant not to say a word unless properly questioned. The small ostrich feather standing upright on her hat, which had annoyed Mr. Samsa ever since she was engaged, was waving gaily in all directions. "Well, what is it then?" asked Mrs. Samsa, who obtained more respect from the charwoman than the others. "Oh," said the charwoman, giggling so amiably that she could not at once continue, "just this, you don't need to bother about how to get rid of the thing next door. It's been seen to already." Mrs. Samsa and Grete bent over their letters again, as if preoccupied; Mr. Samsa, who perceived that she was eager to begin describing it all in detail, stopped her with a decisive hand. But since she was not allowed to tell her story, she remembered the great hurry she was in, being obviously deeply huffed: "Bye, everybody," she said, whirling off violently, and departed with a frightful slamming of doors.

"She'll be given notice tonight," said Mr. Samsa, but neither from his wife nor his daughter did he get any answer, for the charwoman seemed to have shattered again the composure they had barely achieved. They rose, went to the window and stayed there, clasping each other tight. Mr. Samsa turned in his chair to look at them and quietly observed them for a little. Then he called out: "Come along, now, do. Let bygones be bygones. And you might have some consideration for me." The two of them complied at once, hastened to him, caressed him and quickly finished their letters.

Then they all three left the apartment together, which was more than they had done for months, and went by tram into the open country outside the town. The tram, in which they were the only passengers, was filled with warm sunshine. Leaning comfortably back in their seats they canvassed their prospects for the future, and it appeared on closer inspection that these were not at all bad, for the jobs they had got, which so far they had never really discussed with each other, were all three admirable and likely to lead to better things later on. The greatest immediate improvement in their condition would of course arise from moving to another house; they wanted to take a smaller and cheaper but also better situated and more easily run apartment than the one they had, which Gregor had selected. While they were thus conversing, it struck both Mr. and Mrs. Samsa, almost at the same moment, as they became aware of their daughter's increasing vivacity, that in spite of all the sorrow of recent times, which had made her cheeks pale, she had bloomed into a pretty girl with a good figure. They grew quieter and half unconsciously exchanged glances of complete agreement, having come to the conclusion that it would soon be time to find a good husband for her. And it was like a confirmation of their new dreams and excellent intentions that at the end of their journey their daughter sprang to her feet first and stretched her young body.

WILLIAM FAULKNER (1897-1962)

A Rose for Emily

1

When Miss Emily Grierson died, our whole town went to her funeral: the men through a sort of respectful affection for a fallen monument, the women mostly out of curiosity to see the inside of her house, which no one save an old man servant—a combined gardener and cook—had seen in at least ten years.

It was a big, squarish frame house that had once been white, decorated with cupolas and spires and scrolled balconies in the heavily lightsome style of the seventies, set on what had once been our most select street. But garages and cotton gins had encroached and obliterated even the august names of that neighborhood; only Miss Emily's house was left, lifting its stubborn and coquettish decay above the cotton wagons and the gasoline pumps—an eyesore among eyesores. And now Miss Emily had gone to join the representatives of those august names where they lay in the cedar-bemused cemetery among the ranked and anonymous graves of Union and Confederate soldiers who fell at the battle of Jefferson.

Alive, Miss Emily had been a tradition, a duty, and a care; a sort of hereditary obligation upon the town, dating from that day in 1894 when Colonel Sartoris, the mayor—he who fathered the edict that no Negro woman should appear on the streets without an apron—remitted her taxes, the dispensation dating from the death of her father on into perpetuity. Not that Miss Emily would have accepted charity. Colonel Sartoris invented an involved tale to the effect that Miss Emily's father had loaned money to the town, which the town, as a matter of business, preferred this way of repaying. Only a man of Colonel Sartoris' generation and thought would have invented it, and only a woman could have believed it.

When the next generation, with its more modern ideas, became mayors and aldermen, this arrangement created some little dissatisfaction. On the first of the year they mailed her a tax notice. February came, and there was no reply. They wrote her a formal letter, asking her to call at the sheriff's office at her convenience. A week later the mayor wrote her himself, offering to call or to send his car for her, and received in reply a note on paper of an archaic shape, in a thin, flowing calligraphy in faded ink, to the effect that she no longer went out at all. The tax notice was also enclosed, without comment.

They called a special meeting of the Board of Aldermen. A deputation waited upon her, knocked at the door through which no visitor had passed since she ceased giving china-painting lessons eight or ten years earlier. They were admitted by the old Negro in a dim hall from which a stairway mounted into still more shadow. It smelled of dust and disuse—a close, dank smell. The Negro led them into the parlor. It was furnished in heavy, leather-covered furniture. When the Negro opened the blinds of one window, they could see that the leather was cracked; and when they sat down, a faint dust rose sluggishly about their thighs, spinning with slow motes in the single sun-ray. On a tarnished gilt easel before the fireplace stood a crayon portrait of Miss Emily's father.

They rose when she entered—a small, fat woman in black, with a thin gold chain descending to her waist and vanishing into her belt, leaning on an ebony cane with a tarnished gold head. Her skeleton was small and spare; perhaps that was why what would have been merely plumpness in another was obesity in her. She looked bloated, like a body long submerged in motionless water, and of that pallid hue. Her eyes, lost in the fatty ridges of her face, looked like two small pieces of coal pressed into a lump of dough as they moved from one face to another while the visitors stated their errand.

She did not ask them to sit. She just stood in the door and listened quietly until the spokesman came to a stumbling halt. Then they could hear the invisible watch ticking at the end of the gold chain.

Her voice was dry and cold. "I have no taxes in Jefferson. Colonel Sartoris explained it to me. Perhaps one of you can gain access to the city records and satisfy yourselves."

"But we have. We are the city authorities, Miss Emily. Didn't you get a notice from the sheriff, signed by him?"

"I received a paper, yes," Miss Emily said. "Perhaps he considers himself the sheriff . . . I have no taxes in Jefferson."

"But there is nothing on the books to show that, you see. We must go by the—"

"See Colonel Sartoris. I have no taxes in Jefferson."

"But, Miss Emily—"

"See Colonel Sartoris." (Colonel Sartoris had been dead almost ten years.) "I have no taxes in Jefferson. Tobe!" The Negro appeared. "Show these gentlemen out."

2

So she vanquished them, horse and foot, just as she had vanquished their fathers thirty years before about the smell. That was two years after her father's death and a short time after her sweetheart—the one we believed would marry her—had deserted her. After her father's death she went out very little; after her sweetheart went away, people hardly saw her at all. A few of the ladies had the temerity to call, but were not received, and the only sign of life about the place was the Negro man—a young man then—going in and out with a market basket.

"Just as if a man—any man—could keep a kitchen properly," the ladies said; so they were not surprised when the smell developed. It was another link between the gross, teeming world and the high and mighty Griersons.

A neighbor, a woman, complained to the mayor, Judge Stevens, eighty years old.

"But what will you have me do about it, madam?" he said.

"Why, send her word to stop it," the woman said. "Isn't there a law?"

"I'm sure that won't be necessary," Judge Stevens said. "It's probably just a snake or a rat that nigger of hers killed in the yard. I'll speak to him about it."

The next day he received two more complaints, one from a man who came in diffident deprecation. "We really must do something about it, Judge. I'd be the last one in the world to bother Miss Emily, but we've got to do something." That night the Board of Aldermen met—three graybeards and one younger man, a member of the rising generation.

"It's simple enough," he said. "Send her word to have her place cleaned up. Give her a certain time to do it in, and if she don't . . ."

"Dammit, sir," Judge Stevens said, "will you accuse a lady to her face of smelling bad?"

So the next night, after midnight, four men crossed Miss Emily's lawn and slunk about the house like burglars, sniffing along the base of the brickwork and at the cellar openings while one of them performed a regular sowing motion with his hand out of a sack slung from his shoulder. They broke open the cellar door and sprinkled lime there, and in all the outbuildings. As they recrossed the lawn, a window that had been dark was lighted and Miss Emily sat in it, the light behind her, and her upright torso motionless as that of an idol. They crept quietly across the lawn and into the shadow of the locusts that lined the street. After a week or two the smell went away.

That was when people had begun to feel really sorry for her. People in our town, remembering how old lady Wyatt, her great-aunt, had gone completely crazy at last, believed that the Griersons held themselves a little too high for what they really were. None of the young men were quite good enough for Miss Emily and such. We had long thought of them as a tableau, Miss Emily a slender figure in white in the background, her father a spraddled silhouette in the foreground, his back to her and clutching a horsewhip, the two of them framed by the back-flung front door. So when she got to be thirty and was still single, we were not pleased exactly, but vindicated; even with insanity in the family she wouldn't have turned down all of her chances if they had really materialized.

When her father died, it got about that the house was all that was left to her; and in a way, people were glad. At last they could pity Miss Emily. Being left alone, and a pauper, she had become humanized. Now she too would know the old thrill and the old despair of a penny more or less.

The day after his death all the ladies prepared to call at the house and offer condolence and aid, as is our custom. Miss Emily met them at the door, dressed as usual and with no trace of grief on her face. She told them that her father was not dead. She did that for three days, with the ministers calling on her, and the doctors, trying to persuade her to let them dispose of the body. Just as they were about to resort to law and force, she broke down, and they buried her father quickly.

We did not say she was crazy then. We believed she had to do that. We remembered all the young men her father had driven away, and we knew that with nothing left, she would have to cling to that which had robbed her, as people will.

3

She was sick for a long time. When we saw her again, her hair was cut short, making her look like a girl, with a vague resemblance to those angels in colored church windows—sort of tragic and serene.

The town had just let the contracts for paving the sidewalks, and in the summer after her father's death they began the work. The construction company came with niggers and mules and machinery, and a foreman named Homer Barron, a Yankee —a big, dark, ready man, with a big voice and eyes lighter than his face. The little boys would follow in groups to hear him cuss the niggers, and the niggers singing in time to the rise and fall of picks. Pretty soon he knew everybody in town. Whenever you heard a lot of laughing anywhere about the square, Homer Barron would be in the center of the group. Presently we began to see him and Miss Emily on Sunday afternoons driving in the yellow-wheeled buggy and the matched team of bays from the livery stable.

At first we were glad that Miss Emily would have an interest, because the ladies all said, "Of course a Grierson would not think seriously of a Northerner, a day laborer." But there were still others, older people, who said that even grief could not cause a real lady to forget *noblesse oblige**—without calling it *noblesse oblige.* They just said, "Poor Emily. Her kinsfolk should come to her." She had some kin in Alabama; but years ago her father had fallen out with them over the estate of old lady Wyatt, the crazy woman, and there was no communication between the two families. They had not even been represented at the funeral.

And as soon as the old people said, "Poor Emily," the whispering began. "Do you suppose it's really so?" they said to one another. "Of course it is. What else could . . ." This behind their hands; rustling of craned silk and satin behind jalousies closed upon the sun of Sunday afternoon as the thin, swift clop-clop-clop of the matched team passed: "Poor Emily."

She carried her head high enough—even when we believed that she was fallen. It was as if she demanded more than ever the recognition of her dignity as the last Grierson; as if it had wanted that touch of earthiness to reaffirm her imperviousness. Like when she bought the rat poison, the arsenic. That was over a year after they had begun to say "Poor Emily," and while the two female cousins were visiting her.

"I want some poison," she said to the druggist. She was over thirty then, still a slight woman, though thinner than usual, with cold, haughty black eyes in a face the flesh of which was strained across the temples and about the eye-sockets as you imagine a lighthouse-keeper's face ought to look. "I want some poison," she said.

"Yes, Miss Emily. What kind? For rats and such? I'd recom—"

"I want the best you have. I don't care what kind."

The druggist named several. "They'll kill anything up to an elephant. But what you want is—"

"Arsenic," Miss Emily said. "Is that a good one?"

"Is . . . arsenic? Yes, ma'am. But what you want—"

"I want arsenic."

The druggist looked down at her. She looked back at him, erect, her face like a strained flag. "Why, of course," the druggist said. "If that's what you want. But the law requires you to tell what you are going to use it for."

Miss Emily just stared at him, her head tilted back in order to look him eye for

---

* *noblesse oblige:* the obligation of a member of the nobility to behave with honor and dignity.

eye, until he looked away and went and got the arsenic and wrapped it up. The Negro delivery boy brought her the package; the druggist didn't come back. When she opened the package at home there was written on the box, under the skull and bones: "For rats."

4

So the next day we all said, "She will kill herself"; and we said it would be the best thing. When she had first begun to be seen with Homer Barron, we had said, "She will marry him." Then we said, "She will persuade him yet," because Homer himself had remarked—he liked men, and it was known that he drank with the younger men in the Elks' Club—that he was not a marrying man. Later we said, "Poor Emily" behind the jalousies as they passed on Sunday afternoon in the glittering buggy, Miss Emily with her head high and Homer Barron with his hat cocked and a cigar in his teeth, reins and whip in a yellow glove.

Then some of the ladies began to say that it was a disgrace to the town and a bad example to the young people. The men did not want to interfere, but at last the ladies forced the Baptist minister—Miss Emily's people were Episcopal—to call upon her. He would never divulge what happened during that interview, but he refused to go back again. The next Sunday they again drove about the streets, and the following day the minister's wife wrote to Miss Emily's relations in Alabama.

So she had blood-kin under her roof again and we sat back to watch developments. At first nothing happened. Then we were sure that they were to be married. We learned that Miss Emily had been to the jeweler's and ordered a man's toilet set in silver, with the letters H. B. on each piece. Two days later we learned that she had bought a complete outfit of men's clothing, including a nightshirt, and we said, "They are married." We were really glad. We were glad because the two female cousins were even more Grierson than Miss Emily had ever been.

So we were not surprised when Homer Barron—the streets had been finished some time since—was gone. We were a little disappointed that there was not a public blowing-off, but we believed that he had gone on to prepare for Miss Emily's coming, or to give her a chance to get rid of the cousins. (By that time it was a cabal, and we were all Miss Emily's allies to help circumvent the cousins.) Sure enough, after another week they departed. And, as we had expected all along, within three days Homer Barron was back in town. A neighbor saw the Negro man admit him at the kitchen door at dusk one evening.

And that was the last we saw of Homer Barron. And of Miss Emily for some time. The Negro man went in and out with the market basket, but the front door remained closed. Now and then we would see her at a window for a moment, as the men did that night when they sprinkled the lime, but for almost six months she did not appear on the streets. Then we knew that this was to be expected too; as if that quality of her father which had thwarted her woman's life so many times had been too virulent and too furious to die.

When we next saw Miss Emily, she had grown fat and her hair was turning gray. During the next few years it grew grayer and grayer until it attained an even pepper-

and-salt iron-gray, when it ceased turning. Up to the day of her death at seventy-four it was still that vigorous iron-gray, like the hair of an active man.

From that time on her front door remained closed, save for a period of six or seven years, when she was about forty, during which she gave lessons in china-painting. She fitted up a studio in one of the downstairs rooms, where the daughters and granddaughters of Colonel Sartoris' contemporaries were sent to her with the same regularity and in the same spirit that they were sent to church on Sundays with a twenty-five-cent piece for the collection plate. Meanwhile her taxes had been remitted.

Then the newer generation became the backbone and the spirit of the town, and the painting pupils grew up and fell away and did not send their children to her with boxes of color and tedious brushes and pictures cut from the ladies' magazines. The front door closed upon the last one and remained closed for good. When the town got free postal delivery, Miss Emily alone refused to let them fasten the metal numbers above her door and attach a mailbox to it. She would not listen to them.

Daily, monthly, yearly we watched the Negro grow grayer and more stooped, going in and out with the market basket. Each December we sent her a tax notice, which would be returned by the post office a week later, unclaimed. Now and then we would see her in one of the downstairs windows—she had evidently shut up the top floor of the house—like the carven torso of an idol in a niche, looking or not looking at us, we could never tell which. Thus she passed from generation to generation—dear, inescapable, impervious, tranquil, and perverse.

And so she died. Fell ill in the house filled with dust and shadows, with only a doddering Negro man to wait on her. We did not even know she was sick; we had long since given up trying to get any information from the Negro. He talked to no one, probably not even to her, for his voice had grown harsh and rusty, as if from disuse.

She died in one of the downstairs rooms, in a heavy walnut bed with a curtain, her gray head propped on a pillow yellow and moldy with age and lack of sunlight.

5

The Negro met the first of the ladies at the front door and let them in, with their hushed, sibilant voices and their quick, curious glances, and then he disappeared. He walked right through the house and out the back and was not seen again.

The two female cousins came at once. They held the funeral on the second day, with the town coming to look at Miss Emily beneath a mass of bought flowers, with the crayon face of her father musing profoundly above the bier and the ladies sibilant and macabre; and the very old men—some in their brushed Confederate uniforms—on the porch and the lawn, talking of Miss Emily as if she had been a contemporary of theirs, believing that they had danced with her and courted her perhaps, confusing time with its mathematical progression, as the old do, to whom all the past is not a diminishing road but, instead, a huge meadow which no winter ever quite touches, divided from them now by the narrow bottle-neck of the most recent decade of years.

Already we knew that there was one room in that region above stairs which no one had seen in forty years, and which would have to be forced. They waited until Miss Emily was decently in the ground before they opened it.

The violence of breaking down the door seemed to fill this room with pervading dust. A thin, acrid pall as of the tomb seemed to lie everywhere upon this room decked and furnished as for a bridal: upon the valance curtains of faded rose color, upon the rose-shaded lights, upon the dressing table, upon the delicate array of crystal and the man's toilet things backed with tarnished silver, silver so tarnished that the monogram was obscured. Among them lay collar and tie, as if they had just been removed, which, lifted, left upon the surface a pale crescent in the dust. Upon a chair hung the suit, carefully folded; beneath it the two mute shoes and the discarded socks.

The man himself lay in the bed.

For a long while we just stood there, looking down at the profound and fleshless grin. The body had apparently once lain in the attitude of an embrace, but now the long sleep that outlasts love, that conquers even the grimace of love, had cuckolded him. What was left of him, rotted beneath what was left of the nightshirt, had become inextricable from the bed in which he lay; and upon him and upon the pillow beside him lay that even coating of the patient and biding dust.

Then we noticed that in the second pillow was the indentation of a head. One of us lifted something from it, and leaning forward, that faint and invisible dust dry and acrid in the nostrils, we saw a long strand of iron-gray hair.

ERNEST HEMINGWAY (1898–1961)

Hills Like White Elephants

The hills across the valley of the Ebro were long and white. On this side there was no shade and no trees and the station was between two lines of rails in the sun. Close against the side of the station there was the warm shadow of the building and a curtain, made of strings of bamboo beads, hung across the open door into the bar, to keep out flies. The American and the girl with him sat at a table in the shade, outside the building. It was very hot and the express from Barcelona would come in forty minutes. It stopped at this junction for two minutes and went on to Madrid.

"What should we drink?" the girl asked. She had taken off her hat and put it on the table.

"It's pretty hot," the man said.

"Let's drink beer."

"Dos cervezas," the man said into the curtain.

"Big ones?" a woman asked from the doorway.

"Yes. Two big ones."

The woman brought two glasses of beer and two felt pads. She put the felt pads and the beer glasses on the table and looked at the man and the girl. The girl was looking off at the line of hills. They were white in the sun and the country was brown and dry.

"They look like white elephants," she said.

"I've never seen one," the man drank his beer.

"No, you wouldn't have."

"I might have," the man said. "Just because you say I wouldn't have doesn't prove anything."

The girl looked at the bead curtain. "They've painted something on it," she said. "What does it say?"

"Anis del Toro. It's a drink."

"Could we try it?"

The man called "Listen" through the curtain. The woman came out from the bar.

"Four reales."

"We want two Anis del Toro."

"With water?"

"Do you want it with water?"

"I don't know," the girl said. "Is it good with water?"

"It's all right."

"You want them with water?" asked the woman.

"Yes, with water."

"It tastes like licorice," the girl said and put the glass down.

"That's the way with everything."

"Yes," said the girl. "Everything tastes of licorice. Especially all the things you've waited so long for, like absinthe."

"Oh, cut it out."

"You started it," the girl said. "I was being amused. I was having a fine time."

"Well, let's try and have a fine time."

"All right. I was trying. I said the mountains looked like white elephants. Wasn't that bright?"

"That was bright."

"I wanted to try this new drink. That's all we do, isn't it—look at things and try new drinks?"

"I guess so."

The girl looked across at the hills.

"They're lovely hills," she said. "They don't really look like white elephants. I just meant the coloring of their skin through the trees."

"Should we have another drink?"

"All right."

The warm wind blew the bead curtain against the table.

"The beer's nice and cool," the man said.

"It's lovely," the girl said.

"It's really an awfully simple operation, Jig," the man said. "It's not really an operation at all."

The girl looked at the ground the table legs rested on.

"I know you wouldn't mind it, Jig. It's really not anything. It's just to let the air in."

The girl did not say anything.

"I'll go with you and I'll stay with you all the time. They just let the air in and then it's all perfectly natural."

"Then what will we do afterward?"

"We'll be fine afterward. Just like we were before."

"What makes you think so?"

"That's the only thing that bothers us. It's the only thing that's made us unhappy."

The girl looked at the bead curtain, put her hand out and took hold of two of the strings of beads.

"And you think then we'll be all right and be happy."

"I know we will. You don't have to be afraid. I've known lots of people that have done it."

"So have I," said the girl. "And afterward they were all so happy."

"Well," the man said, "if you don't want to you don't have to. I wouldn't have you do it if you didn't want to. But I know it's perfectly simple."

"And you really want to?"

"I think it's the best thing to do. But I don't want you to do it if you don't really want to."

"And if I do it you'll be happy and things will be like they were and you'll love me?"

"I love you now. You know I love you."

"I know. But if I do it, then it will be nice again if I say things are like white elephants, and you'll like it?"

"I'll love it. I love it now but I just can't think about it. You know how I get when I worry."

"If I do it you won't ever worry?"

"I won't worry about that because it's perfectly simple."

"Then I'll do it. Because I don't care about me."

"What do you mean?"

"I don't care about me."

"Well, I care about you."

"Oh, yes. But I don't care about me. And I'll do it and then everything will be fine."

"I don't want you to do it if you feel that way."

The girl stood up and walked to the end of the station. Across, on the other side, were fields of grain and trees along the banks of the Ebro. Far away, beyond the river, were mountains. The shadow of a cloud moved across the field of grain and she saw the river through the trees.

"And we could have all this," she said. "And we could have everything and every day we make it more impossible."

"What did you say?"

"I said we could have everything."

"We can have everything."

"No, we can't."

"We can have the whole world."

"No, we can't."

"We can go everywhere."

"No, we can't. It isn't ours any more."

"It's ours."

"No, it isn't. And once they take it away, you never get it back."

"But they haven't taken it away."

"We'll wait and see."

"Come on back in the shade," he said. "You mustn't feel that way."

"I don't feel any way," the girl said. "I just know things."

"I don't want you to do anything that you don't want to do—"

"Nor that isn't good for me," she said. "I know. Could we have another beer?"

"All right. But you've got to realize—"

"I realize," the girl said. "Can't we maybe stop talking?"

They sat down at the table and the girl looked across at the hills on the dry side of the valley and the man looked at her and at the table.

"You've got to realize," he said, "that I don't want you to do it if you don't want to. I'm perfectly willing to go through with it if it means anything to you."

"Doesn't it mean anything to you? We could get along."

"Of course it does. But I don't want anybody but you. I don't want any one else. And I know it's perfectly simple."

"Yes, you know it's perfectly simple."

"It's all right for you to say that, but I do know it."

"Would you do something for me now?"

"I'd do anything for you."

"Would you please please please please please please please stop talking?"

He did not say anything but looked at the bags against the wall of the station. There were labels on them from all the hotels where they had spent nights.

"But I don't want you to," he said, "I don't care anything about it."

"I'll scream," the girl said.

The woman came out through the curtains with two glasses of beer and put them down on the damp felt pads. "The train comes in five minutes," she said.

"What did she say?" asked the girl.

"That the train is coming in five minutes."

The girl smiled brightly at the woman, to thank her.

"I'd better take the bags over to the other side of the station," the man said. She smiled at him.

"All right. Then come back and we'll finish the beer."

He picked up the two heavy bags and carried them around the station to the other tracks. He looked up the tracks but could not see the train. Coming back, he walked through the barroom, where people waiting for the train were drinking. He drank an Anis at the bar and looked at the people. They were all waiting reasonably for the train. He went out through the bead curtain. She was sitting at the table and smiled at him.

"Do you feel better?" he asked.

"I feel fine," she said. "There's nothing wrong with me. I feel fine."

ANN PETRY (b. 1912)

Like a Winding Sheet

He had planned to get up before Mae did and surprise her by fixing breakfast. Instead he went back to sleep and she got out of bed so quietly he didn't know she wasn't there beside him until he woke up and heard the queer soft gurgle of water running out of the sink in the bathroom.

He knew he ought to get up but instead he put his arms across his forehead to shut the afternoon sunlight out of his eyes, pulled his legs up close to his body, testing them to see if the ache was still in them.

Mae had finished in the bathroom. He could tell because she never closed the door when she was in there and now the sweet smell of talcum powder was drifting down the hall and into the bedroom. Then he heard her coming down the hall.

"Hi, babe," she said affectionately.

"Hum," he grunted, and moved his arms away from his head, opened one eye.

"It's a nice morning."

"Yeah." He rolled over and the sheet twisted around him, outlining his thighs, his chest. "You mean afternoon, don't ya?"

Mae looked at the twisted sheet and giggled. "Looks like a winding sheet," she said. "A shroud—" Laughter tangled with her words and she had to pause for a moment before she could continue. "You look like a huckleberry—in a winding sheet—"

"That's no way to talk. Early in the day like this," he protested.

He looked at his arms silhouetted against the white of the sheets. They were inky black by contrast and he had to smile in spite of himself and he lay there smiling and savoring the sweet sound of Mae's giggling.

"Early?" She pointed a finger at the alarm clock on the table near the bed and giggled again. "It's almost four o'clock. And if you don't spring up out of there, you're going to be late again."

"What do you mean 'again'?"

"Twice last week. Three times the week before. And once the week before and—"

"I can't get used to sleeping in the daytime," he said fretfully. He pushed his legs out from under the covers experimentally. Some of the ache had gone out of them but they weren't really rested yet. "It's too light for good sleeping. And all that standing beats the hell out of my legs."

"After two years you oughta be used to it," Mae said.

He watched her as she fixed her hair, powdered her face, slipped into a pair of blue denim overalls. She moved quickly and yet she didn't seem to hurry.

"You look like you'd had plenty of sleep," he said lazily. He had to get up but he kept putting the moment off, not wanting to move, yet he didn't dare let his legs go completely limp because if he did he'd go back to sleep. It was getting later and later but the thought of putting his weight on his legs kept him lying there.

When he finally got up he had to hurry, and he gulped his breakfast so fast that he wondered if his stomach could possibly use food thrown at it at such a rate of speed. He was still wondering about it as he and Mae were putting their coats on in the hall.

Mae paused to look at the calendar. "It's the thirteenth," she said. Then a faint excitement in her voice, "Why, it's Friday the thirteenth." She had one arm in her coat sleeve and she held it there while she stared at the calendar. "I oughta stay home," she said. "I shouldn't go outa the house."

"Aw, don't be a fool," he said. "Today's payday. And payday is a good luck day everywhere, any way you look at it." And as she stood hesitating he said, "Aw, come on."

And he was late for work again because they spent fifteen minutes arguing before he could convince her she ought to go to work just the same. He had to talk persuasively, urging her gently, and it took time. But he couldn't bring himself to talk to her roughly or threaten to strike her like a lot of men might have done. He wasn't made that way.

So when he reached the plant he was late and he had to wait to punch the time clock because the day-shift workers were streaming out in long lines, in groups and bunches that impeded his progress.

Even now just starting his workday his legs ached. He had to force himself to struggle past the outgoing workers, punch the time clock, and get the little cart he pushed around all night, because he kept toying with the idea of going home and getting back in bed.

He pushed the cart out on the concrete floor, thinking that if this was his plant he'd make a lot of changes in it. There were too many standing-up jobs for one thing. He'd figure out some way most of 'em could be done sitting down and he'd put a lot more benches around. And this job he had—this job that forced him to walk ten hours a night, pushing this little cart, well, he'd turn it into a sitting-down job. One of those little trucks they used around railroad stations would be good for a job like this. Guys sat on a seat and the thing moved easily, taking up little room and turning in hardly any space at all like on a dime.

He pushed the cart near the foreman. He never could remember to refer to her as the forelady even in his mind. It was funny to have a white woman for a boss in a plant like this one.

She was sore about something. He could tell by the way her face was red and her eyes were half-shut until they were slits. Probably been out late and didn't get enough sleep. He avoided looking at her and hurried a little, head down, as he passed her though he couldn't resist stealing a glance at her out of the corner of his eye. He saw the edge of the light-colored slacks she wore and the tip end of a big tan shoe.

"Hey, Johnson!" the woman said.

The machines had started full blast. The whirr and the grinding made the building shake, made it impossible to hear conversations. The men and women at the machines talked to each other but looking at them from just a little distance away, they appeared to be simply moving their lips because you couldn't hear what they were saying. Yet the woman's voice cut across the machine sounds—harsh, angry.

He turned his head slowly. "Good evenin', Mrs. Scott," he said, and waited.

"You're late again."

"That's right. My legs were bothering me."

The woman's face grew redder, angrier looking. "Half this shift comes in late," she said. "And you're the worst one of all. You're always late. Whatsa matter with ya?"

"It's my legs," he said. "Somehow they don't ever get rested. I don't seem to get used to sleeping days. And I just can't get started."

"Excuses. You guys always got excuses," her anger grew and spread. "Every guy comes in here late always has an excuse. His wife's sick or his grandmother died or somebody in the family had to go to the hospital," she paused, drew a deep breath. "And the niggers is the worse. I don't care what's wrong with your legs. You get in here on time. I'm sick of you niggers—"

"You got the right to get mad," he interrupted softly. "You got the right to cuss me four ways to Sunday but I ain't letting nobody call me a nigger."

He stepped closer to her. His fists were doubled. His lips were drawn back in a thin narrow line. A vein in his forehead stood out swollen, thick.

And the woman backed away from him, not hurriedly but slowly—two, three steps back.

"Aw, forget it," she said. "I didn't mean nothing by it. It slipped out. It was an accident." The red of her face deepened until the small blood vessels in her cheeks were purple. "Go on and get to work," she urged. And she took three more slow backward steps.

He stood motionless for a moment and then turned away from the sight of the red lipstick on her mouth that made him remember that the foreman was a woman. And he couldn't bring himself to hit a woman. He felt a curious tingling in his fingers and he looked down at his hands. They were clenched tight, hard, ready to smash some of those small purple veins in her face.

He pushed the cart ahead of him, walking slowly. When he turned his head, she was staring in his direction, mopping her forehead with a dark blue handkerchief. Their eyes met and then they both looked away.

He didn't glance in her direction again but moved past the long work benches, carefully collecting the finished parts, going slowly and steadily up and down, and back and forth the length of the building, and as he walked he forced himself to swallow his anger, get rid of it.

And he succeeded so that he was able to think about what had happened without getting upset about it. An hour went by but the tension stayed in his hands. They were clenched and knotted on the handles of the cart as though ready to aim a blow.

And he thought he should have hit her anyway, smacked her hard in the face, felt the soft flesh of her face give under the hardness of his hands. He tried to make his hands relax by offering them a description of what it would have been like to strike her because he had the queer feeling that his hands were not exactly a part of him anymore—they had developed a separate life of their own over which he had no control. So he dwelt on the pleasure his hands would have felt—both of them cracking at her, first one and then the other. If he had done that his hands would have felt good now—relaxed, rested.

And he decided that even if he'd lost his job for it, he should have let her have it and it would have been a long time, maybe the rest of her life, before she called anybody else a nigger.

The only trouble was he couldn't hit a woman. A woman couldn't hit back the same way a man did. But it would have been a deeply satisfying thing to have cracked her narrow lips wide open with just one blow, beautifully timed and with all his weight in back of it. That way he would have gotten rid of all the energy and tension his anger had created in him. He kept remembering how his heart had started pumping blood so fast he had felt it tingle even in the tips of his fingers.

With the approach of night, fatigue nibbled at him. The corners of his mouth drooped, the frown between his eyes deepened, his shoulders sagged; but his hands stayed tight and tense. As the hours dragged by he noticed that the women workers had started to snap and snarl at each other. He couldn't hear what they said because of the sound of machines but he could see the quick lip movements that sent words tumbling from the sides of their mouths. They gestured irritably with their hands and scowled as their mouths moved.

Their violent jerky motions told him that it was getting close on to quitting time but somehow he felt that the night still stretched ahead of him, composed of endless hours of steady walking on his aching legs. When the whistle finally blew he went on pushing the cart, unable to believe that it had sounded. The whirring of the machines died away to a murmur and he knew then that he'd really heard the whistle. He stood still for a moment, filled with a relief that made him sigh.

Then he moved briskly, putting the cart in the storeroom, hurrying to take his place in the line forming before the paymaster. That was another thing he'd change, he thought. He'd have the pay envelopes handed to the people right at their benches so there wouldn't be ten or fifteen minutes lost waiting for the pay. He always got home about fifteen minutes late on payday. They did it better in the plant where Mae worked, brought the money right to them at their benches.

He stuck his pay envelope in his pants' pocket and followed the line of workers heading for the subway in a slow-moving stream. He glanced up at the sky. It was a nice night, the sky looked packed full to running over with stars. And he thought if he and Mae would go right to bed when they got home from work they'd catch a few hours of darkness for sleeping. But they never did. They fooled around—cooking and eating and listening to the radio and he always stayed in a big chair in the living room and went almost but not quite to sleep and when they finally got to bed it was five or six in the morning and daylight was already seeping around the edges of the sky.

He walked slowly, putting off the moment when he would have to plunge into the crowd hurrying toward the subway. It was a long ride to Harlem and tonight the thought of it appalled him. He paused outside an all-night restaurant to kill time, so that some of the first rush of workers would be gone when he reached the subway.

The lights in the restaurant were brilliant, enticing. There was life and motion inside. And as he looked through the window he thought that everything within range of his eyes gleamed—the long imitation marble counter, the tall stools, the white porcelain-topped tables and especially the big metal coffee urn right near the window. Steam issued from its top and a gas flame flickered under it—a lively, dancing, blue flame.

A lot of the workers from his shift—men and women—were lining up near the coffee urn. He watched them walk to the porcelain-topped tables carrying steaming cups of coffee and he saw that just the smell of the coffee lessened the fatigue lines in their faces. After the first sip their faces softened, they smiled, they began to talk and laugh.

On a sudden impulse he shoved the door open and joined the line in front of the coffee urn. The line moved slowly. And as he stood there the smell of the coffee, the sound of the laughter and the voices, helped dull the sharp ache in his legs.

He didn't pay any attention to the white girl who was serving the coffee at the urn. He kept looking at the cups in the hands of the men who had been ahead of him. Each time a man stepped out of the line with one of the thick white cups the fragrant steam got in his nostrils. He saw that they walked carefully so as not to spill a single drop. There was a froth of bubbles at the top of each cup and he thought about how he would let the bubbles break against his lips before he actually took a big deep swallow.

Then it was his turn. "A cup of coffee," he said, just as he had heard the others say.

The white girl looked past him, put her hands up to her head and gently lifted her hair away from the back of her neck, tossing her head back a little. "No more coffee for a while," she said.

He wasn't certain he'd heard her correctly and he said "What?" blankly.

"No more coffee for a while," she repeated.

There was silence behind him and then uneasy movement. He thought someone would say something, ask why or protest, but there was only silence and then a faint shuffling sound as though the men standing behind him had simultaneously shifted their weight from one foot to the other.

He looked at the girl without saying anything. He felt his hands begin to tingle and the tingling went all the way down to his finger tips so that he glanced down at them. They were clenched tight, hard, into fists. Then he looked at the girl again. What he wanted to do was hit her so hard that the scarlet lipstick on her mouth would smear and spread over her nose, her chin, out toward her cheeks, so hard that she would never toss her head again and refuse a man a cup of coffee because he was black.

He estimated the distance across the counter and reached forward, balancing his weight on the balls of his feet, ready to let the blow go. And then his hands fell back down to his sides because he forced himself to lower them, to unclench them and make them dangle loose. The effort took his breath away because his hands fought against him. But he couldn't hit her. He couldn't even now bring himself to hit a woman, not even this one, who had refused him a cup of coffee with a toss of her head. He kept seeing the gesture with which she had lifted the length of her blond hair from the back of her neck as expressive of her contempt for him.

When he went out the door he didn't look back. If he had he would have seen the flickering blue flame under the shiny coffee urn being extinguished. The line of men who had stood behind him lingered a moment to watch the people drinking coffee at the tables and then they left just as he had without having had the coffee they wanted so badly. The girl behind the counter poured water in the urn and swabbed it out and as she waited for the water to run out, she lifted her hair gently from the back of her neck and tossed her head before she began making a fresh lot of coffee.

But he had walked away without a backward look, his head down, his hands in his pockets, raging at himself and whatever it was inside of him that had forced him to stand quiet and still when he wanted to strike out.

The subway was crowded and he had to stand. He tried grasping an overhead strap and his hands were too tense to grip it. So he moved near the train door and stood there swaying back and forth with the rocking of the train. The roar of the train beat inside his head, making it ache and throb, and the pain in his legs clawed up into his groin so that he seemed to be bursting with pain and he told himself that it was due to all that anger-born energy that had piled up in him and not been used and so it had spread through him like a poison—from his feet and legs all the way up to his head.

Mae was in the house before he was. He knew she was home before he put the key in the door of the apartment. The radio was going. She had it tuned up loud and she was singing along with it.

"Hello, babe," she called out, as soon as he opened the door.

He tried to say "hello" and it came out half grunt and half sigh.

"You sure sound cheerful," she said.

She was in the bedroom and he went and leaned against the doorjamb. The denim overalls she wore to work were carefully draped over the back of a chair by the bed. She was standing in front of the dresser, tying the sash of a yellow housecoat around her waist and chewing gum vigorously as she admired her reflection in the mirror over the dresser.

"Whatsa matter?" she said. "You get bawled out by the boss or somep'n?"

"Just tired," he said slowly. "For God's sake, do you have to crack that gum like that?"

"You don't have to lissen to me," she said complacently. She patted a curl in place near the side of her head and then lifted her hair away from the back of her neck, ducking her head forward and then back.

He winced away from the gesture. "What you got to be always fooling with your hair for?" he protested.

"Say, what's the matter with you anyway?" She turned away from the mirror to face him, put her hands on her hips. "You ain't been in the house two minutes and you're picking on me."

He didn't answer her because her eyes were angry and he didn't want to quarrel with her. They'd been married too long and got along too well and so he walked all the way into the room and sat down in the chair by the bed and stretched his legs out in front of him, putting his weight on the heels of his shoes, leaning way back in the chair, not saying anything.

"Lissen," she said sharply. "I've got to wear those overalls again tomorrow. You're going to get them all wrinkled up leaning against them like that."

He didn't move. He was too tired and his legs were throbbing now that he had sat down. Besides the overalls were already wrinkled and dirty, he thought. They couldn't help but be for she'd worn them all week. He leaned farther back in the chair.

"Come on, get up," she ordered.

"Oh, what the hell," he said wearily, and got up from the chair. "I'd just as soon live in a subway. There'd be just as much place to sit down."

He saw that her sense of humor was struggling with her anger. But her sense of humor won because she giggled.

"Aw, come on and eat," she said. There was a coaxing note in her voice. "You're nothing but an old hungry nigger trying to act tough and—" she paused to giggle and then continued, "You—"

He had always found her giggling pleasant and deliberately said things that might amuse her and then waited, listening for the delicate sound to emerge from her throat. This time he didn't even hear the giggle. He didn't let her finish what she was saying. She was standing close to him and that funny tingling started in his finger tips, went fast up his arms and sent his fist shooting straight for her face.

There was the smacking sound of soft flesh being struck by a hard object and it wasn't until she screamed that he realized he had hit her in the mouth—so hard that the dark red lipstick had blurred and spread over her full lips, reaching up toward the tip of her nose, down toward her chin, out toward her cheeks.

The knowledge that he had struck her seeped through him slowly and he was appalled but he couldn't drag his hands away from her face. He kept striking her and he thought with horror that something inside him was holding him, binding him to this act, wrapping and twisting about him so that he had to continue it. He had lost all control over his hands. And he groped for a phrase, a word, something to describe what this thing was like that was happening to him and he thought it was like being enmeshed in a winding sheet—that was it—like a winding sheet. And even as the thought formed in his mind, his hands reached for her face again and yet again.

RALPH ELLISON (b. 1914)

Battle Royal

It goes a long way back, some twenty years. All my life I had been looking for something, and everywhere I turned someone tried to tell me what it was. I accepted their answers too, though they were often in contradiction and even self-contradictory. I was naïve. I was looking for myself and asking everyone except myself questions which I, and only I, could answer. It took me a long time and much painful boomer-anging of my expectations to achieve a realization everyone else appears to have been born with: That I am nobody but myself. But first I had to discover that I am an invisible man!

And yet I am no freak of nature, nor of history. I was in the cards, other things having been equal (or unequal) eighty-five years ago. I am not ashamed of my grandparents for having been slaves. I am only ashamed of myself for having at one time been ashamed. About eighty-five years ago they were told that they were free, united with others of our country in everything pertaining to the common good, and, in everything social, separate like the fingers of the hand. And they believed it. They exulted in it. They stayed in their place, worked hard, and brought up my fa-ther to do the same. But my grandfather is the one. He was an odd old guy, my grandfather, and I am told I take after him. It was he who caused the trouble. On his deathbed he called my father to him and said, "Son, after I'm gone I want you to keep up the good fight. I never told you, but our life is a war and I have been a traitor all my born days, a spy in the enemy's country ever since I give up my gun back in the Reconstruction. Live with your head in the lion's mouth. I want you to over-come 'em with yeses, undermine 'em with grins, agree 'em to death and destruction, let 'em swoller you till they vomit or bust wide open." They thought the old man had gone out of his mind. He had been the meekest of men. The younger children were rushed from the room, the shades drawn and the flame of the lamp turned so low that it sputtered on the wick like the old man's breathing. "Learn it to the young-uns," he whispered fiercely; then he died.

But my folks were more alarmed over his last words than over his dying. It was as though he had not died at all, his words caused so much anxiety. I was warned em-phatically to forget what he had said and, indeed, this is the first time it has been mentioned outside the family circle. It had a tremendous effect upon me, however. I could never be sure of what he meant. Grandfather had been a quiet old man who never made any trouble, yet on his deathbed he had called himself a traitor and a spy, and he had spoken of his meekness as a dangerous activity. It became a constant puzzle which lay unanswered in the back of my mind. And whenever things went well for me I remembered my grandfather and felt guilty and uncomfortable. It was as though I was carrying out his advice in spite of myself. And to make it worse, ev-eryone loved me for it. I was praised by the most lily-white men of the town. I was considered an example of desirable conduct—just as my grandfather had been. And what puzzled me was that the old man had defined it as *treachery*. When I was praised for my conduct I felt a guilt that in some way I was doing something that was really against the wishes of the white folks, that if they had understood they would have desired me to act just the opposite, that I should have been sulky and mean, and that that really would have been what they wanted, even though they were fooled and thought they wanted me to act as I did. It made me afraid that some day they would look upon me as a traitor and I would be lost. Still I was more afraid to act any other way because they didn't like that at all. The old man's words were like a curse. On my graduation day I delivered an oration in which I showed that humility was the secret, indeed, the very essence of progress. (Not that I believed this— how could I, remembering my grandfather?—I only believed that it worked.) It was a great success. Everyone praised me and I was invited to give the speech at a gathering of the town's leading white citizens. It was a triumph for our whole community.

It was in the main ballroom of the leading hotel. When I got there I discovered that it was on the occasion of a smoker, and I was told that since I was to be there anyway I might as well take part in the battle royal to be fought by some of my schoolmates as part of the entertainment. The battle royal came first.

All of the town's big shots were there in their tuxedoes, wolfing down the buffet foods, drinking beer and whiskey and smoking black cigars. It was a large room with a high ceiling. Chairs were arranged in neat rows around three sides of a portable boxing ring. The fourth side was clear, revealing a gleaming space of polished floor. I had some misgivings over the battle royal, by the way. Not from a distaste for fighting, but because I didn't care too much for the other fellows who were to take part. They were tough guys who seemed to have no grandfather's curse worrying their minds. No one could mistake their toughness. And besides, I suspected that fighting a battle royal might detract from the dignity of my speech. In those pre-invisible days I visualized myself as a potential Booker T. Washington. But the other fellows didn't care too much for me either, and there were nine of them. I felt superior to them in my way, and I didn't like the manner in which we were all crowded together into the servants' elevator. Nor did they like my being there. In fact, as the warmly lighted floors flashed past the elevator we had words over the fact that I, by taking part in the fight, had knocked one of their friends out of a night's work.

We were led out of the elevator through a rococo hall into an anteroom and told to get into our fighting togs. Each of us was issued a pair of boxing gloves and ushered out into the big mirrored hall, which we entered looking cautiously about us and whispering, lest we might accidentally be heard above the noise of the room. It was foggy with cigar smoke. And already the whiskey was taking effect. I was shocked to see some of the most important men of the town quite tipsy. They were all there—bankers, lawyers, judges, doctors, fire chiefs, teachers, merchants. Even one of the more fashionable pastors. Something we could not see was going on up front. A clarinet was vibrating sensuously and the men were standing up and moving eagerly forward. We were a small tight group, clustered together, our bare upper bodies touching and shining with anticipatory sweat; while up front the big shots were becoming increasingly excited over something we still could not see. Suddenly I heard the school superintendent, who had told me to come, yell, "Bring up the shines gentlemen! Bring up the little shines!"

We were rushed up to the front of the ballroom, where it smelled even more strongly of tobacco and whiskey. Then we were pushed into place. I almost wet my pants. A sea of faces, some hostile, some amused, ringed around us, and in the center, facing us, stood a magnificent blonde—stark naked. There was dead silence. I felt a blast of cold air chill me. I tried to back away, but they were behind me and around me. Some of the boys stood with lowered heads, trembling. I felt a wave of irrational guilt and fear. My teeth chattered, my skin turned to goose flesh, my knees knocked. Yet I was strongly attracted and looked in spite of myself. Had the price of looking been blindness, I would have looked. The hair was yellow like that of a circus kewpie doll, the face heavily powdered and rouged, as though to form an abstract mask, the eyes hollow and smeared a cool blue, the color of a baboon's butt. I felt a desire to spit upon her as my eyes brushed slowly over her body. Her breasts were firm and round as the domes of East Indian temples, and I stood so close as to see the fine skin texture and beads of pearly perspiration glistening like dew around the pink and erected buds of her nipples. I wanted at one and the same time to run from the room, to sink through the floor, or go to her and cover her from my eyes and the eyes of the others with my body; to feel the soft thighs, to caress her and destroy her, to love her and murder her, to hide from her, and yet to stroke where below the small American flag tatooed upon her belly her thighs formed a capital V. I had a notion that of all in the room she saw only me with her impersonal eyes.

And then she began to dance, a slow sensuous movement; the smoke of a hundred cigars clinging to her like the thinnest of veils. She seemed like a fair bird-girl girdled in veils calling to me from the angry surface of some gray and threatening sea. I was transported. Then I became aware of the clarinet playing and the big shots yelling at us. Some threatened us if we looked and others if we did not. On my right I saw one boy faint. And now a man grabbed a silver pitcher from a table and stepped close as he dashed ice water upon him and stood him up and forced two of us to support him as his head hung and moans issued from his thick bluish lips. Another boy began to plead to go home. He was the largest of the group, wearing dark red fighting trunks much too small to conceal the erection which projected from him as though in answer to the insinuating low-registered moaning of the clarinet. He tried to hide himself with his boxing gloves.

And all the while the blonde continued dancing, smiling faintly at the big shots who watched her with fascination, and faintly smiling at our fear. I noticed a certain merchant who followed her hungrily, his lips loose and drooling. He was a large man who wore diamond studs in a shirtfront which swelled with the ample paunch underneath, and each time the blonde swayed her undulating hips he ran his hand through the thin hair of his bald head and, with his arms upheld, his posture clumsy like that of an intoxicated panda, wound his belly in a slow and obscene grind. This creature was completely hypnotized. The music had quickened. As the dancer flung herself about with a detached expression on her face, the men began reaching out to touch her. I could see their beefy fingers sink into her soft flesh. Some of the others tried to stop them and she began to move around the floor in graceful circles, as they gave chase, slipping and sliding over the polished floor. It was mad. Chairs went crashing, drinks were spilt, as they ran laughing and howling after her. They caught her just as she reached a door, raised her from the floor, and tossed her as college boys are tossed at a hazing, and above her red, fixed-smiling lips I saw the terror and disgust in her eyes, almost like my own terror and that which I saw in some of the other boys. As I watched, they tossed her twice and her soft breasts seemed to flatten against the air and her legs flung wildly as she spun. Some of the more sober ones helped her to escape. And I started off the floor, heading for the anteroom with the rest of the boys.

Some were still crying and in hysteria. But as we tried to leave we were stopped and ordered to get into the ring. There was nothing to do but what we were told. All ten of us climbed under the ropes and allowed ourselves to be blindfolded with broad bands of white cloth. One of the men seemed to feel a bit sympathetic and tried to cheer us up as we stood with our backs against the ropes. Some of us tried to grin. "See that boy over there?" one of the men said. "I want you to run across at the bell and give it to him right in the belly. If you don't get him, I'm going to get you. I don't like his looks." Each of us was told the same. The blindfolds were put on. Yet even then I had been going over my speech. In my mind each word was as bright as flame. I felt the cloth pressed into place, and frowned so that it would be loosened when I relaxed.

But now I felt a sudden fit of blind terror. I was unused to darkness. It was as though I had suddenly found myself in a dark room filled with poisonous cottonmouths. I could hear the bleary voices yelling insistently for the battle royal to begin.

"Get going in there!"

"Let me at that big nigger!"

I strained to pick up the school superintendent's voice, as though to squeeze some security out of that slightly more familiar sound.

"Let me at those black sonsabitches!" someone yelled.

"No, Jackson, no!" another voice yelled. "Here, somebody, help me hold Jack."

"I want to get at that ginger-colored nigger. Tear him limb from limb," the first voice yelled.

I stood against the ropes trembling. For in those days I was what they called ginger-colored, and he sounded as though he might crunch me between his teeth like a crisp ginger cookie.

Quite a struggle was going on. Chairs were being kicked about and I could hear voices grunting as with a terrific effort. I wanted to see, to see more desperately than ever before. But the blindfold was as tight as a thick skin-puckering scab and when I raised my gloved hands to push the layers of white aside a voice yelled, "Oh, no you don't, black bastard! Leave that alone!"

"Ring the bell before Jackson kills him a coon!" someone boomed in the sudden silence. And I heard the bell clang and the sound of the feet scuffling forward.

A glove smacked against my head. I pivoted, striking out stiffly as someone went past, and felt the jar ripple along the length of my arm to my shoulder. Then it seemed as though all nine of the boys had turned upon me at once. Blows pounded me from all sides while I struck out as best I could. So many blows landed upon me that I wondered if I were not the only blindfolded fighter in the ring, or if the man called Jackson hadn't succeeded in getting me after all.

Blindfolded, I could no longer control my motions. I had no dignity. I stumbled about like a baby or a drunken man. The smoke had become thicker and with each new blow it seemed to sear and further restrict my lungs. My saliva became like hot bitter glue. A glove connected with my head, filling my mouth with warm blood. It was everywhere. I could not tell if the moisture I felt upon my body was sweat or blood. A blow landed hard against the nape of my neck. I felt myself going over, my head hitting the floor. Streaks of blue light filled the black world behind the blind-fold. I lay prone, pretending that I was knocked out, but felt myself seized by hands and yanked to my feet. "Get going, black boy! Mix it up!" My arms were like lead, my head smarting from blows. I managed to feel my way to the ropes and held on, trying to catch my breath. A glove landed in my mid-section and I went over again, feeling as though the smoke had become a knife jabbed into my guts. Pushed this way and that by the legs milling around me, I finally pulled erect and discovered that I could see the black, sweat-washed forms weaving in the smoky-blue atmosphere like drunken dancers weaving to the rapid drum-like thuds of blows.

Everyone fought hysterically. It was complete anarchy. Everybody fought every-body else. No group fought together for long. Two, three, four, fought one, then turned to fight each other, were themselves attacked. Blows landed below the belt and in the kidney, with the gloves open as well as closed, and with my eye partly opened now there was not so much terror. I moved carefully, avoiding blows, al-though not too many to attract attention, fighting from group to group. The boys groped about like blind, cautious crabs crouching to protect their mid-sections, their heads pulled in short against their shoulders, their arms stretched nervously before them, with their fists testing the smoke-filled air like the knobbed feelers of hyper-sensitive snails. In one corner I glimpsed a boy violently punching the air and heard him scream in pain as he smashed his hand against a ring post. For a second I saw him bent over holding his hand, then going down as a blow caught his unprotected head. I played one group against the other, slipping in and throwing a punch then stepping out of range while pushing the others into the melee to take the blows blindly aimed at me. The smoke was agonizing and there were no rounds, no bells at three minute intervals to relieve our exhaustion. The room spun round me, a swirl of lights, smoke, sweating bodies surrounded by tense white faces. I bled from both nose and mouth, the blood spattering upon my chest.

The men kept yelling, "Slug him, black boy! Knock his guts out!"

"Uppercut him! Kill him! Kill that big boy!"

Taking a fake fall, I saw a boy going down heavily beside me as though we were felled by a single blow, saw a sneaker-clad foot shoot into his groin as the two who had knocked him down stumbled upon him. I rolled out of range, feeling a twinge of nausea.

The harder we fought the more threatening the men became. And yet, I had begun to worry about my speech again. How would it go? Would they recognize my ability? What would they give me?

I was fighting automatically and suddenly I noticed that one after another of the boys was leaving the ring. I was surprised, filled with panic, as though I had been left alone with an unknown danger. Then I understood. The boys had arranged it among themselves. It was the custom for the two men left in the ring to slug it out for the winner's prize. I discovered this too late. When the bell sounded two men in tuxedoes leaped into the ring and removed the blindfold. I found myself facing Tatlock, the biggest of the gang. I felt sick at my stomach. Hardly had the bell stopped ringing in my ears than it clanged again and I saw him moving swiftly toward me. Thinking of nothing else to do I hit him smash on the nose. He kept coming, bringing the rank sharp violence of stale sweat. His face was a black blank of a face, only his eyes alive—with hate of me and aglow with a feverish terror from what had happened to us all. I became anxious. I wanted to deliver my speech and he came at me as though he meant to beat it out of me. I smashed him again and again, taking his blows as they came. Then on a sudden impulse I struck him lightly and as we clinched, I whispered, "Fake like I knocked you out, you can have the prize."

"I'll break your behind," he whispered hoarsely.

"For *them?*"

"For *me,* sonofabitch!"

They were yelling for us to break it up and Tatlock spun me half around with a blow, and as a joggled camera sweeps in a reeling scene, I saw the howling red faces crouching tense beneath the cloud of blue-gray smoke. For a moment the world wavered, unraveled, flowed, then my head cleared and Tatlock bounced before me. That fluttering shadow before my eyes was his jabbing left hand. Then falling forward, my head against his damp shoulder, I whispered,

"I'll make it five dollars more."

"Go to hell!"

But his muscles relaxed a trifle beneath my pressure and I breathed, "Seven!"

"Give it to your ma," he said, ripping me beneath the heart.

And while I still held him I butted him and moved away. I felt myself bombarded with punches. I fought back with hopeless desperation. I wanted to deliver my speech more than anything else in the world, because I felt that only these men could judge truly my ability, and now this stupid clown was ruining my chances. I began fighting carefully now, moving in to punch him and out again with my greater speed. A lucky blow to his chin and I had him going too—until I heard a loud voice yell, "I got my money on the big boy."

Hearing this, I almost dropped my guard. I was confused: Should I try to win against the voice out there? Would not this go against my speech, and was not this a moment for humility, for nonresistance? A blow to my head as I danced about sent my right eye popping like a jack-in-the-box and settled my dilemma. The room went red as I fell. It was a dream fall, my body languid and fastidious as to where to land, until the floor became impatient and smashed up to meet me. A moment later I came to. An hypnotic voice said FIVE emphatically. And I lay there, hazily watching a dark red spot of my own blood shaping itself into a butterfly, glistening and soaking into the soiled gray world of the canvas.

When the voice drawled TEN I was lifted up and dragged to a chair. I sat dazed. My eye pained and swelled with each throb of my pounding heart and I wondered if now I would be allowed to speak. I was wringing wet, my mouth still bleeding. We were grouped along the wall now. The other boys ignored me as they congratulated Tatlock and speculated as to how much they would be paid. One boy whimpered over his smashed hand. Looking up front, I saw attendants in white jackets rolling the portable ring away and placing a small square rug in the vacant space surrounded by chairs. Perhaps, I thought, I will stand on the rug to deliver my speech.

Then the M.C. called to us, "Come on up here boys and get your money."

We ran forward to where the men laughed and talked in their chairs, waiting. Everyone seemed friendly now.

"There it is on the rug," the man said. I saw the rug covered with coins of all dimensions and a few crumpled bills. But what excited me, scattered here and there, were the gold pieces.

"Boys, it's all yours," the man said. "You get all you grab."

"That's right, Sambo," a blond man said, winking at me confidentially.

I trembled with excitement, forgetting my pain. I would get the gold and the bills, I thought. I would use both hands. I would throw my body against the boys nearest me to block them from the gold.

"Get down around the rug now," the man commanded, "and don't anyone touch it until I give the signal."

"This ought to be good," I heard.

As told, we got around the square rug on our knees. Slowly the man raised his freckled hand as we followed it upward with our eyes.

I heard, "These niggers look like they're about to pray!"

Then, "Ready," the man said. "Go!"

I lunged for a yellow coin lying on the blue design of the carpet, touching it and sending a surprised shriek to join those rising around me. I tried frantically to remove my hand but could not let go. A hot, violent force tore through my body, shaking me like a wet rat. The rug was electrified. The hair bristled up on my head as I shook myself free. My muscles jumped, my nerves jangled, writhed. But I saw that this was not stopping the other boys. Laughing in fear and embarrassment, some were holding back and scooping up the coins knocked off by the painful contortions of the others. The men roared above us as we struggled.

"Pick it up, goddamnit, pick it up!" someone called like a bass-voiced parrot. "Go on, get it!"

I crawled rapidly around the floor, picking up the coins, trying to avoid the coppers and to get greenbacks and the gold. Ignoring the shock by laughing, as I brushed the coins off quickly, I discovered that I could contain the electricity—a contradiction, but it works. Then the men began to push us onto the rug. Laughing embarrassedly, we struggled out of their hands and kept after the coins. We were all wet and slippery and hard to hold. Suddenly I saw a boy lifted into the air, glistening with sweat like a circus seal, and dropped, his wet back landing flush upon the charged rug, heard him yell and saw him literally dance upon his back, his elbows beating a frenzied tatoo upon the floor, his muscles twitching like the flesh of a horse stung by many flies. When he finally rolled off, his face was gray and no one stopped him when he ran from the floor amid booming laughter.

"Get the money," the M.C. called. "That's good hard American cash!"

And we snatched and grabbed, snatched and grabbed. I was careful not to come too close to the rug now, and when I felt the hot whiskey breath descend upon me like a cloud of foul air I reached out and grabbed the leg of a chair. It was occupied and I held on desperately.

"Leggo, nigger! Leggo!"

The huge face wavered down to mine as he tried to push me free. But my body was slippery and he was too drunk. It was Mr. Colcord, who owned a chain of movie houses and "entertainment palaces." Each time he grabbed me I slipped out of his hands. It became a real struggle. I feared the rug more than I did the drunk, so I held on, surprising myself for a moment by trying to topple *him* upon the rug. It was such an enormous idea that I found myself actually carrying it out. I tried not to be obvious, yet when I grabbed his leg, trying to tumble him out of the chair, he raised up roaring with laughter, and, looking at me with soberness dead in the eye, kicked me viciously in the chest. The chair leg flew out of my hand. I felt myself going and rolled. It was as though I had rolled through a bed of hot coals. It seemed a whole century would pass before I would roll free, a century in which I was seared through the deepest levels of my body to the fearful breath within me and the breath seared and heated to the point of explosion. It'll all be over in a flash, I thought as I rolled clear. It'll all be over in a flash.

But not yet, the men on the other side were waiting, red faces swollen as though from apoplexy as they bent forward in their chairs. Seeing their fingers coming toward me I rolled away as a fumbled football rolls off the receiver's fingertips, back into the coals. That time I luckily sent the rug sliding out of place and heard the coins ringing against the floor and the boys scuffling to pick them up and the M.C. calling, "All right, boys, that's all. Go get dressed and get your money."

I was limp as a dish rag. My back felt as though it had been beaten with wires.

When we had dressed the M.C. came in and gave us each five dollars, except Tatlock, who got ten for being last in the ring. Then he told us to leave. I was not to get a chance to deliver my speech, I thought. I was going out into the dim alley in despair when I was stopped and told to go back. I returned to the ballroom, where the men were pushing back their chairs and gathering in groups to talk.

The M.C. knocked on a table for quiet. "Gentlemen," he said, "we almost forgot an important part of the program. A most serious part, gentlemen. This boy was brought here to deliver a speech which he made at his graduation yesterday. . . ."

"Bravo!"

"I'm told that he is the smartest boy we've got out there in Greenwood. I'm told that he knows more big words than a pocket-sized dictionary."

Much applause and laughter.

"So now, gentlemen, I want you to give him your attention."

There was still laughter as I faced them, my mouth dry, my eye throbbing. I began slowly, but evidently my throat was tense, because they began shouting, "Louder! Louder!"

"We of the younger generation extol the wisdom of that great leader and educator," I shouted, "who first spoke these flaming words of wisdom: 'A ship lost at sea for many days suddenly sighted a friendly vessel. From the mast of the unfortunate vessel was seen a signal: "Water, water; we die of thirst!" The answer from the friendly vessel came back: "Cast down your bucket where you are." The captain of the distressed vessel, at last heeding the injunction, cast down his bucket, and it came up full of fresh sparkling water from the mouth of the Amazon River.' And like him I say, and in his words, 'To those of my race who depend upon bettering their condition in a foreign land, or who underestimate the importance of cultivating friendly relations with the Southern white man, who is his next-door neighbor, I would say: "Cast down your bucket where you are"—cast it down in making friends in every manly way of the people of all races by whom we are surrounded. . . .' "

I spoke automatically and with such fervor that I did not realize that the men were still talking and laughing until my dry mouth, filling up with blood from the cut, almost strangled me. I coughed, wanting to stop and go to one of the tall brass, sand-filled spittoons to relieve myself, but a few of the men, especially the superintendent, were listening and I was afraid. So I gulped it down, blood, saliva, and all, and continued. (What powers of endurance I had during those days! What enthusiasm! What a belief in the rightness of things!) I spoke even louder in spite of the pain. But still they talked and still they laughed, as though deaf with cotton in dirty ears. So I spoke with greater emotional emphasis. I closed my ears and swallowed blood until I was nauseated. The speech seemed a hundred times as long as before, but I could not leave out a single word. All had to be said, each memorized nuance considered, rendered. Nor was that all. Whenever I uttered a word of three or more syllables a group of voices would yell for me to repeat it. I used the phrase "social responsibility" and they yelled:

"What's the word you say, boy?"

"Social responsibility," I said.

"What?"

"Social . . ."

"Louder."

". . . responsibility."

"More!"

"Respon—"

"Repeat!"

"—sibility."

The room filled with the uproar of laughter until, no doubt, distracted by having to gulp down my blood, I made a mistake and yelled a phrase I had often seen denounced in newspaper editorials, heard debated in private.

"Social . . ."

"What?" they yelled.

". . . equality—"

The laughter hung smokelike in the sudden stillness. I opened my eyes, puzzled. Sounds of displeasure filled the room. The M.C. rushed forward. They shouted hostile phrases at me. But I did not understand.

A small dry mustached man in the front row blared out, "Say that slowly, son!"

"What sir?"

"What you just said!"

"Social responsibility, sir," I said.

"You weren't being smart, were you, boy?" he said, not unkindly.

"No, sir!"

"You sure that about 'equality' was a mistake?"

"Oh, yes, sir," I said. "I was swallowing blood."

"Well, you had better speak more slowly so we can understand. We mean to do right by you, but you've got to know your place at all times. All right, now, go on with your speech."

I was afraid. I wanted to leave but I wanted also to speak and I was afraid they'd snatch me down.

"Thank you, sir," I said, beginning where I had left off, and having them ignore me as before.

Yet when I finished there was a thunderous applause. I was surprised to see the superintendent come forth with a package wrapped in white tissue paper, and, gesturing for quiet, address the men.

"Gentlemen, you see that I did not overpraise this boy. He makes a good speech and some day he'll lead his people in the proper paths. And I don't have to tell you that that is important in these days and times. This is a good, smart boy, and so to encourage him in the right direction, in the name of the Board of Education I wish to present him a prize in the form of this . . ."

He paused, removing the tissue paper and revealing a gleaming calf-skin brief case.

". . . in the form of this first-class article from Shad Whitmore's shop."

"Boy," he said, addressing me, "take this prize and keep it well. Consider it a badge of office. Prize it. Keep developing as you are and some day it will be filled with important papers that will help shape the destiny of your people."

I was so moved that I could hardly express my thanks. A rope of bloody saliva forming a shape like an undiscovered continent drooled upon the leather and I wiped it quickly away. I felt an importance that I had never dreamed.

"Open it and see what's inside," I was told.

My fingers a-tremble, I complied, smelling the fresh leather and finding an official-looking document inside. It was a scholarship to the state college for Negroes. My eyes filled with tears and I ran awkwardly off the floor.

I was overjoyed; I did not even mind when I discovered that the gold pieces I had scrambled for were brass pocket tokens advertising a certain make of automobile.

When I reached home everyone was excited. Next day the neighbors came to congratulate me. I even felt safe from grandfather, whose deathbed curse usually spoiled my triumphs. I stood beneath his photograph with my brief case in hand and smiled triumphantly into his stolid black peasant's face. It was a face that fascinated me. The eyes seemed to follow everywhere I went.

That night I dreamed I was at a circus with him and that he refused to laugh at the clowns no matter what they did. Then later he told me to open my brief case and read what was inside and I did, finding an official envelope stamped with the state seal; and inside the envelope I found another and another, endlessly, and I thought I would fall of weariness. "Them's years," he said. "Now open that one." And I did and in it I found an engraved document containing a short message in letters of gold. "Read it," my grandfather said. "Out loud."

"To Whom It May Concern," I intoned. "Keep This Nigger-Boy Running."

I awoke with the old man's laughter ringing in my ears.

(It was a dream I was to remember and dream again for many years after. But at the time I had no insight into its meaning. First I had to attend college.)

JOHN BARTH (b. 1930)

Lost in the Funhouse

For whom is the funhouse fun? Perhaps for lovers. For Ambrose it is *a place of fear and confusion.* He has come to the seashore with his family for the holiday, *the occasion of their visit is Independence Day, the most important secular holiday of the United States of America.* A single straight underline is the manuscript mark for italic type, *which in turn* is the printed equivalent to oral emphasis of words and phrases as well as the customary type for titles of complete works, not to mention. Italics are also employed, in fiction stories especially, for "outside," intrusive, or artificial voices, such as radio announcements, the texts of telegrams and newspaper articles, et cetera. They should be used *sparingly.* If passages originally in roman type are italicized by someone repeating them, it's customary to acknowledge the fact. *Italics mine.*

Ambrose was "at that awkward age." His voice came out high-pitched as a child's if he let himself get carried away; to be on the safe side, therefore, he moved and spoke with *deliberate calm* and *adult gravity.* Talking soberly of unimportant or irrelevant matters and listening consciously to the sound of your own voice are useful habits for maintaining control in this difficult interval. *En route* to Ocean City he sat in the back seat of the family car with his brother Peter, age fifteen, and Magda G————, age fourteen, a pretty girl and exquisite young lady, who lived not far from them on B———— Street in the town of D————, Maryland. Initials, blanks, or both were often substituted for proper names in nineteenth-century fiction to enhance the illusion of reality. It is as if the author felt it necessary to delete the names for reasons of tact or legal liability. Interestingly, as with other aspects of realism, it is an *illusion* that is being enhanced, by purely artificial means. Is it likely, does it violate the principle of verisimilitude, that a thirteen-year-old boy could make such a sophisticated observation? A girl of fourteen is *the psychological coeval* of a boy of fifteen or sixteen; a thirteen-year-old boy, therefore, even one precocious in some other respects, might be three years *her emotional junior.*

Thrice a year—on Memorial, Independence, and Labor Days—the family visits Ocean City for the afternoon and evening. When Ambrose and Peter's father was their age, the excursion was made by train, as mentioned in the novel *The 42nd Parallel* by John Dos Passos. Many families from the same neighborhood used to travel together, with dependent relatives and often with Negro servants; schoolfuls of children swarmed through the railway cars; everyone shared everyone else's Maryland fried chicken, Virginia ham, deviled eggs, potato salad, beaten biscuits, iced tea. Nowadays (that is, in 19—, the year of our story) the journey is made by automobile—more comfortably and quickly though without the extra fun though without the *camaraderie* of a general excursion. It's all part of the deterioration of American life, their father declares; Uncle Karl supposes that when the boys take *their* families to Ocean City for the holidays they'll fly in Autogiros. Their mother, sitting in the middle of the front seat like Magda in the second, only with her arms on the seat-back behind the men's shoulders, wouldn't want the good old days back again, the steaming trains and stuffy long dresses; on the other hand she can do without Autogiros, too, if she has to become a grandmother to fly in them.

Description of physical appearance and mannerisms is one of several standard methods of characterization used by writers of fiction. It is also important to "keep the senses operating"; when a detail from one of the five senses, say visual, is "crossed" with a detail from another, say auditory, the reader's imagination is oriented to the scene, perhaps unconsciously. This procedure may be compared to the way surveyors and navigators determine their positions by two or more compass bearings, a process known as triangulation. The brown hair on Ambrose's mother's forearms gleamed in the sun like. Though right-handed, she took her left arm from the seat-back to press the dashboard cigar lighter for Uncle Karl. When the glass bead in its handle glowed red, the lighter was ready for use. The smell of Uncle Karl's cigar smoke reminded one of. The fragrance of the ocean came strong to the picnic ground where they always stopped for lunch, two miles inland from Ocean City. Having to pause for a full hour almost within sound of the breakers was difficult for Peter and Ambrose when they were younger; even at their present age it was not easy to keep their anticipation, *stimulated by the briny spume,* from turning into short temper. The Irish author James Joyce, in his unusual novel entitled *Ulysses,* now available in this country, uses the adjectives *snot-green* and *scrotum-tightening* to describe the sea. Visual, auditory, tactile, olfactory, gustatory. Peter and Ambrose's father, while steering their black 1936 LaSalle sedan with one hand, could with the other remove the first cigarette from a white pack of Lucky Strikes and, more remarkably, light it with a match forefingered from its book and thumbed against the flint paper without being detached. The matchbook cover merely advertised U. S. War Bonds and Stamps. A fine metaphor, simile, or other figure of speech, in addition to its obvious "first-order" relevance to the thing it describes, will be seen upon reflection to have a second order of significance: it may be drawn from the *milieu* of the action, for example, or be particularly appropriate to the sensibility of the narrator, even hinting to the reader things of which the narrator is unaware; or it may cast further and subtler lights upon the thing it describes, sometimes ironically qualifying the more evident sense of the comparison.

To say that Ambrose's and Peter's mother was *pretty* is to accomplish nothing; the reader may acknowledge the proposition, but his imagination is not engaged. Besides, Magda was also pretty, yet in an altogether different way. Although she lived on B_____ Street she had very good manners and did better than average in school. Her figure was very well developed for her age. Her right hand lay casually on the plush upholstery of the seat, very near Ambrose's left leg, on which his own hand rested. The space between their legs, between her right and his left leg, was out of the line of sight of anyone sitting on the other side of Magda, as well as anyone glancing into the rear-view mirror. Uncle Karl's face resembled Peter's—rather, vice versa. Both had dark hair and eyes, short husky statures, deep voices. Magda's left hand was probably in a similar position on her left side. The boy's father is difficult to describe; no particular feature of his appearance or manner stood out. He wore glasses and was principal of a T——— County grade school. Uncle Karl was a masonry contractor.

Although Peter must have known as well as Ambrose that the latter, because of his position in the car, would be the first to see the electrical towers of the power plant at V———, the halfway point of their trip, he leaned forward and slightly toward the center of the car and pretended to be looking for them through the flat pinewoods and tuckahoe creeks along the highway. For as long as the boys could remember, "looking for the Towers" had been a feature of the first half of their excursions to Ocean City, "looking for the standpipe" of the second. Though the game was childish, their mother preserved the tradition of rewarding the first to see the Towers with a candy-bar or piece of fruit. She insisted now that Magda play the game; the prize, she said, was "something hard to get nowadays." Ambrose decided not to join in; he sat far back in his seat. Magda, like Peter, leaned forward. Two sets of straps were discernible through the shoulders of her sun dress; the inside right one, a brassiere-strap, was fastened or shortened with a small safety pin. The right armpit of her dress, presumably the left as well, was damp with perspiration. The simple strategy for being first to espy the Towers, which Ambrose had understood by the age of four, was to sit on the right-hand side of the car. Whoever sat there, however, had also to put up with the worst of the sun, and so Ambrose, without mentioning the matter, chose sometimes the one and sometimes the other. Not impossibly Peter had never caught on to the trick, or thought his brother hadn't simply because Ambrose on occasion preferred shade to a Baby Ruth or tangerine.

The shade-sun situation didn't apply to the front seat, owing to the windshield; if anything the driver got more sun, since the person on the passenger side not only was shaded below by the door and dashboard but might swing down his sunvisor all the way too.

"Is that them?" Magda asked. Ambrose's mother teased the boys for letting Magda win, insinuating that "somebody [had] a girlfriend." Peter and Ambrose's father reached a long thin arm across their mother to butt his cigarette in the dashboard ashtray, under the lighter. The prize this time for seeing the Towers first was a banana. Their mother bestowed it after chiding their father for wasting a half-smoked cigarette when everything was so scarce. Magda, to take the prize, moved her hand from so near Ambrose's that he could have touched it as though accidentally. She offered to share the prize, things like that were so hard to find; but everyone insisted it was hers alone. Ambrose's mother sang an iambic trimeter couplet from a popular song, femininely rhymed:

> *"What's good is in the Army;*
> *What's left will never harm me."*

Uncle Karl tapped his cigar ash out the ventilator window; some particles were sucked by the slipstream back into the car through the rear window on the passenger side. Magda demonstrated her ability to hold a banana in one hand and peel it with her teeth. She still sat forward; Ambrose pushed his glasses back onto the bridge of his nose with his left hand, which he then negligently let fall to the seat cushion immediately behind her. He even permitted the single hair, gold, on the second joint of his thumb to brush the fabric of her skirt. Should she have sat back at that instant, his hand would have been caught under her.

Plush upholstery prickles uncomfortably through gabardine slacks in the July sun. The function of the *beginning* of a story is to introduce the principal characters, establish their initial relationships, set the scene for the main action, expose the background of the situation if necessary, plant motifs and foreshadowings where appropriate, and initiate the first complication or whatever of the "rising action." Actually, if one imagines a story called "The Funhouse," or "Lost in the Funhouse," the details of the drive to Ocean City don't seem especially relevant. The *beginning* should recount the events between Ambrose's first sight of the funhouse early in the afternoon and his entering it with Magda and Peter in the evening. The *middle* would narrate all relevant events from the time he goes in to the time he loses his way; middles have the double and contradictory function of delaying the climax while at the same time preparing the reader for it and fetching him to it. Then the *ending* would tell what Ambrose does while he's lost, how he finally finds his way out, and what everybody makes of the experience. So far there's been no real dialogue, very little sensory detail, and nothing in the way of a *theme*. And a long time has gone by already without anything happening; it makes a person wonder. We haven't even reached Ocean City yet: we will never get out of the funhouse.

The more closely an author identifies with the narrator, literally or metaphorically, the less advisable it is, as a rule, to use the first-person narrative viewpoint. Once three years previously the young people *aforementioned* played Niggers and Masters in the backyard; when it was Ambrose's turn to be the Master and theirs to be Niggers Peter had to go serve his evening papers; Ambrose was afraid to punish Magda alone, but she led him to the whitewashed Torture Chamber between the woodshed and the privy in the Slaves Quarters; there she knelt sweating among bamboo rakes and dusty Mason jars, pleadingly embraced his knees, and while bees droned in the lattice as if on an ordinary summer afternoon, purchased clemency at a surprising price set by herself. Doubtless she remembered nothing of this event; Ambrose on the other hand seemed unable to forget the least detail of his life. He even recalled how, standing beside himself with awed impersonality in the reeky heat, he'd stared the while at an empty cigar box in which Uncle Karl kept stone-cutting chisels: beneath the words *El Producto,* a laureled, loose-toga'd lady regarded the sea from a marble bench; beside her, forgotten or not yet turned to, was a five-stringed lyre. Her chin reposed on the back of her right hand; her left depended negligently from the bench-arm. The lower half of scene and lady was peeled away; the words EXAMINED BY _____ were inked there into the wood. Nowadays cigar boxes are made of pasteboard. Ambrose wondered what Magda would have done, Ambrose wondered what Magda would do when she sat back on his hand as he resolved she should. Be angry. Make a teasing joke of it. Give no sign at all. For a long time she leaned forward, playing cow-poker with Peter against Uncle Karl and Mother and watching for the first sign of Ocean City. At nearly the same instant, picnic ground and Ocean City standpipe hove into view; an Amoco filling station on their side of the road cost Mother and Uncle Karl fifty cows and the game; Magda bounced back, clapping her right hand on Mother's right arm. Ambrose moved clear "in the nick of time."

At this rate our hero, at this rate our protagonist will remain in the funhouse forever. Narrative ordinarily consists of alternating dramatization and summarization. One symptom of nervous tension, paradoxically, is repeated and violent yawning; neither Peter nor Magda nor Uncle Karl nor Mother reacted in this manner. Although they were no longer small children, Peter and Ambrose were each given a dollar to spend on boardwalk amusements in addition to what money of their own they'd brought along. Magda too, though she protested she had ample spending money. The boys' mother made a little scene out of distributing the bills; she pretended that her sons and Magda were small children and cautioned them not to spend the sum too quickly or in one place. Magda promised with a merry laugh and, having both hands free, took the bill with her left. Peter laughed also and pledged in a falsetto to be a good boy. His imitation of a child was not clever. The boys' father was tall and thin, balding, fair-complexioned. Assertions of that sort are not effective; the reader may acknowledge the proposition, but. We should be much farther along than we are; something has gone wrong; not much of this preliminary rambling seems relevant. Yet everyone begins in the same place; how is it that most go along without difficulty but a few lose their way?

"Stay out from under the boardwalk," Uncle Karl growled from the side of his mouth. The boys' mother pushed his shoulder *in mock annoyance.* They were all standing before Fat May the Laughing Lady who advertised the funhouse. Larger than life, Fat May mechanically shook, rocked on her heels, slapped her thighs while recorded laughter—uproarious, female—came amplified from a hidden loudspeaker. It chuckled, wheezed, wept; tried in vain to catch its breath; tittered, groaned, exploded raucous and anew. You couldn't hear it without laughing yourself, no matter how you felt. Father came back from talking to a Coast-Guardsman on duty and reported that the surf was spoiled with crude oil from tankers recently torpedoed offshore. Lumps of it, difficult to remove, made tarry tidelines on the beach and stuck on swimmers. Many bathed in the surf nevertheless and came out speckled; others paid to use a municipal pool and only sunbathed on the beach. We would do the latter. We would do the latter. We would do the latter.

Under the boardwalk, matchbook covers, grainy other things. What is the story's theme? Ambrose is ill. He perspires in the dark passages; candied apples-on-a-stick, delicious-looking, disappointing to eat. Funhouses need men's and ladies' rooms at intervals. Others perhaps have also vomited in corners and corridors; may even have had bowel movements liable to be stepped in in the dark. The word *fuck* suggests suction and/or and/or flatulence. Mother and Father, grandmothers and grandfathers on both sides; great-grandmothers and great-grandfathers on four sides, et cetera. Count a generation as thirty years: in approximately the year when Lord Baltimore was granted charter to the province of Maryland by Charles I, five hundred twelve women—English, Welsh, Bavarian, Swiss—of every class and character, received into themselves the penises the intromittent organs of five hundred twelve men, ditto, in every circumstance and posture, to conceive the five hundred twelve ancestors of the two hundred fifty-six ancestors of the et cetera et cetera et cetera et cetera et cetera et cetera et cetera et cetera of the author, of the narrator, of this story, *Lost in the Funhouse*. In alleyways, ditches, canopy beds, pinewoods, bridal suites, ship's cabins, coach-and-fours, coaches-and-four, sultry toolsheds; on the cold sand under boardwalks, littered with *El Producto* cigar butts, treasured with Lucky Strike cigarette stubs, Coca-Cola caps, gritty turds, cardboard lollipop sticks, matchbook covers warning that A Slip of the Lip Can Sink a Ship. The shluppish whisper, continuous as seawash round the globe, tidelike falls and rises with the circuit of dawn and dusk.

Magda's teeth. She *was* left-handed. Perspiration. They've gone all the way, through, Magda and Peter, they've been waiting for hours with Mother and Uncle Karl while Father searches for his lost son; they draw french-fried potatoes from a paper cup and shake their heads. They've named the children they'll one day have and bring to Ocean City on holidays. Can spermatozoa properly be thought of as male animalcules when there are no female spermatozoa? They grope through hot, dark windings, past Love's Tunnel's fearsome obstacles. Some perhaps lose their way.

Peter suggested then and there that they do the funhouse; he had been through it before, so had Magda, Ambrose hadn't and suggested, his voice cracking on account of Fat May's laughter, that they swim first. All were chuckling, couldn't help it; Ambrose's father, Ambrose's and Peter's father came up grinning like a lunatic with two boxes of syrup-coated popcorn, one for Mother, one for Magda; the men were to help themselves. Ambrose walked on Magda's right; being by nature left-handed, she carried the box in her left hand. Up front the situation was reversed.

"What are you limping for?" Magda inquired of Ambrose. He supposed in a husky tone that his foot had gone to sleep in the car. Her teeth flashed. "Pins and needles?" It was the honeysuckle on the lattice of the former privy that drew the bees. Imagine being stung there. How long is this going to take?

The adults decided to forgo the pool; but Uncle Karl insisted they change into swimsuits and do the beach. "He wants to watch the pretty girls," Peter teased, and ducked behind Magda from Uncle Karl's pretended wrath. "You've got all the pretty girls you need right here," Magda declared, and Mother said: "Now that's the gospel truth." Magda scolded Peter, who reached over her shoulder to sneak some popcorn. "Your brother and father aren't getting any." Uncle Karl wondered if they were going to have fireworks that night, what with the shortages. It wasn't the shortages, Mr. M_____ replied; Ocean City had fireworks from pre-war. But it was too risky on account of the enemy submarines, some people thought.

"Don't seem like Fourth of July without fireworks," said Uncle Karl. The inverted tag in dialogue writing is still considered permissible with proper names or epithets, but sounds old-fashioned with personal pronouns. "We'll have 'em again soon enough," predicted the boys' father. Their mother declared she could do without fireworks: they reminded her too much of the real thing. Their father said all the more reason to shoot off a few now and again. Uncle Karl asked *rhetorically* who needed reminding, just look at people's hair and skin.

"The oil, yes," said Mrs. M———.

Ambrose had a pain in his stomach and so didn't swim but enjoyed watching the others. He and his father burned red easily. Magda's figure was exceedingly well developed for her age. She too declined to swim, and got mad, and became angry when Peter attempted to drag her into the pool. She always swam, he insisted; what did she mean not swim? Why did a person come to Ocean City?

"Maybe I want to lay here with Ambrose," Magda teased.

Nobody likes a pedant.

"Aha," said Mother. Peter grabbed Magda by one ankle and ordered Ambrose to grab the other. She squealed and rolled over on the beach blanket. Ambrose pretended to help hold her back. Her tan was darker than even Mother's and Peter's. "Help out, Uncle Karl!" Peter cried. Uncle Karl went to seize the other ankle. Inside the top of her swimsuit, however, you could see the line where the sunburn ended and, when she hunched her shoulders and squealed again, one nipple's auburn edge. Mother made them behave themselves. "*You* should certainly know," she said to Uncle Karl. Archly. "That when a lady says she doesn't feel like swimming, a gentleman doesn't ask questions." Uncle Karl said excuse *him;* Mother winked at Magda; Ambrose blushed; stupid Peter kept saying "Phooey on *feel like!*" and tugging at Magda's ankle; then even he got the point, and cannonballed with a holler into the pool.

"I swear," Magda said, in mock *in feigned* exasperation.

The diving would make a suitable literary symbol. To go off the high board you had to wait in a line along the poolside and up the ladder. Fellows tickled girls and goosed one another and shouted to the ones at the top to hurry up, or razzed them for bellyfloppers. Once on the springboard some took a great while posing or clowning or deciding on a dive or getting up their nerve; others ran right off. Especially among the younger fellows the idea was to strike the funniest pose or do the craziest stunt as you fell, a thing that got harder to do as you kept on and kept on. But whether you hollered *Geronimo!* or *Sieg heil!*, held your nose or "rode a bicycle," pretended to be shot or did a perfect jackknife or changed your mind halfway down and ended up with nothing, it was over in two seconds, after all that wait. Spring, pose, splash. Spring, neat-o, splash. Spring, aw fooey, splash.

The grown-ups had gone on. Ambrose wanted to converse with Magda; she was remarkably well developed for her age; it was said that that came from rubbing with a turkish towel, and there were other theories. Ambrose could think of nothing to say except how good a diver Peter was, who was showing off for her benefit. You could pretty well tell by looking at their bathing suits and arm muscles how far along the different fellows were. Ambrose was glad he hadn't gone in swimming, the cold water shrank you up so. Magda pretended to be uninterested in the diving; she probably weighed as much as he did. If you knew your way around in the funhouse like your own bedroom, you could wait until a girl came along and then slip away without ever getting caught, even if her boyfriend was right with her. She'd think *he* did it! It would be better to be the boyfriend, and act outraged, and tear the funhouse apart.

Not act; *be.*

"He's a master diver," Ambrose said. In feigned admiration. "You really have to slave away at it to get that good." What would it matter anyhow if he asked her right out whether she remembered, even teased her with it as Peter would have?

There's no point in going farther; this isn't getting anybody anywhere; they haven't even come to the funhouse yet. Ambrose is off the track, in some new or old part of the place that's not supposed to be used; he strayed into it by some one-in-a-million chance, like the time the roller-coaster car left the tracks in the nineteen-teens against all the laws of physics and sailed over the boardwalk in the dark. And they can't locate him because they don't know where to look. Even the designer and operator have forgotten this other part, that winds around on itself like a whelk shell. That winds around the right part like the snakes on Mercury's caduceus. Some people, perhaps, don't "hit their stride" until their twenties, when the growing-up business is over and women appreciate other things besides wisecracks and teasing and strutting. Peter didn't have one-tenth the imagination *he* had, not one-tenth. Peter did this naming-their-children as a joke, making up names like Aloysius and Murgatroyd, but Ambrose knew *exactly* how it would feel to be married and have children of your own, and be a loving husband and father, and go comfortably to work in the mornings and to bed with your wife at night, and wake up with her there. With a breeze coming through the sash and birds and mockingbirds singing in the Chinese-cigar trees. His eyes watered, there aren't enough ways to say that. He would be quite famous in his line of work. Whether Magda was his wife or not, one evening when he was wise-lined and gray at the temples she'd smile gravely, at a fashionable dinner party, and remind her of his youthful passion. The time they went with his family to Ocean City; the *erotic fantasies* he used to have about her. How long ago it seemed, and childish! Yet tender, too, *n'est-ce pas?* Would she have imagined that the world-famous whatever remembered how many strings were on the lyre on the bench beside the girl on the label of the cigar box he'd stared at in the toolshed at age ten while she, age eleven. Even then he had felt *wise beyond his years;* he'd stroked her hair and said in his deepest voice and correctest English, as to a dear child: "I shall never forget this moment."

But though he had breathed heavily, groaned as if ecstatic, what he'd really felt throughout was an odd detachment, as though someone else were Master. Strive as he might to be transported, he heard his mind take notes upon the scene: *This is what they call* passion. *I am experiencing it.* Many of the digger machines were out of order in the penny arcades and could not be repaired or replaced for the duration. Moreover the prizes, made now in USA, were less interesting than formerly, pasteboard items for the most part, and some of the machines wouldn't work on white pennies. The gypsy fortuneteller machine might have provided a foreshadowing of the climax of this story if Ambrose had operated it. It was even dilapidateder than most: the silver coating was worn off the brown metal handles, the glass windows around the dummy were cracked and taped, her kerchiefs and silks long-faded. If a man lived by himself, he could take a department-store mannequin with flexible joints and modify her in certain ways. *However:* by the time he was that old he'd have a real woman. There was a machine that stamped your name around a white-metal coin with a star in the middle: *A———*. His son would be the second, and when the lad reached thirteen or so he would put a strong arm around his shoulder and tell him calmly: "It is perfectly normal. We have all been through it. It will not last forever." Nobody knew how to be what they were right. He'd smoke a pipe, teach his son how to fish and softcrab, assure him he needn't worry about himself. Magda would certainly give, Magda would certainly yield a great deal of milk, although guilty of occasional solecisms. It don't taste so bad. Suppose the lights came on now!

The day wore on. You think you're yourself, but there are other persons in you. Ambrose gets hard when Ambrose doesn't want to, *and obversely.* Ambrose watches them disagree; Ambrose watches him watch. In the funhouse mirror room you can't see yourself go on forever, because no matter how you stand, your head gets in the way. Even if you had a glass periscope, the image of your eye would cover up the thing you really wanted to see. The police will come; there'll be a story in the papers. That must be where it happened. Unless he can find a surprise exit, an unofficial backdoor escape hatch opening on an alley, say, and then stroll up to the family in front of the funhouse and ask where everybody's been; *he's* been out of the place for ages. That's just where it happened, in that last lighted room: Peter and Magda found the right exit; he found one that you weren't supposed to find and strayed off into the works somewhere. In a perfect funhouse you'd be able to go only one way, like the divers off the high board; getting lost would be impossible; the doors and halls would work like minnow traps or the valves in veins.

On account of German U-boats, Ocean City was "browned out": street-lights were shaded on the seaward side; shopwindows and boardwalk amusement places were kept dim, not to silhouette tankers and Liberty-ships for torpedoing. In a short story about Ocean City, Maryland, during World War II, the author could make use of the image of sailors on leave in the penny arcades and shooting galleries, sighting through the crosshairs of toy machine guns at swastika'd subs, while out in the black Atlantic a U-boat skipper squints through his periscope at real ships outlined by the glow of penny arcades. After dinner the family strolled back to the amusement end of the boardwalk. The boys' father had burnt red as always and was masked with Noxzema, a minstrel in reverse. The grown-ups stood at the end of the boardwalk where the Hurricane of '33 had cut an inlet from the ocean to Assawoman Bay.

"Pronounced with a long *o*," Uncle Karl reminded Magda with a wink. His shirt sleeves were rolled up; Mother punched his brown biceps with the arrowed heart on it and said his mind was naughty. Fat May's laugh came suddenly from the funhouse, as if she'd just got the joke; the family laughed too at the coincidence. Ambrose went under the boardwalk to search for out-of-town matchbook covers with the aid of his pocket flashlight; he looked out from the edge of the North American continent and wondered how far their laughter carried over the water. Spies in rubber rafts; survivors in lifeboats. If the joke had been beyond his understanding, he could have said: *"The laughter was over his head."* And let the reader see the serious wordplay on second reading.

He turned the flashlight on and then off at once even before the woman whooped. He sprang away, heart athud, dropping the light. What had the man grunted? Perspiration drenched and chilled him by the time he scrambled up to the family. "See anything?" his father asked. His voice wouldn't come; he shrugged and violently brushed sand from his pants legs.

"Let's ride the old flying horses!" Magda cried. I'll never be an author. It's been forever already, everybody's gone home, Ocean City's deserted, the ghost-crabs are tickling across the beach and down the littered cold streets. And the empty halls of clapboard hotels and abandoned funhouses. A tidal wave; an enemy air raid; a monster-crab swelling like an island from the sea. *The inhabitants fled in terror.* Magda clung to his trouser leg: he alone knew the maze's secret. "He gave his life that we might live," said Uncle Karl with a scowl of pain, as he. The fellow's hands had been tattooed; the woman's legs, the woman's fat white legs had. *An astonishing coincidence.* He yearned to tell Peter. He wanted to throw up for excitement. They hadn't even chased him. He wished he were dead.

One possible ending would be to have Ambrose come across another lost person in the dark. They'd match their wits together against the funhouse, struggle like Ulysses past obstacle after obstacle, help and encourage each other. Or a girl. By the time they found the exit they'd be closest friends, sweethearts if it were a girl; they'd know each other's inmost souls, be bound together *by the cement of shared adventure;* then they'd emerge into the light and it would turn out that his friend was a Negro. A blind girl. President Roosevelt's son. Ambrose's former archenemy.

Shortly after the mirror room he'd groped along a musty corridor, his heart already misgiving him at the absence of phosphorescent arrows and other signs. He'd found a crack of light—not a door, it turned out, but a seam between the plyboard wall panels—and squinting up to it, espied a small old man, *in appearance not unlike* the photographs at home of Ambrose's late grandfather, nodding upon a stool beneath a bare, speckled bulb. A crude panel of toggle- and knife-switches hung beside the open fuse box near his head; elsewhere in the little room were wooden levers and ropes belayed to boat cleats. At the time, Ambrose wasn't lost enough to rap or call; later he couldn't find that crack. Now it seemed to him that he'd possibly dozed off for a few minutes somewhere along the way; certainly he was exhausted from the afternoon's sunshine and the evening's problems; he couldn't be sure he hadn't dreamed part or all of the sight. Had an old black wall fan droned like bees and shimmied two flypaper streamers? Had the funhouse operator—gentle, somewhat sad and tired-appearing, in expression not unlike the photographs at home of Ambrose's late Uncle Konrad—murmured in his sleep? Is there really such a person as Ambrose, or is he a figment of the author's imagination? Was it Assawoman Bay or Sinepuxent? Are there other errors of fact in this fiction? Was there another sound besides the little slap slap of thigh on ham, like water sucking at the chine-boards of a skiff?

When you're lost, the smartest thing to do is stay put till you're found, hollering if necessary. But to holler guarantees humiliation as well as rescue; keeping silent permits some saving of face—you can act surprised at the fuss when your rescuers find you and swear you weren't lost, if they do. What's more you might find your own way yet, *however belatedly.*

"Don't tell me your foot's still asleep!" Magda exclaimed as the three young people walked from the inlet to the area set aside for ferris wheels, carrousels, and other carnival rides, they having decided in favor of the vast and ancient merry-go-round instead of the funhouse. What a sentence, everything was wrong from the outset. People don't know what to make of him, he doesn't know what to make of himself, he's only thirteen, *athletically and socially inept,* not astonishingly bright, but there are antennae; he has . . . some sort of receivers in his head; things speak to him, he understands more than he should, the world winks at him through its objects, grabs grinning at his coat. Everybody else is in on some secret he doesn't know; they've forgotten to tell him. Through simple *procrastination* his mother put off his baptism until this year. Everyone else had it done as a baby; he'd assumed the same of himself, as had his mother, so she claimed, until it was time for him to join Grace Methodist-Protestant and the oversight came out. He was mortified, but pitched sleepless through his private catechizing, intimidated by the ancient mysteries, a thirteen year old would never say that, resolved to experience conversion like St. Augustine. When the water touched his brow and Adam's sin left him, he contrived by a strain like defecation to bring tears into his eyes—but felt nothing. There was some simple, radical difference about him; he hoped it was genius, feared it was madness, devoted himself to amiability and inconspicuousness. Alone on the seawall near his house he was seized by the terrifying transports he'd thought to find in toolshed, in Communion-cup. The grass was alive! The town, the river, himself, were not imaginary; time roared in his ears like wind; the world was *going on!* This part ought to be dramatized. The Irish author James Joyce once wrote. Ambrose M———— is going to scream.

There is no *texture of rendered sensory detail,* for one thing. The faded distorting mirrors beside Fat May; the impossibility of choosing a mount when one had but a single ride on the great carrousel; the *vertigo attendant on his recognition* that Ocean City was worn out, the place of fathers and grandfathers, straw-boatered men and parasoled ladies survived by their amusements. Money spent, the three paused at Peter's insistence beside Fat May to watch the girls get their skirts blown up. The object was to tease Magda, who said: "I swear, Peter M————, you've got a one-track mind! Amby and me aren't *interested* in such things." In the tumbling-barrel, too, just inside the Devil's mouth entrance to the funhouse, the girls were upended and their boyfriends and others could see up their dresses if they cared to. Which was the whole point, Ambrose realized. Of the entire funhouse! If you looked around, you noticed that almost all the people on the boardwalk were paired off into couples except the small children; in a way, that was the whole point of Ocean City! If you had X-ray eyes and could see everything going on at that instant under the boardwalk and in all the hotel rooms and cars and alleyways, you'd realize that all that normally *showed,* like restaurants and dance halls and clothing and test-your-strength machines, was merely preparation and intermission. Fat May screamed.

Because he watched the goings-on from the corner of his eye, it was Ambrose who spied the half-dollar on the boardwalk near the tumbling-barrel. Losers weepers. The first time he'd heard some people moving through a corridor not far away, just after he'd lost sight of the crack of light, he'd decided not to call to them, for fear they'd guess he was scared and poke fun; it sounded like roughnecks; he'd hoped they'd come by and he could follow in the dark without their knowing. Another time he'd heard just one person, unless he imagined it, bumping along as if on the other side of the plywood; perhaps Peter coming back for him, or Father, or Magda lost too. Or the owner and operator of the funhouse. He'd called out once, as though merrily: "Anybody know where the heck we are?" But the query was too stiff, his voice cracked, when the sounds stopped he was terrified: maybe it was a queer who waited for fellows to get lost, or a longhaired filthy monster that lived in some cranny of the funhouse. He stood rigid for hours it seemed like, scarcely respiring. His future was shockingly clear, in outline. He tried holding his breath to the point of unconsciousness. There ought to be a button you could push to end your life absolutely without pain; disappear in a flick, like turning out a light. He would push it instantly! He despised Uncle Karl. But he despised his father too, for not being what he was supposed to be. Perhaps his father hated *his* father, and so on, and his son would hate him, and so on. Instantly!

Naturally he didn't have nerve enough to ask Magda to go through the funhouse with him. With incredible nerve and to everyone's surprise he invited Magda, quietly and politely, to go through the funhouse with him. "I warn you, I've never been through it before," he added, *laughing easily;* "but I reckon we can manage somehow. The important thing to remember, after all, is that it's meant to be a *fun*-house; that is, a place of amusement. If people really got lost or injured or too badly frightened in it, the owner'd go out of business. There'd even be lawsuits. No character in a work of fiction can make a speech this long without interruption or acknowledgment from the other characters."

Mother teased Uncle Karl: "Three's a crowd, I always heard." But actually Ambrose was relieved that Peter now had a quarter too. Nothing was what it looked like. Every instant, under the surface of the Atlantic Ocean, millions of living animals devoured one another. Pilots were falling in flames over Europe; women were being forcibly raped in the South Pacific. His father should have taken him aside and said: "There is a simple secret to getting through the funhouse, as simple as being first to see the Towers. Here it is. Peter does not know it; neither does your Uncle Karl. You and I are different. Not surprisingly, you've often wished you weren't. Don't think I haven't noticed how unhappy your childhood has been! But you'll understand, when I tell you, why it had to be kept secret until now. And you won't regret not being like your brother and your uncle. *On the contrary!*" If you knew all the stories behind all the people on the boardwalk, you'd see that *nothing* was what it looked like. Husbands and wives often hated each other; parents didn't necessarily love their children; et cetera. A child took things for granted because he had nothing to compare his life to and everybody acted as if things were as they should be. Therefore each saw himself as the hero of the story, when the truth might turn out to be that he's the villain, or the coward. And there wasn't one thing you could do about it!

Hunchbacks, fat ladies, fools—that no one chose what he was was unbearable. In the movies he'd meet a beautiful young girl in the funhouse; they'd have hairsbreadth escapes from real dangers; he'd do and say the right things; she also; in the end they'd be lovers; their dialogue lines would match up; he'd be perfectly at ease; she'd not only like him well enough, she'd think he was *marvelous;* she'd lie awake thinking about *him,* instead of vice versa—the way *his* face looked in different lights and how he stood and exactly what he'd said—and yet that would be only one small episode in his wonderful life, among many many others. Not a *turning point* at all. What had happened in the toolshed was nothing. He hated, he loathed his parents! One reason for not writing a lost-in-the-funhouse story is that either everybody's felt what Ambrose feels, in which case it goes without saying, or else no normal person feels such things, in which case Ambrose is a freak. "Is anything more tiresome, in fiction, than the problems of sensitive adolescents?" And it's all too long and rambling, as if the author. For all a person knows the first time through, the end could be just around any corner; perhaps, *not impossibly* it's been within reach any number of times. On the other hand he may be scarcely past the start, with everything yet to get through, an intolerable idea.

Fill in: His father's raised eyebrows when he announced his decision to do the funhouse with Magda. Ambrose understands now, but didn't then, that his father was wondering whether he knew what the funhouse was *for*—especially since he didn't object, as he should have, when Peter decided to come along too. The ticket-woman, witchlike, mortifying him when inadvertently he gave her his name-coin instead of the half-dollar, then unkindly calling Magda's attention to the birthmark on his temple: "Watch out for him, girlie, he's a marked man!" She wasn't even cruel, he understood, only vulgar and insensitive. Somewhere in the world there was a young woman with such splendid understanding that she'd see him entire, like a poem or story, and find his words so valuable after all that when he confessed his apprehensions she would explain why they were in fact the very things that made him precious to her . . . and to Western Civilization! There was no such girl, the simple truth being. Violent yawns as they approached the mouth. Whispered advice from an old-timer on a bench near the barrel: "Go crabwise and ye'll get an eyeful without upsetting!" Composure vanished at the first pitch: Peter hollered joyously, Magda tumbled, shrieked, clutched her skirt; Ambrose scrambled crabwise, tight-lipped with terror, was soon out, watched his dropped name-coin slide among the couples. Shamefaced he saw that to get through expeditiously was not the point; Peter feigned assistance in order to trip Magda up, shouted "I see Christmas!" when her legs went flying. The old man, his latest betrayer, cackled approval. A dim hall then of black-thread cobwebs and recorded gibber: he took Magda's elbow to steady her against revolving discs set in the slanted floor to throw your feet out from under, and explained to her in a calm, deep voice his theory that each phase of the funhouse was triggered either automatically, by a series of photoelectric devices, or else manually by operators stationed at peepholes. But he lost his voice thrice as the discs unbalanced him; Magda was anyhow squealing: but at one point she clutched him about the waist to keep from falling, and her right cheek pressed for a moment against his belt-buckle. Heroically he drew her up, it was his chance to clutch her close as if for support and say: "I love you." He even put an arm lightly about the small of her back before a sailor-and-girl pitched into them from behind, sorely treading his left big toe and knocking Magda asprawl with them. The sailor's girl was a string-haired hussy with a loud laugh and light blue drawers; Ambrose realized that he wouldn't have said "I love you" anyhow, and was smitten with self-contempt. How much better it would be to be that common sailor! A wiry little Seaman 3rd, the fellow squeezed a girl to each side and stumbled hilarious into the mirror room, closer to Magda in thirty seconds than Ambrose had got in thirteen years. She giggled at something the fellow said to Peter; she drew her hair from her eyes with a movement so womanly it struck Ambrose's heart; Peter's smacking her backside then seemed particularly coarse. But Magda made a pleased indignant face and cried, "All right for *you,* mister!" and pursued Peter into the maze without a backward glance. The sailor followed after, leisurely, drawing his girl against his hip; Ambrose understood not only that they were all so relieved to be rid of his burdensome company that they didn't even notice his absence, but that he himself shared their relief. Stepping from the treacherous passage at last into the mirror-maze, he saw once again, more clearly than ever, how readily he deceived himself into supposing he was a person. He even foresaw, wincing at his dreadful self-knowledge, that he would repeat the deception, at ever-rarer intervals, all his wretched life, so fearful were the alternatives. Fame, madness, suicide; perhaps all three. It's not believable that so young a boy could articulate that reflection, and in fiction the merely true must always yield to the plausible. Moreover, the symbolism is in places heavy-footed. Yet Ambrose M _____ understood, as few adults do, that the famous loneliness of the great was no popular myth but a general truth—furthermore, that it was as much cause as effect.

All the preceding except the last few sentences is exposition that should've been done earlier or interspersed with the present action instead of lumped together. No reader would put up with so much with such *prolixity:* It's interesting that Ambrose's father, though presumably an intelligent man (as indicated by his role as grade-school principal), neither encouraged nor discouraged his sons at all in any way—as if he either didn't care about them or cared all right but didn't know how to act. If this fact should contribute to one of them's becoming a celebrated but wretchedly unhappy scientist, was it a good thing or not? He too might someday face the question; it would be useful to know whether it had tortured his father for years, for example, or never once crossed his mind.

In the maze two important things happened. First, our hero found a name-coin someone else had lost or discarded: *AMBROSE,* suggestive of the famous lightship and of his late grandfather's favorite dessert, which his mother used to prepare on special occasions out of coconut, oranges, grapes, and what else. Second, as he wondered at the endless replication of his image in the mirrors, second, as he *lost himself in the reflection* that the necessity for an observer makes perfect observation impossible, better make him eighteen at least, yet that would render other things unlikely, he heard Peter and Magda chuckling somewhere together in the maze. "Here!" "No, here!" they shouted to each other; Peter said, "Where's Amby?" Magda murmured, "Amb?" Peter called. In a pleased, friendly voice. He didn't reply. The truth was, his brother was a *happy-go-lucky youngster* who'd've been better off with a regular brother of his own, but who seldom complained of his lot and was generally cordial. Ambrose's throat ached; there aren't enough different ways to say that. He stood quietly while the two young people giggled and thumped through the glittering maze, hurrah'd their discovery of its exit, cried out in joyful alarm at what next beset them. Then he set his mouth and followed after, as he supposed, took a wrong turn, strayed into the pass *wherein he lingers yet.*

The action of conventional dramatic narrative may be represented by a diagram called Freitag's Triangle:

or more accurately by a variant of that diagram:

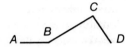

in which *AB* represents the exposition, *B* the introduction of conflict, *BC* the "rising action," complication, or development of the conflict, *C* the climax, or turn of the action, *CD* the dénouement, or resolution of the conflict. While there is no reason to regard this pattern as an absolute necessity, like many other conventions it became conventional because great numbers of people over many years learned by trial and error that it was effective; one ought not to forsake it, therefore, unless one wishes to forsake as well the effect of drama or has clear cause to feel that deliberate violation of the "normal" pattern can better can better effect that effect. This can't go on much longer; it can go on forever. He died telling stories to himself in the dark; years later, when that vast unsuspected area of the funhouse came to light, the first expedition found his skeleton in one of its labyrinthine corridors and mistook it for part of the entertainment. He died of starvation telling himself stories in the dark; but unbeknownst unbeknownst to him, an assistant operator of the funhouse, happening to overhear him, crouched just behind the plyboard partition and wrote down his every word. The operator's daughter, an exquisite young woman with a figure unusually well developed for her age, crouched just behind the partition and transcribed his every word. Though she had never laid eyes on him, she recognized that here was one of Western Culture's truly great imaginations, the eloquence of whose suffering would be an inspiration to unnumbered. And her heart was torn between her love for the misfortunate young man (yes, she loved him, though she had never laid though she knew him only—but how well!—through his words, and the deep, calm voice in which he spoke them) between her love et cetera and her womanly intuition that only in suffering and isolation could he give voice et cetera. Lone dark dying. Quietly she kissed the rough plyboard, and a tear fell upon the page. Where she had written in shorthand *Where she had written in shorthand* Where she had written in shorthand *Where she* et cetera. A long time ago we should have passed the apex of Freitag's Triangle and made brief work of the *dénouement;* the plot doesn't rise by meaningful steps but winds upon itself, digresses, retreats, hesitates, sighs, collapses, expires. The climax of the story must be its protagonist's discovery of a way to get through the funhouse. But he has found none, may have ceased to search.

What relevance does the war have to the story? Should there be fireworks outside or not?

Ambrose wondered, languished, dozed. Now and then he fell into his habit of rehearsing to himself the unadventurous story of his life, narrated from the third-person point of view, from his earliest memory parenthesis of maple leaves stirring in the summer breath of tidewater Maryland end of parenthesis to the present moment. Its principal events, on this telling, would appear to have been *A, B, C,* and *D.*

He imagined himself years hence, successful, married, at ease in the world, the trials of his adolescence far behind him. He has come to the seashore with his family for the holiday: how Ocean City has changed! But at one seldom at one ill-frequented end of the boardwalk a few derelict amusements survive from times gone by: the great carrousel from the turn of the century, with its monstrous griffins and mechanical concert band; the roller coaster rumored since 1916 to have been condemned; the mechanical shooting gallery in which only the image of our enemies changed. His own son laughs with Fat May and wants to know what a funhouse is; Ambrose hugs the sturdy lad close and smiles around his pipestem at his wife.

The family's going home. Mother sits between Father and Uncle Karl, who teases him good-naturedly who chuckles over the fact that the comrade with whom he'd fought his way shoulder to shoulder through the funhouse had turned out to be a blind Negro girl—to their mutual discomfort, as they'd opened their souls. But such are the walls of custom, which even. Whose arm is where? How must it feel. He dreams of a funhouse vaster by far than any yet constructed; but by then they may be out of fashion, like steamboats and excursion trains. Already quaint and seedy: the draperied ladies on the frieze of the carrousel are his father's father's moon-cheeked dreams; if he thinks of it more he will vomit his apple-on-a-stick.

He wonders: will he become a regular person? Something has gone wrong: his vaccination didn't take; at the Boy-Scout initiation campfire he only pretended to be deeply moved, as he pretends to this hour that it is not so bad after all in the funhouse, and that he has a little limp. How long will it last? He envisions a truly astonishing funhouse, incredibly complex yet utterly controlled from a great central switchboard like the console of a pipe organ. Nobody had enough imagination. He could design such a place himself, wiring and all, and he's only thirteen years old. He would be its operator: panel lights would show what was up in every cranny of its cunning of its multifarious vastness; a switch-flick would ease this fellow's way, complicate that's, to balance things out; if anyone seemed lost or frightened, all the operator had to do was.

He wishes he had never entered the funhouse. But he has. Then he wishes he were dead. But he's not. Therefore he will construct funhouses for others and be their secret operator—though he would rather be among the lovers for whom funhouses are designed.

ALICE MUNRO (b. 1931)

Lives of Girls and Women

The snow banks along the main street got to be so high that an archway was cut in one of them, between the street and the sidewalk, in front of the post office. A picture was taken of this and published in the Jubilee *Herald-Advance,* so that people could cut it out and send it to relatives and acquaintances living in less heroic climates, in England or Australia or Toronto. The red-brick clocktower of the post office was sticking up above the snow and two women were standing in the archway, to show it was no trick. Both these women worked in the post office, had put their coats on without buttoning them. One was Fern Dogherty, my mother's boarder.

My mother cut this picture out, because it had Fern in it, and because she said I should keep it, to show to my children.

"They will never see a thing like that," she said. "By then the snow will all be collected in machines and—dissipated. Or people will be living under transparent domes, with a controlled temperature. There will be no such thing as seasons anymore."

How did she collect all her unsettling information about the future? She looked forward to a time when towns like Jubilee would be replaced by domes and mushrooms of concrete, with moving skyways to carry you from one to the other, when the countryside would be bound and tamed forever under broad sweeping ribbons of pavement. Nothing would be the same as we knew it today, no frying pans or bobby pins or printed pages or fountain pens would remain. My mother would not miss a thing.

Her speaking of my children amazed me too, for I never meant to have any. It was glory I was after, walking the streets of Jubilee like an exile or a spy, not sure from which direction fame would strike, or when, only convinced from my bones out that it had to. In this conviction my mother had shared, she had been my ally, but now I would no longer discuss it with her; she was indiscreet, and her expectations took too blatant a form.

Fern Dogherty. There she was in the paper, both hands coquettishly holding up the full collar of her good winter coat, which through pure luck she had worn to work that day. "I look the size of a watermelon," she said. "In that coat."

Mr. Chamberlain, looking with her, pinched her arm above the bracelet wrinkle of the wrist.

"Tough rind, tough old watermelon."

"Don't get vicious," said Fern. "I mean it." Her voice was small for such a big woman, plaintive, put-upon, but in the end good-humored, yielding. All those qualities my mother had developed for her assault on life—sharpness, smartness, determination, selectiveness—seemed to have their opposites in Fern, with her diffuse complaints, lazy movements, indifferent agreeableness. She had a dark skin, not olive but dusty looking, dim, with brown-pigmented spots as large as coins; it was like the dappled ground under a tree on a sunny day. Her teeth were square, white, slightly protruding, with little spaces between them. These two characteristics, neither of which sounds particularly attractive in itself, did give her a roguish, sensual look.

She had a ruby-colored satin dressing gown, a gorgeous garment, fruitily molding, when she sat down, the bulges of her stomach and thighs. She wore it Sunday mornings, when she sat in our dining room smoking, drinking tea, until it was time to get ready for church. It parted at the knees to show some pale clinging rayon—a nightgown. Nightgowns were garments I could not bear, because of the way they twisted around and worked up on you while you slept and also because they left you uncovered between the legs. Naomi and I when we were younger used to draw pictures of men and women with startling gross genitals, the women's fat, bristling with needly hair, like a porcupine's back. Wearing a nightgown one could not help being aware of this vile bundle, which pajamas could decently shroud and contain. My mother at the same Sunday breakfast table wore large striped pajamas, a faded rust-colored kimono with a tasseled tie, the sort of slippers that are woolly socks, with a sole sewn in.

Fern Dogherty and my mother were friends in spite of differences. My mother valued in people experience of the world, contact with any life of learning or culture, and finally any suggestion of being dubiously received in Jubilee. And Fern had not always worked for the post office. No; at one time she had studied singing, she had studied at the Royal Conservatory of Music. Now she sang in the United Church choir, sang "I Know that My Redeemer Liveth" on Easter Sunday, and at weddings she sang "Because" and "O Promise Me" and "The Voice that Breathed O'er Eden." On Saturday afternoons, the post office being closed, she and my mother would listen to the broadcasts of the Metropolitan Opera. My mother had a book of operas. She would get it out and follow the story, identifying the arias, for which translations were provided. She had questions for Fern, but Fern did not know as much about operas as you would think she might; she would even get mixed up about which one it was they were listening to. But sometimes she would lean forward with her elbows on the table, not now relaxed, but alertly supported, and sing, scorning the foreign words. "*Do*—daa—do—da, *do*, da do-do—" The force, the seriousness of her singing voice always came as a surprise. It didn't embarrass her, letting loose those grand, inflated emotions she paid no attention to in life.

"Did you plan to be an opera singer?" I asked.

"No. I just planned to be the lady working in the post office. Well, I did and I didn't. The work, the *training*. I just didn't have the ambition for it, I guess that was my trouble. I always preferred having a good time." She wore slacks on Saturday afternoons, and sandals that showed her pudgy, painted toes. She was dropping ashes on her stomach, which, ungirdled, popped out in a pregnant curve. "Smoking is ruining my voice," she said meditatively.

Fern's style of singing, though admired, was regarded in Jubilee as being just a hair's breadth from showing off, and sometimes children did screech or warble after her, in the street. My mother could take this for persecution. She would construct such cases out of the flimsiest evidence, seeking out the Jewish couple who ran the

Army Surplus store, or the shrunken silent Chinese in the laundry, with bewildering compassion, loud slow-spoken overtures of friendship. They did not know what to make of her. Fern was not persecuted, that I could see. Though my old aunts, my father's aunts, would say her name in a peculiar way, as if it had a stone in it, that they would have to suck, and spit out. And Naomi did tell me, "That Fern Dogherty had a baby."

"She never did," I said, automatically defensive.

"She did so. She had it when she was nineteen years old. That's why she got kicked out of the Conservatory."

"How do you know?"

"My mother knows."

Naomi's mother had spies everywhere, old childbed cases, deathbed companions, keeping her informed. In her nursing job, going from one house to another, she was able to operate like an underwater vacuum tube, sucking up what nobody else could get at. I felt I had to argue with Naomi about it because Fern was our boarder, and Naomi was always saying things about people in our house. ("Your mother's an atheist," she would say with black relish, and I would say, "No she isn't, she's an agnostic," and all through my reasoned hopeful explanation Naomi would chant *same difference, same difference.*) I was not able to retaliate, either out of delicacy or cowardice, though Naomi's own father belonged to some odd and discredited religious sect, and wandered all over town talking prophecies without putting his false teeth in.

I took to noticing pictures of babies in the paper, or in magazines, when Fern was around, saying, "Aw, isn't it *cute?*" and then watching her closely for a flicker of remorse, maternal longing, as if someday she might actually be persuaded to burst into tears, fling out her empty arms, struck to the heart by an ad for talcum powder or strained meat.

Furthermore, Naomi said Fern did everything with Mr. Chamberlain, just the same as if they were married.

It was Mr. Chamberlain who got Fern boarding with us in the first place. We rented the house from his mother, now in her third year, blind and bedridden, in the Wawanash County Hospital. Fern's mother was in the same place; it was there, in fact, on a visiting day, that they had met. She was working in the Blue River post office at that time. Mr. Chamberlain worked at the Jubilee radio station and lived in a small apartment in the same building, not wanting the trouble of a house. My mother spoke of him as "Fern's friend," in a clarifying tone of voice, as if to insist that the word friend in this case meant no more than it was supposed to mean.

"They enjoy each other's company," she said. "They don't bother about any nonsense."

Nonsense meant romance; it meant vulgarity; it meant sex.

I tried out on my mother what Naomi said.

"Fern and Mr. Chamberlain might just as well be married."

"What? What do you mean? Who said that?"

"Everybody knows it."

"I don't. Everybody does not. Nobody ever said such a thing in my hearing. It's that Naomi said it, isn't it?"

Naomi was not popular in my house, nor I in hers. Each of us was suspected of carrying the seeds of contamination—in my case, of atheism, in Naomi's, of sexual preoccupation.

"It's dirty mindedness that is just rampant in this town, and will never let people alone."

"If Fern Dogherty was not a good woman," my mother concluded, with a spacious air of logic, "do you think I would have her living in my house?"

This year, our first year in high school, Naomi and I held almost daily discussions on the subject of sex, but took one tone, so that there were degrees of candor we could never reach. This tone was ribald, scornful, fanatically curious. A year ago we had liked to imagine ourselves victims of passion; now we were established as on-lookers, or at most cold and gleeful experimenters. We had a book Naomi had found in her mother's old hope chest, under the moth-balled best blankets.

Care should be taken during the initial connection, we read aloud, *particularly if the male organ is of an unusual size. Vaseline may prove a helpful lubricant.*

"I prefer butter myself. Tastier."

Intercourse between the thighs is often resorted to in the final stages of pregnancy.
"You mean they still do it *then?*"

The rear-entry position is sometimes indicated in cases where the female is considerably obese.

"Fern," Naomi said. "That's how he does it to Fern. She's considerably obese."

"Aggh! This book makes me sick."

The male sexual organ in erection, we read, had been known to reach a length of fourteen inches. Naomi spat out her chewing gum and rolled it between her palms, stretching it longer and longer, then picked it up by one end and dangled it in the air.

"Mr. Chamberlain, the record breaker!"

Thereafter whenever she came to my place, and Mr. Chamberlain was there, one of us, or both, if we were chewing gum, would take it out and roll it this way and dangle it innocently, till even the adults noticed and Mr. Chamberlain said, "That's quite a game you got there," and my mother said, "Stop that, it's filthy." (She meant the gum.) We watched Mr. Chamberlain and Fern for signs of passion, wantonness, lustful looks, or hands up the skirt. We were not rewarded, my defense of them turning out to be truer than I wished it to be. For I as much as Naomi liked to entertain myself with thoughts of their grunting indecencies, their wallowing in jingly beds (in tourist cabins, Naomi said, every time they drove to Tupperton *to have a look at the lake*). Disgust did not rule out enjoyment, in my thoughts; indeed they were inseparable.

Mr. Chamberlain, Art Chamberlain, read the news on the Jubilee radio. He also did all the more serious and careful announcing. He had a fine professional voice, welcome as dark chocolate flowing in and out of the organ music on the Sunday afternoon program *In Memoriam,* sponsored by a local funeral parlor. He sometimes got Fern singing on this program, sacred songs—"I Wonder as I Wander"—and nonsacred but mournful songs—"The End of a Perfect Day." It was not hard to get on the Jubilee radio; I myself had recited a comic poem, on the *Saturday Morning Young Folks Party,* and Naomi had played "The Bells of St. Mary's" on the piano. Every time you turned it on there was a good chance of hearing someone you knew, or at least of hearing the names of people you knew mentioned in the dedications. ("We are going to play this piece also for Mr. and Mrs. Carl Otis on the occasion of their twenty-eighth wedding anniversary, requested by their son George and wife Etta, and their three grandchildren, Lorraine, Mark, and Lois, also by Mrs. Otis' sister Mrs. Bill Townley of the Porterfield Road.") I had phoned up myself and dedicated a song to Uncle Benny on his fortieth birthday; my mother would not have her name mentioned. She preferred listening to the Toronto station, which brought us the Metropolitan Opera, and news with no commercials, and a quiz program in which she competed with four gentlemen who, to judge from their voices, would all have little, pointed beards.

Mr. Chamberlain had to read commercials, too, and he did it with ripe concern, recommending Vick's Nose Drops from Cross' Drugstore, and Sunday dinner at the Brunswick Hotel, and Lee Wickert and Sons for dead-livestock removal. "How's the dead livestock, soldier?" Fern would greet him, and he might slap her lightly on the rump. "I'll tell them you need their services!" "Looks to me more like you do," said Fern without much malice, and he would drop into a chair and smile at my mother for pouring him tea. His light blue-green eyes had no expression, just that color, so pretty you would want to make a dress out of it. He was always tired.

Mr. Chamberlain's white hands, his nails cut straight across, his graying, thinning, nicely-combed hair, his body that did not in any way disturb his clothes but seemed to be made of the same material as they were, so that he might have been shirt and tie and suit all the way through, were strange to me in a man. Even Uncle Benny, so skinny and narrow-chested, with his damaged bronchial tubes, had some look or way of moving that predicted chance or intended violence, something that would make disorder; my father had this too, though he was so moderate in his ways. Yet it was Mr. Chamberlain, tapping his ready-made cigarette in the ashtray, Mr. Chamberlain who had been in the war, he had been in the Tank Corps. If my father was there when he came to see us—to see Fern, really, but he did not quickly make that apparent—my father would ask him questions about the war. But it was clear that they saw the war in different ways. My father saw it as an overall design, marked off in campaigns, which had a purpose, which failed or succeeded. Mr. Chamberlain saw it as a conglomeration of stories, leading nowhere in particular. He made his stories to be laughed at.

For instance he told us about the first time he went into action, what confusion there was. Some tanks had gone into a wood, got turned around, were coming out the wrong way, where they expected the Germans to come from. So the first shots they fired were at one of their own tanks.

"Blew it up!" said Mr. Chamberlain blithely, unapologetically.

"Were there soldiers in that tank?"

He looked at me in mocking surprise as he always did when I said anything; you would think I had just stood on my head for him. "Well, I wouldn't be too surprised if there were!"

"Were they—killed, then?"

"Something happened to them. I certainly never saw them around again. Poof!"

"Shot by their own side, what a terrible thing," said my mother, scandalized but less than ordinarily sure of herself.

"Things like that happen in a war," said my father quietly but with some severity, as if to object to any of this showed a certain female naiveté. Mr. Chamberlain just laughed. He went on to tell about what they did on the last day of the war. They blew up the cookhouse, turned all the guns on it in the last jolly blaze they would get.

"Sounds like a bunch of kids," said Fern. "Sounds like you weren't grown-up enough to fight a *war*. It just sounds like you had one big, idiotic, good time."

"What I always try to have, isn't it? A good time."

Once it came out that he had been in Florence, which was not surprising, since he had fought the war in Italy. But my mother sat up, she jumped a little in her chair, she quivered with attention.

"Were *you* in Florence?"

"Yes, ma'am," said Mr. Chamberlain without enthusiasm.

"In Florence, you were in Florence," repeated my mother, confused and joyful. I had an inkling of what she felt, but hoped she would not reveal too much. "I never thought," she said. "Well, of course I knew it was Italy but it seems so strange—" She meant that this Italy we had been talking about, where the war was fought, was the same place history happened, in the very place, where the old Popes were, and the Medici, and Leonardo. The Cenci. The cypresses. Dante Alighieri.

Rather oddly, in view of her enthusiasm for the future, she was excited by the past. She hurried into the front room and came back with the art-and-architecture supplement to the encyclopedia, full of statues, paintings, buildings, mostly photographed in a cloudy, cool, museum-gray light.

"There!" she opened it up on the table in front of him. "There's your Florence. Michelangelo's statue of David. Did you see that?"

A naked man. His marble thing hanging on him for everybody to look at; like a drooping lily petal. Who but my mother in her staunch and dreadful innocence would show a man, would show us all, a picture like that? Fern's mouth was swollen, with the effort to contain her smile.

"I never got to see it, no. The place is full of statues. Famous this and famous that. You can't turn around for them."

I could see he was not a person to talk to, about things like this. But my mother kept on.

"Well surely you saw the bronze doors? The magnificent bronze doors? It took the artist his whole life to do them. Look at them, they're here. What was his name —Ghiberti. Ghiberti. His whole life."

Some things Mr. Chamberlain admitted he had seen, some he had not. He looked at the book with a reasonable amount of patience, then said he had not cared for Italy.

"Well, Italy, maybe that was all right. It was the Italians."

"Did you think they were decadent?" said my mother regretfully.

"Decadent, I don't know. I don't know what they were. They don't care. On the streets in Italy I've had a man come up to me and offer to sell me his own daughter. It happened all the time."

"What would they want to sell a girl for?" I said, adopting as I easily could my bold and simple façade of innocence. "For a slave?"

"In a manner of speaking," said my mother, and she shut the book, relinquishing Michelangelo and the bronze doors.

"No older than Del here," said Mr. Chamberlain, with a disgust that in him seemed faintly fraudulent. "Not so old, some of them."

"They mature earlier," Fern said. "Those hot climates."

"Del. You take this book, put it away." Alarm in my mother's voice was like the flap of rising wings.

Well, I had heard. I did not come back to the dining room but went upstairs and undressed. I put on my mother's black rayon dressing gown, splattered with bunches of pink and white flowers. Impractical gift she never wore. In her room I stared, goose-pimpled and challenging, into the three-way mirror. I pulled the material off my shoulders and bunched it over my breasts, which were just about big enough to fit those wide, shallow cones of paper laid in sundae dishes. I had turned on the light beside the dressing table; it came meekly, warmly through a bracket of butterscotch glass, and laid a kind of glow on my skin. I looked at my high round forehead, pink freckled skin, my face as innocent as an egg, and my eyes managed to alter what was there, to make me sly and creamy, to change my hair, which was light brown, fine as a crackling bush, into rich waves more gold than muddy. Mr. Chamberlain's voice in my mind, saying *no older than Del here,* acted on me like the touch of rayon silk on my skin, surrounded me, made me feel endangered and desired. I thought of girls in Florence, girls in Rome, girls my age that a man could buy. Black Italian hair under their arms. Black down at the corners of their mouths. *They mature earlier in those hot climates.* Roman Catholics. A man paid you to let him do it. What did he say? Did he take your clothes off or did he expect you to do that yourself? Did he take down his pants or did he simply unzip himself and point his thing at you? It was the stage of transition, bridge between what was possible, known and normal behavior, and the magical, bestial act, that I could not imagine. Nothing about that was in Naomi's mother's book.

There was a house in Jubilee with three prostitutes in it. That is, three if you counted Mrs. McQuade who ran it; she was at least sixty years old. The house was at the north end of the main street, in a yard all run to hollyhocks and dandelions, beside the B.A. service station. On sunny days the two younger women would sometimes come out and sit in canvas chairs. Naomi and I had made several trips past and had once seen them. They wore print dresses and slippers; their white legs were bare. One of them was reading the *Star Weekly.* Naomi said that this one's name was Peggy, and that one night in the men's toilet at the Gay-la dance hall she had been persuaded to serve a line-up, standing up. Was such a thing possible? (I heard this story another time, only now it was Mrs. McQuade herself who performed or endured this feat, and it was not at the Gay-la dance hall but against the back wall of the Blue Owl Cafe.) I wished I had seen more of this Peggy than the soft, mouse-brown nest of curls above the paper; I wished I had seen her face. I did expect something—a foul shimmer of corruption, some emanation, like marsh gas. I was surprised, in a way, that she would read a paper, that the words in it would mean the same things to her, presumably, as they did to the rest of us, that she ate and drank, was human still. I thought of her as having gone right beyond human functioning into a condition of perfect depravity, at the opposite pole from sainthood but similarly isolated, unknowable. What appeared to be ordinariness here—the *Star Weekly,* dotted curtains looped back, geraniums growing hopefully out of tin cans in the whorehouse window, seemed to me deliberate and tantalizing deception—the skin of everyday appearances stretched over such shamelessness, such consuming explosions of lust.

I rubbed my hipbones through the cool rayon. If I had been born in Italy my flesh would already be used, bruised, knowing. It would not be my fault. The thought of whoredom, not my fault, bore me outward for a moment; a restful, alluring thought, because it was so final, and did away with ambition and anxiety.

After this I constructed in several halting imperfect installments a daydream. I imagined that Mr. Chamberlain saw me in my mother's black flowered dressing gown, pulled down off the shoulders, as I had seen myself in the mirror. Then I proposed to have the dressing gown come off, let him see me with nothing on at all. How could it happen? Other people who would ordinarily be in the house with us would have to be got rid of. My mother I sent out to sell encyclopedias; my brother I banished to the farm. It would have to be in the summer holidays, when I was home from school. Fern would not yet be home from the post office. I would come downstairs in the heat of the late afternoon, a sulphurous still day, wearing only this dressing gown. I would get a drink of water at the sink, not seeing Mr. Chamberlain sitting quietly in the room, and then—what? A strange dog, introduced into our house for this occasion only, might jump on me, pulling the dressing gown off. I might turn and somehow catch the material on the nail of a chair, and the whole thing would just slither to my feet. The thing was that it had to be an accident; no effort on my part, and certainly none on Mr.Chamberlain's. Beyond the moment of revelation my dream did not go. In fact it often did not get that far, but lingered among the preliminary details, solidifying them. The moment of being seen naked could not be solidified, it was a stab of light. I never pictured Mr. Chamberlain's reaction, I never very clearly pictured him. His presence was essential but blurred; in the corner of my daydream he was featureless but powerful, humming away electrically like a blue fluorescent light.

Naomi's father caught us, as we raced past his door on our way downstairs.

"You young ladies come in and visit me a minute, make yourselves comfortable."

It was spring by this time, windy yellow evening. Nevertheless he was burning garbage in a round tin stove in his room, it was hot and smelly. He had washed his socks and underwear and hung them on strings along the wall. Naomi and her mother treated him unceremoniously. When her mother was away, as now, Naomi would open a can of spaghetti and dump it on a plate, for his dinner. I would say, "Aren't you going to heat it?" and she would say, "Why bother? He wouldn't know the difference anyway."

In his room, on the floor, he had stacks of newsprint pamphlets which I supposed had to do with the religion he believed in. Naomi sometimes had to bring them from the post office. Taking her cue from her mother, she had great contempt for his beliefs. "It's all prophecies and prophecies," she said. "They have prophesied the end of the world three times now."

We sat on the edge of the bed, which had no spread on it, only a rough, rather dirty blanket, and he sat in his rocker opposite us. He was an old man. Naomi's mother had nursed him before she married him. Between his words there were usually large gaps, during which he would not forget about you, however, but fix his pale eyes on your forehead as if he expected to find the rest of his thought written out there.

"Reading from the Bible," he said genially and unnecessarily, and rather in the manner of one who chooses not to see objections he knows are there. He opened a large-print Bible with the place already marked and began to read in a piercing elderly voice, with some odd stops, and difficulties of phrasing.

> *Then shall the kingdom of heaven be likened unto ten virgins, which took their lamps, and went forth to meet the bridegroom.*
> *And five of them were wise, and five were foolish.*
> *They that were foolish took their lamps, and took no oil with them:*
> *But the wise took oil in their vessels with their lamps.*
> *While the bridegroom tarried, they all slumbered and slept.*
> *And at midnight there was a cry made, Behold, the bridegroom cometh; go ye out to meet him.*
> *Then all those virgins arose, and trimmed their lamps.*
> *And the foolish said unto the wise, Give us of your oil; for our lamps are gone out.*

Then it turned out of course—now I remembered hearing all this before—that the wise virgins would not give up any of their oil for fear they would not have enough, and the foolish virgins had to go out and buy some, and so missed the bridegroom coming and were shut out. I had always supposed this parable, which I did not like, had to do with prudence, preparedness, something like that. But I could see that Naomi's father believed it to be about sex. I looked sideways at Naomi to catch that slight sucking in of the corners of the mouth, the facial drollery with which she always recognized this subject, but she was looking obstinate and miserable, disgusted by the very thing that was my secret pleasure—poetic flow of words, archaic expressions. *Said unto; tarried; Behold the bridegroom cometh.* She was so offended by all this that she could not even enjoy the word *virgins.*

His toothless mouth shut. Sly and proper as a baby's.

"No more for now. Think about it when the time comes. There's a lesson for young girls."

"Stupid old bugger," said Naomi, on the stairs.

"I feel—sorry for him."

She jabbed me in the kidney.

"Hurry up, let's get out of here. He's liable to find something else. Reads the Bible till his eyes fall out. Serve him right."

We ran outside, up Mason Street. These long light evenings we visited every part of town. We loitered past the Lyceum Theatre, the Blue Owl Cafe, the poolroom. We sat on the benches by the cenotaph, and if any car honked at us we waved. Dismayed by our greenness, our leggy foolishness, they drove on by; they laughed out their windows. We went into the ladies' toilet in the Town Hall—wet floor, sweating cement walls, harsh ammoniac smell—and there on the toilet door where only bad brainless girls wrote up their names, we wrote the names of the two reigning queens of our class—Marjory Coutts, Gwen Mundy. We wrote in lipstick and drew tiny obscene figures underneath. Why did we do this? Did we hate those girls, to whom we were unfailingly obsequiously pleasant? No. Yes. We hated their immunity, well-bred lack of curiosity, whatever kept them floating, charitable and pleased, on the surface of life in Jubilee, and would float them on to sororities, engagements, marriages to doctors or lawyers in more prosperous places far away. We hated them just because they could never be imagined entering the Town Hall toilets.

Having done this, we ran away, not sure whether or not we had committed a criminal act.

We dared each other. Walking under street lights still as pale as flowers cut out of tissue paper, walking past unlighted windows from which we hoped the world watched, we did dares.

"Be like you have cerebral palsy. *Dare.*"

At once I came unjointed, lolled my head, rolled my eyes, began to talk incomprehensively, in a cross insistent babble.

"Do it for a block. Never mind who we meet. Don't stop. *Dare.*"

We met old Dr. Comber, spindly and stately, beautifully dressed. He stopped, and tapped his stick, and objected.

"What is this performance?"

"A fit, sir," said Naomi plaintively. "She's always having these fits."

Making fun of poor, helpless, afflicted people. The bad taste, the heartlessness, the joy of it.

We went to the park, which was neglected, deserted, a triangle of land made too gloomy, by its big cedar trees, for children's play, and not attracting people who went for walks. Why should anybody in Jubilee walk to see more grass and dirt and trees, the same thing that pushed in on the town from every side? They would walk downtown, to look at stores, meet on the double sidewalks, feel the hope of activity. Naomi and I all by ourselves climbed the big cedar trees, scraped our knees on the bark, screamed as we never needed to when we were younger, seeing the branches part, revealing the tilted earth. We hung from the branches by our locked hands, by our ankles; we pretended to be baboons, prattling and gibbering. We felt the whole town lying beneath us, gaping, ready to be astounded.

There were noises peculiar to the season. Children on the sidewalks, skipping and singing in their clear, devout voices.

On the mountain stands a lady
Who she is I do not know.
All she wears is gold and silver.
All she needs is a new pair of shoes!

And the peacocks crying. We dropped from the trees and set off to look at them, down past the park, down a poor unnamed street running to the river. The peacocks belonged to a man named Pork Childs who drove the town garbage truck. The street had no sidewalks. We walked around puddles, gleaming in the soft mud. Pork Childs had a barn behind his house for his fowl. Neither barn nor house was painted.

There were the peacocks, walking around under the bare oak trees. How could we forget them, from one spring to the next?

The hens were easily forgotten, the sullen colors of their yard. But the males were never disappointing. Their astonishing, essential color, blue of breasts and throats and necks, darker feathers showing there like ink blots, or soft vegetation under tropical water. One had his tail spread, to show the blind eyes, painted satin. The little kingly, idiotic heads. Glory in the cold spring, a wonder of Jubilee.

The noise beginning again did not come from any of them. It pulled eyes up to what it was hard to believe we had not seen immediately—the one white peacock up in a tree, his tail full out, falling down through the branches like water over rock. Pure white, pure blessing. And hidden up above, his head gave out these frantic and upbraiding and disorderly cries.

"It's sex makes them scream," said Naomi.

"Cats scream," I said, remembering something from the farm. "They will scream like anything when a tomcat is doing it to them."

"Wouldn't you?" said Naomi.

Then we had to go, because Pork Childs appeared among his peacocks, walking quickly, rocking forward. All his toes had been amputated, we knew, after being frozen when he lay in a ditch long ago, too drunk to get home, before he joined the Baptist Church. "Good evening, boys!" he hollered at us, his old greeting, his old joke. *Hello, boys! Hello, girls!* yelled from the cab of the garbage truck, yelled down all streets bleak or summery, never getting any answer. We ran.

Mr. Chamberlain's car was parked in front of our house.

"Let's go in," said Naomi. "I want to see what he's doing to old Fern."

Nothing. In the dining room Fern was trying on the flowered chiffon dress my mother was helping her to make for Donna Carling's wedding, at which she would be the soloist. My mother was sitting sideways on the chair in front of the sewing machine, while Fern revolved, like a big half-opened parasol, in front of her.

Mr. Chamberlain was drinking a real drink, whiskey and water. He drove to Porterfield to buy his whisky, Jubilee being dry. I was both proud and ashamed to have Naomi see the bottle on the sideboard, a thing that would never appear in her house. My mother excused his drinking, because he had been through the war.

"Here come these two lovely young ladies," said Mr. Chamberlain with great insincerity. "Full of springtime and grace. All fresh from the out-of-doors."

"Give us a drink," I said, showing off in front of Naomi. But he laughed and put a hand over his glass.

"Not until you tell us where you've been."

"We went down to Pork Childs' to look at the peacocks."

"Down to see the pea-cocks. To see the pretty pea-cocks," said Mr. Chamberlain. "Give us a drink."

"Del, behave ourself," said my mother with a mouth full of pins.

"All I want is to find out what it tastes like."

"Well I can't give you a drink for nothing. I don't see you doing any tricks for me. I don't see you sitting up and begging like a good doggie."

"I can be a seal. Do you want to see me be a seal?"

This was one thing I loved to do. I never felt worried that it might not be perfect, that I might not be able to manage it; I was never afraid that anybody would think me a fool. I had even done it at school, for the Junior Red Cross amateur hour, and everyone laughed; this marveling laughter was so comforting, so absolving that I could have gone on being a seal forever.

I went down on my knees and held my elbows at my sides and worked my hands like flippers, meanwhile barking, my wonderful braying bark. I had copied it from an old Mary Martin movie where Mary Martin sings a song beside a turquoise pool and the seals bark in a chorus.

Mr. Chamberlain gradually lowered his glass and brought it close to my lips, withdrawing it, however, every time I stopped barking. I was kneeling by his chair. Fern had her back to me, her arms raised; my mother's head was hidden, as she pinned the material at Fern's waist. Naomi who had seen the seal often enough before and had an interest in dressmaking was looking at Fern and my mother. Mr. Chamberlain at last allowed my lips to touch the rim of the glass which he held in one hand. Then with the other hand he did something nobody could see. He rubbed against the damp underarm of my blouse and then inside the loose armhole of the jumper I was wearing. He rubbed quick, hard against the cotton over my breast. So hard he pushed the yielding flesh up, flattened it. And at once withdrew. It was like a slap, to leave me stung.

"Well, what does it taste like?" Naomi asked me afterwards.

"Like piss."

"You never tasted piss." She gave me a shrewd baffled look; she could always sense secrets.

I meant to tell her, but I did not, I held it back. If I told her, it would have to be re-enacted.

"How? How did he have his hand when he started? How did he get it under your jumper? Did he rub or squeeze, or both? With his fingers or his palm? Like *this?*"

There was a dentist in town, Dr. Phippen, brother of the deaf librarian, who was supposed to have put his hand up a girl's leg while looking at her back teeth. Naomi and I passing under his window would say loudly, "Don't you wish you had an appointment with Dr. Phippen? Dr. Feely Phippen. He's a thorough man!" It would be like that with Mr. Chamberlain; we would turn it into a joke, and hope for scandal, and make up schemes to entrap him, and that was not what I wanted.

"It was beautiful," said Naomi, sounding tired.

"What?"

"That peacock. In the tree."

I was surprised, and a little annoyed, to hear her use the word *beautiful,* about something like that, and to have her remember it, because I was used to have her act in a certain way, be aware of certain things, nothing else. I had already thought, running home, that I would write a poem about the peacock. To have her thinking about it too was almost like trespassing; I never let her or anyone in that part of my mind.

I did start writing my poem when I went upstairs to bed.

What in the trees is crying these veiled
  nights?
The peacocks crying or the winter's ghost?

That was the best part of it.

I also thought about Mr. Chamberlain, his hand which was different from anything he had previously shown about himself, in his eyes, his voice, his laugh, his stories. It was like a signal, given where it will be understood. Impertinent violation, so perfectly sure of itself, so authoritative, clean of sentiment.

Next time he came I made it easy for him to do something again, standing near him while he was getting his rubbers on in the dark hall. Every time, then, I waited for the signal, and got it. He did not bother with a pinch on the arm or a pat on the arm or a hug around the shoulders, fatherly or comradely. He went straight for the breasts, the buttocks, the upper thighs, brutal as lightning. And this was what I expected sexual communication to be—a flash of insanity, a dreamlike, ruthless, contemptuous breakthrough in a world of decent appearances. I had discarded those ideas of love, consolation, and tenderness, nourished by my feelings for Frank Wales; all that now seemed pale and extraordinarily childish. In the secret violence of sex would be recognition, going away beyond kindness, beyond good will or persons.

Not that I was planning on sex. One stroke of lightning does not have to lead anywhere, but to the next stroke of lightning.

Nevertheless my knees weakened, when Mr. Chamberlain honked the horn at me. He was waiting half a block from the school. Naomi was not with me; she had tonsillitis.

"Where's your girl friend?"

"She's sick."

"That's a shame. Want a lift home?"

In the car I trembled. My tongue was dry, my whole mouth was dry so I could hardly speak. Was this what desire was? Wish to know, fear to know, amounting to anguish? Being alone with him, no protection of people or circumstances, made a difference. What could he want to do here, in broad daylight, on the seat of his car?

He did not make a move towards me. But he did not head for River Street; he drove sedately along various side streets, avoiding winter-made potholes.

"You think you're the girl to do me a favor, if I asked you?"

"All right."

"What do you think it might be?"

"I don't know."

He parked the car behind the creamery, under the chestnut tree with the leaves just out, bitter yellowy green. Here?

"You get into Fern's room? You could get into her room when everybody was out of the house?"

I brought my mind back, slowly, from expectations of rape.

"You could get in her room and do a little investigation for me on what she's got there. Something that might interest me. What do you think it would be, eh? What do you think interests me?"

"What?"

"Letters," said Mr. Chamberlain with a sudden drop in tone, becoming matter-of-fact, depressed by some reality he could look into and I couldn't. "See if she has got any old letters. They might be in her drawers. Might be in her closet. Probably keeps them in an old box of some kind. Tied up in bundles, that's what women do."

"Letters from who?"

"From me. What do you think? You don't need to read them, just look at the signature. Written some time ago, the paper might be showing age. I don't know. Written in pen I recall so they're probably still legible. Here. I'll give you a sample of my handwriting, that'll help you out." He took an envelope out of the glove compartment and wrote on it: *Del is a bad girl.*

I put it in my Latin book.

"Don't let Fern see that, she'd recognize the writing. And not your Mama. She might wonder about what I wrote. Be a surprise to her, wouldn't it?"

He drove me home. I wanted to get out at the corner of River Street but he said no. "That just looks as if we've got something to hide. Now, how are you going to let me know? How about Sunday night, when I come around for supper, I'll ask you whether you've got your homework done! If you've found them, you'll say yes. If you've looked and you haven't found them, you'll say no. If for some reason you never got a chance to take a look, you say you forget whether you had any."

He made me repeat, "Yes means found them, no means didn't find them, forget means didn't get a chance to look." This drill insulted me; I was famous for my memory.

"All right. Cheers." Below the level that anybody could see, looking at the car, he bounced his fist off my leg, hard enough to hurt. I hauled myself and my books out, and once I was alone, my thigh still tingling, I took out the envelope and read what he had written. *Del is a bad girl.* Mr. Chamberlain assumed without any trouble at all that there was treachery in me, as well as criminal sensuality, waiting to be used. He had known I would not cry out when he flattened my breast, he had known I would not mention it to my mother; he knew now I would not report this conversation to Fern, but would spy on her as he had asked. Could he have hit upon my true self? It was true that in the dullness of school I had worked with my protractor and compass, I had written out Latin sentences [*having pitched camp and slaughtered the horses of the enemy by means of stealth, Vercingetorix prepared to give battle on the following day*] and all the time been conscious of my depravity vigorous as spring wheat, my body flowering with invisible bruises in those places where it had been touched. Wearing blue rompers, washing with soap that would nearly take your skin off, after a volleyball game, I had looked in the mirror of the girls' washroom and smiled secretly at my ruddy face, to think what lewdness I had been invited to, what deceits I was capable of.

I got into Fern's room on Saturday morning, when my mother had gone out to do some cleaning at the farm. I looked around at leisure, at the koala bear sitting on her pillow, powder spilled on the dresser, jars with a little bit of dried-up deodorant, salve, night cream, old lipstick, and nail polish with the top stuck on. A picture of a lady in a dress of many dripping layers, like an arrangement of scarves, probably Fern's mother, holding a fat woollied baby, probably Fern. Fern for sure in soft focus with butterfly sleeves, holding a sheaf of roses, curls laid in layers on her head. And snapshots stuck around the mirror, their edges curling. Mr. Chamberlain in a sharp straw hat, white pants, looking at the camera as if he knew more than it did. Fern not so plump as now, but plump, wearing shorts, sitting on a log in some vacationtime woods. Mr. Chamberlain and Fern dressed up—she with a corsage—snapped by a street photographer in a strange city, walking under the marquee of a movie house where *Anchors Aweigh!* was showing. The post office employees' picnic in the park at Tupperton, a cloudy day, and Fern, jolly in slacks, holding a baseball bat.

I did not find any letters. I looked through her drawers, on her closet shelves, under her bed, even inside her suitcases. I did find three separate saved bundles of paper, with elastic bands around them.

One bundle contained a chain letter and a great many copies of the same verse, in pencil or ink, different handwritings, some typewritten or mimeographed.

This prayer has already been around the world six times. It was originated in the Isle of Wight by a clairvoyant seer who saw it in a dream. Copy this letter out six times and mail it to six friends, then copy the attached prayer out and mail it to six names at the top of the attached list. Six days from the time you receive this letter you will begin to get copies of this prayer from all corners of the earth and they will bring you blessings and good luck IF YOU DO NOT BREAK THE CHAIN. *If you break the chain you may expect something sad and unpleasant to happen to you six months to the day from the day when you receive this letter.* DO NOT BREAK THE CHAIN, DO NOT OMIT THE SECRET WORD

AT THE END. BY MEANS OF THIS PRAYER HAPPINESS AND GOOD LUCK ARE
BEING SPREAD THROUGHOUT THE WORLD.

Peace and love, O Lord I pray
Shower on this friend today.

Heal his (her) troubles, bless his (her) heart,
From the source of strength and love may he (she) never have to part.

KARKAHMD

Another bundle was made up of several sheets of smudgy printing broken by
blurred gray illustrations of what I thought at first were enema bags with tangled
tubes, but which on reading the text I discovered to be cross sections of the male and
female anatomy, with such things as pessaries, tampons, condoms (these proper
terms were all new to me) being inserted or fitted on. I could not look at these illustrations without feeling alarm and a strong local discomfort, so I started reading. I
read about a poor farmer's wife in North Carolina throwing herself under a wagon
when she discovered she was going to have her ninth child, about women dying in
tenements from complications of pregnancy or childbirth or terrible failed abortions
which they performed with hatpins, knitting needles, bubbles of air. I read, or
skipped, statistics about the increase in population, laws which had been passed in
various countries for and against birth control, women who had gone to jail for advocating it. Then there were the instructions on using different devices. Naomi's
mother's book had had a chapter about this too, but we never got around to reading
it, being bogged down in "Case Histories and Varieties of Intercourse." All I read
now about foam and jelly, even the use of the word "vagina," made the whole business seem laborious and domesticated, somehow connected with ointments and
bandages and hospitals, and it gave me the same feeling of disgusted, ridiculous
helplessness I had when it was necessary to undress at the doctor's.

In the third bundle were typewritten verses. Some had titles. "Homemade
Lemon Squeeze." "The Lament of the Truck Driver's Wife."

Husband, dear husband, what am I to do?
I'm wanting some hard satisfaction from you.
You're never at home or you're never awake.
(A big cock in my pussy is all it would take!)

I was surprised that any adult would know, or still remember, these words. The
greedy progression of verses, the short chunky words set in shameless type, fired up
lust at a great rate, like squirts of kerosene on bonfires. But they were repetitive, elaborate; after awhile the mechanical effort needed to contrive them began to be felt,
and made them heavy going; they grew bewilderingly dull. But the words themselves
still gave off flashes of power, particularly *fuck,* which I had never been able to really
look at on fences or sidewalks. I had never been able to contemplate before its thrust
of brutality, hypnotic swagger.

I said no to Mr. Chamberlain, when he asked me if I had got my homework done.

He did not touch me all evening. But when I came out of school on Monday, he was there.

"Girl friend still sick? That's too bad. Nice though. Isn't it nice?"

"What?"

"Birds are nice. Trees are nice. Nice you can come for a drive with me, do my little investigations for me." He said this in an infantile voice. Evil would never be grand, with him. His voice suggested that it would be possible to do anything, anything at all, and pass it off as a joke, a joke on all the solemn and guilty, all the moral and emotional people in the world, the people who "took themselves seriously." That was what he could not stand in people. His little smile was repulsive; self-satisfaction stretched over quite an abyss of irresponsibility, or worse. This did not give me second thoughts about going with him, and doing whatever it was he had in mind to do. His moral character was of no importance to me there; perhaps it was even necessary that it should be black.

Excitement owing something to Fern's dirty verses had got the upper hand of me, entirely.

"Did you get a good look?" he said in a normal voice.

"Yes."

"Didn't find a thing? Did you look in all her drawers? I mean her *dresser* drawers. Hatboxes, suitcases? Went through her closet?"

"I looked and looked everywhere," I said demurely.

"She must have got rid of them."

"I guess she isn't sentimental."

"Sennamenal? I don't know what dose big words mean, little dirl."

We were driving out of town. We drove south on the No. 4 Highway and turned down the first side road. "Beautiful morning," said Mr. Chamberlain. "Pardon me —beautiful afterno-on, beautiful day." I looked out of the window; the countryside I knew was altered by his presence, his voice, overpowering fore-knowledge of the errand we were going on together. For a year or two I had been looking at trees, fields, landscape with a secret, strong exaltation. In some moods, some days, I could feel for a clump of grass, a rail fence, a stone pile, such pure unbounded emotion as I used to hope for, and have inklings of, in connection with God. I could not do it when I was with anybody, of course, and now with Mr. Chamberlain I saw that the whole nature became debased, maddeningly erotic. It was just now the richest, greenest time of year; ditches sprouted coarse daisies, toadflax, buttercups, hollows were full of nameless faintly golden bushes and the gleam of high creeks. I saw all this as a vast arrangement of hiding places, ploughed fields beyond rearing up like shameless mattresses. Little paths, opening in the bushes, crushed places in the grass, where no doubt a cow had lain, seemed to me specifically, urgently inviting as certain words or pressures.

"Hope we don't meet your mama, driving along here."

I did not think it possible. My mother inhabited a different layer of reality from the one I had got into now.

Mr. Chamberlain drove off the road, following a track that ended soon, in a field half gone to brush. The stopping of the car, cessation of that warm flow of sound and motion in which I had been suspended, jarred me a little. Events were becoming real.

"Let's take a little walk down to the creek."

He got out on his side, I got out on mine. I followed him, down a slope between some hawthorn trees, in bloom, yeasty smelling. This was a traveled route, with cigarette packages, a beer bottle, a Chiclet box lying on the grass. Little trees, bushes closed around us.

"Why don't we call a halt here?" said Mr. Chamberlain in a practical way. "It gets soggy down by the water."

Here in the half-shade above the creek I was cold, and so violently anxious to know what would be done to me that all the heat and dancing itch between my legs had gone dead, numb as if a piece of ice had been laid to it. Mr. Chamberlain opened his jacket and loosened his belt, then unzipped himself. He reached in to part some inner curtains, and "Boo!" he said.

Not at all like marble David's, it was sticking straight out in front of him, which I knew from my reading was what they did. It had a sort of head on it, like a mushroom, and its color was reddish purple. It looked blunt and stupid, compared, say, to fingers and toes with their intelligent expressiveness, or even to an elbow or a knee. It did not seem frightening to me, though I thought this might have been what Mr. Chamberlain intended, standing there with his tightly watching look, his hands holding his pants apart to display it. Raw and blunt, ugly-colored as a wound, it looked to me vulnerable, playful and naive, like some strong-snouted animal whose grotesque simple looks are some sort of guarantee of good will. (The opposite of what beauty usually is.) It did not bring back any of my excitement, though. It did not seem to have anything to do with me.

Still watching me, and smiling, Mr. Chamberlain placed his hand around this thing and began to pump up and down, not too hard, in a controlled efficient rhythm. His face softened; his eyes, still fixed on me, grew glassy. Gradually, almost experimentally, he increased the speed of his hand; the rhythm became less smooth. He crouched over, his smile opened out and drew the lips back from his teeth and his eyes rolled slightly upward. His breathing became loud and shaky, now he worked furiously with his hand, moaned, almost doubled over in spasmodic agony. The face he thrust out at me, from his crouch, was blind and wobbling like a mask on a stick, and those sounds coming out of his mouth, involuntary, last-ditch human noises, were at the same time theatrical, unlikely. In fact the whole performance, surrounded by calm flowering branches, seemed imposed, fantastically and predictably exaggerated, like an Indian dance. I had read about the body being in extremities of pleasure, possessed, but these expressions did not seem equal to the terrible benighted effort, deliberate frenzy, of what was going on here. If he did not soon get to where he wanted to be, I thought he would die. But then he let out a new kind of moan, the most desperate and the loudest yet; it quavered as if somebody was hitting him on the voice box. This died, miraculously, into a peaceful grateful whimper, as stuff shot out of him, the real whitish stuff, the seed, and caught the hem of my skirt. He straightened up, shaky, out of breath, and tucked himself quickly back inside his trousers. He got out a handkerchief and wiped first his hands then my skirt.

"Lucky for you? Eh?" He laughed at me, though he still had not altogether got his breath back.

After such a convulsion, such a revelation, how could a man just put his handkerchief in his pocket, check his fly, and start walking back—still somewhat flushed and bloodshot—the way we had come?

The only thing he said was in the car, when he sat for a moment composing himself before he turned the key.

"Quite a sight, eh?" was what he said.

The landscape was postcoital, distant and meaningless. Mr. Chamberlain may have felt some gloom too, or apprehension, for he made me get down on the floor of the car as we re-entered town, and then he drove around and let me out in a lonely place, where the road dipped down near the CNR station. He felt enough like himself, however, to tap me in the crotch with his fist, as if testing a coconut for soundness.

That was a valedictory appearance for Mr. Chamberlain, as I ought to have guessed it might be. I came home at noon to find Fern sitting at the dining-room table, which was set for dinner, listening to my mother calling from the kitchen over the noise of the potato masher.

"Doesn't matter what anybody says. You weren't married. You weren't engaged. It's nobody's business. Your life is your own."

"Want to see my little love letter?" said Fern, and fluttered it under my nose.

Dear Fern, Owing to circumstances beyond my control, I am taking off this evening in my trusty Pontiac and heading for points west. There is a lot of the world I haven't seen yet and no sense getting fenced in. I may send you a postcard from California or Alaska, who knows? Be a good girl as you always were and keep licking those stamps and steaming open the mail, you may find a hundred-dollar-bill yet. When Mama dies I will probably come home, but not for long. Cheers, Art.

The same hand that had written: *Del is a bad girl.*

"Tampering with the mails is a Federal offense," said my mother, coming in. "I don't think that is very witty, what he says."

She distributed canned carrots, mashed potatoes, meat loaf. No matter what the season, we ate a heavy meal in the middle of the day.

"Looks like it hasn't put me off my food, anyway," said Fern, sighing. She poured ketchup. "I could have had him. Long ago, if I'd wanted. He even wrote me letters mentioning marriage. I should have kept them, I could have breach-of-promised him."

"A good thing you didn't," said my mother spiritedly, "or where would you be today?"

"Didn't what? Breach-of-promised him or married him?"

"Married him. Breach-of-promise is a degradation to women."

"Oh, I wasn't in danger of marriage."

"You had your singing. You had your interest in life."

"I was just usually having too good a time. I knew enough about marriage to know that's when your good times stop."

When Fern talked about having a good time she meant going to dances at the Lakeshore Pavilion, going to the Regency Hotel in Tupperton for drinks and dinner, being driven from one roadhouse to another on Saturday night. My mother did try to understand such pleasures, but she could not, any more than she could understand why people go on rides at a fair, and will get off and throw up, then go on rides again.

Fern was not one to grieve, in spite of her acquaintance with opera. Her expressed feeling was that men always went, and better they did before you got sick of them. But she grew very talkative; she was never silent.

"As bad as Art was," she said to Owen, eating supper. "He wouldn't touch any yellow vegetable. His mother should have taken the paddle to him when he was little. That's what I used to tell him."

"You're built the opposite from Art," she told my father. "The trouble with getting his suits fitted was he was so long in the body, short in the leg. Ransom's in Tupperton was the only place that could fit him."

"Only one time I saw him lose his temper. At the Pavilion when we went to a dance there, and a fellow asked me to dance, and I got up with him because what can you do, and he put his face down, right away down on my neck. Guzzling me up like I was chocolate icing! Art said to him, if you have to slobber don't do it on my girl-friend, I might want her myself! And he yanked him off. He did so!"

I would come into a room where she was talking to my mother and there would be an unnatural, waiting silence. My mother would be listening with a trapped, determinedly compassionate, miserable face. What could she do? Fern was her good, perhaps her only, friend. But there were things she never thought she would have to hear. She may have missed Mr. Chamberlain.

"He treated you shabbily," she said to Fern, against Fern's shrugs and ambiguous laugh. "He did. He did. My estimation of a person has never gone down so fast. But nevertheless I miss him when I hear them trying to read the radio news."

For the Jubilee station had not found anybody else who could read the news the way it was now, full of Russian names, without panicking, and they had let somebody call Bach *Batch* on *In Memoriam,* when they played "Jesu Joy of Man's Desiring." It made my mother wild.

I had meant to tell Naomi all about Mr. Chamberlain, now it was over. But Naomi came out of her illness fifteen pounds lighter, with a whole new outlook on life. Her forthrightness was gone with her chunky figure. Her language was purified. Her daring had collapsed. She had a new delicate regard for herself. She sat under a tree with her skirt spread around her, watching the rest of us play volleyball, and kept feeling her forehead to see if she was feverish. She was not even interested in the fact that Mr. Chamberlain had gone, so preoccupied was she with herself and her illness. Her temperature had risen to over a hundred and five degrees. All the grosser aspects of sex had disappeared from her conversation and apparently from her mind although she talked a good deal about Dr. Wallis, and how he had sponged her legs himself, and she had been quite helplessly exposed to him, when she was sick.

So I had not the relief of making what Mr. Chamberlain had done into a funny, though horrifying, story. I did not know what to do with it. I could not get him back to his old role, I could not make him play the single-minded, simple-minded, vigorous, obliging lecher of my daydreams. My faith in simple depravity had weakened. Perhaps nowhere but in daydreams did the trap door open so sweetly and easily, plunging bodies altogether free of thought, free of personality, into self-indulgence, mad bad license. Instead of that, Mr. Chamberlain had shown me, people take along a good deal—flesh that is not overcome but has to be thumped into ecstasy, all the stubborn puzzle and dark turns of themselves.

In June there was the annual strawberry supper on the lawns behind the United Church. Fern went down to sing at it, wearing the flowered chiffon dress my mother had helped her make. It was not very tight at the waist. Since Mr. Chamberlain had gone Fern had put on weight, so that she was not now soft and bulgy but really fat, swollen up like a boiled pudding, her splotched skin not shady any more but stretched and shiny.

She patted herself around the midriff. "Anyway they won't be able to say I'm pining, will they? It'll be a scandal if I split the seams."

We heard her high heels going down the sidewalk. On leafy, cloudy, quiet evenings under the trees, sounds carried a long way. Sociable noise of the United Church affair washed as far as our steps. Did my mother wish she had a hat and a summer sheer dress on, and was going? Her agnosticism and sociability were often in conflict in Jubilee, where social and religious life were apt to be one and the same. Fern had told her to come ahead. "You're a member. Didn't you tell me you joined when you got married?"

"My ideas weren't formed then. Now I'd be a hypocrite. I'm not a believer."

"Think all of them are?"

I was on the veranda reading *Arch of Triumph,* a book I had got out of the library. The library had been left some money and had bought a supply of new books, mostly on the recommendation of Mrs. Wallis, the doctor's wife, who had a college degree but not perhaps the tastes the Council had been counting on. There had been complaints, people had said it should have been left up to Bella Phippen, but only one book—*The Hucksters*—had actually been removed from the shelves. I had read it first. My mother had picked it up and read a few pages and been saddened.

"I never expected to see such a use made of the printed word."

"It's about the advertising business, how corrupt it is."

"That's not the only thing is corrupt, I'm afraid. Next they will be telling about how they go to the toilet, why do they leave that out? There isn't any of that in *Silas Marner.* There isn't in the classic writers. They were good writers, they didn't need it."

I had turned away from my old favorites, *Kristin Lavransdatter,* historical novels. I read modern books now. Somerset Maugham. Nancy Mitford. I read about rich and titled people who despised the very sort of people who in Jubilee were at the top of society—druggists, dentists, storekeepers. I learned names like Balenciaga, Schiaparelli. I knew about drinks. Whisky and soda. Gin and tonic. Cinzano, Benedictine, Grand Marnier. I knew the names of hotels, streets, restaurants, in London,

Paris, Singapore. In these books people did go to bed together, they did it all the time, but the descriptions of what they were up to there were not thorough, in spite of what my mother thought. One book compared having sexual intercourse to going through a train tunnel (presumably if you were the whole train) and blasting out into a mountain meadow so high, so blest and beautiful, you felt as if you were in the sky. Books always compared it to something else, never told about it by itself.

"You can't read there," my mother said. "You can't read in that light. Come down on the steps."

So I came, but she did not want me to read at all. She wanted company.

"See, the lilacs are turning. Soon we'll be going out to the farm."

Along the front of our yard, by the sidewalk, were purple lilacs gone pale as soft, delicate scrub rags, rusty specked. Beyond them the road, already dusty, and banks of wild blackberry bushes growing in front of the boarded-up factory, on which we could still read the big, faded, vainglorious letters: MUNDY PIANOS.

"I'm sorry for Fern," my mother said. "I'm sorry for her life."

Her sad confidential tone warned me off.

"Maybe she'll find a new boy friend tonight."

"What do you mean? She's not after a new boy friend. She's had enough of all that. She's going to sing 'Where'er You Walk.' She's got a lovely voice, still."

"She's getting fat."

My mother spoke to me in her grave, hopeful, lecturing voice.

"There is a change coming I think in the lives of girls and women. Yes. But it is up to us to make it come. All women have had up till now has been their connection with men. All we have had. No more lives of our own, really, than domestic animals. *He shall hold thee, when his passion shall have spent its novel force, a little closer than his dog, a little dearer than his horse.* Tennyson wrote that. It's true. *Was* true. You will want to have children, though."

That was how much she knew me.

"But I hope you will—use your brains. Use your brains. Don't be distracted. Once you make that mistake, of being—distracted, over a man, your life will never be your own. You will get the burden, a woman always does."

"There is birth control nowadays," I reminded her, and she looked at me startled, though it was she herself who had publicly embarrassed our family, writing to the Jubilee *Herald-Advance* that "prophylactic devices should be distributed to all women on public relief in Wawanash County, to help them prevent any further increase in their families." Boys at school had yelled at me, "Hey, when is your momma giving out the proplastic devices?"

"That is not enough, though of course it is a great boon and religion is the enemy of it as it is of everything that might ease the pangs of life on earth. It is self-respect I am really speaking of. Self-respect."

I did not quite get the point of this, or if I did get the point I was set up to resist it. I would have had to resist anything she told me with such earnestness, such stubborn hopefulness. Her concern about my life, which I needed and took for granted, I could not bear to have expressed. Also I felt that it was not so different from all the other advice handed out to women, to girls, advice that assumed being female made you damageable, that a certain amount of carefulness and solemn fuss and self-protection were called for, whereas men were supposed to be able to go out and take on all kinds of experiences and shuck off what they didn't want and come back proud. Without even thinking about it, I had decided to do the same.

DONALD BARTHELME (b. 1931)

Porcupines at the University

"And now the purple dust of twilight time/steals across the meadows of my heart," the Dean said.

His pretty wife, Paula, extended her long graceful hands full of Negronis.

A scout burst into the room, through the door. "Porcupines!" he shouted.

"Porcupines what?" the Dean asked.

"Thousands and thousands of them. Three miles down the road and comin' fast!"

"Maybe they won't enroll," the Dean said. "Maybe they're just passing through."

"You can't be sure," his wife said.

"How do they look?" he asked the scout, who was pulling porcupine quills out of his ankles.

"Well, you know. Like porcupines."

"Are you going to bust them?" Paula asked.

"I'm tired of busting people," the Dean said.

"They're not people," Paula pointed out.

"De bustibus non est disputandum," the scout said.

"I suppose I'll have to do something," the Dean said.

* * *

Meanwhile the porcupine wrangler was wrangling the porcupines across the dusty and overbuilt West.

Dust clouds. Yips. The lowing of porcupines.

"Git along theah li'l porcupines."

And when I reach the great porcupine canneries of the East, I will be rich, the wrangler reflected. I will sit on the front porch of the Muehlebach Hotel in New York City and smoke me a big seegar. Then, the fancy women.

"All right you porcupines step up to that yellow line."

There was no yellow line. This was just an expression the wrangler used to keep the porcupines moving. He had heard it in the army. The damn-fool porcupines didn't know the difference.

The wrangler ambled along reading the ads in a copy of *Song Hits* magazine. PLAY HARMONICA IN 5 MINS. and so forth.

The porcupines scuffled along making their little hops. There were four-five thousand in the herd. Nobody had counted exactly.

An assistant wrangler rode in from the outskirts of the herd. He too had a copy of *Song Hits* magazine, in his hip pocket. He looked at the head wrangler's arm, which had a lot of little holes in it.

"Hey Griswold."

"Yeah?"

"How'd you get all them little holes in your arm?"

"You ever try to slap a brand on a porky-pine?"

Probably the fancy women will be covered with low-cut dresses and cheap perfume, the wrangler thought. Probably there will be hundreds of them, hundreds and hundreds. All after my medicine bundle containing my gold and my lucky drill bit. But if they try to rush me I will pull out my guitar. And sing them a song of prairie virility.

* * *

"Porcupines at the university," the Dean's wife said. "Well, why not?"

"We don't have *facilities* for four or five thousand porcupines," the Dean said. "I can't get a dial tone."

"They could take Alternate Life Styles," Paula said.

"We've already got too many people in Alternate Life Styles," the Dean said, putting down the telephone. "The hell with it. I'll bust them myself. Single-handed. Ly."

"You'll get hurt."

"Nonsense, they're only porcupines. I'd better wear my old clothes."

"Bag of dirty shirts in the closet," Paula said.

The Dean went into the closet.

Bags and bags of dirty shirts.

"Why doesn't she ever take these shirts to the laundry?"

* * *

Griswold, the wrangler, wrote a new song in the saddle.

Fancy woman fancy woman
How come you don't do right
I oughta rap you in the mouth for the way you acted
In the porte cochère of the Trinity River Consolidated
General High last Friday
Nite.

I will sit back and watch it climbing the charts, he said to himself. As recorded by Merle Travis. First, it will be a Bell Ringer. Then, the Top Forty. Finally a Golden Oldie.

"All right you porcupines. Git along."

The herd was moving down a twelve-lane trail of silky-smooth concrete. Signs along the trail said things like NEXT EXIT 5 MI. and RADAR IN USE.

"Griswold, some of them motorists behind us is gettin' awful pissed."

"I'm runnin' this-here porky-pine drive," Griswold said, "and I say we better gettum off the road."

The herd was turned onto a broad field of green grass. Green grass with white lime lines on it at ten-yard intervals.

The Sonny and Cher show, the wrangler thought. Well, Sonny, how I come to write this song. I was on a porky-pine drive. The last of the great porky-pine drives you might say. We had four-five thousand head we'd fatted up along the Tuscalora and we was headin' for New York City.

* * *

The Dean loaded a gleaming Gatling gun capable of delivering 360 rounds a minute. The Gatling gun sat in a mule-drawn wagon and was covered with an old piece of canvas. Formerly it had sat on a concrete slab in front of the ROTC Building.

First, the Dean said to himself, all they see is this funky old wagon pulled by this busted-up old mule. Then, I whip off the canvas. There stands the gleaming Gatling gun capable of delivering 360 rounds a minute. My hand resting lightly, confidently on the crank. They shall not pass, I say. Ils ne passeront pas. Then, the porcupine hide begins to fly.

I wonder if these rounds are still good?

* * *

The gigantic Gatling gun loomed over the herd like an immense piece of bad news.

"Hey Griswold."

"What?"

"He's got a gun."

"I *see* it," Griswold said. "You think I'm blind?"

"What we gonna do?"

"How about vamoose-ing?"

"But the herd . . ."

"Them li'l porcupines can take care of their own selves," Griswold said. "God-damn it, I guess we better parley." He got up off the grass, where he had been stretched full-length, and walked toward the wagon.

"What say potner?"

"Look," the Dean said. "You can't enroll those porcupines. It's out of the question."

"That so?"

"It's out of the question," the Dean repeated. "We've had a lot of trouble around here. The cops won't even speak to me. We can't *take* any more trouble." The Dean glanced at the herd. "That's a mighty handsome herd you have there."

"Kind of you," Griswold said. "That's a mighty handsome mule *you* got."

They both gazed at the Dean's terrible-looking mule.

Griswold wiped his neck with a red bandanna. "You don't want no porky-pines over to your place, is that it?"

"That's it."

"Well, we don't *go* where we ain't wanted," the wrangler said. "No call to throw down on us with that . . . *machine* there."

The Dean looked embarrassed.

"You don't know Mr. Sonny Bono, do you?" Griswold asked. "He lives around here somewheres, don't he?"

"I haven't had the pleasure," the Dean said. He thought for a moment. "I know a booker in Vegas, though. He was one of our people. He was a grad student in comparative religion."

"Maybe we can do a deal," the wrangler said. "Which-away is New York City?"

* * *

"Well?" the Dean's wife asked. "What were their demands?"

"I'll tell you in a minute," the Dean said. "My mule is double-parked."

* * *

The herd turned onto the Cross Bronx Expressway. People looking out of their cars saw thousands and thousands of porcupines. The porcupines looked like badly engineered vacuum-cleaner attachments.

Vegas, the wrangler was thinking. Ten weeks at Caesar's Palace at a sock 15 G's a week. The Ballad of the Last Drive. Leroy Griswold singing his smash single, The Ballad of the Last Drive.

"Git along theah, li'l porcupines."

The citizens in their cars looked at the porcupines, thinking: What is wonderful? Are these porcupines wonderful? Are they significant? Are they what I need?

JOYCE CAROL OATES (b. 1938)

How I Contemplated the World from the Detroit House of Correction and Began My Life Over Again

Notes for an essay for an English class at Baldwin Country Day School; Poking around in debris; Disgust and curiosity; A revelation of the meaning of life; A happy ending . . .

I EVENTS

1. The girl (myself) is walking through Branden's, that excellent store. Suburb of a large famous city that is a symbol for large famous American cities. The event sneaks up on the girl, who believes she is herding it along with a small fixed smile, a girl of fifteen, innocently experienced. She dawdles in a certain style by a counter of costume jewelry. Rings, earrings, necklaces. Prices from $5 to $50, all within reach. All ugly. She eases over to the glove counter, where everything is ugly too. In her close-fitted coat with its black fur collar she contemplates the luxury of Branden's, which she has known for many years: its many mild pale lights, easy on the eye and the soul, its elaborate tinkly decorations, its women shoppers with their excellent shoes and coats and hairdos, all dawdling gracefully, in no hurry.

Who was ever in a hurry here?

2. The girl seated at home. A small library, paneled walls of oak. Someone is talking to me. An earnest, husky, female voice drives itself against my ears, nervous,

frightened, groping around my heart, saying, "If you wanted gloves, why didn't you say so? Why didn't you ask for them?" That store, Branden's, is owned by Raymond Forrest who lives on Du Maurier Drive. We live on Sioux Drive. Raymond Forrest. A handsome man? An ugly man? A man of fifty or sixty, with gray hair, or a man of forty with earnest, courteous eyes, a good golf game; who is Raymond Forrest, this man who is my salvation? Father has been talking to him. Father is not his physician; Dr. Berg is his physician. Father and Dr. Berg refer patients to each other. There is a connection. Mother plays bridge with . . . On Mondays and Wednesdays our maid Billie works at . . . The strings draw together in a cat's cradle, making a net to save you when you fall. . . .

3. *Harriet Arnold's.* A small shop, better than Branden's. Mother in her black coat, I in my close-fitted blue coat. Shopping. Now look at this, isn't this cute, do you want this, why don't you want this, try this on, take this with you to the fitting room, take this also, what's wrong with you, what can I do for you, why are you so strange . . . ? "I wanted to steal but not to buy," I don't tell her. The girl droops along in her coat and gloves and leather boots, her eyes scan the horizon, which is pastel pink and decorated like Branden's, tasteful walls and modern ceilings with graceful glimmering lights.

4. Weeks later, the girl at a bus stop. Two o'clock in the afternoon, a Tuesday; obviously she has walked out of school.

5. The girl stepping down from a bus. Afternoon, weather changing to colder. Detroit. Pavement and closed-up stores; grillwork over the windows of a pawnshop. What is a pawnshop, exactly?

II CHARACTERS

1. The girl stands five feet five inches tall. An ordinary height. Baldwin Country Day School draws them up to that height. She dreams along the corridors and presses her face against the Thermoplex glass. No frost or steam can ever form on that glass. A smudge of grease from her forehead . . . could she be boiled down to grease? She wears her hair loose and long and straight in suburban teen-age style, 1968. Eyes smudged with pencil, dark brown. Brown hair. Vague green eyes. A pretty girl? An ugly girl? She sings to herself under her breath, idling in the corridor, thinking of her many secrets (the thirty dollars she once took from the purse of a friend's mother, just for fun, the basement window she smashed in her own house just for fun) and thinking of her brother who is at Susquehanna Boys' Academy, an excellent preparatory school in Maine, remembering him unclearly . . . he has long manic hair and a squeaking voice and he looks like one of the popular teen-age singers of 1968, one of those in a group, *The Certain Forces, The Way Out, The Maniacs Responsible.* The girl in her turn looks like one of those fieldsful of girls who listen to the boys' singing, dreaming and mooning restlessly, breaking into high sullen laughter, innocently experienced.

2. The mother. A Midwestern woman of Detroit and suburbs. Belongs to the Detroit Athletic Club. Also the Detroit Golf Club. Also the Bloomfield Hills Country Club. The Village Women's Club at which lectures are given each winter on Genet and Sartre and James Baldwin, by the Director of the Adult Education Program at Wayne State University.... The Bloomfield Art Association. Also the Founders Society of the Detroit Institute of Arts. Also ... Oh, she is in perpetual motion, this lady, hair like blown-up gold and finer than gold, hair and fingers and body of inestimable grace. Heavy weighs the gold on the back of her hairbrush and hand mirror. Heavy heavy the candlesticks in the dining room. Very heavy is the big car, a Lincoln, long and black, that on one cool autumn day split a squirrel's body in two unequal parts.

3. The father. Dr. _____. He belongs to the same clubs as #2. A player of squash and golf; he has a golfer's umbrella of stripes. Candy stripes. In his mouth nothing turns to sugar, however; saliva works no miracles here. His doctoring is of the slightly sick. The sick are sent elsewhere (to Dr. Berg?), the deathly sick are sent back for more tests and their bills are sent to their homes, the unsick are sent to Dr. Coronet (Isabel, a lady), an excellent psychiatrist for unsick people who angrily believe they are sick and want to do something about it. If they demand a male psychiatrist, the unsick are sent by Dr. _____ (my father) to Dr. Lowenstein, a male psychiatrist, excellent and expensive, with a limited practice.

4. Clarita. She is twenty, twenty-five, she is thirty or more? Pretty, ugly, what? She is a woman lounging by the side of a road, in jeans and a sweater, hitchhiking, or she is slouched on a stool at a counter in some roadside diner. A hard line of jaw. Curious eyes. Amused eyes. Behind her eyes processions move, funeral pageants, cartoons. She says, "I never can figure out why girls like you bum around down here. What are you looking for anyway?" An odor of tobacco about her. Unwashed underclothes, or no underclothes, unwashed skin, gritty toes, hair long and falling into strands, not recently washed.

5. Simon. In this city the weather changes abruptly, so Simon's weather changes abruptly. He sleeps through the afternoon. He sleeps through the morning. Rising, he gropes around for something to get him going, for a cigarette or a pill to drive him out to the street, where the temperature is hovering around 35°. Why doesn't it drop? Why, why doesn't the cold clean air come down from Canada; will he have to go up into Canada to get it? will he have to leave the Country of his Birth and sink into Canada's frosty fields . . . ? Will the F.B.I. (which he dreams about constantly) chase him over the Canadian border on foot, hounded out in a blizzard of broken glass and horns . . . ?

"Once I was Huckleberry Finn," Simon says, "but now I am Roderick Usher." Beset by frenzies and fears, this man who makes my spine go cold, he takes green pills, yellow pills, pills of white and capsules of dark blue and green . . . he takes other things I may not mention, for what if Simon seeks me out and climbs into my girl's bedroom here in Bloomfield Hills and strangles me, what then . . . ? (As I write this I begin to shiver. Why do I shiver? I am now sixteen and sixteen is not an age for shivering.) It comes from Simon, who is always cold.

III WORLD EVENTS

Nothing.

IV PEOPLE & CIRCUMSTANCES
CONTRIBUTING TO THIS DELINQUENCY

Nothing.

V SIOUX DRIVE

George, Clyde G. 240 Sioux. A manufacturer's representative; children, a dog, a wife. Georgian with the usual columns. You think of the White House, then of Thomas Jefferson, then your mind goes blank on the white pillars and you think of nothing. Norris, Ralph W. 246 Sioux. Public relations. Colonial. Bay window, brick, stone, concrete, wood, green shutters, sidewalk, lantern, grass, trees, blacktop drive, two children, one of them my classmate Esther (Esther Norris) at Baldwin. Wife, cars. Ramsey, Michael D. 250 Sioux. Colonial. Big living room, thirty by twenty-five, fireplaces in living room, library, recreation room, paneled walls wet bar five bathrooms five bedrooms two lavatories central air conditioning automatic sprinkler automatic garage door three children one wife two cars a breakfast room a patio a large fenced lot fourteen trees a front door with a brass knocker never knocked. Next is our house. Classic contemporary. Traditional modern. Attached garage, attached Florida room, attached patio, attached pool and cabana, attached roof. A front door mail slot through which pour *Time Magazine, Fortune, Life, Business Week,* the *Wall Street Journal,* the *New York Times,* the *New Yorker,* the *Saturday Review, M.D., Modern Medicine, Disease of the Month* . . . and also. . . . And in addition to all this, a quiet sealed letter from Baldwin saying: *Your daughter is not doing work compatible with her performance on the Stanford-Binet* . . . And your son is not doing well, not well at all, very sad. Where is your son anyway? Once he stole trick-and-treat candy from some six-year-old kids, he himself being a robust ten. The beginning. Now your daughter steals. In the Village Pharmacy she made off with, yes she did, don't deny it, she made off with a copy of *Pageant Magazine* for no reason, she swiped a roll of Life Savers in a green wrapper and was in no need of saving her life or even in need of sucking candy; when she was no more than eight years old she stole, don't blush, she stole a package of Tums only because it was out on the counter and available, and the nice lady behind the counter (now dead) said nothing. . . . Sioux Drive. Maples, oaks, elms. Diseased elms cut down. Sioux Drive runs into Roosevelt Drive. Slow, turning lanes, not streets, all drives and lanes and ways and passes. A private police force. Quiet private police, in unmarked cars. Cruising on Saturday evenings with paternal smiles for the residents who are streaming in and out of houses, going to and from parties, a thousand parties, slightly staggering, the women in their furs alighting from automobiles bought of Ford and General Motors and Chrysler, very heavy automobiles. No foreign cars. Detroit. In 275 Sioux, down the block in that magnificent French-Normandy mansion, lives _____ himself, who has the C_____ account itself, imagine that! Look at where he lives and look at the enormous trees and chimneys, imagine his many fireplaces, imagine his wife and children, imagine his wife's hair, imagine her fingernails, imagine her bathtub of smooth clean glowing pink, imagine their embraces, his trouser pockets filled with odd coins and keys and dust and peanuts, imagine their ecstasy on Sioux Drive, imagine their income tax returns, imagine their little boy's pride in his experimental car, a scaled down C_____, as he roars round the neighborhood on the sidewalks frightening dogs and Negro maids, oh imagine all these things, imagine everything, let your mind roar out all over Sioux Drive and Du Maurier Drive and Roosevelt Drive and Ticonderoga Pass and Burning Bush Way and Lincolnshire Pass and Lois Lane.

When spring comes, its winds blow nothing to Sioux Drive, no odors of hollyhocks or forsythia, nothing Sioux Drive doesn't already possess, everything is planted and performing. The weather vanes, had they weather vanes, don't have to turn with the wind, don't have to contend with the weather. There is no weather.

VI DETROIT

There is always weather in Detroit. Detroit's temperature is always 32°. Fast-falling temperatures. Slow-rising temperatures. Wind from the north-northeast four to forty miles an hour, small-craft warnings, partly cloudy today and Wednesday changing to partly sunny through Thursday . . . small warnings of frost, soot warnings, traffic warnings, hazardous lake conditions for small craft and swimmers, restless Negro gangs, restless cloud formations, restless temperatures aching to fall out the very bottom of the thermometer or shoot up over the top and boil everything over in red mercury.

Detroit's temperature is 32°. Fast-falling temperatures. Slow-rising temperatures. Wind from the north-northeast four to forty miles an hour. . . .

VII EVENTS

1. The girl's heart is pounding. In her pocket is a pair of gloves! In a plastic bag! Airproof breathproof plastic bag, gloves selling for twenty-five dollars on Branden's counter! In her pocket! Shoplifted! . . . In her purse is a blue comb, not very clean. In her purse is a leather billfold (a birthday present from her grandmother in Philadelphia) with snapshots of the family in clean plastic windows, in the billfold are bills, she doesn't know how many bills. . . . In her purse is an ominous note from her friend Tykie *What's this about Joe H. and the kids hanging around at Louise's Sat. night? You heard anything?* . . . passed in French class. In her purse is a lot of dirty yellow Kleenex, her mother's heart would break to see such very dirty Kleenex, and at the bottom of her purse are brown hairpins and safety pins and a broken pencil and a ballpoint pen (blue) stolen from somewhere forgotten and a purse-size compact of Cover Girl Make-Up, Ivory Rose. . . . Her lipstick is Broken Heart, a corrupt pink; her fingers are trembling like crazy; her teeth are beginning to chatter; her insides are alive; her eyes glow in her head; she is saying to her mother's astonished face *I want to steal but not to buy.*

2. At Clarita's. Day or night? What room is this? A bed, a regular bed, and a mattress on the floor nearby. Wallpaper hanging in strips. Clarita says she tore it like that with her teeth. She was fighting a barbaric tribe that night, high from some pills; she was battling for her life with men wearing helmets of heavy iron and their faces no more than Christian crosses to breathe through, every one of those bastards looking like her lover Simon, who seems to breathe with great difficulty through the slits of mouth and nostrils in his face. Clarita has never heard of Sioux Drive. Raymond Forrest cuts no ice with her, nor does the C_____ account and its millions; Harvard Business School could be at the corner of Vernor and 12th Street for all she cares, and Vietnam might have sunk by now into the Dead Sea under its tons of debris, for all the amazement she could show ... her face is overworked, overwrought, at the age of twenty (thirty?) it is already exhausted but fanciful and ready for a laugh. Clarita says mournfully to me *Honey somebody is going to turn you out let me give you warning.* In a movie shown on late television Clarita is not a mess like this but a nurse, with short neat hair and a dedicated look, in love with her doctor and her doctor's patients and their diseases, enamored of needles and sponges and rubbing alcohol. . . . Or no: she is a private secretary. Robert Cummings is her boss. She helps him with fantastic plots, the canned audience laughs, no, the audience doesn't laugh because nothing is funny, instead her boss is Robert Taylor and they are not boss and secretary but husband and wife, she is threatened by a young starlet, she is grim, handsome, wifely, a good companion for a good man. . . . She is Claudette Colbert. Her sister too is Claudette Colbert. They are twins, identical. Her husband Charles Boyer is a very rich handsome man and her sister, Claudette Colbert, is plotting her death in order to take her place as the rich man's wife, no one will know because they are *twins.* . . . All these marvelous lives Clarita might have lived, but she fell out the bottom at the age of thirteen. At the age when I was packing my overnight case for a slumber party at Toni Deshield's she was tearing filthy sheets off a bed and scratching up a rash on her arms. . . . Thirteen is uncommonly young for a white girl in Detroit, Miss Brock of the Detroit House of Correction said in a sad newspaper interview for the *Detroit News,* fifteen and sixteen are more likely. Eleven, twelve, thirteen are not surprising in colored . . . they are more precocious. What can we do? Taxes are rising and the tax base is falling. The temperature rises slowly but falls rapidly. Everything is falling out the bottom, Woodward Avenue is filthy, Livernois Avenue is filthy! Scraps of paper flutter in the air like pigeons, dirt flies up and hits you right in the eye, oh Detroit is breaking up into dangerous bits of newspaper and dirt, watch out. . . .

Clarita's apartment is over a restaurant. Simon her lover emerges from the cracks at dark. Mrs. Olesko, a neighbor of Clarita's, an aged white wisp of a woman, doesn't complain but sniffs with contentment at Clarita's noisy life and doesn't tell the cops, hating cops, when the cops arrive. I should give more fake names, more blanks, instead of telling all these secrets. I myself am a secret; I am a minor.

3. My father reads a paper at a medical convention in Los Angeles. There he is, on the edge of the North American continent, when the unmarked detective put his hand so gently on my arm in the aisle of Branden's and said, "Miss, would you like to step over here for a minute?"

And where was he when Clarita put her hand on my arm, that wintry dark sulphurous aching day in Detroit, in the company of closed-down barber shops, closed-down diners, closed-down movie houses, homes, windows, basements, faces ... she put her hand on my arm and said, "Honey, are you looking for somebody down here?"

And was he home worrying about me, gone for two weeks solid, when they carried me off. . . ? It took three of them to get me in the police cruiser, so they said, and they put more than their hands on my arm.

4. I work on this lesson. My English teacher is Mr. Forest, who is from Michigan State. Not handsome, Mr. Forest, and his name is plain, unlike Raymond Forrest's, but he is sweet and rodentlike, he has conferred with the principal and my parents, and everything is fixed . . . treat her as if nothing has happened, a new start, begin again, only sixteen years old, what a shame, how did it happen?—nothing happened, nothing could have happened, a slight physiological modification known only to a gynecologist or to Dr. Coronet. I work on my lesson. I sit in my pink room. I look around the room with my sad pink eyes. I sigh, I dawdle, I pause, I eat up time, I am limp and happy to be home, I am sixteen years old suddenly, my head hangs heavy as a pumpkin on my shoulders, and my hair has just been cut by Mr. Faye at the Crystal Salon and is said to be very becoming.

(Simon too put his hand on my arm and said, "Honey, you have got to come with me," and in his six-by-six room we got to know each other. Would I go back to Simon again? Would I lie down with him in all that filth and craziness? Over and over again,

a Clarita is being betrayed as in front of a Cunningham Drug Store she is nervously eying a colored man who may or may not have money, or a nervous white boy of twenty with sideburns and an Appalachian look, who may or may not have a knife hidden in his jacket pocket, or a husky red-faced man of friendly countenance who may or may not be a member of the Vice Squad out for an early twilight walk.)

I work on my lesson for Mr. Forest. I have filled up eleven pages. Words pour out of me and won't stop. I want to tell everything . . . what was the song Simon was always humming, and who was Simon's friend in a very new trench coat with an old high school graduation ring on his finger . . . ? Simon's bearded friend? When I was down too low for him, Simon kicked me out and gave me to him for three days, I think, on Fourteenth Street in Detroit, an airy room of cold cruel drafts with newspapers on the floor. . . . Do I really remember that or am I piecing it together from what they told me? Did they tell the truth? Did they know much of the truth?

VIII CHARACTERS

1. Wednesdays after school, at four; Saturday mornings at ten. Mother drives me to Dr. Coronet. Ferns in the office, plastic or real, they look the same. Dr. Coronet is queenly, an elegant nicotine-stained lady who would have studied with Freud had

circumstances not prevented it, a bit of a Catholic, ready to offer you some mystery if your teeth will ache too much without it. Highly recommended by Father! Forty dollars an hour, Father's forty dollars! Progress! Looking up! Looking better! That new haircut is so becoming, says Dr. Coronet herself, showing how normal she is for a woman with an I.Q. of 180 and many advanced degrees.

2. Mother. A lady in a brown suede coat. Boots of shiny black material, black gloves, a black fur hat. She would be humiliated could she know that of all the people in the world it is my ex-lover Simon who walks most like her . . . self-conscious and unreal, listening to distant music, a little bowlegged with craftiness. . . .

3. Father. Tying a necktie. In a hurry. On my first evening home he put his hand on my arm and said, "Honey, we're going to forget all about this."

4. Simon. Outside, a plane is crossing the sky, in here we're in a hurry. Morning. It must be morning. The girl is half out of her mind, whimpering and vague; Simon her dear friend is wretched this morning . . . he is wretched with morning itself . . . he forces her to give him an injection with that needle she knows is filthy, she had a dread of needles and surgical instruments and the odor of things that are to be sent into the blood, thinking somehow of her father. . . . This is a bad morning, Simon says that his mind is being twisted out of shape, and so he submits to the needle that he usually scorns and bites his lip with his yellowish teeth, his face going very pale. *Ah baby!* he says in his soft mocking voice, which with all women is a mockery of love, *do it like this—Slowly—*And the girl, terrified, almost drops the precious needle but manages to turn it up to the light from the window . . . is it an extension of herself then? She can give him this gift then? *I wish you wouldn't do this to me,* she says, wise in her terror, because it seems to her that Simon's danger—in a few minutes he may be dead—is a way of pressing her against him that is more powerful than any other embrace. She has to work over his arm, the knotted corded veins of his arm, her forehead wet with perspiration as she pushes and releases the needle, staring at that mixture of liquid now stained with Simon's bright blood. . . . When the drug hits him she can feel it herself, she feels that magic that is more than any woman can give him, striking the back of his head and making his face stretch as if with the impact of a terrible sun. . . . She tries to embrace him but he pushes her aside and stumbles to his feet. *Jesus Christ,* he says. . . .

5. Princess, a Negro girl of eighteen. What is her charge? She is closed-mouthed about it, shrewd and silent, you know that no one had to wrestle her to the sidewalk to get her in here; she came with dignity. In the recreation room she sits reading *Nancy Drew and the Jewel Box Mystery,* which inspires in her face tiny wrinkles of alarm and interest: what a face! Light brown skin, heavy shaded eyes, heavy eyelashes, a serious sinister dark brow, graceful fingers, graceful wristbones, graceful legs, lips, tongue, a sugar-sweet voice, a leggy stride more masculine than Simon's and my mother's, decked out in a dirty white blouse and dirty white slacks; vaguely nautical is Princess' style. . . . At breakfast she is in charge of clearing the table and leans over me, saying, *Honey you sure you ate enough?*

6. The girl lies sleepless, wondering. Why here, why not there? Why Bloomfield Hills and not jail? Why jail and not her pink room? Why downtown Detroit and not Sioux Drive? What is the difference? Is Simon all the difference? The girl's head is a parade of wonders. She is nearly sixteen, her breath is marvelous with wonders, not long ago she was coloring with crayons and now she is smearing the landscape with paints that won't come off and won't come off her fingers either. She says to the matron *I am not talking about anything,* not because everyone has warned her not to talk but because, because she will not talk; because she won't say anything about Simon, who is her secret. And she says to the matron, *I won't go home,* up until that night in the lavatory when everything was changed.... "No, I won't go home I want to stay here," she says, listening to her own words with amazement, thinking that weeds might climb everywhere over that marvelous $180,000 house and dinosaurs might return to muddy the beige carpeting, but never never will she reconcile four o'clock in the morning in Detroit with eight o'clock breakfasts in Bloomfield Hills. ... oh, she aches still for Simon's hands and his caressing breath, though he gave her little pleasure, he took everything from her (five-dollar bills, ten-dollar bills, passed into her numb hands by men and taken out of her hands by Simon) until she herself was passed into the hands of other men, police, when Simon evidently got tired of her and her hysteria.... *No, I won't go home, I don't want to be bailed out.* The girl thinks as a *Stubborn and Wayward Child* (one of several charges lodged against her), and the matron understands her crazy white-rimmed eyes that are seeking out some new violence that will keep her in jail, should someone threaten to let her out. Such children try to strangle the matrons, the attendants, or one another ... they want the locks locked forever, the doors nailed shut ... and this girl is no different up until that night her mind is changed for her. ...

IX THAT NIGHT

Princess and Dolly, a little white girl of maybe fifteen, hardy however as a sergeant and in the House of Correction for armed robbery, corner her in the lavatory at the farthest sink and the other girls look away and file out to bed, leaving her. God, how she is beaten up! Why is she beaten up? Why do they pound her, why such hatred? Princess vents all the hatred of a thousand silent Detroit winters on her body, this girl whose body belongs to me, fiercely she rides across the Midwestern plains on this girl's tender bruised body ... revenge on the oppressed minorities of America! revenge on the slaughtered Indians! revenge on the female sex, on the male sex, revenge on Bloomfield Hills, revenge revenge. ...

X DETROIT

In Detroit, weather weighs heavily upon everyone. The sky looms large. The horizon shimmers in smoke. Downtown the buildings are imprecise in the haze. Perpetual haze. Perpetual motion inside the haze. Across the choppy river is the city of Windsor, in Canada. Part of the continent has bunched up here and is bulging outward, at the tip of Detroit; a cold hard rain is forever falling on the expressways. ... Shoppers shop grimly, their cars are not parked in safe places, their windshields may be smashed and graceful ebony hands may drag them out through their shatterproof smashed windshields, crying, *Revenge for the Indians!* Ah, they all fear leaving Hudson's and being dragged to the very tip of the city and thrown off the parking roof of Cobo Hall, that expensive tomb, into the river. . . .

XI CHARACTERS WE ARE FOREVER ENTWINED WITH

1. Simon drew me into his tender rotting arms and breathed gravity into me. Then I came to earth, weighed down. He said, *You are such a little girl,* and he weighed me down with his delight. In the palms of his hands were teeth marks from his previous life experiences. He was thirty-five, they said. Imagine Simon in this room, in my pink room: he is about six feet tall and stoops slightly, in a feline cautious way, always thinking, always on guard, with his scuffed light suede shoes and his clothes that are anyone's clothes, slightly rumpled ordinary clothes that ordinary men might wear to not-bad jobs. Simon has fair long hair, curly hair, spent languid curls that are like . . . exactly like the curls of wood shavings to the touch, I am trying to be exact . . . and he smells of unheated mornings and coffee and too many pills coating his tongue with a faint green-white scum. . . . Dear Simon, who would be panicked in this room and in this house (right now Billie is vacuuming next door in my parents' room; a vacuum cleaner's roar is a sign of all good things), Simon who is said to have come from a home not much different from this, years ago, fleeing all the carpeting and the polished banisters . . . Simon has a deathly face, only desperate people fall in love with it. His face is bony and cautious, the bones of his cheeks prominent as if with the rigidity of his ceaseless thinking, plotting, for he has to make money out of girls to whom money means nothing, they're so far gone they can hardly count it, and in a sense money means nothing to him either except as a way of keeping on with his life. *Each Day's Proud Struggle,* the title of a novel we could read at jail. . . . Each day he needs a certain amount of money. He devours it. It wasn't love he uncoiled in me with his hollowed-out eyes and his courteous smile, that remnant of a prosperous past, but a dark terror that needed to press itself flat against him, or against another man . . . but he was the first, he came over to me and took my arm, a claim. We struggled on the stairs and I said, *Let me loose, you're hurting my neck, my face,* it was such a surprise that my skin hurt where he rubbed it, and afterward we lay face to face and he breathed everything into me. In the end I think he turned me in.

2. Raymond Forrest. I just read this morning that Raymond Forrest's father, the chairman of the board at _____, died of a heart attack on a plane bound for London. I would like to write Raymond Forrest a note of sympathy. I would like to thank him for not pressing charges against me one hundred years ago, saving me, being so generous . . . well, men like Raymond Forrest are generous men, not like Simon. I would like to write him a letter telling of my love, or of some other emotion that is positive and healthy. Not like Simon and his poetry, which he scrawled down when he was high and never changed a word . . . but when I try to think of something to say, it is Simon's language that comes back to me, caught in my head like a bad song, it is always Simon's language:

There is no reality only dreams
Your neck may get snapped when you wake
My love is drawn to some violent end
She keeps wanting to get away
My love is heading downward
And I am heading upward
She is going to crash on the sidewalk
And I am going to dissolve into the clouds

XII EVENTS

1. Out of the hospital, bruised and saddened and converted, with Princess' grunts still tangled in my hair . . . and Father in his overcoat, looking like a prince himself, come to carry me off. Up the expressway and out north to home. Jesus Christ, but the air is thinner and cleaner here. Monumental houses. Heartbreaking sidewalks, so clean.

2. Weeping in the living room. The ceiling is two stories high and two chandeliers hang from it. Weeping, weeping, though Billie the maid is *probably listening.* I will never leave home again. Never. Never leave home. Never leave this home again, never.

3. Sugar doughnuts for breakfast. The toaster is very shiny and my face is distorted in it. Is that my face?

4. The car is turning in the driveway. Father brings me home. Mother embraces me. Sunlight breaks in movieland patches on the roof of our traditional-contemporary home, which was designed for the famous automotive stylist whose identity, if I told you the name of the famous car he designed, you would all know, so I can't tell you because my teeth chatter at the thought of being sued . . . or having someone climb into my bedroom window with a rope to strangle me. . . . The car turns up the blacktop drive. The house opens to me like a doll's house, so lovely in the sunlight, the big living room beckons to me with its walls falling away in a delirium of joy at my return, Billie the maid is *no doubt* listening from the kitchen as I burst into tears and the hysteria Simon got so sick of. Convulsed in Father's arms, I say I will never leave again, never, why did I leave, where did I go, what happened, my mind is gone wrong, my body is one big bruise, my backbone was sucked dry, it wasn't the men who hurt me and Simon never hurt me but only those girls . . . my God, how they hurt me . . . I will never leave home again. . . . The car is perpetually turning up the drive and I am perpetually breaking down in the living room and we are perpetually taking the right exit from the expressway (Lahser Road) and the wall of the rest room is perpetually banging against my head and perpetually are Simon's hands moving across my body and adding everything up and so too are Father's hands on my shaking bruised back, far from the surface of my skin on the surface of my good blue cashmere coat (dry-cleaned for my release). . . . I weep for all the money here, for

God in gold and beige carpeting, for the beauty of chandeliers and the miracle of a clean polished gleaming toaster and faucets that run both hot and cold water, and I tell them, *I will never leave home, this is my home, I love everything here, I am in love with everything here. . . .*

I am home.

RAYMOND CARVER (b. 1939)

Cathedral

This blind man, an old friend of my wife's, he was on his way to spend the night. His wife had died. So he was visiting the dead wife's relatives in Connecticut. He called my wife from his in-laws'. Arrangements were made. He would come by train, a five-hour trip, and my wife would meet him at the station. She hadn't seen him since she worked for him one summer in Seattle ten years ago. But she and the blind man had kept in touch. They made tapes and mailed them back and forth. I wasn't enthusiastic about his visit. He was no one I knew. And his being blind bothered me. My idea of blindness came from the movies. In the movies, the blind moved slowly and never laughed. Sometimes they were led by seeing-eye dogs. A blind man in my house was not something I looked forward to.

That summer in Seattle she had needed a job. She didn't have any money. The man she was going to marry at the end of the summer was in officers' training school. He didn't have any money, either. But she was in love with the guy, and he was in love with her, etc. She'd seen something in the paper: HELP WANTED—*Reading to Blind Man,* and a telephone number. She phoned and went over, was hired on the spot. She'd worked with this blind man all summer. She read stuff to him, case studies, reports, that sort of thing. She helped him organize his little office in the county social-service department. They'd become good friends, my wife and the blind man. How do I know these things? She told me. And she told me something else. On her last day in the office, the blind man asked if he could touch her face. She agreed to this. She told me he touched his fingers to every part of her face, her nose —even her neck! She never forgot it. She even tried to write a poem about it. She was always trying to write a poem. She wrote a poem or two every year, usually after something really important had happened to her.

When we first started going out together, she showed me the poem. In the poem, she recalled his fingers and the way they had moved around over her face. In the poem, she talked about what she had felt at the time, about what went through her mind when the blind man touched her nose and lips. I can remember I didn't think much of the poem. Of course, I didn't tell her that. Maybe I just don't understand poetry. I admit it's not the first thing I reach for when I pick up something to read.

Anyway, this man who'd first enjoyed her favors, the officer-to-be, he'd been her childhood sweetheart. So okay. I'm saying that at the end of the summer she let the blind man run his hands over her face, said goodbye to him, married her childhood etc., who was now a commissioned officer, and she moved away from Seattle. But they'd kept in touch, she and the blind man. She made the first contact after a year or so. She called him up one night from an Air Force base in Alabama. She wanted to talk. They talked. He asked her to send him a tape and tell him about her life. She did this. She sent the tape. On the tape, she told the blind man about her husband and about their life together in the military. She told the blind man she loved her husband but she didn't like it where they lived and she didn't like it that he was a part of the military-industrial thing. She told the blind man she'd written a poem and he was in it. She told him that she was writing a poem about what it was like to be an Air Force officer's wife. The poem wasn't finished yet. She was still writing it. The blind man made a tape. He sent her the tape. She made a tape. This went on for years. My wife's officer was posted to one base and then another. She sent tapes from Moody AFB, McGuire, McConnell, and finally Travis, near Sacramento, where one night she got to feeling lonely and cut off from people she kept losing in that moving-around life. She got to feeling she couldn't go it another step. She went in and swallowed all the pills and capsules in the medicine chest and washed them down with a bottle of gin. Then she got into a hot bath and passed out.

But instead of dying, she got sick. She threw up. Her officer—why should he have a name? he was the childhood sweetheart, and what more does he want?—came home from somewhere, found her, and called the ambulance. In time, she put it all on a tape and sent the tape to the blind man. Over the years, she put all kinds of stuff on tapes and sent the tapes off lickety-split. Next to writing a poem every year, I think it was her chief means of recreation. On one tape, she told the blind man she'd decided to live away from her officer for a time. On another tape, she told him about her divorce. She and I began going out, and of course she told her blind man about it. She told him everything, or so it seemed to me. Once she asked me if I'd like to hear the latest tape from the blind man. This was a year ago. I was on the tape, she said. So I said okay, I'd listen to it. I got us drinks and we settled down in the living room. We made ready to listen. First she inserted the tape into the player and adjusted a couple of dials. Then she pushed a lever. The tape squeaked and someone began to talk in this loud voice. She lowered the volume. After a few minutes of harmless chitchat, I heard my own name in the mouth of this stranger, this blind man I didn't even know! And then this: "From all you've said about him, I can only conclude—" But we were interrupted, a knock at the door, something, and we didn't ever get back to the tape. Maybe it was just as well. I'd heard all I wanted to.

Now this same blind man was coming to sleep in my house.

"Maybe I could take him bowling," I said to my wife. She was at the draining board doing scalloped potatoes. She put down the knife she was using and turned around.

"If you love me," she said, "you can do this for me. If you don't love me, okay. But if you had a friend, any friend, and the friend came to visit, I'd make him feel comfortable." She wiped her hands with the dish towel.

"I don't have any blind friends," I said.

"You don't have *any* friends," she said. "Period. Besides," she said, "goddamn it, his wife's just died! Don't you understand that? The man's lost his wife!"

I didn't answer. She'd told me a little about the blind man's wife. Her name was Beulah. Beulah! That's a name for a colored woman.

"Was his wife a Negro?" I asked.

"Are you crazy?" my wife said. "Have you just flipped or something?" She picked up a potato. I saw it hit the floor, then roll under the stove. "What's wrong with you?" she said. "Are you drunk?"

"I'm just asking," I said.

Right then my wife filled me in with more detail than I cared to know. I made a drink and sat at the kitchen table to listen. Pieces of the story began to fall into place.

Beulah had gone to work for the blind man the summer after my wife had stopped working for him. Pretty soon Beulah and the blind man had themselves a church wedding. It was a little wedding—who'd want to go to such a wedding in the first place?—just the two of them, plus the minister and the minister's wife. But it was a church wedding just the same. It was what Beulah had wanted, he'd said. But even then Beulah must have been carrying the cancer in her glands. After they had been inseparable for eight years—my wife's word, *inseparable*—Beulah's health went into a rapid decline. She died in a Seattle hospital room, the blind man sitting beside the bed and holding on to her hand. They'd married, lived and worked together, slept together—had sex, sure—and then the blind man had to bury her. All this without his having ever seen what the goddamned woman looked like. It was beyond my understanding. Hearing this, I felt sorry for the blind man for a little bit. And then I found myself thinking what a pitiful life this woman must have led. Imagine a woman who could never see herself as she was seen in the eyes of her loved one. A woman who could go on day after day and never receive the smallest compliment from her beloved. A woman whose husband could never read the expression on her face, be it misery or something better. Someone who could wear makeup or not—what difference to him? She could, if she wanted, wear green eyeshadow around one eye, a straight pin in her nostril, yellow slacks and purple shoes, no matter. And then to slip off into death, the blind man's hand on her hand, his blind eyes streaming tears—I'm imagining now—her last thought maybe this: that he never even knew what she looked like, and she on an express to the grave. Robert was left with a small insurance policy and half of a twenty-peso Mexican coin. The other half of the coin went into the box with her. Pathetic.

So when the time rolled around, my wife went to the depot to pick him up. With nothing to do but wait—sure, I blamed him for that—I was having a drink and watching the TV when I heard the car pull into the drive. I got up from the sofa with my drink and went to the window to have a look.

I saw my wife laughing as she parked the car. I saw her get out of the car and shut the door. She was still wearing a smile. Just amazing. She went around to the other side of the car to where the blind man was already starting to get out. This blind man, feature this, he was wearing a full beard! A beard on a blind man! Too much, I say. The blind man reached into the back seat and dragged out a suitcase. My wife took his arm, shut the car door, and, talking all the way, moved him down the drive and then up the steps to the front porch. I turned off the TV. I finished my drink, rinsed the glass, dried my hands. Then I went to the door.

My wife said, "I want you to meet Robert. Robert, this is my husband. I've told you all about him." She was beaming. She had this blind man by his coat sleeve.

The blind man let go of his suitcase and up came his hand. I took it. He squeezed hard, held my hand, and then he let it go.

"I feel like we've already met," he boomed.

"Likewise," I said. I didn't know what else to say. Then I said, "Welcome. I've heard a lot about you." We began to move then, a little group, from the porch into the living room, my wife guiding him by the arm. The blind man was carrying his suitcase in his other hand. My wife said things like, "To your left here, Robert. That's right. Now watch it, there's a chair. That's it. Sit down right here. This is the sofa. We just bought this sofa two weeks ago."

I started to say something about the old sofa. I'd liked that old sofa. But I didn't say anything. Then I wanted to say something else, small-talk, about the scenic ride along the Hudson. How going *to* New York, you should sit on the right-hand side of the train, and coming *from* New York, the left-hand side.

"Did you have a good train ride?" I said. "Which side of the train did you sit on, by the way?"

"What a question, which side!" my wife said. "What's it matter which side?" she said.

"I just asked," I said.

"Right side," the blind man said. "I hadn't been on a train in nearly forty years. Not since I was a kid. With my folks. That's been a long time. I'd nearly forgotten the sensation. I have winter in my beard now," he said. "So I've been told, anyway. Do I look distinguished, my dear?" the blind man said to my wife.

"You look distinguished, Robert," she said. "Robert," she said. "Robert, it's just so good to see you."

My wife finally took her eyes off the blind man and looked at me. I had the feeling she didn't like what she saw. I shrugged.

I've never met, or personally known, anyone who was blind. This blind man was late forties, a heavy-set, balding man with stooped shoulders, as if he carried a great weight there. He wore brown slacks, brown shoes, a light-brown shirt, a tie, a sports coat. Spiffy. He also had this full beard. But he didn't use a cane and he didn't wear dark glasses. I'd always thought dark glasses were a must for the blind. Fact was, I wished he had a pair. At first glance, his eyes looked like anyone else's eyes. But if you looked close, there was something different about them. Too much white in the iris, for one thing, and the pupils seemed to move round in the sockets without his knowing it or being able to stop it. Creepy. As I stared as his face, I saw the left pupil turn in toward his nose while the other made an effort to keep in one place. But it was only an effort, for that eye was on the roam without knowing it or wanting it to be.

I said, "Let me get you a drink. What's your pleasure? We have a little of everything. It's one of our pastimes."

"Bub, I'm a Scotch man myself," he said fast enough in this big voice.

"Right," I said. Bub! "Sure you are. I knew it."

He let his fingers touch his suitcase, which was sitting alongside the sofa. He was taking his bearings. I didn't blame him for that.

"I'll move that up to your room," my wife said.

"No, that's fine," the blind man said loudly. "It can go up when I go up."

"A little water with the Scotch?" I said.

"Very little," he said.

"I knew it," I said.

He said, "Just a tad. The Irish actor, Barry Fitzgerald? I'm like that fellow. When I drink water, Fitzgerald said, I drink water. When I drink whiskey, I drink whiskey." My wife laughed. The blind man brought his hand up under his beard. He lifted his beard slowly and let it drop.

I did the drinks, three big glasses of Scotch with a splash of water in each. Then we made ourselves comfortable and talked about Robert's travels. First the long flight from the West Coast to Connecticut, we covered that. Then from Connecticut up here by train. We had another drink concerning that leg of the trip.

I remembered having read somewhere that the blind didn't smoke because, as speculation had it, they couldn't see the smoke they exhaled. I thought I knew that much and that much only about blind people. But this blind man smoked his cigarette down to the nubbin and then lit another one. This blind man filled his ashtray and my wife emptied it.

When we sat down at the table for dinner, we had another drink. My wife heaped Robert's plate with cube steak, scalloped potatoes, green beans. I buttered him up two slices of bread. I said, "Here's bread and butter for you." I swallowed some of my drink. "Now let us pray," I said, and the blind man lowered his head. My wife looked at me, her mouth agape. "Pray the phone won't ring and the food doesn't get cold," I said.

We dug in. We ate everything there was to eat on the table. We ate like there was no tomorrow. We didn't talk. We ate. We scarfed. We grazed that table. We were into serious eating. The blind man had right away located his foods, he knew just where everything was on his plate. I watched with admiration as he used his knife and fork on the meat. He'd cut two pieces of meat, fork the meat into his mouth, and then go all out for the scalloped potatoes, the beans next, and then he'd tear off a hunk of buttered bread and eat that. He'd follow this up with a big drink of milk. It didn't seem to bother him to use his fingers once in a while, either.

We finished everything, including half a strawberry pie. For a few moments, we sat as if stunned. Sweat beaded on our faces. Finally, we got up from the table and left the dirty plates. We didn't look back. We took ourselves into the living room and sank into our places again. Robert and my wife sat on the sofa. I took the big chair. We had us two or three more drinks while they talked about the major things that had come to pass for them in the past ten years. For the most part, I just listened. Now and then I joined in. I didn't want him to think I'd left the room, and I didn't want her to think I was feeling left out. They talked of things that had happened to them—to them!—these past ten years. I waited in vain to hear my name on my wife's sweet lips: "And then my dear husband came into my life"—something like that. But I heard nothing of the sort. More talk of Robert. Robert had done a little of everything, it seemed, a regular blind jack-of-all-trades. But most recently he and his wife had had an Amway distributorship, from which, I gathered, they'd earned their living, such as it was. The blind man was also a ham radio operator. He talked in his loud voice about conversations he'd had with fellow operators in Guam, in the Philippines, in Alaska, and even in Tahiti. He said he'd have a lot of friends there if he ever wanted to go visit those places. From time to time, he'd turn his blind face toward me, put his hand under his beard, ask me something. How long had I been in my present position? (Three years.) Did I like my work? (I didn't.) Was I going to stay with it? (What were the options?) Finally, when I thought he was beginning to run down, I got up and turned on the TV.

My wife looked at me with irritation. She was heading toward a boil. Then she looked at the blind man and said, "Robert, do you have a TV?"

The blind man said, "My dear, I have two TVs. I have a color set and a black-and-white thing, an old relic. It's funny, but if I turn the TV on, and I'm always turning it on, I turn on the color set. It's funny, don't you think?"

I didn't know what to say to that. I had absolutely nothing to say to that. No opinion. So I watched the news program and tried to listen to what the announcer was saying.

"This is a color TV," the blind man said. "Don't ask me how, but I can tell."

"We traded up a while ago," I said.

The blind man had another taste of his drink. He lifted his beard, sniffed it, and let it fall. He leaned forward on the sofa. He positioned his ashtray on the coffee table, then put the lighter to his cigarette. He leaned back on the sofa and crossed his legs at the ankles.

My wife covered her mouth, and then she yawned. She stretched. She said, "I think I'll go upstairs and put on my robe. I think I'll change into something else. Robert, you make yourself comfortable," she said.

"I'm comfortable," the blind man said.

"I want you to feel comfortable in this house," she said.

"I am comfortable," the blind man said.

After she'd left the room, he and I listened to the weather report and then to the sports roundup. By that time, she'd been gone so long I didn't know if she was going to come back. I thought she might have gone to bed. I wished she'd come back downstairs. I didn't want to be left alone with a blind man. I asked him if he wanted another drink, and he said sure. Then I asked if he wanted to smoke some dope with me. I said I'd just rolled a number. I hadn't, but I planned to do so in about two shakes.

"I'll try some with you," he said.

"Damn right," I said. "That's the stuff."

I got our drinks and sat down on the sofa with him. Then I rolled us two fat numbers. I lit one and passed it. I brought it to his fingers. He took it and inhaled.

"Hold it as long as you can," I said. I could tell he didn't know the first thing.

My wife came back downstairs wearing her pink robe and her pink slippers.

"What do I smell?" she said.

"We thought we'd have us some cannabis," I said.

My wife gave me a savage look. Then she looked at the blind man and said, "Robert, I didn't know you smoked."

He said, "I do now, my dear. There's a first time for everything. But I don't feel anything yet."

"This stuff is pretty mellow," I said. "This stuff is mild. It's dope you can reason with," I said. "It doesn't mess you up."

"Not much it doesn't, bub," he said, and laughed.

My wife sat on the sofa between the blind man and me. I passed her the number. She took it and toked and then passed it back to me. "Which way is this going?" she said. Then she said, "I shouldn't be smoking this. I can hardly keep my eyes open as it is. That dinner did me in. I shouldn't have eaten so much."

"It was the strawberry pie," the blind man said. "That's what did it," he said, and he laughed his big laugh. Then he shook his head.

"There's more strawberry pie," I said.

"Do you want some more, Robert?" my wife said.

"Maybe in a little while," he said.

We gave our attention to the TV. My wife yawned again. She said, "Your bed is made up when you feel like going to bed, Robert. I know you must have had a long day. When you're ready to go to bed, say so." She pulled his arm. "Robert?"

He came to and said, "I've had a real nice time. This beats tapes, doesn't it?"

I said, "Coming at you," and I put the number between his fingers. He inhaled, held the smoke, and then let it go. It was like he'd been doing it since he was nine years old.

"Thanks, bub," he said. "But I think this is all for me. I think I'm beginning to feel it," he said. He held the burning roach out for my wife.

"Same here," she said. "Ditto. Me, too." She took the roach and passed it to me. "I may just sit here for a while between you two guys with my eyes closed. But don't let me bother you, okay? Either one of you. If it bothers you, say so. Otherwise, I may just sit here with my eyes closed until you're ready to go to bed," she said. "Your bed's made up, Robert, when you're ready. It's right next to our room at the top of the stairs. We'll show you up when you're ready. You wake me up now, you guys, if I fall asleep," She said that and then she closed her eyes and went to sleep.

The news program ended. I got up and changed the channel. I sat back down on the sofa. I wished my wife hadn't pooped out. Her head lay across the back of the sofa, her mouth open. She'd turned so that her robe had slipped away from her legs, exposing a juicy thigh. I reached to draw her robe back over her, and it was then that I glanced at the blind man. What the hell! I flipped the robe open again.

"You say when you want some strawberry pie," I said.

"I will," he said.

I said, "Are you tired? Do you want me to take you up to your bed? Are you ready to hit the hay?"

"Not yet," he said. "No, I'll stay up with you, bub. If that's all right. I'll stay up until you're ready to turn in. We haven't had a chance to talk. Know what I mean? I feel like me and her monopolized the evening." He lifted his beard and he let it fall.

338   *Cathedral*

He picked up his cigarettes and his lighter.

"That's all right," I said. Then I said, "I'm glad for the company."

And I guess I was. Every night I smoked dope and stayed up as long as I could before I fell asleep. My wife and I hardly ever went to bed at the same time. When I did go to sleep, I had these dreams. Sometimes I'd wake up from one of them, my heart going crazy.

Something about the church and the Middle Ages was on the TV. Not your run-of-the-mill TV fare. I wanted to watch something else. I turned to the other channels. But there was nothing on them, either. So I turned back to the first channel and apologized.

"Bub, it's all right," the blind man said. "It's fine with me. Whatever you want to watch is okay. I'm always learning something. Learning never ends. It won't hurt me to learn something tonight. I got ears," he said.

We didn't say anything for a time. He was leaning forward with his head turned at me, his right ear aimed in the direction of the set. Very disconcerting. Now and then his eyelids drooped and then they snapped open again. Now and then he put his fingers into his beard and tugged, like he was thinking about something he was hearing on the television.

On the screen, a group of men wearing cowls was being set upon and tormented by men dressed in skeleton costumes and men dressed as devils. The men dressed as devils wore devil masks, horns, and long tails. This pageant was part of a procession. The Englishman who was narrating the thing said it took place in Spain once a year. I tried to explain to the blind man what was happening.

"Skeletons," he said. "I know about skeletons," he said, and he nodded.

The TV showed this one cathedral. Then there was a long, slow look at another one. Finally, the picture switched to the famous one in Paris, with its flying buttresses and its spires reaching up to the clouds. The camera pulled away to show the whole of the cathedral rising above the skyline.

There were times when the Englishman who was telling the thing would shut up, would simply let the camera move around over the cathedrals. Or else the camera would tour the countryside, men in fields walking behind oxen. I waited as long as I could. Then I felt I had to say something. I said, "They're showing the outside of this cathedral now. Gargoyles. Little statues carved to look like monsters. Now I guess they're in Italy. Yeah, they're in Italy. There's paintings on the walls of this one church."

"Are those fresco paintings, bub?" he asked, and he sipped from his drink.

I reached for my glass. But it was empty. I tried to remember what I could remember. "You're asking me are those frescoes?" I said. "That's a good question. I don't know."

The camera moved to a cathedral outside Lisbon. The differences in the Portuguese cathedral compared with the French and Italian were not that great. But they were there. Mostly the interior stuff. Then something occurred to me, and I said, "Something has occurred to me. Do you have any idea what a cathedral is? What they look like, that is? Do you follow me? If somebody says cathedral to you, do you have any notion what they're talking about? Do you know the difference between that and a Baptist church, say?"

He let the smoke dribble from his mouth. "I know they took hundreds of workers fifty or a hundred years to build," he said. "I just heard the man say that, of course. I know generations of the same families worked on a cathedral. I heard him say that, too. The men who began their life's work on them, they never lived to see the completion of their work. In that wise, bub, they're no different from the rest of us, right?" He laughed. Then his eyelids drooped again. His head nodded. He seemed to be snoozing. Maybe he was imagining himself in Portugal. The TV was showing another cathedral now. This one was in Germany. The Englishman's voice droned on. "Cathedrals," the blind man said. He sat up and rolled his head back and forth. "If you want the truth, bub, that's about all I know. What I just said. What I heard him say. But maybe you could describe one to me? I wish you'd do it. I'd like that. If you want to know, I really don't have a good idea."

I stared hard at the shot of the cathedral on the TV. How could I even begin to describe it? But say my life depended on it. Say my life was being threatened by an insane guy who said I had to do it or else.

I stared some more at the cathedral before the picture flipped off into the countryside. There was no use. I turned to the blind man and said, "To begin with, they're very tall." I was looking around the room for clues. "They reach way up. Up and up. Toward the sky. They're so big, some of them, they have to have these supports. To help hold them up, so to speak. These supports are called buttresses. They remind me of viaducts, for some reason. But maybe you don't know viaducts, either? Sometimes the cathedrals have devils and such carved into the front. Sometimes lords and ladies. Don't ask me why this is," I said.

He was nodding. The whole upper part of his body seemed to be moving back and forth.

"I'm not doing so good, am I?" I said.

He stopped nodding and leaned forward on the edge of the sofa. As he listened to me, he was running his fingers through his beard. I wasn't getting through to him, I could see that. But he waited for me to go on just the same. He nodded, like he was trying to encourage me. I tried to think what else to say. "They're really big," I said. "They're massive. They're built of stone. Marble, too, sometimes. In those olden days, when they built cathedrals, men wanted to be close to God. In those olden days, God was an important part of everyone's life. You could tell this from their cathedral-building. I'm sorry," I said, "but it looks like that's the best I can do for you. I'm just no good at it."

"That's all right, bub," the blind man said. "Hey, listen. I hope you don't mind my asking you. Can I ask you something? Let me ask you a simple question, yes or no. I'm just curious and there's no offense. You're my host. But let me ask if you are in any way religious? You don't mind my asking?"

I shook my head. He couldn't see that, though. A wink is the same as a nod to a blind man. "I guess I don't believe in it. In anything. Sometimes it's hard. You know what I'm saying?"

"Sure, I do," he said.

"Right," I said.

The Englishman was still holding forth. My wife sighed in her sleep. She drew a long breath and went on with her sleeping.

"You'll have to forgive me," I said. "But I can't tell you what a cathedral looks like. It just isn't in me to do it. I can't do any more than I've done."

The blind man sat very still, his head down, as he listened to me.

I said, "The truth is, cathedrals don't mean anything special to me. Nothing. Cathedrals. They're something to look at on late-night TV. That's all they are."

It was then that the blind man cleared his throat. He brought something up. He took a handkerchief from his back pocket. Then he said. "I get it, bub. It's okay. It happens. Don't worry about it," he said. "Hey, listen to me. Will you do me a favor? I got an idea. Why don't you find us some heavy paper? And a pen. We'll do something. We'll draw one together. Get us a pen and some heavy paper. Go on, bub, get the stuff," he said.

So I went upstairs. My legs felt like they didn't have any strength in them. They felt like they did after I'd done some running. In my wife's room, I looked around. I found some ballpoints in a little basket on her table. And then I tried to think where to look for the kind of paper he was talking about.

Downstairs, in the kitchen, I found a shopping bag with onion skins in the bottom of the bag. I emptied the bag and shook it. I brought it into the living room and sat down with it near his legs. I moved some things, smoothed the wrinkles from the bag, spread it out on the coffee table.

The blind man got down from the sofa and sat next to me on the carpet.

He ran his fingers over the paper. He went up and down the sides of the paper. The edges, even the edges. He fingered the corners.

"All right," he said. "All right, let's do her."

He found my hand, the hand with the pen. He closed his hand over my hand. "Go ahead, bub, draw," he said. "Draw. You'll see. I'll follow along with you. It'll be okay. Just begin now like I'm telling you. You'll see. Draw," the blind man said.

So I began. First I drew a box that looked like a house. It could have been the house I lived in. Then I put a roof on it. At either end of the roof, I drew spires. Crazy.

"Swell," he said. "Terrific. You're doing fine," he said. "Never thought anything like this could happen in your lifetime, did you, bub? Well, it's a strange life, we all know that. Go on now. Keep it up."

I put in windows with arches. I drew flying buttresses. I hung great doors. I couldn't stop. The TV station went off the air. I put down the pen and closed and opened my fingers. The blind man felt around over the paper. He moved the tips of his fingers over the paper, all over what I had drawn, and he nodded.

"Doing fine," the blind man said.

I took up the pen again, and he found my hand. I kept at it. I'm no artist. But I kept drawing just the same.

My wife opened up her eyes and gazed at us. She sat up on the sofa, her robe hanging open. She said, "What are you doing? Tell me, I want to know."

I didn't answer her.

The blind man said, "We're drawing a cathedral. Me and him are working on it. Press hard," he said to me. "That's right. That's good," he said. "Sure. You got it, bub. I can tell. You didn't think you could. But you can, can't you? You're cooking with gas now. You know what I'm saying? We're going to really have us something here in a minute. How's the old arm?" he said. "Put some people in there now. What's a cathedral without people?"

My wife said, "What's going on? Robert, what are you doing? What's going on?"

"It's all right," he said to her. "Close your eyes now," the blind man said to me. I did it. I closed them just like he said.

"Are they closed?" he said. "Don't fudge."

"They're closed," I said.

"Keep them that way," he said. He said, "Don't stop now. Draw."

So we kept on with it. His fingers rode my fingers as my hand went over the paper. It was like nothing else in my life up to now.

Then he said, "I think that's it. I think you got it," he said. "Take a look. What do you think?"

But I had my eyes closed. I thought I'd keep them that way for a little longer. I thought it was something I ought to do.

"Well?" he said. "Are you looking?"

My eyes were still closed. I was in my house. I knew that. But I didn't feel like I was inside anything.

"It's really something," I said.

MARGARET ATWOOD (b. 1939)

Loulou; or, The Domestic Life of the Language

Loulou is in the coach-house, wedging clay. She's wearing a pair of running shoes, once white, now grey, over men's wool work socks, a purple Indian-print cotton skirt, and a rust-coloured smock, so heavy with clay dust it hangs on her like brocade, the sleeves rolled up past the elbow. This is her favourite working outfit. To the music of *The Magic Flute,* brought to her by CBC stereo, she lifts the slab of clay and slams it down, gives a half-turn, lifts and slams. This is to get the air bubbles out, so nothing will explode in the kiln. Some potters would hire an apprentice to do this, but not Loulou.

It's true she has apprentices, two of them; she gets them through the government as free trainees. But they make plates and mugs from her designs, about all they're fit for. She doesn't consider them suitable for wedging clay, with their puny little biceps and match-stick wrists, so poorly developed compared with her own solid, smoothly muscled arms and broad, capable but shapely hands, so often admired by the poets. *Marmoreal,* one of them said—wrote, actually—causing Loulou to make one of her frequent sorties into the dictionary, to find out whether or not she'd been insulted.

Once she had done this openly, whenever they'd used a word about her she didn't understand, but when they'd discovered she was doing it they'd found it amusing and had started using words like that on purpose. "Loulou is so geomorphic," one of them would say, and when she would blush and scowl, another would take it up. "Not only that, she's fundamentally chthonic." "Telluric," a third would pipe up. Then they would laugh. She's decided that the only thing to do is to ignore them. But she's not so dumb as they think, she remembers the words, and when they aren't watching she sneaks a look at the Shorter Oxford (kept in the study which really belongs to only one of them but which she thinks of as *theirs*), washing her hands first so she won't leave any tell-tale signs of clay on the page.

She reads their journals, too, taking the same precautions. She suspects they know she does this. It's her way of keeping up with what they are really thinking about her, or maybe only with what they want her to think they're thinking. The journals are supposed to be secret, but Loulou considers it her right and also a kind of duty to read them. She views it in the same light as her mother viewed going through the family's sock and underwear drawers, to sort out the clean things from the ones they'd already worn and stuffed back in. This is what the poets' journals are like. Socks, mostly, but you never know what you will find.

"Loulou is becoming more metonymous," she's read recently. This has been bothering her for days. Sometimes she longs to say to them, "Now just what in hell did you mean by that?" But she knows she would get nowhere.

"Loulou is the foe of abstract order," one would say. This is a favourite belief of theirs.

"Loulou is the foe of abstract ordure."

"Loulou is the Great Goddess."

"Loulou is the great mattress."

It would end up with Loulou telling them to piss off. When that didn't stop them, she would tell them they couldn't have any more baked chicken if they went on like that. Threatening to deprive them of food usually works.

Overtly, Loulou takes care to express scorn for the poets; though not for them, exactly—they have their points—but for their pickiness about words. Her mother would have said they were finicky eaters. "Who cares what a thing's called?" she says to them. "A piece of bread is a piece of bread. You want some or not?" And she bends over to slide three of her famous loaves, high and nicely browned, out of the oven, and the poets admire her ass and haunches. Sometimes they do this openly, like other men, growling and smacking their lips, pretending to be construction workers. They like pretending to be other things; in the summers they play baseball games together and make a big fuss about having the right hats. Sometimes, though, they do it silently, and Loulou only knows about it from the poems they write afterwards. Loulou can tell these poems are about her, even though the nouns change: "my lady," "my friend's lady," "my woman," "my friend's woman," "my wife," "my friend's wife," and, when necessary for the length of the line, "the wife of my friend." Never "girl" though, and never her name. *Ass* and *haunches* aren't Loulou's words either; she would say *butt*.

Loulou doesn't know anything about music but she likes listening to it. Right now, the Queen of the Night runs up her trill, and Loulou pauses to see if she'll make it to the top. She does, just barely, and Loulou, feeling vicarious triumph, rams her fist into the mound of clay. Then she covers it with a sheet of plastic and goes to the sink to wash her hands. Soon the oven timer will go off and one of the poets, maybe her husband but you never know, will call her on the intercom to come and see about the bread. It isn't that they wouldn't take it out themselves, if she asked them to. Among the four or five of them they'd likely manage. It's just that Loulou doesn't trust them. She decided long ago that none of them knows his left tit from a hole in the ground when it comes to the real world. If she wants the bread taken out when it's done but not overdone, and she does, she'll have to do it herself.

She wonders who will be in the kitchen at the main house by now: her first husband for sure, and the man she lived with after that for three years without being married, and her second husband, the one she has now, and two ex-lovers. Half a dozen of them maybe, sitting around the kitchen table, drinking her coffee and eating her hermit cookies and talking about whatever they talk about when she isn't there. In the past there have been periods of strain among them, especially during the times when Loulou has been switching over, but they're all getting along well enough now. They run a collective poetry magazine, which keeps them out of trouble mostly. The name of this magazine is *Comma,* but among themselves the poets refer to it as *Coma.* At parties they enjoy going up to young female would-be poets ("proupies," they call them behind their backs, which means "poetry groupies"), and saying, "I'd like to put you in a *Coma.*" A while ago *Comma* published mostly poems without commas, but this is going out now, just as beards are going out in favour of moustaches and even shaving. The more daring poets have gone so far as to cut off their sideburns. Loulou is not quite sure whether or not she approves of this.

She doesn't know whether the poets are good poets, whether the poems they write in such profusion are any good. Loulou has no opinion on this subject: all that matters is what they are writing about her. Their poems get published in books, but what does that mean? Not money, that's for sure. You don't make any money with poetry, the poets tell her, unless you sing and play the guitar too. Sometimes they give readings and make a couple of hundred bucks. For Loulou that's three medium-sized casseroles, with lids. On the other hand, they don't have her expenses. Part of her expenses is them.

Loulou can't remember exactly how she got mixed up with the poets. It wasn't that she had any special thing for poets as such: it just happened that way. After the first one, the others seemed to follow along naturally, almost as if they were tied onto each other in a long line with a piece of string. They were always around, and she was so busy most of the time that she didn't go out much to look for other kinds of men. Now that her business is doing so well you'd think she would have more leisure time, but this isn't the case. And any leisure time she does have, she spends with the poets. They're always nagging her about working too hard.

Bob was the first one, and also her first husband. He was in art school at the same time she was, until he decided he wasn't suited for it. He wasn't practical enough, he let things dry out: paint, clay, even the leftovers in his tiny refrigerator, as Loulou discovered the first night she'd slept with him. She devoted the next morning to cleaning up his kitchen, getting rid of the saucers of mummified cooked peas and the shrivelled, half-gnawed chicken legs and the warped, cracked quarter-packages of two-month-old sliced bacon, and the bits of cheese, oily on the outside and hard as tiles. Loulou has always hated clutter, which she defines, though not in so many words, as matter out of its proper place. Bob looked on, sullen but appreciative, as she hurled and scoured. Possibly this was why he decided to love her: because she would do this sort of thing. What he said though was, "You complete me."

What he also said was that he'd fallen in love with her name. All the poets have done this, one after the other. The first symptom is that they ask her whether Loulou is short for something—Louise, maybe? When she says no, they look at her in that slightly glazed way she recognizes instantly, as if they've never paid proper attention to her or even seen her before. This look is her favourite part of any new relationship with a man. It's even better than the sex, though Loulou likes sex well enough and all the poets have been good in bed. But then, Loulou has never slept with a man she did not consider good in bed. She's beginning to think this is because she has low standards.

At first Loulou was intrigued by this obsession with her name, mistaking it for an obsession with her, but it turned out to be no such thing. It was the gap that interested them, one of them had explained (not Bob though; maybe Phil, the second and most linguistic of them all).

"What gap?" Loulou asked suspiciously. She knew her upper front teeth were a little wide apart and had been self-conscious about it when she was younger.

"The gap between the word and the thing signified," Phil said. His hand was on her breast and he'd given it an absent-minded squeeze, as if to illustrate what he meant. They were in bed at the time. Mostly Loulou doesn't like talking in bed. But she's not that fond of talking at other times, either.

Phil went on to say that Loulou, as a name, conjured up images of French girls in can-can outfits, with corseted wasp-waists and blonde curls and bubbly laughs. But then there was the real Loulou—dark, straight-haired, firmly built, marmoreal, and well, not exactly bubbly. More earthy, you might say. (Loulou hadn't known then what he meant by "earthy," though by now she's learned that for him, for all of them, it means "functionally illiterate.") The thing was, Phil said, what existed in the space between Loulou and her name?

Loulou didn't know what he was talking about. What space? Once she'd resented her mother for having saddled her with this name; she would rather have been called Mary or Ann. Maybe she suspected that her mother would really have preferred a child more like the name—blonde, thin, curly-headed—but had disappointingly got Loulou instead, short, thick, stubborn-jawed, not much interested in the frilly dolls' clothes her mother had painstakingly crocheted for her. Instead, Loulou was fond of making mud pies on the back porch, placing them carefully along the railing where people wouldn't step on them and ruin them. Her mother's response to these pies was to say, "Oh, Loulou!," as if *Loulou* itself meant mud, meant trouble and dismay.

"It's just a name," she said. "Phil is kind of a dumb name too if you ask me."

Phil said that wasn't the point, he wasn't *criticizing* her, but Loulou had stopped the conversation by climbing on top of him, letting her long hair fall down over his face.

That was early on; he'd liked her hair then. "Rank," he'd called it in a poem, quite a lot later. Loulou hadn't thought much of that when she looked it up. It could mean *too luxuriant* or *offensive and foul-smelling.* The effect of this poem on Loulou was to cause her to wash her hair more often. Sooner or later all the poets got into her hair, and she was tired of having it compared to horse's tails, Newfoundland dog fur, black holes in space and the insides of caves. When Loulou was feeling particularly enraged by the poets she would threaten to get a brushcut, though she knew it would be pushing her luck.

When she has dried her hands, Loulou takes off her smock. Underneath it she's wearing a mauve sweatshirt with RAVING OPTIMIST stencilled across the front. The poets gave it to her, collectively, one Christmas, because a few weeks before one of them had said, "Why are you so grumpy, Loulou?" and Loulou had said, "I'm only grumpy when you pick on me," and then, after a pause, "Compared to you guys I'm a raving optimist." This was true, though they made fun of her for it. In a group they can laugh, but it's only Loulou who has seen them one at a time, sitting in chairs for hours on end with their heads down on their arms, almost unable to move. It's Loulou who's held their hands when they couldn't make it in bed and told them that other things are just as important, though she's never been able to specify what. It's Loulou who has gone out and got drunk with them and listened to them talking about the void and about the terrifying blankness of the page and about how any art form is just a way of evading suicide. Loulou thinks this is a load of b.s.: she herself does not consider the making of casseroles with lids or the throwing of porcelain fruit bowls as an evasion of suicide, but then, as they have often pointed out, what she's doing isn't an art form, it only a craft. Bob once asked her when she was going to branch out into macramé, for which she emptied the dust-pan on him. But she matches them beer for beer; she's even gone so far as to throw up right along with them, if that seemed required. One of them once told her she was a soft touch.

The intercom buzzes as Loulou is hanging up her smock. She buzzes back to show she has heard, takes her hair out of the elastic band and smooths it down, looking in the round tin-framed Mexican mirror that hangs over the sink, and checks up on little Marilyn, her new apprentice, before heading out the door.

Marilyn is still having trouble with cup handles. Loulou will have to spend some time with her later and explain them to her. If the cup handles aren't on straight, she will say, the cup will be crooked when you pick it up and then the people drinking out of it will spill things and burn themselves. That's the way you have to put it for trainees: in terms of physical damage. It's important to Loulou that the production pieces should be done right. They're her bread and butter, though what she most likes to work on are the bigger things, the amphora-like vases, the tureens a size larger than anyone ought to be able to throw. Another potter once said that you'd need a derrick to give a dinner party with Loulou's stuff, but that was jealousy. What they say about her mostly is that she doesn't fool around.

Loulou flings her pink sweater-coat across her shoulders, bangs the coach-house door behind her to make it shut, and walks towards the house, whistling between her teeth and stomping her feet to get the clay dust off. The kitchen is filled with the yeasty smell of baking bread. Loulou breathes it in, revelling in it: a smell of her own creation.

The poets are sitting around the kitchen table, drinking coffee. Maybe they're having a meeting, it's hard to tell. Some nod at her, some grin. Two of the female poets are here today and Loulou isn't too pleased about that. As far as she's concerned they don't have a lot to offer: they're almost as bad as the male poets, but without the saving grace of being men. They wear black a lot and have cheekbones.

Piss on their cheekbones, thinks Loulou. She knows what cheekbones mean. The poets, *her* poets, consider these female poets high-strung and interesting. Sometimes they praise their work, a little too extravagantly, but sometimes they talk about their bodies, though not when they are there of course, and about whether or not they would be any good in bed. Either of these approaches drives Loulou wild. She doesn't like the female poets—they eat her muffins and condescend to her, and Loulou suspects them of having designs on the poets, some of which may already have been carried out, judging from their snotty manner—but she doesn't like hearing them put down, either. What really gets her back up is that, during these discussions, the poets act as if she isn't there.

Really, though, the female poets don't count. They aren't even on the editorial board of *Comma;* they are only on the edges, like mascots, and today Loulou all but ignores them.

"You could've put on more coffee," she says in her grumpiest voice.

"What's the matter, Loulou?" says Phil, who has always been the quickest on the uptake when it comes to Loulou and her bad moods. Not that Loulou goes in for fine tuning.

"Nothing *you* can fix," says Loulou rudely. She takes off her sweater-coat and sticks out her chest. *Marmoreal,* she thinks. So much for the female poets, who are flatchested as well as everything else.

"Hey Loulou, how about a little nictitation?" says one of the poets.

"Up your nose," says Loulou.

"She thinks it's something dirty," says a second one. "She's confusing it with micturition."

"All it means is winking, Loulou," says the first one.

"He got it out of Trivial Pursuit," says a third.

Loulou takes one loaf out of the oven, turns it out, taps the bottom, puts it back into the pan and into the oven. They can go on like that for hours. It's enough to drive you right out of your tree, if you pay any attention to them at all.

"Why do you put up with us, Loulou?" Phil asked her once. Loulou sometimes wonders, but she doesn't know. She knows why they put up with her though, apart from the fact that she pays the mortgage: she's solid, she's predictable, she's always there, she makes them feel safe. But lately she's been wondering: who is there to make her feel safe?

It's another day, and Loulou is on her way to seduce her accountant. She's wearing purple boots, several years old and with watermarks on them from the slush, a cherry-coloured dirndl she made out of curtain material when she was at art school, and a Peruvian wedding shirt dyed mauve; this is the closest she ever comes to getting dressed up. Because of the section of the city she's going to, which is mostly middle-European shops, bakeries and clothing stores with yellowing embroidered blouses in the windows and places where you can buy hand-painted wooden Easter eggs and chess sets with the pawns as Cossacks, she's draped a black wool shawl over her head. This, she thinks, will make her look more ethnic and therefore more inconspicuous: she's feeling a little furtive. One of the poets has said that Loulou is to *subdued* as Las Vegas at night is to a sixty-watt light bulb, but in fact, with her long off-black hair and her large dark eyes and the strong planes of her face, she does have a kind of peasant look. This is enhanced by the two plastic shopping bags she carries, one in either hand. These do not contain groceries, however, but her receipts and cheque stubs for the two previous years. Loulou is behind on her income tax, which is why she got the accountant in the first place. She doesn't see why she shouldn't kill two birds with one stone.

Loulou is behind on her income tax because of her fear of money. When she was married to Bob, neither of them had any money anyway, so the income tax wasn't a problem. Phil, the man she lived with after that, was good with numbers, and although he had no income and therefore no income tax, he treated hers as a game, a kind of superior Scrabble. But her present husband, Calvin, considers money boring. It's all right to have some—as Loulou does, increasingly—but talking about it is sordid and a waste of time. Calvin claims that those who can actually read income-tax forms, let alone understand them, have already done severe and permanent damage to their brains. Loulou has taken to sending out her invoices and toting up her earnings in the coachhouse, instead of at the kitchen table as she used to, and adding and subtracting are acquiring overtones of forbidden sex. Perhaps this is what has led her to the step she is now about to take. You may as well be hung, thinks Loulou, for a sheep as a lamb.

In addition, Loulou has recently been feeling a wistful desire to be taken care of. It comes and goes, especially on cloudy days, and mostly Loulou pays scant attention to it. Nevertheless it's there. Everyone depends on her, but when she needs help, with her income tax for instance, nobody's within call. She could ask Phil to do it again, but Calvin might make a fuss about it. She wants to be able to turn her two plastic shopping bags over to some man, some quiet methodical man with inner strength, and not too ugly, who could make sense of their contents and tell her she has nothing to worry about and, hopefully, nothing to pay.

Before Loulou found this particular accountant, she spent several afternoons window-shopping for one down at King and Bay. When it came right down to it, however, she was so intimidated by the hermetically sealed glass towers and the thought of receptionists with hair-dos and nail polish that she didn't even go in through the doors at any of the addresses she'd looked up in the Yellow Pages. Instead, she stood at street corners as if waiting for the light to change, watching the businessmen hurry past, sometimes in overcoats of the kind the poets never wear, solid-looking and beige or navy blue but slit provocatively up the back, or in three-piece suits, challengingly done up with hundreds of buttons and zippers, their tight tennis-playing butts concealed under layers of expensive wool blend, their ties waving enticingly under their chins like the loose ends of macramé wall hangings: one pull and the whole thing would unravel. The poets, in their track suits or jeans, seem easier of access, but they are hedged with paradox and often moody. The businessmen would be simple and unspoiled, primary reds and blues rather than puce and lilac, potatoes rather than, like the poets, slightly over-ripe avocadoes.

The sight of them filled Loulou with unspecific lust, though she found them touching also. She was like a middle-aged banker surrounded by sixteen-year-old virgins: she longed to be the first, though the first of what she wasn't sure. But she knew she knew lots of things they were unlikely to know: the poets, on their good days, have been nothing if not inventive.

Loulou doesn't think of the accountant she has now as a real one, by which she means a frightening one. He is not in a glass tower, he has no polished receptionist, though he does have a certificate on the wall and even a three-piece suit (though, Loulou suspects, only one). She discovered him by accident when she was down on Queen Street buying fresh chicken from A. Stork, the best place for it in her opinion, especially when you need a lot, as she did that day because all of the poets were coming for dinner. Heading for the streetcar stop with her sackful of tender flesh, Loulou saw a hand-lettered sign in the window of a dry-goods store: INCOME TAX, and underneath it some foreign language. It was the hand-lettered sign that did it for Loulou: badly lettered at that, she could do much better. On impulse she'd pushed open the door and gone in.

There was a tiny bald-headed man behind the counter, barricaded in with bolts of maroon cloth, a rack of cheesy-looking buttons on the wall behind him, but he turned out not to be the accountant. The accountant was in a separate room at the back, with nothing in it except a wooden desk of the sort Loulou associated with her grade-school teachers, and one other chair and a filing cabinet. He stood up when Loulou came in and offered to take her sack of chicken and put it somewhere for her. "No thanks," said Loulou, because she could see there was nowhere for him to put it—there was a fern on the filing cabinet, obviously on its last legs—and that he would merely get more flustered than he already was if she said yes; so she went through their first interview with a bag of still-warm cut-up chicken in her lap.

She's seen him twice since then. He takes more time with her than he really needs to, maybe because he's not what you would call all that busy. He also talks to her more than he needs to. By now, Loulou knows quite a lot about him. Getting started is harder than it used to be, he's told her. The dry-goods store belongs to his father, who gives him the office rent-free, in return for doing the accounts. The father is first-generation Czech, and he himself knows two other languages besides English. In this district—he spread his hands in a kind of resigned shrug while saying this—it helps. He does a couple of local bakeries and a hardware store and a second-hand jeweller's and a few of his father's old friends. Maybe when the recession is over things will pick up. He has volunteered, too, that his hobby is weight-lifting. Loulou has not asked whether or not he's married; she suspects not. If he were married, his fern would be in better shape.

While he talks, Loulou nods and smiles. She isn't sure how old he is. Young, she thinks, though he tries to make himself look older by wearing silver-rimmed glasses. She thinks he has nice hands, not like an accountant's at all, not spindly. The second time, he went out into the main store and came back with cups of tea, which Loulou found thoughtful. Then he asked her advice about a carpet. Already she felt sorry for him. He hardly even goes out for lunch, she's discovered; mostly he just gets take-out from the deli across the street. She's considered bringing him some muffins.

These topics—carpets, weight-lifting, food—are easy for Loulou. What is more difficult is that he's decided she's not just a potter but an artist, and his idea of an artist does not at all accord with Loulou's view of herself. He wants her to be wispy and fey, impractical, unearthly almost; he talks, embarrassingly, about "the creative impulse." This is far too close to the poets for Loulou. She's tried to explain that she works with clay, which is hardly ethereal. "It's like mud pies," she said, but he didn't want to hear that. Nor could she find the words to make him understand what she meant: that when she's throwing a pot she feels exhilaration, exactly the same kind she felt as a child while making a terrible mess of her mother's back porch. If he could see her the way she really is when she's working, guck all over her hands, he'd know she's not exactly essence of roses.

The second time she saw him, the accountant said he envied her freedom. He would like to do something more creative himself, he said, but you have to make a living. Loulou refrained from pointing out that she seems to be doing a sight better at it than he is. She's much more tactful with him than she's ever been with the poets. The fact is that she's starting to enjoy his version of her. Sometimes she even believes it, and thinks she might be on the verge of learning something new about herself. She's beginning to find herself mysterious. It's partly for this reason she wants to sleep with the accountant; she thinks it will change her.

The poets would laugh if they knew, but then she's not about to tell them. She did announce his advent though, that first night, while the poets were all sitting around the table eating chicken and discussing something they called "the language." They do this frequently these days and Loulou is getting bored with it. "The language" is different from just words: it has this mystical aura around it, like religion, she can tell by the way their voices drop reverently whenever they mention it. That night they had all just finished reading a new book. "I'm really getting into the language," one said, and the others chewed in silent communion.

"I've got myself an accountant," Loulou said loudly, to break the spell.

"You've *got* him, but have you *had* him yet?" Bob said. The others laughed, all except Calvin, and began discussing the accountant's chances of escape from Loulou, which they rated at nil. They went on to detail the positions and locations in which Loulou could be expected to finally entrap him—under the desk, on top of the filing cabinet—and the injuries he would sustain. They pictured him fending her off with pens.

Loulou gnawed grimly at a chicken leg. They didn't believe any of this would happen, of course. They were too conceited: having known them, how could she stoop so low? Little did they know.

Loulou approaches the door of the dry-goods store, whistling Mozart between her teeth. Partly she's thinking about the accountant and what his body might be like under his suit, but partly she's thinking about tomorrow, when she has to start work on an order of twelve slab planters for one of her good customers. Either way, it's a question of the right placement of the feet. Like a Judo expert, which she is not, Loulou is always conscious of the position of her feet in relation to the rest of her.

The accountant is waiting for her, shadowy behind the dust-filmed glass of the door. It's after six and the store is closed. Loulou said, slyly, that she couldn't make it any earlier. She didn't want the little bald-headed man lurking around.

The accountant unlocks the door and lets her in. They go back through the smell of wool and freshly torn cotton into his office, and Loulou dumps out her bag of receipts (done up in bundles, with elastic bands: she's not without a sense of decency), all over his desk. He looks pleased, and says they certainly do have a lot of things to catch up on.

He brings in some cups of tea, sits down, picks up a newly sharpened pencil, and asks her how much of her living space can be written off as working space. Loulou explains about the coach-house. She doesn't use any of the actual house herself, she says, not for working, because the poets are always using it. Sometimes they live there too, though it depends.

"On what?" says the accountant, frowning a little.

"On whether they're living anywhere else," says Loulou.

When he hears that they don't pay rent, the accountant makes a tut-tutting sound and tells Loulou that she should not let things go on like this. Loulou says that the poets never have any money, except sometimes from grants. The accountant gets out of his chair and paces around the room, which is difficult for him because Loulou is taking up a lot of space in it. He says that Loulou is allowing herself to be imposed upon and she should get herself out of this situation, which is doing her no good at all.

Loulou may have felt this herself from time to time, but hearing the accountant say it right out in the open air disturbs her. Where would the poets go? Who would take care of them? She doesn't wish to dwell on this right now, it's far too complicated, and perhaps even painful. Instead she stands up, plants her feet firmly apart, intercepts the accountant as he strides past, and, with a tug here and a little pressure there, ends up with his arms more or less around her. She backs herself up against the desk for balance, puts one hand behind her, and upsets his cup of tea into the wastepaper basket. He doesn't notice a thing; luckily it isn't hot.

After a short time the accountant takes off his silver-rimmed glasses, and after another short time he says, in a voice half an octave lower than his normal one, "I wasn't expecting this." Loulou says nothing—she lies only when absolutely necessary—and starts undoing his vest buttons. When she's down to the shirt he lifts his head, glances around the room, and murmurs, "Not here." Which is just as well, because he hasn't got his carpet yet and the floor is painted concrete.

He leads her into the darkened dry-goods store and begins sorting through the bolts of cloth. Loulou can't figure out what he's doing until he selects a roll of dark-pink velvet, unfurls it, and lays it out on the floor behind the counter, with a little flourish, like a cloak over a mud puddle. Loulou admires the way he does this; he's too deft not to have done it before. She lies down on the pink velvet, reaches up for him, and after a few minutes of shaky-fingered fumbling with the clothes they make love, somewhat rapidly. This floor is concrete too and the pink velvet isn't very thick. Loulou worries about his knees.

"Well," says the accountant. Then he sits up and starts putting on his clothes. He does this very skillfully. Loulou wishes he would wait a few minutes—it would be friendlier—but already he's doing up his buttons. Maybe he's afraid someone will come in. He rolls up the pink velvet and inserts the bolt back into its proper slot on the shelf. They go back to his office and he locates his glasses and puts them on, and tells her he'll have some figures for her in maybe two weeks. He doesn't say anything about seeing her in the meantime: perhaps his image of her as a delicate artistic flower has been shaken. He kisses her good-bye, though. The last thing he says to her is, "You shouldn't let people take advantage of you." Loulou knows he thinks he's just done this very thing himself. He's like the poets: he thinks she can't see through him.

Loulou decides to walk back to her house, which is at least a mile away, instead of taking the streetcar. She needs time to calm down. On the one hand she's elated, as she always is when she accomplishes something she's set out to do, but on the other hand she's disoriented. Is she different now, or not? Apart from the actual sex, which Loulou would never knock, and it was fine though a little on the swift side, what has it all boiled down to? She doesn't feel more known, more understood. Instead she feels less understood. She feels nameless. It's as if all those words which the poets have attached to her over the years have come undone and floated off into the sky, like balloons. If she were one of the poets, she would get something out of this: this is exactly the sort of thing they like to write about. A non-event, says Phil, is better to write about than an event, because with a non-event you can make up the meaning yourself, it means whatever you say it means. For the poets nothing is wasted, because even if it is, they can write about the waste. What she ought to do is throw them all out on their ears.

Loulou reaches her three-storey red-brick house and notes, as she always does, the mangy state of the lawn. The poets are divided on the subject of the lawn: some of them think lawns are bourgeois, others think that to say lawns are bourgeois is outdated. Loulou says she'll be damned if she'll cut it herself. The lawn is a stand-off. She goes up the front walk, not whistling, and unlocks her front door. In the hallway the familiar smell of the house envelops her, but it's like a smell from childhood. It's the smell of something left behind.

The poets are in the kitchen, sitting around the table, which is littered with papers and coffee cups and plates with crumbs and smears of butter on them. Loulou looks from one poet to another as if they are figures in a painting, as if she's never seen them before. She could walk out of this room, right this minute, and never come back, and fifty years later they would all still be in there, with the same plates, the same cups, the same crumby butter. Only she doesn't know where she would go.

"We're out of muffins," says Bob.

Loulou stares at him. "Piss on the muffins," she says at last, but without conviction. He looks tired, she thinks. He is showing signs of age, they all are. This is the first time she's noticed it. They won't go on forever.

"Where've you been?" says Calvin. "It's past seven-thirty." This is his way of saying they want their dinner.

"My God, you're helpless," says Loulou. "Why didn't you just phone out for some pizza?" To her knowledge they have never phoned out for pizza. They've never had to.

She sits down heavily at the table. The life she's led up to now seems to her entirely crazed. How did she end up in this madhouse? By putting one foot in front of the other and never taking her eyes off her feet. You could end up anywhere that way. It isn't that the accountant is normal, any more than the poets are; nor is he a possible alternative. She won't even sleep with him again, not on purpose anyway. But he is other, he is another. She too could be other. But which other? What, underneath it all, is Loulou really like? How can she tell? Maybe she is what the poets say she is, after all; maybe she has only their word, their words, for herself.

"Pizza," Bob is beginning, in an injured tone. "Pig of a dog. . . ." But the others shut him up. They can see that something is wrong, and they very much don't want to know what.

"Reify the pizza," says Calvin to Phil. "You use phone. Is modern western invention of technology." Now they're pretending to be foreigners of some kind. This is a game they play more frequently when there is tension in the air than when there isn't.

"Insert finger in possible small hole," says Calvin. "Twist wrist."

"With anchovies then," says Bob, not joining in. Loulou hears their voices coming to her across space, as if they're in another room. What she sees is the grain of the wood in the table right by her hand.

"Loulou thinks *to reify* means *to make real,*" says Phil to everyone, when he's hung up the phone. They're always talking about her in the third person like that, telling each other what she thinks. The truth is that she's never heard the word before in her life.

"So what is it, smartass?" says Loulou with an effort, squeezing out a little belligerence to set them at ease.

"If Loulou didn't exist, God would have to invent her," says Bob.

"God, hell," says Phil. "*We* would. We did it the first time, right?"

This is going too far for Loulou. Nobody invented her, thank you very much. They make things up about her, but that's a whole other story. "Up your nose," says Loulou.

"To reify is to make into a thing," says Phil, "which, as I'm sure most of us will agree, is hardly the same."

Loulou looks around the room. They are all in place, they're all watching her, to see what she will say next. She sticks out her chin at them. "Why not?" she says. "What's the big difference?" and they relax, they laugh, they give each other little punches on the shoulder as if they're part of a team and they've just scored a point. That, they tell each other, is just like Loulou, and suddenly she sees that this is what they require of her, possibly all they require: that she should be *just like Loulou.* No more, but certainly no less. Maybe it's not so bad.

ANN BEATTIE (b. 1947)

Shifting

The woman's name was Natalie, and the man's name was Larry. They had been childhood sweethearts; he had first kissed her at an ice-skating party, when they were ten. She had been unlacing her skates and had not expected the kiss. He had not expected to do it, either—he had some notion of getting his face out of the wind that was blowing across the iced-over lake, and he found himself ducking his head toward her. Kissing her seemed the natural thing to do. When they graduated from high school he was named "class clown" in the yearbook, but Natalie didn't think of him as being particularly funny. He spent more time than she thought he needed to studying chemistry, and he never laughed when she joked. She really did not think of him as funny. They went to the same college, in their home town, but he left after a year to go to a larger, more impressive university. She took the train to be with him on weekends, or he took the train to see her. When he graduated, his parents gave him a car. If they had given it to him when he was still in college it would have made things much easier. They waited to give it to him until graduation day, forcing him into attending the graduation exercises. He thought his parents were wonderful people, and Natalie liked them in a way, too, but she resented their perfect timing, their careful smiles. They were afraid that he would marry her. Eventually, he did. He had gone on to graduate school after college, and he set a date six months ahead for their marriage, so that it would take place after his first-semester final exams. That way, he could devote his time to studying for the chemistry exams.

When she married him, he had had the car for eight months. It still smelled like a brand-new car. There was never any clutter in the car. Even the ice scraper was kept in the glove compartment. There was not even a sweater or a lost glove in the back seat. He vacuumed the car every weekend, after washing it at the car wash. On Friday nights, on their way to some cheap restaurant and a dollar movie, he would stop at the car wash, and she would get out, so he could vacuum all over the inside of the car. She would lean against the metal wall of the car wash and watch him clean it.

It was expected that she would not become pregnant. She did not. It had also been expected that she would keep their apartment clean, and keep out of the way as much as possible in such close quarters while he was studying. The apartment was messy, though, and when he was studying late at night she would interrupt him and try to talk him into going to sleep. He gave a chemistry-class lecture once a week, and she would often tell him that over-preparing was as bad as under-preparing. She did not know if she believed this, but it was a favorite line of hers. Sometimes he listened to her.

On Tuesdays, when he gave the lecture, she would drop him off at school and then drive to a supermarket to do the week's shopping. Usually she did not make a list before she went shopping, but when she got to the parking lot she would take a tablet out of her purse and write a few items on it, sitting in the car in the cold. Even having a few things written down would stop her from wandering aimlessly in the store and buying things that she would never use. Before this, she had bought several pans and cans of food that she had not used, or that she could have done without. She felt better when she had a list.

She would drop him at school again on Wednesdays, when he had two seminars that together took up all the afternoon. Sometimes she would drive out of town then, to the suburbs, and shop there if any shopping needed to be done. Otherwise, she would go to the art museum, which was not far away but was hard to get to by bus. There was one piece of sculpture in there that she wanted very much to touch, but the guard was always nearby. She came so often that in time the guard began to nod hello. She wondered if she could ever persuade the man to turn his head for a few seconds—only that long—so she could stroke the sculpture. Of course she would never dare ask. After wandering through the museum and looking at least twice at the sculpture, she would go to the gift shop and buy a few postcards and then sit on one of the museum benches, padded with black vinyl, with a Calder mobile hanging overhead, and write notes to friends. (She never wrote letters.) She would tuck the postcards in her purse and mail them when she left the museum. But before she left, she often had coffee in the restaurant: she saw mothers and children struggling there, and women dressed in fancy clothes talking with their faces close together, as quietly as lovers.

On Thursdays he took the car. After his class, he would drive to visit his parents and his friend Andy, who had been wounded in Vietnam. About once a month she would go with him, but she had to feel up to it. Being with Andy embarrassed her. She had told him not to go to Vietnam—told him that he could prove his patriotism in some other way—and finally, after she and Larry had made a visit together and she had seen Andy in the motorized bed in his parents' house, Larry had agreed that she need not go again. Andy had apologized to her. It embarrassed her that this man, who had been blown sky-high by a land mine and had lost a leg and lost the full use of his arms, would smile up at her ironically and say, "You were right." She also felt as though he wanted to hear what she would say now, and that now he would listen. Now she had nothing to say. Andy would pull himself up, relying on his right arm, which was the stronger, gripping the rails at the side of the bed, and sometimes he would take her hand. His arms were still weak, but the doctors said he would regain complete use of his right arm with time. She had to make an effort not to squeeze his hand when he held hers, because she found herself wanting to squeeze energy back into him. She had a morbid curiosity about what it felt like to be blown from the ground—to go up, and to come crashing down. During their visits, Larry put on the class-clown act for Andy, telling funny stories and laughing uproariously.

Once or twice, Larry had talked Andy into getting in his wheelchair and had loaded him into the car and taken him to a bar. Larry called her once, late, pretty drunk, to say that he would not be home that night—that he would sleep at his parents' house. "My God, " she said. "Are you going to drive Andy home when you're drunk?" "What the hell else can happen to him?" he said.

Larry's parents blamed her for Larry's not being happy. His mother could only be pleasant with her for a short while, and then she would veil her criticisms by putting them as questions. "I know that one thing that helps enormously is good nutrition, " his mother said. "He works so hard that he probably needs quite a few vitamins as well, don't you think?" Larry's father was the sort of man who found hobbies in order to avoid his wife. His hobbies were building model boats, repairing clocks, and photography. He took pictures of himself building the boats and fixing the clocks, and gave the pictures, in cardboard frames, to Natalie and Larry for Christmas and birthday presents. Larry's mother was very anxious to stay on close terms with her son, and she knew that Natalie did not like her very much. Once she had visited them during the week, and Natalie, not knowing what to do with her, had taken her to the museum. She had pointed out the sculpture, and his mother had glanced at it and then ignored it. Natalie hated her for her bad taste. She had bad taste in the sweaters she gave Larry, too, but he wore them. They made him look collegiate. That whole world made her sick.

When Natalie's uncle died and left her his 1965 Volvo, they immediately decided to sell it and use the money for a vacation. They put an ad in the paper, and there were several callers. There were some calls on Tuesday, when Larry was in class, and Natalie found herself putting the people off. She told one woman that the car had too much mileage on it, and mentioned body rust, which it did not have; she told another caller, who was very persistent, that the car was already sold. When Larry returned from school, she explained that the phone was off the hook because so many people were calling about the car and she had decided not to sell it after all. They could take a little money from their savings account and go on the trip, if he wanted. But she did not want to sell the car. "It's not an automatic shift," he said. "You don't know how to drive it." She told him that she could learn. "It will cost money to insure it," he said, "and it's old and probably not even dependable." She wanted to keep the car. "I know," he said, "but it doesn't make sense. When we have more money, you can have a car. You can have a newer, better car."

The next day, she went out to the car, which was parked in the driveway of an old lady next door. Her name was Mrs. Larsen and she no longer drove a car, and she told Natalie she could park their second car there. Natalie opened the car door and got behind the wheel and put her hands on it. The wheel was covered with a flaky yellow-and-black plastic cover. She eased it off. A few pieces of foam rubber stuck to the wheel. She picked them off. Underneath the cover, the wheel was a dull red. She ran her fingers around and around the circle of the wheel. Her cousin Burt had delivered the car—a young opportunist, sixteen years old, who said he would drive it the hundred miles from his house to theirs for twenty dollars and a bus ticket home. She had not even invited him to stay for dinner, and Larry had driven him to the bus station. She wondered if it was Burt's cigarette in the ashtray or her dead uncle's. She could not even remember if her uncle smoked. She was surprised that he had left her his car. The car was much more comfortable than Larry's, and it had a nice smell inside. It smelled a little the way a field smells after a spring rain. She rubbed the side of her head back and forth against the window and then got out of the car and went in to see Mrs. Larsen. The night before, she had suddenly thought of the boy who brought the old lady the evening newspaper every night; he looked old enough to drive, and he would probably know how to shift. Mrs. Larsen agreed with her—she was sure that he could teach her. "Of course, everything has its price, " the old lady said.

"I know that. I meant to offer him money," Natalie said, and was surprised, listening to her voice, that she sounded old too.

She took an inventory and made a list of things in their apartment. Larry had met an insurance man one evening while playing basketball at the gym, who told him that they should have a list of their possessions, in case of theft. "What's worth anything?" she said when he told her. It was their first argument in almost a year—the first time in a year, anyway, that their voices were raised. He told her that several of the pieces of furniture his grandparents gave them when they got married were antiques, and the man at the gym said that if they weren't going to get them appraised every year, at least they should take snapshots of them and keep the pictures in a safe-deposit box. Larry told her to photograph the pie safe (which she used to store linen), the piano with an inlaid mother-of-pearl decoration on the music rack (neither of them knew how to play), and the table with hand-carved wooden handles and a marble top. He bought her an Instamatic camera at the drugstore, with film and flashbulbs. "Why can't you do it?" she said, and an argument began. He said that she had no respect for his profession and no understanding of the amount of study that went into getting a master's degree in chemistry.

That night, he went out to meet two friends at the gym, to shoot baskets. She put the little flashcube into the top of the camera, dropped in the film, and closed the back. She went first to the piano. She leaned forward so that she was close enough to see the inlay clearly, but she found that when she was that close the whole piano wouldn't fit into the picture. She decided to take two pictures. Then she photographed the pie safe, with one door open, showing the towels and sheets stacked inside. She did not have a reason for opening the door, except that she remembered a Perry Mason show in which detectives photographed everything with the doors hanging open. She photographed the table, lifting the lamp off it first. There were still eight pictures left. She went to the mirror in their bedroom and held the camera above her head, pointing down at an angle, and photographed her image in the mirror. She took off her slacks and sat on the floor and leaned back, aiming the camera down at her legs. Then she stood up and took a picture of her feet, leaning over and aiming down. She put on her favorite record: Stevie Wonder singing "For Once in My Life." She found herself wondering what it would be like to be blind, to have to feel things to see them. She thought about the piece of sculpture in the museum— the two elongated mounds intertwined, the smooth gray stone as shiny as sea pebbles. She photographed the kitchen, bathroom, bedroom, and living room. There was one picture left. She put her left hand on her thigh, palm up, and with some difficulty—with the camera nestled into her neck like a violin—snapped a picture of it with her right hand. The next day would be her first driving lesson.

He came to her door at noon, as he said he would. He had on a long maroon scarf, which made his deep blue eyes very striking. She had only seen him from her window when he carried the paper in to the old lady. He was a little nervous. She hoped that it was just the anxiety of any teen-ager confronting an adult. She needed to have him like her. She did not learn about mechanical things easily (Larry had told her that he would have invested in a "real" camera, except that he did not have the time to teach her about it), so she wanted him to be patient. He sat on the foot-stool in her living room, still in coat and scarf, and told her how a stick shift operated. He moved his hand through the air. The motion he made reminded her of the salute spacemen gave to earthlings in a science-fiction picture she had recently watched on late-night television. She nodded. "How much—" she began, but he interrupted and said, "You can decide what it was worth when you've learned." She was surprised and wondered if he meant to charge a great deal. Would it be her fault and would she have to pay him if he named his price when the lessons were over? But he had an honest face. Perhaps he was just embarrassed to talk about money.

He drove for a few blocks, making her watch his hand on the stick shift. "Feel how the car is going?" he said. "Now you shift." He shifted. The car jumped a little, hummed, moved into gear. It was an old car and didn't shift too easily, he said. She had been sitting forward, so that when he shifted she rocked back hard against the seat—harder than she needed to. Almost unconsciously, she wanted to show him what a good teacher he was. When her turn came to drive, the car stalled. "Take it easy, " he said. "Ease up on the clutch. Don't just raise your foot off of it like that." She tried it again. "That's it," he said. She looked at him when the car was in third. He sat in the seat, looking out the window. Snow was expected. It was Thursday. Although Larry was going to visit his parents and would not be back until late Friday afternoon, she decided she would wait until Tuesday for her next lesson. If he came home early, he would find out that she was taking lessons, and she didn't want him to know. She asked the boy, whose name was Michael, whether he thought she would forget all he had taught her in the time between lessons. "You'll remember," he said.

When they returned to the old lady's driveway, the car stalled going up the incline. She had trouble shifting. The boy put his hand over hers, and kicked the heel of his hand forward. "You'll have to treat this car a little roughly, I'm afraid," he said. That afternoon, after he left, she made spaghetti sauce, chopping little pieces of pepper and onion and mushroom. When the sauce had cooked down, she called Mrs. Larsen and said that she would bring over dinner. She usually ate with the old lady once a week. The old lady often added a pinch of cinnamon to her food, saying that it brought out the flavor better than salt, and that since she was losing her sense of smell, food had to be strongly flavored for her to taste it. Once, she had sprinkled cinnamon on a knockwurst. This time, as they ate, Natalie asked the old lady how much she paid the boy to bring the paper.

"I give him a dollar a week," the old lady said.

"Did he set the price, or did you?"

"He set the price. He told me he wouldn't take much, because he has to walk this street to get to his apartment anyway."

"He taught me a lot about the car today," Natalie said.

"He's very handsome, isn't he?" the old lady said.

She asked Larry, "How were your parents?"

"Fine," he said. "But I spent almost all the time with Andy. It's almost his birthday, and he's depressed. We went to see Mose Allison."

"I think it stinks that hardly anyone else ever visits Andy," she said.

"He doesn't make it easy. He tells you everything that's on his mind, and there's no way you can pretend that his troubles don't amount to much. You just have to sit there and nod."

She remembered that Andy's room looked like a gymnasium. There were handgrips and weights scattered on the floor. There was even a psychedelic pink hula hoop that he was to put inside his elbow and then move his arm in circles wide enough to make the hoop spin. He couldn't do it. He would lie in bed with the hoop in back of his neck and, holding the sides, lift his neck off the pillow. His arms were barely strong enough to do that, really, but he could raise his neck with no trouble, so he just pretended that his arms pulling the loop were raising it. His parents thought that it was a special exercise that he had mastered.

"What did you do today?" Larry said now.

"I made spaghetti," she said. She had made it the day before, but she thought that since he was mysterious about the time he spent away from her ("in the lab" and "at the gym" became interchangeable), she did not owe him a straight answer. That day she had dropped off the film and then she had sat at the drugstore counter to have a cup of coffee. She bought some cigarettes, though she had not smoked since high school. She smoked one mentholated cigarette and then threw the pack away in a garbage container outside the drugstore. Her mouth still felt cool inside.

He asked if she had planned anything for the weekend.

"No," she said.

"Let's do something you'd like to do. I'm a little ahead of myself in the lab right now."

That night they ate spaghetti and made plans, and the next day they went for a ride in the country, to a factory where wooden toys were made. In the showroom, he made a bear marionette shake and twist. She examined a small rocking horse, rhythmically pushing her finger up and down on the back rung of the rocker to make it rock. When they left they took with them a catalogue of toys they could order. She knew that they would never look at the catalogue again. On their way to the museum, he stopped to wash the car. Because it was the weekend there were quite a few cars lined up waiting to go in. They were behind a blue Cadillac that seemed to inch forward of its own accord, without a driver. When the Cadillac moved into the washing area, a tiny man hopped out. He stood on tiptoe to reach the coin box to start the washing machine. She doubted if he was five feet tall.

"Look at that poor son of a bitch," he said.

The little man was washing his car.

"If Andy could get out more," Larry said. "If he could get rid of that feeling he has that he's the only freak . . . I wonder if it wouldn't do him good to come spend a week with us."

"Are you going to take him in the wheelchair to the lab with you?" she said. "I'm not taking care of Andy all day."

His face changed. "Just for a week was all I meant," he said.

"I'm not doing it," she said. She was thinking of the boy, and of the car. She had almost learned how to drive the car.

"Maybe in the warm weather," she said. "When we could go to the park or something."

He said nothing. The little man was rinsing his car. She sat inside when their turn came. She thought that Larry had no right to ask her to take care of Andy. Water flew out of the hose and battered the car. She thought of Andy, in the woods at night, stepping on the land mine, being blown into the air. She wondered if it threw him in an arc, so he ended up somewhere away from where he had been walking, or if it just blasted him straight up, if he went up the way an umbrella opens. Andy had been a wonderful ice skater. They all envied him his long sweeping turns, with his legs somehow neatly together and his body at the perfect angle. She never saw him have an accident on the ice. Never once. She had known Andy, and they had skated at Parker's pond, for eight years before he was drafted.

The night before, as she and Larry were finishing dinner, he had asked her if she intended to vote for Nixon or McGovern in the election. "McGovern," she said. How could he not have known that? She knew then that they were farther apart than she had thought. She hoped that on Election Day she could drive herself to the polls —not go with him and not walk. She planned not to ask the old lady if she wanted to come along, because that would be one vote she could keep Nixon from getting.

At the museum, she hesitated by the sculpture but did not point it out to him. He didn't look at it. He gazed to the side, above it, at a Francis Bacon painting. He could have shifted his eyes just a little and seen the sculpture, and her, standing and staring.

After three more lessons, she could drive the car. The last two times, which were later in the afternoon than their first lesson, they stopped at the drugstore to get the old lady's paper, to save him from having to make the same trip back on foot. After the final lesson, when he came out of the drugstore with the paper she asked him if he'd like to have a beer to celebrate.

"Sure," he said.

They walked down the street to a bar that was filled with college students. She wondered if Larry ever came to this bar. He had never said that he did.

She and Michael talked. She asked why he wasn't in high school. He told her that he had quit. He was living with his brother, and his brother was teaching him carpentry, which he had been interested in all along. On his napkin he drew a picture of the cabinets and bookshelves he and his brother had spent the last week constructing and installing in the house of two wealthy old sisters. He drummed the side of his thumb against the edge of the table in time with the music. They each drank beer, from heavy glass mugs.

"Mrs. Larsen said your husband was in school," the boy said. "What's he studying?"

She looked up, surprised. Michael had never mentioned her husband to her before. "Chemistry," she said.

"I liked chemistry pretty well," he said. "Some of it."

"My husband doesn't know you've been giving me lessons. I'm just going to tell him that I can drive the stick shift, and surprise him."

"Yeah?" the boy said. "What will he think about that?"

"I don't know," she said. "I don't think he'll like it."

"Why?" the boy said.

His question made her remember that he was sixteen. What she had said would never have provoked another question from an adult. The adult would have nodded, or said, "I know."

She shrugged. The boy took a long drink of beer. "I thought it was funny that he didn't teach you himself, when Mrs. Larsen told me you were married," he said.

They had discussed her. She wondered why Mrs. Larsen wouldn't have told her that, because the night she ate dinner with her she had talked to Mrs. Larsen about what an extraordinarily patient teacher Michael was. Had Mrs. Larsen told him that Natalie talked about him?

On the way back to the car, she remembered the photographs and went back to the drugstore and picked up the prints. As she took money out of her wallet, she remembered that today was the day she would have to pay him. She looked around at him, at the front of the store, where he was flipping through magazines. He was tall and he was wearing a very old black jacket. One end of his long, thick maroon scarf was hanging down his back.

"What did you take pictures of?" he said when they were back in the car.

"Furniture. My husband wanted pictures of our furniture, in case it was stolen."

"Why?" he said.

"They say if you have proof that you had valuable things the insurance company won't hassle you about reimbursing you."

"You have a lot of valuable stuff?" he said.

"My husband thinks so," she said.

A block from the driveway, she said, "What do I owe you?"

"Four dollars," he said.

"That's nowhere near enough, " she said, and looked over at him. He had opened the envelope with the pictures in it while she was driving. He was staring at the picture of her legs. "What's this?" he said.

She turned into the driveway and shut off the engine. She looked at the picture. She could not think what to tell him it was. Her hands and heart felt heavy.

"Wow," the boy said. He laughed. "Never mind. Sorry. I'm not looking at any more of them."

He put the pack of pictures back in the envelope and dropped it on the seat between them.

She tried to think what to say, of some way she could turn the pictures into a joke. She wanted to get out of the car and run. She wanted to stay, not to give him the money, so he would sit there with her. She reached into her purse and took out her wallet and removed four one-dollar bills.

"How many years have you been married?" he asked.

"One," she said. She held the money out to him. He said, "Thank you," and leaned across the seat and put his right arm over her shoulder and kissed her. She felt his scarf bunched up against their cheeks. She was amazed at how warm his lips were in the cold car.

He moved his head away and said, "I didn't think you'd mind if I did that." She shook her head no. He unlocked the door and got out.

"I could drive you to your brother's apartment," she said. Her voice sounded hollow. She was extremely embarrassed, but she couldn't let him go.

He got back in the car. "You could drive me and come in for a drink," he said. "My brother's working."

When she got back to the car two hours later she saw a white parking ticket clamped under the windshield wiper, flapping in the wind. When she opened the car door and sank into the seat, she saw that he had left the money, neatly folded, on the floor mat on his side of the car. She did not pick up the money. In a while, she started the car. She stalled it twice on the way home. When she had pulled into the driveway she looked at the money for a long time, then left it lying there. She left the car unlocked, hoping the money would be stolen. If it disappeared she could tell herself that she had paid him. Otherwise, she would not know how to deal with the situation.

When she got into the apartment, the phone rang.

"I'm at the gym to play basketball," Larry said. "Be home in an hour."

"I was at the drugstore," she said. "See you then."

She examined the pictures. She sat on the sofa and laid them out, the twelve of them, in three rows on the cushion next to her. The picture of the piano was between the picture of her feet and the picture of herself that she had shot by aiming into the mirror. She picked up the four pictures of their furniture and put them on the table. She picked up the others and examined them closely. She began to understand why she had taken them. She had photographed parts of her body, fragments of it, to study the pieces. She had probably done it because she thought so much about Andy's body and the piece that was gone—the leg, below the knee, on his left side. She had had two bourbon-and-waters at the boy's apartment, and drinking always depressed her. She felt very depressed looking at the pictures, so she put them down and went into the bedroom. She undressed. She looked at her body—whole, not a bad figure—in the mirror. It was an automatic reaction with her to close the curtains when she was naked, so she turned quickly and went to the window and did that. She went back to the mirror; the room was darker now and her body looked better. She ran her hands down her sides, wondering if the feel of her skin was anything like the way the sculpture would feel. She was sure that the sculpture would be smoother— her hands would move more quickly down the slopes of it than she wanted—that it would be cool, and that somehow she could feel the grayness of it. Those things seemed preferable to her hands lingering on her body, the imperfection of her skin, the overheated apartment. If she were the piece of sculpture and if she could feel, she would like her sense of isolation.

This was in 1972, in Philadelphia.

ALICE WALKER (b. 1955)

Nineteen Fifty-five

1955

The car is a brandnew red Thunderbird convertible, and it's passed the house more than once. It slows down real slow now, and stops at the curb. An older gentleman dressed like a Baptist deacon gets out on the side near the house, and a young fellow who looks about sixteen gets out on the driver's side. They are white, and I wonder what in the world they doing in this neighborhood.

Well, I say to J. T., put your shirt on, anyway, and let me clean these glasses offa the table.

We had been watching the ballgame on TV. I wasn't actually watching, I was sort of daydreaming, with my foots up in J. T.'s lap.

I seen 'em coming on up the walk, brisk, like they coming to sell something, and then they rung the bell, and J. T. declined to put on a shirt but instead disappeared into the bedroom where the other television is. I turned down the one in the living room; I figured I'd be rid of these two double quick and J. T. could come back out again.

Are you Gracie Mae Still? asked the old guy, when I opened the door and put my hand on the lock inside the screen.

And I don't need to buy a thing, said I.

What makes you think we're sellin'? he asks, in that heavy Southern way that makes my eyeballs ache.

Well, one way or another and they're inside the house and the first thing the young fellow does is raise the TV a couple of decibels. He's about five feet nine, sort of womanish looking, with real dark white skin and a red pouting mouth. His hair is black and curly and he looks like a Loosianna creole.

About one of your songs, says the deacon. He is maybe sixty, with white hair and beard, white silk shirt, black linen suit, black tie and black shoes. His cold gray eyes look like they're sweating.

One of my songs?

Traynor here just *loves* your songs. Don't you, Traynor? He nudges Traynor with his elbow. Traynor blinks, says something I can't catch in a pitch I don't register.

The boy learned to sing and dance livin' round you people out in the country. Practically cut his teeth on you.

Traynor looks up at me and bites his thumbnail.

I laugh.

Well, one way or another they leave with my agreement that they can record one of my songs. The deacon writes me a check for five hundred dollars, the boy grunts his awareness of the transaction, and I am laughing all over myself by the time I rejoin J. T.

Just as I am snuggling down beside him though I hear the front door bell going off again.

Forgit his hat? asks J. T.

I hope not, I say.

The deacon stands there leaning on the door frame and once again I'm thinking of those sweaty-looking eyeballs of his. I wonder if sweat makes your eyeballs pink because his are sure pink. Pink and gray and it strikes me that nobody I'd care to know is behind them.

I forgot one little thing, he says pleasantly. I forgot to tell you Traynor and I would like to buy up all of those records you made of the song. I tell you we sure do love it.

Well, love it or not, I'm not so stupid as to let them do that without making 'em pay. So I says, Well, that's gonna cost you. Because, really, that song never did sell all that good, so I was glad they was going to buy it up. But on the other hand, them two listening to my songs by themselves, and nobody else getting to hear me sing it, give me a pause.

Well, one way or another the deacon showed me where I would come out ahead on any deal he had proposed so far. Didn't I give you five hundred dollars? he asked. What white man—and don't even need to mention colored—would give you more? We buy up all your records of that particular song: first, you git royalties. Let me ask you, how much you sell that song for in the first place? Fifty dollars? A hundred, I say. And no royalties from it yet, right? Right. Well, when we buy up all of them records you gonna git royalties. And that's gonna make all them race record shops sit up and take notice of Gracie Mae Still. And they gonna push all them other records of yourn they got. And you no doubt will become one of the big name colored recording artists. And then we can offer you another five hundred dollars for letting us do all this for you. And by God you'll be sittin' pretty! You can go out and buy you the kind of outfit a star should have. Plenty sequins and yards of red satin.

I had done unlocked the screen when I saw I could get some more money out of him. Now I held it wide open while he squeezed through the opening between me and the door. He whipped out another piece of paper and I signed it.

He sort of trotted out to the car and slid in beside Traynor, whose head was back against the seat. They swung around in a u-turn in front of the house and they was gone.

J. T. was putting his shirt on when I got back to the bedroom. Yankees beat the Orioles 10–6, he said. I believe I'll drive out to Paschal's pond and go fishing. Wanta go?

While I was putting on my pants J. T. was holding the two checks.

I'm real proud of a woman that can make cash money without leavin' home, he said. And I said *Umph*. Because we met on the road with me singing in first one little low-life jook after another, making ten dollars a night for myself if I was lucky, and sometimes bringin' home nothing but my life. And J. T. just loved them times. The way I was fast and flashy and always on the go from one town to another. He loved the way my singin' made the dirt farmers cry like babies and the womens shout Honey, hush! But that's mens. They loves any style to which you can get 'em accustomed.

1956

My little grandbaby called me one night on the phone: Little Mama, Little Mama, there's a white man on the television singing one of your songs! Turn on channel 5.

Lord, if it wasn't Traynor. Still looking half asleep from the neck up, but kind of awake in a nasty way from the waist down. He wasn't doing too bad with my song either, but it wasn't just the song the people in the audience was screeching and screaming over, it was that nasty little jerk he was doing from the waist down.

Well, Lord have mercy, I said, listening to him. If I'da closed my eyes, it could have been me. He had followed every turning of my voice, side streets, avenues, red lights, train crossings and all. It gave me a chill.

Everywhere I went I heard Traynor singing my song, and all the little white girls just eating it up. I never had so many ponytails switched across my line of vision in my life. They was so *proud.* He was a *genius.*

Well, all that year I was trying to lose weight anyway and that and high blood pressure and sugar kept me pretty well occupied. Traynor had made a smash from a song of mine, I still had seven hundred dollars of the original one thousand dollars in the bank, and I felt if I could just bring my weight down, life would be sweet.

1957

I lost ten pounds in 1956. That's what I give myself for Christmas. And J. T. and me and the children and their friends and grandkids of all description had just finished dinner—over which I had put on nine and a half of my lost ten—when who should appear at the front door but Traynor. Little Mama, Little Mama! It's that white man who sings —— —— ——. The children didn't call it my song anymore. Nobody did. It was funny how that happened. Traynor and the deacon had bought up all my records, true, but on his record he had put "written by Gracie Mae Still." But that was just another name on the label, like "produced by Apex Records."

On the TV he was inclined to dress like the deacon told him. But now he looked presentable.

Merry Christmas, said he.

And same to you, Son.

I don't know why I called him Son. Well, one way or another they're all our sons. The only requirement is that they be younger than us. But then again, Traynor seemed to be aging by the minute.

You looks tired, I said. Come on in and have a glass of Christmas cheer.

J. T. ain't never in his life been able to act decent to a white man he wasn't working for, but he poured Traynor a glass of bourbon and water, then he took all the children and grandkids and friends and whatnot out to the den. After while I heard Traynor's voice singing the song, coming from the stereo console. It was just the kind of Christmas present my kids would consider cute.

I looked at Traynor, complicit. But he looked like it was the last thing in the world he wanted to hear. His head was pitched forward over his lap, his hands holding his glass and his elbows on his knees.

I done sung that song seem like a million times this year, he said. I sung it on the Grand Ole Opry, I sung it on the Ed Sullivan show. I sung it on Mike Douglas, I sung it at the Cotton Bowl, the Orange Bowl. I sung it at Festivals. I sung it at Fairs. I sung it overseas in Rome, Italy, and once in a submarine *underseas.* I've sung it and sung it, and I'm making forty thousand dollars a day offa it, and you know what, I don't have the faintest notion what that song means.

Whatchumean, what do it mean? It mean what it says. All I could think was: These suckers is making forty thousand a *day* offa my song and now they gonna come back and try to swindle me out of the original thousand.

It's just a song, I said. Cagey. When you fool around with a lot of no count mens you sing a bunch of 'em. I shrugged.

Oh, he said. Well. He started brightening up. I just come to tell you I think you are a great singer.

He didn't blush, saying that. Just said it straight out.

And I brought you a little Christmas present too. Now you take this little box and hold it until I drive off. Then you take it outside under that first streetlight back up the street aways in front of that green house. Then you open the box and see . . . Well, just *see.*

What had come over this boy, I wondered, holding the box. I looked out the window in time to see another white man come up and get in the car with him and then two more cars full of white mens start out behind him. They was all in long black cars that looked like a funeral procession.

Little Mama, Little Mama, what it is? One of my grandkids come running up and started pulling at the box. It was wrapped in gay Christmas paper—the thick, rich kind that it's hard to picture folks making just to throw away.

J. T. and the rest of the crowd followed me out the house, up the street to the streetlight and in front of the green house. Nothing was there but somebody's gold-grilled white Cadillac. Brandnew and most distracting. We got to looking at it so till I almost forgot the little box in my hand. While the others were busy making 'miration I carefully took off the paper and ribbon and folded them up and put them in my pants pocket. What should I see but a pair of genuine solid gold caddy keys.

Dangling the keys in front of everybody's nose, I unlocked the caddy, motioned for J. T. to git in on the other side, and us didn't come back home for two days.

1960

Well, the boy was sure nuff famous by now. He was still a mite shy of twenty but already they was calling him the Emperor of Rock and Roll.

Then what should happen but the draft.

Well, says J. T. There goes all this Emperor of Rock and Roll business.

But even in the army the womens was on him like white on rice. We watched it on the News.

Dear Gracie Mae [he wrote from Germany],

How you? Fine I hope as this leaves me doing real well. Before I come in the army I was gaining a lot of weight and gitting jittery from making all them dumb movies. But now I exercise and eat right and get plenty of rest. I'm more awake than I been in ten years.

I wonder if you are writing any more songs?

Sincerely,
Traynor

I wrote him back:

Dear Son,

We is all fine in the Lord's good grace and hope this finds you the same. J. T. and me be out all times of the day and night in that car you give me—which you know you didn't have to do. Oh, and I do appreciate the mink and the new self-cleaning oven. But if you send anymore stuff to eat from Germany I'm going to have to open up a store in the neighborhood just to get rid of it. Really, we have more than enough of everything. The Lord is good to us and we don't know Want.

Glad to hear you is well and gitting your right rest. There ain't nothing like exercising to help that along. J. T. and me work some part of every day that we don't go fishing in the garden.

Well, so long Soldier.

Sincerely,
Gracie Mae

He wrote:

Dear Gracie Mae,

I hope you and J. T. like that automatic power tiller I had one of the stores back home send you. I went through a mountain of catalogs looking for it—I wanted something that even a woman could use.

I've been thinking about writing some songs of my own but every time I finish one it don't seem to be about nothing I've actually lived myself. My agent keeps sending me other people's songs but they just sound mooney. I can hardly git through 'em without gagging.

Everybody still loves that song of yours. They ask me all the time what do I think it means, really. I mean, they want to know just what I want to know. Where out of your life did it come from?

Sincerely,
Traynor

1968

I didn't see the boy for seven years. No. Eight. Because just about everybody was dead when I saw him again. Malcolm X, King, the president and his brother, and even J. T. J. T. died of a head cold. It just settled in his head like a block of ice, he said, and nothing we did moved it until one day he just leaned out the bed and died.

His good friend Horace helped me put him away, and then about a year later Horace and me started going together. We was sitting out on the front porch swing one summer night, dusk-dark, and I saw this great procession of lights winding to a stop.

Holy Toledo! said Horace. (He's got a real sexy voice like Ray Charles.) Look *at* it. He meant the long line of flashy cars and the white men in white summer suits jumping out on the drivers' sides and standing at attention. With wings they could pass for angels, with hoods they could be the Klan.

Traynor comes waddling up the walk.

And suddenly I know what it is he could pass for. An Arab like the ones you see in the storybooks. Plump and soft and with never a care about weight. Because with so much money, who cares? Traynor is almost dressed like someone from a storybook too. He has on, I swear, about ten necklaces. Two sets of bracelets on his arms, at least one ring on every finger, and some kind of shining buckles on his shoes, so that when he walks you get quite a few twinkling lights.

Gracie Mae, he says, coming up to give me a hug. J. T.

I explain that J. T. passed. That this is Horace.

Horace, he says, puzzled but polite, sort of rocking back on his heels, Horace.

That's it for Horace. He goes in the house and don't come back.

Looks like you and me is gained a few, I say.

He laughs. The first time I ever heard him laugh. It don't sound much like a laugh and I can't swear that it's better than no laugh a'tall.

He's gitting fat for sure, but he's still slim compared to me. I'll never see three hundred pounds again and I've just about said (excuse me) fuck it. I got to thinking about it one day an' I thought: aside from the fact that they say it's unhealthy, my fat ain't never been no trouble. Mens always have loved me. My kids ain't never complained. Plus they's fat. And fat like I is I looks distinguished. You see me coming and know somebody's *there*.

Gracie Mae, he says, I've come with a personal invitation to you to my house tomorrow for dinner. He laughed. What did it sound like? I couldn't place it. See them men out there? he asked me. I'm sick and tired of eating with them. They don't never have nothing to talk about. That's why I eat so much. But if you come to dinner tomorrow we can talk about the old days. You can tell me about that farm I bought you.

I sold it, I said.

You did?

Yeah, I said, I did. Just cause I said I liked to exercise by working in a garden didn't mean I wanted five hundred acres! Anyhow, I'm a city girl now. Raised in the country it's true. Dirt poor—the whole bit—but that's all behind me now.

Oh well, he said, I didn't mean to offend you.

We sat a few minutes listening to the crickets.

Then he said: You wrote that song while you was still on the farm, didn't you, or was it right after you left?

You had somebody spying on me? I asked.

You and Bessie Smith got into a fight over it once, he said.

You *is* been spying on me!

But I don't know what the fight was about, he said. Just like I don't know what happened to your second husband. Your first one died in the Texas electric chair. Did you know that? Your third one beat you up, stole your touring costumes and your car and retired with a chorine to Tuskegee. He laughed. He's still there.

I had been mad, but suddenly I calmed down. Traynor was talking very dreamily.

It was dark but seems like I could tell his eyes weren't right. It was like some*thing* was sitting there talking to me but not necessarily with a person behind it.

You gave up on marrying and seem happier for it. He laughed again. I married but it never went like it was supposed to. I never could squeeze any of my own life either into it or out of it. It was like singing somebody else's record. I copied the way it was sposed to be *exactly* but I never had a clue what marriage meant.

I bought her a diamond ring big as your fist. I bought her clothes. I built her a mansion. But right away she didn't want the boys to stay there. Said they smoked up the bottom floor. Hell, there were *five* floors.

No need to grieve, I said. No need to. Plenty more where she come from.

He perked up. That's part of what the song means, ain't it? No need to grieve. Whatever it is, there's plenty more down the line.

I never really believed that way back when I wrote that song, I said. It was all bluffing then. The trick is to live long enough to put your young bluffs to use. Now if I was to sing that song today I'd tear it up. 'Cause I done lived long enough to know it's *true.* Them words could hold me up.

I ain't lived that long, he said.

Look like you on your way, I said. I don't know why, but the boy seemed to need some encouraging. And I don't know, seem like one way or another you talk to rich white folks and you end up reassuring *them.* But what the hell, by now I feel something for the boy. I wouldn't be in his bed all alone in the middle of the night for nothing. Couldn't be nothing worse than being famous the world over for something you don't even understand. That's what I tried to tell Bessie. She wanted that same song. Overheard me practicing it one day, said, with her hands on her hips: Gracie Mae, I'ma sing your song tonight. I *likes* it.

Your lips be too swole to sing, I said. She was mean and she was strong, but I trounced her.

Ain't you famous enough with your own stuff? I said. Leave mine alone. Later on, she thanked me. By then she was Miss Bessie Smith to the World, and I was still Miss Gracie Mae Nobody from Notasulga.

The next day all these limousines arrived to pick me up. Five cars and twelve bodyguards. Horace picked that morning to start painting the kitchen.

Don't paint the kitchen, fool, I said. The only reason that dumb boy of ours is going to show me his mansion is because he intends to present us with a new house.

What you gonna do with it? he asked me, standing there in his shirtsleeves stirring the paint.

Sell it. Give it to the children. Live in it on weekends. It don't matter what I do. He sure don't care.

Horace just stood there shaking his head. Mama you sure looks *good,* he says. Wake me up when you git back.

Fool, I say, and pat my wig in front of the mirror.

The boy's house is something else. First you come to this mountain, and then you commence to drive and drive up this road that's lined with magnolias. Do magnolias grow on mountains? I was wondering. And you come to ponds and you come to deer and you come up on some sheep. And I figure these two is sposed to represent England and Wales. Or something out of Europe. And you just keep on coming to stuff. And it's all pretty. Only the man driving my car don't look at nothing but the road. Fool. And then *finally*, after all this time, you begin to go up the driveway. And there's more magnolias—only they're not in such good shape. It's sort of cool up this high and I don't think they're gonna make it. And then I see this building that looks like if it had a name it would be The Tara Hotel. Columns and steps and outdoor chandeliers and rocking chairs. Rocking chairs? Well, and there's the boy on the steps dressed in a dark green satin jacket like you see folks wearing on TV late at night, and he looks sort of like a fat dracula with all that house rising behind him, and standing beside him there's this little white vision of loveliness that he introduces as his wife.

He's nervous when he introduces us and he says to her: This is Gracie Mae Still, I want you to know me. I mean . . . and she gives him a look that would fry meat.

Won't you come in, Gracie Mae, she says, and that's the last I see of her.

He fishes around for something to say or do and decides to escort me to the kitchen. We go through the entry and the parlor and the breakfast room and the dining room and the servants' passage and finally get there. The first thing I notice is that, altogether, there are five stoves. He looks about to introduce me to one.

Wait a minute, I say. Kitchens don't do nothing for me. Let's go sit on the front porch.

Well, we hike back and we sit in the rocking chairs rocking until dinner.

Gracie Mae, he says down the table, taking a piece of fried chicken from the woman standing over him, I got a little surprise for you.

It's a house, ain't it? I ask, spearing a chitlin.

You're getting *spoiled,* he says. And the way he says *spoiled* sounds funny. He slurs it. It sounds like his tongue is too thick for his mouth. Just that quick he's finished the chicken and is now eating chitlins *and* a pork chop. *Me* spoiled, I'm thinking.

I already got a house. Horace is right this minute painting the kitchen. I bought that house. My kids feel comfortable in that house.

But this one I bought you is just like mine. Only a little smaller.

I still don't need no house. And anyway who would clean it?

He looks surprised.

Really, I think, some peoples advance *so* slowly.

I hadn't thought of that. But what the hell, I'll get you somebody to live in.

I don't want other folks living 'round me. Makes me nervous.

You *don't?* It *do?*

What I want to wake up and see folks I don't even know for?

He just sits there downtable staring at me. Some of that feeling is in the song, ain't it? Not the words, the *feeling.* What I want to wake up and see folks I don't even know for? But I see twenty folks a day I don't even know, including my wife.

This food wouldn't be bad to wake up to though, I said. The boy had found the genius of corn bread.

He looked at me real hard. He laughed. Short. They want what you got but they don't want you. They want what I got only it ain't mine. That's what makes 'em so hungry for me when I sing. They getting the flavor of something but they ain't getting the thing itself. They like a pack of hound dogs trying to gobble up a scent.

You talking 'bout your fans?

Right. Right. He says.

Don't worry 'bout your fans, I say. They don't know their asses from a hole in the ground. I doubt there's a honest one in the bunch.

That's the point. Dammit, that's the point! He hits the table with his fist. It's so solid it don't even quiver. You need a honest audience! You can't have folks that's just gonna lie right back to you.

Yeah, I say, it was small compared to yours, but I had one. It would have been worth my life to try to sing 'em somebody else's stuff that I didn't know nothing about.

He must have pressed a buzzer under the table. One of his flúnkies zombies up.

Git Johnny Carson, he says.

On the phone? asks the zombie.

On the phone, says Traynor, what you think I mean, git him offa the front porch? Move your ass.

So two weeks later we's on the Johnny Carson show.

Traynor is all corseted down nice and looks a little bit fat but mostly good. And all the women that grew up on him and my song squeal and squeal. Traynor says: The lady who wrote my first hit record is here with us tonight, and she's agreed to sing it for all of us, just like she sung it forty-five years ago. Ladies and Gentlemen, the great Gracie Mae Still!

Well, I had tried to lose a couple of pounds my own self, but failing that I had me a very big dress made. So I sort of rolls over next to Traynor, who is dwarfted by me, so that when he puts his arm around back of me to try to hug me it looks funny to the audience and they laugh.

I can see this pisses him off. But I smile out there at 'em. Imagine squealing for twenty years and not knowing why you're squealing? No more sense of endings and beginnings than hogs.

It don't matter, Son, I say. Don't fret none over me.

I commence to sing. And I sound—wonderful. Being able to sing good ain't all about having a good singing voice a'tall. A good singing voice helps. But when you come up in the Hard Shell Baptist church like I did you understand early that the fellow that sings is the singer. Them that waits for programs and arrangements and letters from home is just good voices occupying body space.

So there I am singing my own song, my own way. And I give it all I got and enjoy every minute of it. When I finish Traynor is standing up clapping and clapping and beaming at first me and then the audience like I'm his mama for true. The audience claps politely for about two seconds.

Traynor looks disgusted.

He comes over and tries to hug me again. The audience laughs.

Johnny Carson looks at us like we both weird.

Traynor is mad as hell. He's supposed to sing something called a love ballad. But instead he takes the mike, turns to me and says: Now see if my imitation still holds up. He goes into the same song, *our* song, I think, looking out at his flaky audience. And he sings it just the way he always did. My voice, my tone, my inflection, everything. But he forgets a couple of lines. Even before he's finished the matronly squeals begin.

He sits down next to me looking whipped.

It don't matter, Son, I say, patting his hand. You don't even know those people. Try to make the people you know happy.

Is that in the song? he asks.

Maybe. I say.

1977

For a few years I hear from him, then nothing. But trying to lose weight takes all the attention I got to spare. I finally faced up to the fact that my fat is the hurt I don't admit, not even to myself, and that I been trying to bury it from the day I was born. But also when you git real old, to tell the truth, it ain't as pleasant. It gits lumpy and slack. Yuck. So one day I said to Horace, I'ma git this shit offa me.

And he fell in with the program like he always try to do and Lord such a procession of salads and cottage cheese and fruit juice!

One night I dreamed Traynor had split up with his fifteenth wife. He said: *You meet 'em for no reason. You date 'em for no reason. You marry 'em for no reason. I do it all but I swear it's just like somebody else doing it. I feel like I can't remember Life.*

The boy's in trouble, I said to Horace.

You've always said that, he said.

I have?

Yeah. You always said he looked asleep. You can't sleep through life if you wants to live it.

You not such a fool after all, I said, pushing myself up with my cane and hobbling over to where he was. Let me sit down on your lap, I said, while this salad I ate takes effect.

In the morning we heard Traynor was dead. Some said fat, some said heart, some said alcohol, some said drugs. One of the children called from Detroit. Them dumb fans of his is on a crying rampage, she said. You just ought to turn on the t.v.

But I didn't want to see 'em. They was crying and crying and didn't even know what they was crying for. One day this is going to be a pitiful country, I thought.

 *Poetry*

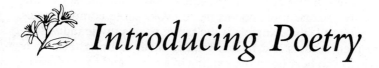

Introducing Poetry

Poetry and the Reader's Experience

Poetry surrounds everybody. It is part of the background of people's lives in more ways than they sometimes realize—in rock lyrics, nursery rhymes, advertising, football songs, graffiti, church hymns, patriotic songs, folk songs, and demonstration chants. But the main kind of poetry that students encounter in a college literature class is, of course, something different: it is the poetry sanctioned by the "high" cultural tradition from the past.

In English, this "high" cultural poetry was written from the Middle Ages onwards by such British poets as Chaucer, Shakespeare, Sidney, Milton, Pope, Wordsworth, and Tennyson, and from the seventeenth century onwards by such American poets as Whitman, Dickinson, and Stevens. Such poetry is "serious"—intellectually demanding, giving its readers (or so it has been traditionally argued) access to the insights of especially gifted men and women.

But reading poetry can be like listening to a favorite song on the radio or on an album. Certain song lyrics have rich emotional associations: Bruce Springsteen's "Born to Run" may remind you of the time you drove one hundred miles an hour along a country road, and every time you hear the song it may invoke that feeling of dangerous freedom. Or hearing Cyndi Lauper's song "Girls Just Want to Have Fun," you may recall the particular afternoon when you first heard it, the person you were with, what you were doing. Everyone fastens his or her own personal associations onto the music, the words, the voice, the emotions, so that whenever the song is played, something of those associations comes back.

Listeners don't generally ask what a song lyric *means* in general so much as what it means *to them* as individuals. Yet when these same listeners turn to poetry, they frequently feel inhibited about having strong personal reactions. Of course not all poetry has the same kind of immediacy as the latest song—partly because most poems try to evoke more complex reactions and responses. But the principle is the same: poems invite individual reactions from their readers and in fact require them to bring their own personal experiences to bear upon the reading of a poem and to participate deeply in the experience of reading.

We believe you can respond to and enjoy poetry on any subject from any period so long as you can, in some way, integrate it with your own experiences. We also believe that the formal **conventions** of the poem (such as its meter, rhyme scheme, imagery) matter less than your responses to the poem. The conventions of a poem definitely contribute to your response to it, and they should not be ignored; however, they are generally not the primary elements to which you respond. And an excessive focus on them can lead to a sterile and often tedious treatment of a poem that may stifle your most deeply felt reactions to the text. In this anthology you will find poetry that is regarded as part of the **canon**—that is, the sanctioned masterpieces, generally agreed upon by critics as the best works of the best poets. But you will find also a selection of more recent poetry and some examples from what is loosely called *popular* poetry, including song lyrics. Poetry is not only a significant part of our cultural past, but it is also written, read, and enjoyed in the present. In fact, poetry is one of our society's great cottage industries. Many thousands of little poetry magazines are published every year, and hundreds of small presses publish books of poetry. Rarely do any of these make the best-seller list, but the fact that they are written and published indicates the lively, though marginal, place that poetry has in our culture.

Why do readers sometimes feel that poetry is solemn, obscure, or esoteric? If you ever go to a poetry reading at your college, the atmosphere can sometimes be like that—a distinguished person, often a middle-aged man, is introduced as the winner of awards and citations, and reads poems about his own personal experiences in a serious tone and in obscure language. But some poetry is not like that at all but rather is entertaining, witty, and appealing. For instance, read the following poem—preferably aloud and with other people around to listen (always a good idea with a poem).

JIM DANIELS (b. 1956)

Short-Order Cook

An average joe comes in and orders
30 cheeseburgers and 30 fries.

I wait for him to pay before I start cooking.
He pays—
he ain't no average joe.   5

The grill is just big enough for 10 rows of 3.
I slap the burgers down,
throw two buckets of fries in the deep frier
and they pop pop spit spit . . .
psss. . . .   10
The counter girls laugh.
I concentrate.
It is the crucial point:
they are ready for the cheese.

My fingers shake as I tear off slices, toss   15
them on the burgers/fries done/dump/
refill buckets/burgers ready/flip
into buns, beat that melting cheese/wrap
burgers in plastic/into paper bags/fries done/
dump/fill 30 bags/bring them to the counter girls.   20
I puff my chest out and bellow:
"30 cheeseburgers, 30 fries."
They look at me funny.
I grab a handful of ice, toss it in my mouth,
do a little dance, and walk back to the grill.   25
Pressure, responsibility, success.
30 cheeseburgers, 30 fries.

What is your response to this poem? Do you like it? Would you describe it as *serious* poetry? Is it poetry at all? Does it conform to your conventional expectations about poetry? "Short-Order Cook" looks like a poem, but it lacks a number of traditional conventions that you may commonly associate with poetry. For example, it doesn't have a particular meter or rhyme scheme. On one level it seems to be about a very common set of experiences—grilling cheeseburgers and cooking fries in a restaurant. On another level, it may be about a serious subject—challenge and achievement—but both its **setting** and its **voice** are far from being elitist or esoteric.

The poem is clearly designed to get you to laugh and to sympathize, as you recognize the emotions—the challenge, the pride of achievement, the energy that is evoked. These emotions may seem more immediate and appealing to you because of the everyday nature of the event in the poem. Your own **general repertoire** probably matches that of the poem, and thus you may easily respond favorably to the familiar scene of a frantic fast-food counter. It could almost be as if the poem is about your own experience, so you make the "I" of the poem temporarily your own. Note also how ordinary the poem's language is: it is very close to everyday conversation ("They look at me funny"), the conversation of an ordinary working person just talking to a bunch of friends. Most ordinary conversations are not perhaps as concentrated and lively as this poem; and the concentration—the economy of language and the intensity of experience—may constitute the difference between ordinary conversation and the language of this poem.

Therefore, when you read a poem, we suggest you ask yourself initially: What does it mean? What does the poet intend? Does it scan easily or have a regular rhythmic pattern? But more important, ask: How do I respond to it? What does it say to me directly? Does it tell me something important about life—or about my life?

A poem is a set of words asking to be read and responded to by you, its reader. As the reader, your repertoire—your interests, memories, beliefs, assumptions—comes into play, and you recreate the poem in terms of it. The poem's repertoire interacts with yours, and from that interaction emerges your reading. With a poem like "Short-Order Cook," your repertoire will probably match harmoniously with the text's: you are familiar with the scene and the feelings the poem evokes. With other poems, however, the matching of repertoires may be less harmonious: their repertoires may not so fully and richly intersect with yours.

The "Author's Intentions"

Some readers may also assume that the poem's author is the final authority for its meaning, or that authors have in mind a single, unchangeable meaning. But readers should not be overwhelmed by what they believe to be the *author's intentions.* Bear in mind that, although the poet wrote the poem, he or she is just one reader of that poem and may be completely unconscious of a number of significant relationships you discover or create when reading the poem. Further, if the poem was written in a period earlier than your own, you will probably respond to it in ways that the poet could never have anticipated simply because of changing cultural assumptions. Don't try to suppress your reactions to the poem in deference to its "author's intentions" since you can never know, with certainty, what those intentions were.

Investigating the historical period in which the poem was written constitutes a more productive way of trying to take the author into account without losing the sense of your own response to the text. Then you can more easily compare how your culture differs from the poet's and hence how your reaction to the poem is influenced by your own repertoire and cultural situation. But you should do so only *after* you have developed your own responses to the poem. A poem is an invitation to its readers to bring it to life. If you can give the words significance as you read them and think about that significance afterwards, then and only then does the poem come to life. Otherwise it remains just words, just meaningless black marks on the page. A poem expresses its power only if it is read and responded to actively.

In the model of the reading process outlined on page 7, it becomes clear that both the *text* and the *reader* contribute to the reading experience. In particular, readers need to be active and involved, and to see their own contributions to the making of meaning as a vital part of reading. On the following pages, we want to provide you with some models and strategies for reading poems in this active and engaged way.

Building a Response to the Poem

A particularly useful device for developing the reader's contribution to the reading process is the **response statement,** discussed fully on page 15. Writing response statements can help you get away from the common presupposition that there is *one* fixed meaning to a text. In preparing to write one, you gather raw materials and sort out your initial reactions to a text. Sometimes response statements can be used simply as preliminary steps towards writing more formal papers or essays—but that is probably their least important function. Far more, they help readers explore and record their own reactions to the text, speculate on how their own literary and general repertoires inform those reactions, and then use those reactions to develop a detailed written statement about their response to the text.

Before you determine even your initial response to a poem, you usually need to read it a number of times. If possible, reread the poem aloud: reading aloud enables you to "hear" the poem become more and more familiar, and poems thereby often make more sense. For example, the rhythm, particularly if it is regular, might seem more evident to you when you read the poem aloud. Often if you listen for the strong stresses, you can work out the pattern of strong and weak beats and see if the poem scans in any traditional meter. Remember, however, there is no one correct way to read a poem aloud: most poems can be read with varied voice inflections, pauses, and emphases. Poems certainly provide us with clues and hints about how they might best be read, but there is always a lot of leeway, just as singers can interpret the same song lyrics with interesting personal variations, conveying very different moods to different audiences. Reading aloud, therefore, helps to underscore the important general point that readers, in many ways, create the text to which they are responding. A poem can be seen as a kind of script, with implied directions for producing its meaning: the reader gets a sense of those directions by paying careful attention to the text.

As you continue to read to build a response statement, you should take notes on those details you discover to be most insistent—the strong verbal signals that help you develop a reading. You might use your *annotations*—those you made in the margins next to the poem or those you recorded in a journal. You might look up in your dictionary any unfamiliar words or check any puzzling familiar words for other senses in which they might be being used. Then incorporate what you discover into your reading.

You may want to pause over the connotations or suggestiveness of certain words and phrases—either for the making of meaning or the generating of feelings, or both. Try playing with the text, thinking of other possible connotations of words or phrases; ask yourself what certain key phrases might mean in the broadest possible sense. *This initial phase of careful rereading and developing a response is something that should not be rushed.* Play freely with the poem and become fully familiar with the text; memorize some key phrases; let the poem work on you; be patient and don't settle for instant gratification or superficial understanding. Often the most interesting poems are those whose effects work only gradually upon their readers. The repertoire of the poem and reader never totally match, but the initial reading is an opportunity for the two to be brought together more productively.

The Poem's Voice

The **voice** of the poem in part arises from what you bring to reading it and in part from what the text suggests to you. A poem has a voice of its own only because you give it one: you interpret certain voices to be friendly, loving, angry, or imperious, based on how you perceive that the poem and its subject matter affect you or direct you. You may think that you have merely *found* the poet's voice in doing this, but in fact you have used your own knowledge of language to interpret specific clues from the text to *create* a voice for the poet. You may have the illusion that you are reading objectively or that you are trying to be "faithful" to what the author wanted you to grasp; however, the reading that you finally settle on as being your "best" one is that which most clearly articulates *your sense* of the poem.

Thus rereading and reading aloud are seemingly elementary but crucial ways of moving into the atmosphere of a poem. Rereading is also a way of going beyond just the obvious meanings of a poem and digging deeper. The first time you read a poem, you may be just puzzling out its surface, finding out the straightforward dictionary meanings of words and trying to establish some kind of appropriate voice for your reading, such as the likable voice in "Short-Order Cook," with its ironic patter. Once you have established a preliminary sense of the whole, you can concentrate on what the poem suggests to you, how it affects you emotionally, and what kind of matching is occurring between your repertoire and the poem's. There may be parallels and similarities—or great differences between your repertoire and that of the poem. Gradually, through careful rereading and making notes, building up your responses, and listening to the opinions of others, you will become aware that rather than simply summarizing the poem and letting that stand for your reading of it, you are now starting to explain the poem self-consciously in terms of your own literary and wider cultural repertoire.

Connotation and the Reader's Participation: Blake, "The Tyger"

We want to illustrate our suggestions for producing a strong reading by turning from a contemporary work to a powerful text by an English poet of the high cultural tradition. William Blake is considered one of the foremost romantic poets, along with Wordsworth and Coleridge.

WILLIAM BLAKE (1757–1827)

The Tyger

Tyger! Tyger! burning bright
In the forests of the night,
What immortal hand or eye
Could frame thy fearful symmetry?

In what distant deeps or skies   5
Burnt the fire of thine eyes?
On what wings dare he aspire?
What the hand dare seize the fire?

And what shoulder, and what art,
Could twist the sinews of thy heart?   10
And when thy heart began to beat,
What dread hand? and what dread feet?

What the hammer? what the chain?
In what furnace was thy brain?
What the anvil? what dread grasp   15
Dare its deadly terrors clasp?

When the stars threw down their spears
And watered heaven with their tears,
Did he smile his work to see?
Did he who made the Lamb make thee?   20

Tyger! Tyger! burning bright
In the forests of the night,
What immortal hand or eye
Dare frame thy fearful symmetry?

When you read Blake's poem, you soon realize that it consists of a series of questions. Are the answers to these questions given? If so, where are they? And what is the "tyger" that the poem is asking about? Readers play a crucial role in filling in such **gaps** or indeterminacies as these in the text, and they do so on the basis of their own general and literary repertoires. The way readers respond to texts (and gaps in them) depends in part on their recognizing certain text cues. "The Tyger" has words of great suggestiveness, such as "fearful symmetry," "distant deeps or skies," "dread hand." Because these words do not seem to have an obvious literal meaning in the poem, readers are called on to use their imaginations to think up various *connotations*—what the words suggest to them. The connotations that you come up with are yours. That you are looking for them in the first place is because you, along with most readers, find the language evocative. Further, all those question marks, exclamation points, and the insistent strong rhythms demand that the poem be read with vigor and emotion. Look at the opening lines, for instance:

/ — / — / — — /
Tyger Tyger burning bright
/ — / — / — /
In the forests of the Night

Here the / sign stands for a strong, emphatic beat that most readings would emphasize—like an insistent drumbeat. The effect of the rhythmical beat may suggest something of the insistence or the power of the "tyger." But what precisely *is* the "tyger"? You know what "tigers" are: you've seen them in zoos, in the movies, and maybe even in the wild. So you have some general knowledge in your repertoire about the animal, but a real tiger in a real jungle seems very different from this tyger "burning bright/in the forests of the night."

In constructing a strong reading, readers should concentrate on the *suggestiveness* of the words, their rich connotations, not their literal or dictionary meaning (their denotations). The tyger seems to be a powerful physical figure or looming force from a dream, a nightmare, a horror story, or another planet. The tyger stands for something that you might describe, perhaps, as being "like . . ." But like what? This is where you, as the reader of the poem, must bring in your own examples to fill out what is indeterminate in the poem. "Tyger" is a **gap** in the text, and since you can't *find* precisely what the word means by reading the poem closely, you must instead *create* its meaning from the text's cues or prompts.

To continue to build up your reading, ask yourself what *impact* the questions of the poem have on you. Is it curiosity? Fear? Awe? Hope? What, in particular, is the effect of that fifth stanza, where the power of this beast, this force, the tyger, makes the whole of creation afraid? In reflecting on your reactions, you might think, say, of the tyger as nuclear energy, something in our own time that is powerful, awe-inspiring, and frightening. If you thought of the tyger as something "like" nuclear energy, would that make the awe—the combination of attractiveness and fearfulness of the poem—relevant for you?

Developing such an interpretation doesn't mean that the tyger *means* "nuclear energy." You aren't trying to establish a single fixed meaning of the poem: you are only suggesting some ways in which you might go about creating a meaning or strong reading for yourself. Blake didn't, of course, know about nuclear energy. Nor did any of his early readers. Instead, they found other significances in his poem—religious or natural. Most readers of the poem have seen the "tyger" as representing some primeval force, some untameable power, or else the sublime creation of humankind's imaginative powers. You may find such readings attractive; but you may also see the parallel with nuclear energy. A knowledge of the awesome but potentially destructive power of nuclear fission is, after all, inevitably part of your general repertoire. So if such a comparison is suggestive to you, you should not try to repress or exorcise this knowledge from your mind just because it was not part of Blake's repertoire. Whatever kind of interpretation readers develop, whatever voice they give to a poem, they will highlight certain text features and ignore others. And therefore you will always be creating your own poem because you will be establishing a dialogue between the text's repertoire and your own individual repertoire.

Metaphor and Other Figurative Language

Metaphor, simile, symbolism, and *allegory* are all "figures" of reading and writing—means by which we express or interpret language to make it more vivid, powerful, and satisfying. Metaphor is most often associated with poetry, but it is in fact found in all kinds of writing and all uses of language, so much so that it constitutes one of our most basic ways of thinking.

To write or to read *metaphorically* is to describe one thing in terms of another, or to transfer one thing's characteristics to another in order to extend, compress, intensify, or make vivid what we want to say. The phrase "my heart is an open book," for example, is a vivid way of explaining that my feelings are honest and sincere. The features of an "open" (accessible, obvious to read) book are transferred to my "heart," metaphorically the *seat* (yet another metaphor) of my emotions. When we suggest, as we do throughout this anthology, that you read texts "against the grain," we are speaking metaphorically: we are transferring to reading the characteristics of cutting timber—cutting *with* the grain is the easier and seemingly "natural" way of cutting timber. To read against the grain, therefore, like cutting timber against the grain, is to go against the dominant or seemingly natural way of reading a text.

But no use of language is intrinsically metaphorical. A meaning is said to be "literal" if it is the dominant and most accepted one in a given cultural community. It is said to be "figurative" or metaphorical if it diverges from the dominant meaning. Even a seemingly factual sentence like "My aunt is a butcher" can be seen as metaphorical depending on the context in which it is used—literal usage cannot be separated from figurative usage when one tries to figure out the meaning of this sentence. Does my aunt cut meat? Or is she a manager who ruthlessly fires people under her who do not perform their jobs according to her expectations? The context will determine what the literal meaning is. What we want you to keep in mind is that while we will talk about metaphor throughout this book, the literal/metaphorical distinction is not absolute but is contingent upon language context and cultural contexts.

Closely connected with *metaphor* are *simile, symbol,* and *allegory.* A *simile* is grammatically distinguishable from a metaphor. While a metaphor is an implied comparison, a simile makes the comparison explicit by using *like* or *as*: "my love is like a red, red rose," "he is as good as gold."

Symbol tends to be used much more generically. To read symbolically is to find broad, even universal, significance in the associations of the words you read and the events they portray. Some words convey conventional symbolism, meanings that have been socially or culturally produced and that thus represent some widely agreed significance. If your general repertoire includes such knowledge, you will recognize such conventional symbols as the cross (standing for Christianity) or a national flag (standing for allegiance to a country). Other symbolic readings are deeply rooted in common associations of natural phenomena: the sun symbolizes light, heat, or hopefulness; falling leaves symbolize old age or decay; darkness symbolizes mystery, fear, or obscurity. Recognizing such widely shared, symbolic associations often seems so "natural" a part of our repertoires that we take them for granted

A *symbol* can be distinguished from an *allegorical* figure by two characteristics. First, it has a natural "reality status" of its own. For example, the whale in *Moby-Dick* can be seen as just a whale, that is, it can be read nonsymbolically. Second, when it is read symbolically, it is seen to have multiple meanings. The whale can symbolize such things as the abyss in which all people exist, the inability of nature to be tamed, or the desire in people to conquer the unconquerable.

An allegorical figure, in contrast, does not possess a "reality status" of its own apart from its symbolic function. For example, the name of the character "Faith" in Hawthorne's story "Young Goodman Brown" seems to force the reader to see her as representing Goodman Brown's faith rather than as representing his earthly wife. Faith is an *allegorical* rather than a symbolic figure because the way she is depicted limits rather than opens up interpretive options. She symbolizes *faith*, not greed, despair, or love. If you read a story with characters named "Faith" and "Goodman," you are strongly directed by clues in the text about how to interpret it. Such clues are a distinctive characteristic of allegory. All the clues of an allegory usually fit into a well-organized system. Therefore, to read an allegory against the grain requires you to be a very strong reader, indeed. However, if your literary repertoire includes a strong liking for reading allegorically, you will habitually ask what each key word or phrase "stands for," and in that way you may be able to construct systematic allegorical readings for many texts you read.

The Harmonious Matching of Repertoires: Hopkins, "Spring and Fall"

Some poems deal with such common issues that it seems relatively easy to match our repertoires to theirs. Seemingly "universal" concerns like love, time, and death encourage readers to relate to them easily, harmoniously. You may think you have a distinctive viewpoint on such matters, but you probably share it with many readers. Poems that share it can be easily assimilated into your existing repertoire. Their effect on you is likely to be one of reinforcing your existing beliefs and assumptions or, at best, of making you more sensitive to them. We can speak therefore in such cases of a harmonious *matching of repertoires* between text and reader.

Take for instance this poem:

GERARD MANLEY HOPKINS (1844–1889)

Spring and Fall

To a Young Child

Márgarét, are you gríeving
Over Goldengrove unleaving?
Leáves, like the things of man, you
With your fresh thoughts care for, can you?
Áh! aś the heart grows older   5
It will come to such sights colder
By and by, nor spare a sigh
Though worlds of wanwood leafmeal lie:
And yet you will weep and know why.
Now no matter, child, the name: 10
Sórrow's spríngs áre the same.
Nor mouth had, no nor mind, expressed
What heart heard of, ghost guessed:
It ís the blight man was born for,
It is Margaret you mourn for.   15

This short, evocative poem announces itself in the title as being about something very ordinary—the seasons. But as you read carefully, it becomes clear that it repays close attention because of its finely drawn argument and the development of the voice. Even though the voice addresses a particular person, a young child named Margaret, the discussion is on a subject familiar to most readers—the change of seasons when trees lose their leaves ("unleaving").

One useful strategy for interpreting a poem is to generalize from the particular details or situations presented in the text. Using this strategy, many of you may decide that Margaret can be interpreted as representing all young children and perhaps all things that are now young but that will inevitably grow old. The poem, in short, can be seen to broaden out to consider one of the most universal and inexplicable topics—the individual's awareness of change, time, and death.

Let us construct in more detail the *surface picture* the poem paints, focusing on its language and voice. A young child grieves over the fallen leaves—the "worlds of wanwood leafmeal." Note how suggestive those last two strange words are: "wanwood" combines two words, *wan* meaning "sad" with *wood*, and *leafmeal* suggests the chopped up, random pattern of the fallen leaves. But the poem does not just present a scene; it also introduces a voice, who is a kind of character in the poem. The child is being observed and consoled by that voice; the effect is one of melancholy sympathy. This poem benefits from being read aloud. The gentle rhymes of "grieving" and "unleaving" contrast with the harsher sounds of "older" and "colder." The rhyming words also suggest equivalences between such phrases as "born for" and "mourn for."

But something else very interesting is going on. When you read the poem, you temporarily become the "I." So on the one hand, as you read it, you become an observer of the scene, standing outside Margaret and the leaves, and sympathizing with her. But on the other hand, you are not only the subject (the "I") of the poem, but you become its subject in another sense: what the poem is about is you. Part of you identifies with the speaker and voices sympathy with Margaret; another part identifies with Margaret and sees that you, like her, are as temporary as the leaves.

Having constructed such a surface picture of the poem, you should next try to construct its *surface argument,* bearing in mind that such an attempt provides not a single final or fixed meaning, but one selectively constructed by a particular reader. Here is one such reading of the poem's argument: If when people are young they are caring or sensitive or moved enough to cry over fallen leaves, as they get older, they grow more indifferent, "colder"— and learn not even to "spare a sigh" for such commonplace occurrences. And yet there is a truth, a spiritual truth, that the "ghost" (an old-fashioned word for "spirit" or "soul") knows. What does it know? That we are right to weep for such things, for our weeping acknowledges our awareness of our transience and our own inevitable "fall":

It is the blight man was born for
It is Margaret you mourn for.

We, as it were, know what the child cannot know but can only sense. We mourn not just for the leaves but for ourselves because we too are like the leaves: it is in the nature of leaves and humans to die.

This "reading" of the poem allows at least some of its powerful concerns to emerge. But the above prose restatement is by no means objective: inevitably it reflects the reader's own repertoire, in this case the editors of this anthology. In fact, when the editor who drafted this section suggested one particular reading of this poem, the others either were skeptical about some points or wanted the focus altered. Even so-called experts disagree on what is supposedly "there," in the text.

But with a poem like "Spring and Fall," which brings into discussion many issues that are commonly felt in our culture, there is probably a generally shared range of readings. That is, most modern readers' repertoires will match relatively harmoniously with the poem's. This does not mean that the poem has an "objective" meaning: different readers will bring different attitudes to the issues the poem raises. You might identify strongly with its anxiety about change, especially about growing old, and fear of death, all of which are nearly universal feelings. If you responded to that anxiety, you might have already experienced how your own or your loved ones' mortality can be reflected in natural phenomena, like the change of the seasons. Everyone has had the experience of looking at old photographs of oneself or one's parents or grandparents, then marveling at the changes. As people get older, they always find an occasion to laugh or fret at the first gray hair. They laugh, but they may be laughing uneasily.

Your own concerns about mortality can be introduced into your reading if you develop a strong philosophical or religious interpretation. Do you feel threatened by old age? By the passing of time? Time is certainly widely felt to be one of the greatest mysteries of our lives. What does the poem suggest? Is there a solution to these uneasy feelings? What do you as an individual feel is the answer to fears about passing time? What place does, say, religion play in dealing with such a question? All these, and other, questions can be provoked by the poem. Some are implied by the text; others may be brought to bear by different readers. But if you do find this poem provocative or moving, it is in part because of what you as a reader contribute to your reading.

You can see that even when you read a poem where there is likely to be a harmonious matching of repertoires, it is easy to develop a strong reading. You focus on your *own* repertoire and account for it by reference to the general ideology of your time, and read the poem in terms of your own deeply felt concerns.

Suggested Approach to Reading a Poem

1. Do a *preliminary reading* of the poem:
   (a) Try to create a clear sense of atmosphere, subject matter, voice
   (b) Examine the text's general and literary repertoires, including denotations of unknown or strange words, connotations of powerfully emotional words and phrases, historical detail, setting, characters, gaps, indeterminacies
   (c) Reread (aloud, if possible), looking to integrate your preliminary discoveries
   (d) Restate the poem in your own words
   (e) Remind yourself that even though you have seemingly concentrated on the "text," you are not producing an objective reading: your own repertoire is already influencing your reading

2. Formulate an *initial response* to the poem:
   (a) Ask yourself what immediate effects the poem has upon you
   (b) Account for those effects by relating them both to your own literary and general repertoires and to those of the text
   (c) Ask yourself about the kind of matching of repertoires that is occurring in your response
   (d) Remind yourself that you now have the basis for developing a strong reading of the poem

3. Do a *strong reading* of the poem:
   (a) Choose one or more issues that reading the poem raises for you and pursue your own perspective of them in relation to the poem. Some possible perspectives for a strong reading include philosophical, religious, feminist, masculinist, psychological, Freudian, political, elitist, populist, and many others
   (b) Make your reading as convincing as you can by analyzing the assumptions that give rise to it, placing them in a larger social context, and acknowledging the possibility of alternative readings
   (c) Remind yourself that yours is not, and there can never be, a final reading

The Problematic Matching of Repertoires: Wayman, "Unemployment"

Now let us look at a different kind of matching of repertoires, where the poem raises issues that may easily provoke widely differing responses:

TOM WAYMAN (b. 1945)

Unemployment

The chrome lid of the coffee pot
twists off, and the glass knob rinsed.
Lift out the assembly, dump
the grounds out. Wash the pot and
fill with water, put everything back with
fresh grounds and snap the top down.   5
Plug in again and wait.

Unemployment is also
a great snow deep around the house
choking the street, and the City.
Nothing moves. Newspaper photographs   10
show the traffic backed up for miles.
Going out to shovel the walk
I think how in a few days the sun will clear this.
No one will know I worked here.

This is like whatever I do.   15
How strange that so magnificent a thing as a body
with its twinges, its aches
should have all that chemistry, that bulk
the intricate electrical brain
subjected to something as tiny   20
as buying a postage stamp.
Or selling it.

Or waiting.

A very different kind of poem from the one by Hopkins, this poem uses a
series of pictures to evoke the frustration and helplessness of being unemployed. We suggested that you might well feel a sense of involvement in
reading "Spring and Fall" because the poem, though addressed to one person, describes a nearly universal human situation. The matching of repertoires will probably be relatively harmonious because the text's argument is
shared by nearly all its modern readers. "Unemployment" is more problematic: it tries to involve you by asking for your compassion for something
about which you may or may not have strong feelings. The poem may have
the power to change your mind about unemployment—but only if you let
it. The poem does not *insist* emphatically that you take up any one attitude,
but it does try very hard to make you sympathetic to the unemployed—to
sense the anger, the helplessness, the loss of dignity as well as of earnings.
But do you? And if not, does your reaction make the poem a failure?

Can you imagine yourself in such a situation? If not, does your reaction
make the poem of little interest to you? This is an excellent poem for work-

ing out a comparison of *your* repertoire of attitudes and beliefs with that of the text and for studying how the two intersect in your reading. For example, if you have had a parent who was unemployed, you are likely to be sympathetic. On the other hand, you may be tough-minded and think that the unemployed are the necessary casualties of a free-enterprise system and that people who find themselves without a job should look for another one. Has this poem changed your attitude in any way? Do you think your age or socioeconomic class makes a difference in your reading? If you do wish to argue with the poem or to lay out a more detailed case about the complexities of unemployment, then clearly the poem has done its work; it has stimulated you to start producing a strong reading, regardless of whether that reading is sympathetic to the poem's argument or not.

In constructing such a strong reading, you become aware of how words constitute a site of struggle for more than "literary" values. One of the key words in "Unemployment" is "City." Note how it is capitalized, as if it stands for something more than a particular city, more than a New York or a St. Louis. Words, after all, are not simple signs that have only one meaning: as we saw with "The Tyger," they carry *connotations*—suggestions and associations ultimately traceable to society's deep-seated beliefs and practices—its *ideology*. What does "City" connote? For some, a city is a place of excitement, stimulation, possibility; for others, a place of risk, danger, oppression. We might say that these very different understandings of "City" are struggling here, almost for the control of the word.

Words are like little battlegrounds: they are sites where separate meanings struggle for supremacy. In this poem different philosophies of life—different "ideological" beliefs and practices about work, capitalism, labor, unions, unemployment—struggle. And you, as readers, become part of that struggle. "City" is another *gap* or indeterminacy that you flesh out with your own contributions to the debate, and in doing so, you develop your individual strong reading of this poem. Reading, therefore, is not just an aesthetic activity. Language is not just confined to poems; it is what we use to locate ourselves within the great issues of the world. Reading some poems can help us to do that; some poems speak to us more passionately than others, depending on the repertoires of both text and reader.

Note how active you must become as a reader of this poem. In constructing your own text in response to it, you are a bit like a psychoanalyst, probing at the contradictions in the text, offering some explanations, filling gaps, and then giving a diagnosis. You become strong readers when you choose—for clear intellectual reasons—to confront a strong text.

Different Repertoires, Different Readings

You have seen how strong readings can be developed on two quite different poems—one where the issues seem common and uncontroversial, one where they might well seem arguable. You may agree with what you perceive as the poem's general repertoire; or you may choose to read the poem differently. In the first instance, a strong reading consists of elaborating on the issues raised by the matching of your repertoire with the text's; in the second, it means producing a self-consciously different reading, in which, while acknowledging the dominant perspective of the poem, you choose to adopt an alternative one. Different repertoires will produce different readings.

Why do readers adopt alternative perspectives in this manner? First, they may discover that their repertoire is at such odds with that of the poem that they cannot passively accept the poem's position and must read the poem "against the grain"—that is, against what it seems to want. Second, readers may perceive significances when they are reading a poem, particularly one of an earlier century, that they know were not part of the poet's repertoire, such as the nuclear energy interpretation of Blake's "Tyger." Third, readers may deliberately try to read as if they were someone else, that is, from perspectives other than their own (for example, from a feminist, a socialist, or a fundamentalist position).

Strong readings may also be prompted by the gaps or indeterminacies within the text, the places that the reader must "fill in" in order to make sense of the poem. Readers often disagree about how to fill in these gaps. This disagreement arises not from the text itself but rather from what readers bring to it—their repertoire of beliefs, values, assumptions; in short, they arise from readers' positions within their culture's ideology. In the study of any text, it is most important for readers to articulate and discuss their differences. Then they should try to understand from where such differences arise and what they imply about beliefs.

We are not suggesting, however, that strong readings allow the reader to produce bizarre, subjective readings of poems for their own sake. For example, we are not advocating that readers arbitrarily decide all poems they read are about baseball just because they are baseball fans. Strong readings, because they may go against the grain of the poem and because they may also go against the readings of your classmates, must be justified by a clear analysis of how your interests, beliefs, and preoccupations inform—and for you, perhaps *demand*—the strong reading that you present. To learn to produce strong readings often involves hard digging. You must look at your repertoires closely. You may also have to do library research; you may have to discuss and argue for your position in detail. The more you bring to a reading, the more your readings become powerful and *yours*.

At this point we pose some important questions: What limits are there to interpretation? Can one, in fact, say just *anything* about a poem? How can we tell a good from a bad interpretation? In a very serious sense, *no* interpretation should be ruled out so long as it is interestingly argued, well developed, concretely supported, and engaging to hear or read. Readers cannot be "faithful to what the text says": what the text says depends in part on what readers want it to say. This approach to the question of "legitimate" versus "illegitimate" or "valid" versus "invalid" readings acknowledges that no pure or objective readings exist, and asks that strong readers try, as explicitly as possible, to make their perspective and its implications clear. But in practice some readings will certainly seem too bizarre, too removed from our experience, too improbable, too unfamiliar—and therefore less acceptable to us. In the drama section, we discuss how readers have interpreted *Hamlet* very differently over the centuries and how seemingly "bizarre" readings have come to be seen as perfectly acceptable. That same principle applies to poems. Why should that be?

A Strong Reading:
Wyatt, "They Flee from Me"

To help address these questions, we will look at an example of how "different" readings come from actual classroom practice in regard to a well-known poem written by a Renaissance courtier.

THOMAS WYATT (1503–1542)

They Flee from Me

They flee from me, that sometime did me seek,
With naked foot stalking in my chamber.
I have seen them, gentle, tame, and meek,
That now are wild, and do not remember
That sometime they put themselves in danger   5
To take bread at my hand; and now they range,
Busily seeking with a continual change.

Thanked be fortune it hath been otherwise.
Twenty times better; but once in special,
In thin array, after a pleasant guise,   10
When her loose gown from her shoulders did fall,
And she me caught in her arms long and small,
Therewithall sweetly did me kiss
And softly said, "Dear heart, how like you this?"

It was no dream, I lay broad waking.   15
But all is turned, through my gentleness,
Into a strange fashion of forsaking;
And I have leave to go, of her goodness,
And she also to use newfangleness.
But since that I so kindely am served,   20
I fain would know what she hath deserved.

Students in our class were asked to do a series of tasks, as they gradually turned an initial response statement into a more formal paper. They were first asked to write a response statement to clarify for themselves something of their individual reactions to the poem. To do so, they had to investigate both the text's repertoire and their own. With the text, they were encouraged to do research on the period in which the poem was written—looking at books on Wyatt or on sixteenth-century poetry. Then they had to develop a strong reading by analyzing their own repertoires as well as those parts of the general cultural ideology of our own time that produced their readings. In the first part of their responses, students looked at the ways that the text had been produced—its subject matter, its language, conventions, organization, poetic devices. They worked out the *argument* that the poem seemed to put forward, looking in particular at the powerful metaphor of the hunt, the description of the "once in special" incident in the second stanza, and the question at the poem's end. They then investigated carefully the poem's assumptions and values—its ideological position. To do this, they asked these questions: Is the stalking of wild animals or birds an appropriate metaphor for love? What does such a metaphor say about the view of love prevailing when the poem was written? What can be discovered from doing research on the social context at the time of the poem's writing and first reception? The first part of their responses, therefore, concentrated on what went into the production of the text—the way the general and literary ideology of a historical period informs the poem.

What emerged over a class period was that some students had found after some research that the *kind* of love depicted in the poem was different in some—though not all—respects from what they themselves thought of as love. The kind of *courtly* or *Petrarchan* love described in the poem was typical of Renaissance England in the court of King Henry VIII when Wyatt wrote it in about 1530. Love was seen as a kind of game, involving contradictory and paradoxical experiences; it emphasized flirtation, not fulfillment. For the most part, students argued that the Petrarchan view of love directly contrasts with their own views of love, which give priority to honesty, simplicity, and fulfillment. Students acknowledged the differences between their own views of love and those of the Renaissance; however, they did not dismiss the poem as trivial or outdated because the "I" of the poem seems almost as confused by the Petrarchan ideal of love as the students are by that ideal. The "I" is very puzzled by his particular experience with one woman, which seems to have contradicted all he had learned about Petrarchan love. His experience with her appears different from others, unpredictable, "once in special."

Exploring the differences between the courtly view of love and their own contemporary view, the students addressed these questions: Do I feel differently about love after reading this poem? Do I think frustration is a stimulus to love or something to be overcome? Is anticipation more powerful than fulfillment? Who is the dominant person in a love relationship? Answering questions such as these strengthens the reader's repertoire. They led to the final stage of the exercise in which students were asked to *account for* their different readings of the poems.

After two class periods of investigation, explanation, and discussion, it became clear that individuals in the class differed significantly in their responses to the poem. Most of the men in the group identified with the "I" of the poem—with the wounded male ego—rejected by a woman with whom he has unexpectedly fallen in love, told by her that it was all an enjoyable but superficial flirtation.

Though amused by such a reading, women in the class tended to be derisive. Knowing that they did not have to restrict their readings to the viewpoint articulated by that hurt male "I," they asked about the woman's viewpoint. In such a society, and with such a philosophy of love, both so male-centered, why shouldn't a woman get what she could out of this so-called game of love? Wasn't survival crucial to her in a world so overwhelmingly dominated by men? Why should the man be so upset that the woman, in order to protect herself, took on the dominant value system of the period, one that he would have endorsed had he not fallen in love with her? The women in the class were able to read against the grain of this poem to develop sympathy for the female rather than for the male in a way that Wyatt's own readers probably could not have.

Many of the women in the class, therefore, developed a powerful, shared reading of the poem from the viewpoint of the late-twentieth-century young woman. There were disagreements—on the degree of sympathy for that male ego, on the culpability of a man as opposed to the social system in which he finds himself, and on the degree of helplessness of the woman. But by and large they produced a shared, distinctive, powerful reading of the poem, one that clearly and systematically was "different" from the reading that the poem may have asked its readers to accept passively. It was, if you like, a "feminist" reading, just as some men in the class had produced a "masculinist" reading. The women felt compelled to produce a different reading because they felt that their repertoires could not match that of the text. And to be fair, some of the men in the class who chose to read the poem from a feminist perspective developed readings quite similar to the readings of the women. Here are some sample responses the class produced, the first by one of the men in the class:

> I sympathize with the speaker. Women today tend to like to play at love, and when a man falls in love, especially "once in special," it comes as a real shock when he is rejected. The woman in this poem is a flirt, and I feel by the end of the poem he is seeing this, and is confused about the way he should respond to her. He had treated her "kindly," and she is rejecting him.

In this reading, what we termed above a "masculinist" reading, the student did what the poem seemed to ask its readers to do—to develop a sense of understanding and compassion for the speaker. The reader picked out the parts of the poem that reinforced views with which he felt comfortable while bringing his own presuppositions about sexual relationships and gender roles into play.

Here, by contrast, is part of a response statement by a woman in the class:

> At first, I felt sorry for the speaker of the poem, but eventually I realized he was indulging himself in a power play. He has everything on his side: he is a male in an environment that favors men; he regards women as frightened little animals; and he sees love as a pursuit, like a hunt. What power does she have? She probably has her reputation at stake, and her withdrawal from him is a kind of self-protection. He is an egotist, thinking only of his injured feelings and saying nothing about her state of mind. What kind of relationship is he really after?

The reader is responding to the same lines but is clearly bringing quite different assumptions to bear on those lines. This response is gender-specific in ways that are obviously very different from those of our male reader.

Most important, both readers related their readings of this poem to their own lives, the kind of identification that leads to the final phase in the construction of a strong reading. The students were then asked to consider what implications for their lives, commitments, and beliefs does such a reading have. Does how you treat someone suggest your moral position? Does poetry *matter?* The question became not did they *like* poetry or this particular poem, but rather how does the reading they did of the poem affect their behavior in the world, their choice of a lifestyle, and their political, moral, or other commitments. Such questions, of course, may easily turn into an engaged and serious debate about feminism or other issues raised in their readings. This is exactly where the study of poetry should lead—not to just "liking" poetry but to the development of a sharper and more committed perspective on your own position within your society and culture.

Finally, we want to stress three points about our approach to reading any text. First, the different readings produced by members of our classes were created in the relationship between readers and the text, and between the ideologies that produced the poem and those that produced the readers. They were not unambiguously or objectively "in" the text. Second, none of the readings was in itself inherently bad or good, valid or invalid. Students judged their own interpretations on the intelligence, vigor, detail, organization, and persuasiveness of what they had to say—not on whether they had developed the supposedly *correct* interpretation. Third, what individual students developed was *their own* interpretation: they had worked toward it by starting with their early reactions to a poem. Then they allowed the text and its ideological assumptions to have their say while teasing out what the text left unsaid or assumed. Only then did students articulate their own perspective on issues raised by the poem. They thereby produced powerful readings that were partly a collective discovery and partly an individual one. They produced what the greatest and the most powerful poems are designed to evoke—powerful readings and powerful readers.

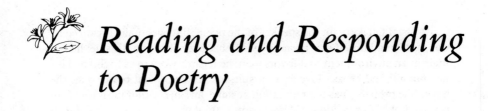

Reading and Responding to Poetry

Read the following poems and the questions that follow them.

PHILIP LARKIN (1922–1984)

Church Going

Once I am sure there's nothing going on
I step inside, letting the door thud shut.
Another church: matting, seats, and stone,
And little books; sprawlings of flowers, cut
For Sunday, brownish now; some brass and stuff   5
Up at the holy end; the small neat organ;
And a tense, musty, unignorable silence,
Brewed God knows how long. Hatless, I take off
My cycle-clips in awkward reverence,

Move forward, run my hand around the font.   10
From where I stand, the roof looks almost new—
Cleaned, or restored? Someone would know: I don't.
Mounting the lectern, I peruse a few
Hectoring large-scale verses, and pronounce
'Here endeth' much more loudly than I'd meant.   15
The echoes snigger briefly. Back at the door
I sign the book, donate an Irish sixpence,
Reflect the place was not worth stopping for.

Yet stop I did: in fact I often do,
And always end much at a loss like this,   20
Wondering what to look for; wondering, too,

When churches fall completely out of use
What we shall turn them into, if we shall keep
A few cathedrals chronically on show,
Their parchment, plate and pyx° in locked cases,   25
And let the rest rent-free to rain and sheep.
Shall we avoid them as unlucky places?

Or, after dark, will dubious women come
To make their children touch a particular stone;
Pick simples° for a cancer; or on some   30
Advised night see walking a dead one?
Power of some sort or other will go on
In games, in riddles, seemingly at random;
But superstition, like belief, must die,
And what remains when disbelief has gone?   35
Grass, weedy pavement, brambles, buttress, sky,

A shape less recognisable each week,
A purpose more obscure. I wonder who
Will be the last, the very last, to seek
This place for what it was; one of the crew   40
That tap and jot and know what rood-lofts° were?
Some ruin-bibber,° randy for antique,
Or Christmas-addict, counting on a whiff
Of gown-and-bands and organ-pipes and myrrh?
Or will he be my representative,   45

Bored, uninformed, knowing the ghostly silt
Dispersed, yet tending to this cross of ground
Through suburb scrub because it held unspilt
So long and equably what since is found
Only in separation—marriage, and birth,   50
And death, and thoughts of these—for whom was built
This special shell? For, though I've no idea
What this accoutred° frowsty barn is worth,
It pleases me to stand in silence here;

A serious house on serious earth it is,   55
In whose blent air all our compulsions meet,
Are recognised, and robed as destinies.
And that much never can be obsolete,
Since someone will forever be surprising
A hunger in himself to be more serious,   60
And gravitating with it to this ground,
Which, he once heard, was proper to grow wise in,
If only that so many dead lie round.

---

25 **pyx:** containers in which Eucharistic wafers are kept.   30 **simples:** medicinal herbs.   41
rood-lofts: church galleries.   42 **ruin-bibber:** enthusiast for ruins.   53 **accoutred:** dressed up.

Response Statement Assignment

After rereading the general guidelines for response statements (pp. 15–20), consider the following questions.

1. What is your response to the poem's tone? Do you find it ironic? Serious? Flippant? Do you have a mixture of reactions? Attempt to account for these reactions by reference to specific lines of the poem and to your own **general** and **literary repertoires.**
2. Pick out an aspect of the poem's argument about religion that is especially noteworthy. What kinds of attitudes does it put forward? How do these views match your own? Account for your own position on the issues raised.

Sample Student Response Statement

Here is our student's initial response statement:

> I found ''Church Going'' a puzzling mixture of tedium and mild interest. It seemed to move very slowly, as if the speaker wasn't quite sure of what he wanted to say. I think a poem should keep its reader's interest, but this seemed very low key. There's almost a lack of interest in lines like ''Hatless, I take off/My cycle-clips in awkward reverence,'' or ''Reflect the place was not worth stopping for.'' I like poetry to be uplifting and not end in a kind of puzzlement. There doesn't seem to be much point to the poem.
>
> The poet appears to be unsure of why he is in the church. Perhaps this reflects a modern disbelief about religion. As a Christian, I feel I know what truth is. As far as I'm concerned, I have no doubts about the place of the church in my life, but I know there are many people who do not agree with me. They are equally entitled to their opinions, but I don't believe that churches will fall down. I think the poet is, to use his own words, ''bored, uninformed.''

Discussion

This initial response is a fairly negative one, yet we found it promising and provocative because, however briefly, the writer focuses on his own views and tries to analyze them by referring to both his literary ("I like poetry to be uplifting") and general repertoires. We did not ask our student to change his opinion of the poem, as he stated it in this initial response, but we did ask him in his revision to try to develop additional connections with the poem. The matching of repertoires that occurs in this response is somewhat narrowly focused—on his view of poetry and on a very strong (though underdeveloped) statement about his own religious views.

Religious ideology plays a very large part in his reading: noting that the poem concerns religion, churches, and personal belief, he is immediately stimulated to draw on his ingrained assumptions about the truth of his religion. But note how contradictory he is when he asserts, on the one hand, that he has "no doubts" about the truth of his religion but that, on the other hand, other people are "equally entitled to their opinions." Response statements are especially useful for drawing out such ideological contradictions —whether or not the student will want to explore these contradictions or try to reconcile them is difficult to know with such an emotionally laden subject as religion. But at least in the discussion of his response statement, he can become aware that they exist.

So far as his literary repertoire is concerned, it is interesting that he finds not "much point" to the poem since, in his view, poetry should be "uplifting." Here his analysis could be intensified if he would ask himself whether the exploration of doubt, indecision, and puzzlement can be a legitimate subject for poetry. To admirers of Larkin, one of the great virtues of his poetry is that he makes us become more sensitive to our own intimate, private moments of doubt, ambiguity, or moral complexity. Another much praised aspect of Larkin's work is his quiet ironical humor. In "Church Going," we suggested to the student that the slight foolishness of the narrator, caught between acknowledging the power of traditional religion and being skeptical and embarrassed by it, is another possible interpretation. Where the student mentions the line, "Reflect the place was not worth stopping for," we asked him to explain why the poem then continues for so long. Perhaps the speaker contradicts himself. Perhaps underneath, he is fascinated with the place—despite himself.

In fact, when we talked to this student about his initial written response to the poem, we discovered that his perception of the poet's confusion resulted from his adopting some **reading strategies** that proved to be quite self-defeating. For example, he told us that he had decided not to read the poem closely because he did not like its subject matter. He read it quickly just to "get the gist," a common strategy for a first reading, but when he decided that the gist was anti-religious, he wanted simply to dismiss the poem rather than to try to trace its argument carefully. Because he did not adopt the strategy of reading the poem closely, he was not able to argue with the poem's pivotal ideas in his initial response statement. Rather, he had to resort, to a certain extent, to some name calling in the first paragraph. He told us that he had argued the poem was pointless when what he really meant was that he didn't *agree* with its point. We asked this student to use a *close reading* strategy for his revision so that he could get a better sense of the religious position of the poem and then develop a stronger, more detailed reading of it.

We also discovered another strategy he had used that prevented him from doing a strong reading of the poem. He noted in paragraph 2 of his initial response statement that the narrator "appears to be unsure about why he is in the church," but he had not elaborated on this point. When we asked him about this, he said that he felt that the poet contradicts himself in the poem, but he wasn't sure whether he should actually write this. He had been told previously that an interpretation always *resolves* contradictions, points of confusion, or ambiguities, and he therefore felt that he "wouldn't look good" if his response statement made these contradictions more apparent. Consequently one of his reading strategies was to develop an interpretation that "makes the poem appear coherent." This strategy prevented him from writing about the tensions in the poem (and possibly relating them to the tensions in society at large) over the role of religion in our lives. For his revision we suggested that he should adopt a reading strategy in which, rather than trying to resolve ambiguities or contradictions, he tries to explore the cultural forces that might engender such contradictions in people.

In short, our student's initial response statement had potential for further development, but it should not be seen as a first "subjective" step towards an "objective" reading of the poem. Again, we do not want to encourage readers to change their minds so much as *broaden* their minds, and so become more self-conscious about both their reading strategies and their literary and general repertoires. In the process (and this almost invariably happens), the reader may come to change, or at least deepen, his or her reading of the poem.

Response Statement: First Revision

Now look at what this initial response statement became:

> Initially I found ''Church Going'' a puzzling mixture, both mildly tedious and mildly interesting. I was responding to the mixture of eager interest and doubt and puzzlement I sensed in the speaker. He clearly isn't sure about what he wants to say about entering a church. There are even lines when he laughs at himself for his embarrassment at being in a place that other people revere, but that he does not. This leads him to a long consideration of why churches still impose a sense of awe, even on him, and what future ages might think of them. On a second reading, lines expressing the speaker's perplexity, like ''Hatless, I take off/my cycle-clips in awkward reverence,'' become quite funny, when I realized the speaker knows he is in a holy place and thinks he should do something reverent to show it. Rereading the poem, I got a better sense of him as a genuine truth seeker--someone trying to be honest about himself.
>
> While the poet seems to be unsure about why he is in the church, as a Christian I have no doubt about the place of the church in my life. In his doubt, the speaker is a product of

the modern age. Skepticism about religion is typical of today's world, and therefore the poem evokes quite well what it is like to be an unbeliever or, more accurately, a half-believer. I myself am not exactly sure what all the religious objects and actions the poem refers to are, so my unfamiliarity with church rituals suggests I too have been influenced by the twentieth century. I would guess that the speaker is an example of the so-called decentered self of the modern age, caught between contradictory ideological views. He's quite amusing to me in this respect, since I have no doubts about the place of the church in my life, yet I know there are many people (like the speaker) who do. But I don't believe churches will fall down.

On rereading the poem, I changed my strategies for reading the text. Temperamentally I don't like ambiguity; that's probably one reason that I don't have doubts about religion. But I realize that other people, like the speaker in this poem, may not like to doubt but find that they have serious doubts anyway. When I read this poem the first time, I tried to pin the speaker down as an anti-religious type. I wanted to get a single meaning out of the poem because I thought this would make my reading stronger, but I also realize that this particular reading strategy is part of my general approach to life--to pigeonhole people into right and wrong. I think this is a useful way of operating in the world, but I think I've learned both from reading this poem and from trying to change my strategies, that I can't always either categorize people or impose my values on them. If people are confused, like this poet, maybe it's best to let them be confused; and maybe their confusion can give the rest of us a better sense of what the issues are. People who are sure, like myself, often see only <u>one</u> side of a situation. Thus I think that I might in time develop a greater tolerance for ambiguity, though I still don't like it.

On a second reading, therefore, I think the poem gives its reader insight into a distinctive modern sensibility, one that I'm sympathetic to, even if I don't show it.

Discussion

Clearly this revised response is not only longer but also sharper; it is much more analytical about the student's cultural situation and reading strategies —even if the student has not fully explored his own ideological position. Note that this second version does not strive for "objectivity" but rather attempts to deepen the insights already articulated in the initial response. We suggested that a third revision might include material on historical or religious backgrounds of both the text and the reader, more detailed accounts of the "decentered" modern self, or the notion of the student being "written" by different discourses. It might also raise the question of the kind of poetry the writer prefers—and why. By developing these points, the reader would move from a rough personal first response towards a deliberately chosen and well-developed strong reading.

Clearly the student wishes to develop what he calls a "Christian" reading of a skeptical poem—an emphasis his next revision should strengthen. His next draft, in fact, did something of this, as he tried to create a strong reading, making much more explicit his own distinctive viewpoint on religion. He substituted the following section for the opening sentence of paragraph 2 of his first revision.

Response Statement: Second Revision

While the poet seems to be unsure about why he is in the church, as a Christian I have no doubt of the place of the church in my life. Here there is a genuine clash between the poem's skepticism or disbelief and my own faith. The speaker, wandering about the church, unaware of the significance of ''brass and stuff/Up at the holy end,'' or mockingly reading ''a few/Hectoring large-scale verses'' is representative of modern skepticism. Like a vast proportion of modern men and women, he doesn't see the certainty of a transcendent faith. When you are assured of salvation and firm in your faith, such skepticism isn't possible. Something greater than your own weak powers takes over and speaks through you. The speaker obviously doesn't have this--and hence he wanders aimlessly around the church, bored, his pilgrimage without point.

And yet coming through his boredom, the truth nonetheless indirectly appears. As stanza 3 puts it: ''Yet stop I did: in fact I often do.'' One of the marks of the modern world is the way God's grace comes through our skepticism. The speaker looks forward to a time when churches will be abandoned, ruined, not understood, and he asks himself ''who/Will be the last, the very last, to seek/This place for what it was.'' Even in such a question, there is a desire for the truth to be showing through.

And what finally convinces him? Death. The last great reality of our lives. Surrounding the churches are the graves. They show him (and the poem's reader) where the truth lies. What a Christian knows that the poet doesn't is that the ''hunger in himself to be more serious'' is satisfied by the Lord. Therefore the poem evokes quite well what it is like to be an unbeliever.

In this the speaker is a product of . . .

And so he continued where his first revision left off, making only minor changes. The added paragraph makes clear where the writer's position is coming from. He was starting to produce a very compelling strong reading. His response statement uses details from the poem but, above all, it brings out a distinct perspective on it. It is an intelligent reading of the poem "against the grain," one that is interesting and provocative because it belongs to the reader.

Additional Response Assignments

1. What were your initial reactions to the poem's title? As you read the poem, were they confirmed or changed?
2. The poem is written by a poet living in England where churches built hundreds of years ago still are used. Do you think it makes a difference to your **reading strategies** that you don't live in such an environment?
3. The narrative voice of the poem is clearly puzzled, skeptical, and occasionally bored. Do you find his reactions a help or a hindrance as you read the poem? Discuss your reactions to and interpretation of narrative **voice.**

SIR PHILIP SIDNEY (1554–1586)

From *Astrophil and Stella*
Sonnet 52

A strife is grown between Virtue and Love,
  While each pretends° that Stella must be his:
  Her eyes, her lips, her all, saith Love do° this,
Since they do wear his badge,° most firmly prove.
But Virtue thus that title doth disprove,   5
  That° Stella (O dear name) that Stella is
  That virtuous soul, sure heir of heav'nly bliss:
Not this fair outside, which our hearts doth move.
  And therefore, though her beauty and her grace
Be Love's indeed, in Stella's self he may   10
By no pretense claim any manner place.
Well, Love, since this demur° our suit° doth stay,
  Let Virtue have that Stella's self; yet thus,
  That Virtue but that body grant to us.

2 **pretends:** in law, bring a charge or action.   3 **do:** auxiliary verb with "prove" (line 4).   4 **his badge:** Love's livery.   6 **That:** i.e., claiming that.   12 **demur:** legal plea, creating delay; it acknowledges facts stated by opponent, but denies his right to relief.   12 **suit:** (1) legal; (2) courtship of Stella.

Response Statement Assignments

1. How do you respond to the poem's **argument?**
2. Does an understanding of the sonnet form help you organize the poem's argument? Were you conscious of poetic form while reading?
3. Briefly note the shifts in dialogue in the poem. Who is speaking at each point? What, in particular, is the effect of the last three lines in the dialogue?
4. Do you find yourself convinced by any or all of the protagonists? Try to account for your agreement (or lack of it). What are your own views about the subject they are debating?
5. Does this poem fit your view of what love poetry should be? Sidney himself criticized the love poetry written in his time for being unpersuasive, saying that such poets would "never persuade me they were in love." Do you think this poem escaped that criticism by his contemporaries? Do you think it does so *today?*

WILLIAM SHAKESPEARE (1564–1616)

Sonnet 18

Shall I compare thee to a summer's day?
Thou art more lovely and more temperate:
Rough winds do shake the darling buds of May,
And summer's lease hath all too short a date:
Sometimes too hot the eye of heaven shines,   5
And often is his gold complexion dimmed;
And every fair from fair sometimes declines,
By chance or nature's changing course untrimmed;°
But thy eternal summer shall not fade,
Nor lose possession of that fair thou ow'st;   10
Nor shall death brag thou wander'st in his shade,
When in eternal lines to time thou grow'st:
So long as men can breathe, or eyes can see,
So long lives this, and this gives life to thee.

8 **untrimmed:** unchecked.

Response Statement Assignment

1. Trace, as closely as you can, your process of reading and researching this poem. What lines did you respond to most powerfully on a first reading? How did this response influence your second reading?

2. Do you, living in the late twentieth century, find the views of love implied by this poem attractive? Do you think they are compatible with the modern world? Or are they archaic?
3. This poem is written in sonnet form. Do you think the regular pattern of rhymes helps to express its insights? In particular, how do you respond to the rhymed couplet at the end?

ROBERT HERRICK (1591–1674)

Delight in Disorder

A sweet disorder in the dress
Kindles in clothes a wantonness.
A lawn° about the shoulders thrown
Into a fine distraction;
An erring lace, which here and there   5
Enthralls the crimson stomacher,°
A cuff neglectful, and thereby
Ribbons to flow confusedly;
A winning wave, deserving note,
In the tempestuous petticoat;   10
A careless shoestring, in whose tie
I see a wild civility;
Do more bewitch me than when art
Is too precise in every part.

3 **lawn:** a scarf of linen.   6 **stomacher:** an ornamental piece of clothing (worn over women's breasts).

Response Statement Assignments

1. What is your response to the poem's concern with a "sweet" or slight disorder in dress? Are you amused? Unconvinced? How do you respond to the sexual overtones? Account for your reaction.
2. The poem emphasizes how the "I" of the poem (presumably a male "I") constructs the object of his attention (presumably a female) by his gaze, treating her as a kind of object. How does your own gender affect your response to that situation?
3. Can you imagine what a reader of the opposite sex might feel reading this text? Or do you feel that a gender-specific reading is not relevant?
4. Although the descriptions seem to refer to clothing and fashion—especially women's clothing and fashion—do you feel that the arguments are applicable to other areas of your experience? Concentrate especially on the impact of the last two lines.

JONATHAN SWIFT (1667–1745)

A Description of a City Shower

October, 1710.

Careful Observers may foretel the Hour
(By sure Prognosticks) when to dread a Show'r;
While Rain depends,° the pensive Cat gives o'er
Her Frolicks, and pursues her Tail no more.
Returning Home at Night, you'll find the Sink°   5
Strike your offended Sense with double Stink.
If you be wise, then go not far to dine,
You'll spend in Coach-hire more than save in Wine.
A coming Show'r your shooting Corns presage,
Old Aches throb, your hollow Tooth will rage.   10
Sauntring in Coffee-house is *Dulman* seen;
He damns the Climate, and complains of Spleen.°

Mean while the South rising with dabbled Wings,
A Sable Cloud a-thawrt the Welkin° flings,
That swill'd more Liquor than it could contain,   15
And like a Drunkard gives it up again.
Brisk *Susan* whips her Linen from the Rope,
While the first drizzling Show'r is born aslope.°
Such is that Sprinkling which some careless Quean°
Flirts on you from her Mop, but not so clean.   20
You fly, invoke the Gods; then turning, stop
To rail; she singing, still whirls on her Mop.
Not yet, the Dust had shun'd th'unequal Strife,
But aided by the Wind, fought still for Life;
And wafted with its Foe by violent Gust,   25
'Twas doubtful which was Rain, and which was Dust.
Ah! where must needy Poet seek for Aid,
When Dust and Rain at once his Coat invade;
His only Coat, where Dust confus'd with Rain,
Roughen the Nap, and leave a mingled Stain.   30

Now in contiguous Drops the Flood comes down,
Threat'ning with Deluge this *Devoted*° Town.
To Shops in Crowds the daggled° Females fly,
Pretend to cheapen Goods, but nothing buy.
The Templer° spruce, while ev'ry Spout's a-broach,°   35
Stays till 'tis fair, yet seems to call a Coach.

---

3 **depends:** threatens.   5 **Sink:** sewer.   12 **spleen:** moodiness.   14 **Welkin:** sky.   18 **aslope:**
slanting.   19 **Quean:** woman.   32 **Devoted:** doomed.   33 **daggled:** rain-spattered.
35 **Templer:** law student (at the Temple, London).   35 **a-broach:** running.

The tuck'd-up Sempstress walks with hasty Strides,
While Streams run down her oil'd Umbrella's Sides.
Here various Kinds by various Fortunes led,
Commence Acquaintance underneath a Shed.   40
Triumphant Tories, and desponding Whigs,°
Forget their Fewds, and join to save their Wigs.
Box'd in a Chair° the Beau impatient sits,
While Spouts run clatt'ring o'er the Roof by Fits;
And ever and anon with frightful Din   45
The Leather sounds, he trembles from within.
So when *Troy* Chair-men bore the Wooden Steed,
Pregnant with *Greeks,* impatient to be freed.
(Those Bully *Greeks,* who, as the Moderns do,
Instead of paying Chair-men, run them thro'.)   50
Laoco'n° struck the Outside with his Spear,
And each imprison'd Hero quak'd for Fear.

    Now from all Parts the swelling Kennels° flow,
And bear their Trophies with them as they go:
Filth of all Hues and Odours seem to tell   55
What Street they sail'd from, by their Sight and Smell.
They, as each Torrent drives, with rapid Force
From *Smithfield*° or St. *Pulchre's* shape their Course,
And in huge Confluent join at *Snow-Hill* Ridge,
Fall from the *Conduit* prone to *Holborn-Bridge.*   60
Sweepings from Butchers Stalls, Dung, Guts, and Blood,
Drown'd Puppies, stinking Sprats, all drench'd in Mud,
Dead Cats and Turnip-Tops come tumbling down the Flood.

41 **Tories . . . Whigs:** political parties in 18th-century England.   43 **Chair:** sedan chair (equivalent to a modern taxi).   51 **Laoco'n:** Laocoon was a Trojan soldier whose spear hit the outside of the Wooden Horse, frightening the Greeks inside.   53 **Kennels:** gutters.   58
Smithfield . . . St. Pulchre . . . Snow-Hill . . . Holborn-Bridge: areas of London.

Response Statement Assignments

1. How do you respond to the title of the poem (and its subsequent development)?
2. Do you think "a description of a city shower" is an appropriate topic for
   poetry? Try to account for why you hold your opinion; refer to educational, institutional, or personal factors.
3. Account for the effect of the rhymed couplets in your reading of the
   poem, referring to individual examples and to your expectations about
   poetic form.
4. What are the effects of rhymed and unrhymed verse? And which do you
   prefer?

WALT WHITMAN (1819–1892)

Song of Myself (Selection)

A child said What is the grass? fetching it to me with full hands;
How could I answer the child? I do not know what it is anymore than he.

I guess it must be the flag of my disposition, out of hopeful green stuff
   woven.

Or I guess it is the handkerchief of the Lord,
A scented gift and remembrancer designedly dropt,   5
Bearing the owner's name someway in the corners, that we may see and
   remark, and say Whose?

Or I guess the grass is itself a child, the produced babe of the vegetation.

Or I guess it is a uniform hieroglyphic,
And it means, Sprouting alike in broad zones and narrow zones.
Growing among black folks as among white,   10
Kanuck,° Tuckahoe,° Congressman, Cuff,° I give them the same, I receive
   them the same.

And now it seems to me the beautiful uncut hair of graves.

11 **Kanuck:** French Canadian; **Tuckahoe:** Virginian of eastern lowlands; **Cuff:** a black.

Response Statement Assignments

1. What are the differences between "free" verse and formal verse? How do you respond to the informal free verse of this poem? Do you find it intimate or "unpoetic"? Do you find the effect repetitive or meditative? How would you characterize your reactions to it?
2. As you build up your reading, focus on your own expectations about poetry. Do you think the poem should have traditional form? Should it rhyme?
3. Do you find the subject of the grass an appropriate one for poetry? What are appropriate subjects for poetry?
4. What expectations did you have when you read the poem's opening line, and were they fulfilled as you read on?
5. What is the effect of the metaphors of this poem on you? Stimulating? Imaginative? Unconvincing?

ROBERT FROST (1874–1963)

The Road Not Taken

Two roads diverged in a yellow wood,
And sorry I could not travel both
And be one traveler, long I stood

And looked down one as far as I could
To where it bent in the undergrowth;   5

Then took the other, as just as fair,
And having perhaps the better claim,
Because it was grassy and wanted wear;
Though as for that the passing there
Had worn them really about the same,   10

And both that morning equally lay
In leaves no step had trodden black.
Oh, I kept the first for another day!
Yet knowing how way leads on to way,
I doubted if I should ever come back.   15

I shall be telling this with a sigh
Somewhere ages and ages hence:
Two roads diverged in a wood, and I—
I took the one less traveled by,
And that has made all the difference.   20

Response Statement Assignments

1. What is your predominant response to the poem? Do you find it solemn?
   Profound? Trivial?
2. Is it true that people miss most poignantly those experiences that they
   almost had? Are you ever haunted by what might have been?
3. Do you think your particular religious or philosophical beliefs (or choice
   of lifestyle) affected your response?
4. What **reading strategies** did you use to read this poem: Did you find
   yourself working hard to follow the poem's argument? Did you make almost immediate associations to your own life? Did you look for the
   rhyme scheme of the poem? Any other strategies? (a) How are those
   strategies influenced by your literary repertoire, that is, your past experiences with poetry? (b) How did the reading strategies you used influence
   your response to the poem? How did certain expectations you have
   about poetry in general or about the subject matter of this poem direct
   your reading of and reaction to the poem?

LANGSTON HUGHES (1902–1967)

Theme for English B

The instructor said,

> *Go home and write*
> *a page tonight.*
> *And let that page come out of you—*
> *Then, it will be true.*   5

I wonder if it's that simple?
I am twenty-two, colored, born in Winston-Salem.
I went to school there, then Durham, then here
to this college on the hill above Harlem.
I am the only colored student in my class.   10
The steps from the hill lead down into Harlem,
through a park, then I cross St. Nicholas,°
Eighth Avenue, Seventh, and I come to the Y,
the Harlem Branch Y, where I take the elevator
up to my room, sit down, and write this page: 15

It's not easy to know what is true for you or me
at twenty-two, my age. But I guess I'm what
I feel and see and hear, Harlem, I hear you:
hear you, hear me—we two—you, me, talk on this page.
(I hear New York, too.) Me—who?   20

Well, I like to eat, sleep, drink, and be in love.
I like to work, read, learn, and understand life.
I like a pipe for a Christmas present,
or records—Bessie,° bop, or Bach.
I guess being colored doesn't make me *not* like   25
the same things other folks like who are other races.
So will my page be colored that I write?

Being me, it will not be white.
But it will be
a part of you, instructor.   30
You are white—
yet a part of me, as I am a part of you.
That's American.
Sometimes perhaps you don't want to be a part of me.
Nor do I often want to be a part of you.   35
But we are, that's true!
As I learn from you,
I guess you learn from me—
although you're older—and white—
and somewhat more free.   40

This is my page for English B.

12–15 place names mentioned are all in New York.   24 **Bessie:** Bessie Smith, famous black
singer.

Response Statement Assignments

1. How does your **general repertoire,** specifically your knowledge about
   writing "themes" or papers for English classes, influence your response
   to the poem?
2. The instructor says, "let that page come out of you. Then it will be true."

The speaker replies "I wonder if it's that simple?" Does this debate sound like anything that has occurred in your English classes?

3. This poem clearly brings to the foreground the speaker's racial background. Does your own background affect your reading of the poem?

4. Think about the possibilities of creating very different strong readings of this poem. Can you envisage the differences between a male and female reading of this poem? What would be the crucial differences?

W. H. AUDEN (1907–1973)

Musée des Beaux Arts°

About suffering they were never wrong,
The Old Masters: how well they understood
Its human position; how it takes place
While someone else is eating or opening a window or just walking dully
    along;
How, when the aged are reverently, passionately waiting   5
For the miraculous birth, there always must be
Children who did not specially want it to happen, skating
On a pond at the edge of the wood:
They never forgot
That even the dreadful martyrdom must run its course   10
Anyhow in a corner, some untidy spot
Where the dogs go on with their doggy life and the torturer's horse
Scratches its innocent behind on a tree.
In Brueghel's *Icarus,*° for instance: how everything turns away
Quite leisurely from the disaster; the ploughman may   15
Have heard the splash, the forsaken cry,
But for him it was not an important failure; the sun shone
As it had to on the white legs disappearing into the green
Water; and the expensive delicate ship that must have seen
Something amazing, a boy falling out of the sky,   20
Had somewhere to get to and sailed calmly on.

Title: The Museum of Fine Arts, Brussels.   14 **Brueghel's *Icarus:*** painting by 16th-century Dutch painter.

Response Statement Assignments

1. Characterize your experience of reading this poem. Did you find it difficult to read? Challenging? Exciting? Remote from your experiences?

2. As you develop your interpretation, consider the **matching of repertoires** that is occurring. What aspects of the *text's* repertoire, for instance, contributed to your response? What aspects of *your* repertoire contributed to your response?

3. Our century is characterized by widespread suffering—the holocaust, World War II, famine in Africa, possible nuclear conflagration, and so forth. In 1986, NASA's space vehicle Challenger exploded just after launch, killing all the astronauts. Yet life goes on. Does art or poetry help us deal with that realization? Can pain or suffering or evil be somehow contained by art?
4. Use this poem to develop your own view of art. On the basis of what experiences have your views been formed? How do they relate to the poet's?

THEODORE ROETHKE (1908–1963)

I Knew a Woman

I knew a woman, lovely in her bones,
When small birds sighed, she would sigh back at them;
Ah, when she moved, she moved more ways than one:
The shapes a bright container can contain!
Of her choice virtues only gods should speak,   5
Or English poets who grew up on Greek
(I'd have them sing in chorus, cheek to cheek).

How well her wishes went! She stroked my chin,
She taught me Turn, and Counter-turn, and Stand,°
She taught me Touch, that undulant white skin;   10
I nibbled meekly from her proffered hand;
She was the sickle; I, poor I, the rake,
Coming behind her for her pretty sake
(But what prodigious mowing we did make).

Love likes a gander, and adores a goose: 15
Her full lips pursed, the errant note to seize;
She played it quick, she played it light and loose;
My eyes, they dazzled at her flowing knees;
Her several parts could keep a pure repose,
Or one hip quiver with a mobile nose   20
(She moved in circles, and those circles moved).

Let seed be grass, and grass turn into hay:
I'm martyr to a motion not my own;
What's freedom for? To know eternity.
I swear she cast a shadow white as stone.   25
But who would count eternity in days?
These old bones live to learn her wanton ways:
(I measure time by how a body sways).

9 **Turn . . . counter-turn . . . stand:** the three parts of the Pindaric ode.

Reading Statement Assignments

1. What is your impression of the overall *mood* of this poem? Which of your **reading strategies** help you determine such an ambiguous characteristic as mood?
2. Love poetry frequently uses metaphors and images from nature. Why do you think this is? What comparisons from nature do you find most appropriate for love poetry?
3. Most love poems in our language have been written by men. Why do you think that is? What is there in this poem that is characteristic of the way men traditionally think about women? Consider, in particular, the tone and the comparisons with nature.

DYLAN THOMAS (1914–1953)

Do Not Go Gentle into That Good Night

Do not go gentle into that good night,
Old age should burn and rave at close of day;
Rage, rage against the dying of the light.

Though wise men at their end know dark is right,
Because their words had forked no lightning they   5
Do not go gentle into that good night.

Good men, the last wave by, crying how bright
Their frail deeds might have danced in a green bay,
Rage, rage against the dying of the light.

Wild men who caught and sang the sun in flight   10
And learn, too late, they grieved it on its way,
Do not go gentle into that good night.

Grave men, near death, who see with blinding sight
Blind eyes could blaze like meteors and be gay,
Rage, rage against the dying of the light.   15

And you, my father, there on the sad height,
Curse, bless, me now with your fierce tears, I pray.

Do not go gentle into that good night.
Rage, rage against the dying of the light.

Response Statement Assignments

1. How do you respond to the formal, tightly organized rhyme scheme of this poem? How does this **text strategy** work for you with regard to the poem's subject matter?

2. This poem was written during the final illness of the poet's father. Does this knowledge change your reading of the poem or your response to its careful construction? If so, why?
3. Compare and contrast the attitudes to death in this poem with those in John Donne's "Death, Be Not Proud" (p. 446). What is the clearest difference between them? What ideological differences lie behind these poems? Which poem engages your attention most and why?

GWENDOLYN BROOKS (b. 1917)

We Real Cool

The Pool Players.
Seven at the Golden Shovel.

We real cool. We
Left school. We

Lurk late. We   5
Strike straight. We

Sing sin. We
Thin gin. We

Jazz June. We
Die soon.   10

Response Statement Assignments

1. What is your initial response to this poem? What **text strategies** most influenced your response to this poem?
2. Describe the situation this poem evokes for you. What assumptions from your own **general repertoire** most influenced your response?
3. What distinctive ethnic, class, or lifestyle attitudes did you focus on in your reading? Do they have their origins in your personal experience or in what you perceive "in" the poem?
4. Now describe the speaker's attitude to the scene you have created. Do you share it?

KENDRICK SMITHYMAN (b. 1922)

King's College Chapel°

Wonderful! basses growled to fan
vaulting. Wonderful! wonderful! altos sighed.
The little dog laughed—to see an old sow

Title: King's College, Cambridge, England, famous for the architecture of its 16th-century chapel.

laid on her back, dugs up for the cloud
farrow? But that's no little dog.   5

That is Hound, of whom you should go
mainly chary. Know him, by the company
he keeps. Gryphons,° fabulous, louche,° world-weary
beasts, sensual, fiercesome, remote or too close,
altogether too close, to your bone.   10
If here Hound sleeps, one eye is not
quite shut. Otherwise, avidly stares.
You are not alone, unobserved.
Your track won't be lost
in the Parade, down Silver Street, or Bridge.   15
Not misplaced in mystifying fog.

Fog or fine, Calvinist air at the Backs.
Made uneasy, splendid pochards or mandarins,
preveniently assured, study a certain
presence in the air, not merely winter   20
rough from the fens. A cry disappears
without being seen behind Clare,° is
(you think) answered behind John's° or goes
pattering, nail-clicking on pavings, after
your marketing, soft-foots through King Street   25
to watercoloured Midsummer Common unseen.
Unheard, is alert, when you double Jesus Green.

A change in aspect of History Building glass,
cold spot between two Library stacks,   30
he holds the hand of a riverside barmaid.
At Churchill,° a bump on the road, is shocking to
taxis, jars axles and teeth. Boys
singing *a capella* feel his eyes'
virtue at their throats. Sinuous, anarch,   35
wit's counterpoise to antic faith,
are you ever prepared for him?
He is smart. Besides, he is more old.

8 **Gryphons:** mythical medieval animals; **louche:** cross-eyed, squinting.   15–17 **Parade, Silver Street, Bridge [Street], the Backs:** areas in Cambridge.   22, 23, 31: **Clare, Johns, Churchill:** refer to Cambridge colleges.   33 **a capella:** unaccompanied by instrument.

Response Statement Assignments

1. The last line of this poem suggests a mixture of awe and derision; contrast it with the attitudes voiced by the speaker in Philip Larkin's "Church Going" (p. 396). Both poems are about visiting a church. Do you think these poets' responses are similar? Why?
2. Are your own responses to these two poems similar?

3. What **text strategies** and what **reader strategies** influence your responses?
4. In your reading, do you find yourself taking a view similar to that of the student writer on "Church Going" (p. 396)? What parts of your general repertoire influence your attitudes to these two poems?

FRANK O'HARA (1926–1966)

The Day Lady Died

It is 12:20 in New York a Friday
three days after Bastille day,° yes
it is 1959 and I go get a shoeshine
because I will get off the 4:19 in Easthampton°
at 7:15 and then go straight to dinner   5
and I don't know the people who will feed me

I walk up the muggy street beginning to sun
and have a hamburger and a malted and buy
an ugly NEW WORLD WRITING to see what the poets
in Ghana are doing these days   10
                              I go on to the bank
and Miss Stillwagon (first name Linda I once heard)
doesn't even look up my balance for once in her life
and in the GOLDEN GRIFFIN I get a little Verlaine°
for Patsy with drawings by Bonnard° although I do   15
think of Hesiod,° trans. Richmond Lattimore or
Brendan Behan's new play° or *Le Balcon* or *Les Nègres*
of Genet,° but I don't, I stick with Verlaine
after practically going to sleep with quandariness

and for Mike I just stroll into the PARK LANE   20
Liquor Store and ask for a bottle of Strega° and
then I go back where I came from to 6th Avenue
and the tobacconist in the Ziegfeld Theatre and
casually ask for a carton of Gauloises° and a carton
of Picayunes, and a NEW YORK POST with her° face on it   25

and I am sweating a lot by now and thinking of
leaning on the john door in the 5 SPOT
while she whispered a song along the keyboard
to Mal Waldron° and everyone and I stopped breathing

2 **Bastille Day:** July 14, a day celebrating the French revolution.   4 **Easthampton:** town on Long Island.   14 **Verlaine:** French poet (1844–1896).   15 **Bonnard:** French painter (1867–1947).   16 **Hesiod:** Roman poet.   17 **Brendan Behan:** Irish playwright.   18 **Genet:** Jean Genet, modern French dramatist.   21 **Strega:** an Italian liquor.   24–25 **Gauloises . . . Picayunes:** cigarettes.   25 **her:** Billie Holiday ("Lady"), who died in 1959.   29 **Mal Waldron:** Billie Holiday's pianist.

1. Have you ever tried to hide from yourself the fact that something dreadful has just happened to you? Or that some public catastrophe has just occurred? Respond to the poem in those terms.
2. What is the effect on you of all the details mentioned—details of New York streets, plays, personal events? Do they fill out the scene or convey a mood?
3. Do your personal feelings about and experiences of cities help you relate to the mood of the poem?

ADRIENNE RICH (b. 1929)

Living in Sin

She had thought the studio would keep itself;
no dust upon the furniture of love.
Half heresy, to wish the taps less vocal,
the panes relieved of grime. A plate of pears,
a piano with a Persian shawl, a cat   5
stalking the picturesque amusing mouse
had risen at his urging.
Not that at five each separate stair would writhe
under the milkman's tramp; that morning light
so coldly would delineate the scraps   10
of last night's cheese and three sepulchral bottles;
that on the kitchen shelf among the saucers
a pair of beetle-eyes would fix her own—
envoy from some village in the moldings . . .
Meanwhile, he, with a yawn,   15
sounded a dozen notes upon the keyboard,
declared it out of tune, shrugged at the mirror,
rubbed at his beard, went out for cigarettes;
while she, jeered by the minor demons,
pulled back the sheets and made the bed and found   20
a towel to dust the table-top,
and let the coffee-pot boil over on the stove.
By evening she was back in love again,
though not so wholly but throughout the night
she woke sometimes to feel the daylight coming   25
like a relentless milkman up the stairs.

Response Statement Assignments

1. Many of the details in this poem can be read either literally or metaphorically. Explain why you chose to adopt either a literal or a figurative reading. You might consult the discussion of metaphor (pp. 383).

2. Adrienne Rich has often supported radical feminist positions. Do you think you should adopt a different attitude or develop different reading strategies because you know this?
3. What parts of contemporary life do you find especially relevant to your reading of this poem?
4. How does your own position on feminism influence your response to the poem?

MARGARET ATWOOD (b. 1939)

This Is a Photograph of Me

It was taken some time ago.
At first it seems to be
a smeared
print: blurred lines and gray flecks
blended with the paper;   5

then, as you scan
it, you see in the left-hand corner
a thing that is like a branch: part of a tree
(balsam or spruce) emerging
and, to the right, halfway up   10
what ought to be a gentle
slope, a small frame house.

In the background there is a lake,
and beyond that, some low hills.
(The photograph was taken   15
the day after I drowned.

I am in the lake, in the center
of the picture, just under the surface.

It is difficult to say where
precisely, or to say   20
how large or small I am:
the effect of water
on light is a distortion

but if you look long enough,
eventually   25
you will be able to see me.)

Response Statement Assignments

1. Reading is a process of discovery. At what particular points in your reading of this poem did you find yourself making important discoveries that eventually produced your reading?

2. Many readers of this poem find that it offers some moral or philosophical insights. Do you agree? What parts of your own **general repertoire** are relevant to your interpretation?

ROBERT HASS (b. 1941)

Meditation at Lagunitas

All the new thinking is about loss.
In this it resembles all the old thinking.
The idea, for example, that each particular erases
the luminous clarity of a general idea. That the clown-
faced woodpecker probing the dead sculpted trunk   5
of that black birch is, by his presence,
some tragic falling off from a first world
of undivided light. Or the other notion that,
because there is in this world no one thing
to which the bramble of *blackberry* corresponds,   10
a word is elegy to what it signifies.
We talked about it late last night and in the voice
of my friend, there was a thin wire of grief, a tone
almost querulous. After a while I understood that,
talking this way, everything dissolves: *justice,*   15
pine, hair, woman, you and *I.* There was a woman
I made love to and I remembered how, holding
her small shoulders in my hands sometimes,
I felt a violent wonder at her presence
like a thirst for salt, for my childhood river   20
with its island willows, silly music from the pleasure boat,
muddy places where we caught the little orange-silver fish
called *pumpkinseed.* It hardly had to do with her.
Longing, we say, because desire is full
of endless distances. I must have been the same to her.   25
But I remember so much, the way her hands dismantled bread,
the thing her father said that hurt her, what
she dreamed. There are moments when the body is as numinous
as words, days that are the good flesh continuing.
Such tenderness, those afternoons and evenings,   30
saying *blackberry, blackberry, blackberry.*

Response Statement Assignments

1. This poem mixes very concrete details with some quite abstract philosophizing. Read the poem carefully. What philosophical issues does it raise and how do they relate to the concrete details? Do you find it easier to respond to the concrete details or the abstract ideas?

2. What in your own **general repertoire** helps you respond to the poem's ideas? Does the poem raise questions that affect your life?
3. Language is one important issue raised in the poem. Do you ever feel frustrated at language's inability to say exactly what you want it to say—especially at moments of high emotion? Or as the poem puts it, do you ever feel "a word is elegy to what it signifies"? Can you account for this frustration in terms of social—and not just individual—factors?

GERALD COSTANZO (b. 1946)

Dinosaurs of the Hollywood Delta

Joe DiMaggio, who was married for three years to
Marilyn Monroe, has ended a 20-year standing order
for thrice-weekly delivery of roses to her crypt.
The florist said Mr. DiMaggio gave no explanation.
                    —New York Times, Sept. 30, 1982

In times of plenty
they arrived from everywhere
to forage among the palmettos
of Beverly and Vine, to roam
the soda fountains and dime stores   5
of paradise. For every Miss Tupelo

who got a break, whose blonde
tresses made it to the silver screen,
whose studio sent her on a whirlwind
tour to Chicago, and to the Roxy   10
in Manhattan where she'd chat
with an audience, do a little tap

dance, and answer questions
about the morality of the jitterbug,
thousands became extinct.   15
Their beauty, it was said, drove
men to wallow in dark
booths in the Florentine

Lounge dreaming of voluptuous
vanilla, though the rumor persists   20
that they were dumb.
They were called *Jean, Rita, Jayne,*
Mae, and *Betty.* The easy names.
No one remembers now
how the waning of their kind   25
began. Theories have pointed
to our own growing sophistication—

as if that were a part of natural
selection. At first we missed
them little, and only in that detached 　　　　　　　　30

manner one laments the passing
of any passing thing. Then posters
began to appear. Whole boutiques
adoring their fashion: heavy rouge,
thick lipstick. The sensuous puckering 　　　　　35
of lips. Surreptitious giggling.

We began to congregate on street corners
at night, Santa Monica and La Brea,
to erect searchlights
and marquees announcing premieres 　　　　　40
for which there were no shows.
We looked upward,

as if what had been taken from us
were somehow etched in starlight above
their sacred city. We began 　　　　　　　　45
to chant, demanding their return—
to learn, for once, the meaning
of their desperate, flagrant love.

Response Statement Assignments

1. What parts of contemporary American life that you know well are relevant to your reading of this poem? From your own experience, do you
think the poem gives a fair interpretation of them?
2. The "myth" of Hollywood is clearly relevant to the reading of this poem.
What are your own views of Hollywood?
3. What parts of your repertoire lead you to react negatively and positively
to Hollywood? How do they affect your reading of the poem?

JIM DANIELS (b. 1956)

At the Poetry Reading: "This Is a Poem about That"

This will be my *last* poem tonight.
I want to share this experience with you.
When I read this poem, many people wonder
if this is a true story. Well,
it's true. This really happened. 　　　　　　　　5
This is dedicated to someone in this room.
Is this mike on?
There's a couple words in this poem you may not know:

formication: a spontaneous abnormal sensation of ants
or other insects running over the skin.   10
fubsy: somewhat fat and squat.
When I was at Iowa.
The 'I' in this poem isn't me.
The 'you' in this poem isn't me.
The you in this poem isn't the same you   15
as in the other poems.
At my last reading.
This is about a place I used to live
and people I used to know:
you don't know them.   20
My agent told me.
At dinner before the reading.
For this poem, I'll play my dulcimer
one octave lower.
I mailed this to my ex-wife   25
but got no response.
This is a light poem.
There is a famous unnamed writer in this poem.
When I was at Breadloaf.
Or was it Provincetown.   30
This is a long poem.
It's divided into sections.
When I run my hand through my hair
it's a new section.
We're negotiating movie rights.   35
I wrote this when I was depressed.
Please applaud.
Would you like to hear more?

Response Statement Assignments

1. Have you ever been to a public poetry reading? Do you remember poets
   introducing their poems in similar ways?
2. Add three or four more lines to the poem. Do you get the sense it could
   go on forever?
3. What do you think makes this text a poem? What prior expectations
   (from your **literary repertoire**) about reading a poem inform your response?
4. Do you find its informality and humor attractive?

Anthology of Poetry

ANONYMOUS (Anglo-Saxon, 8th Century)

The Seafarer

(Modern version by Ezra Pound)

May I for my own self song's truth reckon,
Journey's jargon, how I in harsh days
Hardship endured oft.
Bitter breast-cares have I abided,
Known on my keel many a care's hold,   5
And dire sea-surge, and there I oft spent
Narrow nightwatch nigh the ship's head
While she tossed close to cliffs. Coldly afflicted,
My feet were by frost benumbed.
Chill its chains are; chafing signs   10
Hew my heart round and hunger begot.
Mere-weary° mood. Lest man know not
That he on dry land loveliest liveth,
List how I, care-wretched, on ice-cold sea,
Weathered the winter, wretched outcast   15
Deprived of my kinsmen;
Hung with hard ice-flakes, where hail-scur flew,
There I heard naught save the harsh sea
And ice-cold wave, at whiles the swan cries,
Did for my games the gannet's clamor,   20
Sea-fowls' loudness was for me laughter,
The mews' singing all my mead-drink.

12 **Mere-weary:** weary of the sea.

Storms, on the stone-cliffs beaten, fell on the stern
In icy feathers; full oft the eagle screamed
With spray on his pinion.   25
                              Not any protector
May make merry man faring needy.
This he little believes, who aye in winsome life
Abides 'mid burghers some heavy business,
Wealthy and wine-flushed, how I weary oft
Must bide above brine.   30
Neareth nightshade, snoweth from north,
Frost froze the land, hail fell on earth then,
Corn of the coldest. Nathless there knocketh now
The heart's thought that I on high streams
The salt-wavy tumult traverse alone.   35
Moaneth alway my mind's lust
That I fare forth, that I afar hence
Seek out a foreign fastness.
For this there's no mood-lofty man over earth's midst,
Not though he be given his good, but will have in his youth greed;   40
Nor his deed to the daring, nor his king to the faithful
But shall have his sorrow for sea-fare
Whatever his lord will.
He hath not heart for harping, nor in ring-having
Nor winsomeness to wife, nor world's delight   45
Nor any whit else save the wave's slash,
Yet longing comes upon him to fare forth on the water.
Bosque taketh blossom, cometh beauty of berries,
Fields to fairness, land fares brisker,
All this admonisheth man eager of mood,   50
The heart turns to travel so that he then thinks
On flood-ways to be far departing.
Cuckoo calleth with gloomy crying,
He singeth summerward, bodeth sorrow,
The bitter heart's blood. Burgher knows not—   55
He the prosperous man—what some perform
Where wandering them widest draweth.
So that but now my heart burst from my breastlock,
My mood 'mid the mere-flood,
Over the whale's acre, would wander wide.   60
On earth's shelter cometh oft to me,
Eager and ready, the crying lone-flyer,
Whets for the whale-path the heart irresistibly,
O'er tracks of ocean; seeing that anyhow
My lord deems to me this dead life   65
On loan and on land, I believe not
That any earth-weal° eternal standeth
Save there be somewhat calamitous
That, ere a man's tide go, turn it to twain.

67 **earth-weal:** earthly society.

Disease or oldness or sword-hate   70
Beats out the breath from doom-gripped body.
And for this, every earl whatever, for those speaking after—
Laud of the living, boasteth some last word,
That he will work ere he pass onward,
Frame on the fair earth 'gainst foes his malice,   75
Daring ado, . . .
So that all men shall honor him after
And his laud beyond them remain 'mid the English,
Aye, for ever, a lasting life's-blast,
Delight 'mid the doughty.   80
                         Days little durable,
And all arrogance of earthen riches,
There come now no kings nor Caesars
Nor gold-giving lords like those gone.
Howe'er in mirth most magnified,
Whoe'er lived in life most lordliest,   85
Drear all this excellence, delights undurable!
Waneth the watch, but the world holdeth.
Tomb hideth trouble. The blade is layed low.
Earthly glory ageth and seareth.
No man at all going the earth's gait.   90
But age fares against him, his face paleth,
Grey-haired he groaneth, knows gone companions,
Lordly men, are to earth o'ergiven,
Nor may he then the flesh-cover, whose life ceaseth,
Nor eat the sweet nor feel the sorry,   95
Nor stir hand nor think in mid heart,
And though he strew the grave with gold,
His born brothers, their buried bodies
Be an unlikely treasure hoard.

ANONYMOUS ENGLISH LYRIC (13th–15th Centuries)

The Three Ravens

There were three ravens sat on a tree,
  Downe a downe, hay down, hay downe
There were three ravens sat on a tree,
  With a downe
There were three ravens sat on a tree,   5
They were as black as they might be,
  With a downe derrie, derrie, derrie, downe, downe.

The one of them said to his mate,
"Where shall we our breakfast take?"

"Down in yonder greene field,   10
There lies a knight slain under his shield.

"His hounds they lie downe at his feete,
So well they can their master keepe.

"His haukes they flie so eagerly,
There's no fowle dare him come nie."   15

Downe there comes a fallow doe,
As great with yong as she might goe.
She lift up his bloudy hed,
And kist his wounds that were so red.

She got him up upon her backe,   20
And carried him to earthen lake.

She buried him before the prime,
She was dead herselfe ere even-song time.

God send every gentleman
Such haukes, such hounds, and such a leman.°   25

25 **leman**: lover.

ANONYMOUS MEDIEVAL ENGLISH LYRIC (15th Century)

I Sing of a Maiden

I sing of a maiden
 That is makeless:°
King of alle kinges
 To her son she ches.°

He came also° stille   5
 Where his mother was
As dew in Aprille
 That falleth on the grass.

He came also stille
 To his mother's bower   10
As dew in Aprille
 That falleth on the flower.

He came also stille
 Where his mother lay
As dew in Aprille   15
 That falleth on the spray.

Mother and maiden
 Was never none but she—
Well may such a lady
 Godes mother be.   20

2 **makeless**: matchless, without a mate. 4 **ches**: chose. 5 **also**: just as.

ANONYMOUS ENGLISH LYRIC (15th Century)

I Have a Gentle Cock

I have a gentle° cock,
   Croweth me day;
He doth me risen° early
   My matins° for to say.

I have a gentle cock,
   Comen he is of great;°
His comb is of red coral,
   His tail is of jet.

I have a gentle cock,
   Comen he is of kind;°
His comb is of red coral,
   His tail is of inde.°

His legges be of azure,
   So gentle and so small;
His spurres are of silver white
   Into the wortewale.°

His eyen are of crystal,
   Locked° all in amber;
And every night he percheth him
   In my lady's chamber.

5

10

15

20

1 **gentle:** noble.   3 **me risen:** makes me rise.   4 **matins:** morning prayer.   6 **of great:** from great ancestry.   10 **kind:** good stock.   12 **inde:** indigo.   16 **Into the wortewale:** up to the root.   18 **Locked:** set.

ANONYMOUS ENGLISH LYRIC (15th Century)

Western Wind

Western wind, when will thou blow,
   The small rain down can rain?
Christ, if my love were in my arms
   And I in my bed again!

ANONYMOUS ENGLISH LYRIC (15th Century)

Adam Lay Ibounden

Adam lay ibounden,°
Bounden in a bond:
Foure thousand winter

1 **ibounden:** bound.

Thought he not too long.
And all was for an apple, 5
And apple that he tok,
As clerkes° finden
Wreten in here book.

Ne hadde the apple take ben,
The apple taken ben, 10
Ne hadde never our Lady
A ben Hevene Quen.
Blissed be the time
That apple take was!
Therfore we moun singen, 15
'Deo gracias!'°

7 **clerkes:** learned men.   15 **moun:** may   16 **Deo gracias:** God be praised.

THOMAS WYATT (1503–1542)

Whoso List To Hunt

Whoso list° to hunt, I know where is an hind,
   But as for me, alas, I may no more;
   The vain travail hath wearied me so sore,
   I am of them that furthest come behind.
Yet may I by no means my wearied mind 5
   Draw from the deer, but as she fleeth afore
   Fainting I follow; I leave off therefore,
   Since in a net I seek to hold the wind.
Who list° her hunt, I put him out of doubt,
   As well as I, may spend his time in vain. 10
   And graven with diamonds in letters plain,
There is written her fair neck round about,
   "Noli me tangere,° for Caesar's I am,
   And wild for to hold, though I seem tame."

1, 9 **list:** wants.   13 ***Noli me tangere:*** do not touch me.

SIR WALTER RALEIGH (1552–1618)

The Nymph's Reply to the Shepherd

If all the world and love were young,
And truth in every shepherd's tongue,
Those pretty pleasures might me move
To live with thee and be thy love.

Time drives the flocks from field to fold, 5
When rivers rage, and rocks grow cold,

And Philomel° becometh dumb;
The rest complain of cares to come.

The flowers do fade, and wanton fields
To wayward winter reckoning yields: 10
A honey tongue, a heart of gall,
Is fancy's spring, but sorrow's fall.

Thy gowns, thy shoes, thy beds of roses,
Thy cap, thy kirtle,° and thy posies
Soon break, soon wither, soon forgotten;   15
In folly ripe, in reason rotten.

Thy belt of straw and ivy buds,
Thy coral clasps and amber studs,
All these in me no means can move
To come to thee and be thy love.   20

But could youth last, and love still breed,
Had joys no date, nor age no need,
Then these delights my mind might move
To live with thee and be thy love.

7 **Philomel:** mythological name for the nightingale.   14 **kirtle:** skirt.

As You Came from the Holy Land

As you came from the holy land,
    Of Walsingham,
Met you not with my true love
    By the way as you came?

How shall I know your true love   5
    That have met many one
As I went to the holy land
    That have come, that have gone?

She is neither white nor brown
    But as the heavens fair,   10
There is none hath a form so divine
    In the earth or the air.

Such an one did I meet, good sir,
    Such an angel-like face,
Who like a queen, like a nymph, did appear   15
    By her gait, by her grace.

She hath left me here all alone,
    All alone, as unknown,
Who sometime did me lead with herself,
    And me loved as her own.   20

What's the cause that she leaves you alone,
  And a new way doth take;
Who loved you once as her own
  And her joy did you make?

I have loved her all my youth,   25
  But now old, as you see,
Love likes not the falling fruit
  From the withered tree.

Know that love is a careless child
  And forgets promise past,   30
He is blind, he is deaf when he list
  And in faith never fast.

His desire is a dureless content
  And a trustless joy,
He is won with a world of despair   35
  And is lost with a toy.

Of womenkind such indeed is the love
  Or the word Love abused,
Under which many childish desires
  And conceits are excused.   40

But true Love is a durable fire
  In the mind ever burning;
Never sick, never old, never dead,
  From its self never turning.

Nature, That Washed Her Hands in Milk

Nature, that washed her hands in milk,
And had forgot to dry them,
Instead of earth took snow and silk,
At love's request to try them,
If she a mistress could compose   5
To please love's fancy out of those.

Her eyes he would should be of light,
A violet breath, and lips of jelly;
Her hair not black, nor overbright,
And of the softest down her belly;   10
As for her inside he'd have it
Only of wantonness and wit.

At love's entreaty such a one
Nature made, but with her beauty
She hath framed a heart of stone;   15
So as love, by ill destiny,
Must die for her whom nature gave him,
Because her darling would not save him.

But time (which nature doth despise,
And rudely gives her love the lie,   20
Makes hope a fool, and sorrow wise)
His hands do neither wash nor dry;
But being made of steel and rust,
Turns snow and silk and milk to dust.

The light, the belly, lips, and breath,   25
He dims, discolors, and destroys;
With those he feeds but fills not death,
Which sometimes were the food of joys.
Yea, time doth dull each lively wit,
And dries all wantonness with it.   30

Oh, cruel time! which takes in trust
Our youth, our joys, and all we have,
And pays us but with age and dust;
Who in the dark and silent grave
When we have wandered all our ways   35
Shuts up the story of our days.

[And from which earth and grave and dust
The Lord shall raise me up, I trust.]°

37–38 Lines added approximately 25 years after the poem was written, probably on the night
before the poet was executed.

SIR PHILIP SIDNEY (1554–1586)

From *Astrophil and Stella*
Sonnet 1

Loving in truth, and fain° in verse my love to show,
That the dear she might take some pleasure of my pain,
Pleasure might cause her read, reading might make her know,
Knowledge might pity win, and pity grace obtain,
I sought fit words to paint the blackest face of woe: 5
Studying inventions fine, her wits to entertain,
Oft turning others' leaves, to see if thence would flow
Some fresh and fruitful showers upon my sunburned brain.
But words came halting forth, wanting Invention's stay;
Invention, Nature's child, fled stepdame Study's blows;   10
And others' feet still seemed but strangers in my way.
Thus, great with child to speak, and helpless in my throes,
Biting my truant pen, beating myself for spite:
"Fool," said my Muse to me, "look in thy heart, and write."

1 **fain:** eager.

Sonnet 31

With how sad steps, Oh Moon, thou climb'st the skies,
How silently, and with how wan a face!
What, may it be that even in heav'nly place
That busy archer° his sharp arrows tries?
Sure, if that long-with-love-acquainted eyes   5
Can judge of love, thou feel'st a lover's case;
I read it in thy looks: thy languished grace,
To me that feel the like, thy state descries.
Then even of fellowship, Oh Moon, tell me,
Is constant love deemed there but want of wit?   10
Are beauties there as proud as here they be?
Do they above love to be loved, and yet
Those lovers scorn whom that love doth possess?
Do they call virtue there ungratefulness?

4 **That busy archer:** Cupid, god of love.

Sonnet 33

I might (unhappy word), O me, I might,
And then would not, or could not, see my bliss:
Till now, wrapped in a most infernal night,
I find how heavenly day, wretch, I did miss.
    Heart, rend thyself, thou dost thyself but right;   5
No lovely Paris made thy Helen° his;
No force, no fraud, robbed thee of thy delight;
Nor Fortune of thy fortune author is;
    But to myself myself did give the blow,
While too much wit (forsooth) so troubled me   10
That I respects for both our sakes must show:
And yet could not by rising morn foresee
    How fair a day was near. O punished eyes,
    That I had been more foolish, or more wise!

6 **Paris . . . Helen:** famous classical Greek lovers.

Sonnet 45

Stella oft sees the very face of woe
    Painted in my beclouded stormy face;
    But cannot skill to pity my disgrace,
Not though thereof the cause herself she know;
Yet hearing late a fable, which did show   5
    Of lovers never known a grievous case,

Pity thereof gat in her breast such place
That, from that sea derived, tears' springs did flow.
   Alas, if fancy drawn by imaged things,
Though false, yet with free scope more grace doth breed   10
Than servant's wrack, where new doubts honour brings;
Then think, my dear, that you in me do read
   Of lover's ruin some sad tragedy:
   I am not I, pity the tale of me.

Sonnet 71

Who will in fairest book of nature know
   How virtue may best lodged in beauty be,
   Let him but learn of love to read in thee,
Stella, those fair lines which true goodness show.
There shall he find all vices' overthrow,   5
   Not by rude force, but sweetest sovereignty
   Of reason, from whose light those night-birds fly,
That inward sun in thine eyes shineth so.
   And not content to be perfection's heir
Thy self, dost strive all minds that way to move,   10
Who mark in thee what is in thee most fair;
So while thy beauty draws the heart to love,
   As fast thy virtue bends that love to good.
   But ah, desire still cries: 'Give me some food.'

MICHAEL DRAYTON (1563–1631)

From *Idea*
Sonnet 7

Since there's no help, come, let us kiss and part.
Nay, I have done, you get no more of me,
And I am glad, yea glad with all my heart
That thus so cleanly I myself can free;
Shake hands forever, cancel all our vows,   5
And when we meet at any time again
Be it not seen in either of our brows
That we one jot of former love retain.
Now at the last gasp of Love's latest breath,
When, his pulse failing, Passion speechless lies,   10
When Faith is kneeling by his bed of death
And Innocence is closing up his eyes,
   Now if thou would'st, when all have given him over,
   From death to life thou might'st him yet recover.

CHRISTOPHER MARLOWE (1564–1593)

The Passionate Shepherd to His Love

Come live with me and be my love,
And we will all the pleasures prove
That valleys, groves, hills, and fields,
Woods, or steepy mountain yields.

And we will sit upon the rocks,   5
Seeing the shepherds feed their flocks,
By shallow rivers to whose falls
Melodious birds sing madrigals.°

And I will make thee beds of roses
And a thousand fragrant posies,   10
A cap of flowers, and a kirtle°
Embroidered all with leaves of myrtle;

A gown made of the finest wool
Which from our pretty lambs we pull;
Fair lined slippers for the cold,   15
With buckles of the purest gold;

A belt of straw and ivy buds,
With coral clasps and amber studs:
And if these pleasures may thee move,
Come live with me, and be my love.   20

The shepherd swains shall dance and sing
For thy delight each May morning:
If these delights thy mind may move,
Then live with me and be my love.

8 **madrigals:** five- or six-part songs.   11 **kirtle:** skirt.

FULKE GREVILLE, LORD BROOKE (1564–1626)

Caelica, 45

Absence, the noble truce
Of Cupid's war:
Where though desires want use,
They honour'd are.
Thou art the just protection,   5
Of prodigal affection,
Have thou the praise;

When bankrupt Cupid braveth,°
Thy mines his credit saveth,
With sweet delays.   10

Of wounds which presence makes
With beauty's shot,
Absence the anguish slakes,
But healeth not:
Absence records the stories,   15
Wherein Desire glories,
Although she burn;
She cherisheth the spirits
Where Constancy inherits
And passions mourn.   20

Absence, like dainty clouds,
On glorious bright,
Nature weak senses shrouds,
From harming light.
Absence maintains the treasure   25
Of pleasure unto pleasure,
Sparing with praise;
Absence doth nurse the fire,
Which starves and feeds desire
With sweet delays.   30

Presence to every part
Of beauty ties,
Where wonder rules the heart
There pleasure dies:
Presence plagues mind and senses   35
With modesty's defences,
Absence is free:
Thoughts do in absence venter
On Cupid's shadowed centre,
They wink and see.   40

But thoughts be not so brave,
With absent joy;
For you with that you have
Yourself destroy:
The absence which you glory,   45
Is that which makes you sorry,
And burn in vain:
For thought is not the weapon,
Wherewith thought's ease men cheapen,
Absence is pain.   50

8 **braveth**: boasts.

MARY SIDNEY, COUNTESS OF PEMBROKE (1566–1620)

Psalm 51

O Lord, whose grace no limits comprehend;
  Sweet Lord, whose mercies stand from measure free;
To mee that grace, to mee that mercie send,
    And wipe O Lord, my sinnes from sinfull mee
    O clense, O wash my foule iniquitie: 5
Clense still my spotts, still wash awaie my staynings,
Till staines and spotts in me leave no remaynings.

For I, alas, acknowledging doe know
  My filthie fault, my faultie filthiness
To my soules eye uncessantly doth show.   10
    Which done to thee, to thee I doe confesse,
    Just judge, true witness; that for righteousness,
Thy doome may passe against my guilt awarded,
Thy evidence for truth maie be regarded.

My mother, loe! when I began to be,   15
  Conceaving me, with me did sinne conceave:
And as with living heate she cherisht me,
    Corruption did like cherishing receave
    But loe, thy love to purest good doth cleave,
And inward truth which hardlie els discerned,   20
My trewand soule in thy hid schoole hath learned.

Then as thy self to leapers hast assign'd,
  With hisop, Lord, thy Hisop,° purge me soe:
And that shall clense the leaprie° of my mind;
Make over me thy mercies streames to flow,   25
Soe shall my whiteness scorn the whitest snow.
To eare and hart send soundes and thoughts of gladness,
That brused bones maie daunce awaie their sadness.

Thy ill-pleas'd eye from my misdeedes avert:
  Cancell the registers my sinns containe: 30
Create in me a pure, cleane, spottless hart:
    Inspire a sprite where love of right maie raigne.
    Ah! cast me not from thee: take not againe
Thy breathing grace! againe thy comfort send me,
And let the guard of thy free sp'rite attend me.   35

Soe I to them a guiding hand wilbe,
  Whose faultie feete have wandred from thy way:
And turn'd from sinne will make retorne to thee,
    Whom, turn'd from thee, sinne erst had ledd astraie.
    O God, God of my health, O doe away   40
My bloody crime: soe shall my tongue be raised
To praise thy truth, enough can not be praised.

23 **hisop:** a medicinal and purifying herb.   24 **leaprie:** leprosy.

Unlock my lipps, shut up with sinnfull shame:
   Then shall my mouth, O Lord, thy honor sing;
For bleeding fuell for thy alters flame,   45
    To gaine thy grace what bootes it me to bring?
    Burnt-offrings are to thee no pleasant thing.
The sacrifice that God will holde respected,
Is the heart-broken soule, the sprite dejected.

Lastly, O Lord, how soe I stand or fall,   50
   Leave not thy loved Sion° to embrace:
But with thy favour build up Salems° wall,
    And still in peace, maintaine that peacefull place.
    Then shalt thou turne a well-accepting face
To sacred fires with offred giftes perfumed: 55
Till ev'n whole calves on alters be consumed.

51 **Sion:** Jerusalem, the Heavenly City.   52 **Salems:** Jerusalem.

WILLIAM SHAKESPEARE (1564–1616)

Sonnet 29

When, in disgrace with fortune and men's eyes,
I all alone beweep my outcast state
And trouble deaf heaven with my bootless° cries
And look upon myself and curse my fate,
Wishing me like to one more rich in hope,   5
Featured like him, like him with friends possess'd,
Desiring this man's art and that man's scope,°
With what I most enjoy contented least;
Yet in these thoughts myself almost despising
Haply I think on thee, and then my state,   10
Like to the lark at break of day arising
From sullen earth, sings hymns at heaven's gate;
   For thy sweet love remember'd such wealth brings
   That then I scorn to change my state with kings.

3 **bootless:** helpless.   7 **scope:** opportunities.

Sonnet 30

When to the sessions° of sweet silent thought
I summon up remembrance of things past,
I sigh the lack of many a thing I sought,
And with old woes new wail my dear time's waste:
Then can I drown an eye, unused to flow,   5

1 **sessions:** formal (usually legal) meetings.

For precious friends hid in death's dateless° night,
And weep afresh love's long since canceled woe,
And moan the expense° of many a vanished sight:
Then can I grieve at grievances foregone,
And heavily from woe to woe tell o'er   10
The sad account of fore-bemoanéd moan,
Which I new pay as if not paid before.
But if the while I think on thee, dear friend,
All losses are restored and sorrows end.

6 **dateless:** endless.   8 **expense:** loss.

Sonnet 60

Like as the waves make towards the pebbled shore,
So do our minutes hasten to their end,
Each changing place with that which goes before,
In sequent toil all forwards do contend.
Nativity, once in the main of light,   5
Crawls to maturity, wherewith being crowned,
Crooked° eclipses 'gainst his glory fight,
And time that gave doth now his gift confound.
Time doth transfix the flourish set on youth,
And delves the parallels in beauty's brow,   10
Feeds on the rarities of nature's truth,
And nothing stands but for his scythe to mow.
    And yet to times in hope my verse shall stand,
    Praising thy worth, despite his cruel hand.

7 **crooked:** malevolent.

Sonnet 64

When I have seen by time's fell° hand defaced
The rich proud cost of outworn buried age;
When sometime° lofty towers I see down-razed,
And brass eternal slave to mortal rage;
When I have seen the hungry ocean gain   5
Advantage on the kingdom of the shore,
And the firm soil win of the watery main,°
Increasing store with loss, and loss with store;
When I have seen such interchange of state,
Or state itself confounded to decay,   10
Ruin hath taught me thus to ruminate,

1 **fell:** destructive.   3 **sometime:** formerly.   7 **main:** the high sea.

That time will come and take my love away.
This thought is as a death, which cannot choose
But weep to have that which it fears to lose.

Sonnet 65

Since brass, nor stone, nor earth, nor boundless sea
But sad mortality o'er-sways their power,
How with this rage shall beauty hold a plea,
Whose action is no stronger than a flower?
O, how shall summer's honey breath hold out   5
Against the wreckful siege of battering days,
When rocks impregnable are not so stout,
Nor gates of steel so strong, but Time decays?
O fearful meditation! where, alack,
Shall Time's best jewel from Time's chest lie hid?   10
Or what strong hand can hold his swift foot back?
Or who his spoil of beauty can forbid?
O, none, unless this miracle have might,
That in black ink my love may still shine bright.

Sonnet 73

That time of year thou mayst in me behold
When yellow leaves, or none, or few, do hang
Upon those boughs which shake against the cold,
Bare ruined choirs, where late the sweet birds sang.
In me thou see'st the twilight of such day   5
As after sunset fadeth in the west;
Which by and by black night doth take away,
Death's second self, that seals up all in rest.
In me thou see'st the glowing of such fire,
That on the ashes of his youth doth lie,   10
As the deathbed whereon it must expire,
Consumed with that which it was nourished by.
This thou perceiv'st, which makes thy love more strong,
To love that well which thou must leave ere long.

Sonnet 116

Let me not to the marriage of true minds
Admit impediments. Love is not love
Which alters when it alteration finds,
Or bends with the remover to remove:
Oh, no! it is an ever-fixéd mark,   5

That looks on tempests and is never shaken;
It is the star to every wandering bark,
Whose worth's unknown, although his height be taken.°
Love's not Time's fool, though rosy lips and cheeks
Within his bending sickle's compass come;   10
Love alters not with his brief hours and weeks.
But bears it out even to the edge of doom.°
If this be error and upon me proved,
I never writ, nor no man ever loved.

8 **taken:** calculated.   12 **doom:** the end of the world.

Sonnet 129

Th' expense of spirit in a waste of shame
Is lust in action; and till action, lust
Is perjured, murderous, bloody, full of blame,
Savage, extreme, rude, cruel, not to trust;
Enjoyed no sooner but despiséd straight: 5
Past reason hunted; and no sooner had,
Past reason hated, as a swallowed bait,
On purpose laid to make the taker mad:
Mad in pursuit, and in possession so;
Had, having, and in quest to have, extreme;   10
A bliss in proof, and proved, a very woe;
Before, a joy proposed; behind, a dream.
All this the world well knows; yet none knows well
To shun the heaven that leads men to this hell.

Sonnet 130

My mistress' eyes are nothing like the sun;
Coral is far more red than her lips' red;
If snow be white, why then her breasts are dun;
If hairs be wires, black wires grow on her head.
I have seen roses damasked,° red and white,   5
But no such roses see I in her cheeks;
And in some perfumes is there more delight
Than in the breath that from my mistress reeks.
I love to hear her speak, yet well I know
That music hath a far more pleasing sound;   10
I grant I never saw a goddess go;
My mistress, when she walks, treads on the ground.
And yet, by heaven, I think my love as rare
As any she belied with false compare.

5 **damasked:** dappled.

THOMAS CAMPION (1567–1619)

There Is a Garden in Her Face

There is a garden in her face,
Where roses and white lilies grow,
A heavenly paradise is that place,
Wherein all pleasant fruits do flow.
There cherries grow, which none may buy   5
Till "Cherry ripe!"° themselves do cry.

Those cherries fairly do enclose
Of orient pearl a double row,
Which when her lovely laughter shows,
They look like rosebuds filled with snow.   10
Yet them nor peer nor prince can buy,
Till "Cherry ripe!" themselves do cry.

Her eyes like angels watch them still;
Her brows like bended bows do stand,
Threatening with piercing frowns to kill   15
All that attempt with eye or hand
Those sacred cherries to come nigh,
Till "Cherry ripe!" themselves do cry.

6, 12, 18 **"Cherry ripe!":** cry of street fruit seller.

MARY SIDNEY, LADY WROTH (1586–1640)

Lindamira's Complaint

Leave me vaine Hope, too long thou hast possest
  My mind, made subject to thy flattring skill,
While Aprill mornings did my pleasures fill,
But cloudy dayes soone changd me from that rest;

And weeping afternoones to me adrest,   5
  My utter ruine framd by Fortunes will,
  When knowledge said Hope did but breed, and kill,
  Producing only shadowes at the best.

Yet Hope tis true, thy faults did faire appeare
  And therefore loth to thinke thou counseldst me   10
  Or wilfully thy errors would not see
  But catch at Sunne moates which I held most deare

Till now alas with true felt losse I know,
  Thy selfe a Bubble each faire face can blow.

12 **moates:** faults, weaknesses.

JOHN DONNE (1572–1631)

Song

Go and catch a falling star,
 Get with child a mandrake° root,
Tell me where all past years are,
 Or who cleft the Devil's foot,
Teach me to hear mermaids singing,   5
Or to keep off envy's stinging,
    And find
    What wind
Serves to advance an honest mind.

If thou beest born to strange sights,   10
 Things invisible to see,
Ride ten thousand days and nights,
 Till age snow white hairs on thee.
Thou, when thou return'st, wilt tell me
All strange wonders that befell thee,   15
    And swear
    Nowhere
Lives a woman true, and fair.

If thou find'st one, let me know,
 Such a pilgrimage were sweet;   20
Yet do not, I would not go,
 Though at next door we might meet;
Though she were true when you met her,
And last till you write your letter,
    Yet she   25
    Will be
False, ere I come, to two, or three.

2 **mandrake root:** root of the Mandragora plant, believed to be infertile.

Woman's Constancy

Now thou hast loved me one whole day,
Tomorrow when thou leav'st, what wilt thou say?
Wilt thou then antedate some new-made vow?
    Or say that now
We are not just those persons which we were?   5
Or, that oaths made in reverential fear
Of love, and his wrath, any may forswear°?
Or, as true deaths true marriages untie,

7 **forswear:** break (promises).

So lovers' contracts, images of those,
Bind but till sleep, death's image, them unloose?
 Or, your own end to justify,
For having purposed change, and falsehood, you
Can have no way but falsehood to be true?
Vain lunatic, against these 'scapes° I could
 Dispute, and conquer, if I would,
 Which I abstain to do,
For by tomorrow, I may think so too.

10

15

14 **scapes:** witty arguments.

The Sun Rising

 Busy old fool, unruly sun,
 Why dost thou thus,
Through windows and through curtains call on us?
Must to thy motions lovers' seasons run?
 Saucy pedantic wretch, go chide
 Late school boys and sour prentices,°
 Go tell court huntsmen that the king will ride,
 Call country ants to harvest offices;
Love, all alike, no season knows nor clime,
Nor hours, days, months, which are the rags of time.

 Thy beams, so reverend and strong
 Why shouldst thou think?
I could eclipse and cloud them with a wink,
But that I would not lose her sight so long;
 If her eyes have not blinded thine,
 Look, and tomorrow late tell me,
 Whether both th' Indias° of spice and mine
 Be where thou leftst them, or lie here with me.
Ask for those kings whom thou saw'st yesterday,
And thou shalt hear, All here in one bed lay.

 She's all states, and all princes, I,
 Nothing else is.
Princes do but play us; compared to this,
All honor's mimic, all wealth alchemy.°
 Thou, sun, art half as happy as we,
 In that the world's contracted thus;
 Thine age asks ease, and since thy duties be
 To warm the world, that's done in warming us.
Shine here to us, and thou art everywhere;
This bed thy center is, these walls, thy sphere.°

5

10

15

20

25

30

6 **prentices:** apprentices.   17 **both th' Indias:** East and West Indies.   24 **alchemy:** fraudulent, counterfeit.   30 **sphere:** path round the heavens (of the sun).

The Flea

Mark but this flea, and mark in this
How little that which thou deny'st me is;
It sucked me first, and now sucks thee,
And in this flea our two bloods mingled be;
Thou know'st that this cannot be said   5
A sin, nor shame, nor loss of maidenhead,
    Yet this enjoys before it woo,
    And pampered swells with one blood made of two,
    And this, alas, is more than we would do.

Oh stay, three lives in one flea spare,   10
Where we almost, yea more than married are.
This flea is you and I, and this
Our marriage bed, and marriage temple is;
Though parents grudge, and you, we're met
And cloistered in these living walls of jet.   15
    Though use° make you apt to kill me,
    Let not to that, self-murder added be,
    And sacrilege, three sins in killing three.

Cruel and sudden, hast thou since
Purpled thy nail in blood of innocence?   20
Wherein could this flea guilty be,
Except in that drop which it sucked from thee?
Yet thou triumph'st, and say'st that thou
Find'st not thyself, nor me, the weaker now;
    'Tis true; then learn how false, fears be;   25
    Just so much honor, when thou yield'st to me,
    Will waste, as this flea's death took life from thee.

16 **use:** familiarity.

Elegy 19. To His Mistress Going to Bed

Come, madam, come, all rest my powers defy,
Until I labor, I in labor lie.
The foe oft-times having the foe in sight,
Is tired with standing though he never fight.
Off with that girdle, like heaven's zone glistering,   5
But a far fairer world encompassing.
Unpin that spangled breastplate which you wear,
That the eyes of busy fools may be stopped there.
Unlace yourself, for that harmonious chime
Tells me from you that now 'tis your bed time.   10
Off with that happy busk,° which I envy,
That still can be, and still can stand so nigh.

11 **busk:** corset.

Your gown, going off, such beauteous state reveals,
As when from flowry meads the hill's shadow steals.
Off with that wiry coronet° and show   15
The hairy diadem which on you doth grow:
Now off with those shoes, and then safely tread
In this love's hallowed temple, this soft bed.
In such white robes, heaven's angels used to be
Received by men; thou, Angel, bring'st with thee   20
A heaven like Mahomet's Paradise; and though
Ill° spirits walk in white, we easily know
By this these angels from an evil sprite:
Those set our hairs, but these our flesh upright.
    License my roving hands, and let them go   25
Before, behind, between, above, below.
O my America! my new-found-land,
My kingdom, safeliest when with one man manned,
My mine of precious stones, my empery,°
How blest am I in this discovering thee!   30
To enter in these bonds is to be free;
Then where my hand is set, my seal shall be.
    Full nakedness!   All joys are due to thee,
As souls unbodied, bodies unclothed must be
To taste whole joys.°   Gems which you women use   35
Are like Atlanta's balls,° cast in men's views,
That when a fool's eye lighteth on a gem,
His earthly soul may covet theirs, not them.
    Like pictures, or like books' gay coverings made
For lay-men, are all women thus arrayed;   40
Themselves are mystic books, which only we
(Whom their imputed grace will dignify)
Must see revealed. Then, since that I may know,
As liberally as to a midwife, show
Thyself: cast all, yea, this white linen hence,   45
Here is no penance, much less innocence,
    To teach thee, I am naked first; why than,
What needst thou have more covering than a man.

15 **coronet:** headpiece.   22 **ill:** evil.   29 **empery:** empire.   34–35 Just as souls must leave their bodies to gain the joy of heaven, so bodies must undress to gain theirs.   35–36 In the Greek myth, Hippomenes raced with Atlanta, dropping heavy golden balls in her way to distract her so he could win the race.

A Valediction: Forbidding Mourning

As virtuous men pass mildly away,
   And whisper to their souls to go,
Whilst some of their sad friends do say
   The breath goes now, and some say no:

So let us melt, and make no noise,   5
    No tear-floods, nor sigh-tempests move;
'Twere profanation of our joys
    To tell the laity° our love.

Moving of th' earth brings harms and fears;
    Men reckon what it did and meant;   10
But trepidation of the spheres,°
    Though greater far, is innocent.

Dull sublunary° lovers' love
    (Whose soul is sense)° cannot admit
Absence, because it doth remove   15
    Those things which elemented° it.

But we, by a love so much refined
    That ourselves know not what it is,
Inter-assurèd of the mind,
    Care less, eyes, lips, and hands to miss.   20

Our two souls, therefore, which are one,
    Though I must go, endure not yet
A breach, but an expansion,
    Like gold to airy thinness beat.

If they be two, they are two so   25
    As stiff twin compasses are two:
Thy soul, the fixed foot, makes no show
    To move, but doth, if th' other do.

And though it in the center sit,
    Yet when the other far doth roam,   30
It leans, and hearkens after it,
    And grows erect, as that comes home.

Such wilt thou be to me, who must
    Like the other foot, obliquely run;
Thy firmness makes my circle just,   35
    And makes me end, where I begun.

8 **laity:** the uninitiated, ignorant.   11 **trepidation of the spheres:** movement of the planets (which we can't perceive, i.e., it is "innocent," line 12).   13 **sublunary:** beneath the moon, i.e., inconstant.   14 **soul is sense:** essential principle is sensuality.   16 **elemented:** made up of.

Holy Sonnet 14

Death, be not proud, though some have callèd thee
Mighty and dreadful, for thou art not so;
For those whom thou think'st thou dost overthrow
Die not, poor Death, nor yet canst thou kill me.
From rest and sleep, which but thy pictures be,   5
Much pleasure; then from thee much more must flow,

And soonest our best men with thee do go,
Rest of their bones, and soul's delivery.
Thou art slave to fate, chance, kings, and desperate men,
And dost with poison, war, and sickness dwell,   10
And poppy° or charms can make us sleep as well
And better than thy stroke; why swell'st thou then?
One short sleep past, we wake eternally
And death shall be no more: Death, thou shalt die.

11 **poppy:** opium.

BEN JONSON (1573–1637)

Song: To Celia

Drink to me only with thine eyes,
And I will pledge with mine;
Or leave a kiss but in the cup,
And I'll not look for wine.
The thirst that from the soul doth rise,   5
Doth ask a drink divine:
But might I of Jove's nectar sup,
I would not change for thine.
I sent thee late a rosy wreath,
Not so much honoring thee,   10
As giving it a hope, that there
It could not withered be.
But thou thereon did'st only breathe,
And sent'st it back to me;
Since when it grows and smells, I swear,   15
Not of itself, but thee.

Inviting a Friend to Supper

Tonight, grave sir, both my poor house, and I
Do equally desire your company;
Not that we think us worthy such a guest,
But that your worth will dignify our feast
With those that come, whose grace may make that seem   5
Something, which else could hope for no esteem.
It is the fair acceptance, sir, creates
The entertainment perfect, not the cates.°
Yet shall you have, to rectify your palate,
An olive, capers, or some better salad   10
Ushering the mutton; with a short-legged hen,

8 **cates:** food.

If we can get her, full of eggs, and then
Lemons, and wine for sauce; to these a cony°
Is not to be despaired of, for our money;
And, though fowl now be scarce, yet there are clerks,°   15
The sky not falling, think we may have larks
I'll tell you of more, and lie, so you will come:
Of partridge, pheasant, woodcock, of which some
May yet be there, and godwit,° if we can;
Knot, rail, and ruff too. Howsoe'er, my man   20
Shall read a piece of Virgil,° Tacitus,
Livy, or of some better book to us,
Of which we'll speak our minds, amidst our meat;
And I'll profess no verses to repeat.
To this, if aught appear which I not know of,   25
That will the pastry, not my paper, show of.
Digestive cheese and fruit there sure will be;
But that which most doth take my Muse and me,
Is a pure cup of rich Canary wine,
Which is the Mermaid's° now, but shall be mine;   30
Of which had Horace,° or Anacreon tasted,
Their lives, as do their lines, till now had lasted.
Tobacco, nectar, or the Thespian spring,
Are all but Luther's beer° to this I sing.
Of this we will sup free, but moderately,   35
And we will have no Pooley,° or Parrot° by,
Nor shall our cups make any guilty men;
But, at our parting we will be as when
We innocently met. No simple word
That shall be uttered at our mirthful board,°   40
Shall make us sad next morning or affright
The liberty that we'll enjoy tonight.

13 **cony:** rabbit.   15 **clerks:** learned scholars.   19 **godwit:** a game bird.   21–22 **Virgil, Taci-tus, Livy:** ancient Roman writers   30 **Mermaid:** a well-known London tavern.   31 **Horace, Anacreon:** Roman poets.   34 **Luther's beer:** weak beer.   36 **Pooley, Parrot:** notorious spies in Jonson's time.   40 **board:** table.

ROBERT HERRICK (1591-1674)

To the Virgins, to Make Much of Time

Gather ye rosebuds while ye may,
    Old time is still a-flying;
And this same flower that smiles today
    Tomorrow will be dying.

The glorious lamp of heaven, the sun,   5
    The higher he's a-getting,

The sooner will his race be run,
　　And nearer he's to setting.

That age is best which is the first,
　　When youth and blood are warmer;　　　　　　　10
But being spent, the worse, and worst
　　Times still succeed the former.

Then be not coy, but use your time,
　　And, while ye may, go marry;
For, having lost but once your prime,　　　　　　15
　　You may forever tarry.

To Daffodils

Fair daffodils, we weep to see
　　You haste away so soon:
As yet the early-rising sun
　　Has not attained his noon.
　　　Stay, stay,　　　　　　　　　　　　　5
　　Until the hasting day
　　　Has run
　　But to the evensong;
And, having prayed together, we
　　Will go with you along.　　　　　　　　　10

We have short time to stay as you;
　We have as short a spring;
As quick a growth to meet decay,
　　As you or anything.
　　　We die,　　　　　　　　　　　　　15
　As your hours do, and dry
　　　Away
　　Like to the summer's rain;
Or as the pearls of morning's dew,
　　Ne'er to be found again.　　　　　　　　20

Upon Julia's Clothes

Whenas in silks my Julia goes,
Then, then, methinks, how sweetly flows
That liquefaction of her clothes.

Next, when I cast mine eyes and see
That brave vibration each way free,　　　　　　5
O how that glittering taketh me!

GEORGE HERBERT (1593–1633)

The Pulley

When God at first made man,
Having a glass of blessings standing by,
  "Let us," said he, "pour on him all we can:
Let the world's riches, which dispersèd lie,
  Contract into a span."   5

  So Strength first made a way;
Then Beauty flowed; then Wisdom, Honor, Pleasure.
  When almost all was out, God made a stay,
Perceiving that alone of all his treasure
  Rest in the bottom lay.   10

  "For if I should," said he,
"Bestow this jewel also on my creature,
  He would adore my gifts instead of me,
And rest in Nature, not the God of Nature;
  So both should losers be.   15

  "Yet let him keep the rest,
But keep them with repining restlessness:
  Let him be rich and weary, that at least,
If goodness lead him not, yet weariness
  May toss him to my breast."   20

The Collar

I struck the board° and cried, "No more!
    I will abroad!
What, shall I ever sigh and pine?
My lines and life are free: free as the road,
  Loose as the wind, as large as store.   5
    Shall I be still in suit?°
Have I no harvest but a thorn
To let me blood, and not restore
What I have lost with cordial fruit?
    Sure there was wine   10
Before my sighs did dry it; there was corn
  Before my tears did drown it.
  Is the year only lost to me?
    Have I no bays° to crown it,
No flowers, no garlands gay? all blasted?   15
    All wasted?
Not so, my heart; but there is fruit,
    And thou hast hands.

1 **board**: table (also in the sense of altar, or communion table).   6 **in suit**: begging.   9 **cordial**: medicinal.   14 **bays**: wreath of laurel, worn to show fame, often of a poet.

Recover all thy sigh-blown age
On double pleasures. Leave thy cold dispute   20
Of what is fit and not. Forsake thy cage,
      Thy rope of sands,
Which petty thoughts have made and made to thee
    Good cable, to enforce and draw,
        And be thy law,   25
While thou didst wink and wouldst not see.
      Away! take heed!
      I will abroad!
Call in thy death's-head there! Tie up thy fears!
      He that forbears   30
    To suit and serve his need,
      Deserves his load."
But as I raved, and grew more fierce and wild
      At every word,
Methought I heard one calling, "Child!"   35
    And I replied, "My Lord."

Jordan (I)°

Who says that fictions only and false hair
Become a verse? Is there in truth no beauty?
Is all good structure in a winding stair?
May no lines pass, except they do their duty
    Not to a true, but painted chair?   5

Is it no verse, except enchanted groves
And sudden arbors° shadow coarse-spun lines?
Must purling streams refresh a lover's loves?
Must all be veiled while he that reads, divines,°
    Catching the sense at two removes?   10

Shepherds are honest people; let them sing:
Riddle who list, for me, and pull for prime:°
I envy no man's nightingale or spring;
Nor let them punish me with loss of rhyme,
    Who plainly say, *My God, My King.*   15

Title: river of Jordan, traditionally symbolizing baptism.   **7 arbors:** grove of trees,   **9 divines:**
interprets with difficulty.   12 the line refers to moves in a game of whist.

Love (III)

Love bade me welcome: yet my soul drew back,
    Guilty of dust and sin.
But quick-eyed Love, observing me grow slack
    From my first entrance in,

Drew nearer to me, sweetly questioning 5
If I lacked anything.

"A guest," I answered, "worthy to be here":
Love said, "You shall be he."
"I, the unkind, ungrateful? Ah, my dear,
I cannot look on thee." 10
Love took my hand, and smiling did reply,
"Who made the eyes but I?"

"Truth, Lord: but I have marred them; let my shame
Go where it doth deserve."
"And know you not," says Love, "who bore the blame?" 15
"My dear, then I will serve."
"You must sit down," says Love, "and taste my meat."
So I did sit and eat.

THOMAS CAREW (1595?–1639?)

Mediocrity in Love Rejected

Give me more love, or more disdain;
The torrid or the frozen zone
Bring equal ease unto my pain;
The temperate affords me none:
Either extreme, of love or hate, 5
Is sweeter than a calm estate.

Give me a storm; if it be love,
Like Danaë° in that golden shower,
I swim in pleasure; if it prove
Disdain, that torrent will devour 10
My vulture hopes; and he's possessed
Of heaven that's but from hell released.
Then crown my joys, or cure my pain;
Give me more love or more disdain.

8 **Danaë:** goddess pursued by Jove who showered her with gold.

EDMUND WALLER (1606–1687)

Go, Lovely Rose

Go, lovely rose,
Tell her that wastes her time and me,
That now she knows,
When I resemble her to thee,
How sweet and fair she seems to be. 5

Tell her that's young,
And shuns to have her graces spied,
  That hadst thou sprung
In deserts, where no men abide,
  Thou must have uncommended died.   10

  Small is the worth
Of beauty from the light retired;
  Bid her come forth,
Suffer herself to be desired,
  And not blush so to be admired.   15

  Then die, that she
The common fate of all things rare
  May read in thee;
How small a part of time they share,
  That are so wondrous sweet and fair.   20

JOHN MILTON (1608–1674)

How Soon Hath Time

How soon hath Time, the subtle thief of youth,
Stolen on his wing my three-and-twentieth year!
My hasting days fly on with full career,
But my late spring no bud or blossom shew'th.
Perhaps my semblance might deceive the truth   5
That I to manhood am arrived so near;

And inward ripeness doth much less appear,
That some more timely-happy spirits endu'th.°
Yet be it less or more, or soon or slow,
It shall be still in strictest measure even   10
To that same lot, however mean or high,
Toward which Time leads me, and the will of Heaven;
All is, if I have grace to use it so,
As ever in my great Taskmaster's eye.

8 **endu'th:** that endows some more fortunate people.

On His Blindness

When I consider how my light is spent,
Ere half my days, in this dark world and wide,
And that one talent which is death to hide
Lodged with me useless, though my soul more bent
To serve therewith my Maker, and present   5

My true account, lest he returning chide,
"Doth God exact day labor, light denied?"
I fondly ask; but Patience, to prevent
That murmur, soon replies: "God doth not need
Either man's work or his own gifts; who best   10
Bear his mild yoke, they serve him best. His state
Is kingly: thousands at his bidding speed
And post o'er land and ocean without rest.
They also serve who only stand and wait."

SIR JOHN SUCKLING (1609–1642)

Song

Why so pale and wan, fond lover?
    Prithee, why so pale?
Will, when looking well can't move her,
    Looking ill prevail?
    Prithee, why so pale?   5

Why so dull and mute, young sinner?
    Prithee, why so mute?
Will, when speaking well can't win her,
    Saying nothing do 't?
    Prithee, why so mute?   10

Quit, quit, for shame; this will not move,
    This cannot take her.
If of herself she will not love,
    Nothing can make her:
    The devil take her!   15

Out upon It!

Out upon it! I have loved
    Three whole days together;
And am like to love three more,
    If it prove fair weather.

Time shall molt away his wings,   5
    Ere he shall discover
In the whole wide world again
    Such a constant lover.

But the spite on 't is, no praise
    Is due at all to me: 10
Love with me had made no stays
    Had it any been but she.

Had it any been but she,
   And that very face,
There had been at least ere this   15
   A dozen dozen in her place.

ANNE BRADSTREET (1612–1672)

A Letter to Her Husband, Absent upon Public Employment

My head, my heart, mine eyes, my life, nay, more,
My joy, my magazine of earthly store,
If two be one, as surely thou and I,
How stayest thou there, whilst I at Ipswich lie?
So many steps, head from the heart to sever,   5
If but a neck, soon should we be together.
I, like the Earth this season, mourn in black,
My Sun is gone so far in's zodiac,
Whom whilst I' joyed, nor storms, nor frost I felt,
His warmth such frigid colds did cause to melt.   10
My chilled limbs now numbed lie forlorn;
Return, return, sweet Sol, from Capricorn;°
In this dead time, alas, what can I more
Than view those fruits which through thy heat I bore?
Which sweet contentment yield me for a space,   15
True living pictures of their father's face.
O strange effect! now thou art southward gone,
I weary grow the tedious day so long;
But when thou northward to me shalt return,
I wish my Sun may never set, but burn   20
Within the Cancer° of my glowing breast,
The welcome house of him my dearest guest.
Where ever, ever stay, and go not thence,
Till nature's sad decree shall call thee hence;
Flesh of thy flesh, bone of thy bone,   25
I here, thou there, yet both but one.

12 **Sol, . . . Capricorn:** the sun returning from the cold climatic zone.   21 **Cancer:** the warm, torrid zone.

RICHARD LOVELACE (1618–1658)

To Althea, from Prison

When Love with unconfinéd wings
Hovers within my gates,
And my divine Althea brings
To whisper at the grates;

When I lie tangled in her hair   5
And fettered to her eye,
The gods that wanton° in the air
Know no such liberty.

When flowing cups run swiftly round,
With no allaying Thames,°   10
Our careless heads with roses bound,
Our hearts with loyal flames;
When thirsty grief in wine we steep,
When healths and draughts go free,
Fishes, that tipple in the deep,   15
Know no such liberty.

When, like committed° linnets, I
With shriller throat shall sing
The sweetness, mercy, majesty,
And glories of my King;   20
When I shall voice aloud how good
He is, how great should be,
Enlargéd winds, that curl the flood,
Know no such liberty.

Stone walls do not a prison make,   25
Nor iron bars a cage;
Minds innocent and quiet take
That for an hermitage.
If I have freedom in my love,
And in my soul am free,   30
Angels alone, that soar above,
Enjoy such liberty.

7 **wanton:** play, relax.   9 **Thames:** river Thames, i.e., water.   17 **committed:** dedicated.

ANDREW MARVELL (1621–1678)

Bermudas

Where the remote Bermudas ride,
In th' ocean's bosom unespied,
From a small boat that rowed along,
The listening winds received this song:
    "What should we do but sing His praise,   5
That led us through the watery maze
Unto an isle so long unknown,
And yet far kinder than our own?
Where He the huge sea monsters wracks,
That lift the deep upon their backs;   10
He lands us on a grassy stage,
Safe from the storms, and prelate's° rage.

12 **prelate's:** bishop's.

He gave us this eternal spring
Which here enamels everything,
And sends the fowls to us in care, 15
On daily visits through the air;
He hangs in shades the orange bright,
Like golden lamps in a green night,
And does in the pomegranates close
Jewels more rich than Ormus° shows; 20
He makes the figs our mouths to meet,
And throws the melons at our feet;
But apples° plants of such a price,
No tree could ever bear them twice;
With cedars, chosen by His hand, 25
From Lebanon, He stores the land;
And makes the hollow seas, that roar,
Proclaim the ambergris° on shore;
He cast (of which we rather boast)
The Gospel's pearl upon our coast, 30
And in these rocks for us did frame
A temple, where to sound His name.
O! let our voice His praise exalt,
Till it arrive at heaven's vault,
Which, thence (perhaps) rebounding, may 35
Echo beyond the Mexique Bay."
    Thus sung they in the English boat,
An holy and a cheerful note;
And all the way, to guide their chime,
With falling oars they kept the time. 40

20 **Ormus:** Hormuz, an island in the Persian Gulf, famous as a jewel mart.   23 **apples:** here, probably pomegranate.   28 **ambergris:** secretion of the sperm whale, used in perfumes.

To His Coy Mistress

    Had we but world enough, and time,
This coyness, lady, were no crime.
We would sit down, and think which way
To walk, and pass our long love's day.
Thou by the Indian Ganges'° side 5
Shoudst rubies° find; I by the tide
Of Humber° would complain. I would
Love you ten years before the flood,
And you should, if you please, refuse
Till the conversion of the Jews.° 10
My vegetable° love should grow

5 **Ganges:** river in India.   6 **rubies:** jewel supposedly protecting virginity.   7 **Humber:** river in Marvell's hometown of Kingston-upon-Hull.   10 **conversion of the Jews:** just before the end of the world.   11 **vegetable:** organically growing.

Vaster than empires and more slow;
An hundred years should go to praise
Thine eyes, and on thy forehead gaze;
Two hundred to adore each breast,   15
But thirty thousand to the rest;
An age at least to every part,
And the last age should show your heart.
For, lady, you deserve this state,°
Nor would I love at lower rate.   20
    But at my back I always hear
Time's wingéd chariot hurrying near;
And yonder all before us lie
Deserts of vast eternity.
Thy beauty shall no more be found;   25
Nor, in thy marble vault, shall sound
My echoing song; then worms shall try
That long-preserved virginity,
And your quaint° honor turn to dust,
And into ashes all my lust: 30
The grave's a fine and private place,
But none, I think, do there embrace.
    Now therefore, while the youthful hue
Sits on thy skin like morning dew
And while thy willing soul transpires°   35
At every pore with instant fires,
Now let us sport us while we may,
And now, like amorous birds of prey,
Rather at once our time devour
Than languish in his slow-chapped° power.   40
Let us roll all our strength and all
Our sweetness up into one ball,
And tear our pleasures with rough strife
Thorough° the iron gates of life:
Thus, though we cannot make our sun   45
Stand still, yet we will make him run.

19 **state:** honor.   29 **quaint:** subtle (pun on "cunt").   35 **transpires:** breathes.   40 **slow-chapped:** slowly devouring (chaps: jaws).   44 **Thorough:** through.

JOHN DRYDEN (1631–1700)

A Song for St. Cecilia's Day

I
From harmony, from heavenly harmony
    This universal frame began:
    When Nature underneath a heap

Title: St. Cecilia, the patron saint of music.

Of jarring atoms lay,
    And could not heave her head,   5
The tuneful voice was heard from high:
    "Arise, ye more than dead."
Then cold, and hot, and moist, and dry,
 In order to their stations leap,
    And Music's power obey.   10
From harmony, from heavenly harmony
    This universal frame began:
    From harmony to harmony
Through all the compass of the notes it ran,
The diapason closing full in man.   15

II

What passion cannot Music raise and quell!
    When Jubal° struck the corded shell,
    His listening brethren stood around,
    And, wondering, on their faces fell
    To worship that celestial sound.   20
Less than a god they thought there could not dwell
    Within the hollow of that shell
    That spoke so sweetly and so well.
What passion cannot Music raise and quell!

III

The trumpet's loud clangor   25
    Excites us to arms,
  With shrill notes of anger,
    And mortal alarms.
The double double double beat
    Of the thundering drum   30
Cries: "Hark! the foes come;
Charge, charge, 'tis too late to retreat."

IV

The soft complaining flute
In dying notes discovers
The woes of hopeless lovers,   35
Whose dirge is whispered by the warbling lute.

V

Sharp violins proclaim
Their jealous pangs, and desperation,
Fury, frantic indignation,
Depth of pains, and height of passion,   40
    For the fair, disdainful dame.

VI

But O! what art can teach,
  What human voice can reach,
The sacred organ's praise?

---

17 **Jubal:** descendant of Cain, "father of all such as handle the harp and organ." (Gen. 4:21)

Notes inspiring holy love, 45
Notes that wing their heavenly ways
To mend the choirs above.

VII

Orpheus° could lead the savage race;
And trees unrooted left their place,
Sequacious of the lyre; 50
But bright Cecilia raised the wonder higher:
When to her organ vocal breath was given,
An angel heard, and straight appeared
Mistaking earth for heaven.

GRAND CHORUS

As from the power of sacred lays 55
The spheres began to move,
And sung the great Creator's praise
To all the blest above;
So, when the last and dreadful hour
This crumbling pageant shall devour, 60
The trumpet shall be heard on high,
The dead shall live, the living die,
And Music shall untune the sky.

48 **Orpheus:** god of music and poetry.

THOMAS TRAHERNE (1637–1674)

Shadows in the Water

In unexperienced infancy
Many a sweet mistake doth lie:
Mistake though false, intending° true;
A seeming somewhat more than view;
   That doth instruct the mind 5
   In things that lie behind,
And many secrets to us show
Which afterwards we come to know.

Thus did I by the water's brink
Another world beneath me think; 10
And while the lofty spacious skies
Reverséd there, abused mine eyes,
   I fancied other feet
   Came mine to touch or meet;
As by some puddle I did play 15
Another world within it lay.

3 **intending:** meaning.

Beneath the water people drowned,
Yet with another heaven crowned,
In spacious regions seemed to go
As freely moving to and fro: 20
   In bright and open space
   I saw their very face;
Eyes, hands, and feet they had like mine;
Another sun did with them shine.

'Twas strange that people there should walk,   25
And yet I could not hear them talk:
That through a little watery chink,
Which one dry ox or horse might drink,
   We other worlds should see,
   Yet not admitted be;   30
And other confines there behold
Of light and darkness, heat and cold.

I called them oft, but called in vain;
No speeches we could entertain:
Yet did I there expect to find   35
Some other world, to please my mind.
   I plainly saw by these
   A new antipodes,
Whom, though they were so plainly seen,
A film kept off that stood between.   40

By walking men's reversèd feet
I chanced another world to meet;
Though it did not to view exceed
A phantom, 'tis a world indeed,
   Where skies beneath us shine,   45
   And earth by art divine
Another face presents below,
Where people's feet against ours go.

Within the regions of the air,
Compassed about with heavens fair,   50
Great tracts of land there may be found
Enriched with fields and fertile ground;
   Where many numerous hosts
   In those far distant coasts,
For other great and glorious ends   55
Inhabit, my yet unknown friends.

O ye that stand upon the brink,
Whom I so near me through the chink
With wonder see: what faces there,
Whose feet, whose bodies, do ye wear?   60
   I my companions see
   In you, another me.
They seeméd others, but are we;
Our second selves these shadows be.

Look how far off those lower skies   65
Extend themselves! scarce with mine eyes
I can them reach. O ye my friends,
What secret borders on those ends?
    Are lofty heavens hurled
        'Bout your inferior world?   70
Are yet the representatives
Of other peoples' distant lives?

Of all the playmates which I knew
That here I do the image view
In other selves, what can it mean?   75
But that below the purling stream
    Some unknown joys there be
    Laid up in store for me:
To which I shall, when that thin skin
Is broken, be admitted in.   80

EDWARD TAYLOR (1642–1729)

Meditation 8

I kenning° through astronomy divine
    The world's bright battlement, wherein I spy
A golden path my pencil cannot line,
    From that bright throne unto my threshold lie.
    And while my puzzled thoughts about it pore   5
    I find the bread of life in it at my door.

When that this bird of paradise put in
    This wicker cage (my corpse) to tweedle° praise
Had pecked the fruit forbad, and so did fling
    Away its food, and lost its golden days,   10
    It fell into celestial famine sore,
    And never could attain a morsel more.

Alas! alas! Poor bird, what wilt thou do?
    The creatures' field no food for souls e'er gave.
And if thou knock at angels' doors they show   15
    An empty barrel; they no soul bread have.
    Alas! Poor bird, the world's white loaf is done,
    And cannot yield thee here the smallest crumb.

In this sad state, God's tender bowels° run
    Out streams of grace; and he to end all strife   20
The purest wheat in heaven, his dear, dear son
    Grinds, and kneads up into this bread of life.
    Which bread of life from heaven down came and stands
    Dished on my table up by angels' hands.

1 **kenning**: learning.   8 **tweedle**: sing.   19 **bowels**: in the 17th century, seat of compassion.

Or drest in smiles of sweet Cecilia shine,
With simp'ring Angels, Palms, and Harps divine;
Whether the Charmer sinner it, or saint it,   15
If Folly grows romantic,° I must paint it.
    Come then, the colours and the ground prepare!
Dip in the Rainbow, trick her off in Air,
Chuse a firm Cloud, before it fall, and in it
Catch, ere she change, the Cynthia of this minute.   20
    Rufa,° whose eye quick-glancing o'er the Park,
Attracts each light gay meteor of a Spark,
Agrees as ill with Rufa studying Locke,°
As Sappho's diamonds with her dirty smock,
Or Sappho at her toilet's greazy task,   25
With Sappho fragrant at an ev'ning Mask:
So morning Insects that in muck begun,
Shine, buzz, and fly-blow in the setting-sun.
    How soft is Silia! fearful to offend,
The Frail one's advocate, the Weak one's friend: 30
To her, Calista prov'd her conduct nice,°
And good Simplicius asks of her advice.
Sudden, she storms! she raves! You tip the wink,
But spare your censure; Silia does not drink.
All eyes may see from what the change arose,   35
All eyes may see—a Pimple on her nose.
    Papillia, wedded to her doating spark,
Sighs for the shades—'How charming is a Park!'
A Park is purchas'd, but the Fair he sees
All bath'd in tears—'Oh odious, odious Trees!'   40
    Ladies, like variegated Tulips, show,
'Tis to their Changes that their charms they owe;
Their happy Spots the nice admirer take,
Fine by defect, and delicately weak.
'Twas thus Calypso once each heart alarm'd,   45
Aw'd without Virtue, without Beauty charm'd;
Her Tongue bewitch'd as odly as her Eyes,
Less Wit than Mimic, more a Wit than wise:
Strange graces still, and stranger flights she had,
Was just not ugly, and was just not mad;   50
Yet ne'er so sure our passion to create,
As when she touch'd the brink of all we hate.
  Narcissa's nature, tolerably mild,
To make a wash, would hardly stew a child,
Has ev'n been prov'd to grant a Lover's pray'r,   55
And paid a Tradesman once to make him stare,
Gave alms at Easter, in a Christian trim,
And made a Widow happy, for a whim.

---

16 **romantic:** exaggerated.   21 **Rufa:** redhead.   23 **Locke:** 17th-century British philosopher.   31 **nice:** fussy.

Why then declare Good-nature is her scorn,
When 'tis by that alone she can be born?   60
Why pique° all mortals, yet affect a name?
A fool to Pleasure, and a slave to Fame:
Now deep in Taylor° and the Book of Martyrs,
Now drinking citron with his Grace and Chartres.
Now Conscience chills her, and now Passion burns;   65
And Atheism and Religion take their turns;
A very Heathen in the carnal part,
Yet still a sad, good Christian at her heart.
    See Sin in State, majestically drunk,
Proud as a Peeress, prouder as a Punk;
Chaste to her Husband, frank to all beside,   70
A teeming Mistress, but a barren Bride.
What then? let Blood and Body bear the fault,
Her Head's untouch'd, that noble Seat of Thought:
Such this day's doctrine—in another fit
She sins with Poets thro' pure Love of Wit.   75
What has not fir'd her bosom or her brain?
Caesar and Tall-boy, Charles and Charlema'ne.
As Helluo,° late Dictator of the Feast,
The Nose of Hautgout,° and the Tip of Taste,   80
Critick'd your wine, and analyz'd your meat,
Yet on plain Pudding deign'd at-home to eat;
So Philomedé, lect'ring all mankind
On the soft Passion, and the Taste refin'd,
Th' Address, the Delicacy—stoops at once,   85
And makes her hearty meal upon a Dunce.
    Flavia's a Wit, has too much sense to Pray,
To Toast our wants and wishes, is her way;
Nor asks of God, but of her Stars to give
The mighty blessing, 'while we live, to live.'   90
Then all for Death, that Opiate of the soul!
Lucretia's dagger, Rosamonda's bowl.
Say, what can cause such impotence of mind?
A Spark too fickle, or a Spouse too kind.
Wise Wretch! with Pleasures too refin'd to please,   95
With too much Spirit to be e'er at ease,
With too much Quickness ever to be taught,
With too much Thinking to have common Thought:
Who purchase Pain with all that Joy can give,
And die of nothing but a Rage to live.   100
    Turn then from Wits; and look on Simo's Mate,
No Ass so meek, no Ass so obstinate:
Or her, that owns her Faults, but never mends,
Because she's honest, and the best of Friends:
Or her, whose life the Church and Scandal share,   105

61 **pique:** annoy.   63 **Taylor:** 17th-century religious writer.   79 **Helluo:** Glutton.   80 **Hautgout:** over-ripe food.

For ever in a Passion, or a Pray'r:
Or her, who laughs at Hell, but (like her Grace)
Cries, 'Ah! how charming if there's no such place!'
Or who in sweet vicissitude appears
Of Mirth and Opium, Ratafie° and Tears,   110
The daily Anodyne,° and nightly Draught,
To kill those foes to Fair ones, Time and Thought.
Woman and Fool are two hard things to hit,
For true No-meaning puzzles more than Wit.
   But what are these to great Atossa's mind?   115
Scarce once herself, by turns all Womankind!
Who, with herself, or others, from her birth
Finds all her life one warfare upon earth:
Shines, in exposing Knaves, and painting Fools,
Yet is, whate'er she hates and ridicules.   120
No Thought advances, but her Eddy Brain
Whisks it about, and down it goes again.
Full sixty years the World has been her Trade,
The wisest Fool much Time has ever made.
From loveless youth to unrespected age,   125
No Passion gratify'd except her Rage.
So much the Fury still out-ran the Wit,
The Pleasure miss'd her, and the Scandal hit.
Who breaks with her, provokes Revenge from Hell,
But he's a bolder man who dares be well: 130
Her ev'ry turn with Violence pursu'd,
Nor more a storm her Hate than Gratitude.
To that each Passion turns, or soon or late;
Love, if it makes her yield, must make her hate:
Superiors? death! and Equals? what a curse!   135
But an Inferior not dependant? worse.
Offend her, and she knows not to forgive;
Oblige her, and she'll hate you while you live:
But die, and she'll adore you—Then the Bust
And Temple rise—then fall again to dust.   140
Last night, her Lord was all that's good and great,
A Knave this morning, and his Will a Cheat.
Strange! by the Means defeated of the Ends,
By Spirit robb'd of Pow'r, by Warmth of Friends,
By Wealth of Follow'rs! without one distress   145
Sick of herself thro' very selfishness!
Atossa, curs'd with ev'ry granted pray'r,
Childless with all her Children, wants an Heir.
To Heirs unknown descends th' unguarded store
Or wanders, Heav'n-directed, to the Poor.   150
   Pictures like these, dear Madam, to design,
Asks no firm hand, and no unerring line;
Some wand'ring touch, or some reflected light,

110 **Ratafie:** liquor made from the stones of fruit.   111 **Anodyne:** painkiller.

Some flying stroke alone can hit 'em right:
For how should equal Colours do the knack?   155
Chameleons who can paint in white and black?
　'Yet Cloe sure was form'd without a spot—'
Nature in her then err'd not, but forgot.
'With ev'ry pleasing, ev'ry prudent part,
Say, what can Cloe want?'—she wants a Heart.   160
She speaks, behaves, and acts just as she ought;
But never, never, reach'd one gen'rous Thought.
Virtue she finds too painful an endeavour,
Content to dwell in Decencies for ever.
So very reasonable, so unmov'd,   165
As never yet to love, or to be lov'd.
She, while her Lover pants upon her breast,
Can mark the figures on an Indian chest;
And when she sees her Friend in deep despair,
Observes how much a Chintz exceeds Mohair.°   170
Forbid it Heav'n, a Favour or a Debt
She e'er should cancel—but she may forget.
Safe is your Secret still in Cloe's ear;
But none of Cloe's shall you ever hear.
Of all her Dears she never slander'd one,   175
But cares not if a thousand are undone.
Would Cloe know if you're alive or dead?
She bids her Footman put it in her head.
Cloe is prudent—would you too be wise?
Then never break your heart when Cloe dies.   180
　One certain Portrait may (I grant) be seen,
Which Heav'n has varnish'd out,° and made a *Queen:*
The same for ever! and describ'd by all
With Truth and Goodness, as with Crown and Ball:
Poets heap Virtues, Painters Gems at will,   185
And show their zeal, and hide their want of skill.
'Tis well—but, Artists! who can paint or write,
To draw the Naked is your true delight:
That Robe of Quality so struts and swells,
None see what Parts of Nature it conceals.   190
Th' exactest traits of Body or of Mind,
We owe to models of an humble kind.
If QUEENSBERRY to strip there's no compelling,
'Tis from a Handmaid we must take a Helen.
From Peer or Bishop 'tis no easy thing   195
To draw the man who loves his God, or King:
Alas! I copy (or my draught° would fail)
From honest Mah'met,° or plain Parson Hale°
　But grant, in Public Men sometimes are shown,

---

170 **Chintz . . . Mohair:** fashionable fabrics.　182 **varnished out:** completed and varnished.
197 **draught:** drawing.　198 **Mah'met:** Mahomet;　**Parson Hale:** typical honest village clergyman.

A Woman's seen in Private life alone: 200
Our bolder Talents in full light display'd,
Your Virtues open fairest in the shade.
Bred to disguise, in Public 'tis you hide;
There, none distinguish 'twixt your Shame or Pride,
Weakness or Delicacy; all so nice,   205
That each may seem a Virtue, or a Vice.
    In Men, we various Ruling Passions find,
In Women, two almost divide the kind;
Those, only fix'd, they first or last obey,
The Love of Pleasure, and the Love of Sway.°   210
    That, Nature gives; and where the lesson taught
Is but to please, can Pleasure seem a fault?
Experience, this; by Man's oppression curst,
They seek the second not to lose the first.
    Men, some to Bus'ness, some to Pleasure take;   215
But ev'ry Woman is at heart a Rake:°
Men, some to Quiet, some to public Strife;
But ev'ry Lady would be Queen for life.
    Yet mark the fate of a whole Sex of Queens!
Pow'r all their end, but Beauty all the means.   220
In Youth they conquer, with so wild a rage,
As leaves them scarce a Subject in their Age:
For foreign glory, foreign joy, they roam;
No thought of Peace or Happiness at home.
But Wisdom's Triumph is well-tim'd Retreat,   225
As hard a science to the Fair as Great!
Beauties, like Tyrants, old and friendless grown,
Yet hate to rest, and dread to be alone,
Worn out in public, weary ev'ry eye,
Nor leave one sigh behind them when they die.   230
    Pleasures the sex, as children Birds, pursue,
Still out of reach, yet never out of view,
Sure, if they catch, to spoil the Toy at most,
To covet flying, and regret when lost:
At last, to follies Youth could scarce defend,   235
'Tis half their Age's prudence to pretend;
Asham'd to own they gave delight before,
Reduc'd to feign it, when they give no more:
As Hags hold Sabbaths,° less for joy than spight,
So these their merry, miserable Night;°   240
Still round and round the Ghosts of Beauty glide,
And haunt the places where their Honour dy'd.
    See how the World its Veterans rewards!
A Youth of frolicks, an old Age of Cards,
Fair to no purpose, artful to no end,   245
Young without Lovers, old without a Friend,

210 **Sway:** power.   216 **Rake:** immoral person.   239 **Hags . . . Sabbaths:** witches' rituals.
240 **Night:** night for visits.

A Fop their Passion, but their Prize a Sot,
Alive, ridiculous, and dead, forgot!
   Ah Friend! to dazzle let the Vain design,
To raise the Thought and touch the Heart, be thine!   250
That Charm shall grow, while what fatigues the Ring
Flaunts and goes down, an unregarded thing.
So when the Sun's broad beam has tir'd the sight,
All mild ascends the Moon's more sober light,
Serene in Virgin Modesty she shines,   255
And unobserv'd the glaring Orb declines.
   Oh! blest with Temper, whose unclouded ray
Can make to morrow chearful as to day;
She, who can love a Sister's charms, or hear
Sighs for a Daughter with unwounded ear;   260
She, who ne'er answers till a Husband cools,
Or, if she rules him, never shows she rules;
Charms by accepting, by submitting sways,
Yet has her humour most, when she obeys;
Lets Fops or Fortune fly which way they will;   265
Disdains all loss of Tickets, or Codille;°
Spleen, Vapours, or Small-pox, above them all,
And Mistress of herself, tho' China fall.
   And yet, believe me, good as well as ill,
Woman's at best a Contradiction still.   270
Heav'n, when it strives to polish all it can
Its last best work, but forms a softer Man;
Picks from each sex, to make its Fav'rite blest,
Your love of Pleasure, our desire of Rest,
Blends, in exception to all gen'ral rules,   275
Your Taste of Follies, with our Scorn of Fools,
Reserve with Frankness, Art with Truth ally'd,
Courage with Softness, Modesty with Pride,
Fix'd Principles, with Fancy ever new;
Shakes all together, and produces—You.   280
   Be this a Woman's Fame: with this unblest,
Toasts live a scorn, and Queens may die a jest.
This Phoebus° promis'd (I forget the year)
When those blue eyes first open'd on the sphere;
Ascendant Phoebus watch'd that hour with care,   285
Averted half your Parents simple Pray'r,
And gave you Beauty, but deny'd the Pelf
Which buys your sex a Tyrant o'er itself.
The gen'rous God, who Wit and Gold refines,
And ripens Spirits as he ripens Mines,   290
Kept Dross° for Duchesses, the world shall know it,
To you gave Sense, Good-humour, and a Poet.

---

266 **Tickets ... Codille:** lottery tickets, card game.   283 **Phoebus:** god of the sun.
291 **Dross:** rubbish, impurity.

THOMAS GRAY (1716–1771)

Ode

On the Death of a Favorite Cat,
Drowned in a Tub of Goldfishes

'Twas on a lofty vase's side,
Where China's gayest art had dyed
   The azure flowers that blow;°
Demurest of the tabby kind,
The pensive Selima, reclined,   5
   Gazed on the lake below.

Her conscious tail her joy declared;
The fair round face, the snowy beard,
   The velvet of her paws,
Her coat, that with the tortoise vies,   10
Her ears of jet, and emerald eyes,
   She saw; and purred applause.

Still had she gazed; but 'midst the tide
Two angel forms were seen to glide,
   The genii° of the stream: 15
Their scaly armor's Tyrian hue°
Through richest purple to the view
   Betrayed a golden gleam.

The hapless nymph with wonder saw:
A whisker first and then a claw,   20
   With many an ardent wish,
She stretched in vain to reach the prize.
What female heart can gold despise?
   What cat's averse to fish?

Presumptuous maid! with looks intent   25
Again she stretched, again she bent,
   Nor knew the gulf between.
(Malignant Fate sat by and smiled)
The slippery verge her feet beguiled,
   She tumbled headlong in.   30

Eight times emerging from the flood
She mewed to every watery god,
   Some speedy aid to send.
No dolphin came, no Nereid° stirred;
Nor cruel Tom, nor Susan heard;   35
   A favorite has no friend!

3 **blow:** bloom.   15 **genii:** guardian angels.   16 **Tyrian hue:** rich purple.   34 **Nereid:** sea-nymph.

From hence, ye beauties, undeceived,
Know, one false step is ne'er retrieved,
    And be with caution bold.
Not all that tempts your wandering eyes   40
And heedless hearts is lawful prize.
    Nor all that glisters, gold.

Elegy Written in a Country Churchyard

The curfew tolls the knell° of parting day,
    The lowing herd wind slowly o'er the lea,°
The plowman homeward plods his weary way,
    And leaves the world to darkness and to me.

Now fades the glimmering landscape on the sight,   5
    And all the air a solemn stillness holds,
Save where the beetle wheels his droning flight,
    And drowsy tinklings lull the distant folds;

Save that from yonder ivy-mantled tower
    The moping owl does to the moon complain   10
Of such, as wandering near her secret bower,
    Molest her ancient solitary reign.

Beneath those rugged elms, that yew tree's shade,
    Where heaves the turf in many a moldering heap,
Each in his narrow cell forever laid,   15
    The rude° forefathers of the hamlet sleep.

The breezy call of incense-breathing morn,
    The swallow twittering from the straw-built shed,
The cock's shrill clarion, or the echoing horn,
    No more shall rouse them from their lowly bed.   20

For them no more the blazing hearth shall burn,
    Or busy housewife ply her evening care;
No children run to lisp their sire's return,
    Or climb his knees the envied kiss to share.

Oft did the harvest to their sickle yield,   25
    Their furrow oft the stubborn glebe° has broke;
How jocund did they drive their team afield!
    How bowed the woods beneath their sturdy stroke!

Let not Ambition mock their useful toil,
    Their homely joys, and destiny obscure;   30
Nor Grandeur hear with a disdainful smile
    The short and simple annals of the poor.

1 **knell:** tolling (of a bell).   2 **lea:** fields.   16 **rude:** rustic.   26 **glebe:** earth.

The boast of heraldry,° the pomp of power,
    And all that beauty, all that wealth e'er gave,
Awaits alike the inevitable hour.   35
    The paths of glory lead but to the grave.

Nor you, ye proud, impute to these the fault,
    If Memory o'er their tomb no trophies raise,
Where through the long-drawn aisle and fretted° vault
    The pealing anthem swells the note of praise.   40

Can storied° urn or animated bust
    Back to its mansion call the fleeting breath?
Can Honor's voice provoke the silent dust,
    Or Flattery soothe the dull cold ear of Death?

Perhaps in this neglected spot is laid   45
    Some heart once pregnant with celestial fire;
Hands that the rod of empire might have swayed,
    Or waked to ecstasy the living lyre.

But Knowledge to their eyes her ample page
    Rich with the spoils of time did ne'er unroll;   50
Chill Penury repressed their noble rage,
    And froze the genial current of the soul.

Full many a gem of purest ray serene,
    The dark unfathomed caves of ocean bear:
Full many a flower is born to blush unseen,   55
    And waste its sweetness on the desert air.

Some village Hampden,° that with dauntless breast
    The little tyrant of his fields withstood;
Some mute inglorious Milton here may rest,
    Some Cromwell guiltless of his country's blood.   60

The applause of listening senates to command,
    The threats of pain and ruin to despise,
To scatter plenty o'er a smiling land,
    And read their history in a nation's eyes,

Their lot forbade: nor circumscribed alone   65
    Their growing virtues, but their crimes confined;
Forbade to wade through slaughter to a throne,
    And shut the gates of mercy on mankind.

The struggling pangs of conscious truth to hide,
    To quench the blushes of ingenuous shame,   70
Or heap the shrine of Luxury and Pride
    With incense kindled at the Muse's flame.

Far from the madding° crowd's ignoble strife,
    Their sober wishes never learned to stray;

33 **heraldry:** nobility.   39 **fretted:** decorated.   41 **storied:** engraved.   57 **Hampden:** parlia-
mentary leader in the English Civil War.   73 **madding:** swarming.

Along the cool sequestered vale of life   75
    They kept the noiseless tenor of their way.

Yet even these bones from insult to protect
    Some frail memorial still erected nigh,
With uncouth rhymes and shapeless sculpture decked,
    Implores the passing tribute of a sigh.   80

Their name, their years, spelt by the unlettered Muse,
    The place of fame and elegy supply:
And many a holy text around she strews,
    That teach the rustic moralist to die.

For who to dumb Forgetfulness a prey,   85
    This pleasing anxious being e'er resigned,
Left the warm precincts of the cheerful day,
    Nor cast one longing lingering look behind?

On some fond breast the parting soul relies,
    Some pious drops the closing eye requires;   90
Even from the tomb the voice of Nature cries,
    Even in our ashes live their wonted fires.

For thee, who mindful of the unhonored dead
    Dost in these lines their artless tale relate;
If chance, by lonely contemplation led,   55
    Some kindred spirit shall inquire thy fate,

Haply some hoary-headed swain may say,
    "Oft have we seen him at the peep of dawn
Brushing with hasty steps the dews away
    To meet the sun upon the upland lawn.   100

"There at the foot of yonder nodding beech
    That wreathes its old fantastic roots so high,
His listless length at noontide would he stretch,
    And pore upon the brook that babbles by.

"Hard by yon wood, now smiling as in scorn,   105
    Muttering his wayward fancies he would rove,
Now drooping, woeful wan, like one forlorn,
    Or crazed with care, or crossed in hopeless love.

"One morn I missed him on the customed hill,
    Along the heath and near his favorite tree;   110
Another came; nor yet beside the rill,
    Nor up the lawn, nor at the wood was he;

"The next with dirges due in sad array
    Slow through the churchway path we saw him borne.
Approach and read (for thou canst read) the lay,   115
    Graved on the stone beneath yon aged thorn."

The Epitaph

Here rests his head upon the lap of Earth
    A youth to Fortune and to Fame unknown.

Fair Science frowned not on his humble birth,
    And Melancholy marked him for her own.   120

Large was his bounty, and his soul sincere,
    Heaven did a recompense as largely send:
He gave to Misery all he had, a tear,
    He gained from Heaven ('twas all he wished) a friend.

No farther seek his merits to disclose,   125
    Or draw his frailties from their dread abode
(There they alike in trembling hope repose),
    The bosom of his Father and his God.

CHRISTOPHER SMART (1722–1771)

Jubilate Agno (Selection)

For I will consider my Cat Jeoffry.
For he is the servant of the Living God, duly and daily serving him.
For at the first glance on the glory of God in the East he worships in his
    way.
For is this done by wreathing his body seven times around with elegant
    quickness.
For then he leaps up to catch the musk,° which is the blessing of God
    upon his prayer.   5
For he rolls upon prank to work it in.
For having done duty and received blessing he begins to consider himself.
For this he performs in ten degrees.
For first he looks upon his forepaws to see if they are clean.
For secondly he kicks up behind to clear away there.   10
For thirdly he works it upon stretch with the forepaws extended.
For fourthly he sharpens his paws by wood.
For fifthly he washes himself.
For sixthly he rolls upon wash.
For seventhly he fleas himself, that he may not be interrupted upon the
    beat.°   15
For eighthly he rubs himself against a post.
For ninthly he looks up for his instructions.
For tenthly he goes in quest of food.
For having considered God and himself he will consider his neighbor.
For if he meets another cat he will kiss her in kindness.
For when he takes his prey he plays with it to give it a chance.   20
For one mouse in seven escapes by his dallying.
For when his day's work is done his business more properly begins.
For he keeps the Lord's watch in the night against the adversary.
For he counteracts the powers of darkness by his electrical skin and glaring
    eyes.
For he counteracts the Devil, who is death, by brisking about the life.   25

Title: Rejoice in the lamb of God.   5 **musk:** aromatic plant.   15 **the beat:** his rounds.

For in his morning orisons he loves the sun and the sun loves him.
For he is of the tribe of Tiger.
For the Cherub Cat is a term° of the Angel Tiger.
For he has the subtlety and hissing of a serpent, which in goodness he
    suppresses.
For he will not do destruction if he is well-fed, neither will he spit without
    provocation.   30
For he purrs in thankfulness when God tells him he's a good Cat.
For he is an instrument for the children to learn benevolence upon.
For every house is incomplete without him, and a blessing is lacking in the
    spirit.
For the Lord commanded Moses concerning the cats at the departure of
    the Children of Israel from Egypt.   35
For every family had one cat at least in the bag.°
For the English Cats are the best in Europe.
For he is the cleanest in the use of his forepaws of any quadruped.
For the dexterity of his defense is an instance of the love of God to him
    exceedingly.
For he is the quickest to his mark of any creature.   40
For he is tenacious of his point.
For he is a mixture of gravity and waggery.°
For he knows that God is his Saviour.
For there is nothing sweeter than his peace when at rest.
For there is nothing brisker than his life when in motion.   45
For he is of the Lord's poor, and so indeed is he called by benevolence
    perpetually—Poor Jeoffry! poor Jeoffry! the rat has bit thy throat.
For I bless the name of the Lord Jesus that Jeoffry is better.
For the divine spirit comes about his body to sustain it in complete cat.
For his tongue is exceeding pure so that it has in purity what it wants in
    music.
For he is docile and can learn certain things.   50
For he can sit up with gravity, which is patience upon approbation.
For he can fetch and carry, which is patience in employment.
For he can jump over a stick, which is patience upon proof positive.
For he can spraggle upon waggle at the word of command.
For he can jump from an eminence into his master's bosom.   55
For he can catch the cork and toss it again.
For he is hated by the hypocrite and miser.
For the former is afraid of detection.
For the latter refuses the charge.
For he camels his back to bear the first notion of business.   60
For he is good to think on, if a man would express himself neatly.
For he made a great figure in Egypt for his signal services.
For he killed the Icneumon° rat, very pernicious by land.
For his ears are so acute that they sting again.
For from this proceeds the passing quickness of his attention.   65

28 **term:** sub-species.   36 **in the bag:** in their possession.
42 **waggery:** playfulness.   63 **Icneumon:** mongoose.

For by stroking of him I have found out electricity.

For I perceived God's light about him both wax and fire.

For the electrical fire is the spiritual substance which God sends from
   heaven to sustain the bodies both of man and beast.

For God has blessed him in the variety of his movements.

For, though he cannot fly, he is an excellent clamberer.°   70

For his motions upon the face of the earth are more than any other
   quadruped.

For he can tread to all the measures upon the music.

For he can swim for life.

For he can creep.

70 **clamberer:** climber.

OLIVER GOLDSMITH (1728–1774)

When Lovely Woman Stoops to Folly

When lovely woman stoops to folly,
   And finds too late that men betray,
What charm can soothe her melancholy,
   What art can wash her guilt away?

The only art her guilt to cover,   5
   To hide her shame from every eye,
To give repentance to her lover,
   And wring his bosom—is to die.

WILLIAM BLAKE (1757–1827)

The Sick Rose

O Rose, thou art sick!
The invisible worm
That flies in the night,
In the howling storm,

Has found out thy bed   5
Of crimson joy,
And his dark secret love
Does thy life destroy.

The Garden of Love

I went to the Garden of Love,
And saw what I never had seen:
A Chapel was built in the midst,
Where I used to play on the green.

And the gates of this Chapel were shut,   5
And "Thou shalt not" writ over the door;
So I turn'd to the Garden of Love,
That so many sweet flowers bore,

And I saw it was filled with graves,
And tomb-stones where flowers should be: 10
And Priests in black gowns were walking their rounds,
And binding with briars° my joys & desires.

12 **briars:** thorns.

The Lamb

Little Lamb, who made thee?
Dost thou know who made thee?
Gave thee life & bid thee feed,
By the stream & o'er the mead;°
Gave thee clothing of delight,   5
Softest clothing wooly bright;
Gave thee such a tender voice,
Making all the vales rejoice!
Little Lamb who made thee?
Dost thou know who made thee?   10

Little Lamb I'll tell thee,
Little Lamb I'll tell thee!
He is callèd by thy name,
For he calls himself a Lamb:
He is meek & he is mild,
He became a little child:
I a child & thou a lamb,
We are callèd by his name.
Little Lamb God bless thee.
Little Lamb God bless thee.   20

4 **mead:** field.

The Little Black Boy

My mother bore me in the southern wild,
And I am black, but O! my soul is white;
White as an angel is the English child:
But I am black as if bereav'd of light.

My mother taught me underneath a tree,   5
And sitting down before the heat of day,

She took me on her lap and kisséd me,
And pointing to the east, began to say:

"Look on the rising sun: there God does live,
And gives his light, and gives his heat away;   10
And flowers and trees and beasts and men receive
Comfort in morning, joy in the noon day.

"And we are put on earth a little space,
That we may learn to bear the beams of love,
And these black bodies and this sun-burnt face   15
Is but a cloud, and like a shady grove.

"For when our souls have learn'd the heat to bear,
The cloud will vanish; we shall hear his voice,
Saying: 'Come out from the grove, my love & care,
And round my golden tent like lambs rejoice.'"   20

Thus did my mother say, and kisséd me;
And thus I say to little English boy:
When I from black and he from white cloud free,
And round the tent of God like lambs we joy,

I'll shade him from the heat till he can bear   25
To lean in joy upon our father's knee;
And then I'll stand and stroke his silver hair,
And be like him, and he will then love me.

London

I wander thro' each charter'd° street,
Near where the charter'd Thames does flow,
And mark in every face I meet
Marks of weakness, marks of woe.

In every cry of every man,   5
In every Infant's cry of fear,
In every voice, in every ban,°
The mind-forg'd manacles° I hear.

How the Chimney-sweeper's cry
Every blackning Church appalls;   10
And the hapless Soldier's sigh
Runs in blood down Palace walls.

But most thro' midnight streets I hear
How the youthful Harlot's° curse
Blasts the new-born Infant's tear,   15
And blights with plagues the Marriage hearse.

1 **charter'd:** legally mapped out.   7 **ban:** prohibition.   8 **manacles:** handcuffs.   14 **Harlot's:** prostitute's.

And Did Those Feet

And did those feet in ancient time
Walk upon England's mountains green?
And was the holy Lamb of God
On England's pleasant pastures seen?

And did the Countenance Divine   5
Shine forth upon our clouded hills?
And was Jerusalem° builded here,
Among these dark Satanic Mills?°

Bring me my Bow of burning gold:
Bring me my Arrows of desire: 10
Bring me my Spear: O clouds unfold!
Bring me my Chariot of fire!

I will not cease from Mental Fight,
Nor shall my Sword sleep in my hand,
Till we have built Jerusalem   15
In England's green & pleasant Land.

7 **Jerusalem:** the Holy City.   8 **Satanic Mills:** diabolical factories.

ROBERT BURNS (1759–1796)

Holy Willie's Prayer

O Thou, wha in the heavens dost dwell,
Wha, as it pleases best thysel',
Sends ane to heaven and ten to hell,
    A' for thy glory,
And no for ony guid or ill   5
    They've done afore thee!

I bless and praise thy matchless might,
Whan thousands thou hast left in night,
That I am here afore thy sight,
    For gifts an' grace   10
A burnin' an' a shinin' light,
    To a' this place.

What was I, or my generation,
That I should get sic exaltation?
I, wha deserve most just damnation,   15
    For broken laws,
Sax thousand years 'fore my creation,
    Thro' Adam's cause.

When frae my mither's womb I fell,
Thou might hae plungéd me in hell,   20
To gnash my gums, to weep and wail,

In burnin lakes,
Where damnéd devils roar and yell,
        Chained to their stakes;

Yet I am here a chosen sample,   25
To show thy grace is great and ample;
I'm here a pillar in thy temple,
        Strong as a rock,
A guide, a buckler, an example
        To a' thy flock.   30

O Lord, thou kens what zeal I bear,
When drinkers drink, and swearers swear.
And singin' there and dancin' here,
        Wi' great an' sma':
For I am keepit by thy fear   35
        Free frae them a'.

But yet, O Lord! confess I must
At times I'm fashed° wi' fleshy lust;
An' sometimes too, wi' warldly trust,
        Vile self gets in;   40
But thou remembers we are dust,
        Defiled in sin.

O Lord! yestreen,° thou kens, wi' Meg—
Thy pardon I sincerely beg;
O! may't ne'er be a livin' plague   45
        To my dishonour,
An' I'll ne'er lift a lawless leg
        Again upon her.

Besides I farther maun allow,
Wi' Lizzie's lass, three times I trow—   50
But, Lord, that Friday I was fou,°
        When I cam near her,
Or else thou kens thy servant true
        Wad never steer° her.

May be thou lets this fleshly thorn   55
Beset thy servant e'en and morn
Lest he owre high and proud should turn,
        That he's sae gifted;
If sae, thy hand maun e'en be borne,
        Until thou lift it.   60

Lord, bless thy chosen in this place,
For here thou hast a chosen race;
But God confound their stubborn face,
        And blast their name,
Wha bring thy elders to disgrace   65
        An' public shame.

---

38 **fashed:** annoyed.   43 **yestreen:** last night.   51 **fou:** drunk.   54 **steer:** touch.

Lord, mind Gawn Hamilton's deserts,
He drinks, an' swears, an' plays at cartes,
Yet has sae mony takin arts
      Wi' great an' sma',   70
Frae God's ain priest the people's hearts
      He steals awa'.

An' when we chastened him therefor,
Thou kens how he bred sic a splore°
As set the warld in a roar   75
      O' laughin' at us;
Curse thou his basket and his store,
      Kail° and potatoes.

Lord, hear my earnest cry an' pray'r,
Against that presbytery o' Ayr;   80
Thy strong right hand, Lord, make it bare
      Upo' their heads;
Lord, weigh it down, and dinna spare,
      For their misdeeds.

O Lord my God, that glib-tongued Aiken,   85
My very heart and soul are quakin',
To think how we stood sweatin, shakin,
      An' pissed wi' dread,
While he, wi' hingin° lips and snakin,°
      Held up his head.   90

Lord in the day of vengeance try him;
Lord, visit them wha did employ him,
And pass not in thy mercy by them,
      Nor hear their pray'r:
But, for thy people's sake, destroy them,   95
      And dinna spare.

But, Lord, remember me and mine
Wi' mercies temp'ral and divine,
That I for gear° and grace may shine
      Excelled by nane,   100
And a' the glory shall be thine,
      Amen, Amen!

74 **splore:** noise.   78 **Kail:** cabbage.   89 **snakin:** sneering.   99 **gear:** riches.

O My Luve's like a Red, Red Rose

O My Luve's like a red, red rose,
    That's newly sprung in June;
O My Luve's like the melodie
    That's sweetly played in tune.

As Fair art thou, my bonnie lass,
  So deep in luve am I;
And I will luve thee still, my dear,
  Till a' the seas gang° dry.

Till a' the seas gang dry, my dear,
  And the rocks melt wi' the sun:
O I will love thee still, my dear,
  While the sands o' life shall run.

And fare thee weel, my only luve,
  And fare thee weel awhile!
And I will come again, my luve,
  Though it were ten thousand mile.

8 **gang:** become.

WILLIAM WORDSWORTH (1770–1850)

She Dwelt Among the Untrodden Ways

She dwelt among the untrodden ways
  Beside the springs of Dove.°
A Maid whom there were none to praise
  And very few to love;

A violet by a mossy stone
  Half hidden from the eye!
—Fair as a star, when only one
  Is shining in the sky.

She lived unknown, and few could know
  When Lucy ceased to be;
But she is in her grave, and, oh,
  The difference to me!

2 **Dove:** river in the Lake District, England.

Three Years She Grew

Three years she grew in sun and shower,
Then Nature said, "A lovelier flower
On earth was never sown;
This Child I to myself will take;
She shall be mine, and I will make
A Lady of my own.

"Myself will to my darling be
Both law and impulse: and with me
The Girl, in rock and plain,

In earth and heaven, in glade and bower,   10
Shall feel an overseeing power
To kindle or restrain.

"She shall be sportive as the fawn
That wild with glee across the lawn
Or up the mountain springs;   15
And hers shall be the breathing balm,
And hers the silence and the calm
Of mute insensate things.

"The floating clouds their state shall lend
To her; for her the willow bend;   20
Nor shall she fail to see
Even in the motions of the Storm
Grace that shall mold the Maiden's form
By silent sympathy.

"The stars of midnight shall be dear   25
To her; and she shall lean her ear
In many a secret place
Where rivulets dance their wayward round,
And beauty born of murmuring sound
Shall pass into her face.   30

"And vital feelings of delight
Shall rear her form to stately height,
Her virgin bosom swell;
Such thoughts to Lucy I will give
While she and I together live   35
Here in this happy dell."

Thus Nature spake—the work was done—
How soon my Lucy's race was run!
She died, and left to me
This heath, this calm, and quiet scene;   40
The memory of what has been,
And never more will be.

A Slumber Did My Spirit Seal

A slumber did my spirit seal;
    I had no human fears:
She seemed a thing that could not feel
    The touch of earthly years.

No motion has she now, no force;   5
    She neither hears nor sees;
Rolled round in earth's diurnal° course,
    With rocks, and stones, and trees.

7 **diurnal**: daily.

I Wandered Lonely as a Cloud

I wandered lonely as a cloud
That floats on high o'er vales and hills,
When all at once I saw a crowd,
A host, of golden daffodils;
Beside the lake, beneath the trees,   5
Fluttering and dancing in the breeze.

Continuous as the stars that shine
And twinkle on the milky way,
They stretched in never-ending line
Along the margin of a bay: 10
Ten thousand saw I at a glance,
Tossing their heads in sprightly dance.

The waves beside them danced; but they
Outdid the sparkling waves in glee;
A poet could not but be gay,   15
In such a jocund° company;
I gazed—and gazed—but little thought
What wealth the show to me had brought:

For oft, when on my couch I lie
In vacant or in pensive mood,   20
They flash upon that inward eye
Which is the bliss of soltitude;
And then my heart with pleasure fills,
And dances with the daffodils.

16 **jocund:** joyful.

SAMUEL TAYLOR COLERIDGE (1772–1834)

Dejection: An Ode

Late, late yestreen I saw the new Moon,
With the old Moon in her arms;
And I fear, I fear, my master dear!
We shall have a deadly storm.

> *Ballad of Sir Patrick Spence*

I

Well! If the bard was weather-wise, who made
  The grand old ballad of Sir Patrick Spence,
  This night, so tranquil now, will not go hence
Unroused by winds, that ply a busier trade
Than those which mold yon cloud in lazy flakes,   5
Or the dull sobbing draft, that moans and rakes

Upon the strings of this Aeolian lute,
    Which better far were mute.
    For lo! the New-moon winter-bright!
    And overspread with phantom light,   10
    (With swimming phantom light o'erspread
    But rimmed and circled by a silver thread)
I see the old Moon in her lap, foretelling
    The coming-on of rain and squally blast.
And oh! that even now the gust were swelling,   15
    And the slant night shower driving loud and fast!
Those sounds which oft have raised me, whilst they awed,
    And sent my soul abroad,
Might now perhaps their wonted impulse give,
Might startle this dull pain, and make it move and live!   20

II

A grief without a pang, void, dark, and drear,
    A stifled, drowsy, unimpassioned grief,
    Which finds no natural outlet, no relief,
        In word, or sigh, or tear—
O Lady! in this wan and heartless mood,   25
To other thoughts by yonder throstle wooed,
    All this long eve, so balmy and serene,
Have I been gazing on the western sky,
    And its peculiar tint of yellow green:
And still I gaze—and with how blank an eye!   30
And those thin clouds above, in flakes and bars,
That give away their motion to the stars;
Those stars, that glide behind them or between,
Now sparkling, now bedimmed, but always seen:
Yon crescent Moon, as fixed as if it grew   35
In its own cloudless, starless lake of blue;
I see them all so excellently fair,
I see, not feel, how beautiful they are!

III

    My genial spirits fail;
    And what can these avail   40
To lift the smothering weight from off my breast?
    It were a vain endeavor,
        Though I should gaze forever
On that green light that lingers in the west:
I may not hope from outward forms to win   45
The passion and the life, whose fountains are within.

IV

O Lady! we receive but what we give,
And in our life alone does Nature live:
Ours is her wedding garment, ours her shroud!
    And would we aught behold, of higher worth,   50
Than that inanimate cold world allowed
To the poor loveless ever-anxious crowd,

Ah! from the soul itself must issue forth
A light, a glory, a fair luminous cloud
    Enveloping the Earth—
And from the soul itself must there be sent
  A sweet and potent voice, of its own birth,
Of all sweet sounds the life and element!

V

O pure of heart! thou need'st not ask of me
What this strong music in the soul may be!
What, and wherein it doth exist,
This light, this glory, this fair luminous mist,
This beautiful and beauty-making power.
    Joy, virtuous Lady! Joy that ne'er was given,
Save to the pure, and in their purest hour,
Life, and Life's effluence,° cloud at once and shower,
Joy, Lady! is the spirit and the power,
Which wedding Nature to us gives in dower
    A new Earth and new Heaven,
Undreamt of by the sensual and the proud—
Joy is the sweet voice, Joy the luminous cloud—
    We in ourselves rejoice!
And thence flows all that charms or ear or sight,
  All melodies the echoes of that voice,
All colors a suffusion from that light.

VI

There was a time when, though my path was rough,
  This joy within me dallied with distress,
And all misfortunes were but as the stuff
  Whence Fancy made me dreams of happiness:
For hope grew round me, like the twining vine,
And fruits, and foliage, not my own, seemed mine.
But now afflictions bow me down to earth:
Nor care I that they rob me of my mirth;
    But oh! each visitation
Suspends what nature gave me at my birth,
  My shaping spirit of Imagination.
For not to think of what I needs must feel,
  But to be still and patient, all I can;
And happly by abstruse research to steal
  From my own nature all the natural man—
  This was my sole resource, my only plan:
Till that which suits a part infects the whole,
And now is almost grown the habit of my soul.

VII

Hence, viper thoughts, that coil around my mind,
    Reality's dark dream!
I turn from you, and listen to the wind,

66 **effluence:** overflowing.

Which long has raved unnoticed. What a scream
Of agony by torture lengthened out
That lute sent forth! Thou Wind, that rav'st without,
    Bare crag, or mountain tairn,° or blasted tree,   100
Or pine grove whither woodman never clomb,
Or lonely house, long held—the witches' home,
    Methinks were fitter instruments for thee,
Mad lutanist! who in this month of showers,
Of dark-brown gardens, and of peeping flowers,   105
Mak'st devils' yule,° with worse than wintry song,
The blossoms, buds, and timorous leaves among.
    Thou actor, perfect in all tragic sounds!
Thou mighty poet, e'en to frenzy bold!
        What tell'st thou now about?   110
        'Tis of the rushing of an host in rout,
    With groans, of trampled men, with smarting wounds—
At once they groan with pain, and shudder with the cold!
But hush! there is a pause of deepest silence!
    And all that noise, as of a rushing crowd,   115
With groans, and tremulous shudderings—all is over—
    It tells another tale, with sounds less deep and loud!
        A tale of less affright,
        And tempered with delight,
As Otway's° self had framed the tender lay—   120
        'Tis of a little child
        Upon a lonesome wild,
Not far from home, but she hath lost her way:
And now moans low in bitter grief and fear,
And now screams loud, and hopes to make her mother hear.   125

VIII

'Tis midnight, but small thoughts have I of sleep:
Full seldom may my friend such vigils keep!
Visit her, gentle Sleep! with wings of healing,
    And may this storm be but a mountain birth,
May all the stars hang bright above her dwelling,   130
    Silent as though they watched the sleeping Earth!
        With light heart may she rise,
        Gay fancy, cheerful eyes,
    Joy lift her spirit, joy attune her voice;
To her may all things live, from pole to pole,   135
Their life the eddying of her living soul!
    O simple spirit, guided from above,
Dear Lady! friend devoutest of my choice,
Thus mayest thou ever, evermore rejoice.

100 **tairn:** pond.   106 **devils' yule:** winter storm in springtime.   120 **Otway:** 18th-century
poet.

Kubla Khan°

or A Vision in a Dream. A Fragment

In Xanadu did Kubla Khan
A stately pleasure dome decree:
Where Alph, the sacred river, ran
Through caverns measureless to man
   Down to a sunless sea.   5
So twice five miles of fertile ground
With walls and towers were girdled round:
And there were gardens bright with sinuous rills,°
Where blossomed many an incense-bearing tree;
And here were forests ancient as the hills,   10
Enfolding sunny spots of greenery.

But oh! that deep romantic chasm which slanted
Down the green hill athwart a cedarn cover!
A savage place! as holy and enchanted
As e'er beneath a waning moon was haunted   15
By woman wailing for her demon lover!
And from this chasm, with ceaseless turmoil seething,
As if this earth in fast thick pants were breathing,
A mighty fountain momently was forced:
Amid whose swift half-intermitted burst   20
Huge fragments vaulted like rebounding hail,
Or chaffy grain beneath the thresher's flail:
And 'mid these dancing rocks at once and ever
It flung up momently the sacred river.
Five miles meandering with a mazy motion   25
Through wood and dale the sacred river ran,
Then reached the caverns measureless to man,
And sank in tumult to a lifeless ocean:
And 'mid this tumult Kubla heard from far
Ancestral voices prophesying war!   30

   The shadow of the dome of pleasure
   Floated midway on the waves;
   Where was heard the mingled measure
   From the fountain and the caves.
It was a miracle of rare device,   35
A sunny pleasure dome with caves of ice!

   A damsel with a dulcimer°
   In a vision once I saw:
   It was an Abyssinian maid,
   And on her dulcimer she played,   40
   Singing of Mount Abora.

Title—Kubla Khan: 13th-century Chinese emperor.   8 **sinuous rills:** curving streams.
37 **dulcimer:** musical instrument like a harp.

Could I revive within me
Her symphony and song,
To such a deep delight 'twould win me,
That with music loud and long,   45
I would build that dome in air,
That sunny dome! those caves of ice!
And all who heard should see them there,
And all should cry, Beware! Beware!
His flashing eyes, his floating hair!   50
Weave a circle round him thrice,
And close your eyes with holy dread,
For he on honey-dew hath fed,
And drunk the milk of Paradise.

GEORGE GORDON, LORD BYRON (1788–1824)

So We'll Go No More A-Roving

So we'll go no more a-roving
    So late into the night,
Though the heart be still as loving,
    And the moon be still as bright.

For the sword outwears its sheath,   5
    And the soul wears out the breast,
And the heart must pause to breathe,
    And Love itelf have rest.

Though the night was made for loving,
    And the day returns too soon,   10
Yet we'll go no more a-roving
    By the light of the moon.

She Walks in Beauty

She walks in beauty, like the night
    Of cloudless climes and starry skies;
And all that's best of dark and bright
    Meet in her aspect and her eyes:
Thus mellowed to that tender light   5
    Which heaven to gaudy day denies.

One shade the more, one ray the less,
    Had half impaired the nameless grace
Which waves in every raven tress,
    Or softly lightens o'er her face;   10
Where thoughts serenely sweet express
    How pure, how dear their dwelling place.

And on that cheek, and o'er that brow,
    So soft, so calm, yet eloquent,
The smiles that win, the tints that glow, 15
    But tell of days in goodness spent,
A mind at peace with all below,
    A heart whose love is innocent!

PERCY BYSSHE SHELLEY (1792–1822)

Ozymandias°

I met a traveler from an antique land
Who said: Two vast and trunkless legs of stone
Stand in the desert . . . Near them, on the sand,
Half sunk, a shattered visage lies, whose frown,
And wrinkled lip, and sneer of cold command, 5
Tell that its sculptor well those passions read
Which yet survive, stamped on these lifeless things,
The hand that mocked them, and the heart that fed:
And on the pedestal these words appear:
"My name is Ozymandias, king of kings: 10
Look on my works, ye Mighty, and despair!"
Nothing beside remains. Round the decay
Of that colossal wreck, boundless and bare
The lone and level sands stretch far away.

Title: Ozymandias (Rameses II) was a 13th-century B.C. Egyptian king.

Ode to the West Wind

I

O wild West Wind, thou breath of Autumn's being,
Thou, from whose unseen presence the leaves dead
Are driven, like ghosts from an enchanter fleeing,

Yellow, and black, and pale, and hectic red,
Pestilence-stricken multitudes: O thou, 5
Who chariotest to their dark wintry bed

The wingéd seeds, where they lie cold and low,
Each like a corpse within its grave, until
Thine azure sister of the Spring shall blow

Her clarion o'er the dreaming earth, and fill 10
(Driving sweet buds like flocks to feed in air)
With living hues and odors plain and hill:

Wild Spirit, which art moving everywhere;
Destroyer and preserver; hear, oh, hear!

II

Thou on whose stream, mid the steep sky's commotion,   15
Loose clouds like earth's decaying leaves are shed,
Shook from the tangled boughs of Heaven and Ocean,

Angels of rain and lightning: there are spread
On the blue surface of thine aëry surge,
Like the bright hair uplifted from the head   20

Of some fierce Maenad,° even from the dim verge
Of the horizon to the zenith's height,
The locks of the approaching storm. Thou dirge

Of the dying year, to which this closing night
Will be the dome of a vast sepulcher,   25
Vaulted with all thy congregated might

Of vapors, from whose solid atmosphere
Black rain, and fire, and hail will burst: oh, hear!

III

Thou who didst waken from his summer dreams
The blue Mediterranean, where he lay,   30
Lulled by the coil of his crystálline streams,

Beside a pumice isle in Baiae's° bay,
And saw in sleep old palaces and towers
Quivering within the wave's intenser day,

All overgrown with azure° moss and flowers   35
So sweet, the sense faints picturing them! Thou
For whose path the Atlantic's level powers

Cleave themselves into chasms, while far below
The sea-blooms and the oozy woods which wear
The sapless foliage of the ocean, know   40

Thy voice, and suddenly grow gray with fear,
And tremble and despoil themselves: oh, hear!

IV

If I were a dead leaf thou mightest bear;
If I were a swift cloud to fly with thee;
A wave to pant beneath thy power, and share   45

The impulse of thy strength, only less free
Than thou, O uncontrollable! If even
I were as in my boyhood, and could be

The comrade of thy wanderings over Heaven,
As then, when to outstrip thy skyey speed   50
Scarce seem a vision; I would ne'er have striven

---

21 **Maenad:** drunken dancer.   32 **Baiae:** near Naples, Italy.   35 **azure:** The blue color of the clear sky.

As thus with thee in prayer in my sore need.
Oh, lift me as a wave, a leaf, a cloud!
I fall upon the thorns of life! I bleed!

A heavy weight of hours has chained and bowed   55
One too like thee: tameless, and swift, and proud.

V

Make me thy lyre,° even as the forest is:
What if my leaves are falling like its own!
The tumult of thy mighty harmonies

Will take from both a deep, autumnal tone,   60
Sweet though in sadness. Be thou, Spirit fierce,
My spirit! Be thou me, impetuous one!

Drive my dead thoughts over the universe
Like withered leaves to quicken a new birth!
And, by the incantation of this verse,   65

Scatter, as from an unextinguished hearth
Ashes and sparks, my words among mankind!
Be through my lips to unawakened earth

The trumpet of a prophecy! O Wind,
If Winter comes, can Spring be far behind?   70

57 **lyre:** harp.

JOHN KEATS (1795–1821)

The Eve of St. Agnes°

I

St. Agnes' Eve—Ah, bitter chill it was!
The owl, for all his feathers, was a-cold;
The hare limped trembling through the frozen grass,
And silent was the flock in woolly fold:
Numb were the Beadsman's° fingers, while he told   5
His rosary, and while his frosted breath,
Like pious incense from a censer old,
Seemed taking flight for heaven, without a death,
Past the sweet Virgin's picture, while his prayer he saith.

II

His prayer he saith, this patient, holy man;   10
Then takes his lamp, and riseth from his knees,
And back returneth, meager, barefoot, wan,
Along the chapel aisle by slow degrees:

Title: January 20, dedicated to St. Agnes, patron saint of virgins.   5 **Beadsman:** A man paid to
pray for a patron.

The sculptured dead, on each side, seem to freeze,
Imprisoned in black, purgatorial rails: 15
Knights, ladies, praying in dumb orat'ries,°
He passeth by; and his weak spirit fails
To think how they may ache in icy hoods and mails.

III

Northward he turneth through a little door,
And scarce three steps, ere Music's golden tongue 20
Flattered to tears this aged man and poor;
But no—already had his deathbell rung:
The joys of all his life were said and sung:
His was harsh penance on St. Agnes' Eve:
Another way he went, and soon among 25
Rough ashes sat he for his soul's reprieve,
And all night kept awake, for sinners' sake to grieve.

IV

That ancient Beadsman heard the prelude soft;
And so it chanced, for many a door was wide,
From hurry to and fro. Soon, up aloft, 30
The silver, snarling trumpets 'gan to chide:
The level chambers, ready with their pride,
Were glowing to receive a thousand guests:
The carvéd angels, ever eager-eyed,
Stared, where upon their heads the cornice° rests, 35
With hair blown back, and wings put crosswise on their breasts.

V

At length burst in the argent revelry,°
With plume, tiara, and all rich array,
Numerous as shadows haunting faerily°
The brain, new stuffed, in youth, with triumphs gay 40
Of old romance. These let us wish away,
And turn, sole-thoughted, to one Lady there,
Whose heart had brooded, all that wintry day,
On love, and winged St. Agnes' saintly care,
As she had heard old dames full many times declare. 45

VI

They told her how, upon St. Agnes' Eve,
Young virgins might have visions of delight,
And soft adorings from their loves receive
Upon the honeyed middle of the night,
If ceremonies due they did aright; 50
As, supperless to bed they must retire,
And couch supine their beauties, lily white;
Nor look behind, nor sideways, but require
Of Heaven with upward eyes for all that they desire.

16 **orat'ries:** small chapels.   35 **cornice:** ornamental wall moulding.   37 **argent revelry:**
brightly dressed revelers.   39 **faerily:** like fairies.

VII

Full of this whim was thoughtful Madeline: 55
The music, yearning like a God in pain,
She scarcely heard: her maiden eyes divine,
Fixed on the floor, saw many a sweeping train
Pass by—she heeded not at all: in vain
Came many a tiptoe, amorous cavalier,   60
And back retired; not cooled by high disdain;
But she saw not: her heart was otherwhere:
She sighed for Agnes' dreams, the sweetest of the year.

VIII

She danced along with vague, regardless eyes,
Anxious her lips, her breathing quick and short: 65
The hallowed hour was near at hand: she sighs
Amid the timbrels,° and the thronged resort
Of whisperers in anger, or in sport;
'Mid looks of love, defiance, hate, and scorn,
Hoodwinked with faery fancy; all amort,°   70
Save to St. Agnes and her lambs unshorn,
And all the bliss to be before tomorrow morn.

IX

So, purposing each moment to retire,
She lingered still. Meantime, across the moors,
Had come young Porphyro, with heart on fire   75
For Madeline. Beside the portal doors,
Buttressed from moonlight, stands he, and implores
All saints to give him sight of Madeline,
But for one moment in the tedious hours,
That he might gaze and worship all unseen;   80
Perchance speak, kneel, touch, kiss—in sooth such things have been.

X

He ventures in: let no buzzed whisper tell:
All eyes be muffled, or a hundred swords
Will storm his heart, Love's fev'rous citadel:
For him, those chambers held barbarian hordes,   85
Hyena foemen, and hot-blooded lords,
Whose very dogs would execrations howl
Against his lineage: not one breast affords
Him any mercy, in that mansion foul,
Save one old beldame,° weak in body and in soul.   90

XI

Ah, happy chance! the aged creature came,
Shuffling along with ivory-headed wand,
To where he stood, hid from the torch's flame,

---

67 **timbrels:** snare drums.   70 **amort:** insensible.   90 **beldame:** old woman, hag.

Behind a broad hall-pillar, far beyond
The sound of merriment and chorus bland: 95
He startled her; but soon she knew his face,
And grasped his fingers in her palsied hand,
Saying, "Mercy, Porphyro! hie thee from this place;
They are all here tonight, the whole bloodthirsty race!

XII

"Get hence! get hence! there's dwarfish Hildebrand;   100
He had a fever late, and in the fit
He cursèd thee and thine, both house and land:
Then there's that old Lord Maurice, not a whit
More tame for his gray hairs—Alas me! flit!
Flit like a ghost away."—"Ah, Gossip° dear,   105
We're safe enough; here in this armchair sit,
And tell me how"—"Good Saints! not here, not here;
Follow me, child, or else these stones will be thy bier."

XIII

He followed through a lowly archèd way,
Brushing the cobwebs with his lofty plume,   110
And as she muttered "Well-a—well-a-day!"
He found him in a little moonlight room,
Pale, latticed, chill, and silent as a tomb.
"Now tell me where is Madeline," said he,
"O tell me, Angela, by the holy loom   115
Which none but secret sisterhood may see,
When they St. Agnes' wool are weaving piously."

XIV

"St. Agnes! Ah! it is St. Agnes' Eve—
Yet men will murder upon holy days:
Thou must hold water in a witch's sieve,   120
And be liege lord of all the Elves and Fays,
To venture so: it fills me with amaze
To see thee, Porphyro!—St. Agnes' Eve!
God's help! my lady fair the conjuror plays°
This very night: good angels her deceive!   125
But let me laugh awhile, I've mickle° time to grieve."

XV

Feebly she laugheth in the languid moon,
While Porphyro upon her face doth look,
Like puzzled urchin on an aged crone
Who keepeth closed a wondrous riddle-book,   130
As spectacled she sits in chimney nook.
But soon his eyes grew brilliant, when she told
His lady's purpose; and he scarce could brook°

---

105 **Gossip:** term of endearment for an old woman.   124 **plays:** confuses.   126 **mickle:**
much   133 **brook:** check.

Tears, at the thought of those enchantments cold,
And Madeline asleep in lap of legends old.   135

XVI

Sudden a thought came like a full-blown rose,
Flushing his brow, and in his painéd heart
Made purple riot: then doth he propose
A stratagem, that makes the beldame start:
"A cruel man and impious thou art: 140
Sweet lady, let her pray, and sleep, and dream
Alone with her good angels, far apart
From wicked men like thee. Go, go!—I deem
Thou canst not surely be the same that thou didst seem."

XVII

"I will not harm her, by all saints I swear,"   145
Quoth Porphyro: "O may I ne'er find grace
When my weak voice shall whisper its last prayer,
If one of her soft ringlets I displace,
Or look with ruffian passion in her face:
Good Angela, believe me by these tears;   150
Or I will, even in a moment's space,
Awake, with horrid shout, my foemen's ears,
And beard them, though they be more fanged than wolves and bears."

XVIII

"Ah! why wilt thou affright a feeble soul?
A poor, weak, palsy-stricken, churchyard thing,   155
Whose passing bell may ere the midnight toll;
Whose prayers for thee, each morn and evening,
Were never missed."—Thus plaining,° doth she bring
A gentler speech from burning Porphyro;
So woeful and of such deep sorrowing,   160
That Angela gives promise she will do
Whatever he shall wish, betide her weal or woe.

XIX

Which was, to lead him, in close secrecy,
Even to Madeline's chamber, and there hide
Him in a closet, of such privacy   165
That he might see her beauty unespied,
And win perhaps that night a peerless bride,
While legioned faeries paced the coverlet,
And pale enchantment held her sleepy-eyed.
Never on such a night have lovers met,   170
Since Merlin paid his Demon all the monstrous debt.°

XX

"It shall be as thou wishest," said the Dame:
"All cates° and dainties shall be storéd there

---

158 **plaining:** complaining.   171 the Demon was a temptress who trapped Merlin after coaxing his spoils from him.   173 **cates:** delicacies.

Quickly on this feast night: by the tambour frame
Her own lute thou wilt see: no time to spare,   175
For I am slow and feeble, and scarce dare
On such a catering trust my dizzy head.
Wait here, my child, with patience; kneel in prayer
The while: Ah! thou must needs the lady wed,
Or may I never leave my grave among the dead."   180

XXI

So saying, she hobbled off with busy fear.
The lover's endless minutes slowly passed:
The dame returned, and whispered in his ear
To follow her; with aged eyes aghast
From fright of dim espial. Safe at last,   185
Through many a dusky gallery, they gain
The maiden's chamber, silken, hushed, and chaste;
Where Porphyro took covert, pleased amain.°
His poor guide hurried back with agues in her brain.

XXII

Her falt'ring hand upon the balustrade,   190
Old Angela was feeling for the stair,
When Madeline, St. Agnes' charméd maid,
Rose, like a missioned spirit, unaware:
With silver taper's light, and pious care,
She turned, and down the aged gossip led   195
To a safe level matting. Now prepare,
Young Porphyro, for gazing on that bed;
She comes, she comes again, like ringdove frayed° and fled.

XXIII

Out went the taper as she hurried in;
Its little smoke, in pallid moonshine, died: 200
She closed the door, she panted, all akin
To spirits of the air, and visions wide:
No uttered syllable, or, woe betide!
But to her heart, her heart was voluble,
Paining with eloquence her balmy side;   205
As though a tongueless nightingale should swell
Her throat in vain, and die, heart-stifled, in her dell.

XXIV

A casement high and triple-arched there was,
All garlanded with carven imag'ries
Of fruits, and flowers, and bunches of knot-grass,   210
And diamonded with panes of quaint device,
Innumerable of stains and splendid dyes,
As are the tiger-moth's deep-damasked wings;

188 **amain:** much.   198 **frayed:** frightened.

And in the midst, 'mong thousand heraldries,
And twilight saints, and dim emblazonings,   215
A shielded scutcheon° blushed with blood of queens and kings.

XXV

Full on this casement shone the wintry moon,
And threw warm gules° on Madeline's fair breast,
As down she knelt for heaven's grace and boon;°
Rose-bloom fell on her hands, together pressed,   220
And on her silver cross soft amethyst,
And on her hair a glory, like a saint:
She seemed a splendid angel, newly dressed,
Save wings, for heaven—Porphyro grew faint:
She knelt, so pure a thing, so free from mortal taint.   225

XXVI

Anon his heart revives: her vespers done,
Of all its wreathéd pearls her hair she frees;
Unclasps her warméd jewels one by one;
Loosens her fragrant bodice; by degrees
Her rich attire creeps rustling to her knees;   230
Half-hidden, like a mermaid in sea-weed,
Pensive awhile she dreams awake, and sees,
In fancy, fair St. Agnes in her bed,
But dares not look behind, or all the charm is fled.

XXVII

Soon, trembling in her soft and chilly nest,   235
In sort of wakeful swoon, perplexed she lay,
Until the poppied warmth of sleep oppressed
Her soothéd limbs, and soul fatigued away;
Flown, like a thought, until the morrow-day;
Blissfully havened both from joy and pain;   240
Clasped like a missal where swart Paynims° pray;
Blinded alike from sunshine and from rain,
As though a rose should shut, and be a bud again.

XXVIII

Stol'n to this paradise, and so entranced,
Porphyro gazed upon her empty dress,   245
And listened to her breathing, if it chanced
To wake into a slumberous tenderness;
Which when he heard, that minute did he bless,
And breathed himself: then from the closet crept,
Noiseless as fear in a wide wilderness,   250
And over the hushed carpet, silent, stepped,
And 'tween the curtains peeped, where, lo!—how fast she slept.

---

216 **scutcheon:** coat of arms; **blushed:** colored red.   218 **gules:** red light.   219 **boon:** gift.
241 **swart Paynims:** dark pagans.

XXIX

Then by the bedside, where the faded moon
Made a dim, silver twilight, soft he set
A table, and, half anguished, threw thereon   255
A cloth of woven crimson, gold, and jet—
O for some drowsy Morphean amulet!°
The boisterous, midnight, festive clarion,
The kettledrum, and far-heard clarinet,
Affray his ears, though but in dying tone—   260
The hall door shuts again, and all the noise is gone.

XXX

And still she slept an azure-lidded sleep,
In blanchéd linen, smooth, and lavendered,
While he from forth the closet brought a heap
Of candied apple, quince, and plum, and gourd;   265
With jellies soother than the creamy curd,
And lucent syrups, tinct with cinnamon;
Manna° and dates, in argosy transferred
From Fez;° and spicéd dainties, every one,
From silken Samarcand to cedared Lebanon.°   270

XXXI

These delicates he heaped with glowing hand
On golden dishes and in baskets bright
Of wreathéd silver: sumptuous they stand
In the retiréd quiet of the night,
Filling the chilly room with perfume light.—   275
"And now, my love, my seraph° fair, awake!
Thou art my heaven, and I thine eremite:°
Open thine eyes, for meek St. Agnes' sake,
Or I shall drowse beside thee, so my soul doth ache."

XXXII

Thus whispering, his warm, unnerved arm   280
Sank in her pillow. Shaded was her dream
By the dusk curtains: 'twas a midnight charm
Impossible to melt as icéd stream:
The lustrous salvers° in the moonlight gleam;
Broad golden fringe upon the carpet lies: 285
It seemed he never, never could redeem
From such a steadfast spell his lady's eyes;
So mused awhile, entoiled in wooféd° fantasies.

XXXIII

Awakening up, he took her hollow lute—
Tumultuous—and, in chords that tenderest be,   290

---

257 **Morphean amulet:** bracelet dedicated to Morpheus, the god of sleep.   268 **Manna:** holy
food.   269–70 **Fez, Samarcand, Lebanon:** Middle Eastern places associated with luxurious
goods.   276 **seraph:** angel.   277 **eremite:** worshiper.   284 **salvers:** dishes.   288 **woofed:**
woven.

He played an ancient ditty, long since mute,
In Provence called "*La belle dame sans merci*"
Close to her ear touching the melody;
Wherewith disturbed, she uttered a soft moan:
He ceased—she panted quick—and suddenly
Her blue affrayéd eyes wide open shone:
Upon his knees he sank, pale as smooth-sculptured stone.

XXXIV

Her eyes were open, but she still beheld,
Now wide awake, the vision of her sleep:
There was a painful change, that nigh expelled
The blisses of her dream so pure and deep,
At which fair Madeline began to weep,
And moan forth witless words with many a sigh;
While still her gaze on Porphyro would keep,
Who knelt, with joinéd hands and piteous eye,
Fearing to move or speak, she looked so dreamingly.

XXXV

"Ah, Porphyro!" said she, "but even now
Thy voice was at sweet tremble in mine ear,
Made tunable with every sweetest vow;
And those sad eyes were spiritual and clear:
How changed thou art! how pallid, chill, and drear!
Give me that voice again, my Porphyro,
Those looks immortal, those complainings dear!
Oh leave me not in this eternal woe,
For if thou diest, my Love, I know not where to go."

XXXVI

Beyond a mortal man impassioned far
At these voluptuous accents, he arose,
Ethereal, flushed, and like a throbbing star
Seen mid the sapphire heaven's deep repose;
Into her dream he melted, as the rose
Blendeth its odor with the violet—
Solution sweet: meantime the frost-wind blows
Like Love's alarum pattering the sharp sleet
Against the windowpanes; St. Agnes' moon hath set.

XXXVII

'Tis dark: quick pattereth the flaw-blown° sleet:
"This is no dream, my bride, my Madeline!"
'Tis dark: the icéd gusts still rave and beat:
"No dream, alas! alas! and woe is mine!
Porphyro will leave me here to fade and pine.—
Cruel! what traitor could thee hither bring?
I curse not, for my heart is lost in thine,

295

300

305

310

315

320

325

330

325 **flaw-blown:** blown by gusts of wind.

Though thou forsakest a deceivéd thing—
A dove forlorn and lost with sick unprunéd wing."

XXXVIII

"My Madeline! sweet dreamer! lovely bride!
Say, may I be for aye thy vassal blest?   335
Thy beauty's shield, heart-shaped and vermcil° dyed?
Ah, silver shrine, here will I take my rest
After so many hours of toil and quest,
A famished pilgrim—saved by miracle.
Though I have found, I will not rob thy nest   340
Saving of thy sweet self; if thou think'st well
To trust, fair Madeline, to no rude infidel.

XXXIX

"Hark! 'tis an elfin-storm from faery land,
Of haggard seeming, but a boon indeed:
Arise—arise! the morning is at hand—   345
The bloated wassaillers° will never heed—
Let us away, my love, with happy speed;
There are no ears to hear, or eyes to see—
Drowned all in Rhenish and the sleepy mead:
Awake! arise! my love, and fearless be,   350
For o'er the southern moors I have a home for thee."

XL

She hurried at his words, beset with fears,
For there were sleeping dragons all around,
At glaring watch, perhaps, with ready spears—
Down the wide stairs a darkling way they found.—   355
In all the house was heard no human sound.
A chain-dropped lamp was flickering by each door;
The arras, rich with horseman, hawk, and hound,
Fluttered in the besieging wind's uproar;
And the long carpets rose along the gusty floor.   360

XLI

They glide, like phantoms, into the wide hall;
Like phantoms, to the iron porch, they glide;
Where lay the Porter, in uneasy sprawl,
With a huge empty flagon by his side:
The wakeful bloodhound rose, and shook his hide,   365
But his sagacious eye an inmate owns:°
By one, and one, the bolts full easy slide:
The chains lie silent on the footworn stones;
The key turns, and the door upon its hinges groans.

XLII

And they are gone: aye, ages long ago   370
These lovers fled away into the storm.

---

336 **vermcil:** scarlet, vermilion.   346 **wassaillers:** drunken revelers   366 **owns:** acknowledges.

That night the Baron dreamt of many a woe,
And all his warrior-guests, with shade and form
Of witch, and demon, and large coffin-worm,
Were long be-nightmared. Angela the old
Died palsy-twitched, with meager face deform;
The Beadsman, after thousand aves told,
For aye unsought for slept among his ashes cold.

375

JOHN KEATS

La Belle Dame sans Merci°

O what can ail thee, Knight at arms,
   Alone and palely loitering?
The sedge has withered from the Lake
   And no birds sing!

O what can ail thee, Knight at arms,   5
   So haggard, and so woebegone?
The squirrel's granary is full
   And the harvest's done.

I see a lily on thy brow
   With anguish moist and fever dew,   10
And on thy cheeks a fading rose
   Fast withereth too.

"I met a Lady in the Meads,°
   Full beautiful, a faery's child,
He hair was long, her foot was light   15
   And her eyes were wild.

"I made a Garland for her head,
   And bracelets too, and fragrant Zone;°
She looked at me as she did love
   And made sweet moan.   20

"I set her on my pacing steed
   And nothing else saw all day long,
For sidelong would she bend and sing
   A faery's song.

"She found me roots of relish sweet,   25
   And honey wild, and manna° dew,
And sure in language strange she said
   'I love thee true.'

"She took me to her elfin grot
   And there she wept and sighed full sore,   30

Title: the beautiful merciless woman.   13 **Meads:** meadows.   18 **Zone:** girdle, belt.
26 **manna:** holy food.

And there I shut her wild wild eyes
  With kisses four.

"And there she lulléd me asleep,
  And there I dreamed, Ah Woe betide!
The latest° dream I ever dreamt   35
  On the cold hill side.

"I saw pale Kings, and Princes too,
  Pale warriors, death-pale were they all;
They cried, 'La belle dame sans merci
  Thee hath in thrall!'   40

"I saw their starved lips in the gloom
  With horrid warning gapéd wide,
And I awoke, and found me here
  On the cold hill's side.

"And this is why I sojourn here,   45
  Alone and palely loitering;
Though the sedge is withered from the Lake
  And no birds sing."

35 **latest:** last.

Ode on a Grecian Urn°

I

Thou still unravished bride of quietness,
  Thou foster child of silence and slow time,
Sylvan historian, who canst thus express
  A flowery tale more sweetly than our rhyme:
What leaf-fringed legend haunts about thy shape   5
  Of deities or mortals, or of both,
    In Tempe or the dales of Arcady?°
  What men or gods are these? What maidens loath?
What mad pursuit? What struggle to escape?   10
    What pipes and timbrels? What wild ecstasy?

II

Heard melodies are sweet, but those unheard
  Are sweeter; therefore, ye soft pipes, play on;
Not to the sensual ear, but, more endeared,
  Pipe to the spirit ditties of no tone:
Fair youth, beneath the trees, thou canst not leave   15
  Thy song, nor ever can those trees be bare;
    Bold Lover, never, never canst thou kiss,

Title: Greek vase decorated with paintings of mythological scenes.   7 **Tempe . . . Arcady:** regions in Greece.

Though winning near the goal—yet, do not grieve;
   She cannot fade, though thou hast not thy bliss,
   Forever wilt thou love, and she be fair!   20

III

Ah, happy, happy boughs! that cannot shed
   Your leaves, nor ever bid the Spring adieu;
And, happy melodist, unwearièd,
   Forever piping songs forever new;
More happy love! more happy, happy love!   25
   Forever warm and still to be enjoyed,
      Forever panting, and forever young;
All breathing human passion far above,
   That leaves a heart high-sorrowful and cloyed,
      A burning forehead, and a parching tongue.   30

IV

Who are these coming to the sacrifice?
   To what green altar, O mysterious priest,
Lead'st thou that heifer lowing at the skies,
   And all her silken flanks with garlands dressed?
What little town by river or sea shore,   35
   Or mountain-built with peaceful citadel,
      Is emptied of this folk, this pious morn?
And, little town, thy streets forevermore
   Will silent be; and not a soul to tell
      Why thou art desolate, can e'er return.   40

V

O Attic° shape! Fair attitude! with brede°
   Of marble men and maidens overwrought,
With forest branches and the trodden weed;
   Thou, silent form, dost tease us out of thought
As doth eternity: Cold Pastoral!   45
   When old age shall this generation waste,
      Thou shalt remain, in midst of other woe
Than ours, a friend to man, to whom thou say'st,
   "Beauty is truth, truth beauty,"—that is all
      Ye know on earth, and all ye need to know.   50

41 **Attic:** Greek, mainly Athenian; **brede:** woven pattern

On First Looking into Chapman's Homer°

Much have I traveled in the realms of gold,
   And many goodly states and kingdoms seen;
   Round many western islands have I been

Title: translation of Homer's poetry by the Elizabethan poet George Chapman.

Which bards in fealty° to Apollo° hold.
Oft of one wide expanse had I been told   5
    That deep-browed Homer° ruled as his demesne;°
    Yet did I never breathe its pure serene
Till I heard Chapman speak out loud and bold:
Then felt I like some watcher of the skies
    When a new planet swims into his ken;   10
Or like stout Cortez° when with eagle eyes
    He stared at the Pacific—and all his men
Looked at each other with a wild surmise—
    Silent, upon a peak in Darien.°

4 **fealty:** allegiance; **Apollo:** god of poetry and music.   6 **Homer:** Greek poet; **demesne:** property.   11 an error or poetic liberty; it was Balboa who discovered the Pacific in 1513.
14 **Darien:** area of Central America.

When I Have Fears

When I have fears that I may cease to be
    Before my pen has gleaned my teeming brain,
Before high-piléd books, in charact'ry,
    Hold like rich garners the full-ripened grain;
When I behold, upon the night's starred face,   5
    Huge cloudy symbols of a high romance,
And think that I may never live to trace
    Their shadows, with the magic hand of chance;
And when I feel, fair creature of an hour,
    That I shall never look upon thee more,   10
Never have relish in the faery power
    Of unreflecting love!—then on the shore
Of the wide world I stand alone, and think
Till Love and Fame to nothingness do sink.   15

ELIZABETH BARRETT BROWNING (1806–1861)

Sonnet 43

How do I love thee? Let me count the ways.
I love thee to the depth and breadth and height
My soul can reach, when feeling out of sight
For the ends of Being and ideal Grace.
I love thee to the level of everyday's   5
Most quiet need, by sun and candle-light.
I love thee freely, as men strive for Right;
I love thee purely, as they turn from Praise.

I love thee with the passion put to use
In my old griefs, and with my childhood's faith.   10
I love thee with a love I seemed to lose
With my lost saints,—I love thee with the breath,
Smiles, tears, of all my life!—and, if God choose,
I shall but love thee better after death.

RALPH WALDO EMERSON (1803–1882)

Days

Daughters of Time, the hypocritic Days,
Muffled and dumb like barefoot dervishes,
And marching single in an endless file,
Bring diadems and fagots in their hands.
To each they offer gifts after his will,   5
Bread, kingdoms, stars, and sky that holds them all.
I, in my pleached garden, watched the pomp,
Forgot my morning wishes, hastily
Took a few herbs and apples, and the Day
Turned and departed silent. I, too late,   10
Under her solemn fillet saw the scorn.

ALFRED, LORD TENNYSON (1809–1892)

Break, Break, Break

Break, break, break,
    On thy cold gray stones, O Sea!
And I would that my tongue could utter
    The thoughts that arise in me.

O well for the fisherman's boy,   5
    That he shouts with his sister at play!
O well for the sailor lad,
    That he sings in his boat on the bay!

And the stately ships go on
    To their haven under the hill;   10
But O for the touch of a vanished hand,
    And the sound of a voice that is still!

Break, break, break,
    At the foot of thy crags, O Sea!
But the tender grace of a day that is dead   15
    Will never come back to me.

Tears, Idle Tears

'Tears, idle tears, I know not what they mean,
Tears from the depth of some divine despair
Rise in the heart, and gather to the eyes,
In looking on the happy Autumn-fields,
And thinking of the days that are no more.   5

'Fresh as the first beam glittering on a sail,
That brings our friends up from the underworld,
Sad as the last which reddens over one
That sinks with all we love below the verge;
So sad, so fresh, the days that are no more.   10

'Ah, sad and strange as in dark summer dawns
The earliest pipe of half-awakened birds
To dying ears, when unto dying eyes
The casement slowly grows a glimmering square;
So sad, so strange, the days that are no more.   15

'Dear as remembered kisses after death,
And sweet as those by hopeless fancy feigned
On lips that are for others; deep as love,
Deep as first love, and wild with all regret;
O Death in Life, the days that are no more.'   20

Tithonus°

The woods decay, the woods decay and fall,
The vapors weep their burthen to the ground,
Man comes and tills the field and lies beneath,
And after many a summer dies the swan.
Me only cruel immortality   5
Consumes; I wither slowly in thine arms,
Here at the quiet limit of the world,
A white-haired shadow roaming like a dream
The ever-silent spaces of the East,
Far-folded mists, and gleaming halls of morn.   10
    Alas! for this gray shadow, once a man—
So glorious in his beauty and thy choice,
Who madest him thy chosen, that he seemed
To his great heart none other than a God!
I asked thee, "Give me immortality."   15
Then didst thou grant mine asking with a smile,

Title: a Trojan prince loved by the goddess of the dawn. Zeus, the king of the gods, gave him
immortal life at her request, but she neglected to ask as well for eternal youth.

Like wealthy men who care not how they give.
But thy strong Hours indignant worked their wills,
And beat me down and marred and wasted me,
And though they could not end me, left me maimed   20
To dwell in presence of immortal youth.
Immortal age beside immortal youth,
And all I was in ashes. Can thy love,
Thy beauty, make amends, though even now,
Close over us, the silver star° thy guide,   25
Shines in those tremulous eyes that fill with tears
To hear me? Let me go; take back thy gift.
Why should a man desire in any way
To vary from the kindly race of men,
Or pass beyond the goal of ordinance   30
Where all should pause, as is most meet for all?
   A soft air fans the cloud apart; there comes
A glimpse of that dark world where I was born.
Once more the old mysterious glimmer steals
From thy pure brows, and from thy shoulders pure,   35
And bosom beating with a heart renewed.
Thy cheek begins to redden through the gloom,
Thy sweet eyes brighten slowly close to mine,
Ere yet they blind the stars, and the wild team
Which love thee, yearning for thy yoke, arise,   40
And shake the darkness from their loosened manes,
And beat the twilight into flakes of fire.
   Lo! ever thus thou growest beautiful
In silence, then before thine answer given
Departest, and thy tears are on my cheek.   45
   Why wilt thou ever scare me with thy tears,
And make me tremble lest a saying learnt,
In days far-off, on that dark earth, be true?
"The Gods themselves cannot recall their gifts."
   Ay me! ay me! with what another heart   50
In days far-off, and with what other eyes
I used to watch—if I be he that watched—
The lucid outline forming round thee; saw
The dim curls kindle into sunny rings;
Changed with thy mystic change, and felt my blood   55
Glow with the glow that slowly crimsoned all
Thy presence and thy portals, while I lay,
Mouth, forehead, eyelids, growing dewy-warm
With kisses balmier than half-opening buds
Of April, and could hear the lips that kissed   60
Whispering I knew not what of wild and sweet,
Like that strange song I heard Apollo sing,

25 **silver star:** morning star.

While Ilion like a mist rose into towers.°
   Yet hold me not for ever in thine East;
How can my nature longer mix with thine?   65
Coldly thy rosy shadows bathe me, cold
Are all thy lights, and cold my wrinkled feet
Upon thy glimmering thresholds, when the steam
Floats up from those dim fields about the homes
Of happy men that have the power to die,   70
And grassy barrows of the happier dead.
Release me, and restore me to the ground.
Thou seest all things, thou wilt see my grave;
Thou wilt renew thy beauty morn by morn,
I earth in earth forget these empty courts,   75
And thee returning on thy silver wheels.

63 the walls of Troy (Ilion) were magically built by the power of Apollo's song.

Ulysses°

It little profits that an idle king,
By this still hearth, among these barren crags,
Matched with an agéd wife, I mete and dole
Unequal laws unto a savage race,
That hoard, and sleep, and feed, and know not me.   5
I cannot rest from travel; I will drink
Life to the lees. All times I have enjoyed
Greatly, have suffered greatly, both with those
That loved me, and alone; on shore, and when
Thro' scudding drifts the rainy Hyades°   10
Vext the dim sea. I am become a name;
For always roaming with a hungry heart
Much have I seen and known,—cities of men
And manners, climates, councils, governments,
Myself not least, but honored of them all,—   15
And drunk delight of battle with my peers,
Far on the ringing plains of windy Troy.
I am a part of all that I have met;
Yet all experience is an arch wherethro'
Gleams that untravelled world whose margin fades   20
For ever and for ever when I move.
How dull it is to pause, to make an end,
To rust unburnished, not to shine in use!
As tho' to breathe were life! Life piled on life

Title: famous Greek hero, returning home after twenty years.   10 **Hyades:** constellation of stars.

Were all too little, and of one to me 25
Little remains; but every hour is saved
From that eternal silence, something more,
A bringer of new things; and vile it were
For some three suns to store and hoard myself,
And this gray spirit yearning in desire 30
To follow knowledge like a sinking star,
Beyond the utmost bound of human thought.
    This is my son, mine own Telemachus,
To whom I leave the sceptre and the isle,
Well-loved of me, discerning to fulfill 35
This labor, by slow prudence to make mild
A rugged people, and thro' soft degrees
Subdue them to the useful and the good.
Most blameless is he, centred in the sphere
Of common duties, decent not to fail 40
In offices of tenderness, and pay
Meet adoration to my household gods,
When I am gone. He works his work, I mine.
    There lies the port; the vessel puffs her sail;
There gloom the dark, broad seas. My mariners, 45
Souls that have toiled, and wrought, and thought with me,—
That ever with a frolic welcome took
The thunder and the sunshine, and opposed
Free hearts, free foreheads,—you and I are old;
Old age hath yet his honor and his toil. 50
Death closes all; but something ere the end,
Some work of noble note, may yet be done,
Not unbecoming men that strove with Gods.
The lights begin to twinkle from the rocks;
The long day wanes; the slow moon climbs; the deep 55
Moans round with many voices. Come, my friends.
'Tis not too late to seek a newer world.
Push off, and sitting well in order smite
The sounding furrows; for my purpose holds
To sail beyond the sunset, and the baths 60
Of all the western stars, until I die.
It may be that the gulfs will wash us down;
It may be we shall touch the Happy Isles,°
And see the great Achilles, whom we knew.
Tho' much is taken, much abides; and tho' 65
We are not now that strength which in old days
Moved earth and heaven, that which we are, we are,—
One equal temper of heroic hearts,
Made weak by time and fate, but strong in will
To strive, to seek, to find, and not to yield.

63 **Happy Isles:** mythical place where soldiers' souls were sent.

ROBERT BROWNING (1812–1889)

My Last Duchess

Ferrara

That's my last duchess painted on the wall,
Looking as if she were alive. I call
That piece a wonder, now: Frà Pandolf's hands
Worked busily a day, and there she stands.
Will't please you sit and look at her? I said   5
"Frà Pandolf" by design, for never read
Strangers like you that pictured countenance,
The depth and passion of its earnest glance,
But to myself they turned (since none puts by
The curtain I have drawn for you, but I)   10
And seemed as they would ask me, if they durst,
How such a glance came there; so, not the first
Are you to turn and ask thus. Sir, 'twas not
Her husband's presence only, called that spot
Of joy into the Duchess' cheek: perhaps   15
Frà Pandolf chanced to say "Her mantle laps
"Over my lady's wrist too much," or "Paint
"Must never hope to reproduce the faint
"Half-flush that dies along her throat": such stuff
Was courtesy, she thought, and cause enough   20
For calling up that spot of joy. She had
A heart—how shall I say?—too soon made glad,
Too easily impressed; she liked whate'er
She looked on, and her looks went everywhere.
Sir, 'twas all one! My favor at her breast,   25
The dropping of the daylight in the West,
The bough of cherries some officious fool
Broke in the orchard for her, the white mule
She rode with round the terrace—all and each
Would draw from her alike the approving speech,   30
Or blush, at least. She thanked men—good! but thanked
Somehow—I know not how—as if she ranked
My gift of a nine-hundred-years-old name
With anybody's gift. Who'd stoop to blame
This sort of trifling? Even had you skill   35
In speech—which I have not—to make your will
Quite clear to such an one, and say, "Just this
"Or that in you disgusts me; here you miss,
"Or there exceed the mark"—and if she let
Herself be lessoned so, nor plainly set   40
Her wits to yours, forsooth, and made excuse,
—E'en then would be some stooping; and I choose
Never to stoop. Oh sir, she smiled, no doubt,
Whene'er I passed her; but who passed without

Much the same smile? This grew; I gave commands;   45
Then all smiles stopped together. There she stands
As if alive. Will't please you rise? We'll meet
The company below, then. I repeat,
The Count your master's known munificence
Is ample warrant that no just pretense   50
Of mine for dowry will be disallowed;
Though his fair daughter's self, as I avowed
At starting, is my object. Nay, we'll go
Together down, sir. Notice Neptune, though,
Taming a sea-horse, thought a rarity,   55
Which Claus of Innsbruck cast in bronze for me!

WALT WHITMAN (1819–1892)

Out of the Cradle Endlessly Rocking

Out of the cradle endlessly rocking,
Out of the mocking-bird's throat, the musical shuttle,
Out of the Ninth-month midnight,
Over the sterile sands and the fields beyond, where the child leaving his
    bed wander'd alone, bareheaded, barefoot,
Down from the shower'd halo   5
Up from the mystic play of shadows twining and twisting as if they were
    alive,
Out from the patches of briers and blackberries,
From the memories of the bird that chanted to me,
From your memories sad brother, from the fitful risings and fallings I
    heard,
From under that yellow half-moon late-risen and swollen as if with tears,   10
From those beginning notes of yearning and love there in the mist,
From the thousand responses of my heart never to cease,
From the myriad thence-arous'd words,
From the word stronger and more delicious than any,
From such as now they start the scene revisiting,   15
As a flock, twittering, rising, or overhead passing,
Borne hither, ere all eludes me, hurriedly,
A man, yet by these tears a little boy again,
Throwing myself on the sand, confronting the waves,
I, chanter of pains and joys, uniter of here and hereafter,   20
Taking all hints to use them, but swiftly leaping beyond them,
A reminiscence sing.

Once Paumanok,
When the lilac-scent was in the air and Fifth-month grass was growing,
Up this seashore in some briers,   25
Two feather'd guests from Alabama, two together,
And their nest, and four light-green eggs spotted with brown,

And every day the he-bird to and fro near at hand,
And every day the she-bird crouch'd on her nest, silent, with bright eyes,
And every day I, a curious boy, never too close, never disturbing them,   30
Cautiously peering, absorbing, translating.

Shine! shine! shine!
Pour down your warmth, great sun!
While we bask, we two together.

Two together!   35
Winds blow south, or winds blow north,
Day come white, or night come black,
Home, or rivers and mountains from home,
Singing all time, minding no time,
While we two keep together.   40

Till of a sudden,
May-be kill'd, unknown to her mate,
One forenoon the she-bird crouch'd not on the nest,
Nor return'd that afternoon, nor the next,
Nor ever appear'd again.   45

And thenceforward all summer in the sound of the sea,
And at night under the full of the moon in calmer weather,
Over the hoarse surging of the sea,
Or flitting from brier to brier by day,
I saw, I heard at intervals the remaining one, the he-bird,   50
The solitary guest from Alabama.

Blow! blow! blow!
Blow up sea-winds along Paumanok's shore;
I wait and I wait till you blow my mate to me.

Yes, when the stars glisten'd,   55
All night long on the prong of a moss-scallop'd stake,
Down almost amid the slapping waves,
Sat the lone singer wonderful causing tears.

He call'd on his mate,
He pour'd forth the meanings which I of all men know.   60

Yes my brother I know,
The rest might not, but I have treasur'd every note,
For more than once dimly down to the beach gliding,
Silent, avoiding the moonbeams, blending myself with the shadows,
Recalling now the obscure shapes, the echoes, the sounds and sights after
    their sorts,   65
The white arms out in the breakers tirelessly tossing,
I, with bare feet, a child, the wind wafting my hair,
Listen'd long and long.

Listen'd to keep, to sing, now translating the notes,
Following you my brother.   70

Soothe! soothe! soothe!
Close on its wave soothes the wave behind,
And again another behind embracing and lapping, every one close,
But my love soothes not me, not me.

Low hangs the moon, it rose late,   75
It is lagging—O I think it is heavy with love, with love.

O madly the sea pushes upon the land,
With love, with love.

O night! do I not see my love fluttering out among the breakers?
What is that little black thing I see there in the white?   80

Loud! loud! loud!
Loud I call to you, my love!
High and clear I shoot my voice over the waves,
Surely you must know who is here, is here,
You must know who I am, my love.   85

Low-hanging moon!
What is that dusky spot in your brown yellow?
O it is the shape, the shape of my mate!
O moon do not keep her from me any longer.

Land! land! O land!   90
Whichever way I turn, O I think you could give me my mate back again if
*   you only would,*
For I am almost sure I see her dimly whichever way I look.

O rising stars!
Perhaps the one I want so much will rise, will rise with some of you.

O throat! O trembling throat!   95
Sound clearer through the atmosphere!
Pierce the woods, the earth,
Somewhere listening to catch you must be the one I want.

Shake out carols!
Solitary here, the night's carols!   100
Carols of lonesome love! death's carols!
Carols under that lagging, yellow, waning moon!
O under that moon where she droops almost down into the sea!
O reckless despairing carols.

But soft! sink low!   105
Soft! let me just murmur,
And do you wait a moment you husky-nois'd sea,
For somewhere I believe I heard my mate responding to me,
So faint, I must be still, be still to listen,
But not altogether still, for then she might not come immediately to me.   110

Hither my love!
Here I am! here!

With this just-sustain'd note I announce myself to you,
This gentle call is for you my love, for you.

Do not be decoy'd elsewhere, 115
That is the whistle of the wind, it is not my voice,
That is the fluttering, the fluttering of the spray,
Those are the shadows of leaves.

O darkness! O in vain!
O I am very sick and sorrowful. 120

O brown halo in the sky near the moon, drooping upon the sea!
O troubled reflection in the sea!
O throat! O throbbing heart!
And I singing uselessly, uselessly all the night.

O past! O happy life! O songs of joy! 125
In the air, in the woods, over fields,
Loved! loved! loved! loved! loved!
But my mate no more, no more with me!
We two together no more.

The aria sinking,
All else continuing, the stars shining,
The winds blowing, the notes of the bird continuous echoing,
With angry moans the fierce old mother incessantly moaning,
On the sands of Paumanok's shore gray and rustling,
The yellow half-moon enlarged, sagging down, drooping, the face of the
 sea almost touching, 135
The boy ecstatic, with his bare feet the waves, with his hair the atmosphere
 dallying,
The love in the heart long pent, now loose, now at last tumultuously
 bursting,
The aria's meaning, the ears, the soul, swiftly depositing,
The strange tears down the cheeks coursing,
The colloquy there, the trio, each uttering, 140
The undertone, the savage old mother incessantly crying,
To the boy's soul's questions sullenly timing, some drown'd secret hissing,
To the outsetting bard.

Demon or bird! (said the boy's soul,)
Is it indeed toward your mate you sing? or is it really to me? 145
For I, that was a child, my tongue's use sleeping, now I have heard you,
Now in a moment I know what I am for, I awake,
And already a thousand singers, a thousand songs, clearer, louder and
 more sorrowful than yours,
A thousand warbling echoes have started to life within me, never to die.

O you singer solitary, singing by yourself, projecting me, 150
O solitary me listening, never more shall I cease perpetuating you,
Never more shall I escape, never more the reverberations,
Never more the cries of unsatisfied love be absent from me,

Never again leave me to be the peaceful child I was before what there in
   the night,
By the sea under the yellow and sagging moon,   155
The messenger there arous'd, the fire, the sweet hell within,
The unknown want, the destiny of me.

O give me the clew! (it lurks in the night here somewhere,)
O if I am to have so much, let me have more!

A word then, (for I will conquer it,)   160
The word final, superior to all,
Subtle, sent up—what is it?—I listen;
Are you whispering it, and have been all the time, you sea-waves?
Is that it from your liquid rims and wet sands?

Whereto answering, the sea,   165
Delaying not, hurrying not,
Whisper'd me through the night, and very plainly before daybreak,
Lisp'd to me the low and delicious word death,
And again death, death, death, death,
Hissing melodious, neither like the bird nor like my arous'd child's heart, 170
But edging near as privately for me rustling at my feet,
Creeping thence steadily up to my ears and laving me softly all over,
Death, death, death, death, death.

Which I do not forget,
But fuse the song of my dusky demon and brother,   175
That he sang to me in the moonlight on Paumanok's gray beach,
With the thousand responsive songs at random,
My own songs awaked from that hour,
And with them the key, the word up from the waves,
The word of the sweetest song and all songs,
That strong and delicious word which, creeping to my feet,   180
(Or like some old crone rocking the cradle, swathed in sweet garments,
   bending aside,)
The sea whisper'd me.

The Dalliance of the Eagles

Skirting the river road, (my forenoon walk, my rest,)
Skyward in air a sudden muffled sound, the dalliance of the eagles,
The rushing amorous contact high in space together,
The clinching interlocking claws, a living, fierce, gyrating wheel,
Four beating wings, two beaks, a swirling mass tight grappling,   5
In tumbling turning clustering loops, straight downward falling,
Till o'er the river pois'd, the twain yet one, a moment's lull,
A motionless still balance in the air, then parting, talons loosing,
Upward again on slow-firm pinions slanting, their separate diverse flight,
She hers, he his, pursuing.   10

A Noiseless Patient Spider

A noiseless patient spider,
I mark'd where on a little promontory it stood isolated,
Mark'd how to explore the vacant vast surrounding,
It launch'd forth filament, filament, filament, out of itself,
Ever unreeling them, ever tirelessly speeding them.   5

And you O my soul where you stand,
Surrounded, detached, in measureless oceans of space,
Ceaselessly musing, venturing, throwing, seeking the spheres to connect
     them,
Till the bridge you will need be form'd, till the ductile anchor hold,
Till the gossamer thread you fling catch somewhere, O my soul.   10

Cavalry Crossing a Ford

A line in long array where they wind betwixt green islands,
They take a serpentine course, their arms flash in the sun—hark to the
     musical clank,
Behold the silvery river, in it the splashing horses loitering stop to drink,
Behold the brown-faced men, each group, each person a picture, the
     negligent rest on the saddles,
Some emerge on the opposite bank, others are just entering the
     ford—while,   5
Scarlet and blue and snowy white,
The guidon flags flutter gayly in the wind.

I Saw in Louisiana a Live-Oak Growing

I saw in Louisiana a live-oak growing,
All alone stood it and the moss hung down from the branches,
Without any companion it grew there uttering joyous leaves of dark green,
And its look, rude, unbending, lusty, made me think of myself,
But I wonder'd how it could utter joyous leaves standing alone there
     without its friend near, for I knew I could not,   5
And I broke off a twig with a certain number of leaves upon it, and twined
     around it a little moss,
And brought it away, and I have placed it in sight in my room,
It is not needed to remind me as of my own dear friends,
(For I believe lately I think of little else than of them,)
Yet it remains to me a curious token, it makes me think of manly love;   10

For all that, and though the live-oak glistens there in Louisiana solitary in
    a wide flat space,
Uttering joyous leaves all its life without a friend a lover near,
I know very well I could not.

MATTHEW ARNOLD (1822–1888)

Dover Beach

The sea is calm tonight,
The tide is full, the moon lies fair
Upon the straits;—on the French coast the light
Gleams and is gone; the cliffs of England stand,
Glimmering and vast, out in the tranquil bay. 5
Come to the window, sweet is the night-air!
Only, from the long line of spray
Where the sea meets the moon-blanched land,
Listen! you hear the grating roar
Of pebbles which the waves draw back, and fling, 10
At their return, up the high strand,
Begin, and cease, and then again begin,
With tremulous cadence slow, and bring
The eternal note of sadness in.

Sophocles long ago 15
Heard it on the Aegean, and it brought
Into his mind the turbid ebb and flow
Of human misery; we
Find also in the sound a thought,
Hearing it by this distant northern sea. 20

The Sea of Faith
Was once, too, at the full, and round earth's shore
Lay like the folds of a bright girdle furled.
But now I only hear
Its melancholy, long, withdrawing roar, 25
Retreating, to the breath
Of the night-wind, down the vast edges drear
And naked shingles of the world.

Ah, love, let us be true
To one another! for the world, which seems 30
To lie before us like a land of dreams,
So various, so beautiful, so new,
Hath really neither joy, nor love, nor light,
Nor certitude, nor peace, nor help for pain;
And we are here as on a darkling plain 35
Swept with confused alarms of struggle and flight,
Where ignorant armies clash by night.

To Marguerite

Yes! in the sea of life enisled,
With echoing straits between us thrown,
Dotting the shoreless watery wild,
We mortal millions live *alone.*
The islands feel the enclasping flow,   5
And then their endless bounds they know.

But when the moon their hollows lights,
And they are swept by balms of spring,
And in their glens, on starry nights,
The nightingales divinely sing;   10
And lovely notes, from shore to shore,
Across the sounds and channels pour—

Oh! then a longing like despair
Is to their farthest caverns sent;
For surely once, they feel, we were   15
Parts of a single continent!
Now round us spreads the watery plain—
Oh might our marges meet again!

Who ordered, that their longing's fire
Should be, as soon as kindled, cooled?   20
Who renders vain their deep desire?—
A God, a God their severance ruled!
And bade betwixt their shores to be
The unplumbed, salt, estranging sea.

EMILY DICKINSON (1830–1886)

67 [Success is counted sweetest]

Success is counted sweetest
By those who ne'er succeed.
To comprehend a nectar
Requires sorest need.

Not one of all the purple Host   5
Who took the Flag today
Can tell the definition
So clear of Victory

As he defeated—dying—
On whose forbidden ear   10
The distant strains of triumph
Burst agonized and clear!

214 [I taste a liquor never brewed—]

I taste a liquor never brewed—
From Tankards scooped in Pearl—
Not all the Vats upon the Rhine
Yield such an Alcohol!

Inebriate of Air—am I—   5
And Debauchee of Dew—
Reeling—thro endless summer days—
From inns of Molten Blue—

When "Landlords" turn the drunken Bee
Out of the Foxglove's door—   10
When Butterflies—renounce their "drams"—
I shall but drink the more!

Till Seraphs swing their snowy Hats—
And Saints—to windows run—
To see the little Tippler   15
Leaning against the—Sun—

303 [The Soul selects her own Society—]

The Soul selects her own Society—
Then—shuts the Door—
To her divine Majority—
Present no more—

Unmoved—she notes the Chariots—pausing—   5
At her low Gate—
Unmoved—an Emperor be kneeling
Upon her Mat—

I've known her—from an ample nation—
Choose One—   10
Then—close the Valves of her attention—
Like Stone—

449 [I died for Beauty—but was scarce]

I died for Beauty—but was scarce
Adjusted in the Tomb
When One who died for Truth, was lain
In an adjoining Room—

He questioned softly "Why I failed"?   5
"For Beauty", I replied—
"And I—for Truth—Themself are One—
We Brethren, are", He said—

And so, as Kinsmen, met a Night—
We talked between the Rooms—   10
Until the Moss had reached our lips—
And covered up—our names—

465 [I heard a Fly buzz—when I died—]

I heard a Fly buzz—when I died—
The Stillness in the Room
Was like the Stillness in the Air—
Between the Heaves of Storm—

The Eyes around—had wrung them dry—   5
And Breaths were gathering firm
For that last Onset—when the King
Be witnessed—in the Room—

I willed my Keepsakes—Signed away
What portion of me be   10
Assignable—and then it was
There interposed a Fly—

With Blue—uncertain stumbling Buzz—
Between the light—and me—
And then the Windows failed—and then   15
I could not see to see—

585 [I like to see it lap the miles—]

I like to see it lap the Miles—
And lick the Valleys up—
And stop to feed itself at Tanks—
And then—prodigious step

Around a Pile of Mountains—   5
And supercilious peer
In Shanties—by the sides of Roads—
And then a Quarry pare

To fit its Ribs
And crawl between   10
Complaining all the while
In horrid—hooting stanza—
Then chase itself down Hill—

And neigh like Boanerges°—
Then—punctual as a Star
Stop—docile and omnipotent
At its own stable door—

15

14 **Boanerges:** a term for thundering loud-voiced preachers and orators.

712 [Because I could not stop for Death—]

Because I could not stop for Death—
He kindly stopped for me—
The Carriage held but just Ourselves—
And Immortality.

We slowly drove—He knew no haste   5
And I had put away
My labor and my leisure too,
For His Civility—

We passed the School, where Children strove
At Recess—in the Ring—   10
We passed the Fields of Gazing Grain—
We passed the Setting Sun—

Or rather—He passed Us—
The Dews drew quivering and chill—
For only Gossamer, my Gown—   15
My Tippet—only Tulle—

We paused before a House that seemed
A Swelling of the Ground—
The Roof was scarcely visible—
The Cornice—in the Ground—   20

Since then—'tis Centuries—and yet
Feels shorter than the Day
I first surmised the Horses' Heads
Were toward Eternity—

986 [A narrow Fellow in the Grass]

A narrow Fellow in the Grass
Occasionally rides—
You may have met Him—did you not
His notice sudden is—

The Grass divides as with a Comb—   5
A spotted shaft is seen—
And then it closes at your feet
And opens further on—

He likes a Boggy Acre
A Floor too cool for Corn—
Yet when a Boy, and Barefoot—
I more than once at Noon
Have passed, I thought, a Whip lash
Unbraiding in the Sun
When stooping to secure it
It wrinkled, and was gone—

Several of Nature's People
I know, and they know me—
I feel for them a transport
Of cordiality—

But never met this Fellow
Attended, or alone
Without a tighter breathing
And Zero at the Bone—

10

15

20

25

1052 [I never saw a Moor—]

I never saw a Moor—
I never saw the Sea—
Yet know I how the Heather looks
And what a Billow be.

I never spoke with God
Nor visited in Heaven—
Yet certain am I of the spot
As if the Checks were given—

5

CHRISTINA ROSSETTI (1830–1894)

Song

When I am dead, my dearest,
   Sing no sad songs for me;
Plant thou no roses at my head,
   Nor shady cypress tree:
Be the green grass above me
   With showers and dewdrops wet:
And if thou wilt, remember,
   And if thou wilt, forget.

I shall not see the shadows,
   I shall not feel the rain;
I shall not hear the nightingale
   Sing on as if in pain:

5

10

And dreaming through the twilight
    That doth not rise nor set,
Haply I may remember,   15
    And haply may forget.

Remember

Remember me when I am gone away,
    Gone far away into the silent land;
    When you can no more hold me by the hand,
Nor I half turn to go yet turning stay.
Remember me when no more day by day   5
    You tell me of our future that you planned:
Only remember me: you understand
It will be late to counsel then or pray.
Yet if you should forget me for a while
    And afterwards remember, do not grieve: 10
    For if the darkness and corruption leave
    A vestige of the thoughts that once I had,
Better by far you should forget and smile
    Than that you should remember and be sad.

LEWIS CARROLL (1832–1898)

Jabberwocky

'Twas brillig, and the slithy toves
    Did gyre and gimble in the wabe;
All mimsy were the borogoves,
    And the mome raths outgrabe.

"Beware the Jabberwock, my son!   5
    The jaws that bite, the claws that catch!
Beware the Jubjub bird, and shun
    The frumious Bandersnatch!"

He took his vorpal sword in hand
    Long time the manxome foe he sought—   10
So rested he by the Tumtum tree,
    And stood awhile in thought.

And, as in uffish thought he stood,
    The Jabberwock, with eyes of flame,
Came whiffling through the tulgey wood,   15
    And burbled as it came!

One, two! One, two! And through and through
    The vorpal blade went snicker-snack!

He left it dead, and with its head
    He went galumphing back.   20

"And hast thou slain the Jabberwock?
    Come to my arms, my beamish boy!
O frabjous day! Callooh! Callay!"
    He chortled in his joy.

'Twas brillig, and the slithy toves   25
    Did gyre and gimble in the wabe;
All mimsy were the borogoves,
    And the mome raths outgrabe.

THOMAS HARDY (1840–1928)

Neutral Tones

We stood by a pond that winter day,
And the sun was white, as though chidden of God,
And a few leaves lay on the starving sod;
    —They had fallen from an ash, and were gray.

Your eyes on me were as eyes that rove   5
Over tedious riddles of years ago;
And some words played between us to and fro
    On which lost the more by our love.

The smile on your mouth was the deadest thing
Alive enough to have strength to die;   10
And a grin of bitterness swept thereby
    Like an ominous bird a-wing. . . .

Since then, keen lessons that love deceives,
And wrings with wrong, have shaped to me
Your face, and the God-curst sun, and a tree,   15
    And a pond edged with grayish leaves.

Channel Firing

That night your great guns, unawares,
Shook all our coffins as we lay,
And broke the chancel window-squares,
We thought it was the Judgment-day

And sat upright. While drearisome   5
Arose the howl of wakened hounds:
The mouse let fall the altar-crumb,
The worms drew back into the mounds,

The glebe cow° drooled. Till God called, "No;
It's gunnery practice out at sea   10
Just as before you went below;
The world is as it used to be:

"All nations striving strong to make
Red war yet redder. Mad as hatters
They do no more for Christés sake   15
Than you who are helpless in such matters.

"That this is not the judgment-hour
For some of them's a blessed thing,
For if it were they'd have to scour
Hell's floor for so much threatening. . . .   20

"Ha, ha. It will be warmer when
I blow the trumpet (if indeed
I ever do; for you are men,
And rest eternal sorely need)."

So down we lay again. "I wonder,   25
Will the world ever saner be,"
Said one, "than when He sent us under
In our indifferent century!"

And many a skeleton shook his head.
"Instead of preaching forty year,"   30
My neighbor Parson Thirdly said,
"I wish I had stuck to pipes and beer."

Again the guns disturbed the hour,
Roaring their readiness to avenge,
As far inland as Stourton Tower,   35
And Camelot, and starlit Stonehenge.°

9 **glebe cow:** cow owned by the village clergyman.   35–36 **Stourton Tower . . . Camelot . . .
Stonehenge:** ancient monuments in southern England.

Ah, Are You Digging on My Grave?

"Ah, are you digging on my grave
   My loved one?—planting rue?"
      —*"No: yesterday he went to wed*
      One of the brightest wealth has bred.
      'It cannot hurt her now,' he said,   5
        'That I should not be true.'"

"Then who is digging on my grave?
   My nearest, dearest kin?"
      —*"Ah, no: they sit and think, 'What use!*
      What good will planting flowers produce?   10
      No tendance of her mound can loose
        Her spirit from Death's gin.'"

"But someone digs upon my grave?
  My enemy?—prodding sly?"
    —*"Nay: when she heard you had passed the Gate*   15
    That shuts on all flesh soon or late,
    She thought you no more worth her hate,
      She cares not where you lie."

"Then, who is digging on my grave?
  Say—since I have not guessed!"   20
    —*"O it is I, my mistress dear,*
    Your little dog, who still lives near,
    And much I hope my movements here
      Have not disturbed your rest?"

"Ah, yes! *You* dig upon my grave. . . .   25
  Why flashed it not on me
That one true heart was left behind!
What feeling do we ever find
To equal among human kind
  A dog's fidelity!"   30

    "Mistress, I dug upon your grave
      To bury a bone, in case
    I should be hungry near this spot
    When passing on my daily trot.
    I am sorry, but I quite forgot   35
      It was your resting-place."

The Man He Killed

  "Had he and I but met
    By some old ancient inn,
  We should have sat us down to wet
    Right many a nipperkin!°

  "But ranged as infantry,   5
    And staring face to face,
  I shot at him as he at me,
    And killed him in his place."

4 **nipperkin:** half-pint container (for beer).

Drummer Hodge

                  I
  They throw in Drummer Hodge, to rest
    Uncoffined—just as found:
  His landmark is a kopje-crest°

3 **kopje:** small hill.

That breaks the veldt° around;
 And foreign constellations west   5
 Each night above his mound.

                            II

 Young Hodge the Drummer never knew—
 Fresh from his Wessex° home—
 The meaning of the broad Karoo,°
 The Bush,° the dusty loam,   10
 And why uprose to nightly view
 Strange stars amid the gloam.

                            III

 Yet portion of that unknown plain
 Will Hodge for ever be;
 His homely Northern breast and brain   15
 Grow to some Southern tree,
 And strange-eyed constellations reign
 His stars eternally.

4 **veldt:** plain.   8 **Wessex:** a region of southern England.   9 **Karoo:** barren plateau.
10 **Bush:** outback.

GERARD MANLEY HOPKINS (1844–1889)

The Windhover°

To Christ Our Lord

 I caught this morning morning's minion,° king-
     dom of daylight's dauphin,° dapple-dawn-drawn Falcon, in his riding
   Of the rolling level underneath him steady air, and striding
 High there, how he rung upon the rein of a wimpling° wing
 In his ecstasy! then off, off forth on swing,   5
     As a skate's heel sweeps smooth on a bow-bend: the hurl and gliding
   Rebuffed the big wind. My heart in hiding
 Stirred for a bird,—the achieve of, the mastery of the thing!

 Brute beauty and valor and act, oh, air, pride, plume, here
     Buckle! AND the fire that breaks from thee then, a billion   10
 Times told lovelier, more dangerous, O my chevalier!°

   No wonder of it: sheer plod makes plough down sillion°
 Shine, and blue-bleak embers, ah my dear,
     Fall, gall themselves, and gash gold-vermilion.

Title: a windhover is a kestrel, or small hawk.   1 **minion:** darling, beloved.   2 **dauphin:** heir
(to a kingdom).   4 **wimpling:** rippling.   11 **chevalier:** champion.   12 **sillion:** furrow.

God's Grandeur

The world is charged with the grandeur of God.
  It will flame out, like shining from shook foil;
  It gathers to a greatness, like the ooze of oil
Crushed. Why do men then now not reck his rod?
Generations have trod, have trod, have trod;   5
  And all is seared with trade; bleared, smeared with toil;
  And wears man's smudge and shares man's smell: the soil
Is bare now, nor can foot feel, being shod.

And for all this, nature is never spent;
  There lives the dearest freshness deep down things;   10
And though the last lights off the black West went
  Oh, morning, at the brown brink eastward, springs—
Because the Holy Ghost over the bent
  World broods with warm breast and with ah! bright wings.

Pied Beauty

Glory be to God for dappled° things—
  For skies of couple-colour as a brinded° cow;
    For rose-moles all in stipple° upon trout that swim;
Fresh-firecoal chestnut-falls; finches' wings;
  Landscape plotted and pieced—fold, fallow, and plow;   5
    And all trades, their gear and tackle and trim.
All things counter, original, spare, strange;
  Whatever is fickle, freckled (who knows how?)
    With swift, slow; sweet, sour; adazzle, dim;
He fathers-forth whose beauty is past change: 10
          Praise him.

1 **dappled:** patchy colored.   2 **brinded:** streaked.   3 **stipple:** colored dots.

A. E. HOUSMAN (1859–1936)

Loveliest of Trees, the Cherry Now

Loveliest of trees, the cherry now
Is hung with bloom along the bough,
And stands about the woodland ride
Wearing white for Eastertide.

Now, of my threescore years and ten,   5
Twenty will not come again,
And take from seventy springs a score,
It only leaves me fifty more.

And since to look at things in bloom
Fifty springs are little room,   10
About the woodlands I will go
To see the cherry hung with snow.

WILLIAM BUTLER YEATS (1865–1939)

A Prayer for My Daughter

Once more the storm is howling, and half hid
Under this cradle-hood and coverlid
My child sleeps on. There is no obstacle
But Gregory's wood and one bare hill
Whereby the haystack- and roof-levelling wind,   5
Bred on the Atlantic, can be stayed;
And for an hour I have walked and prayed
Because of the great gloom that is in my mind.

I have walked and prayed for this young child an hour
And heard the sea-wind scream upon the tower,   10
And under the arches of the bridge, and scream
In the elms above the flooded stream;
Imagining in excited reverie
That the future years had come,
Dancing to a frenzied drum.   15
Out of the murderous innocence of the sea.

May she be granted beauty and yet not
Beauty to make a stranger's eye distraught,
Or hers before a looking-glass, for such,
Being made beautiful overmuch,   20
Consider beauty a sufficient end,
Lose natural kindness and maybe
The heart-revealing intimacy
That chooses right, and never find a friend.

Helen° being chosen found life flat and dull   25
And later had much trouble from a fool,
While that great Queen,° that rose out of the spray,
Being fatherless could have her way
Yet chose a bandy-leggéd smith° for man.
It's certain that fine women eat   30
A crazy salad with their meat
Whereby the Horn of Plenty° is undone.

25 **Helen:** the beautiful Helen of Troy.   27 **Queen:** Aphrodite, Greek goddess of love.   29
bandy-legged smith: Hephaestus (Vulcan), husband of Aphrodite.   32 **Horn of Plenty:** cornucopia, source of all good things.

In courtesy I'd have her chiefly learned;
Hearts are not had as a gift but hearts are earned
By those that are not entirely beautiful;   35
Yet many, that have played the fool
For beauty's very self, has charm made wise,
And many a poor man that has roved,
Loved and thought himself beloved,
From a glad kindness cannot take his eyes.   40

May she become a flourishing hidden tree
That all her thoughts may like the linnet be,
And have no business but dispensing round
Their magnanimities of sound,
Nor but in merriment begin a chase,   45
Nor but in merriment a quarrel.
O may she live like some green laurel
Rooted in one dear perpetual place.

My mind, because the minds that I have loved,
The sort of beauty that I have approved,   50
Prosper but little, has dried up of late,
Yet knows that to be choked with hate
May well be of all evil chances chief.
If there's no hatred in a mind
Assault and battery of the wind   55
Can never tear the linnet from the leaf.

An intellectual hatred is the worst,
So let her think opinions are accursed.
Have I not seen the loveliest woman born
Out of the mouth of Plenty's horn,   60
Because of her opinionated mind
Barter that horn and every good
By quiet natures understood
For an old bellows full of angry wind?

Considering that, all hatred driven hence,   65
The soul recovers radical innocence
And learns at last that it is self-delighting,
Self-appeasing, self-affrighting,
And that its own sweet will is Heaven's will;
She can, though every face should scowl   70
And every windy quarter howl
Or every bellows burst, be happy still.

And may her bridegroom bring her to a house
Where all's accustomed, ceremonious;
For arrogance and hatred are the wares   75
Peddled in the thoroughfares.
How but in custom and in ceremony
Are innocence and beauty born?
Ceremony's a name for the rich horn,
And custom for the spreading laurel tree.   80

Leda and the Swan°

A sudden blow: the great wings beating still
Above the staggering girl, her thighs caressed
By the dark webs, her nape caught in his bill
He holds her helpless breast upon his breast.

How can those terrified vague fingers push   5
The feathered glory from her loosening thighs?
And how can body, laid in that white rush,
But feel the strange heart beating where it lies?

A shudder in the loins engenders there
The broken wall, the burning roof and tower   10
And Agamemnon dead.
                 Being so caught up,
So mastered by the brute blood of the air,
Did she put on his knowledge with his power
Before the indifferent beak could let her drop?   15 ·

Title: Leda, mother of Helen of Troy, was raped by Zeus, father of the gods, disguised as a swan.

When You Are Old

When you are old and gray and full of sleep,
And nodding by the fire, take down this book,
And slowly read, and dream of the soft look
Your eyes had once, and of their shadows deep;

How many loved your moments of glad grace,   5
And loved your beauty with love false or true;
But one man loved the pilgrim soul in you,
And loved the sorrows of your changing face.

And bending down beside the glowing bars
Murmur, a little sadly, how love fled   10
And paced upon the mountains overhead
And hid his face amid a crowd of stars.

Among School Children

I

I walk through the long schoolroom questioning;
  A kind old nun in a white hood replies;
The children learn to cipher° and to sing,
To study reading-books and history,
To cut and sew, be neat in everything   5
In the best modern way—the children's eyes

3 **to cipher:** to learn arithmetic.

In momentary wonder stare upon
A sixty-year-old smiling public man.

II

I dream of a Ledaean° body, bent
Above a sinking fire, a tale that she   10
Told of a harsh reproof, or trivial event
That changed some childish day to tragedy—
Told, and it seemed that our two natures blent
Into a sphere from youthful sympathy,
Or else, to alter Plato's parable,°   15
Into the yolk and white of the one shell.

III

And thinking of that fit of grief or rage
I look upon one child or t'other there
And wonder if she stood so at that age—
For even daughters of the swan can share   20
Something of every paddler's heritage—
And had that colour upon cheek or hair,
And thereupon my heart is driven wild:
She stands before me as a living child.

IV

Her present image floats into the mind—   25
Did Quattrocento° finger fashion it
Hollow of cheek as though it drank the wind
And took a mess of shadows for its meat?
And I though never of Ledaean kind
Had pretty plumage once—enough of that,   30
Better to smile on all that smile, and show
There is a comfortable kind of old scarecrow.

V

What youthful mother, a shape upon her lap
Honey of generation° had betrayed,
And that must sleep, shriek, struggle to escape   35
As recollection or the drug decide,
Would think her son, did she but see that shape
With sixty or more winters on its head,
A compensation for the pang of his birth,
Or the uncertainty of his setting forth?   40

VI

Plato° thought nature but a spume that plays
Upon a ghostly paradigm of things;

---

9 **Ledaean:** as beautiful as Leda.   15 **Plato's parable:** the story told by Plato that we were originally dual in nature, were cut in two (like an egg), and have ever since looked for our lost
halves.   26 **Quattrocento:** fifteenth century, famous for its painting.   34 **Honey of generation:** the sweetness of procreation.   41–44: Plato saw the world as merely a false copy of an
ideal world; Aristotle, a tutor of Alexander the Great, had a much more materialistic view of
things.

Solider Aristotle played the taws
Upon the bottom of a king of kings;
World-famous golden-thighed Pythagoras°   45
Fingered upon a fiddle-stick or strings
What a star sang and careless Muses heard:
Old clothes upon old sticks to scare a bird.

VII

Both nuns and mothers worship images,
But those the candles light are not as those   50
That animate a mother's reveries,
But keep a marble or a bronze repose.
And yet they too break hearts—O Presences
That passion, piety or affection knows,
And that all heavenly glory symbolise—   55
O self-born mockers of man's enterprise;

VIII

Labour is blossoming or dancing where
The body is not bruised to pleasure soul,
Nor beauty born out of its own despair,
Nor blear-eyed wisdom out of midnight oil.   60
O chestnut-tree, great-rooted blossomer,
Are you the leaf, the blossom or the bole?
O body swayed to music, O brightening glance,
How can we know the dancer from the dance?

45–46: Pythagoras speculated about the underlying harmony of the universe.

ROBERT FROST (1874–1963)

Mending Wall

Something there is that doesn't love a wall,
That sends the frozen-ground-swell under it
And spills the upper boulders in the sun,
And makes gaps even two can pass abreast.
The work of hunters is another thing: 5
I have come after them and made repair
Where they have left not one stone on a stone,
But they would have the rabbit out of hiding,
To please the yelping dogs. The gaps I mean,
No one has seen them made or heard them made,   10
But at spring mending-time we find them there.
I let my neighbor know beyond the hill;
And on a day we meet to walk the line
And set the wall between us once again.
We keep the wall between us as we go.   15

To each the boulders that have fallen to each.
And some are loaves and some so nearly balls
We have to use a spell to make them balance:
"Stay where you are until our backs are turned!"
We wear our fingers rough with handling them.   20
Oh, just another kind of outdoor game,
One on a side. It comes to little more:
There where it is we do not need the wall:
He is all pine and I am apple orchard.
My apple trees will never get across   25
And eat the cones under his pines, I tell him.
He only says, "Good fences make good neighbors."
Spring is the mischief in me, and I wonder
If I could put a notion in his head:
"*Why* do they make good neighbors? Isn't it   30
Where there are cows? But here there are no cows.
Before I built a wall I'd ask to know
What I was walling in or walling out,
And to whom I was like to give offense.
Something there is that doesn't love a wall,   35
That wants it down." I could say "Elves" to him,
But it's not elves exactly, and I'd rather
He said it for himself. I see him there,
Bringing a stone grasped firmly by the top
In each hand, like an old-stone savage armed.   40
He moves in darkness as it seems to me,
Not of woods only and the shade of trees.
He will not go behind his father's saying,
And he likes having thought of it so well
He says again, "Good fences make good neighbors."   45

Stopping by Woods on a Snowy Evening

Whose woods these are I think I know.
His house is in the village, though:
He will not see me stopping here
To watch his woods fill up with snow.

My little horse must think it queer   5
To stop without a farmhouse near
Between the woods and frozen lake
The darkest evening of the year.

He gives his harness bells a shake
To ask if there is some mistake.   10
The only other sound's the sweep
Of easy wind and downy flake.

The woods are lovely, dark and deep,
But I have promises to keep,
And miles to go before I sleep,   15
And miles to go before I sleep.

Birches

When I see birches bend to left and right
Across the lines of straighter darker trees,
I like to think some boy's been swinging them.
But swinging doesn't bend them down to stay
As ice-storms do. Often you must have seen them   5
Loaded with ice a sunny winter morning
After a rain. They click upon themselves
As the breeze rises, and turn many-colored
As the stir cracks and crazes their enamel.
Soon the sun's warmth makes them shed crystal shells   10
Shattering and avalanching on the snow-crust—
Such heaps of broken glass to sweep away
You'd think the inner dome of heaven had fallen.
They are dragged to the withered bracken by the load,
And they seem not to break; though once they are bowed   15
So low for long, they never right themselves:
You may see their trunks arching in the woods
Years afterwards, trailing their leaves on the ground
Like girls on hands and knees that throw their hair
Before them over their heads to dry in the sun.   20
But I was going to say when Truth broke in
With all her matter-of-fact about the ice-storm,
I should prefer to have some boy bend them
As he went out and in to fetch the cows—
Some boy too far from town to learn baseball,   25
Whose only play was what he found himself,
Summer or winter, and could play alone.
One by one he subdued his father's trees
By riding them down over and over again
Until he took the stiffness out of them,   30
And not one but hung limp, not one was left
For him to conquer. He learned all there was
To learn about not launching out too soon
And so not carrying the tree away
Clear to the ground. He always kept his poise   35
To the top branches, climbing carefully
With the same pains you use to fill a cup
Up to the brim, and even above the brim.

Then he flung outward, feet first, with a swish,
Kicking his way down through the air to the ground.   40
So was I once myself a swinger of birches.
And so I dream of going back to be.
It's when I'm weary of considerations,
And life is too much like a pathless wood
Where your face burns and tickles with the cobwebs   45
Broken across it, and one eye is weeping
From a twig's having lashed across it open.
I'd like to get away from earth awhile
And then come back to it and begin over.
May no fate willfully misunderstand me   50
And half grant what I wish and snatch me away
Not to return. Earth's the right place for love:
I don't know where it's likely to go better.
I'd like to go by climbing a birch tree,
And climb black branches up a snow-white trunk   55
Toward heaven, till the tree could bear no more,
But dipped its top and set me down again.
That would be good both going and coming back.
One could do worse than be a swinger of birches.

WALLACE STEVENS (1879–1955)

The Emperor of Ice-Cream

Call the roller of big cigars,
The muscular one, and bid him whip
In kitchen cups concupiscent curds.
Let the wenches dawdle in such dress
As they are used to wear, and let the boys   5
Bring flowers in last month's newspapers.
Let be be finale of seem.
The only emperor is the emperor of ice-cream.

Take from the dresser of deal,°
Lacking the three glass knobs, that sheet   10
On which she embroidered fantails° once
And spread it so as to cover her face.
If her horny feet protrude, they come
To show how cold she is, and dumb.
Let the lamp affix its beam.   15
The only emperor is the emperor of ice-cream.

9 **dresser of deal:** pine sideboard.   11 **fantails:** fan-shaped patterns, resembling the tails of birds.

Anecdote of the Jar

I placed a jar in Tennessee,
And round it was, upon a hill.
It made the slovenly wilderness
Surround that hill.

The wilderness rose up to it,   5
And sprawled around, no longer wild.
The jar was round upon the ground
And tall and of a port in air.

It took dominion everywhere.
The jar was gray and bare.   10
It did not give of bird or bush,
Like nothing else in Tennessee.

Thirteen Ways of Looking at a Blackbird

I
Among twenty snowy mountains,
The only moving thing
Was the eye of the blackbird.

II
I was of three minds,
Like a tree   5
In which there are three blackbirds.

III
The blackbird whirled in the autumn winds.
It was a small part of the pantomime.

IV
A man and a woman
Are one.   10
A man and a woman and a blackbird
Are one.

V
I do not know which to prefer,
The beauty of inflections,
Or the beauty of innuendoes,   15
The blackbird whistling
Or just after.

VI
Icicles filled the long window
With barbaric glass.

The shadow of the blackbird   20
Crossed it, to and fro.
The mood
Traced in the shadow
An indecipherable cause.

VII

O thin men of Haddam,°   25
Why do you imagine golden birds?
Do you not see how the blackbird
Walks around the feet
Of the women about you?

VIII

I know noble accents   30
And lucid, inescapable rhythms;
But I know, too,
That the blackbird is involved
In what I know.

IX

When the blackbird flew out of sight,   35
It marked the edge
Of one of many circles.

X

At the sight of blackbirds
Flying in a green light,
Even the bawds of euphony   40
Would cry out sharply.

XI

He rode over Connecticut
In a glass coach.
Once, a fear pierced him,
In that he mistook   45
The shadow of his equipage°
For blackbirds.

XII

The river is moving.
The blackbird must be flying.

XIII

It was evening all afternoon.   50
It was snowing
And it was going to snow.
The blackbird sat
In the cedar-limbs.

25 **Haddam:** town in Connecticut.   46 **equipage:** carriage.

WILLIAM CARLOS WILLIAMS (1883–1963)

This Is Just to Say

I have eaten
the plums
that were in
the icebox

and which
you were probably
saving
for breakfast

Forgive me
they were delicious
so sweet
and so cold

5

10

The Red Wheelbarrow

so much depends
upon

a red wheel
barrow

glazed with rain
water

beside the white
chickens.

5

EZRA POUND (1885–1972)

In a Station of the Metro

The apparition of these faces in the crowd;
Petals on a wet, black bough.

MARIANNE MOORE (1887–1972)

The Fish

wade
through black jade.
   Of the crow-blue mussel shells, one keeps

adjusting the ash heaps;
    opening and shutting itself like   5

an
injured fan.
  The barnacles which encrust the side
  of the wave, cannot hide
    there for the submerged shafts of the   10

sun,
split like spun
  glass, move themselves with spotlight swiftness
  into the crevices—
    in and out, illuminating   15

the
turquoise sea
  of bodies. The water drives a wedge
  of iron through the iron edge
    of the cliff; whereupon the stars,°   20

pink
rice-grains, ink-
  bespattered jellyfish, crabs like green
  lilies, and submarine
    toadstools, slide each on the other.   25

All
external
  marks of abuse are present on this
  defiant edifice—
    all the physical features of   30

ac-
cident—lack
  of cornice, dynamite grooves, burns, and
  hatchet strokes, these things stand
    out on it; the chasm side is   35

dead.
Repeated
  evidence has proved that it can live
  on what can not revive
    its youth. The sea grows old in it.   40

20 **stars:** starfish.

Poetry

I, too, dislike it: there are things that are important beyond all this fiddle.
  Reading it, however, with a perfect contempt for it, one discovers in
  it after all, a place for the genuine.

Hands that can grasp, eyes
   that can dilate, hair that can rise   5
      if it must, these things are important not because a

high-sounding interpretation can be put upon them but because they are
   useful. When they become so derivative as to become unintelligible,
   the same thing may be said for all of us, that we
      do not admire what   10
      we cannot understand: the bat
         holding on upside down or in quest of something to

eat, elephants pushing, a wild horse taking a roll, a tireless wolf under
   a tree, the immovable critic twitching his skin like a horse that feels a
   flea, the base-
      ball fan, the statistician—   15
      nor is it valid
         to discriminate against 'business documents and

school-books'; all these phenomena are important. One must make a
   distinction
   however: when dragged into prominence by half poets, the result is not
   poetry,
   nor till the poets among us can be   20
      'literalists of
      the imagination'—above
         insolence and triviality and can present

for inspection, 'imaginary gardens with real toads in them', shall we have
   it. In the meantime, if you demand on the one hand,   25
   the raw material of poetry in
      all its rawness and
      that which is on the other hand
         genuine, you are interested in poetry.

T. S. ELIOT (1888–1965)

Rhapsody on a Windy Night

Twelve o'clock.
Along the reaches of the street
Held in a lunar synthesis,
Whispering lunar incantations
Dissolve the floors of memory   5
And all its clear relations,
Its divisions and precisions,
Every street lamp that I pass
Beats like a fatalistic drum,
And through the spaces of the dark   10
Midnight shakes the memory
As a madman shakes a dead geranium.

Half-past one,
The street-lamp sputtered,
The street-lamp muttered, 15
The street-lamp said, 'Regard that woman
Who hesitates toward you in the light of the door
Which opens on her like a grin.
You see the border of her dress
Is torn and stained with sand, 20
And you see the corner of her eye
Twists like a crooked pin.'

The memory throws up high and dry
A crowd of twisted things;
A twisted branch upon the beach 25
Eaten smooth, and polished
As if the world gave up
The secret of its skeleton,
Stiff and white.
A broken spring in a factory yard, 30
Rust that clings to the form that the strength has left
Hard and curled and ready to snap.

Half-past two,
The street-lamp said,
'Remark the cat which flattens itself in the gutter, 35
Slips out its tongue
And devours a morsel of rancid butter.'
So the hand of the child, automatic,
Slipped out and pocketed a toy that was running along the quay.

I could see nothing behind that child's eye. 40
I have seen eyes in the street
Trying to peer through lighted shutters,
And a crab one afternoon in a pool,
An old crab with barnacles on his back,
Gripped the end of a stick which I held him. 45

Half-past three,
The lamp sputtered,
The lamp muttered in the dark.
The lamp hummed:
'Regard the moon, 50
La lune ne garde aucune rancune,°
She winks a feeble eye,
She smiles into corners.
She smooths the hair of the grass.
The moon has lost her memory. 55
A washed-out smallpox cracks her face,
Her hand twists a paper rose,

51 **La lune ne garde aucune rancune:** the moon looks on without malice.

That smells of dust and eau de Cologne,
She is alone
With all the old nocturnal smells
That cross and cross across her brain.'   60
The reminiscence comes
Of sunless dry geraniums
And dust in crevices,
Smells of chestnuts in the streets,
And female smells in shuttered rooms,   65
And cigarettes in corridors
And cocktail smells in bars.

The lamp said,
'Four o'clock,   70
Here is the number on the door.
Memory!
You have the key,
The little lamp spreads a ring on the stair.
Mount.   75
The bed is open; the tooth-brush hangs on the wall,
Put your shoes at the door, sleep, prepare for life.'

The last twist of the knife.

The Love Song of J. Alfred Prufrock

S'io credessi che mia risposta fosse
a persona che mai tornasse al mondo,
questa fiamma staria senza più scosse.
Ma per ciò che giammai di questo fondo
non tornò vivo alcun, s'i'odo il vero,
senza tema d'infamia ti rispondo.°

Let us go then, you and I,
When the evening is spread out against the sky
Like a patient etherised upon a table;
Let us go, through certain half-deserted streets,
The muttering retreats   5
Of restless nights in one-night cheap hotels
And sawdust restaurants with oyster-shells:
Streets that follow like a tedious argument
Of insidious intent
To lead you to an overwhelming question . . .   10
Oh, do not ask, 'What is it?'
Let us go and make our visit.

Epigraph: from Dante, *Inferno*, 27:61–66: "If I thought my reply were given to anyone who
would ever be returned to the world, this flame would stand still without further movement;
but since, if what I am told is true, nobody has ever returned alive from this abyss, then I will
answer you without fear of infamy."

In the room the women come and go
Talking of Michelangelo.°

The yellow fog that rubs its back upon the window-panes,   15
The yellow smoke that rubs its muzzle on the window-panes,
Licked its tongue into the corners of the evening,
Lingered upon the pools that stand in drains,
Let fall upon its back the soot that falls from chimneys,
Slipped by the terrace, made a sudden leap,   20
And seeing that it was a soft October night,
Curled once about the house, and fell asleep.

And indeed there will be time
For the yellow smoke that slides along the street
Rubbing its back upon the window-panes;   25
There will be time, there will be time
To prepare a face to meet the faces that you meet;
There will be time to murder and create,
And time for all the works and days of hands
That lift and drop a question on your plate;   30
Time for you and time for me,
And time yet for a hundred indecisions,
And for a hundred visions and revisions,
Before the taking of a toast and tea.

In the room the women come and go   35
Talking of Michelangelo.

And indeed there will be time
To wonder, 'Do I dare?' and, 'Do I dare?'
Time to turn back and descend the stair,
With a bald spot in the middle of my hair—   40
(They will say: 'How his hair is growing thin!')
My morning coat, my collar mounting firmly to the chin,
My necktie rich and modest, but asserted by a simple pin—
(They will say: 'But how his arms and legs are thin!')
Do I dare   45
Disturb the universe?
In a minute there is time
For decisions and revisions which a minute will reverse.

For I have known them all already, known them all—
Have known the evenings, mornings, afternoons,   50
I have measured out my life with coffee spoons;
I know the voices dying with a dying fall
Beneath the music from a farther room.
    So how should I presume?

And I have known the eyes already, known them all—   55
The eyes that fix you in a formulated phrase,

14 **Michelangelo:** celebrated 16th-century painter and sculptor.

And when I am formulated, sprawling on a pin,
When I am pinned and wriggling on the wall,
Then how should I begin
To spit out all the butt-ends of my days and ways?   60
    And how should I presume?

And I have known the arms already, known them all—
Arms that are braceleted and white and bare
(But in the lamplight, downed with light brown hair!)
Is it perfume from a dress   65
That makes me so digress?
Arms that lie along a table, or wrap about a shawl.
    And should I then presume?
    And how should I begin?
          * * *
Shall I say, I have gone at dusk through narrow streets   70
And watched the smoke that rises from the pipes
Of lonely men in shirt-sleeves, leaning out of windows? . . .

I should have been a pair of ragged claws
Scuttling across the floors of silent seas.
          * * *
And the afternoon, the evening, sleeps so peacefully!   75
Smoothed by long fingers,
Asleep . . . tired . . . or it malingers,
Stretched on the floor, here beside you and me.
Should I, after tea and cakes and ices,
Have the strength to force the moment to its crisis?   80
But though I have wept and fasted, wept and prayed,
Though I have seen my head (grown slightly bald) brought in upon a
    platter,°
I am no prophet—and here's no great matter;
I have seen the moment of my greatness flicker,
And I have seen the eternal Footman hold my coat, and snicker,   85
And in short, I was afraid.
And would it have been worth it, after all,
After the cups, the marmalade, the tea,
Among the porcelain, among some talk of you and me,
Would it have been worth while,   90
To have bitten off the matter with a smile,
To have squeezed the universe into a ball
To roll it towards some overwhelming question,
To say: 'I am Lazarus, come from the dead,
Come back to tell you all, I shall tell you all'—   95
If one, settling a pillow by her head,
    Should say: 'That is not what I meant at all.
    That is not it, at all.'

82 **head. . .platter:** refers to the story of John the Baptist, whose head was presented on a plate
to Salome as a reward for her dance before Herod.

And would it have been worth it, after all,   100
Would it have been worth while,
After the sunsets and the dooryards and the sprinkled streets,
After the novels, after the teacups, after the skirts that trail along the floor—
And this, and so much more?—
It is impossible to say just what I mean!
But as if a magic lantern threw the nerves in patterns on a screen: 105
Would it have been worth while
If one, settling a pillow or throwing off a shawl,
And turning toward the window, should say:
      'That is not it at all,   110
      That is not what I meant, at all.'
                              *   *   *
No! I am not Prince Hamlet, nor was meant to be;
Am an attendant lord, one that will do
To swell a progress,° start a scene or two,
Advise the prince; no doubt, an easy tool,
Deferential, glad to be of use,   115
Politic, cautious, and meticulous;
Full of high sentence, but a bit obtuse;
At times, indeed, almost ridiculous—
Almost, at times, the Fool.

I grow old . . . I grow old . . .   120
I shall wear the bottoms of my trousers rolled.

Shall I part my hair behind? Do I dare to eat a peach?
I shall wear white flannel trousers, and walk upon the beach.
I have heard the mermaids singing, each to each.

I do not think that they will sing to me.   125

I have seen them riding seaward on the waves
Combing the white hair of the waves blown back
When the wind blows the water white and black.

We have lingered in the chambers of the sea
By sea-girls wreathed with seaweed red and brown   130
Till human voices wake us, and we drown.

113 **swell a progress:** join a stately procession.

Gerontion°

Thou hast nor youth nor age
But as it were an after dinner sleep
Dreaming of both.°

Title: little old man.   Epigraph: Shakespeare, *Measure for Measure.*

Here I am, an old man in a dry month,
Being read to by a boy, waiting for rain.
I was neither at the hot gates
Nor fought in the warm rain
Nor knee deep in the salt marsh, heaving a cutlass,   5
Bitten by flies, fought.
My house is a decayed house,
And the jew squats on the window sill, the owner,
Spawned in some estaminet° of Antwerp,
Blistered in Brussels, patched and peeled in London.   10
The goat coughs at night in the field overhead;
Rocks, moss, stonecrop, iron, merds.
The woman keeps the kitchen, makes tea,
Sneezes at evening, poking the peevish gutter.
          I an old man,   15
A dull head among windy spaces.

Signs are taken for wonders. "We would see a sign!"
The word within a word, unable to speak a word,
Swaddled with darkness. In the juvescence of the year
Came Christ the tiger   20

In depraved May, dogwood and chestnut, flowering judas,
To be eaten, to be divided, to be drunk
Among whispers; by Mr. Silvero
With caressing hands, at Limoges
Who walked all night in the next room;   25

By Hakagawa, bowing among the Titians;
By Madame de Tornquist, in the dark room
Shifting the candles; Fräulein von Kulp
Who turned in the hall, one hand on the door. Vacant shuttles
Weave the wind. I have no ghosts,   30
An old man in a draughty house
Under a windy knob.

After such knowledge, what forgiveness? Think now
History has many cunning passages, contrived corridors
And issues, deceives with whispering ambitions,   35
Guides us by vanities. Think now
She gives when our attention is distracted
And what she gives, gives with such supple confusions
That the giving famishes the craving. Gives too late
What's not believed in, or if still believed,   40
In memory only, reconsidered passion. Gives too soon
Into weak hands, what's thought can be dispensed with
Till the refusal propagates a fear. Think
Neither fear nor courage saves us. Unnatural vices
Are fathered by our heroism. Virtues   45

9 **estaminet:** cheap café.

Are forced upon us by our impudent crimes.
These tears are shaken from the wrath-bearing tree.

The tiger springs in the new year. Us he devours.
  Think at last
We have not reached conclusion, when I   50
Stiffen in a rented house. Think at last
I have not made this show purposelessly
And it is not by any concitation
Of the backward devils
I would meet you upon this honestly.   55
I that was near your heart was removed therefrom
To lose beauty in terror, terror in inquisition.
I have lost my passion: why should I need to keep it
Since what is kept must be adulterated?
I have lost my sight, smell, hearing, taste and touch: 60
How should I use them for your closer contact?

These with a thousand small deliberations
Protract the profit of their chilled delirium,
Excite the membrane, when the sense has cooled,
With pungent sauces, multiply variety   65
In a wilderness of mirrors. What will the spider do,
Suspend its operations, will the weevil
Delay? De Bailhache, Fresca, Mrs. Cammel, whirled
Beyond the circuit of the shuddering Bear
In fractured atoms. Gull against the wind, in the windy straits   70
Of Belle Isle, or running on the Horn,
White feathers in the snow, the Gulf claims,
And an old man driven by the Trades
To a sleepy corner.

                            Tenants of the house,   75
Thoughts of a dry brain in a dry season.

E. E. CUMMINGS (1894–1962)

[my sweet old etcetera]

my sweet old etcetera
aunt lucy during the recent

war could and what
is more did tell you just
what everybody was fighting   5

for,
my sister

isabel created hundreds
(and
hundreds) of socks not to   10
mention shirts fleaproof earwarmers

etcetera wristers etcetera, my
mother hoped that

i would die etcetera
bravely of course my father used   15
to become hoarse talking about how it was
a privilege and if only he
could meanwhile my

self etcetera lay quietly
in the deep mud et   20

cetera
(dreaming,
et
    cetera, of
Your smile   25
eyes knees and of your Etcetera)

[somewhere i have never travelled,gladly beyond]

somewhere i have never travelled,gladly beyond
any experience,your eyes have their silence:
in your most frail gesture are things which enclose me,
or which i cannot touch because they are too near

your slightest look easily will unclose me   5
though i have closed myself as fingers,
you open always petal by petal myself as Spring opens
(touching skilfully,mysteriously) her first rose

or if your wish be to close me,i and
my life will shut very beautifully,suddenly,   10
as when the heart of this flower imagines
the snow carefully everywhere descending;

nothing which we are to perceive in this world equals
the power of your intense fragility:whose texture
compels me with the colour of its countries,   15
rendering death and forever with each breathing

(i do not know what it is about you that closes
and opens;only something in me understands
the voice of your eyes is deeper than all roses)
nobody,not even the rain,has such small hands   20

[O sweet spontaneous]

O sweet spontaneous
earth how often have
the
doting

      fingers of 5
prurient philosophers pinched
and
poked

thee
, has the naughty thumb 10
of science prodded
thy
    beauty   how
often have religions taken
thee upon their scraggy knees 15
squeezing and

buffeting thee that thou mightest conceive
gods
    (but
true 20

to the incomparable
couch of death thy
rhythmic
lover

     thou answerest 25

them only with
         spring)

[she being Brand]

she being Brand

-new;and you
know consequently a
little stiff i was
careful of her and (having 5

thoroughly oiled the universal
joint tested my gas felt of
her radiator made sure her springs were O.

K.) i went right to it flooded-the-carburetor cranked her

up,slipped the 10
clutch (and then somehow got into reverse she

552   *[she being Brand]*

kicked what
the hell) next
minute i was back in neutral tried and

again slo-wly; bare,ly nudg.   ing (my   15

lev-er Right-
oh and her gears being in
A 1 shape passed
from low through
second-in-to-high like   20
greasedlightning) just as we turned the corner of Divinity

avenue i touched the accelerator and give
her the juice,good

                  (it
was the first ride and believe i we was   25
happy to see how nice she acted right up to
the last minute coming back down by the Public
Gardens i slammed on
the

internalexpanding   30
&
externalcontracting
brakes Bothatonce and

brought allofher tremB
-ling
 to a:dead.   35

stand-
;Still)

COUNTÉE CULLEN (1903–1946)

Yet Do I Marvel

I doubt not God is good, well-meaning, kind,
And did He stoop to quibble could tell why
The little buried mole continues blind,
Why flesh that mirrors Him must some day die,
Make plain the reason tortured Tantalus°   5
Is baited by the fickle fruit, declare
If merely brute caprice dooms Sisyphus°
To struggle up a never-ending stair.

5 **Tantalus:** in Greek mythology, Tantalus was made to stand forever with food and drink
beyond his grasp.   7 **Sisyphus:** also in Greek mythology, Sisyphus was condemned to push a
huge stone up a hill forever.

Inscrutable His ways are, and immune
To catechism by a mind too strewn   10
With petty cares to slightly understand
What awful brain compels His awful hand.
Yet do I marvel at this curious thing:
To make a poet black, and bid him sing!

EARLE BIRNEY (b. 1904)

For George Lamming

To you
   I can risk words about this

Mastering them   you know
   they are dull
      servants   5
who say less
   and worse
     than we feel

That party above Kingston Town°
   we stood   five (six?) couples   10
linked singing
    more than rum happy

I was giddy
   from sudden friendship
wanted   undeserved   15

   black tulip faces
self swaying forgotten
   laughter in dance

Suddenly on a wall mirror
   my face assaulted me   20
stunned to see itself
   like a white snail
     in the supple dark flowers

Always now I move grateful
   to all of you   25
who let me walk thoughtless
   and unchallenged
in the gardens
   in the castles
    of your skins   30

9 **Kingston Town:** Kingston, Jamaica.

RICHARD EBERHART (b. 1904)

The Fury of Aerial Bombardment

You would think the fury of aerial bombardment
Would rouse God to relent; the infinite spaces
Are still silent. He looks on shock-pried faces.
History, even, does not know what is meant.

You would feel that after so many centuries   5
God would give man to repent; yet he can kill
As Cain could, but with multitudinous will,
No farther advanced than in his ancient furies.

Was man made stupid to see his own stupidity?
Is God by definition indifferent, beyond us all?   10
Is the eternal truth man's fighting soul
Wherein the Beast ravens in its own avidity?

Of Van Wettering I speak, and Averill,
Names on a list, whose faces I do not recall
But they are gone to early death, who late in school   15
Distinguished the belt feed lever from the belt holding pawl.

KENNETH REXROTH (1905–1982)

Proust's Madeleine

Somebody has given my
Baby daughter a box of
Old poker chips to play with.
Today she hands me one while
I am sitting with my tired   5
Brain at my desk. It is red.
On it is a picture of
An elk's head and the letters
B.P.O.E.—a chip from
A small town Elks' Club. I flip   10
It idly in the air and
Catch it and do a coin trick
To amuse my little girl.
Suddenly everything slips aside.
I see my father   15
Doing the very same thing,
Whistling "Beautiful Dreamer,"
His breath smelling richly
Of whiskey and cigars. I can
Hear him coming home drunk   20
From the Elks' Club in Elkhart

Indiana, bumping the
Chairs in the dark. I can see
Him dying of cirrhosis
Of the liver and stomach   25
Ulcers and pneumonia,
Or, as he said on his deathbed, of
Crooked cards and straight whiskey,
Slow horses and fast women.

ROBERT PENN WARREN (b. 1905)

Small Eternity

The time comes when you count the names—whether
Dim or flaming in the head's dark, or whether
In stone cut, time-crumbling or moss-glutted.
You count the names to reconstruct yourself.

But a face remembered may blur, even as you stare   5
At a headstone. Or sometimes a face, as though from air,
Will stare at you with a boyish smile—but, not
Stone-moored, blows away like dandelion fuzz.

It is very disturbing. It is as though you were
The idiot boy who ventures out on pond ice   10
Too thin, and hears here—hears there—the creak
And crackling spread. That is the sound Reality

Makes as it gives beneath your metaphysical
Poundage. Memory dies. Or lies. Time
Is a wind that never shifts airt. Pray only   15
That, in the midst of selfishness, some

Small act of careless kindness, half-unconscious, some
Unwitting smile or brush of lips, may glow
In some other mind's dark that's lost your name, but stumbles
Upon that momentary Eternity.   20

Rumor Verified

Since the rumor has been verified, you can, at least,
Disappear. You will no longer be seen at the Opera,
With your head bowed studiously, to one side a little,
Nor at your unadvertised and very exclusive
Restaurant, discussing wine with the sommelier,   5
Nor at your club, setting modestly forth your subtle opinion.

Since the rumor has been verified, you can try, as in dream,
To have lived another life—not with the father
Of rigid self-discipline, and x-ray glance,
Not with the mother, overindulgent and pretty,   10
Who toyed with your golden locks, slipped money on the side,
And waved a witch's wand for success, and a rich marriage.

Since the rumor has been verified, you may secretly sneak
Into El Salvador, or some such anguished spot,
Of which you speak the language, dreaming, trying to believe   15
That, orphaned, you grew up in poverty and vision, struggling
For learning, for mankind's sake. Here you pray with the sick, kiss lepers.

Since the rumor has been verified, you yearn to hold
A cup of cold water for the dying man to sip.
You yearn to look deep into his eyes and learn wisdom.   20
Or perhaps you have a practical streak and seek
Strange and derelict friends, and for justification lead
A ragtag squad to ambush the uniformed patrol.

Well, assuming the rumor verified—that may be
The only logical course: at any price,   25
Even bloodshed, however ruthless, to change any dominant order
And the secret corruption of power that makes us what we seem.
Yes, what is such verification against a strength of will?

But even in face of the rumor, you sometimes shudder,
Seeing men as old as you who survive the terror   30
Of knowledge. You watch them slyly. What is their trick?
Do they wear a Halloween face? But what can you do?
Perhaps pray to God for strength to face the verification
That you are simply a man, with a man's dead reckoning, nothing more.

You Sort Old Letters

Some are pure business, land deals, receipts, a contract,
Bank statements, dead policies, demand for some payment.
But a beach-party invite!—yes, yes, that tease
Of a hostess and you, withdrawn beyond dunes, lay,
The laughter far off, and for contact   5
Of tongue and teeth, she let you first loosen a breast.
You left town soon after—and now wonder what
Might that day have meant.

Suppose you hadn't left town—well, she's dead anyway.
Three divorces, three children, all born for the sludge of the pit.   10
It was Number One, nice fellow, when she took you to the dunes,
And gasped: "Harder, bite harder!" And you did
In the glare of day. When she scrambled up,

She cried: "Oh, don't you hate me!" And wept
Like a child. You patted, caressed her.   15
Cuddled and kissed her. She said: "I'm a shit."

Do you seem to remember that, for a moment,
Your heart stirred? But you shrug now, remembering
How, in the end, she shacked up
With a likker-head plumber, who, now and then,   20
Would give her a jolt to the jaw, or with heel of a palm
Would flatten lips to the teeth, then slam
Her the works, blood
On her swollen lips—as was common gossip.

You married a little late—and now in this mess   25
Of old papers the words at you stare:
You were smart to blow town. Keep your pecker up!
Signed only: *Yours, maybe.*

Of course, she had everything—money, looks,
Wit, breeding, a charm   30
Of defenseless appeal—the last what trapped, no doubt,
The three near middle-aged fall guys, who got only
Horns for their pains. Yes, she threw all away.
And as you've guessed, by struggling
Sank deeper and deeper into   35
A slough of self-hate. However, you
Are no psychiatrist, and couldn't say
What or why, as you, far away, lay

By the warm and delicious body you loved
So well, in the dark ashamed of   40
Recurring speculations, as though this
Betrayed your love. Years passed. The end, you heard,
Was sleeping pills. You felt some confusion, or guilt—
But how could you be blamed?—Even if
Knees once were grinding sand as sun once smote
Your bare back, or, in a dream, lips,
Bloody, lifted for your kiss.

W. H. AUDEN (1907–1973)

Lullaby

Lay your sleeping head, my love,
Human on my faithless arm;
Time and fevers burn away
Individual beauty from
Thoughtful children, and the grave   5
Proves the child ephemeral:
But in my arms till break of day

Let the living creature lie,
Mortal, guilty, but to me
The entirely beautiful.   10

Soul and body have no bounds:
To lovers as they lie upon
Her tolerant enchanted slope
In their ordinary swoon,
Grave the vision Venus sends   15
Of supernatural sympathy,
Universal love and hope;
While an abstract insight wakes
Among the glaciers and the rocks
The hermit's carnal ecstasy.   20

Certainty, fidelity
On the stroke of midnight pass
Like vibrations of a bell
And fashionable madmen raise
Their pedantic boring cry: 25
Every farthing of the cost,
All the dreaded cards foretell,
Shall be paid, but from this night
Not a whisper, not a thought,
Not a kiss nor look be lost.   30

Beauty, midnight, vision dies:
Let the winds of dawn that blow
Softly round your dreaming head
Such a day of welcome show
Eye and knocking heart may bless,   35
Find our mortal world enough;
Noons of dryness find you fed
By the involuntary powers,
Nights of insult let you pass
Watched by every human love.   40

THEODORE ROETHKE (1908–1963)

Dolor

I have known the inexorable sadness of pencils,
Neat in their boxes, dolor of pad and paper-weight,
All the misery of manilla folders and mucilage,
Desolation in immaculate public places,
Lonely reception room, lavatory, switchboard,   5
The unalterable pathos of basin and pitcher,
Ritual of multigraph, paper-clip, comma,

Endless duplication of lives and objects.
And I have seen dust from the walls of institutions,
Finer than flour, alive, more dangerous than silica,   10
Sift, almost invisible, through long afternoons of tedium,
Dropping a fine film on nails and delicate eyebrows,
Glazing the pale hair, the duplicate grey standard faces.

My Papa's Waltz

The whiskey on your breath
Could make a small boy dizzy;
But I hung on like death:
Such waltzing was not easy.

We romped until the pans   5
Slid from the kitchen shelf;
My mother's countenance
Could not unfrown itself.

The hand that held my wrist
Was battered on one knuckle;   10
At every step you missed
My right ear scraped a buckle.

You beat time on my head
With a palm caked hard by dirt,
Then waltzed me off to bed
Still clinging to your shirt.

DOROTHY LIVESAY (b. 1909)

The Unquiet Bed

The woman I am
is not what you see
I'm not just bones
and crockery

the woman I am   5
knew love and hate
hating the chains
that parents make

longing that love
might set men free   10
yet hold them fast
in loyalty

the woman I am
is not what you see
move over love   15
make room for me

ELIZABETH BISHOP (1911–1979)

The Fish

I caught a tremendous fish
and held him beside the boat
half out of water, with my hook
fast in a corner of his mouth.
He didn't fight.   5
He hadn't fought at all.
He hung a grunting weight,
battered and venerable
and homely. Here and there
his brown skin hung in strips   10
like ancient wallpaper,
and its pattern of darker brown
was like wallpaper:
shapes like full-blown roses
stained and lost through age.   15
He was speckled with barnacles,
fine rosettes of lime,
and infested
with tiny white sea-lice,
and underneath two or three   20
rags of green weed hung down.
While his gills were breathing in
the terrible oxygen
—the frightening gills,
fresh and crisp with blood,   25
that can cut so badly—
I thought of the coarse white flesh
packed in like feathers,
the big bones and the little bones,
the dramatic reds and blacks   30
of his shiny entrails,
and the pink swim-bladder
like a big peony.
I looked into his eyes
which were far larger than mine   35
but shallower, and yellowed,
the irises backed and packed
with tarnished tinfoil

seen through the lenses
of old scratched isinglass.° 40
They shifted a little, but not
to return my stare.
—It was more like the tipping
of an object toward the light.
I admired his sullen face, 45
the mechanism of his jaw,
and then I saw
that from his lower lip
—if you could call it a lip—
grim, wet, and weaponlike, 50
hung five old pieces of fish-line,
or four and a wire leader
with the swivel still attached,
with all their five big hooks
grown firmly in his mouth. 55
A green line, frayed at the end
where he broke it, two heavier lines,
and a fine black thread
still crimped from the strain and snap
when it broke and he got away. 60
Like medals with their ribbons
frayed and wavering,
a five-haired beard of wisdom
trailing from his aching jaw.
I stared and stared 65
and victory filled up
the little rented boat,
from the pool of bilge
where oil had spread a rainbow
around the rusted engine 70
to the bailer rusted orange,
the sun-cracked thwarts,°
the oarlocks on their strings,
the gunnels—until everything
was rainbow, rainbow, rainbow! 75
And I let the fish go.

40 **isinglass:** mica glass.   72 **thwarts:** benches in a small boat.

Varick Street°

> At night the factories
> struggle awake,
> wretched uneasy buildings

Title: street in lower Manhattan, New York City.

veined with pipes
attempt their work.
Trying to breathe,
the elongated nostrils
haired with spikes
give off such stenches, too.
And I shall sell you sell you
sell you of course, my dear, and you'll sell me.

On certain floors
certain wonders.
Pale dirty light,
some captured iceberg
being prevented from melting.
See the mechanical moons,
sick, being made
to wax and wane
at somebody's instigation.
And I shall sell you sell you
sell you of course, my dear, and you'll sell me.

Lights music of love
work on. The presses
print calendars
I suppose; the moons
make medicine
or confectionery. Our bed
shrinks from the soot
and hapless odors
hold us close.
And I shall sell you sell you
sell you of course, my dear, and you'll sell me.

Letter to N.Y.

For Louise Crane

In your next letter I wish you'd say
where you are going and what you are doing;
how are the plays, and after the plays
what other pleasures you're pursuing:

taking cabs in the middle of the night,   5
driving as if to save your soul
where the road goes round and round the park
and the meter glares like a moral owl,

and the trees look so queer and green
standing alone in big black caves   10

and suddenly you're in a different place
where everything seems to happen in waves,

and most of the jokes you just can't catch,
like dirty words rubbed off a slate,
and the songs are loud but somehow dim   15
and it gets so terribly late,

and coming out of the brownstone house
to the gray sidewalk, the watered street,
one side of the buildings rises with the sun
like a glistening field of wheat.   20

—Wheat, not oats, dear. I'm afraid
if it's wheat it's none of your sowing,
nevertheless I'd like to know
what you are doing and where you are going.

KENNETH PATCHEN (1911–1972)

Do the Dead Know What Time It Is?

The old guy put down his beer.
Son, he said,
   (and a girl came over to the table where we were:
   asked us by Jack Christ to buy her a drink.)
Son, I am going to tell you something   5
The like of which nobody ever was told.
   (and the girl said, I've got nothing on tonight;
   how about you and me going to your place?)
I am going to tell you the story of my mother's
Meeting with God.   10
   (and I whispered to the girl: I don't have a room,
   but maybe . . .)
She walked up to where the top of the world is
And He came right up to her and said
So at last you've come home.   15
   (but maybe what?
   I thought I'd like to stay here and talk to you.)
My mother started to cry and God
Put His arms around her.
   (about what?   20
   Oh, just talk . . . we'll find something.)
She said it was like a fog coming over her face
And light was everywhere and a soft voice saying
You can stop crying now.

(what can we talk about that will take all night?   25
and I said that I didn't know.)
You can stop crying now.

IRVING LAYTON (b. 1912)

The Bull Calf

The thing could barely stand. Yet taken
from his mother and the barn smells
he still impressed with his pride,
with the promise of sovereignty in the way
his head moved to take us in.   5
The fierce sunlight tugging the maize from the ground
licked at his shapely flanks.
He was too young for all that pride.
I thought of the deposed Richard II.

'No money in bull calves,' Freeman had said.   10
The visiting clergyman rubbed the nostrils
now snuffing pathetically at the windless day.
'A pity,' he sighed.
My gaze slipped off his hat toward the empty sky
that circled over the black knot of men,   15
over us and the calf waiting for the first blow.

Struck,
the bull calf drew in his thin forelegs
as if gathering strength for a mad rush . . .
tottered . . . raised his darkening eyes to us,   20
and I saw we were at the far end
of his frightened look, growing smaller and smaller
till we were only the ponderous mallet
that flicked his bleeding ear
and pushed him over on his side, stiffly,   25
like a block of wood.

Below the hill's crest
the river snuffled on the improvised beach.
We dug a deep pit and threw the dead calf into it.
It made a wet sound, a sepulchral gurgle,   30
as the warm sides bulged and flattened.
Settled, the bull calf lay as if asleep,
one foreleg over the other;
bereft of pride and so beautiful now,
without movement, perfectly still in the cool pit,   35
I turned away and wept.

Keine Lazarovitch

1870–1959

When I saw my mother's head on the cold pillow,
Her white waterfalling hair in the cheeks' hollows,
I thought, quietly circling my grief, of how
She had loved God but cursed extravagantly his creatures.

For her final mouth was not water but a curse,   5
A small black hole, a black rent in the universe,
Which damned the green earth, stars and trees in its stillness
And the inescapable lousiness of growing old.

And I record she was comfortless, vituperative,
Ignorant, glad, and much else besides; I believe   10
She endlessly praised her black eyebrows, their thick weave,
Till plagiarizing Death leaned down and took them for his mould.

And spoiled a dignity I shall not again find,
And the fury of her stubborn limited mind;
Now none will shake her amber beads and call God blind,   15
Or wear them upon a breast so radiantly.

O fierce she was, mean and unaccommodating;
But I think now of the toss of her gold earrings,
Their proud carnal assertion, and her youngest sings
While all the rivers of her red veins move into the sea.   20

Berry Picking

Silently my wife walks on the still wet furze
Now darkgreen the leaves are full of metaphors
Now lit up is each tiny lamp of blueberry.
The white nails of rain have dropped and the sun is free.

And whether she bends or straightens to each bush   5
To find the children's laughter among the leaves
Her quiet hands seem to make the quiet summer hush—
Berries or children, patient she is with these.

I only vex and perplex her; madness, rage
Are endearing perhaps put down upon the page;   10
Even silence daylong and sullen can then
Enamour as restraint or classic discipline.

So I envy the berries she puts in her mouth,
The red and succulent juice that stains her lips;
I shall never taste that good to her, nor will they   15
Displease her with a thousand barbarous jests.

How they lie easily for her hand to take,
Part of the unoffending world that is hers;

Here beyond complexity she stands and stares
And leans her marvellous head as if for answers.   20

No more the easy soul my childish craft deceives
Nor the simpler one for whom yes is always yes;
No, now her voice comes to me from a far way off
Though her lips are redder than the raspberries.

DELMORE SCHWARTZ (1913–1966)

The Heavy Bear Who Goes with Me

"the withness of the body"

The heavy bear who goes with me,
A manifold honey to smear his face,
Clumsy and lumbering here and there,
The central ton of every place,
The hungry beating brutish one   5
In love with candy, anger, and sleep,
Crazy factotum,° dishevelling all,
Climbs the building, kicks the football,
Boxes his brother in the hate-ridden city.

Breathing at my side, that heavy animal,   10
That heavy bear who sleeps with me,
Howls in his sleep for a world of sugar,
A sweetness intimate as the water's clasp,
Howls in his sleep because the tight-rope
Trembles and shows the darkness beneath.   15
—The strutting show-off is terrified,
Dressed in his dress-suit, bulging his pants,
Trembles to think that his quivering meat
Must finally wince to nothing at all.

That inescapable animal walks with me,   20
Has followed me since the black womb held,
Moves where I move, distorting my gesture,
A caricature, a swollen shadow,
A stupid clown of the spirit's motive,
Perplexes and affronts with his own darkness,   25
The secret life of belly and bone,
Opaque, too near, my private, yet unknown,
Stretches to embrace the very dear
With whom I would walk without him near,
Touches her grossly, although a word   30
Would bare my heart and make me clear,

7 **factotum:** servant.

Stumbles, flounders, and strives to be fed
Dragging me with him in his mouthing care,
Amid the hundred million of his kind,
The scrimmage of appetite everywhere.   35

JOHN BERRYMAN (1914–1972)

A Professor's Song

(. . rabid or dog-dull.) Let me tell you how
The Eighteenth Century couplet ended. Now
Tell me. Troll me the sources of that Song—
Assigned last week—by Blake. Come, come along,
Gentlemen. (Fidget and huddle, do. Squint soon.)   5
I want to end these fellows all by noon.

"That deep romantic chasm"°—an early use;
The word is from the French, by our abuse
Fished out a bit. (Red all your eyes. O when?)
'A poet is a man speaking to men':°   10
But I am then a poet, am I not?—
Ha ha. The radiator, please. Well, what?

Alive now—no—Blake would have written prose,
But movement following movement crisply flows,
So much the better, better the much so,   15
As burbleth Mozart. Twelve. The class can go.
Until I meet you, then, in Upper Hell
Convulsed, foaming immortal blood: farewell.

7 **"That . . . chasm"**: quotation from Coleridge's "Kubla Khan" (see p. 489).   10 **"A poet . . .
men"**: quotation from Wordsworth's preface to *Lyrical Ballads* (1798).

The Dream Songs

4

Filling her compact & delicious body
with chicken páprika, she glanced at me
twice.

Fainting with interest, I hungered back
and only the fact of her husband & four other people   5
kept me from springing on her

or falling at her little feet and crying
"You are the hottest one for years of night

Henry's dazed eyes
have enjoyed, Brilliance." I advanced upon   10
(despairing) my spumoni.—Sir Bones: is stuffed,
de world, wif feeding girls.

—Black hair, complexion Latin, jeweled eyes
downcast . . . The slob beside her   feasts . . . What wonders is
she sitting on, over there?   15
The restaurant buzzes. She might as well be on Mars.
Where did it all go wrong? The ought to be a law against Henry.
—Mr. Bones: there is.

The Dream Songs
14

Life, friends, is boring. We must not say so.
After all, the sky flashes, the great sea yearns,
we ourselves flash and yearn,
and moreover my mother told me as a boy
(repeatingly) 'Ever to confess you're bored   5
means you have no

Inner Resources.' I conclude now I have no
inner resources, because I am heavy bored.
Peoples bore me,
literature bores me, especially great literature,   10
Henry bores me, with his plights & gripes
as bad as achilles,

who loves people and valiant art, which bores me.
And the tranquil hills, & gin, look like a drag
and somehow a dog   15
has taken itself & its tail considerably away
into mountains or sea or sky, leaving
behind: me, wag.

The Dream Songs
375. His Helplessness

I know a young lady's high-piled ashen hair
and she is miserable, threatened a thoroughfare
for pants in their desire
fondless: she drinks too dear, & feels put down,

"no one is friendly to me" she scribbles here,   5
of all them griefs the crown

having been her lay by her father agèd ten
from which she grew up slowly into the world of men
who headed ha for her.
She put her soul in jeopardy with pills   10
a week ago, she writes—Henry would offer,
only it's thousands of miles,
help to the delicate lady far in her strait,
counsel she needs, needs one to pace her fate.
I cannot spot a hole,   15
& I look with my heart, in her darkness over there:
dark shroud the clouds on her disordered soul
whose last letter flew like a prayer.

RANDALL JARRELL (1914–1965)

A Girl in a Library

An object among dreams, you sit here with your shoes off
And curl your legs up under you; your eyes
Close for a moment, your face moves toward sleep . . .
You are very human.
                   But my mind, gone out in tenderness,   5
Shrinks from its object with a thoughtful sigh.
This is a waist the spirit breaks its arm on.
The gods themselves, against you, struggle in vain.
This broad low strong-boned brow; these heavy eyes;
These calves, grown muscular with certainties;   10
This nose, three medium-sized pink strawberries
—But I exaggerate. In a little you will leave:
I'll hear, half squeal, half shriek, your laugh of greeting—
Then, *decrescendo*, bars of that strange speech
In which each sound sets out to seek each other,   15
Murders its own father, marries its own mother,
And ends as one grand transcendental vowel.
(Yet for all I know, the Egyptian Helen spoke so.)
As I look, the world contracts around you:
I see Brünnhilde had brown braids and glasses   20
She used for studying; Salome straight brown bangs,
A calf's brown eyes, and sturdy light-brown limbs
Dusted with cinnamon, an apple-dumpling's . . .
Many a beast has gnawn a leg off and got free,
Many a dolphin curved up from Necessity—   25
The trap has closed about you, and you sleep:

If someone questioned you, *What doest thou here?*
You'd knit your brows like an orangoutang
(But not so sadly; not so thoughtfully)
And answer with a pure heart, guilelessly: 30
I'm studying. . . .
                    If only you were not!
Assignments,
            recipes,
                    the *Official Rulebook*   35
Of Basketball—ah, let them go; you needn't mind.
The soul has no assignments, neither cooks
Nor referees: it wastes its time.
                              It wastes its time.
Here is this enclave there are centuries   40
For you to waste: the short and narrow stream
Of Life meanders into a thousand valleys
Of all that was, or might have been, or is to be.
The books, just leafed through, whisper endlessly . . .
Yet it is hard. One sees in your blurred eyes   45
The "uneasy half-soul" Kipling saw in dogs'.
One sees it, in the glass, in one's own eyes.
In rooms alone, in galleries, in libraries,
In tears, in searchings of the heart, in staggering joys
We memorize once more our old creation,   50
Humanity: with what yawns the unwilling
Flesh puts on its spirit, O my sister!

So many dreams! And not one troubles
Your sleep of life? no self stares shadowily
From these worn hexahedrons, beckoning   55
With false smiles, tears? . . .
                    Meanwhile Tatyana
Larina (gray eyes nickel with the moonlight
That falls through the willows onto Lensky's tomb;
Now young and shy, now old and cold and sure)   60
Asks, smiling: "But what is she dreaming of, fat thing?"
I answer: She's not fat. She isn't dreaming.
She purrs or laps or runs, all in her sleep;
Believes, awake, that she is beautiful;
She never dreams.   65
                    Those sunrise-colored clouds
Around man's head—that inconceivable enchantment
From which, at sunset, we come back to life
To find our graves dug, families dead, selves dying:
Of all this, Tanya, she is innocent.   70
For nineteen years she's faced reality:
They look alike already.
                    They say, man wouldn't be
The best thing in this world—and isn't he?—

If he were not too good for it. But she   75
—She's good enough for it.
                        And yet sometimes
Her sturdy form, in its pink strapless formal,
Is as if bathed in moonlight—modulated
Into a form of joy, a Lydian mode;   80
This Wooden Mean's a kind, furred animal
That speaks, in the Wild of things, delighting riddles
To the soul that listens, trusting . . .
                        Poor senseless Life:
When, in the last light sleep of dawn, the messenger   85
Comes with his message, you will not awake.
He'll give his feathery whistle, shake you hard,
You'll look with wide eyes at the dewy yard
And dream, with calm slow factuality:
"Today's Commencement. My bachelor's degree   90
In Home Ec., my doctorate of philosophy
In Phys. Ed.
            [Tanya, they won't even *scan*]
Are waiting for me. . . ."
                        Oh, Tatyana,   95
The Angel comes: better to squawk like a chicken
Than to say with truth, "But I'm a *good* girl,"
And Meet his Challenge with a last firm strange
Uncomprehending smile; and—then, then!—see
The blind date that has stood you up: your life.   100
(For all this, if it isn't perhaps, life,
Has yet, at least, a language of its own
Different from the books'; worse than the books'.)
And yet, the ways we miss our lives are life.
Yet . . . yet . . .   105
            to have one's life add up to *yet!*

You sigh a shuddering sigh. Tatyana murmurs,
"Don't cry, little peasant"; leaves us with a swift
"Good-bye, good-bye . . . Ah, don't think ill of me . . ."
Your eyes open: you sit here thoughtlessly.   110
I love you—and yet—and yet—I love you.

Don't cry, little peasant. Sit and dream.
One comes, a finger's width beneath your skin,
To the braided maidens singing as they spin;
There sound the shepherd's pipe, the watchman's rattle   115
Across the short dark distance of the years.
I am a thought of yours: and yet, you do not think . . .
The firelight of a long, blind, dreaming story
Lingers upon your lips; and I have seen
Firm, fixed forever in your closing eyes,   120
The Corn King beckoning to his Spring Queen.

DYLAN THOMAS (1914–1953)

The Force That Through the Green Fuse Drives the Flower

The force that through the green fuse drives the flower
Drives my green age; that blasts the roots of trees
Is my destroyer.
And I am dumb to tell the crooked rose
My youth is bent by the same wintry fever.   5

The force that drives the water through the rocks
Drives my red blood; that dries the mouthing streams
Turns mine to wax.
And I am dumb to mouth unto my veins
How at the mountain spring the same mouth sucks.   10

The hand that whirls the water in the pool
Stirs the quicksand; that ropes the blowing wind
Hauls my shroud sail.
And I am dumb to tell the hanging man
How of my clay is made the hangman's lime.   15

The lips of time leech to the fountain head;
Love drips and gathers, but the fallen blood
Shall calm her sores.
And I am dumb to tell a weather's wind
How time has ticked a heaven round the stars.   20
And I am dumb to tell the lover's tomb
How at my sheet goes the same crooked worm.

Fern Hill

Now as I was young and easy under the apple boughs
About the lilting house and happy as the grass was green,
    The night above the dingle° starry,
        Time let me hail and climb
      Golden in the heydays of his eyes,   5
And honoured among wagons I was prince of the apple towns
And once below a time I lordly had the trees and leaves
      Trail with daisies and barley
    Down the rivers of the windfall light.

And as I was green and carefree, famous among the barns   10
About the happy yard and singing as the farm was home,
    In the sun that is young once only,
      Time let me play and be
      Golden in the mercy of his means,
And green and golden I was huntsman and herdsman, the calves   15
Sang to my horn, the foxes on the hills barked clear and cold,

3 **dingle:** woods.

And the sabbath rang slowly
In the pebbles of the holy streams.

All the sun long it was running, it was lovely, the hay
Fields high as the house, the tunes from the chimneys, it was air   20
    And playing, lovely and watery
        And fire green as grass.
    And nightly under the simple stars
As I rode to sleep the owls were bearing the farm away,
All the moon long I heard, blessed among stables, the night-jars   25
    Flying with the ricks,° and the horses
        Flashing into the dark.

And then to awake, and the farm, like a wanderer white
With the dew, come back, the cock on his shoulder: it was all
    Shining, it was Adam and maiden,   30
        The sky gathered again
    And the sun grew round that very day.
So it must have been after the birth of the simple light
In the first, spinning place, the spellbound horses walking warm
    Out of the whinnying green stable   35
        On to the fields of praise.

And honoured among foxes and pheasants by the gay house
Under the new made clouds and happy as the heart was long,
    In the sun born over and over,
        I ran my heedless ways,   40
    My wishes raced through the house high hay
And nothing I cared, at my sky blue trades, that time allows
In all his tuneful turning so few and such morning songs
    Before the children green and golden
        Follow him out of grace,   45

Nothing I cared, in the lamb white days, that time would take me
Up to the swallow thronged loft by the shadow of my hand,
    In the moon that is always rising,
        Nor that riding to sleep
    I should hear him fly with the high fields   50
And wake to the farm forever fled from the childless land.
Oh as I was young and easy in the mercy of his means,
        Time held me green and dying
        Though I sang in my chains like the sea.

26 **ricks:** haystacks.

ROBERT LOWELL (1917–1977)

"To Speak of Woe That Is in Marriage"

*"It is the future generation that presses into being by means of these
exuberant feelings and supersensible soap bubbles of ours."*

—Schopenhauer

"The hot night makes us keep our bedroom windows open.
Our magnolia blossoms. Life begins to happen.
My hopped up husband drops his home disputes,
and hits the streets to cruise for prostitutes,
free-lancing out along the razor's edge.   5
This screwball might kill his wife, then take the pledge.
Oh the monotonous meanness of his lust. . . .
It's the injustice . . . he is so unjust—
whiskey-blind, swaggering home at five.
My only thought is how to keep alive.   10
What makes him tick? Each night now I tie
ten dollars and his car key to my thigh. . . .
Gored by the climacteric° of his want,
he stalls above me like an elephant."

13 **climacteric:** declining period of life.

For the Union Dead°

"Relinquunt Omnia Servare Rem Publicam."°

The old South Boston Aquarium stands
in a Sahara of snow now. Its broken windows are boarded.
The bronze weathervane cod has lost half its scales.
The airy tanks are dry.

Once my nose crawled like a snail on the glass;   5
my hand tingled
to burst the bubbles
drifting from the noses of the cowed, compliant fish.

My hand draws back. I often sigh still
for the dark downward and vegetating kingdom   10
of the fish and reptile. One morning last March,
I pressed against the new barbed and galvanized

fence on the Boston Common. Behind their cage,
yellow dinosaur steamshovels were grunting
as they cropped up tons of mush and grass   15
to gouge their underworld garage.

Parking spaces luxuriate like civic
sandpiles in the heart of Boston.
A girdle of orange, Puritan-pumpkin colored girders
braces the tingling Statehouse,   20

shaking over the excavations, as it faces Colonel Shaw°
and his bell-cheeked Negro infantry

Title: refers to a Civil War momument in Boston Common.   Epigraph: "They gave up everything to serve the republic."   21 **Colonel Shaw:** commander of a black regiment in the Civil
War.

on St. Gaudens' shaking Civil War relief,°
propped by a plank splint against the garage's earthquake.

Two months after marching through Boston,   25
half the regiment was dead;
at the dedication,
William James° could almost hear the bronze Negroes breathe.

Their monument sticks like a fishbone
in the city's throat.   30
Its Colonel is as lean
as a compass-needle.

He has an angry wrenlike vigilance,
a greyhound's gentle tautness;
he seems to wince at pleasure,   35
and suffocate for privacy.

He is out of bounds now. He rejoices in man's lovely,
peculiar power to choose life and die—
when he leads his black soldiers to death,
he cannot bend his back.

On a thousand small town New England greens,   40
the old white churches hold their air
of sparse, sincere rebellion; frayed flags
quilt the graveyards of the Grand Army of the Republic.

The stone statues of the abstract Union Soldier
grow slimmer and younger each year—   45
wasp-waisted, they doze over muskets
and muse through their sideburns . . .

Shaw's father wanted no monument
except the ditch,
where his son's body was thrown   50
and lost with his "niggers."

The ditch is nearer.
There are no statues for the last war here;
on Boylston Street, a commercial photograph
shows Hiroshima boiling   55

over a Mosler Safe, the "Rock of Ages"
that survived the blast. Space is nearer.
When I crouch to my television set,
the drained faces of Negro school-children rise like balloons.

Colonel Shaw   60
is riding on his bubble,
he waits
for the blesséd break.

23 **St. Gaudens:** American sculptor of monument to Colonel Shaw and his regiment.
28 **William James:** 19th-century Harvard philosopher.

The Aquarium is gone. Everywhere,
giant finned cars nose forward like fish;   65
a savage servility
slides by on grease.

AL PURDY (b. 1918)

Song of the Impermanent Husband

Oh I would
I would in a minute
if the cusswords and bitter anger couldn't—
if the either/or quarrel didn't—
and the fat around my middle wasn't—
if I was young if
        I wasn't so damn sure
I couldn't find another maddening bitch
like you holding on for dear life to
all the different parts of me for   10
twenty or twenty
        thousand years
I'd leave in the night like
a disgraced caviar salesman
        descend the moonlight   15
stairs to Halifax°
        (uh-no-not Halifax)
well then Toronto
        ah
I guess not Toronto either/or   20
rain-soaked Vancouver down
                        down
                                down
the dark stairs to
the South Seas' sunlit milky reefs and   25
    the jungle's green
        unending bank account with
all the brown girls being brown
        as they can be and all
the one piece behinds stretched tight tonight   30
in small sarongs gawd not to be touched tho Oh
beautiful as an angel's ass
—without the genitals
And me
    in Paris like a smudged Canadian postcard and   35
(dear me)
    all the importuning white and lily girls

16–21 **Halifax, Toronto, Vancouver:** cities in Canada.

of Rue Pigalle
       and stroll
the sodden London streets and   40
          find a sullen foggy woman who
enjoyed my odd colonial ways and send
a postcard back to you about my faithfulness and
talk about the lovely beastly English weather
I'd be the slimiest most uxorious wife deserter   45
          my shrunk amoeba self absurd inside
a saffron girl's geography and
hating me between magnetic nipples
but
    fooling no one   50
in all the sad and much emancipated world
Why then I'll stay
          at least for tea for
all the brownness is too brown and
all the whiteness too damned white   55
and I'm afraid
          afraid of being
any other woman's man
who might be me
          afraid   60
the unctuous and uneasy self I glimpse
sometimes might lose my faint and yapping cry
for being anything
                    was never quite what I intended
And you you   65
          bitch no irritating
questions re love and permanence only
          an unrolling lifetime here
between your rocking thighs

          and the semblance of motion   70

LAWRENCE FERLINGHETTI (b. 1919)

[In Goya's greatest scenes we seem to see]

In Goya's° greatest scenes we seem to see
                     the people of the world
   exactly at the moment when
       they first attained the title of
               'suffering humanity'   5
    They writhe upon the page
              in a veritable rage
                  of adversity

1 **Goya:** eminent Spanish painter (1746–1828).

Heaped up
   groaning with babies and bayonets   10
       under cement skies
  in an abstract landscape of blasted trees
   bent statues bats wings and beaks
    slippery gibbets
  cadavers and carnivorous cocks   15
  and all the final hollering monsters
   of the
     'imagination of disaster'
  they are so bloody real
     it is as if they really still existed   20

And they do

  Only the landscape is changed

They still are ranged along the roads
  plagued by legionnaires
     false windmills and demented roosters 25
They are the same people
     only further from home
  on freeways fifty lanes wide
   on a concrete continent
     spaced with bland billboards   30
    illustrating imbecile illusions of happiness
The scene shows fewer tumbrils
    but more maimed citizens
      in painted cars
  and they have strange license plates   35
  and engines
   that devour America

Underwear

I didn't get much sleep last night
thinking about underwear
Have you ever stopped to consider
underwear in the abstract
When you really dig into it   5
some shocking problems are raised
Underwear is something
we all have to deal with
Everyone wears
some kind of underwear   10
Even Indians
wear underwear
Even Cubans
wear underwear

The Pope wears underwear I hope   15
Underwear is worn by Negroes
The Governor of Louisiana
wears underwear
I saw him on TV
He must have had tight underwear   20
He squirmed a lot
Underwear can really get you in a bind
Negroes often wear
white underwear
which may lead to trouble   25
You have seen the underwear ads
for men and women
so alike but so different
Women's underwear holds things up
Men's underwear holds things down   30
Underwear is one thing
men and women have in common
Underwear is all we have between us
You have seen the three-color pictures
with crotches encircled   35
to show the areas of extra strength
and three-way stretch
promising full freedom of action
Don't be deceived
It's all based on the two-party system   40
which doesn't allow much freedom of choice
the way things are set up
America in its Underwear
struggles thru the night
Underwear controls everything in the end   45
Take foundation garments for instance
They are really fascist forms
of underground government
making people believe
something but the truth   50
telling you what you can or can't do
Did you ever try to get around a girdle
Perhaps Non-Violent Action
is the only answer
Did Gandhi wear a girdle?   55
Did Lady Macbeth wear a girdle?
Was that why Macbeth murdered sleep?
And that spot she was always rubbing—
Was it really in her underwear?
Modern anglosaxon ladies   60
must have huge guilt complexes
always washing and washing and washing
Out damned spot—rub don't blot—
Underwear with spots very suspicious

Underwear with bulges very shocking   65
Underwear on clothesline a great flag of freedom
Someone has escaped his Underwear
May be naked somewhere
Help!
But don't worry   70
Everybody's still hung up in it
There won't be no real revolution
And poetry still the underwear of the soul
And underwear still covering
a multitude of faults   75
in the geological sense—
strange sedimentary stones, inscrutable cracks!
And that only the beginning
For does not the body stay alive
after death   80
and still need its underwear
or outgrow it
some organs said to reach full maturity
only after the head stops holding them back?
If I were you I'd keep aside   85
an oversize pair of winter underwear
Do not go naked into that good night
And in the meantime
keep calm and warm and dry
No use stirring ourselves up prematurely   90
'over Nothing'
Move forward with dignity
hand in vest
Don't get emotional
And death shall have no dominion   95
There's plenty of time my darling
Are we not still young and easy
Don't shout

HOWARD NEMEROV (b. 1920)

The Goose Fish

On the long shore, lit by the moon
To show them properly alone,
Two lovers suddenly embraced
So that their shadows were as one.
The ordinary night was graced   5
For them by the swift tide of blood
That silently they took at flood,
And for a little time they prized
    Themselves emparadised.

Then, as if shaken by stage-fright
Beneath the hard moon's bony light,
They stood together on the sand
Embarrassed in each other's sight
But still conspiring hand in hand,
Until they saw, there underfoot,
As though the world had found them out,
The goose fish turning up, though dead,
    His hugely grinning head.

There in the china light he lay,
Most ancient and corrupt and gray
They hesitated at his smile,
Wondering what it seemed to say
To lovers who a little while
Before had thought to understand,
By violence upon the sand,
The only way that could be known
    To make a world their own.

It was a wide and moony grin
Together peaceful and obscene;
They knew not what he would express,
So finished a comedian
He might mean failure or success,
But took it for an emblem of
Their sudden, new and guilty love
To be observed by, when they kissed,
    That rigid optimist.

So he became their patriarch,
Dreadfully mild in the half-dark.
His throat that the sand seemed to choke,
His picket teeth, these left their mark
But never did explain the joke
That so amused him, lying there
While the moon went down to disappear
Along the still and tilted track
    That bears the zodiac.

RICHARD WILBUR (b. 1921)

The Writer

In her room at the top of the house
Where light breaks, and the windows are tossed with linden,
My daughter is writing a story.

I pause in the stairwell, hearing
From her shut door a commotion of typewriter-keys
Like a chain hauled over a gunwale.

10

15

20

25

30

35

40

45

5

Young as she is, the stuff
Of her life is a great cargo, and some of it heavy:
I wish her a lucky passage.

But now it is she who pauses,   10
As if to reject my thought and its easy figure.
A stillness greatens, in which

The whole house seems to be thinking,
And then she is at it again with a bunched clamor
Of strokes, and again is silent.   15

I remember the dazed starling
Which was trapped in that very room, two years ago;
How we stole in, lifted a sash

And retreated, not to affright it;
And how for a helpless hour, through the crack of the door,   20
We watched the sleek, wild, dark

And iridescent creature
Batter against the brilliance, drop like a glove
To the hard floor, or the desk-top,

And wait then, humped and bloody,   25
For the wits to try it again; and how our spirits
Rose when, suddenly sure,

It lifted off from a chair-back,
Beating a smooth course for the right window
And clearing the sill of the world.   30

It is always a matter, my darling,
Of life or death, as I had forgotten. I wish
What I wished you before, but harder.

PHILIP LARKIN (1922–1984)

An Arundel Tomb°

Side by side, their faces blurred,
The earl and countess lie in stone,
Their proper habits vaguely shown
As jointed armor, stiffened pleat,
And that faint hint of the absurd—   5
The little dogs under their feet.

Such plainness of the pre-baroque
Hardly involves the eye, until
It meets his left-hand gauntlet, still
Clasped empty in the other; and   10

Title: Arundel, the home of the Dukes of Norfolk.

One sees, with a sharp tender shock,
His hand withdrawn, holding her hand.

They would not think to lie so long.
Such faithfulness in effigy
Was just a detail friends would see: 15
A sculptor's sweet commissioned grace
Thrown off in helping to prolong
The Latin names around the base.

They would not guess how early in
Their supine stationary voyage   20
The air would change to soundless damage,
Turn the old tenantry away;
How soon succeeding eyes begin
To look, not read. Rigidly they

Persisted, linked, through lengths and breadths   25
Of time. Snow fell, undated. Light
Each summer thronged the glass. A bright
Litter of birdcalls strewed the same
Bone-riddled ground. And up the paths
The endless altered people came,   30

Washing at their identity.
Now, helpless in the hollow of
An unarmorial age, a trough
Of smoke in slow suspended skeins
Above their scrap of history,   35
Only an attitude remains:

Time has transfigured them into
Untruth. The stone fidelity
They hardly meant has come to be
Their final blazon, and to prove   40
Our almost-instinct almost true:
What will survive of us is love.

The Whitsun Weddings

That Whitsun,° I was late getting away:
    Not till about
One-twenty on the sunlit Saturday
Did my three-quarters-empty train pull out,
All windows down, all cushions hot, all sense   5
Of being in a hurry gone. We ran
Behind the backs of houses, crossed a street

1 **Whitsun:** seventh Sunday after Easter, a long weekend in England, popular for weddings.

Of blinding windscreens,° smelt the fish-dock; thence
The river's level drifting breadth began,
Where sky and Lincolnshire and water meet.   10

All afternoon, through the tall heat that slept
   For miles inland,
A slow and stopping curve southwards we kept.
Wide farms went by, short-shadowed cattle, and
Canals with floatings of industrial froth;   15
A hothouse flashed uniquely: hedges dipped
And rose: and now and then a smell of grass
Displaced the reek of buttoned carriage-cloth
Until the next town, new and nondescript,
Approached with acres of dismantled cars.   20

At first, I didn't notice what a noise
   The weddings made
Each station that we stopped at: sun destroys
The interest of what's happening in the shade,
And down the long cool platforms whoops and skirls   25
I took for porters larking with the mails,
And went on reading. Once we started, though,
We passed them, grinning and pomaded, girls
In parodies of fashion, heels and veils,
All posed irresolutely, watching us go,   30

As if out on the end of an event
   Waving goodbye
To something that survived it. Struck, I leant
More promptly out next time, more curiously,
And saw it all again in different terms: 35
The fathers with broad belts under their suits
And seamy foreheads; mothers loud and fat;
An uncle shouting smut; and then the perms,
The nylon gloves and jewellery-substitutes,
The lemons, mauves, and olive-ochres that   40

Marked off the girls unreally from the rest.
   Yes, from cafés
And banquet-halls up yards, and bunting-dressed
Coach-party annexes, the wedding-days
Were coming to an end. All down the line   45
Fresh couples climbed aboard: the rest stood round;
The last confetti and advice were thrown,
And, as we moved, each face seemed to define
Just what it saw departing: children frowned
At something dull; fathers had never known   50

Success so huge and wholly farcical;
   The women shared

8 **windscreens:** windshields.

The secret like a happy funeral;
While girls, gripping their handbags tighter, stared
At a religious wounding. Free at last,   55
And loaded with the sum of all they saw,
We hurried towards London, shuffling gouts of steam.
Now fields were building-plots, and poplars cast
Long shadows over major roads, and for
Some fifty minutes, that in time would seem   60

Just long enough to settle hats and say
   I nearly died,
A dozen marriages got under way.
They watched the landscape, sitting side by side
—An Odeon° went past, a cooling tower,   65
And someone running up to bowl°—and none
Thought of the others they would never meet
Or how their lives would all contain this hour.
I thought of London spread out in the sun,
Its postal districts packed like squares of wheat: 70

There we were aimed. And as we raced across
   Bright knots of rail
Past standing Pullmans,° walls of blackened moss
Came close, and it was nearly done, this frail
Travelling coincidence; and what it held   75
Stood ready to be loosed with all the power
That being changed can give. We slowed again,
And as the tightened brakes took hold, there swelled
A sense of falling, like an arrow-shower
Sent out of sight, somewhere becoming rain.   80

65 **Odeon:** cinema.   66 **running up to bowl:** playing cricket.   73 **Pullmans:** railway cars.

ANTHONY HECHT (b. 1923)

The Dover Bitch: A Criticism of Life°
for Andrews Wanning

So there stood Matthew Arnold and this girl
With the cliffs of England crumbling away behind them,
And he said to her, "Try to be true to me,
And I'll do the same for you, for things are bad
All over, etc., etc."   5
Well now, I knew this girl. It's true she had read
Sophocles in a fairly good translation
And caught that bitter allusion to the sea,

Title: refers to two works by Matthew Arnold, the poem "Dover Beach" (p. 519) and an essay
that describes poetry's function as "a criticism of life."

But all the time he was talking she had in mind
The notion of what his whiskers would feel like 10
On the back of her neck. She told me later on
That after a while she got to looking out
At the lights across the channel, and really felt sad,
Thinking of all the wine and enormous beds
And blandishments in French and the perfumes. 15
And then she got really angry. To have been brought
All the way down from London, and then be addressed
As a sort of mournful cosmic last resort
Is really tough on a girl, and she was pretty.
Anyway, she watched him pace the room 20
And finger his watch-chain and seem to sweat a bit,
And then she said one or two unprintable things.
But you mustn't judge her by that. What I mean to say is,
She's really all right. I still see her once in a while
And she always treats me right. We have a drink 25
And I give her a good time, and perhaps it's a year
Before I see her again, but there she is,
Running to fat, but dependable as they come.
And sometimes I bring her a bottle of *Nuit d'Amour.*°

29 ***Nuit d'Amour:*** brand of perfume.

CAROLYN KIZER (b. 1925)

Afternoon Happiness

At a party I spy a handsome psychiatrist
And wish, as we all do, to get her advice for free:
Doctor, I'll say, I'm supposed to be a poet;
All life's awfulness has been grist to me.
We learn that happiness is a Chinese meal 5
While sorrow is a nourishment forever.
My new environment is California Dreamer;
I'm fearful I'm forgetting how to brood.
And, Doctor, another thing has got me worried:
I'm not drinking as much as I should . . . 10

At home, I want to write a happy poem
On love, or a love poem of happiness.
But they won't do, the tensions of everyday,
The rub, the minor abrasions of any two
Who share one space. Ah, there's no substitute for tragedy!
But in this chapter, tragedy belongs
To that other life, the old life before *us.*
Here is my aphorism of the day:
Happy people are monogamous
Even in California. So how does the poem play 20

Without the paraphernalia of betrayal and loss?
I don't have a jealous eye or fear
And neither do you. In truth, I'm fond
Of your ex-mate, whom I name, "my wife-in-law."
My former husband, that old disaster, is now just funny,   25
So laugh we do, in what Cyril Connolly°
Has called the endless nocturnal conversation
Of marriage. Which may be the best part.
Darling, must I love you in light verse
Without the tribute of profoundest art?   30
Of course it won't last. You will break my heart
Or I yours, by dying. I could weep over that.
But now it seems forced, here in these heaven-hills,
The mourning doves mourning, the squirrels mating,
My old cat warm on my lap—here on our terrace   35
As from below comes a musical cursing
As you mend my favorite plate. Later of course
I could pick a fight. There is always material in that.
But we don't come from fighting people, those
Who scream out red-hot iambs in their hate.   40

No, love, the heavy poems will have to come
From *temps perdu,*° fertile with pain, or perhaps
Detonated by terrors far beyond this place
Where the world rends itself, and its tainted waters
Rise in the east, to erode our safety here.   45
Much as I want to gather a lifetime thrift
And craft, my cunning skills tied in a knot for you,
There is only this useless happiness as gift.

26 **Cyril Connolly:** well-known modern journalist and essayist.   42 **temps perdu:** lost time.

KENNETH KOCH (b. 1925)

Mending Sump

"Hiram, I think the sump is backing up.
The bathroom floor boards for above two weeks
Have seemed soaked through. A little bird, I think,
Has wandered in the pipes, and all's gone wrong."
"Something there is that doesn't hump a sump,"   5
He said; and through his head she saw a cloud
That seemed to twinkle. "Hiram, well," she said,
"Smith is come home! I saw his face just now
While looking through your head. He's come to die
Or else to laugh, for hay is dried-up grass   10
When you're alone." He rose, and sniffed the air.
"We'd better leave him in the sump," he said.

MIKE DOYLE (b. 1922)

Growing a Beard

it's a full time
occupation, he said

there's my work cut out
for the summer

since he's a man of discrimination   5
I imagine it so

him growing it
carefully, hair by hair

ROBERT CREELEY (b. 1926)

I Know a Man

As I sd to my
friend, because I am
always talking,—John, I

sd, which was not his
name, the darkness sur-   5
rounds us, what

can we do against
it, or else, shall we &
why not, buy a goddamn big car,
drive, he sd, for   10
christ's sake, look
out where yr going.

If You

If you were going to get a pet
what kind of animal would you get.

A soft bodied dog, a hen—
feathers and fur to begin it again.

When the sun goes down and it gets dark   5
I saw an animal in a park.

Bring it home, to give it to you.
I have seen animals break in two.

You were hoping for something soft
and loyal and clean and wondrously careful—   10

a form of otherwise vicious habit
can have long ears and be called a rabbit.

Dead. Died. Will die. Want.
Morning, midnight. I asked you

if you were going to get a pet   15
what kind of animal would you get.

The Way

My love's manners in bed
are not to be discussed by me,
as mine by her
I would not credit comment upon gracefully.

Yet I ride by the margin of that lake in   5
the wood, the castle,
and the excitement of strongholds;
and have a small boy's notion of doing good.

Oh well, I will say here,
knowing each man,   10
let you find a good wife too,
and love her as hard as you can.

A. R. AMMONS (b. 1926)
Auto Mobile

For the bumps bangs & scratches of
collisive encounters
madam
I through time's ruts and weeds
sought you, metallic, your   5
stainless steel flivver:
I have banged you, bumped
and scratched, side-swiped,
momocked & begommed you &
your little flivver still   10
works so well.

FRANK O'HARA (1926–1966)

Why I Am Not a Painter

I am not a painter, I am a poet.
Why? I think I would rather be
a painter, but I am not. Well,

for instance, Mike Goldberg°
is starting a painting. I drop in.   5
"Sit down and have a drink" he
says. I drink; we drink. I look
up. "You have SARDINES in it."
"Yes, it needed something there."
"Oh." I go and the days go by   10
and I drop in again. The painting
is going on, and I go, and the days
go by. I drop in. The painting is
finished. "Where's SARDINES?"
All that's left is just   15
letters, "It was too much," Mike says.

But me? One day I am thinking of
a color: orange. I write a line
about orange. Pretty soon it is a
whole page of words, not lines.   20
Then another page. There should be
so much more, not of orange, of
words, of how terrible orange is
and life. Days go by. It is even in
prose, I am a real poet. My poem   25
is finished and I haven't mentioned
orange yet. It's twelve poems, I call
it ORANGES. And one day in a gallery
I see Mike's painting, called SARDINES.

4 **Mike Goldberg:** New York artist.

JOHN ASHBERY (b. 1927)

And *Ut Pictura Poesis* Is Her Name°

You can't say it that way any more.
Bothered about beauty you have to
Come out into the open, into a clearing,
And rest. Certainly whatever funny happens to you
Is OK. To demand more than this would be strange   5
Of you, you who have so many lovers,
People who look up to you and are willing
To do things for you, but you think
It's not right, that if they really knew you . . .
So much for self-analysis. Now,   10
About what to put in your poem-painting:
Flowers are always nice, particularly delphinium.
Names of boys you once knew and their sleds,
Skyrockets are good—do they still exist?

Title: *Ut Pictura Poesis:* As in painting, so in poetry.

There are a lot of other things of the same quality   15
As those I've mentioned. Now one must
Find a few important words, and a lot of low-keyed,
Dull-sounding ones. She approached me
About buying her desk. Suddenly the street was
Bananas and the clangor of Japanese instruments.   20
Humdrum testaments were scattered around. His head
Locked into mine. We were a seesaw. Something
Ought to be written about how this affects
You when you write poetry:
The extreme austerity of an almost empty mind   25
Colliding with the lush, Rousseau-like foliage of its desire to communicate
Something between breaths, if only for the sake
Of others and their desire to understand you and desert you
For other centers of communication, so that understanding
May begin, and in doing so be undone.   30

Decoy

We hold these truths to be self-evident:
That ostracism, both political and moral, has
Its place in the twentieth-century scheme of things;
That urban chaos is the problem we have been seeing into and seeing into,
For the factory, deadpanned by its very existence into a   5
Descending code of values, has moved right across the road from total
    financial upheaval
And caught regression head-on. The descending scale does not imply
A corresponding deterioration of moral values, punctuated
By acts of corporate vandalism every five years,
Like a bunch of violets pinned to a dress, that knows and ignores its own
    standing.   10
There is every reason to rejoice with those self-styled prophets of
    commercial disaster, those harbingers of gloom,
Over the imminent lateness of the denouement that, advancing slowly,
    never arrives,
At the same time keeping the door open to a tongue-and-cheek attitude on
    the part of the perpetrators,
The men who sit down to their vast desks on Monday to begin planning
    the week's notations, jotting memoranda that take
Invisible form in the air, like flocks of sparrows   15
Above the city pavements, turning and wheeling aimlessly
But on the average directed by discernible motives.

To sum up: We are fond of plotting itineraries
And our pyramiding memories, alert as dandelion fuzz, dart from one
    pretext to the next
Seeking in occasions new sources of memories, for memory is profit   20

Until the day it spreads out all its accumulation, delta-like, on the plain
For that day no good can come of remembering, and the anomalies cancel
    each other out.   30
But until then foreshortened memories will keep us going, alive, one to the
    other.

There was never any excuse for this and perhaps there need be none,
For kicking out into the morning, on the wide bed,   25
Waking far apart on the bed, the two of them:
Husband and wife
Man and wife

Crazy Weather

It's this crazy weather we've been having:
Falling forward one minute, lying down the next
Among the loose grasses and soft, white, nameless flowers.
People have been making a garment out of it,
Stitching the white of lilacs together with lightning   5
At some anonymous crossroads. The sky calls
To the deaf earth. The proverbial disarray
Of morning corrects itself as you stand up.
You are wearing a text. The lines
Droop to your shoelaces and I shall never want or need   10
Any other literature than this poetry of mud
And ambitious reminiscences of times when it came easily
Through the then woods and ploughed fields and had
A simple unconscious dignity we can never hope to
Approximate now except in narrow ravines nobody   15
Will inspect where some late sample of the rare,
Uninteresting specimen might still be putting out shoots,
    for all we know.

ROBERT KROETSCH (b. 1927)

Mile Zero: being some account of a journey through western Canada in the dead of six nights

   1.
I looked at the dust
on the police car hood.
I looked around the horizon.
(Insert here passage on
nature—   5
   try: The sun was blight
       enough for the wild rose.

       A musky flavour on the milk
       foretold the cracked earth . . .
try One crow foresaw my fright,
       leaned out of the scalding
       air, and ate a grasshopper's
       warning . . .
try: A whirlwind of gulls
       burned the black field white,
       burned white the dark ploughman
       and the coming night . . .)

I AM A SIMPLE POET
I wrote in the dust
on the police car hood.

   2.
Where did the virgin come from
on my second night west?
   Let me, prosaically, parenthetically, remark
   upon what I observed: the lady in question took
   from the left (or was it right?) pocket of her
   coffee-stained apron a small square pad of lined
   sheets of paper. She bit the wood back from
   the lead of a stub of pencil. And she wrote,
   without once stopping to think, the loveliest
   goddamned (I had gauged her breasts when she
   wiped the table) poem that Christ ever read.
She had a clean mind.

   3.
On the third night west
a mountain stopped us.
The mountains were lined up
to dance. I raised my baton:
rooted in earth, the lightning
rod of the roof of the barn,
on my soul's body. A crow
flew over the moon. I raised
my baton, a moon, a mountain.
(Verily, I insist: I did
not raise the purple crow.)
The crow flew over the mountain.

   4.
Order, gentlemen. Order
(her breasts were paradigms)
is the ultimate
mountain. I raised my baton.

   5.
The bindertwine of place—
The mansource of the man—
The natural odour of stinkweed—

The ache at the root of
            the spinal thrust—
(Despair is   not writing the poem,
say what you will about despair.)   55

        6.
What I took to be an eagle
turned out to be a gull.
We glimpsed the sea.
The road ended
but it did not end: 60
the crying gulls turned
on the moon. The moon
was in the sea.
Despair that had sought the moon's
meaning found now the moon.   65
(Mile Zero is everywhere.)
the roar of the sea was the sea's roar.

PHILIP LEVINE (b. 1928)

They Feed They Lion

Out of burlap sacks, out of bearing butter,
Out of black bean and wet slate bread,
Out of the acids of rage, the candor of tar,
Out of creosote, gasoline, drive shafts, wooden dollies,
They Lion grow.   5
        Out of the gray hills
Of industrial barns, out of rain, out of bus ride,
West Virginia to Kiss My Ass, out of buried aunties,
Mothers hardening like pounded stumps, out of stumps,
Out of the bones' need to sharpen and the muscles' to stretch,   10
They Lion grow.
        Earth is eating trees, fence posts,
Gutter cars, earth is calling in her little ones,
"Come home, Come home!" From pig balls,
From the ferocity of pig driven to holiness,   15
From the furred ear and the full jowl come
The repose of the hung belly, from the purpose
They Lion grow.
        From the sweet glues of the trotters
Come the sweet kinks of the fist, from the full flower   20
Of the hams the thorax of caves,
From "Bow Down" come "Rise Up,"
Come they Lion from the reeds of shovels,
The grained arm that pulls the hands,
They Lion grow.   25
        From my five arms and all my hands,

From all my white sins forgiven, they feed,
From my car passing under the stars,
They Lion, from my children inherit,
From the oak turned to a wall, they Lion,   30
From the sack and they belly opened
And all that was hidden burning on the oil-stained earth
They feed they Lion and he comes.

ADRIENNE RICH (b. 1929)

A Clock in the Square

This handless clock stares blindly from its tower,
Refusing to acknowledge any hour.
But what can one clock do to stop the game
When others go on striking just the same?
Whatever mite of truth the gesture held,   5
Time may be silenced but will not be stilled,
Nor we absolved by any one's withdrawing
From all the restless ways we must be going
And all the rings in which we're spun and swirled,
Whether around a clockface or a world.   10

Aunt Jennifer's Tigers

Aunt Jennifer's tigers prance across a screen,
Bright topaz denizens of a world of green.
They do not fear the men beneath the tree;
They pace in sleek chivalric certainty.

Aunt Jennifer's fingers fluttering through her wool   5
Find even the ivory needle hard to pull.
The massive weight of Uncle's wedding band
Sits heavily upon Aunt Jennifer's hand.

When Aunt is dead, her terrified hands will lie
Still ringed with ordeals she was mastered by.   10
The tigers in the panel that she made
Will go on prancing, proud and unafraid.

TED HUGHES (b. 1930)

Crow's First Lesson

God tried to teach Crow how to talk.
"Love," said God. "Say, Love."
Crow gaped, and the white shark crashed into the sea
And went rolling downwards, discovering its own depth.

"No, no," said God, "Say Love. Now try it. LOVE."   5
Crow gaped, and a bluefly, a tsetse,° a mosquito
Zoomed out and down
To their sundry flesh-pots.

"A final try," said God. "Now, LOVE."
Crow convulsed, gaped, retched and   10
Man's bodiless prodigious head
Bulbed out onto the earth, with swivelling eyes,
Jabbering protest—

And Crow retched again, before God could stop him.
And woman's vulva dropped over man's neck and tightened.   15
The two struggled together on the grass.
God struggled to part them, cursed, wept—

Crow flew guiltily off.

6 **tsetse:** malaria-bearing mosquito.

Crow's Theology

Crow realized God loved him—
Otherwise, he would have dropped dead.
So that was proved.
Crow reclined, marvelling, on his heart-beat.

And he realized that God spoke Crow—   5
Just existing was His revelation.

But what
Loved the stones and spoke stone?
They seemed to exist too.
And what spoke that strange silence   10
After his clamour of caws faded?

And what loved the shot-pellets
That dribbled from those strung-up mummifying crows?
What spoke the silence of lead?

Crow realized there were two Gods—   15

One of them much bigger than the other
Loving his enemies
And having all the weapons.

The Thought-Fox

I imagine this midnight moment's forest:
Something else is alive
Beside the clock's loneliness
And this blank page where my fingers move.

Through the window I see no star: 5
Something more near
Though deeper within darkness
Is entering the loneliness:

Cold, delicately as the dark snow,
A fox's nose touches twig, leaf;   10
Two eyes serve a movement, that now
And again now, and now, and now

Sets neat prints into the snow
Between trees, and warily a lame
Shadow lags by stump and in hollow   15
Of a body that is bold to come

Across clearings, an eye,
A widening deepening greenness,
Brilliantly, concentratedly,
Coming about its own business   20

Till, with sudden sharp hot stink of fox
It enters the dark hole of the head.
The window is starless still; the clock ticks,
The page is printed.

GARY SNYDER (b. 1930)

Looking at Pictures to Be Put Away

Who was this girl
In her white night gown
Clutching a pair of jeans

On a foggy redwood deck.
She looks up at me tender,   5
Calm, surprised,

What will we remember
Bodies thick with food and lovers
After twenty years.

Marin-An°

sun breaks over the eucalyptus
grove below the wet pasture,
water's about hot,

Title: refers to Marin County, California.

I sit in the open window
& roll a smoke.   5

distant dogs bark, a pair of
cawing crows; the twang
of a pygmy nuthatch high in a pine—
from behind the cypress windrow
the mare moves up, grazing.   10

a soft continuous roar
comes out of the far valley
of the six-lane highway—thousands
and thousands of cars
driving men to work.   15

SYLVIA PLATH (1932–1963)

The Applicant

First, are you our sort of a person?
Do you wear
A glass eye, false teeth or a crutch,
A brace or a hook,
Rubber breasts or a rubber crotch,   5

Stitches to show something missing?
    No, no? Then
How can we give you a thing?
Stop crying.
Open your hand.
Empty? Empty. Here is a hand   10

To fill it and willing
To bring teacups and roll away
    headaches
And do whatever you tell it.
Will you marry it?
It is guaranteed   15

To thumb shut your eyes at the end
And dissolve of sorrow.
We make new stock from the salt.
I notice you are stark naked.
How about this suit—   20

Black and stiff, but not a bad fit.
Will you marry it?
It is waterproof, shatterproof, proof
Against fire and bombs through the roof.
Believe me, they'll bury you in it.   25

Now your head, excuse me, is empty.
I have the ticket for that.
Come here, sweetie, out of the closet.
Well, what do you think of *that?*
Naked as paper to start   30

But in twenty-five years she'll be silver,
In fifty, gold
A living doll, everywhere you look.
It can sew, it can cook,
It can talk, talk, talk.   35

It works, there is nothing wrong with it.
You have a hole, it's a poultice.
You have an eye, it's an image.
My boy, it's your last resort.
Will you marry it, marry it, marry it.   40

Tulips

The tulips are too excitable, it is winter here.
Look how white everything is, how quiet, how snowed-in.
I am learning peacefulness, lying by myself quietly
As the light lies on these white walls, this bed, these hands.
I am nobody; I have nothing to do with explosions.   5
I have given my name and my day-clothes up to the nurses
And my history to the anaesthetist and my body to surgeons.

They have propped my head between the pillow and the sheet-cuff
Like an eye between two white lids that will not shut.
Stupid pupil, it has to take everything in.   10
The nurses pass and pass, they are no trouble,
They pass the way gulls pass inland in their white caps,
Doing things with their hands, one just the same as another,
So it is impossible to tell how many there are.

My body is a pebble to them, they tend it as water   15
Tends to the pebbles it must run over, smoothing them gently.
They bring me numbness in their bright needles, they bring me sleep.
Now I have lost myself I am sick of baggage—
My patent leather overnight case like a black pillbox,
My husband and child smiling out of the family photo;   20
Their smiles catch onto my skin, little smiling hooks.

I have let things slip, a thirty-year-old cargo boat
Stubbornly hanging on to my name and address.
They have swabbed me clear of my loving associations
Scared and bare on the green plastic-pillowed trolley   25
I watched my tea-set, my bureaus of linen, my books

Sink out of sight, and the water went over my head.
I am a nun now, I have never been so pure.

I didn't want any flowers, I only wanted
To lie with my hands turned up and be utterly empty.   30
How free it is, you have no idea how free—
The peacefulness is so big it dazes you,
And it asks nothing, a name tag, a few trinkets.
It is what the dead close on, finally; I imagine them
Shutting their mouths on it, like a Communion tablet.   35

The tulips are too red in the first place, they hurt me.
Even through the gift paper I could hear them breathe
Lightly, through their white swaddlings, like an awful baby.
Their redness talks to my wound, it corresponds.
They are subtle: they seem to float, though they weigh me down,   40
Upsetting me with their sudden tongues and their color,
A dozen red lead sinkers round my neck.

Nobody watched me before, now I am watched.
The tulips turn to me, and the window behind me
Where once a day the light slowly widens and slowly thins,   45
And I see myself, flat, ridiculous, a cut-paper shadow
Between the eye of the sun and the eyes of the tulips,
And I have no face, I have wanted to efface myself.
The vivid tulips eat my oxygen.

Before they came the air was calm enough,   50
Coming and going, breath by breath, without any fuss.
Then the tulips filled it up like a loud noise.
Now the air snags and eddies round them the way a river
Snags and eddies round a sunken rust-red engine.
They concentrate my attention, that was happy   55
Playing and resting without committing itself.

The walls, also, seem to be warming themselves.
The tulips should be behind bars like dangerous animals;
They are opening like the mouth of some great African cat,
And I am aware of my heart: it opens and closes   60
Its bowl of red blooms out of sheer love of me.
The water I taste is warm and salt, like the sea,
And comes from a country far away as health.

Morning Song

Love set you going like a fat gold watch.
The midwife slapped your footsoles, and your bald cry
Took its place among the elements.

Our voices echo, magnifying your arrival. New statue.
In a drafty museum, your nakedness   5
Shadows our safety. We stand round blankly as walls.

I'm no more your mother
Than the cloud that distils a mirror to reflect its own slow
Effacement at the wind's hand.

All night your moth-breath   10
Flickers among the flat pink roses. I wake to listen:
A far sea moves in my ear.

One cry, and I stumble from bed, cow-heavy and floral
In my Victorian nightgown.
Your mouth opens clean as a cat's. The window square   15

Whitens and swallows its dull stars. And now you try
Your handful of notes;
The clear vowels rise like balloons.

ALDEN NOWLAN (b. 1933)

The Mysterious Naked Man

A mysterious naked man has been reported
on Cranston Avenue. The police are performing
the usual ceremonies with coloured lights and sirens.
Almost everyone is outdoors and strangers are conversing excitedly
as they do during disasters when their involvement is peripheral.   5
"What did he look like?" the lieutenant is asking.
"I don't know," says the witness. "He was naked."
There is talk of dogs—this is no ordinary case
of indecent exposure, the man has been seen
a dozen times since the milkman spotted him and now   10
the sky is turning purple and voices
carry a long way and the children
have gone a little crazy as they often do at dusk
and cars are arriving
from other sections of the city.   15
And the mysterious naked man
is kneeling behind a garbage can or lying on his belly
in somebody's garden
or maybe even hiding in the branches of a tree,
where the wind from the harbour   20
whips at his naked body,
and by now he's probably done
whatever it was he wanted to do
and wishes he could go to sleep

or die
or take to the air like Superman.   25

Untitled Poem

Welcome to these lines
There is a war on
but I'll try to make you comfortable
Don't follow my conversation
it's just nervousness   5
Didn't I make love to you
when we were students of the East
Yes the house is different
the village will be taken soon
I've removed whatever   10
might give comfort to the enemy
We are alone
until the times change
and those who have been betrayed
come back like pilgrims to this moment   15
when we did not yield
and call the darkness poetry

MARGE PIERCY (b. 1936)

Barbie Doll

This girlchild was born as usual
and presented dolls that did pee-pee
and miniature GE stoves and irons
and wee lipsticks the color of cherry candy.
Then in the magic of puberty, a classmate said: 5
You have a great big nose and fat legs.

She was healthy, tested intelligent,
possessed strong arms and back,
abundant sexual drive and manual dexterity.
She went to and fro apologizing.   10
Everyone saw a fat nose on thick legs.

She was advised to play coy,
exhorted to come on hearty,
exercise, diet, smile and wheedle.
Her good nature wore out   15
like a fan belt.
So she cut off her nose and her legs
and offered them up.

In the casket displayed on satin she lay
with the undertaker's cosmetics painted on,   20
a turned-up putty nose,
dressed in a pink and white nightie.
Doesn't she look pretty? everyone said.
Consummation at last.
To every woman a happy ending.   25

ROGER McGOUGH (b. 1937)

My Busconductor

My busconductor tells me
he only has one kidney
and that may soon go on strike
through overwork.
Each busticket   5
takes on now a different shape
and texture.
He holds a ninepenny single
as if it were a rose
and puts the shilling in his bag   10
as a child into a gasmeter.
His thin lips
have no quips
for fat factorygirls
and he ignores   15
the drunk who snores
and the oldman who talks to himself
and gets off at the wrong stop.
He goes gently to the bedroom
of the bus   20
to collect
and watch familiar shops and pubs passby
(perhaps for the last time?)
The sameold streets look different now
more distinct   25
as through new glasses.
And the sky
was it ever so blue?

And all the time
deepdown in the deserted busshelter of his mind   30
he thinks about his journey nearly done.
One day he'll clock on and never clock off
or clock off and never clock on.

At Lunchtime: A Story of Love

When the busstopped suddenly to avoid
damaging a mother and child in the road, the
younglady in the greenhat sitting opposite
was thrown across me, and not being one to
miss an opportunity i started to makelove   5
with all my body.

   At first she resisted saying that it
was tooearly in the morning and toosoon
after breakfast and that anyway she found
me repulsive. But when i explained that   10
this being a nuclearage, the world was going
to end at lunchtime, she tookoff her
greenhat, put her busticket in her pocket
and joined in the exercise.

   The buspeople, and therewere many of   15
them, were shockedandsurprised and amused-
andannoyed, but when the word got around
that the world was coming to an end at lunchtime, they put their pride in their pockets
with their bustickets and madelove one with   20
the other. And even the busconductor, being
over, climbed into the cab and struck up
some sort of relationship with the driver.

   Thatnight, on the bus coming home,
wewere all alittle embarrassed, especially me   25
and the younglady in the greenhat, and we
all started to say in different ways howhasty
and foolish we had been. Butthen, always
having been a bitofalad, i stood up and
said it was a pity that the world didn't nearly   30
end every lunchtime and that we could always
pretend. And then it happened . . .

   Quick asa crash we all changed partners
and soon the bus was aquiver with white
mothballbodies doing naughty things.   35

        And the next day
        And everyday
        In everybus
        In everystreet
        In everytown   40
        In everycountry

people pretended that the world was coming
to an end at lunchtime. It still hasn't.
Although in a way it has.

JAY MEEK (b. 1937)

The Week the Dirigible Came

After the third day it began to be familiar,
an analogue by which one could find
himself in finding it, so whenever it came
outside the window what came to mind was how
marvellous and common the day was, and how expert   5
I'd become at dirigibles. And when
it stayed, one felt the agreeable confidence
that comes with having a goldfish
live four days. So I began to watch its shadow
passing through back yards, only once   10
looked at the tie-line swinging from its nose.
How much it seemed to want an effigy, a fish,
something that might save it from being simply a theory
about itself, and on the fifth day
old ladies came stomping out in their gardens   15
as the shadow passed under them,
and in the woods hunters
fired at the ground. The sixth day rained,
but morning broke clear and the air seemed grand
and empty as a palace, and I went out,   20
looked up, and the sun crossing my nose
cast such shadows as sun-dials make,
and I knew whatever time
had come was our time and it was like nothing else.

JOHN NEWLOVE (b. 1938)

Crazy Riel°

Time to write a poem
or something.
Fill up a page.
The creature noise.
Huge massed forces of men   5
hating each other.
What young men do not know.
To keep quiet,
contemporaneously.
Contempt. The robin diligently   10
on the lawn sucks up worms,
hopping from one to another.
Youthfully. Sixteen miles
from my boyhood home

Title: refers to Louis Riel, 19th-century Canadian rebel leader.

the frogs sit in the grassy marsh 15
that looks like a golf course
by the lake. Green frogs.
Boys catch them for bait or sale.
Or caught them. Time.
To fill up a page. 20
To fill up a hole.
To make things feel better. Noise.
The noise of the images
that are people I will never understand.
Admire them though I may. 25
Poundmaker. Big Bear. Wandering Spirit,
those miserable men.
Riel. Crazy Riel. Riel hanged.
Politics must have its way.
The way of noise. To fill up. 30
The definitions bullets make,
and field guns.
The noise your dying makes,
to which you are the only listener.
The noise the frogs hesitate 35
to make as the metal hook
breaks through the skin
and slides smoothly into place
in the jaw. The noise
the fish makes caught in the jaw, 40
which is only an operation
of the body and the element,
which a stone would make
thrown in the same water, thrashing,
not its voice. 45
The lake is not displaced
with one less jackfish body.
In the slough that looks like a golf course
the family of frogs sings. Metal throats.
The images of death hang upside-down. 50
Grey music.
It is only the listening for death,
fingering the paraphernalia,
the noise of the men you admire.
And cannot understand. 55
Knowing little enough about them.
The knowledge waxing.
The wax that paves hell's road,
slippery as the road to heaven.
So that as a man slips 60
he might as easily slide
into being a saint as destroyer.
In his ears the noise magnifies.
He forgets men.

ISHMAEL REED (b. 1938)

beware :   do not read this poem

        tonite ,   thriller was
        abt an ol woman   , so vain she
        surrounded herself w/
            many mirrors

        it got so bad that finally she   5
        locked herself indoors & her
        whole life became the
            mirrors

        one day the villagers broke
        into her house ,   but she was too   10
        swift for them   .   she disappeared
            into a mirror

        each tenant who bought the house
        after that   ,   lost a loved one to
            the ol woman in the mirror   :   15
            first a little girl
            then a young woman
            then the young woman/s husband

        the hunger of this poem is legendary
        it has taken in many victims   20
        back off from this poem
        it has drawn in yr feet
        back off from this poem
        it has drawn in yr legs

        you are into this poem   from   25
            the waist down
        nobody can hear you can they   ?
        this poem has had you up to here
            belch
        this poem aint got no manners   30
        you cant call out frm this poem
        relax now & go w/ this poem
        move & roll on to this poem
        do not resist this poem
        this poem has yr eyes   35
        this poem has his head
        this poem has his arms
        this poem has his fingers
        this poem has his fingertips

        this poem is the reader & the   40
        reader this poem

statistic :   the us bureau of missing persons reports
        that in 1968 over 100,000 people disappeared

        leaving no solid clues
                nor trace   only   45
    a space   in the lives of their friends

MARGARET ATWOOD (b. 1939)

The Animals in That Country

In that country the animals
have the faces of people:

the ceremonial
cats possessing the streets

the fox run   5
politely to earth, the huntsmen
standing around him, fixed
in their tapestry of manners

the bull, embroidered
with blood and given   10
an elegant death, trumpets, his name
stamped on him, heraldic brand
because

(when he rolled
on the sand, sword in his heart, the teeth   15
in his blue mouth were human)

he is really a man

even the wolves, holding resonant
conversations in their
forests thickened with legend.   20

    In this country the animals
    have the faces of
    animals.

    Their eyes
    flash once in car headlights   25
    and are gone.

    Their deaths are not elegant.

    They have the faces of
    no-one.

You Fit into Me

you fit into me
like a hook into an eye

a fish hook
an open eye

STEPHEN DUNN (b. 1939)

Day and Night Handball

I think of corner shots, the ball
hitting and dying like a butterfly
on a windshield, shots so fine
and perverse they begin to live

alongside weekends of sex   5
in your memory. I think of serves
delivered deep to the left hand,
the ball sliding off the side wall

into the blindnesses of one's body,
and diving returns that are impossible   10
except on days when your body is all
rubber bands and dreams

unfulfilled since childhood.
I think of a hand slicing the face
of a ball, so much english   15
that it comes back drunk

to your opponent who doesn't have
enough hands to hit it,
who hits it anyway, who makes you think
of "God!" and "Goddam!",   20

The pleasure of falling to your knees
for what is superb, better than you.
But it's position I think of most,
the easy slam and victory

because you have a sense of yourself   25
and the court, the sense that old men
gone in the knees have,
one step in place of five,

finesse in place of power,
and all the time   30
the four walls around you
creating the hardship, the infinite variety.

RAYMOND CARVER (b. 1939)

Prosser

In winter two kinds of fields on the hills
outside Prosser: fields of new green wheat, the slips
rising overnight out of the plowed ground,

and waiting,
and then rising again, and budding.   5
Geese love this green wheat.
I ate some of it once too, to see.

And wheat stubble-fields that reach to the river.
These are the fields that have lost everything.
At night they try to recall their youth,   10
but their breathing is slow and irregular as
their life sinks into dark furrows.
Geese love this shattered wheat also.
They will die for it.

But everything is forgotten, nearly everything,   15
and sooner rather than later, please God—
fathers, friends, they pass
into your life and out again, a few women stay
a while, then go, and the fields
turn their backs, disappear in rain.   20
Everything goes, but Prosser.

Those nights driving back through miles of wheat fields—
headlamps raking the fields on the curves—
Prosser, that town, shining as we break over hills,
heater rattling, tired through to bone,   25
the smell of gunpowder on our fingers still:
I can barely see him, my father, squinting
through the windshield in that cab, saying, Prosser.

PATRICK LANE (b. 1939)

Passing into Storm

Know him for a white man.
He walks sideways into wind
allowing the left of him

to forget what the right
knows as cold. His ears   5
turn into death what

his eyes can't see. All day
he walks away from the sun
passing into storm. Do not

mistake him for the howl you hear   10
or the track you think you
follow. Finding a white man
in snow is to look for the dead.
He has been burned by the wind.
He has left too much   15

flesh on winter's white metal
to leave his colour as a sign.
Cold white. Cold flesh. He leans

into wind sideways; kills without
mercy anything to the left of him   20
coming like madness in the snow.

DENNIS LEE (b. 1939)

Thursday

Powerful men can fuck up too. It is Thursday,
a mean old lady has died, she got him his
paper route and there is still that whiff of
ju-jube and doilies from her front hall; a stroke; he can
taste them going soggy; some in his pocket too, they always picked up   5
lint; anyway, she is dead.
And tonight there are things to do in the study, he has a
report, he has the kids, it is
almost too much. Forty-five years, and
still the point eludes him whenever he stops to think.   10
Next morning,
hacking the day into shape on the phone, there is still no
way—routine & the small ache,
he cannot accommodate both.
At Hallowe'en too, in her hall.   15
And I know which one he takes and that
night at six, while the kids are tackling his legs with their small tussling,
how he fends them off, tells them "Play upstairs"; one day
they will be dead also with their jelly beans.
In her kitchen, she had a parrot that said "Down the hatch!"   20

ROBERT HASS (b. 1941)

Picking Blackberries with a Friend
Who Has Been Reading Jacques Lacan°

August is dust here. Drought
stuns the road,
but juice gathers in the berries.

Title: refers to Jacques Lacan, famous French psychoanalyst, who writes about how language is
the only reality we know and how the unconscious is structured like a language.

We pick them in the hot
slow-motion of midmorning.   5
Charlie is exclaiming:

for him it is twenty years ago
and raspberries and Vermont.
We have stopped talking

about *L'Histoire de la vérité,*   10
about subject and object
and the mediation of desire.

Our ears are stoppered
in the bee-hum. And Charlie,
laughing wonderfully,   15

beard stained purple
by the word *juice,*
goes to get a bigger pot.

WILLIAM PITT ROOT (b. 1941)

Under the Umbrella of Blood

In the shower not ten minutes ago and blind from the vinegar rinse
I was thinking 40, I'm 40
when the stinging reminded me of how Turks used to bet on
just how far a headless man could run.
                              —It was orderly, in its way,   5
with a band of selected prisoners, troops in attendance, distance markers,
the executioner with his two-handed sword and another man holding
a hammered copper plate glowing like the sun at the end of a pole;
as the prisoners one at a time ran past, the sword took off their heads
and the plate scorched the neckstumps shut to keep blood pressure up   10
so the runners ran farther, each stumbling on under the umbrella of blood
until the disfigured collapse, all legs and loose elbows.

Do you suppose as each head fell staring and revolving
that it could hear the tossed coins clink on the outspread blanket?
Could it see the body running off without it?   15
As it lay speechless, facing dirt or the sky, as chance would have it,
would it know whether it won or lost for its learned critics?

I wonder, and I rush off to the typewriter wiping my eyes clear,
knowing if I am to get it right
the images under the final downpour must be running   20
faster than the applauding coins of the world can ever fall.

PAUL SIMON (b. 1941)

America

"Let us be lovers,
We'll marry our fortunes together.
I've got some real estate
Here in my bag."
So we bought a pack of cigarettes.   5
And Mrs. Wagner's pies,
And walked off
To look for America.
"Kathy," I said.
As we boarded a Greyhound in Pittsburgh,   10
"Michigan seems like a dream to me now.
It took me four days
To hitchhike from Saginaw.
I've come to look for America."

Laughing on the bus,   15
Playing games with the faces,
She said the man in the gabardine suit
Was a spy.
I said. "Be careful.
His bowtie is really a camera."   20
"Toss me a cigarette.
I think there's one in my raincoat."
"We smoked the last one
An hour ago."

So I looked at the scenery.   25
She read her magazine;
And the moon rose over an open field.
"Kathy, I'm lost," I said.
Though I knew she was sleeping.
"I'm empty and aching and   30
I don't know why."
Counting the cars
On the New Jersey Turnpike.
They've all come
To look for America.   35
All come to look for America.

BOB DYLAN (b. 1941)

The Times They Are A-Changin'

Come gather 'round people
Wherever you roam
And admit that the waters

Around you have grown
And accept it that soon   5
You'll be drenched to the bone.
If your time to you
Is worth savin'
Then you better start swimmin'
Or you'll sink like a stone   10
For the times they are a-changin'.

Come writers and critics
Who prophesize with your pen
And keep your eyes wide
The chance won't come again   15
And don't speak too soon
For the wheel's still in spin
And there's no tellin' who
That it's namin'.
For the loser now   20
Will be later to win
For the times they are a-changin'.

Come senators, congressmen
Please heed the call
Don't stand in the doorway   25
Don't block up the hall
For he that gets hurt
Will be he who has stalled
There's a battle outside
And it is ragin'.   30
It'll soon shake your windows
And rattle your walls
For the times they are a-changin'.

Come mothers and fathers
Throughout the land   35
And don't criticize
What you can't understand
Your sons and your daughters
Are beyond your command
Your old road is   40
Rapidly agin'.
Please get out of the new one
If you can't lend your hand
For the times they are a-changin'.

The line it is drawn   45
The curse it is cast
The slow one now
Will later be fast
As the present now
Will later be past   50

The order is
Rapidly fadin'.
And the first one now
Will later be last
For the times they are a-changin'.   55

I Shall Be Released

They say ev'rything can be replaced,
Yet ev'ry distance is not near.
So I remember ev'ry face
Of ev'ry man who put me here.
I see my light come shining   5
From the west unto the east.
Any day now, any day now,
I shall be released.

They say ev'ry man needs protection,
They say ev'ry man must fall.   10
Yet I swear I see my reflection
Some place so high above this wall.
I see my light come shining
From the west unto the east.
Any day now, any day now,   15
I shall be released.

Standing next to me in this lonely crowd,
Is a man who swears he's not to blame.
All day long I hear him shout so loud,
Crying out that he was framed.   20
I see my light come shining
From the west unto the east.
Any day now, any day now,
I shall be released.

NIKKI GIOVANNI (b. 1943)

Nikki Rosa

childhood remembrances are always a drag
if you're Black
you always remember things like living in Woodlawn
with no inside toilet
and if you become famous or something   5
they never talk about how happy you were to have your mother
all to yourself and
how good the water felt when you got your bath from one of those

big tubs that folk in chicago barbecue in
and somehow when you talk about home
it never gets across how much you
understood their feelings
as the whole family attended meetings about Hollydale
and even though you remember
your biographers never understand
your father's pain as he sells his stock
and another dream goes
and though you're poor it isn't poverty that
concerns you
and though they fought a lot
it isn't your father's drinking that makes any difference
but only that everybody is together and you
and your sister have happy birthdays and very good christ-
masses and I really hope no white person ever has cause to
write about me because they never understand Black love
is Black wealth and they'll probably talk about my hard
childhood and never understand that all the while I was
quite happy

10

15

20

25

MICHAEL ONDAATJE (b. 1945)

King Kong Meets Wallace Stevens

Take two photographs—
Wallace Stevens and King Kong
(Is it significant that I eat bananas as I write this?)

Stevens is portly, benign, a white brush cut
striped tie. Businessman but
for the dark thick hands, the naked brain
the thought in him.

5

Kong is staggering
lost in New York streets again
a spawn of annoyed cars at his toes.
The mind is nowhere.
Fingers are plastic, electric under the skin.
He's at the call of Metro-Goldwyn-Mayer.

10

Meanwhile W. S. in his suit
is thinking chaos is thinking fences.
In his head—the seeds of fresh pain
his exorcising,
the bellow of locked blood.

15

The hands drain from his jacket,
pose in the murderer's shadow.

20

PIER GIORGIO DI CICCO (b. 1949)

The Man Called Beppino

When a man loses his barbershop during the war
as well as an only son, and his wife and
daughter sing the blues of starvation, the man

believes in the great white hope, now the red white
and blue. The man ventures overseas, and lands finally   5
in Baltimore, Maryland, USA—destined to be the
finest barber at eastpoint shopping plaza.

That man works for nothing, because his english is
less than fine; the customers like him,
and the man is easily duped, he believes in the
honest dollar, and is offered peanuts in return.

This while the general manager runs to Las Vegas
to take porno pictures of himself between
tall whores.

The man who lost his barbershop during the war   15
loves great white roses at the back of a house beside
a highway. The roses dream with him,
of being understood in clear english, or of a large
Italian sun, or of walking forever on a
Sunday afternoon.   20

Never mind the new son, the family. It is this man, whose
hospital cheques are being spent in Las Vegas,
it is this man whose hair will shine like
olive leaves at noon; it is this man who will sit
on his front lawn, after the fifth hemorrhage, having   25
his last picture taken,
because he drank too much.

It is this man who will sit under his mimosa
by the highway, fifty pounds underweight, with no
hospital, and look   30

there are great white roses in his eyes.

BRUCE SPRINGSTEEN (b. 1949)

Darkness on the Edge of Town

They're still racing out at the Trestles,
But that blood it never burned in her veins,
Now I hear she's got a house up in Fairview,
And a style she's trying to maintain.

Well, if she wants to see me,   5
You can tell her that I'm easily found,
Tell her there's a spot out 'neath Abram's Bridge,
And tell her, there's a darkness on the edge of town.

Everybody's got a secret, Sonny,
Something that they just can't face,   10
Some folks spend their whole lives trying to keep it,
They carry it with them every step that they take.
Till some day they just cut it loose
Cut it loose or let it drag 'em down,
Where no one asks any questions,   15
or looks too long in your face,
In the darkness on the edge of town.

Some folks are born into a good life,
Other folks get it anyway, anyhow,
I lost my money and I lost my wife,
Them things don't seem to matter much to me now.
Tonight I'll be on that hill 'cause I can't stop,
I'll be on that hill with everything I got,
Lives on the line where dreams are found and lost,
I'll be there on time and I'll pay the cost,   25
For wanting things that can only be found
In the darkness on the edge of town.

LAURIE ANDERSON (b. 1950)

O Superman (For Massenet)

O Superman, O Judge. O Mom and Dad. Mom and Dad.
O Superman. O Judge. O Mom and Dad. Mom and Dad.
Hi. I'm not home right now. But if you want to leave a message, just start
    talking at the sound of the tone.
Hello? This is your Mother. Are you there? Are you coming home?
Hello? Is anybody home? Well, you don't know me, but I know you.   5
And I've got a message to give to you.
    Here come the planes.
So you better get ready. Ready to go. You can come as you are, but pay as
    you go. Pay as you go.

And I said: OK. Who is this really? And the voice said:
This is the hand, the hand that takes. This is the hand, the hand that
    takes
This is the hand, the hand that takes.   10
    Here come the planes.
They're American planes. Made in America.
Smoking or non-smoking?
And the voice said: Neither snow or rain nor gloom of night shall stay
    these couriers from the swift completion of their appointed rounds.   15

'Cause when love is gone, there's always justice,
   And when justice is gone, there's always force.
   And when force is gone, there's always Mom. Hi Mom!

So hold me, Mom, in your long arms. So hold me,
   Mom, in your long arms.   20
In your automatic arms, Your electronic arms, in your arms.
So hold me, Mom, in your long arms.
Your petrochemical arms, Your military arms,
In your electronic arms.

Drama

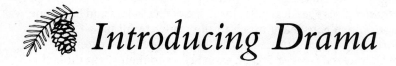 *Introducing Drama*

Dramatic Performance and Multiple Meanings

Of all the major literary forms, plays are distinctive in that they are primarily written not to be read but to be watched. People can be spectators of a play as well as readers. The plays themselves are written as *scripts,* sets of directions and lines of dialogue that must be performed on a stage before an audience.

The public character of drama generates a wide diversity of interpretations. Audiences react both individually and collectively to what they experience in the theater, and professional reviewers and literary critics argue about the significance of both live performances and printed texts. Both spectators and readers bring their own **literary** and **general repertoires**— their historical and cultural backgrounds as well as their immediate expectations—to their experiences of a play. Especially in the theater, they are participants in the performance. Drama therefore lends itself more obviously than any other literary form to being studied in terms of the reader's experiences and the broader cultural contexts of writing and reading.

Even when reading by ourselves, we are aware of important differences between reading a play and reading fiction or poetry. Plays do not usually provide explicit descriptions or discussions of such parts of the text's repertoire as characters or setting. Thus Hansberry's play, *A Raisin in the Sun,* starts with the rather vague direction that it is set "in Chicago's Southside, sometime between World War II and the present"—"the present" presumably about 1959 when the play was first acted. There are some thirty lines that discuss the living room in which the opening scene is set, and then about five lines on the character Ruth. Meant primarily as a working script for actors, *Hamlet* gives even less help, just a list of characters and barebone stage directions. Such gaps leave much to the reader to fill in.

In a short story, by contrast, you can usually count on extended descriptions of characters' faces or voices, even access to their silent thoughts. In *realistic* stories, like those of Chekhov or James, the texts try to persuade you that the characters exist and that the words you read are like a mirror of the world you see around you. You may also be guided by detailed descriptions of places or background accounts of events. Your literary repertoire—your expectations and previous experiences with such descriptions in other texts—helps you to build up mental pictures of the settings and you people them with the kinds of characters you expect. But most plays are much more indeterminate: they are scripts, offering mainly the dialogue among the dramatic personages and usually little ongoing description.

The reason a play doesn't read like a short story or a poem is that the dramatist often wrote it to be performed—to be seen and heard rather than read. So the crowd of spectators around the stage in the open-air Globe Theatre outside London in the early 1600s didn't need written words to tell them whether Hamlet was passive or aggressive or whether the "something rotten in the state of Denmark" was Claudius, or politics, or Hamlet himself (some of the various interpretations offered by modern critics). Members of Shakespeare's audience would see and hear for themselves. In fact, over the course of different performances, they might witness quite different interpretations of the play—even significantly rewritten versions of the play. The same indeterminacy occurs today: different casts of actors will interpret the same play very differently, and a director may have a particular "reading" of the play he or she wants to convey and so may cut or emphasize parts of the script accordingly. The director may set the play in contemporary America to emphasize its relevance or may stage it in sumptuous Elizabethan dress.

Often modern-day readers or audiences assume, wrongly, that some absolute standard or model of the "true" *Hamlet* existed in Shakespeare's time. Like all plays, *Hamlet* has always been produced differently according to different directors' and actors' conceptions of the play. That a text is always interpreted differently—and often with very "strong" readings—is not of course peculiar to drama, but is more obvious in drama than with other literary forms.

In part the different interpretations are more obvious with drama because of the public nature of its performances. The theater possesses a repertoire of devices to make performances gripping, or entertaining, or memorable. These include costumes, sets, music, lighting, as well as the varied talents of the actors. Shakespeare's theater had neither stage curtains nor lights, and made do with a very bare stage; many modern theaters have very elaborate lighting and make the stage look as realistic or fantastic as the director's conception of the play demands.

Above all, each performance of a play has a different audience. Performance is always interactive, a mutual creation of actors and audiences and their different intersecting repertoires. Sometimes a production will not work: a director's interpretation may alienate an audience or may seem too trite. The actors always hope for favorable reactions and are buoyed up when they get them. But it doesn't always work like that. Sometimes their jokes are greeted by dead silence whereas a seriously intended remark might strike the audience as incongruous and bring a roar of unexpected laughter.

Of all the plays in this anthology, *Hamlet* exemplifies most clearly how the same play has been produced in a great variety of ways. *Hamlet* is particularly focused on its leading actor who must be on the stage most of the time. Throughout its stage and critical history, the interpretation of the play has centered largely on the interpretation of the leading character. As you will see from reading Raymond Williams's essay on the meaning of the word "individual" (p. 1106), ours is a culture that has placed enormous importance on being individual, and of all our literary works it is perhaps *Hamlet* on which that concern for individuality has been most obviously concentrated. Even trends in production reflect our views of individuality. The contemporary director Jonathan Miller says, "I think of *Hamlet* as a series of lines to which a series of claimants arrives and competes for." In our predominantly youth-oriented culture, it is rare for Hamlet to be played by an actor over fifty, as happened frequently in the past.

A typical modern production was that by the Royal Shakespeare Company at Stratford-on-Avon in the 1965–1966 season on which a reviewer commented that the actor playing Hamlet "reminds us of a drama student or an inconspicuous undergraduate, or a worried young man leaving a coffee bar . . .his lank blond hair ruffled, a rust red scarf looped about his neck, and cloak rucked up like a belted grey mackintosh." The reviewer went on, "If there is one personage he does not resemble, it is Hamlet, Prince of Denmark," mistakenly assuming that there really might be an ideal model of Hamlet somewhere. In a Stratford, Ontario, production in 1976, two quite different actors alternated the role, one playing Hamlet as emotionally closer to his mother Queen Gertrude, the other playing him as emotionally closer to his dead father, the former king.

If productions today vary so much, they will inevitably vary even more widely between different historical eras and different cultural settings. Imagine the possible differences between a production of *Hamlet* in London in the sixteenth century, in Shanghai in the eighteenth, or in Dallas in the twentieth. You can do this most readily by imagining the kinds of questions a culture very different from your own might ask about *Hamlet*. Earlier in this century, an anthropologist wrote of how he explained *Hamlet* to a group of Indonesian natives. When he explained that King Claudius had married his dead brother's widow, the Indonesians commented on how satisfying and comforting that must have been to young Hamlet—to see his mother take her place among the new king's wives. Having studied earlier parts of this anthology, you know that such a reading of *Hamlet* arises from this particular audiences's cultural assumptions—and ultimately from its dominant ideology. Of course, as usual, it is always easier to see another culture's ideological predispositions than it is to see one's own.

A Fixed Text or a Working Script?

Plays are therefore distinctively malleable because individuals, with their own purposes and cultural assumptions, repeatedly *remake* the plays in the process of producing new performances. And by performance we now refer not only to those literally on the stage but in readers' minds as they read the plays. This process begins with the playwright. Shakespeare probably started the first rehearsal of *Hamlet* by passing out handwritten copies of the script to the director and actors of the players' company to which he belonged. That text probably started to change immediately. Actors may have made suggestions about lines or scenes. The script would have changed during rehearsals, at offstage meetings, and perhaps backstage as the responses of a live audience were noted—and again at later performances by other theatrical companies.

Still later, when the play was finally edited and printed by his friends after Shakespeare's death, the editors of that first printed edition had to reconstruct the parts of the play for which they had various conflicting versions. Thus the original draft of the play was modified both to suit the tastes of the various people involved and to increase its chances for success at theaters in different locations where it was performed. Different versions of *Hamlet* have survived, and scholars still argue which is the "best" or most authentic.

Today a playwright may publish his or her new play just as it opens, yet this text may differ from what is actually used in different live productions. It may be an earlier version, with a different ending, that the producer and director have discarded in favor of one they believe will have better success at the box office. Or the author may offer a newer version in print, one that has not yet been performed, to reflect his or her latest thoughts and to serve as the text the author hopes will be used in the future. Printing the text does not mean that the playwright will be able to keep his or her preferred version intact: nothing is less likely. Producers and directors using the play in the future will also have their own ideas on how to improve it; they will take the author's version as plastic rather than rigid.

There is often much heated controversy over such changes. There are those who believe that plays, especially older ones, should be staged to resemble as closely as possible what a director believes were their original versions. Others think that older plays can best be realized by producing them in radically changed form, to make them more accessible to modern audiences. While no one can say how Shakespeare might react if he saw how modern productions have presented his character Julius Caesar as a fascist and have cast Hamlet as a woman, living playwrights often react with outrage when innovative producers and directors take too many liberties with their texts. In 1984 three world-famous authors threatened or brought legal actions to block significant changes imposed on their plays in new productions. Edward Albee stopped a company in Texas from turning the two husband-wife couples in *Who's Afraid of Virginia Woolf* into male homosexual pairs; Arthur Miller blocked a New York theater's use of segments of his play *The Crucible* in a larger work entitled *L.S.D.;* and Samuel Beckett forced a theater company in Cambridge, Massachusetts, to modify its presentation of his *Endgame.* Where the poem or story usually remains in a relatively fixed form once published, the play remains remarkably fluid.

Now we suggest you examine some of these issues by reading one of the most controversial and open-ended dramas in the canon, Shakespeare's *Hamlet* (text on p. 678)

Multiple Readings of Hamlet

We can illustrate the open-endedness of the dramatic text by looking at a question that has long preoccupied interpretations of *Hamlet:* Why does it apparently take Hamlet so long to get his revenge? In one sense, to speak of "Hamlet's delay" is an interpretation in itself. Shakespeare may have just wanted to write a full-length five-act play to give his audience its money's worth, and perhaps he reasoned that it would spoil the plot to have Hamlet kill his father's murderer in the middle of the play instead of at the end.

Samuel Taylor Coleridge, a leading British poet and critic of the early nineteenth century, explained Hamlet's delay in a distinctively strong reading. He described Hamlet as a romantic, depressed, brooding, isolated figure who had difficulty making decisions, as someone overwhelmed by great impersonal forces. He also argued that Shakespeare was taking a strongly moral position when he made Hamlet procrastinate. Coleridge believed that to think, to wait, to suffer the agony of indecision for a certain period of time was morally superior to acting too hastily, and he saw Hamlet in similar terms. We could term his a *moralistic interpretation.* Nonetheless, since the nineteenth century, critics and spectators have tended to see Hamlet's delaying tactics differently in understanding his character and the overall play. They focus on such speeches as the famous soliloquy (act 2, scene 2) after he has seen an actor moved to tears by pretending to be mourning the death of Hecuba:

> O, what a rogue and peasant slave am I!
> It is not monstrous that this player here,

But in a fiction, in a dream of passion,
Could force his soul so to his own conceit
That from her working all the visage wann'd,
Tears in his eyes, distraction in his aspect,
A broken voice, and his whole function suiting
With forms to his conceit? And all for nothing,
For Hecuba!
What's Hecuba to him, or he to Hecuba,
That he should weep for her? What would he do
Had he the motive and the cue for passion
That I have? He would drown the stage with tears,
And cleave the general ear with horrid speech,
Make mad the guilty, and appall the free,
Confound the ignorant, and amaze indeed
The very faculties of eyes and ears. Yet I,
A dull and muddy-mettled rascal, peak,
Like John-a-dreams, unpregnant of my cause,
And can say nothing—no, not for a king
Upon whose property and most dear life
A damn'd defeat was made.

Other strong interpretations of Hamlet's delay are based on psychological theories. Since the development of psychoanalysis nearly a century ago, it has seemed increasingly plausible that the insights of Freud and his followers into the complexities of the human psyche can be applied to literary texts. Can we apply such insights to *Hamlet?* For many modern readers, to interpret Hamlet in such terms seems natural because psychology has given us powerful language with which to understand and discuss the psyche.

But when readers interpret any text from the past, can they legitimately use ideas and insights that have been developed *after* the work was originally written? This seems to be what inevitably happens. For most readers in the twentieth century, the question of Hamlet's psychological state has become a prominent concern. One result has been an interpretation that assumes that the prince was a "normal" person who unexpectedly found himself in a situation so bizarre and threatening as to affect anyone's mood and behavior. Such readers point to Hamlet's melancholy, his avoidance of old friends, his irritability, and his almost savage treatment of Ophelia. Hamlet's behavior, with its unpredictable moodiness, whether caused by genes or circumstance, suggests a deep neurosis, one which would inhibit actions.

One of the most powerful Freudian readings of *Hamlet* is by Ernest Jones, an early follower of Freud. It constitutes another and a particularly good example of a **strong reading.** Jones sees Hamlet as paralyzed by neurosis and in classic Freudian fashion seeks its causes in early childhood. What if, he asks, Hamlet as a child had bitterly resented having had to share his mother's affection even with his own father, had regarded him as a rival, and had secretly wished him out of the way, so that he might enjoy undisputed and undisturbed the monopoly of that affection? If such thoughts had been present in his mind in childhood they evidently would have been "repressed" and all traces of them obliterated, by filial piety and other educative influences.

In this case, says Jones, the sudden death of his father would reactivate Hamlet's inner conflict, making his unconscious mind somehow responsible for willing that death through his childish wishes, even though those wishes and memories remained repressed. His resulting guilt might well incline him to depression and explain his inability to move quickly to avenge his father. And to Ernest Jones, the complexity of Hamlet's relationship with his mother, and his ambivalent feelings about her, would compound the conflict:

> The explanation, therefore, of the delay and self-frustration exhibited in the endeavor to fulfill his father's demand for vengeance is that to Hamlet the thought of incest and parricide combined is too intolerable to be borne. One part of him tries to carry out the task, the other flinches inexorably from the thought of it.

Jones understood, of course, that Hamlet was a character in a play, not an actual historical figure or a real medical case. But his assumption is that Hamlet's predicament constitutes a reflection of Shakespeare's life experience—and perhaps of some "universal" experience. Clearly Jones's interpretation is not "in" the script; Shakespeare had not read Freud. Yet consider just how natural it seems for most people in the twentieth century to accept some kind of belief in an "unconscious," in the influence of childhood experiences on adult behavior, and to accept such commonly used terms as an *Oedipus complex*. Now that you have read some of Jones's interpretation, does it start to color your own?

Jones's argument is a strong reading not only because it is detailed, well argued, and persuasive, but because it comes to the text with very specific assumptions, with a series of questions that he wishes to put to the text. When you read *Hamlet,* is there something in your repertoire that makes you sympathetic or hostile to Jones's views? And why? Your response to *his* strong reading should provide you with the opportunity to become aware of your own prior assumptions and how you can formulate your own strong reading.

Many important modern critics have produced distinctively strong readings of *Hamlet*. We might consider two in particular, George Wilson Knight, a well-known director as well as a critic, and L. C. Knights, both of whom argued that the source of evil in the play is not Claudius at all but Hamlet, that the prince is not the morally sensitive, noble person of Coleridge's interpretation, but a weak man overwhelmed by the task he finds himself given and increasingly corrupted by it. At the play's end, rather than at last triumphantly overcoming all the obstacles and achieving his revenge, Hamlet has given in to the evil that lies within him from the start.

As you develop your own perspective on *Hamlet,* remember that you do not have to find an interpretation in line with others, or even one with which most of your class agrees. Rather, you should only try to understand the various *assumptions* underlying different interpretations of the play (whether by Coleridge, Ernest Jones, or your classmates) and then, exploring your own assumptions, start to produce your own strong reading of it. The multiple and diverse readings of *Hamlet* reveal both the openness of this literary text to interpretation and the extent to which the text is necessarily produced by the reader.

Creating Strong Readings: An Assignment on Hamlet

In teaching *Hamlet,* we have made an interesting discovery. For the most part, and despite its lengthy history of varied interpretations, most of our students did not find *Hamlet* particularly ambiguous on a first reading. They assumed, by and large, that a literary work almost by definition was unified and somehow contained a single meaning. That was the way they had been previously taught to read literature, and even when they were familiar with a more open-ended, or *perspectival,* approach to reading like the one we advocate in this anthology, they still expected a shared, objective meaning. That a classic like *Hamlet* does not have a definitive, generally agreed-upon meaning is often disconcerting to students.

When such readers come to realize that *Hamlet* has been interpreted in so many different ways, what happens? We have asked a number of our own classes to do some research into the many diverse interpretations of *Hamlet* produced over the past three hundred and more years. By reading both earlier and more recent critical discussions of *Hamlet,* students are confronted with the notion that critics are merely other readers whose responses are conditioned by their own particular cultural assumptions. The questions we must address are (1) how can we evaluate these various critical responses, and (2) do expert readers read with any more authority than student readers?

In preparing response statements on *Hamlet,* we ask you first to record your reading strategies and reactions to the play: Did you find the play ambiguous or confusing? Did you reread any sections of the play? Do you identify particularly with any of the characters? Do you think that Hamlet delayed in killing Claudius?

After you record your initial responses, do some research on the play; for example, read extracts from essays by Ernest Jones and A. C. Bradley, and a review article by John Jump[1] on the history of *Hamlet* criticism from the seventeenth century to the 1960s. Based on this material, which enlarges your literary repertoire, answer the following:

1. Do you agree with any of the varied, often contradictory, interpretations of *Hamlet?* Have any of these interpretations changed your own original interpretation of *Hamlet?*
2. How can you account for so many interpretations of a single play? Is it possible that Freud's theories can apply to a play written in the seventeenth century? What do all these different interpretations suggest about the status of a text?
3. Are there any meanings, or constraints on the making of meaning, *in* the text? If you think there are, give examples. Or is meaning determined solely by a reader's repertoires?
4. Having read a survey of *Hamlet* criticism, comment on the influences of literary criticism on the interpretation and production of a play.

Reading diverse critical positions on *Hamlet* forced our students to ask how one text can support so many interpretations without seeming incoherent or fragmented. The many plausible interpretations of *Hamlet* paradoxically support the notion that texts both do and do not constrain interpretation. One student wrote in a response statement:

> Many of the texts we have read in class seemed to allow for two or three possible interpretations, but none so far have allowed for as many interpretations that make sense as *Hamlet.* Perhaps it's the evocative power of Shakespeare's language, or perhaps the fact that the text deals with so many moral issues enables readers to read it in such diverse ways.

Some students argued, on the other hand, that reading criticism on *Hamlet* demonstrates that readers *create* rather than discover meanings in texts. As another student wrote: "Everyone writing on *Hamlet* seems to think they're getting a certain meaning *out of* the text when actually they're getting it out of their own repertoire of knowledge."

One student, for example, arguing that the text limits interpretive possibilities, asserted that if one were to say something seemingly stupid, that Hamlet was something absurd—like a whale—one would be "wrong." But other students suggested that if enough evidence could be put forth, which largely would have to be "extra-textual," and if the argument were sufficiently persuasive, it might *become* plausible to think that Hamlet is a whale. They further argued that it is only because we cannot currently think of any evidence that this position seems implausible. These students used

---

[1] See Ernest Jones, "Hamlet Diagnosed," in *Four Centuries of Shakespeare Criticism,* ed. by Frank Kermode (New York: Avon, 1956); A. C. Bradley, *Shakespearean Tragedy* (London: Macmillan, 1904); John Jump, *"Hamlet,"* in *Shakespeare: Selected Bibliographical Guides,* ed. by Stanley Wells (Oxford: Oxford UP, 1973) 145–157.

their experience of reading Ernest Jones's Freudian interpretation as a case in point: to most of them Jones's argument had initially seemed nearly as implausible as the suggestion that Hamlet is a whale. None of them felt that they would have tried to psychoanalyze a character, largely because they had read little or nothing of Freud. Nonetheless, they were able to entertain Jones's interpretation of Hamlet simply because he offered a persuasive argument in its defense. Thus notions of "correct" and "incorrect" interpretation came to be seen as constrained much more by a given reader's knowledge and by the persuasiveness of an interpretation rather than by "the text."

These students recognized that critics, like themselves, are influenced by cultural and literary assumptions and consequently have no greater access to the "true" meaning of a text than do student readers. In fact, by studying the many different interpretations of *Hamlet,* many students began to recognize that paradigms for determining what truth is are always relative to different historical periods and are never absolute. Thus many began to argue that meaning cannot be said to be "in" a text. While students recognized that their interpretations, like those of expert readers, are always conditioned by their historical situation, they nonetheless argued that, because expert readers have a greater knowledge base from which to draw, they can write more complex and potentially persuasive analyses of texts than can students. Finally, students argued that their judgments on whether one critic's interpretation seemed better or more correct than another were always influenced by their own prior knowledge; for many, this recognition provided an incentive to learn more about a given text before reading and judging critical interpretations about it.

So you can easily see there are limits on the amount of control that a playwright can exercise, especially given the ease with which readers (and performers) can induce multiple interpretations from a script. What can you learn from the dialogue? Think about how you respond when you overhear a conversation. Do you judge the meaning or implications of the words from just what is said or from a whole host of other factors such as voice tone, gestures, previous knowledge about the speakers, or your own repertoire?

Conventions of Dramatic Texts

Recall that most of our students did not initially regard *Hamlet* as ambiguous. Other types of plays, however, may often seem quite strange, confusing, or ambiguous to you particularly on a first reading. Ionesco's *The Gap* attempts to create a feeling of uneasiness as well as amusement by making its spectators and readers aware that something odd and "unreal" is going on. Like the plays of Samuel Beckett, Edward Albee, and Harold Pinter, Ionesco's plays evoke in their audiences a sense of the irrationality that threatens to disrupt their lives. It gets its effects by a clever mixture of ordinary, seemingly rational, everyday language and absurd and sinister situations. A distinguished senior academic has discovered that by an oversight he has never completed his bachelor's degree. Once this "gap" in his career has been revealed, all of his subsequent honors and distinctions somehow become invalid. His intellect seems to degenerate; he fails his examination and seems to be reduced to stupidity and ridicule. Reading the play may make you think of the frustration of dealing with bureaucracies, filling out seemingly unnecessary and stupid forms—much of which, we often say, seems "absurd." The effect is a strange mixture of logic and illogicality, all the more effective because the absurd events proceed so logically and because the play's characters don't seem to notice what, for the audience, is the main effect—the "unrealistic," absurd nature of the events.

The effect of such plays is often very disturbing. If you approach such a play with expectations that a play ought to be a realistic mirror of everyday events, then *The Gap* may irritate you. What is occurring is that the play is drawing attention to the *theatricality* of performance. It will probably have different effects on you from those of *Hamlet* because it is using different theatrical conventions.

Reading *Hamlet* should show you that the interpretation of plays depends on both the reader's (or spectator's) experiences and culturally specific factors that have produced the text (or performance). But while plays are relatively "open" texts and so provide their readers with an unusual degree of flexibility in interpretation, conventions do exist that try to guide playwrights, director, actors and, through them, spectators and readers. In this section, we will introduce you to some of the conventional textual strategies typically found in drama texts.

We have already discussed drama's most important feature, its performative nature: "The medium of drama," the poet Ezra Pound noted, "is not words, but persons moving about on a stage using words"—and, we emphasize, doing so in the presence of an audience. Particular features that affect an audience's response are the stage and its setting, costume, gestures, and sound effects; these elements constitute the basic repertoire of the dramatic text. The script itself also has distinctive characteristics. *Dialogue* is the most significant (some plays, normally termed *mimes* or, as in *Hamlet,* "dumb shows," have no dialogue). From the dialogue, readers and spectators gain not just random information but telling language that reveals character, furthers the plot, or produces distinctive theatrical effects.

Most plays have a main plot, often accompanied by minor or *sub*plots. Traditional plays, by Shakespeare or Sophocles, usually follow a fairly recognizable pattern with distinctive points of crisis and resolution, where expectations are built up and then resolved or dissipated. In printed versions, and often in performance, plays will be conventionally divided for the audience by acts (and scenes) to indicate breaks in the time, place, or action on stage. The end of an act is usually shown by lowering a curtain, by dimming the lights that illuminate the stage, or by some other suggestion of a break in the continuity. In Shakespeare's time, when most theaters were outdoors and did not have lights or curtains, the ending of a scene or act would often be presented by a concluding rhymed couplet, like the one at the end of *Hamlet*. When you read the plays in this section, ask yourself what effect the divisions in a play make on the level of tension and thus on your interpretation. Would you, as a director, perhaps not have a production take a break where an author requested it? What effect would your alternative breaks have? In Shakespeare's time, *Hamlet* was probably acted without a break from start to finish. Most productions today have at least two intervals. Where would you place the breaks in *Hamlet?* Your answer to that question will undoubtedly show something of your interpretation. Where would you want your audience to be left in suspense, anticipating new and exciting developments? You might consider alternative possibilities—a production taking only *one* break as opposed to two, for instance. Where would this break come and what would its different effects be?

With plays, there are enormous gaps and indeterminacies in the script for readers to fill. Nearly all that the audience or its readers know comes from either the actions or the dialogue of the players. In ancient Greek drama, participants called the *chorus,* who appeared on stage but took no part in either the main action or the dialogue, addressed the audience periodically with descriptions of the action and comments on it. In the later English theater of Shakespeare's time, one convention sometimes used by playwrights, who could not describe the silent thoughts of a character as a storyteller could and who did not want to use a chorus, was to have the actor speak such thoughts directly to the audience, or off to one side, while the others on stage ignore the speech as if it were not audible. Such a convention is called a **soliloquy.** In the famous soliloquies of Hamlet where he berates himself ("Oh, what a rogue and peasant slave am I! . . .") and then puzzles over his course of action ("To be, or not to be: that is the question: . . ."), he is voicing his silent train of thought for the benefit of the audience. *Rosencrantz and Guildenstern Are Dead* fills in certain gaps in *Hamlet* by presenting dialogue that might have occurred offstage in Shakespeare's play. By doing so, it creates further gaps for its audience. Do ordinary people like Rosencrantz and Guildenstern matter? Can you reconcile the depiction of them here with your visualization of them in *Hamlet?*

As we have seen, some plays are much more explicit than others in their instructions to readers. Their authors want to try to control as much as possible the way their readers see settings, hear actors, and understand the meanings of the action. This approach to drama gained favor in the late nineteenth century, as playwrights, like other writers in the Western world, fell under the influence of **realism,** the attempt to produce art and literature that supposedly mirrored the world of nature and society. In Ibsen's *The Wild Duck,* for example, the author provides extensive descriptions of his characters and settings for the reader and for those staging the play in order to shape, as much as possible, their thinking about the play.

Whatever the style in which the play you are studying is written, as you develop *your* reading of it, never forget that it is written to be performed, not merely to be read. Try to analyze your own preferences and expectations about drama. For Shakespeare, do you prefer "realistic" performances or costume performances (in so-called authentic costumes) or do you prefer your Shakespeare in twentieth-century dress? What kind of emotional effects do you want from "your" production of *Raisin in the Sun* or *Death of a Salesman?* What kind of theatrical space would you prefer to have? Do you envisage a particular theater—perhaps your own college theater or maybe an outdoor venue, such as many summer theaters use? How would you adapt *The Wild Duck* or *Rosencrantz and Guildenstern Are Dead* to such theater spaces? How would you produce Stoppard's play in the light of what you know of *Hamlet?* What would it be like to consider producing *both* plays? In short, as you study the plays that we have chosen, read them but also think of them as performances. That will be easier to do if you act out small parts when you discuss them with friends or in class. Attending productions of plays, whether of these plays or others, will also offer you immediate experience of the ways drama takes place, of the possibilities for staging, and of various interpretations of the text.

Ideological Differences in Reading: Death of a Salesman

Miller's *Death of a Salesman* gives its readers the opportunity to explore another important issue in reading and interpreting dramatic texts—the different ways in which the **general repertoires** of text and readers can match. Even in the same society, different readers will inevitably take different positions on issues and so will ask quite different questions of the play because of their distinct general repertoires. Our students, in reading this play, do not come to many resolutions; in fact, they often disagree violently over it.

The play is subtitled *Certain Private Conversations in Two Acts and a Requiem.* "Requiem" suggests death and tragedy, and yet if readers assume the play is a tragedy like *Hamlet,* with noble characters and elegant language, they may well be disappointed. Willy Loman, the main character, is a salesman, not a prince, and his death might easily be seen as unheroic, even trivial.

But as readers of *Death of a Salesman,* you may be more struck by the ordinariness of Willy Loman and the "realism" of his actions, dilemmas, and failures. The play can, in fact, be just as disturbing and "tragic" to its audience as an aristocratic play like *Hamlet* with aristocratic characters, probably because as late twentieth-century readers, you are caught up in many of the same ideological pressures as the play's characters. It is therefore particularly interesting to examine your own assumptions as you read the play and try to construct your initial response to it. When Willy boasts of his success as a salesman ("When I went north the first time, the Wagner Company didn't know where New England was!") and when his insecurity and fear begin to emerge, your interpretations will be conditioned by your own feelings about the American economic system, with its unemployment, private enterprise, and consumerism. You may have strong views about such issues, and they will determine your interpretation of the play —whether you see Willy as a victim of a cruel and unpredictable system, as a little man who tried as hard as he could, or as a morally weak man who deserves his fate.

Both personal and social factors operate in such assumptions. When Willy complains, "Figure it out. Work a lifetime to pay off a house. You finally own it, and there's nobody to live in it," a reader who has undergone a similar experience may be immediately sympathetic and become personally caught up in Willy's problem. But at a more profound level, your discussion might be directed to the American system of doing business that provides Willy with these experiences. Willy's remark on Biff, "I'll get him a job selling. He could be big in no time," idealizes such values as individual enterprise, the work ethic, the self-made man, and unlimited opportunity, all values to which Willy subscribes. How an individual reader responds to Willy's "ideals and plans" is determined by that reader's commitment to and awareness of such values.

It is perfectly possible, for instance, to see Willy's fate as just as tragic as that of Antigone or Hamlet—a man of ideals destroyed by forces he neither controls nor understands. For instance, one of our students wrote:

> Willy Loman's wife claims that "a small man can be just as exhausted as a great man. He works for a company thirty-six years this March, opens up unheard-of territories to their trademark, and now in his old age they take his salary away." She sees the unfairness of a system that ignores someone when it has no use for him any longer. The ideals that Willy Loman has as a salesman leave him open to exploitation by people stronger than he is, people who are more part of the system. As I read the play, I became more and more indignant about "them" and "it."

It would be easy to take another view—to argue, for instance, that the essence of the salesman's life is risk, opportunism, knowing when to cheat "legitimately," and knowing that a salesman is "a man out there in the blue, riding on a smile and a shoeshine. And when they start not smiling back— that's an earthquake. And then you get yourself a couple of spots on your hat, and you're finished." According to such a reading, risk is what makes life worthwhile—a view that reflects the central values of what is called the

American dream, even if it finally becomes destructive. "A salesman has got to dream, boy. It comes with the territory," says Willy, and those who agree would say that Willy's tragedy exists in his inability to make the risk pay off.

These two opposing interpretations arise from the different ideological assumptions that readers bring to the play. These assumptions are the product of the readers' involvement in, detachment from, or skepticism about "the American dream." As you read, you can become conscious of how your own ideological conditioning will lead you inevitably to take up your own attitudes towards Willy and his family.

Expanding Reading Strategies:
Six Characters in Search of an Author

We suggested above that you may be puzzled by Ionesco's *The Gap* because it employs unfamiliar conventions. Often encountering a play with **text strategies** that are new to you can help to enlarge your repertoire of **reading strategies.** We suggest you read *Six Characters in Search of an Author* (p. 859) with this goal in mind.

With this nontraditional play, the notion of "character" may be especially difficult. The characters in this play are not presented as real people but as discarded figments of their author's imagination. How can you relate to characters who describe themselves as imaginary? While the characters are not "real," neither are ghosts; yet most viewers don't question the status of the ghost in *Hamlet.* Why is this? Most people do not believe in ghosts, but they are familiar enough with their depiction in literature, art, and popular culture: in short, they are familiar with ghosts as conventions. But they do not usually find characters announcing on stage that they are characters in a play. This goes against the deeply ingrained convention of realistic presentation of characters. In other words, it is readers' familiarity with conventions, not the conventions themselves, that determines their responses. Reading a play like *Six Characters* can help you expand your literary repertoire and so create a more interesting reading in which your reading strategies more fully intersect with the strategies of the text.

Once your expectations about "character" in *Six Characters* expand, you can begin to recognize the many levels of reality in the play—the characters, the actors, the actors playing characters, and the fact that all of the "persons" in the play are actors, some of whom are playing characters and some of whom are playing actors. Realizing that the focus of the play can be the multiple perspectives that people inevitably find themselves caught up in rather than the presentation of conventionally unified characters can help you enjoy a great variety of drama, especially works written in the last fifty years.

Reading and Responding to Drama

TOM STOPPARD

Rosencrantz and Guildenstern Are Dead

The text for Stoppard's *Rosencrantz and Guildenstern Are Dead* begins on page 1030.

Response Statement Assignment

After rereading the general guidelines for writing response statements (pp. 15–20), write a response statement on *Rosencrantz and Guildenstern Are Dead,* based on the following topic:

Stoppard's play can be seen as a *strong reading* of Shakespeare's *Hamlet,* a commentary that projects its own perspective upon the earlier play, perhaps adapting some of *Hamlet's* issues to twentieth-century concerns. One concern seems to be especially insistent—that Rosencrantz and Guildenstern are taking part in a play they don't quite understand—and by extension so are the play's spectators and readers. The "play" is therefore not just *Rosencrantz and Guildenstern Are Dead* by Tom Stoppard—but our own lives.

How do you respond to the play's constant emphasis on the theatrical nature of experience, and on the suggestion that you (like Rosencrantz and Guildenstern) are actors in a world that keeps you "intrigued without ever quite being enlightened." Do you agree? What parts of your own **general repertoire** influence your response to the play on this issue?

Sample Student Response Statement

Here is what one of our students wrote as a response statement.

> I found the parts of this play where the "real" Hamlet came
> in the most intriguing. It was as if we were seeing behind the
> scenes to what was actually going on. But when the curtain was
> lifted, what in fact did we see? Not much. Just two very
> ordinary people trying to understand a mystery that is beyond
> them.
>
> Rosencrantz and Guildenstern, who seem confused about who is
> really who (just as I was), arrive in Denmark, summoned by the
> king to investigate Hamlet's strange behavior. That much
> background we know from the play Hamlet, and we find the same
> state of affairs in Stoppard's play. They meet the players,
> talk to the king, watch Hamlet and Ophelia--all of which
> happens in Shakespeare's play. What we see in Stoppard's play
> seems to fit.
>
> What is different is the way we get some idea of the
> "ordinary" person's point of view as distinct from Hamlet's.
> Rosencrantz and Guildenstern are out of their depth from the
> start. Guildenstern remarks:
>
> > I am the essence of a man spinning double-headed coins,
> > and betting against himself in private atonement for an
> > unremembered past.
>
> They are "kept intrigued without ever quite being
> enlightened." When they interview Hamlet all they get is
> "evasions":
>
> > It was question and answer, all right. Twenty-seven
> > questions he got out in ten minutes, and answered three. I
> > was waiting for you to delve. "When is he going to start
> > delving?" I asked myself.
>
> What does that tell them? More important, what does that
> tell us? I thought Hamlet was supposed to be very ambiguous,
> but this play is even more obscure. Stoppard's play conveys the
> sense that life is ambiguous and complicated, and we can't tell
> much about it. Once Rosencrantz says "Ha! it's beginning to
> make sense," but it isn't.

Discussion

This response statement has great potential but, as a *response* statement, it
is too text-centered: the student puts too much emphasis on a plot summary
and on trying to find an objective meaning. And almost no attention is
given to the reader's repertoire.

If you feel you need to summarize or paraphrase a text that you are reading, you should (1) regard it very much as a preliminary step only and (2) be aware that inevitably you will bring some of your own repertoire into it. There is *no* "objective" or "correct" summary of a text. Moreover, your views are always involved in your reading strategies.

When revised, this initial response statement should become much more self-conscious and focused—the student's own contribution to the reading that is developing should, in particular, be brought out. Creating a sense of the atmosphere, establishing plot and characters, and restating the play's ideas are all merely *preliminary* stages in developing a reading. What is more important is to become aware of (and discuss) your own part in the building up of your reading. You do this by focusing on your response and then working to create your own strong reading of the play. There are important strategies you can adopt: you can first note your predominant response to the play (which this response statement, as yet, does not do). Then you can explore what in your repertoire caused you to respond as you did. Only with this level of self-awareness and literary awareness can you begin to develop a strong reading of the play.

The response statement assignment gives hints on the direction in which a strong reading might develop: it suggests that the reader examine Stoppard's play as a commentary on *Hamlet* and assess to what extent a late twentieth-century reader shares, or differs from, Stoppard's perspective.

First Revision

Here is a revised version of the initial response statement in which you can see some of these improvements:

> Stoppard's play is a commentary on Shakespeare's Hamlet, in which Stoppard tries to represent a "modern" reading of Hamlet. That it is written for a modern audience makes it more relevant to us. When the "real" Hamlet comes in, the play reaches its most intriguing point. It is as if we are privileged to see what is going on behind the scenes. But when the curtain is lifted, what in fact do we see? Not much. Just two very ordinary people trying to understand a mystery that is beyond them.
>
> As to Stoppard's play as a reading of Hamlet, I wonder whether other ages, between Shakespeare's time and ours, would have seen Rosencrantz and Guildenstern in the same way. Probably not. Their language is very informal, more like modern speech. More important, their ideas sound suspiciously like a lot of modern literature. They are concerned with personal identity, with the distinction between fact and fiction, with the randomness of experience, all themes of modern life--though perhaps they were concerns of Shakespeare's time as well.

Another "modern" aspect of the play is that we get some idea of the "ordinary" person's point of view. Rosencrantz and Guildenstern are out of their depth from the start. Guildenstern remarks:

> I am the essence of a man spinning double-headed coins, and betting against himself in private atonement for an unremembered past.

They are "kept intrigued without ever quite being enlightened." When they interview Hamlet, all they get is "evasions":

> It was question and answer, all right. Twenty-seven questions he got out in ten minutes, and answered three. I was waiting for you to delve. "When is he going to start delving?" I asked myself.

How do I respond to this? From a great deal of modern literature, especially the drama of the absurd, we learn to explain how we feel life is ambiguous, dislocated, and unpredictable. These are certainly common feelings, and in fact we don't need literature to tell us. But a play like Stoppard's gives us a way of expressing something of these feelings, and it also shows how Hamlet, long thought to be a great classic of the language, is such a powerful work that it can deal with the questions we raise as well as those of Shakespeare's time. We often feel today that the modern world is tragically perplexing. Hamlet could become a hero for our time--if only we could understand him. We respond to Rosencrantz and Guildenstern because these two ordinary men are like us. They are ordinary people caught in a world bigger than both of them--rather like the way many of us feel.

Our student in this revision made a real effort to relate her *experience* of reading the play to the interpretation that she developed. She could develop her reading even further by investigating whether *Hamlet's* original readers might have experienced the same kind of ambiguity or dislocation that a modern reader experiences—and whether Stoppard's play is merely bringing out, in its "strong reading" of *Hamlet,* something that would have been perceived similarly then.

Or our student could contrast the apparent restoration of political order at the end of *Hamlet* with the way events just trickle to a stop in *Rosencrantz and Guildenstern Are Dead.* The latter ending, too, might be felt to be a more "modern" experience. Which of the two kinds of endings would be more or less satisfying to you? Why might you choose one view rather than the other? What emotional or intellectual effect would a firm ending as opposed to an indecisive ending have in Stoppard's play?

Additional Response Assignments

1. Why do you think Stoppard chose these two characters to write about and not others in Shakespeare's play?
2. Consider the ending of this play and the ending of *Hamlet*. Do you sense any difference in tone or direction? Is one more open-ended? Which do you prefer and why?
3. Choose one aspect of the staging of the play—costume, scenery, action —and discuss the problems and possibilities it poses for a modern director. How might you deal with these matters? How could they reinforce your reading of the play?
4. Many students contend that they cannot develop a reading of Stoppard's play using such traditional expectations about drama as: (1) the plot will come to a climax; (2) the characters will be clearly developed and will change over time; (3) some closure or unity or message will seem evident near the end of the play. Do you, like many other students, find yourself frustrated by imposing these traditional expectations on the play? If so, then a mismatching of repertoire has occurred between your reading strategies and the play's text strategies. What new expectations can you develop about plot, character, and meaning that might help you interact more productively with the text?

SOPHOCLES (496–406 B.C.)

Antigone

Translated by Elizabeth Wyckoff

CHARACTERS

ANTIGONE	TEIRESIAS
ISMENE	A SENTRY
EURYDICE	A MESSENGER
CREON	CHORUS
HAEMON	

SCENE: *Thebes, before the royal palace.* ANTIGONE *and* ISMENE *emerge from its great central door.*

ANTIGONE
    My sister, my Ismene, do you know
    of any suffering from our father sprung
    that Zeus does not achieve for us survivors?
    There's nothing grievous, nothing free from doom,
    not shameful, not dishonored, I've not seen.   5
    Your sufferings and mine.
    And now, what of this edict which they say
    the commander has proclaimed to the whole people?

Have you heard anything? Or don't you know
that the foes' trouble comes upon our friends? 10

ISMENE

I've heard no word, Antigone, of our friends.
Not sweet nor bitter, since that single moment
when we two lost two brothers
who died on one day by a double blow.
And since the Argive army went away 15
this very night, I have no further news
of fortune or disaster for myself.

ANTIGONE

I knew it well, and brought you from the house
for just this reason, that you alone may hear.

ISMENE

What is it? Clearly some news has clouded you. 20

ANTIGONE

It has indeed. Creon will give the one
of our two brothers honor in the tomb;
the other none.
Eteocles, with just entreatment treated,
as law provides he has hidden under earth 25
to have full honor with the dead below.
But Polyneices' corpse who died in pain,
they say he has proclaimed to the whole town
that none may bury him and none bewail,
but leave him unwept, untombed, a rich sweet sight 30
for the hungry birds' beholding.
Such orders they say the worthy Creon gives
to you and me—yes, yes, I say to *me*—
and that he's coming to proclaim it clear
to those who know it not. 35
Further: he has the matter so at heart
that anyone who dares attempt the act
will die by public stoning in the town.
So there you have it and you soon will show
if you are noble, or fallen from your descent. 40

ISMENE

If things have reached this stage, what can I do,
poor sister, that will help to make or mend?

ANTIGONE

Think will you share my labor and my act.

ISMENE

What will you risk? And where is your intent?

ANTIGONE

Will you take up that corpse along with me? 45

ISMENE

>To bury him you mean, when it's forbidden?

ANTIGONE

>My brother, and yours, though you may wish he were not.
>I never shall be found to be his traitor.

ISMENE

>O hard of mind! When Creon spoke against it!

ANTIGONE

>It's not for him to keep me from my own. 50

ISMENE

>Alas. Remember, sister, how our father
>perished abhorred, ill-famed.
>Himself with his own hand, through his own curse
>destroyed both eyes.
>Remember next his mother and his wife 55
>finishing life in the shame of the twisted strings.
>And third two brothers on a single day,
>poor creatures, murdering, a common doom
>each with his arm accomplished on the other.
>And now look at the two of us alone. 60
>We'll perish terribly if we force law
>and try to cross the royal vote and power.
>We must remember that we two are women
>so not to fight with men.
>And that since we are subject to strong power 65
>we must hear these orders, or any that may be worse.
>So I shall ask of them beneath the earth
>forgiveness, for in these things I am forced,
>and shall obey the men in power. I know
>that wild and futile action makes no sense. 70

ANTIGONE

>I wouldn't urge it. And if now you wished
>to act, you wouldn't please me as a partner.
>Be what you want to; but that man shall I
>bury. For me, the doer, death is best.
>Friend shall I lie with him, yes friend with friend, 75
>when I have dared the crime of piety.
>Longer the time in which to please the dead
>than that for those up here.
>There shall I lie forever. You may see fit
>to keep from honor what the gods have honored. 80

ISMENE

>I shall do no dishonor. But to act
>against the citizens. I cannot.

ANTIGONE

>That's your protection. Now I go, to pile
>the burial-mound for him, my dearest brother.

ISMENE

    Oh my poor sister. How I fear for you!   85

ANTIGONE

    For me, don't borrow trouble. Clear your fate.

ISMENE

    At lest give no one warning of this act;
    you keep it hidden, and I'll do the same.

ANTIGONE

    Dear God! Denounce me. I shall hate you more
    if silent, not proclaiming this to all.   90

ISMENE

    You have a hot mind over chilly things.

ANTIGONE

    I know I please those whom I most should please.

ISMENE

    If but you can. You crave what can't be done.

ANTIGONE

    And so, when strength runs out, I shall give over.

ISMENE

    Wrong from the start, to chase what cannot be.   95

ANTIGONE

    If that's your saying, I shall hate you first,
    and next the dead will hate you in all justice.
    But let me and my own ill-counselling
    suffer this terror. I shall suffer nothing
    as great as dying with a lack of grace.   100

ISMENE

    Go, since you want to. But know this: you go
    senseless indeed, but loved by those who love you.

ISMENE *returns to the palace;* ANTIGONE *leaves by one of the side entrances. The* CHORUS *now enters from the other side.*

CHORUS

    Sun's own radiance, fairest light ever shone on the gates of Thebes,
    then did you shine, O golden day's
    eye, coming over Dirce's stream,   105
    on the Man who had come from Argos with all his armor
    running now in headlong fear as you shook his bridle free.

        He was stirred by the dubious quarrel of Polyneices.
        So, screaming shrill,
        like an eagle over the land he flew,   110
        covered with white-snow wing,
        with many weapons,
        with horse-hair crested helms.

He who had stood above our halls, gaping about our seven gates,
with that circle of thirsting spears. 115
Gone, without our blood in his jaws,
before the torch took hold on our tower-crown
Rattle of war at his back; hard the fight for the dragon's foe.

The boasts of a proud tongue are for Zeus to hate.
So seeing them streaming on 120
in insolent clangor of gold,
he struck with hurling fire him who rushed
for the high wall's top,
to cry conquest abroad.

Swinging, striking the earth he fell 125
fire in hand, who in mad attack,
had raged against us with blasts of hate.
He failed. He failed of his aim.
For the rest great Ares dealt his blows about,
first in the war-team. 130

The captains stationed at seven gates
fought with seven and left behind
their brazen arms as an offering
to Zeus who is turner of battle.
All but those wretches, sons of one man, 135
one mother's sons, who sent their spears
each against each and found the share
of a common death together.

Great-named Victory comes to us
answering Thebe's warrior-joy. 140
Let us forget the wars just done
and visit the shrines of the gods.
All, with night-long dance which Bacchus will lead,
who shakes Thebe's acres.

CREON *enters from the palace.*

Now here he comes, the king of the land, 145
Creon, Menoeceus' son,
newly named by the gods' new fate.
What plan that beats about his mind
has made him call this council-session,
sending his summons to all? 150

CREON
My friends, the very gods who shook the state
with mighty surge have set it straight again.
So now I sent for you, chosen from all,
first that I knew you constant in respect
to Laius' royal power; and again 155
when Oedipus had set the state to rights,

and when he perished, you were faithful still
in mind to the descendants of the dead.
When they two perished by a double fate,
on one day struck and striking and defiled 160
each by his own hand, now it comes that I
hold all the power and the royal throne
through close connection with the perished men.
You cannot learn of any man the soul,
the mind, and the intent until he shows 165
his practise of the government and law.
For I believe that who controls the state
and does not hold to the best plans of all,
but locks his tongue up through some kind of fear,
that he is worst of all who are or were. 170
And he who counts another greater friend
than his own fatherland, I put him nowhere.
So I—may Zeus all-seeing always know it—
could not keep silent as disaster crept
upon the town, destroying hope of safety. 175
Nor could I count the enemy of the land
friend to myself, not I who know so well
that she it is who saves us, sailing straight,
and only so can we have friends at all.
With such good rules shall I enlarge our state. 180
And now I have proclaimed their brother-edict.
In the matter of the sons of Oedipus,
citizens, know: Eteocles who died,
defending this our town with champion spear,
is to be covered in the grave and granted 185
all holy rites we give the noble dead.
But his brother Polyneices whom I name
the exile who came back and sought to burn
his fatherland, the gods who were his kin,
who tried to gorge on blood he shared, and lead 190
the rest of us as slaves—
it is announced that no one in this town
may give him burial or mourn for him.
Leave him unburied, leave his corpse disgraced,
a dinner for the birds and for the dogs. 195
Such is my mind. Never shall I, myself,
honor the wicked and reject the just.
The man who is well-minded to the state
from me in death and life shall have his honor.

CHORUS
This resolution, Creon, is your own, 200
in the matter of the traitor and the true.
For you can make such rulings as you will
about the living and about the dead.

CREON

Now you be sentinels of the decree.

CHORUS

Order some younger man to take this on. 205

CREON

Already there are watchers of the corpse.

CHORUS

What other order would you give us, then?

CREON

Not to take sides with any who disobey.

CHORUS

No fool is fool as far as loving death.

CREON

Death is the price. But often we have known 210
men to be ruined by the hope of profit.

Enter, from the side, a guard.

GUARD

Lord, I can't claim that I am out of breath
from rushing here with light and hasty step,
for I had many haltings in my thought
making me double back upon my road. 215
My mind kept saying many things to me:
"Why go where you will surely pay the price?"
"Fool, are you halting? And if Creon learns
from someone else, how shall you not be hurt?"
Turning this over, on I dilly-dallied. 220
And so a short trip turns itself to long.
Finally, though, my coming here won out.
If what I say is nothing, still I'll say it.
For I come clutching to one single hope
that I can't suffer what is not my fate. 225

CREON

What is it that brings on this gloom of yours?

GUARD

I want to tell you first about myself.
I didn't do it, didn't see who did it.
It isn't right for me to get in trouble.

CREON

Your aim is good. You fence the fact around. 230
It's clear you have some shocking news to tell.

GUARD

Terrible tidings make for long delays.

CREON

    Speak out the story, and then get away.

GUARD

    I'll tell you. Someone left the corpse just now,
    burial all accomplished, thirsty dust   235
    strewn on the flesh, the ritual complete.

CREON

    What are you saying? What man has dared to do it?

GUARD

    I wouldn't know. There were no marks of picks,
    no grubbed-out earth. The ground was dry and hard,
    no trace of wheels. The doer left no sign.   240
    When the first fellow on the day-shift showed us,
    we all were sick with wonder.
    For he was hidden, not inside a tomb,
    light dust upon him, enough to turn the curse,
    no wild beast's track, nor track of any hound   245
    having been near, nor was the body torn.
    We roared bad words about, guard against guard,
    and came to blows. No one was there to stop us.
    Each man had done it, nobody had done it
    so as to prove it on him—we couldn't tell.   250
    We were prepared to hold to red-hot iron,
    to walk through fire, to swear before the gods
    we hadn't done it, hadn't shared the plan,
    when it was plotted or when it was done.
    And last, when all our sleuthing came out nowhere,   255
    one fellow spoke, who made our heads to droop
    low toward the ground. We couldn't disagree.
    We couldn't see a chance of getting off.
    He said we had to tell you all about it.
    We couldn't hide the fact.   260
    So he won out. The lot chose poor old me
    to win the prize. So here I am unwilling,
    quite sure you people hardly want to see me.
    Nobody likes the bringer of bad news.

CHORUS

    Lord, while he spoke, my mind kept on debating.   265
    Isn't this action possibly a god's?

CREON

    Stop now, before you fill me up with rage,
    or you'll prove yourself insane as well as old,
    Unbearable, your saying that the gods
    take any kindly forethought for this corpse.   270
    Would it be they had hidden him away,
    honoring his good service, his who came

to burn their pillared temples and their wealth,
even their land, and break apart their laws?
Or have you seen them honor wicked men?   275
It isn't so.
No, from the first there were some men in town
who took the edict hard, and growled against me,
who hid the fact that they were rearing back,
not rightly in the yoke, no way my friends.   280
These are the people—oh it's clear to me—
who have bribed these men and brought about the deed.
No current custom among men as bad
as silver currency. This destroys the state;
this drives men from their homes; this wicked teacher   285
drives solid citizens to acts of shame.
It shows men how to practise infamy
and know the deeds of all unholiness.
Every least hireling who helped in this
brought about then the sentence he shall have.   290
But further, as I still revere great Zeus,
understand this, I tell you under oath,
if you don't find the very man whose hands
buried the corpse, bring him for me to see,
not death alone shall be enough for you   295
till living, hanging, you make clear the crime.
For any future grabbings you'll have learned
where to get pay, and that it doesn't pay
to squeeze a profit out of every source.
For you'll have felt that more men come to doom   300
through dirty profits than are kept by them.

GUARD
May I say something? Or just turn and go?

CREON
Aren't you aware your speech is most unwelcome?

GUARD
Does it annoy your hearing or your mind?

CREON
Why are you out to allocate my pain?   305

GUARD
The doer hurts your mind. I hurt your ears.

CREON
You are a quibbling rascal through and through.

GUARD
But anyhow I never did the deed.

CREON
And you the man who sold your mind for money!

GUARD

   Oh! 310

   How terrible to guess, and guess at lies!

CREON

   Go pretty up your guesswork. If you don't
   show me the doers you will have to say
   that wicked payments work their own revenge.

GUARD

   Indeed, I pray he's found, but yes or no, 315
   taken or not as luck may settle it,
   you won't see me returning to this place.
   Saved when I neither hoped nor thought to be,
   I owe the gods a mighty debt of thanks.

CREON *enters the palace. The Guard leaves by the way he came.*

CHORUS

   Many the wonders but nothing walks stranger than man. 320
   This thing crosses the sea in the winter's storm,
   making his path through the roaring waves.
   And she, the greatest of gods, the earth—
   ageless she is, and unwearied—he wears her away
   as the ploughs go up and down form year to year 325
   and his mules turn up the soil.

   Gay nations of birds he snares and leads,
   wild beast tribes and the salty brood of the sea,
   with the twisted mesh of his nets, this clever man.
   He controls with craft the beasts of the open air, 330
   walkers on hills. The horse with his shaggy mane
   he holds and harnesses, yoked about the neck,
   and the strong bull of the mountain.

   Language, and thought like the wind
   and the feelings that make the town, 335
   he has taught himself, and shelter against the cold,
   refuge from rain. He can always help himself.
   He faces no future helpless. There's only death
   that he cannot find an escape from. He has contrived
   refuge from illnesses once beyond all cure. 340

   Clever beyond all dreams
   the inventive craft that he has
   which may drive him one time or another to well or ill.
   When he honors the laws of the land and the god's sworn right
   high indeed is his city; but stateless the man 345
   who dares to dwell with dishonor. Not by my fire,
   never to share my thoughts, who does these things.

The Guard enters with ANTIGONE.

My mind is split at this awful sight.
I know her. I cannot deny
Antigone is here. 350
Alas, the unhappy girl,
her unhappy father's child.
Oh what is the meaning of this?
It cannot be you that they bring
for breaking the royal law, 355
caught in open shame.

GUARD

This is the woman who has done the deed.
We caught her at the burying. Where's the king?

CREON *enters.*

CHORUS

Back from the house again just when he's needed.

CREON

What must I measure up to? What has happened? 360

GUARD

Lord, one should never swear off anything.
Afterthought makes the first resolve a liar.
I could have vowed I wouldn't come back here
after your threats, after the storm I faced.
But joy that comes beyond the wildest hope 365
is bigger than all other pleasure known.
I'm here, though I swore not to be, and bring
this girl. We caught her burying the dead.
This time we didn't need to shake the lots;
mine was the luck, all mine. 370
So now, lord, take her, you, and question her
and prove her as you will. But I am free.
And I deserve full clearance on this charge.

CREON

Explain the circumstance of the arrest.

GUARD

She was burying the man. You have it all. 375

CREON

Is this the truth? And do you grasp its meaning?

GUARD

I saw her burying the very corpse
you had forbidden. Is this adequate?

CREON

How was she caught and taken in the act?

GUARD

It was like this: when we got back again 380

struck with those dreadful threatenings of yours,
we swept away the dust that hid the corpse.
We stripped it back to slimy nakedness.
And then we sat to windward on the hill
so as to dodge the smell. 385
We poked each other up with growling threats
if anyone was careless of his work.
For some time this went on, till it was noon.
The sun was high and hot. Then from the earth
up rose a dusty whirlwind to the sky, 390
filling the plain, smearing the forest-leaves,
clogging the upper air. We shut our eyes,
sat and endured the plague the gods had sent.
So the storm left us after a long time.
We saw the girl. She cried the sharp and shrill 395
cry of a bitter bird which sees the nest
bare where the young birds lay.
So this same girl, seeing the body stripped,
cried with great groanings, cried a dreadful curse
upon the people who had done the deed. 400
Soon in her hands she brought the thirsty dust,
and holding high a pitcher of wrought bronze
she poured the three libations for the dead.
We saw this and surged down. We trapped her fast;
and she was calm. We taxed her with the deeds 405
both past and present. Nothing was denied.
And I was glad, and yet I took it hard.
One's own escape from trouble makes one glad;
but bringing friends to trouble is hard grief.
Still, I care less for all these second thoughts 410
than for the fact that I myself am safe.

CREON
  You there, whose head is drooping to the ground,
  do you admit this, or deny you did it?

ANTIGONE
  I say I did it and I don't deny it.

CREON *(to the guard)*
  Take yourself off wherever you wish to go 415
  free of a heavy charge.

CREON *(to ANTIGONE)*
  You—tell me not at length but in a word.
  You knew the order not to do this thing?

ANTIGONE
  I knew, of course I knew. The word was plain.

CREON
  And still you dared to overstep these laws? 420

ANTIGONE

>For me it was not Zeus who made that order.
Nor did that Justice who lives with the gods below
mark out such laws to hold among mankind.
Nor did I think your orders were so strong
that you, a mortal man, could over-run   425
the gods' unwritten and unfailing laws.
Not now, nor yesterday's, they always live,
and no one knows their origin in time.
So not through fear of any man's proud spirit
would I be likely to neglect these laws,   430
draw on myself the gods' sure punishment.
I knew that I must die; how could I not?
even without your warning. If I die
before my time, I say it is a gain.
Who lives in sorrows many as are mine   435
how shall he not be glad to gain his death?
And so, for me to meet this fate, no grief.
But if I left that corpse, my mother's son,
dead and unburied I'd have cause to grieve
as now I grieve not.   440
And if you think my acts are foolishness
the foolishness may be in a fool's eye.

CHORUS

>The girl is bitter. She's her father's child.
She cannot yield to trouble; nor could he.

CREON

>These rigid spirits are the first to fall.   445
The strongest iron, hardened in the fire,
most often ends in scraps and shatterings.
Small curbs bring raging horses back to terms.
Slave to his neighbor, who can think of pride?
This girl was expert in her insolence   450
when she broke bounds beyond established law.
Once she had done it, insolence the second,
to boast her doing, and to laugh in it.
I am no man and she the man instead
if she can have this conquest without pain.   455
She is my sister's child, but were she child
of closer kin than any at my hearth,
she and her sister should not so escape
their death and doom. I charge Ismene too.
She shared the planning of this burial.   460
Call her outside. I saw her in the house,
maddened, no longer mistress of herself.
The sly intent betrays itself sometimes
before the secret plotters work their wrong.

I hate it too when someone caught in crime   465
then wants to make it seem a lovely thing.

ANTIGONE
Do you want more than my arrest and death?

CREON
No more than that. For that is all I need.

ANTIGONE
Why are you waiting? Nothing that you say
fits with my thought. I pray it never will.   470
Nor will you ever like to hear my words.
And yet what greater glory could I find
than giving my own brother funeral?
All these would say that they approved my act
did fear not mute them.   475
(A king is fortunate in many ways,
and most, that he can act and speak at will.)

CREON
None of these others see the case this way.

ANTIGONE
They see, and do not say. You have them cowed.

CREON
And you are not ashamed to think alone?   480

ANTIGONE
No, I am not ashamed. When was it shame
to serve the children of my mother's womb?

CREON
It was not your brother who died against him, then?

ANTIGONE
Full brother, on both sides, my parents' child.

CREON
Your act of grace, in his regard, is crime.   485

ANTIGONE
The corpse below would never say it was.

CREON
When you honor him and the criminal just alike?

ANTIGONE
It was a brother, not a slave, who died.

CREON
Died to destroy this land the other guarded.

ANTIGONE
Death yearns for equal law for all the dead.   490

CREON
  Not that the good and bad draw equal shares.

ANTIGONE
  Who knows that this is holiness below?

CREON
  Never the enemy, even in death, a friend.

ANTIGONE
  I cannot share in hatred, but in love.

CREON
  Then go down there, if you must love, and love   495
  the dead. No woman rules me while I live.

ISMENE *is brought from the palace under guard.*

CHORUS
  Look there! Ismene is coming out.
  She loves her sister and mourns,
  with clouded brow and bloodied cheeks,
  tears on her lovely face.   500

CREON
  You, lurking like a viper in the house,
  who sucked me dry. I looked the other way
  while twin destruction planned against the throne.
  Now tell me, do you say you shared this deed?
  Or will you swear you didn't even know?   505

ISMENE
  I did the deed, if she agrees I did.
  I am accessory and share the blame.

ANTIGONE
  Justice will not allow this. You did not
  wish for a part, nor did I give you one.

ISMENE
  You are in trouble, and I'm not ashamed   510
  to sail beside you into suffering.

ANTIGONE
  Death and the dead, they know whose act it was.
  I cannot love a friend whose love is words.

ISMENE
  Sister, I pray, don't fence me out from honor,
  from death with you, and honor done the dead.   515

ANTIGONE
  Don't die along with me, nor make your own
  that which you did not do. My death's enough.

ISMENE
  When you are gone what life can be my friend?

ANTIGONE

Love Creon. He's your kinsman and your care.

ISMENE

Why hurt me, when it does yourself no good?   520

ANTIGONE

I also suffer, when I laugh at you.

ISMENE

What further service can I do you now?

ANTIGONE

To save yourself. I shall not envy you.

ISMENE

Alas for me. Am I outside your fate?

ANTIGONE

Yes. For you chose to live when I chose death.   525

ISMENE

At least I was not silent. You were warned.

ANTIGONE

Some will have thought you wiser. Some will not.

ISMENE

And yet the blame is equal for us both.

ANTIGONE

Take heart. You live. My life died long ago.
And that has made me fit to help the dead.   530

CREON

One of these girls has shown her lack of sense
just now. The other had it from her birth.

ISMENE

Yes, lord. When people fall in deep distress
their native sense departs, and will not stay.

CREON

You chose your mind's distraction when you chose   535
to work out wickedness with this wicked girl.

ISMENE

What life is there for me to live without her?

CREON

Don't speak of her. For she is here no more.

ISMENE

But will you kill your own son's promised bride?

CREON

Oh, there are other furrows for his plough.   540

ISMENE
But where the closeness that has bound these two?

CREON
Not for my sons will I choose wicked wives.

ISMENE
Dear Haemon, your father robs you of your rights.

CREON
You and your marriage trouble me too much.

ISMENE
You will take away his bride from your own son?   545

CREON
Yes. Death will help me break this marriage off.

CHORUS
It seems determined that the girl must die.

CREON
You helped determine it. Now, no delay!
Slaves, take them in. They must be women now.
No more free running.   550
Even the bold will fly when they see Death
drawing in close enough to end their life.

ANTIGONE *and* ISMENE *are taken inside.*

CHORUS
Fortunate they whose lives have no taste of pain.
For those whose house is shaken by the gods
escape no kind of doom. It extends to all the kin   555
like the wave that comes when the winds of Thrace
run over the dark of the sea.
The black sand of the bottom is brought from the depth;
the beaten capes sound back with a hollow cry.

Ancient the sorrow of Labdacus' house, I know.   560
Dead men's grief comes back, and falls on grief.
No generation can free the next.
One of the gods will strike. There is no escape.
So now the light goes out
for the house of Oedipus, while the bloody knife   565
cuts the remaining root. Folly and Fury have done this.

What madness of man, O Zeus, can bind your power?
Not sleep can destroy it who ages all,
nor the weariless months the gods have set. Unaged in time
monarch you rule of Olympus' gleaming light.   570
Near time, far future, and the past,
one law controls them all:
any greatness in human life brings doom.

Wandering hope brings help to many men.
But others she tricks from their giddy loves, 575
and her quarry knows nothing until he has walked into flame.
Word of wisdom it was when someone said,
"The bad becomes the good
to him a god would doom."
Only briefly is that one from under doom. 580

HAEMON *enters from the side.*

Here is your one surviving son.
Does he come in grief at the fate of his bride,
in pain that he's tricked of his wedding?

CREON
Soon we shall know more than a seer could tell us.
Son, have you heard the vote condemned your bride? 585
And are you here, maddened against your father,
or are we friends, whatever I may do?

HAEMON
My father, I am yours. You keep me straight
with your good judgment, which I shall ever follow.
Nor shall a marriage count for more with me 590
than your kind leading.

CREON
There's my good boy. So should you hold at heart
and stand behind your father all the way.
It is for this men pray they may beget
households of dutiful obedient sons, 595
who share alike in punishing enemies,
and give due honor to their father's friends.
Whoever breeds a child that will not help
what has he sown but trouble for himself,
and for his enemies laughter full and free? 600
Son, do not let your lust mislead your mind,
all for a woman's sake, for well you know
how cold the thing he takes into his arms
who has a wicked woman for his wife.
What deeper wounding than a friend no friend? 605
Oh spit her forth forever, as your foe.
Let the girl marry somebody in Hades.
Since I have caught her in the open act,
the only one in town who disobeyed.
I shall not now proclaim myself a liar, 610
but kill her. Let her sing her song of Zeus
who guards the kindred.
If I allow disorder in my house
I'd surely have to licence it abroad.
A man who deals in fairness with his own, 615
he can make manifest justice in the state.

But he who crosses law, or forces it,
or hopes to bring the rulers under him,
shall never have a word of praise from me.
The man the state has put in place must have   620
obedient hearing to his least command
when it is right, and even when it's not.
He who accepts this teaching I can trust,
ruler, or ruled, to function in his place,
to stand his ground even in the storm of spears,   625
a mate to trust in battle at one's side.
There is no greater wrong than disobedience.
This ruins cities, this tears down our homes,
this breaks the battle-front in panic-rout.
If men live decently it is because   630
discipline saves their very lives for them.
So I must guard the men who yield to order,
not let myself be beaten by a woman.
Better, if it must happen, that a man
should overset me.   635
I won't be called weaker than womankind.

CHORUS
We think—unless our age is cheating us—
that what you say is sensible and right.

HAEMON
Father, the gods have given men good sense,
the only sure possession that we have.   640
I couldn't find the words in which to claim
that there was error in your late remarks.
Yet someone else might bring some further light.
Because I am your son I must keep watch
on all men's doing where it touches you,   645
their speech, and most of all, their discontents.
Your presence frightens any common man
from saying things you would not care to hear.
But in dark corners I have heard them say
how the whole town is grieving for this girl,   650
unjustly doomed, if ever woman was,
to die in shame for glorious action done.
She would not leave her fallen, slaughtered brother
there, as he lay, unburied, for the birds
and hungry dogs to make an end of him.   655
Isn't her real desert a golden prize?
This is the undercover speech in town.
Father, your welfare is my greatest good.
What loveliness in life for any child
outweighs a father's fortune and good fame?   660
And so a father feels his children's faring.
Then, do not have one mind, and one alone

that only your opinion can be right.
Whoever thinks that he alone is wise,
his eloquence, his mind, above the rest, 665
come the unfolding, shows his emptiness.
A man, though wise, should never be ashamed
of learning more, and must unbend his mind.
Have you not seen the trees beside the torrent, 670
the ones that bend them saving every leaf,
while the resistant perish root and branch?
And so the ship that will not slacken sail,
the sheet drawn tight, unyielding, overturns.
She ends the voyage with her keel on top. 675
No, yield your wrath, allow a change of stand.
Young as I am, if I may give advice,
I'd say it would be best if men were born
perfect in wisdom, but that failing this
(which often fails) it can be no dishonor 680
to learn from others when they speak good sense.

CHORUS
Lord, if your son has spoken to the point
you should take his lesson. He should do the same.
Both sides have spoken well.

CREON
At my age I'm to school my mind by his? 685
This boy instructor is my master, then?

HAEMON
I urge no wrong. I'm young, but you should watch
my actions, not my years, to judge of me.

CREON
A loyal action, to respect disorder?

HAEMON
I wouldn't urge respect for wickedness. 690

CREON
You don't think she is sick with that disease?

HAEMON
Your fellow-citizens maintain she's not.

CREON
Is the town to tell me how I ought to rule?

HAEMON
Now there you speak just like a boy yourself.

CREON
Am I to rule by other mind than mine? 695

HAEMON
No city is property of a single man.

CREON
But custom gives possession to the ruler.

HAEMON
You'd rule a desert beautifully alone.

CREON *(to the* CHORUS*)*
It seems he's firmly on the woman's side.

HAEMON
If you're a woman. It is you I care for.   700

CREON
Wicked, to try conclusions with your father.

HAEMON
When you conclude unjustly, so I must.

CREON
Am I unjust, when I respect my office?

HAEMON
You tread down the gods' due. Respect is gone.

CREON
Your mind is poisoned. Weaker than a woman!   705

HAEMON
At least you'll never see me yield to shame.

CREON
Your whole long argument is but for her.

HAEMON
And you, and me, and for the gods below.

CREON
You shall not marry her while she's alive.

HAEMON
Then she shall die. Her death will bring another.   710

CREON
Your boldness has made progress. Threats, indeed!

HAEMON
No threat, to speak against your empty plan.

CREON
Past due, sharp lessons for your empty brain.

HAEMON
If you weren't father, I should call you mad.

CREON
Don't flatter me with "father," you woman's slave.   715

HAEMON
You wish to speak but never wish to hear.

CREON
    You think so? By Olympus, you shall not
    revile me with these tauntings and go free.
    Bring out the hateful creature; she shall die
    full in his sight, close at her bridegroom's side.   720

HAEMON
    Not at my side her death, and you will not
    ever lay eyes upon my face again.
    Find other friends to rave with after this.

HAEMON *leaves, by one of the side entrances.*

CHORUS
    Lord, he has gone with all the speed of rage.
    When such a man is grieved his mind is hard.   725

CREON
    Oh, let him go, plan superhuman action.
    In any case the girls shall not escape.

CHORUS
    You plan for both the punishment of death?

CREON
    Not her who did not do it. You are right.

CHORUS
    And what death have you chosen for the other?   730

CREON
    To take her where the foot of man comes not.
    There shall I hide her in a hollowed cave
    living, and leave her just so much to eat
    as clears the city from the guilt of death.
    There, if she prays to Death, the only god   735
    of her respect, she may manage not to die.
    Or she may learn at last and even then
    how much too much her labor for the dead.

CREON *returns to the palace.*

CHORUS
    Love unconquered in fight, love who falls on our havings.
    You rest in the bloom of a girl's unwithered face.   740
    You cross the sea, you are known in the wildest lairs.
    Not the immortal gods can fly,
    nor men of a day. Who has you within him is mad.

    You twist the minds of the just. Wrong they pursue and are ruined.
    You made this quarrel of kindred before us now.   745
    Desire looks clear from the eyes of a lovely bride:
    power as strong as the founded world.
    For there is the goddess at play with whom no man can fight.

ANTIGONE *is brought from the palace under guard.*

Now I am carried beyond all bounds.
My tears will not be checked. 750
I see Antigone depart
to the chamber where all men sleep.

ANTIGONE

Men of my fathers' land, you see me go
my last journey. My last sight of the sun,
then never again. Death who brings all to sleep 755
takes me alive to the shore
of the river underground.
Not for me was the marriage-hymn, nor will anyone start the song
at a wedding of mine. Acheron is my mate.

CHORUS

With praise as your portion you go 760
in fame to the vault of the dead.
Untouched by wasting disease,
not paying the price of the sword,
of your own motion you go.
Alone among mortals will you descend 765
in life to the house of Death.

ANTIGONE

Pitiful was the death that stranger died,
our queen once, Tantalus' daughter. The rock
it covered her over, like stubborn ivy it grew.
Still, as she wastes, the rain 770
and snow companion her.
Pouring down from her mourning eyes comes the water that soaks the stone.
My own putting to sleep a god has planned like hers.

CHORUS

God's child and god she was.
We are born to death. 775
Yet even in death you will have your fame,
to have gone like a god to your fate,
in living and dying alike.

ANTIGONE

Laughter against me now. In the name of our fathers' gods,
could you not wait till I went? Must affront be thrown in my face? 780
O city of wealthy men.
I call upon Dirce's spring,
I call upon Thebe's grove in the armored plain,
to be my witnesses, how with no friend's mourning,
by what decree I go to the fresh-made prison-tomb. 785
Alive to the place of corpses, an alien still,
never at home with the living nor with the dead.

CHORUS

You went to the furthest verge
of daring, but there you found
the high foundation of justice, and fell.
Perhaps you are paying your father's pain.   790

ANTIGONE

You speak of my darkest thought, my pitiful father's fame,
spread through all the world, and the doom that haunts our house,
the royal house of Thebes.
My mother's marriage-bed.   795
Destruction where she lay with her husband-son,
my father. These are my parents and I their child.
I go to stay with them. My curse is to die unwed.
My brother, you found your fate when you found your bride,
found it for me as well. Dead, you destroy my life.   800

CHORUS

You showed respect for the dead.
So we for you: but power
is not to be thwarted so.
Your self-sufficiency has brought you down.

ANTIGONE

Unwept, no wedding-song, unfriended, now I go   805
the road laid down for me.
No longer shall I see this holy light of the sun.
No friend to bewail my fate.

CREON *enters from the palace.*

CREON

When people sing the dirge for their own deaths
ahead of time, nothing will break them off   810
if they can hope that this will buy delay.
Take her away at once, and open up
the tomb I spoke of. Leave her there alone.
There let her choose: death, or a buried life.
No stain of guilt upon us in this case,   815
but she is exiled from our life on earth.

ANTIGONE

O tomb, O marriage-chamber, hollowed out
house that will watch forever, where I go.
To my own people, who are mostly there;
Persephone has taken them to her.   820
Last of them all, ill-fated past the rest,
shall I descend, before my course is run.
Still when I get there I may hope to find
I come as a dear friend to my dear father,
to you, my mother, and my brother too.   825

All three of you have known my hand in death.
I washed your bodies, dressed them for the grave,
poured out the last libation at the tomb.
Last, Polyneices knows the price I pay
for doing final service to his corpse. 830
And yet the wise will know my choice was right.
Had I had children or their father dead,
I'd let them moulder. I should not have chosen
in such a case to cross the state's decree.
What is the law that lies behind these words? 835
One husband gone, I might have found another,
or a child from a new man in first child's place,
but with my parents hid away in death,
no brother, ever, could spring up for me.
Such was the law by which I honored you. 840
But Creon thought the doing was a crime,
a dreadful daring, brother of my heart.
So now he takes and leads me out by force.
No marriage-bed, no marriage-song for me,
and since no wedding, so no child to rear. 845
I go, without a friend, struck down by fate,
live to the hollow chambers of the dead.
What divine justice have I disobeyed?
Why, in my misery, look to the gods for help?
Can I call any of them my ally? 850
I stand convicted of impiety,
the evidence my pious duty done.
Should the gods think that this is righteousness,
in suffering I'll see my error clear.
But if it is the others who are wrong 855
I wish them no greater punishment than mine.

CHORUS
The same tempest of mind
as ever, controls the girl.

CREON
Therefore her guards shall regret
the slowness with which they move. 860

ANTIGONE
That word comes close to death.

CREON
You are perfectly right in that.

ANTIGONE
O town of my fathers in Thebe's land,
O gods of our house.
I am led away at last. 865
Look, leaders of Thebes,

I am last of your royal line.
Look what I suffer, at whose command,
because I respected the right.

ANTIGONE *is led away. The slow procession should begin during the preceding passage.*

CHORUS
Danaë suffered too.   870
She went from the light to the brass-built room,
chamber and tomb together. Like you, poor child,
she was of great descent, and more, she held and kept
the seed of the golden rain which was Zeus.
Fate has terrible power.   875
You cannot escape it by wealth or war.
No fort will keep it out, no ships outrun it.

Remember the angry king,
son of Dryas, who raged at the god and paid,
pent in a rock-walled prison. His bursting wrath   880
slowly went down. As the terror of madness went,
he learned of his frenzied attack on the god.
Fool, he had tried to stop
the dancing women possessed of god,
the fire of Dionysus, the songs and flutes.   885

Where the dark rocks divide
sea from sea in Thrace
is Salmydessus whose savage god
beheld the terrible blinding wounds
dealt to Phineus' sons by their father's wife.   890
Dark the eyes that looked to avenge their mother.
Sharp with her shuttle she struck, and blooded her hands.

Wasting they wept their fate,
settled when they were born
to Cleopatra, unhappy queen.   895
She was a princess too, of an ancient house.
reared in the cave of the wild north wind, her father.
Half a goddess but, child, she suffered like you.

Enter, from the side TEIRESIAS, *the blind prophet, led by a boy attendant.*

TEIRESIAS
Elders of Thebes, we two have come one road,
two of us looking through one pair of eyes.
This is the way of walking for the blind.   900

CREON
Teiresias, what news has brought you here?

TEIRESIAS
I'll tell you. You in turn must trust the prophet.

CREON
I've always been attentive to your counsel.

TEIRESIAS
And therefore you have steered this city straight.

CREON
So I can say how helpful you have been.   905

TEIRESIAS
But now you are balanced on a razor's edge.

CREON
What is it? How I shudder at your words!

TEIRESIAS
You'll know, when you hear the signs that I have marked.
I sat where every bird of heaven comes
in my old place of augury, and heard   910
bird-cries I'd never known. They screeched about
goaded by madness, inarticulate.
I marked that they were tearing one another
with claws of murder. I could hear the wing-beats.
I was afraid, so straight away I tried   915
burnt sacrifice upon the flaming altar.
No fire caught my offerings. Slimy ooze
dripped on the ashes, smoked and sputtered there.
Gall burst its bladder, vanished into vapor;
the fat dripped from the bones and would not burn.   920
These are the omens of the rites that failed,
as my boy here has told me. He's my guide
as I am guide to others.
Why has this sickness struck against the state?
Through your decision.   925
All of the altars of the town are choked
with leavings of the dogs and birds; their feast
was on that fated, fallen Polyneices.
So the gods will have no offering from us,
not prayer, nor flame of sacrifice. The birds   930
will not cry out a sound I can distinguish,
gorged with the greasy blood of that dead man.
Think of these things, my son. All men may err
but error once committed, he's no fool
nor yet unfortunate, who gives up his stiffness   935
and cures the trouble he has fallen in.
Stubbornness and stupidity are twins.
Yield to the dead. Why goad him where he lies?
What use to kill the dead a second time?
I speak for your own good. And I am right.   940
Learning from a wise counsellor is not pain
if what he speaks are profitable words.

CREON

    Old man, you all, like bowmen at a mark,
    have bent your bows at me. I've had my share
    of seers. I've been an item in your accounts.   945
    Make profit, trade in Lydian silver-gold,
    pure gold of India; that's your chief desire.
    But you will never cover up that corpse.
    Not if the very eagles tear their food
    from him, and leave it at the throne of Zeus.   950
    I wouldn't give him up for burial
    in fear of that pollution. For I know
    no mortal being can pollute the gods.
    O old Teiresias, human beings fall;
    the clever ones the furthest, when they plead   955
    a shameful case so well in hope of profit.

TEIRESIAS

    Alas!
    What man can tell me, has he thought at all ...

CREON

    What hackneyed saw is coming from your lips?

TEIRESIAS

    How better than all wealth is sound good counsel.   960

CREON

    And so is folly worse than anything.

TEIRESIAS

    And you're infected with that same disease.

CREON

    I'm reluctant to be uncivil to a seer ...

TEIRESIAS

    You're that already. You have said I lie.

CREON

    Well, the whole crew of seers are money-mad.   965

TEIRESIAS

    And the whole tribe of tyrants grab at gain.

CREON

    Do you realize you are talking to a king?

TEIRESIAS

    I know. Who helped you save this town you hold?

CREON

    You're a wise seer, but you love wickedness.

TEIRESIAS

    You'll bring me to speak the unspeakable, very soon.   970

CREON
Well, speak it out. But do not speak for profit.

TEIRESIAS
No, there's no profit in my words for you.

CREON
You'd better realise that you can't deliver
my mind, if you should sell it, to the buyer.

TEIRESIAS
Know well, the sun will not have rolled its course   975
many more days, before you come to give
corpse for these corpses, child of your own loins.
For you've confused the upper and lower worlds.
You sent a life to settle in a tomb;
you keep up here that which belongs below   980
the corpse unburied, robbed of its release.
Not you, nor any god that rules on high
can claim him now.
You rob the nether gods of what is theirs.
So the pursuing horrors lie in wait   985
to track you down. The Furies sent by Hades
and by all gods will even you with your victims.
Now say that I am bribed! At no far time
shall men and women wail within your house.
And all the cities that you fought in war   990
whose sons had burial from wild beasts, or dogs,
or birds that brought the stench of your great wrong
back to each hearth, they move against you now.
A bowman, as you said, I send my shafts,
now you have moved me, straight. You'll feel the wound.   995
Boy, take me home now. Let him spend his rage
on younger men, and learn to calm his tongue,
and keep a better mind than now he does.

Exit.

CHORUS
Lord, he has gone. Terrible prophecies!
And since the time when I first grew grey hair   1000
his sayings to the city have been true.

CREON
I also know this. And my mind is torn.
To yield is dreadful. But to stand against him.
Dreadful to strike my spirit to destruction.

CHORUS
Now you must come to counsel, and take advice.   1005

CREON
What must I do? Speak, and I shall obey.

CHORUS

Go free the maiden from that rocky house.
Bury the dead who lies in readiness.

CREON

This is your counsel? You would have me yield?

CHORUS

Quick as you can. The gods move very fast   1010
when they bring ruin on misguided men.

CREON

How hard, abandonment of my desire.
But I can fight necessity no more.

CHORUS

Do it yourself. Leave it to no one else.

CREON

I'll go at once. Come, followers, to your work.   1015
You that are here round up the other fellows.
Take axes with you, hurry to that place
that overlooks us.
Now my decision has been overturned
shall I, who bound her, set her free myself.
I've come to fear it's best to hold the laws   1020
of old tradition to the end of life.

Exit.

CHORUS

God of the many names, Semele's golden child,
child of Olympian thunder, Italy's lord.
Lord of Eleusis, where all men come
to mother Demeter's plain.   1025
Bacchus, who dwell in Thebes,
by Ismenus' running water,
where wild Bacchic women are at home,
on the soil of the dragon seed.

Seen in the glaring flame, high on the double mount, 1030
with the nymphs of Parnassus at play on the hill,
seen by Kastalia's flowing stream.
You come from the ivied heights,
from green Euboea's shore.
In immortal words we cry   1035
your name, lord, who watch the ways,
the many ways of Thebes.

This is your city, honored beyond the rest,
the town of your mother's miracle-death.
Now, as we wrestle our grim disease,   1040
come with healing step from Parnassus' slope
or over the moaning sea.

Leader in dance of the fire-pulsing stars,
overseer of the voices of night,
child of Zeus, be manifest,   1045
with due companionship of Maenad maids
whose cry is but your name.

Enter one of those who left with CREON, *as messenger.*

MESSENGER
Neighbors of Cadmus, and Amphion's house,
there is no kind of state in human life
which I now dare to envy or to blame.   1050
Luck sets it straight, and luck she overturns
the happy or unhappy day by day.
No prophecy can deal with men's affairs.
Creon was envied once, as I believe,
for having saved this city from its foes   1055
and having got full power in this land.
He steered it well. And he had noble sons.
Now everything is gone.
Yes, when a man has lost all happiness,
he's not alive. Call him a breathing corpse.   1060
Be very rich at home. Live as a king.
But once your joy has gone, though these are left
they are smoke's shadow to lost happiness.

CHORUS
What is the grief of princes that you bring?

MESSENGER
They're dead. The living are responsible.   1065

CHORUS
Who died? Who did the murder? Tell us now.

MESSENGER
Haemon is gone. One of his kin drew blood.

CHORUS
But whose arm struck? His father's or his own?

MESSENGER
He killed himself. His blood is on his father.

CHORUS
Seer, all too true the prophecy you told!   1070

MESSENGER
This is the state of things. Now make your plans.

Enter, from the palace, EURYDICE.

CHORUS
Eurydice is with us now, I see.
Creon's poor wife. She may have come by chance.
She may have heard something about her son.

EURYDICE

    I heard your talk as I was coming out   1075
to greet the goddess Pallas with my prayer.
And as I moved the bolts that held the door
I heard of my own sorrow.
I fell back fainting in my women's arms.
But say again just what the news you bring.   1080
I, whom you speak to, have known grief before.

MESSENGER

    Dear lady, I was there, and I shall tell,
leaving out nothing of the true account.
Why should I make it soft for you with tales
to prove myself a liar? Truth is right.   1085
I followed your husband to the plain's far edge,
where Polyneices' corpse was lying still
unpitied. The dogs had torn him all apart.
We prayed the goddess of all journeyings,
and Pluto, that they turn their wrath to kindness, 1090
we gave the final purifying bath,
then burned the poor remains on new-cut boughs,
and heaped a high mound of his native earth.
Then turned we to the maiden's rocky bed,
death's hollow marriage-chamber.   1095
But, still far off, one of us heard a voice
in keen lament by that unblest abode.
He ran and told the master. As Creon came
he heard confusion crying. He groaned and spoke:
"Am I a prophet now, and do I tread   1100
the saddest of all roads I ever trod?
My son's voice crying! Servants, run up close,
stand by the tomb and look, push through the crevice
where we built the pile of rock, right to the entry.
Find out if that is Haemon's voice I hear   1105
or if the gods are tricking me indeed."
We obeyed the order of our mournful master.
In the far corner of the tomb we saw
her, hanging by the neck, caught in a noose
of her own linen veiling.   1110
Haemon embraced her as she hung, and mourned
his bride's destruction, dead and gone below,
his father's actions, the unfated marriage.
When Creon saw him, he groaned terribly,
and went toward him, and called him with lament: 1115
"What have you done, what plan have you caught up,
what sort of suffering is killing you?
Come out, my child, I do beseech you, come!"
The boy looked at him with his angry eyes,
spat in his face and spoke no further word.   1120
He drew his sword, but as his father ran,

he missed his aim. Then the unhappy boy,
in anger at himself, leant on the blade.
It entered, half its length, into his side.
While he was conscious he embraced the maiden,   1125
holding her gently. Last, he gasped out blood,
red blood on her white cheek.
Corpse on a corpse he lies. He found his marriage.
Its celebration in the halls of Hades.
So he has made it very clear to men   1130
that to reject good counsel is a crime.

EURYDICE *returns to the house.*

CHORUS
What do you make of this? The queen has gone
in silence. We know nothing of her mind.

MESSENGER
I wonder at her, too. But we can hope
that she has gone to mourn her son within   1135
with her own women, not before the town.
She knows discretion. She will do no wrong.

CHORUS
I am not sure. This muteness may portend
as great disaster as a loud lament.

MESSENGER
I will go in and see if some deep plan   1140
hides in her heart's wild pain. You may be right.
There can be heavy danger in mute grief.

The messenger goes into the house. CREON *enters with his followers. They are carry-ing* HAEMON'*s body on a bier.*

CHORUS
But look, the king draws near.
His own hand brings
the witness of his crime,   1145
the doom he brought on himself.

CREON
O crimes of my wicked heart,
harshness bringing death.
You see the killer, you see the kin he killed.
My planning was all unblest.   1150
Son, you have died too soon.
Oh, you have gone away
through my fault, not your own.

CHORUS
You have learned justice, though it comes too late.

CREON

Yes, I have learned in sorrow. It was a god who struck,   1155
who has weighted my head with disaster; he drove me to wild strange ways,
his heavy heel on my joy.
Oh sorrows, sorrows of men.

Re-enter the MESSENGER, *from a side door of the palace.*

MESSENGER

Master, you hold one sorrow in your hands
but you have more, stored up inside the house.   1160

CREON

What further suffering can come on me?

MESSENGER

Your wife has died. The dead man's mother in deed,
poor soul, her wounds are fresh.

CREON

Hades, harbor of all,
you have destroyed me now.   1165
Terrible news to hear, horror the tale you tell.
I was dead, and you kill me again.
Boy, did I hear you right?
Did you say the queen was dead,
slaughter on slaughter heaped?   1170

The central doors of the palace begin to open.

CHORUS

Now you can see. Concealment is all over.

The doors are open, and the corpse of EURYDICE *is revealed.*

CREON

My second sorrow is here. Surely no fate remains
which can strike me again. Just now, I held my son in my arms.
And now I see her dead.
Woe for the mother and son.   1175

MESSENGER

There, by the altar, dying on the sword,
her eyes fell shut. She wept her older son
who died before, and this one. Last of all
she cursed you as the killer of her children.

CREON

I am mad with fear. Will no one strike   1180
and kill me with cutting sword?
Sorrowful, soaked in sorrow to the bone!

MESSENGER

Yes, for she held you guilty in the death
of him before you, and the elder dead.

CREON
How did she die? 1185

MESSENGER
Struck home at her own heart
when she had heard of Haemon's suffering.

CREON
This is my guilt, all mine. I killed you, I say it clear.
Servants, take me away, out of the sight of men.
I who am nothing more than nothing now. 1190

CHORUS
Your plan is good—if any good is left.
Best to cut short our sorrow.

CREON
Let me go, let me go. May death come quick,
bringing my final day.
O let me never see tomorrow's dawn. 1195

CHORUS
That is the future's. We must look to now.
What will be is in other hands than ours.

CREON
All my desire was in that prayer of mine.

CHORUS
Pray not again. No mortal can escape
the doom prepared for him. 1200

CREON
Take me away at once, the frantic man who killed
my son, against my meaning. I cannot rest.
My life is warped past cure. My fate has struck me down.

CREON *and his attendants enter the house.*

CHORUS
Our happiness depends
on wisdom all the way. 1205
The gods must have their due.
Great words by men of pride
bring greater blows upon them.
So wisdom comes to the old.

Response Statement Assignments

1. Discuss some of the problems involved in reading a play that comes to us
   from a very distant and alien culture.
2. What efforts do you feel you must make to have the play mean anything
   significant to you?

3. Do you find the beliefs about duty and absolute rule asserted in this play too extreme to be believable?
4. Construct a feminist reading of the play. Do you think such a reading that supports Antigone's stand might be a way of interpreting the play?
5. Clearly the *Antigone* that you read or see produced today has been read and interpreted in extremely diverse ways throughout history. If "meanings" of a text change over time, can you argue that something "true" and "timeless" exists in the play to which audiences of all historical periods have responded? How do you account for the play's endurance and continued popularity?

WILLIAM SHAKESPEARE (1564–1616)

The Tragedy of Hamlet, Prince of Denmark

DRAMATIS PERSONAE

CLAUDIUS, *King of Denmark*
HAMLET, *son to the late King Hamlet,*
and nephew to the present King
POLONIUS, *Lord Chamberlain*
HORATIO, *friend to Hamlet*
LAERTES, *son to Polonius*
MARCELLUS ⎫ *officers*
BARNARDO ⎭
FRANCISCO, *a soldier*
REYNALDO, *servant to Polonius*
FORTINBRAS, *Prince of Norway*
NORWEGIAN CAPTAIN
DOCTOR OF DIVINITY
PLAYERS
Two CLOWNS, *grave-diggers*

VOLTEMAND ⎫
CORNELIUS ⎪
ROSENCRANTZ ⎪ *courtiers*
GUILDENSTERN ⎬
OSRIC ⎪
GENTLEMAN ⎭
ENGLISH AMBASSADORS
GERTRUDE, *Queen of Denmark, and*
mother to Hamlet
OPHELIA, *daughter to Polonius*
GHOST *of Hamlet's Father*
LORDS, LADIES, OFFICERS, SOLDIERS,
SAILORS, MESSENGERS, *and*
ATTENDANTS

SCENE. *Denmark*

ACT I

SCENE I.

Enter BARNARDO *and* FRANCISCO, *two sentinels, [meeting].*

BAR.   Who's there?
FRAN.   Nay, answer me. Stand and unfold yourself.
BAR.   Long live the King!
FRAN.   Barnardo.
BAR.   He.   5
FRAN.   You come most carefully upon your hour.
BAR.   'Tis now strook twelf. Get thee to bed, Francisco.
FRAN.   For this relief much thanks. 'Tis bitter cold,
    And I am sick at heart.
BAR.   Have you had quiet guard?
FRAN.   Not a mouse stirring.   10

Words and passages enclosed in square brackets in the text above are either emendations of the
copy-text or additions to it.

I.i. Location: Elsinore. A guard-platform of the castle.
² **answer me:** i.e. *you* answer *me*. Francisco is on watch; Barnardo has come to relieve
   him. **unfold yourself:** make known who you are.
³ **Long . . . King.** Perhaps a password, perhaps simply an utterance to allow the voice to be recognized.
⁷ **strook twelf:** struck twelve.
⁹ **sick at heart:** in low spirits.

BAR. Well, good night.
  If you do meet Horatio and Marcellus,
  The rivals of my watch, bid them make haste.

Enter HORATIO *and* MARCELLUS.

FRAN. I think I hear them. Stand ho! Who is there?
HOR. Friends to this ground.
MAR.   And liegemen to the Dane.   15
FRAN. Give you good night.
MAR.   O, farewell, honest [soldier].
  Who hath reliev'd you?
FRAN.   Barnardo hath my place.
  Give you good night.

Exit FRANCISCO.

MAR.   Holla, Barnardo!
BAR.   Say—
  What, is Horatio there?
HOR.   A piece of him.
BAR. Welcome, Horatio, welcome, good Marcellus.   20
HOR. What, has this thing appear'd again to-night?
BAR. I have seen nothing.
MAR. Horatio says 'tis but our fantasy,
  And will not let belief take hold of him
  Touching this dreaded sight twice seen of us;   25
  Therefore I have entreated him along,
  With us to watch the minutes of this night,
  That if again this apparition come,
  He may approve our eyes and speak to it.
HOR. Tush, tush, 'twill not appear.
BAR.   Sit down a while,   30
  And let us once again assail your ears,
  That are so fortified against our story,
  What we have two nights seen.
HOR.   Well, sit we down,
  And let us hear Barnardo speak of this.
BAR. Last night of all,   35
  When yond same star that's westward from the pole
  Had made his course t' illume that part of heaven
  Where now it burns, Marcellus and myself,
  The bell then beating one—

Enter GHOST.

[13] **rivals:** partners.
[15] **liegemen . . . Dane:** loyal subjects to the King of Denmark.
[16] **Give:** God give.
[23] **fantasy:** imagination.
[29] **approve:** corroborate.
[36] **pole:** pole star.
[37] **his:** its (the commonest form of the neuter possessive singular in Shakespeare's day).

MAR. Peace, break thee off! Look where it comes again! 40
BAR. In the same figure like the King that's dead.
MAR. Thou art a scholar, speak to it, Horatio.
BAR. Looks 'a not like the King? Mark it, Horatio.
HOR. Most like; it [harrows] me with fear and wonder.
BAR. It would be spoke to.
MAR.   Speak to it, Horatio. 45
HOR. What art thou that usurp'st this time of night,
  Together with that fair and warlike form
  In which the majesty of buried Denmark
  Did sometimes march? By heaven I charge thee speak!
MAR. It is offended.
BAR.   See, it stalks away! 50
HOR. Stay! Speak, speak, I charge thee speak!

Exit GHOST.

MAR. 'Tis gone, and will not answer.
BAR. How now, Horatio? you tremble and look pale.
  Is not this something more than fantasy?
  What think you on't? 55
HOR. Before my God, I might not this believe
  Without the sensible and true avouch
  Of mine own eyes.
MAR.   Is it not like the King?
HOR. As thou art to thyself.
  Such was the very armor he had on 60
  When he the ambitious Norway combated.
  So frown'd he once when in an angry parle
  He smote the sledded [Polacks] on the ice.
  'Tis strange.
MAR. Thus twice before, and jump at this dead hour, 65
  With martial stalk hath he gone by our watch.
HOR. In what particular thought to work I know not,
  But in the gross and scope of mine opinion,
  This bodes some strange eruption to our state.

41 **like:** in the likeness of.
42 **a scholar:** i.e. one who knows how best to address it.
43 **'a:** he.
45 **It . . . to.** A ghost had to be spoken to before it could speak.
46 **ursurp'st.** The ghost, a supernatural being, has invaded the realm of nature.
48 **majesty . . . Denmark.** late King of Denmark.
49 **sometimes:** formerly.
57 **sensible:** relating to the senses. **avouch:** guarantee.
61 **Norway:** King of Norway.
62 **parle:** parley.
63 **sledded:** using sleds or sledges. **Polacks:** Poles.
65 **jump:** precisely.
67–68 **In . . . opinion:** while I have no precise theory about it, my general feeling is that. *Gross =* wholeness, totality; *scope =* range.
69 **eruption:** upheaval.

MAR.   Good now, sit down, and tell me, he that knows,   70
        Why this same strict and most observant watch
        So nightly toils the subject of the land,
        And [why] such daily [cast] of brazen cannon,
        And foreign mart for implements of war,
        Why such impress of shipwrights, whose sore task   75
        Does not divide the Sunday from the week,
        What might be toward, that this sweaty haste
        Doth make the night joint-laborer with the day:
        Who is't that can inform me?
HOR.   That can I,
        At least the whisper goes so: our last king,   80
        Whose image even but now appear'd to us,
        Was, as you know, by Fortinbras of Norway,
        Thereto prick'd on by a most emulate pride,
        Dar'd to the combat; in which our valiant Hamlet
        (For so this side of our known word esteem'd him)   85
        Did slay this Fortinbras, who, by a seal'd compact
        Well ratified by law and heraldy,
        Did forfeit (with his life) all [those] his lands
        Which he stood seiz'd of, to the conqueror;
        Against the which a moi'ty competent   90
        Was gaged by our king, which had [return'd]
        To the inheritance of Fortinbras,
        Had he been vanquisher; as by the same comart
        And carriage of the article [design'd],
        His fell to Hamlet. Now, sir, young Fortinbras,   95
        Of unimproved mettle hot and full,
        Hath in the skirts of Norway here and there
        Shark'd up a list of lawless resolutes
        For food and diet to some enterprise
        That hath a stomach in't, which is no other,   100
        As it doth well appear unto our state,
        But to recover of us, by strong hand

---

[72] **toils:** causes to work. **subject:** subjects.
[74] **foreign mart:** dealing with foreign markets.
[75] **impress:** forced service.
[77] **toward:** in preparation.
[83] **emulate:** emulous, proceeding from rivalry.
[87] **law and heraldy:** heraldic law (governing combat). *Heraldy* is a variant of *heraldry*.
[89] **seiz'd of:** possessed of.
[90] **moi'ty:** portion. **competent:** adequate, i.e. equivalent.
[91] **gaged:** pledged. **had:** would have.
[92] **inheritance:** possession.
[93] **comart:** bargain.
[94] **carriage:** tenor. **design'd:** drawn up.
[96] **unimproved:** untried (?) or not directed to any useful end (?).
[97] **skirts:** outlying territories.
[98] **Shark'd up:** gathered up hastily and indiscriminately.
[100] **stomach:** relish of danger (?) or demand for courage (?).

And terms compulsatory, those foresaid lands
So by his father lost; and this, I take it,
Is the main motive of our preparations,   105
The source of this our watch, and the chief head
Of this post-haste and romage in the land.
BAR.   I think it be no other but e'en so.
Well may it sort that this portentous figure
Comes armed through our watch so like the King   110
That was and is the question of these wars.
HOR.   A mote it is to trouble the mind's eye.
In the most high and palmy state of Rome,
A little ere the mightiest Julius fell,
The graves stood [tenantless] and the sheeted dead   115
Did squeak and gibber in the Roman streets.
As stars with trains of fire, and dews of blood,
Disasters in the sun; and the moist star
Upon whose influence Neptune's empire stands
Was sick almost to doomsday with eclipse.   120
And even the like precurse of [fear'd] events,
As harbingers preceding still the fates
And prologue to the omen coming on,
Have heaven and earth together demonstrated
Unto our climatures and countrymen.   125

Enter GHOST.

But soft, behold! lo where it comes again!

It spreads his arms.

I'll cross it though it blast me. Stay, illusion!
If thou hast any sound or use of voice,
Speak to me.
If there be any good thing to be done   130
That may to thee do ease, and grace to me,
Speak to me.
If thou art privy to thy country's fate,

---

[106] **head:** source.
[107] **romage:** rummage, bustling activity.
[109] **sort:** fit.   **portentous:** ominous.
[116] One or more lines may have been lost between this line and the next.
[118] **Disasters:** ominous signs.   **moist star:** moon.
[119] **Neptune's empire stands:** the seas are dependent.
[120] **sick ... doomsday:** i.e. almost totally darkened. When the Day of Judgment is imminent, says Matthew 24:29, "the moon shall not give her light."   **eclipse.** There were a solar and two total lunar eclipses visible in England in 1598; they caused gloomy speculation.
[121] **precurse:** foreshadowing.
[122] **harbingers:** advance messengers.   **still:** always.
[123] **omen:** i.e. the events portended.
[125] **climatures:** regions.
[126] s.d. **his:** its.
[127] **cross it:** cross its path, confront it directly.   **blast:** wither (by supernatural means).

Which happily foreknowing may avoid,
O speak!   135
Or if thou hast uphoarded in thy life
Extorted treasure in the womb of earth,
For which, they say, your spirits oft walk in death,
Speak of it, stay and speak! (*The cock crows.*) Stop it, Marcellus.
MAR.   Shall I strike it with my partisan?   140
HOR.   Do, if it will not stand.
BAR.   'Tis here!
HOR.   'Tis here!
MAR.   'Tis gone!

[Exit GHOST.*]*

We do it wrong, being so majestical,
To offer it the show of violence,
For it is as the air, invulnerable,   145
And our vain blows malicious mockery.
BAR.   It was about to speak when the cock crew.
HOR.   And then it started like a guilty thing
Upon a fearful summons. I have heard
The cock, that is the trumpet to the morn,   150
Doth with his lofty and shrill-sounding throat
Awake the god of day, and at his warning,
Whether in sea or fire, in earth or air,
Th' extravagant and erring spirit hies
To his confine; and of the truth herein   155
This present object made probation.
MAR.   It faded on the crowing of the cock.
Some say that ever 'gainst that season comes
Wherein our Saviour's birth is celebrated,
This bird of dawning singeth all night long,   160
And then they say no spirit dare stir abroad,
The nights are wholesome, then no planets strike,
No fairy takes, nor witch hath power to charm,
So hallowed, and so gracious, is that time.
HOR.   So have I heard and do in part believe it.   165
But look, the morn in russet mantle clad

¹³⁴ **happily:** haply, perhaps.
¹³⁸ **your.** Colloquial and impersonal; cf. I.v.167, IV.iii.20–21. Most editors adopt *you* from Fl.
¹⁴⁰ **partisan:** long-handled spear.
¹⁴⁶ **malicious mockery:** mockery of malice, i.e. empty pretenses of harming it.
¹⁵⁰ **trumpet:** trumpeter.
¹⁵⁴ **extravagant:** wandering outside its proper bounds. **erring:** wandering abroad. **hies:** hastens.
¹⁵⁶ **object:** sight. **probation:** proof.
¹⁵⁸ **'gainst:** just before.
¹⁶² **strike:** exert malevolent influence.
¹⁶³ **takes:** bewitches, charms.
¹⁶⁴ **gracious:** blessed.
¹⁶⁶ **russet:** coarse greyish-brown cloth.

Walks o'er the dew of yon high eastward hill.
Break we our watch up, and by my advice
Let us impart what we have seen to-night
Unto young Hamlet, for, upon my life,   170
This spirit, dumb to us, will speak to him.
Do you consent we shall acquaint him with it,
As needful in our loves, fitting our duty?
MAR.   Let's do't, I pray, and I this morning know
Where we shall find him most convenient.   175

Exeunt.

SCENE II.

Flourish. Enter CLAUDIUS, KING OF DENMARK, GERTRUDE THE QUEEN; COUNCIL:
as POLONIUS; *and his son* LAERTES, HAMLET, *cum aliis [including* VOLTEMAND *and*
CORNELIUS*]*.

KING   Though yet of Hamlet our dear brother's death
The memory be green, and that it us befitted
To bear our hearts in grief, and our whole kingdom
To be contracted in one brow of woe,
Yet so far hath discretion fought with nature   5
That we with wisest sorrow think on him
Together with remembrance of ourselves.
Therefore our sometime sister, now our queen,
Th' imperial jointress to this warlike state,
Have we, as 'twere with a defeated joy,   10
With an auspicious, and a dropping eye,
With mirth in funeral, and with dirge in marriage,
In equal scale weighing delight and dole,
Taken to wife; nor have we herein barr'd
Your better wisdoms, which have freely gone   15
With this affair along. For all, our thanks.
Now follows that you know young Fortinbras,
Holding a weak supposal of our worth,
Or thinking by our late dear brother's death
Our state to be disjoint and out of frame,   20
Co-leagued with this dream of his advantage,

I.ii Location: The castle.
o.s.d. **Flourish:** trumpet fanfare.   **cum aliis:** with others.
[2] **befitted:** would befit.
[4] **contracted in:** (1) reduced to; (2) knit or wrinkled in.   **brow of woe:** mournful brow.
[9] **jointress:** joint holder.
[10] **defeated:** impaired.
[11] **auspicious ... dropping:** cheerful ... weeping.
[15] **freely:** fully, without reservation.
[17] **know:** be informed, learn.
[18] **supposal:** conjecture, estimate.
[21] **Co-leagued:** joined.

He hath not fail'd to pester us with message
Importing the surrender of those lands
Lost by his father, with all bands of law,
To our most valiant brother. So much for him.   25
Now for ourself, and for this time of meeting,
Thus much the business is: we have here writ
To Norway, uncle of young Fortinbras—
Who, impotent and bedred, scarcely hears
Of this his nephew's purpose—to suppress   30
His further gait herein, in that the levies,
The lists, and full proportions are all made
Out of his subject; and we here dispatch
You, good Cornelius, and you, Voltemand,
For bearers of this greeting to old Norway,   35
Giving to you no further personal power
To business with the King, more than the scope
Of these delated articles allow.

[Giving a paper.]

Farewell, and let our haste commend your duty.
COR., VOL.   In that, and all things, will we show our duty.   40
KING   We doubt it nothing; heartily farewell.

[Exeunt VOLTEMAND *and* CORNELIUS.*]*

And now, Laertes, what's the news with you?
You told us of some suit, what is't, Laertes?
You cannot speak of reason to the Dane
And lost your voice. What wouldst thou beg, Laertes,   45
That shall not be my offer, not thy asking?
The head is not more native to the heart,
The hand more instrumental to the mouth,
Than is the throne of Denmark to thy father.
What wouldst thou have, Laertes?
LAER.   My dread lord,   50
Your leave and favor to return to France,
From whence though willingly I came to Denmark

---

²² **pester . . . message:** trouble me with persistent messages (the original sense of *pester* is "overcrowd").
²³ **Importing:** having as import.
²⁴ **bands:** bonds, binding terms.
²⁹ **impotent and bedred:** feeble and bedridden.
³¹ **gait:** proceeding.
³¹⁻³³ **in . . . subject:** since the troops are all drawn from his subjects.
³⁸ **delated:** extended, detailed (a variant of *dilated*).
⁴¹ **nothing:** not at all.
⁴⁵ **lose:** waste.
⁴⁷ **native:** closely related.
⁴⁸ **instrumental:** serviceable.
⁵¹ **leave and favor:** gracious permission.

To show my duty in your coronation
Yet now I must confess, that duty done,
My thoughts and wishes bend again toward France,   55
And bow them to your gracious leave and pardon.
KING   Have you your father's leave? What says Polonius?
POL.   H'ath, my lord, wrung from me my slow leave
  By laborsome petition, and at last
  Upon his will I seal'd my hard consent.   60
  I do beseech you give him leave to go.
KING   Take thy fair hour, Laertes, time be thine,
  And thy best graces spend it at thy will!
  But now, my cousin Hamlet, and my son—
HAM. *[Aside.]*   A little more than kin, and less than kind.   65
KING   How is it that the clouds still hang on you?
HAM.   Not so, my lord, I am too much in the sun.
QUEEN   Good Hamlet, cast thy nighted color off,
  And let thine eye look like a friend on Denmark.
  Do not for ever with thy vailed lids   70
  Seek for thy noble father in the dust.
  Thou know'st 'tis common, all that lives must die,
  Passing through nature to eternity.
HAM.   Ay, madam, it is common.
QUEEN   If it be,
  Why seems it so particular with thee?   75
HAM.   Seems, madam? nay, it is, I know not "seems."
  'Tis not alone my inky cloak, [good] mother,
  Nor customary suits of solemn black,
  Nor windy suspiration of forc'd breath,
  No, nor the fruitful river in the eye,   80
  Nor the dejected havior of the visage,
  Together with all forms, moods, [shapes] of grief,
  That can [denote] me truly. These indeed seem,
  For they are actions that a man might play,
  But I have that within which passes show,   85
  These but the trappings and the suits of woe.
KING   'Tis sweet and commendable in your nature, Hamlet,
  To give these mourning duties to your father.
  But you must know your father lost a father,

---

56 **pardon:** permission to depart.
59 **H'ath:** he hath.
60 **hard:** reluctant.
64 **cousin:** kinsman (used in familiar address to any collateral relative more distant than a brother or sister; here to a nephew).
65 **A little . . . kind:** closer than a nephew, since you are my mother's husband; yet more distant than a son, too (and not well disposed to you).
67 **sun.** With obvious quibble on *son.*
70 **vailed:** downcast.
72 **common:** general, universal;.
75 **particular:** individual, personal.
80 **fruitful:** copious.

That father lost, lost his, and the survivor bound 90
In filial obligation for some term
To do obsequious sorrow. But to persever
In obstinate condolement is a course
Of impious stubborness, 'tis unmanly grief,
It shows a will most incorrect to heaven, 95
A heart unfortified, or mind impatient,
An understanding simple and unschool'd:
For what we know must be, and is as common
As any the most vulgar thing to sense,
Why should we in our peevish opposition 100
Take it to heart? Fie, 'tis a fault to heaven,
A fault against the dead, a fault to nature,
To reason most absurd, whose common theme
Is death of fathers, and who still hath cried,
From the first corse till he that died to-day, 105
"This must be so." We pray you throw to earth
This unprevailing woe, and think of us
As of a father, for let the world take note
You are the most immediate to our throne,
And with no less nobility of love 110
Than that which dearest father bears his son
Do I impart toward you. For your intent
In going back to school in Wittenberg,
It is most retrograde to our desire,
And we beseech you bend you to remain 115
Here in the cheer and comfort of our eye,
Our chiefest courtier, cousin, and our son.
QUEEN Let not thy mother lose her prayers, Hamlet,
I pray thee stay with us, go not to Wittenberg.
HAM. I shall in all my best obey you, madam. 120
KING Why, 'tis a loving and a fair reply.
Be as ourself in Denmark. Madam, come.
This gentle and unforc'd accord of Hamlet
Sits smiling to my heart, in grace whereof,
No jocund health that Denmark drinks to-day, 125
But the great cannon to the clouds shall tell,
And the King's rouse the heaven shall bruit again,
Respeaking earthly thunder. Come away.

92 **obsequious:** proper to obsequies.
93 **condolement:** grief.
95 **incorrect:** unsubmissive.
99 **any . . . sense:** what is perceived to be commonest.
101 **to:** against.
103 **absurd:** contrary.
107 **unprevailing:** unavailing.
111 **dearest:** most loving.
112 **impart:** i.e. impart love.
127 **rouse:** bumper, drink. **bruit:** loudly declare.

Flourish. Exeunt all but HAMLET.

HAM.   O that this too too sallied flesh would melt,
  Thaw, and resolve itself into a dew!   130
  Or that the Everlasting had not fix'd
  His canon 'gainst [self-]slaughter! O God, God,
  How [weary], stale, flat, and unprofitable
  Seem to me all the uses of this world!
  Fie on't, ah fie! 'tis an unweeded garden   135
  That grows to seed, things rank and gross in nature
  Possess it merely. That it should come [to this]!
  But two months dead, nay, not so much, not two.
  So excellent a king, that was to this
  Hyperion to a satyr, so loving to my mother   140
  That he might not beteem the winds of heaven
  Visit her face too roughly. Heaven and earth,
  Must I remember? Why, she should hang on him
  As if increase of appetite had grown
  By what it fed on, and yet, within a month—   145
  Let me not think on't! Frailty, thy name is woman!—
  A little month, or ere those shoes were old
  With which she followed my poor father's body,
  Like Niobe, all tears—why, she, [even she]—
  O God, a beast that wants discourse of reason   150
  Would have mourn'd longer—married with my uncle,
  My father's brother, but no more like my father
  Than I to Hercules. Within a month,
  Ere yet the salt of most unrighteous tears
  Had left the flushing in her galled eyes,   155
  She married—O most wicked speed: to post
  With such dexterity to incestious sheets,
  It is not, nor it cannot come to good,
  But break my heart, for I must hold my tongue.

Enter HORATIO, MARCELLUS, *and* BARNARDO.

---

[129] **sallied:** sullied. Many editors prefer the Fl reading, *solid.*
[132] **canon:** law.
[134] **uses:** customs.
[137] **merely:** utterly.
[139] **to:** in comparison with.
[140] **Hyperion:** the sun-god.
[141] **beteem:** allow.
[147] **or ere:** before.
[149] **Niobe.** She wept endlessly for her children, whom Apollo and Artemis had killed.
[150] **wants . . . reason:** lacks the power of reason (which distinguishes men from beasts).
[154] **unrighteous:** i.e. hypocritical.
[155] **flushing:** redness.   **galled:** inflamed.
[157] **incestious:** incestuous. The marriage of a man to his brother's widow was so regarded until long after Shakespeare's day.

HOR. Hail to your lordship!

HAM.   I am glad to see you well.   160
    Horatio—or do I forget myself.

HOR. The same, my lord, and your poor servant ever.

HAM. Sir, my good friend—I'll change that name with you.
    And what make you from Wittenberg, Horatio?
    Marcellus.   165

MAR. My good lord.

HAM. I am very glad to see you. *[To* BARNARDO.*]* Good even, sir.—
    But what, in faith, make you from Wittenberg?

HOR. A truant disposition, good my lord.

HAM. I would not hear your enemy say so,   170
    Nor shall you do my ear that violence
    To make it truster of your own report
    Against yourself. I know you are no truant.
    But what is your affair in Elsinore?
    We'll teach you to drink [deep] ere you depart.   175

HOR. My lord, I came to see your father's funeral.

HAM. I prithee do not mock me, fellow student,
    I think it was to [see] my mother's wedding.

HOR. Indeed, my lord, it followed hard upon.

HAM. Thrift, thrift, Horatio, the funeral bak'd-meats   180
    Did coldly furnish forth the marriage tables.
    Would I had met my dearest foe in heaven
    Or ever I had seen that day, Horatio!
    My father—methinks I see my father.

HOR. Where, my lord?

HAM.   In my mind's eye, Horatio.   185

HOR. I saw him once, 'a was a goodly king.

HAM. 'A was a man, take him for all in all,
    I shall not look upon his like again.

HOR. My lord, I think I saw him yesternight.

HAM. Saw, who?   190

HOR. My lord, the King your father.

HAM.   The King my father?

HOR. Season your admiration for a while
    With an attent ear, till I may deliver,
    Upon the witness of these gentlemen,
    This marvel to you.

---

[163] **change:** exchange.

[164] **what . . . from:** what are you doing away from.

[169] **truant disposition:** inclination to play truant.

[177] **studient:** student.

[181] **coldly:** when cold.

[182] **dearest:** most intensely hated.

[183] **Or:** ere, before.

[192] **Season:** temper. **admiration:** wonder.

[193] **deliver:** report.

HAM.   For God's love let me hear!   195
HOR.   Two nights together had these gentlemen,
       Marcellus and Barnardo, on their watch,
       In the dead waste and middle of the night,
       Been thus encount'red: a figure like your father,
       Armed at point exactly, cap-a-pe,   200
       Appears before them, and with solemn march
       Goes slow and stately by them; thrice he walk'd
       By their oppress'd and fear-surprised eyes
       Within his truncheon's length, whilst they, distill'd
       Almost to jelly with the act of fear,   205
       Stand dumb and speak not to him. This to me
       In dreadful secrecy impart they did,
       And I with them the third night kept the watch,
       Where, as they had delivered, both in time,
       Form of the thing, each word made true and good,   210
       The apparition comes. I knew your father,
       These hands are not more like.
HAM.   But where was this?
MAR.   My lord, upon the platform where we watch.
HAM.   Did you not speak to it?
HOR.   My lord, I did,
       But answer made it none. Yet once methought   215
       It lifted up it head and did address
       Itself to motion like as it would speak;
       But even then the morning cock crew loud,
       And at the sound it shrunk in haste away
       And vanish'd from our sight.
HAM.   'Tis very strange.   220
HOR.   As I do live, my honor'd lord, 'tis true,
       And we did think it writ down in our duty
       To let you know of it.
HAM.   Indeed, [indeed,] sirs. But this troubles me.
       Hold you the watch to-night?
[MAR., BAR.]   We do, my lord.   225
HAM.   Arm'd, say you?
[MAR., BAR.]   Arm'd, my lord.
HAM.   From top to toe?
[MAR., BAR.]   My lord, from head to foot.

---

198 **waste:** empty expanse.
200 **at point exactly:** in every particular.   **cap-a-pe:** from head to foot.
203 **fear-surprised:** overwhelmed by fear.
204 **truncheon:** short staff carried as a symbol of military command.
205 **act:** action, operation.
207 **dreadful:** held in awe, i.e. solemnly sworn.
212 **are . . . like:** i.e. do not resemble each other more closely than the apparition resembled him.
216 **it:** its.
216–17 **address . . . motion:** begin to make a gesture.

HAM.   Then saw you not his face.

HOR.   O yes, my lord, he wore his beaver up.   230

HAM.   What, look'd he frowningly?

HOR.   A countenance more
In sorrow than in anger.

HAM.   Pale, or red?

HOR.   Nay, very pale.

HAM.   And fix'd his eyes upon you?

HOR.   Most constantly.

HAM.   I would I had been there.

HOR.   It would have much amaz'd you.   235

HAM.   Very like, [very like]. Stay'd it long?

HOR.   While one with moderate haste might tell a hundreth.

BOTH [MAR., BAR.]   Longer, longer.

HOR.   Not when I saw't.

HAM.   His beard was grisl'd, no?

HOR.   It was, as I have seen it in his life   240
A sable silver'd.

HAM.   I will watch to-night,
Perchance 'twill walk again.

HOR.   I warr'nt it will.

HAM.   If it assume my noble father's person,
I'll speak to it though hell itself should gape
And bid me hold my peace. I pray you all,   245
If you have hitherto conceal'd this sight,
Let it be tenable in your silence still,
And whatsomever else shall hap to-night,
Give it an understanding but no tongue.
I will requite your loves. So fare you well.   250
Upon the platform 'twixt aleven and twelf
I'll visit you.

ALL   Our duty to your honor.

HAM.   Your loves, as mine to you; farewell.

Exeunt [all but HAMLET].

My father's spirit—in arms! All is not well,
I doubt some foul play. Would the night were come!   255
Till then sit still, my soul. [Foul] deeds will rise,
Though all the earth o'erwhelm them, to men's eyes.

Exit.

---

230 **beaver:** visor.
237 **tell a hundreth:** count a hundred.
239 **grisl'd:** grizzled, mixed with grey.
247 **tenable:** held close.
251 **aleven:** eleven.
255 **doubt:** suspect.

Scene III.

Enter LAERTES *and* OPHELIA, *his sister.*

LAER. My necessaries are inbark'd. Farewell.
And, sister, as the winds give benefit
And convey [is] assistant, do not sleep,
But let me hear from you.

OPH.   Do you doubt that?

LAER. For Hamlet, and the trifling of his favor,   5
Hold it a fashion and a toy in blood,
A violet in the youth of primy nature,
Forward, not permanent, sweet, not lasting,
The perfume and suppliance of a minute—
No more.

OPH.   No more but so?

LAER.   Think it no more: 10
For nature crescent does not grow alone
In thews and [bulk], but as this temple waxes,
The inward service of the mind and soul
Grows wide withal. Perhaps he loves you now,
And now no soil nor cautel doth besmirch   15
The virtue of his will, but you must fear,
His greatness weigh'd, his will is not his own,
[For he himself is subject to his birth:]
He may not, as unvalued persons do,
Carve for himself, for on his choice depends   20
The safety and health of this whole state,
And therefore must his choice be circumscrib'd
Unto the voice and yielding of that body
Whereof he is the head. Then if he says he loves you,
It fits your wisdom so far to believe it   25
As he in his particular act and place

I.iii. Location: Polonius' quarters in the castle.
¹ **inbark'd:** embarked, abroad.
³ **convey is assistant:** means of transport is available.
⁶ **a fashion:** i.e. standard behavior for a young man.   **toy in blood:** idle fancy of youthful passion.
⁷ **primy:** springlike.
⁸ **Forward:** early of growth.
⁹ **suppliance:** pastime.
¹¹ **crescent:** growing, increasing.
¹² **thews:** muscles, sinews.
¹²⁻¹⁴ **as ... withal:** as the body develops, the powers of mind and spirit grow along with it.
¹⁵ **soil:** stain.   **cautel:** deceit.
¹⁶ **will:** desire.
¹⁷ **His greatness weigh'd:** considering his princely status.
¹⁹ **unvalued:** of low rank.
²⁰ **Carve for himself:** indulge his own wishes.
²³ **voice:** vote, approval.   **yielding:** consent.   **that body:** i.e. the state.
²⁶ **in ... place:** i.e. acting as he must act in the position he occupies.

May give his saying deed, which is no further
Than the main voice of Denmark goes withal.
Then weigh what loss your honor may sustain
If with too credent ear you list his songs,   30
Or lose your heart, or your chaste treasure open
To his unmast'red importunity.
Fear it, Ophelia, fear it, my dear sister,
And keep you in the rear of your affection,
Out of the shot and danger of desire.   35
The chariest maid is prodigal enough
If she unmask her beauty to the moon.
Virtue itself scapes not calumnious strokes.
The canker galls the infants of the spring
Too oft before their buttons be disclos'd,   40
And in the morn and liquid dew of youth
Contagious blastments are most imminent.
Be wary then, best safety lies in fear:
Youth to itself rebels, though none else near.
OPH.   I shall the effect of this good lesson keep   45
As watchman to my heart. But, good my brother,
Do not, as some ungracious pastors do,
Show me the steep and thorny way to heaven,
Whiles, [like] a puff'd and reckless libertine,
Himself the primrose path of dalliance treads,   50
And reaks not his own rede.
LAER.   O, fear me not.

Enter POLONIUS.

I stay too long—but here my father comes.
A double blessing is a double grace,
Occasion smiles upon a second leave.
POL.   Yet here, Laertes? Aboard, aboard, for shame!   55
  The wind sits in the shoulder of your sail,
And you are stay'd for. There—*[laying his hand on* LAERTES' *head]* my blessing
with thee!
And these few precepts in thy memory
Look thou character. Give thy thoughts no tongue,

28 **main:** general.   **goes withal:** accord with.
30 **credent:** credulous.
35 **shot:** range.
39 **canker:** canker-worm.
40 **buttons:** buds.   **disclos'd:** opened.
42 **blastments:** withering blights.
44 **to:** of.
47 **ungracious:** graceless.
49 **puff'd:** bloated.
51 **reaks:** recks, heeds.   **rede:** advice.   **fear me not:** don't worry about me.
54 **Occasion:** opportunity (here personified, as often).   **smiles upon:** i.e. graciously bestows.
59 **character:** inscribe.

Nor any unproportion'd thought his act.   60
Be thou familiar, but by no means vulgar:
Those friends thou hast, and their adoption tried,
Grapple them unto thy soul with hoops of steel,
But do not dull thy palm with entertainment
Of each new-hatch'd, unfledg'd courage. Beware   65
Of entrance to a quarrel, but being in,
Bear't that th' opposed may beware of thee.
Give every man thy ear, but few thy voice,
Take each man's censure, but reserve thy judgment.
Costly thy habit as thy purse can buy,   70
But not express'd in fancy, rich, not gaudy,
For the apparel oft proclaims the man,
And they in France of the best rank and station
[Are] of a most select and generous chief in that.
Neither a borrower nor a lender [be],   75
For [loan] oft loses both itself and friend,
And borrowing dulleth [th'] edge of husbandry.
This above all: to thine own self be true,
And it must follow, as the night the day,
Thou canst not then be false to any man.   80
Farewell, my blessing season this in thee!
LAER.   Most humbly do I take my leave, my lord.
POL.   The time invests you, go, your servants tend.
LAER.   Farewell, Ophelia, and remember well
What I have said to you.
OPH.   'Tis in my memory lock'd,   85
And you yourself shall keep the key of it.
LAER.   Farewell.

Exit LAERTES.

POL.   What is't, Ophelia, he hath said to you?
OPH.   So please you, something touching the Lord Hamlet.
POL.   Marry, well bethought.   90
'Tis told me, he hath very oft of late
Given private time to you, and you yourself
Have of your audience been most free and bounteous.

[60] **unproportion'd:** unfitting.
[61] **familiar:** affable, sociable.   **vulgar:** friendly with everybody.
[62] **their adoption tried:** their association with you tested and proved.
[65] **courage:** spirited, young blood.
[67] **Bear't that:** manage it in such a way that.
[69] **Take:** listen to.   **censure:** opinion.
[74] **generous:** noble.   **chief:** eminence (?). But the line is probably corrupt. Perhaps *of a* is intrusive, in which case *chief* = chiefly.
[77] **husbandry:** thrift.
[81] **season:** preserve (?) or ripen, make fruitful (?).
[83] **invests:** besieges.   **tend:** wait.
[90] **Marry:** indeed (originally the name of the Virgin Mary used as an oath).

If it be so—as so 'tis put on me,
And that in way of caution—I must tell you,   95
You do not understand yourself so clearly
As it behooves my daughter and your honor.
What is between you? Give me up the truth.
OPH.   He hath, my lord, of late made many tenders
Of his affection to me.   100
POL.   Affection, puh! You speak like a green girl,
Unsifted in such perilous circumstance.
Do you believe his tenders, as you call them?
OPH.   I do not know, my lord, what I should think.
POL.   Marry, I will teach you: think yourself a baby   105
That you have ta'en these tenders for true pay,
Which are not sterling. Tender yourself more dearly,
Or (not to crack the wind of the poor phrase,
[Wringing] it thus) you'll tender me a fool.
OPH.   My lord, he hath importun'd me with love   110
In honorable fashion.
POL.   Ay, fashion you may call it. Go to, go to.
OPH.   And hath given countenance to his speech, my lord,
With almost all the holy vows of heaven.
POL.   Ay, springes to catch woodcocks, I do know,   115
When the blood burns, how prodigal the soul
Lends the tongue vows. These blazes, daughter,
Giving more light than heat, extinct in both
Even in their promise, as it is a-making,
You must not take for fire. From this time   120
Be something scanter of your maiden presence,
Set your entreatments at a higher rate
Than a command to parle. For Lord Hamlet,
Believe so much in him, that he is young,
And with a larger teder may he walk   125
Than may be given you. In few, Ophelia,

⁹⁴ **put on:** told to.
⁹⁹ **tenders:** offers.
¹⁰² **Unsifted:** untried.
¹⁰⁶ **tenders.** With play on the sense "money offered in payment" (as in *legal tender*).
¹⁰⁷ **Tender:** hold, value.
¹⁰⁹ **Wringing:** straining, forcing to the limit. **tender . . . fool:** (1) show me that you are a fool;
(2) make me look like a fool; (3) present me with a (bastard) grandchild.
¹¹² **fashion.** See note on line 6.
¹¹³ **countenance:** authority.
¹¹⁵ **springes:** snares. **woodcocks.** Proverbially gullible birds.
¹²²⁻²³ **Set . . . parle:** place a higher value on your favors; do not grant interviews simply because
he asks for them. Polonius uses a military figure: *entreatments* = negotiations for surrender; *parle* = parley, discuss terms.
¹²⁴ **so . . . him:** no more than this with respect to him.
¹²⁵ **larger teder:** longer tether.

Do not believe his vows, for they are brokers,
Not of that dye which their investments show,
But mere [implorators] of unholy suits,
Breathing like sanctified and pious bonds,   130
The better to [beguile]. This is for all:
I would not, in plain terms, from this time forth
Have you so slander any moment leisure
As to give words or talk with the Lord Hamlet.
Look to't, I charge you. Come your ways.   135
OPH.   I shall obey, my lord.

Exeunt.

SCENE IV.

Enter HAMLET, HORATIO, *and* MARCELLUS.

HAM.   The air bites shrowdly, it is very cold.
HOR.   It is [a] nipping and an eager air.
HAM.   What hour now?
HOR.   I think it lacks of twelf.
MAR.   No, it is strook.
HOR.   Indeed? I heard it not. It then draws near the season   5
Wherein the spirit held his wont to walk.

A flourish of trumpets, and two pieces goes off [within].

What does this mean, my lord?
HAM.   The King doth wake to-night and takes his rouse,
Keeps wassail, and the swagg'ring up-spring reels;
And as he drains his draughts of Rhenish down,   10
The kettle-drum and trumpet thus bray out
The triumph of his pledge.
HOR.   Is it a custom?
HAM.   Ay, marry, is't,
But to my mind, though I am native here

---

¹²⁷ **brokers:** procurers.
¹²⁸ **Not . . . show:** not of the color of their garments (*investments*) exhibit, i.e. not what they
seem.
¹²⁹ **mere:** out-and-out.
¹³⁰ **bonds:** (lover's) vows or assurances. Many editors follow Theobald in reading *bawds.*
¹³³ **slander:** disgrace. **moment:** momentary.
¹³⁵ **Come your ways:** come along.

I.iv. Location: The guard-platform of the castle.
¹ **shrowdly:** shrewdly, wickedly.
² **eager:** sharp.
⁶ s.d. **pieces:** cannon.
⁸ **doth . . . rouse:** i.e. holds revels far into the night.
⁹ **wassail:** carousal. **up-spring:** wild dance.
¹⁰ **Rhenish:** Rhine wine.
¹² **triumph . . . pledge:** accomplishment of his toast (by draining his cup at a single draft).

And to the manner born, it is a custom 15
More honor'd in the breach than the observance.
This heavy-headed revel east and west
Makes us traduc'd and tax'd of other nations.
They clip us drunkards, and with swinish phrase
Soil our addition, and indeed it takes 20
From our achievements, though perform'd at height,
The pith and marrow of our attribute.
So, oft it chances in particular men,
That for some vicious mole of nature in them,
As in their birth, wherein they are not guilty 25
(Since nature cannot choose his origin),
By their o'ergrowth of some complexion
Oft breaking down the pales and forts of reason,
Or by some habit, that too much o'er-leavens
The form of plausive manners—that these men, 30
Carrying, I say, the stamp of one defect,
Being nature's livery, or fortune's star,
His virtues else, be they as pure as grace,
As infinite as man may undergo,
Shall in the general censure take corruption 35
From that particular fault: the dram of [ev'l]
Doth all the noble substance of a doubt
To his own scandal.

Enter GHOST.

HOR.   Look, my lord, it comes!

[15] **manner:** custom (of carousing).
[16] **More . . . observance:** which it is more honorable to break than to observe.
[18] **tax'd of:** censured by.
[19] **clip:** clepe, call.
[20] **addition:** titles of honor.
[21] **at height:** most excellently.
[22] **attribute:** reputation.
[23] **particular:** individual.
[24] **vicious . . . nature:** small natural blemish.
[26] **his:** its.
[27] **By . . . complexion:** by the excess of some one of the humors (which were thought to govern the disposition).
[28] **pales:** fences.
[29] **o'er-leavens:** makes itself felt throughout (as leaven works in the whole mass of dough).
[30] **plausive:** pleasing.
[32] **Being . . . star:** i.e. whether they were born with it, or got it by misfortune. *Star* means "blemish."
[34] **undergo:** carry the weight of, sustain.
[35] **general censure:** popular opinion.
[36] **dram:** minute amount.   **ev'l:** evil, with a pun on *eale*, "yeast" (cf. *o'er-leavens* in line 29).
[37] **of a doubt.** A famous crux, for which many emendations have been suggested, the most widely accepted being Steevens' *often dout* (i.e. extinguish).
[38] **To . . . scandal:** i.e. so that it all shares in the disgrace.

HAM.   Angels and ministers of grace defend us!
Be thou a spirit of health, or goblin damn'd,   40
Bring with thee airs from heaven, or blasts from hell,
Be thy intents wicked, or charitable,
Thou com'st in such a questionable shape
That I will speak to thee. I'll call thee Hamlet,
King, father, royal Dane. O, answer me!   45
Let me not burst in ignorance, but tell
Why thy canoniz'd bones, hearsed in death,
Have burst their cerements; why the sepulchre,
Wherein we saw thee quietly interr'd,
Hath op'd his ponderous and marble jaws   50
To cast thee up again. What may this mean,
That thou, dead corse, again in complete steel
Revisits thus the glimpses of the moon,
Making night hideous, and we fools of nature
So horridly to shake our disposition   55
With thoughts beyond the reaches of our souls?
Say why is this? wherefore? what should we do?

[GHOST] *beckons* [HAMLET].

HOR.   It beckons you to go away with it,
As if it some impartment did desire
To you alone.
MAR.   Look with what courteous action   60
It waves you to a more removed ground,
But do not go with it.
HOR.   No, by no means.
HAM.   It will not speak, then I will follow it.
HOR.   Do not, my lord.
HAM.   Why, what should be the fear?
I do not set my life at a pin's fee,   65
And for my soul, what can it do to that,
Being a thing immortal as itself?
It waves me forth again, I'll follow it.
HOR.   What if it tempt you toward the flood, my lord,
Or to the dreadful summit of the cliff   70
That beetles o'er his base into the sea,

---

[40] **of health:** wholesome, good.
[43] **questionable:** inviting talk.
[47] **canoniz'd:** buried with the prescribed rites.
[48] **cerements:** grave clothes.
[52] **complete steel:** full armor.
[53] **Revisits.** The *-s* ending in the second person singular is common.
[54] **fools of nature:** the children (or the dupes) of a purely natural order, baffled by the supernatural.
[55] **disposition:** nature.
[59] **impartment:** communication.
[65] **fee:** worth.

And there assume some other horrible form
Which might deprive your sovereignty of reason,
And draw you into madness? Think of it.
The very place puts toys of desperation, 75
Without more motive, into every brain
That looks so many fadoms to the sea
And hears it roar beneath.
HAM.   It waves me still.—
    Go on, I'll follow thee
MAR.   You shall not go, my lord.
HAM.   Hold off your hands. 80
HOR.   Be rul'd, you shall not go.
HAM.   My fate cries out,
And makes each petty artere in this body
As hardy as the Nemean lion's nerve.
Still am I call'd. Unhand me, gentlemen.
By heaven, I'll make a ghost of him that lets me! 85
I say away—Go on, I'll follow thee.

Exeunt GHOST *and* HAMLET.

HOR.   He waxes desperate with [imagination].
MAR.   Let's follow. 'Tis not fit thus to obey him.
HOR.   Have after. To what issue will this come?
MAR.   Something is rotten in the state of Denmark. 90
HOR.   Heaven will direct it.
MAR.   Nay, let's follow him.

Exeunt.

SCENE V.

Enter GHOST *and* HAMLET

HAM.   Whither wilt thou lead me? Speak, I'll go no further.
GHOST   Mark me.
HAM.   I will.
GHOST   My hour is almost come
    When I to sulph'rous and tormenting flames
    Must render up myself.
HAM.   Alas, poor ghost!
GHOST   Pity me not, but lend thy serious hearing 5
    To what I shall unfold.

---

[73] **deprive . . . reason:** unseat reason from the rule of your mind.
[75] **toys of desperation:** fancies of desperate action, i.e. inclinations to jump off.
[77] **fadoms:** fathoms.
[82] **artere:** variant spelling of *artery;* here, ligament, sinew.
[83] **Nemean lion.** Slain by Hercules as one of his twelve labors. **nerve:** sinew.
[85] **lets:** hinders.
[91] **it:** i.e. the issue.
I.v. Location: On the battlements of the castle.

HAM.   Speak, I am bound to hear.

GHOST   So art thou to revenge, when thou shalt hear.

HAM.   What?

GHOST   I am thy father's spirit.
Doom'd for a certain term to walk the night,   10
And for the day confin'd to fast in fires,
Till the foul crimes done in my days of nature
Are burnt and purg'd away. But that I am forbid
To tell the secrets of my prison-house,
I could a tale unfold whose lightest word   15
Would harrow up thy soul, freeze thy young blood,
Make thy two eyes like stars start from their spheres,
Thy knotted and combined locks to part,
And each particular hair to stand an end,
Like quills upon the fearful porpentine.   20
But this eternal blazon must not be
To ears of flesh and blood. List, list, O, list!
If thou didst ever thy dear father love—

HAM.   O God!

GHOST   Revenge his foul and most unnatural murther.   25

HAM.   Murther!

GHOST   Murther most foul, as in the best it is,
But this most foul, strange, and unnatural.

HAM.   Haste me to know't, that I with wings as swift
As meditation, or the thoughts of love,   30
May sweep to my revenge.

GHOST   I find thee apt,
And duller shouldst thou be than the fat weed
That roots itself in ease on Lethe wharf,
Wouldst thou not stir in this. Now, Hamlet, hear:
'Tis given out that, sleeping in my orchard,   35
A serpent stung me, so the whole ear of Denmark
Is by a forged process of my death
Rankly abus'd; but know, thou noble youth,
The serpent that did sting thy father's life
Now wears his crown.

---

[11] **fast:** do penance.

[12] **crimes:** sins.

[17] **spheres:** eye sockets; with allusion to the revolving spheres in which, according to the Ptolemaic astronomy, the stars were fixed.

[19] **an end:** on end.

[20] **fearful porpentine:** frightened porcupine.

[21] **eternal blazon:** revelation of eternal things.

[30] **meditation:** thought.

[33] **Lethe:** river of Hades, the water of which made the drinker forget the past.   **wharf:** bank.

[35] **orchard:** garden.

[37] **forged process:** false account.

[38] **abus'd:** deceived.

HAM.   O my prophetic soul!   40
    My uncle?
GHOST   Ay, that incestuous, that adulterate beast,
    With witchcraft of his wits, with traitorous gifts—
    O wicked wit and gifts that have the power
    So to seduce!—won to his shameful lust   45
    The will of my most seeming virtuous queen.
    O Hamlet, what [a] falling-off was there
    From me, whose love was of that dignity
    That it went hand in hand even with the vow
    I made to her in marriage, and to decline   50
    Upon a wretch whose natural gifts were poor
    To those of mine!
    But virtue, as it never will be moved,
    Though lewdness court it in a shape of heaven,
    So [lust], though to a radiant angel link'd,   55
    Will [sate] itself in a celestial bed
    And prey on garbage.
    But soft, methinks I scent the morning air,
    Brief let me be. Sleeping within my orchard,
    My custom always of the afternoon,   60
    Upon my secure hour thy uncle stole,
    With juice of cursed hebona in a vial,
    And in the porches of my ears did pour
    The leprous distillment, whose effect
    Holds such an enmity with blood of man   65
    That swift as quicksilver it courses through
    The natural gates and alleys of the body,
    And with a sudden vigor it doth [posset]
    And curd, like eager droppings into milk,
    The thin and wholesome blood. So did it mine,   70
    And a most instant tetter bark'd about,
    Most lazar-like, with vile and loathsome crust
    All my smooth body.
    Thus was I, sleeping, by a brother's hand
    Of life, of crown, of queen, at once dispatch'd,   75
    Cut off even in the blossoms of my sin,

---

[42] **adulterate:** adulterous.
[54] **shape of heaven:** angelic form.
[61] **secure:** carefree.
[62] **hebona:** ebony (which Shakespeare, following a literary tradition, and perhaps also associat-
ing the word with *henbane,* thought the name of a poison).
[68] **posset:** curdle.
[69] **eager:** sour.
[71] **tetter:** scabby eruption.   **bark'd:** formed a hard covering, like bark on a tree.
[72] **lazar-like:** leperlike.
[75] **at once:** all at the same time.   **dispatch'd:** deprived.

Unhous'led, disappointed, unanel'd,
No reck'ning made, but sent to my account
With all my imperfections on my head.
O, horrible, O, horrible, most horrible!   80
If thou hast nature in thee, bear it not,
Let not the royal bed of Denmark be
A couch for luxury and damned incest.
But howsomever thou pursues this act,
Taint not thy mind, nor let thy soul contrive   85
Against thy mother aught. Leave her to heaven,
And to those thorns that in her bosom lodge
To prick and sting her. Fare thee well at once!
The glow-worm shows the matin to be near,
And gins to pale his uneffectual fire.   90
Adieu, adieu, adieu! remember me.

[Exit.]

HAM.   O all you host of heaven! O earth! What else?
And shall I couple hell? O fie, hold, hold, my heart,
And you, my sinows, grow not instant old,
But bear me [stiffly] up. Remember thee!   95
Ay, thou poor ghost, whiles memory holds a seat
In this distracted globe. Remember thee!
Yea, from the table of my memory
I'll wipe away all trivial fond records,
All saws of books, all forms, all pressures past   100
That youth and observation copied there,
And thy commandment all alone shall live
Within the book and volume of my brain,
Unmix'd with baser matter. Yes, by heaven!
O most pernicious woman!   105
O villain, villain, smiling, damned villain!
My tables—meet it is I set it down
That one may smile, and smile, and be a villain!
At least I am sure it may be so in Denmark.

[He writes.]

---

[77] **Unhous'led:** without the Eucharist. **disappointed:** without (spiritual) preparation. **unanel'd:** unanointed, without extreme unction.
[81] **nature:** natural feeling.
[83] **luxury:** lust.
[89] **matin:** morning.
[90] **gins:** begins.
[94] **sinows:** sinews.
[97] **globe:** head.
[98] **table:** writing tablet.
[99] **fond:** foolish.
[100] **saws:** wise sayings. **forms:** shapes, images. **pressures:** impressions.

So, uncle, there you are. Now to my word: 110
It is "Adieu, adieu! remember me."
I have sworn't.
HOR. *[Within.]* My lord, my lord!
MAR. *[Within.]*   Lord Hamlet!

Enter HORATIO *and* MARCELLUS.

HOR.   Heavens secure him!
HAM.   So be it!
MAR.   Illo, ho, ho, my lord!   115
HAM.   Hillo, ho, ho, boy! come, [bird,] come.
MAR.   How is't, my noble lord?
HOR.   What news, my lord?
HAM.   O, wonderful!
HOR.   Good my lord, tell it.
HAM.   No, you will reveal it.
HOR.   Not I, my lord, by heaven.
MAR.   Nor I, my lord.   120
HAM.   How say you then, would heart of man once think it?—
But you'll be secret?
BOTH [HOR., MAR.] Ay, by heaven, [my lord].
HAM.   There's never a villain dwelling in all Denmark
But he's an arrant knave.
HOR.   There needs no ghost, my lord, come from the grave   125
To tell us this.
HAM.   Why, right, you are in the right,
And so, without more circumstance at all,
I hold it fit that we shake hands and part,
You, as your business and desire shall point you,
For every man hath business and desire,   130
Such as it is, and for my own poor part,
I will go pray.
HOR.   These are but wild and whirling words, my lord.
HAM.   I am sorry they offend you, heartily,
Yes, faith, heartily.
HOR.   There's no offense, my lord.   135
HAM.   Yes, by Saint Patrick, but there is, Horatio,
And much offense too. Touching this vision here,
It is an honest ghost, that let me tell you.
For your desire to know what is between us,
O'ermaster't as you may. And now, good friends,   140
As you are friends, scholars, and soldiers,
Give me one poor request.

---

110 **word:** i.e. word of command from the Ghost.
116 **Hillo ... come.** Hamlet answers Marcellus' halloo with a falconer's cry.
127 **circumstance:** ceremony.
138 **honest:** true, genuine.

HOR.   What is't, my lord, we will.

HAM.   Never make known what you have seen tonight.

BOTH [HOR., MAR.]   My lord, we will not.

HAM.   Nay, but swear't.

HOR.   In faith.   145
    My lord, not I.

MAR.   Nor I, my lord, in faith.

HAM.   Upon my sword.

MAR.   We have sworn, my lord, already.

HAM.   Indeed, upon my sword, indeed.

GHOST *cries under the stage.*

GHOST   Swear.

HAM.   Ha, ha, boy, say'st thou so? Art thou there, truepenny?   150
    Come on, you hear this fellow in the cellarage,
    Consent to swear.

HOR.   Propose the oath, my lord.

HAM.   Never to speak of this that you have seen,
    Swear by my sword.

GHOST *[Beneath.]*   Swear.   155

HAM.   *Hic et ubique?* Then we'll shift our ground.
    Come hither, gentlemen,
    And lay your hands again upon my sword.
    Swear by my sword
    Never to speak of this that you have heard.   160

GHOST *[Beneath.]*   Swear by his sword.

HAM.   Well said, old mole, canst work i' th' earth so fast?
    A worthy pioner! Once more remove, good friends.

HOR.   O day and night, but this is wondrous strange!

HAM.   And therefore as a stranger give it welcome.   165
    There are more things in heaven and earth, Horatio,
    Than are dreamt of in your philosophy.
    But come—
    Here, as before, never, so help you mercy,
    How strange or odd some'er I bear myself—   170
    As I perchance hereafter shall think meet
    To put an antic disposition on—
    That you, at such times seeing me, never shall,
    With arms encumb'red thus, or this headshake,

---

[143] **What is't:** whatever it is.

[147] **Upon my sword:** i.e. on the cross formed by the hilt.

[150] **truepenny:** trusty fellow.

[156] **Hic et ubique:** here and everywhere.

[163] **pioner:** digger, miner (variant of *pioneer*).

[165] **as . . . welcome:** give it the welcome due in courtesy to strangers.

[167] **your.** See note on I.i.138.   **philosophy:** i.e. natural philosophy, science.

[172] **put . . . on:** behave in some fantastic manner, act like a madman.

[174] **encumb'red:** folded.

Or by pronouncing of some doubtful phrase,   175
As "Well, well, we know," or "We could, and if we would,"
Or "If we list to speak," or "There be, and if they might,"
Or such ambiguous giving out, to note
That you know aught of me—this do swear,
So grace and mercy at your most need help you.   180

GHOST *[Beneath.]*   Swear.

[They swear.]

HAM.   Rest, rest, perturbed spirit! So gentlemen,
With all my love I do commend me to you,
And what so poor a man as Hamlet is
May do t' express his love and friending to you,   185
God willing, shall not lack. Let us go in together,
And still your fingers on your lips, I pray.
The time is out of joint—O cursed spite,
The ever I was born to set it right!
Nay, come, let's go together.   190

Exeunt.

ACT II

SCENE I.

Enter old POLONIUS *and his man* [REYNALDO].

POL.   Give him this money and these notes, Reynaldo.
REY.   I will, my lord.
POL.   You shall do marvell's wisely, good Reynaldo,
Before you visit him, to make inquire
Of his behavior.
REY.   My lord, I did intend it.   5
POL.   Marry, well said, very well said. Look you, sir,
Inquire me first what Danskers are in Paris,
And how, and who, what means, and where they keep,
What company, at what expense; and finding
By this encompassment and drift of question   10
That they do know my son, come you more nearer

---

¹⁷⁶ **and if:** if.
¹⁷⁷ **list:** cared, had a mind.
¹⁷⁸ **note:** indicate.
¹⁸⁷ **still:** always.
¹⁹⁰ **Nay . . . together.** They are holding back to let him go first.

II.i. Location: Polonius' quarters in the castle.
³ **marvell's:** marvelous(ly).
⁷ **Danskers:** Danes.
⁸ **keep:** lodge.
¹⁰ **encompassment:** circuitousness.   **drift of question:** directing of the conversation.

Than your particular demands will touch it.
Take you as 'twere some distant knowledge of him,
As thus, "I know his father and his friends,
And in part him." Do you mark this, Reynaldo? 15
REY.   Ay, very well, my lord.
POL.   "And in part him—but," you may say, "not well.
But if't be he I mean, he's very wild,
Addicted so and so," and there put on him
What forgeries you please: marry, none so rank 20
As may dishonor him, take heed of that,
But, sir, such wanton, wild, and usual slips
As are companions noted and most known
To youth and liberty.
REY.   As gaming, my lord.
POL.   Ay, or drinking, fencing, swearing, quarrelling, 25
Drabbing—you may go so far.
REY.   My lord, that would dishonor him.
POL.   Faith, as you may season it in the charge:
You must not put another scandal on him,
That he is open to incontinency— 30
That's not my meaning. But breathe his faults so quaintly
That they may seem the taints of liberty,
The flash and outbreak of a fiery mind,
A savageness in unreclaimed blood,
Of general assault.
REY.   But, my good lord— 35
POL.   Wherefore should you do this?
REY.   Ay, my lord,
I would know that.
POL.   Marry, sir, here's my drift,
And I believe it is a fetch of wit:
You laying these slight sallies on my son,
As 'twere a thing a little soil'd [wi' th'] working, 40
Mark you,
Your party in converse, him you would sound,

---

¹² **particular demands:** direct questions.
²⁰ **forgeries:** invented charges.
²² **wanton:** sportive.
²⁶ **Drabbing:** whoring.
²⁸ **Faith.** Most editors read *Faith, no,* following Fl; this makes easier sense.   **season:** qualify, temper.
³⁰ **open to incontinency:** habitually profligate.
³¹ **quaintly:** artfully.
³⁴ **unreclaimed:** untamed.
³⁵ **Of general assault:** i.e. to which young men are generally subject.
³⁸ **fetch of wit:** ingenious device.
³⁹ **sallies:** sullies, blemishes.
⁴⁰ **soil'd . . . working:** i.e. shopworn.

Having ever seen in the prenominate crimes
The youth you breathe of guilty, be assur'd
He closes with you in this consequence: 45
"Good sir," or so, or "friend," or "gentleman,"
According to the phrase or the addition
Of man and country.
REY.   Very good, my lord.
POL.   And then, sir, does 'a this—'a does—what was I about to say?
By the mass, I was about to say something.   50
Where did I leave?
REY.   At "closes in the consequence."
POL.   At "closes in the consequence," ay, marry.
He closes thus: "I know the gentleman.
I saw him yesterday, or th' other day,
Or then, or then, with such or such, and as you say,   55
There was 'a gaming, there o'ertook in 's rouse,
There falling out at tennis"; or, perchance,
"I saw him enter such a house of sale,"
Videlicet, a brothel, or so forth. See you now,
Your bait of falsehood take this carp of truth,   60
And thus do we of wisdom and of reach,
With windlasses and with assays of bias,
By indirections find directions out;
So by my former lecture and advice
Shall you my son. You have me, have you not?   65
REY.   My lord, I have.
POL.   God buy ye, fare ye well.
REY.   Good my lord.
POL.   Observe his inclination in yourself.
REY.   I shall, my lord.
POL.   And let him ply his music.
REY.   Well, my lord.   70
POL.   Farewell.

Exit REYNALDO.

Enter OPHELIA.

[43] **Having:** if he has.   **prenominate crimes:** aforementioned faults.
[45] **closes:** falls in.   **in this consequence:** as follows.
[47] **addition:** style of address.
[56] **o'ertook in 's rouse:** overcome by drink.
[61] **reach:** capacity, understanding.
[62] **windlasses:** roundabout methods.   **assays of bias:** indirect attempts (a figure from the game of bowls, in which the player must make allowance for the curving course his bowl will take toward its mark).
[63] **directions:** the way things are going.
[65] **have me:** understand me.
[66] **God buy ye:** good-bye (a contraction of *God be with you*).
[68] **in:** by. Polonius asks him to observe Laertes directly, as well as making inquiries.
[70] **let him ply:** see that he goes on with.

How now, Ophelia, what's the matter?

OPH. O my lord, my lord, I have been so affrighted!

POL. With what, i' th' name of God?

OPH. My lord, as I was sewing in my closet,
Lord Hamlet, with his doublet all unbrac'd,   75
No hat upon his head, his stockins fouled,
Ungart'red, and down-gyved to his ankle,
Pale as his shirt, his knees knocking each other,
And with a look so piteous in purport
As if he had been loosed out of hell   80
To speak of horrors—he comes before me.

POL. Mad for thy love?

OPH.   My lord, I do not know,
But truly I do fear it.

POL.   What said he?

OPH. He took me by the wrist, and held me hard,
Then goes he to the length of all his arm,   85
And with his other hand thus o'er his brow,
He falls to such perusal of my face
As 'a would draw it. Long stay'd he so.
At last, a little shaking of mine arm,
And thrice his head thus waving up and down,   90
He rais'd a sigh so piteous and profound
As it did seem to shatter all his bulk
And end his being. That done, he lets me go,
And with his head over his shoulder turn'd,
He seem'd to find his way without his eyes,   95
For out a' doors he went without their helps,
And to the last bended their light on me.

POL. Come, go with me. I will go seek the King.
This is the very ecstasy of love,
Whose violent property fordoes itself,   100
And leads the will to desperate undertakings
As oft as any passions under heaven
That does afflict our natures. I am sorry—
What, have you given him any hard words of late?

OPH. No, my good lord, but as you did command   105
I did repel his letters, and denied
His access to me.

POL.   That hath made him mad.
I am sorry that with better heed and judgment

---

[74] **closet:** private room.
[75] **unbrac'd:** unlaced.
[76] **stockins fouled:** stockings dirty.
[77] **down-gyved:** hanging down like fetters on a prisoner's legs.
[92] **bulk:** body.
[99] **ecstasy:** madness.
[100] **property:** quality. **fordoes:** destroys.

I had not coted him. I fear'd he did but trifle
And meant to wrack thee, but beshrow my jealousy!   110
By heaven, it is as proper to our age
To cast beyond ourselves in our opinions,
As it is common for the younger sort
To lack discretion. Come, go we to the King.
This must be known, which, being kept close, might move   115
More grief to hide, than hate to utter love.
Come.

Exeunt.

SCENE II.

Flourish. Enter KING *and* QUEEN, ROSENCRANTZ *and* GUILDENSTERN *[cum aliis].*

KING   Welcome, dear Rosencrantz and Guildenstern!
Moreover that we much did long to see you,
The need we have to use you did provoke
Our hasty sending. Something have you heard
Of Hamlet's transformation; so call it,   5
Sith nor th' exterior nor the inward man
Resembles that it was. What it should be,
More than his father's death, that thus hath put him
So much from th' understanding of himself,
I cannot dream of. I entreat you both   10
That, being of so young days brought up with him,
And sith so neighbored to his youth and havior,
That you voutsafe your rest here in our court
Some little time, so by your companies
To draw him on to pleasures, and to gather   15
So much as from occasion you may glean,
Whether aught to us unknown afflicts him thus,
That, open'd, lies within our remedy.
QUEEN   Good gentlemen, he hath much talk'd of you,
And sure I am two men there is not living   20
To whom he more adheres. If it will please you

[109] **coted:** observed.
[110] **beshrow:** beshrew, plague take. **jealousy:** suspicious mind.
[111] **proper . . . age:** characteristic of men of my age.
[112] **cast beyond ourselves:** overshoot, go too far (by way of caution).
[115] **close:** secret.
[115-16] **move . . . love:** cause more grievous consequences by its concealment than we shall incur displeasure by making it known.

II.ii. Location: The castle.
[2] **Moreover . . . you:** besides the fact that we wanted to see you for your own sakes.
[6] **Sith:** since.
[11] **of:** from.
[13] **voutsafe your rest:** vouchsafe to remain.
[21] **more adheres:** is more attached.

To show us so much gentry and good will
As to expend your time with us a while
For the supply and profit of our hope,
Your visitation shall receive such thanks   25
As fits a king's remembrance.
ROS.   Both your Majesties
Might, by the sovereign power you have of us,
Put your dread pleasures more into command
Than to entreaty.
GUIL.   But we both obey,
And here give up ourselves, in the full bent,   30
To lay our service freely at your feet,
To be commanded.
KING   Thanks, Rosencrantz and gentle Guildenstern.
QUEEN   Thanks, Guildenstern and gentle Rosencrantz.
And I beseech you instantly to visit   35
My too much changed son. Go some of you
And bring these gentlemen where Hamlet is.
GUIL.   Heavens make our presence and our practices
Pleasant and helpful to him!
QUEEN   Ay, amen!

Exeunt ROSENCRANTZ *and* GUILDENSTERN *[with some* ATTENDANTS*]*.

Enter POLONIUS.

POL.   Th' embassadors from Norway, my good lord,   40
Are joyfully return'd.
KING   Thou still hast been the father of good news.
POL.   Have I, my lord? I assure my good liege
I hold my duty as I hold my soul,
Both to my God and to my gracious king;   45
And I do think, or else this brain of mine
Hunts not the trail of policy so sure
As it hath us'd to do, that I have found
The very cause of Hamlet's lunacy.
KING   O, speak of that, that do I long to hear.   50
POL.   Give first admittance to th' embassadors;
My news shall be the fruit to that great feast.
KING   Thyself do grace to them, and bring them in.

[Exit POLONIUS*]*.

---

²² **gentry:** courtesy.
²⁴ **supply and profit:** support and advancement.
³⁰ **in . . . bent:** to our utmost.
⁴⁰ **embassadors:** ambassadors.
⁴² **still:** always.
⁴³ **liege:** sovereign.
⁴⁷ **policy:** statecraft.
⁵² **fruit:** dessert.

He tells me, my dear Gertrude, he hath found
The head and source of all your son's distemper.   55
QUEEN   I doubt it is no other but the main,
His father's death and our [o'erhasty] marriage.

Enter [POLONIUS *with* VOLTEMAND *and* CORNELIUS, THE] EMBASSADORS.

KING   Well, we shall sift him.—Welcome, my good friends!
Say Voltemand, what from our brother Norway?
VOL.   Most fair return of greetings and desires.   60
Upon our first, he sent out to suppress
His nephew's levies, which to him appear'd
To be a preparation 'gainst the Polack;
But better look'd into, he truly found
It was against your Highness. Whereat griev'd,   65
That to his sickness, age, and impotence
Was falsely borne in hand, sends out arrests
On Fortinbras, which he, in brief, obeys,
Receives rebuke from Norway, and in fine,
Makes vow before his uncle never more   70
To give th' assay of arms against your Majesty.
Whereon old Norway, overcome with joy,
Gives him threescore thousand crowns in annual fee,
And his commission to employ those soldiers,
So levied, as before, against the Polack,   75
With an entreaty, herein further shown,

[Giving a paper.]

That it might please you to give quiet pass
Through your dominions for this enterprise,
On such regards of safety and allowance
As therein are set down.
KING   It likes us well,   80
And at our more considered time we'll read,
Answer, and think upon this business.
Mean time, we thank you for your well-took labor.
Go to your rest, at night we'll feast together.
Most welcome home!

Exeunt EMBASSADORS *[and* ATTENDANTS*]*.

---

⁵⁵ **head.** Synonymous with *source.*   **distemper:** (mental) illness.
⁵⁶ **doubt:** suspect.   **main:** main cause.
⁶¹ **Upon our first:** at our first representation.
⁶⁵ **griev'd:** aggrieved, offended.
⁶⁷ **borne in hand:** taken advantage of.
⁶⁹ **in fine:** in the end.
⁷¹ **assay:** trial.
⁷⁹ **On . . . allowance:** with such safeguards and provisos.
⁸⁰ **likes:** pleases.
⁸¹ **consider'd:** suitable for consideration.

POL.   This business is well ended   85
     My liege, and madam, to expostulate
     What majesty should be, what duty is,
     Why day is day, night night, and time is time,
     Were nothing but to waste night, day, and time;
     Therefore, [since] brevity is the soul of wit,   90
     And tediousness the limbs and outward flourishes,
     I will be brief. Your nobel son is mad:
     Mad call I it, for to define true madness,
     What is't but to be nothing else but mad?
     But let that go.
QUEEN   More matter with less art.   95
POL.   Madam, I swear I use no art at all.
     That he's mad, 'tis true, 'tis true 'tis pity,
     And pity 'tis 'tis true— a foolish figure,
     But farewell it, for I will use no art.
     Mad let us grant him then, and now remains   100
     That we find out the cause of this effect,
     Or rather say, the cause of this defect,
     For this effect defective comes by cause:
     Thus it remains, and the remainder thus.
     Perpend.   105
     I have a daughter—have while she is mine—
     Who in her duty and obedience, mark,
     Hath given me this. Now gather, and surmise.

[Reads the salutation of the letter.]

     "To the celestial and my soul's idol, the most beautified Ophelia"—
     That's an ill phrase, a vile phrase, "beautified" is a vile phrase. But you shall hear.   110
     Thus:
     "In her excellent white bosom, these, etc."
QUEEN   Came this from Hamlet to her?
POL.   Good madam, stay awhile. I will be faithful.

[Reads the] letter.

     "Doubt thou the stars are fire,   115
     Doubt that the sun doth move,
     Doubt truth to be a liar,
     But never doubt I love.

---

86 **expostulate:** expound.
90 **wit:** understanding, wisdom.
95 **art:** i.e. rhetorical art.
98 **figure:** figure of speech.
103 **For . . . cause:** for this effect (which shows as a defect in Hamlet's reason) is not merely acci-
     dental, and has a cause we may trace.
105 **Perpend:** consider.
110 **beautified:** beautiful (not an uncommon usage).
117 **Doubt:** suspect.

O dear Ophelia, I am ill at these numbers. I have not art to reckon my groans, but
that I love thee best, O most best, believe it. Adieu.   120
Thine evermore, most dear lady,
   whilst this machine is to him, Hamlet."
This in obedience hath my daughter shown me,
And more [above], hath his solicitings,
As they fell out by time, by means, and place,   125
All given to mine ear.
KING   But how hath she
   Receiv'd his love?
POL.   What do you think of me?
KING   As of a man faithful and honorable.
POL.   I would fain prove so. But what might you think,
   When I had seen this hot love on the wing—   130
   As I perceiv'd it (I must tell you that)
   Before my daughter told me—what might you,
   Or my dear Majesty your queen here, think,
   If I had play'd the desk or table-book,
   Or given my heart a [winking,] mute and dumb,   135
   Or look'd upon this love with idle sight,
   What might you think? No, I went round to work,
   And my young mistress thus I did bespeak:
   "Lord Hamlet is a prince out of thy star;
   This must not be"; and then I prescripts gave her,   140
   That she should lock herself from [his] resort,
   Admit no messengers, receive no tokens.
   Which done, she took the fruits of my advice;
   And he repell'd, a short tale to make,
   Fell into a sadness, then into a fast,   145
   Thence to a watch, thence into a weakness,
   Then to [a] lightness, and by this declension,
   Into the madness wherein now he raves,
   And all we mourn for.
KING   Do you think ['tis] this?
QUEEN   It may be, very like.   150

[119] **ill . . . numbers:** bad at versifying.   **reckon:** count (with a quibble on *numbers*).
[122] **machine:** body.
[124] **more above:** furthermore.
[129] **fain:** willingly, gladly.
[134] **play'd . . . table-book:** i.e. noted the matter secretly.
[135] **winking:** closing of the eyes.
[136] **idle sight:** uncomprehending eyes.
[137] **round:** straightforwardly.
[138] **bespeak:** address.
[139] **star:** i.e. sphere, lot in life.
[143] **took . . . of:** profited by, i.e. carried out.
[144] **repell'd:** repulsed.
[146] **watch:** sleeplessness.
[147] **lightness:** lightheadedness.

POL.   Hath there been such a time—I would fain know that—
That I have positively said, "Tis so,"
When it prov'd otherwise?
KING   Not that I know.
POL. *[Points to his head and shoulder.]*   Take this from this, if this be otherwise.
If circumstances lead me, I will find   155
Where truth is hid, though it were hid indeed
Within the centre.
KING   How may we try it further?
POL.   You know sometimes he walks four hours together
Here in the lobby.
QUEEN   So he does indeed.
POL.   At such a time I'll loose my daughter to him.   160
Be you and I behind an arras then,
Mark the encounter: if he love her not,
And be not from his reason fall'n thereon,
Let me be no assistant for a state,
But keep a farm and carters.
KING   We will try it.   165

Enter HAMLET *[reading on a book].*

QUEEN   But look where sadly the poor wretch comes reading.
POL.   Away, I do beseech you, both away.
I'll board him presently.

Exeunt KING *and* QUEEN.

                    O, give me leave,
How does my good Lord Hamlet?
HAM.   Well, God-a-mercy.   170
POL.   Do you know me, my lord?
HAM.   Excellent well, you are a fishmonger.
POL.   Not I, my lord.
HAM.   Then I would you were so honest a man.
POL.   Honest, my lord?   175
HAM.   Ay, sir, to be honest, as this world goes, is to be one man pick'd out of ten
thousand.
POL.   That's very true, my lord.
HAM.   For if the sun breed maggots in a dead dog, being a good kissing carrion—
Have you a daughter?
POL.   I have, my lord.   180

---

[157] **centre:** i.e. of the earth (which in the Ptolemaic system is also the center of the universe).
[161] **arras:** hanging tapestry.
[163] **thereon:** because of that.
[168] **board:** accost. **presently:** at once.
[170] **God-a-mercy:** thank you.
[172] **fishmonger.** Usually explained as slang for "bawd," but no evidence has been produced for
such a usage in Shakespeare's day.
[178] **good kissing carrion:** flesh good enough for the sun to kiss.

HAM. Let her not walk i' th' sun. Conception is a blessing, but as your daughter may conceive, friend, look to't.

POL. *[Aside.]* How say you by that? still harping on my daughter. Yet he knew me not at first, 'a said I was a fishmonger. 'A is far gone. And truly in my youth I suff'red much extremity for love—very near this. I'll speak to him again.—What do you read, my lord? 185

HAM. Words, words, words.

POL. What is the matter, my lord?

HAM. Between who?

POL. I mean, the matter that you read, my lord. 190

HAM. Slanders, sir; for the satirical rogue says here that old men have grey beards, that their faces are wrinkled, their eyes purging thick amber and plum-tree gum, and that they have a plentiful lack of wit, together with most weak hams; all which, sir, though I most powerfully and potently believe, yet I hold it not honesty to have it thus set down, for yourself, sir, I shall grow old as I am, if like a crab you 195 could go backward.

POL. *[Aside.]* Though this be madness, yet there is method in't.—Will you walk out of the air, my lord?

HAM. Into my grave.

POL. Indeed that's out of the air. *[Aside.]* How pregnant sometimes his replies are! 200 a happiness that often madness hits on, which reason and [sanity] could not so prosperously be deliver'd of. I will leave him, [and suddenly contrive the means of meeting between him] and my daughter.—My lord, I will take my leave of you.

HAM. You cannot take from me any thing that I will not more willingly part withal—except my life, except my life, except my life. 205

POL. Fare you well, my lord.

HAM. These tedious old fools!

Enter GUILDENSTERN *and* ROSENCRANTZ.

POL. You go to seek the Lord Hamlet, there he is.

ROS. *[To* POLONIUS.*]* God save you, sir!

[Exit POLONIUS.*]*

GUIL. My honor'd lord! 210

ROS. My most dear lord!

HAM. My [excellent] good friends! How dost thou, Guildenstern? Ah, Rosencrantz! Good lads, how do you both?

ROS. As the indifferent children of the earth.

GUIL. Happy, in that we are not [over-]happy, on Fortune's [cap] we are not the 215 very button.

---

[181] **Conception:** understanding (with following play on the sense "conceiving a child").

[188] **matter:** subject; but Hamlet replies as if he had understood Polonius to mean "cause for a quarrel."

[194] **honesty:** a fitting thing.

[197] **method:** orderly arrangement, sequence of ideas.

[198] **out . . . air:** Outdoor air was thought to be bad for invalids.

[200] **pregnant:** apt.

[202] **suddenly:** at once.

[214] **indifferent:** average.

HAM.   Nor the soles of her shoe?

ROS.   Neither, my lord.

HAM.   Then you live about her waist, or in the middle of her favors?

GUIL.   Faith, her privates we.   220

HAM.   In the secret parts of Fortune? O, most true, she is a strumpet. What news?

ROS.   None, my lord, but the world's grown honest.

HAM.   Then is doomsday near. But your news is not true. [Let me question more in particular. What have you, my good friends, deserv'd at the hands of Fortune, that she sends you to prison hither?   225

GUIL.   Prison, my lord?

HAM.   Denmark's a prison.

ROS.   Then is the world one.

HAM.   A goodly one, in which there are many confines, wards, and dungeons, Denmark being one o' th' worst.   230

ROS.   We think not so, my lord.

HAM.   Why then 'tis none to you; for there is nothing either good or bad, but thinking makes it so. To me it is a prison.

ROS.   Why then your ambition makes it one. 'Tis too narrow for your mind.

HAM.   O God, I could be bounded in a nutshell, and count myself a king of infinite   235
space—were it not that I have bad dreams.

GUIL.   Which dreams indeed are ambition, for the very substance of the ambitious is merely the shadow of a dream.

HAM.   A dream itself is but a shadow.

ROS.   Truly, and I hold ambition of so airy and light a quality that it is but a   240
shadow's shadow.

HAM.   Then are our beggars bodies, and our monarchs and outstretch'd heroes the beggars' shadows. Shall we to th' court? for, by my fay, I cannot reason.

BOTH [ROS., GUIL.]   We'll wait upon you.

HAM.   No such matter. I will not sort you with the rest of my servants; for to speak   245
to you like an honest man, I am most dreadfully attended.] But in the beaten way of friendship, what make you at Elsinore?

ROS.   To visit you, my lord, no other occasion.

HAM.   Beggar that I am, I am [even] poor in thanks—but I thank you, and sure, dear friends, my thanks are too dear a halfpenny. Were you not sent for? is it your   250
own inclining? is it a free visitation? Come, come, deal justly with me. Come, come—nay, speak.

GUIL.   What should we say, my lord?

---

220 **privates:** (1) intimate friends, (2) genitalia.

221 **strumpet.** A common epithet for Fortune, because she grants favors to all men.

229 **wards:** cells.

242 **bodies:** i.e. not shadows (since they lack ambition).   **outstrech'd:** i.e. with their ambition extended to the utmost (and hence producing stretched-out or elongated shadows).

243 **fay:** faith.

244 **wait upon you:** attend you thither.

245 **sort:** associate.

246 **dreadfully:** execrably.

250 **too . . . halfpenny:** too expensive priced at a halfpenny, i.e. not worth much.

251 **justly:** honestly.

HAM. Any thing but to th' purpose. You were sent for, and there is a kind of confession in your looks, which your modesties have not craft enough to color. 255
I know the good King and Queen have sent for you.

ROS. To what end, my lord?

HAM. That you must teach me. But let me conjure you, by the rights of our fellowship, by the consonancy of our youth, by the obligation of our ever-preserv'd love, and by what more dear a better proposer can charge you withal, be even and direct 260
with me, whether you were sent for or no!

ROS. *[Aside to* GUILDENSTERN.*]* What say you?

HAM. *[Aside.]* Nay then I have an eye of you!—If you love me, hold not off.

GUIL. My lord, we were sent for.

HAM. I will tell you why, so shall my anticipation prevent your discovery, and your 265
secrecy to the King and Queen moult no feather. I have of late—but wherefore I know not—lost all my mirth, forgone all custom of exercises; and indeed it goes so heavily with my disposition, that this goodly frame, the earth, seems to me a sterile promontory; this most excellent canopy, the air, look you, this brave o'erhanging firmament, this majestical roof fretted with golden fire, why, it appeareth 270
nothing to me but a foul and pestilent congregation of vapors. What [a] piece of work is a man, how noble in reason, how infinite in faculties, in form and moving, how express and admirable in action, how like an angel in apprehension, how like a god! the beauty of the world; the paragon of animals; and yet to me what is this quintessence of dust? Man delights not me—nor women neither, though by 275
your smiling you seem to say so.

ROS. My lord, there was no such stuff in my thoughts.

HAM. Why did ye laugh then, when I said, "Man delights not me"?

ROS. To think, my lord, if you delight not in man, what lenten entertainment the players shall receive from you. We coted them on the way, and hither are they 280
coming to offer you service.

HAM. He that plays the king shall be welcome—his Majesty shall have tribute on me, the adventerous knight shall use his foil and target, the lover shall not sigh

---

254 **but.** Ordinarily punctuated with a comma preceding, to give the sense "provided that it is"; but Q2 has no comma, and Hamlet may intend, or include, the sense "except."

255 **modesties:** sense of shame.

259 **consonancy . . . youth:** similarity of our ages.

260 **charge:** urge, adjure. **even:** frank, honest (cf. modern "level with me").

263 **of:** on.

265 **prevent your discovery:** forestall your disclosure (of what the King and Queen have said to you in confidence).

266 **moult no feather:** not be impaired in the least.

267 **custom of exercises:** my usual athletic activities.

269 **brave:** splendid.

270 **fretted:** ornamented as with fretwork.

271-72 **piece of work:** masterpiece.

273 **express:** exact.

275 **quintessence:** finest and purest extract.

279 **lenten entertainment:** meager reception.

280 **coted:** outstripped.

282 **on:** of, from.

283 **adventerous:** adventurous, i.e. wandering in search of adventure. **foil and target:** light fencing sword and small shield.

gratis, the humorous man shall end his part in peace, [the clown shall make those laugh whose lungs are [tickle] a' th' sere,] and the lady shall say her mind freely, or   285
the [blank] verse shall halt for't. What players are they?

ROS.   Even those you were wont to take such delight in, the tragedians of the city.

HAM.   How chances it they travel? Their residence, both in reputation and profit, was better both ways.

ROS.   I think their inhibition comes by the means of the late innovation.   290

HAM.   Do they hold the same estimation they did when I was in the city? Are they so follow'd?

ROS.   No indeed are they not.

[HAM.   *How comes it? do they grow rusty?*

ROS.   Nay, their endeavor keeps in the wonted pace; but there is, sir, an aery of   295 children, little eyases, that cry out on the top of question, and are most tyranni- cally clapp'd for't. These are now the fashion, and so [berattle] the common stages—so they call them—that many wearing rapiers are afraid of goose-quills and dare scarce come thither.

HAM.   What, are they children? Who maintains 'em? How are they escoted? Will   300 they pursue the quality no longer than they can sing? Will they not say afterwards, if they should grow themselves to common players (as it is [most like], if their means are [no] better), their writers do them wrong, to make them exclaim against their own succession?

---

²⁸⁴ **gratis:** without reward.   **humorous:** dominated by some eccentric trait (like the melancholy Jaques in *As You Like It*).

²⁸⁵ **tickle . . . sere:** i.e. easily made to laugh (literally, describing a gun that goes off easily; *sere* = a catch in the gunlock; *tickle* = easily affected, highly sensitive to stimulus).

²⁸⁶ **halt:** limp, come off lamely (the verse will not scan if she omits indecent words).

²⁹⁰ **inhibition:** hindrance (to playing in the city). The word could be used of an official prohibi- tion. See next note.   **innovation.** Shakespeare elsewhere uses this word of a political upris- ing or revolt, and line 290 is often explained as meaning that the company had been forbidden to play in the city as the result of some disturbance. It is commonly conjectured that the allusion is to the Essex rebellion of 1601, but it is known that Shakespeare's com- pany, though to some extent involved on account of the special performance of *Richard II* it was commissioned to give on the eve of the rising, was not in fact punished by inhibition. A second intepretation explains *innovation* as referring to the new theatrical vogue described in lines 295 ff., and conjectures that *inhibition* may allude to a Privy Council order of 1600 restricting the number of London playhouses to two and the number of performances to two a week.

²⁹⁴⁻³¹¹ **How . . . too.** This passage refers topically to the "War of the Theatres" between the child actors and their poet Jonson on the one side, and on the other the adults, with Dekker, Marston, and possibly Shakespeare as spokesmen, in 1600–1601.

²⁹⁵ **aery:** nest.

²⁹⁶ **eyases:** unfledged hawks.   **cry . . . question:** cry shrilly above others in controversy.   **tyr- annically:** outrageously.

²⁹⁷ **berattle:** cry down, satirize.   **common stages:** public theaters (the children played at the Blackfriars, a private theater).

²⁹⁸ **goose-quills:** pens (of satirical playwrights).

³⁰⁰ **escoted:** supported.

³⁰¹ **quality:** profession (of acting).   **no . . . sing:** i.e. only until their voices change.

³⁰⁴ **succession:** future.

ROS.   Faith, there has been much to do on both sides, and the nation holds it no sin   305
to tarre them to controversy. There was for a while no money bid for argument,
unless the poet and the player went to cuffs in the question.

HAM.   Is't possible?

GUIL.   O, there has been much throwing about of brains.

HAM.   Do the boys carry it away?   310

ROS.   Ay, that they do, my lord—Hercules and his load too.]

HAM.   It is not very strange, for my uncle is King of Denmark, and those that would
make mouths at him while my father liv'd, give twenty, forty, fifty, a hundred
ducats apiece for his picture in little. 'Sblood, there is something in this more than
natural, if philosophy could find it out.   315

A flourish [for the PLAYERS*]*.

GUIL.   There are the players.

HAM.   Gentlemen, you are welcome to Elsinore. Your hands, come then: th' appurtenance of welcome is fashion and ceremony. Let me comply with you in this
garb, [lest my] extent to the players, which, I tell you, must show fairly outwards,
should more appear like entertainment than yours. You are welcome; but my   320
uncle-father and aunt-mother are deceiv'd.

GUIL.   In what, my dear lord?

HAM.   I am but mad north-north-west. When the wind is southerly I know a hawk
from a hand-saw.

Enter POLONIUS.

POL.   Well be with you, gentlemen!   325

HAM. *[Aside to them.]*   Hark you, Guildenstern, and you too—at each ear a hearer
—that great baby you see there is not yet out of his swaddling-clouts.

ROS.   Happily he is the second time come to them, for they say an old man is twice
a child.

HAM.   I will prophesy, he comes to tell me of the players, mark it. *[Aloud.]* You say   330
right, sir, a' Monday morning, 'twas then indeed.

POL.   My lord, I have news to tell you.

---

[305] **to do:** ado
[306] **tarre:** incite.
[307] **argument:** plot of a play.   **in the question:** i.e. as part of the script.
[310] **carry it away:** win.
[311] **Hercules . . . too.** Hercules in the course of one of his twelve labors supported the world for
Atlas; the children do better, for they carry away the world and Hercules as well. There is an
allusion to the Globe playhouse, which reportedly had for its sign the figure of Hercules
upholding the world.
[313] **mouths:** derisive faces.
[314] **'Sblood:** by God's (Christ's) blood.
[318] **comply:** observe the formalities.
[319] **garb:** fashion, manner.   **my extent:** i.e. the degree of courtesy I show.
[320] **more . . . yours:** seem to be a warmer reception that I have given you.
[323-24] **hawk, hand-saw.** Both cutting tools; but also both birds, if *hand-saw* quibbles on *hern-
shaw,* "heron," a bird preyed upon by the hawk.
[327] **swaddling-clouts:** swaddling clothes.
[328] **Happily:** haply, perhaps.   **twice:** i.e. for the second time.

HAM. My lord, I have news to tell you. When Roscius was an actor in Rome—
POL. The actors are come hither, my lord.
HAM. Buzz, buzz! 335
POL. Upon my honor—
HAM. "Then came each actor on his ass"—
POL. The best actors in the world, either for tragedy, comedy, history, pastoral, pastoral-comical, historical-pastoral, [tragical-historical, tragical-comical-historical-pastoral,] scene individable, or poem unlimited; Seneca cannot be too heavy, nor 340 Plautus too light, for the law of writ and the liberty: these are the only men.
HAM. O Jephthah, judge of Israel, what a treasure hadst thou!
POL. What a treasure had he, my lord?
HAM. Why—

    "One fair daughter, and no more, 345
      The which he loved passing well."

POL. *[Aside.]* Still on my daughter.
HAM. Am I not i' th' right, old Jephthah?
POL. If you call me Jephthah, my lord, I have a daughter that I love passing well.
HAM. Nay, that follows not. 350
POL. What follows then, my lord?
HAM. Why—

    "As by lot, God wot,"

and then, you know,

    "It came to pass, as most like it was"— 355

the first row of the pious chanson will show you more, for look where my abridgment comes.

Enter the PLAYERS, *[four or five].*

You are welcome, masters, welcome all. I am glad to see thee well. Welcome, good friends. O, old friend! why, thy face is valanc'd since I saw thee last; com'st thou to beard me in Denmark? What, my young lady and mistress! by' lady, your ladyship 360 is nearer to heaven than when I saw you last, by the altitude of a chopine. Pray

---

³³³ **Roscius:** the most famous of Roman actors (died 62 B.C.). News about him would be stale news indeed.
³³⁵ **Buzz:** exclamation of impatience at someone who tells news already known.
³⁴⁰ **scene individable:** play observing the unity of place.   **poem unlimited:** play ignoring rules such as the three unities.   **Seneca:** Roman writer of tragedies.   **Plautus:** Roman writer of comedies.
³⁴¹ **for . . . liberty:** for strict observance of the rules, or for freedom from them (with possible allusion to the location of playhouses, which were not built in properties under city jurisdiction, but in the "liberties"—land once monastic and now outside the jurisdiction of the city authorities).   **only:** very best (a frequent use).
³⁴² **Jephthah . . . Israel:** title of a ballad, from which Hamlet goes on to quote. For the story of Jephthah and his daughter, see Judges 11.
³⁵⁶ **row:** stanza.   **chanson:** song, ballad.   **abridgment:** (1) interruption; (2) pastime.
³⁵⁹ **valanc'd:** fringed, i.e. bearded.
³⁶⁰ **beard:** confront boldly (with obvious pun).   **by' lady:** by Our Lady.
³⁶¹ **chopine:** thick-soled shoe.

God your voice, like a piece of uncurrent gold, be not crack'd within the ring. Masters, you are all welcome. We'll e'en to't like [French] falc'ners—fly at any thing we see; we'll have a speech straight. Come give us a taste of your quality, come, a passionate speech.   365

[1] PLAY. What speech, my good lord?

HAM. I heard thee speak me a speech once, but it was never acted, or if it was, not above once; for the play, I remember, pleas'd not the million, 'twas caviary to the general, but it was—as I receiv'd it, and others, whose judgments in such matters cried in the top of mine—an excellent play, well digested in the scenes, set down   370 with as much modesty as cunning. I remember one said there were sallets in the lines to make the matter savory, nor no matter in the phrase that might indict the author of affection, but call'd it an honest method, as wholesome as sweet, and by very much more handsome than fine. One speech in't I chiefly lov'd, 'twas Aeneas' [tale] to Dido, and thereabout of it especially when he speaks of Priam's   375 slaughter. If it live in your memory, begin at this line—let me see, let me see: "The rugged Pyrrhus, like th' Hyrcanian beast—" 'Tis not so, it begins with Pyrrhus: "The rugged Pyrrhus, he whose sable arms, Black as his purpose, did the night resemble   380 When he lay couched in th' ominous horse, Hath now this dread and black complexion smear'd With heraldy more dismal: head to foot Now is he total gules, horridly trick'd With blood of fathers, mothers, daughters, sons,   385 Bak'd and impasted with the parching streets, That lend a tyrannous and a damned light To their lord's murther. Roasted in wrath and fire, And thus o'er-sized with coagulate gore, With eyes like carbuncles, the hellish Pyrrhus   390

---

362 **crack'd . . . ring:** i.e. broken to the point where you can no longer play female roles. A coin with a crack extending far enough in from the edge to cross the circle surrounding the stamp of the sovereign's head was unacceptable in exchange (*uncurrent*).

364 **straight:** straightway. **quality:** professional skill.

368-69 **caviary . . . general:** caviar to the common people, i.e. too choice for the multitude.

370 **cried . . . of:** were louder than, i.e. carried more authority than.

371 **sallet:** salads, i.e. spicy jokes.

372 **savory:** zesty.

373 **affection:** affectation.

374 **fine:** showily dressed (in language).

375-76 **Priam's slaughter:** the slaying of Priam (at the fall of Troy).

377 **Pyrrhus:** another name for Neoptolemus, Achilles' son. **Hyrcanian beast.** Hyrcania in the Caucasus was notorious for its tigers.

379 **sable arms.** The Greeks within the Trojan horse had blackened their skin so as to be inconspicuous when they emerged at night.

383 **heraldy:** heraldry. **dismal:** ill-boding.

384 **gules:** red (heraldic term). **trick'd:** adorned.

386 **Bak'd:** caked. **impasted:** crusted. **with . . . streets:** i.e. by the heat from the burning streets.

389 **o'er-sized:** covered over as with a coat of sizing.

390 **carbuncles:** jewels believed to shine in the dark.

Old grandsire Priam seeks."
So proceed you.

POL. 'Fore God, my lord, well spoken, with good accent and good discretion.

[1] PLAY. "Anon he finds him
  Striking too short at Greeks. His antique sword,   395
  Rebellious to his arm, lies where it falls,
  Repugnant to command. Unequal match'd,
  Pyrrhus at Priam drives, in rage strikes wide,
  But with the whiff and wind of his fell sword
  Th' unnerved father falls. [Then senseless Ilium,]   400
  Seeming to feel this blow, with flaming top
  Stoops to his base, and with a hideous crash
  Takes prisoner Pyrrhus' ear; for lo his sword,
  Which was declining on the milky head
  Of reverent Priam, seem'd i' th' air to stick.   405
  So as a painted tyrant Pyrrhus stood
  [And,] like a neutral to his will and matter,
  Did nothing.
  But as we often see, against some storm,
  A silence in the heavens, the rack stand still,   410
  The bold winds speechless, and the orb below
  As hush as death, anon the dreadful thunder
  Doth rend the region; so after Pyrrhus' pause,
  A roused vengeance sets him new a-work,
  And never did the Cyclops' hammers fall   415
  On Mars's armor forg'd for proof eterne
  With less remorse than Pyrrhus' bleeding sword
  Now falls on Priam.
  Out, out, thou strumpet Fortune! All you gods,
  In general synod take away her power!   420
  Break all the spokes and [fellies] from her wheel,
  And bowl the round nave down the hill of heaven
  As low as to the fiends!"

POL. This is too long.

HAM. It shall to the barber's with your beard. Prithee say on, he's for a jig or a tale   425
of bawdry, or he sleeps. Say on, come to Hecuba.

---

[397] **Repugnant:** resistant, hostile.
[399] **fell:** cruel.
[400] **unnerved:** drained of strength. **senseless:** insensible. **Ilium:** the citadel of Troy.
[405] **reverent:** reverend, aged.
[407] **like . . . matter:** i.e. poised midway between intention and performance.
[409] **against:** just before.
[410] **rack:** cloud mass.
[413] **region:** i.e. air.
[415] **Cyclops:** giants who worked in Vulcan's smithy, where armor was made for the gods.
[416] **proof eterne:** eternal endurance.
[417] **remorse:** pity.
[421] **fellies:** rims.
[422] **nave:** hub.
[425] **jig:** song-and-dance entertainment performed after the main play.

[1] PLAY. "But who, ah woe, had seen the mobled queen"—
HAM. "The mobled queen"?
POL. That's good, ["[mobled] queen" is good].
[1] PLAY. "Run barefoot up and down, threat'ning the flames   430
  With bisson rheum, a clout upon that head
  Where late the diadem stood, and for a robe,
  About her lank and all o'er-teemed loins,
  A blanket, in the alarm of fear caught up—
  Who this had seen, with tongue in venom steep'd,   435
  'Gainst Fortune's state would treason have pronounc'd.
  But if the gods themselves did see her then,
  When she saw Pyrrhus make malicious sport
  In mincing with his sword her [husband's] limbs,
  The instant burst of clamor that she made,   440
  Unless things mortal move them not at all,
  Would have made milch the burning eyes of heaven,
  And passion in the gods."
POL. Look whe'er he has not turn'd his color and has tears in 's eyes. Prithee no
  more.   445
HAM. 'Tis well, I'll have thee speak out the rest of this soon. Good my lord, will you
  see the players well bestow'd? Do you hear, let them be well us'd, for they are the
  abstract and brief chronicles of the time. After your death you were better have a
  bad epitaph than their ill report while you live.
POL. My lord, I will use them according to their desert.   450
HAM. God's bodkin, man, much better: use every man after his desert, and who
  shall scape whipping? Use them after your own honor and dignity—the less they
  deserve, the more merit is in your bounty. Take them in.
POL. Come, sirs.

[Exit.]

HAM. Follow him, friends, we'll hear a play tomorrow.   455

[Exeunt all the PLAYERS *but the* FIRST.*]*

  Dost thou hear me, old friend? Can you play "The Murther of Gonzago"?
[1] PLAY. Ay, my lord.
HAM. We'll ha't to-morrow night. You could for need study a speech of some
  dozen lines, or sixteen lines, which I would set down and insert in't, could you
  not?   460
[1] PLAY. Ay, my lord.

427 **mobled:** muffled.
431 **bisson rheum:** blinding tears.   **clout:** cloth.
433 **o'er-teemed:** worn out by childbearing.
436 **state:** rule, government.
442 **milch:** moist (literally, milky).
443 **passion:** grief.
444 **Look . . . not:** i.e. note how he has.
447 **bestow'd:** lodged.   **us'd:** treated.
451 **God's bodkin:** by God's (Christ's) little body.
458 **for need:** if necessary.

HAM. Very well. Follow that lord, and look you mock him not. *[Exit* FIRST
      PLAYER.*]* My good friends, I'll leave you [till] night. You are welcome to Elsinore.
ROS. Good my lord!
HAM. Ay so, God buy to you.

Exeunt [ROSENCRANTZ *and* GUILDENSTERN].

465

                          Now I am alone.
O, what a rogue and peasant slave am I!
It is not monstrous that this player here,
But in a fiction, in a dream of passion,
Could force his soul so to his own conceit
That from her working all the visage wann'd,   470
Tears in his eyes, distraction in his aspect,
A broken voice, an' his whole function suiting
With forms to his conceit? And all for nothing,
For Hecuba!
What's Hecuba to him, or he to [Hecuba],   475
That he should weep for her? What would he do
Had he the motive and [the cue] for passion
That I have? He would drown the stage with tears,
And cleave the general ear with horrid speech,
Make mad the guilty, and appall the free,   480
Confound the ignorant, and amaze indeed
The very faculties of eyes and ears. Yet I,
A dull and muddy-mettled rascal, peak
Like John-a-dreams, unpregnant of my cause,
And can say nothing; no, not for a king,   485
Upon whose property and most dear life
A damn'd defeat was made. Am I a coward?
Who calls me villain, breaks my pate across,
Plucks off my beard and blows it in my face,
Tweaks me by the nose, gives me the lie i' th' throat   490
As deep as to the lungs? Who does me this?
Hah, 'swounds, I should take it; for it cannot be
But I am pigeon-liver'd, and lack gall
To make oppression bitter, or ere this
I should 'a' fatted all the region kites   495

---

469 **conceit:** imaginative conception.
472 **his whole function:** the operation of his whole body.
473 **forms:** actions, expressions.
480 **free:** innocent.
481 **amaze:** confound.
483 **muddy-mettled:** dull-spirited. **peak:** mope.
484 **John-a-dreams:** a sleepy fellow. **unpregnant of:** unquickened by.
487 **defeat:** destruction.
490–91 **gives . . . lungs:** calls me a liar in the extremest degree.
492 **'swounds:** by God's (Christ's) wounds. **should:** would certainly.
493 **am . . . gall:** i.e. am constitutionally incapable of resentment. That doves were mild because
     they had no gall was a popular belief.
495 **region kites:** kites of the air.

With this slave's offal. Bloody, bawdy villain!
Remorseless, treacherous, lecherous, kindless villain!
Why, what an ass am I! This is most brave,
That I, the son of a dear [father] murthered,
Prompted to my revenge by heaven and hell,   500
Must like a whore unpack my heart with words,
And fall a-cursing like a very drab,
A stallion. Fie upon't, foh!
About, my brains! Hum—I have heard
That guilty creatures sitting at a play   505
Have by the very cunning of the scene
Been strook so to the soul, that presently
They have proclaim'd their malefactions:
For murther, though it have no tongue, will speak
With most miraculous organ. I'll have these players   510
Play something like the murther of my father
Before mine uncle. I'll observe his looks,
I'll tent him to the quick. If 'a do blench,
I know my course. The spirit that I have seen
May be a [dev'l], and the [dev'l] hath power   515
T' assume a pleasing shape, yea, and perhaps,
Out of my weakness and my melancholy,
As he is very potent with such spirits,
Abuses me to damn me. I'll have grounds
More relative than this—the play's the thing   520
Wherein I'll catch the conscience of the King.

Exit.

ACT III

SCENE I.

Enter KING, QUEEN, POLONIUS, OPHELIA, ROSENCRANTZ, GUILDENSTERN, LORDS.

KING   An' can you by no drift of conference
Get from him why he puts on this confusion,
Grating so harshly all his days of quiet
With turbulent and dangerous lunacy?

---

496 **offal:** entrails.
497 **kindless:** unnatural.
503 **stallion:** male whore. Most editors adopt the Fl reading *scullion,* "kitchen menial."
504 **About:** to work.
507 **presently:** at once, then and there.
513 **tent:** probe.   **blench:** flinch.
518 **spirits:** states of temperament.
519 **Abuses:** deludes.
520 **relative:** closely related (to fact), i.e. conclusive.

III.i. Location: The castle.
¹ **An':** and.   **drift of conference:** leading on of conversation.

ROS.   He does confess he feels himself distracted,   5
   But from what cause 'a will by no means speak.
GUIL.   Nor do we find him forward to be sounded,
   But with a crafty madness keeps aloof
   When we would bring him on to some confession
   Of his true state.
QUEEN   Did he receive you well?   10
ROS.   Most like a gentleman.
GUIL.   But with much forcing of his disposition.
ROS.   Niggard of question, but of our demands
   Most free in his reply.
QUEEN   Did he assay him
   To any pastime?   15
ROS.   Madam, it so fell out that certain players
   We o'erraught on the way; of these we told him,
   And there did seem in him a kind of joy
   To hear of it. They are here about the court,
   And as I think, they have already order   20
   This night to play before him.
POL.   'Tis most true,
   And he beseech'd me to entreat your Majesties
   To hear and see the matter.
KING   With all my heart, and it doth much content me
   To hear him so inclin'd.   25
   Good gentlemen, give him a further edge,
   And drive his purpose into these delights.
ROS.   We shall, my lord.

Exeunt ROSENCRANTZ *and* GUILDENSTERN.

KING   Sweet Gertrude, leave us two,
   For we have closely sent for Hamlet hither,
   That he, as 'twere by accident, may here   30
   Affront Ophelia. Her father and myself,
   We'll so bestow ourselves that, seeing unseen,
   We may of their encounter frankly judge,
   And gather by him, as he is behav'd,
   If't be th' affliction of his love or no   35
   That thus he suffers for.

---

[7] **forward:** readily willing.   **sounded:** plumbed, probed.
[8] **crafty madness:** i.e. mad craftiness, the shrewdness that mad people sometimes exhibit.
[12] **disposition:** inclination.
[13] **question:** conversation.   **demands:** questions.
[14] **assay:** attempt to win.
[17] **o'erraught:** passed (literally, overreached).
[26] **edge:** stimulus.
[27] **into:** on to.
[29] **closely:** privately.
[31] **Affront:** meet.
[33] **frankly:** freely.

QUEEN   I shall obey you.
And for your part, Ophelia, I do wish
That your good beauties be the happy cause
Of Hamlet's wildness. So shall I hope your virtues
Will bring him to his wonted way again,   40
To both your honors.
OPH.   Madam, I wish it may.

[Exit QUEEN.*]*

POL.   Ophelia, walk you here.—Gracious, so please you,
We will bestow ourselves. *[To* OPHELIA.*]* Read on this book,
That show of such an exercise may color
Your [loneliness]. We are oft to blame in this—   45
'Tis too much prov'd—that with devotion's visage
And pious action we do sugar o'er
The devil himself.

KING   *[Aside.]*   O, 'tis too true!
How smart a lash that speech doth give my conscience!
The harlot's cheek, beautified with plast'ring art,   50
Is not more ugly to the thing that helps it
Than is my deed to my most painted word.
O heavy burthen!

POL.   I hear him coming. Withdraw, my lord.

[Exeunt KING *and* POLONIUS.*]*

Enter HAMLET.

HAM.   To be, or not to be, that is the question: 55
Whether 'tis nobler in the mind to suffer
The slings and arrows of outrageous fortune,
Or to take arms against a sea of troubles,
And by opposing, end them. To die, to sleep—
No more, and by a sleep to say we end   60
The heart-ache and the thousand natural shocks
That flesh is heir to; 'tis a consummation
Devoutly to be wish'd. To die, to sleep—
To sleep, perchance to dream—ay, there's the rub,
For in that sleep of death what dreams may come,   65
When we have shuffled off this mortal coil,
Must give us pause; there's the respect

---

[44] **exercise:** i.e. religious exercise (as the next sentence makes clear).
[44-45] **color Your loneliness:** make your solitude seem natural.
[46] **too much prov'd:** too often proved true.
[47] **action:** demeanor.
[51] **to . . . it:** in comparison with the paint that makes it look beautiful.
[56] **suffer:** submit to, endure patiently.
[62] **consummation:** completion, end.
[64] **rub:** obstacle (a term from the game of bowls).
[66] **shuffled off:** freed ourselves from.   **this mortal coil:** the turmoil of this mortal life.
[67] **respect:** consideration.

That makes calamity of so long life:
For who would bear the whips and scorns of time,
Th' oppressor's wrong, the proud man's contumely,   70
The pangs of despis'd love, the law's delay,
The insolence of office, and the spurns
That patient merit of th' unworthy takes,
When he himself might his quietus make
With a bare bodkin; who would fardels bear,   75
To grunt and sweat under a weary life,
But that the dread of something after death,
The undiscover'd country, from whose bourn
No traveller returns, puzzles the will,
And makes us rather bear those ills we have,   80
Than fly to others that we know not of?
Thus conscience does make cowards [of us all],
And thus the native hue of resolution
Is sicklied o'er with the pale cast of thought,
And enterprises of great pitch and moment   85
With this regard their currents turn awry,
And lose the name of action.—Soft you now,
The fair Ophelia. Nymph, in thy orisons
Be all my sins rememb'red.
OPH.   Good my lord,
How does your honor for this many a day?   90
HAM.   I humbly thank you, well, [well, well].
OPH.   My lord, I have remembrances of yours
That I have longed long to redeliver.
I pray you now receive them.
HAM.   No, not I,
I never gave you aught.   95
OPH.   My honor'd lord, you know right well you did,
And with them words of so sweet breath compos'd
As made these things more rich. Their perfume lost,
Take these again, for to the noble mind
Rich gifts wax poor when givers prove unkind.   100
There, my lord.

---

68 **of . . . life:** so long-lived.
69 **time:** the world.
74 **his quietus make:** write paid to his account.
75 **bare bodkin:** mere dagger.   **fardels:** burdens.
78 **undiscover'd:** not disclosed to knowledge; about which men have no information.   **bourn:** boundary, i.e. region.
79 **puzzles:** paralyzes.
82 **conscience:** reflection (but with some of the modern sense, too).
83 **native hue:** natural (ruddy) complexion.
84 **pale cast:** pallor.   **thought:** i.e. melancholy thought, brooding.
85 **pitch:** loftiness (a term from falconry, signifying the highest point of a hawk's flight).
88 **orisons:** prayers.

HAM.   Ha, ha! are you honest?

OPH.   My lord?

HAM.   Are you fair?

OPH.   What means your lordship?   105

HAM.   That if you be honest and fair, [your honesty] should admit no discourse to your beauty.

OPH.   Could beauty, my lord, have better commerce than with honesty?

HAM.   Ay, truly, for the power of beauty will sooner transform honesty from what it is to a bawd than the force of honesty can translate beauty into his likeness. This   110
was sometime a paradox, but now the time gives it proof. I did love you once.

OPH.   Indeed, my lord, you made me believe so.

HAM.   You should not have believ'd me, for virtue cannot so [inoculate] our old stock but we shall relish of it. I lov'd you not.

OPH.   I was the more deceiv'd.   115

HAM.   Get thee [to] a nunn'ry, why wouldst thou be a breeder of sinners? I am my- self indifferent honest, but yet I could accuse me of such things that it were better my mother had not borne me: I am very proud, revengeful, ambitious, with more offenses at my beck than I have thoughts to put them in, imagination to give them shape, or time to act them in. What should such fellows as I do crawling between   120
earth and heaven? We are arrant knaves, believe none of us. Go thy ways to a nunn'ry. Where's your father?

OPH.   At home, my lord.

HAM.   Let the doors be shut upon him, that he may play the fool no where but in 's own house. Farewell.   125

OPH.   O, help him, you sweet heavens!

HAM.   If thou dost marry, I'll give thee this plague for thy dowry: be thou as chaste as ice, as pure as snow, thou shalt not escape calumny. Get thee to a nunn'ry, fare- well. Or if thou wilt needs marry, marry a fool, for wise men know well enough what monsters you make of them. To a nunn'ry, go, and quickly too. Farewell.   130

OPH.   Heavenly powers, restore him!

HAM.   I have heard of your paintings, well enough. God hath given you one face, and you make yourselves another. You jig and amble, and you [lisp,] you nick- name God's creatures and make your wantonness [your] ignorance. Go to, I'll no more on't, it hath made me mad. I say we will have no moe marriage. Those that   135
are married already (all but one) shall live, the rest shall keep as they are. To a nunn'ry, go.

Exit.

---

[102] **honest:** chaste.

[111] **sometime:** formerly.   **paradox:** tenet contrary to accepted belief.

[113–14] **virtue . . . it:** virtue, engrafted on our old stock (of viciousness), cannot so change the na- ture of the plant that no trace of the original will remain.

[117] **indifferent honest:** tolerably virtuous.

[130] **monsters.** Alluding to the notion that the husbands of unfaithful wives grew horns.   **you:** you women.

[133–34] **You . . . creatures:** i.e. you walk and talk affectedly.

[134] **make . . . ignorance:** excuse your affectation as ignorance.

[135] **moe:** more.

OPH.   O, what a noble mind is here o'erthrown!
   The courtier's, soldier's, scholar's, eye, tongue, sword,
   Th' expectation and rose of the fair state,   140
   The glass of fashion and the mould of form,
   Th' observ'd of all observers, quite, quite down!
   And I, of ladies most deject and wretched.
   That suck'd the honey of his [music] vows,
   Now see [that] noble and most sovereign reason   145
   Like sweet bells jangled out of time, and harsh;
   That unmatch'd form and stature of blown youth
   Blasted with ecstasy. O, woe is me
   T' have seen what I have seen, see what I see!

[OPHELIA withdraws.]

Enter KING *and* POLONIUS.

KING   Love? his affections do not that way tend,   150
   Nor what he spake, though it lack'd form a little,
   Was not like madness. There's something in his soul
   O'er which his melancholy sits on brood,
   And I do doubt the hatch and the disclose
   Will be some danger; which for to prevent,   155
   I have in quick determination
   Thus set it down: he shall with speed to England
   For the demand of our neglected tribute.
   Haply the seas, and countries different,
   With variable objects, shall expel   160
   This something-settled matter in his heart,
   Whereon his brains still beating puts him thus
   From fashion of himself. What think you on't?
POL.   It shall do well; but yet do I believe
   The origin and commencement of his grief   165
   Sprung from neglected love. *[OPHELIA comes forward.]* How now, Ophelia?
   You need not tell us what Lord Hamlet said,
   We heard it all. My lord, do as you please,
   But if you hold it fit, after the play
   Let his queen-mother all alone entreat him   170
   To show his grief. Let her be round with him,
   And I'll be plac'd (so please you) in the ear

---

140 **expectation:** hope.   **rose:** ornament.   **fair.** Probably proleptic: "(the kingdom) made fair by his presence."
141 **glass:** mirror.   **mould of form:** pattern of (courtly) behavior.
142 **observ'd ... observers.** Shakespeare uses *observe* to mean not only "behold, mark attentively" but also "pay honor to."
147 **blown:** in full bloom.
148 **Blasted:** withered.   **ecstasy:** madness.
150 **affections:** inclinations, feelings.
154 **doubt:** fear.   **disclose.** Synonymous with *hatch;* see also V.i.231.
166 **neglected:** unrequited.
171 **his grief:** what is troubling him.   **round:** blunt, outspoken.

Of all their conference. If she find him not,
To England send him, or confine him where
Your wisdom best shall think.

KING   It shall be so.   175
Madness in great ones must not [unwatch'd] go.

Exeunt.

SCENE II.

Enter HAMLET *and three of the* PLAYERS.

HAM. Speak the speech, I pray you, as I pronounc'd it to you, trippingly on the
tongue, but if you mouth it, as many of our players do, I had as live the town-crier
spoke my lines. Nor do not saw the air too much with your hand, thus, but use all
gently, for in the very torrent, tempest, and, as I may say, whirlwind of your passion, you must acquire and beget a temperance that may give it smoothness. O, it   5
offends me to the soul to hear a robustious periwig-pated fellow tear a passion to
totters, to very rags, to spleet the ears of the groundlings, who for the most part are
capable of nothing but inexplicable dumb shows and noise. I would have such a
fellow whipt for o'erdoing Termagant, it out-Herods Herod, pray you avoid it.
[1] PLAY. I warrant your honor.   10
HAM. Be not too tame neither, but let your own discretion be your tutor. Suit the
action to the word, the word to the action, with this special observance, that you
o'erstep not the modesty of nature: for any thing so o'erdone is from the purpose
of playing, whose end, both at the first and now, was and is, to hold as 'twere the
mirror up to nature: to show virtue her feature, scorn her own image, and the very   15
age and body of the time his form and pressure. Now this overdone, or come tardy
off, though it makes the unskillful laugh, cannot but make the judicious grieve;
the censure of which one must in your allowance o'erweigh a whole theatre of
others. O, there be players that I have seen play—and heard others [praise], and
that highly—not to speak it profanely, that, neither having th' accent of Christians   20
nor the gait of Christian, pagan, nor man, have so strutted and bellow'd that I
have thought some of Nature's journeymen had made men, and not made them
well, they imitated humanity so abominably.

[173] **find him:** learn the truth about him.

III.ii. Location: The castle.
[2] **mouth:** pronounce with exaggerated distinctness or declamatory effect. **live:** lief, willingly.
[7] **totters:** tatters. **spleet:** split. **groundlings:** those who paid the lowest admission price and
stood on the ground in the "yard" or pit of the theater.
[8] **capable of:** able to take in.
[9] **Termagant:** a supposed god of the Saracens, whose role in medieval drama, like that of Herod,
was noisy and violent.
[13] **modesty:** moderation. **from:** contrary to.
[15] **scorn:** i.e. that which is worthy of scorn.
[16] **pressure:** impression (as of a seal), exact image. **tardy:** inadequately.
[17] **censure:** judgment.
[18] **which one:** (even) one of whom. **allowance:** estimation.
[20] **profanely:** irreverently.
[22-23]**some . . . abominably:** i.e. they were so unlike men that it seemed Nature had not made
them herself, but had delegated the task to mediocre assistants.

[1] PLAY.   I hope we have reform'd that indifferently with us, [sir].

HAM.   O, reform it altogether. And let those that play your clowns speak no more   25
than is set down for them, for there be of them that will themselves laugh to set on
some quantity of barren spectators to laugh too, though in the mean time some
necessary question of the play be then to be consider'd. That's villainous, and
shows a most pitiful ambition in the fool that uses it. Go make you ready.

[Exeunt PLAYERS.]

Enter POLONIUS, GUILDENSTERN, and ROSENCRANTZ.

How now, my lord? Will the King hear this piece of work?   30
POL.   And the Queen too, and that presently.
HAM.   Bid the players make haste.

[Exit POLONIUS.]

Will you two help to hasten them?
ROS.   Ay, my lord.

Exeunt they two.

HAM.   What ho, Horatio!   35

Enter HORATIO.

HOR.   Here sweet lord, at your service.
HAM.   Horatio, thou art e'en as just a man
As e'er my conversation cop'd withal.
HOR.   O my dear lord—
HAM.   Nay, do not think I flatter,
For what advancement may I hope from thee   40
That no revenue hast but thy good spirits
To feed and clothe thee? Why should the poor be flatter'd?
No, let the candied tongue lick absurd pomp,
And crook the pregnant hinges of the knee
Where thrift may follow fawning. Dost thou hear?   45
Since my dear soul was mistress of her choice
And could of men distinguish her election,
Sh' hath seal'd thee for herself, for thou hast been
As one in suff'ring all that suffers nothing,
A man that Fortune's buffets and rewards   50
Hast ta'en with equal thanks; and blest are those

---

²⁴ **indifferently:** pretty well.
²⁶ **of them:** some of them.
²⁹ **fool:** (1) stupid person; (2) actor playing a fool's role.
³⁰ **piece of work:** masterpiece (said jocularly).
³¹ **presently:** at once.
³⁷ **thou . . . man:** i.e. you come as close to being what a man should be (*just* = exact, precise).
³⁸ **my . . . withal:** my association with people has brought me into contact with.
⁴³ **candied:** sugared, i.e. flattering.   **absurd:** tasteless (Latin sense).
⁴⁴ **pregnant:** moving readily.
⁴⁵ **thrift:** thriving, profit.

Whose blood and judgment are so well co-meddled,
That they are not a pipe for Fortune's finger
To sound what stop she please. Give me that man
That is not passion's slave, and I will wear him   55
In my heart's core, ay, in my heart of heart,
As I do thee. Something too much of this.
There is a play to-night before the King,
One scene of it comes near the circumstance
Which I have told thee of my father's death.   60
I prithee, when thou seest that act afoot,
Even with the very comment of thy soul
Observe my uncle. If his occulted guilt
Do not itself unkennel in one speech,
It is a damned ghost that we have seen,   65
And my imaginations are as foul
As Vulcan's stithy. Give him heedful note,
For I mine eyes will rivet to his face.
And after we will both our judgments join
In censure of his seeming.
HOR.   Well, my lord.   70
If 'a steal aught the whilst this play is playing,
And scape [detecting], I will pay the theft.

[Sound a flourish. Danish march.] Enter Trumpets and Kettle-drums, KING, QUEEN,
POLONIUS, OPHELIA, [ROSENCRANTZ, GUILDENSTERN, *and other* LORDS *attendant,
with his* GUARD *carrying torches].*

HAM.   They are coming to the play. I must be idle;
  Get you a place.
KING   How fares our cousin Hamlet?   75
HAM.   Excellent, i' faith, of the chameleon's dish: I eat the air, promise-cramm'd—
  you cannot feed capons so.
KING   I have nothing with this answer, Hamlet, these words are not mine.
HAM.   No, nor mine now. *[To* POLONIUS.*]* My lord, you play'ed once i' th' univer-
  sity, you say?   80
POL.   That did I, my lord, and was accounted a good actor.
HAM.   What did you enact?

---

[52] **blood:** passions.   **co-meddled:** mixed, blended.
[56] **my heart of heart:** the heart of my heart.
[62] **very . . . soul:** your most intense critical observation.
[63] **occulted:** hidden.
[64] **unkennel:** bring into the open.
[65] **damned ghost:** evil spirit, devil.
[67] **stithy:** forge.
[70] **censure . . . seeming:** reaching a verdict on his behavior.
[73] **be idle:** act foolish, pretend to be crazy.
[75] **fares.** Hamlet takes up this word in another sense.
[76] **chameleon's dish.** Chameleons were thought to feed on air. Hamlet says that he subsists on
  an equally nourishing diet, the promise of succession. There is probably a pun on *air/heir.*
[78] **have nothing with:** do not understand.   **mine:** i.e. an answer to my question.

POL. I did enact Julius Caesar. I was kill'd i' th' Capitol; Brutus kill'd me.

HAM. It was a brute part of him to kill so capital a calf there. Be the players ready?

ROS. Ay, my lord, they stay upon your patience. 85

QUEEN Come hither, my dear Hamlet, sit by me.

HAM. No, good mother, here's metal more attractive.

[Lying down at OPHELIA's *feet.]*

POL. *[To the* KING.*]* O ho, do you mark that?

HAM. Lady, shall I lie in your lap?

OPH. No, my lord 90

[HAM. I mean, my head upon your lap?

OPH. Ay, my lord.]

HAM. Do you think I meant country matters?

OPH. I think nothing, my lord.

HAM. That's a fair thought to lie between maids' legs. 95

OPH. What is, my lord?

HAM. Nothing.

OPH. You are merry, my lord.

HAM. Who, I?

OPH. Ay, my lord. 100

HAM. O God, your only jig-maker. What should a man do but be merry, for look
you how cheerfully my mother looks, and my father died within 's two hours.

OPH. Nay, 'tis twice two months, my lord.

HAM. So long? Nay then let the dev'l wear black, for I'll have a suit of sables. O
heavens, die two months ago, and not forgotten yet? Then there's hope a great 105
man's memory may outlive his life half a year, but, by'r lady, 'a must build
churches then, or else shall 'a suffer not thinking on, with the hobby-horse, whose
epitaph is, "For O, for O, the hobby-horse is forgot."

The trumpets sound. Dumb show follows.
Enter a King and a Queen [very lovingly], the Queen embracing him and he her.
[She kneels and makes show of protestation unto him.] He takes her up and declines
his head upon her neck. He lies down upon a bank of flowers. She, seeing him asleep,
leaves him. Anon come in another man, takes off his crown, kisses it, pours poison in
the sleeper's ears and leaves him. The Queen returns, finds the King dead, makes
passionate action. The pois'ner with some three or four [mutes] come in again, seem
to condole with her. The dead body is carried away. The pois'ner woos the Queen
with gifts; she seems harsh [and unwilling] awhile, but in the end accepts love.
[Exeunt.]

84 **part:** action.
93 **country matters:** indecency.
101 **only:** very best. **jig-maker:** one who composed or played in the farcical song-and-dance
entertainments that followed plays.
102 **'s:** this.
104 **let . . . sables:** i.e. to the devil with my garments; after so long a time I am ready for the old
man's garb of sables (fine fur).
107 **not thinking on:** not being thought of, i.e. being forgotten.
108 **For . . . forgot:** line from a popular ballad lamenting puritanical suppression of such country
sports as the May-games, in which the hobby-horse, a character costumed to resemble a
horse, traditionally appeared.

OPH.   What means this, my lord?

HAM.   Marry, this' [miching] mallecho, it means mischief.   110

OPH.   Belike this show imports the argument of the play.

Enter PROLOGUE.

HAM.   We shall know by this fellow. The players cannot keep [counsel], they'll tell all.

OPH.   Will 'a tell us what this show meant?

HAM.   Ay, or any show that you will show him. Be not you asham'd to show, he'll   115
not shame to tell you what it means.

OPH.   You are naught, you are naught. I'll mark the play.

PRO.   For us, and for our tragedy,
   Here stooping to your clemency,
   We beg your hearing patiently.   120

[Exit.]

HAM.   Is this a prologue, or the posy of a ring?

OPH.   'Tis brief, my lord.

HAM.   As woman's love.

Enter [two PLAYERS,*]* KING *and* QUEEN.

[P.] KING   Full thirty times hath Phoebus' cart gone round
   Neptune's salt wash and Tellus' orbed ground.   125
   And thirty dozen moons with borrowed sheen
   About the world have times twelve thirties been,
   Since love our hearts and Hymen did our hands
   Unite comutual in most sacred bands.

[P.] QUEEN   So many journeys may the sun and moon   130
   Make us again count o'er ere love be done!
   But woe is me, you are so sick of late,
   So far from cheer and from [your] former state,
   That I distrust you. Yet though I distrust,
   Discomfort you, my lord, it nothing must,   135
   [For] women's fear and love hold quantity
   In neither aught, or in extremity.
   Now what my [love] is, proof hath made you know,

---

[110] **this' miching mallecho:** this is sneaking mischief.

[111] **argument:** subject, plot.

[112] **counsel:** secrets.

[114] **Be not you:** if you are not.

[116] **naught:** wicked.

[121] **posy . . . ring:** verse motto inscribed in a ring (necessarily short).

[124] **Phoebus' cart:** the sun-god's chariot.

[125] **Tellus:** goddess of the earth.

[128] **Hymen:** god of marriage.

[129] **bands:** bonds.

[134] **distrust:** fear for.

[136] **hold quantity:** are related in direct proportion.

[138] **proof:** experience.

And as my love is siz'd, my fear is so.
Where love is great, the littlest doubts are fear; 140
Where little fears grow great, great love grows there.
[P.] KING   Faith, I must leave thee, love, and shortly too;
My operant powers their functions leave to do,
And thou shalt live in this fair world behind,
Honor'd, belov'd, and haply one as kind 145
For husband shalt thou—
[P.] QUEEN   O, confound the rest!
Such love must needs be treason in my breast.
In second husband let me be accurs'd!
None wed the second but who kill'd the first.
HAM. *[Aside.]*   That's wormwood! 150
[P.] QUEEN   The instances that second marriage move
Are base respects of thrift, but none of love.
A second time I kill my husband dead,
When second husband kisses me in bed.
[P.] KING   I do believe you think what now you speak, 155
But what we do determine, oft we break.
Purpose is but the slave to memory,
Of violent birth, but poor validity,
Which now, the fruit unripe, sticks on the tree,
But fall unshaken when they mellow be. 160
Most necessary 'tis that we forget
To pay ourselves what ourselves is debt.
What to ourselves in passion we propose,
The passion ending, doth the purpose lose.
The violence of either grief or joy 165
Their own enactures with themselves destroy.
Where joy most reveals, grief doth most lament;
Grief [joys], joy grieves, on slender accident.
This world is not for aye, nor 'tis not strange
That even our loves should with our fortunes change: 170
For 'tis a question left us yet to prove,
Whether love lead fortune, or else fortune love.
The great man down, you mark his favorite flies,

---

143 **operant:** active, vital.   **leave to do:** cease to perform.
146 **confound the rest:** may destruction befall what you are about to speak of—a second marriage on my part.
151 **instances:** motives.   **move:** give rise to.
152 **respects of thrift:** considerations of advantage.
158 **validity:** strength, power to last.
161-62 **Most . . . debt:** i.e. such resolutions are debts we owe to ourselves, and it would be foolish to pay such debts.
163 **passion:** violent emotion.
165-66 **The violence . . . destroy:** i.e. both violent grief and violent joy fail of their intended acts because they destroy themselves by their very violence.
168 **slender accident:** slight occasion.

The poor advanc'd makes friends of enemies.
And hitherto doth love on fortune tend, 175
For who not needs shall never lack a friend,
And who in want a hollow friend doth try,
Directly seasons him his enemy.
But orderly to end where I begun,
Our wills and fates do so contrary run 180
That our devices still are overthrown,
Our thoughts are ours, their ends none of our own:
So think thou wilt no second husband wed,
But die thy thoughts when thy first lord is dead.

[P.] QUEEN   Nor earth to me give food, nor heaven light, 185
Sport and repose lock from me day and night,
To desperation turn my trust and hope,
[An] anchor's cheer in prison be my scope!
Each opposite that blanks the face of joy
Meet what I would have well and it destroy! 190
Both here and hence pursue me lasting strife,
If once I be a widow, ever I be a wife!

HAM.   If she should break it now!

[P.] KING   'Tis deeply sworn. Sweet, I leave me here a while,
My spirits grow dull, and fain I would beguile 195
The tedious day with sleep.

[Sleeps.]

[P.] QUEEN   Sleep rock thy brain,
And never come mischance between us twain!

Exit.

HAM.   Madam, how like you this play?

QUEEN   The lady doth protest too much, methinks.

HAM.   O but she'll keep her word. 200

KING   Have you heard the argument? is there no offense in't?

HAM.   No, no, they do but jest, poison in jest—no offense i' th' world.

KING   What do you call the play?

HAM.   "The Mouse-trap." Marry, how? tropically: this play is the image of a
murther done in Vienna; Gonzago is the duke's name, his wife, Baptista. You 205
shall see anon. 'Tis a knavish piece of work, but what of that? Your Majesty, and

---

178 **seasons:** ripens, converts into.
181 **devices:** devisings, intentions.   **still:** always.
188 **anchor's cheer:** hermit's fare.   **my scope:** the extent of my comforts.
189 **blanks:** blanches, makes pale (a symptom of grief).
201 **offense:** offensive matter (but Hamlet quibbles on the sense "crime").
202 **jest:** i.e. pretend.
204 **tropically:** figuratively (with play on *trapically*—which is the reading of Q1—and probably
with allusion to the children's saying *marry trap,* meaning "now you're caught").   **image:**
representation.

we that have free souls, it touches us not. Let the gall'd jade winch, our withers are unwrung.

Enter LUCIANUS.

This is one Lucianus, nephew to the king.

OPH.   You are as good as a chorus, my lord.   210

HAM.   I could interpret between you and your love, if I could see the puppets dallying.

OPH.   You are keen, my lord, you are keen.

HAM.   It would cost you a groaning to take off mine edge.

OPH.   Still better, and worse.   215

HAM.   So you mistake your husbands. Begin, murtherer, leave thy damnable faces and begin. Come, the croaking raven doth bellow for revenge.

LUC.   Thoughts black, hands apt, drugs fit, and time agreeing.
        [Confederate] season, else no creature seeing,
        Thou mixture rank, of midnight weeds collected,   220
        With Hecat's ban thrice blasted, thrice [infected],
        Thy natural magic and dire property
        On wholesome life usurps immediately.

[Pours the poison in his ears.]

HAM.   'A poisons him i' th' garden for his estate. His name's Gonzago, the story is extant, and written in very choice Italian. You shall see anon how the murtherer   225
        gets the love of Gonzago's wife.

OPH.   The King rises.

[HAM.   What frighted with false fire?]

QUEEN   How fares my lord?

POL.   Give o'er the play.   230

KING   Give me some light. Away!

POL.   Lights, lights, lights!

Exeunt all but HAMLET *and* HORATIO.

HAM.   "Why, let the strooken deer go weep,
                The hart ungalled play,

207 **free souls:** clear consciences. **gall'd jade:** chafed horse. **winch:** wince. **withers:** ridge between a horse's shoulders.
208 **unwrung:** not rubbed sore.
210 **chorus:** i.e. one who explains the forthcoming action.
211-12 **I . . . dallying:** I could speak the dialogue between you and your lover like a puppet-master (with an indecent jest).
213 **keen:** bitter, sharp.
215 **better, and worse:** i.e. more pointed and less decent.
216 **So:** i.e. "for better, for worse," in the words of the marriage service. **mistake:** i.e. mis-take, take wrongfully. Their vows, Hamlet suggests, prove false. **faces:** facial expressions.
217 **the croaking . . . revenge.** Misquoted from an old play, *The True Tragedy of Richard III.*
219 **Confederate season:** the time being my ally.
221 **Hecat's ban:** the curse of Hecate, goddess of witchcraft.
228 **false fire:** i.e. a blank cartridge.
233 **strooken:** struck, i.e. wounded.
234 **ungalled:** unwounded.

> For some must watch while some must sleep, 235
>> Thus runs the world away."

Would not this, sir, and a forest of feathers—if the rest of my fortunes turn Turk with me—with [two] Provincial roses on my raz'd shoes, get me a fellowship in a cry of players?

HOR. Half a share. 240

HAM. A whole one, I.

>> "For thou dost know, O Damon dear,
>>> This realm dismantled was
>>> Of Jove himself, and now reigns here
>>> A very, very"—pajock. 245

HOR. You might have rhym'd.

HAM. O good Horatio, I'll take the ghost's word for a thousand pound. Didst perceive?

HOR. Very well, my lord.

HAM. Upon the talk of the pois'ning? 250

HOR. I did very well note him.

HAM. Ah, ha! Come, some music! Come the recorders!
For if the King like not the comedy,
Why then belike he likes it not, perdy.
Come, some music! 255

Enter ROSENCRANTZ *and* GUILDENSTERN.

GUIL. Good my lord, voutsafe me a word with you.

HAM. Sir, a whole history.

GUIL. The King, sir—

HAM. Ay, sir, what of him?

GUIL. Is in his retirement marvellous distemp'red. 260

HAM. With drink, sir?

GUIL. No, my lord, with choler.

HAM. Your wisdom should show itself more richer to signify this to the doctor, for for me to put him to his purgation would perhaps plunge him into more choler.

GUIL. Good my lord, put your discourse into some frame, and [start] not so wildly 265
from my affair.

HAM. I am tame, sir. Pronounce.

GUIL. The Queen, your mother, in most great affliction of spirit, hath sent me to
you.

HAM. You are welcome. 270

---

235 **watch:** stay awake.

237 **feathers:** the plumes worn by tragic actors.   **turn Turk:** i.e. go to the bad.

238-39 **Provincial roses:** rosettes designed to look like a variety of French rose.   **raz'd:** with decorating slashing.   **fellowship:** partnership.   **cry:** company.

243 **dismantled:** divested, deprived.

245 **pajock:** peacock (substituting for the rhyme-word *ass*). The natural history of the time attributed many vicious qualities to the peacock.

254 **perdy:** assuredly (French *pardieu*, "by God").

262 **choler:** anger (but Hamlet willfully takes up the word in the sense "biliousness").

264 **put ... purgation:** i.e. prescribe for what's wrong with him.

265 **frame:** logical structure.

GUIL.   Nay, good my lord, this courtesy is not of the right breed. If it shall please you to make me a wholesome answer, I will do your mother's commandment; if not, your pardon and my return shall be the end of [my] business.

HAM.   Sir, I cannot.

ROS.   What, my lord?   275

HAM.   Make you a wholesome answer—my wit's diseas'd. But, sir, such answer as I can make; you shall command, or rather, as you say, my mother. Therefore no more, but to the matter: my mother, you say—

ROS.   Then thus she says: your behavior hath strook her into amazement and admiration.   280

HAM.   O wonderful son, that can so stonish a mother! But is there no sequel at the heels of this mother's admiration? Impart.

ROS.   She desires to speak with you in her closet ere you go to bed.

HAM.   We shall obey, were she ten times our mother. Have you any further trade with us?   285

ROS.   My lord, you once did love me.

HAM.   And do still, by these pickers and stealers.

ROS.   Good my lord, what is your cause of distemper? You do surely bar the door upon your own liberty if you deny your griefs to your friend.

HAM.   Sir, I lack advancement.   290

ROS.   How can that be, when you have the voice of the King himself for your succession in Denmark?

HAM.   Ay, sir, but "While the grass grows"—the proverb is something musty.

Enter the PLAYERS *with recorders.*

O, the recorders! Let me see one.—To withdraw with you—why do you go about to recover the wind of me, as if you would drive me into a toil?   295

GUIL.   O my lord, if my duty be too bold, my love is too unmannerly.

HAM.   I do not well understand that. Will you play upon this pipe?

GUIL.   My lord, I cannot.

HAM.   I pray you.

GUIL.   Believe me, I cannot.   300

HAM.   I do beseech you.

GUIL.   I know no touch of it, my lord.

HAM.   It is as easy as lying. Govern these ventages with your fingers and [thumbs], give it breath with your mouth, and it will discourse most eloquent music. Look you, these are the stops.   305

GUIL.   But these cannot I command to any utt'rance of harmony. I have not the skill.

---

272 **wholesome:** sensible, rational.
273 **pardon:** permission for departure.
279 **amazement and admiration:** bewilderment and wonder.
281 **stonish:** astound.
283 **closet:** private room.
287 **pickers and stealers:** hands; which, as the Catechism says, we must keep "from picking and stealing."
293 **proverb:** i.e. "While the grass grows, the steed starves."   **something musty:** somewhat stale.
295 **recover the wind:** get to windward.   **toil:** snare.
303 **ventages:** stops.

HAM. Why, look you now, how unworthy a thing you make of me! You would play
upon me, you would seem to know my stops, you would pluck out the heart of my
mystery, you would sound me from my lowest note to [the top of] my compass;   310
and there is much music, excellent voice, in this little organ, yet cannot you make
it speak. 'Sblood, do you think I am easier to be play'd on than a pipe? Call me
what instrument you will, though you fret me, [yet] you cannot play upon me.

Enter POLONIUS.

God bless you, sir.   315
POL. My lord, the Queen would speak with you, and presently.
HAM. Do you see yonder cloud that's almost in shape of a camel?
POL. By th' mass and 'tis, like a camel indeed.
HAM. Methinks it is like a weasel.
POL. It is back'd like a weasel.
HAM. Or like a whale.   320
POL. Very like a whale.
HAM. Then I will come to my mother by and by. *[Aside.]* They fool me to the top of
my bent.—I will come by and by.
[POL.] I will say so.

[Exit.]

HAM. "By and by" is easily said. Leave me, friends.   325

[Exeunt all but HAMLET.*]*

'Tis now the very witching time of night,
When churchyards yawn and hell itself [breathes] out
Contagion to this world. Now could I drink hot blood,
And do such [bitter business as the] day
Would quake to look on. Soft, now to my mother.   330
O heart, lose not thy nature! let not ever
The soul of Nero enter this firm bosom,
Let me be cruel, not unnatural;
I will speak [daggers] to her, but use none.
My tongue and soul in this be hypocrites—   335
How in my words somever she be shent,
To give them seals never my soul consent!

Exit.

---

³¹² **organ:** instrument.
³¹³ **fret:** (1) finger (an instrument); (2) vex.
³¹⁶ **presently:** at once.
³²²⁻²³ **They . . . bent:** they make me play the fool to the limit of my ability.
³²⁵ **by and by:** at once.
³²⁶ **witching:** i.e. when the powers of evil are at large.
³³¹ **nature:** natural affection, filial feeling.
³³² **Nero:** Murderer of his mother.
³³⁶ **shent:** rebuked.
³³⁷ **give them seals:** confirm them by deeds.

SCENE III.

Enter KING, ROSENCRANTZ, *and* GUILDENSTERN.

KING   I like him not, nor stands it safe with us
    To let his madness range. Therefore prepare you.
    I your commission will forthwith dispatch,
    And he to England shall along with you.
    The terms of our estate may not endure   5
    Hazard so near 's as doth hourly grow
    Out of his brows.
GUIL.   We will ourselves provide.
    Most holy and religious fear it is
    To keep those many many bodies safe
    That live and feed upon your Majesty.   10
ROS.   The single and peculiar life is bound
    With all the strength and armor of the mind
    To keep itself from noyance, but much more
    That spirit upon whose weal depends and rests
    The lives of many. The cess of majesty   15
    Dies not alone, but like a gulf doth draw
    What's near it with it. Or it is a massy wheel
    Fix'd on the summit of the highest mount,
    To whose [huge] spokes ten thousand lesser things
    Are mortis'd and adjoin'd, which when it falls,   20
    Each small annexment, petty consequence,
    Attends the boist'rous [ruin]. Never alone
    Did the King sigh, but [with] a general groan.
KING   Arm you, I pray you, to this speedy viage,
    For we will fetters put about this fear,   25
    Which now goes too free-footed.
ROS.   We will haste us.

Exeunt GENTLEMEN [ROSENCRANTZ *and* GUILDENSTERN].

Enter POLONIUS.

III.iii. Location: The castle.
¹ **him:** i.e. his state of mind, his behavior.
³ **dispatch:** have drawn up.
⁵ **terms:** conditions, nature.   **our estate:** my position (as king).
⁷ **his brows:** the madness visible in his face (?).
⁸ **fear:** concern.
¹¹ **single and peculiar:** individual and private.
¹³ **noyance:** injury.
¹⁵ **cess:** cessation, death.
¹⁶ **gulf:** whirlpool.
²⁰ **mortis'd:** fixed.
²² **Attends:** accompanies.   **ruin:** fall.
²⁴ **Arm:** prepare.   **viage:** voyage
²⁵ **fear:** object of fear.

POL. My lord, he's going to his mother's closet.
   Behind the arras I'll convey myself
   To hear the process. I'll warrant she'll tax him home,
   And as you said, and wisely was it said,   30
   'Tis meet that some more audience than a mother,
   Since nature makes them partial; should o'erhear
   The speech, of vantage. Fare you well, my liege,
   I'll call upon you ere you go to bed.
   And tell you what I know.
KING   Thanks, dear my lord.   35

Exit [POLONIUS].

   O, my offense is rank, it smells to heaven,
   It hath the primal eldest curse upon't,
   A brother's murther. Pray can I not,
   Though inclination be as sharp as will.
   My stronger guilt defeats my strong intent,   40
   And, like a man to double business bound,
   I stand in pause where I shall first begin,
   And both neglect. What if this cursed hand
   Were thicker than itself with brother's blood,
   Is there not rain enough in the sweet heavens   45
   To wash it white as snow? Whereto serves mercy
   But to confront the visage of offense?
   And what's in prayer but this twofold force,
   To be forestalled ere we come to fall,
   Or [pardon'd] being down? then I'll look up.   50
   My fault is past, but, O, what form of prayer
   Can serve my turn? "Forgive me my foul murther"?
   That cannot be, since I am still possess'd
   Of those effects for which I did the murther:
   My crown, mine own ambition, and my queen.   55
   May one be pardon'd and retain th' offense?
   In the corrupted currents of this world
   Offense's gilded hand may [shove] by justice,
   And oft 'tis seen the wicked prize itself
   Buys out the law, but 'tis not so above: 60

---

[29] **process:** course of the talk. **tax him home:** take him severely to task
[33] **of vantage:** from an advantageous position (?) or in addition(?).
[37] **primal eldest curse:** i.e. God's curse on Cain, who also slew his brother.
[39] **Though . . . will:** though my desire is as strong as my resolve to do so.
[41] **bound:** committed.
[43] **neglect:** omit.
[46–47] **Whereto . . . offense:** i.e. what function has mercy except when there has been sin.
[56] **th' offense:** i.e. the "effects" or fruits of the offense.
[57] **currents:** courses.
[58] **gilded:** i.e. bribing.
[59] **wicked prize:** rewards of vice.

There is no shuffling, there the action lies
In his true nature, and we ourselves compell'd,
Even to the teeth and forehead of our faults,
To give in evidence. What then? What rests?
Try what repentance can. What can it not?   65
Yet what can it, when one can not repent?
O wretched state! O bosom black as death!
O limed soul, that struggling to be free
Art more engag'd! Help, angels! Make assay,
Bow, stubborn knees, and heart, with strings of steel,   70
Be soft as sinews of the new-born babe!
All may be well.

[He kneels.]

Enter HAMLET.

HAM.   Now might I do it [pat], now 'a is a-praying;
And now I'll do't—and so 'a goes to heaven,
And so am I [reveng'd]. That would be scann'd: 75
A villain kills my father, and for that
I, his sole son, do this same villain send
To heaven.
Why, this is [hire and salary], not revenge.
'A took my father grossly, full of bread,   80
With all his crimes broad blown, as flush as May,
And how his audit stands who knows save heaven?
But in our circumstance and course of thought
'Tis heavy with him. And am I then revenged,
To take him in the purging of his soul,   85
When he is fit and season'd for his passage?
No!
Up, sword, and know thou a more horrid hent:
When he is drunk asleep, or in his rage,
Or in th' incestious pleasure of his bed,   90
At game a-swearing, or about some act
That has no relish of salvation in't—
Then trip him, that his heels may kick at heaven,

---

61 **shuffling:** evasion   **the action lies:** the charge comes for legal consideration.
63 **Even . . . forehead:** i.e. fully recognizing their features, extenuating nothing.
64 **rests:** remains.
68 **limed:** caught (as in birdlime, a sticky substance used for catching birds).
69 **engag'd:** entangled.
75 **would be scann'd:** must be carefully considered.
80 **grossly:** in a gross state; not spiritually prepared.
81 **crimes:** sins.   **broad blown:** in full bloom.   **flush:** lusty, vigorous.
82 **audit:** account.
83 **in . . . thought:** i.e. to the best of our knowledge and belief.
88 **Up:** into the sheath.   **know . . . hent:** be grasped at a more dreadful time.
92 **relish:** trace.

And that his soul may be as damn'd and black
As hell, whereto it goes. My mother stays,   95
This physic but prolongs thy sickly days.

Exit.

KING *[Rising.]*   My words fly up, my thoughts remain below:
Words without thoughts never to heaven go.

Exit.

SCENE IV.

Enter [QUEEN] GERTRUDE *and* POLONIUS.

POL.   'A will come straight. Look you lay home to him.
Tell him his pranks have been too broad to bear with,
And that your Grace hath screen'd and stood between
Much heat and him. I'll silence me even here;
Pray you be round [with him].   5
QUEEN   I'll [warr'nt] you, fear me not. Withdraw,
I hear him coming.

[POLONIUS hides behind the arras.]

Enter HAMLET.

HAM.   Now, mother, what's the matter?
QUEEN   Hamlet, thou hast thy father much offended.
HAM.   Mother, you have my father much offended.   10
QUEEN   Come, come, you answer with an idle tongue.
HAM.   Go, go, you question with a wicked tongue.
QUEEN   Why, how now, Hamlet?
HAM.   What's the matter now?
QUEEN   Have you forgot me?
HAM.   No, by the rood, not so:
You are the Queen, your husband's brother's wife,   15
And would it were not so, you are my mother.
QUEEN   Nay, then I'll set those to you that can speak.
HAM.   Come, come, and sit you down, you shall not boudge;
You go not till I set you up a glass
Where you may see the [inmost] part of you.   20
QUEEN   What wilt thou do? Thou wilt not murther me?
Help ho!

---

⁹⁶ **physic:** (attempted) remedy, i.e. prayer.

III.iv. Location: The Queen's closet in the castle.
¹ **lay . . . him:** reprove him severely.
² **broad:** unrestrained.
⁵ **round:** plain-spoken.
⁶ **fear me not:** have no fears about my handling of the situation.
¹¹ **idle:** foolish.
¹⁴ **rood:** cross.
¹⁸ **boudge:** budge.

POL. *[Behind.]* What ho, help!

HAM. *[Drawing.]* How now? A rat? Dead, for a ducat, dead!

[Kills POLONIUS through the arras.]

POL. *[Behind.]* O, I am slain.

QUEEN   O me, what hast thou done?   25

HAM. Nay, I know not, is it the King?

QUEEN O, what a rash and bloody deed is this!

HAM. A bloody deed! almost as bad, good mother,
As kill a king, and marry with his brother.

QUEEN As kill a king!

HAM.   Ay, lady, it was my word.   30

[Parts the arras and discovers POLONIUS.]

Thou wretched, rash, intruding fool, farewell!
I took thee for thy better. Take thy fortune;
Thou find'st to be too busy is some danger.—
Leave wringing of your hands. Peace, sit you down,
And let me wring your heart, for so I shall   35
If it be made of penetrable stuff,
If damned custom have not brass'd it so
That it be proof and bulwark against sense.

QUEEN What have I done, that thou dar'st wag thy tongue
In noise so rude against me?

HAM.   Such an act   40
That blurs the grace and blush of modesty,
Calls virtue hypocrite, takes off the rose
From the fair forehead of an innocent love
And sets a blister there, makes marriage vows
As false as dicers' oaths, O, such a deed   45
As from the body of contraction plucks
The very soul, and sweet religion makes
A rhapsody of words. Heaven's face does glow
O'er this solidity and compound mass
With heated visage, as against the doom;   50
Is thought-sick at the act.

QUEEN   Ay me, what act
That roars so loud and thunders in the index?

HAM. Look here upon this picture, and on this,

---

[24] **for a ducat:** I'll wager a ducat.

[33] **busy:** officious, meddlesome.

[37] **damned custom:** i.e. the habit of ill-doing. **brass'd:** hardened, literally, plated with brass.

[38] **proof:** armor. **sense:** feeling.

[44] **blister:** brand of shame.

[46] **contraction:** the making of contracts, i.e. the assuming of solemn obligation.

[47] **religion:** i.e. sacred vows.

[48] **rhapsody:** miscellaneous collection, jumble. **glow:** i.e. with anger.

[49] **this . . . mass:** i.e. the earth. *Compound* = compounded of the four elements.

[50] **as . . . doom:** as if for Judgment Day.

[52] **index:** i.e. table of contents. The index was formerly placed at the beginning of a book.

The counterfeit presentment of two brothers.
See what a grace was seated on this brow: 55
Hyperion's curls, the front of Jove himself,
An eye like Mars, to threaten and command,
A station like the herald Mercury
New lighted on a [heaven-]kissing hill,
A combination and a form indeed,   60
Where every god did seem to set his seal
To give the world assurance of a man.
This was your husband. Look you now what follows:
Here is your husband, like a mildewed ear,
Blasting his wholesome brother. Have you eyes?   65
Could you on this fair mountain leave to feed,
And batten on this moor? ha, have you eyes?
You cannot call it love, for at your age
The heyday in the blood is tame, it's humble,
And waits upon the judgment, and what judgment   70
Would step from this to this? Sense sure you have,
Else could you not have motion, but sure that sense
Is apoplex'd, for madness would not err,
Nor sense to ecstasy was ne'er so thrall'd
But it reserv'd some quantity of choice   75
To serve in such a difference. What devil was't
That thus hath cozen'd you at hoodman-blind?
Eyes without feeling, feeling without sight,
Ears without hands or eyes, smelling sans all,
Or but a sickly part of one true sense   80
Could not so mope. O shame, where is thy blush?
Rebellious hell,
If thou canst mutine in a matron's bones,
To flaming youth let virtue be as wax
And melt in her own fire. Proclaim no shame   85

⁵⁴ **counterfeit presentment:** painted likenesses.
⁵⁶ **Hyperion's:** the sun-god's. **front:** forehead.
⁵⁸ **station:** bearing.
⁶⁴ **ear:** i.e. of grain.
⁶⁷ **batten:** gorge.
⁶⁹ **heyday:** excitement.
⁷¹ **Sense:** sense perception, the five senses.
⁷³ **apoplex'd:** paralyzed.
^{73–76} **madness . . . difference:** i.e. madness itself could not go so far astray, nor were the senses
   ever so enslaved by lunacy that they did not retain the power to make so obvious a distinction.
⁷⁷ **cozen'd:** cheated. **hoodman-blind:** blindman's bluff.
⁷⁹ **sans:** without.
⁸¹ **mope:** be dazed.
⁸³ **mutine:** rebel.
^{85–88} **Proclaim . . . will:** do not call it sin when the hot blood of youth is responsible for lechery,
   since here we see people of calmer age on fire for it; and reason acts as procurer for desire,
   instead of restraining it. *Ardure* = ardor.

When the compulsive ardure gives the charge,
Since frost itself as actively doth burn,
And reason [panders] will.
QUEEN   O Hamlet, speak no more!
Thou turn'st my [eyes into my very] soul,
And there I see such black and [grained] spots   90
As will [not] leave their tinct.
HAM.   Nay, but to live
In the rank sweat of an enseamed bed,
Stew'd in corruption, honeying and making love
Over the nasty sty!
QUEEN   O, speak to me no more!
These words like daggers enter in my ears.   95
No more, sweet Hamlet!
HAM.   A murtherer and a villain!
A slave that is not twentith part the [tithe]
Of your precedent lord, a Vice of kings,
A cutpurse of the empire and the rule,
That from a shelf the precious diadem stole,   100
And put it in his pocket—
QUEEN   No more!

Enter GHOST *[in his night-gown].*

HAM.   A king of shreds and patches—
Save me, and hover o'er me with your wings,
You heavenly guards! What would your gracious figure!
QUEEN   Alas, he's mad!   105
HAM.   Do you not come your tardy son to chide,
That, laps'd in time and passion, lets go by
Th' important acting of your dread command?
O, say!
GHOST   Do not forget! This visitation   110
Is but to whet thy almost blunted purpose.
But look, amazement on thy mother sits,
O, step between her and her fighting soul.

---

90 **grained:** fast-dyed, indelible.
91 **leave their tinct:** lose their color.
92 **enseamed:** greasy.
97 **twentith:** twentieth.
98 **precedent:** former.   **Vice:** buffoon (like the Vice of the morality plays).
101 s.d. **night-gown:** dressing gown.
102 **of . . . patches:** clownish (alluding to the motley worn by jesters) (?) or patched up, beggarly (?).
107 **laps'd . . . passion:** "having suffered time to slip and passion to cool" (Johnson)
108 **important:** urgent.
112 **amazement:** utter bewilderment.

Conceit in weakest bodies strongest works,
Speak to her, Hamlet.
HAM.   How is it with you, lady?   115
QUEEN   Alas, how is't with you.
That you do bend your eye on vacancy,
And with th' incorporal air do hold discourse?
Forth at your eyes your spirits wildly peep,
And as the sleeping soldiers in th' alarm,   120
Your embedded hair, like life in excrements,
Start up and stand an end. O gentle son,
Upon the heat and flame of thy distemper
Sprinkle cool patience. Whereon do you look?
HAM.   On him, on him! look you how pale he glares!   125
His form and cause conjoin'd, preaching to stones,
Would make them capable.—Do not look upon me,
Lest with this piteous action you convert
My stern effects, then what I have to do
Will want true color—tears perchance for blood.   130
QUEEN   To whom do you speak this?
HAM.   Do you see nothing there?
QUEEN   Nothing at all, yet all that is I see.
HAM.   Nor did you nothing hear?
QUEEN   No, nothing but ourselves.
HAM.   Why, look you there, look how it steals away!
My father, in his habit as he lived!   135
Look where he goes, even now, out at the portal!

Exit GHOST.

QUEEN   This is the very coinage of your brain,
This bodiless creation ecstasy
Is very cunning in.
HAM.   [Ecstasy?]
My pulse as yours doth temperately keep time,   140
And makes as healthful music. It is not madness
That I have utt'red. Bring me to the test,
And [I] the matter will reword, which madness

---

114 **Conceit:** imagination.
120 **in th' alarm:** when the call to arms is sounded.
121 **excrements:** outgrowths; here, hair (also used of nails).
122 **an end:** on end.
124 **patience:** self-control.
126 **His . . . cause:** his appearance and what he has to say.
127 **capable:** sensitive, receptive.
128 **convert:** alter.
129 **effects:** (purposed) actions.
130 **want true color:** lack its proper appearance.
135 **habit:** dress.
138 **ecstasy:** madness.

Would gambol from. Mother, for love of grace,
Lay not that flattering unction to your soul,   145
That not your trespass but my madness speaks;
It will but skin and film the ulcerous place,
Whiles rank corruption, mining all within,
Infects unseen. Confess yourself to heaven,
Repent what's past, avoid what is to come,   150
And do not spread the compost on the weeds
To make them ranker. Forgive me this my virtue,
For in the fatness of these pursy times
Virtue itself of vice must pardon beg,
Yea, curb and woo for leave to do him good.   155
QUEEN   O Hamlet, thou hast cleft my heart in twain.
HAM.   O, throw away the worser part of it,
And [live] the purer with the other half.
Good night, but go not to my uncle's bed—
Assume a virtue, if you have it not.   160
That monster custom, who all sense doth eat,
Of habits devil, is angel yet in this,
That to the use of actions fair and good
He likewise gives a frock or livery
That aptly is put on. Refrain [to-]night,   165
And that shall lend a kind of easiness
To the next abstinence, the next more easy;
For use almost can change the stamp of nature,
And either [. . . .] the devil or throw him out
With wondrous potency. Once more good night,   170
And when you are desirous to be blest,
I'll blessing beg of you. For this same lord,

[Pointing to POLONIUS.*]*

I do repent; but heaven hath pleas'd it so
To punish me with this, and this with me,
That I must be their scourge and minister.   175

---

[144] **gambol:** start, jerk away.

[145] **flattering unction:** soothing ointment.

[151] **compost:** manure.

[153] **pursy:** puffy, out of condition.

[155] **curb and woo:** bow and entreat.

[161] **all . . . eat:** wears away all natural feeling.

[162] **Of habits devil:** i.e. though it acts like a devil in establishing bad habits. Most editors read (in lines 161–62) *eat / Of habits evil,* following Theobald.

[164-65] **frock . . . on:** i.e. a "habit" or customary garment, readily put on without need of any decision.

[168] **use:** habit.

[169] A word seems to be wanting after *either.*

[171] **desirous . . . blest:** i.e. repentant.

[175] **scourge and minister:** the agent of heavenly justice against human crime. *Scourge* suggests a permissive cruelty (Tamburlaine was the "scourge of God"), but "woe to him by whom the offense cometh"; the scourge must suffer for the evil it performs.

I will bestow him, and will answer well
The death I gave him. So again good night.
I must be cruel only to be kind.
This bad begins and worse remains behind.
On word more, good lady.   180
QUEEN   What shall I do?
HAM.   Not this, by no means, that I bid you do:
Let the bloat king tempt you again to bed,
Pinch wanton on your cheek, call you his mouse,
And let him, for a pair of reechy kisses,
Or paddling in your neck with his damn'd fingers,   185
Make you to ravel all this matter out,
That I essentially am not in madness,
But mad in craft. 'Twere good you let him know,
For who that's but a queen, fair, sober, wise,
Would from a paddock, from a bar, a gib,   190
Such dear concernings hide? Who would do so?
No, in despite of sense and secrecy,
Unpeg the basket on the house's top,
Let the birds fly, and like the famous ape,
To try conclusions in the basket creep,   195
And break your own neck down.
QUEEN   Be thou assur'd, if words be made of breath,
And breath of life, I have no life to breathe
What thou hast said to me.
HAM.   I must to England, you know that?
QUEEN   Alack,   200
I had forgot. 'Tis so concluded on.
HAM.   There's letters seal'd, and my two schoolfellows,
Whom I trust as I will adders fang'd,
They bear the mandate, they must sweep my way
And marshal me to knavery. Let it work,   205
For 'tis the sport to have the enginer
Hoist with his own petar, an't shall go hard
But I will delve one yard below their mines,
And blow them at the moon. O, 'tis most sweet

---

[176] **bestow:** dispose of.   **answer:** answer for.
[179] **behind:** to come.
[184] **reechy:** filthy.
[190] **paddock:** toad.   **gib:** tomcat.
[191] **dear concernings:** matters of intense concern.
[193] **Unpeg the basket:** open the door of the cage.
[194] **famous ape.** The actual story has been lost.
[195] **conclusions:** experiments (to see whether he too can fly if he enters the cage and then leaps out).
[196] **down:** by the fall.
[205] **knavery:** some knavish scheme against me.
[206] **enginer:** deviser of military "engines" or contrivances.
[207] **Hoist with:** blown up by.   **petar:** petard, bomb.

When in one line two crafts directly meet.   210
This man shall set me packing;
I'll lug the guts into the neighbor room.
Mother, good night indeed. This counsellor
Is now most still, most secret, and most grave,
Who was in life a foolish prating knave.   215
Come sir, to draw toward an end with you.
Good night, mother.

Exeunt [severally, HAMLET *tugging in* POLONIUS].

ACT IV

SCENE I.

Enter KING *and* QUEEN *with* ROSENCRANTZ *and* GUILDENSTERN.

KING   There's matter in these sighs, these profound heaves—
    You must translate, 'tis fit we understand them.
    Where is your son?
QUEEN   Bestow this place on us a little while.

[Exeunt ROSENCRANTZ *and* GUILDENSTERN.*]*

    Ah, mine own lord, what have I seen to-night!   5
KING   What, Gertrude? How does Hamlet?
QUEEN   Mad as the sea and wind when both contend
    Which is the mightier. In his lawless fit,
    Behind the arras hearing something stir,
    Whips out his rapier, cries, "A rat, a rat!"   10
    And in this brainish apprehension kills
    The unseen good old man.
KING   O heavy deed!
    It had been so with us had we been there.
    His liberty is full of threats to all,
    To you yourself, to us, to every one.
    Alas, how shall this bloody deed be answer'd?   15
    It will be laid to us, whose providence
    Should have kept short, restrain'd, and out of haunt
    This mad young man; but so much was our love,
    We would not understand what was most fit,   20
    But like the owner of a foul disease,

---

[210] **crafts:** plots.
[211] **packing:** (1) taking on a load; (2) leaving in a hurry.
[216] **draw . . . end:** finish my conversation.

IV.i. Location: The castle.
[11] **brainish apprehension:** crazy notion.
[16] **answer'd:** i.e. satisfactorily accounted for to the public.
[17] **providence:** foresight.
[18] **short:** on a short leash. **out of haunt:** away from other people.

To keep it from divulging, let it feed
Even on the pith of life. Where is he gone?
QUEEN   To draw apart the body he hath kill'd,
O'er whom his very madness, like some ore   25
Among a mineral of metals base,
Shows itself pure: 'a weeps for what is done.
KING   O Gertrude, come away!
The sun no sooner shall the mountains touch,
But we will ship him hence, and this vile deed   30
We must with all our majesty and skill
Both countenance and excuse. Ho, Guildenstern!

Enter ROSENCRANTZ *and* GUILDENSTERN.

Friends both, go join you with some further aid:
Hamlet in madness hath Polonius slain,
And from his mother's closet hath he dragg'd him.   35
Go seek him out, speak fair, and bring the body
Into the chapel. I pray you haste in this.

[Exeunt ROSENCRANTZ *and* GUILDENSTERN.*]*

Come, Gertrude, we'll call up our wisest friends
And let them know both what we mean to do
And what's untimely done, [. . . .]   40
Whose whisper o'er the world's diameter,
As level as the cannon to his blank,
Transports his pois'ned shot, may miss our name,
And hit the woundless air. O, come away!
My soul is full of discord and dismay.

Exeunt.

SCENE II.

Enter HAMLET.

HAM.   Safely stow'd.
[GENTLEMEN *(Within.)*   Hamlet! Lord Hamlet!]
[HAM.]   But soft, what noise? Who calls on Hamlet?
O, here they come.

Enter ROSENCRANTZ *and* [GUILDENSTERN].

ROS.   What have you done, my lord, with the dead body?   5

---

²² **divulging:** being revealed.
²⁵ **ore:** vein of gold.
²⁶ **mineral:** mine.
⁴⁰ Some words are wanting at the end of the line. Capell's conjecture, *so, haply, slander,* probably indicates the intended sense of the passage.
⁴² **As level:** with aim as good.   **blank:** target.
⁴⁴ **woundless:** incapable of being hurt.

IV.ii. Location: The castle.

HAM. [Compounded] it with dust, whereto 'tis kin.

ROS. Tell us where 'tis, that we may take it thence,
And bear it to the chapel.

HAM. Do not believe it.

ROS. Believe what? 10

HAM. That I can keep your counsel and not mine own. Besides, to be demanded of a spunge, what replication should be made by the son of a king?

ROS. Take you me for a spunge, my lord?

HAM. Ay, sir, that soaks up the King's countenance, his rewards, his authorities. But such officers do the King best service in the end: he keeps them, like [an ape] 15 an apple, in the corner of his jaw, first mouth'd, to be last swallow'd. When he needs what you have glean'd, it is but squeezing you, and, spunge, you shall be dry again.

ROS. I understand you not, my lord.

HAM. I am glad of it, a knavish speech sleeps in a foolish ear. 20

ROS. My lord, you must tell us where the body is, and go with us to the King.

HAM. The body is with the King, but the King is not with the body. The King is a thing—

GUIL. A thing, my lord?

HAM. Of nothing, bring me to him. [Hide fox, and all after.] 25

Exeunt.

SCENE III.

Enter KING *and two or three.*

KING I have sent to seek him, and to find the body.
How dangerous is it that this man goes loose!
Yet must not we put the strong law on him.
He's lov'd of the distracted multitude,
Who like not in their judgment, but their eyes, 5
And where 'tis so, th' offender's scourge is weigh'd,
But never the offense. To bear all smooth and even,
This sudden sending him away must seem
Deliberate pause. Diseases desperate grown

---

11 **demanded of:** questioned by.

12 **spunge:** sponge. **replication:** reply.

14 **countenance:** favor.

20 **sleeps:** is meaningless.

21-22 **The body . . . the body.** Possibly alluding to the legal fiction that the king's dignity is separate from his mortal body.

25 **Of nothing:** of no account. Cf. "Man is like a thing of nought, his time passeth away like a shadow" (Psalm 144:4 in the Prayer Book version). "Hamlet at once insults the King and hints that his days are numbered" (Dover Wilson). **Hide . . . after.** Probably a cry in some game resembling hide-and-seek.

IV.iii. Location: The castle
4 **distracted:** unstable.
6 **scourge:** i.e. punishment.
7 **bear:** manage.
8-9 **must . . . pause:** i.e. must be represented as a maturely considered decision.

By desperate appliance are reliev'd,   10
Or not at all.

Enter ROSENCRANTZ.

                    How now, what hath befall'n?
ROS.   Where the dead body is bestow'd, my lord,
   We cannot get from him.
KING   But where is he?
ROS.   Without, my lord, guarded, to know your pleasure.
KING   Bring him before us.
ROS.   Ho, bring in the Lord.   15

They [HAMLET *and* GUILDENSTERN] *enter.*

KING   Now, Hamlet, where's Polonius?
HAM.   At supper.
KING   At supper? where?
HAM.   Not where he eats, but where 'a is eaten; a certain convocation of politic
   worms are e'en at him. Your worm is your only emperor for diet: we fat all crea- 20
   tures else to fat us, and we fat ourselves for maggots; your fat king and your lean
   beggar is but variable service, two dishes, but to one table—that's the end.
KING   Alas, alas!
HAM.   A man may fish with the worm that hath eat of a king, and eat of the fish that
   hath fed of that worm.   25
KING   What dost thou mean by this?
HAM.   Nothing but to show you how a king may go a progress through the guts of a
   beggar.
KING   Where is Polonius?
HAM.   In heaven, send thither to see; if your messenger find him not there, seek   30
   him i' th' other place yourself. But if indeed you find him not within this month,
   you shall nose him as you go up the stairs into the lobby.
KING *[To* ATTENDANTS.*]*   Go seek him there.
HAM.   'A will stay till you come.

[Exeunt ATTENDANTS.*]*

KING   Hamlet, this deed, for thine especial safety—   35
   Which we do tender, as we dearly grieve
   For that which thou hast done—must send thee hence
   [With fiery quickness]; therefore prepare thyself,
   The bark is ready, and the wind at help,
   Th' associates tend, and every thing is bent   40
   For England.
HAM.   For England.

---

[19] **politic:** crafty, prying; "such worms as might breed in a politician's corpse" (Dowden).
[20] **e'en:** even now.   **for diet:** with respect to what it eats.
[22] **variable service:** different courses of a meal.
[27] **progress:** royal journey of state.
[36] **tender:** regard with tenderness, hold dear.   **dearly:** with intense feeling.
[39] **at help:** favorable.
[40] **Th':** thy.   **tend:** await.   **bent:** made ready.

KING   Ay, Hamlet.

HAM.   Good.

KING   So is it, if thou knew'st our purposes.

HAM.   I see a cherub that sees them. But come, for England! Farewell, dear mother.

KING   Thy loving father, Hamlet.

HAM.   My mother: father and mother is man and wife, man and wife is one flesh—   45
so, my mother. Come, for England!

Exit.

KING   Follow him at foot, tempt him with speed aboard.
       Delay it not, I'll have him hence to-night.
       Away, for every thing is seal'd and done
       That else leans on th' affair. Pray you make haste.   50

[Exeunt ROSENCRANTZ *and* GUILDENSTERN.*]*

       And, England, if my love thou hold'st at aught—
       As my great power thereof may give thee sense,
       Since yet thy cicatrice looks raw and red
       After the Danish sword, and thy free awe
       Pays homage to us—thou mayst not coldly set   55
       Our sovereign process, which imports at full,
       By letters congruing to that effect,
       The present death of Hamlet, Do it, England,
       For like the hectic in my blood he rages,
       And thou must cure me. Till I know 'tis done,   60
       How e'er my haps, my joys [were] ne'er [begun].

Exit.

SCENE IV.

Enter FORTINBRAS *with his army over the stage.*

FORT.   Go, captain, from me greet the Danish king.
        Tell him that by his license Fortinbras
        Craves the conveyance of a promis'd march

---

⁴³ **I . . . them:** i.e. heaven sees them.

⁴⁷ **at foot:** at his heels, close behind.

⁵⁰ **leans on:** relates to.

⁵¹ **England:** King of England.

⁵³ **cicatrice:** scar.

⁵⁴⁻⁵⁵ **thy . . . Pays:** your fear makes you pay voluntarily.

⁵⁵ **coldly set:** undervalue, disregard.

⁵⁶ **process:** command.

⁵⁷ **congruing to:** in accord with.

⁵⁸ **present:** immediate.

⁵⁹ **hectic:** continuous fever.

⁶¹ **haps:** fortunes.

IV.iv. Location: The Danish coast, near the castle.

³ **conveyance of:** escort for.

Over his kingdom. You know the rendezvous.
If that his Majesty would aught with us,
We shall express our duty in his eye,
And let him know so.
CAP.   I will do't my lord.
FORT.   Go softly on.

[Exeunt all but the CAPTAIN.*]*

Enter HAMLET, ROSENCRANTZ, [GUILDENSTERN,] *etc.*

HAM.   Good sir, whose powers are these?
CAP.   They are of Norway, sir.
HAM.   How purpos'd, sir, I pray you?
CAP.   Against some part of Poland.
HAM.   Who commands them, sir?
CAP.   The nephew to old Norway, Fortinbras.
HAM.   Goes it against the man of Poland, sir,
Or for some frontier?
CAP.   Truly to speak, and with no addition,
We go to gain a little patch of ground
That hath in it no profit but the name.
To pay five ducats, five, I would not farm it;
Nor will it yield to Norway or the Pole
A ranker rate, should it be sold in fee.
HAM.   Why then the Polack never will defend it.
CAP.   Yes, it is already garrison'd.
HAM.   Two thousand souls and twenty thousand ducats
Will not debate the question of this straw.
This is th' imposthume of much wealth and peace,
That inward breaks, and shows no cause without
Why the man dies. I humbly thank you, sir.
CAP.   God buy you, sir.

[Exit.]

ROS.   Will't please you go, my lord?
HAM.   I'll be with you straight—go a little before.

Exeunt all but HAMLET.*]*

How all occasions do inform against me,
And spur my dull revenge! What is a man,

---

⁶ **eye:** presence.
⁸ **softly:** slowly.
⁹ **powers:** forces.
¹⁵ **main:** main territory.
²⁰ **To pay:** i.e. for an annual rent of.   **farm:** lease.
²² **ranker:** higher.   **in fee:** outright.
²⁶ **Will not debate:** i.e. will scarcely be enough to fight out.
²⁷ **imposthume:** abscess.
³² **inform against:** denounce, accuse.

If his chief good and market of his time
Be but to sleep and feed? a beast, no more.   35
Sure He that made us with such large discourse,
Looking before and after, gave us not
That capability and godlike reason
To fust in us unus'd. Now whether it be
Bestial oblivion, or some craven scruple   40
Of thinking too precisely on th' event—
A thought which quarter'd hath but one part wisdom
And ever three parts coward—I do not know
Why yet I live to say, "This thing's to do,"
Sith I have cause, and will, and strength, and means   45
To do't. Examples gross as earth exhort me:
Witness this army of such mass and charge,
Led by a delicate and tender prince,
Whose spirit with divine ambition puff'd
Makes mouths at the invisible event,   50
Exposing what is mortal and unsure
To all that fortune, death, and danger dare,
Even for an egg-shell. Rightly to be great
Is not to stir without great argument,
But greatly to find quarrel in a straw   55
When honor's at the stake. How stand I then,
That have a father kill'd, a mother stain'd,
Excitements of my reason and my blood,
And let all sleep, while to my shame I see
The imminent death of twenty thousand men,   60
That for a fantasy and trick of fame
Go to their graves like beds, fight for a plot
Whereon the numbers cannot try the cause,
Which is not tomb enough and continent
To hide the slain? O, from this time forth,   65
My thoughts be bloody, or be nothing worth!

Exit.

³⁴ **market:** purchase, profit.
³⁶ **discourse:** reasoning power.
³⁹ **fust:** grow mouldy.
⁴⁰ **oblivion:** forgetfulness.
⁴¹ **event:** outcome.
⁴⁶ **gross:** large, obvious.
⁴⁷ **mass and charge:** size and expense.
⁵⁰ **Makes mouths at:** treats scornfully.   **invisible:** i.e. unforeseeable.
⁵⁴ **Is not to:** i.e. is *not* not to.   **argument:** cause.
⁵⁵ **greatly:** nobly.
⁵⁸ **Excitements of:** urgings by.
⁶¹ **fantasy:** caprice.   **trick:** trifle.
⁶³ **Whereon . . . cause:** which isn't large enough to let the opposing armies engage upon it.
⁶⁴ **continent:** container.

Scene V.

Enter HORATIO, [QUEEN] GERTRUDE, *and a* GENTLEMAN.

QUEEN I will not speak with her.
GENT. She is importunate, indeed distract.
  Her mood will needs be pitied.
QUEEN   What would she have?
GENT. She speaks much of her father, says she hears
  There's tricks i' th' world, and hems, and beats her heart,   5
  Spurns enviously at straws, speaks things in doubt
  That carry but half sense. Her speech is nothing,
  Yet the unshaped use of it doth move
  The hearers to collection; they yawn at it,
  And botch the words up fit to their own thoughts,   10
  Which as her winks and nods and gestures yield them,
  Indeed would make one think there might be thought,
  Though nothing sure, yet much unhappily.
HOR. 'Twere good she were spoken with, for she may strew
  Dangerous conjectures in ill-breeding minds.   15
[QUEEN] Let her come in.

[Exit GENTLEMAN.*]*

  [Aside.] To my sick soul, as sin's true nature is,
  Each toy seems prologue to some great amiss,
  So full of artless jealousy is guilt,
  It spills itself in fearing to be spilt.   20

Enter OPHELIA *[distracted, with her hair down, playing on a lute].*

OPH. Where is the beauteous majesty of Denmark?
QUEEN How now, Ophelia?
OPH. *(She sings)*

        "How should I your true-love know
          From another one?

IV.v. Location: The castle.
⁶ **Spurns . . . straws:** spitefully takes offense at trifles. **in doubt:** obscurely.
⁷ **Her speech:** what she says.
⁸ **unshaped use:** distracted manner.
⁹ **collection:** attempts to gather the meaning. **yawn at:** strive, as if openmouthed, to grasp (?).
  Most editors adopt the Fl reading *aim at.*
¹⁰ **botch:** patch.
¹¹ **Which:** i.e. the words.
¹² **thought:** inferred, conjectured.
¹⁵ **ill-breeding:** conceiving ill thoughts, prone to think the worst.
¹⁸ **toy:** trifle. **amiss:** calamity.
¹⁹ **artless jealousy:** uncontrolled suspicion.
²⁰ **spills:** destroys.
₂₃⁻²⁴ These lines resemble a passage in an earlier ballad beginning "As you came from the holy
  land / Of Walsingham." Probably all the song fragments sung by Ophelia were familiar to
  the Globe audience, but only one other line (178) is from a ballad still extant.

    By his cockle hat and staff,   25
    And his sandal shoon."
QUEEN Alas, sweet lady, what imports this song?
OPH. Say you? Nay, pray you mark.

Song.

    "He is dead and gone, lady,
     He is dead and gone,   30
    At his head a grass-green turf,
     At his heels a stone."

 O ho!
QUEEN Nay, but, Ophelia—
OPH. Pray you mark.   35

[Sings.]

    "White his shroud as the mountain snow"—

Enter KING.

QUEEN Alas, look here, my lord.
OPH.

Song.

    "Larded all with sweet flowers,
    Which bewept to the ground did not go
     With true-love showers."   40

KING How do you, pretty lady?
OPH. Well, God dild you! They say the owl was a baker's daughter. Lord, we know what we are, but know not what we may be. God be at your table!
KING Conceit upon her father.
OPH. Pray let's have no words of this, but when they ask you what it means, say 45
you this:

Song.

    "To-morrow is Saint Valentine's day
     All in the morning betime,
    And I a maid at your window,
     To be your Valentine.

    "Then up he rose and donn'd his clo'es,   50
     And dupp'd the chamber-door,

---

[25] **cockle hat:** hat bearing a cockle shell, the badge of a pilgrim to the shrine of St. James of Compostela in Spain. **staff.** Another mark of a pilgrim.

[26] **shoon:** shoes (already an archaic form in Shakespeare's day).

[38] **Larded:** adorned.

[39] **not.** Contrary to the expected sense, and unmetrical: explained as Ophelia's alteration of the line to accord with the facts of Polonius' burial (see line 80).

[42] **dild:** yield, reward. **owl.** Alluding to the legend of a baker's daughter whom Jesus turned into an owl because she did not respond generously to his request for bread.

[44] **Conceit:** fanciful brooding.

[51] **dupp'd:** opened.

Let in the maid, that out a maid
Never departed more."

KING   Pretty Ophelia!
OPH.   Indeed without an oath I'll make an end on't.   55

[Sings.]

"By Gis, and by Saint Charity,
    Alack, and fie for shame!
Young men will do't if they come to't,
    By Cock, they are to blame.

"Quoth she, 'Before you tumbled me,   60
    You promis'd me to wed.'"

(He answers.)

"'So would I 'a' done, by yonder sun,
    And thou hadst not come to my bed.'"

KING   How long hath she been thus?   65
OPH.   I hope all will be well. We must be patient, but I cannot choose but weep to
think they would lay him i' th' cold ground. My brother shall know of it, and so I
thank you for your good counsel. Come, my coach! Good night, ladies, good
night. Sweet ladies, good night, good night.

[Exit.]

KING   Follow her close, give her good watch, I pray you.   70

[Exit HORATIO.]

O, this the poison of deep grief, it springs
All from her father's death—and now behold!
O Gertrude, Gertrude,
When sorrows come, they come not single spies,
But in battalions: first, her father slain;   75
Next, your son gone, and he most violent author
Of his own just remove; the people muddied,
Thick and unwholesome in [their] thoughts and whispers
For good Polonius' death; and we have done but greenly
In hugger-mugger to inter him; poor Ophelia   80
Divided from herself and her fair judgment,
Without the which we are pictures, or mere beasts;
Last, and as much containing as all these,
Her brother is in secret come from France,

---

⁵⁶ **Gis:** contraction of *Jesus.*
⁵⁹ **Cock:** corruption of *God.*
⁶⁴ **And:** if.
⁷⁴ **spies:** i.e. soldiers sent ahead of the main force to reconnoiter, scouts.
⁷⁷ **muddied:** confused.
⁷⁹ **greenly:** unwisely.
⁸⁰ **In hugger-mugger:** secretly and hastily.

Feeds on this wonder, keeps himself in clouds,   85
And wants not buzzers to infect his ear
With pestilent speeches of his father's death,
Wherein necessity, of matter beggar'd,
Will nothing stick our person to arraign
In ear and ear, O my dear Gertrude, this,   90
Like to a murd'ring-piece, in many places
Gives me superfluous death.

A noise within.

[QUEEN   Alack, what noise is this?]
KING Attend!
    Where is my Swissers? Let them guard the door.

Enter a MESSENGER.

    What is the matter?
MESS.   Save yourself, my lord!   95
    The ocean, overpeering of his list,
    Eats not the flats with more impiteous haste
    Than young Laertes, in a riotous head,
    O'erbears your officers. The rabble call him lord,
    And as the world were now but to begin,   100
    Antiquity forgot, custom not known,
    The ratifiers and props of every word,
    [They] cry, "Choose we, Laertes shall be king!"
    Caps, hands, and tongues applaud it to the clouds,
    "Laertes shall be king, Laertes king!"   105

A noise within.

QUEEN How cheerfully on the false trail they cry!
    O, this is counter, you false Danish dogs!

Enter LAERTES *with others.*

KING The doors are broke.
LAER. Where is this king? Sirs, stand you all without.
ALL No, let's come in.
LAER.   I pray you give me leave.   110
ALL We will, we will.

---

⁸⁵ **in clouds:** i.e. in cloudy surmise and suspicion (rather than the light of fact).
⁸⁶ **wants:** lacks. **buzzers:** whispering informers.
⁸⁸ **of matter beggar'd:** destitute of facts.
⁸⁹ **nothing . . . arraign:** scruple not at all to charge me with the crime.
⁹¹ **murd'ring-piece:** cannon firing a scattering charge.
⁹⁴ **Swissers:** Swiss guards.
⁹⁶ **overpeering . . . list:** rising higher than its shores.
⁹⁸ **in . . . head:** with a rebellious force.
¹⁰⁰ **as:** as if.
¹⁰² **word:** pledge, promise.
¹⁰⁷ **counter:** on the wrong scent (literally, following the scent backward).

LAER. I thank you, keep the door. *[Exeunt* LAERTES' *followers.]* O thou vile king,
   Give me my father!
QUEEN   Calmly, good Laertes.
LAER. That drop of blood that's calm proclaims me bastard,
   Cries cuckold to my father, brands the harlot   115
   Even here between the chaste unsmirched brow
   Of my true mother.
KING   What is the cause, Laertes,
   That thy rebellion looks so giant-like?
   Let him go, Gertrude, do not fear our person:
   There's such divinity doth hedge a king   120
   That treason can but peep to what it would,
   Acts little of his will. Tell me, Laertes,
   Why thou art thus incens'd. Let him go, Gertrude.
   Speak, man.
LAER. Where is my father?
KING   Dead.
QUEEN   But not by him.   125
KING   Let him demand his fill.
LAER. How came he dead? I'll not be juggled with.
   To hell, allegiance! vows, to the blackest devil!
   Conscience and grace, to the profoundest pit!
   I dare damnation. To this point I stand,   130
   That both the worlds I give to negligence,
   Let come what comes, only I'll be reveng'd
   Most throughly for my father.
KING   Who shall stay you?
LAER. My will, not all the world's:
   And for my means, I'll husband them so well,   135
   They shall go far with little.
KING   Good Laertes,
   If you desire to know the certainty
   Of your dear father, is't writ in your revenge
   That, swoopstake, you will draw both friend and foe,
   Winner and loser?   140
LAER. None but his enemies.
KING   Will you know them then?
LAER. To his good friends thus wide I'll ope my arms,
   And like the kind life-rend'ring pelican,
   Repast them with my blood.

---

[119] **fear:** fear for.
[121] **would:** i.e. would like to do.
[131] **both . . . negligence:** i.e. I don't care what the consequences are in this world or in the next.
[133] **throughly:** thoroughly.
[134] **world's:** i.e. world's will.
[139] **swoopstake:** sweeping up everything without discrimination (modern *sweepstake).*
[143] **pelican.** The female pelican was believed to draw blood from her own breast to nourish her young.

KING   Why, now you speak
  Like a good child and true gentleman.   145
  That I am guiltless of your father's death,
  And am most sensibly in grief for it,
  It shall as level to your judgment 'pear
  As day does to your eyes.

A noise within.

                              "Let her come in!"
LAER.   How now, what noise is that?   150

Enter OPHELIA.

  O heat, dry up my brains! tears seven times salt
  Burn out the sense and virtue of mine eye!
  By heaven, thy madness shall be paid with weight
  [Till] our scale turn the beam. O rose of May!
  Dear maid, kind sister, sweet Ophelia!   155
  O heavens, is't possible a young maid's wits
  Should be as mortal as [an old] man's life?
  [Nature is fine in love, and where 'tis fine,
  It sends some precious instance of itself
  After the thing it loves.]   160
OPH.

Song.

            "They bore him barefac'd on the bier,
              [Hey non nonny, nonny, hey nonny,]
            And in his grave rain'd many a tear"—

  Fare you well, my dove!
LAER.   Hadst thou thy wits and didst persuade revenge,   165
  It could not move thus.
OPH.   You must sing, "A-down, a-down," and you call him a-down-a. O how the
  wheel becomes it! It is the false steward, that stole his master's daughter.
LAER.   This nothing's more than matter.
OPH.   There's rosemary, that's for remembrance; pray you, love, remember. And   170
  there is pansies, that's for thoughts.
LAER.   A document in madness, thoughts and remembrance fitted.

---

¹⁴⁵ **good child:** faithful son.
¹⁴⁷ **sensibly:** feelingly.
¹⁴⁸ **level:** plain.
¹⁵² **virtue:** faculty.
¹⁵⁸ **fine in:** refined or spiritualized by.
¹⁵⁹ **instance:** proof, token. So delicate is Ophelia's love for her father that her sanity has pursued
  him into the grave.
¹⁶⁵ **persuade:** argue logically for.
¹⁶⁷ **and ... a-down-a:** "if he indeed agrees that Polonius is 'a-down,' i.e. fallen low" (Dover
  Wilson). **wheel:** refrain (?) or spinning wheel, at which women sang ballads(?).
¹⁶⁹ **matter:** lucid speech.
¹⁷² **A document in madness:** a lesson contained in mad talk.

OPH. *[To* CLAUDIUS.*]* There's fennel for you, and columbines. *[To* GERTRUDE.*]*
There's rue for you, and here's some for me; we may call it herb of grace a' Sundays. You may wear your rue with a difference. There's a daisy. I would give you   175
some violets, but they wither'd all when my father died. They say 'a made a good
end—

[Sings.]

             "For bonny sweet Robin is all my joy."

LAER.   Thought and afflictions, passion, hell itself,
  She turns to favor and to prettiness.   180
OPH.

Song.

        "And will 'a not come again?
        And will 'a not come again?
          No, no, he is dead,
          Go to thy death-bed,
        He never will come again.   185

        "His beard was as white as snow,
        [All] flaxen was his pole,
          He is gone, he is gone,
          And we cast away moan,
        God 'a' mercy on his soul!"   190

And of all Christians' souls, [I pray God]. God buy you.

[Exit.]

LAER.   Do you [see] this, O God?
KING   Laertes, I must commune with your grief,
  Or you deny me right. Go but apart,
  Make choice of whom your wisest friends you will,   195
  And they shall hear and judge 'twixt you and me.
  If by direct or by collateral hand
  They find us touch'd, we will our kingdom give,
  Our crown, our life, and all that we call ours,
  To you in satisfaction; but if not,   200
  Be you content to lend your patience to us,

---

[173] **fennel, columbines.** Symbols respectively of flattery and ingratitude.
[174] **rue.** Symbolic of sorrow and repentance.
[175] **with a difference:** i.e. to represent a different cause of sorrow. *Difference* is a term from heraldry, meaning a variation in a coat of arms made to distinguish different members of a family. **daisy, violets.** Symbolic respectively of dissembling and faithfulness. It is not clear who
are the recipients of these.
[179] **Thought:** melancholy.
[180] **favor:** grace, charm.
[187] **flaxen:** white. **pole:** poll, head.
[197] **collateral:** i.e. indirect.
[198] **touch'd:** guilty.

And we shall joinly labor with your soul
To give it due content.
LAER.   Let this be so.
His means of death, his obscure funeral—
No trophy, sword, nor hatchment o'er his bones,   205
No noble rite nor formal ostentation—
Cry to be heard, as 'twere from heaven to earth,
That I must call't in question.
KING   So you shall,
And where th' offense is, let the great axe fall.
I pray you go with me.   210

Exeunt.

SCENE VI.

Enter HORATIO *and others.*

HOR.   What are they that would speak with me?
GENTLEMAN   Sea-faring men, sir. They say they have letters for you.
HOR.   Let them come in.

[Exit GENTLEMAN.*]*

I do not know from what part of the world
I should be greeted, if not from Lord Hamlet.   5

Enter SAILORS.

[1] SAIL.   God bless you, sir.
HOR.   Let him bless thee too.
[1] SAIL.   'A shall, sir, and ['t] please him. There's a letter for you, sir—it came from
th' embassador that was bound for England—if your name be Horatio, as I am let
to know it is.   10
HOR. *[Reads.]* "Horatio, when thou shalt have overlook'd this, give these fellows
some means to the King, they have letters for him. Ere we were two days old at
sea, a pirate of very warlike appointment gave us chase. Finding ourselves too
slow of sail, we put on a compell'd valor, and in the grapple I boarded them. On
the instant they got clear of our ship, so I alone became their prisoner. They have   15
dealt with me like thieves of mercy, but they knew what they did: I am to do a
[good] turn for them. Let the King have the letters I have sent, and repair thou to
me with as much speed as thou wouldest fly death. I have words to speak in thine
ear will make thee dumb, yet are they much too light for the [bore] of the matter.
These good fellows will bring thee where I am. Rosencrantz and Guildenstern   20
hold their course for England, of them I have much to tell thee. Farewell.

---

205 **trophy:** memorial.   **hatchment:** heraldic memorial tablet.
206 **formal ostentation:** fitting and customary ceremony.
208 **That:** so that.

IV.iv. Location: The castle.
16 **thieves of mercy:** merciful thieves.
19 **bore:** caliber, size (gunnery term).

[He] that thou knowest thine,
                                        Hamlet."
Come, I will [give] you way for these your letters,
And do't the speedier that you may direct me   25
To him from whom you brought them.

Exeunt.

SCENE VII.

Enter KING *and* LAERTES.

KING   Now must your conscience my acquittance seal,
        And you must put me in your heart for friend,
        Sith you have heard, and with a knowing ear,
        That he which hath your noble father slain
        Pursued my life.

LAER.   It well appears. But tell me   5
        Why you [proceeded] not against these feats
        So criminal and so capital in nature,
        As by your safety, greatness, wisdom, all things else
        You mainly were stirr'd up.

KING   O, for two special reasons,
        Which may to you perhaps seem much unsinow'd,   10
        But yet to me th' are strong. The Queen his mother
        Lives almost by his looks, and for myself—
        My virtue or my plague, be it either which—
        She is so [conjunctive] to my life and soul,
        That, as the star moves not but in his sphere,   15
        I could not but by her. The other motive,
        Why to a public count I might not go,
        Is the great love the general gender bear him,
        Who, dipping all his faults in their affection,
        Work like the spring that turneth wood to stone,   20
        Convert his gyves to graces, so that my arrows,
        Too slightly timber'd for so [loud a wind],
        Would have reverted to my bow again,
        But not where I have aim'd then.

IV.vii. Location: The castle.
[1] **my acquittance seal:** ratify my acquittal, i.e. acknowledge my innocence in Polonius' death.
[6] **feats:** acts.
[8] **safety:** i.e. regard for your own safety.
[9] **mainly:** powerfully.
[10] **unsinow'd:** unsinewed, i.e. weak.
[13] **either which:** one or the other.
[14] **conjunctive:** closely joined.
[15] **in his sphere:** by the movement of the sphere in which it is fixed (as the Ptolemaic astronomy taught).
[17] **count:** reckoning.
[18] **the general gender:** everybody.
[21] **gyves:** fetters.

LAER.   And so have I a noble father lost,   25
   A sister driven into desp'rate terms,
   Whose worth, if praises may go back again,
   Stood challenger on mount of all the age
   For her perfections—but my revenge will come.
KING   Break not your sleeps for that. You must not think   30
   That we are made of stuff so flat and dull
   That we can let our beard be shook with danger
   And think it pastime. You shortly shall hear more.
   I lov'd your father, and we love ourself,
   And that, I hope, will teach you to imagine—   35

Enter a MESSENGER *with letters.*

   [How now? What news?
MESS.   Letters, my lord, from Hamlet:]
   These to your Majesty, this to the Queen.
KING   From Hamlet? Who brought them?
MESS.   Sailors, my lord, they say, I saw them not.
   They were given me by Claudio. He receiv'd them   40
   Of him that brought them.
KING   Laertes, you shall hear them.
   —Leave us.

[Exit MESSENGER.*]*

[Reads.]

   "High and mighty, You shall know I am set naked on your kingdom. To-morrow
   shall I beg leave to see your kingly eyes, when I shall, first asking you pardon there-
   unto, recount the occasion of my sudden [and more strange] return.   45
            [Hamlet.]"
   What should this mean? Are all the rest come back?
   Or is it some abuse, and no such thing?
LAER.   Know you the hand?
KING   'Tis Hamlet's character. "Naked"!
   And in a postscript here he says "alone."   50
   Can you devise me?
LAER.   I am lost in it, my lord. But let him come,
   It warms the very sickness in my heart

---

²⁶ **terms:** condition.

²⁷ **go back again:** i.e. refer to what she was before she went mad.

²⁸ **on mount:** preeminent.

³⁰ **for that:** i.e. for fear of losing your revenge.

³¹ **flat:** spiritless.

³² **let . . . shook.** To ruffle or tweak a man's beard was an act of insolent defiance that he could
   not disregard without loss of honor. Cf. II.ii. 489. **with:** by.

⁴³ **naked:** destitute.

⁴⁴ **pardon thereunto:** permission to do so.

⁴⁸ **abuse:** deceit.

⁴⁹ **character:** handwriting.

⁵¹ **devise me:** explain it to me.

That I [shall] live and tell him to his teeth,
"Thus didst thou."
KING   If it be so, Laertes—   55
As how should it be so? how otherwise?—
Will you be rul'd by me?
LAER.   Ay, my lord,
So you will not o'errule me to a peace.
KING   To thine own peace. If he be now returned
As [checking] at his voyage, and that he means   60
No more to undertake it, I will work him
To an exploit, now ripe in my device,
Under the which he shall not choose but fall;
And for his death no wind of blame shall breathe,
But even his mother shall uncharge the practice,   65
And call it accident.
LAER.   My lord, I will be rul'd,
The rather if you could devise it so
That I might be the organ.
KING   It falls right.
You have been talk'd of since your travel much,
And that in Hamlet's hearing, for a quality   70
Wherein they say you shine. Your sum of parts
Did not together pluck such envy from him
As did that one, and that, in my regard,
Of the unworthiest siege.
LAER.   What part is that, my lord?
KING   A very riband in the cap of youth,   75
Yet needful too, for youth no less becomes
The light and careless livery that it wears
Than settled age his sables and his weeds,
Importing health and graveness. Two months since
Here was a gentleman of Normandy: 80
I have seen myself, and serv'd against, the French,
And they can well on horseback, but this gallant
Had witchcraft in't, he grew unto his seat,
And to such wondrous doing brought his horse,
As had he been incorps'd and demi-natur'd   85

56 **As ... otherwise:** How can he have come back? Yet he obviously has.
58 **So:** provided that.
60 **checking at:** turning from (like a falcon diverted from its quarry by other prey).
65 **uncharge the practice:** adjudge the plot no plot, i.e. fail to see the plot.
68 **organ:** instrument, agent.
70 **quality:** skill.
71 **Your ... parts:** all your (other) accomplishments put together.
74 **unworthiest:** i.e. least important (with no implication of unsuitableness).   **siege:** status, position.
78 **weeds:** (characteristic) garb.
79 **Importing ... graveness:** signifying prosperity and dignity.
82 **can ... horseback:** are excellent riders.
85 **incorps'd:** made one body.   **demi-natur'd:** i.e. become half of a composite animal.

With the brave beast. So far he topp'd [my] thought,
That I in forgery of shapes and tricks
Come short of what he did.

LAER.   A Norman was't?

KING   A Norman.

LAER.   Upon my life, Lamord.

KING   The very same.   90

LAER.   I know him well. He is the brooch indeed
And gem of all the nation.

KING   He made confession of you,
And gave you such a masterly report
For art and exercise in your defense,   95
And for your rapier most especial,
That he cried out 'twould be a sight indeed
If one could match you. The scrimers of their nation
He swore had neither motion, guard, nor eye,
If you oppos'd them. Sir, this report of his   100
Did Hamlet so envenom with his envy
That he could nothing do but wish and beg
Your sudden coming o'er to play with you.
Now, out of this—

LAER.   What out of this, my lord?

KING   Laertes, was your father dear to you?   105
Or are you like the painting of a sorrow,
A face without a heart?

LAER.   Why ask you this?

KING   Not that I think you did not love your father,
But that I know love is begun by time,
And that I see, in passages of proof,   110
Time qualifies the spark and fire of it.
There lives within the very flame of love
A kind of week or snuff that will abate it,
And nothing is at a like goodness still,
For goodness, growing to a plurisy,   115
Dies in his own too much. That we would do,
We should do when we would; for this "would" changes,

---

[87] **forgery:** mere imagining.

[91] **brooch:** ornament (worn in the hat).

[93] **made . . . you:** acknowledged your excellence.

[98] **scrimers:** fencers.

[103] **sudden:** speedy.

[109] **time:** i.e. a particular set of circumstances.

[110] **in . . . proof:** i.e. by the test of experience, by actual examples.

[111] **qualifies:** moderates.

[113] **week:** wick.

[114] **nothing . . . still:** nothing remains forever at the same pitch of perfection.

[115] **plurisy:** plethora (a variant spelling of *pleurisy,* which was erroneously related to *plus,* stem *plur-,* "more, overmuch."

[116] **too much:** excess.

And hath abatements and delays as many
As there are tongues, are hands, are accidents,
And then this "should" is like a spendthrift's sigh,   120
That hurts by easing. But to the quick of th' ulcer:
Hamlet comes back. What would you undertake
To show yourself indeed your father's son
More than in words?

LAER.   To cut his throat i' th' church.

KING   No place indeed should murther sanctuarize,   125
Revenge should have no bounds. But, good Laertes,
Will you do this, keep close within your chamber.
Hamlet return'd shall know you are come home.
We'll put on those shall praise your excellence,
And set a double varnish on the fame   130
The Frenchman gave you, bring you in fine together,
And wager o'er your heads. He, being remiss,
Most generous, and free from all contriving,
Will not peruse the foils, so that with ease,
Or with a little shuffling, you may choose   135
A sword unbated, and in a [pass] of practice
Requite him for your father.

LAER.   I will do't,
And for [that] purpose I'll anoint my sword.
I bought an unction of a mountebank,
So mortal that, but dip a knife in it,   140
Where it draws blood, no cataplasm so rare,
Collected from all simples that have virtue
Under the moon, can save the thing from death
That is but scratch'd withal. I'll touch my point
With this contagion, that if I gall him slightly,   145
It may be death.

KING   Let's further think of this,

---

¹²⁰ **spendthrift's sigh:** A sigh was supposed to draw blood from the heart.
¹²¹ **hurts by easing:** injures us at the same time that it gives us relief.
¹²⁵ **sanctuarize:** offer asylum to.
¹²⁷ **Will . . . this:** if you want to undertake this.
¹²⁹ **put on those:** incite those who.
¹³⁰ **double varnish:** second coat of varnish.
¹³¹ **in fine:** finally.
¹³² **remiss:** careless, overtrustful.
¹³³ **generous:** noble-minded. **free . . . contriving:** innocent of sharp practices.
¹³⁴ **peruse:** examine.
¹³⁵ **shuffling:** cunning exchange.
¹³⁶ **unbated:** not blunted. **pass of practice:** tricky thrust.
¹³⁹ **unction:** ointment. **mountebank:** traveling quack-doctor.
¹⁴⁰ **mortal:** deadly.
¹⁴¹ **cataplasm:** poultice.
¹⁴² **simples:** medicinal herbs. **virtue:** curative power.
¹⁴⁵ **gall:** graze.

Weight what convenience both of time and means
May fit us to our shape. If this should fail,
And that our drift look through our bad performance,
'Twere better not assay'd; therefore this project   150
Should have a back or second, that might hold
If this did blast in proof. Soft, let me see.
We'll make a solemn wager on your cunnings—
I ha't!
When in your motion you are hot and dry—   155
As make your bouts more violent to that end—
And that he calls for drink, I'll have preferr'd him
A chalice for the nonce, whereon but sipping,
If he by chance escape your venom'd stuck,
Our purpose may hold there. But stay, what noise?   160

Enter QUEEN.

QUEEN   One woe doth tread upon another's heel,
    So fast they follow. Your sister's drown'd, Laertes.
LAER.   Drown'd! O, where?
QUEEN   There is a willow grows askaunt the brook,
    That shows his hoary leaves in the glassy stream,   165
    Therewith fantastic garlands did she make
    Of crow-flowers, nettles, daisies, and long purples
    That liberal shepherds give a grosser name,
    But our cull-cold maids do dead men's fingers call them.
    There on the pendant boughs her crownet weeds   170
    Clamb'ring to hang, an envious sliver broke,
    When down her weedy trophies and herself
    Fell in the weeping brook. Her clothes spread wide,
    And mermaid-like awhile they bore her up,
    Which time she chaunted snatches of old lauds,   175

148 **fit . . . shape:** i.e. suit our purposes best.
149 **drift:** purpose.   **look through:** become visible, be detected.
151 **back or second:** i.e. a second plot in reserve for emergency.
152 **blast in proof:** blow up while being tried (an image from gunnery).
156 **As:** i.e. and you should.
157 **preferr'd:** offered to. Most editors adopt the Fl reading *prepar'd.*
158 **nonce:** occasion.
159 **stuck:** thrust (from *stoccado,* a fencing term).
164 **askaunt:** sideways over.
165 **hoary:** grey-white.
166 **Therewith:** i.e. with willow branches.
167 **long purples:** wild orchids.
168 **liberal:** free-spoken.
169 **cull-cold:** chaste.
170 **crownet:** made into coronets.
171 **envious sliver:** malicious branch.
175 **lauds:** hymns.

As one incapable of her own distress,
Or like a creature native and indued
Unto that element. But long it could not be
Till that her garments, heavy with their drink,
Pull'd the poor wretch from her melodious lay   180
To muddy death.

LAER.   Alas, then she is drown'd?

QUEEN Drown'd, drown'd.

LAER.   Too much of water hast thou, poor Ophelia,
And therefore I forbid my tears; but yet
It is our trick, Nature her custom holds,   185
Let shame say what it will; when these are gone,
The woman will be out. Adieu, my lord,
I have a speech a' fire that fain would blaze,
But that this folly drowns it.

Exit.

KING   Let's follow Gertrude.
How much I had to do to calm his rage!   190
Now fear I this will give it start again,
Therefore let's follow.

Exeunt.

ACT V

SCENE I.

Enter two CLOWNS *[with spades and mattocks].*

1 CLO. Is she to be buried in Christian burial when she willfully seeks her own salvation?

2 CLO. I tell thee she is, therefore make her grave straight. The crowner hath sate on her, and finds it Christian burial.

1 CLO. How can that be, unless she drown'd herself in her own defense?   5

2 CLO. Why, 'tis found so.

1 CLO. It must be *[se offendendo]*, it cannot be else. For here lies the point: if I drown myself wittingly, it argues an act, and an act hath three branches—it is to act, to do, to perform; [argal], she drown'd herself wittingly.

---

[176] **incapable:** insensible.
[177] **indued:** habituated.
[185] **It:** i.e. weeping. **trick:** natural way.
[186] **these:** these tears.
[187] **The woman ... out:** my womanish traits will be gone for good.

V.i. Location: A churchyard.
o.s.d. **Clowns:** rustics.
[3] **straight:** immediately. **crowner:** coroner.
[7] **se offendendo:** blunder for *se defendendo,* "in self-defense."
[9] **argal:** blunder for *ergo,* "therefore."

2 CLO. Nay, but hear you, goodman delver— 10

1 CLO. Give me leave. Here lies the water; good. Here stands the man; good. If the man go to this water and drown himself, it is, will he, nill he, he goes, mark you that. But if the water come to him and drown him, he drowns not himself; argal, he that is not guilty of his own death shortens not his own life.

2 CLO. But is this law? 15

1 CLO. Ay, marry, is't—crowner's quest law.

2 CLO. Will you ha' the truth an't? If this had not been a gentlewoman, she should have been buried out a' Christian burial.

1 CLO. Why, there thou say'st, and the more pity that great folk should have count'nance in this world to drown or hang themselves, more than their even- 20 Christen. Come, my spade. There is no ancient gentlemen but gard'ners, ditchers, and grave-makers; they hold up Adam's profession.

2 CLO. Was he a gentleman?

1 CLO. 'A was the first that ever bore arms.

[2 CLO. Why, he had none. 25

1 CLO. What, art a heathen? How dost thou understand the Scripture? The Scripture says Adam digg'd; could he dig without arms?] I'll put another question to thee. If thou answerest me not to the purpose, confess thyself—

2 CLO. Go to.

1 CLO. What is he that builds stronger than either the mason, the shipwright, or the 30 carpenter?

2 CLO. The gallows-maker, for that outlives a thousand tenants.

1 CLO. I like thy wit well, in good faith. The gallows does well; but how does it well? It does well to those that do ill. Now thou dost ill to say the gallows is built stronger than the church; argal, the gallows may do well to thee. To't again, come. 35

2 CLO. Who builds stronger than a mason, a shipwright, or a carpenter?

1 CLO. Ay, tell me that, and unyoke.

2 CLO. Marry, now I can tell.

1 CLO. To't.

2 CLO. Mass, I cannot tell. 40

Enter HAMLET *and* HORATIO *[afar off].*

1 CLO. Cudgel thy brains no more about it, for your dull ass will not mend his pace with beating, and when you are ask'd this question next, say "a grave-maker": the houses he makes lasts till doomsday. Go get thee in, and fetch me a sup of liquor.

[Exit SECOND CLOWN. FIRST CLOWN *digs.]*

Song.

11-14 **Here . . . life:** Alluding to a very famous suicide case, that of Sir James Hales, a judge who drowned himself in 1554; it was long cited in the courts. The clown gives a garbled account of the defense summing-up and the verdict.

12 **nill he:** he will not.

16 **quest:** inquest.

20-21 **even-Christen:** fellow Christians.

25 **none:** i.e. no coat of arms.

37 **unyoke:** i.e. cease to labor, call it a day.

40 **Mass:** by the mass.

"In youth when I did love, did love,
    Methought it was very sweet,
To contract—O—the time for—a—my behove,   45
    O, methought there—a—was nothing—a—meet."

HAM.   Has this fellow no feeling of his business? 'a sings in grave-making.
HOR.   Custom hath made it in him a property of easiness.
HAM.   'Tis e'en so, the hand of little employment hath the daintier sense.   50
1 CLO.

Song.

"But age with his stealing steps
    Hath clawed me in his clutch,
And hath shipped me into the land,
    As if I had never been such."

[Throws up a shovelful of earth with a skull in it.]

HAM.   That skull had a tongue in it, and could sing once. How the knave jowls it to   55
the ground, as if 'twere Cain's jaw-bone, that did the first murder! This might be
the pate of a politician, which this ass now o'erreaches, one that would circumvent
God, might it not?
HOR.   It might, my lord.
HAM.   Or of a courtier, which could say, "Good morrow, sweet lord! How dost   60
thou, sweet lord?" This might be my Lord Such-a-one, that prais'd my Lord
Such-a-one's horse when 'a [meant] to beg it, might it not?
HOR.   Ay, my lord.
HAM.   Why, e'en so, and now my Lady Worm's, chopless, and knock'd about the
[mazzard] with a sexton's spade. Here's fine revolution, and we had the trick to   65
see't. Did these bones cost no more the breeding, but to play at loggats with them?
Mine ache to think on't.
1 CLO.

Song.

"A pickaxe and a spade, a spade,
    For and a shrouding sheet:
O, a pit of clay for to be made   70
    For such a guest is meet."

---

[46] **contract . . . behove:** shorten, i.e. spend agreeably . . . advantage. The song, punctuated by
the grunts of the clown as he digs, is a garbled version of a poem by Thomas Lord Vaux,
entitled "The Aged Lover Renounceth Love."
[49] **Custom:** habit.   **a property of easiness:** i.e. a thing he can do with complete ease of mind.
[50] **daintier sense:** more delicate sensitivity.
[55] **jowls:** dashes.
[57] **politician:** schemer, intriguer.   **o'erreaches:** gets the better of (with play on the literal
sense).   **circumvent God:** bypass God's law.
[64–65] **chopless:** lacking the lower jaw.   **mazzard:** head.
[65] **revolution:** change.   **and:** if.   **trick:** knack, ability.
[66] **Did . . . cost:** were . . . worth.   **loggats:** a game in which blocks of wood were thrown at a
stake.

[Throws up another skull.]

HAM.　There's another. Why may not that be the skull of a lawyer? Where be his quiddities now, his quillities, his cases, his tenures, and his tricks? Why does he suffer this mad knave now to knock him about the sconce with a dirty shovel, and will not tell him of his action of battery? Hum! This fellow might be in 's time a 75 great buyer of land, with his statutes, his recognizances, his fines, his double vouchers, his recoveries. [Is this the fine of his fines, and the recovery of his recoveries,] to have his fine pate full of fine dirt? Will [his] vouchers vouch him no more of his purchases, and [double ones too], than the length and breadth of a pair of indentures? The very conveyances of his lands will scarcely lie in this box, and 80 must th' inheritor himself have no more, ha?

HOR.　Not a jot more, my lord.

HAM.　Is not parchment made of sheep-skins?

HOR.　Ay, my lord, and of calves'-skins too.

HAM.　They are sheep and calves which seek out assurance in that. I wil speak to 85 this fellow. Whose grave's this, sirrah?

1 CLO.　Mine, sir.

[Sings.]

> "[O], a pit of clay for to be made
> [For such a guest is meet]."

HAM.　I think it be thine indeed, for thou liest in't. 90

1 CLO.　You lie out on't, sir, and therefore 'tis not yours; for my part, I do not lie in't, yet it is mine.

HAM.　Thou dost lie in't, to be in't and say it is thine. 'Tis for the dead, not for the quick; therefore thou liest.

1 CLO.　'Tis a quick lie, sir, 'twill away again from me to you. 95

HAM.　What man dost thou dig it for?

1 CLO.　For no man, sir.

HAM.　What woman then?

1 CLO.　For none neither.

HAM.　Who is to be buried in't? 100

1 CLO.　One that was a woman, sir, but, rest her soul, she's dead.

HAM.　How absolute the knave is! we must speak by the card, or equivocation will undo us. By the Lord, Horatio, this three years I have took note of it: the age is

---

[73] **quiddities:** subtleties, quibbles.　**quillities:** fine distinctions.　**tenures:** titles to real estate.
[74] **sconce:** head.
[76-77] **statutes, recognizances:** bonds securing debts by attaching land and property.　**fines, recoveries:** procedures for converting an entailed estate to freehold.　**double vouchers:** documents guaranteeing title to real estate, signed by two persons.
[77] **fine:** end.
[79-80] **pair of indentures:** legal document cut into two parts that fit together on a serrated edge. Perhaps Hamlet thus refers to the two rows of teeth in the skull, or to the bone sutures.　**conveyances:** documents relating to transfer of property.
[80-81] **this box:** i.e. the skull itself.　**inheritor:** owner.
[86] **sirrah:** term of address to inferiors.
[102] **absolute:** positive.　**by the card:** by the compass, i.e. punctiliously.　**equivocation:** ambiguity.

grown so pick'd that the toe of the peasant comes so near the heel of the courtier, he galls his kibe. How long hast thou been grave-maker? 105

1 CLO.   Of [all] the days i' th' year, I came to't that day that our last king Hamlet overcame Fortinbras.

HAM.   How long is that since?

1 CLO.   Cannot you tell that? Every fool can tell that. It was that very day that young Hamlet was born—he that is mad, and sent into England. 110

HAM.   Ay, marry, why was he sent into England?

1 CLO.   Why, because 'a was mad. 'A shall recover his wits there, or if 'a do not, 'tis no great matter there.

HAM.   Why?

1 CLO.   'Twill not be seen in him there, there the men are as mad as he. 115

HAM.   How came he mad?

1 CLO.   Very strangely, they say.

HAM.   How strangely?

1 CLO.   Faith, e'en with losing his wits.

HAM.   Upon what ground? 120

1 CLO.   Why, here in Denmark. I have been sexton here, man and boy, thirty years.

HAM.   How long will a man lie i' th' earth ere he rot?

1 CLO.   Faith, if 'a be not rotten before 'a die—as we have many pocky corses, that will scarce hold the laying in—'a will last you some eight year or nine year. A tanner will last you nine year. 125

HAM.   Why he more than another?

1 CLO.   Why, sir, his hide is so tann'd with his trade that 'a will keep out water a great while, and your water is a sore decayer of your whoreson dead body. Here's a skull now hath lien you i' th' earth three and twenty years.

HAM.   Whose was it? 130

1 CLO.   A whoreson mad fellow's it was. Whose do you think it was?

HAM.   Nay, I know not.

1 CLO.   A pestilence on him for a mad rogue! 'a pour'd a flagon of Rhenish on my head once. This same skull, sir, was, sir, Yorick's skull, the King's jester.

HAM.   This? 135

[Takes the skull.]

1 CLO.   E'en that.

HAM.   Alas, poor Yorick! I knew him, Horatio, a fellow of infinite jest, of most excellent fancy. He hath bore me on his back a thousand times, and now how abhorr'd in my imagination it is! my gorge rises at it. Here hung those lips that I have kiss'd I know not how oft. Where be your gibes now, your gambols, your songs, 140 your flashes of merriment, that were wont to set the table on a roar? Not one now to mock your own grinning—quite chop-fall'n. Now get you to my lady's [chamber], and tell her, let her paint an inch thick, to this favor she must come; make her laugh at that. Prithee, Horatio, tell me one thing.

[104] **pick'd:** refined.
[105] **galls his kibe:** rubs the courtier's chilblain.
[123] **pocky:** rotten with venereal disease.
[124] **hold . . . in:** last out the burial.
[142] **chop-fall'n:** (1) lacking the lower jaw; (2) downcast.
[143] **favor:** appearance.

HOR.   What's that, my lord?   145
HAM.   Dost thou think Alexander look'd a' this fashion i' th' earth?
HOR.   E'en so.
HAM.   And smelt so? pah!

[Puts down the skull.]

HOR.   E'en so, my lord.
HAM.   To what base uses we may return, Horatio! Why may not imagination trace   150
the noble dust of Alexander, til 'a find it stopping a bunghole?
HOR.   'Twere to consider too curiously, to consider so.
HAM.   No, faith, not a jot, but to follow him thither with modesty enough and like-
lihood to lead it: Alexander died, Alexander was buried, Alexander returneth to
dust, the dust is earth, of earth we make loam, and why of that loam whereto   155
he was converted might they not stop a beer-barrel?
Imperious Caesar, dead and turn'd to clay,
Might stop a hole to keep the wind away.
O that that earth which kept the world in awe
Should patch a wall t' expel the [winter's] flaw!   160
But soft, but soft awhile, here comes the King,

Enter KING, QUEEN, LAERTES, *and [a* DOCTOR OF DIVINITY, *following] the corse,*
[with LORDS *attendant].*

The Queen, the courtiers. Who is this they follow?
And with such maimed rites? This doth betoken
The corse they follow did with desp'rate hand
Foredo it own life. 'Twas of some estate.   165
Couch we a while and mark.

[Retiring with HORATIO.*]*

LAER.   What ceremony else?
HAM.   That is Laertes, a very noble youth. Mark.
LAER.   What ceremony else?
DOCTOR   Her obsequies have been as far enlarg'd   170
As we have warranty. He death was doubtful,
And but that great command o'ersways the order,
She should in ground unsanctified been lodg'd
Till the last trumpet; for charitable prayers,

---

[152] **curiously:** closely, minutely.
[153] **modesty:** moderation.
[155] **loam:** a mixture of moistened clay with sand, straw, etc.
[157] **Imperious:** imperial.
[160] **flaw:** gust.
[163] **maimed rites:** lack of customary ceremony.
[165] **Foredo:** fordo, destroy. **it:** its. **estate:** rank.
[166] **Couch we:** let us conceal ourselves.
[171] **doubtful:** i.e. the subject of an "open verdict."
[172] **order:** customary procedure.
[173] **should:** would certainly.
[174] **for:** instead of.

[Shards,] flints, and pebbles should be thrown on her.   175
Yet here she is allow'd her virgin crants,
Her maiden strewments, and the bringing home
Of bell and burial.
LAER.   Must there no more be done?
DOCTOR   No more be done:
We should profane the service of the dead   180
To sing a requiem and such rest to her
As to peace-parted souls.
LAER.   Lay her i' th' earth,
And from her fair and unpolluted flesh
May violets spring! I tell thee, churlish priest,
A minist'ring angel shall my sister be   185
When thou liest howling.
HAM.   What, the fair Ophelia!
QUEEN *[Scattering flowers.]*   Sweets to the sweet, farewell!
I hop'd thou shouldst have been my Hamlet's wife.
I thought thy bride-bed to have deck'd, sweet maid,
And not have strew'd thy grave.
LAER.   O, treble woe   190
Fall ten times [treble] on that cursed head
Whose wicked deed thy most ingenious sense
Depriv'd thee of! Hold off the earth a while,
Till I have caught her once more in mine arms.

[Leaps in the grave.]

Now pile your dust upon the quick and dead,   195
Till of this flat a mountain you have made
T' o'ertop old Pelion, or the skyish head
Of blue Olympus.
HAM. *[Coming forward.]*   What is he whose grief
Bears such an emphasis, whose phrase of sorrow   200
Conjures the wand'ring stars and makes them stand
Like wonder-wounded hearers? This is I,
Hamlet the Dane!

*[*HAMLET *leaps in after* LAERTES.]*

LAER.   The devil take thy soul!

---

¹⁷⁶ **crants:** garland.
¹⁷⁷ **maiden strewments:** flowers scattered on the grave of an unmarried girl.
¹⁷⁷⁻⁷⁸ **bringing . . . burial:** i.e. burial in consecrated ground, with the bell tolling.
¹⁸¹ **requiem:** dirge.
¹⁸⁷ **Sweets:** flowers.
¹⁹² **ingenious:** intelligent.
^{197, 98} **Pelion, Olympus:** mountains in northeastern Greece.
²⁰⁰ **emphasis, phrase:** Rhetorical terms, here used in disparaging reference to Laertes' inflated language.
²⁰¹ **Conjures:** puts a spell upon. **wand'ring stars:** planets.
²⁰³ **the Dane:** This title normally signifies the King.

[Grappling with him.]

HAM.   Thou pray'st not well.
    I prithee take thy fingers from my throat.   205
    For though I am not splenitive [and] rash,
    Yet have I in me something dangerous,
    Which let thy wisdom fear. Hold off thy hand!
KING   Pluck them asunder.
QUEEN   Hamlet, Hamlet!
ALL   Gentlemen!
HOR.   Good my lord, be quiet.   210

[The ATTENDANTS *part them, and they come out of the grave.]*

HAM.   Why, I will fight with him upon this theme
    Until my eyelids will no longer wag.
QUEEN   O my son, what theme?
HAM.   I lov'd Ophelia. Forty thousand brothers
    Could not with all their quantity of love   215
    Make up my sum. What wilt thou do for her?
KING   O, he is mad, Laertes.
QUEEN   For love of God, forbear him.
HAM.   'Swounds, show me what thou't do.
    Woo't weep, woo't fight, woo't fast, woo't tear thyself?   220
    Woo't drink up eisel, eat a crocadile?
    I'll do't. Dost [thou] come here to whine?
    To outface me with leaping in her grave?
    Be buried quick with her, and so will I.
    And if thou prate of mountains, let them throw   225
    Millions of acres on us, till our ground,
    Singeing his pate against the burning zone,
    Make Ossa like a wart! Nay, and thou'lt mouth,
    I'll rant as well as thou.
QUEEN   This is mere madness,
    And [thus] a while the fit will work in him;   230
    Anon, as patient as the female dove,
    When that her golden couplets are disclosed,
    His silence will sit drooping.
HAM.   Hear you, sir,
    What is the reason that you use me thus?

[206] **splenitive:** impetuous.
[219] **thou't:** thou wilt.
[220] **Woo't:** wilt thou.
[221] **eisel:** vinegar. **crocadile:** crocodile.
[225] **if . . . mountains:** Referring to lines 195–98.
[227] **burning zone:** sphere of the sun.
[228] **Ossa:** another mountain in Greece, near Pelion and Olympus. **mouth:** talk bombast (synonymous with *rant* in the next line).
[229] **mere:** utter.
[231] **patient:** calm.
[232] **golden couplets:** pair of baby birds, covered with yellow down. **disclosed:** hatched.

I lov'd you ever. But it is no matter.   235
Let Hercules himself do what he may,
The cat will mew, and dog will have his day.

Exit HAMLET.

KING   I pray thee, good Horatio, wait upon him.

[Exit] HORATIO.

[To LAERTES.*]*   Strengthen your patience in our last night's speech,
We'll put the matter to the present push.—   240
Good Gertrude, set some watch over your son.
This grave shall have a living monument.
An hour of quiet [shortly] shall we see,
Till then in patience our proceeding be.

Exeunt.

SCENE II.

Enter HAMLET *and* HORATIO.

HAM.   So much for this, sir, now shall you see the other—
You do remember all the circumstance?
HOR.   Remember it, my lord!
HAM.   Sir, in my heart there was a kind of fighting
That would not let me sleep. [Methought] I lay   5
Worse than the mutines in the [bilboes]. Rashly—
And prais'd be rashness for it—let us know
Our indiscretion sometime serves us well
When our deep plots do pall, and that should learn us
There's a divinity that shapes our ends,   10
Rough-hew them how we will—
HOR.   That is most certain.
HAM.   Up from my cabin,
My sea-gown scarf'd about me, in the dark
Grop'd I to find out them, had my desire,

236-37 **Let . . . day:** i.e. nobody can prevent another from making the scenes he feels he has a
    right to.
239 **in:** i.e. by recalling.
240 **present push:** immediate test.
242 **living:** enduring (?) or in the form of a lifelike effigy (?).

V.ii. Location: The castle.
1 **see the other:** i.e. hear the other news I have to tell you (hinted at in the letter to Horatio,
    (IV.vi.18).
6 **mutines:** mutineers (but the term *mutiny* was in Shakespeare's day used of almost any act of
    rebellion against authority).   **bilboes:** fetters attached to a heavy iron bar.   **Rashly:** on im-
    pulse.
7 **know:** recognize, acknowledge.
9 **pall:** lose force, come to nothing.   **learn:** teach.
10 **shapes our ends:** gives final shape to our designs.
11 **Rough-hew them:** block them out in initial form.

Finger'd their packet, and in fine withdrew   15
To mine own room again, making so bold,
My fears forgetting manners, to [unseal]
Their grand commission; where I found, Horatio—
Ah, royal knavery!—an exact command,
Larded with many several sorts of reasons,   20
Importing Denmark's health and England's too,
With, ho, such bugs and goblins in my life,
That, on the supervise, no leisure bated,
No, not to stay the grinding of the axe,
My head should be strook off.
HOR.   Is't possible?   25
HAM.   Here's the commission, read it at more leisure.
But wilt thou hear now how I did proceed?
HOR.   I beseech you.
HAM.   Being thus benetted round with [villainies],
Or I could make a prologue to my brains,   30
They had begun the play. I sat me down,
Devis'd a new commission, wrote it fair.
I once did hold it, as our statists do,
A baseness to write fair, and labor'd much
How to forget that learning, but, sir, now   35
It did me yeman's service. Wilt thou know
Th' effect of what I wrote?
HOR.   Ay, good my lord.
HAM.   An earnest conjuration from the King,
As England was his faithful tributary,
As love between them like the palm might flourish,   40
As peace should still her wheaten garland wear
And stand a comma 'tween their amities,
And many such-like [as's] of great charge,
That on the view and knowing of these contents,
Without debatement further, more or less,   45

¹⁵ **Finger'd:** filched, "pinched."
²⁰ **Larded:** garnished.
²¹ **Importing:** relating to.
²² **bugs . . . life:** terrifying things in prospect if I were permitted to remain alive. *Bugs* = buga-boos.
²³ **supervise:** perusal.   **bated:** deducted (from the stipulated speediness).
²⁴ **stay:** wait for.
³⁰ **Or:** before.
³² **fair:** i.e. in a beautiful hand (such as a professional scribe would use).
³³ **statists:** statesmen, public officials.
³⁴ **A baseness:** i.e. a skill befitting men of low rank.
³⁶ **yeman's:** yeoman's, i.e. solid, substantial.
³⁷ **effect:** purport, gist.
⁴² **comma:** connective, link.
⁴³ **as's . . . charge:** (1) weighty clauses beginning with *as;* (2) asses with heavy loads.

He should those bearers put to sudden death,
Not shriving time allow'd.
HOR.   How was this seal'd?
HAM.   Why, even in that was heaven ordinant.
I had my father's signet in my purse,
Which was the model of that Danish seal;   50
Folded the writ up in the form of th' other,
[Subscrib'd] it, gave't th' impression, plac'd it safely,
The changeling never known. Now the next day
Was our sea-fight, and what to this was sequent
Thou knowest already.   55
HOR.   So Guildenstern and Rosencrantz go to't.
HAM.   [Why, man, they did make love to this employment.]
They are not near my conscience. Their defeat
Does by their own insinuation grow.
'Tis dangerous when the baser nature comes   60
Between the pass and fell incensed points
Of mighty opposites.
HOR.   Why, what a king is this!
HAM.   Does it not, think thee, stand me now upon—
He that hath kill'd my king and whor'd my mother,
Popp'd in between th' election and my hopes,   65
Thrown out his angle for my proper life,
And with such coz'nage—is't not perfect conscience
[To quit him with this arm? And is't not to be damn'd,
To let this canker of our nature come
In further evil?   70
HOR.   It must be shortly known to him from England
What is the issue of the business there.

---

[47] **shriving time:** time for confession and absolution.
[48] **ordinant:** in charge, guiding.
[50] **model:** small copy.
[52] **Subscrib'd:** signed.
[53] **changeling:** i.e. Hamlet's letter, substituted secretly for the genuine letter, as fairies substituted their children for human children.   **never known:** never recognized as a substitution (unlike the fairies' changelings).
[56] **go to't:** i.e. are going to their death.
[58] **defeat:** ruin, overthrow.
[59] **insinuation:** winding their way into the affair.
[60] **baser:** inferior.
[61] **pass:** thrust.   **fell:** fierce.
[63] **stand . . . upon:** i.e. rest upon me as a duty.
[65] **election:** i.e. as King of Denmark.
[66] **angle:** hook and line.   **proper:** very.
[67] **coz'nage:** trickery.
[68] **quit him:** pay him back.
[69] **canker:** cancerous sore.
[69-70] **come In:** grow into.

HAM.   It will be short; the interim's mine,
And a man's life's no more than to say "one."
But I am very sorry, good Horatio,   75
That to Laertes I forgot myself,
For by the image of my cause I see
The portraiture of his. I'll [court] his favors.
But sure the bravery of his grief did put me
Into a tow'ring passion.
HOR.   Peace, who comes here?]   80

Enter [young OSRIC,*] a courtier.*

OSR.   Your lordship is right welcome back to Denmark.
HAM.   I humbly thank you, sir.—Dost know this water-fly?
HOR.   No, my good lord.
HAM.   Thy state is the more gracious, for 'tis a vice to know him. He hath much
land, and fertile; let a beast be lord of beasts, and his crib shall stand at the King's   85
mess. 'Tis a chough, but, as I say, spacious in the possession of dirt.
OSR.   Sweet lord, if your lordship were at leisure, I should impart a thing to you
from his Majesty.
HAM.   I will receive it, sir, with all diligence of spirit. [Put] your bonnet to his right
use, 'tis for the head.   90
OSR.   I thank your lordship, it is very hot.
HAM.   No, believe me, 'tis very cold, the wind is northerly.
OSR.   It is indifferent cold, my lord, indeed.
HAM.   But yet methinks it is very [sultry] and hot [for] my complexion.
OSR.   Exceedingly, my lord, it is very sultry—as 'twere—I cannot tell how. My lord,   95
his Majesty bade me signify to you that 'a has laid a great wager on your head. Sir,
this is the matter—
HAM.   I beseech you remember.

*[*HAMLET *moves him to put on his hat.]*

OSR.   Nay, good my lord, for my ease, in good faith. Sir, here is newly come to court
Laertes, believe me, an absolute [gentleman], full of most excellent differences, of   100

---

[74] **a man's . . . more:** i.e. to kill a man takes no more time.   **say "one."** Perhaps this is equivalent to "deliver one sword thrust"; see line 239 below, where Hamlet says "One" as he makes
the first hit.
[77] **image:** likeness.
[79] **bravery:** ostentatious expression.
[82] **water-fly:** i.e. tiny, vainly agitated creature.
[84] **gracious:** virtuous.
[85] **let . . . mess:** i.e. if a beast owned as many cattle as Osric, he could feast with the King.
[86] **chough:** jackdaw, a bird that could be taught to speak.
[89] **bonnet:** hat.
[93] **indifferent:** somewhat.
[94] **complexion:** temperament.
[99] **for my ease:** i.e. I am really more comfortable with my hat off (a polite insistence on maintaining ceremony).
[100] **absolute:** complete, possessing every quality a gentleman should have.   **differences:** distinguishing characteristics, personal qualities.

very soft society, and great showing; indeed, to speak sellingly of him, he is the card or calendar of gentry; for you shall find in him the continent of what part a gentleman would see.

HAM. Sir, his definement suffers no perdition in you, though I know to divide him inventorially would dozy th' arithmetic of memory, and yet but yaw neither in 105 respect of his quick sail; but in the verity of extolment, I take him to be a soul of great article, and his infusion of such dearth and rareness as, to make true diction of him, his semblable is his mirror, and who else would trace him, his umbrage, nothing more.

OSR. Your lordship speaks most infallibly of him. 110

HAM. The concernancy, sir? Why do we wrap the gentleman in our more rawer breath?

OSR. Sir?

HOR. Is't not possible to understand in another tongue? You will to't, sir, really.

HAM. What imports the nomination of this gentleman? 115

OSR. Of Laertes?

HOR. His purse is empty already: all 's golden words are spent.

HAM. Of him, sir.

OSR. I know you are not ignorant—

HAM. I would you did, sir, yet, in faith, if you did, it would not much approve me. 120 Well, sir?

OSR. You are not ignorant of what excellence Laertes is—

HAM. I dare not confess that, lest I should compare with him in excellence, but to know a man well were to know himself.

OSR. I mean, sir, for [his] weapon, but in the imputation laid on him by them, in 125 his meed he's unfellow'd.

---

[101] **soft:** agreeable. **great showing:** splendid appearance. **sellingly:** i.e. like a seller to a prospective buyer; in a fashion to do full justice. Most editors follow Q3 in reading *feelingly* = with exactitude, as he deserves.

[102] **card or calendar:** chart or register, i.e. compendious guide. **gentry:** gentlemanly behavior. **the continent . . . part:** one who contains every quality.

[104] **perdition:** loss.

[105] **dozy:** make dizzy. **yaw:** keep deviating erratically from its course (said of a ship). **neither:** for all that.

[105–06] **in respect of:** compared with.

[106] **in . . . extolment:** to praise him truly.

[107] **article:** scope (?) or importance (?). **infusion:** essence, quality. **dearth:** scarceness. **make true diction:** speak truly.

[108] **his semblable:** his only likeness or equal. **who . . . him:** anyone else who tries to follow him. **umbrage:** shadow.

[111] **concernancy:** relevance. **more rawer breath:** i.e. words too crude to describe him properly.

[114] **in another tongue:** i.e. when someone else is the speaker. **You . . . really:** i.e. you can do it if you try.

[115] **nomination:** naming, mention.

[120] **approve:** commend.

[123] **compare . . . excellence:** i.e. seem to claim the same degree of excellence for myself. **but:** The sense seems to require *for*.

[124] **himself:** i.e. oneself.

[125] **in . . . them:** i.e. in popular estimation.

[126] **meed:** merit.

HAM.   What's his weapon?

OSR.   Rapier and dagger.

HAM.   That's two of his weapons—but well.

OSR.   The King, sir, hath wager'd with him six Barbary horses, against the which he   130
has impawn'd, as I take it, six French rapiers and poniards, with their assigns, as
girdle, [hangars], and so. Three of the carriages, in faith, are very dear to fancy,
very responsive to the hilts, most delicate carriages, and of very liberal conceit.

HAM.   What call you the carriages?

HOR.   I knew you must be edified by the margent ere you had done.   135

OSR.   The [carriages], sir, are the hangers.

HAM.   The phrase would be more germane to the matter if we could carry a cannon
by our sides; I would it [might be] hangers till then. But on: six Barb'ry horses
against six French swords, their assigns, and three liberal-conceited carriages;
that's the French bet against the Danish. Why is this all [impawn'd, as] you call it?   140

OSR.   The King, sir, hath laid, sir, that in a dozen passes between yourself and him,
he shall not exceed you three hits; he hath laid on twelve for nine; and it would
come to immediate trial, if your lordship would vouchsafe the answer.

HAM.   How if I answer no?

OSR.   I mean, my lord, the opposition of your person in trial.   145

HAM.   Sir, I will walk here in the hall. If it please his Majesty, it is the breathing time
of day with me. Let the foils be brought, the gentleman willing, and the King hold
his purpose, I will win for him and I can; if not, I will gain nothing but my shame
and the odd hits.

OSR.   Shall I deliver you so?   150

HAM.   To this effect, sir—after what flourish your nature will.

OSR.   I commend my duty to your lordship.

HAM.   Yours. *[Exit* OSRIC.*]* ['A] does well to commend it himself, there are no
tongues else for 's turn.

HOR.   This lapwing runs away with the shell on his head.   155

HAM.   'A did [comply], sir, with his dug before 'a suck'd it. Thus has he, and many

---

131 **impawn'd:** staked. **assigns:** appurtenances.

132 **hangers:** straps on which the swords hang from the girdle. **carriages:** properly, gun carriages; here used affectedly in place of *hangers*. **fancy:** taste.

133 **very responsive to:** matching well. **liberal conceit:** elegant design.

135 **must . . . margent:** would require enlightenment from a marginal note.

141 **laid:** wagered.

142 **he . . . hits:** Laertes must win by at least eight to four (if none of the "passes" or bouts are
draws), since at seven to five he would be only two up. **he . . . nine:** Not satisfactorily explained despite much discussion. One suggestion is that Laertes has raised the odds against
himself by wagering that out of twelve bouts he will win nine.

143 **answer:** encounter (as Hamlet's following quibble forces Osric to explain in his next speech).

146–47 **breathing . . . me:** my usual hour for exercise.

151 **after what flourish:** with whatever embellishment of language.

152 **commend my duty:** offer my dutiful respects (but Hamlet picks up the phrase in the sense
"praise my manner of bowing").

155 **lapwing:** a foolish bird that upon hatching was supposed to run with part of the eggshell still
over its head. (Osric has put his hat on at last.)

156 **comply . . . dug:** bow politely to his mother's nipple.

156–57 **drossy:** i.e. worthless. **tune . . . time:** i.e. fashionable ways of talk.

more of the same breed that I know the drossy age dotes on, only got the tune of the time, and out of an habit of encounter, a kind of [yesty] collection, which carries them through and through the most [profound] and [winnow'd] opinions, and do but blow them to their trial, the bubbles are out.   160

Enter a LORD.

LORD   My lord, his Majesty commended him to you by young Osric, who bring back to him that you attend him in the hall. He sends to know if your pleasure hold to play with Laertes, or that you will take longer time.

HAM.   I am constant to my purposes, they follow the King's pleasure. If his fitness speaks, mine is ready; now or whensoever, provided I be so able as now.   165

LORD   The King and Queen and all are coming down.

HAM.   In happy time.

LORD   The Queen desires you to use some gentle entertainment to Laertes before you fall to play.

HAM.   She well instructs me.   170

[Exit LORD.*]*

HOR.   You will lose, my lord.

HAM.   I do not think so; since he went into France I have been in continual practice. I shall win at the odds. Thou wouldst not think how ill all's here about my heart—but it is no matter.

HOR.   Nay, good my lord—   175

HAM.   It is but foolery, but it is such a kind of [gain-]giving, as would perhaps trouble a woman.

HOR.   If your mind dislike any thing, obey it. I will forestall their repair hither, and say you are not fit.

HAM.   Not a whit, we defy augury. There is special providence in the fall of a sparrow. If it be [now], 'tis not to come; if it be not to come, it will be now; if it be not now, yet it [will] come—the readiness is all. Since no man, of aught he leaves, knows what is't to leave betimes, let be.   180

A table prepar'd, [and flagons of wine on it. Enter] Trumpets. Drums, and OFFICERS *with cushions, foils, daggers;* KING, QUEEN, LAERTES, *[*OSRIC,*] and all the State.*

KING   Come, Hamlet, come, and take this hand from me.

[The KING *puts* LAERTES' *hand into* HAMLET'*s.]*

---

[158] **habit of encounter:** mode of social intercourse.   **yesty:** yeasty, frothy.   **collection:** i.e. anthology of fine phrases.

[159] **winnow'd:** sifted, choice.   **opinions:** judgments.

[160] **blow . . . trial:** test them by blowing on them, i.e. make even the least demanding trial of them.   **out:** blown away (?) or at an end, done for (?).

[164–65] **If . . . ready:** i.e. if this is a good moment for him, it is for me also.

[168] **gentle entertainment:** courteous greeting.

[176] **gain-giving:** misgiving.

[180] **special . . . sparrow:** See Matthew 10:29.

[182] **of aught:** i.e. whatever.

[183] **knows . . . betimes:** knows what is the best time to leave it.

[183] s.d. **State:** nobles.

HAM.   Give me your pardon, sir. I have done you wrong,   185
  But pardon't as you are a gentleman.
  This presence knows,
  And you must needs have heard, how I am punish'd
  With a sore distraction. What I have done
  That might your nature, honor, and exception   190
  Roughly awake, I here proclaim was madness.
  Was't Hamlet wrong'd Laertes? Never Hamlet!
  If Hamlet from himself be ta'en away,
  And when he's not himself does wrong Laertes,
  Then Hamlet does it not, Hamlet denies it.   195
  Who does it then? His madness. If't be so,
  Hamlet is of the faction that is wronged,
  His madness is poor Hamlet's enemy.
  [Sir, in this audience,]
  Let my disclaiming from a purpos'd evil   200
  Free me so far in your most generous thoughts,
  That I have shot my arrow o'er the house
  And hurt my brother.
LAER.   I am satisfied in nature,
  Whose motive in this case should stir me most
  To my revenge, but in my terms of honor   205
  I stand aloof, and will no reconcilement
  Till by some elder masters of known honor
  I have a voice and president of peace
  To [keep] my name ungor'd. But [till] that time
  I do receive your offer'd love like love,   210
  And will not wrong it.
HAM.   I embrace it freely,
  And will this brothers' wager frankly play.
  Give us the foils. [Come on.]
LAER.   Come, one for me.
HAM.   I'll be your foil, Laertes; in mine ignorance
  Your skill shall like a star i' th' darkest night   215
  Stick fiery off indeed.
LAER.   You mock me, sir.
HAM.   No, by this hand.

---

187 **presence:** assembled court.
188 **punish'd:** afflicted.
190 **exception:** objection.
200 **my ... evil:** my declaration that I intended no harm.
201 **Free:** absolve.
203 **in nature:** so far as my personal feelings are concerned.
205 **in ... honor:** i.e. as a man governed by an established code of honor.
208-09 **have ... ungor'd:** can secure an opinion backed by precedent that I can make peace with
    you without injury to my reputation.
212 **brothers':** i.e. amicable, as if between brothers.   **frankly:** freely, without constraint.
214 **foil:** thin sheet of metal placed behind a jewel to set it off.
216 **Stick ... off:** blaze out in contrast.

KING   Give them the foils, young Osric. Cousin Hamlet,
    You know the wager?
HAM.   Very well, my lord.
    Your Grace has laid the odds a' th' weaker side.   220
KING   I do not fear it, I have seen you both;
    But since he is [better'd], we have therefore odds.
LAER.   This is too heavy; let me see another.
HAM.   This likes me well. These foils have all a length?

[Prepare to play.]

OSR.   Ay, my good lord.   225
KING   Set me the stoups of wine upon that table.
    If Hamlet give the first or second hit,
    Or quite in answer of the third exchange,
    Let all the battlements their ord'nance fire.
    The King shall drink to Hamlet's better breath,   230
    And in the cup an [union] shall he throw,
    Richer than that which four successive kings
    In Denmark's crown have worn. Give me the cups,
    And let the kettle to the trumpet speak,
    The trumpet to the cannoneer without,   235
    The cannons to the heavens, the heaven to earth,
    "Now the King drinks to Hamlet." Come begin;

Trumpets the while.

    And you, the judges, bear a wary eye.
HAM.   Come on, sir.
LAER.   Come, my lord.

[They play and HAMLET *scores a hit.]*

HAM.   One.
LAER.   No.
HAM.   Judgment.
OSR.   A hit, a very palpable hit.
LAER.   Well, again.   240
KING   Stay, give me drink. Hamlet, this pearl is thine,
    Here's to thy health! Give him the cup.

Drum, trumpets [sound] flourish. A piece goes off [within].

---

²²⁰ **laid the odds:** i.e. wagered a higher stake (horses to rapiers).
²²² **is better'd:** has perfected his skill. **odds:** i.e. the arrangement that Laertes must take more
    bouts than Hamlet to win.
²²⁴ **likes:** pleases. **a length:** the same length.
²²⁶ **stoups:** tankards.
²²⁹ **quit ... exchange:** pays back wins by Laertes in the first and second bouts by taking the
    third.
²³¹ **union:** an especially fine pearl.
²³⁴ **kettle:** kettledrum.

HAM. I'll play this bout first, set it by a while.
  Come. *[They play again.]* Another hit; what say you?
LAER. [A touch, a touch,] I do confess't.   245
KING Our son shall win.
QUEEN   He's fat, and scant of breath.
  Here, Hamlet, take my napkin, rub thy brows.
  The Queen carouses to thy fortune, Hamlet.
HAM. Good madam!
KING   Gertrude, do not drink.
QUEEN I will, my lord, I pray you pardon me.   250
KING *[Aside.]* It is the pois'ned cup, it is too late.
HAM. I dare not drink yet, madam; by and by.
QUEEN Come, let me wipe thy face.
LAER. My lord, I'll hit him now.
KING   I do not think't.
LAER. *[Aside.]* And yet it is almost against my conscience.   255
HAM. Come, for the third, Laertes, you do but dally.
  I pray you pass with your best violence;
  I am sure you make a wanton of me.
LAER. Say you so? Come on.

[They play.]

OSR. Nothing, neither way.   260
LAER. Have at you now!

[LAERTES wounds HAMLET; then, in scuffling, they change rapiers.]

KING   Part them, they are incens'd.
HAM. Nay, come again.

[HAMLET wounds LAERTES. The QUEEN falls.]

OSR.   Look to the Queen there ho!
HOR. They bleed on both sides. How is it, my lord?
OSR. How is't, Laertes?
LAER. Why, as a woodcock to mine own springe, Osric: 265
  I am justly kill'd with mine own treachery.
HAM. How does the Queen?
KING   She sounds to see them bleed.
QUEEN No, no, the drink, the drink—O my dear Hamlet—
  The drink, the drink! I am pois'ned.

[Dies.]

HAM. O villainy! Ho, let the door be lock'd!   270
  Treachery! Seek it out.

---

[246] **fat:** sweaty. **carouses:** drinks a toast.
[256] **make . . . me:** i.e. are holding back in order to let me win, as one does with a spoiled child
  (wanton).
[265] **springe:** snare.
[267] **sounds:** swoons.

LAER.   It is here, Hamlet. [Hamlet,] thou art slain.
No med'cine in the world can do thee good;
In thee there is not half an hour's life.
The treacherous instrument is in [thy] hand,   275
Unbated and envenom'd. The foul practice
Hath turn'd itself on me. Lo here I lie,
Never to rise again. Thy mother's pois'ned.
I can no more—the King, the King's to blame.
HAM.   The point envenom'd too!   280
Then, venom, to thy work.

[Hurts the KING.]

ALL   Treason! treason!
KING   O, yet defend me, friends, I am but hurt.
HAM.   Here, thou incestious, [murd'rous], damned Dane,
Drink [off] this potion! Is [thy union] here?   285
Follow my mother!

[KING dies.]

LAER.   He is justly served,
It is a poison temper'd by himself.
Exchange forgiveness with me, noble Hamlet.
Mine and my father's death come not upon thee,
Nor thine on me!   290

[Dies.]

HAM.   Heaven make thee free of it! I follow thee.
I am dead, Horatio. Wretched queen, adieu!
You that look pale, and tremble at this chance,
That are but mutes or audience to this act,
Had I but time—as this fell sergeant, Death,   295
Is strict in his arrest—O, I could tell you—
But let it be. Horatio, I am dead,
Thou livest. Report me and my cause aright
To the unsatisfied.
HOR.   Never believe it;
I am more an antique Roman than a Dane.   300
Here's yet some liquor left.
HAM.   As th' art a man,
Give me the cup. Let go! By heaven, I'll ha't!
O God, Horatio, what a wounded name,
Things standing thus unknown, shall I leave behind me!

276 **Unbated:** not blunted.   **foul practice:** vile plot.
281 s.d. **Hurts:** wounds.
287 **temper'd:** mixed.
291 **make thee free:** absolve you.
294 **mutes or audience:** silent spectators.
295 **fell:** cruel.   **sergeant:** sheriff's officer.
300 **antique Roman:** i.e. one who will commit suicide on such an occasion.

If thou didst ever hold me in thy heart, 305
Absent thee from felicity a while,
And in this harsh world draw thy breath in pain
To tell my story.

A march afar off [and a shot within].

What warlike noise is this?

[OSRIC goes to the door and returns.]

OSR.   Young Fortinbras, with conquest come from Poland,
To th' embassadors of England gives 310
This warlike volley.
HAM.   O, I die, Horatio,
The potent poison quite o'er-crows my spirit.
I cannot live to hear the news from England,
But I do prophesy th' election lights
On Fortinbras, he has my dying voice. 315
So tell him, with th' occurrents more and less
Which have solicited—the rest is silence.

[Dies.]

HOR.   Now cracks a noble heart. Good night, sweet prince,
And flights of angels sing thee to thy rest!

[March within.]

Why does the drum come hither? 320

Enter FORTINBRAS *with the* [ENGLISH] EMBASSADORS, *[with Drum, Colors, and* AT-
TENDANTS*].*

FORT.   Where is this sight?
HOR.   What is it you would see?
If aught of woe or wonder, cease your search.
FORT.   This quarry cries on havoc. O proud death,
What feast is toward in thine eternal cell,
That thou so many princes at a shot 325
So bloodily hastily hast strook?
[1] EMB.   The sight is dismal,
And our affairs from England come too late.
The ears are senseless that should give us hearing,
To tell him his commandement is fulfill'd,
That Rosencrantz and Guildenstern are dead. 330
Where should we have our thanks?

---

³¹² **o'er-crows:** triumphs over (a term derived from cockfighting).   **spirit:** vital energy.
³¹⁵ **voice:** vote.
³¹⁶ **occurrents:** occurrences.
³¹⁷ **solicited:** instigated.
³²³ **This . . . havoc:** this heap of corpses proclaims a massacre.
³²⁴ **toward:** in preparation.

HOR.   Not from his mouth,
    Had it th' ability of life to thank you.
    He never gave commandement for their death,
    But since so jump upon this bloody question,
    You from the Polack wars, and you from England,   335
    Are here arrived, give order that these bodies
    High on a stage be placed to the view,
    And let me speak to [th'] yet unknowing world
    How these things came about. So shall you hear
    Of carnal, bloody, and unnatural acts,   340
    Of accidental judgments, casual slaughters,
    Of deaths put on by cunning and [forc'd] cause,
    And in this upshot, purposes mistook
    Fall'n on th' inventors' heads: all this can I
    Truly deliver.
FORT.   Let us haste to hear it,   345
    And call the noblest to the audience.
    For me, with sorrow I embrace my fortune.
    I have some rights, of memory in this kingdom,
    Which now to claim my vantage doth invite me.
HOR. Of that I shall have also cause to speak,   350
    And from his mouth whose voice will draw [on] more.
    But let this same be presently perform'd
    Even while men's minds are wild, lest more mischance
    On plots and errors happen.
FORT.   Let four captains
    Bear Hamlet like a soldier to the stage,   355
    For he was likely, had he been put on,
    To have prov'd most royal; and for his passage,
    The soldiers' music and the rite of war
    Speak loudly for him.   360
    Take up the bodies. Such a sight as this
    Becomes the field, but here shows much amiss.
    Go bid the soldiers shoot.

Exeunt [marching; after the which a peal of ordinance are shot off].

[331] **his:** i.e. the King's.
[334] **jump:** precisely, pat. **question:** matter.
[337] **stage:** platform.
[341] **judgments:** retributions. **casual:** happening by chance.
[342] **put on:** instigated.
[348] **of memory:** unforgotten.
[349] **my vantage:** i.e. my opportune presence at a moment when the throne is empty.
[351] **his ... more:** the mouth of one (Hamlet) whose vote will induce others to support your claim.
[352] **presently:** at once.
[353] **wild:** distraught.
[356] **put on:** put to the test (by becoming king).
[357] **passage:** death.
[361] **Becomes ... amiss:** befits the battlefield, but appears very much out of place here.

Response Statement Assignments

1. Over the centuries, the character of Hamlet has been interpreted in many ways; he has been described as a noble prince, a cruel avenger, a victim of an Oedipal complex, a foolish procrastinator. Explain what you thought of Hamlet as you were reading the play.
2. Explore the aspects of your literary and cultural **repertoire** that caused you to react to Hamlet as you did.
3. Although *Hamlet* is considered to be a classic text, how can you account for the fact that its "meanings" have changed over time for its readers? How do you reconcile these changes in interpretation with the notion that a classic text is generally thought to have a "timeless" message?
4. When you were reading the play, did you find it to be particularly ambiguous? If so, in what specific scenes? For example, there is much debate among readers as to whether Hamlet is sane or insane, whether Ophelia is pregnant or not, or whether Hamlet knows when he first speaks to Ophelia that Polonius is listening. Examine some of the **reading strategies** you used that caused you to detect such ambiguities.
5. How do you respond to the presence of a ghost in the play, particularly since you probably don't believe in ghosts? If you don't find the ghost difficult to accept, this is one example of your **naturalizing** a strange event in a literary text. What conventions do you call upon from your **literary repertoire** that help you naturalize the ghost?
6. Compare and contrast some of the reading strategies you used for resolving ambiguities in *Hamlet* with those you used for *Rosencrantz and Guildenstern Are Dead*. What assumptions and expectations of yours about the nature of drama were confirmed or challenged by these two plays? Did you develop any new reading strategies or expectations while reading either play?

HENRIK IBSEN (1828–1906)

The Wild Duck

Translated by R. Farquharson Sharp

DRAMATIS PERSONAE

WERLE, *a merchant and manufacturer.*
GREGERS WERLE, *his son.*
Old EKDAL.
HJALMAR EKDAL, *his son, a photographer.*
GINA EKDAL, *Hjalmar's wife.*
HEDVIG, *their daughter, aged fourteen.*

GRAABERG, *a bookkeeper in Werle's office.*
PETTERSEN, *Werle's servant.*
JENSEN, *a hired waiter.*
a flabby, fat GUEST.
a thin-haired GUEST.
a short-sighted GUEST.
Six other GUESTS *at Werle's dinner-party.*

MRS. SÖRBY, *the elder Werle's housekeeper.*
RELLING, *a doctor.*
MOLVIK, *an ex-student of theology.*

Several hired SERVANTS.

The first Act takes place in the elder Werle's house; the other four at Hjalmar Ekdal's.

ACT I

SCENE. *A handsomely and comfortably furnished study in* WERLE'S *house. Bookcases and upholstered furniture; a desk, covered with papers and documents, in the middle of the floor; the lamps are lit and have green shades, producing a soft light in the room. At the back are folding doors which have been thrown open and the portières drawn back. Through these is visible a large and well-appointed room, brightly lit with lamps and branch candlesticks. A small private door, on the right-hand side of the study, leads to the office. On the left is a fireplace, with a cheerful fire, and beyond it folding doors leading to the dining-room.*

WERLE'S *servant* PETTERSEN, *in livery, and the hired waiter* JENSEN *in black, are setting the study in order. In the large room at the back two or three other waiters are moving about, tidying the room and lighting more candles. From within the dining-room the noise of the guests' talking and laughing can be heard; someone raps on a glass with a knife, silence follows and a toast is proposed; applause follows and the hum of conversation begins again.*

PETTERSEN *(lighting a lamp on the mantelpiece and putting a shade over it)*   Hark at 'em, Jensen; the old man's up now, making a long speech to propose Mrs. Sörby's health.

JENSEN *(moving a chair forward)*   Do you think what people say about those two is true, that there's something between them?

PETTERSEN   Goodness knows.

JENSEN   He's been a gay old dog in his time, hasn't he?

PETTERSEN   Maybe.

JENSEN   They say this dinner-party is in honour of his son.

PETTERSEN   Yes, he came home yesterday.

JENSEN   I never knew old Werle had a son.

PETTERSEN   Oh yes, he has a son, but he sticks up at the works at Höidal; he hasn't once been in the town all the years I have been in service here.

A WAITER *(in the doorway to the other room)*   Pettersen, there is an old chap here who—

PETTERSEN *(muttering)*   Devil take him, what is anyone coming now for!

Old EKDAL *appears from the inner room. He is dressed in a weather-worn greatcoat with a high collar, carries a stick and a fur cap in his hands, and a paper parcel under his arm. He wears a dirty reddish-brown wig and a small grey moustache.*

PETTERSEN *(going towards him)*   Good Lord!—what do you want in here?

EKDAL *(in the doorway)*   I want so badly to get into the office, Pettersen.

PETTERSEN   The office was closed an hour ago, and—

EKDAL   They told me that at the door, old man. But Graaberg is still there. Be a good chap, Pettersen, and let me slip in that way. *(Points to the private door.)* I've been that way before.

PETTERSEN   All right, you can go in. *(Opens the door.)* But, whatever you do, don't forget to go out the proper way, because we have got guests here.

EKDAL   Yes, yes—I know. Thanks, dear old Pettersen! My good old friend! Thanks! *(Under his breath.)* Old codfish! *(Goes into the office.* PETTERSEN *shuts the door after him.)*

JENSEN   Is that fellow one of the clerks?

PETTERSEN   No, he only does odd jobs of copying when there is any wanted. But I can tell you old Ekdal was a fine fellow in his day.

JENSEN   He looks as if he had seen better times.

PETTERSEN   That he has. He was a lieutenant, though you wouldn't think it.

JENSEN   The deuce he was!

PETTERSEN   True as I'm alive. But he took to the timber trade, or something. They say he played old Werle a remarkably dirty trick once. The two of them were in partnership up at Höidal at that time. Oh, I know all about old Ekdal, I do. Many's the glass of bitters or bottle of beer we've drunk together at Mother Eriksen's.

JENSEN   I shouldn't have thought he had much to stand treat with.

PETTERSEN   Good Lord, Jensen, it's me that's stood the treat! Besides, I think one ought to be a bit civil to gentry that have come down in the world.

JENSEN   Did he go bankrupt, then?

PETTERSEN   No, it was a deal worse than that. He went to gaol.

JENSEN   To gaol!

PETTERSEN   Or perhaps it was the penitentiary—. *(Listens.)* Sh! they are getting up from the table now.

The dining-room doors are thrown open by a couple of servants. MRS. SÖRBY *comes out, talking to two of the guests. The others follow her by degrees, with the elder* WERLE *amongst them.* HJALMAR EKDAL *and* GREGERS WERLE *come last.*

MRS. SÖRBY *(to the* SERVANT, *in passing)*   We will take coffee in the music-room, Pettersen.

PETTERSEN   Very good, ma'am.

MRS. SÖRBY *and the two gentlemen go into the inner room and out to the right of it.* PETTERSEN *and* JENSEN *follow them.*

THE FLABBY GUEST *(to the* THIN-HAIRED GUEST*)*   Whew!—it's hard work eating through a dinner like that!

THE THIN-HAIRED GUEST   Oh, with a little good-will, it's amazing what you can get through in three hours.

THE FLABBY GUEST   Yes, but afterwards, my dear sir, afterwards!

ANOTHER GUEST   I believe the coffee and liqueurs are to be served in the music-room.

THE FLABBY GUEST   Good! Then perhaps Mrs. Sörby will play us something.

THE THIN-HAIRED GUEST *(in a low voice)*   So long as she doesn't make us dance to a tune we don't like.

THE FLABBY GUEST   Not a bit of it; Bertha would never go back on her old friends.

They laugh and go into the inner room.

WERLE *(in a low and depressed voice)*   I don't think anybody noticed it, Gregers.

GREGERS *(looking at him)*   What?

WERLE Didn't you notice it either?

GREGERS What was there to notice?

WERLE We were thirteen at table.

GREGERS Really? Were we?

WERLE *(with a look towards* HJALMAR EKDAL*)* We are always accustomed to sit down twelve. *(Turns to the other guests.)* Come along in here, gentlemen.

He leads the way out through the inner room, and is followed by all the others except HJALMAR *and* GREGERS.

HJALMAR *(who has heard what they were saying)* You shouldn't have invited me, Gregers.

GREGERS What? This party is supposed to be in my honour. Why should I not invite my best and only friend?

HJALMAR But I don't believe your father likes it. I never come to the house.

GREGERS So I understand. But I wanted to see you and talk to you, because I expect to be going away again directly.—Well, we two old schoolfellows have drifted a long way apart from each other, haven't we? We have not met for sixteen or seventeen years.

HJALMAR Is it so long?

GREGERS It is indeed. And how is the world treating you? You look well. You have almost become corpulent!

HJALMAR Well, I should hardly call it corpulent; but probably I look more of a man than I did then.

GREGERS That you do; there is certainly more of your outer man.

HJALMAR *(sadly)* But the inner man, Gregers! Believe me, there is a vast difference there. You know what a disastrous blow has fallen on me and mine, since we two last met.

GREGERS *(lowering his voice)* How is your father getting on now?

HJALMAR My dear fellow, don't let us talk about it. My poor unfortunate father lives at home with me, of course. He has not another creature in the world to cling to. But you can understand what torture it is to me to speak about it. Tell me, rather, how you have been getting on up there at the works.

GREGERS It has been splendidly lonely. I have had a fine opportunity to ruminate over all sorts of things. Come here, let us make ourselves more comfortable.

He sits down in an armchair by the fire and pushes HJALMAR *into another beside him.*

HJALMAR *(with feeling)* Anyway, Gregers, I am grateful to you for asking me here; it shows that you no longer bear me any grudge.

GREGERS *(astonished)* What should make you think I had any grudge against you?

HJALMAR Just at first you certainly had.

GREGERS When?

HJALMAR After that miserable affair happened. And it was perfectly natural that you should, seeing that your own father was within a hair's breadth of being drawn into this—this terrible business.

GREGERS Was that any reason for my bearing you a grudge? Who put that idea into your head?

HJALMAR I know you did, Gregers; your father himself told me so.

GREGERS *(with a start)* My father! Did he, indeed? Ah!—And so that's why you never let me hear from you—not a single word?

HJALMAR Yes.

GREGERS Not even when you went and turned yourself into a photographer?

HJALMAR Your father said I had better not write to you about anything at all.

GREGERS *(looking straight in front of him)* Well, perhaps he was right. But tell me now, Hjalmar, are you tolerably content with your present position?

HJALMAR *(with a slight sigh)* Oh yes, oh yes; I may say so, certainly. It was a bit difficult for me at first, as you can understand. It was such an entirely new life to take up. But then the old life could never have been the same any more. My father's hopeless disaster—the shame and disgrace, Gregers—

GREGERS *(feelingly)* Yes, yes—of course, of course.

HJALMAR It was impossible to think of going on with my studies; we hadn't a shilling left—worse than that, there were debts, most of them owed to your father, I believe—

GREGERS Hm!—

HJALMAR So that it seemed to me the best thing was to drop the old life and all its associations, once and for all. It was chiefly due to your father's advice that I did so; and as he was so kind in helping me—

GREGERS My father was?

HJALMAR Surely you know he was? Where do you suppose I could find the money to learn photography and set myself up in a studio? That costs a bit, I can tell you.

GREGERS And did my father pay for all this?

HJALMAR Yes, my dear fellow, didn't you know that? I understood that he had written to you about it.

GREGERS He never said a word about its being his doing. He must have forgotten. We have never written anything but business letters to each other. So it was really my father—!

HJALMAR Yes, that it was, indeed. He has never wanted anyone to know anything about it, but it was he. And it was thanks to him, too, that I was able to marry. But perhaps that is news to you too?

GREGERS I knew nothing whatever about it. *(Takes him by the arm.)* I can't tell you, my dear Hjalmar, how glad all this makes me—and how it pains me at the same time. I may have been unjust to my father after all, in some things. It shows at any rate that he has a heart. There is evidence of a conscience about it—

HJALMAR Of a conscience—?

GREGERS Well, call it what you like. I can't tell you how glad I am to hear this about my father.—And so you are a married man, Hjalmar. It will be a long time before I shall be able to say that of myself. Well, I hope you are happy in your marriage.

HJALMAR Very happy. I have as pretty and as capable a wife as a man could wish, and she is by no means without education either.

GREGERS *(slightly surprised)* I should hope not!

HJALMAR Well, life is an education, you see. Her daily companionship with me—and we see a few clever people now and then. I can assure you, you would hardly know it was the same Gina.

GREGERS Gina?

HJALMAR Yes, don't you remember her name was Gina?

GREGERS What Gina? I don't know—

HJALMAR Have you forgotten that she had a place in this house once?

GREGERS *(glancing at him)*   Is it Gina Hansen?

HJALMAR   Of course it is Gina Hansen.

GREGERS   Who kept house for us that last year when my mother was ill?

HJALMAR   Certainly. But I thought, my dear fellow, that your father had written to you about my marriage.

GREGERS *(rising)*   Yes, he did; but not that it was—. *(Walks up and down.)* Yes, wait a bit. I expect he did, now that I think of it. My father always writes me such brief letters. *(Sits down on the arm of* HJALMAR's *chair.)* Tell me, Hjalmar—it's curious—how did you come to make Gina's—your wife's acquaintance?

HJALMAR   It was quite simple. Gina was not here any longer. Everything was upside down in the house then with your mother's illness; Gina could not put up with it, so she took herself off. That was the year before your mother died—or I daresay it was the same year.

GREGERS   It was the same year. I was up at the works then. And after that?

HJALMAR   Well, Gina went home to her mother, a very active and hard-working woman, who kept a small restaurant. And she had a room to let, a very nice, comfortable room—

GREGERS   And you were fortunate enough to get it, I suppose?

HJALMAR   Yes, and in fact it was your father who put the idea into my head. And that, you see, was the way I came to know Gina.

GREGERS   And it ended in your falling in love?

HJALMAR   Yes. Young people don't take long to fall in love, you know.

GREGERS *(rise again and walks about)*   Tell me, was it when you were engaged that my father induced you—I mean, was it then that you began to think of taking up photography?

HJALMAR   Certainly. I was so anxious to get some settled occupation, and both your father and I thought photography offered the best chances. And Gina thought so too. Yes, and there was another reason, I must tell you; it turned out that, fortunately, Gina had taken some lessons in retouching photography.

GREGERS   It was extraordinarily lucky altogether.

HJALMAR *(in a pleased voice as he rises)*   Yes, wasn't it! Don't you think everything happened wonderfully luckily for me?

GREGERS   I do, indeed. It looks as if my father had been a sort of providence to you.

HJALMAR *(heartily)*   He did not forsake his old friend's son in the day of trouble. He has a heart, you see.

MRS. SÖRBY *(coming in on the elder* WERLE's *arm)*   Don't be obstinate, dear Mr. Werle. You must not stay in there any longer staring at all those lights. It is bad for your eyes.

WERLE *(slips his arm out of hers and passes his hand over his eyes)*   Well, I really believe you are right.

MRS. SÖRBY *(to the guests, who are in the other room)*   If anyone would like a glass of punch, he must come in here and get it.

THE FAT GUEST *(coming up to her)*   Is it really true that you are determined to deprive us of the sacred right of smoking?

MRS. SÖRBY   Yes, it's forbidden in here, in Mr. Werle's sanctum.

THE THIN-HAIRED GUEST   When did you enact this cruel law about tobacco, Mrs. Sörby?

MRS. SÖRBY   After our last dinner, when certain persons allowed themselves to overstep the mark altogether.

THE THIN-HAIRED GUEST   Mayn't we overstep it just a wee bit?—not the least bit?

MRS. SÖRBY   Not the least bit in any direction, Mr. Balle.

Most of the GUESTS *have come in by this time. The* SERVANTS *hand round the punch.*

WERLE *(to* HJALMAR, *who is standing apart by a table)*   What are you looking at there, Ekdal?

HJALMAR   I was just looking at an album, Mr. Werle.

THE THIN-HAIRED GUEST *(who is wandering about the room)*   Ah, photographs! They must interest you, of course.

THE FAT GUEST *(who has settled himself in an armchair)*   Haven't you brought any of your own with you?

HJALMAR   No, I haven't.

THE FAT GUEST   You should have; it's an excellent thing for the digestion to sit and look at pictures.

THE THIN-HAIRED GUEST   And it contributes to the general entertainment, you know.

THE SHORT-SIGHTED GUEST   And all contributions are thankfully received.

MRS. SÖRBY   They think that when one is asked out to dinner one ought to do something to earn it, Mr. Ekdal.

THE FAT GUEST   Which is a real pleasure when one gets a good dinner for it.

THE THIN-HAIRED GUEST   And when it is a case of a struggle for existence, then—

MRS. SÖRBY   You are right there! *(They go on laughing and joking.)*

GREGERS *(aside, to* HJALMAR)   You must join in, Hjalmar.

HJALMAR *(wincing)*   How on earth am I to join in?

THE FAT GUEST   Don't you think, Mr. Werle, that Tokay may be considered a comparatively wholesome drink?

WERLE *(standing by the fire)*   I can vouch for the Tokay you had today, anyway; it is of one of the very finest years. But I have no doubt you noticed that.

THE FAT GUEST   Yes, it had a wonderfully delicate flavour.

HJALMAR *(hesitatingly)*   Is there a difference between the years then?

THE FAT GUEST *(laughing)*   Well, that's good!

WERLE *(with a smile)*   It's evidently waste of money to give him a fine wine.

THE THIN-HAIRED GUEST   Tokay grapes are like photographs, Mr. Ekdal; they need sunshine. Isn't that so?

HJALMAR   Yes, the light is a great point, certainly.

MRS. SÖRBY   Then it is just the same with all you gentlemen in official positions; you all like to bask in the sunshine of Court favour.

THE THIN-HAIRED GUEST   Come, come!—that's a very ancient joke!

THE SHORT-SIGHTED GUEST   Mrs. Sörby is coming out!

THE FAT GUEST   And at our expense. *(Wags his finger.)* Madam Bertha! Madam Bertha!

MRS. SÖRBY   Another thing that is true of you, too, is that different years' vintages may differ vastly. The old vintages are the best.

THE SHORT-SIGHTED GUEST   Do you reckon me among the old ones?

MRS. SÖRBY   Far from it.

THE THIN-HAIRED GUEST   Listen to that! But what about me, dear Mrs. Sörby?

THE FAT GUEST   Yes, and me! What vintage do you consider us?

MRS. SÖRBY   Very sweet years, both of you!

She puts a glass of punch to her lips; the GUESTS *continue laughing and joking with her.*

WERLE Mrs. Sörby can always get neatly out of a difficult position, if she likes. Don't put your glasses down; Pettersen, fill them up!—Gregers, come and have a glass with me. *(GREGERS does not move.)* Won't you join us, Ekdal? I had no opportunity of drinking with you at dinner.

GRAABERG, *the bookkeeper, peeps into the room through the private door.*

GRAABERG I beg your pardon, sir, but I can't get out.
WERLE Have you got locked in again?
GRAABERG Yes, and Flagstad has gone off with the keys.
WERLE All right, come out this way.
GRAABERG But I have someone with me—
WERLE Come along, come along, both of you. Don't mind us.

GRAABERG *and old* EKDAL *come out of the office.* WERLE *gives an involuntary exclamation of disgust; the laughing and joking stops suddenly.* HJALMAR *starts at the sight of his father, puts down his glass and turns towards the fireplace.*

EKDAL *(keeping his eyes on the ground and bowing awkwardly from side to side as he goes out, mumbling)* Excuse me! Come the wrong way—door's locked—door's locked—Excuse me!

Exit at the back, with GRAABERG.

WERLE *(between his teeth)* Confound that Graaberg!
GREGERS *(with mouth hanging open and eyes staring, to* HJALMAR*)* Surely that was never—!
THE FAT GUEST What is it? Who was that?
GREGERS Nothing; only the bookkeeper and another man.
THE THIN-HAIRED GUEST *(to* HJALMAR*)* Was he a friend of yours?
HJALMAR I don't know—I didn't notice—
THE FAT GUEST *(rising)* What the deuce is all this about?

He joins some of the others, who are talking below their breath.

MRS. SÖRBY *(whispers to the* SERVANT*)* Give him something to take away with him—something good.
PETTERSEN *(nodding)* I will. *(Exit.)*
GREGERS *(in a low and shaking voice, to* HJALMAR*)* So it was really he?
HJALMAR Yes.
GREGERS And yet you stood there and said you didn't know him!
HJALMAR *(in a loud whisper)* How could I—
GREGERS Acknowledge your own father?
HJALMAR *(bitterly)* If you were in my place, you would—

The GUESTS, *who have been talking in low tones, now raise their voices with an obvious effort.*

THE THIN-HAIRED GUEST *(coming up genially to* HJALMAR *and* GREGERS*)* Well, I suppose you two are talking over old times at College, eh? Won't you smoke, Mr. Ekdal? Shall I give you a light? Ah, I forgot, we mustn't smoke.
HJALMAR Thank you, I don't care to.
THE FAT GUEST Can't you recite some charming little poem to us, Mr. Ekdal? You used to have a great talent for that.
HJALMAR I am sorry I cannot remember anything.

THE FAT GUEST   What a pity. Well, what shall we do, Balle?

The two GUESTS *go together into the other room.*

HJALMAR *(sadly)*   Gregers, I must go away. When Fate has dealt a man such a blow as it has done to me, you know—. Say good-night to your father from me.

GREGERS   Yes, yes. Are you going straight home?

HJALMAR   Yes. Why?

GREGERS   Well, perhaps I may come along and see you presently.

HJALMAR   No, you mustn't do that. Don't come to my house. Mine is a sad home, Gregers—especially after a splendid entertainment like this. We can always find some place in the town to meet.

MRS. SÖRBY *(coming up to them, and speaking low)*   Are you going, Mr. Ekdal?

HJALMAR   Yes.

MRS. SÖRBY   Remember me to Gina.

HJALMAR   Thank you.

MRS. SÖRBY   And tell her I shall be up to see her some day soon.

HJALMAR   Yes, thanks. *(To* GREGERS*)* Stay here. I will slip out unobserved.

He goes out through the other room.

MRS. SÖRBY *(to the* SERVANT *who has come back)*   Well, did you give the old man something to take with him?

PETTERSEN   Yes, ma'am; I gave him a bottle of brandy.

MRS. SÖRBY   Oh, you might have found something better than that to give him.

PETTERSEN   No, indeed, ma'am. Brandy is what he likes best, I know.

THE FAT GUEST *(standing in the doorway with a piece of music in his hand)*   Shall we play a duet, Mrs. Sörby?

MRS. SÖRBY   Certainly.

THE GUESTS   Bravo! Bravo!

They and all the GUESTS *go out of the room.* GREGERS *remains standing by the fire. His father is looking for something on the writing-table and seems anxious for* GREGERS *to go; as* GREGERS *does not move,* WERLE *goes toward the door.*

GREGERS   Father, will you wait a moment?

WERLE *(stopping)*   What is it?

GREGERS   I want a word with you.

WERLE   Can't it wait till we are alone?

GREGERS   No, it can't. Perhaps we shall never find ourselves alone.

WERLE *(coming nearer him)*   What do you mean by that?

During the following conversation the sound of the piano is heard faintly from the other room.

GREGERS   How could you let that family come so miserably to grief?

WERLE   You mean the Ekdals, I presume.

GREGERS   Yes, I mean the Ekdals. Lieutenant Ekdal and you were once so intimate.

WERLE   A great deal too intimate, unfortunately, and I have been paying for it these many years. It is him I have to thank for the fact that my good name and reputation have suffered to some extent too.

GREGERS *(in a low voice)*   Was he really the only one guilty?

WERLE Who else, if you please!

GREGERS He and you were in partnership over that big purchase of timber—

WERLE But you know that it was Ekdal who made the map of the ground—that misleading map. He was responsible for the illegal felling of timber on Government property. In fact, he was responsible for the whole business. I had no knowledge of what Lieutenant Ekdal was undertaking.

GREGERS Lieutenant Ekdal seems to have had no knowledge himself of what he was undertaking.

WERLE Maybe. But the fact remains that he was found guilty and I was acquitted.

GREGERS Yes, I am quite aware there were no proofs.

WERLE An acquittal is an acquittal. Why are you raking up these horrible old stories, which have whitened my hair before its time? Is this what your mind has been brooding upon up there all these years? I can assure you, Gregers, that here in town the whole story has been forgotten long ago, as far as I am concerned.

GREGERS But what about that wretched family?

WERLE What could you have expected me to do for them? When Ekdal regained his freedom he was a broken man, absolutely past help. There are some men who go under entirely if Fate hits them ever so little, and never come to the surface again. Believe me, Gregers, I could have done no more than I have, without exposing myself to all sorts of suspicion and gossip—

GREGERS Suspicion—? Quite so.

WERLE I got Ekdal copying to do at the office, and I pay him a great deal more for his work than it is worth.

GREGERS *(without looking at him)* I have no doubt of that.

WERLE You smile? Perhaps you don't believe it is true? I am quite aware it doesn't appear in my accounts; I never enter such payments as that.

GREGERS *(with a cold smile)* I quite agree that there are certain expenses it is better not to enter in one's accounts.

WERLE *(with a start)* What do you mean?

GREGERS *(in a more confident tone)* Have you entered in your accounts what it cost you to have Hjalmar Ekdal taught photography?

WERLE I? Why should I have entered that?

GREGERS I know now that it was you who paid it. And I know, too, that it was you who made it possible for him to settle down as he has done.

WERLE And, after all that, you say I have done nothing for the Ekdals! I can assure you that family has caused me enough expense, in all conscience.

GREGERS Have you entered any one item of it in your accounts?

WERLE Why do you ask that?

GREGERS I have my reasons. Tell me this—didn't your great solicitude for your old friend's son begin just at the time he was contemplating getting married?

WERLE Good Lord!—after all these years, how can I—?

GREGERS You wrote to me at the time—a business letter, naturally—and in a postscript, in just one or two words, you told me Hjalmar Ekdal had married a Miss Hansen.

WERLE Well, that was true; that was her name.

GREGERS But you never mentioned the fact that this Miss Hansen was Gina Hansen, our former housekeeper.

WERLE *(laughs ironically, but in a constrained manner)* No, I didn't suppose you were so specially interested in our former housekeeper.

GREGERS   Nor was I. But *(lowering his voice)* there was someone else in this house who *was* specially interested in her.

WERLE   What do you mean? *(In an angry voice.)* You don't mean that you refer to me?

GREGERS *(in a low voice, but firmly)*   Yes, I refer to you.

WERLE   And you dare—! You have the audacity to—! And as for this ungrateful photographer fellow—how dare he presume to come here and make such accusations!

GREGERS   Hjalmar has never said a single word of the kind. I don't believe that he has even a suspicion of anything of the sort.

WERLE   Then where have you got it from? Who could have told you such a thing?

GREGERS   My poor unhappy mother told me, the last time I saw her.

WERLE   Your mother! I might have thought as much! She and you were always together in everything. It was she from the very first who drew you apart from me.

GREGERS   No, it was the suffering and humiliation she had to undergo, till at last it broke her down and drove her to such a miserable end.

WERLE   She had not the least suffering or humiliation to undergo—not more than many others, anyway! But there is no dealing with sickly and hysterical folk. I have good reason to know that. And so you have been brooding over such a suspicion as this!—you have been raking up all sorts of ancient rumours and slanders about your own father!—Let me tell you, Gregers, I really think at your age you might find something more useful to do.

GREGERS   Yes, I think it is quite time I did.

WERLE   And perhaps, if you did, you would be easier in your mind than you appear to be at present. What possible point is there in your drudging away at the works, year in and year out, like the merest clerk, and refusing to accept a shilling more than the ordinary wages? It is simply folly on your part.

GREGERS   Ah, if only I were as certain of that as you are!

WERLE   I think I understand. You want to be independent, not to be under the slightest obligation to me. Well, now there happens to be an opportunity for you to become independent, to be your own master entirely.

GREGERS   Indeed? and what may that be?

WERLE   When I wrote to you that I had urgent reasons for asking you to come to town at once—well—

GREGERS   Well, what is it exactly that you want? I have been waiting all day for you to tell me.

WERLE   I propose to offer you a partnership in the firm.

GREGERS   I!—a partner in your firm?

WERLE   Yes. It need not necessitate our always being together. You might manage the business here in town, and I would go up to the works.

GREGERS   You?

WERLE   Yes. You see, I am no longer as fit for my work as I used to be. I am obliged to be careful of my eyes, Gregers; they have begun to get a bit weak.

GREGERS   They were always that.

WERLE   Not as weak as they are now. And, besides that, circumstances might make it desirable for me to live up there, at any rate for a while.

GREGERS   Such an idea has never entered into my mind.

WERLE   Listen, Gregers; we seem to stand apart from each other in very many ways, but after all we are father and son. It seems to me we ought to be able to come to some kind of an understanding with one another.

GREGERS   To outward appearance, I suppose you mean?

WERLE   Well, at any rate that would be something. Think over it, Gregers. Doesn't it appear to you as a possibility? Eh?

GREGERS *(looking at him coldly)*   There is something at the bottom of all this.

WERLE   What do you mean?

GREGERS   You probably intend to make use of me in some way.

WERLE   Two people as closely connected as we are can always be of use to one another.

GREGERS   Possibly.

WERLE   I want you to stay at home with me for a bit. I am a lonely man, Gregers; I have always felt lonely, all my life, and I feel it more than ever now that I am no longer young. I need some companionship.

GREGERS   You have Mrs. Sörby.

WERLE   Yes, that is true; and she has, to tell you the truth, become almost indispensable to me. She is clever and easy-going, and livens up the house—and I need that sort of thing badly.

GREGERS   Quite so; you seem to me to have just what you want.

WERLE   Yes, but I am afraid it can't last. Under such circumstances a woman is easily put into a false position in the eyes of the world. Indeed, one might almost say that the man is not much safer.

GREGERS   Oh, when a man gives such good dinners as you do, he can take considerable liberties with public opinion.

WERLE   Yes, but what about her, Gregers? I am so afraid she won't put up with it any longer. And even if she did—if out of attachment to me she were to disregard gossip and scandal, and so on—? You have a very strong sense of justice, Gregers; doesn't it seem to you that—

GREGERS *(interrupting him)*   Tell me this, without beating about the bush; are you thinking of marrying her?

WERLE   And if I were, what then?

GREGERS   Exactly. What then?

WERLE   Would it be a thing you would find it impossible to countenance?

GREGERS   Not in the least. Not by any means.

WERLE   Well, I was not sure whether perhaps, out of respect for your mother's memory, you—

GREGERS   I am not sentimental.

WERLE   Well, whether you are or not, you have at any rate lifted a heavy weight off my mind. It is an immense pleasure to me that I can count on your sympathy in this matter.

GREGERS *(looking intently at him)*   Now I understand how it is you want to make use of me.

WERLE   Make use of you? What an expression!

GREGERS   Oh, don't let us be so nice in our choice of words—at any rate when we are alone. *(With a short laugh.)* I see! This was the reason why it was absolutely necessary for me to come to town—to help you to make a pretence of family life here for Mrs. Sörby's edification!—a touching tableau, father and son! That would be something new.

WERLE   How dare you take that tone with me!

GREGERS   When was there any family life here? Never, as long as I can remember. But now, if you please, a little of that sort of thing is desirable. It would undeniably have a splendid effect if it could get about that the son has hastened home, on the wings of filial piety, to attend his old father's wedding. What becomes then of all the rumours of what his poor dead mother had suffered and endured? They are absolutely silenced; her son's action would do that.

WERLE   Gregers—I don't believe there is anyone living towards whom you feel as bitterly as you do to me.

GREGERS *(in a low voice)*   I have seen you at too close quarters.

WERLE   You have seen me through your mother's eyes. *(Lowering his voice a little.)* But you ought to remember that her eyes were—were—clouded now and then.

GREGERS *(trembling)*   I understand what you mean. But who is to blame for my mother's unfortunate weakness? You, and all your—! The last of them was this woman that was foisted upon Hjalmar Ekdal when you were tired of her. Faugh!

WERLE *(shrugging his shoulders)*   Just the way your mother used to talk.

GREGERS *(without paying any attention to him)*   And there he is now, like a big unsuspecting child, in the middle of all this deceit; living under the same roof with a woman like that, without the slightest idea that what he calls his home is built on a lie. *(Taking a step nearer his father.)* When I look back on all you have done, it is like looking at a battle-field strewn on every side with ruined lives.

WERLE   I am beginning to think the gulf between us two is too wide to be bridged.

GREGERS *(controls himself and bows)*   I agree with you; and therefore I will take my hat and go.

WERLE   Go? Out of the house?

GREGERS   Yes, I see at last some object to live for.

WERLE   What may that be?

GREGERS   You would only laugh, if I told you.

WERLE   A lonely man doesn't laugh so readily, Gregers.

GREGERS *(pointing to the back of the room)*   Look, father—Mrs. Sörby is playing blind man's buff with your guests. Good-night, and good-bye.

He goes out. The GUESTS *are heard merrily laughing as they come into the other room.*

WERLE *(muttering scornfully after* GREGERS*)*   Ha! Ha! Poor chap—and he says he is not sentimental!

Act II

SCENE. HJALMAR EKDAL'S *studio, a fairly large attic room. On the right, a sloping roof with large glass windows, half covered by a blue curtain. The door leading into the room is in the right-hand corner, and further forward on the same side is a door leading to a sitting-room. In the left-hand wall are two doors, with a stove between them. In the back wall are wide double doors, arranged so as to slide back on either side. The studio is simply but comfortably furnished. Between the doors on the right, near the wall, stands a sofa with a table and some chairs; on the table a shaded lamp is lit. An old armchair is drawn up by the stove. Photographic apparatus and instruments are scattered here and there about the room. Against the back wall, to the left of the double doors, is a bookcase, containing some books, boxes, bottles of chemicals, and a variety of instruments and tools. On the table are lying photographs, paint-brushes, paper, and so forth.* GINA EKDAL *is sitting on a chair by the table, sewing.* HEDVIG *is on the sofa reading a book, with her thumbs in her ears and her hands shading her eyes.*

GINA *(who has glanced several times at* HEDVIG *with restrained anxiety, calls to her)* Hedvig!

HEDVIG *does not hear her.*

GINA *(louder)* Hedvig!
HEDVIG *(puts her hands down and looks up)* Yes, mother?
GINA Hedvig, you must be good and not sit there reading any longer.
HEDVIG Mayn't I read a little more, mother? Just a little?
GINA No, no, you must put your book away. Your father doesn't like it; he don't ever read in the evening himself.
HEDVIG *(shutting her book)* No, father doesn't care so much about reading.
GINA *(puts down her sewing and takes up a pencil and a little note-book)* Do you remember how much we paid for the butter to-day?
HEDVIG One and ninepence.
GINA That's right. *(Writes it down.)* It's frightful, the amount of butter we get through in this house. And then there was the smoked sausage and the cheese—let me see—*(writes)*—and then there was the ham—*(adds up)*—there, that lot alone come to—
HEDVIG And then there's the beer.
GINA Yes, of course. *(Puts it down.)* It soon mounts up, but it can't be helped.
HEDVIG But then you and I didn't need anything hot for dinner, as father was out.
GINA No, that was lucky. And, what's more, I have taken eight and sixpence for photographs.
HEDVIG As much as that!
GINA Yes, eight and sixpence exactly.

Silence. GINA *resumes her sewing.* HEDVIG *takes a piece of paper and a pencil and begins drawing, shading her eyes with her left hand.*

HEDVIG Isn't it funny to think of father at a big dinner-party at Mr. Werle's?
GINA He is not, strictly speaking, Mr. Werle's guest, it was the son who invited him. *(After a pause.)* We have nothing to do with Mr. Werle.
HEDVIG I wish most awfully he would come home. He promised to ask Mrs. Sörby for something nice to bring back to me.
GINA Ah, there's plenty of good things going in that house, I can tell you.
HEDVIG *(resuming her drawing)* And I believe I am a bit hungry too.

Old EKDAL *comes in, a roll of papers under his arm and a parcel sticking out of his pocket.*

GINA How late you are tonight, grandfather—
EKDAL They had locked up the office. I had to wait for Graaberg; and then I was obliged to go through—hm!
HEDVIG Did they give you some more copying, grandfather?
EKDAL All this lot. Just look!
GINA That's splendid.
HEDVIG And you have got a parcel in your pocket, too.
EKDAL Have I? Oh, that's nothing, that's nothing. *(Puts down his stick in a corner of the room.)* This will keep me busy for a long time, Gina. *(Pulls one of the sliding doors at the back a little open.)* Hush! *(He looks in through the door for a moment*

and then shuts it again carefully.) Ha, ha! They are all asleep together in there. And she has gone into the basket of her own accord. Ha, ha!

HEDVIG   Are you quite sure she isn't cold in the basket, grandfather?

EKDAL   What an idea! Cold? In all that straw? *(Goes to the farther door on the left.)* Are there matches here?

GINA   There's some on the chest of drawers. *(EKDAL goes into his room.)*

HEDVIG   Isn't it nice that grandfather has got all this fresh copying to do!

GINA   Yes, poor old grandfather; he will be able to make a little pocket-money.

HEDVIG   And won't be able to sit all the morning at that horrid restaurant of Mrs. Eriksen's over there.

GINA   Yes, that's another thing.

HEDVIG   *(after a short pause)*   Do you think they are still at dinner?

GINA   Goodness knows. Very likely they are.

HEDVIG   Just think what a lovely dinner father must be having. I know he will be in such a good temper when he comes home. Don't you think so, mother?

GINA   Yes, but just think how nice it would be if we could tell him we had let the room.

HEDVIG   We don't need that tonight.

GINA   Oh, every little bit helps. And the room is standing empty.

HEDVIG   I mean that we don't need to be able to tell him that tonight. He will be in good spirits anyway. We shall be all the better for the news about the room for another time.

GINA   *(looking at her)*   Do you like having some good news to tell your father when he comes home of an evening?

HEDVIG   Yes, because things seem to go pleasanter then.

GINA   *(thoughtfully)*   There's something in that, certainly.

Old EKDAL *comes in again, and is going out by the nearer door on the left.*

GINA   *(turning in her chair)*   Do you want something in the kitchen, grandfather?

EKDAL   Yes, I do. Don't get up. *(Exit.)*

GINA   I hope he is not poking the fire, in there. *(After a short pause.)* Hedvig, do see what he is up to.

EKDAL *returns with a little jug of hot water.*

HEDVIG   Have you been getting some hot water, grandfather?

EKDAL   Yes, I have. I want it for something—I have got some writing to do, and my ink is all dried up as thick as porridge—hm!

GINA   But you ought to have your supper first. It is all laid in there.

EKDAL   I can't bother about supper, Gina. I'm dreadfully busy, I tell you. I won't have anyone coming into my room, not anyone—hm! *(Goes into his room.)*

GINA *and* HEDVIG *exchange glances.*

GINA   *(in a low voice)*   Can you imagine where he has got the money from?

HEDVIG   I expect he has got it from Graaberg.

GINA   Not a bit of it. Graaberg always sends his pay to me.

HEDVIG   Then he must have got a bottle on credit somewhere.

GINA   Poor grandfather, no one would give him credit.

Enter HJALMAR EKDAL, *wearing an overcoat and a grey felt hat.*

GINA *(throws down her sewing and gets up)* Back already, Hjalmar?

HEDVIG *(at the same time, jumping up)* Fancy your coming now, father!

HJALMAR *(taking off his hat)* Oh, most of the guests were leaving.

HEDVIG So early?

HJALMAR Yes, it was a dinner-party, you know. *(Begins taking off his coat.)*

GINA Let me help you.

HEDVIG And me too. *(They take off his coat, Gina hangs it on the wall.)* Were there many there, father?

HJALMAR Oh no, not many. We were just twelve or fourteen at table.

GINA And you had a chat with all of them?

HJALMAR A little, yes; but Gregers practically monopolised me.

GINA Is Gregers as ugly as ever?

HJALMAR Well, he's not particularly handsome. Isn't the old man in yet?

HEDVIG Yes, grandfather is busy writing.

HJALMAR Did he say anything?

GINA No, what about?

HJALMAR Didn't he say anything about—? I fancied I heard he had been to Graaberg. I will go in and see him for a moment.

GINA No, no, it's not worth while.

HJALMAR Why not? Did he say he didn't want me to go in?

GINA He doesn't want anyone to go in tonight.

HEDVIG *(making signs to her)* Hm—hm!

GINA *(taking no notice)* He came in and fetched himself some hot water.

HJALMAR Then I suppose he is—?

GINA Yes, that's it.

HJALMAR Good heavens—my poor old grey-haired father! Well, anyway, let him have what little pleasure he can.

Old EKDAL *comes out of his room wearing a dressing-gown and smoking a pipe.*

EKDAL Ah, you are back. I thought I heard your voice.

HJALMAR I have just come in.

EKDAL You didn't see me, then?

HJALMAR No, but they told me you had gone through—and so I thought I would come after you.

EKDAL Nice of you, Hjalmar—hm! What were all those people?

HJALMAR Oh, all sorts. Flor was there, and Balle, and Kaspersen, and what's-his-name—I don't remember—all of them men about the Court, you know.

EKDAL *(nodding)* Do you hear that, Gina? All of 'em men about the Court!

GINA Yes, they are very fine in that house now.

HEDVIG Did any of them sing, father—or recite?

HJALMAR No, they only talked nonsense. They wanted me to recite to them, but I wasn't going to do that.

EKDAL You weren't going to do that, eh?

GINA I think you might have done that.

HJALMAR No, I don't think one ought to be at everybody's beck and call. *(Walking up and down.)* Anyway, I am not going to be.

EKDAL No, no, Hjalmar's not that sort.

HJALMAR I fail to see why I should be expected to amuse others if I happen to go out for once. Let the others exert themselves a little. These fellows go from one house to another, eating and drinking, every day of their lives. I think they should take the trouble to do something in return for all the excellent meals they get.

GINA   But you didn't tell them that?

HJALMAR   *(humming)*   Hm—hm—hm; they heard something that astonished them, I can tell you.

EKDAL   And all of 'em men about the Court!

HJALMAR   That didn't save them. *(Casually.)* And then we had a little argument about Tokay.

EKDAL   Tokay, did you say? That's a grand wine, if you like!

HJALMAR   It *can* be a grand wine. But of course, you know, all vintages are not of the same quality; it entirely depends how much sunshine the vines have had.

GINA   There isn't anything you don't know, Hjalmar.

EKDAL   And did they want to argue about that?

HJALMAR   They tried to; but they were informed that it was just the same with Court officials. All years are not equally good in their case either, they were told.

GINA   I don't know how you think of such things!

EKDAL   Ha—ha! They had to put that in their pipes and smoke it?

HJALMAR   We let them have it straight between the eyes.

EKDAL   Do you hear that, Gina? Straight between the eyes!—and men about the Court too!

GINA   Fancy that, straight between the eyes!

HJALMAR   Yes, but I don't want you to talk about it. One doesn't repeat such things as that. The whole thing passed off quite amicably, of course. They were very genial, pleasant fellows. Why should I want to hurt their feelings? Not I.

EKDAL   But straight between the eyes—

HEDVIG   *(coaxingly)*   How funny it is to see you in dress clothes. You look very nice in dress clothes, father.

HJALMAR   Yes, don't you think so? And this really fits me beautifully. It looks almost as if it had been made for me—a little tight in the armholes, perhaps—help me, Hedvig. *(Takes off the coat.)* I would rather put on my jacket. Where have you put my jacket, Gina?

GINA   Here it is. *(Brings the jacket and helps him on with it.)*

HJALMAR   That's better! Be sure you don't forget to let Molvik have the suit back tomorrow morning.

GINA   *(folding it up)*   I will see to it.

HJALMAR   *(stretching himself)*   Ah, that's more comfortable. And I rather fancy a loose, easy coat like this suits my style better. Don't you think so, Hedvig?

HEDVIG   Yes, father.

HJALMAR   Especially if I tie my cravat with flowing ends, like this—what do you think?

HEDVIG   Yes, it goes so well with your beard and your thick curly hair.

HJALMAR   I don't know that I should call it curly; I should think "wavy" was a better word.

HEDVIG   Yes, it has beautiful waves in it.

HJALMAR   That's it—wavy.

HEDVIG   *(after a little pause, pulling his coat)*   Father!

HJALMAR   Well, what is it?

HEDVIG   You know quite well.

HJALMAR   No, indeed I don't.

HEDVIG *(half laughing and half crying)* Father, you mustn't tease me any longer.

HJALMAR But what is it?

HEDVIG *(shaking him)* Don't pretend! Out with them, father—the good things you promised to bring home to me.

HJALMAR There, just fancy my having forgotten all about it!

HEDVIG No, you are only making fun of me, father! It's too bad. Where have you hidden it?

HJALMAR Upon my word, I forgot all about it! But wait a bit, Hedvig, I have got something else for you. *(Rises, and hunts in the pockets of the dress coat.)*

HEDVIG *(jumping and clapping her hands)* Oh, mother! mother!

GINA You see, if you only give him time—

HJALMAR *(holding out a bit of paper)* Look, here it is.

HEDVIG That! It is only a piece of paper.

HJALMAR It is the bill of fare, my dear—the whole bill of fare. Here is "Menu" at the top, that means the bill of fare.

HEDVIG Is that all you have got?

HJALMAR I forgot to bring anything else, I tell you. But I can tell you all these good things were a great treat. Sit down at the table now and read the list, and I will describe the taste of all the dishes to you. Look, Hedvig.

HEDVIG *(gulping down her tears)* Thank you.

She sits down, but does not read it. GINA *makes signs to her, and* HJALMAR *notices it.*

HJALMAR *(walking up and down)* It is incredible what the father of a family is expected to be able to think about; and if he forgets the slightest little thing, he is sure to see glum faces at once. Well, one gets accustomed even to that. *(Stands by the stove beside his father.)* Have you taken a peep in there this evening, father?

EKDAL Of course I have. She has gone into the basket.

HJALMAR Has she gone into the basket? She is beginning to get accustomed to it, then.

EKDAL Yes, I told you she would. But, you know, there are some little matters—

HJALMAR Little improvements, eh?

EKDAL Yes, but we must see to them.

HJALMAR Very well, let us talk over these improvements, father. Come and sit on the sofa.

EKDAL Quite so. But I think I will just attend to my pipe first—it wants cleaning. Hm! *(Goes into his room.)*

GINA *(smiling at* HJALMAR*)* Clean his pipe!

HJALMAR Come, come, Gina—let him be. Poor, broken-down old fellow. Yes, these improvements—we had better get them off our hands tomorrow.

GINA You won't have time tomorrow, Ekdal.

HEDVIG *(interrupting)* Oh yes, he will, mother!

GINA Remember those prints that have got to be retouched. They have asked for them over and over again.

HJALMAR Bless my soul, those prints again! I'll finish those off easily enough. Are there any new orders?

GINA No, worse luck, there are only the two appointments you booked for tomorrow.

HJALMAR Nothing else? Well, of course, if people won't exert themselves—

GINA But what am I to do? I am sure I advertise as much as I can.

HJALMAR   Yes, you advertise!—and you see how much good it does. I suppose no-body has been to look at the room either?

GINA   Not yet.

HJALMAR   What else could you expect? If people won't keep their wits about them—. You really must pull yourself together, Gina.

HEDVIG *(coming forward)*   Shall I get you your flute, father?

HJALMAR   No, no; I have no room for pleasures in my life. *(Walking about.)* Work, work—I will show you what work means to-morrow, you may be sure of that. I shall go on working as long as my strength holds out—

GINA   My dear Hjalmar, I didn't mean you to take me up that way.

HEDVIG   Wouldn't you like me to bring you a bottle of beer, father?

HJALMAR   Certainly not, I don't want anything. *(Stops suddenly.)* Beer?—did you say beer?

HEDVIG *(briskly)*   Yes, father, lovely cool beer.

HJALMAR   Well, if you insist on it, I don't mind if you bring me a bottle.

GINA   Yes, do, Hedvig; then we shall feel cosy.

HEDVIG *runs towards the kitchen.* HJALMAR, *who is standing by the stove, stops her, looks at her, and draws her towards him.*

HJALMAR   My little Hedvig!

HEDVIG *(with tears of joy in her eyes)*   Dear, kind father!

HJALMAR   No, you mustn't call me that. There was I, sitting at the rich man's table, enjoying myself, sitting there filling myself with all his good things—. I might at least have remembered—!

GINA *(sitting down at the table)*   Don't be absurd, Hjalmar.

HJALMAR   It's true. But you mustn't think too much of that. You know, anyway, how much I love you.

HEDVIG *(throwing her arms round him)*   And we love you so awfully, father!

HJALMAR   And if sometimes I am unreasonable with you, you will remember—won't you—that I am a man beset by a host of cares. There, there! *(Wipes his eyes.)* No beer at such a moment as this. Give me my flute.

HEDVIG *runs to the bookcase and gets it for him.*

HJALMAR   Thank you. That's better. With my flute in my hand, and you two be-side me—!

HEDVIG *sits down at the table beside* GINA. HJALMAR *walks up and down, then reso-lutely begins playing a Bohemian country dance, but in very slow time and very sen-timentally. He soon stops, stretches out his left hand to* GINA *and says in a voice full of emotion.*

HJALMAR   No matter if we have to live poorly and frugally, Gina—this is our home; and I will say this, that it is good to be at home again.

He resumes his playing; shortly afterwards a knock is heard at the door.

GINA *(getting up)*   Hush, Hjalmar—I think there is some one at the door.

HJALMAR *(laying down his flute)*   Of course!

GINA *goes and opens the door.*

GREGERS WERLE *(speaking outside the door)*   I beg your pardon—

GINA *(retreating a little)* Ah!

GREGERS *(outside)* Is this where Mr. Ekdal the photographer lives?

GINA Yes, it is.

HJALMAR *(going to the door)* Gregers! Is it you after all? Come in, come in.

GREGERS *(coming in)* I told you I would come up and see you.

HJALMAR But to-night—? Have you left all your guests?

GREGERS I have left my guests and my home. Good evening, Mrs. Ekdal. I don't suppose you recognise me?

GINA Of course, I do; you are not so difficult to recognise, Mr. Werle.

GREGERS I suppose not; I am like my mother, and no doubt you remember her a little.

HJALMAR Did you say that you had left your home?

GREGERS Yes, I have gone to an hotel.

HJALMAR Indeed? Well, as you are here, take off your things and sit down.

GREGERS Thank you.

He takes off his coat. He has changed his clothes, and is dressed in a plain grey suit of provincial cut.

HJALMAR Sit down here on the sofa. Make yourself at home.

GREGERS *sits on the sofa and* HJALMAR *on the chair by the table.*

GREGERS *(looking round him)* So this is where you live, Hjalmar. Do you work here too?

HJALMAR This is the studio, as you can see—

GINA It is our largest room, and so we prefer sitting in here.

HJALMAR We used to live in better quarters, but these have one great advantage, there is such a splendid amount of space—

GINA And we have a room on the other side of the passage, which we can let.

GREGERS *(to* HJALMAR*)* Ah!—have you any lodgers?

HJALMAR No, not yet. It is not so easy, you know; one has to make an effort to get them. *(To* HEDVIG*)* What about that beer?

HEDVIG *nods and goes into the kitchen.*

GREGERS Is that your daughter?

HJALMAR Yes, that is Hedvig.

GREGERS Your only child?

HJALMAR Our only child, yes. She is the source of our greatest happiness and—*(lowering his voice)* also of our keenest sorrow.

GREGERS What do you mean?

HJALMAR She is dangerously threatened with the loss of her sight.

GREGERS Going blind!

HJALMAR Yes. There are only the first symptoms of it at present, and all may go well for some time yet. But the doctor has warned us. It is inevitable.

GREGERS What a terrible misfortune! What is the cause of it?

HJALMAR *(sighing)* It is hereditary, apparently.

GREGERS *(starting)* Hereditary?

GINA Hjalmar's mother had weak eyes too.

HJALMAR Yes, so my father tells me; I can't remember her, you know.

GREGERS Poor child! And how does she take it?

HJALMAR   Oh well, you will understand that we have not had the heart to tell her anything about it. She suspects nothing. She is as happy and careless as a bird, singing about the house, and so she is flitting through her life into the blackness that awaits her. *(Despairingly.)* It is terribly hard for me, Gregers.

HEDVIG *comes in, bringing a tray with beer and glasses, and sets it down on the table.*

HJALMAR *(stroking her hair)*   Thank you, dear, thank you.

HEDVIG *puts her arms round his neck and whispers in his ear.*

HJALMAR   No—no bread and butter, thanks—unless perhaps you would take some, Gregers?

GREGERS *(shaking his head)*   No, thanks.

HJALMAR *(still speaking in a melancholy tone)*   Well, you may as well bring in a little, all the same. If you have a crusty piece, I should prefer it—and be sure to see that there is enough butter on it.

HEDVIG *nods happily and goes into the kitchen again.*

GREGERS *(who has followed her with his eyes)*   She seems well and strong in other respects.

GINA   Yes, thank heaven, she is quite well in every other way.

GREGERS   She looks as if she will be like you when she grows up, Mrs. Ekdal. How old is she now?

GINA   Hedvig is just fourteen; her birthday is the day after to-morrow.

GREGERS   She is tall for her age.

GINA   Yes, she has grown a lot this last year.

GREGERS   These young people growing up make us realise our own age. How long have you been married now?

GINA   We have been married—let me see—just fifteen years.

GREGERS   Can it be so long as that!

GINA *(looks at him watchfully)*   It is indeed.

HJALMAR   Yes, that it is. Fifteen years all but a few months. *(Changes the subject.)* They must have seemed long years to you up at the works, Gregers.

GREGERS   They did seem so while I was getting through them; but now, looking back on them, I can scarcely believe it is all that time.

Old EKDAL *comes in from his room, without his pipe, and wearing his old military cap. He walks a little unsteadily.*

EKDAL   Now then, Hjalmar, we can sit down and talk over those—hm! What is it —what is it?

HJALMAR *(going towards him)*   Father, some one is here—Gregers Werle. I don't know whether you remember him?

EKDAL *(looking at* GREGERS, *who has risen)*   Werle? Do you mean the son? What does he want with me?

HJALMAR   Nothing; it is me he has come to see.

EKDAL   Oh, then there is nothing the matter?

HJALMAR   No, of course not.

EKDAL *(swinging his arms)*   I don't mind, you know; I am not afraid, but—

GREGERS *(going up to him)*   I only want to bring you a greeting from your old hunting-ground, Lieutenant Ekdal.

EKDAL   My hunting-ground?

GREGERS   Yes, from up there round the Höidal works.

EKDAL   Ah, up there. I was well known up there once.

GREGERS   You were a mighty hunter in those days.

EKDAL   Ah, that I was, I believe you. You are looking at my cap. I need ask no one's leave to wear it here indoors. So long as I don't go into the streets with it on—

HEDVIG *brings in a plate of bread and butter, and puts it on the table.*

HJALMAR   Sit down, father, and have a glass of beer. Help yourself, Gregers.

EKDAL *totters over to the sofa, mumbling.* GREGERS *sits down on a chair beside him.* HJALMAR *sits on the other side of* GREGERS. GINA *sits a little way from the table and sews;* HEDVIG *stands beside her* FATHER.

GREGERS   Do you remember, Lieutenant Ekdal, how Hjalmar and I used to come up and see you in the summertime and at Christmas?

EKDAL   Did you? No—no—I don't remember that. But I can tell you I was a fine sportsman in those days. I have shot bears, too—nine of 'em, I have shot.

GREGERS *(looking at him sympathetically)*   And now you get no more shooting.

EKDAL   Oh, I don't know about that. I get some sport still now and then. Not that sort of sport, of course. In the forests, you know—the forests, the forests—! *(Drinks.)* Are the forests looking fine up there now?

GREGERS   Not so fine as in your day. A lot of them have been cut down.

EKDAL *(lowering his voice, as if afraid)*   That's a dangerous thing to do. That brings trouble. The forests avenge themselves.

HJALMAR *(filling his* FATHER's *glass)*   Now, father—a little more.

GREGERS   How can a man like you, who were always accustomed to be in the open, live in a stuffy town, boxed in by four walls like this?

EKDAL *(looking at* HJALMAR *with a quiet smile)*   Oh, it is not so bad here, not at all so bad.

GREGERS   But think of all you were always accustomed to—the cool, refreshing breezes, the free life in the woods and on the moors, among the beasts and birds—

EKDAL *(smiling)*   Hjalmar, shall we show it to him?

HJALMAR *(hastily and with some embarrassment)*   No, no, father—not to-night.

GREGERS   What does he want to show me?

HJALMAR   Oh, it is only a sort of—. You can see it some other time.

GREGERS *(continues talking to* EKDAL*)*   What I had in my mind, Lieutenant Ekdal, was that you should come back up to the works with me; I am going back there very soon. You could easily get some copying to do up there too; and here you haven't a single thing to give you pleasure or to amuse you.

EKDAL *(staring at him in amazement)*   I haven't a single thing to—!

GREGERS   Well, of course, you have Hjalmar; but then he has his own family ties. But a man like you, who has always felt so strongly the call of a free, unfettered life—

EKDAL *(striking the table)*   Hjalmar, he *shall* see it!

HJALMAR   But, father, is it worth while now? It is dark, you know.

EKDAL   Nonsense, there is moonlight. *(Gets up.)* He *shall* see it, I say. Let me pass—and you come and help me, Hjalmar.

HEDVIG   Yes, do, father!

HJALMAR *(getting up)*   Very well.

GREGERS *(to* GINA*)* What does he want me to see?

GINA Oh, you mustn't expect to see anything very wonderful.

EKDAL *and* HJALMAR *have gone to the back of the stage, and each of them pushes back one side of the sliding doors.* HEDVIG *helps the old man;* GREGERS *remains standing by the sofa;* GINA *sits quietly sewing. The open doors disclose a large, irregularly-shaped attic, full of recesses and with two stove-pipes running up through it. Through the little roof-windows the bright moonlight is pouring in upon certain spots in the attic; the rest of it is in deep shadow.*

EKDAL *(to* GREGERS*)* Come close and have a look.

GREGERS *(going to him)* What is there for me to see?

EKDAL Come and take a good look. Hm!

HJALMAR *(in a slightly constrained tone)* This is all my father's, you know.

GREGERS *(comes to the door and looks into the attic)* You keep poultry then, Lieutenant Ekdal!

EKDAL I should think we did keep poultry. They are roosting now; but you should just see them in the daytime!

HEDVIG And we have got a—

EKDAL Hush! Hush! Don't say anything yet.

GREGERS You have got pigeons too, I see.

EKDAL Yes, I shouldn't wonder if we had got pigeons too! They have nesting-boxes up there under the eaves, you see; pigeons like to roost well above ground, you know.

GREGERS They are not common pigeons, though.

EKDAL Common pigeons! No, I should think not! We have got tumblers, and a pair of pouters too. But come and look here! Can you see that hutch over there against the wall?

GREGERS Yes, what is it for?

EKDAL That's where the rabbits sleep at night.

GREGERS What, have you got rabbits too?

EKDAL Yes, you bet we have rabbits! He is asking if we have got rabbits, Hjalmar! Hm! But now I will show you the great sight! Now you shall see it! Get out of the way, Hedvig. Just stand there; that's it; now look in there. Don't you see a basket with straw in it?

GREGERS Yes. And I can see a bird lying in the basket.

EKDAL Hm!—a bird!

GREGERS Isn't it a duck?

HJALMAR But what kind of a duck, should you say.

HEDVIG It isn't an ordinary duck.

EKDAL Sh!

GREGERS It isn't a foreign bird either.

EKDAL No, Mr.—Werle, that is no foreign bird, because it is a wild duck.

GREGERS No! is it really? A wild duck?

EKDAL Yes, that it is. The "bird," as you call it, is a wild duck. That's our wild duck.

HEDVIG My wild duck. It belongs to me.

GREGERS Is it possible it can live up here in the attic? Does it do well?

EKDAL Of course it has a trough of water to splash about in.

HJALMAR And gets fresh water every other day.

GINA *(turning to* HJALMAR*)*   Hjalmar, dear, it is getting icy cold in here, you know.

EKDAL   Hm! we will shut it up then. We mustn't disturb their night's rest. Catch hold, Hedvig. *(*HJALMAR *and* HEDVIG *push the doors together.)* Some other time you shall see it properly. *(Sits down in the armchair by the stove.)* They are most remarkable birds, wild ducks, I can tell you.

GREGERS   But how did you manage to capture it?

EKDAL   I didn't capture it. It is a certain person in the town here, that we have to thank for it.

GREGERS *(with a slight start)*   I suppose that man is not my father, by any chance?

EKDAL   You have hit it. Your father and no one else. Hm!

HJALMAR   It is funny you should guess that, Gregers.

GREGERS   You told me you were indebted to my father for so many different things; so I thought very likely—

GINA   But we didn't get the duck from Mr. Werle himself—

EKDAL   It is Haakon Werle we have to thank for it all the same, Gina. *(To* GREGERS.*)* He was out in a boat, you see, and shot it. But your father's sight isn't good, you know, and it was only wounded.

GREGERS   I see, it was only slightly hit.

HJALMAR   Yes, only in two or three places.

HEDVIG   It was hit in the wing, so it couldn't fly.

GREGERS   I see; then I suppose it dived down to the bottom?

EKDAL *(sleepily in a thick voice)*   Naturally. Wild duck always do that. They stick down at the bottom—as deep as they can get—bite fast hold of the weed and wrack and all the rubbish that is down there. And so they never come up again.

GREGERS   But, Lieutenant Ekdal, your wild duck came up again.

EKDAL   He had an extraordinarily clever dog, your father. And the dog—it dived after it and hauled it up again.

GREGERS *(turning to* HJALMAR*)*   And then you got it?

HJALMAR   Not directly. It was brought to your father's house first, but it didn't thrive there; so Pettersen asked leave to kill it—

EKDAL *(half asleep)*   Hm!—Pettersen—yes—old codfish!—

HJALMAR *(lowering his voice)*   That was how we got it, you see. Father knows Pettersen a little, and heard this about the wild duck, and managed to get it handed over to him.

GREGERS   And now it thrives quite well in the attic there?

HJALMAR   Yes, perfectly well. It has grown fat. It has been so long in there now that it has forgotten all about its own wild life; and that was all that was necessary.

GREGERS   You are right there, Hjalmar. Only, never let it see the sky and the water.
—But I mustn't stay any longer. I think your father has gone to sleep.

HJALMAR   Oh, don't go on that account.

GREGERS   But, by the way—you said you had a room to let, a room you don't use?

HJALMAR   Yes—why? Do you happen to know any one—?

GREGERS   Can I have the room?

HJALMAR   You?

GINA   What, you, Mr. Werle?

GREGERS   Can I have the room? If so, I will move in early to-morrow morning.

HJALMAR   Certainly, by all means—

GINA   But, Mr. Werle, it really isn't the sort of room to suit you.

HJALMAR   Gina, how can you say that!

GINA   Well, it isn't big enough or light enough, and—

GREGERS   That doesn't matter at all, Mrs. Ekdal.

HJALMAR   I should call it a very nice room, and not so badly furnished either.

GINA   But remember the couple that are lodging underneath.

GREGERS   Who are they?

GINA   One of them used to be a private tutor—

HJALMAR   Mr. Molvik—he has taken a degree—

GINA   And the other is a doctor of the name of Relling.

GREGERS   Relling? I know him a little; he used to practise up at Höidal at one time.

GINA   They are a regular pair of good-for-nothings. They are often out on the spree in the evening, and they come home late at night and not always quite—

GREGERS   I should easily get accustomed to that. I hope I shall settle down like the wild duck.

GINA   Well, I think you ought to sleep over it first, anyway.

GREGERS   You don't seem to like the idea of having me in the house, Mrs. Ekdal.

GINA   Gracious me! what makes you think that?

HJALMAR   I must say it is extremely odd of you, Gina. *(To* GREGERS.*)* Tell me, do you propose remaining here in town for the present?

GREGERS *(putting on his overcoat)*   Yes, now I propose to remain here.

HJALMAR   But not at home with your father? What do you intend to do with yourself?

GREGERS   Ah, if only I knew that, it would be all plain sailing. But when one has had the misfortune to be christened "Gregers"—"Gregers," and "Werle" to follow—did you ever hear anything so hideous?—

HJALMAR   It doesn't sound so to me.

GREGERS *(shuddering)*   I should feel inclined to spit on any fellow with a name like that. Once a man has had the misfortune to find himself saddled with the name of Gregers Werle, as I have—

HJALMAR *(laughing)*   Ha, ha! Well, but if you weren't Gregers Werle, what would you like to be?

GREGERS   If I could choose, I would rather be a clever dog than anything else.

GINA   A dog!

HEDVIG *(involuntarily)*   Oh no!

GREGERS   Yes, an extraordinarily clever dog; the sort of dog that would go down to the bottom after wild duck, when they dive down and bite fast hold of the weed and wrack in the mud.

HJALMAR   I will tell you what it is, Gregers—I don't understand a word of all this.

GREGERS   No, and I daresay the meaning is not very pretty either. Well, then, early tomorrow morning I will move in. *(To* GINA.*)* I shan't give you any trouble; I do everything for myself. *(To* HJALMAR.*)* We will finish our chat tomorrow. Good-night, Mrs. Ekdal. *(Nods to* HEDVIG.*)* Good-night.

GINA   Good-night, Mr. Werle.

HEDVIG   Good-night.

HJALMAR *(who has lit a candle)*   Wait a moment, I must give you a light; it is sure to be dark on the stair. *(*GREGERS *and* HJALMAR *go out by the outer room.)*

GINA *(staring in front of her, with her sewing lying on her lap)*   A funny idea, to want to be a dog!

HEDVIG   Do you know, mother—I believe he meant something quite different by that.

GINA   What else could he mean?

HEDVIG   I don't know; but I thought he seemed to mean something quite different from what he said—all the time

GINA   Do you think so? It certainly was queer.

HJALMAR *(coming back)*   The lamp was still lit. *(Puts out the candle and lays it down.)* Now, at last one can get a chance of something to eat. *(Begins to eat the bread and butter.)* Well, you see, Gina—if only you keep your wits about you—

GINA   How do you mean, keep your wits about you?

HJALMAR   Well, anyway we have had a bit of luck, to succeed in letting the room at last. And, besides, to a man like Gregers—a dear old friend.

GINA   Well, I really don't know what to say about it.

HEDVIG   Oh mother, you will see it will be lovely.

HJALMAR   You certainly are very odd. A little while ago you were so bent on letting the room, and now you don't like it.

GINA   Oh, I do, Hjalmar—if only it had been to some one else. What do you suppose his father will say?

HJALMAR   Old Werle? It is no business of his.

GINA   But you may be sure things have gone wrong between them again, as the young man is leaving his father's house. You know the sort of terms those two are on.

HJALMAR   That may be all very true, but—

GINA   And it is quite likely his father may think that you are at the bottom of it all.

HJALMAR   Let him think what he likes! Mr. Werle has done a wonderful lot for me; I am the last to want to deny it. But that is no reason why I should think myself bound to consult him in everything all my life.

GINA   But, Hjalmar dear, it might end in grandfather's suffering for it; he might lose the little bit of money he gets from Graaberg.

HJALMAR   I feel almost inclined to say I wish he might! Don't you suppose it is a humiliating thing for a man like me, to see his grey-haired old father treated like an outcast? But I think that sort of thing is nearly at an end. *(Takes another piece of bread and butter.)* I have a mission in life, and I shall fulfil it!

HEDVIG   Oh yes, father, do!

HJALMAR *(lowering his voice)*   I *shall* fulfil it, I say. The day will come when—when—. And that is why it is a good thing we got the room let; it puts me in a more independent position. And a man who has a mission in life must be independent of others. *(Stands by his father's chair and speaks with emotion.)* Poor old white-haired father! You may depend on your Hjalmar! He has broad shoulders—strong shoulders, at any rate. Some fine day you shall wake up, and—. *(To* GINA.*)* Don't you believe it?

GINA *(getting up)*   Of course I do; but the first thing is to see about getting him to bed.

HJALMAR   Yes, come along then.

They lift the old man carefully.

ACT III

SCENE. HJALMAR EKDAL'S *studio, the following morning. The sun is shining in through the big window in the sloping roof, where the curtain has been drawn back.* HJALMAR *is sitting at the table busy retouching a photograph. Various other portraits are lying in front of him. After a few moments* GINA *comes in by the outer door, in hat and cloak, and carrying a covered basket.*

HJALMAR   Back already, Gina?

GINA   Yes, I've no time to waste.

She puts the basket down on a chair and takes her things off.

HJALMAR   Did you look in on Gregers?

GINA   Yes, that I did; and a nice sight too! He had made the room in a pretty state as soon as he arrived.

HJALMAR   How?

GINA   He said he wanted to do everything for himself, you know. So he tried to set the stove going; and what must he do but shut the register, so that the whole room was filled with smoke. Ouf!—there was a stink like—

HJALMAR   You don't mean it!

GINA   But that's not the best of it. He wanted to put the fire out then, so he emptied his ewer into the stove, and flooded the whole floor with a filthy mess.

HJALMAR   What a nuisance!

GINA   I have just got the porter's wife to clean up after him, the pig; but the room won't be fit to go into till the afternoon.

HJALMAR   What is he doing with himself in the meantime?

GINA   He said he would go out for a bit.

HJALMAR   I went to see him, too, for a minute, after you went out.

GINA   So he told me. You have asked him to lunch.

HJALMAR   Just for a snack of lunch, you know. The first day he is here—we could hardly do less. You are sure to have something in the house.

GINA   I will go and see what I can find.

HJALMAR   Don't be too scrimpy, though; because I fancy Relling and Molvik are coming up too. I happened to meet Relling on the stair, you see, and so I had to—

GINA   Are we to have those two as well?

HJALMAR   Bless my soul!—a little bit more or less can't make much difference.

Old EKDAL *opens his door and looks in.*

EKDAL   Look here, Hjalmar—*(Seeing* GINA.*)* Oh!

GINA   Do you want something, grandfather?

EKDAL   No, no—it doesn't matter. Hm! *(Goes into his room again.)*

GINA *(taking up her basket)*   Keep your eye on him, and see he doesn't go out.

HJALMAR   Yes, yes, I will. Look here, Gina—a little herring salad would be rather nice; I rather fancy Relling and Molvik were making a night of it last night.

GINA   So long as they don't come before I am ready—

HJALMAR   They won't do that. Take your time.

GINA   Very well, and you can get a little work done in the meantime.

HJALMAR   Don't you see I *am* working? I am working as hard as I can.

GINA   You will be able to get those off your hands, you see.

Takes her basket into the kitchen. HJALMAR *resumes his work on the photographs with evident reluctance.*

EKDAL *(peeps in, and, after looking round the studio, says in a low voice)*   Have you finished that work?

HJALMAR   I am working away at these portraits—

EKDAL   Well, well, it doesn't matter—if you are so busy—Hm!

Goes in again, but leaves his door open. HJALMAR *goes on working for a little in silence; then lays down his brush and goes to the door.*

HJALMAR   Are you busy, father?

EKDAL *(from within, in an aggrieved voice)*   If you are busy, I'm busy too. Hm!

HJALMAR   Quite so, quite so.

Returns to his work. After a few moments EKDAL *comes out of his room again.*

EKDAL   Hm! Look here, Hjalmar, I am not so busy as all that.

HJALMAR   I thought you were doing your copying.

EKDAL   Deuce take Graaberg! Can't he wait a day or two? It's not a matter of life and death, I suppose.

HJALMAR   No; and you are not his slave, anyway.

EKDAL   And there is that other matter in there—

HJALMAR   Quite so. Do you want to go in? Shall I open the doors for you?

EKDAL   I don't think it would be a bad idea.

HJALMAR *(rising)*   And then we shall have got *that* off our hands.

EKDAL   Just so, yes. It must be ready by tomorrow morning early. We did say to-morrow, didn't we? Eh?

HJALMAR   Yes, tomorrow.

HJALMAR *and* EKDAL *each pull back a division of the sliding-door. The morning sun is shining in through the top-lights of the attic; some of the pigeons are flying about, others sitting cooing on the rafters; from time to time the sound of hens cackling is heard from the recesses of the attic.*

HJALMAR   There—now you can start, father.

EKDAL *(going in)*   Aren't you coming, too?

HJALMAR   Well, I don't know—I think I—. *(Seeing* GINA *at the kitchen door.)* No, I haven't time; I must work. But we must use our patent arrangement.

He pulls a cord and lowers a curtain, of which the bottom part is made out of a strip of old sailcloth, while the upper part is a fisherman's net stretched out. When it is down, the floor of the attic is no longer visible.

HJALMAR   That's it. Now I can sit down in peace for a little.

GINA   Is he rummaging about in there again?

HJALMAR   Would you rather he had gone straight to the wine-shop? *(Sitting down.)* Is there anything you want? You look so—

GINA   I only wanted to ask if you thought we could have lunch in here?

HJALMAR   Yes; I suppose we have no sitters coming as early as that?

GINA   No, I don't expect anyone except the engaged couple who want to be taken together.

HJALMAR   Why the devil can't they be taken together some other day!

GINA   It is all right, Hjalmar dear; I arranged to take them in the afternoon, when you are having your nap.

HJALMAR   That's capital! Yes, then, we will have lunch in here.

GINA   Very well, but there is no hurry about laying the lunch; you can have the table for a good while yet.

HJALMAR   Can't you see that I am taking every opportunity that I can to use the table!

GINA   Then you will be free afterwards, you see. *(Goes into the kitchen again. Short pause.)*

EKDAL *(standing in the attic doorway, behind the net)*   Hjalmar!

HJALMAR   Well?

EKDAL   I am afraid we shall be obliged to move the water-trough after all.

HJALMAR   Exactly what I have said all along.

EKDAL   Hm—hm—hm! *(Moves away from the door.)*

HJALMAR *goes on with his work for a little, then glances at the attic, and is just getting up when* HEDVIG *comes in from the kitchen; thereupon he sits down again promptly.*

HJALMAR   What do you want?

HEDVIG   Only to come in to you, father.

HJALMAR *(after a moment's pause)*   You seem to be very inquisitive. Were you sent to watch me?

HEDVIG   Of course not.

HJALMAR   What is your mother doing in there now?

HEDVIG   She's busy making a herring salad. *(Goes up to the table.)* Isn't there any little thing I could help you with, father?

HJALMAR   No, no. It is right that I should be the one to work away at it all—as long as my strength holds out. There is no fear of my wanting help, Hedvig—at any rate so long as my health doesn't give way.

HEDVIG   Oh, father—don't say such horrid things!

She wanders about the room, then stands in the attic doorway and looks in.

HJALMAR   What is he about in there?

HEDVIG   I fancy he is making a new path to the water-trough.

HJALMAR   He will never be able to manage that by himself. What a nuisance it is that I am obliged to sit here and—

HEDVIG *(going to him)*   Let me have the brush, father; I can do it, you know.

HJALMAR   Nonsense, you would only hurt your eyes.

HEDVIG   Not a bit of it. Give me the brush.

HJALMAR *(getting up)*   Well, certainly it wouldn't take me more than a minute or two.

HEDVIG   Pooh! What harm can it do me? *(Takes the brush from him.)* Now then. *(Sits down.)* I have got one here as a model, you know.

HJALMAR   But don't hurt your eyes! Do you hear? I won't be responsible; you must take the responsibility yourself, understand that.

HEDVIG *(going on with the work)*   Yes, yes, I will.

HJALMAR   Clever little girl! Just for a minute or two, you understand.

He stoops under the net and goes into the attic. HEDVIG *sits still, working.* HJALMAR'S *voice and his* FATHER'S *are heard discussing something.*

HJALMAR *(coming to the net)*   Hedvig, just give me the pincers; they are on the shelf. And the chisel. *(Looks back into the attic.)* Now you will see, father. Just let me show you first what I mean. (HEDVIG *has fetched the tools, and gives them to him.)* Thanks. I think it was a good thing I came, you know. *(Goes into the attic.)*

Sounds of carpentering and talking are heard from within. HEDVIG *stands looking after him. A moment later a knock is heard at the outer door, but she does not notice it.*

GREGERS WERLE *(who is bareheaded and without an overcoat, comes in and stands for a moment in the doorway)*   Ahem!

HEDVIG *(turns round and goes to him)* Oh, good-morning! Won't you come in?

GREGERS Thanks. *(Glances towards the attic.)* You seem to have workmen in the house.

HEDVIG No, it's only father and grandfather. I will go and tell them.

GREGERS No, no, don't do that; I would rather wait a little. *(Sits down on the sofa.)*

HEDVIG It's so untidy here—*(Begins to collect the photographs.)*

GREGERS Oh, let them be. Are they portraits that want finishing?

HEDVIG. Yes, just a little job I was helping father with.

GREGERS Any way, don't let me disturb you.

HEDVIG Oh, you don't.

She draws the things to her again and sits down to her work. GREGERS *watches her for a time without speaking.*

GREGERS Has the wild duck had a good night?

HEDVIG Yes, thanks, I think it had.

GREGERS *(turning towards the attic)* In the daylight it looks quite a different place from what it did in moonlight.

HEDVIG Yes, it has such a different look at different times. In the morning it looks quite different from in the evening, and when it rains you wouldn't think it was the same place as on a fine day.

GREGERS Ah, have you noticed that?

HEDVIG You couldn't help noticing it.

GREGERS Are you fond of being in there with the wild duck, too?

HEDVIG Yes, when I can—

GREGERS But I expect you haven't much time for that. I suppose you go to school?

HEDVIG No, I don't go to school any more. Father is afraid of my hurting my eyes.

GREGERS I see; I suppose he reads with you himself, then?

HEDVIG He has promised to read with me, but he hasn't had time so far.

GREGERS But isn't there anyone else to give you a little help?

HEDVIG Yes, there is Mr. Molvik, but he isn't always exactly—quite—that is to say—

GREGERS Not quite sober?

HEDVIG That's it.

GREGERS I see; then you have a good deal of time to yourself. And, in there, I suppose, it is like a little world of its own, isn't it?

HEDVIG Yes, exactly. And there are such lots of wonderful thing in there.

GREGERS Are there?

HEDVIG Yes, there are great cupboards full of books, and in lots of the books there are pictures.

GREGERS I see.

HEDVIG And then there is an old desk with drawers and flaps in it, and a great clock with figures that ought to come out when it strikes. But the clock isn't going any longer.

GREGERS So time has ceased to exist in there—beside the wild duck.

HEDVIG Yes. And there is an old paint-box and things—and all the books.

GREGERS And you like reading the books?

HEDVIG Yes, when I can manage it. But the most of them are in English, and I can't read that; so then I look at the pictures. There is a great big book called *Harrison's History of London;* it is quite a hundred years old, and there's a tremendous lot of pictures in it. At the beginning there's a picture of Death, with an hour-glass, and a girl. I don't like that. But there are all the other pictures of churches, and castles, and streets, and big ships sailing on the sea.

GREGERS   But, tell me, where did you get all these wonderful things from?

HEDVIG   Oh, an old sea-captain lived here once, and he used to bring them home with him. They called him the Flying Dutchman; it was a funny thing to call him, because he wasn't a Dutchman at all.

GREGERS   Wasn't he?

HEDVIG   No. But one day he never came back, and all these things were left here.

GREGERS   Tell me this—when you are sitting in there looking at the pictures, don't you want to get away out into the big world and see it for yourself?

HEDVIG   Not I! I want to stay at home here always and help father and mother.

GREGERS   To finish photographs?

HEDVIG   No, not only that. What I should like best of all would be to learn to engrave pictures like those in the English books.

GREGERS   Hm! what does your father say to that?

HEDVIG   I don't think father likes it; he is so funny about that. Just fancy, he wants me to learn such absurd things as basket-making and straw-plaiting! I don't see any good in my doing that.

GREGERS   Nor do I.

HEDVIG   But father is right so far, that if I had learnt to make baskets, I could have made the new basket for the wild duck.

GREGERS   Yes, so you could; and it was your business to see it was comfortable, wasn't it?

HEDVIG   Yes, because it is my wild duck

GREGERS   Of course it is.

HEDVIG   Yes, it's my very own. But I lend it to father and grandfather as long as they like.

GREGERS   I see, but what do they want with it?

HEDVIG   Oh, they look after it, and build places for it, and all that sort of thing.

GREGERS   I see; it is the most important person in there.

HEDVIG   That it is, because it is a real, true wild duck. Poor thing, it hasn't anyone to make friends with; isn't it a pity!

GREGERS   It has no brothers and sisters, as the rabbits have.

HEDVIG   No. The hens have got lots of others there, that they were chickens with; but it has come right away from all its friends, poor thing. It is all so mysterious about the wild duck. It has got no friends—and no one knows where it came from either.

GREGERS   And then it has been down to the ocean's depths.

HEDVIG   (looks quickly at him, half smiles and asks)   Why do you say "the ocean's depths"?

GREGERS   What else should I say?

HEDVIG   You might have said "the bottom of the sea."

GREGERS   Isn't it just the same if I say "the ocean's depths"?

HEDVIG   It sounds so funny to me to hear anyone else say "the ocean's depths."

GREGERS   Why? Tell me why.

HEDVIG   No, I won't; it's only foolishness.

GREGERS   It isn't. Tell me why you smiled.

HEDVIG   It is because whenever I happen to think all at once—all in a moment—of what is in there, the whole room and all that is in it make me think of "the ocean's depths." But that's all nonsense.

GREGERS   No, don't say that.

HEDVIG   Well, it's nothing but an attic.

GREGERS *(looking earnestly at her)*   Are you so sure of that?

HEDVIG *(astonished)*   Sure that it's an attic?

GREGERS   Yes; are you so sure of that?

HEDVIG *is silent and looks at him open-mouthed.* GINA *comes in from the kitchen to lay the table.*

GREGERS *(rising)*   I am afraid I have come too early.

GINA   Oh, well, you have got to be somewhere; and we shall very soon be ready. Clear up the table, Hedvig.

HEDVIG *gathers up the things; she and* GINA *lay the table during the following dialogue.* GREGERS *sits down in the armchair and turns over the pages of an album.*

GREGERS   I hear you can retouch photos, Mrs. Ekdal.

GINA *(glancing at him)*   Mhm! I can.

GREGERS   That must have come in very handy.

GINA   How do you mean?

GREGERS   As Hjalmar has taken to photography, I mean.

HEDVIG   Mother can take photographs too.

GINA   Oh, yes, of course I got taught to do that.

GREGERS   I suppose it is you who run the business, then?

GINA   Well, when Hjalmar hasn't time himself, I—

GREGERS   His old father takes up a great deal of his time, I suppose?

GINA   Yes, and it isn't the sort of work for a man like Hjalmar to go taking rubbishin' portraits all day long.

GREGERS   Quite so; but still, when he had once gone in for the thing—

GINA   I will ask you to understand, Mr. Werle, that Hjalmar is not an ordinary photographer.

GREGERS   Just so, just so; but—*(A shot is fired within the attic.* GREGERS *starts up.)* What's that!

GINA   Bah! now they are at their firing again.

GREGERS   Do they use guns in there too?

HEDVIG   They go out shooting.

GREGERS   What on earth—? *(Goes to the attic door.)* Have you gone out shooting, Hjalmar?

HJALMAR *(inside the net)*   Oh, are you there? I didn't know. I was so busy—*(To* HEDVIG.*)* To think of your not telling us! *(Comes into the studio.)*

GREGERS   Do you go shooting in there in the attic?

HJALMAR *(showing a double-barrelled pistol)*   Oh, only with this old thing.

GINA   Yes, you and grandfather will do yourselves a mischief some day with that there gun.

HJALMAR *(angrily)*   I think I have mentioned that a firearm of this kind is called a pistol.

GINA   Well, that doesn't make it much better, that I can see.

GREGERS   So you have become a sportsman too, Hjalmar?

HJALMAR Oh, we only go after a rabbit or two now and then. It is principally to please my father, you know.

GINA Men are funny creatures, they must always have something to bemuse them.

HJALMAR *(irritably)* Quite so, quite so; men must always have something to *a*muse them.

GINA. Well, that's exactly what I said.

HJALMAR Well,—ahem! *(To* GREGERS.*)* It happens very fortunately, you see, that the attic is so situated that no one can hear us shooting. *(Lays down the pistol on the top shelf of the bookcase.)* Don't touch the pistol, Hedvig; one barrel is loaded, remember.

GREGERS *(looking through the net)* You have got a sporting gun too, I see.

HJALMAR That is father's old gun. It won't shoot any longer, there is something gone wrong with the lock. But it is rather fun to have it there all the same; we can take it to pieces now and then and clean it, and grease it, and put it together again. Of course it's my father's toy, really.

HEDVIG *(going to* GREGERS*)* Now you can see the wild duck properly.

GREGERS I was just looking at it. It seems to me to trail one wing a little.

HJALMAR Well, no wonder; it was wounded.

GREGERS And it drags one foot a little—isn't that so?

HJALMAR Perhaps just a tiny bit.

HEDVIG Yes, that was the foot the dog fixed its teeth into.

HJALMAR But otherwise it hasn't the slightest blemish; and that is really remarkable when you consider that it has had a charge of shot in its wing and has been between a dog's teeth—

GREGERS *(glancing at* HEDVIG*)* And has been down so long in the ocean's depths.

HEDVIG *(with a smile)* Yes.

GINA *(standing by the table)* That blessed wild duck! The whole place is turned upside down for it.

HJALMAR Ahem!—shall you soon have finished laying the table?

GINA Yes, very soon. Come and help me, Hedvig. *(She and* HEDVIG *go into the kitchen.)*

HJALMAR *(in an undertone)* I think perhaps you had better not stand there watching my father; he doesn't like it. *(*GREGERS *comes away from the attic door.)* And I had better shut the doors, before the others arrive. Sh! sh! Get in with you! *(He hoists up the netting and pulls the doors together.)* That contrivance is my own invention. It is really quite an amusement to have things to contrive and to repair when they go wrong. Besides, it is an absolute necessity, you see, because Gina wouldn't like to have rabbits and fowls wandering about the studio.

GREGERS Of course not, and I suppose the studio is really your wife's domain?

HJALMAR I hand over the ordinary business as much as possible to her, for that enables me to shut myself up in the sitting-room and give my mind to more important matters.

GREGERS What are they, Hjalmar?

HJALMAR I wonder you haven't asked that before. But perhaps you haven't heard anyone speak of the invention?

GREGERS The invention? No.

HJALMAR Really? You haven't heard of it? Oh well, of course, up there in those outlandish parts—

GREGERS Then you have made an invention?

HJALMAR   Not exactly made it yet, but I am working hard at it. You can surely understand that when I decided to take up photography, it was not with the idea of merely taking ordinary portraits.

GREGERS   No, that is what your wife was saying to me just now.

HJALMAR   I vowed to myself that, if I devoted my powers to this trade, I would so dignify it, that it should become both an art and a science. And so I decided to make this remarkable invention.

GREGERS   And what is the nature of the invention? What is the idea?

HJALMAR   My dear fellow, you mustn't ask me for details yet. It takes time, you know. And you mustn't suppose it is vanity that impels me. I assure you I don't work for my own sake. No, no; it is the object of my life that is in my thoughts night and day.

GREGERS   What object is that?

HJALMAR   Do you forget that poor old white-haired man?

GREGERS   Your poor father? Yes, but what exactly can you do for him?

HJALMAR   I can revive his dead self-respect by restoring the name of Ekdal to honour and dignity.

GREGERS   So that is the object of your life.

HJALMAR   Yes. I mean to rescue that poor shipwrecked being; for shipwrecked he was, when the storm broke over him. As soon as those horrible investigations were begun, he was no longer himself. That very pistol there—the same that we use to shoot rabbits with—has played its part in the tragedy of the Ekdals.

GREGERS   That pistol! Indeed?

HJALMAR   When the sentence of imprisonment was pronounced, he had his pistol in his hand—

GREGERS   Did he mean to—?

HJALMAR   Yes, but he did not dare. He was a coward; so dazed and so broken in spirit was he by that time. Can you conceive it? He, a soldier, a man who had shot nine bears and was the descendant of two lieutenant-colonels—one after the other, of course—. Can you conceive it, Gregers?

GREGERS   Yes, I can conceive it very well.

HJALMAR   I can't. And I will tell you how the pistol a second time played a part in the history of our house. When they had dressed him in prison clothes and put him under lock and key—that was a terrible time for me, my friend. I kept the blinds down on both my windows. When I peeped out, I saw the sun shining as usual. I could not understand it. I saw people going along the street, laughing and talking about casual matters. I could not understand that. It seemed to me as if the whole universe must be standing still as if it were eclipsed.

GREGERS   I felt exactly that when my mother died.

HJALMAR   It was at one of those moments that Hjalmar Ekdal pointed the pistol at his own heart.

GREGERS   Then you too meant to—?

HJALMAR   Yes.

GREGERS   But you didn't shoot?

HJALMAR   No. At that critical moment I gained the victory over myself. I went on living. But I can tell you it makes a call upon a man's courage to choose life under such conditions.

GREGERS   Well, that depends how you look at it.

HJALMAR   No, there is no question about it. But it was best so, for now I shall soon have completed my invention; and Relling thinks, and so do I, that my father will be allowed to wear his uniform again. I shall claim that as my only reward.

GREGERS   It is the matter of the uniform, then, that he—

HJALMAR   Yes, that is what he covets and yearns for most of all. You can't imagine how it cuts me to the heart. Every time we keep any little anniversary—such as our wedding-day, or anything of that sort—the old man comes in dressed in the uniform he used to wear in his happier days. But if he hears so much as a knock at the door, he hurries into his room again as fast as his poor old legs will carry him —because, you see, he daren't show himself like that to strangers. It is enough to break a son's heart to see it, I can tell you!

GREGERS   And about when do you suppose the invention will be ready?

HJALMAR   Oh, bless my soul!—you can't expect me to tell you to a day! A man who has the inventive genius can't control it exactly as he wishes. Its working depends in great measure on inspiration—on a momentary suggestion—and it is almost impossible to tell beforehand at what moment it will come.

GREGERS   But I suppose it is making good progress?

HJALMAR   Certainly it is making progress. Not a day passes without my turning it over in my mind. It possesses me entirely. Every afternoon, after I have had my lunch, I lock myself in the sitting-room where I can ruminate in peace. But it is no use trying to hurry me! that can do no good—Relling says so, too.

GREGERS   But don't you think all those arrangements in the attic there, distract you and divert your attention too much?

HJALMAR   Not a bit, not a bit; quite the contrary. You mustn't say that. It is impossible for me to be perpetually poring over the same exhausting train of ideas. I must have something as a secondary occupation, to fill in the blank hours when I am waiting for inspiration. Nothing that I am doing can prevent the flash of inspiration coming when it has to come.

GREGERS   My dear Hjalmar, I am beginning to think you have something of the wild duck in you.

HJALMAR   Something of the wild duck? How do you mean?

GREGERS   You have dived down and bitten yourself fast in the weeds.

HJALMAR   I suppose you refer to that well-nigh fatal blow that crippled my father, and me as well?

GREGERS   Not exactly that. I won't say that you have been wounded, like the duck; but you have got into a poisonous marsh, Hjalmar; you have contracted an insidious disease and have dived down to the bottom to die in the dark.

HJALMAR   I? Die in the dark? Look here, Gregers, you really must stop talking such nonsense.

GREGERS   Make your mind easy, I shall find a way to get you up to the surface again. I have got an object in life too, now; I discovered it yesterday.

HJALMAR   Maybe, but you will have the goodness to leave me out of it. I can assure you that—apart, of course, from my very natural melancholy—I feel as well as any man could wish to be.

GREGERS   That very fact is a result of the poison.

HJALMAR   Now, my dear Gregers, be good enough not to talk any more nonsense about diseases and poisons. I am not accustomed to conversation of that sort; in my house no one ever speaks to me about ugly things.

GREGERS   I can well believe it.

HJALMAR   Yes, that sort of thing doesn't suit me at all. And there *are* no marsh poisons, as you call them, here. The photographer's home is a humble one—that I know; and my means are small. But I am an inventor, let me tell you, and the breadwinner of a family. That raises me up above my humble circumstances.— Ah, here they come with the lunch!

GINA *and* HEDVIG *bring in bottles of beer, a decanter of brandy, glasses, and so forth. At the same time* RELLING *and* MOLVIK *come in from the passage. They neither of them have hats or overcoats on;* MOLVIK *is dressed in black.*

GINA *(arranging the table)* Ah, you have just come at the right moment.

RELLING Molvik thought he could smell herring-salad, and then there was no holding him. Good-morning again, Ekdal.

HJALMAR Gregers, let me introduce Mr. Molvik, and Doctor—ah, of course you know Relling?

GREGERS Slightly, yes.

RELLING Mr. Werle junior, isn't it? Yes, we have had one or two passages-at-arms up at the Höidal works. Have you just moved in?

GREGERS I only moved in this morning.

RELLING Molvik and I live just below you; so you haven't far to go for a doctor or a parson, if you should need them!

GREGERS Thanks, it is quite possible I may; because yesterday we were thirteen at table.

HJALMAR Oh, come—don't get on to ugly topics again!

RELLING You may make your mind easy, Ekdal; it isn't you that events point to.

HJALMAR I hope not, for my family's sake. But now let us sit down, and eat, drink, and be merry.

GREGERS Shall we not wait for your father?

HJALMAR No, he likes to have his lunch in his own room later. Come along!

The men sit down at table, and eat and drink. GINA *and* HEDVIG *move about, waiting on them.*

RELLING Molvik was disgracefully drunk again yesterday, Mrs. Ekdal.

GINA What? Yesterday again?

RELLING Didn't you hear him when I came home with him last night?

GINA No, I can't say I did.

RELLING It is just as well; Molvik was disgusting last night.

GINA Is that true, Mr. Molvik?

MOLVIK Let us draw a veil over last night's doings. Such things have no connection with my better self.

RELLING *(to* GREGERS*)* It comes over him like a spell; and then I have to go out on the spree with him. Mr. Molvik is a demoniac, you see.

GREGERS A demoniac?

RELLING Molvik is a demoniac, yes.

GREGERS Hm!

RELLING And demoniacs are not capable of keeping to a perfectly straight line through life; they have to stray a little bit now and then.—Well, and so you can still stand it up at those disgustingly dirty works?

GREGERS I have stood it till now.

RELLING And has your "demand," that you used to go about presenting, been met?

GREGERS   My demand? *(Understanding him.)* Oh, I see.

HJALMAR   What is this demand of yours, Gregers?

GREGERS   He is talking nonsense.

RELLING   It is perfectly true. He used to go round to all the cottagers' houses presenting what he called "the demand of the ideal."

GREGERS   I was young then.

RELLING   You are quite right, you were very young. And as for the "demand of the ideal," I never heard of your getting anyone to meet it while I was up there.

GREGERS   Nor since, either.

RELLING   Ah, I expect you have learnt enough to make you reduce the amount of your demand.

GREGERS   Never when I am dealing with a man who *is* a man.

HJALMAR   That seems to me very reasonable. A little butter, Gina.

RELLING   And a piece of pork for Molvik.

MOLVIK   Ugh! not pork!

Knocking is heard at the attic door.

HJALMAR   Open the door, Hedvig; father wants to come out.

HEDVIG *opens the door a little.* Old EKDAL *comes in holding a fresh rabbit-skin. He shuts the door after him.*

EKDAL   Good-morning, gentlemen. I have had good sport; shot a big one.

HJALMAR   And you have skinned it without me—!

EKDAL   Yes, and salted it too. Nice, tender meat, rabbit's meat; and sweet, too; tastes like sugar. I hope you will enjoy your lunch, gentlemen! *(Goes into his room.)*

MOLVIK *(getting up)*   Excuse me—I can't—I must go downstairs at once—

RELLING   Have some soda-water, you duffer!

MOLVIK *(hurrying up)*   Ugh!—Ugh! *(Goes out by the outer door.)*

RELLING *(to* HJALMAR*)*   Let us drink to the old sportsman's health.

HJALMAR *(clinking glasses with him)*   To the old sportsman on the brink of the grave!—yes.

RELLING   To the grey-haired—*(drinks)*—tell me, is it grey hair he has got, or white?

HJALMAR   As a matter of fact, it is between the two; but, as far as that goes, he hasn't much hair of any kind left.

RELLING   Oh, well—a wig will take a man through the world. You are really very fortunate, you know, Ekdal. You have got a splendid object in life to strive after—

HJALMAR   And you may be sure I *do* strive after it.

RELLING   And you have got your clever wife, paddling about in her felt slippers, with that comfortable waddle of hers, making everything easy and cosy for you.

HJALMAR   Yes, Gina—*(nodding—to her)* you are an excellent companion to go through life with, my dear.

GINA   Oh, don't sit there making fun of me.

RELLING   And then your little Hedvig, Ekdal!

HJALMAR *(with emotion)*   My child, yes! My child first and foremost. Come to me, Hedvig. *(Stroking her hair.)* What day is tomorrow?

HEDVIG *(shaking him)*   No, you mustn't say anything about it, father.

HJALMAR   It makes my heart bleed to think what a meagre affair it will be—just a little festive gathering in the attic there—

HEDVIG   But that will be just lovely, father!

RELLING   Only wait till the great invention is finished, Hedvig!

HJALMAR   Yes, indeed—then you will see! Hedvig, I am determined to make your future safe. You shall live in comfort all your life. I shall demand something for you—something or other; and that shall be the poor inventor's only reward.

HEDVIG *(throwing her arms round his neck)*   Dear, dear father!

RELLING *(to GREGERS)*   Well, don't you find it very pleasant, for a change, to sit at a well-furnished table in the midst of a happy family circle?

GREGERS   As far as I am concerned, I don't thrive in a poisonous atmosphere.

RELLING   A poisonous atmosphere?

HJALMAR   Oh, don't begin that nonsense again!

GINA   Goodness knows there's no poisonous atmosphere here, Mr. Werle; I air the place thoroughly every mortal day.

GREGERS *(rising from table)*   No airing will drive away the foulness I refer to.

HJALMAR   Foulness!

GINA   What do you think of that, Hjalmar!

RELLING   Excuse me, but isn't it more likely that you yourself have brought the foulness with you from the mines up there?

GREGERS   It is just like you to suggest that what I bring to a house is foulness.

RELLING *(going up to him)*   Listen to me, Mr. Werle junior. I have a strong suspicion that you are going about still with the original unabridged "demand of the ideal" in your pocket.

GREGERS   I carry it in my heart.

RELLING   Carry the damned thing where you like; but I advise you not to play at presenting demand notes here, as long as I am in the house.

GREGERS   And suppose I do, nevertheless?

RELLING   Then you will go downstairs head first. Now you know.

HJALMAR *(rising)*   Really, Relling!

GREGERS   Well, throw me out, then—

GINA *(interposing)*   You mustn't do any such thing, Mr. Relling. But this I will say, Mr. Werle; it doesn't come well from you, who made all that filthy mess with your stove, to come in here and talk about foulness. *(A knock is heard at the outer door.)*

HEDVIG   Somebody is knocking, mother.

HJALMAR   There now, I suppose we are going to be pestered with people!

GINA   Let me go and see. *(She goes to the door and opens it, starts, shudders and draws back.)* Oh, my goodness!

The elder WERLE, *wearing a fur coat, steps into the doorway.*

WERLE   Pardon me, but I fancy my son is living in this house.

GINA *(breathlessly)*   Yes.

HJALMAR *(coming up to them)*   Mr. Werle, won't you be so good as to—

WERLE   Thanks. I only want to speak to my son.

GREGERS   What do you want? Here I am.

WERLE   I want to speak to you in your own room.

GREGERS   In my own room—very well. *(Turns to go.)*

GINA   No, goodness knows it is not in a state for you to—

WERLE   Well, outside in the passage, then. I want to see you alone.

HJALMAR   You can do so here, Mr. Werle. Come into the sitting-room, Relling.

HJALMAR *and* RELLING *go out to the right.* GINA *takes* HEDVIG *with her into the kitchen.*

GREGERS *(after a short pause)* Well, here we are, alone now.

WERLE You made use of certain expressions last night—and, seeing that now you have taken up your abode with the Ekdals, I am driven to suppose that you are meditating some scheme or other against me.

GREGERS I am meditating opening Hjalmar Ekdal's eyes. He shall see his position as it really is; that is all.

WERLE Is this the object in life that you spoke of yesterday?

GREGERS Yes. You have left me no other.

WERLE Is it I that have upset your mind, Gregers?

GREGERS You have upset my whole life. I am not thinking of what we said about my mother—but it is you I have to thank for the fact that I am harried and tortured by a guilt-laden conscience.

WERLE Oh, it's your conscience that you are crazy about, is it?

GREGERS I ought to have taken a stand against you long ago, when the trap was laid for Lieutenant Ekdal. I ought to have warned him, for I suspected then what the outcome of it would be.

WERLE Yes, you should have spoken then.

GREGERS I had not the courage to; I was so cowed and so scared of you. I can't tell you how afraid I was of you, both then and long after.

WERLE You are not afraid of me now, apparently.

GREGERS No, fortunately. The wrong that both I and—others have done to old Ekdal can never be undone; but I can set Hjalmar free from the falsehood and dissimulation that are dragging him down.

WERLE Do you imagine you will do any good by that?

GREGERS I am confident of it.

WERLE Do you really think Hjalmar Ekdal is the sort of man to thank you for such a service?

GREGERS Certainly.

WERLE Hm!—we shall see.

GREGERS And, besides, if I am to go on living, I must do something to cure my sick conscience.

WERLE You will never cure it. Your conscience has been sickly from childhood. It is an inheritance from your mother, Gregers—the only thing she did leave you.

GREGERS *(with a bitter smile)* Haven't you managed yet to get over your mistaken calculation in thinking a fortune was coming to you with her?

WERLE Don't let us talk about irrelevant matters. Are you determined on this course?—to set Hjalmar Ekdal on what you suppose to be the right scent?

GREGERS Yes, quite determined.

WERLE Well, in that case, I might have spared myself the trouble of coming here; because I suppose it isn't any use asking you to come home again.

GREGERS No.

WERLE And you won't come into the firm, either?

GREGERS No.

WERLE So be it. But now that I propose to make a new marriage, the estate will be divided between us.

GREGERS *(quickly)* No, I won't have that.

WERLE You won't have it?

GREGERS No, I won't have it. My conscience forbids it.

WERLE *(after a short pause)* Shall you go up to the works again?

GREGERS No. I don't consider myself in your service any longer.

WERLE But what are you going to do?

GREGERS Only attain the object of my life; nothing else.

WERLE Yes—but afterwards? What will you live on?

GREGERS I have saved a little out of my pay.

WERLE That won't last you long.

GREGERS I think it will last out my time.

WERLE What do you mean?

GREGERS I shall answer no more questions.

WERLE Good-bye, then, Gregers.

GREGERS Good-bye. *(*WERLE *goes out.)*

HJALMAR *(peeping in)* Has he gone?

GREGERS Yes.

HJALMAR *and* RELLING *come in; at the same time* GINA *and* HEDVIG *come from the kitchen.*

RELLING That lunch was a failure.

GREGERS Get your things on, Hjalmar; you must come for a long walk with me.

HJALMAR With pleasure. What did your father want? Was it anything to do with me?

GREGERS Come along out; we must have a little talk. I will go and get my coat. *(Goes out.)*

GINA You oughtn't to go out with him, Hjalmar.

RELLING No, don't. Stay where you are.

HJALMAR *(taking his hat and coat)* What do you mean! When an old friend feels impelled to open his mind to me in private—?

RELLING But, devil take it, can't you see the fellow is mad, crazy, out of his senses!

GINA It is quite true. His mother had fits of that kind from time to time.

HJALMAR Then he has all the more need of a friend's watchful eye. *(To* GINA.*)* Be sure and see that dinner is ready in good time. Good-bye just now. *(Goes out by the outer door.)*

RELLING It's a great pity the fellow didn't go to hell in one of the mines at Höidal.

GINA Good lord!—what makes you say that?

RELLING *(muttering)* Oh, I have my own reasons.

GINA Do you think he is really mad?

RELLING No, unfortunately. He is not madder than most people. But he has got a disease in his system, right enough.

GINA What is the matter with him?

RELLING I will tell you, Mrs. Ekdal. He is suffering from acute rectitudinal fever.

GINA Rectitudinal fever?

HEDVIG Is that a kind of disease?

RELLING Indeed it is; it is a national disease; but it only crops up sporadically. *(Nods to* GINA.*)* Thanks for my lunch. *(Goes out by the outer door.)*

GINA *(walking about uneasily)* Ugh!—that Gregers Werle—he was always a horrid creature.

HEDVIG *(standing at the table and looking searchingly at her)* It all seems to me very odd.

ACT IV

THE SAME SCENE. *A photograph has just been taken; the camera, with a cloth thrown over it, a stand, a couple of chairs and a small table are in the middle of the floor. Afternoon light; the sun is on the point of setting; a little later it begins to grow dark.* GINA *is standing at the open door, with a small box and a wet glass plate in her hands, speaking to someone outside.*

GINA Yes, without fail. If I promise a thing, I keep my word. The first dozen shall be ready by Monday. Good-morning!

Steps are heard going down the stair. GINA *shuts the door, puts the plate in the box and replaces the whole in the camera.* HEDVIG *comes in from the kitchen.*

HEDVIG Are they gone?

GINA *(tidying the room)* Yes, thank goodness I have finished with them at last.

HEDVIG Can you imagine why father hasn't come home yet?

GINA Are you sure he is not downstairs with Relling?

HEDVIG No, he isn't. I went down the back-stair just now to see.

GINA And there is the dinner standing and getting cold for him.

HEDVIG Think of father being so late! He is always so particular to come home in time for dinner.

GINA Oh, he will come directly, no doubt.

HEDVIG I wish he would; it seems so odd here to-day, somehow.

GINA *(calls out)* Here he is!

HJALMAR *comes in from the passage.*

HEDVIG *(going to him)* Father, we have been waiting such a time for you!

GINA *(glancing at him)* What a long time you have been out, Hjalmar.

HJALMAR *(without looking at her)* I was rather long, yes.

He takes off his overcoat. GINA *and* HEDVIG *offer to help him, but he waves them aside.*

GINA Perhaps you have had your dinner with Mr. Werle.

HJALMAR *(hanging up his coat)* No.

GINA *(going towards the kitchen)* I will bring it in for you, then.

HJALMAR No let it be. I don't want anything to eat now.

HEDVIG *(going up to him)* Aren't you well, father?

HJALMAR Well? Oh, yes, well enough. Gregers and I had a very exhausting walk.

GINA You shouldn't have done that, Hjalmar; you are not accustomed to it.

HJALMAR Ah!—one has to get accustomed to a great many things in this world. *(Walks up and down.)* Has anyone been here while I was out?

GINA No one but the engaged couple.

HJALMAR No new orders?

GINA No, not today.

HEDVIG Someone is sure to come tomorrow, father, you will see.

HJALMAR Let us hope so. Tomorrow I intend to set to work as hard as I can.

HEDVIG Tomorrow! But—have you forgotten what day tomorrow is?

HJALMAR Ah, that is true. Well, the day after tomorrow then. For the future I mean to do everything myself; I don't wish anyone to help me in the work at all.

GINA But what's the good of that, Hjalmar? It will only make your life miserable. I can do the photographing all right, and you can give your time to the invention.

HEDVIG And to the wild duck, father—and all the hens and rabbits.

HJALMAR Don't talk such nonsense! From tomorrow I am never going to set foot in the attic again.

HEDVIG But, father, you know you promised me that tomorrow we should have a little festivity—

HJALMAR That's true. Well, from the day after tomorrow, then. As for that confounded wild duck, I should have great pleasure in wringing its neck!

HEDVIG *(with a scream)* The wild duck!

GINA Did you ever hear such a thing!

HEDVIG *(pulling him by the arm)* Yes, but, father, it is my wild duck!

HJALMAR That is why I won't do it. I haven't the heart—haven't the heart to do it, for your sake, Hedvig. But I feel in the bottom of my heart that I ought to do it. I ought not to tolerate under my roof a single creature that has been in that man's hands.

GINA But, good heavens, as it was from that ass Pettersen that grandfather got it—

HJALMAR *(walking up and down)* But there are certain claims—what shall I call them?—let us say claims of the ideal—absolute demands on a man, that he cannot set aside without injuring his soul.

HEDVIG *(following him about)* But think, father, the wild duck—the poor wild duck!

HJALMAR *(standing still)* Listen. I will spare it—for your sake. I will not hurt a hair of its head—well, as I said, I will spare it. There are greater difficulties than that to be tackled. Now you must go out for a little, as usual, Hedvig; it is dark enough now for you.

HEDVIG No, I don't want to go out now.

HJALMAR Yes, you must go out. Your eyes seem to me to be watering. All these vapours in here are not good for you. There is a bad atmosphere in this house.

HEDVIG All right; I will run down the back-stair and go for a little stroll. My cloak and hat—? Oh, they are in my room. Father—promise you won't do the wild duck any harm while I am out.

HJALMAR It shall not lose a feather of its head. *(Drawing her to him.)* You and I, Hedvig—we two!—now run along, dear.

HEDVIG *nods to her parents and goes out through the kitchen.* HJALMAR *walks up and down without raising his eyes.*

HJALMAR Gina!

GINA Yes?

HJALMAR From tomorrow—or let us say from the day after tomorrow—I should prefer to keep the household books myself.

GINA You want to keep the household books too!

HJALMAR Yes, or at any rate to keep account of what our income is.

GINA Bless the man—that's simple enough!

HJALMAR I am not sure; you seem to me to make what I give you go an astonishingly long way. *(Stands still and looks at her.)* How do you manage it?

GINA Because Hedvig and I need so little.

HJALMAR Is it true that father is so liberally paid for the copying he does for old Mr. Werle?

GINA I don't know about its being so liberal. I don't know what is usually paid for that kind of work.

HJALMAR Well, roughly speaking, what does he make? Tell me.

GINA   It varies; roughly speaking, I should say it is about what he costs us and a little pocket-money over.

HJALMAR   What he costs us! And you have never told me that before?

GINA   No, I couldn't. You seemed so pleased to think that he had everything from you.

HJALMAR   And in reality he had it from old Werle!

GINA   Oh, well, Mr. Werle has got plenty to spare.

HJALMAR   Light the lamp for me, please.

GINA *(lighting it)*   Besides, we don't really know if it is Mr. Werle himself; it might be Graaberg—

HJALMAR   Why do you want to shift it on to Graaberg?

GINA   I know nothing about it; I only thought—

HJALMAR   Hm!

GINA   It wasn't me that got the copying for grandfather, remember that. It was Bertha, when she came to the house.

HJALMAR   Your voice seems to me to be unsteady.

GINA *(putting the shade on the lamp)*   Does it?

HJALMAR   And your hands are shaking, aren't they?

GINA *(firmly)*   Tell me straight, Hjalmar, what nonsense has he been telling you about me?

HJALMAR   Is it true—can it possibly be true—that there was anything between you and old Mr. Werle when you were in service there?

GINA   It's not true. Not then. Mr. Werle was always after me, true enough. And his wife thought there was something in it; and then there was the devil's own fuss. Not a moment's peace did she give me, that woman—and so I threw up my place.

HJALMAR   But afterwards?

GINA   Well, then I went home. And my mother—she wasn't what you thought her, Hjalmar; she talked a heap of nonsense to me about this, that and the other. Mr. Werle was a widower by that time, you know.

HJALMAR   Well, and then?

GINA   It's best you should know it. He never let me alone, till he had had his way.

HJALMAR *(clasping his hands)*   And this is the mother of my child! How could you conceal such a thing from me?

GINA   It was wrong of me, I know. I ought to have told you about it long ago.

HJALMAR   You ought to have told me at the first,—then I should have known what sort of a woman you were.

GINA   But would you have married me, all the same?

HJALMAR   How can you suppose such a thing!

GINA   No; and that's why I didn't dare to tell you anything then. I had got to love you so dearly, as you know. And I couldn't make myself utterly wretched—

HJALMAR *(walking about)*   And this is my Hedvig's mother! And to know that I owe everything I see here—*(kicks at a chair)*—my whole home—to a favoured predecessor! Ah, that seducer, Werle!

GINA   Do you regret the fourteen—the fifteen years we have lived together?

HJALMAR *(standing in front of her)*   Tell me this. Haven't you regretted every day —every hour—this web of lies you have enmeshed me in? Answer me! Haven't you really suffered agonies of regret and remorse?

GINA   My dear Hjalmar, I have had plenty to do thinking about the housekeeping and all the work there was to do every day—

HJALMAR   Then you never wasted a thought on what your past had been!

GINA   No—God knows I had almost forgotten all about that old trouble.

HJALMAR   Oh, this callous, insensate content! There is something so shocking about it, to me. Just think of it!—not a moment's regret.

GINA   But you tell me this, Hjalmar—what would have become of you if you hadn't found a wife like me?

HJALMAR   A wife like you!

GINA   Yes; I have always been a better business man than you, so to speak. Of course, it is true I am a year or two older than you.

HJALMAR   What would have become of me?

GINA.   Yes, you had got into all sorts of bad ways when you first met me; you can't deny that.

HJALMAR   You talk about bad ways? You can't understand how a man feels when he is overcome with grief and despair—especially a man of my ardent temperament.

GINA   No, very likely not. And I oughtn't to say much about it anyway, because you made a real good husband as soon as you had a home of your own. And here we had got such a comfortable, cosy home, and Hedvig and I were just beginning to be able to spend a little bit on ourselves for food and clothes—

HJALMAR   In a swamp of deceit, yes.

GINA   If only that hateful fellow hadn't poked his nose in here!

HJALMAR   I used to think, too, that I had a happy home. It was a delusion. Where am I to look now for the necessary incentive to bring my invention into existence? Perhaps it will die with me; and then it will be your past, Gina, that has killed it.

GINA *(on the brink of tears)*   Don't talk about such things, Hjalmar. I, that have all along only wanted what was best for you!

HJALMAR   I ask you—what has become of the dream of the bread-winner now? When I lay in there on the sofa, thinking over my invention, I used to have a presentiment that it would use up all my powers. I used to feel that when the great day came when I should hold my patent in my hands, that day would be the day of my—departure. And it was my dream, too, that you would be left as the well-to-do widow of the departed inventor.

GINA *(wiping away her tears)*   You mustn't talk such nonsense, Hjalmar. I pray God I never may live to see the day when I am left a widow!

HJALMAR   Well, it is of no consequence now. It is all over now, anyway—all over now!

GREGERS WERLE *opens the outer door cautiously and looks in.*

GREGERS   May I come in?

HJALMAR   Yes, come in.

GREGERS *(advances with a beaming, happy face, and stretches out his hand to them)*   Well, you dear people—! *(Looks alternately at one and the other, and whispers to* HJALMAR.*)* Haven't you done it yet?

HJALMAR *(aloud)*   It is done.

GREGERS   It is?

HJALMAR   I have passed through the bitterest moment of my life.

GREGERS   But the most elevating too, I expect.

HJALMAR   Well, we have got it off our hands for the present, anyway.

GINA   God forgive you, Mr. Werle.

GREGERS *(greatly surprised)* But, I don't understand.

HJALMAR   What don't you understand?

GREGERS   After such a momentous enlightenment—an enlightenment that is to be the starting-point of a completely new existence—a real companionship, founded on truth and purged of all falsehood—

HJALMAR   Yes, I know; I know.

GREGERS   I certainly expected, when I came in, to be met by the light of transfiguration in the faces of you both. And yet I see nothing but gloomy, dull, miserable—

GINA *(taking off the lampshade)* Quite so.

GREGERS   I daresay you won't understand me, Mrs. Ekdal. Well, well—you will in time. But you, Hjalmar? You must feel consecrated afresh by this great enlightenment?

HJALMAR   Yes, of course I do. This is to say—in a sort of way.

GREGERS   Because there is surely nothing in the world that can compare with the happiness of forgiveness and of lifting up a guilty sinner in the arms of love.

HJALMAR   Do you think it is so easy for a man to drink the bitter cup that I have just drained?

GREGERS   No, not for an ordinary man, I daresay. But for a man like you—!

HJALMAR   Good heavens, I know that well enough. But you mustn't rush me, Gregers. It takes time, you know.

GREGERS   You have a lot of the wild duck in you, Hjalmar.

RELLING *has come in by the outer door.*

RELLING   Hullo! are you talking about the old wild duck again?

HJALMAR   Yes, the one old Mr. Werle winged.

RELLING   Old Mr. Werle—? Is it him you are talking about?

HJALMAR   Him and—the rest of us.

RELLING *(half aloud, to* GREGERS*)* I wish the devil would fly away with you!

HJALMAR   What are you saying?

RELLING   I was breathing an earnest wish that this quack doctor would take himself off home. If he stays here he is capable of being the death of both of you.

GREGERS   No harm is coming to these two, Mr. Relling. I won't speak about Hjalmar; we know him. And as for his wife, I have little doubt that she, too, has the springs of trustworthiness and sincerity deep down in her heart.

GINA *(nearly crying)* Then you ought to have let me be as I was.

RELLING *(to* GREGERS*)* Would it be indiscreet to ask precisely what you think you are doing here?

GREGERS   I am trying to lay the foundation of a true marriage.

RELLING   Then you don't think Ekdal's marriage is good enough as it is?

GREGERS   Oh, it is as good a marriage as many others, I daresay. But a true marriage it has never yet been.

HJALMAR   You have never had your eyes opened to the demands of the ideal, Relling.

RELLING   Rubbish, my dear chap!—But, excuse me, Mr. Werle, how many "true marriages," roughly speaking, have you seen in your life?

GREGERS   I scarcely think I have seen a single one.

RELLING   Nor I either.

GREGERS   But I have seen such hundreds of marriages of the opposite kind, and I have had the opportunity of watching at close quarters the mischief such a marriage may do to both parties.

HJALMAR   A man's moral character may be completely sapped; that is the dreadful part of it.

RELLING   Well, I have never exactly been married, so I can't lay down the law on the matter. But this I do know, that the child is part of the marriage too—and you must leave the child in peace.

HJALMAR   Ah—Hedvig! My poor little Hedvig!

RELLING   Yes, you will have the goodness to keep Hedvig out of the matter. You two are grown people; goodness knows, you may play ducks and drakes with your happiness, for all I care. But you must walk warily with Hedvig, believe me; otherwise it may end in your doing her a great mischief.

HJALMAR   A great mischief?

RELLING   Yes, or it may end in her doing a great mischief to herself—and perhaps to others too.

GINA   But how can you know anything about it, Mr. Relling?

HJALMAR   There is no imminent danger for her eyes, is there?

RELLING   What I mean has nothing to do with her eyes at all. But Hedvig is at a critical age. She may take all sorts of strange fancies into her head.

GINA.   There!—and to be sure she is doing that already! She has begun to be very fond of meddling with the fire, out in the kitchen. She calls it playing at houses-on-fire. Often and often I have been afraid she *would* set the house on fire.

RELLING   There you are. I knew it.

GREGERS *(to* RELLING*)*   But how do you explain such a thing?

RELLING *(sulkily)*   She is becoming a woman, my friend.

HJALMAR   So long as the child has me—! So long as my life lasts—!

A knock is heard at the door.

GINA   Hush, Hjalmar; there is someone outside. *(Calls out.)* Come in!

MRS. SÖRBY, *dressed in outdoor clothes, comes in.*

MRS. SÖRBY   Good-evening!

GINA *(going to her)*   Bertha!—is it you!

MRS. SÖRBY   Certainly it's me! But perhaps I have come at an inconvenient time?

HJALMAR   Not at all; a messenger from *that* house—

MRS. SÖRBY *(to* GINA*)*   To tell you the truth, I rather hoped I shouldn't find your men-folk at home just now; I just ran up to have a little chat with you and say good-bye.

GINA   Oh? Are you going away?

MRS. SÖRBY   Early to-morrow morning, yes—up to Höidal. Mr. Werle went this afternoon. *(Meaningly, to* GREGERS.*)* He asked to be remembered to you.

GINA   Just fancy—!

HJALMAR   So Mr. Werle has gone away?—and now you are going to join him?

MRS. SÖRBY   Yes, what do you say to that, Mr. Ekdal?

HJALMAR   Be careful what you are doing, I say.

GREGERS   I can explain. My father and Mrs. Sörby are going to be married!

HJALMAR   Going to be married!

GINA   Oh, Bertha! Has it come to that?

RELLING *(his voice faltering a little)* Is this really true?

MRS. SÖRBY Yes, my dear Relling, it is perfectly true.

RELLING Are you going to marry again?

MRS. SÖRBY Yes, that's what it has come to. Mr. Werle has got a special licence, and we are going to be married very quietly up at the works.

GREGERS Then I suppose I must wish you happiness, like a good stepson.

MRS. SÖRBY Many thanks—if you mean it. And I am sure I hope it will mean happiness, both for Mr. Werle and for me.

RELLING You can confidently hope that. Mr. Werle never gets drunk—so far as I know; and I don't imagine he is in the habit of ill-treating his wives, either, as the late lamented horse-doctor used to do.

MRS. SÖRBY Sörby is dead; let him alone. And even he had his good points.

RELLING Mr. Werle has points that are better, I expect.

MRS. SÖRBY At any rate he hasn't wasted all that was best in him. A man who does that must take the consequences.

RELLING To-night I shall go out with Molvik.

MRS. SÖRBY That is wrong of you. Don't do that—for my sake, don't.

RELLING There is nothing else for it. *(To* HJALMAR.*)* You can come too, if you like.

GINA No, thank you. Hjalmar is not going with you to places of *that* kind.

HJALMAR *(half aloud in an irritated voice)* Oh, do hold your tongue!

RELLING Good-bye, Mrs.—Werle. *(Goes out at the outer door.)*

GREGERS *(to* MRS. SÖRBY*)* You and Doctor Relling seem to know each other pretty well.

MRS. SÖRBY Yes, we have known each other many years. At one time it looked as if our friendship were going to ripen into something warmer.

GREGERS But, luckily for you, I suppose, it didn't.

MRS. SÖRBY You may well say so. But I have always been chary of giving way to impulse. A woman mustn't absolutely throw herself away, either.

GREGERS Are you not in the least afraid of my letting my father get a hint of this old acquaintance?

MRS. SÖRBY Of course I have told him about it myself.

GREGERS Indeed?

MRS. SÖRBY Your father knows every single thing with a grain of truth in it that anyone could find to tell him about me. I have told him absolutely everything; it was the first thing I did when he made it evident what his intentions were.

GREGERS Then you have been more frank than is usually the case, I expect.

MRS. SÖRBY I always have been frank. It is the best way for us women.

HJALMAR What do you say to that, Gina?

GINA Oh, women are all so different. Some are built that way; some aren't.

MRS. SÖRBY Well, Gina, I believe now that the wisest line to take is the one I have taken. And Mr. Werle hasn't concealed anything on his side, either. It is that, you see, that knits us so closely together. Now he can sit and talk to me as fearlessly as a child. That is a thing he has never had a chance of doing yet. All his young days, and for the best years of his life, when he was a healthy and vigorous man, he had to sit and listen to nothing but sermons on his sins. And very often the point of the sermons turned on the most imaginary offences—at least, so it seems to me.

GINA Yes, it's quite certain that's true.

GREGERS If you ladies are going into those subjects, I had better take my leave.

MRS. SÖRBY   Oh, you can stay, for that matter. I won't say a word more. But I
wanted you to understand that I have done nothing deceitful or in the least degree
underhand. Very likely you think I am coming in for a great slice of luck; and so I
am, in a way. But, all the same, I don't believe I shall be taking more than I shall be
giving. At any rate I shall never forsake him; and what I *can* do is to look after him
and care for him as no one else can, now that he will soon be helpless.
HJALMAR   Soon be helpless?
GREGERS *(to* MRS. SÖRBY*)*   Don't speak of that here.
MRS. SÖRBY   There is no use concealing it any longer, however much he would like
to. He is going blind.
HJALMAR *(with a start)*   Going blind? That is extraordinary. Is he going blind too?
GINA   A great many people do.
MRS. SÖRBY   And one can well imagine what that means to a business man. Well, I
shall try to use my eyes for him as well as I can. But I mustn't stay any longer; I am
frightfully busy just now.—Oh, I was to tell you this, Mr. Ekdal, that if there were
anything in which Mr. Werle could be of service to you, you were just to go to
Graaberg about it.
GREGERS   A message that I should think Hjalmar Ekdal would be *very* grateful for!
MRS. SÖRBY   Really? I rather think there was a time when—
GINA   He's quite right, Bertha. Hjalmar doesn't need to take anything from Mr.
Werle now.
HJALMAR *(slowly and weightily)*   Will you give my kind regards to your future hus-
band, and say that I mean as soon as possible to call on Graaberg—
GREGERS   What! Do you really mean to do that?
HJALMAR   To call on Graaberg, I say, and ask for an account of the sum I owe his
employer. I will pay that debt of honour—ha! ha! debt of honour is a good name
for it!— but enough of that. I will pay the whole sum, with five per cent, interest.
GINA.   But, my dear Hjalmar, we have no money to do that with, Heaven knows!
HJALMAR   Will you tell your *fiancé* that I am working busily at my invention. Will
you tell him that what keeps up my strength for this exhausting task is the desire to
be quit of a painful burden of debt. That is why I am working at this invention.
The whole proceeds of it shall be devoted to freeing myself from the obligation
under which your future husband's pecuniary advances have laid me.
MRS. SÖRBY   Something or other has happened in this house.
HJALMAR   You are right.
MRS. SÖRBY   Well—good-bye, then. I had something I wanted to talk over with
you, Gina; but that must wait till another time. Good-bye!

HJALMAR *and* GREGERS *bow silently;* GINA *follows her to the door.*

HJALMAR   Not farther than the door, Gina!

MRS. SÖRBY *goes out;* GINA *shuts the door after her.*

HJALMAR   There, Gregers. Now I have got that load of debt off my hands.
GREGERS   Soon you will, any way.
HJALMAR   I think my attitude may be called correct.
GREGERS   You are the man I always took you for.
HJALMAR   In certain cases it is impossible to overlook the claim of the ideal. As
breadwinner of the family, I have to writhe and smart under this. I can tell you it is

by no means a joke for a man, who is not well off, to get free from a debt of many years' standing, over which the dust of oblivion, so to speak, has collected. But that makes no difference; the manhood in me demands its rights too.

GREGERS *(putting his hands on his shoulders)* Dear Hjalmar, wasn't it a good thing I came?

HJALMAR Yes.

GREGERS Hasn't it been a good thing that you have got a clear knowledge of the whole situation?

HJALMAR *(a little impatiently)* Of course it's a good thing. But there is one thing that goes against my sense of what is right.

GREGERS What is that?

HJALMAR It is this. I—well, I don't know whether I ought to speak so freely about your father?

GREGERS Don't think of me in the matter at all.

HJALMAR Very well. It seems to me a very aggravating thought that now it isn't I, but he, that will realise the true marriage.

GREGERS How can you say such a thing?

HJALMAR It certainly is so. Your father and Mrs. Sörby are entering upon a marriage which is based upon complete confidence, based upon an entire and unrestricted frankness on both sides; they conceal nothing from each other; there is no dissimulation at the back of things; they have proclaimed, if I may so express myself, a mutual forgiveness of sins.

GREGERS Well, what if they have?

HJALMAR Well, surely that is the whole thing. That is all that this difficult position needs, to lay the foundations of a true marriage—you said so yourself.

GREGERS But this is a different thing altogether, Hjalmar. Surely you are not going to compare either you or your wife with these two—well, you know what I mean?

HJALMAR Still I can't help feeling that in all this there is something that sorely injures my sense of justice. It looks for all the world as though there were no such thing as a just Providence at all.

GINA Gracious, Hjalmar!—for heaven's sake don't say such a thing.

GREGERS Ahem!—I think we had better not enter into that question.

HJALMAR But, on the other hand, I certainly seem to see the directing finger of destiny in it, all the same: He is going blind.

GINA Perhaps it isn't certain that he is.

HJALMAR There is no doubt he is. We ought not to doubt that he will, anyway; for it is just that very fact that constitutes the just retribution. He himself, in his time, has blinded the eyes of a credulous fellow-creature.

GREGERS Alas, he has done that to a good many!

HJALMAR And now comes the inexorable, mysterious power, and demands this man's own eyes.

GINA Hjalmar, how can you dare say such dreadful things! You make me all of a tremble.

HJALMAR It is good for one sometimes to plunge down into the dark side of life.

HEDVIG, *in her hat and coat, comes in at the outer door, breathless and looking happy.*

GINA Are you back again?

HEDVIG   Yes, I didn't want to stay out any longer; and it was lucky I didn't, for I have just met some one at the door.

HJALMAR   Mrs. Sörby, I suppose.

HEDVIG   Yes.

HJALMAR *(walking up and down)*   I hope you have seen her for the last time.

A pause. HEDVIG, *obviously disheartened, looks first at one and then at the other of them, as if to try and read their thoughts.*

HEDVIG *(going up to her father coaxingly)*   Father!

HJALMAR   Well, what is it, Hedvig?

HEDVIG   Mrs. Sörby had something with her for me.

HJALMAR *(standing still)*   For you?

HEDVIG   Yes, it is something for to-morrow.

GINA   Bertha has always sent some little thing for her birthday.

HJALMAR   What is it?

HEDVIG   You mustn't know anything about it yet. Mother is to give it to me in bed the first thing to-morrow morning.

HJALMAR   All this mystery!—and I am to be kept in the dark, I suppose.

HEDVIG *(quickly)*   No, you may see it if you like. It is a big letter. *(Takes a letter out of the pocket of her coat.)*

HJALMAR   A letter, too?

HEDVIG   She only gave me the letter. The rest of it is coming afterwards, I suppose. Just fancy—a letter! I have never had a letter before. And there is "Miss" on the envelope. *(Reads.)* "Miss Hedvig Ekdal." Think of it—that's me!

HJALMAR   Let me see the letter.

HEDVIG *(giving it to him)*   There you are.

HJALMAR   It is old Mr. Werle's writing.

GINA   Are you sure, Hjalmar?

HJALMAR   See for yourself.

GINA   Do you suppose I know anything about such things?

HJALMAR   Hedvig, may I open the letter—and read it?

GINA   Not to-night, Hjalmar. It is for tomorrow, you know.

HEDVIG *(softly)*   Oh, can't you let him read it! It is sure to be something nice, and then father will be happy and things will get pleasant again.

HJALMAR   Then I have leave to open it?

HEDVIG   Yes, please, father. It will be such fun to see what it is.

HJALMAR   Very well. *(He opens the letter, takes out a paper that is in it, and reads it through with evident astonishment.)* What on earth is this?

GINA.   What does it say?

HEDVIG   Yes, father—do tell us.

HJALMAR   Be quiet. *(Reads it through again; he has turned pale, but collects himself.)* It is a deed of gift, Hedvig.

HEDVIG   Really? What am I getting?

HJALMAR   Read it for yourself. (HEDVIG *goes to the lamp and reads.* HJALMAR *clasps his hands and says half aloud.)* The eyes! The eyes!—and then this letter.

HEDVIG *(who stops reading)*   Yes, but it seems to me it is grandfather who is getting it.

HJALMAR *(taking the letter from her)*   Gina—can you understand this?

GINA   I know nothing whatever about it. Tell me what it is.

HJALMAR   Old Mr. Werle writes to Hedvig that her old grandfather need not bother himself with copying work any longer, but that for the future he will be entitled to five pounds a month paid from the office—

GREGERS   Aha!

HEDVIG   Five pounds, mother!—I read that.

GINA   How nice for grandfather!

HJALMAR   Five pounds a month, as long as he needs it; that means, naturally, till his death.

GINA   Well, then, he is provided for, poor old man.

HJALMAR   But that is not all. You didn't read the rest, Hedvig. Afterwards the gift is to be transferred to you.

HEDVIG   To me! All that?

HJALMAR   You are assured the same amount for the whole of your life, it says. Do you hear that, Gina?

GINA   Yes, yes, I hear.

HEDVIG   Just think of it—I am to get all that money. *(Shakes him.)* Father, father, aren't you glad?

HJALMAR *(moving away from her)*   Glad! *(Walks up and down.)* What a future— what a picture it calls up to my eyes! It is Hedvig for whom he provides so liberally—Hedvig!

GINA   Yes, it's Hedvig's birthday—

HEDVIG   You shall have it all the same, father! Of course I shall give all the money to you and mother.

HJALMAR   To your mother, yes!—that's just the point.

GREGERS   Hjalmar, this is a trap he is laying for you.

HJALMAR   Do you think this is another trap?

GREGERS   When he was here this morning, he said: "Hjalmar Ekdal is not the man you imagine he is."

HJALMAR   Not the man—!

GREGERS   "You will see," he said.

HJALMAR   You will see whether I allow myself to be put off with a bribe—

HEDVIG   Mother, what does it all mean?

GINA   Go away and take your things off.

HEDVIG *goes out by the kitchen door, half in tears.*

GREGERS   Yes, Hjalmar—now we shall see who is right, he or I.

HJALMAR *(tears the paper slowly across, and lays the two pieces on the table)*   That is my answer.

GREGERS   That is what I expected.

HJALMAR *(goes over to* GINA, *who is standing by the stove, and speaks to her in a low voice)*   No more lies, now. If everything was over between you and him when you—when you began to love me, as you call it, why was it that he put us in a position to marry?

GINA   I suppose he thought he would get a footing in the house.

HJALMAR   Only that? Wasn't he afraid of a certain possibility?

GINA   I don't understand what you mean.

HJALMAR   I want to know, whether—whether your child has the right to live under my roof.

GINA *(drawing herself up, with eyes flashing)* Can you ask that!

HJALMAR You shall answer this question. Does Hedvig belong to me—or to—? Well?

GINA *(looking at him with cold bravado)* I don't know.

HJALMAR *(in a trembling voice)* You don't know?

GINA How should I know? A woman like me—

HJALMAR *(quietly, as he turns away from her)* Then I have no longer any part in this house.

GREGERS Think well what you are doing, Hjalmar!

HJALMAR *(putting on his overcoat)* There is nothing here for a man like me to think about.

GREGERS Indeed there is a tremendous lot here for you to think about. You three must be together, if you are going to reach the goal of self-sacrificing forgiveness.

HJALMAR I have no desire for that. Never! Never! My hat! *(Takes his hat.)* My home has fallen into ruins round me. *(Bursts into tears.)* Gregers, I have no child now!

HEDVIG *(who has opened the kitchen door)* What are you saying! *(Goes to him.)* Father! Father!

GINA Now, what's to happen!

HJALMAR Don't come near me, Hedvig! Go away—go away! I can't bear to see you. Ah—the eyes! Good-bye. *(Goes towards the door.)*

HEDVIG *(clings to him, screaming)* No, no! Don't turn away from me.

GINA *(crying out)* Look at the child, Hjalmar! Look at the child!

HJALMAR I won't! I can't! I must get out of here—away from all this!

He tears himself away from HEDVIG *and goes out by the outer door.*

HEDVIG *(with despair in her eyes)* He is going away from us, mother! He is going away! He will never come back!

GINA Don't cry, Hedvig. Father will come back.

HEDVIG *(throws herself on the sofa, sobbing)* No, no,—he will never come back any more.

GREGERS Will you believe that I meant all for the best, Mrs. Ekdal?

GINA I almost believe you did; but, God forgive you, all the same.

HEDVIG *(lying on the sofa)* I think this will kill me! What have I done to him? Mother, you *must* get him home again!

GINA Yes, yes; only be quiet, and I will go out and look for him. *(Puts on her coat.)* Perhaps he has gone down to Relling. But, if I go, you mustn't lie there crying. Will you promise me that?

HEDVIG *(sobbing convulsively)* Yes, I won't cry—if only father comes back.

GREGERS *(to* GINA, *as she goes out)* Would it not be better, anyway, to let him first fight his bitter fight to the end?

GINA He can do that afterwards. First and foremost we must get the child quiet. *(Goes out.)*

HEDVIG *(sitting upright and wiping away her tears)* Now you must tell me what is the matter. Why won't father have anything to do with me any more?

GREGERS You mustn't ask that until you are a big girl and grown up.

HEDVIG *(gulping down her tears)* But I can't go on being so wretchedly miserable till I am a big girl and grown up. I believe I know what it is—perhaps I am not really father's child.

GREGERS *(uneasily)* How on earth can that be?

HEDVIG Mother might have found me. And now perhaps father has found that out; I have read of such things.

GREGERS Well, even if it were so—

HEDVIG Yes, it seems to me he might love me just as much in spite of that—even more. We had the wild duck sent us as a present, too, but all the same I love it very dearly.

GREGERS *(to divert her thoughts)* The wild duck—that's true! Let's talk about the wild duck a little, Hedvig.

HEDVIG The poor wild duck!—he can't bear to look at it any more, either. Just fancy, he wanted to wring its neck.

GREGERS Oh, he won't do that.

HEDVIG No, but he said so. And I think it was so unkind of him to say so, because I say a prayer every night for the wild duck, and pray that it may be preserved from death and anything that will harm it.

GREGERS *(looking at her)* Do you say your prayers at night?

HEDVIG Of course.

GREGERS Who taught you?

HEDVIG I taught myself. It was once when father was very ill and had leeches on his neck, and said he was at the point of death.

GREGERS Really?

HEDVIG So I said a prayer for him when I had got into bed—and since then I have gone on doing it.

GREGERS And now you pray for the wild duck too?

HEDVIG I thought it would be best to put the wild duck in the prayer too, because it was so sickly at first.

GREGERS Do you say prayers in the morning, too?

HEDVIG No, of course I don't.

GREGERS Why don't you say them in the morning as well?

HEDVIG Because in the morning it is light, and there is nothing to be afraid of.

GREGERS And your father wanted to wring the neck of the wild duck that you love so dearly?

HEDVIG No, he said it would be a great pleasure to him to do it, but that he would spare it for my sake; and I think that was very nice of father.

GREGERS *(coming nearer to her)* But now, suppose you sacrificed the wild duck, of your own free will, for his sake?

HEDVIG *(getting up)* The wild duck?

GREGERS Suppose now you gave up for him, as a free-will offering, the dearest possession you have in the world?

HEDVIG Do you think it would help?

GREGERS Try it Hedvig.

HEDVIG *(gently, with glistening eyes)* Yes, I will try it.

GREGERS Have you really the strength of mind to do it, do you think?

HEDVIG I will ask grandfather to shoot the wild duck for me.

GREGERS Yes, do. But not a word about anything of the kind to your mother.

HEDVIG Why not?

GREGERS She doesn't understand us.

HEDVIG The wild duck! I will try it the first thing tomorrow morning. *(GINA comes in by the outer door.* HEDVIG *goes to her.)* Did you find him, mother?

GINA   No, but I heard he had gone out and taken Relling with him.

GREGERS   Are you certain?

GINA   Yes, the porter's wife said so. Molvik has gone with them too, she said.

GREGERS   And this, when his mind is so sorely in need of fighting in solitude—!

GINA *(taking off her things)*   Oh, you never know what men are going to do. Heaven knows where Relling has taken him off to! I ran over to Mrs. Eriksen's, but they weren't there.

HEDVIG *(struggling with her tears)*   Oh, suppose he never comes back any more!

GREGERS   He'll come back. I have a message to give him in the morning, and you will see how he will come home. You may go to sleep quite hopefully about that, Hedvig. Good-night. *(Goes out.)*

HEDVIG *(throws herself into GINA's arms, sobbing).*   Mother! Mother!

GINA *(patting her on the back and sighing)*   Yes, yes,—Relling was right. This is what happens when mad folk come presenting these demands that no one can make head or tail of.

ACT V

THE SAME SCENE. *The cold grey light of morning is shining in; wet snow is lying on the large panes of the skylight.* GINA *comes in from the kitchen wearing a high apron and carrying a broom and a duster, and goes towards the sitting-room door. At the same moment* HEDVIG *comes hurriedly in from the passage.*

GINA *(stopping)*   Well?

HEDVIG   Mother, I rather think he is downstairs with Relling—

GINA   Look at that, now!

HEDVIG   Because the porter's wife said she heard two people come in with Relling when he came home last night.

GINA   That's just what I thought.

HEDVIG   But that is no good if he won't come up to us.

GINA   At any rate I shall be able to go down and have a talk with him.

Old EKDAL *comes in from his room, in dressing-gown and slippers and smoking his pipe.*

EKDAL   Look here, Hjalmar—. Isn't Hjalmar at home?

GINA   No, he has gone out.

EKDAL   So early? and in such a heavy snowstorm? Well, well; that's his affair. I can take my morning stroll by myself.

He opens the attic door; HEDVIG *helps him. He goes in, and she shuts the door after him.*

HEDVIG *(in an undertone)*   Just think, mother—when poor grandfather hears that father wants to go away from us!

GINA   Nonsense—grandfather mustn't hear anything about it. It's God's mercy he wasn't here yesterday when all that rumpus was going on.

HEDVIG   Yes, but—

GREGERS *comes in by the outer door.*

GREGERS   Well? Have you any trace of him yet?

GINA   He is most likely downstairs with Relling, I am told.

GREGERS With Relling! Can he really have been out with that fellow?

GINA That he has, evidently.

GREGERS Yes, but he—who so urgently needed solitude to pull himself seriously together—!

GINA You may well say so.

RELLING *comes in from the passage.*

HEDVIG *(going up to him)* Is father in your rooms?

GINA *(at the same time)* Is he there?

RELLING Certainly he is.

HEDVIG And you never told us!

RELLING Yes, I know I'm a beast. But first of all I had the other beast to keep in order—our demoniac gentleman, I mean—and after that I fell so dead asleep that—

GINA What does Hjalmar say to-day?

RELLING He doesn't say anything at all.

HEDVIG Hasn't he talked to you at all?

RELLING Not a blessed word.

GREGERS Of course not; I can understand that very well.

GINA But what is he doing with himself, then?

RELLING He is lying on the sofa, snoring.

GINA Is he? Hjalmar's a fine hand at snoring.

HEDVIG Is he asleep? Can he sleep?

RELLING Well, it looks like it.

GREGERS It is easy to understand that; after the conflict of soul that has torn him—

GINA Besides, he has never been accustomed to rambling out at night.

HEDVIG I daresay it is a good thing he is getting some sleep, mother.

GINA I think so, too; and it would be a pity to wake him up too soon. Many thanks, Mr. Relling. Now first of all I must get the house cleaned up and tidied a bit, and then—. Come and help me, Hedvig.

She goes with HEDVIG *into the sitting-room.*

GREGERS *(turning to* RELLING*)* What do you think of the spiritual upheaval that is going on in Hjalmar Ekdal?

RELLING As far as I am concerned, I haven't noticed any spiritual upheaval going on in him at all.

GREGERS What! After such a crisis, when the whole of his life has been shifted on to a new basis? How can you suppose that a personality like Hjalmar's—

RELLING Personality!—he? Even if he ever had any tendency to any such abnormality as you call "personality," it has been absolutely rooted out of him and destroyed when he was a boy. I can assure you of that.

GREGERS It would certainly be very strange if that were true, in the case of a man brought up with such loving care as he was.

RELLING By those two crazy hysterical maiden aunts of his, do you mean?

GREGERS Let me tell you that they were women who were never oblivious to the demands of the ideal—but if I say that, you will only begin making fun of me again.

RELLING No, I am in no humour for that. Besides, I know all about them. He has delivered himself to me of any amount of rhetoric about these two "soul-mothers" of his. But I don't think he has much to thank them for. Ekdal's misfortune is that all his life he has been looked upon as a shining light in his own circle—

GREGERS   And is he not that?—in profundity of mind, I mean?

RELLING   I have never noticed anything of the sort. His father believed it, I daresay; the poor old lieutenant has been a simpleton all his days.

GREGERS   He has been a man with a childlike mind all his days; that is a thing you can't understand.

RELLING   All right! But when our dear sweet Hjalmar became a student of sorts, he was at once accepted amongst his fellow-students as the great light of the future. Good-looking he was, too, the nincompoop—pink and white—just what common girls like for a lover; and with his susceptible disposition and that sympathetic voice of his, and the facility with which he declaimed other people's verses and other people's thoughts—

GREGERS   *(indignantly)*   Is it Hjalmar Ekdal that you are speaking of like this?

RELLING   Yes, by your leave; for that is the real man, instead of the idol you have been falling on your knees to.

GREGERS   I venture to think I was not so blind as all that.

RELLING   Well, it's not far from the truth, anyway. You are a sick man too, you see.

GREGERS   You are right there.

RELLING   Quite so. You are suffering from a complicated complaint. First of all there is that debilitating rectitudinal fever of yours; and then, what's worse, you are always in a raving delirium of hero-worship—you must always have some object of admiration that you really have no concern with.

GREGERS   I certainly can only find that by looking outside of my own concerns.

RELLING   But you are so monstrously mistaken as to these miraculous beings you think you find around you. This is just another case of your coming to a workman's cottage to present your "demands of the ideal"; but the people in this house are all insolvent.

GREGERS   If you haven't any higher opinion of Hjalmar Ekdal than that, how can you find any pleasure in being always hand-in-glove with him?

RELLING   Bless your heart—I am supposed to be a kind of doctor, though you mightn't think it; and it is only my duty to pay some attention to the poor invalids I live in the house with.

GREGERS   Really! Is Hjalmar Ekdal a sick man too, then?

RELLING   All the world is sick, pretty nearly—that's the worst of it.

GREGERS   And what treatment are you using for Hjalmar?

RELLING   My usual one. I am trying to keep up the make-believe of life in him.

GREGERS   The make-believe? I don't think I heard you aright?

RELLING   Yes, I said make-believe. That is the stimulating principle of life, you know.

GREGERS   May I ask what sort of a make-believe enters into the scheme of Hjalmar's life?

RELLING   No, you mayn't. I never disclose secrets like that to quacks. You were making an even worse mess of his case than I. My method has stood the test of trial. I have applied it in Molvik's case too. I have made a "demoniac" of him. That is the blister I have put on *his* neck.

GREGERS   Isn't he a demoniac, then?

RELLING   What in heaven's name do you mean by "being a demoniac"? That is only a bit of make-believe I invented to keep the life in him. If I hadn't done that, the poor honest wretch would have given way to self-contempt and despair years ago. And the same with the old lieutenant there! But he has happened to hit upon the cure by himself.

GREGERS   Lieutenant Ekdal? what of him?

RELLING   Well, what do you make of an old bear-stalker, like him, going into that dark attic there to shoot rabbits? There isn't a happier sportsman in the world than that poor old man playing about in there in that scrap-heap. The four or five withered Christmas trees that he has kept are the same to him as the great tall live trees in the Höidal forests; the cocks and hens are the wild-fowl in the tree-tops; and the rabbits, that lop about all over the attic floor, are the big game this famous backwoodsman used to pit himself against.

GREGERS   Poor old man! Yes, he has indeed had to endure the quenching of all his youthful ideals.

RELLING   And, while I think of it, Mr. Werle junior—don't use that outlandish word "ideals." There is a good home-grown word—"falsehoods."

GREGERS   Do you really think the two things are the same?

RELLING   Just as nearly as typhus and putrid fever are.

GREGERS   Doctor Relling, I won't give in till I have rescued Hjalmar from your clutches.

RELLING   So much the worse for him. If you take away make-believe from the average man, you take away his happiness as well. *(To* HEDVIG, *who has come in from the sitting-room.)* Well, little wild-duck mother, I am going down now to see whether your daddy is still lying pondering over the wonderful invention. *(Goes out by the outer door.)*

GREGERS *(going up to* HEDVIG*)*   I can see by your face that the deed isn't done yet.

HEDVIG   What deed? Oh, the wild duck. No.

GREGERS   Your courage failed you when the time came to do it, I suppose?

HEDVIG   No, it's not that. But when I woke up early this morning and remembered all we said, it all seemed so strange to me.

GREGERS   Strange?

HEDVIG   Yes, I don't know—. Last night, when we were talking about it, it seemed such a splendid idea; but, after my sleep, when I remembered it again, it all seemed different.

GREGERS   I see; I suppose it was impossible for you to grow up here without something being injured in you.

HEDVIG   I don't care anything about that; if only father would come up, then—

GREGERS   Ah, if only your eyes had been opened to what makes life worth living— if you possessed the true, happy, courageous spirit of self-sacrifice—you would see how you would be able to bring him up to you. But I have faith in you still, Hedvig. *(Goes out by the outer door.)*

HEDVIG *walks up and down; she is just going into the kitchen, but at the same moment a knock is heard on the attic door; she goes and opens it a little, and old* EKDAL *comes out, after which she shuts the door again.*

EKDAL   Hm! There's not much pleasure in taking one's morning walk alone.

HEDVIG   Haven't you felt inclined for any shooting, grandfather?

EKDAL   It isn't the weather for shooting today. Too dark in there, you can hardly see a hand's length.

HEDVIG   Have you never felt inclined to shoot anything else but the rabbits?

EKDAL   Why? Aren't the rabbits good enough sport?

HEDVIG   Yes, but the wild duck?

EKDAL   Ho! ho!—are you afraid I shall shoot your wild duck for you? Never in the world: I would never do that.

HEDVIG   No, I suppose you couldn't; wild duck must be very hard to shoot.

EKDAL   Couldn't! I should rather think I could.

HEDVIG   How would you manage it, grandfather?—not my wild duck, I mean, but with others?

EKDAL   I would see that I shot them in the breast, you know, because that is the surest place. And you must shoot against the lie of the feathers, do you understand—not with the lie of the feathers.

HEDVIG   Do they die then, grandfather?

EKDAL   Certainly they do, if you shoot properly. Well, I must go in and make myself tidy. Hm!—you understand—hm! *(Goes into his room.)*

HEDVIG *waits a little; glances at the door, then goes to the bookcase, stands on tiptoe, and takes the pistol down from the shelf and looks at it.* GINA *comes in from the sitting-room, with her broom and duster.* HEDVIG *hastily puts down the pistol unnoticed.*

GINA   Don't go rummaging among your father's things, Hedvig.

HEDVIG *(moving away from the bookcase)*   I only wanted to put things straight a little.

GINA   You had much better go into the kitchen and see if the coffee is keeping hot; I will take his tray with me, when I go down to him.

HEDVIG *goes out.* GINA *begins to sweep and clean the studio. After a while the outer door is opened slowly, and* HJALMAR *looks in. He is wearing his overcoat, but is without his hat; he is unwashed and his hair is ruffled and untidy; his eyes are dull and heavy.* GINA *stands still with the broom in her hand and looks at him.*

GINA   Well there, Hjalmar!—have you come after all?

HJALMAR *(walks in and answers in a dull voice)*   I have come—but only to go away again directly.

GINA   Yes, yes—I suppose so. But, mercy me, what a sight you are!

HJALMAR   What a sight?

GINA   And your good overcoat too! It *has* had a doing!

HEDVIG *(from the kitchen doorway)*   Mother, shall I—? *(Sees* HJALMAR, *screams with joy and runs to him.)* Father! father!

HJALMAR *(turning away and waving her back)*   Go away, go away! *(To* GINA.*)* Make her go away from me, I tell you!

GINA *(in an undertone)*   Go into the sitting-room, Hedvig. *(*HEDVIG *goes in silently.)*

HJALMAR *(pulling out the table-drawer, with a show of being busy)*   I must have my books with me. Where are my books?

GINA   What books?

HJALMAR   My scientific works, of course—the technical journals I use for my invention.

GINA *(looking in the bookcase)*   Are they these unbound ones?

HJALMAR   Of course they are.

GINA *(laying a pile of magazines on the table)*   Shan't I get Hedvig to cut them for you?

HJALMAR   I don't need to have them cut. *(Short silence.)*

GINA   Is it settled that you leave us, then, Hjalmar?

HJALMAR *(rummaging among the books)*   I should think that was evident.

GINA   Yes, yes.

HJALMAR *(vehemently)*   I can't come here and get a knife into my heart every hour of the day!

GINA   God forgive you, for saying such hard things of me.

HJALMAR   Prove to me—

GINA   I think it is you should prove to me.

HJALMAR   After a past like yours? There are certain demands—one might almost call them demands of the ideal—

GINA   But what about grandfather? What is to become of him, poor old man?

HJALMAR   I know my duty; the helpless old man will go with me. I shall go into the town and make my arrangements.—Hm—*(hesitatingly)*—has anyone found my hat on the stairs?

GINA   No. Have you lost your hat?

HJALMAR   Of course I must have had it when I came in last night, there's no doubt of that; but this morning I couldn't find it.

GINA   Good Lord!—wherever did you go with those two scamps?

HJALMAR   Don't ask silly questions. Do you suppose I am in a condition to remember details.

GINA   I only hope you haven't caught cold, Hjalmar. *(Goes into the kitchen.)*

HJALMAR *(talks to himself in an angry undertone while he empties the table drawer)*   You are a scoundrel, Relling! You are a blackguard!—a shameless seducer!—I should like to murder you!

He puts some old letters on one side, comes upon the torn paper of the day before, takes it up and looks at the pieces, but puts it down hastily as GINA *comes in.*

GINA *(putting down a breakfast tray on the table)*   Here is a drop of something hot, if you could fancy it. And some bread and butter and a little salt meat with it.

HJALMAR *(glancing at the tray)*   Salt meat? Never under this roof!—It is true I haven't tasted a bit of food for four-and-twenty hours, but that makes no difference.—My notes! The beginning of my memoirs! Where on earth are my diary and my important papers? *(Opens the sitting-room door, but draws back.)* There she is again!

GINA   Good gracious, the child must be somewhere!

HJALMAR   Come out. *(Stands aside, and* HEDVIG *comes out into the studio, looking frightened.* HJALMAR *stands with his hand on the door-handle.)* In these last moments I am spending in my former home, I wish to be protected from those who have no business here. *(Goes into the room.)*

HEDVIG *(goes with a bound towards her mother and speaks in a low trembling voice)*   Does he mean me?

GINA   Stay in the kitchen, Hedvig; or, no—better go into your own room. *(Talks to* HJALMAR, *as she goes in to him.)* Wait a minute, Hjalmar; don't turn all the drawers upside down; I know where all the things are.

HEDVIG *(stands motionless for a moment frightened and irresolute, biting her lips to keep back the tears. Then she clenches her hands convulsively and says softly)*   The wild duck!

She creeps over and takes the pistol from the shelf, opens the attic door a little, slips in and shuts the door after her. HJALMAR *and* GINA *are heard wrangling in the sitting-room.* HJALMAR *comes out carrying some notebooks and and loose papers which he lays on the table.*

HJALMAR   That portmanteau won't nearly hold them! There are a hundred and one things I must take with me.

GINA. *(following him with the portmanteau)*   Well, let the rest wait. Just take a shirt and a pair of drawers with you.

HJALMAR   Poof!—these exhausting preparations—! *(Takes off his overcoat and throws it on the sofa.)*

GINA   And there is the coffee getting all cold, too.

HJALMAR   Hm! *(Drinks a mouthful absently and then another.)*

GINA *(dusting the backs of the chairs)*   You will have a job to find another big attic like this for the rabbits.

HJALMAR   What! Have I got to take all the rabbits with me too?

GINA   Yes, grandfather can't live without his rabbits, I am sure.

HJALMAR   He will have to get accustomed to it. I have got to renounce what is of a deal more vital importance than rabbits.

GINA *(dusting the bookcase)*   Shall I put your flute in the portmanteau for you?

HJALMAR   No. No flute for me. But give me the pistol.

GINA   Are you going to take that there gun with you?

HJALMAR   Yes. My loaded pistol.

GINA *(looking for it)*   It isn't here. He must have taken it in with him.

HJALMAR   Is he in the attic?

GINA   No doubt he is.

HJALMAR   Hm—poor lonely old fellow. *(Takes a piece of bread and butter, eats it and drinks up his cup of coffee.)*

GINA   If only we hadn't let our other room, you might have moved in there.

HJALMAR   I should be living under the same roof with—! Never—never!

GINA   But couldn't you put up for a day or two in the sitting-room? You should have it all to yourself.

HJALMAR   Never within these walls.

GINA   Well, then, downstairs, with Relling and Molvik?

HJALMAR   Don't mention those fellows' names! The very thought of them almost takes my appetite away. No, no—I must go out into the storm and snow—go from house to house seeking shelter for my father and myself.

GINA   But you have no hat, Hjalmar! You know you have lost your hat.

HJALMAR   Oh, those scum of the earth, steeped in every vice!—I must get a hat as I go. *(Takes another piece of bread and butter.)* I must make the necessary arrangements. I am not going to endanger my life. *(Searches for something on the tray.)*

GINA   What are you looking for.

HJALMAR   Butter.

GINA   I will get some in a moment. *(Goes into the kitchen.)*

HJALMAR *(calling after her)*   Oh, it's of no consequence. Dry bread will do just as well for me.

GINA *(bringing in a butter-dish)*   See, this is fresh churned.

She pours out another cup of coffee for him; he sits down on the sofa, puts more butter on his bread, and eats and drinks for a little while in silence.

HJALMAR If I decided to do so, could I—without being exposed to intrusion on anyone's part—put up for a day or two in the sitting-room there?

GINA Of course you could, if only you would.

HJALMAR Because I don't see there is any possibility of getting all father's things out in a moment.

GINA And, besides that, you have got to tell him first that you don't mean to live here with us any longer.

HJALMAR *(pushing his cup away)* Yes, that's another thing; I have got to open up all this complicated question again—I must consider the situation; I must have time to breathe; I cannot sustain all these burdens in a single day.

GINA No, and in such vile weather as it is, too.

HJALMAR *(turning over* MR. WERLE'S *letter)* I see this paper is still lying here.

GINA Yes, I haven't touched it.

HJALMAR The rubbish is no concern of mine—

GINA Well, I am sure *I* had no idea of doing anything with it.

HJALMAR But it might be as well not to let it get out of sight altogether. In all the upset of my moving, it might so easily—

GINA I'll take care of it, Hjalmar.

HJALMAR The deed of gift, after all, belongs first and foremost to my father, and it is his affair whether he chooses to make any use of it.

GINA *(sighing)* Yes, poor old father.

HJALMAR Just for the sake of safety—where can I find some paste?

GINA *(going to the book-shelf)* Here is the paste-pot.

HJALMAR And a brush.

GINA Here is a brush too. *(Brings them to him.)*

HJALMAR *(taking up a pair of scissors)* Just a strip of paper along the back—. *(Cuts and pastes.)* Far be it from me to want to do anything amiss with other people's property—least of all with what belongs to a poor old man—and, indeed, to someone else as well. There we are! Let it lie there for a little. And when it is dry, take it away. I don't wish ever to set eyes on the paper again. Never!

GREGERS WERLE *comes in from the passage.*

GREGERS *(slightly astonished)* What—are you sitting here, Hjalmar?

HJALMAR *(getting up hurriedly)* I had sunk down from exhaustion.

GREGERS You have been having some breakfast, I see.

HJALMAR The body makes its claims felt sometimes, too.

GREGERS What have you decided to do?

HJALMAR For a man like me, there is only one thing to be done. I am just engaged in putting my most important things together. But it takes time, as you may suppose.

GINA *(a little impatiently)* Well, am I to get the room ready for you, or pack your portmanteau?

HJALMAR *(with a glance of irritation towards* GREGERS*)* Pack—and get the room ready as well!

GREGERS *(after a short pause)* I should never have thought this would be the end of it. Is there really any necessity for you to leave house and home?

HJALMAR *(walking about uneasily)* What do you want me to do, then?—I am not fit to stand unhappiness, Gregers. I need a sense of security and peace about me.

GREGERS But can't you have that here? Just make the trial. It seems to me that now you have firm ground to build upon—and to begin afresh. Remember, too, you have your invention to live for.

HJALMAR Oh, don't talk to me about my invention. I shouldn't wonder if that were a very long way off.

GREGERS Really?

HJALMAR Good heavens! Yes. Just tell me what you suppose I am going to invent? Other people have invented most things already. It becomes harder every day—

GREGERS But you, who have worked so hard at it—

HJALMAR It was that scoundrel Relling who set me on to it.

GREGERS Relling?

HJALMAR Yes, it was he that first called my attention to my talent for making some remarkable discovery in photography.

GREGERS Aha!—it was Relling!

HJALMAR I got so much happiness out of it, Gregers. Not so much for the sake of the invention itself, as because Hedvig believed in it—believed in it with a child's whole-hearted enthusiasm. Perhaps I should say that I have been fool enough to go and fancy she believed in it.

GREGERS Can you really suppose that Hedvig has not been genuine about it?

HJALMAR I can suppose anything now. It is Hedvig that stands in my way. She has taken all the sunshine out of my life.

GREGERS Hedvig? Can you say that of Hedvig? How can she have done anything of the sort?

HJALMAR *(without answering him)* How unspeakably I have loved that child! How unspeakably happy I have felt every time I came home into my poor room, and she ran to meet me with her sweet little half-closed eyes!—Credulous fool! I loved her so unspeakably, that I deluded myself with the dream that she loved me just as much.

GREGERS Do you say that was a delusion?

HJALMAR How can I tell? I can get nothing whatever out of Gina, and she is so utterly lacking in any sense of the ideal side of all these complications. But to you I feel forced to open my mind, Gregers. There is that terrible doubt—perhaps Hedvig has never really honestly loved me.

GREGERS It is possible you may have proof of that. *(Listens.)* What is that? I thought I heard the wild duck cry.

HJALMAR It is the wild duck quacking. Father is in the attic.

GREGERS Is he? *(A look of happiness lights up his face.)* I tell you, you may have proof yet that your poor misunderstood Hedvig loves you.

HJALMAR What proof can she give me? I daren't believe in any assurances from that quarter.

GREGERS There is not an atom of deceitfulness in Hedvig.

HJALMAR Ah, Gregers, that is just what I am not so certain about. Who knows what Gina and that Mrs. Sörby may have sat here whispering and gossiping about? And Hedvig is generally all ears, I can tell you. Perhaps the deed of gift did not come so unexpectedly, after all. Indeed, I thought I noticed something.

GREGERS What sort of spirit is this that has taken hold of you?

HJALMAR I have had my eyes opened. Just you wait. You will see the deed of gift is only a beginning. Mrs. Sörby has all along been very thick with Hedvig, and now she has it in her power to do whatever she pleases for the child. They can take her from me whenever they like.

GREGERS   Hedvig will never leave you.

HJALMAR   Don't be so sure of that. If they come beckoning to her with their hands full of gifts—. And I have loved her so unspeakably! I, who would have thought it my greatest joy to take her carefully by the hand and lead her through life—just as one leads a child, who is frightened of the dark, through a great empty room! Now I feel such a gnawing certainty that the poor photographer, up in his garret here, has never really and truly been anything to her. She has only been cunningly careful to keep on a good footing with me till the time came.

GREGERS   You don't really believe that, Hjalmar?

HJALMAR   That is just the cruellest part of it—that I don't know what to believe— and that I shall never know. But can you really doubt that it is as I say? Ha! ha! You rely far too much on your "demands of the ideal," my good Gregers! If the others were to come, with their hands full, and call to the child: "Come away from him: you will learn what life is with us—"

GREGERS   *(hastily)*   Well, what then, do you suppose?

HJALMAR   If I asked her then: "Hedvig, are you willing to give up this life they offer you, for my sake?" *(Laughs derisively.)* Thank you!—you would just hear what answer I should get.

A pistol shot is heard from within the attic.

GREGERS   *(with a happy shout)*   Hjalmar!

HJALMAR   Listen to that. He must needs go shooting too.

GINA   *(coming in)*   Hjalmar, I think grandfather is blundering about in the attic by himself.

HJALMAR   I will look in—

GREGERS   *(quickly and with emotion)*   Wait a moment! Do you know what that was?

HJALMAR   Of course I know.

GREGERS   No, but you don't. I know. That was the proof you wanted.

HJALMAR   What proof?

GREGERS   That was a child's act of sacrifice. She has got your father to shoot the wild duck!

HJALMAR   Shoot the wild duck!

GINA   Fancy that, now!

HJALMAR   What for?

GREGERS   She wanted to sacrifice, for your sake, what she prized most in the world; because she believed it would make you love her again.

HJALMAR   *(tenderly with emotion)*   Poor child!

GINA   What things she thinks of!

GREGERS   She only wanted your love again, Hjalmar; she did not feel as if she could live without it.

GINA   *(struggling with her tears)*   There you are, Hjalmar!

HJALMAR   Gina, where is she?

GINA   *(sniffing)*   Poor thing, she is sitting out in the kitchen, I expect.

HJALMAR   *(crosses the room and opens the kitchen door)*   Hedvig—come! Come here to me! *(Looks round.)* No, she is not there.

GINA   Then she must be in her own little room.

HJALMAR   *(who has gone out to look)*   No, she is not here either. *(Comes in.)* She must have gone out.

GINA   Yes, you wouldn't have her anywhere in the house.

HJALMAR   If only she would come home soon, so that I could let her know—. Everything will go well now, Gregers; now I believe we can begin life over again.

GREGERS *(quietly)*   I knew it was through the child that reparation would be made.

Old EKDAL *comes to the door of his room; he is in full uniform, and is occupied in trying to buckle on his sword.*

HJALMAR *(in astonishment)*   Father! are you there!

GINA   Was it in your room that you fired?

EKDAL *(indignantly as he approaches)*   So you go shooting alone, do you, Hjalmar?

HJALMAR *(anxious and perplexed)*   Wasn't it you, then, that was shooting in the attic?

EKDAL   I shooting? Hm!

GREGERS *(calls to* HJALMAR*)*   She has shot the wild duck herself, don't you see?

HJALMAR   What can it mean! *(Hurries to the attic door, tears it aside, looks in, and gives a loud scream.)* Hedvig!

GINA *(running to the door)*   Heavens! what is it?

HJALMAR *(going in)*   She is lying on the floor!

GREGERS   Hedvig on the floor! *(Goes in to* HJALMAR*.)*

GINA *(at the same time)*   Hedvig! *(From within the garret.)* Oh, no! no! no!

EKDAL   Ho! ho! does she go out shooting too!

HJALMAR, GINA *and* GREGERS *carry* HEDVIG *into the studio; the pistol is clasped tight in the fingers of her right hand, which is hanging down.*

HJALMAR *(distractedly)*   The pistol has gone off—and she has been shot. Call for help! Help!

GINA *(runs into the passage and calls out)*   Relling! Relling! Doctor Relling! come up as quickly as ever you can!

HJALMAR *and* GREGERS *lay* HEDVIG *on the sofa.*

EKDAL *(quietly)*   The forests avenge themselves.

HJALMAR *(on his knees beside* HEDVIG*)*   She is coming to now. She is coming to— yes, yes, yes.

GINA *(who has come in again)*   Where has she been shot? I can't see anything.

RELLING *comes in hurriedly with* MOLVIK *at his heels; the latter is without waistcoat or necktie, and with his coat flying open.*

RELLING   What is the matter?

GINA   They say Hedvig has shot herself.

HJALMAR   Come here and help!

RELLING   Shot herself! *(Pushes the table aside and begins to examine her.)*

HJALMAR *(looking anxiously up at him)*   It can't be dangerous, Relling? What? She hardly bleeds at all. It can't be dangerous?

RELLING   How did it happen?

HJALMAR   I can't imagine—!

GINA   She wanted to shoot the wild duck.

RELLING   The wild duck?

HJALMAR   The pistol must have gone off.

RELLING   Hm! Quite so.

EKDAL   The forests avenge themselves. But I am not afraid, anyway. *(Goes into the attic and shuts the door after him.)*

HJALMAR   Well, Relling—why don't you say something?

RELLING   The ball has entered the breast.

HJALMAR   Yes—but she's coming to!

GINA *(bursting into tears)*   My child, my child!

GREGERS *(in a choked voice)*   In the ocean's depths—

HJALMAR *(springing up)*   Yes, yes, she *must* live! Oh, for God's sake, Relling—just for a moment—just long enough for me to let her know how unspeakably I have loved her all the time!

RELLING   The heart has been hit. Internal hemorrhage. She died on the spot.

HJALMAR   And I hunted her away from me! And she crept like a frightened animal into the attic and died for love of me. *(Sobbing.)* I can never make it right now! I can never tell her—! *(Clenches his fists and cries up to heaven.)* Thou who are there above us—if indeed Thou *art* there! Why hast Thou done this to me!

GINA   Hush, hush! you mustn't take on in that terrible way. We had no right to keep her, I suppose.

MOLVIK   The child is not dead, but sleepeth.

RELLING   Rubbish!

HJALMAR *(goes more calmly over to the sofa and, folding his arms, looks down at HEDVIG)*   There she lies, so stiff and still.

RELLING *(trying to take the pistol from her fingers)*   She holds so tight, so tight.

GINA   No, no. Relling, don't hurt her fingers; let the thing alone.

HJALMAR   She shall take it with her.

GINA   Yes, let her. But the child mustn't lie out here for a show. She shall go into her own little room, she shall. Carry her with me, Hjalmar. *(She and HJALMAR take her up.)*

HJALMAR *(as they carry her out)*   Oh, Gina, Gina—can you ever get over this?

GINA   We must help one another. Now, I think, we each have a share in her.

MOLVIK *(stretches out his arms and babbles)*   Blessed he the Lord! Earth to earth, dust to dust—

RELLING *(whispering)*   Shut up, you fool—you're drunk.

HJALMAR and GINA *carry the body out through the kitchen.* RELLING *stands looking after them.* MOLVIK *sneaks out into the passage.*

RELLING *(going over to GREGERS)*   No one will ever persuade me this was an accident.

GREGERS *(who has stood terror-stricken, his face twitching convulsively)*   No one can say how the dreadful thing happened.

RELLING   The flame has scorched her dress. She must have held the pistol to her breast and fired.

GREGERS   Hedvig has not died in vain. You saw how his grief called out all the best that was in him.

RELLING   Most people show their best side in the presence of death. But how long do you suppose this turn for the better will last in this case?

GREGERS   Surely it will last and increase as long as he lives!

RELLING   In eight or nine months little Hedvig will be no more to him than a beautiful theme to declaim upon.

GREGERS   Do you dare to say that of Hjalmar Ekdal?

RELLING   We will talk of it again as soon as the grass has grown over her grave. Then you will hear him pumping up his fine phrases about "the child torn prematurely from her father's loving heart"; you will see him wallowing in emotional fits of self-admiration and self-compassion. Just you wait and see!

GREGERS   If you are right, and I am wrong, life is no longer worth living.

RELLING   Oh, life would be all right if we could only be rid of these infernal fools who come to poor people's doors presenting their "demands of the ideal."

GREGERS *(looking in front of him)*   If that is so, I am glad my destiny is what it is.

RELLING   Excuse me, but—what *is* your destiny?

GREGERS *(turning to go)*   To be the thirteenth at table.

RELLING   So I should imagine!

Response Statement Assignments

1. In Shakespeare's *Hamlet,* the stage directions are minimal. In contrast, Ibsen's stage directions carefully inform the reader about what the Werle house looks like, how the characters look and speak, and even at times how they think. How do you respond to Ibsen's greater influence on your interpretations, to the constraints he imposes, to the limitations on your freedom to see the characters as you wish?

2. As you read the play, did you find that any of the characters were particularly open to multiple interpretations? If so, discuss your interpretations, explaining what **text strategies** and what **reading strategies** influenced you?

3. How do you explain the strange symbol of the wild duck? *Why* a wild duck? Would you have preferred to have the play called something like "Hedvig" or "Hedvig's Sacrifice"? Or does the title *The Wild Duck* create a dramatic force that goes beyond the literal events of the play?

4. *The Wild Duck* is often described as being partly "realistic" and partly "symbolic." What **strategies** did you use to make sense of the play? Did they differ from one part of the play to another?

LUIGI PIRANDELLO (1867–1936)

Six Characters in Search of an Author

An English version by Edward Storer

CHARACTERS
OF THE COMEDY IN THE MAKING

THE FATHER	MADAME PACE
THE MOTHER	THE BOY ⎫
THE STEPDAUGHTER	THE CHILD ⎬ *(These two do not speak)*
THE SON	

ACTORS
OF THE COMPANY

THE MANAGER	OTHER ACTORS AND ACTRESSES
LEADING LADY	PROPERTY MAN
LEADING MAN	PROMPTER
SECOND LADY LEAD	MACHINIST
L'INGÉNUE	MANAGER'S SECRETARY
JUVENILE LEAD	DOORKEEPER
	SCENE-SHIFTERS

DAYTIME: *The Stage of a Theatre.*

N.B. The Comedy is without acts or scenes. The performance is interrupted once, without the curtain being lowered, when THE MANAGER *and the chief characters withdraw to arrange the scenario. A second interruption of the action takes place when, by mistake, the stage hands let the curtain down.*

ACT I

The spectators will find the curtain raised and the stage as it usually is during the daytime. It will be half dark, and empty, so that from the beginning the public may have the impression of an impromptu performance.

PROMPTER'S *box and a small table and chair for* THE MANAGER.

Two other small tables and several chairs scattered about as during rehearsals.

The ACTORS *and* ACTRESSES *of the company enter from the back of the stage:*

First one, then another, then two together: nine or ten in all. They are about to rehearse a Pirandello play: Mixing It Up. *Some of the company move off towards their dressing rooms. The* PROMPTER, *who has the "book" under his arm, is waiting for* THE MANAGER *in order to begin the rehearsal.*

The ACTORS *and* ACTRESSES, *some standing, some sitting, chat and smoke. One perhaps reads a paper; another cons his part.*

Finally, THE MANAGER *enters and goes to the table prepared for him. His* SECRETARY *brings him his mail, through which he glances. The* PROMPTER *takes his seat, turns on a light, and opens the "book."*

THE MANAGER *(Throwing a letter down on the table)* I can't see. *(To* PROPERTY MAN*)* Let's have a little light, please!

PROPERTY MAN Yes sir, yes, at once. *(A light comes down on to the stage.)*

THE MANAGER *(Clapping his hands)* Come along! Come along! Second act of Mixing It Up. *(Sits down.)*

The ACTORS *and* ACTRESSES *go from the front of the stage to the wings, all except the three who are to begin the rehearsal.*

PROMPTER *(Reading the "book")* "Leo Gala's house. A curious room serving as dining-room and study."

THE MANAGER *(To* PROPERTY MAN*)* Fix up the old red room.

PROPERTY MAN *(Noting it down)* Red set. All right!

PROMPTER *(Continuing to read from the "book")* "Table already laid and writing desk with books and papers. Bookshelves. Exit rear to Leo's bedroom. Exit left to kitchen. Principal exit to right."

THE MANAGER *(Energetically)*   Well, you understand: The principal exit over there; here, the kitchen. *(Turning to* ACTOR *who is to play the part of Socrates)* You make your entrances and exits here. *(To* PROPERTY MAN*)* The baize doors at the rear, and curtains.

PROPERTY MAN *(Noting it down)*   Right-o!

PROMPTER *(Reading as before)*   "When the curtain rises, Leo Gala, dressed in cook's cap and apron is busy beating an egg in a cup. Philip, also dressed as a cook, is beating another egg. Guido Venanzi is seated and listening."

LEADING MAN *(To* MANAGER*)*   Excuse me, but must I absolutely wear a cook's cap?

THE MANAGER *(Annoyed)*   I imagine so. It says so there anyway. *(Pointing to the "book")*

LEADING MAN   But it's ridiculous!

THE MANAGER   Ridiculous? Ridiculous? Is it my fault if France won't send us any more good comedies, and we are reduced to putting on Pirandello's work where nobody understands anything, and where the author plays the fool with us all? *(The* ACTORS *grin.* THE MANAGER *goes to* LEADING MAN *and shouts)* Yes sir, you put on the cook's cap and beat eggs. Do you suppose that with all this egg-beating business you are on an ordinary stage? Get that out of your head. You represent the shell of the eggs you are beating! *(Laughter and comments among the* ACTORS*)* Silence! and listen to my explanations, please! *(To* LEADING MAN*)* "The empty form of reason without the fullness of instinct, which is blind"—You stand for reason, your wife is instinct. It's a mixing up of the parts, according to which you who act your own part become the puppet of yourself. Do you understand?

LEADING MAN   I'm hanged if I do.

THE MANAGER   Neither do I. But let's get on with it. It's sure to be a glorious failure anyway. *(Confidentially)* But I say, please face three-quarters. Otherwise, what with the abstruseness of the dialogue, and the public that won't be able to hear you, the whole thing will go to hell. Come on! come on!

PROMPTER   Pardon sir, may I get into my box? There's a bit of a draught.

THE MANAGER   Yes, yes, of course!

At this point, the DOORKEEPER *has entered from the stage door and advances towards* THE MANAGER*'s table, taking off his braided cap. During this maneuver, the* SIX CHARACTERS *enter, and stop by the door at back of stage, so that when the* DOORKEEPER *is about to announce their coming to* THE MANAGER, *they are already on the stage. A tenuous light surrounds them, almost as if irradiated by them—the faint breath of their fantastic reality.*

This light will disappear when they come forward towards the ACTORS. *They preserve, however, something of the dream lightness in which they seem almost suspended; but this does not detract from the essential reality of their forms and expressions.*

He who is known as THE FATHER *is a man of about 50: hair, reddish in color, thin at the temples; he is not bald, however; thick moustaches, falling over his still fresh mouth, which often opens in an empty and uncertain smile. He is fattish, pale; with an especially wide forehead. He has blue, oval-shaped eyes, very clear and piercing.*

Wears light trousers and a dark jacket. He is alternatively mellifluous and violent in his manner.

THE MOTHER *seems crushed and terrified as if by an intolerable weight of shame and abasement. She is dressed in modest black and wears a thick widow's veil of crêpe. When she lifts this, she reveals a wax-like face. She always keeps her eyes downcast.*

THE STEPDAUGHTER *is dashing, almost impudent, beautiful. She wears mourning too, but with great elegance. She shows contempt for the timid half-frightened manner of the wretched* BOY *(14 years old, and also dressed in black); on the other hand, she displays a lively tenderness for her little sister,* THE CHILD *(about four), who is dressed in white, with a black silk sash at the waist.*

THE SON *(22) tall, severe in his attitude of contempt for* THE FATHER, *supercilious and indifferent to* THE MOTHER. *He looks as if he had come on the stage against his will.*

DOORKEEPER *(Cap in hand)* Excuse me, sir. . . .

THE MANAGER *(Rudely)* Eh? What is it?

DOORKEEPER *(Timidly)* These people are asking for you, sir.

THE MANAGER *(Furious)* I am rehearsing, and you know perfectly well no one's allowed to come in during rehearsals! *(Turning to the* CHARACTERS*)* Who are you, please? What do you want?

THE FATHER *(Coming forward a little, followed by the others, who seem embarrassed)* As a matter of fact . . . we have come here in search of an author. . . .

THE MANAGER *(Half angry, half amazed)* An author? What author?

THE FATHER Any author, sir.

THE MANAGER But there's no author here. We are not rehearsing a new piece.

THE STEPDAUGHTER *(Vivaciously)* So much the better, so much the better! We can be your new piece.

AN ACTOR *(Coming forward from the others)* Oh, do you hear that?

THE FATHER *(To* STEPDAUGHTER*)* Yes, but if the author isn't here . . . *(To* MANAGER*)* . . . unless you would be willing. . . .

THE MANAGER You are trying to be funny.

THE FATHER No, for Heaven's sake, what are you saying? We bring you a drama, sir.

THE STEPDAUGHTER We may be your fortune.

THE MANAGER Will you oblige me by going away? We haven't time to waste with mad people.

THE FATHER *(Mellifluously)* Oh sir, you know well that life is full of infinite absurdities, which, strangely enough, do not even need to appear plausible, since they are true.

THE MANAGER What the devil is he talking about?

THE FATHER I say that to reverse the ordinary process may well be considered a madness: that is, to create credible situations, in order that they may appear true. But permit me to observe that if this be madness, it is the sole *raison d'être* of your profession, gentlemen. *(The* ACTORS *look hurt and perplexed.)*

THE MANAGER *(Getting up and looking at him)* So our profession seems to you one worthy of madmen then?

THE FATHER Well, to make seem true that which isn't true . . . without any need

... for a joke as it were ... Isn't that your mission, gentlemen: to give life to fantastic characters on the stage?

THE MANAGER *(Interpreting the rising anger of the* COMPANY*)* But I would beg you to believe, my dear sir, that the profession of the comedian is a noble one. If today, as things go, the playwrights give us stupid comedies to play and puppets to represent instead of men, remember we are proud to have given life to immortal works here on these very boards! *(The* ACTORS, *satisfied, applaud their* MANAGER.*)*

THE FATHER *(Interrupting furiously)* Exactly, perfectly, to living beings more alive than those who breathe and wear clothes: being less real perhaps, but truer! I agree with you entirely. *(The* ACTORS *look at one another in amazement.)*

THE MANAGER But what do you mean? Before, you said ...

THE FATHER No, excuse me, I meant it for you, sir, who were crying out that you had no time to lose with madmen, while no one better than yourself knows that nature uses the instrument of human fantasy in order to pursue her high creative purpose.

THE MANAGER Very well—but where does all this take us?

THE FATHER Nowhere! It is merely to show you that one is born to life in many forms, in many shapes, as tree, or as stone, as water, as butterfly, or as woman. So one may also be born a character in a play.

THE MANAGER *(With feigned comic dismay)* So you and these other friends of yours have been born characters?

THE FATHER Exactly, and alive as you see! *(*MANAGER *and* ACTORS *burst out laughing.)*

THE FATHER *(Hurt)* I am sorry you laugh, because we carry in us a drama, as you can guess from this woman here, veiled in black.

THE MANAGER *(Losing patience at last and almost indignant)* Oh, chuck it! Get away please! Clear out of here! *(To* PROPERTY MAN*)* For Heaven's sake, turn them out!

THE FATHER *(Resisting)* No, no, look here, we....

THE MANAGER *(Roaring)* We come here to work, you know.

LEADING MAN One cannot let oneself be made such a fool of.

THE FATHER *(Determined, coming forward)* I marvel at your incredulity, gentlemen. Are you not accustomed to see the characters created by an author spring to life in yourselves and face each other? Just because there is no "book" *(Pointing to the* PROMPTER'S *box)* which contains us, you refuse to believe....

THE STEPDAUGHTER *(Advances towards* MANAGER, *smiling and coquettish)* Believe me, we are really six most interesting characters, sir; side-tracked however.

THE FATHER Yes, that is the word! *(To* MANAGER *all at once)* In the sense, that is, that the author who created us alive no longer wished, or was no longer able, materially to put us into a work of art. And this was a real crime, sir; because he who has had the luck to be born a character can laugh even at death. He cannot die. The man, the writer, the instrument of the creation will die, but his creation does not die. And to live for ever, it does not need to have extraordinary gifts or to be able to work wonders. Who was Sancho Panza? Who was Don Abbondio? Yet they live eternally because—live germs as they were—they had the fortune to find a fecundating matrix, a fantasy which could raise and nourish them: make them live for ever!

THE MANAGER That is quite all right. But what do you want here, all of you?

THE FATHER   We want to live.

THE MANAGER *(Ironically)*   For Eternity?

THE FATHER   No, sir, only for a moment . . . in you.

AN ACTOR   Just listen to him!

LEADING LADY   They want to live, in us! . . .

JUVENILE LEAD *(Pointing to the* STEPDAUGHTER*)*   I've no objection, as far as that one is concerned!

THE FATHER   Look here! Look here! The comedy has to be made. *(To the* MANAGER*)* But if you and your actors are willing, we can soon concert it among ourselves.

THE MANAGER *(Annoyed)*   But what do you want to concert? We don't go in for concerts here. Here we play dramas and comedies!

THE FATHER   Exactly! That is just why we have come to you.

THE MANAGER   And where is the "book"?

THE FATHER   It is in us! *(The* ACTORS *laugh)* The drama is in us, and we are the drama. We are impatient to play it. Our inner passion drives us on to this.

THE STEPDAUGHTER *(Disdainful, alluring, treacherous, full of impudence)*   My passion, sir! Ah, if you only knew! My passion for him! *(Points to the* FATHER *and makes a pretence of embracing him. Then she breaks out into a loud laugh.)*

THE FATHER *(Angrily)*   Behave yourself! And please don't laugh in that fashion.

THE STEPDAUGHTER   With your permission, gentlemen, I, who am a two months' orphan, will show you how I can dance and sing. *(Sings and then dances* Prenez garde à Tchou-Tchin-Tchou.)

Les chinois sont un peuple malin,
De Shanghaî à Pékin,
Ils ont mis des écriteaux partout:
Prenez garde à Tchou-Tchin-Tchou.

ACTORS AND ACTRESSES   Bravo! Well done! Tip-top!

THE MANAGER   Silence! This isn't a café concert, you know! *(Turning to the* FATHER *in consternation)* Is she mad?

THE FATHER   Mad? No, she's worse than mad.

THE STEPDAUGHTER *(To* MANAGER*)*   Worse? Worse? Listen! Stage this drama for us at once! Then you will see that at a certain moment I . . . when this little darling here . . . *(Takes the* CHILD *by the hand and leads her to the* MANAGER*)* Isn't she a dear? *(Takes her up and kisses her)* Darling! Darling! *(Puts her down again and adds feelingly)* Well, when God suddenly takes this dear little child away from that poor mother there; and this imbecile here *(seizing hold of the* BOY *roughly and pushing him forward)* does the stupidest things, like the fool he is, you will see me run away. Yes, gentlemen, I shall be off. But the moment hasn't arrived yet. After what has taken place between him and me *(indicates the* FATHER *with a horrible wink)* I can't remain any longer in this society, to have to witness the anguish of this mother here for that fool . . . *(Indicates the* SON*)* Look at him! Look at him! See how indifferent, how frigid he is, because he is the legitimate son. He despises me, despises him *(pointing to the* BOY*)*, despises this baby here; because . . .we are bastards. *(Goes to the* MOTHER *and embraces her)* And he doesn't want to recognize her as his mother—she who is the common mother of us all. He looks down upon her as if she were only the mother of us three bastards. Wretch! *(She says all* *this very rapidly, excitedly. At the word "bastards" she raises her voice, and almost spits out the final "Wretch!")*

THE MOTHER *(To the* MANAGER, *in anguish)* In the name of these two little children, I beg you ... *(She grows faint and is about to fall)* Oh God!

THE FATHER *(Coming forward to support her as do some of the* ACTORS*)* Quick, a chair, a chair for this poor widow!

THE ACTORS Is it true? Has she really fainted?

THE MANAGER Quick, a chair! Here!

One of the ACTORS *brings a chair, the others proffer assistance. The* MOTHER *tries to prevent the* FATHER *from lifting the veil which covers her face.*

THE FATHER Look at her! Look at her!

THE MOTHER No, stop; stop it please!

THE FATHER *(Raising her veil)* Let them see you!

THE MOTHER *(Rising and covering her face with her hands, in desperation)* I beg you, sir, to prevent this man from carrying out his plan which is loathsome to me.

THE MANAGER *(Dumbfounded)* I don't understand at all. What is the situation? Is this lady your wife? *(To the* FATHER.*)*

THE FATHER Yes, gentlemen: my wife!

THE MANAGER But how can she be a widow if you are alive? *(The* ACTORS *find relief for their astonishment in a loud laugh.)*

THE FATHER Don't laugh! Don't laugh like that, for Heaven's sake. Her drama lies just here in this: she has had a lover, a man who ought to be here.

THE MOTHER *(With a cry)* No! No!

THE STEPDAUGHTER Fortunately for her, he is dead. Two months ago as I said. We are mourning, as you see.

THE FATHER He isn't here you see, not because he is dead. He isn't here—look at her a moment and you will understand—because her drama isn't a drama of the love of two men for whom she was incapable of feeling anything except possibly a little gratitude—gratitude not for me but for the other. She isn't a woman, she is a mother, and her drama—powerful, sir, I assure you—lies, as a matter of fact, all in these four children she has had by two men.

THE MOTHER I had them? Have you got the courage to say that I wanted them? *(To the* COMPANY*)* It was his doing. It was he who gave me that other man, who forced me to go away with him.

THE STEPDAUGHTER It isn't true.

THE MOTHER *(Startled)* Not true, isn't it?

THE STEPDAUGHTER No, it isn't true, it just isn't true.

THE MOTHER And what can you know about it?

THE STEPDAUGHTER It isn't true. Don't believe it. *(To* MANAGER*)* Do you know why she says so? For that fellow there. *(Indicates the* SON*)* She tortures herself, destroys herself on account of the neglect of that son there; and she wants him to believe that if she abandoned him when he was only two years old, it was because he *(indicates the* FATHER*)* made her do so.

THE MOTHER *(Vigorously)* He forced me to it, and I call God to witness it. *(To the* MANAGER*)* Ask him *(indicates the* FATHER*)* if it isn't true. Let him speak. You *(to* DAUGHTER*)* are not in a position to know anything about it.

THE STEPDAUGHTER I know you lived in peace and happiness with my father while he lived. Can you deny it?

THE MOTHER No, I don't deny it ...

THE STEPDAUGHTER He was always full of affection and kindness for you. *(To the* BOY, *angrily)* It's true, isn't it? Tell them! Why don't you speak, you little fool?

THE MOTHER Leave the poor boy alone. Why do you want to make me appear ungrateful, daughter? I don't want to offend your father. I have answered him that I didn't abandon my house and my son through any fault of mine, nor from any wilful passion.

THE FATHER It is true. It was my doing.

LEADING MAN *(To the* COMPANY*)* What a spectacle!

LEADING LADY We are the audience this time.

JUVENILE LEAD For once, in a way.

THE MANAGER *(Beginning to get really interested)* Let's hear them out. Listen!

THE SON Oh yes, you're going to hear a fine bit now. He will talk to you of the Demon of Experiment.

THE FATHER You are a cynical imbecile. I've told you so already a hundred times. *(To the* MANAGER*)* He tries to make fun of me on account of this expression which I have found to excuse myself with.

THE SON *(With disgust)* Yes, phrases! phrases!

THE FATHER Phrases! Isn't everyone consoled when faced with a trouble or fact he doesn't understand, by a word, some simple word, which tells us nothing and yet calms us?

THE STEPDAUGHTER Even in the case of remorse. In fact, especially then.

THE FATHER Remorse? No, that isn't true. I've done more than use words to quiet the remorse in me.

THE STEPDAUGHTER Yes, there was a bit of money too. Yes, yes, a bit of money. There were the hundred lire he was about to offer me in payment, gentlemen. . . . *(Sensation of horror among the* ACTORS*.)*

THE SON *(To the* STEPDAUGHTER*)* This is vile.

THE STEPDAUGHTER Vile? There they were in a pale blue envelope on a little mahogany table in the back of Madame Pace's shop. You know Madame Pace—one of those ladies who attract poor girls of good family into their ateliers, under the pretext of their selling *robes et manteaux.*

THE SON And he thinks he has bought the right to tyrannize over us all with those hundred lire he was going to pay; but which, fortunately—note this, gentlemen— he had no chance of paying.

THE STEPDAUGHTER It was a near thing, though, you know! *(Laughs ironically.)*

THE MOTHER *(Protesting)* Shame, my daughter, shame!

THE STEPDAUGHTER Shame indeed! This is my revenge! I am dying to live that scene. . . . The room . . . I see it . . . Here is the window with the mantles exposed, there the divan, the looking-glass, a screen, there in front of the window the little mahogany table with the blue envelope containing one hundred lire. I see it. I see it. I could take hold of it . . . But you, gentlemen, you ought to turn your backs now: I am almost nude, you know. But I don't blush: I leave that to him. *(Indicating* FATHER.*)*

THE MANAGER I don't understand this at all.

THE FATHER Naturally enough. I would ask you, sir, to exercise your authority a little here, and let me speak before you believe all she is trying to blame me with. Let me explain.

THE STEPDAUGHTER Ah yes, explain it in your own way.

THE FATHER But don't you see that the whole trouble lies here. In words, words.

Each one of us has within him a whole world of things, each man of us his own special world. And how can we ever come to an understanding if I put in the words I utter the sense and value of things as I see them; while you who listen to me must inevitably translate them according to the conception of things each one of you has within himself. We think we understand each other, but we never really do. Look there! This woman *(indicating the* MOTHER*)* takes all my pity for her as a specially ferocious form of cruelty.

THE MOTHER   But you drove me away.

THE FATHER   Do you hear her? I drove her away! She believes I really sent her away.

THE MOTHER   You know how to talk, and I don't; but, believe me sir *(To* MANAGER*)*, after he had married me . . . who knows why? . . . I was a poor insignificant woman. . . .

THE FATHER   But, good Heaven! it was just for your humility that I married you. I loved this simplicity in you. *(He stops when he sees she makes signs to contradict him, opens his arms wide in sign of desperation, seeing how hopeless it is to make himself understood)* You see she denies it. Her mental deafness, believe me, is phenomenal, the limit *(touches his forehead):* deaf, deaf, mentally deaf! She had plenty of feeling. Oh yes, a good heart for the children; but the brain—deaf, to the point of desperation—!

THE STEPDAUGHTER   Yes, but ask him how his intelligence has helped us.

THE FATHER   If we could see all the evil that may spring from good, what should we do? *(At this point the* LEADING LADY *who is biting her lips with rage at seeing the* LEADING MAN *flirting with the* STEPDAUGHTER, *comes forward and says to the* MANAGER.*)*

LEADING LADY   Excuse me, but are we going to rehearse today?

THE MANAGER   Of course, of course; but let's hear them out.

JUVENILE LEAD   This is something quite new.

L'INGÉNUE   Most interesting!

LEADING LADY   Yes, for the people who like that kind of thing. *(Casts a glance at* LEADING MAN.*)*

THE MANAGER *(To* FATHER*)*   You must please explain yourself quite clearly. *(Sits down.)*

THE FATHER   Very well then: listen! I had in my service a poor man, a clerk, a secretary of mine, full of devotion, who became friends with her. *(Indicating the* MOTHER*)* They understood one another, were kindred souls in fact, without, however, the least suspicion of any evil existing. They were incapable even of thinking of it.

THE STEPDAUGHTER   So he thought of it—for them!

THE FATHER   That's not true. I meant to do good to them—and to myself, I confess, at the same time. Things had come to the point that I could not say a word to either of them without their making a mute appeal, one to the other, with their eyes. I could see them silently asking each other how I was to be kept in countenance, how I was to be kept quiet. And this, believe me, was just about enough of itself to keep me in a constant rage, to exasperate me beyond measure.

THE MANAGER   And why didn't you send him away then—this secretary of yours?

THE FATHER   Precisely what I did, sir. And then I had to watch this poor woman drifting forlornly about the house like an animal without a master, like an animal one has taken in out of pity.

THE MOTHER   Ah yes! . . .

THE FATHER *(Suddenly turning to the* MOTHER*)*   It's true about the son anyway, isn't it?

THE MOTHER   He took my son away from me first of all.

THE FATHER   But not from cruelty. I did so that he should grow up healthy and strong by living in the country.

THE STEPDAUGHTER *(Pointing to him ironically)*   As one can see.

THE FATHER *(Quickly)*   Is it my fault if he has grown up like this? I sent him to a wet nurse in the country, a peasant, as *she* did not seem to me strong enough, though she is of humble origin. That was, anyway, the reason I married her. Unpleasant all this may be, but how can it be helped? My mistake possibly, but there we are! All my life I have had these confounded aspirations towards a certain moral sanity. *(At this point the* STEPDAUGHTER *bursts out into a noisy laugh.)* Oh, stop it! Stop it! I can't stand it.

THE MANAGER   Yes, please stop it, for Heaven's sake.

THE STEPDAUGHTER   But imagine moral sanity from him, if you please—the client of certain ateliers like that of Madame Pace!

THE FATHER   Fool! That is the proof that I am a man! This seeming contradiction, gentlemen, is the strongest proof that I stand here a live man before you. Why, it is just for this very incongruity in my nature that I have had to suffer what I have. I could not live by the side of that woman *(indicating the* MOTHER*)* any longer; but not so much for the boredom she inspired me with as for the pity I felt for her.

THE MOTHER   And so he turned me out—.

THE FATHER   —well provided for! Yes, I sent her to that man, gentlemen . . . to let her go free of me.

THE MOTHER   And to free himself.

THE FATHER   Yes, I admit it. It was also a liberation for me. But great evil has come of it. I meant well when I did it; and I did it more for her sake than mine. I swear it. *(Crosses his arms on his chest; then turns suddenly to the* MOTHER*)* Did I ever lose sight of you until that other man carried you off to another town, like the angry fool he was? And on account of my pure interest in you . . . my pure interest, I repeat, that had no base motive in it . . . I watched with the tenderest concern the new family that grew up around her. She can bear witness to this. *(Points to the* STEPDAUGHTER*)*

THE STEPDAUGHTER   Oh yes, that's true enough. When I was a kiddie, so so high, you know, with plaits over my shoulders and knickers longer than my skirts, I used to see him waiting outside the school for me to come out. He came to see how I was growing up.

THE FATHER   This is infamous, shameful!

THE STEPDAUGHTER   No. Why?

THE FATHER   Infamous! Infamous! *(Then excitedly to* MANAGER, *explaining)* After she *(indicating* MOTHER*)* went away, my house seemed suddenly empty. She was my incubus, but she filled my house. I was like a dazed fly alone in the empty rooms. This boy here *(indicating the* SON*)* was educated away from home, and when he came back, he seemed to me to be no more mine. With no mother to stand between him and me, he grew up entirely for himself, on his own, apart, with no tie of intellect or affection binding him to me. And then—strange but true—I was driven, by curiosity at first and then by some tender sentiment, towards her family, which had come into being through my will. The thought of her began gradually to fill up the emptiness I felt all around me. I wanted to know if she were happy in living out the simple daily duties of life. I wanted to think of her as fortunate and happy because far away from the complicated torments of my spirit. And so, to have proof of this, I used to watch that child coming out of school.

THE STEPDAUGHTER Yes, yes. True. He used to follow me in the street and smiled at me, waved his hand, like this. I would look at him with interest, wondering who he might be. I told my mother, who guessed at once. *(The* MOTHER *agrees with a nod)* Then she didn't want to send me to school for some days; and when I finally went back, there he was again—looking so ridiculous—with a paper parcel in his hands. He came close to me, caressed me, and drew out a fine straw hat from the parcel, with a bouquet of flowers—all for me!

THE MANAGER A bit discursive this, you know!

THE SON *(Contemptuously)* Literature! Literature!

THE FATHER Literature indeed! This is life, this is passion!

THE MANAGER It may be, but it won't act.

THE FATHER I agree. This is only the part leading up. I don't suggest this should be staged. She *(pointing to the* STEPDAUGHTER*),* as you see, is no longer the flapper with plaits down her back—.

THE STEPDAUGHTER —and the knickers showing below the skirt!

THE FATHER The drama is coming now, sir; something new, complex, most interesting.

THE STEPDAUGHTER As soon as my father died. . . .

THE FATHER —there was absolute misery for them. They came back here, unknown to me. Through her stupidity! *(Pointing to the* MOTHER*)* It is true she can barely write her own name; but she could anyhow have got her daughter to write to me that they were in need. . . .

THE MOTHER And how was I to divine all this sentiment in him?

THE FATHER That is exactly your mistake, never to have guessed any of my sentiments.

THE MOTHER After so many years apart, and all that had happened. . . .

THE FATHER Was it my fault if that fellow carried you away? It happened quite suddenly; for after he had obtained some job or other, I could find no trace of them; and so, not unnaturally, my interest in them dwindled. But the drama culminated unforeseen and violent on their return, when I was impelled by my miserable flesh that still lives. . . . Ah! what misery, what wretchedness is that of the man who is alone and disdains debasing *liaisons!* Not old enough to do without women, and not young enough to go and look for one without shame. Misery? It's worse than misery; it's a horror; for no woman can any longer give him love; and when a man feels this . . . One ought to do without, you say? Yes, yes, I know. Each of us when he appears before his fellows is clothed in a certain dignity. But every man knows what unconfessable things pass within the secrecy of his own heart. One gives way to the temptation, only to rise from it again, afterwards, with a great eagerness to reestablish one's dignity, as if it were a tombstone to place on the grave of one's shame, and a monument to hide and sign the memory of our weaknesses. Everybody's in the same case. Some folks haven't the courage to say certain things, that's all!

THE STEPDAUGHTER   All appear to have the courage to do them though.

THE FATHER   Yes, but in secret. Therefore, you want more courage to say these things. Let a man but speak these things out, and folks at once label him a cynic. But it isn't true. He is like all the others, better indeed, because he isn't afraid to reveal with the light of the intelligence the red shame of human bestiality on which most men close their eyes so as not to see it. Woman—for example, look at her case! She turns tantalizing inviting glances on you. You seize her. No sooner does she feel herself in your grasp than she closes her eyes. It is the sign of her mission, the sign by which she says to man: "Blind yourself, for I am blind."

THE STEPDAUGHTER   Sometimes she can close them no more: when she no longer feels the need of hiding her shame to herself, but dry-eyed and dispassionately, sees only that of the man who has blinded himself without love. Oh, all these intellectual complications make me sick, disgust me—all this philosophy that uncovers the beast in man, and then seeks to save him, excuse him . . . I can't stand it, sir. When a man seeks to "simplify" life bestially, throwing aside every relic of humanity, every chaste aspiration, every pure feeling, all sense of ideality, duty, modesty, shame . . . then nothing is more revolting and nauseous than a certain kind of remorse—crocodiles' tears, that's what it is.

THE MANAGER   Let's come to the point. This is only discussion.

THE FATHER   Very good, sir! But a fact is like a sack which won't stand up when it is empty. In order that it may stand up, one has to put into it the reason and sentiment which have caused it to exist. I couldn't possibly know that after the death of that man, they had decided to return here, that they were in misery, and that she *(pointing to the* MOTHER*)* had gone to work as a modiste, and at a shop of the type of that of Madame Pace.

THE STEPDAUGHTER   A real high-class modiste, you must know, gentlemen. In appearance, she works for the leaders of the best society; but she arranges matters so that these elegant ladies serve her purpose . . . without prejudice to other ladies who are . . . well . . . only so so.

THE MOTHER   You will believe me, gentlemen, that it never entered my mind that the old hag offered me work because she had her eye on my daughter.

THE STEPDAUGHTER   Poor mamma! Do you know, sir, what that woman did when I brought her back the work my mother had finished? She would point out to me that I had torn one of my frocks, and she would give it back to my mother to mend. It was I who paid for it, always I; while this poor creature here believed she was sacrificing herself for me and these two children here, sitting up at night sewing Madame Pace's robes.

THE MANAGER   And one day you met there. . . .

THE STEPDAUGHTER   Him, him. Yes, sir, an old client. There's a scene for you to play! Superb!

THE FATHER   She, the Mother arrived just then. . . .

THE STEPDAUGHTER   *(Treacherously)* Almost in time!

THE FATHER   *(Crying out)* No, in time! in time! Fortunately I recognized her . . . in time. And I took them back home with me to my house. You can imagine now her position and mine: she, as you see her; and I who cannot look her in the face.

THE STEPDAUGHTER   Absurd! How can I possibly be expected—after that—to be a modest young miss, a fit person to go with his confounded aspirations for "a solid moral sanity"?

THE FATHER   For the drama lies all in this—in the conscience that I have, that each one of us has. We believe this conscience to be a single thing, but it is many-sided. There is one for this person, and another for that. Diverse consciences. So we have this illusion of being one person for all, of having a personality that is unique in all our acts. But it isn't true. We perceive this when, tragically perhaps, in something we do, we are, as it were, suspended, caught up in the air on a kind of hook. Then we perceive that all of us was not in that act, and that it would be an atrocious injustice to judge us by that action alone, as if all our existence were summed up in that one deed. Now do you understand the perfidy of this girl? She surprised me in a place where she ought not to have known me, just as I could not exist for her; and she now seeks to attach to me a reality such as I could never suppose I should have to assume for her in a shameful and fleeting moment of my life. I feel this above all else. And the drama, you will see, acquires a tremendous value from this point. Then there is the position of the others . . . his . . . *(Indicating the* SON.*)*

THE SON *(Shrugging his shoulders scornfully)* Leave me alone! I don't come into this.

THE FATHER What? You don't come into this?

THE SON I've got nothing to do with it, and don't want to have; because you know well enough I wasn't made to be mixed up in all this with the rest of you.

THE STEPDAUGHTER We are only vulgar folk! He is the fine gentleman. You may have noticed, Mr. Manager, that I fix him now and again with a look of scorn while he lowers his eyes—for he knows the evil he has done me.

THE SON *(Scarcely looking at her)* I?

THE STEPDAUGHTER You! you! I owe my life on the streets to you. Did you or did you not deny us, with your behavior, I won't say the intimacy of home, but even that mere hospitality which makes guests feel at their ease? We were intruders who had come to disturb the kingdom of your legitimacy. I should like to have you witness, Mr. Manager, certain scenes between him and me. He says I have tyrannized over everyone. But it was just his behavior which made me insist on the reason for which I had come into the house—this reason he calls "vile"—into his house, with my mother, who is his mother too. And I came as mistress of the house.

THE SON It's easy for them to put me always in the wrong. But imagine, gentlemen, the position of a son, whose fate it is to see arrive one day at his home a young woman of impudent bearing, a young woman who inquires for his father, with whom who knows what business she has. This young man has then to witness her return bolder than ever, accompanied by that child there. He is obliged to watch her treat his father in an equivocal and confidential manner. She asks money of him in a way that lets one suppose he must give it her, *must,* do you understand, because he has every obligation to do so.

THE FATHER But I have, as a matter of fact, this obligation. I owe it to your mother.

THE SON How should I know? When had I ever seen or heard of her? One day there arrive with her *(indicating* STEPDAUGHTER*)* that lad and this baby here. I am told: "This is *your* mother too, you know." I divine from her manner *(indicating* STEPDAUGHTER *again)* why it is they have come home. I had rather not say what I feel and think about it. I shouldn't even care to confess to myself. No action can therefore be hoped for from me in this affair. Believe me, Mr. Manager, I am an "unrealized" character, dramatically speaking; and I find myself not at all at ease in their company. Leave me out of it, I beg you.

THE FATHER   What? It is just because you are so that . . .

THE SON   How do you know what I am like? When did you ever bother your head about me?

THE FATHER   I admit it. I admit it. But isn't that a situation in itself? This aloofness of yours which is so cruel to me and to your mother, who returns home and sees you almost for the first time grown up, who doesn't recognize you but knows you are her son . . . *(Pointing out the* MOTHER *to the* MANAGER*)* See, she's crying!

THE STEPDAUGHTER   *(Angrily, stamping her foot)*   Like a fool!

THE FATHER   *(Indicating* STEPDAUGHTER*)*   She can't stand him, you know. *(Then referring again to the* SON*)* He says he doesn't come into the affair, whereas he is really the hinge of the whole action. Look at that lad who is always clinging to his mother, frightened and humiliated. It is on account of this fellow here. Possibly his situation is the most painful of all. He feels himself a stranger more than the others. The poor little chap feels mortified, humiliated at being brought into a home out of charity as it were. *(In confidence)*—He is the image of his father. Hardly talks at all. Humble and quiet.

THE MANAGER   Oh, we'll cut him out. You've no notion what a nuisance boys are on the stage . . .

THE FATHER   He disappears soon, you know. And the baby too. She is the first to vanish from the scene. The drama consists finally in this: when that mother re-enters my house, her family born outside of it, and shall we say superimposed on the original, ends with the death of the little girl, the tragedy of the boy and flight of the elder daughter. It cannot go on, because it is foreign to its surroundings. So after much torment, we three remain: I, the mother, that son. Then, owing to the disappearance of that extraneous family, we too find ourselves strange to one an-other. We find we are living in an atmosphere of mortal desolation which is the revenge, as he *(indicating* SON*)* scornfully said of the Demon of Experiment, that unfortunately hides in me. Thus, sir, you see when faith is lacking, it becomes im-possible to create certain states of happiness, for we lack the necessary humility. Vaingloriously, we try to substitute ourselves for this faith, creating thus for the rest of the world a reality which we believe after their fashion, while, actually, it doesn't exist. For each one of us has his own reality to be respected before God, even when it is harmful to one's very self.

THE MANAGER   There is something in what you say. I assure you all this interests me very much. I begin to think there's the stuff for a drama in all this, and not a bad drama either.

THE STEPDAUGHTER   *(Coming forward)*   When you've got a character like me.

THE FATHER   *(Shutting her up, all excited to learn the decision of the* MANAGER*)* You be quiet!

THE MANAGER   *(Reflecting, heedless of interruption)*   It's new . . . hem . . . yes . . .

THE FATHER   Absolutely new!

THE MANAGER   You've got a nerve though, I must say, to come here and fling it at me like this . . .

THE FATHER   You will understand, sir, born as we are for the stage . . .

THE MANAGER   Are you amateur actors then?

THE FATHER   No, I say born for the stage, because . . .

THE MANAGER   Oh, nonsense. You're an old hand, you know.

THE FATHER   No sir, no. We act that rôle for which we have been cast, that rôle which we are given in life. And in my own case, passion itself, as usually happens, becomes a trifle theatrical when it is exalted.

THE MANAGER   Well, well, that will do. But you see, without an author . . . I could give you the address of an author if you like . . .

THE FATHER   No, no. Look here! You must be the author.

THE MANAGER   I? What are you talking about?

THE FATHER   Yes, you, you! Why not?

THE MANAGER   Because I have never been an author: that's why.

THE FATHER   Then why not turn author now? Everybody does it. You don't want any special qualities. Your task is made much easier by the fact that we are all here alive before you . . .

THE MANAGER   It won't do.

THE FATHER   What? When you see us live our drama . . .

THE MANAGER   Yes, that's all right. But you want someone to write it.

THE FATHER   No, no. Someone to take it down, possibly, while we play it, scene by scene! It will be enough to sketch it out at first, and then try it over.

THE MANAGER   Well . . . I am almost tempted. It's a bit of an idea. One might have a shot at it.

THE FATHER   Of course. You'll see what scenes will come out of it. I can give you one, at once . . .

THE MANAGER   By Jove, it tempts me, I'd like to have a go at it. Let's try it out. Come with me to my office. *(Turning to the* ACTORS*)* You are at liberty for a bit, but don't step out of the theatre for long. In a quarter of an hour, twenty minutes, all back here again! *(To the* FATHER*)* We'll see what can be done. Who knows if we don't get something really extraordinary out of it?

THE FATHER   There's no doubt about it. They *(indicating the* CHARACTERS*)* had better come with us too, hadn't they?

THE MANAGER   Yes, yes. Come on! come on! *(Moves away and then turning to the* ACTORS*)* Be punctual, please!

MANAGER *and the* SIX CHARACTERS *cross the stage and go off. The other* ACTORS *remain, looking at one another in astonishment.*

LEADING MAN   Is he serious? What the devil does he want to do?

JUVENILE LEAD   This is rank madness.

THIRD ACTOR   Does he expect to knock up a drama in five minutes?

JUVENILE LEAD   Like the improvisers!

LEADING LADY   If he thinks I'm going to take part in a joke like this . . .

JUVENILE LEAD   I'm out of it anyway.

FOURTH ACTOR   I should like to know who they are. *(Alludes to* CHARACTERS.*)*

THIRD ACTOR   What do you suppose? Madmen or rascals!

JUVENILE LEAD   And he takes them seriously!

L'INGÉNUE   Vanity! He fancies himself as an author now.

LEADING MAN   It's absolutely unheard of. If the stage has come to this . . . well I'm . . .

FIFTH ACTOR   It's rather a joke.

THIRD ACTOR   Well, we'll see what's going to happen next.

Thus talking, the ACTORS *leave the stage; some going out by the little door at the back; others retiring to their dressing-rooms.*

The curtain remains up.

The action of the play is suspended for twenty minutes.

ACT II

The stage call-bells ring to warn the company that the play is about to begin again.

THE STEPDAUGHTER *comes out of the* MANAGER'S *office along with the* CHILD *and the* BOY. *As she comes out of the office, she cries:* Nonsense! Nonsense! Do it yourselves! I'm not going to mix myself up in this mess. *(Turning to the* CHILD *and coming quickly with her on to the stage)* Come on, Rosetta, let's run!

The BOY *follows them slowly, remaining a little behind and seeming perplexed.*

THE STEPDAUGHTER *(Stops, bends over the* CHILD *and takes the latter's face between her hands)* My little darling! You're frightened, aren't you? You don't know where we are, do you? *(Pretending to reply to a question of the* CHILD*)* What is the stage? It's a place, baby, you know, where people play at being serious, a place where they act comedies. We've got to act a comedy now, dead serious, you know; and you're in it also, little one. *(Embraces her, pressing the little head to her breast, and rocking the* CHILD *for a moment)* Oh darling, darling, what a horrid comedy you've got to play! What a wretched part they've found for you! A garden . . . a fountain . . . look . . . just suppose, kiddie, it's here. Where, you say? Why, right here in the middle. It's all pretence you know. That's the trouble, my pet: it's all make-believe here. It's better to imagine it though, because if they fix it up for you, it'll only be painted cardboard, painted cardboard for the rockery, the water, the plants . . . Ah, but I think a baby like this one would sooner have a make-believe fountain than a real one, so she could play with it. What a joke it'll be for the others! But for you, alas! not quite such a joke: you who are real, baby dear, and really play by a real fountain that is big and green and beautiful, with ever so many bamboos around it that are reflected in the water, and a whole lot of little ducks swimming about . . . No, Rosetta, no, your mother doesn't bother about you on account of that wretch of a son there. I'm in the devil of a temper, and as for that lad . . . *(Seizes* BOY *by the arm to force him to take one of his hands out of his pockets)* What have you got there? What are you hiding? *(Pulls his hand out of his pocket, looks into it and catches the glint of a revolver)* Ah, where did you get this?

The BOY, *very pale in the face, looks at her, but does not answer.*

Idiot! If I'd been in your place, instead of killing myself, I'd have shot one of those two, or both of them: father and son.

The FATHER *enters from the office, all excited from his work. The* MANAGER *follows him.*

THE FATHER Come on, come on, dear! Come here for a minute! We've arranged everything. It's all fixed up.

THE MANAGER *(Also excited)* If you please, young lady, there are one or two points to settle still. Will you come along?

THE STEPDAUGHTER *(Following him towards the office)* Ouff! what's the good, if you've arranged everything.

The FATHER, MANAGER *and* STEPDAUGHTER *go back into the office again [off] for a moment. At the same time, the* SON, *followed by the* MOTHER, *comes out.*

THE SON *(Looking at the three entering office)* Oh this is fine, fine! And to think I can't even get away!

The MOTHER *attempts to look at him, but lowers her eyes immediately when he turns away from her. She then sits down. The* BOY *and the* CHILD *approach her. She casts a glance at the* SON, *and speaks with humble tones, trying to draw him into conversation.*

THE MOTHER   And isn't my punishment the worst of all? *(Then seeing from the* SON*'s manner that he will not bother himself about her)* My God! Why are you so cruel? Isn't it enough for one person to support all this torment? Must you then insist on others seeing it also?

THE SON *(Half to himself, meaning the* MOTHER *to hear, however)*   And they want to put it on the stage! If there was at least a reason for it! He thinks he has got at the meaning of it all. Just as if each one of us in every circumstance of life couldn't find his own explanation of it! *(Pauses)* He complains he was discovered in a place where he ought not to have been seen, in a moment of his life which ought to have remained hidden and kept out of the reach of that convention which he has to maintain for other people. And what about my case? Haven't I had to reveal what no son ought ever to reveal: how father and mother live and are man and wife for themselves quite apart from that idea of father and mother which we give them? When this idea is revealed, our life is then linked at one point only to that man and that woman; and as such it should shame them, shouldn't it?

The MOTHER *hides her face in her hands. From the dressing-rooms and the little door at the back of the stage the* ACTORS *and* STAGE MANAGER *return, followed by the* PROPERTY MAN, *and the* PROMPTER. *At the same moment, the* MANAGER *comes out of his office, accompanied by the* FATHER *and the* STEPDAUGHTER.

THE MANAGER   Come on, come on, ladies and gentlemen! Heh! you there, machinist!

MACHINIST   Yes sir?

THE MANAGER   Fix up the white parlor with the floral decorations. Two wings and a drop with a door will do. Hurry up!

The MACHINIST *runs off at once to prepare the scene, and arranges it while the* MANAGER *talks with the* STAGE MANAGER, *the* PROPERTY MAN, *and the* PROMPTER *on matters of detail.*

THE MANAGER *(To* PROPERTY MAN*)*   Just have a look, and see if there isn't a sofa or divan in the wardrobe . . .

PROPERTY MAN   There's the green one.

THE STEPDAUGHTER   No, no! Green won't do. It was yellow, ornamented with flowers—very large! and most comfortable!

PROPERTY MAN   There isn't one like that.

THE MANAGER   It doesn't matter. Use the one we've got.

THE STEPDAUGHTER   Doesn't matter? It's most important!

THE MANAGER   We're only trying it now. Please don't interfere. *(To* PROPERTY MAN*)* See if we've got a shop window—long and narrowish.

THE STEPDAUGHTER   And the little table! The little mahogany table for the pale blue envelope!

PROPERTY MAN *(To* MANAGER*)*   There's that little gilt one.

THE MANAGER   That'll do fine.

THE FATHER   A mirror.

THE STEPDAUGHTER   And the screen! We must have a screen. Otherwise how can I manage?

PROPERTY MAN   That's all right, Miss. We've got any amount of them.

THE MANAGER *(To the* STEPDAUGHTER*)*   We want some clothes pegs too, don't we?

THE STEPDAUGHTER   Yes, several, several!

THE MANAGER   See how many we've got and bring them all.

PROPERTY MAN   All right!

The PROPERTY MAN *hurries off to obey his orders. While he is putting the things in their places, the* MANAGER *talks to the* PROMPTER *and then with the* CHARACTERS *and the* ACTORS.

THE MANAGER *(To* PROMPTER*)*   Take your seat. Look here: this is the outline of the scenes, act by act. *(Hands him some sheets of paper)* And now I'm going to ask you to do something out of the ordinary.

PROMPTER   Take it down in shorthand?

THE MANAGER *(Pleasantly surprised)*   Exactly! Can you do shorthand?

PROMPTER   Yes, a little.

THE MANAGER   Good! *(Turning to a stage hand)* Go and get some paper from my office, plenty, as much as you can find.

The STAGE HAND *goes off, and soon returns with a handful of paper which he gives to the* PROMPTER.

THE MANAGER *(To* PROMPTER*)*   You follow the scenes as we play them, and try and get the points down, at any rate the most important ones. *(Then addressing the* ACTORS*)* Clear the stage, ladies and gentlemen! Come over here *(Pointing to the Left)* and listen attentively.

LEADING LADY   But, excuse me, we . . .

THE MANAGER *(Guessing her thought)*   Don't worry! You won't have to improvise.

LEADING MAN   What have we to do then?

THE MANAGER   Nothing. For the moment you just watch and listen. Everybody will get his part written out afterwards. At present we're going to try the thing as best we can. They're going to act now.

THE FATHER *(As if fallen from the clouds into the confusion of the state)*   We? What do you mean, if you please, by a rehearsal?

THE MANAGER   A rehearsal for them. *(Points to the* ACTORS.*)*

THE FATHER   But since we are the characters . . .

THE MANAGER   All right: "characters" then, if you insist on calling yourselves such. But here, my dear sir, the characters don't act. Here the actors do the acting. The characters are there, in the "book"—*(Pointing towards* PROMPTER'S *box)* when there is a "book"!

THE FATHER   I won't contradict you; but excuse me, the actors aren't the characters. They want to be, they pretend to be, don't they? Now if these gentlemen here are fortunate enough to have us alive before them . . .

THE MANAGER   Oh this is grand! You want to come before the public yourselves then?

THE FATHER   As we are . . .

THE MANAGER   I can assure you it would be a magnificent spectacle!

LEADING MAN   What's the use of us here anyway then?

THE MANAGER   You're not going to pretend that you can act? It makes me laugh! *(The* ACTORS *laugh)* There, you see, they are laughing at the notion. But, by the way, I must cast the parts. That won't be difficult. They cast themselves. *(To the* SECOND LADY LEAD*)* You play the Mother. *(To the* FATHER*)* We must find her a name.

THE FATHER   Amalia, sir.

THE MANAGER   But that is the real name of your wife. We don't want to call her by her real name.

THE FATHER   Why ever not, if it is her name? . . . Still, perhaps, if that lady must . . . *(Makes a slight motion of the hand to indicate the* SECOND LADY LEAD*)* I see this woman here *(means the* MOTHER*)* as Amalia. But do as you like. *(Gets more and more confused)* I don't know what to say to you. Already, I begin to hear my own words ring false, as if they had another sound . . .

THE MANAGER   Don't you worry about it. It'll be our job to find the right tones. And as for her name, if you want her Amalia, Amalia it shall be; and if you don't like it, we'll find another! For the moment though, we'll call the characters in this way: *(to* JUVENILE LEAD*)* You are the Son; *(to the* LEADING LADY*)* You naturally are the Stepdaughter . . .

THE STEPDAUGHTER   *(Excitedly)*   What? what? I, that woman there? *(Bursts out laughing.)*

THE MANAGER   *(Angry)*   What is there to laugh at?

LEADING LADY   *(Indignant)*   Nobody has ever dared to laugh at me. I insist on being treated with respect; otherwise I go away.

THE STEPDAUGHTER   No, no, excuse me . . . I am not laughing at you . . .

THE MANAGER   *(To* STEPDAUGHTER*)*   You ought to feel honored to be played by . . .

LEADING LADY   *(At once, contemptuously)*   "That woman there" . . .

THE STEPDAUGHTER   But I wasn't speaking of you, you know. I was speaking of myself—whom I can't see at all in you! That is all. I don't know . . . but . . . you . . . aren't in the least like me . . .

THE FATHER   True. Here's the point. Look here, sir, our temperaments, our souls . . .

THE MANAGER   Temperament, soul, be hanged. Do you suppose the spirit of the piece is in you? Nothing of the kind!

THE FATHER   What, haven't we our own temperaments, our own souls?

THE MANAGER   Not at all. Your soul or whatever you like to call it takes shape here. The actors give body and form to it, voice and gesture. And my actors—I may tell you—have given expression to much more lofty material than this little drama of yours, which may or may not hold up on the stage. But if it does, the merit of it, believe me, will be due to my actors.

THE FATHER   I don't dare contradict you, sir; but, believe me, it is a terrible suffering for us who are as we are, with these bodies of ours, these features to see . . .

THE MANAGER   *(Cutting him short and out of patience)*   Good heavens! The make-up will remedy all that, man, the make-up . . .

THE FATHER   Maybe. But the voice, the gestures . . .

THE MANAGER   Now, look here! On the stage, you as yourself, cannot exist. The actor here acts you, and that's an end to it!

THE FATHER   I understand. And now I think I see why our author who conceived us as we are, all alive, didn't want to put us on the stage after all. I haven't the least desire to offend your actors. Far from it! But when I think that I am to be acted by . . . I don't know by whom . . .

LEADING MAN *(On his dignity)* By me, if you've no objection!

THE FATHER *(Humbly, mellifluously)* Honored, I assure you, sir. *(Bows)* Still, I must say that try as this gentleman may, with all his good will and wonderful art, to absorb me into himself . . .

LEADING MAN Oh chuck it! "Wonderful art!" Withdraw that, please!

THE FATHER The performance he will give, even doing his best with make-up to look like me . . .

LEADING MAN It will certainly be a bit difficult! *(The* ACTORS *laugh.)*

THE FATHER Exactly! It will be difficult to act me as I really am. The effect will be rather—apart from the make-up—according as to how he supposes I am, as he senses me—if he does sense me—and not as I inside of myself feel myself to be. It seems to me then that account should be taken of this by everyone whose duty it may become to criticize us . . .

THE MANAGER Heavens! The man's starting to think about the critics now! Let them say what they like. It's up to us to put on the play if we can. *(Looking around)* Come on! come on! Is the stage set? *(To the* ACTORS *and* CHARACTERS*)* Stand back—stand back! Let me see, and don't let's lose any more time! *(To the* STEPDAUGHTER*)* Is it all right as it is now?

THE STEPDAUGHTER Well, to tell the truth, I don't recognize the scene.

THE MANAGER My dear lady, you can't possibly suppose that we can construct that shop of Madame Pace piece by piece here? *(To the* FATHER*)* You said a white room with flowered wall paper, didn't you?

THE FATHER Yes.

THE MANAGER Well then. We've got the furniture right, more or less. Bring that little table a bit further forward. *(The* STAGE HANDS *obey the order. To* PROPERTY MAN*)* You go and find an envelope, if possible, a pale blue one; and give it to that gentleman. *(Indicates* FATHER*.)*

PROPERTY MAN An ordinary envelope?

MANAGER *and* FATHER Yes, yes, an ordinary envelope.

PROPERTY MAN At once, sir. *(Exit.)*

THE MANAGER Ready, everyone! First scene—the Young Lady. *(The* LEADING LADY *comes forward)* No, no, you must wait. I meant her. *(Indicating the* STEP-DAUGHTER*)* You just watch—

THE STEPDAUGHTER *(Adding at once)* How I shall play it, how I shall live it! . . .

LEADING LADY *(Offended)* I shall live it also, you may be sure, as soon as I begin!

THE MANAGER *(With his hands to his head)* Ladies and gentlemen, if you please! No more useless discussions! Scene I: the young lady with Madame Pace: Oh! *(Looks around as if lost)* And this Madame Pace, where is she?

THE FATHER She isn't with us, sir.

THE MANAGER Then what the devil's to be done?

THE FATHER But she is alive too.

THE MANAGER Yes, but where is she?

THE FATHER One minute. Let me speak! *(Turning to the* ACTRESSES*)* If these ladies could be so good as to give me their hats for a moment . . .

THE ACTRESSES *(Half surprised, half laughing, in chorus)* What? Why?

Our hats?

What does he say?

THE MANAGER   What are you going to do with the ladies' hats? *(The* ACTORS *laugh.)*

THE FATHER   Oh nothing. I just want to put them on these pegs for a moment. And one of the ladies will be so kind as to take off her mantle . . .

THE ACTORS   Oh, what d'you think of that? Only the mantle? He must be mad.

SOME ACTRESSES   But why?

Mantles as well?

THE FATHER   To hang them up there for a moment. Please be so kind, will you?

THE ACTRESSES *(Taking off their hats, one or two also their cloaks, and going to hang them on the racks)*   After all, why not?

There you are!

This is really funny.

We've got to put them on show.

THE FATHER   Exactly; just like that, on show.

THE MANAGER   May we know why?

THE FATHER   I'll tell you. Who knows if, by arranging the stage for her, she does not come here herself, attracted by the very articles of her trade? *(Inviting the* ACTORS *to look towards the exit at back of stage)* Look! Look!

The door at the back of stage opens and MADAME PACE *enters and takes a few steps forward. She is a fat, oldish woman with puffy oxygenated hair. She is rouged and powdered, dressed with a comical elegance in black silk. Round her waist is a long silver chain from which hangs a pair of scissors. The* STEPDAUGHTER *runs over to her at once amid the stupor of the* ACTORS.

THE STEPDAUGHTER *(Turning towards her)*   There she is! There she is!

THE FATHER *(Radiant)*   It's she! I said so, didn't I? There she is!

THE MANAGER *(Conquering his surprise, and then becoming indignant)*   What sort of a trick is this?

LEADING MAN *(Almost at the same time)*   What's going to happen next?

JUVENILE LEAD   Where does *she* come from?

L'INGÉNUE   They've been holding her in reserve, I guess.

LEADING LADY   A vulgar trick!

THE FATHER *(Dominating the protests)*   Excuse me, all of you! Why are you so anxious to destroy in the name of a vulgar, commonplace sense of truth, this reality which comes to birth attracted and formed by the magic of the stage itself, which has indeed more right to live here than you, since it is much truer than you —if you don't mind my saying so? Which is the actress among you who is to play Madame Pace? Well, here is Madame Pace herself. And you will allow, I fancy, that the actress who acts her will be less true than this woman here, who is herself in person. You see my daughter recognized her and went over to her at once. Now you're going to witness the scene!

But the scene between the STEPDAUGHTER *and* MADAME PACE *has already begun despite the protest of the* ACTORS *and the reply of the* FATHER. *It has begun quietly, naturally, in a manner impossible for the stage. So when the* ACTORS, *called to attention by the* FATHER, *turn round and see* MADAME PACE, *who has placed one hand under the* STEPDAUGHTER'*s chin to raise her head, they observe her at first with great attention, but hearing her speak in an unintelligible manner their interest begins to wane.*

THE MANAGER   Well? well?

LEADING MAN   What does she say?

LEADING LADY   One can't hear a word.

JUVENILE LEAD   Louder! Louder please!

THE STEPDAUGHTER   (*Leaving* MADAME PACE, *who smiles a Sphinxlike smile, and advancing towards the* ACTORS)   Louder? Louder? What are you talking about? These aren't matters which can be shouted at the top of one's voice. If I have spoken them out loud, it was to shame him and have my revenge. (*Indicates* FATHER) But for Madame it's quite a different matter.

THE MANAGER   Indeed? indeed? But here, you know, people have got to make themselves heard, my dear. Even we who are on the stage can't hear you. What will it be when the public's in the theater? And anyway, you can very well speak up now among yourselves, since we shan't be present to listen to you as we are now. You've got to pretend to be alone in a room at the back of a shop where no one can hear you.

The STEPDAUGHTER *coquettishly and with a touch of malice makes a sign of disagreement two or three times with her finger.*

THE MANAGER   What do you mean by no?

THE STEPDAUGHTER   (*Sotto voce, mysteriously*)   There's someone who will hear us if she (*indicating* MADAME PACE) speaks out loud.

THE MANAGER   (*In consternation*)   What? Have you got someone else to spring on us now? (*The* ACTORS *burst out laughing.*)

THE FATHER   No, no sir. She is alluding to me. I've got to be here—there behind that door, in waiting; and Madame Pace knows it. In fact, if you will allow me, I'll go there at once, so I can be quite ready. (*Moves away.*)

THE MANAGER (*Stopping him*)   No! wait! wait! We must observe the conventions of the theater. Before you are ready . . .

THE STEPDAUGHTER (*Interrupting him*)   No, get on with it at once! I'm just dying, I tell you, to act this scene. If he's ready, I'm more than ready.

THE MANAGER (*Shouting*)   But, my dear young lady, first of all, we must have the scene between you and this lady . . . (*Indicates* MADAME PACE) Do you understand? . . .

THE STEPDAUGHTER   Good Heavens! She's been telling me what you know already: that Mamma's work is badly done again, that the material's ruined; and that if I want her to continue to help us in our misery I must be patient . . .

MADAME PACE (*Coming forward with an air of great importance*)   Yes indeed, sir, I no wanta take advantage of her, I no wanta be hard . . .

Note: MADAM PACE *is supposed to talk in a jargon half Italian, half English.*

THE MANAGER (*Alarmed*)   What? What? she talks like that? (*The* ACTORS *burst out laughing again.*)

THE STEPDAUGHTER (*Also laughing*)   Yes, yes, that's the way she talks, half English, half Italian! Most comical it is!

MADAME PACE   Itta seem not verra polite gentlemen laugha atta me eef I trya best speaka English.

THE MANAGER   *Diamine!* Of course! Of course! Let her talk like that! Just what we want. Talk just like that, Madame, if you please! The effect will be certain. Exactly what was wanted to put a little comic relief into the crudity of the situation. Of course she talks like that! Magnificent!

THE STEPDAUGHTER   Magnificent? Certainly! When certain suggestions are made to one in language of that kind, the effect is certain, since it seems almost a joke. One feels inclined to laugh when one hears her talk about an "old signore" "who wanta talka nicely with you." Nice old signore, eh, Madame?

MADAME PACE   Not so old, my dear, not so old! And even if you no lika him, he won't make any scandal!

THE MOTHER   *(Jumping up amid the amazement and consternation of the* ACTORS *who had not been noticing her. They move to restrain her)*   You old devil! You murderess!

THE STEPDAUGHTER   *(Running over to calm her* MOTHER*)*   Calm yourself, mother, calm yourself! Please don't . . .

THE FATHER   *(Going to her also at the same time)*   Calm yourself! Don't get excited! Sit down now!

THE MOTHER   Well then, take that woman away out of my sight!

THE STEPDAUGHTER   *(To* MANAGER*)*   It is impossible for my mother to remain here.

THE FATHER   *(To* MANAGER*)*   They can't be here together. And for this reason, you see: that woman there was not with us when we came . . . If they are on together, the whole thing is given away inevitably, as you see.

THE MANAGER   It doesn't matter. This is only a first rough sketch—just to get an idea of the various points of the scene, even confusedly . . . *(Turning to the* MOTHER *and leading her to her chair)* Come along, my dear lady, sit down now, and let's get on with the scene . . .

Meanwhile, the STEPDAUGHTER, *coming forward again, turns to* MADAME PACE.

THE STEPDAUGHTER   Come on, Madame, come on!

MADAME PACE   *(Offended)*   No, no, *grazie.* I not do anything witha your mother present.

THE STEPDAUGHTER   Nonsense! Introduce this "old signore" who wants to talk nicely to me. *(Addressing the company imperiously)* We've got to do this scene one way or another, haven't we? Come on! *(To* MADAME PACE*)* You can go!

MADAME PACE   Ah yes! I go'way! I go'way! Certainly! *(Exits furious.)*

THE STEPDAUGHTER   *(To the* FATHER*)*   Now you make your entry. No, you needn't go over there. Come here. Let's suppose you've already come in. Like that, yes! I'm here with bowed head, modest-like. Come on! Out with your voice! Say "Good morning, Miss" in that peculiar tone, that special tone . . .

THE MANAGER   Excuse me, but are you the Manager, or am I? *(To the* FATHER, *who looks undecided and perplexed)* Get on with it, man! Go down there to the back of the stage. You needn't go off. Then come right forward here.

The FATHER *does as he is told, looking troubled and perplexed at first. But as soon as he begins to move, the reality of the action affects him, and he begins to smile and to be more natural. The* ACTORS *watch intently.*

THE MANAGER   *(Sotto voce, quickly to the* PROMPTER *in his box)*   Ready! ready? Get ready to write now.

THE FATHER *(Coming forward and speaking in a different tone)* Good afternoon, Miss!

THE STEPDAUGHTER *(Head bowed down slightly, with restrained disgust)* Good afternoon!

THE FATHER *(Looks under her hat which partly covers her face. Perceiving she is very young, he makes an exclamation, partly of surprise, partly of fear lest he compromise himself in a risky adventure)* Ah . . . but . . . ah . . . I say . . . this is not the first time that you have come here, is it?

THE STEPDAUGHTER *(Modestly)* No sir.

THE FATHER You've been here before, eh? *(Then seeing her nod agreement)* More than once? *(Waits for her to answer, looks under her hat, smiles, and then says)* Well then, there's no need to be so shy, is there? May I take off your hat?

THE STEPDAUGHTER *(Anticipating him and with veiled disgust)* No sir . . . I'll do it myself. *(Takes it off quickly.)*

The MOTHER, *who watches the progress of the scene with the* SON *and the other two* CHILDREN *who cling to her, is on thorns; and follows with varying expressions of sorrow, indignation, anxiety, and horror the words and actions of the other two. From time to time she hides her face in her hands and sobs.*

THE MOTHER Oh, my God, my God!

THE FATHER *(Playing his part with a touch of gallantry)* Give it to me! I'll put it down. *(Takes hat from her hands)* But a dear little head like yours ought to have a smarter hat. Come and help me choose one from the stock, won't you?

L'INGÉNUE *(Interrupting)* I say . . . those are our hats, you know.

THE MANAGER *(Furious)* Silence! silence! Don't try and be funny, if you please . . . We're playing the scene now, I'd have you notice. *(To the* STEPDAUGHTER*)* Begin again, please!

THE STEPDAUGHTER *(Continuing)* No thank you, sir.

THE FATHER Oh, come now. Don't talk like that. You must take it. I shall be upset if you don't. There are some lovely little hats here; and then—Madame will be pleased. She expects it, anyway, you know.

THE STEPDAUGHTER No, no! I couldn't wear it!

THE FATHER Oh, you're thinking about what they'd say at home if they saw you come in with a new hat? My dear girl, there's always a way round these little matters, you know.

THE STEPDAUGHTER *(All keyed up)* No, it's not that. I couldn't wear it because I am . . . as you see . . . you might have noticed . . . *(Showing her black dress.)*

THE FATHER . . . in mourning! Of course: I beg your pardon: I'm frightfully sorry . . .

THE STEPDAUGHTER *(Forcing herself to conquer her indignation and nausea)* Stop! Stop! It's I who must thank you. There's no need for you to feel mortified or specially sorry. Don't think any more of what I've said. *(Tries to smile)* I must forget that I'm dressed so . . .

THE MANAGER *(Interrupting and turning to the* PROMPTER*)* Stop a minute! Stop! Don't write that down. Cut out that last bit. *(Then to the* FATHER *and* STEPDAUGHTER*)* Fine! it's going fine! *(To the* FATHER *only)* And now you can go on as we arranged. *(To the* ACTORS*)* Pretty good that scene, where he offers her the hat, eh?

THE STEPDAUGHTER   The best's coming now. Why can't we go on?

THE MANAGER   Have a little patience! *(To the* ACTORS*)* Of course, it must be treated rather lightly.

LEADING MAN   Still, with a bit of go in it!

LEADING LADY   Of course! It's easy enough! *(To* LEADING MAN*)* Shall you and I try it now?

LEADING MAN   Why, yes! I'll prepare my entrance. *(Exit in order to make his entrance.)*

THE MANAGER *(To* LEADING LADY*)*   See here! The scene between you and Madame Pace is finished. I'll have it written out properly after. You remain here . . . oh, where are you going?

LEADING LADY   One minute. I want to put my hat on again. *(Goes over to hatrack and puts her hat on her head.)*

THE MANAGER   Good! You stay here with your head bowed down a bit.

THE STEPDAUGHTER   But she isn't dressed in black.

LEADING LADY   But I shall be, and much more effectively than you.

THE MANAGER *(To* STEPDAUGHTER*)*   Be quiet please, and watch! You'll be able to learn something. *(Clapping his hands)* Come on! come on! Entrance, please!

The door at rear of stage opens, and the LEADING MAN *enters with the lively manner of an old gallant. The rendering of the scene by the* ACTORS *from the very first words is seen to be quite a different thing, though it has not in any way the air of a parody. Naturally, the* STEPDAUGHTER *and the* FATHER, *not being able to recognize themselves in the* LEADING LADY *and the* LEADING MAN, *who deliver their words in different tones and with a different psychology, express, sometimes with smiles, sometimes with gestures, the impression they receive.*

LEADING MAN   Good afternoon, Miss . . .

THE FATHER *(At once unable to contain himself)*   No! no!

The STEPDAUGHTER, *noticing the way the* LEADING MAN *enters, bursts out laughing.*

THE MANAGER *(Furious)*   Silence! And you, please, just stop that laughing. If we go on like this, we shall never finish.

THE STEPDAUGHTER   Forgive me, sir, but it's natural enough. This lady *(indicating* LEADING LADY*)* stands there still; but if she is supposed to be me, I can assure you that if I heard anyone say "Good afternoon" in that manner and in that tone, I should burst out laughing as I did.

THE FATHER   Yes, yes, the manner, the tone . . .

THE MANAGER   Nonsense! Rubbish! Stand aside and let me see the action.

LEADING MAN   If I've got to represent an old fellow who's coming into a house of an equivocal character . . .

THE MANAGER   Don't listen to them, for Heaven's sake! Do it again! It goes fine. *(Waiting for the* ACTORS *to begin again)* Well?

LEADING MAN   Good afternoon, Miss.

LEADING LADY   Good afternoon.

LEADING MAN *(Imitating the gesture of the* FATHER *when he looked under the hat, and then expressing quite clearly first satisfaction and then fear)*   Ah, but . . . I say . . . this is not the first time that you have come here, is it?

THE MANAGER   Good, but not quite so heavily. Like this. *(Acts himself)* "This isn't the first time that you have come here" ... *(To* LEADING LADY*)* And you say: "No, sir."

LEADING LADY   No, sir.

LEADING MAN   You've been here before, more than once.

THE MANAGER   No, no, stop! Let her nod "yes" first. "You've been here before, eh?"

The LEADING LADY *lifts up her head slightly and closes her eyes as though in disgust. Then she inclines her head twice.*

THE STEPDAUGHTER   *(Unable to contain herself)*   Oh my God! *(Puts a hand to her mouth to prevent herself from laughing.)*

THE MANAGER   *(Turning round)*   What's the matter?

THE STEPDAUGHTER   Nothing, nothing!

THE MANAGER   *(To* LEADING MAN*)*   Go on!

LEADING MAN   You've been here before, eh? Well, then, there's no need to be so shy, is there? May I take off your hat?

The LEADING MAN *says this last speech in such a tone and with such gestures that the* STEPDAUGHTER, *though she has her hand to her mouth, cannot keep from laughing.*

LEADING LADY   *(Indignant)*   I'm not going to stop here to be made a fool of by that woman there.

LEADING MAN   Neither am I! I'm through with it!

THE MANAGER   *(Shouting to* STEPDAUGHTER*)*   Silence! for once and all, I tell you!

STEPDAUGHTER   Forgive me! forgive me!

THE MANAGER   You haven't any manners: that's what it is! You go too far.

THE FATHER   *(Endeavoring to intervene)*   Yes, it's true, but excuse her ...

THE MANAGER   Excuse what? It's absolutely disgusting.

THE FATHER   Yes, sir, but believe me, it has such a strange effect when ...

THE MANAGER   Strange? Why strange? Where is it strange?

THE FATHER   No, sir; I admire your actors—this gentleman here, this lady; but they are certainly not us!

THE MANAGER   I should hope not. Evidently they cannot be you, if they are actors.

THE FATHER   Just so: actors! Both of them act our parts exceedingly well. But, believe me, it produces quite a different effect on us. They want to be us, but they aren't, all the same.

THE MANAGER   What is it then anyway?

THE FATHER   Something that is ... that is theirs—and no longer ours ...

THE MANAGER   But naturally, inevitably. I've told you so already.

THE FATHER   Yes, I understand ... I understand ...

THE MANAGER   Well then, let's have no more of it! *(Turning to the* ACTORS*)* We'll have the rehearsals by ourselves, afterwards, in the ordinary way. I never could stand rehearsing with the author present. He's never satisfied! *(Turning to* FATHER *and* STEPDAUGHTER*)* Come on! Let's get on with it again; and try and see if you can't keep from laughing.

THE STEPDAUGHTER   Oh, I shan't laugh any more. There's a nice little bit coming from me now: you'll see.

THE MANAGER   Well then: when she says "Don't think any more of what I've said.

I must forget, etc.," you *(addressing the* FATHER*)* come in sharp with "I understand, I understand"; and then you ask her . . .

THE STEPDAUGHTER *(Interrupting)* What?

THE MANAGER Why she is in mourning.

THE STEPDAUGHTER Not at all! See here: when I told him that it was useless for me to be thinking about my wearing mourning, do you know how he answered me? "Ah well," he said, "then let's take off this little frock."

THE MANAGER Great! Just what we want, to make a riot in the theater!

THE STEPDAUGHTER But it's the truth!

THE MANAGER What does that matter? Acting is our business here. Truth up to a certain point, but no further.

THE STEPDAUGHTER What do you want to do then?

THE MANAGER You'll see, you'll see! Leave it to me.

THE STEPDAUGHTER No sir! What you want to do is to piece together a little romantic sentimental scene out of my disgust, out of all the reasons, each more cruel and viler than the other, why I am what I am. He is to ask me why I'm in mourning; and I'm to answer with tears in my eyes, that it is just two months since papa died. No sir, no! He's got to say to me; as he did say: "Well, let's take off this little dress at once." And I; with my two months' mourning in my heart, went there behind that screen, and with these fingers tingling with shame . . .

THE MANAGER *(Running his hands through his hair)* For Heaven's sake! What are you saying?

THE STEPDAUGHTER *(Crying out excitedly)* The truth! The truth!

THE MANAGER It may be. I don't deny it, and I can understand all your horror; but you must surely see that you can't have this kind of thing on the stage. It won't go.

THE STEPDAUGHTER Not possible, eh? Very well! I'm much obliged to you—but I'm off!

THE MANAGER Now be reasonable! Don't lose your temper!

THE STEPDAUGHTER I won't stop here! I won't! I can see you've fixed it all up with him in your office. All this talk about what is possible for the stage . . . I understand! He wants to get at his complicated "cerebral drama," to have his famous remorses and torments acted; but I want to act my part, *my part!*

THE MANAGER *(Annoyed, shaking his shoulders)* Ah! Just *your* part! But, if you will pardon me, there are other parts than yours: his *(indicating the* FATHER*)* and hers! *(Indicating the* MOTHER*)* On the stage you can't have a character becoming too prominent and overshadowing all the others. The thing is to pack them all into a neat little framework and then act what is actable. I am aware of the fact that everyone has his own interior life which he wants very much to put forward. But the difficulty lies in this fact: to set out just so much as is necessary for the stage, taking the other characters into consideration, and at the same time hint at the unrevealed interior life of each. I am willing to admit, my dear young lady, that from your point of view it would be a fine idea if each character could tell the public all his troubles in a nice monologue or a regular one-hour lecture. *(Good-humoredly)* You must restrain yourself, my dear, and in your own interest, too; because this fury of yours, this exaggerated disgust you show, may make a bad impression, you know. After you have confessed to me that there were others before him at Madame Pace's and more than once . . .

THE STEPDAUGHTER *(Bowing her head, impressed)* It's true. But remember those others mean him for me all the same.

THE MANAGER *(Not understanding)* What? The others? What do you mean?

THE STEPDAUGHTER For one who has gone wrong, sir, he who was responsible for the first fault is responsible for all that follow. He is responsible for my faults, was, even before I was born. Look at him, and see if it isn't true!

THE MANAGER Well, well! And does the weight of so much responsibility seem nothing to you? Give him a chance to act it, to get it over!

THE STEPDAUGHTER How? How can he act all his "noble remorses," all his "moral torments," if you want to spare him the horror of being discovered one day—after he had asked her what he did ask her—in the arms of her, that already fallen woman, that child, sir, that child he used to watch come out of school? *(She is moved.)*

The MOTHER *at this point is overcome with emotion, and breaks out into a fit of crying.*

All are touched. A long pause.

THE STEPDAUGHTER *(As soon as the* MOTHER *becomes a little quieter, adds resolutely and gravely)* At present, we are unknown to the public. Tomorrow, you will act us as you wish, treating us in your own manner. But do you really want to see drama, do you want to see it flash out as it really did?

THE MANAGER Of course! That's just what I do want, so I can use as much of it as is possible.

THE STEPDAUGHTER Well then, ask that Mother there to leave us.

THE MOTHER *(Changing her low plaint into a sharp cry)* No! No! Don't permit it, sir, don't permit it!

THE MANAGER But it's only to try it.

THE MOTHER I can't bear it. I can't.

THE MANAGER But since it has happened already . . . I don't understand!

THE MOTHER It's taking place now. It happens all the time. My torment isn't a pretended one. I live and feel every minute of my torture. Those two children there—have you heard them speak? They can't speak any more. They cling to me to keep my torment actual and vivid for me. But for themselves, they do not exist, they aren't any more. And she *(indicating* STEPDAUGHTER*)* has run away, she has left me, and is lost. If I now see her here before me, it is only to renew for me the tortures I have suffered for her too.

THE FATHER The eternal moment! She *(indicating the* STEPDAUGHTER*)* is here to catch me, fix me, and hold me eternally in the stocks for that one fleeting and shameful moment of my life. She can't give it up! And you sir, cannot either fairly spare me it.

THE MANAGER I never said I didn't want to act it. It will form, as a matter of fact, the nucleus of the whole first act right up to her surprise. *(Indicating the* MOTHER.*)*

THE FATHER Just so! This is my punishment: the passion in all of us that must culminate in her final cry.

THE STEPDAUGHTER I can hear it still in my ears. It's driven me mad, that cry—You can put me on as you like; it doesn't matter. Fully dressed, if you like—provided I have at least the arm bare; because standing like this *(she goes close to the* FATHER *and leans her head on his breast)* with my head so, and my arms round his neck, I saw a vein pulsing in my arm here; and then, as if that live vein had awakened disgust in me, I closed my eyes like this, and let my head sink on his breast. *(Turning to the* MOTHER*)* Cry out, mother! Cry out! *(Buries head in* FA-

THER's breast, and with her shoulders raised as if to prevent her hearing the cry, adds in tones of intense emotion) Cry out as you did then!

THE MOTHER (Coming forward to separate them) No! My daughter, my daughter! (And after having pulled her away from him) You brute! you brute! She is my daughter! Don't you see she's my daughter?

THE MANAGER (Walking backwards towards footlights) Fine! fine! Damned good! And then, of course—curtain!

THE FATHER (Going towards him excitedly) Yes, of course, because that's the way it really happened.

THE MANAGER (Convinced and pleased) Oh, yes, no doubt about it. Curtain here, curtain!

At the reiterated cry of the MANAGER, the MACHINIST lets the curtain down, leaving the MANAGER and the FATHER in front of it before the footlights.

THE MANAGER The darned idiot! I said "curtain" to show the act should end there, and he goes and lets it down in earnest. (To the FATHER, while he pulls the curtain back to go onto the stage again.) Yes, yes, it's all right. Effect certain! That's the right ending. I'll guarantee the first act, at any rate.

ACT III

When the curtain goes up again, it is seen that the stage hands have shifted the bit of scenery used in the last part, and have rigged up instead at the back of the stage a drop, with some trees, and one or two wings. A portion of a fountain basin is visible. THE MOTHER is sitting on the Right with the two children by her side. THE SON is on the same side, but away from the others. He seems bored, angry, and full of shame. THE FATHER and THE STEPDAUGHTER are also seated towards the Right front. On the other side (Left) are the ACTORS, much in the positions they occupied before the curtain was lowered. Only THE MANAGER is standing up in the middle of the stage, with his hand closed over his mouth, in the act of meditating.

THE MANAGER (Shaking his shoulders after a brief pause) Ah yes: the second act! Leave it to me, leave it all to me as we arranged, and you'll see! It'll go fine!

THE STEPDAUGHTER Our entry into his house (indicates FATHER) in spite of him . . . (indicates the SON.)

THE MANAGER (Out of patience) Leave it to me, I tell you!

THE STEPDAUGHTER Do let it be clear, at any rate, that it is in spite of my wishes.

THE MOTHER (From her corner, shaking her head) For all the good that's come of it . . .

THE STEPDAUGHTER (Turning towards her quickly) It doesn't matter. The more harm done to us, the more remorse for him.

THE MANAGER (Impatiently) I understand! Good Heavens! I understand! I'm taking it into account.

THE MOTHER (Supplicatingly) I beg you, sir, to let it appear quite plain that for conscience' sake I did try in every way . . .

THE STEPDAUGHTER (Interrupting indignantly and continuing for the MOTHER). . . . to pacify me, to dissuade me from spiting him. (To MANAGER) Do as she wants: satisfy her, because it is true! I enjoy it immensely. Anyhow, as you can see, the meeker she is, the more she tries to get at his heart, the more distant and aloof does he become.

THE MANAGER   Are we going to begin this second act or not?

THE STEPDAUGHTER   I'm not going to talk any more now. But I must tell you this: you can't have the whole action take place in the garden, as you suggest. It isn't possible!

THE MANAGER   Why not?

THE STEPDAUGHTER   Because he *(indicates the* SON *again)* is always shut up alone in his room. And then there's all the part of that poor dazed-looking boy there which takes place indoors.

THE MANAGER   Maybe! On the other hand, you will understand—we can't change scenes three or four times in one act.

THE LEADING MAN   They used to once.

THE MANAGER   Yes, when the public was up to the level of that child there.

THE LEADING LADY   It makes the illusion easier.

THE FATHER *(Irritated)*   The illusion! For Heaven's sake, don't say illusion. Please don't use that word, which is particularly painful for us.

THE MANAGER *(Astounded)*   And why, if you please?

THE FATHER   It's painful, cruel, really cruel; and you ought to understand that.

THE MANAGER   But why? What ought we to say then? The illusion, I tell you, sir, which we've got to create for the audience . . .

THE LEADING MAN   With our acting.

THE MANAGER   The illusion of a reality.

THE FATHER   I understand; but you, perhaps, do not understand us. Forgive me! You see . . . here for you and your actors, the thing is only—and rightly so . . . a kind of game . . .

LEADING LADY *(Interrupting indignantly)*   A game! We're not children here, if you please! We are serious actors.

THE FATHER   I don't deny it. What I mean is the game, or play, of your art, which has to give, as the gentleman says, a perfect illusion of reality.

THE MANAGER   Precisely——!

THE FATHER   Now, if you consider the fact that we *(indicates himself and the other five* CHARACTERS*)*, as we are, have no other reality outside of this illusion . . .

THE MANAGER *(Astonished, looking at his* ACTORS, *who are also amazed)*   And what does that mean?

THE FATHER *(After watching them for a moment with a wan smile)*   As I say, sir, that which is a game of art for you is our sole reality. *(Brief pause. He goes a step or two nearer the* MANAGER *and adds)* But not only for us, you know, by the way. Just you think it over well. *(Looks him in the eyes)* Can you tell me who you are?

THE MANAGER *(Perplexed, half smiling)*   What? Who am I? I am myself.

THE FATHER   And if I were to tell you that that isn't true, because you are I? . . .

THE MANAGER   I should say you were mad——! *(The* ACTORS *laugh.)*

THE FATHER   You're quite right to laugh: because we are all making believe here. *(To* MANAGER*)* And you can therefore object that it's only for a joke that that gentleman there *(indicates the* LEADING MAN*)*, who naturally is himself, has to be me, who am on the contrary myself—this thing you see here. You see I've caught you in a trap! *(The* ACTORS *laugh.)*

THE MANAGER *(Annoyed)*   But we've had all this over once before. Do you want to begin again?

THE FATHER   No, no! that wasn't my meaning! In fact, I should like to request you to abandon this game of art *(Looking at the* LEADING LADY *as if anticipating her)* which you are accustomed to play here with your actors, and to ask you seriously once again: who are you?

THE MANAGER (*Astonished and irritated, turning to his* ACTORS) If this fellow here hasn't got a nerve! A man who calls himself a character comes and asks me who I am!

THE FATHER (*With dignity, but not offended*) A character, sir, may always ask a man who he is. Because a character has really a life of his own, marked with his especial characteristics; for which reason he is always "somebody." But a man— I'm not speaking of you now—may very well be "nobody."

THE MANAGER Yes, but you are asking these questions of me, the boss, the manager! Do you understand?

THE FATHER But only in order to know if you, as you really are now, see yourself as you once were with all the illusions that were yours then, with all the things both inside and outside of you as they seemed to you—as they were then indeed for you. Well, sir, if you think of all those illusions that mean nothing to you now, of all those things which don't even *seem* to you to exist any more, while once they *were* for you, don't you feel that—I won't say these boards—but the very earth under your feet is sinking away from you when you reflect that in the same way this *you* as you feel it today—all this present reality of yours—is fated to seem a mere illusion to you tomorrow?

THE MANAGER (*Without having understood much, but astonished by the specious argument*) Well, well! And where does all this take us anyway?

THE FATHER Oh, nowhere! It's only to show you that if we (*indicating the* CHARACTERS) have no other reality beyond illusion, you too must not count overmuch on your reality as you feel it today, since, like that of yesterday, it may prove an illusion for you tomorrow.

THE MANAGER (*Determining to make fun of him*) Ah, excellent! Then you'll be saying next that you, with this comedy of yours that you brought here to act, are truer and more real than I am.

THE FATHER (*With the greatest seriousness*) But of course; without doubt!

THE MANAGER Ah, really?

THE FATHER Why, I thought you'd understand that from the beginning.

THE MANAGER More real than I?

THE FATHER If your reality can change from one day to another . . .

THE MANAGER But everyone knows it can change. It is always changing, the same as anyone else's.

THE FATHER (*With a cry*) No, sir, not ours! Look here! That is the very difference! Our reality doesn't change: it can't change! It can't be other than what it is, because it is already fixed for ever. It's terrible. Ours is an immutable reality which should make you shudder when you approach us if you are really conscious of the fact that your reality is a mere transitory and fleeting illusion, taking this form today and that tomorrow, according to the conditions, according to your will, your sentiments, which in turn are controlled by an intellect that shows them to you today in one manner and tomorrow . . . who knows how? . . . Illusions of reality represented in this fatuous comedy of life that never ends, nor can ever end! Because if tomorrow it were to end . . . then why, all would be finished.

THE MANAGER Oh for God's sake, will you *at least* finish with this philosophizing and let us try and shape this comedy which you yourself have brought me here? You argue and philosophize a bit too much, my dear sir. You know you seem to me almost, almost ... *(Stops and looks him over from head to foot)* Ah, by the way, I think you introduced yourself to me as a —what shall ... we say—a "character," created by an author who did not afterwards care to make a drama of his own creations.

THE FATHER   It is the simple truth, sir.

THE MANAGER   Nonsense! Cut that out, please! None of us believes it, because it isn't a thing, as you must recognize yourself, which one can believe seriously. If you want to know, it seems to me you are trying to imitate the manner of a certain author whom I heartily detest—I warn you—although I have unfortunately bound myself to put on one of his works. As a matter of fact, I was just starting to rehearse it, when you arrived. *(Turning to the* ACTORS*)* And this is what we've gained—out of the frying-pan into the fire!

THE FATHER   I don't know to what author you may be alluding, but believe me I feel what I think; and I seem to be philosophizing only for those who do not think what they feel, because they blind themselves with their own sentimen.. I know that for many people this self-blinding seems much more "human"; but the contrary is really true. For man never reasons so much and becomes so introspective as when he suffers; since he is anxious to get at the cause of his sufferings, to learn who has produced them, and whether it is just or unjust that he should have to bear them. On the other hand, when he is happy, he takes his happiness as it comes and doesn't analyze it, just as if happiness were his right. The animals suffer without reasoning about their sufferings. But take the case of a man who suffers and begins to reason about it. Oh no! it can't be allowed! Let him suffer like an animal, and then—ah yes, he is "human!"

THE MANAGER   Look here! Look here! You're off again, philosophizing worse than ever.

THE FATHER   Because I suffer, sir! I'm not philosophizing: I'm crying aloud the reason of my sufferings.

THE MANAGER *(Makes brusque movement as he is taken with a new idea)*   I should like to know if anyone has ever heard of a character who gets right out of his part and perorates and speechifies as you do. Have you ever heard of a case? I haven't.

THE FATHER   You have never met such a case, sir, because authors, as a rule, hide the labor of their creations. When the characters are really alive before their author, the latter does nothing but follow them in their action, in their words, in the situations which they suggest to him; and he has to will them the way they will themselves—for there's trouble if he doesn't. When a character is born, he acquires at once such an independence, even of his own author, that he can be imagined by everybody even in many other situations where the author never dreamed of placing him; and so he acquires for himself a meaning which the author never thought of giving him.

THE MANAGER   Yes, yes, I know this.

THE FATHER   What is there then to marvel at in us? Imagine such a misfortune for characters as I have described to you: to be born of an author's fantasy, and be denied life by him; and then answer me if these characters left alive, and yet without life, weren't right in doing what they did do and are doing now, after they have attempted everything in their power to persuade him to give them their stage life. We've all tried him in turn, I, she *(indicating the* STEPDAUGHTER*)* and she. *(Indicating the* MOTHER.*)*

THE STEPDAUGHTER   It's true. I too have sought to tempt him, many, many times, when he had been sitting at his writing table, feeling a bit melancholy, at the twilight hour. He would sit in his armchair too lazy to switch on the light, and all the shadows that crept into his room were full of our presence coming to tempt him. *(As if she saw herself still there by the writing table, and was annoyed by the presence of the* ACTORS*)* Oh, if you would only go away, go away and leave us alone— mother here with that son of hers—I with that Child—that Boy there always alone—and then I with him—*(just hints at the* FATHER*)*—and then I alone, alone . . . in those shadows! *(Makes a sudden movement as if in the vision she has of herself illuminating those shadows she wanted to seize hold of herself)* Ah! my life! my life! Oh, what scenes we proposed to him—and I tempted him more than any of the others!

THE FATHER   Maybe. But perhaps it was your fault that he refused to give us life: because you were too insistent, too troublesome.

THE STEPDAUGHTER   Nonsense! Didn't he make me so himself? *(Goes close to the* MANAGER *to tell him as if in confidence)* In my opinion he abandoned us in a fit of depression, of disgust for the ordinary theater as the public knows it and likes it.

THE SON   Exactly what it was, sir; exactly that!

THE FATHER   Not at all! Don't believe it for a minute. Listen to me! You'll be doing quite right to modify, as you suggest, the excesses both of this girl here, who wants to do too much, and of this young man, who won't do anything at all.

THE SON   No, nothing!

THE MANAGER   You too get over the mark occasionally, my dear sir, if I may say so.

THE FATHER   I? When? Where?

THE MANAGER   Always! Continuously! Then there's this insistence of yours in trying to make us believe you are a character. And then too, you must really argue and philosophize less, you know, much less.

THE FATHER   Well, if you want to take away from me the possibility of representing the torment of my spirit which never gives me peace, you will be suppressing me: that's all. Every true man, sir, who is a little above the level of the beasts and plants does not live for the sake of living, without knowing how to live; but he lives so as to give a meaning and a value of his own to life. For me this is *everything.* I cannot give up this, just to represent a mere fact as she *(indicating the* STEPDAUGHTER*)* wants. It's all very well for her, since her "vendetta" lies in the "fact." I'm not going to do it. It destroys my *raison d'être.*

THE MANAGER   Your *raison d'être!* Oh, we're going ahead fine! First she starts off, and then you jump in. At this rate, we'll never finish.

THE FATHER   Now, don't be offended! Have it your own way—provided, however, that within the limits of the parts you assign us each one's sacrifice isn't too great.

THE MANAGER   You've got to understand that you can't go on arguing at your own pleasure. Drama is action, sir, action and not confounded philosophy.

THE FATHER   All right. I'll do just as much arguing and philosophizing as everybody does when he is considering his own torments.

THE MANAGER   If the drama permits! But for Heaven's sake, man, let's get along and come to the scene.

THE STEPDAUGHTER   It seems to me we've got too much action with our coming into his house. *(Indicating* FATHER*)* You said, before, you couldn't change the scene every five minutes.

THE MANAGER   Of course not. What we've got to do is to combine and group up all the facts in one simultaneous, close-knit action. We can't have it as you want, with your little brother wandering like a ghost from room to room, hiding behind doors and meditating a project which—what did you say it did to him?

THE STEPDAUGHTER Consumes him, sir, wastes him away!

THE MANAGER Well, it may be. And then at the same time, you want the little girl there to be playing in the garden . . . one in the house, and the other in the garden: isn't that it?

THE STEPDAUGHTER Yes, in the sun, in the sun! That is my only pleasure: to see her happy and careless in the garden after the misery and squalor of the horrible room where we all four slept together. And I had to sleep with her—I, do you understand?—with my vile contaminated body next to hers; with her folding me fast in her loving little arms. In the garden, whenever she spied me, she would run to take me by the hand. She didn't care for the big flowers, only the little ones; and she loved to show me them and pet me.

THE MANAGER Well then, we'll have it in the garden. Everything shall happen in the garden; and we'll group the other scenes there. *(Calls a* STAGE HANL*)* Here, a back-cloth with trees and something to do as a fountain basin. *(Turning round to look at the back of the stage)* Ah, you've fixed it up. Good! *(To* STEPDAUGHTER*)* This is just to give an idea, of course. The Boy, instead of hiding behind the doors, will wander about here in the garden, hiding behind the trees. But it's going to be rather difficult to find a child to do that scene with you where she shows you the flowers. *(Turning to the* BOY*)* Come forward a little, will you please? Let's try it now! Come along! come along! *(Then seeing him come shyly forward, full of fear and looking lost)* It's a nice business, this lad here. What's the matter with him? We'll have to give him a word or two to say. *(Goes close to him, puts a hand on his shoulders, and leads him behind one of the trees)* Come on! come on! Let me see you a little! Hide here . . . yes, like that. Try and show your head just a little as if you were looking for someone . . . *(Goes back to observe the effect, when the* BOY *at once goes through the action)* Excellent! fine! *(Turning to* STEPDAUGHTER*)* Suppose the little girl there were to surprise him as he looks round, and run over to him, so we could give him a word or two to say?

THE STEPDAUGHTER It's useless to hope he will speak, as long as that fellow there is here . . . *(Indicates the* SON*)* You must send him away first.

THE SON *(Jumping up)* Delighted! delighted! I don't ask for anything better. *(Begins to move away.)*

THE MANAGER *(At once stopping him)* No! No! Where are you going? Wait a bit!

The MOTHER *gets up, alarmed and terrified at the thought that he is really about to go away. Instinctively she lifts her arms to prevent him, without, however, leaving her seat.*

THE SON *(To* MANAGER, *who stops him)* I've got nothing to do with this affair. Let me go please! Let me go!

THE MANAGER What do you mean by saying you've got nothing to do with this?

THE STEPDAUGHTER *(Calmly, with irony)* Don't bother to stop him: he won't go away.

THE FATHER He has to act the terrible scene in the garden with his mother.

THE SON *(Suddenly resolute and with dignity)* I shall act nothing at all. I've said so from the very beginning. *(To the* MANAGER*)* Let me go!

THE STEPDAUGHTER *(Going over to the* MANAGER*)* Allow me? *(Puts down the* MANAGER'S *arm which is restraining the* SON*)* Well, go away then, if you want to!

(The SON *looks at her with contempt and hatred. She laughs and says)* You see, he can't, he can't go away! He is obliged to stay here, indissolubly bound to the chain. If I, who fly off when that happens which has to happen, because I can't bear him —if I am still here and support that face and expression of his, you can well imagine that he is unable to move. He has to remain here, has to stop with that nice father of his, and that mother whose only son he is. *(Turning to the* MOTHER*)* Come on, mother, come along! *(Turning to* MANAGER *to indicate her)* You see, she was getting up to keep him back. *(To the* MOTHER, *beckoning her with her hand)* Come on! come on! *(Then to* MANAGER*)* You can imagine how little she wants to show these actors of yours what she really feels; but so eager is she to get near him that . . . There, you see? She is willing to act her part. *(And in fact, the* MOTHER *approaches him; and as soon as the* STEPDAUGHTER *has finished speaking, opens her arms to signify that she consents.)*

THE SON *(Suddenly)*   No! No! If I can't go away, then I'll stop here; but I repeat: I act nothing!

THE FATHER *(To* MANAGER *excitedly)*   You can force him, sir.

THE SON   Nobody can force me.

THE FATHER   I can.

THE STEPDAUGHTER   Wait a minute, wait . . . First of all, the baby has to go to the fountain . . . *(Runs to take the* CHILD *and leads her to the fountain.)*

THE MANAGER   Yes, yes of course; that's it. Both at the same time.

The SECOND LADY LEAD *and the* JUVENILE LEAD *at this point separate themselves from the group of* ACTORS. *One watches the* MOTHER *attentively; the other moves about studying the movements and manner of the* SON *whom he will have to act.*

THE SON *(To* MANAGER*)*   What do you mean by both at the same time? It isn't right. There was no scene between me and her. *(Indicates the* MOTHER*)* Ask her how it was!

THE MOTHER   Yes, it's true. I had come into his room . . .

THE SON   Into my room, do you understand? Nothing to do with the garden.

THE MANAGER   It doesn't matter. Haven't I told you we've got to group the action?

THE SON *(Observing the* JUVENILE LEAD *studying him)*   What do you want?

JUVENILE LEAD   Nothing! I was just looking at you.

THE SON *(Turning towards the* SECOND LADY LEAD*)*   Ah! she's at it too: to re-act her part! *(Indicating the* MOTHER.*)*

THE MANAGER   Exactly! And it seems to me that you ought to be grateful to them for their interest.

THE SON   Yes, but haven't you yet perceived that it isn't possible to live in front of a mirror which not only freezes us with the image of ourselves, but throws our likeness back at us with a horrible grimace?

THE FATHER   That is true, absolutely true. You must see that.

THE MANAGER *(To* SECOND LADY LEAD *and* JUVENILE LEAD*)*   He's right! Move away from them!

THE SON   Do as you like. I'm out of this!

THE MANAGER   Be quiet, you, will you? And let me hear your mother! *(To* MOTHER*)* You were saying you had entered . . .

THE MOTHER   Yes, into his room, because I couldn't stand it any longer. I went to empty my heart to him of all the anguish that tortures me . . . But as soon as he saw me come in . . .

THE SON   Nothing happened! There was no scene. I went away, that's all! I don't care for scenes!

THE MOTHER   It's true, true. That's how it was.

THE MANAGER   Well now, we've got to do this bit between you and him. It's indispensable.

THE MOTHER   I'm ready . . . when you are ready. If you could only find a chance for me to tell him what I feel here in my heart.

THE FATHER *(Going to* SON *in a great rage)*   You'll do this for your mother, for your mother, do you understand?

THE SON *(Quite determined)*   I do nothing!

THE FATHER *(Taking hold of him and shaking him)*   For God's sake, do as I tell you! Don't you hear your mother asking you for a favor? Haven't you even got the guts to be a son?

THE SON *(Taking hold of the* FATHER*)*   No! No! And for God's sake stop it, or else . . . *(General agitation. The* MOTHER, *frightened, tries to separate them.)*

THE MOTHER *(Pleading)*   Please! please!

THE FATHER *(Not leaving hold of the* SON*)*   You've got to obey, do you hear?

THE SON *(Almost crying from rage)*   What does it mean, this madness you've got? *(They separate)* Have you no decency, that you insist on showing everyone our shame? I won't do it! I won't! And I stand for the will of our author in this. He didn't want to put us on the stage, after all!

THE MANAGER   Man alive! You came here . . .

THE SON *(Indicating* FATHER*)*   *He* did! I didn't!

THE MANAGER   Aren't you here now?

THE SON   It was his wish, and he dragged us along with him. He's told you not only the things that did happen, but also things that have never happened at all.

THE MANAGER   Well, tell me then what did happen. You went out of your room without saying a word?

THE SON   Without a word, so as to avoid a scene!

THE MANAGER   And then what did you do?

THE SON   Nothing . . . walking in the garden . . . *(Hesitates for a moment with expression of gloom.)*

THE MANAGER *(Coming closer to him, interested by his extraordinary reserve)*   Well, well . . . walking in the garden . . .

THE SON *(Exasperated)*   Why on earth do you insist? It's horrible! *(The* MOTHER *trembles, sobs, and looks towards the fountain.)*

THE MANAGER *(Slowly observing the glance and turning towards the* SON *with increasing apprehension)*   The baby?

THE SON   There in the fountain . . .

THE FATHER *(Pointing with tender pity to the* MOTHER*)*   She was following him at the moment . . .

THE MANAGER *(To the* SON, *anxiously)*   And then you . . .

THE SON   I ran over to her; I was jumping in to drag her out when I saw something that froze my blood . . . the boy there, standing stock still, with eyes like a madman's, watching his little drowned sister, in the fountain! *(The* STEPDAUGHTER *bends over the fountain to hide the* CHILD. *She sobs)* Then . . . *(A revolver shot rings out behind the trees where the* BOY *is hidden.)*

THE MOTHER *(With a cry of terror runs over in that direction together with several of the* ACTORS *amid general confusion)*   My son! My son! *(Then amid the cries and exclamations one hears her voice)* Help! Help!

THE MANAGER *(Pushing the* ACTORS *aside while they lift up the* BOY *and carry him off)* Is he really wounded?

SOME ACTORS   He's dead, dead!

OTHER ACTORS   No, no, it's only make-believe, it's only pretence!

THE FATHER *(With a terrible cry)* Pretence? Reality, sir, reality!

THE MANAGER   Pretence? Reality? To hell with it all! Never in my life has such a thing happened to me. I've lost a whole day over these people, a whole day!

Curtain

Response Statement Assignments

1. After your first reading of this play, summarize what you think it is about.
2. How many levels of reality is this play working on?
3. Which level(s) did you choose to focus on in your summary (question 1) of the play? Why?
4. Which of your expectations about the nature of life and the nature of drama does this play confirm or challenge?
5. Did you develop any new **reading strategies** when reading the play? If so, did your experiences with other types of texts or art forms help you develop alternative strategies for reading this play?
6. Many readers have trouble with the status of the six characters in this play because they aren't "real." In what ways are these characters different from the ghost of Hamlet's father in *Hamlet,* who also, presumably, isn't real?
7. What does the following quotation, spoken by the father, suggest to you about the relationship between art and reality: "Life is full of infinite absurdities, which, strangely enough, do not even need to appear plausible, since they are true."
8. What does the following quotation suggest to you about the nature of the self: "A character, sir, may always ask a man who he is. Because a character has really a life of his own, marked with his especial characteristics; for which reason he is always 'somebody.' But a man—I'm not speaking of you now—may very well be 'nobody.'"
9. Watch a television news program that presents "experts" offering contradictory views on a given subject. What kinds of listening strategies and assumptions help you process such discussions? Are any of these applicable to your reading *Six Characters in Search of an Author?*
10. Reread the play after you have had a class discussion on various of the above questions. With an enlarged **repertoire** and a different set of expectations, how does your response to the play change?

EUGÈNE IONESCO (b. 1912)

The Gap

An English translation by Rosette Lamont

CHARACTERS

THE FRIEND
THE ACADEMICIAN
THE ACADEMICIAN'S WIFE
THE MAID

SET. *A rich bourgeois living room with artistic pretensions. One or two sofas, a number of armchairs, among which, a green, Régence style one, right in the middle of the room. The walls are covered with framed diplomas. One can make out, written in heavy script at the top of a particularly large one, "Doctor Honoris causa." This is followed by an almost illegible Latin inscription. Another equally impressive diploma states: "Doctorat honoris causa," again followed by a long, illegible text. There is an abundance of smaller diplomas, each of which bears a clearly written "doctorate."*

A door to the right of the audience.

As the curtain rises, one can see THE ACADEMICIAN'S WIFE *dressed in a rather crumpled robe. She has obviously just gotten out of bed, and has not had time to dress.* THE FRIEND *faces her. He is well dressed: hat, umbrella in hand, stiff collar, black jacket and striped trousers, shiny black shoes.*

THE WIFE   Dear friend, tell me all.

THE FRIEND   I don't know what to say.

THE WIFE   I know.

THE FRIEND   I heard the news last night. I did not want to call you. At the same time I couldn't wait any longer. Please forgive me for coming so early with such terrible news.

THE WIFE   He didn't make it! How terrible! We were still hoping. . . .

THE FRIEND   It's hard, I know. He still had a chance. Not much of one. We had to expect it.

THE WIFE   I didn't expect it. He was always so successful. He could always manage somehow, at the last moment.

THE FRIEND   In that state of exhaustion. You shouldn't have let him!

THE WIFE   What can we do, what can we do! . . . How awful!

THE FRIEND   Come on, dear friend, be brave. That's life.

THE WIFE   I feel faint: I'm going to faint. *(She falls in one of the armchairs.)*

THE FRIEND *(holding her, gently slapping her cheeks and hands)*   I shouldn't have blurted it out like that. I'm sorry.

THE WIFE   No, you were right to do so. I had to find out somehow or other.

THE FRIEND   I should have prepared you, carefully.

THE WIFE   I've got to be strong. I can't help thinking of him, the wretched man. I hope they won't put it in the papers. Can we count on the journalists' discretion?

THE FRIEND   Close your door. Don't answer the telephone. It will still get around.

You could go to the country. In a couple of months, when you are better, you'll come back, you'll go on with your life. People forget such things.

THE WIFE People won't forget so fast. That's all they were waiting for. Some friends will feel sorry, but the others, the others. . . .

THE ACADEMICIAN *comes in, fully dressed: uniform, chest covered with decorations, his sword on his side.*

THE ACADEMICIAN Up so early, my dear? (*To* THE FRIEND.) You've come early too. What's happening? Do you have the final results?

THE WIFE What a disgrace!

THE FRIEND You mustn't crush him like this, dear friend. (*To* THE ACADEMICIAN.) You have failed.

THE ACADEMICIAN Are you quite sure?

THE FRIEND You should never have tried to pass the baccalaureate examination.

THE ACADEMICIAN They failed me. The rats! How dare they do this to me!

THE FRIEND The marks were posted late in the evening.

THE ACADEMICIAN Perhaps it was difficult to make them out in the dark. How could you read them?

THE FRIEND They had set up spotlights.

THE ACADEMICIAN They're doing everything to ruin me.

THE FRIEND I passed by in the morning; the marks were still up.

THE ACADEMICIAN You could have bribed the concierge into pulling them down.

THE FRIEND That's exactly what I did. Unfortunately the police were there. Your name heads the list of those who failed. Everyone's standing in line to get a look. There's an awful crush.

THE ACADEMICIAN Who's there? The parents of the candidates?

THE FRIEND Not only they.

THE WIFE All your rivals, all your colleagues must be there. All those you attacked in the press for ignorance: your undergraduates, your graduate students, all those you failed when you were chairman of the board of examiners.

THE ACADEMICIAN I am discredited! But I won't let them. There must be some mistake.

THE FRIEND I saw the examiners. I spoke with them. They gave me your marks. Zero in mathematics.

THE ACADEMICIAN I had no scientific training.

THE FRIEND Zero in Greek, zero in Latin.

THE WIFE *(to her husband)* You, a humanist, the spokesman for humanism, the author of that famous treatise "The Defense of Poesy and Humanism."

THE ACADEMICIAN I beg your pardon, but my book concerns itself with twentieth-century humanism. (*To* THE FRIEND.) What about composition? What grade did I get in composition?

THE FRIEND Nine hundred. You have nine hundred points.

THE ACADEMICIAN That's perfect. My average must be all the way up.

THE FRIEND Unfortunately not. They're marking on the basis of two thousand. The passing grade is one thousand.

THE ACADEMICIAN They must have changed the regulations.

THE WIFE They didn't change them just for you. You have a frightful persecution complex.

THE ACADEMICIAN I tell you they changed them.

THE FRIEND They went back to the old ones, back to the time of Napoleon.

THE ACADEMICIAN Utterly outmoded. Besides, when did they make those changes? It isn't legal. I'm chairman of the Baccalaureate Commission of the Ministry of Public Education. They didn't consult me, and they cannot make any changes without my approval. I'm going to expose them. I'm going to bring government charges against them.

THE WIFE Darling, you don't know what you're doing. You're in your dotage. Don't you recall handing in your resignation just before taking the examination so that no one could doubt the complete objectivity of the board of examiners?

THE ACADEMICIAN I'll take it back.

THE WIFE You should never have taken that test. I warned you. After all, it's not as if you needed it. But you have to collect all the honors, don't you? You're never satisfied. What did you need this diploma for? Now all is lost. You have your Doctorate, your Master's, your high school diploma, your elementary school certificate, and even the first part of the baccalaureate.

THE ACADEMICIAN There was a gap.

THE WIFE No one suspected it.

THE ACADEMICIAN But *I* knew it. Others might have found out. I went to the office of the Registrar and asked for a transcript of my record. They said to me: "Certainly Professor, Mr. President, Your Excellency. . . ." Then they looked up my file, and the Chief Registrar came back looking embarrassed, most embarrassed indeed. He said: "There's something peculiar, very peculiar. You have your Master's, certainly, but it's no longer valid." I asked him why, of course. He answered: "There's a gap behind your Master's. I don't know how it happened. You must have registered and been accepted at the University without having passed the second part of the baccalaureate examination."

THE FRIEND And then?

THE WIFE Your Master's degree is no longer valid?

THE ACADEMICIAN No, not quite. It's suspended. "The duplicate you are asking for will be delivered to you upon completion of the baccalaureate. Of course you will pass the examination with no trouble." That's what I was told, so you see now that I had to take it.

THE FRIEND Your husband, dear friend, wanted to fill the gap. He's a conscientious person.

THE WIFE. It's clear you don't know him as I do. That's not it at all. He wants fame, honors. He never had enough. What does one diploma more or less matter? No one notices them anyway, but he sneaks in at night, on tiptoe, into the living room, just to look at them, and count them.

THE ACADEMICIAN What else can I do when I have insomnia?

THE FRIEND The questions asked at the baccalaureate are usually known in advance. You were admirably situated to get this particular information. You could also have sent in a replacement to take the test for you. One of your students, perhaps. Or if you wanted to take the test without people realizing that you already knew the questions, you could have sent your maid to the black market, where one can buy them.

THE ACADEMICIAN I don't understand how I could have failed in my composition. I filled three sheets of paper, I treated the subject fully, taking into account the historical background. I interpreted the situation accurately . . . at least plausibly. I didn't deserve a bad grade.

THE FRIEND   Do you recall the subject?

THE ACADEMICIAN   Hum . . . let's see. . . .

THE FRIEND   He doesn't even remember what he discussed.

THE ACADEMICIAN   I do . . . wait . . . hum.

THE FRIEND   The subject to be treated was the following: "Discuss the influence of Renaissance painters on novelists of the Third Republic." I have here a photostatic copy of your examination paper. Here is what you wrote.

THE ACADEMICIAN *(grabbing the photostat and reading)*   "The trial of Benjamin: After Benjamin was tried and acquitted, the assessors holding a different opinion from that of the President murdered him, and condemned Benjamin to the suspension of his civic rights, imposing on him a fine of nine hundred francs. . . ."

THE FRIEND   That's where the nine hundred points come from.

THE ACADEMICIAN   "Benjamin appealed his case . . . Benjamin appealed his case. . . ." I can't make out the rest. I've always had bad handwriting. I ought to have taken a typewriter along with me.

THE WIFE   Horrible handwriting, scribbling and crossing out; ink spots didn't help you much.

THE ACADEMICIAN *(goes on with his reading after having retrieved the text his wife had pulled out of his hand)*   "Benjamin appealed his case. Flanked by policemen dressed in zouave uniforms . . . in zouave uniforms. . . ." It's getting dark. I can't see the rest. . . . I don't have my glasses.

THE WIFE   What you've written has nothing to do with the subject.

THE FRIEND   Your wife's quite right, friend. It has nothing to do with the subject.

THE ACADEMICIAN   Yes, it has. Indirectly.

THE FRIEND   Not even indirectly.

THE ACADEMICIAN   Perhaps I chose the second question.

THE FRIEND   There was only one.

THE ACADEMICIAN   Even if there was only that one, I treated another quite adequately. I went to the end of the story. I stressed the important points, explaining the motivations of the characters, highlighting their behavior. I explained the mystery, making it plain and clear. There was even a conclusion at the end. I can't make out the rest. (*To* THE FRIEND.) Can you read it?

THE FRIEND   It's illegible. I don't have my glasses either.

THE WIFE *(taking the text)*   It's illegible and I have excellent eyes. You pretended to write. Mere scribbling.

THE ACADEMICIAN   That's not true. I've even provided a conclusion. It's clearly marked here in heavy print: "Conclusion or sanction . . . Conclusion or sanction. . . ." They can't get away with it. I'll have this examination rendered null and void.

THE WIFE   Since you treated the wrong subject, and treated it badly, setting down only titles, and writing nothing in between, the mark you received is justified. You'd lose your case.

THE FRIEND   You'd most certainly lose. Drop it. Take a vacation.

THE ACADEMICIAN   You're always on the side of the Others.

THE WIFE   After all, these professors know what they're doing. They haven't been granted their rank for nothing. They passed examinations, received serious training. They know the rules of composition.

THE ACADEMICIAN   Who was on the board of examiners?

THE FRIEND   For Mathematics, a movie star. For Greek, one of the Beatles. For Latin, the champion of the automobile race, and many others.

THE ACADEMICIAN   But these people aren't any more qualified than I am. And for composition?

THE FRIEND   A woman, a secretary in the editorial division of the review *Yesterday, the Day Before Yesterday, and Today.*

THE ACADEMICIAN   Now I know. This wretch gave me a poor grade out of spite because I never joined her political party. It's an act of vengeance. But I have ways and means of rendering the examination null and void. I'm going to call the President.

THE WIFE   Don't. You'll make yourself look even more ridiculous. (*To* THE FRIEND.) Please try to restrain him. He listens to you more than to me. (THE FRIEND *shrugs his shoulders, unable to cope with the situation.* THE WIFE *turns to her husband, who has just lifted the receiver off the hook.*) Don't call!

THE ACADEMICIAN (*on the telephone*)   Hello, John? It is I . . . What? . . . What did you say? . . . But, listen, my dear friend . . . but, listen to me . . Hello! Hello! (*Puts down the receiver.*)

THE FRIEND   What did he say?

THE ACADEMICIAN   He said. . .He said. . . . "I don't want to talk to you. My mummy won't let me make friends with boys at the bottom of the class." Then he hung up on me.

THE WIFE   You should have expected it. All is lost. How could you do this to me? How could you do this to me?

THE ACADEMICIAN   Think of it! I lectured at the Sorbonne, at Oxford, at American universities. Ten thousand theses have been written on my work; hundreds of critics have analyzed it. I hold an *honoris causa* doctorate from Amsterdam as well as a secret university Chair with the Duchy of Luxembourg. I received the Nobel Prize three times. The King of Sweden himself was amazed by my erudition. A doctorate *honoris causa, honoris causa* . . . and I failed the baccalaureate examination!

THE WIFE   Everyone will laugh at us!

THE ACADEMICIAN *takes off his sword and breaks it on his knee.*

THE FRIEND (*picking up the two pieces*)   I wish to preserve these in memory of our ancient glory.

THE ACADEMICIAN *meanwhile in a fit of rage is tearing down his decorations, throwing them on the floor, and stepping on them.*

THE WIFE (*trying to salvage the remains*)   Don't do this! Don't! That's all we've got left.

Curtain

Response Statement Assignments

1. How do you respond to the "reality" of the characters and of the situation they find themselves in? Do you find one more apparently "realistic" than the other?
2. Can you imagine an equivalent experience in your own life? What would you mean if you called such a situation "absurd"?

3. This play is very short. How does that affect your response? What parts of your **repertoire** help you read it? Consider, for example, the experience of reading a "short" story, or telling (or listening to) a joke or a story at a party.

4. *The Gap,* unlike *Death of a Salesman,* has no "realistic" situation, story line, or chain of events. How do you read and build consistency in your interpretation of such a play?

5. In what way does the play speak to social problems like those in more realistic plays and films you have read or seen?

6. Does its strange order of events seem unnatural or do you think that your world is as disordered as the play? How do you respond to disorder in drama—as opposed to life?

7. What response do you have to the way in which characters, such as those in the play, communicate with one another? What attitudes about human nature—of how people interact, of how they read one another— exists in *The Gap*?

ARTHUR MILLER (b.1915)

Death of a Salesman

Certain Private Conversations in Two Acts and a Requiem

CHARACTERS

WILLY LOMAN	UNCLE BEN
LINDA	HOWARD WAGNER
BIFF	JENNY
HAPPY	STANLEY
BERNARD	MISS FORSYTHE
THE WOMAN	LETTA
CHARLEY	

The action takes place in WILLY LOMAN'S *house and yard and in various places he visits in the New York and Boston of today.*

Throughout the play, in the stage directions, left and right mean stage left and stage right.

ACT I

AN OVERTURE. A melody is heard, played upon a flute. It is small and fine, telling of grass and trees and the horizon. The curtain rises.

Before us is the Salesman's house. We are aware of towering, angular shapes behind it, surrounding it on all sides. Only the blue light of the sky falls upon the house and forestage; the surrounding area shows an angry glow of orange. As more light appears, we see a solid vault of apartment houses around the small, fragile-seeming home. An air of the dream clings to the place, a dream rising out of reality. The kitchen at center seems actual enough, for there is a kitchen table with three chairs, and a refrigerator. But no other fixtures are seen. At the back of the kitchen there is a draped entrance, which leads to the living room. To the right of the kitchen, on a level raised two feet, is a bedroom furnished only with a brass bedstead and a straight chair. On a shelf over the bed a silver athletic trophy stands. A window opens onto the apartment house at the side.

Behind the kitchen, on a level raised six and a half feet, is the boys' bedroom, at present barely visible. Two beds are dimly seen, and at the back of the room a dormer window. (This bedroom is above the unseen living room.) At the left a stairway curves up to it from the kitchen.

The entire setting is wholly or, in some places, partially transparent. The roof-line of the house is one-dimensional; under and over it we see the apartment buildings. Before the house lies an apron, curving beyond the forestage into the orchestra. This forward area serves as the back yard as well as the locale of all WILLY's imaginings and of his city scenes. Whenever the action is in the present the actors observe the imaginary wall-lines, entering the house only through its door at the left. But in the scenes of the past these boundaries are broken, and characters enter or leave a room by stepping "through" a wall onto the forestage.

From the right, WILLY LOMAN, the Salesman, enters, carrying two large sample cases. The flute plays on. He hears but is not aware of it. He is past sixty years of age, dressed quietly. Even as he crosses the stage to the doorway of the house, his exhaustion is apparent. He unlocks the door, comes into the kitchen, and thankfully lets his burden down, feeling the soreness of his palms. A word-sigh escapes his lips—it might be "Oh, boy, oh, boy." He closes the door, then carries his cases out into the living room, through the draped kitchen doorway.

LINDA, his wife, has stirred in her bed at the right. She gets out and puts on a robe, listening. Most often jovial, she has developed an iron repression of her exceptions to WILLY's behavior—she more than loves him, she admires him, as though his mercurial nature, his temper, his massive dreams and little cruelties, served her only as sharp reminders of the turbulent longings within him, longings which she shares but lacks the temperament to utter and follow to their end.

LINDA (hearing WILLY outside the bedroom, calls with some trepidation) Willy!
WILLY It's all right. I came back.
LINDA Why? What happened? (Slight pause) Did something happen, Willy?
WILLY No, nothing happened.
LINDA You didn't smash the car, did you?
WILLY (with casual irritation) I said nothing happened. Didn't you hear me?
LINDA Don't you feel well?
WILLY I'm tired to the death. (The flute has faded away. He sits on the bed beside her, a little numb) I couldn't make it. I just couldn't make it, Linda.
LINDA (very carefully, delicately) Where were you all day? You look terrible.
WILLY I got as far as a little above Yonkers. I stopped for a cup of coffee. Maybe it was the coffee.
LINDA What?
WILLY (after a pause) I suddenly couldn't drive any more. The car kept going off onto the shoulder, y'know?
LINDA (helpfully) Oh. Maybe it was the steering again. I don't think Angelo knows the Studebaker.

WILLY   No, it's me, it's me. Suddenly I realize I'm goin' sixty miles an hour and I don't remember the last five minutes. I'm—I can't seem to—keep my mind to it.

LINDA   Maybe it's your glasses. You never went for your new glasses.

WILLY   No, I see everything. I came back ten miles an hour. It took me nearly four hours from Yonkers.

LINDA *(resigned)*   Well, you'll just have to take a rest, Willy, you can't continue this way.

WILLY   I just got back from Florida.

LINDA   But you didn't rest your mind. Your mind is overactive, and the mind is what counts, dear.

WILLY   I'll start out in the morning. Maybe I'll feel better in the morning. *(She is taking off his shoes)* These goddam arch supports are killing me.

LINDA   Take an aspirin. Should I get you an aspirin? It'll soothe you.

WILLY *(with wonder)*   I was driving along, you understand? And I was fine. I was even observing the scenery. You can imagine, me looking at scenery, on the road every week of my life. But it's so beautiful up there, Linda, the trees are so thick, and the sun is warm. I opened the windshield and just let the warm air bathe over me. And then all of a sudden I'm goin' off the road! I'm tellin' ya, I absolutely forgot I was driving. If I'd've gone the other way over the white line I might've killed somebody. So I went on again—and five minutes later I'm dreamin' again, and I nearly—*(He presses two fingers against his eyes)* I have such thoughts, I have such strange thoughts.

LINDA   Willy, dear. Talk to them again. There's no reason why you can't work in New York.

WILLY   They don't need me in New York. I'm the New England man. I'm vital in New England.

LINDA   But you're sixty years old. They can't expect you to keep traveling every week.

WILLY   I'll have to send a wire to Portland. I'm supposed to see Brown and Morrison tomorrow morning at ten o'clock to show the line. Goddammit, I could sell them! *(He starts putting on his jacket.)*

LINDA *(taking the jacket from him)*   Why don't you go down to the place tomorrow and tell Howard you've simply got to work in New York? You're too accommodating, dear.

WILLY   If old man Wagner was alive I'd a been in charge of New York now! That man was a prince, he was a masterful man. But that boy of his, that Howard, he don't appreciate. When I went north the first time, the Wagner Company didn't know where New England was!

LINDA   Why don't you tell those things to Howard, dear?

WILLY *(encouraged)*   I will, I definitely will. Is there any cheese?

LINDA   I'll make you a sandwich.

WILLY   No, go to sleep. I'll take some milk. I'll be up right away. The boys in?

LINDA   They're sleeping. Happy took Biff on a date tonight.

WILLY *(interested)*   That so?

LINDA   It was so nice to see them shaving together, one behind the other, in the bathroom. And going out together. You notice? The whole house smells of shaving lotion.

WILLY   Figure it out. Work a lifetime to pay off a house. Finally own it, and there's nobody to live in it.

LINDA   Well, dear, life is a casting off. It's always that way.

WILLY   No, no, some people—some people accomplish something. Did Biff say anything after I went this morning?

LINDA   You shouldn't have criticized him, Willy, especially after he just got off the train. You musn't lose your temper with him.

WILLY   When the hell did I lose my temper? I simply asked him if he was making any money. Is that a criticism?

LINDA   But, dear, how could he make any money?

WILLY   *(worried and angered)*   There's such an undercurrent in him. He became a moody man. Did he apologize when I left this morning?

LINDA   He was crestfallen, Willy. You know how he admires you. I think if he finds himself, then you'll both be happier and not fight any more.

WILLY   How can he find himself on a farm? Is that a life? A farmhand? In the beginning, when he was young, I thought, well, a young man, it's good for him to tramp around, take a lot of different jobs. But it's more than ten years now and he has yet to make thirty-five dollars a week!

LINDA   He's finding himself, Willy.

WILLY   Not finding yourself at the age of thirty-four is a disgrace!

LINDA   Shh!

WILLY   The trouble is he's lazy, goddammit!

LINDA   Willy, please!

WILLY   Biff is a lazy bum!

LINDA   They're sleeping. Get something to eat. Go on down.

WILLY   Why did he come home? I would like to know what brought him home.

LINDA   I don't know. I think he's still lost, Willy. I think he's very lost.

WILLY   Biff Loman is lost. In the greatest country in the world a young man with such—personal attractiveness, gets lost. And such a hard worker. There's one thing about Biff—he's not lazy.

LINDA   Never.

WILLY   *(with pity and resolve)*   I'll see him in the morning; I'll have a nice talk with him. I'll get him a job selling. He could be big in no time. My God! Remember how they used follow him around in high school? When he smiled at one of them their faces lit up. When he walked down the street . . . *(He loses himself in reminiscences)*

LINDA   *(trying to bring him out of it)*   Willy, dear, I got a new kind of American-type cheese today. It's whipped.

WILLY   Why do you get American when I like Swiss?

LINDA   I just thought you'd like a change—

WILLY   I don't want a change! I want Swiss cheese. Why am I always being contradicted?

LINDA   *(with a covering laugh)*   I thought it would be a surprise.

WILLY   Why don't you open a window in here, for God's sake?

LINDA   *(with infinite patience)*   They're all open, dear.

WILLY   The way they boxed us in here. Bricks and windows, windows and bricks.

LINDA   We should've bought the land next door.

WILLY   The street is lined with cars. There's not a breath of fresh air in the neighborhood. The grass don't grow any more, you can't raise a carrot in the back yard. They should've had a law against apartment houses. Remember those two beautiful elm trees out there? When I and Biff hung the swing between them?

LINDA   Yeah, like being a million miles from the city.

WILLY They should've arrested the builder for cutting those down. They mas-sacred the neighborhood. *(Lost)* More and more I think of those days, Linda. This time of year it was lilac and wisteria. And then the peonies would come out, and the daffodils. What fragrance in this room!

LINDA Well, after all, people had to move somewhere.

WILLY No, there's more people now.

LINDA I don't think there's more people. I think—

WILLY There's more people! That's what's ruining this country! Population is get-ting out of control. The competition is maddening! Smell the stink from that apartment house! And another one on the other side . . . How can they whip cheese?

On WILLY'S *last line,* BIFF *and* HAPPY *raise themselves up in their beds, listening.*

LINDA Go down, try it. And be quiet.

WILLY *(turning to* LINDA, *guiltily)* You're not worried about me, are you, sweet-heart?

BIFF What's the matter?

HAPPY Listen!

LINDA You've got too much on the ball to worry about.

WILLY You're my foundation and my support, Linda.

LINDA Just try to relax, dear. You make mountains out of molehills.

WILLY I won't fight with him any more. If he wants to go back to Texas, let him go.

LINDA He'll find his way.

WILLY Sure. Certain men just don't get started till later in life. Like Thomas Edison, I think. Or B. F. Goodrich. One of them was deaf. *(He starts for the bed-room doorway)* I'll put my money on Biff.

LINDA And Willy—if it's warm Sunday we'll drive in the country. And we'll open the windshield, and take lunch.

WILLY No, The windshields don't open on the new cars.

LINDA But you opened it today.

WILLY Me? I didn't. *(He stops)* Now isn't that peculiar! Isn't that a remarkable— *(He breaks off in amazement and fright as the flute is heard distantly)*

LINDA What, darling?

WILLY That is the most remarkable thing.

LINDA What, dear?

WILLY I was thinking of the Chevvy. *(Slight pause)* Nineteen twenty-eight . . . when I had that red Chevvy—*(Breaks off)* That funny? I coulda sworn I was driv-ing that Chevvy today.

LINDA Well, that's nothing. Something must've reminded you.

WILLY Remarkable. Ts. Remember those days? The way Biff used to simonize that car? The dealer refused to believe there was eighty thousand miles on it. *(He shakes his head)* Heh! *(To* LINDA*)* Close your eyes, I'll be right up. *He walks out of the bedroom)*

HAPPY *(to* BIFF*)* Jesus, maybe he smashed up the car again!

LINDA *(calling after* WILLY*)* Be careful on the stairs, dear! The cheese is on the middle shelf! *(She turns, goes over to the bed, takes his jacket, and goes out of the bedroom)*

Light has risen on the boys' room. Unseen, WILLY *is heard talking to himself, "Eighty thousand miles," and a little laugh.* BIFF *gets out of bed, comes downstage a bit, and stands attentively.* BIFF *is two years older than his brother* HAPPY, *well built, but in these days bears a worn air and seems less self-assured. He has succeeded less, and his dreams are stronger and less acceptable than* HAPPY'S. HAPPY *is tall, power-fully made. Sexuality is like a visible color on him, or a scent that many women have discovered. He, like his brother, is lost, but in a different way, for he has never allowed himself to turn his face toward defeat and is thus more confused and hard-skinned, although seemingly more content.*

HAPPY *(getting out of bed)* He's going to get his license taken away if he keeps that up. I'm getting nervous about him, y'know, Biff?

BIFF His eyes are going.

HAPPY No, I've driven with him. He sees all right. He just doesn't keep his mind on it. I drove into the city with him last week. He stops at a green light and then it turns red and he goes. *(He laughs)*

BIFF Maybe he's color-blind.

HAPPY Pop? Why he's got the finest eye for color in the business. You know that.

BIFF *(sitting down on his bed)* I'm going to sleep.

HAPPY You're not still sour on Dad, are you, Biff?

BIFF He's all right, I guess.

WILLY *(underneath them, in the living-room)* Yes, sir, eighty thousand miles—eighty-two thousand!

BIFF You smoking?

HAPPY *(holding out a pack of cigarettes)* Want one?

BIFF *(taking a cigarette)* I can never sleep when I smell it.

WILLY What a simonizing job, heh!

HAPPY *(with deep sentiment)* Funny, Biff, y'know? Us sleeping in here again? The old beds. *(He pats his bed affectionately)* All the talk that went across those two beds, huh? Our whole lives.

BIFF Yeah. Lotta dreams and plans.

HAPPY *(with deep and masculine laugh)* About five hundred women would like to know what was said in this room.

They share a soft laugh.

BIFF Remember that big Betsy something—what the hell was her name—over on Bushwick Avenue?

HAPPY *(combing his hair)* With the collie dog!

BIFF That's the one. I got you in there, remember?

HAPPY Yeah, that was my first time—I think. Boy, there was a pig! *(They laugh, almost crudely)* You taught me everything I know about women. Don't forget that.

BIFF I bet you forgot how bashful you used to be. Especially with girls.

HAPPY Oh, I still am, Biff.

BIFF Oh, go on.

HAPPY I just control it, that's all. I think I got less bashful and you got more so. What happened, Biff? Where's the old humor, the old confidence? *(He shakes* BIFF's *knee.* BIFF *gets up and moves restlessly about the room)* What's the matter?

BIFF Why does Dad mock me all the time?

HAPPY He's not mocking you, he—

BIFF Everything I say there's a twist of mockery on his face. I can't get near him.

HAPPY   He just wants you to make good, that's all. I wanted to talk to you about Dad for a long time, Biff. Something's—happening to him. He—talks to himself.

BIFF   I noticed that this morning. But he always mumbled.

HAPPY   But not so noticeable. It got so embarrassing I sent him to Florida. And you know something? Most of the time he's talking to you.

BIFF   What's he say about me?

HAPPY   I can't make it out.

BIFF   What's he say about me?

HAPPY   I think the fact that you're not settled, that you're still kind of up in the air . . .

BIFF   There's one or two other things depressing him, Happy.

HAPPY   What do you mean?

BIFF   Never mind. Just don't lay it all to me.

HAPPY   But I think if you just got started—I mean—is there any future for you out there?

BIFF   I tell ya, Hap, I don't know what the future is. I don't know—what I'm supposed to want.

HAPPY   What do you mean?

BIFF   Well, I spent six or seven years after high school trying to work myself up. Shipping clerk, salesman, business of one kind or another. And it's a measly manner of existence. To get on that subway on the hot mornings in summer. To devote your whole life to keeping stock, or making phone calls, or selling or buying. To suffer fifty weeks of the year for the sake of a two-week vacation, when all you really desire is to be outdoors, with your shirt off. And always to have to get ahead of the next fella. And still—that's how you build a future.

HAPPY   Well, you really enjoy it on a farm? Are you content out there?

BIFF   *(with rising agitation)*   Hap, I've had twenty or thirty different kinds of jobs since I left home before the war, and it always turns out the same. I just realized it lately. In Nebraska when I herded cattle, and the Dakotas, and Arizona, and now in Texas. It's why I came home now, I guess, because I realized it. This farm I work on, it's spring there now, see? And they've got about fifteen new colts. There's nothing more inspiring or—beautiful than the sight of a mare and a new colt. And it's cool there now, see? Texas is cool now, and it's spring. And whenever spring comes to where I am, I suddenly get the feeling, my God, I'm not gettin' anywhere! What the hell am I doing, playing around with horses, twenty-eight dollars a week! I'm thirty-four years old, I oughta be makin' my future. That's when I come running home. And now, I get here, and I don't know what to do with myself. *(After a pause)* I've always made a point of not wasting my life, and everytime I come back here I know that all I've done is to waste my life.

HAPPY   You're a poet, you know that, Biff? You're a—you're an idealist!

BIFF   No, I'm mixed up very bad. Maybe I oughta get married. Maybe I oughta get stuck into something. Maybe that's my trouble. I'm like a boy. I'm not married, I'm not in business, I just—I'm like a boy. Are you content, Hap? You're a success, aren't you? Are you content?

HAPPY   Hell, no!

BIFF   Why? You're making money, aren't you?

HAPPY   *(moving about with energy, expressiveness)*   All I can do now is wait for the merchandise manager to die. And suppose I get to be merchandise manager? He's a good friend of mine, and he just built a terrific estate on Long Island. And he lived there about two months and sold it, and now he's building another one. He can't enjoy it once it's finished. And I know that's just what I would do. I don't know what the hell I'm workin' for. Sometimes I sit in my apartment—all alone. And I think of the rent I'm paying. And it's crazy. But then, it's what I always wanted. My own apartment, a car, and plenty of women. And still, goddammit. I'm lonely.

BIFF *(with enthusiasm)* Listen, why don't you come out West with me?

HAPPY You and I, heh?

BIFF Sure, maybe we could buy a ranch. Raise cattle, use our muscles. Men built like we are should be working out in the open.

HAPPY *(avidly)* The Loman Brothers, heh?

BIFF *(with vast affection)* Sure, we'd be known all over the counties!

HAPPY *(enthralled)* That's what I dream about, Biff. Sometimes I want to just rip my clothes off in the middle of the store and outbox that goddam merchandise manager. I mean I can outbox, outrun, and outlift anybody in that store, and I have to take orders from those common, petty sons-of-bitches till I can't stand it any more.

BIFF I'm tellin' you, kid, if you were with me I'd be happy out there.

HAPPY *(enthused)* See, Biff, everybody around me is so false that I'm constantly lowering my ideals . . .

BIFF Baby, together we'd stand up for one another, we'd have someone to trust.

HAPPY If I were around you—

BIFF Hap, the trouble is we weren't brought up to grub for money. I don't know how to do it.

HAPPY Neither can I!

BIFF Then let's go!

HAPPY The only thing is—what can you make out there?

BIFF But look at your friend. Builds an estate and then hasn't the peace of mind to live in it.

HAPPY Yeah, but when he walks into the store the waves part in front of him. That's fifty-two thousand dollars a year coming through the revolving door, and I got more in my pinky finger than he's got in his head.

BIFF Yeah, but you just said—

HAPPY I gotta show some of those pompous, self-important executives over there that Hap Loman can make the grade. I want to walk into the store the way he walks in. Then I'll go with you, Biff. We'll be together yet, I swear. But take those two we had tonight. Now weren't they gorgeous creatures?

BIFF Yeah, yeah, most gorgeous I've had in years.

HAPPY I get that any time I want, Biff. Whenever I feel disgusted. The only trouble is, it gets like bowling or something. I just keep knockin' them over and it doesn't mean anything. You still run around a lot?

BIFF Naa. I'd like to find a girl—steady, somebody with substance.

HAPPY That's what I long for.

BIFF Go on! You'd never come home.

HAPPY I would! Somebody with character, with resistance! Like Mom, y'know? You're gonna call me a bastard when I tell you this. That girl Charlotte I was with tonight is engaged to be married in five weeks. *(He tries on his new hat)*

BIFF No kiddin'!

HAPPY   Sure, the guy's in line for the vice-presidency of the store. I don't know what gets into me, maybe I just have an overdeveloped sense of competition or something, but I went and ruined her, and furthermore I can't get rid of her. And he's the third executive I've done that to. Isn't that a crummy characteristic? And to top it all, I go to their weddings! *(Indignantly, but laughing)* Like I'm not supposed to take bribes. Manufacturers offer me a hundred-dollar bill now and then to throw an order their way. You know how honest I am, but it's like this girl, see. I hate myself for it. Because I don't want the girl, and still, I take it and—I love it!

BIFF   Let's go to sleep.

HAPPY   I guess we didn't settle anything, heh?

BIFF   I just got one idea that I think I'm going to try.

HAPPY   What's that?

BIFF   Remember Bill Oliver?

HAPPY   Sure, Oliver is very big now. You want to work for him again?

BIFF   No, but when I quit he said something to me. He put his arm on my shoulder, and he said, "Biff, if you ever need anything, come to me."

HAPPY   I remember that. That sounds good.

BIFF   I think I'll go to see him. If I could get ten thousand or even seven or eight thousand dollars I could buy a beautiful ranch.

HAPPY   I bet he'd back you. 'Cause he thought highly of you, Biff. I mean, they all do. You're well liked, Biff. That's why I say to come back here, and we both have the apartment. And I'm tellin' you, Biff, any babe you want . . .

BIFF   No, with a ranch I could do the work I like and still be something. I just wonder though. I wonder if Oliver still thinks I stole that carton of basketballs.

HAPPY   Oh, he probably forgot that long ago. It's almost ten years. You're too sensitive. Anyway, he didn't really fire you.

BIFF   Well, I think he was going to. I think that's why I quit. I was never sure whether he knew or not. I know he thought the world of me, though. I was the only one he'd let lock up the place.

WILLY   *(below)*   You gonna wash the engine, Biff?

HAPPY   Shh!

BIFF *looks at* HAPPY, *who is gazing down, listening.* WILLY *is mumbling in the parlor.*

HAPPY   You hear that?

They listen. WILLY *laughs warmly.*

BIFF *(growing angry)*   Doesn't he know Mom can hear that?

WILLY   Don't get your sweater dirty, Biff!

A look of pain crosses BIFF's *face.*

HAPPY   Isn't that terrible? Don't leave again, will you? You'll find a job here. You gotta stick around. I don't know what to do about him, it's getting embarrassing.

WILLY   What a simonizing job!

BIFF   Mom's hearing that!

WILLY   No kiddin', Biff, you got a date? Wonderful!

HAPPY   Go on to sleep. But talk to him in the morning, will you?

BIFF *(reluctantly getting into bed)*   With her in the house. Brother!

HAPPY *(getting into bed)*   I wish you'd have a good talk with him.

The light on their room begins to fade.

BIFF *(to himself in bed)* That selfish, stupid . . .

HAPPY Sh . . . Sleep, Biff.

Their light is out. Well before they have finished speaking, WILLY's *form is dimly seen below in the darkened kitchen. He opens the refrigerator, searches in there, and takes out a bottle of milk. The apartment houses are fading out, and the entire house and surroundings become covered with leaves. Music insinuates itself as the leaves appear.*

WILLY Just wanna be careful with those girls, Biff, that's all. Don't make any promises. No promises of any kind. Because a girl, y'know, they always believe what you tell 'em, and you're very young, Biff, you're too young to be talking seriously to girls.

Light rises on the kitchen. WILLY, *talking, shuts the refrigerator door and comes downstage to the kitchen table. He pours milk into a glass. He is totally immersed in himself, smiling faintly.*

WILLY Too young entirely, Biff. You want to watch your schooling first. Then when you're all set, there'll be plenty of girls for a boy like you. *(He smiles broadly at a kitchen chair)* That so? The girls pay for you? *(He laughs)* Boy, you must really be makin' a hit.

WILLY *is gradually addressing—physically—a point offstage, speaking through the wall of the kitchen, and his voice has been rising in volume to that of a normal conversation.*

WILLY I been wondering why you polish the car so careful. Ha! Don't leave the hubcaps, boys. Get the chamois to the hubcaps. Happy, use newspaper on the windows, it's the easiest thing. Show him how to do it, Biff! You see, Happy? Pad it up, use it like a pad. That's it, that's it, good work. You're doin' all right, Hap. *(He pauses, then nods in approbation for few seconds, then looks upward)* Biff, first thing we gotta do when we get time is clip that big branch over the house. Afraid it's gonna fall in a storm and hit the roof. Tell you what. We get a rope and sling her around, and then we climb up there with a couple of saws and take her down. Soon as you finish the car, boys, I wanna see ya. I got a surprise for you, boys.

BIFF *(offstage)* Whatta ya got, Dad?

WILLY No, you finish first. Never leave a job till you're finished—remember that. *(Looking toward the "big trees")* Biff, up in Albany I saw a beautiful hammock. I think I'll buy it next trip, and we'll hang it right between those two elms. Wouldn't that be something? Just swingin' there under those branches. Boy, that would be . . .

YOUNG BIFF *and* YOUNG HAPPY *appear from the direction* WILLY *was addressing.* HAPPY *carries rags and a pail of water.* BIFF, *wearing a sweater with a block "S," carries a football.*

BIFF *(pointing in direction of the car offstage)* How's that, Pop, professional?

WILLY Terrific. Terrific job, boys. Good work, Biff.

HAPPY Where's the surprise, Pop?

WILLY In the back seat of the car.

HAPPY Boy! *(He runs off)*

BIFF   What is it, Dad? Tell me, what'd you buy?

WILLY *(laughing, cuffs him)*   Never mind, something I want you to have.

BIFF *(turns and starts off)*   What is it, Hap?

HAPPY *(offstage)*   It's a punching bag!

BIFF   Oh, Pop!

WILLY   It's got Gene Tunney's signature on it!

HAPPY *runs onstage with a punching bag.*

BIFF   Gee, how'd you know we wanted a punching bag?

WILLY   Well, it's the finest thing for the timing.

HAPPY *(lies down on his back and pedals with his feet)*   I'm losing weight, you notice, Pop?

WILLY *(to HAPPY)*   Jumping rope is good too.

BIFF   Did you see the new football I got?

WILLY *(examining the ball)*   Where'd you get a new ball?

BIFF   The coach told me to practice my passing.

WILLY   That so? And he gave you the ball, heh?

BIFF   Well, I borrowed it from the locker room. *(He laughs confidentially)*

WILLY *(laughing with him at the theft)*   I want you to return that.

HAPPY   I told you he wouldn't like it!

BIFF *(angrily)*   Well, I'm bringing it back!

WILLY *(stopping the incipient argument, to HAPPY)*   Sure, he's gotta practice with a regulation ball, doesn't he? *(To BIFF)* Coach'll probably congratulate you on your initiative!

BIFF   Oh, he keeps congratulating my initiative all the time, Pop.

WILLY   That's because he likes you. If somebody else took that ball there'd be an uproar. So what's the report, boys, what's the report?

BIFF   Where'd you go this time, Dad? Gee we were lonesome for you.

WILLY *(pleased, puts an arm around each boy and they come down to the apron)*   Lonesome, heh?

BIFF   Missed you every minute.

WILLY   Don't say? Tell you a secret, boys. Don't breathe it to a soul. Someday I'll have my own business, and I'll never have to leave home any more.

HAPPY   Like Uncle Charley, heh?

WILLY   Bigger than Uncle Charley! Because Charley is not—liked. He's liked, but he's not—well liked.

BIFF   Where'd you go this time, Dad?

WILLY   Well, I got on the road, and I went north to Providence. Met the Mayor.

BIFF   The Mayor of Providence!

WILLY   He was sitting in the hotel lobby.

BIFF   What'd he say?

WILLY   He said, "Morning!" And I said, "You got a fine city here, Mayor." And then he had coffee with me. And then I went to Waterbury. Waterbury is a fine city. Big clock city, the famous Waterbury clock. Sold a nice bill there. And then Boston—Boston is the cradle of the Revolution. A fine city. And a couple of other towns in Mass., and on to Portland and Bangor and straight home!

BIFF   Gee, I'd love to go with you sometime, Dad.

WILLY   Soon as summer comes.

HAPPY   Promise?

WILLY You and Hap and I, and I'll show you all the towns. America is full of beautiful towns and fine, upstanding people. And they know me, boys, they know me up and down New England. The finest people. And when I bring you fellas up, there'll be open sesame for all of us, 'cause one thing, boys: I have friends. I can park my car in any street in New England, and the cops protect it like their own. This summer, heh?

BIFF AND HAPPY *(together)* Yeah! You bet!

WILLY We'll take our bathing suits.

HAPPY We'll carry your bags, Pop!

WILLY Oh, won't that be something! Me comin' into the Boston stores with you boys carryin' my bags. What a sensation!

BIFF *is prancing around, practicing passing the ball.*

WILLY You nervous, Biff, about the game?

BIFF Not if you're gonna be there.

WILLY What do they say about you in school, now that they made you captain?

HAPPY There's a crowd of girls behind him everytime the classes change.

BIFF *(taking* WILLY's *hand)* This Saturday, Pop, this Saturday—just for you, I'm going to break through for a touchdown.

HAPPY You're supposed to pass.

BIFF I'm takin' one play for Pop. You watch me, Pop, and when I take off my helmet, that means I'm breakin' out. Then you watch me crash through that line!

WILLY *(kisses* BIFF*)* Oh, wait'll I tell this in Boston!

BERNARD *enters in knickers. He is younger than* BIFF, *earnest and loyal, a worried boy.*

BERNARD Biff, where are you? You're supposed to study with me today.

WILLY Hey, looka Bernard. What're you lookin' so anemic about, Bernard?

BERNARD He's gotta study, Uncle Willy. He's got Regents next week.

HAPPY *(tauntingly, spinning* BERNARD *around)* Let's box, Bernard!

BERNARD Biff! *(He gets away from* HAPPY*)* Listen, Biff, I heard Mr. Birnbaum say that if you don't start studyin' math he's gonna flunk you, and you won't graduate. I heard him!

WILLY You better study with him, Biff. Go ahead now.

BERNARD I heard him!

BIFF Oh, Pop, you didn't see my sneakers! *(He holds up a foot for* WILLY *to look at)*

WILLY Hey, that's a beautiful job of printing!

BERNARD *(wiping his glasses)* Just because he printed University of Virginia on his sneakers doesn't mean they've got to graduate him, Uncle Willy!

WILLY *(angrily)* What're you talking about? With scholarships to three universities they're gonna flunk him?

BERNARD But I heard Mr. Birnbaum say—

WILLY Don't be a pest, Bernard! *(To his boys)* What an anemic!

BERNARD Okay, I'm waiting for you in my house, Biff.

BERNARD *goes off. The* LOMANS *laugh.*

WILLY Bernard is not well liked, is he?

BIFF He's liked, but he's not well liked.

HAPPY That's right, Pop.

WILLY That's just what I mean. Bernard can get the best marks in school, y'understand, but when he gets out in the business world, y'understand, you are going to be five times ahead of him. That's why I thank Almighty God you're both built like Adonises. Because the man who makes an appearance in the business world, the man who creates personal interest, is the man who gets ahead. Be liked and you will never want. You take me, for instance. I never have to wait in line to see a buyer. "Willy Loman is here!" That's all they have to know, and I go right through.

BIFF Did you knock them dead, Pop?

WILLY Knocked 'em cold in Providence, slaughtered 'em in Boston.

HAPPY *(on his back, pedaling again)* I'm losing weight, you notice, Pop?

LINDA *enters, as of old, a ribbon in her hair, carrying a basket of washing.*

LINDA *(with youthful energy)* Hello, dear!

WILLY Sweetheart!

LINDA How'd the Chevvy run?

WILLY Chevrolet, Linda, is the greatest car ever built. *(To the boys)* Since when do you let your mother carry wash up the stairs?

BIFF Grab hold there, boy!

HAPPY Where to, Mom?

LINDA Hang them on the line. And you better go down to your friends, Biff. The cellar is full of boys. They don't know what to do with themselves.

BIFF Ah, when Pop comes home they can wait!

WILLY *(laughs appreciatively)* You better go down and tell them what to do, Biff.

BIFF I think I'll have them sweep out the furnace room.

WILLY Good work, Biff.

BIFF *(goes through wall-line of kitchen to doorway at back and calls down)* Fellas! Everybody sweep out the furnace room! I'll be right down!

VOICES All right! Okay, Biff.

BIFF George and Sam and Frank, come out back! We're hangin' up the wash! Come on, Hap, on the double! *(He and HAPPY carry out the basket)*

LINDA The way they obey him!

WILLY Well, that's training, the training. I'm tellin' you, I was sellin' thousands and thousands, but I had to come home.

LINDA Oh, the whole block'll be at that game. Did you sell anything?

WILLY I did five hundred gross in Providence and seven hundred gross in Boston.

LINDA No! Wait a minute, I've got a pencil. *(She pulls pencil and paper out of her apron pocket)* That makes your commission . . .Two hundred—my God! Two hundred and twelve dollars!

WILLY Well, I didn't figure it yet, but . . .

LINDA How much did you do?

WILLY Well, I—I did—about a hundred and eighty gross in Providence. Well, no —it came to—roughly two hundred gross on the whole trip.

LINDA *(without hesitation)* Two hundred gross. That's . . . *(She figures)*

WILLY The trouble was that three of the stores were half closed for inventory in Boston. Otherwise I woulda broke records.

LINDA Well, it makes seventy dollars and some pennies. That's very good.

WILLY What do we owe?

LINDA Well, on the first there's sixteen dollars on the refrigerator—

WILLY   Why sixteen?

LINDA   Well, the fan belt broke, so it was a dollar eighty.

WILLY   But it's brand new.

LINDA   Well, the man said that's the way it is. Till they work themselves in, y'know.

They move through the wall-line into the kitchen.

WILLY   I hope we didn't get stuck on that machine.

LINDA   They got the biggest ads of any of them!

WILLY   I know, it's a fine machine. What else?

LINDA   Well, there's nine-sixty for the washing machine. And for the vacuum cleaner there's three and a half due on the fifteenth. Then the roof, you got twenty-one dollars remaining.

WILLY   It don't leak, does it?

LINDA   No, they did a wonderful job. Then you owe Frank for the carburetor.

WILLY   I'm not going to pay that man! That goddam Chevrolet, they ought to prohibit the manufacture of that car!

LINDA   Well, you owe him three and a half. And odds and ends, comes to around a hundred and twenty dollars by the fifteenth.

WILLY   A hundred and twenty dollars! My God, if business don't pick up I don't know what I'm gonna do!

LINDA   Well, next week you'll do better.

WILLY   Oh, I'll knock 'em dead next week. I'll go to Hartford. I'm very well liked in Hartford. You know, the trouble is, Linda, people don't seem to take to me.

They move on the forestage.

LINDA   Oh, don't be foolish.

WILLY   I know it when I walk in. They seem to laugh at me.

LINDA   Why? Why would they laugh at you? Don't talk that way, Willy.

WILLY *moves to the edge of the stage.* LINDA *goes into the kitchen and starts to darn stockings.*

WILLY   I don't know the reason for it, but they just pass me by. I'm not noticed.

LINDA   But you're doing wonderful, dear. You're making seventy to a hundred dollars a week.

WILLY   But I gotta be at it ten, twelve hours a day. Other men—I don't know—they do it easier. I don't know why—I can't stop myself—I talk too much. A man oughta come in with a few words. One thing about Charley. He's a man of few words, and they respect him.

LINDA   You don't talk too much, you're just lively.

WILLY *(smiling)*   Well, I figure, what the hell, life is short, a couple of jokes. *(To himself)* I joke too much! *(The smile goes)*

LINDA   Why? You're—

WILLY   I'm fat. I'm very—foolish to look at, Linda. I didn't tell you, but Christmas time I happened to be calling on F. H. Stewarts, and a salesman I know, as I was going in to see the buyer I heard him say something about—walrus. And I—I cracked him right across the face. I won't take that. I simply will not take that. But they do laugh at me. I know that.

LINDA   Darling . . .

WILLY   I gotta overcome it. I know I gotta overcome it. I'm not dressing to advantage, maybe.

LINDA   Willy, darling, you're the handsomest man in the world—

WILLY   Oh, no, Linda.

LINDA   To me you are. *(Slight pause)* The handsomest.

From the darkness is heard the laughter of a woman. WILLY *doesn't turn to it, but it continues through* LINDA'S *lines.*

LINDA   And the boys, Willy. Few men are idolized by their children the way you are.

Music is heard as behind a scrim, to the left of the house. THE WOMAN, *dimly seen, is dressing.*

WILLY   *(with great feeling)*   You're the best there is, Linda, you're a pal, you know that? On the road—on the road I want to grab you sometimes and just kiss the life outa you.

The laughter is loud now, and he moves into a brightening area at the left, where THE WOMAN *has come from behind the scrim and is standing, putting on her hat, looking into a "mirror" and laughing.*

WILLY   'Cause I get so lonely—especially when business is bad and there's nobody to talk to. I get the feeling that I'll never sell anything again, that I won't make a living for you, or a business, a business for the boys. *(He talks through* THE WOMAN'S *subsiding laughter;* THE WOMAN *primps at the "mirror")* There's so much I want to make for—

THE WOMAN   Me? You didn't make me, Willy. I picked you.

WILLY   *(pleased)*   You picked me?

THE WOMAN   *(who is quite proper-looking,* WILLY'S *age)*   I did. I've been sitting at that desk watching all the salesmen go by, day in, day out. But you've got such a sense of humor, and we do have such a good time together, don't we?

WILLY   Sure, sure. *(He takes her in his arms)* Why do you have to go now?

THE WOMAN   It's two o'clock . . .

WILLY   No, come on in! *(He pulls her)*

THE WOMAN   . . . my sisters'll be scandalized. When'll you be back?

WILLY   Oh, two weeks about. Will you come up again?

THE WOMAN   Sure thing. You do make me laugh. It's good for me. *(She squeezes his arm, kisses him)* And I think you're a wonderful man.

WILLY   You picked me, heh?

THE WOMAN   Sure. Because you're so sweet. And such a kidder.

WILLY   Well, I'll see you next time I'm in Boston.

THE WOMAN   I'll put you right through to the buyers.

WILLY   *(slapping her bottom)*   Right. Well, bottoms up!

THE WOMAN   *(slaps him gently and laughs)*   You just kill me, Willy. *(He suddenly grabs her and kisses her roughly)* You kill me. And thanks for the stockings. I love a lot of stockings. Well, good night.

WILLY   Good night. And keep your pores open!

THE WOMAN   Oh, Willy!

THE WOMAN *bursts out laughing, and* LINDA's *laughter blends in.* THE WOMAN *disappears into the dark. Now the area at the kitchen table brightens.* LINDA *is sitting where she was at the kitchen table, but now is mending a pair of silk stockings.*

LINDA   You are, Willy. The handsomest man. You've got no reason to feel that—
WILLY   *(coming out of* THE WOMAN's *dimming area and going over to* LINDA*)*   I'll make it all up to you, Linda, I'll—
LINDA   There's nothing to make up, dear. You're doing fine, better than—
WILLY   *(noticing her mending)*   What's that?
LINDA   Just mending my stockings. They're so expensive—
WILLY   *(angrily, taking them from her)*   I won't have you mending stockings in this house! Now throw them out!

LINDA *puts the stockings in her pocket.*

BERNARD   *(entering on the run)*   Where is he? If he doesn't study!
WILLY   *(moving to the forestage, with great agitation)*   You'll give him the answers!
BERNARD   I do, but I can't on a Regents! That's a state exam! They're liable to arrest me!
WILLY   Where is he? I'll whip him, I'll whip him!
LINDA   And he'd better give back that football, Willy, it's not nice.
WILLY   Biff! where is he? Why is he taking everything?
LINDA   He's too rough with the girls, Willy. All the mothers are afraid of him!
WILLY   I'll whip him!
BERNARD   He's driving the car without a license!

THE WOMAN's *laugh is heard.*

WILLY   Shut up!
LINDA   All the mothers—
WILLY   Shut up!
BERNARD *(backing quietly away and out)*   Mr. Birnbaum says he's stuck up.
WILLY   Get outa here!
BERNARD   If he doesn't buckle down he'll flunk math! *(He goes off)*
LINDA   He's right, Willy, you've gotta—
WILLY *(exploding at her)*   There's nothing the matter with him! You want him to be a worm like Bernard? He's got spirit, personality . . .

As he speaks, LINDA, *almost in tears, exits into the living-room.* WILLY *is alone in the kitchen, wilting and staring. The leaves are gone. It is night again, and the apartment houses look down from behind.*

WILLY   Loaded with it. Loaded! What is he stealing? He's giving it back, isn't he? Why is he stealing? What did I tell him? I never in my life told him anything but decent things.

HAPPY *in pajamas has come down the stairs;* WILLY *suddenly becomes aware of* HAPPY's *presence.*

HAPPY   Let's go now, come on.
WILLY *(sitting down at the kitchen table)*   Huh! Why did she have to wax the floors herself? Everytime she waxes the floors she keels over. She knows that!
HAPPY   Shh! Take it easy. What brought you back tonight?

WILLY I got an awful scare. Nearly hit a kid in Yonkers. God! Why didn't I go to Alaska with my brother Ben that time! Ben! That man was a genius, that man was success incarnate! What a mistake! He begged me to go.

HAPPY Well, there's no use in—

WILLY You guys! There was a man started with the clothes on his back and ended up with diamond mines!

HAPPY Boy, someday I'd like to know how he did it.

WILLY What's the mystery? The man knew what he wanted and went out and got it! Walked into a jungle, and comes out, the age of twenty-one, and he's rich! The world is an oyster, but you don't crack it open on a mattress!

HAPPY Pop, I told you I'm gonna retire you for life.

WILLY You'll retire me for life on seventy goddam dollars a week? And your women and your car and your apartment, and you'll retire me for life! Christ's sake, I couldn't get past Yonkers today! Where are you guys, where are you? The woods are burning! I can't drive a car!

CHARLEY *has appeared in the doorway. He is a large man, slow of speech, laconic, immovable. In all he says, despite what he says, there is pity, and, now, trepidation. He has a robe over pajamas, slippers on his feet. He enters the kitchen.*

CHARLEY Everything all right?

HAPPY Yeah, Charley, everything's . . .

WILLY What's the matter?

CHARLEY I heard some noise. I thought something happened. Can't we do something about the walls? You sneeze in here, and in my house hats blow off.

HAPPY Let's go to bed, Dad. Come on.

CHARLEY *signals to* HAPPY *to go.*

WILLY You go ahead, I'm not tired at the moment.

HAPPY *(to* WILLY*)* Take it easy, huh? *(He exits)*

WILLY What're you doin' up?

CHARLEY *(sitting down at the kitchen table opposite* WILLY*)* Couldn't sleep good. I had a heartburn.

WILLY Well, you don't know how to eat.

CHARLEY I eat with my mouth.

WILLY No, you're ignorant. You gotta know about vitamins and things like that.

CHARLEY Come on, let's shoot. Tire you out a little.

WILLY *(hesitantly)* All right. You got cards?

CHARLEY *(taking a deck from his pocket)* Yeah, I got them. Someplace. What is it with those vitamins?

WILLY *(dealing)* They build up your bones. Chemistry.

CHARLEY Yeah, but there's no bones in a heartburn.

WILLY What are you talkin' about? Do you know the first thing about it?

CHARLEY Don't get insulted.

WILLY Don't talk about something you don't know anything about.

They are playing. Pause.

CHARLEY What're you doin' home?

WILLY A little trouble with the car.

CHARLEY Oh. *(Pause)* I'd like to take a trip to California.

WILLY   Don't say.

CHARLEY   You want a job?

WILLY   I got a job, I told you that. *(After a slight pause)* What the hell are you offering me a job for?

CHARLEY   Don't get insulted.

WILLY   Don't insult me.

CHARLEY   I don't see no sense in it. You don't have to go on this way.

WILLY   I got a good job. *(Slight pause)* What do you keep comin' in here for?

CHARLEY   You want me to go?

WILLY *(after a pause, withering)*   I can't understand it. He's going back to Texas again. What the hell is that?

CHARLEY   Let him go.

WILLY   I got nothin' to give him, Charley, I'm clean, I'm clean.

CHARLEY   He won't starve. None of them starve. Forget about him.

WILLY   Then what have I got to remember?

CHARLEY   You take it too hard. To hell with it. When a deposit bottle is broken you don't get your nickel back.

WILLY   That's easy enough for you to say.

CHARLEY   That ain't easy for me to say.

WILLY   Did you see the ceiling I put up in the living-room?

CHARLEY   Yeah, that's a piece of work. To put up a ceiling is a mystery to me. How do you do it?

WILLY   What's the difference?

CHARLEY   Well, talk about it.

WILLY   You gonna put up a ceiling?

CHARLEY   How could I put up a ceiling?

WILLY   Then what the hell are you bothering me for?

CHARLEY   You're insulted again.

WILLY   A man who can't handle tools is not a man. You're disgusting.

CHARLEY   Don't call me disgusting, Willy.

UNCLE BEN, *carrying a valise and an umbrella, enters the forestage from around the right corner of the house. He is a stolid man, in his sixties, with a mustache and an authoritative air. He is utterly certain of his destiny, and there is an aura of far places about him. He enters exactly as* WILLY *speaks.*

WILLY   I'm getting awfully tired, Ben.

BEN*'s music is heard.* BEN *looks around at everything*

CHARLEY   Good, keep playing; you'll sleep better. Did you call me Ben?

BEN *looks at his watch.*

WILLY   That's funny. For a second there you reminded me of my brother Ben.

BEN   I only have a few minutes. *(He strolls, inspecting the place.* WILLY *and* CHARLEY *continue playing)*

CHARLEY   You never heard from him again, heh? Since that time?

WILLY   Didn't Linda tell you? Couple of weeks ago we got a letter from his wife in Africa. He died.

CHARLEY   That so.

BEN *(chuckling)*   So this is Brooklyn, eh?

CHARLEY   Maybe you're in for some of his money.

WILLY   Naa, he had seven sons. There's just one opportunity I had with that man . . .

BEN   I must make a train, William. There are several properties I'm looking at in Alaska.

WILLY   Sure, sure! If I'd gone with him to Alaska that time, everything would've been totally different.

CHARLEY   Go on, you'd froze to death up there.

WILLY   What're you talking about?

BEN   Opportunity is tremendous in Alaska, William. Surprised you're not up there.

WILLY   Sure, tremendous.

CHARLEY   Heh?

WILLY   There was the only man I ever met who knew the answers.

CHARLEY   Who?

BEN   How are you all?

WILLY   *(taking a pot, smiling)*   Fine, fine.

CHARLEY   Pretty sharp tonight.

BEN   Is Mother living with you?

WILLY   No, she died a long time ago.

CHARLEY   Who?

BEN   That's too bad. Fine specimen of a lady, Mother.

WILLY   *(to CHARLEY)*   Heh?

BEN   I'd hoped to see the old girl.

CHARLEY   Who died?

BEN   Heard anything from Father, have you?

WILLY   *(unnerved)*   What do you mean, who died?

CHARLEY   *(taking a pot)*   What're you talkin' about?

BEN   *(looking at his watch)*   William, it's half-past eight!

WILLY   *(as though to dispel his confusion he angrily stops CHARLEY's hand)*   That's my build!

CHARLEY   I put the ace—

WILLY   If you don't know how to play the game I'm not gonna throw my money away on you!

CHARLEY   *(rising)*   It was my ace, for God's sake!

WILLY   I'm through, I'm through!

BEN   When did Mother die?

WILLY   Long ago. Since the beginning you never knew how to play cards.

CHARLEY   *(picks up the cards and goes to the door)*   All right! Next time I'll bring a deck with five aces.

WILLY   I don't play that kind of game!

CHARLEY   *(turning to him)*   You ought to be ashamed of yourself!

WILLY   Yeah?

CHARLEY   Yeah! *(He goes out)*

WILLY   *(slamming the door after him)*   Ignoramus!

BEN   *(as WILLY comes toward him through the wall-line of the kitchen)*   So you're William.

WILLY   *(shaking BEN's hand)*   Ben! I've been waiting for you so long! What's the answer? How did you do it?

BEN   Oh, there's a story in that.

LINDA *enters the forestage, as of old, carrying the wash basket.*

LINDA   Is this Ben?

BEN *(gallantly)*   How do you do, my dear.

LINDA   Where've you been all these years? Willy's always wondered why you—

WILLY *(pulling* BEN *away from her impatiently)*   Where is Dad? Didn't you follow him? How did you get started?

BEN   Well, I don't know how much you remember.

WILLY   Well, I was just a baby, of course, only three or four years old—

BEN   Three years and eleven months.

WILLY   What a memory, Ben!

BEN   I have many enterprises, William, and I have never kept books.

WILLY   I remember I was sitting under the wagon in—was it Nebraska?

BEN   It was South Dakota, and I gave you a bunch of wild flowers.

WILLY   I remember you walking away down some open road.

BEN *(laughing)*   I was going to find Father in Alaska.

WILLY   Where is he?

BEN   At that age I had a very faulty view of geography, William. I discovered after a few days that I was heading due south, so instead of Alaska, I ended up in Africa.

LINDA   Africa!

WILLY   The Gold Coast!

BEN   Principally diamond mines.

LINDA   Diamond mines!

BEN   Yes, my dear. But I've only a few minutes—

WILLY   No! Boys! Boys! (YOUNG BIFF *and* HAPPY *appear*) Listen to this. This is your Uncle Ben, a great man! Tell my boys, Ben!

BEN   Why, boys, when I was seventeen I walked into the jungle, and when I was twenty-one I walked out. *(He laughs)* And by God I was rich.

WILLY *(to the boys)*   You see what I been talking about? The greatest things can happen!

BEN *(glancing at his watch)*   I have an appointment in Ketchikan Tuesday week.

WILLY   No, Ben! Please tell about Dad. I want my boys to hear. I want them to know the kind of stock they spring from. All I remember is a man with a big beard, and I was in Mamma's lap, sitting around a fire, and some kind of high music.

BEN   His flute. He played the flute.

WILLY   Sure, the flute, that's right!

New music is heard, a high, rollicking tune.

BEN   Father was a very great and a very wild-hearted man. We would start in Boston, and he'd toss the whole family into the wagon, and then he'd drive the team right across the country; through Ohio, and Indiana, Michigan, Illinois, and all the Western states. And we'd stop in the towns and sell the flutes that he'd made on the way. Great inventor, Father. With one gadget he made more in a week than a man like you could make in a lifetime.

WILLY   That's just the way I'm bringing them up, Ben—rugged, well liked, all-around.

BEN   Yeah? *(To* BIFF*)* Hit that, boy—hard as you can. *(He pounds his stomach)*

BIFF   Oh, no, sir!

BEN *(taking boxing stance)*   Come on, get to me! *(He laughs)*

WILLY   Go to it, Biff! Go ahead, show him!

BIFF   Okay! *(He cocks his fists and starts in)*

LINDA *(to* WILLY*)*   Why must he fight, dear?

BEN *(sparring with* BIFF*)*   Good boy! Good boy!

WILLY   How's that, Ben, heh?

HAPPY   Give him the left, Biff!

LINDA   Why are you fighting?

BEN   Good boy! *(Suddenly comes in, trips* BIFF, *and stands over him, the point of his umbrella poised over* BIFF*'s eye)*

LINDA   Look out, Biff!

BIFF   Gee!

BEN *(patting* BIFF*'s knee)*   Never fight fair with a stranger, boy. You'll never get out of the jungle that way. *(Taking* LINDA*'s hand and bowing)* It was an honor and a pleasure to meet you, Linda.

LINDA *(withdrawing her hand coldly, frightened)*   Have a nice—trip.

BEN *(to* WILLY*)*   And good luck with your—what do you do?

WILLY   Selling.

BEN   Yes. Well . . . *(He raises his hand in farewell to all)*

WILLY   No, Ben, I don't want you to think . . . *(He takes* BEN*'s arm to show him)* It's Brooklyn, I know, but we hunt too.

BEN   Really, now.

WILLY   Oh, sure, there's snakes and rabbits and—that's why I moved out here. Why, Biff can fell any one of these trees in no time! Boys! Go right over to where they're building the apartment house and get some sand. We're gonna rebuild the entire front stoop right now! Watch this, Ben!

BIFF   Yes, sir! On the double, Hap!

HAPPY *(as he and* BIFF *run off)*   I lost weight, Pop, you notice?

CHARLEY *enters in knickers, even before the boys are gone.*

CHARLEY   Listen, if they steal any more from that building the watchman'll put the cops on them!

LINDA *(to* WILLY*)*   Don't let Biff . . .

BEN *laughs lustily.*

WILLY   You shoulda seen the lumber they brought home last week. At least a dozen six-by-tens worth all kinds a money.

CHARLEY   Listen, if that watchman—

WILLY   I gave them hell, understand. But I got a couple of fearless characters there.

CHARLEY   Willy, the jails are full of fearless characters.

BEN *(clapping* WILLY *on the back, with a laugh at* CHARLEY*)*   And the stock exchange, friend!

WILLY *(joining in* BEN*'s laughter)*   Where are the rest of your pants?

CHARLEY   My wife bought them.

WILLY   Now all you need is a golf club and you can go upstairs and go to sleep. *(To* BEN*)* Great athlete! Between him and his son Bernard they can't hammer a nail!

BERNARD *(rushing in)*   The watchman's chasing Biff!

WILLY *(angrily)*   Shut up! He's not stealing anything!

LINDA *(alarmed, hurrying off left)*   Where is he? Biff, dear! *(She exits)*

WILLY *(moving toward the left, away from* BEN*)* There's nothing wrong. What's the matter with you?

BEN Nervy boy. Good!

WILLY *(laughing)* Oh, nerves of iron, that Biff!

CHARLEY Don't know what it is. My New England man comes back and he's bleedin', they murdered him up there.

WILLY It's contacts, Charley, I got important contacts!

CHARLEY *(sarcastically)* Glad to hear it, Willy. Come in later, we'll shoot a little casino. I'll take some of your Portland money. *(He laughs at* WILLY *and exits)*

WILLY *(turning to* BEN*)* Business is bad, it's murderous. But not for me, of course.

BEN I'll stop by on my way back to Africa.

WILLY *(longingly)* Can't you stay a few days? You're just what I need, Ben, because I—I have a fine position here, but I—well, Dad left when I was such a baby and I never had a chance to talk to him and I still feel—kind of temporary about myself.

BEN I'll be late for my train.

They are at opposite ends of the stage.

WILLY Ben, my boys—can't we talk? They'd go into the jaws of hell for me, see, but I—

BEN William, you're being first-rate with your boys. Outstanding, manly chaps!

WILLY *(hanging on to his words)* Oh, Ben that's good to hear! Because sometimes I'm afraid that I'm not teaching them the right kind of—Ben, how should I teach them?

BEN *(giving great weight to each word, and with a certain vicious audacity)* William, when I walked into the jungle, I was seventeen. When I walked out I was twenty-one. And, by God, I was rich! *(He goes off into darkness around the right corner of the house)*

WILLY . . . was rich! That's just the spirit I want to imbue them with! To walk into a jungle! I was right! I was right! I was right!

BEN *is gone, but* WILLY *is still speaking to him as* LINDA, *in nightgown and robe, enters the kitchen, glances round for* WILLY, *then goes to the door of the house, looks out and sees him. Comes down to his left. He looks at her.*

LINDA Willy, dear? Willy?

WILLY I was right!

LINDA Did you have some cheese? *(He can't answer)* It's very late, darling. Come to bed, heh?

WILLY *(looking straight up)* Gotta break your neck to see a star in this yard.

LINDA You coming in?

WILLY Whatever happened to that diamond watch fob? Remember? When Ben came from Africa that time? Didn't he give me a watch fob with a diamond in it?

LINDA You pawned it, dear. Twelve, thirteen years ago. For Biff's radio correspondence course.

WILLY Gee, that was a beautiful thing. I'll take a walk.

LINDA But you're in your slippers.

WILLY *(starting to go around the house at the left)* I was right1 I was! *(Half to* LINDA, *as he goes, shaking his head)* What a man! There was a man worth talking to. I was right!

LINDA *(calling after* WILLY*)* But in your slippers, Willy!

WILLY *is almost gone when* BIFF, *in his pajamas, comes down the stairs and enters the kitchen.*

BIFF   What is he doing out there?

LINDA   Sh!

BIFF   God Almighty, Mom, how long has he been doing this?

LINDA   Don't, he'll hear you.

BIFF   What the hell is the matter with him?

LINDA   It'll pass by morning.

BIFF   Shouldn't we do anything?

LINDA   Oh, my dear, you should do a lot of things, but there's nothing to do, so go to sleep.

HAPPY *comes down the stairs and sits on the steps.*

HAPPY   I never heard him so loud, Mom.

LINDA   Well, come around more often; you'll hear him. *(She sits down at the table and mends the lining of* WILLY'*s jacket)*

BIFF   Why didn't you ever write me about this, Mom?

LINDA   How would I write to you? For over three months you had no address.

BIFF   I was on the move. But you know I thought of you all the time. You know that, don't you, pal?

LINDA   I know, dear, I know. But he likes to have a letter. Just to know that there's still a possibility for better things.

BIFF   He's not like this all the time, is he?

LINDA   It's when you come home he's always the worst.

BIFF   When I come home?

LINDA   When you write you're coming, he's all smiles, and talks about the future, and—he's just wonderful. And then the closer you seem to come, the more shaky he gets, and then, by the time you get here, he's arguing, and he seems angry at you. I think it's just that maybe he can't bring himself to—to open up to you. Why are you so hateful to each other? Why is that?

BIFF *(evasively)*   I'm not hateful, Mom.

LINDA   But you no sooner come in the door than you're fighting!

BIFF   I don't know why. I mean to change. I'm tryin', Mom, you understand?

LINDA   Are you home to stay now?

BIFF   I don't know. I want to look around, see what's doin'.

LINDA   Biff, you can't look around all your life, can you?

BIFF   I just can't take hold, Mom. I can't take hold of some kind of a life.

LINDA   Biff, a man is not a bird, to come and go with the springtime.

BIFF   Your hair . . . *(He touches her hair)* Your hair got so gray.

LINDA   Oh, its been gray since you were in high school. I just stopped dyeing it, that's all.

BIFF   Dye it again, will ya? I don't want my pal looking old. *(He smiles)*

LINDA   You're such a boy! You think you can go away for a year and . . . You've got to get it into your head now that one day you'll knock on this door and there'll be strange people here—

BIFF   What are you talking about? You're not even sixty, Mom.

LINDA   But what about your father?

BIFF *(lamely)*   Well, I meant him too.

HAPPY   He admires Pop.

LINDA   Biff, dear, if you don't have any feeling for him, then you can't have any feeling for me.

BIFF   Sure I can, Mom.

LINDA   No. You can't just come to see me, because I love him. *(With a threat, but only a threat, of tears)* He's the dearest man in the world to me, and I won't have anyone making him feel unwanted and low and blue. You've got to make up your mind now, darling, there's no leeway any more. Either he's your father and you pay him that respect, or else you're not to come here. I know he's not easy to get along with—nobody knows that better than me—but . . .

WILLY   *(from the left, with a laugh)*   Hey, hey, Biffo!

BIFF   *(starting to go out after WILLY)*   What the hell is the matter with him? (HAPPY *stops him*)

LINDA   Don't—don't go near him!

BIFF   Stop making excuses for him! He always, always wiped the floor with you. Never had an ounce of respect for you.

HAPPY   He's always had respect for—

BIFF   What the hell do you know about it?

HAPPY   *(surlily)*   Just don't call him crazy!

BIFF   He's got no character—Charley wouldn't do this. Not in his own house— spewing out that vomit from his mind.

HAPPY   Charley never had to cope with what he's got to.

BIFF   People are worse off than Willy Loman. Believe me, I've seen them!

LINDA   Then make Charley your father, Biff. You can't do that, can you? I don't say he's a great man. Willy Loman never made a lot of money. His name was never in the paper. He's not the finest character that ever lived. But he's a human being, and a terrible thing is happening to him. So attention must be paid. He's not to be allowed to fall into his grave like an old dog. Attention, attention must be finally paid to such a person. You called him crazy—

BIFF   I didn't mean—

LINDA   No, a lot of people think he's lost his—balance. But you don't have to be very smart to know what his trouble is. The man is exhausted.

HAPPY   Sure!

LINDA   A small man can be just as exhausted as a great man. He works for a company thirty-six years this March, opens up unheard-of territories to their trademark, and now in his old age they take his salary away.

HAPPY   *(indignantly)*   I didn't know that, Mom.

LINDA   You never asked, my dear! Now that you get your spending money someplace else you don't trouble your mind with him.

HAPPY   But I gave you money last—

LINDA   Christmas time, fifty dollars! To fix the hot water it cost ninety-seven fifty! For five weeks he's been on straight commission, like a beginner, an unknown!

BIFF   Those ungrateful bastards!

LINDA   Are they any worse than his sons? When he brought them business, when he was young, they were glad to see him. But now his old friends, the old buyers that loved him so and always found some order to hand him in a pinch—they're all dead, retired. He used to be able to make six, seven calls a day in Boston. Now he takes his valises out of the car and puts them back and takes them out again and he's exhausted. Instead of walking he talks now. He drives seven hundred miles, and when he gets there no one knows him any more, no one welcomes him. And what goes through a man's mind, driving seven hundred miles home without having earned a cent? Why shouldn't he talk to himself? Why? When he has to go to Charley and borrow fifty dollars a week and pretend to me that it's his pay? How long can that go on? How long? You see what I'm sitting here and waiting for? And you tell me he has no character? The man who never worked a day but for your benefit? When does he get the medal for that? Is this his reward—to turn around at the age of sixty-three and find his sons, who he loved better than his life, one a philandering bum—

HAPPY   Mom!

LINDA   That's all you are, my baby! *(To* BIFF*)* And you! What happened to the love you had for him? You were such pals! How you used to talk to him on the phone every night! How lonely he was till he could come home to you!

BIFF   All right, Mom. I'll live here in my room, and I'll get a job. I'll keep away from him, that's all.

LINDA   No, Biff. You can't stay here and fight all the time.

BIFF   He threw me out of this house, remember that.

LINDA   Why did he do that? I never knew why.

BIFF   Because I know he's a fake and he doesn't like anybody around who knows!

LINDA   Why a fake? In what way? What do you mean?

BIFF   Just don't lay it all at my feet. It's between me and him—that's all I have to say. I'll chip in from now on. He'll settle for half my pay check. He'll be all right. I'm going to bed. *(He starts for the stairs)*

LINDA   He won't be all right.

BIFF *(turning on the stairs, furiously)*   I hate this city and I'll stay here. Now what do you want?

LINDA   He's dying, Biff.

HAPPY *turns quickly to her, shocked.*

BIFF *(after a pause)*   Why is he dying?

LINDA   He's been trying to kill himself.

BIFF *(with great horror)*   How?

LINDA   I live from day to day.

BIFF   What're you talking about?

LINDA   Remember I wrote you that he smashed up the car again? In February?

BIFF   Well?

LINDA   The insurance inspector came. He said that they have evidence. That all these accidents in the last year—weren't—weren't—accidents.

HAPPY   How can they tell that? That's a lie.

LINDA   It seems there's a woman . . . *(She takes a breath as . . .)*

⌈BIFF *(sharply but contained)*   What woman?

⌊LINDA *(simultaneously)*   . . . and this woman . . .

LINDA   What?

BIFF   Nothing. Go ahead.

LINDA   What did you say?

BIFF   Nothing. I just said what woman?

HAPPY   What about her?

LINDA   Well, it seems she was walking down the road and saw his car. She says that he wasn't driving fast at all, and that he didn't skid. She says he came to that little bridge, and then deliberately smashed into the railing, and it was only the shallowness of the water that saved him.

BIFF   Oh, no, he probably just fell asleep again.

LINDA   I don't think he fell asleep.

BIFF   Why not?

LINDA   Last month . . . *(With great difficulty)* Oh, boys, it's so hard to say a thing like this! He's just a big stupid man to you, but I tell you there's more good in him than in many other people. *(She chokes, wipes her eyes)* I was looking for a fuse. The lights blew out, and I went down the cellar. And behind the fuse box—it happened to fall out—was a length of rubber pipe—just short.

HAPPY   No kidding?

LINDA   There's a little attachment on the end of it. I knew right away. And sure enough, on the bottom of the water heater there's a new little nipple on the gas pipe.

HAPPY   *(angrily)*   That—jerk.

BIFF   Did you have it taken off?

LINDA   I'm—I'm ashamed to. How can I mention it to him? Every day I go down and take away that little rubber pipe. But, when he comes home, I put it back where it was. How can I insult him that way? I don't know what to do. I live from day to day, boys. I tell you, I know every thought in his mind. It sounds so old-fashioned and silly, but I tell you he put his whole life into you and you've turned your backs on him. *(She is bent over in the chair, weeping, her face in her hands)* Biff, I swear to God! Biff, his life is in your hands!

HAPPY   *(to BIFF)*   How do you like that damned fool!

BIFF   *(kissing her)*   All right, pal, all right. It's all settled now. I've been remiss. I know that, Mom. But now I'll stay, and I swear to you, I'll apply myself. *(Kneeling in front of her, in a fever of self-reproach)* It's just—you see, Mom, I don't fit in business. Not that I won't try. I'll try, and I'll make good.

HAPPY   Sure you will. The trouble with you in business was you never tried to please people.

BIFF   I know, I—

HAPPY   Like when you worked for Harrison's. Bob Harrison said you were tops, and then you go and do some damn fool thing like whistling whole songs in the elevator like a comedian.

BIFF   *(against HAPPY)*   So what? I like to whistle sometimes.

HAPPY   You don't raise a guy to a responsible job who whistles in the elevator!

LINDA   Well, don't argue about it now.

HAPPY   Like when you'd go off and swim in the middle of the day instead of taking the line around.

BIFF   *(his resentment rising)*   Well, don't you run off? You take off sometimes, don't you? On a nice summer day?

HAPPY   Yeah, but I cover myself!

LINDA   Boys!

HAPPY   If I'm going to take a fade the boss can call any number where I'm supposed to be and they'll swear to him that I just left. I'll tell you something that I hate to say, Biff, but in the business world some of them think you're crazy.

BIFF   *(angered)*   Screw the business world!

HAPPY   All right, screw it! Great, but cover yourself!

LINDA   Hap, Hap!

BIFF   I don't care what they think! They've laughed at Dad for years, and you know why? Because we don't belong in this nuthouse of a city! We should be mixing cement on some open plain, or—or carpenters. A carpenter is allowed to whistle!

WILLY *walks in from the entrance of the house, at left.*

WILLY   Even your grandfather was better than a carpenter. *(Pause. They watch him)* You never grew up. Bernard does not whistle in the elevator, I assure you.

BIFF *(as though to laugh* WILLY *out of it)*   Yeah, but you do, pop.

WILLY   I never in my life whistled in an elevator! And who in the business world thinks I'm crazy?

BIFF   I didn't mean it like that, Pop. Now don't make a whole thing out of it, will ya?

WILLY   Go back to the West! Be a carpenter, a cowboy, enjoy yourself!

LINDA   Willy, he was just saying—

WILLY   I heard what he said!

HAPPY *(trying to quiet* WILLY*)*   Hey, Pop, come on now . . .

WILLY *(continuing over* HAPPY*'s line)*   They laugh at me, heh? Go to Filene's, go to the Hub, go to Slattery's, Boston. Call out the name Willy Loman and see what happens! Big shot!

BIFF   All right, Pop.

WILLY   Big!

BIFF   All right!

WILLY   Why do you always insult me?

BIFF   I didn't say a word. *(To* LINDA*)* Did I say a word?

LINDA   He didn't say anything, Willy.

WILLY *(going to the doorway of the living-room)*   All right, good night, good night.

LINDA   Willy, dear, he just decided . . .

WILLY *(to* BIFF*)*   If you get tired hanging around tomorrow, paint the ceiling I put up in the living-room.

BIFF   I'm leaving early tomorrow.

HAPPY   He's going to see Bill Oliver, Pop.

WILLY *(interestedly)*   Oliver? For what?

BIFF *(with reserve, but trying, trying)*   He always said he'd stake me. I'd like to go into business, so maybe I can take him up on it.

LINDA   Isn't that wonderful?

WILLY   Don't interrupt. What's wonderful about it? There's fifty men in the City of New York who'd stake him. *(To* BIFF*)* Sporting goods?

BIFF   I guess so. I know something about it and—

WILLY   He knows something about it! You know sporting goods better than Spalding, for God's sake! How much is he giving you?

BIFF   I don't know, I didn't even see him yet, but—

WILLY   Then what're you talkin' about?

BIFF *(getting angry)*   Well, all I said was I'm gonna see him, that's all!

WILLY *(turning away)*   Ah, you're counting you chickens again.

BIFF *(starting left for the stairs)*   Oh, Jesus, I'm going to sleep!

WILLY *(calling after him)*   Don't curse in this house!

BIFF *(turning)*   Since when did you get so clean?

HAPPY *(trying to stop them)*   Wait a . . .

WILLY   Don't use that language to me! I won't have it!

HAPPY *(grabbing* BIFF, *shouts)* Wait a minute! I got an idea. I got a feasible idea. Come here, Biff, let's talk this over now, let's talk some sense here. When I was down in Florida last time, I thought of a great idea to sell sporting goods. It just came back to me. You and I, Biff—we have a line, the Loman Line. We train a couple of weeks, and put on a couple of exhibitions, see?

WILLY That's an idea!

HAPPY Wait! We form two basketball teams, see? Two waterpolo teams. We play each other. It's a million dollars' worth of publicity. Two brothers, see? The Loman Brothers. Displays in the Royal Palms—all the hotels. And banners over the ring and the basketball court: "Loman Brothers." Baby, we could sell sporting goods!

WILLY That is a one-million-dollar idea!

LINDA Marvelous!

BIFF I'm in great shape as far as that's concerned.

HAPPY And the beauty of it is, Biff, it wouldn't be like a business. We'd be out playin' ball again . . .

BIFF *(enthused)* Yeah, that's . . .

WILLY Million-dollar . . .

HAPPY And you wouldn't get fed up with it, Biff. It'd be the family again. There'd be the old honor, and comradeship, and if you wanted to go off for a swim or somethin'—well, you'd do it! Without some smart cooky gettin' up ahead of you!

WILLY Lick the world! You guys together could absolutely lick the civilized world.

BIFF I'll see Oliver tomorrow. Hap, if we could work that out . . .

LINDA Maybe things are beginning to—

WILLY *(wildly enthused, to* LINDA*)* Stop interrupting! *(To* BIFF*)* But don't wear sport jacket and slacks when you see Oliver.

BIFF No, I'll—

WILLY A business suit, and talk as little as possible, and don't crack any jokes.

BIFF He did like me. Always liked me.

LINDA He loved you!

WILLY *(to* LINDA*)* Will you stop! *(To* BIFF*)* Walk in very serious. You are not applying for a boy's job. Money is to pass. Be quiet, fine, and serious. Everybody likes a kidder, but nobody lends him money.

HAPPY I'll try to get some myself, Biff. I'm sure I can.

WILLY I see great things for you kids, I think your troubles are over. But remember, start big and you'll end big. Ask for fifteen. How much you gonna ask for?

BIF Gee, I don't know—

WILLY And don't say "Gee." "Gee" is a boy's word. A man walking in for fifteen thousand dollars does not say "Gee!"

BIFF Ten, I think, would be top though.

WILLY Don't be so modest. You always started too low. Walk in with a big laugh. Don't look worried. Start off with a couple of your good stories to lighten things up. It's not what you say, it's how you say it—because personality always wins the day.

LINDA Oliver always thought the highest of him—

WILLY Will you let me talk?

BIFF Don't yell at her, Pop, will ya?

WILLY *(angrily)* I was talking, wasn't I?

BIFF I don't like you yelling at her all the time, and I'm tellin' you, that's all.

WILLY What're you, takin' over this house?

LINDA Willy—

WILLY *(turning on her)* Don't take his side all the time, goddammit!

BIFF *(furiously)* Stop yelling at her!

WILLY *(suddenly pulling on his cheek, beaten down, guilt ridden)* Give my best to Bill Oliver—he may remember me. *(He exits through the living-room doorway)*

LINDA *(her voice subdued)* What'd you have to start that for? (BIFF *turns away)* You see how sweet he was as soon as you talked hopefully? *(She goes over to* BIFF*)* Come up and say good night to him. Don't let him go to bed that way.

HAPPY Come on, Biff, let's buck him up.

LINDA Please, dear. Just say good night. It takes so little to make him happy. Come. *(She goes through the living-room doorway, calling upstairs from within the living-room)* Your pajamas are hanging in the bathroom, Willy!

HAPPY *(looking toward where* LINDA *went out)* What a woman! They broke the mold when they made her. You know that, Biff?

BIFF He's off salary. My God, working on commission!

HAPPY Well, let's face it: he's no hot-shot selling man. Except that sometimes, you have to admit, he's a sweet personality.

BIFF *(deciding)* Lend me ten bucks, will ya? I want to buy some new ties.

HAPPY I'll take you to a place I know. Beautiful stuff. Wear one of my striped shirts tomorrow.

BIFF She got gray. Mom got awful old. Gee, I'm gonna go in to Oliver tomorrow and knock him for a—

HAPPY Come on up. Tell that to Dad. Let's give him a whirl. Come on.

BIFF *(steamed up)* You know, with ten thousand bucks, boy!

HAPPY *(as they go into the living-room)* That's the talk, Biff, that's the first time I've heard the old confidence out of you! *(From within the living-room, fading off)* You're gonna live with me, kid, and any babe you want just say the word . . .

The last lines are hardly heard. They are mounting the stairs to their parents' bedroom.

LINDA *(entering her bedroom and addressing* WILLY, *who is in the bathroom. She is straightening the bed for him)* Can you do anything about the shower? It drips.

WILLY *(from the bathroom)* All of a sudden everything falls to pieces! Goddam plumbing, oughta be sued, those people. I hardly finished putting it in and the thing . . . *(His words rumble off)*

LINDA I'm just wondering if Oliver will remember him. You think he might?

WILLY *(coming out of the bathroom in his pajamas)* Remember him? What's the matter with you, you crazy? If he'd've stayed with Oliver he'd be on top by now! Wait'll Oliver gets a look at him. You don't know the average caliber any more. The average young man today—*(he is getting into bed)*—is got a caliber of zero. Greatest thing in the world for him was to bum around.

BIFF *and* HAPPY *enter the bedroom. Slight pause.*

WILLY *(stops short, looking at* BIFF*)* Glad to hear it, boy.

HAPPY He wanted to say good night to you, sport.

WILLY *(to* BIFF*)* Yeah. Knock him dead, boy. What'd you want to tell me?

BIFF Just take it easy, Pop. Good night. *(He turns to go)*

WILLY *(unable to resist)* And if anything falls off the desk while you're talking to him—like a package or something—don't you pick it up. They have office boys for that.

LINDA I'll make a big breakfast—

WILLY Will you let me finish? *(To BIFF)* Tell him you were in the business in the West. Not farm work.

BIFF All right, Dad.

LINDA I think everything—

WILLY *(going right through her speech)* And don't undersell yourself. No less than fifteen thousand dollars.

BIFF *(unable to bear him)* Okay. Good night, Mom. *(He starts moving)*

WILLY Because you got a greatness in you, Biff, remember that. You got all kinds a greatness . . . *(He lies back, exhausted.* BIFF *walks out)*

LINDA *(calling after BIFF)* Sleep well, darling!

HAPPY I'm gonna get married, Mom. I wanted to tell you.

LINDA Go to sleep, dear.

HAPPY *(going)* I just wanted to tell you.

WILLY Keep up the good work. (HAPPY *exits*) God . . . remember that Ebbets Field game? The championship of the city?

LINDA Just rest. Should I sing to you?

WILLY Yeah. Sing to me. (LINDA *hums a soft lullaby*) When that team came out— he was the tallest, remember?

LINDA Oh, yes. And in gold.

BIFF *enters the darkened kitchen, takes a cigarette, and leaves the house. He comes downstage into a golden pool of light. He smokes, staring at the night*

WILLY Like a young god. Hercules—something like that. And the sun, the sun all around him. Remember how he waved to me? Right up from the field, with the representatives of three colleges standing by? And the buyers I brought, and the cheers when he came out—Loman, Loman, Loman! God almighty, he'll be great yet. A star like that, magnificent, can never really fade away!

The light on WILLY *is fading. The gas heater begins to glow through the kitchen wall, near the stairs, a blue flame beneath red coils.*

LINDA *(timidly)* Willy dear, what has he got against you?

WILLY I'm so tired. Don't talk any more.

BIFF *slowly returns to the kitchen. He stops, stares toward the heater.*

LINDA Will you ask Howard to let you work in New York?

WILLY First thing in the morning. Everything'll be all right.

BIFF *reaches behind the heater and draws out a length of rubber tubing. He is horrified and turns his head toward* WILLY's *room, still dimly lit, from which the strains of* LINDA's *desperate but monotonous humming rise.*

WILLY *(staring through the window into the moonlight)* Gee, look at the moon moving between the buildings!

BIFF *wraps the tubing around his hand and quickly goes up the stairs.*

Curtain

Act II

Music is heard, gay and bright. The curtain rises as the music fades away. WILLY, *in shirt sleeves, is sitting at the kitchen table, sipping coffee, his hat in his lap.* LINDA *is filling his cup when she can.*

WILLY Wonderful coffee. Meal in itself.

LINDA Can I make you some eggs?

WILLY No. Take a breath.

LINDA You look so rested, dear.

WILLY I slept like a dead one. First time in months. Imagine, sleeping till ten on a Tuesday morning. Boys left nice and early, heh?

LINDA They were out of here by eight o'clock.

WILLY Good work!

LINDA It was so thrilling to see them leaving together. I can't get over the shaving lotion in this house!

WILLY *(smiling)* Mmm—

LINDA Biff was very changed this morning. His whole attitude seemed to be hopeful. He couldn't wait to get downtown to see Oliver.

WILLY He's heading for a change. There's no question, there simply are certain men that take longer to get—solidified. How did he dress?

LINDA His blue suit. He's so handsome in that suit. He could be a—anything in that suit!

WILLY *gets up from the table.* LINDA *holds his jacket for him.*

WILLY There's no question, no question at all. Gee, on the way home tonight I'd like to buy some seeds.

LINDA *(laughing)* That'd be wonderful. But not enough sun gets back there. Nothing'll grow any more.

WILLY You wait, kid, before it's all over we're gonna get a little place out in the country, and I'll raise some vegetables, a couple of chickens . . .

LINDA You'll do it yet, dear.

WILLY *walks out of his jacket.* LINDA *follows him.*

WILLY And they'll get married, and come for a weekend. I'd build a little guest house. 'Cause I got so many fine tools, all I'd need would be a little lumber and some peace of mind.

LINDA *(joyfully)* I sewed the lining . . .

WILLY I could build two guest houses, so they'd both come. Did he decide how much he's going to ask Oliver for?

LINDA *(getting him into the jacket)* He didn't mention it, but I imagine ten or fifteen thousand. You going to talk to Howard today?

WILLY Yeah. I'll put it to him straight and simple. He'll just have to take me off the road.

LINDA And Willy, don't forget to ask for a little advance, because we've got the insurance premium. It's the grace period now.

WILLY That's a hundred . . . ?

LINDA A hundred and eight, sixty-eight. Because we're a little short again.

WILLY Why are we short?

LINDA Well, you had the motor job on the car . . .

WILLY   That goddam Studebaker!

LINDA   And you got one more payment on the refrigerator . . .

WILLY   But it just broke again!

LINDA   Well, it's old, dear.

WILLY   I told you we should've bought a well-advertised machine. Charley bought a General Electric and it's twenty years old and it's still good, that son-of-a-bitch.

LINDA   But, Willy—

WILLY   Whoever heard of a Hastings refrigerator? Once in my life I would like to own something outright before it's broken! I'm always in a race with the junkyard! I just finished paying for the car and it's on its last legs. The refrigerator consumes belts like a goddam maniac. They time those things. They time them so when you finally paid for them, they're used up.

LINDA   *(buttoning up his jacket as he unbuttons it)*   All told, about two hundred dollars would carry us, dear. But that includes the last payment on the mortgage. After this payment, Willy, the house belongs to us.

WILLY   It's twenty-five years!

LINDA   Biff was nine years old when we bought it.

WILLY   Well, that's a great thing. To weather a twenty-five year mortgage is—

LINDA   It's an accomplishment.

WILLY   All the cement, the lumber, the reconstruction I put in this house! There ain't a crack to be found in it any more.

LINDA   Well, it served its purpose.

WILLY   What purpose? Some stranger'll come along, move in, and that's that. If only Biff would take this house, and raise a family . . . *(He starts to go)* Good-by, I'm late.

LINDA   *(suddenly remembering)*   Oh, I forgot! You're supposed to meet them for dinner.

WILLY   Me?

LINDA   At Frank's Chop House on Forty-eighth near Sixth Avenue.

WILLY   Is that so! How about you?

LINDA   No, just the three of you. They're gonna blow you to a big meal!

WILLY   Don't say! Who thought of that?

LINDA   Biff came to me this morning, Willy, and he said, "Tell Dad, we want to blow him to a big meal." Be there six o'clock. You and your two boys are going to have dinner.

WILLY   Gee whiz! That's really somethin'. I'm gonna knock Howard for a loop, kid. I'll get an advance, and I'll come home with a New York job. Goddammit, now I'm gonna do it!

LINDA   Oh, that's the spirit, Willy!

WILLY   I will never get behind a wheel the rest of my life!

LINDA   It's changing. Willy, I can feel it changing!

WILLY   Beyond a question. G'by, I'm late. *(He starts to go again)*

LINDA   *(calling after him as she runs to the kitchen table for a handkerchief)*   You got your glasses?

WILLY   *(feels for them, then comes back in)*   Yeah, yeah, got my glasses.

LINDA   *(giving him the handkerchief)*   And a handkerchief.

WILLY   Yeah, handkerchief.

LINDA   And your saccharine?

WILLY   Yeah, my saccharine.

LINDA   Be careful on the subway stairs.

She kisses him, and a silk stocking is seen hanging from her hand. WILLY *notices it.*

WILLY   Will you stop mending stockings? At least while I'm in the house. It gets me nervous. I can't tell you. Please.

LINDA *hides the stocking in her hand as she follows* WILLY *across the forestage in front of the house.*

LINDA   Remember, Frank's Chop House.
WILLY *(passing the apron)*   Maybe beets would grow out there.
LINDA *(laughing)*   But you tried so many times.
WILLY   Yeah. Well, don't work hard today. *(He disappears around the right corner of the house)*
LINDA   Be careful!

As WILLY *vanishes,* LINDA *waves to him. Suddenly the phone rings. She runs across the stage and into the kitchen and lifts it.*

LINDA   Hello? Oh, Biff! I'm so glad you called, I just . . . Yes, sure, I told him. Yes, he'll be there for dinner at six o'clock, I didn't forget. Listen, I was just dying to tell you. You know that little rubber pipe I told you about? That he connected to the gas heater? I finally decided to go down the cellar this morning and take it away and destroy it. But it's gone! Imagine? He took it away himself, it isn't there! *(She listens)* When? Oh, then you took it. Oh—nothing, it's just that I'd hoped he'd taken it away himself. Oh, I'm not worried, darling, because this morning he left in such high spirits, it was like the old days! I'm not afraid any more. Did Mr. Oliver see you? . . . Well, you wait there then. And make a nice impression on him, darling. Just don't perspire too much before you see him. And have a nice time with Dad. He may have big news too! . . . That's right, a New York job. And be sweet to him tonight, dear. Be loving to him. Because he's only a little boat looking for a harbor. *(She is trembling with sorrow and joy)* Oh, that's wonderful, Biff, you'll save his life. Thanks, darling. Just put your arm around him when he comes into the restaurant. Give him a smile. That's the boy . . . Good-by, dear. . . . You got your comb? . . . That's fine. Good-by, Biff dear.

In the middle of her speech, HOWARD WAGNER, *thirty-six, wheels on a small type-writer table on which is a wire-recording machine and proceeds to plug it in. This is on the left forestage. Light slowly fades on* LINDA *as it rises on* HOWARD. HOWARD *is intent on threading the machine and only glances over his shoulder as* WILLY *appears.*

WILLY   Pst! Pst!
HOWARD   Hello, Willy, come in.
WILLY   Like to have a little talk with you, Howard.
HOWARD   Sorry to keep you waiting. I'll be with you in a minute.
WILLY   What's that, Howard?
HOWARD   Didn't you ever see one of these? Wire recorder.
WILLY   Oh. Can we talk a minute?
HOWARD   Records things. Just got delivery yesterday. Been driving me crazy, the most terrific machine I ever saw in my life. I was up all night with it.
WILLY   What do you do with it?

HOWARD   I bought it for dictation, but you can do anything with it. Listen to this. I had it home last night. Listen to what I picked up. The first one is my daughter. Get this. *(He flicks the switch and "Roll out the Barrel" is heard being whistled)* Listen to that kid whistle.

WILLY   That is lifelike, isn't it?

HOWARD   Seven years old. Get that tone.

WILLY   Ts, ts. Like to ask a little favor of you . . .

The whistling breaks off, and the voice of HOWARD'S *daughter is heard.*

HIS DAUGHTER   "Now you, Daddy."

HOWARD   She's crazy for me! *(Again the same song is whistled)* That's me! Ha! *(He winks)*

WILLY   You're very good!

The whistling breaks off again. The machine runs silent for a moment.

HOWARD   Sh! Get this now, this is my son.

HIS SON   "The capital of Alabama is Montgomery; the capital of Arizona is Phoenix; the capital of Arkansas is Little Rock; the capital of California is Sacramento . . ." *(and on, and on)*

HOWARD   *(holding up five fingers)*   Five years old, Willy!

WILLY   He'll make an announcer some day!

HIS SON *(continuing)*   "The capital . . ."

HOWARD   Get that—alphabetical order! *(The machine breaks off suddenly)* Wait a minute. The maid kicked the plug out.

WILLY   It certainly is a—

HOWARD   Sh, for God's sake!

HIS SON   "It's nine o'clock, Bulova watch time. So I have to go to sleep."

WILLY   That really is—

HOWARD   Wait a minute! The next is my wife.

They wait.

HOWARD'S VOICE   "Go on, say something." *(Pause)* "Well, you gonna talk?"

HIS WIFE   "I can't think of anything."

HOWARD'S VOICE   "Well, talk—it's turning."

HIS WIFE *(shyly, beaten)*   "Hello." *(Silence)* "Oh, Howard, I can't talk into this . . ."

HOWARD *(snapping the machine off)*   That was my wife.

WILLY   That is a wonderful machine. Can we—

HOWARD   I tell you, Willy, I'm gonna take my camera, and my bandsaw, and all my hobbies, and out they go. This is the most fascinating relaxation I ever found.

WILLY   I think I'll get one myself.

HOWARD   Sure, they're only a hundred and a half. You can't do without it. Supposing you wanna hear Jack Benny, see? But you can't be at home at that hour. So you tell the maid to turn the radio on when Jack Benny comes on, and this automatically goes on with the radio . . .

WILLY   And when you come home you . . .

HOWARD   You can come home twelve o'clock, one o'clock, any time you like, and you get yourself a Coke and sit yourself down, throw the switch, and there's Jack Benny's program in the middle of the night!

WILLY I'm definitely going to get one. Because lots of time I'm on the road, and I think to myself, what I must be missing on the radio!

HOWARD Don't you have a radio in the car?

WILLY Well, yeah, but who ever thinks of turning it on?

HOWARD Say, aren't you supposed to be in Boston?

WILLY That's what I want to talk to you about, Howard. You got a minute? *(He draws a chair in from the wing)*

HOWARD What happened? What're you doing here?

WILLY Well . . .

HOWARD You didn't crack up again, did you?

WILLY Oh, no. No . . .

HOWARD Geez, you had me worried there for a minute. What's the trouble?

WILLY Well, tell you the truth, Howard. I've come to the decision that I'd rather not travel any more.

HOWARD Not travel! Well, what'll you do?

WILLY Remember, Christmas time, when you had the party here? You said you'd try to think of some spot for me here in town.

HOWARD With us?

WILLY Well, sure.

HOWARD Oh, yeah, yeah. I remember. Well, I couldn't think of anything for you, Willy.

WILLY I tell ya, Howard. The kids are all grown up, y'know. I don't need much any more. If I could take home—well, sixty-five dollars a week, I could swing it.

HOWARD Yeah, but Willy, see I—

WILLY I tell ya why, Howard. Speaking frankly and between the two of us, y'know —I'm just a little tired.

HOWARD Oh, I could understand that, Willy. But you're a road man, Willy, and we do a road business. We've only got a half-dozen salesmen on the floor here.

WILLY God knows, Howard, I never asked a favor of any man. But I was with the firm when your father used to carry you in his arms.

HOWARD I know that, Willy, but—

WILLY Your father came to me the day you were born and asked me what I thought of the name of Howard, may he rest in peace.

HOWARD I appreciate that, Willy, but there just is no spot here for you. If I had a spot I'd slam you right in, but I just don't have a single solitary spot.

He looks for his lighter. WILLY *has picked it up and gives it to him. Pause.*

WILLY *(with increasing anger)* Howard, all I need to set my table is fifty dollars a week.

HOWARD But where am I going to put you, kid?

WILLY Look, it isn't a question of whether I can sell merchandise, is it?

HOWARD No, but it's a business, kid, and everybody's gotta pull his own weight.

WILLY *(desperately)* Just let me tell you a story, Howard—

HOWARD 'Cause you gotta admit, business is business.

WILLY *(angrily)* Business is definitely business, but just listen for a minute. You don't understand this. When I was a boy—eighteen, nineteen—I was already on the road. And there was a question in my mind as to whether selling had a future for me. Because in those days I had a yearning to go to Alaska. See, there were three gold strikes in one month in Alaska, and I felt like going out. Just for the ride, you might say.

HOWARD *(barely interested)* Don't say.

WILLY Oh, yeah, my father lived many years in Alaska. He was an adventurous man. We've got quite a little streak of self-reliance in our family. I thought I'd go out with my older brother and try to locate him, and maybe settle in the North with the old man. And I was almost decided to go, when I met a salesman in the Parker House. His name was Dave Singleman. And he was eighty-four years old, and he'd drummed merchandise in thirty-one states. And old Dave, he'd go up to his room, y'understand, put on his green velvet slippers—I'll never forget—and pick up his phone and call the buyers, and without ever leaving his room, at the age of eighty-four, he made his living. And when I saw that, I realized that selling was the greatest career a man could want. 'Cause what could be more satisfying than to be able to go, at the age of eighty-four, into twenty or thirty different cities, and pick up a phone, and be remembered and loved and helped by so many different people? Do you know? when he died—and by the way he died the death of a salesman, in his green velvet slippers in the smoker of the New York, New Haven and Hartford, going into Boston—when he died, hundreds of salesmen and buyers were at his funeral. Things were said on a lotta trains for months after that. *(He stands up.* HOWARD *has not looked at him)* In those days there was personality in it, Howard. There was respect, and comradeship, and gratitude in it. Today, it's all cut and dried, and there's no chance for bringing friendship to bear—or personality. You see what I mean? They don't know me any more.

HOWARD *(moving away, to the right)* That's just the thing, Willy.

WILLY If I had forty dollars a week—that's all I'd need. Forty dollars, Howard.

HOWARD Kid, I can't take blood from a stone, I—

WILLY *(desperation is on him now)* Howard, the year Al Smith was nominated, your father came to me and—

HOWARD *(starting to go off)* I've got to see some people, kid.

WILLY *(stopping him)* I'm talking about your father! There were promises made across this desk! You mustn't tell me you've got people to see—I put thirty-four years into this firm, Howard, and now I can't pay my insurance! You can't eat the orange and throw the peel away—a man is not a piece of fruit! *(After a pause)* Now pay attention. Your father—in 1928 I had a big year. I averaged a hundred and seventy dollars a week in commissions.

HOWARD *(impatiently)* Now, Willy, you never averaged—

WILLY *(banging his hand on the desk)* I averaged a hundred and seventy dollars a week in the year of 1928! And your father came to me—or rather, I was in the office here—it was right over this desk—and he put his hand on my shoulder—

HOWARD *(getting up)* You'll have to excuse me, Willy, I gotta see some people. Pull yourself together. *(Going out)* I'll be back in a little while.

On HOWARD's *exit, the light on his chair grows very bright and strange.*

WILLY Pull myself together! What the hell did I say to him? My God, I was yelling at him! How could I! (WILLY *breaks off, staring at the light, which occupies the chair, animating it. He approaches this chair, standing across the desk from it)* Frank, Frank, don't you remember what you told me that time? How you put your hand on my shoulder, and Frank . . . *(He leans on the desk and as he speaks the dead man's name he accidentally switches on the recorder, and instantly)*

HOWARD'S SON ". . . of New York is Albany. The capital of Ohio is Cincinnati, the capital of Rhode Island is . . ." *(The recitation continues)*

WILLY *(leaping away with fright, shouting)* Ha! Howard! Howard! Howard!

HOWARD *(rushing in)* What happened?

WILLY *(pointing at the machine, which continues nasally, childishly, with the capital cities)* Shut it off! Shut it off!

HOWARD *(pulling the plug out)* Look Willy . . .

WILLY *(pressing his hands to his eyes)* I gotta get myself some coffee. I'll get some coffee . . .

WILLY *starts to walk out.* HOWARD *stops him.*

HOWARD *(rolling up the cord)* Willy, look . . .

WILLY I'll go to Boston.

HOWARD Willy, you can't go to Boston for us.

WILLY Why can't I go?

HOWARD I don't want you to represent us. I've been meaning to tell you for a long time now.

WILLY Howard, are you firing me?

HOWARD I think you need a good long rest, Willy.

WILLY Howard—

HOWARD And when you feel better, come back, and we'll see if we can work something out.

WILLY But I gotta earn money, Howard. I'm in no position to—

HOWARD Where are your sons? Why don't your sons give you a hand?

WILLY They're working on a very big deal.

HOWARD This is no time for false pride, Willy. You go to your sons and you tell them that you're tired. You've got two great boys, haven't you?

WILLY Oh, no question, no question, but in the meantime . . .

HOWARD Then that's that, heh?

WILLY All right, I'll go to Boston tomorrow.

HOWARD No, no.

WILLY I can't throw myself on my sons. I'm not a cripple!

HOWARD Look, kid, I'm busy this morning.

WILLY *(grasping* HOWARD's *arm)* Howard, you've got to let me go to Boston!

HOWARD *(hard, keeping himself under control)* I've got a line of people to see this morning. Sit down, take five minutes, and pull yourself together, and then go home, will ya? I need the office, Willy. *(He starts to go, turns, remembering the recorder, starts to push off the table holding the recorder)* Oh, yeah. Whenever you can this week, stop by and drop off the samples. You'll feel better, Willy, and then come back and we'll talk. Pull yourself together, kid, there's people outside.

HOWARD *exits, pushing the table off left.* WILLY *stares into space, exhausted. Now the music is heard—*BEN's *music—first distantly, then closer, closer. As* WILLY *speaks,* BEN *enters from the right. He carries valise and umbrella.*

WILLY Oh, Ben, how did you do it? What is the answer? Did you wind up the Alaska deal already?

BEN Doesn't take much time if you know what you're doing. Just a short business trip. Boarding ship in an hour. Wanted to say good-by.

WILLY Ben, I've got to talk to you.

BEN *(glancing at his watch)* Haven't the time, William.

WILLY *(crossing the apron to* BEN*)* Ben, nothing's working out. I don't know what to do.

BEN Now, look here, William. I've bought timberland in Alaska and I need a man to look after things for me.

WILLY God, timberland! Me and my boys in those grand outdoors!

BEN You've a new continent at your doorstep, William. Get out of these cities, they're full of talk and time payments and courts of law. Screw on your fists and you can fight for a fortune up there.

WILLY Yes, yes! Linda, Linda!

LINDA *enters as of old, with the wash.*

LINDA Oh, you're back?

BEN I haven't much time.

WILLY No, wait! Linda, he's got a proposition for me in Alaska.

LINDA But you've got—*(To* BEN*)* He's got a beautiful job here.

WILLY But in Alaska, kid, I could—

LINDA You're doing well enough, Willy!

BEN *(to* LINDA*)* Enough for what, my dear?

LINDA *(frightened of* BEN *and angry at him)* Don't say those things to him! Enough to be happy right here, right now. *(To* WILLY, *while* BEN *laughs)* Why must everybody conquer the world? You're well liked, and the boys love you, and someday —*(to* BEN*)*—why, old man Wagner told him just the other day that if he keeps it up he'll be a member of the firm, didn't he, Willy?

WILLY Sure, sure. I am building something with this firm, Ben, and if a man is building something he must be on the right track, mustn't he?

BEN What are you building? Lay your hand on it. Where is it?

WILLY *(hesitantly)* That's true, Linda, there's nothing.

LINDA Why? *(To* BEN*)* There's a man eighty-four years old—

WILLY That's right, Ben, that's right. When I look at that man I say, what is there to worry about?

BEN Bah!

WILLY It's true, Ben. All he has to do is go into any city, pick up the phone, and he's making his living and you know why?

BEN *(picking up his valise)* I've got to go.

WILLY *(holding* BEN *back)* Look at this boy!

BIFF, *in his high school sweater, enters carrying suitcase.* HAPPY *carries* BIFF'S *shoulder guards, gold helmet, and football pants.*

WILLY Without a penny to his name, three great universities are begging for him, and from there the sky's the limit, because it's not what you do, Ben. It's who you know and the smile on your face! It's contacts, Ben, contacts! The whole wealth of Alaska passes over the lunch table at the Commodore Hotel, and that's the wonder, the wonder of this country, that a man can end with diamonds here on the basis of being liked! *(He turns to* BIFF*)* And that's why when you get out on that field today it's important. Because thousands of people will be rooting for you and loving you. *(To* BEN, *who has again begun to leave)* And Ben! when he walks into a business office his name will sound out like a bell and all the doors will open to him! I've seen it, Ben, I've seen it a thousand times! You can't feel it with your hand like timber, but it's there!

BEN   Good-by, William.

WILLY   Ben, am I right? Don't you think I'm right? I value your advice.

BEN   There's a new continent at your doorstep, William. You could walk out rich. Rich! *(He is gone)*

WILLY   We'll do it here, Ben! You hear me? We're gonna do it here!

YOUNG BERNARD *rushes in. The gay music of the boys is heard.*

BERNARD   Oh, gee, I was afraid you left already!

WILLY   Why? What time is it?

BIFF   It's half-past one!

WILLY   Well, come on, everybody! Ebbets Field next stop! Where's the pennants? *(He rushes through the wall-line of the kitchen and out into the living-room)*

LINDA *(to BIFF)*   Did you pack fresh underwear?

BIFF *(who has been limbering up)*   I want to go!

BERNARD   Biff, I'm carrying your helmet, ain't I?

HAPPY   No, I'm carrying the helmet.

BERNARD   Oh, Biff, you promised me.

HAPPY   I'm carrying the helmet.

BERNARD   How am I going to get in the locker room?

LINDA   Let him carry the shoulder guards. *(She puts her coat and hat on in the kitchen)*

BERNARD   Can I, Biff? 'Cause I told everybody I'm going to be in the locker room.

HAPPY   In Ebbets Field it's the clubhouse.

BERNARD   I meant the clubhouse. Biff!

HAPPY   Biff!

BIFF *(grandly, after a slight pause)*   Let him carry the shoulder guards.

HAPPY *(as he gives BERNARD the shoulder guards)*   Stay close to us now.

WILLY *rushes in with the pennants.*

WILLY *(handing them out)*   Everybody wave when Biff comes out on the field. *(*HAPPY *and* BERNARD *run off)* You set now, boy?

The music has died away.

BIFF   Ready to go, Pop. Every muscle is ready.

WILLY *(at the edge of the apron)*   You realize what this means?

BIFF   That's right, Pop.

WILLY *(feeling BIFF's muscles)*   You're comin' home this afternoon captain of the All-Scholastic Championship Team of the City of New York.

BIFF   I got it, Pop. And remember, pal, when I take off my helmet, that touchdown is for you.

WILLY   Let's go! *(He is starting out, with his arm around BIFF, when CHARLEY enters, as of old, in knickers)* I got no room for you, Charley.

CHARLEY   Room? For what?

WILLY   In the car.

CHARLEY   You goin' for a ride? I wanted to shoot some casino.

WILLY *(furiously)*   Casino! *(Incredulously)* Don't you realize what today is?

LINDA   Oh, he knows, Willy. He's just kidding you.

WILLY   That's nothing to kid about!

CHARLEY   No, Linda, what's goin' on?

LINDA   He's playing in Ebbets Field.

CHARLEY   Baseball in this weather?

WILLY   Don't talk to him. Come on, come on! *(He is pushing them out)*

CHARLEY   Wait a minute, didn't you hear the news?

WILLY   What?

CHARLEY   Don't you listen to the radio? Ebbets Field just blew up.

WILLY   You go to hell! *(CHARLEY laughs) (Pushing them out)* Come on, come on! We're late.

CHARLEY *(as they go)*   Knock a homer, Biff, knock a homer!

WILLY *(the last to leave, turning to CHARLEY)*   I don't think that was funny, Charley. This is the greatest day of his life.

CHARLEY   Willy, when are you going to grow up?

WILLY   Yeah, heh? When this game is over, Charley, you'll be laughing out of the other side of your face. They'll be calling him another Red Grange. Twenty-five thousand a year.

CHARLEY *(kidding)*   Is that so?

WILLY   Yeah, that's so.

CHARLEY   Well, then, I'm sorry, Willy. But tell me something.

WILLY   What?

CHARLEY   Who is Red Grange?

WILLY   Put up your hands. Goddam you, put up your hands!

CHARLEY, *chuckling, shakes his head and walks away, around the left corner of the stage.* WILLY *follows him. the music rises to a mocking frenzy.*

WILLY   Who the hell do you think you are, better than everybody else? You don't know everything, you big, ignorant, stupid . . . Put up your hands!

Light rises, on the right side of the forestage, on a small table in the reception room of CHARLEY's *office. Traffic sounds are heard.* BERNARD, *now mature, sits whistling to himself. A pair of tennis rackets and an overnight bag are on the floor beside him.*

WILLY *(offstage)*   What are you walking away for? Don't walk away! If you're going to say something say it to my face! I know you laugh at me behind my back. You'll laugh out of the other side of your goddam face after this game. Touchdown! Touchdown! Eighty thousand people! Touchdown! Right between the goal posts.

BERNARD *is a quiet, earnest, but self-assured young man.* WILLY'S *voice is coming from right upstage now.* BERNARD *lowers his feet off the table and listens.* JENNY, *his father's secretary, enters.*

JENNY *(distressed)*   Say, Bernard, will you go out in the hall?

BERNARD   What is that noise? Who is it?

JENNY   Mr. Loman. He just got off the elevator.

BERNARD *(getting up)*   Who's he arguing with?

JENNY   Nobody. There's nobody with him. I can't deal with him any more and your father gets all upset every time he comes. I've got a lot of typing to do, and your father's waiting to sign it. Will you see him?

WILLY *(entering)*   Touchdown! Touch—*(He sees* JENNY*)* Jenny, Jenny, good to see you. How're ya? Workin'? Or still honest?

JENNY   Fine. How've you been feeling?

WILLY   Not much any more, Jenny. Ha, ha! *(He is surprised to see the rackets)*

BERNARD   Hello, Uncle Willy.

WILLY *(almost shocked)* Bernard! Well, look who's here! *(He comes quickly, guiltily, to* BERNARD *and warmly shakes his hand)*

BERNARD How are you? Good to see you.

WILLY What are you doing here?

BERNARD Oh, just stopped by to see Pop. Get off my feet till my train leaves. I'm going to Washington in a few minutes.

WILLY Is he in?

BERNARD Yes, he's in his office with the accountant. Sit down.

WILLY *(sitting down)* What're you going to do in Washington?

BERNARD Oh, just a case I've got there, Willy.

WILLY That so? *(Indicating the rackets)* You going to play tennis there?

BERNARD I'm staying with a friend who's got a court.

WILLY Don't say. His own tennis court. Must be fine people, I bet.

BERNARD They are, very nice. Dad tells me Biff's in town.

WILLY *(with a big smile)* Yeah, Biff's in. Working on a very big deal, Bernard.

BERNARD What's Biff doing?

WILLY Well, he's been doing very big things in the West. But he decided to establish himself here. Very big. We're having dinner. Did I hear your wife had a boy?

BERNARD That's right. Our second.

WILLY Two boys! What do you know!

BERNARD What kind of a deal has Biff got?

WILLY Well, Bill Oliver—very big sporting-goods man—he wants Biff very badly. Called him in from the West. Long distance, carte blanche, special deliveries. Your friends have their own private tennis court?

BERNARD You still with the old firm, Willy?

WILLY *(after a pause)* I'm—I'm overjoyed to see how you made the grade, Bernard, overjoyed. It's an encouraging thing to see a young man really—really— Looks very good for Biff—very—*(He breaks off, then)* Bernard—*(He is so full of emotion, he breaks off again)*

BERNARD What is it, Willy?

WILLY *(small and alone)* What—what's the secret?

BERNARD What secret?

WILLY How—how did you? Why didn't he ever catch on?

BERNARD I wouldn't know that, Willy.

WILLY *(confidentially, desperately)* You were his friend, his boyhood friend. There's something I don't understand about it. His life ended after that Ebbets Field game. From the age of seventeen nothing good ever happened to him.

BERNARD He never trained himself for anything.

WILLY But he did, he did. After high school he took so many correspondence courses. Radio mechanics; television; God knows what, and never made the slightest mark.

BERNARD *(taking off his glasses)* Willy, do you want to talk candidly?

WILLY *(rising, faces* BERNARD) I regard you as a very brilliant man, Bernard. I value your advice.

BERNARD Oh, the hell with the advice, Willy. I couldn't advise you. There's just one thing I've always wanted to ask you. When he was supposed to graduate, and the math teacher flunked him—

WILLY Oh, that son-of-a-bitch ruined his life.

BERNARD Yeah, but, Willy, all he had to do was go to summer school and make up that subject.

WILLY That's right, that's right.

BERNARD Did you tell him not to go to summer school?

WILLY Me? I begged him to go. I ordered him to go!

BERNARD Then why wouldn't he go?

WILLY Why? Why! Bernard, that question has been trailing me like a ghost for the last fifteen years. He flunked the subject, and laid down and died like a hammer hit him!

BERNARD Take it easy, kid.

WILLY Let me talk to you—I got nobody to talk to. Bernard, Bernard, was it my fault? Y'see? It keeps going around in my mind, maybe I did something to him. I got nothing to give him.

BERNARD Don't take it so hard.

WILLY Why did he lay down? What is the story there? You were his friend!

BERNARD Willy, I remember, it was June, and our grades came out. And he'd flunked math.

WILLY That son-of-a-bitch!

BERNARD No, it wasn't right then. Biff just got very angry, I remember, and he was ready to enroll in summer school.

WILLY *(surprised)* He was?

BERNARD He wasn't beaten by it at all. But then, Willy, he disappeared from the block for almost a month. And I got the idea that he'd gone up to New England to see you. Did he have a talk with you then?

WILLY *stares in silence.*

BERNARD Willy?

WILLY *(with a strong edge of resentment in his voice)* Yeah, he came to Boston. What about it?

BERNARD Well, just that when he came back—I'll never forget this, it always mystifies me. Because I'd thought so well of Biff, even though he'd always taken advantage of me. I loved him, Willy, y'know? And he came back after that month and took his sneakers—remember those sneakers with "University of Virginia" printed on them? He was so proud of those, wore them every day. And he took them down in the cellar, and burned them up in the furnace. We had a fist fight. It lasted at least half an hour. Just the two of us, punching each other down the cellar, and crying right through it. I've often thought of how strange it was that I knew he'd given up his life. What happened in Boston, Willy?

WILLY *looks at him as at an intruder.*

BERNARD I just bring it up because you asked me.

WILLY *(angrily)* Nothing. What do you mean, "What happened?" What's that got to do with anything?

BERNARD Well, don't get sore.

WILLY What are you trying to do, blame it on me? If a boy lays down is that my fault?

BERNARD Now, Willy, don't get—

WILLY Well, don't—don't talk to me that way! What does that mean, "What happened?"

CHARLEY *enters. He is in his vest, and he carries a bottle of bourbon.*

CHARLEY   Hey, you're going to miss that train. *(He waves the bottle)*

BERNARD   Yeah, I'm going. *(He takes the bottle)* Thanks, Pop. *(He picks up his rackets and bag)* Good-by, Willy, and don't worry about it. You know, "If at first you don't succeed . . ."

WILLY   Yes, I believe in that.

BERNARD   But sometimes, Willy, it's better for a man just to walk away.

WILLY   Walk away?

BERNARD   That's right.

WILLY   But if you can't walk away?

BERNARD   *(after a slight pause)*   I guess that's when it's tough. *(Extending his hand)* Good-by, Willy.

WILLY   *(shaking BERNARD's hand)*   Good-by, boy.

CHARLEY   *(an arm on BERNARD's shoulder)*   How do you like this kid? Gonna argue a case in front of the Supreme Court.

BERNARD   *(protesting)*   Pop!

WILLY   *(genuinely shocked, pained, and happy)*   No! The Supreme Court!

BERNARD   I gotta run. 'By, Dad!

CHARLEY   Knock 'em dead, Bernard!

BERNARD *goes off.*

WILLY   *(as CHARLEY takes out his wallet)*   The Supreme Court! And he didn't even mention it!

CHARLEY   *(counting out money on the desk)*   He don't have to—he's gonna do it.

WILLY   And you never told him what to do, did you? You never took any interest in him.

CHARLEY   My salvation is that I never took any interest in anything. There's some money—fifty dollars. I got an accountant inside.

WILLY   Charley, look . . . *(With difficulty)* I got my insurance to pay. If you can manage it—I need a hundred and ten dollars.

CHARLEY *doesn't reply for a moment; merely stops moving.*

WILLY   I'd draw it from my bank but Linda would know, and I . . .

CHARLEY   Sit down, Willy.

WILLY   *(moving toward the chair)*   I'm keeping an account of everything, re-member. I'll pay every penny back. *(He sits)*

CHARLEY   Now listen to me, Willy.

WILLY   I want you to know I appreciate . . .

CHARLEY   *(sitting down on the table)*   Willy, what're you doin'? What the hell is goin' on in your head?

WILLY   Why? I'm simply . . .

CHARLEY   I offered you a job. You can make fifty dollars a week. And I won't send you on the road.

WILLY   I've got a job.

CHARLEY   Without pay? What kind of a job is a job without pay? *(He rises)* Now, look, kid, enough is enough. I'm no genius but I know when I'm being insulted.

WILLY   Insulted!

CHARLEY   Why don't you want to work for me?

WILLY   What's the matter with you? I've got a job.

CHARLEY   Then what're you walkin' in here every week for?

WILLY *(getting up)* Well, if you don't want me to walk in here—

CHARLEY I am offering you a job.

WILLY I don't want your goddam job!

CHARLEY When the hell are you going to grow up?

WILLY *(furiously)* You big ignoramus, if you say that to me again I'll rap you one! I don't care how big you are! *(He's ready to fight)*

Pause.

CHARLEY *(kindly, going to him)* How much do you need, Willy?

WILLY Charley, I'm strapped. I'm strapped. I don't know what to do. I was just fired.

CHARLEY Howard fired you?

WILLY That snotnose. Imagine that? I named him. I named him Howard.

CHARLEY Willy, when're you gonna realize that them things don't mean anything? You named him Howard, but you can't sell that. The only thing you got in this world is what you can sell. And the funny thing is that you're a salesman, and you don't know that.

WILLY I've always tried to think otherwise, I guess. I always felt that if a man was impressive, and well liked, that nothing—

CHARLEY Why must everybody like you? Who liked J. P. Morgan? Was he impressive? In a Turkish bath he'd look like a butcher. But with his pockets on he was very well liked. Now listen, Willy, I know you don't like me, and nobody can say I'm in love with you, but I'll give you a job because—just for the hell of it, put it that way. Now what do you say?

WILLY I—I just can't work for you, Charley.

CHARLEY What're you, jealous of me?

WILLY I can't work for you, that's all, don't ask me why.

CHARLEY *(angered, takes out more bills)* You been jealous of me all your life, you damned fool! Here, pay your insurance. *(He puts the money in* WILLY's *hand)*

WILLY I'm keeping strict accounts.

CHARLEY I've got some work to do. Take care of yourself. And pay your insurance.

WILLY *(moving to the right)* Funny, y'know? After all the highways, and the trains, and the appointments, and the years, you end up worth more dead than alive.

CHARLEY Willy, nobody's worth nothin' dead. *(After a slight pause)* Did you hear what I said?

WILLY *stands still, dreaming.*

CHARLEY Willy!

WILLY Apologize to Bernard for me when you see him. I didn't mean to argue with him. He's a fine boy. They're all fine boys, and they'll end up big—all of them. Someday they'll all play tennis together. Wish me luck, Charley. He saw Bill Oliver today.

CHARLEY Good luck.

WILLY *(on the verge of tears)* Charley, you're the only friend I got. Isn't that a remarkable thing? *(He goes out)*

CHARLEY Jesus!

CHARLEY *stares after him a moment and follows. All light blacks out. Suddenly raucous music is heard, and a red glow rises behind the screen at right.* STANLEY, *a young waiter, appears, carrying a table, followed by* HAPPY, *who is carrying two chairs.*

STANLEY *(putting the table down)*   That's all right, Mr. Loman, I can handle it my-self. *(He turns and takes the chairs from* HAPPY *and places them at the table)*
HAPPY *(glancing around)*   Oh, this is better.
STANLEY   Sure, in the front there you're in the middle of all kinds a noise. When-ever you got a party, Mr. Loman, you just tell me and I'll put you back here. Y'know, there's a lotta people they don't like it private, because when they go out they like to see a lotta action around them because they're sick and tired to stay in the house by theirself. But I know you, you ain't from Hackensack. You know what I mean?
HAPPY *(sitting down)*   So how's it coming, Stanley?
STANLEY   Ah, it's a dog's life. I only wish during the war they'd a took me in the Army. I coulda been dead by now.
HAPPY   My brother's back, Stanley.
STANLEY   Oh, he come back, heh? From the Far West.
HAPPY   Yeah, big cattle man, my brother, so treat him right. And my father's com-ing too.
STANLEY   Oh, your father too!
HAPPY   You got a couple of nice lobsters?
STANLEY   Hundred per cent, big.
HAPPY   I want them with the claws.
STANLEY   Don't worry, I don't give you no mice. *(*HAPPY *laughs)* How about some wine? It'll put a head on the meal.
HAPPY   No. You remember, Stanley, that recipe I brought you from overseas? With the champagne in it?
STANLEY   Oh, yeah, sure. I still got it tacked up yet in the kitchen. But that'll have to cost a buck apiece anyways.
HAPPY   That's all right.
STANLEY   What'd you, hit a number or somethin'?
HAPPY   No, it's a little celebration. My brother is—I think he pulled off a big deal today. I think we're going into business together.
STANLEY   Great! That's the best for you. Because a family business, you know what I mean?—that's the best.
HAPPY   That's what I think.
STANLEY   'Cause what's the difference? Somebody steals? It's in the family. Know what I mean? *(Sotto voce)* Like this bartender here. The boss is goin' crazy what kinda leak he's got in the cash register. You put it in but it don't come out.
HAPPY *(raising his head)*   Sh!
STANLEY   What?
HAPPY   You notice I wasn't lookin' right or left, was I?
STANLEY   No.
HAPPY   And my eyes are closed.
STANLEY   So what's the—?
HAPPY   Strudel's comin'.
STANLEY *(catching on, looks around)*   Ah, no, there's no—

He breaks off as a furred, lavishly dressed girl enters and sits at the next table. Both follow her with their eyes.

STANLEY   Geez, how'd ya know?

HAPPY   I got radar or something. *(Staring directly at her profile)* Oooooooo . . . Stanley.

STANLEY   I think that's for you, Mr. Loman.

HAPPY   Look at that mouth. Oh, God. And the binoculars.

STANLEY   Geez, you got a life, Mr. Loman.

HAPPY   Wait on her.

STANLEY *(going to the* GIRL's *table)*   Would you like a menu, ma'am?

GIRL   I'm expecting someone, but I'd like a—

HAPPY   Why don't you bring her—excuse me, miss, do you mind? I sell champagne, and I'd like you to try my brand. Bring her a champagne, Stanley.

GIRL   That's awfully nice of you.

HAPPY   Don't mention it. It's all company money. *(He laughs)*

GIRL   That's a charming product to be selling, isn't it?

HAPPY   Oh, gets to be like everything else. Selling is selling, y'know.

GIRL   I suppose.

HAPPY   You don't happen to sell, do you?

GIRL   No, I don't sell.

HAPPY   Would you object to a compliment from a stranger? You ought to be on a magazine cover.

GIRL *(looking at him a little archly)*   I have been.

STANLEY *comes in with a glass of champagne.*

HAPPY   What'd I say before, Stanley? You see? She's a cover girl.

STANLEY   Oh, I could see, I could see.

HAPPY *(to the* GIRL*)*   What magazine?

GIRL   Oh, a lot of them. *(She takes her drink)* Thank you.

HAPPY   You know what they say in France, don't you? "Champagne is the drink of the complexion"—Hya, Biff!

BIFF *has entered and sits with* HAPPY.

BIFF   Hello, kid. Sorry I'm late.

HAPPY   I just got here. Uh, Miss—?

GIRL   Forsythe.

HAPPY   Miss Forsythe, this is my brother.

BIFF   Is Dad here?

HAPPY   His name is Biff. You might've heard of him. Great football player.

GIRL   Really? What team?

HAPPY   Are you familiar with football?

GIRL   No, I'm afraid I'm not.

HAPPY   Biff is quarterback with the New York Giants.

GIRL.   Well, that is nice, isn't it? *(She drinks)*

HAPPY   Good health.

GIRL   I'm happy to meet you.

HAPPY   That's my name. Hap. It's really Harold, but at West Point they called me Happy.

GIRL *(now really impressed)*   Oh, I see. How do you do? *(She turns her profile)*

BIFF   Isn't Dad coming?

HAPPY   You want her?

BIFF   Oh, I could never make that.

946   *Death of a Salesman*

HAPPY   I remember the time that idea would never come into your head. Where's the old confidence, Biff?

BIFF   I just saw Oliver—

HAPPY   Wait a minute. I've got to see that old confidence again. Do you want her? She's on call.

BIFF   Oh, no. *(He turns to look at the* GIRL*)*

HAPPY   I'm telling you. Watch this. *(Turning to the* GIRL*)* Honey? *(She turns to him)* Are you busy?

GIRL   Well, I am . . . but I could make a phone call.

HAPPY   Do that, will you, honey? And see if you can get a friend. We'll be here for a while. Biff is one of the greatest football players in the country.

GIRL *(standing up)*   Well, I'm certainly happy to meet you.

HAPPY   Come back soon.

GIRL   I'll try.

HAPPY   Don't try, honey, try hard.

The GIRL *exits.* STANLEY *follows, shaking his head in bewildered admiration.*

HAPPY   Isn't that a shame now? A beautiful girl like that? That's why I can't get married. There's not a good woman in a thousand. New York is loaded with them, kid!

BIFF   Hap, look—

HAPPY   I told you she was on call!

BIFF *(strangely unnerved)*   Cut it out, will ya? I want to say something to you.

HAPPY   Did you see Oliver?

BIFF   I saw him all right. Now look, I want to tell Dad a couple of things and I want you to help me.

HAPPY   What? Is he going to back you?

BIFF   Are you crazy? You're out of your goddam head, you know that?

HAPPY   Why? What happened?

BIFF *(breathlessly)*   I did a terrible thing today, Hap. It's been the strangest day I ever went through. I'm all numb, I swear.

HAPPY   You mean he wouldn't see you?

BIFF   Well, I waited six hours for him, see? All day. Kept sending my name in. Even tried to date his secretary so she'd get me to him, but no soap.

HAPPY   Because you're not showin' the old confidence, Biff. He remembered you, didn't he?

BIFF *(stopping* HAPPY *with a gesture)*   Finally, about five o'clock, he comes out. Didn't remember who I was or anything. I felt like such an idiot, Hap.

HAPPY   Did you tell him my Florida idea?

BIFF   He walked away. I saw him for one minute. I got so mad I could've torn the walls down! How the hell did I ever get the idea I was a salesman there? I even believed myself that I'd been a salesman for him! And then he gave me one look and—I realized what a ridiculous lie my whole life has been! We've been talking in a dream for fifteen years. I was a shipping clerk.

HAPPY   What'd you do?

BIFF *(with great tension and wonder)*   Well, he left, see. And the secretary went out. I was all alone in the waiting-room. I don't know what came over me, Hap. The next thing I know I'm in his office—paneled walls, everything. I can't explain it. I—Hap, I took his fountain pen.

HAPPY   Geez, did he catch you?

BIFF   I ran out. I ran down all eleven flights. I ran and ran and ran.

HAPPY   That was an awful dumb—what'd you do that for?

BIFF *(agonized)*   I don't know, I just—wanted to take something. I don't know. You gotta help me, Hap. I'm gonna tell Pop.

HAPPY   You crazy? What for?

BIFF   Hap, he's got to understand that I'm not the man somebody lends that kind of money to. He thinks I've been spiting him all these years and it's eating him up.

HAPPY   That's just it. You tell him something nice.

BIFF   I can't.

HAPPY   Say you got a lunch date with Oliver tomorrow.

BIFF   So what do I do tomorrow?

HAPPY   You leave the house tomorrow and come back at night and say Oliver is thinking it over. And he thinks it over for a couple of weeks, and gradually it fades away and nobody's the worse.

BIFF   But it'll go on forever!

HAPPY   Dad is never so happy as when he's looking forward to something!

WILLY *enters.*

HAPPY   Hello, scout!

WILLY   Gee, I haven't been here in years!

STANLEY *has followed* WILLY *in and sets a chair for him.* STANLEY *starts off but* HAPPY *stops him.*

HAPPY   Stanley!

STANLEY *stands by, waiting for an order.*

BIFF *(going to* WILLY *with guilt, as to an invalid)*   Sit down, Pop. You want a drink?

WILLY   Sure, I don't mind.

BIFF   Let's get a load on.

WILLY   You look worried.

BIFF   N-no. *(To* STANLEY*)* Scotch all around. Make it doubles.

STANLEY   Doubles, right. *(He goes)*

WILLY   You had a couple already, didn't you?

BIFF   Just a couple, yeah.

WILLY   Well, what happened, boy? *(Nodding affirmatively, with a smile)* Everything go all right?

BIFF *(takes a breath, then reaches out and grasps* WILLY*'s hand)*   Pal ... *(He is smiling bravely, and* WILLY *is smiling too)* I had an experience today.

HAPPY   Terrific, Pop.

WILLY   That so? What happened?

BIFF *(high, slightly alcoholic, above the earth)*   I'm going to tell you everything from first to last. It's been a strange day. *(Silence. He looks around, composes himself as best he can, but his breath keeps breaking the rhythm of his voice)* I had to wait quite a while for him, and—

WILLY   Oliver?

BIFF   Yeah, Oliver. All day, as a matter of cold fact. And a lot of—instances—facts, Pop, facts about my life came back to me. Who was it, Pop? Who ever said I was a salesman with Oliver?

WILLY   Well, you were.

BIFF   No, Dad, I was a shipping clerk.

WILLY But you were practically—

BIFF *(with determination)* Dad, I don't know who said it first, but I was never a salesman for Bill Oliver.

WILLY What're you talking about?

BIFF Let's hold on to the facts tonight, Pop. We're not going to get anywhere bullin' around. I was a shipping clerk.

WILLY *(angrily)* All right, now listen to me—

BIFF Why don't you let me finish?

WILLY I'm not interested in stories about the past or any crap of that kind because the woods are burning, boys, you understand? There's a big blaze going on all around. I was fired today.

BIFF *(shocked)* How could you be?

WILLY I was fired, and I'm looking for a little good news to tell your mother, because the woman has waited and the woman has suffered. The gift of it is that I haven't got a story left in my head, Biff. So don't give me a lecture about facts and aspects. I am not interested. Now what've you got to say to me?

STANLEY *enters with three drinks. They wait until he leaves.*

WILLY Did you see Oliver?

BIFF Jesus, Dad!

WILLY You mean you didn't go up there?

HAPPY Sure he went up there.

BIFF I did. I—saw him. How could they fire you?

WILLY *(on the edge of his chair)* What kind of a welcome did he give you?

BIFF He won't even let you work on commission?

WILLY I'm out! *(Driving)* So tell me, he gave you a warm welcome?

HAPPY Sure, Pop, sure!

BIFF *(driven)* Well, it was kind of—

WILLY I was wondering if he'd remember you. *(To HAPPY)* Imagine, man doesn't see him for ten, twelve years and gives him that kind of a welcome!

HAPPY Damn right!

BIFF *(trying to return to the offensive)* Pop, look—

WILLY You know why he remembered you, don't you? Because you impressed him in those days.

BIFF Let's talk quietly and get this down to the facts, huh?

WILLY *(as though BIFF had been interrupting)* Well, what happened? It's great news, Biff. Did he take you into his office or'd you talk in the waiting-room?

BIFF Well, he came in, see, and—

WILLY *(with a big smile)* What'd he say? Betcha he threw his arm around you.

BIFF Well, he kinda—

WILLY He's a fine man. *(To HAPPY)* Very hard man to see, y'know.

HAPPY *(agreeing)* Oh, I know.

WILLY *(to BIFF)* Is that where you had the drinks?

BIFF Yeah, he gave me a couple of—no, no!

HAPPY *(cutting in)* He told him my Florida idea.

WILLY Don't interrupt. *(To BIFF)* How'd he react to the Florida idea?

BIFF Dad, will you give me a minute to explain?

WILLY I've been waiting for you to explain since I sat down here! What happened? He took you into his office and what?

BIFF Well—I talked. And—and he listened, see.

WILLY   Famous for the way he listens, y'know. What was his answer?

BIFF   His answer was— *(He breaks off, suddenly angry)* Dad, you're not letting me tell you what I want to tell you!

WILLY *(accusing, angered)*   You didn't see him, did you?

BIFF   I did see him!

WILLY   What'd you insult him or something? You insulted him, didn't you?

BIFF   Listen, will you let me out of it, will you just let me out of it!

HAPPY   What the hell!

WILLY   Tell me what happened!

BIFF *(to HAPPY)*   I can't talk to him!

A single trumpet note jars the ear. The light of green leaves stains the house, which holds the air of night and a dream. YOUNG BERNARD *enters and knocks on the door of the house.*

YOUNG BERNARD *(frantically)*   Mrs. Loman, Mrs. Loman!

HAPPY   Tell him what happened!

BIFF *(to HAPPY)*   Shut up and leave me alone!

WILLY   No, no! You had to go and flunk math!

BIFF   What math? What're you talking about?

YOUNG BERNARD   Mrs. Loman, Mrs. Loman!

LINDA *appears in the house, as of old.*

WILLY *(wildly)*   Math, math, math!

BIFF   Take it easy, Pop!

YOUNG BERNARD   Mrs. Loman!

WILLY *(furiously)*   If you hadn't flunked you'd've been set by now!

BIFF   Now, look, I'm gonna tell you what happened, and you're going to listen to me.

YOUNG BERNARD   Mrs. Loman!

BIFF   I waited six hours—

HAPPY   What the hell are you saying?

BIFF   I kept sending in my name but he wouldn't see me. So finally he . . . *(He continues unheard as light fades low on the restaurant)*

YOUNG BERNARD   Biff flunked math!

LINDA   No!

YOUNG BERNARD   Birnbaum flunked him! They won't graduate him!

LINDA   But they have to. He's gotta go to the university. Where is he? Biff! Biff!

YOUNG BERNARD   No, he left. He went to Grand Central.

LINDA   Grand— You mean he went to Boston!

YOUNG BERNARD   Is Uncle Willy in Boston?

LINDA   Oh, maybe Willy can talk to the teacher. Oh, the poor, poor boy!

Light on house area snaps out.

BIFF *(at the table, now audible, holding up a gold fountain pen)*. . . so I'm washed up with Oliver, you understand? Are you listening to me?

WILLY *(at a loss)*   Yeah, sure. If you hadn't flunked—

BIFF   Flunked what? What're you talking about?

WILLY   Don't blame everything on me! I didn't flunk math—you did! What pen?

HAPPY   That was awful dumb, Biff, a pen like that is worth—

WILLY *(seeing the pen for the first time)* You took Oliver's pen?

BIFF *(weakening)* Dad, I just explained it to you.

WILLY You stole Bill Oliver's fountain pen!

BIFF I didn't exactly steal it! That's just what I've been explaining to you!

HAPPY He had it in his hand and just then Oliver walked in, so he got nervous and stuck it in his pocket.

WILLY My God, Biff!

BIFF I never intended to do it, Dad!

OPERATOR'S VOICE Standish Arms, good evening!

WILLY *(shouting)* I'm not in my room!

BIFF *(frightened)* Dad, what's the matter? *(He and HAPPY stand up)*

OPERATOR Ringing Mr. Loman for you!

WILLY I'm not there, stop it!

BIFF *(horrified, gets down on one knee before WILLY)* Dad, I'll make good, I'll make good. *(WILLY tries to get to his feet. BIFF holds him down)* Sit down now.

WILLY No, you're no good, you're no good for anything.

BIFF I am, Dad, I'll find something else, you understand? Now don't worry about anything. *(He holds up WILLY's face)* Talk to me, Dad.

OPERATOR Mr. Loman does not answer. Shall I page him?

WILLY *(attempting to stand, as though to rush and silence the OPERATOR)* No, no, no!

HAPPY He'll strike something, Pop.

WILLY No, no . . .

BIFF *(desperately, standing over WILLY)* Pop, listen! Listen to me! I'm telling you something good. Oliver talked to his partner about the Florida idea. You listening? He—he talked to his partner, and he came to me . . . I'm going to be all right, you hear? Dad, listen to me, he said it was just a question of the amount!

WILLY Then you . . . got it?

HAPPY He's gonna be terrific, Pop!

WILLY *(trying to stand)* Then you got it, haven't you? You got it! You got it!

BIFF *(agonized, holds WILLY down)* No, no. Look, Pop. I'm supposed to have lunch with them tomorrow. I'm just telling you this so you'll know that I can still make an impression, Pop. And I'll make good somewhere, but I can't go tomorrow, see?

WILLY Why not? You simply—

BIFF But the pen, Pop!

WILLY You give it to him and tell him it was an oversight!

HAPPY Sure, have lunch tomorrow!

BIFF I can't say that—

WILLY You were doing a crossword puzzle and accidentally used his pen!

BIFF Listen, kid, I took those balls years ago, now I walk in with his fountain pen? That clinches it, don't you see? I can't face him like that! I'll try elsewhere.

PAGE'S VOICE Paging Mr. Loman!

WILLY Don't you want to be anything?

BIFF Pop, how can I go back?

WILLY You don't want to be anything, is that what's behind it?

BIFF *(now angry at WILLY for not crediting his sympathy)* Don't take it that way! You think it was easy walking into that office after what I'd done to him? A team of horses couldn't have dragged me back to Bill Oliver!

WILLY   Then why'd you go?

BIFF   Why did I go? Why did I go! Look at you! Look at what's become of you!

Off left, THE WOMAN *laughs.*

WILLY   Biff, you're going to go to that lunch tomorrow, or—

BIFF   I can't go. I've got no appointment!

HAPPY   Biff, for . . . !

WILLY   Are you spiting me?

BIFF   Don't take it that way! Goddammit!

WILLY *(strikes* BIFF *and falters away from the table)*   You rotten little louse! Are you spiting me?

THE WOMAN   Someone's at the door, Willy!

BIFF   I'm no good, can't you see what I am?

HAPPY *(separating them)*   Hey, you're in a restaurant! Now cut it out, both of you! *(The girls enter)* Hello, girls, sit down.

THE WOMAN *laughs, off left.*

MISS FORSYTHE   I guess we might as well. This is Letta.

THE WOMAN   Willy, are you going to wake up?

BIFF *(ignoring* WILLY*)*   How're ya, miss, sit down. What do you drink?

MISS FORSYTHE   Letta might not be able to stay long.

LETTA   I gotta get up very early tomorrow. I got jury duty. I'm so excited! Were you fellows ever on a jury?

BIFF   No, but I been in front of them! *(The girls laugh)* This is my father.

LETTA   Isn't he cute? Sit down with us, Pop.

HAPPY   Sit him down, Biff!

BIFF *(going to him)*   Come on, slugger, drink us under the table. To hell with it! Come on, sit down, pal.

On BIFF'S *last insistence,* WILLY *is about to sit.*

THE WOMAN *(now urgently)*   Willy, are you going to answer the door!

THE WOMAN*'s call pulls* WILLY *back. He starts right, befuddled.*

BIFF   Hey, where are you going?

WILLY   Open the door.

BIFF   The door?

WILLY   The washroom . . . the door . . . where's the door?

BIFF *(leading* WILLY *to the left)*   Just go straight down.

WILLY *moves left.*

THE WOMAN   Willy, Willy, are you going to get up, get up, get up, get up?

WILLY *exits left.*

LETTA   I think it's sweet you bring your daddy along.

MISS FORSYTHE   Oh, he isn't really your father!

BIFF *(at left, turning to her resentfully)*   Miss Forsythe, you've just seen a prince walk by. A fine, troubled prince. A hard-working, unappreciated prince. A pal, you understand? A good companion. Always for his boys.

LETTA   That's so sweet.

HAPPY Well, girls, what's the program? We're wasting time. Come on, Biff. Gather round. Where would you like to go?

BIFF Why don't you do something for him?

HAPPY Me!

BIFF Don't you give a damn for him, Hap?

HAPPY What're you talking about? I'm the one who—

BIFF I sense it, you don't give a good goddam about him. *(He takes the rolled-up hose from his pocket and puts it on the table in front of* HAPPY*)* Look what I found in the cellar, for Christ's sake. How can you bear to let it go on?

HAPPY Me? Who goes away? Who runs off and—

BIFF Yeah, but he doesn't mean anything to you. You could help him—I can't! Don't you understand what I'm talking about? He's going to kill himself, Don't you know that?

HAPPY Don't I know it! Me!

BIFF Hap, help him! Jesus . . . help him . . . Help me, help me, I can't bear to look at his face! *(Ready to weep, he hurries out, up right)*

HAPPY *(starting after him)* Where are you going?

MISS FORSYTHE What's he so mad about?

HAPPY Come on, girls, we'll catch up with him.

MISS FORSYTHE *(as* HAPPY *pushes her out)* Say, I don't like that temper of his!

HAPPY He's just a little overstrung, he'll be all right!

WILLY *(off left, as* THE WOMAN *laughs)* Don't answer! Don't answer!

LETTA Don't you want to tell your father—

HAPPY No, that's not my father. He's just a guy. Come on, we'll catch Biff, and, honey, we're going to paint this town! Stanley, where's the check! Hey, Stanley!

They exit. STANLEY *looks toward left.*

STANLEY *(calling to* HAPPY *indignantly)* Mr. Loman! Mr. Loman!

STANLEY *picks up a chair and follows them off. Knocking is heard off left.* THE WOMAN *enters, laughing.* WILLY *follows her. She is in a black slip; he is buttoning his shirt. Raw, sensuous music accompanies their speech.*

WILLY Will you stop laughing? Will you stop?

THE WOMAN Aren't you going to answer the door? He'll wake the whole hotel.

WILLY I'm not expecting anybody.

THE WOMAN Whyn't you have another drink, honey, and stop being so damn self-centered?

WILLY I'm so lonely.

THE WOMAN You know you ruined me, Willy? From now on, whenever you come to the office, I'll see that you go right through to the buyers. No waiting at my desk any more, Willy. You ruined me.

WILLY That's nice of you to say that.

THE WOMAN Gee, you are self-centered! Why so sad? You are the saddest, self-centerdest soul I ever did see-saw. *(She laughs. He kisses her)* Come on inside, drummer boy. It's silly to be dressing in the middle of the night. *(As knocking is heard)* Aren't you going to answer the door?

WILLY They're knocking on the wrong door.

THE WOMAN But I felt the knocking. And he heard us talking in here. Maybe the hotel's on fire!

WILLY *(his terror rising)* It's a mistake.

THE WOMAN Then tell him to go away!

WILLY There's nobody there.

THE WOMAN It's gettin on my nerves, Willy. There's somebody standing out there and it's getting on my nerves!

WILLY *(pushing her away from him)* All right, stay in the bathroom here, and don't come out. I think there's a law in Massachusetts about it, so don't come out. It may be that new room clerk. He looked very mean. So don't come out. It's a mistake, there's no fire.

The knocking is heard again. He takes a few steps away from her, and she vanishes into the wing. The light follows him, and now he is facing YOUNG BIFF, *who carries a suitcase.* BIFF *steps toward him. The music is gone.*

BIFF Why didn't you answer?

WILLY Biff! What are you doing in Boston?

BIFF Why didn't you answer? I've been knocking for five minutes, I called you on the phone—

WILLY I just heard you. I was in the bathroom and had the door shut. Did anything happen home?

BIFF Dad—I let you down.

WILLY What do you mean?

BIFF Dad . . .

WILLY Biffo, what's this about? *(Putting his arm around* BIFF*)* Come on, let's go downstairs and get you a malted.

BIFF Dad, I flunked math.

WILLY Not for the term?

BIFF The term. I haven't got enough credits to graduate.

WILLY You mean to say Bernard wouldn't give you the answers?

BIFF He did, he tried, but I only got a sixty-one.

WILLY And they wouldn't give you four points?

BIFF Birnbaum refused absolutely. I begged him, Pop, but he won't give me those points. You gotta talk to him before they close the school. Because if he saw the kind of man you are, and you just talked to him in your way, I'm sure he'd come through for me. The class came right before practice, see, and I didn't go enough. Would you talk to him? He'd like you, Pop. You know the way you could talk.

WILLY You're on. We'll drive right back.

BIFF Oh, Dad, good work! I'm sure he'll change it for you!

WILLY Go downstairs and tell the clerk I'm checkin' out. Go right down.

BIFF Yes, sir, See, the reason he hates me, Pop—one day he was late for class so I got up at the blackboard and imitated him. I crossed my eyes and talked with a lithp.

WILLY *(laughing)* You did? The kids like it?

BIF They nearly died laughing!

WILLY Yeah? What'd you do?

BIFF The thquare root of thixthy twee is . . . *(*WILLY *burst out laughing;* BIFF *joins him)* And in the middle of it he walked in!

WILLY *laughs and* THE WOMAN *joins in offstage.*

WILLY *(without hesitation)* Hurry downstairs and—

BIFF   Somebody in there?

WILLY   No, that was next door.

THE WOMAN *laughs offstage.*

BIFF   Somebody got in your bathroom!

WILLY   No, it's the next room, there's a party—

THE WOMAN *(enters, laughing. She lisps this)*   Can I come in? There's something in the bathtub, Willy, and it's moving!

WILLY *looks at* BIFF, *who is staring open-mouthed and horrified at* THE WOMAN.

WILLY   Ah—you better go back to your room. They must be finished painting by now. They're painting her room so I let her take a shower here. Go back, go back . . . *(He pushes her)*

THE WOMAN *(resisting)*   But I've got to get dressed, Willy, I can't—

WILLY   Get out of here! Go back, go back . . . *(Suddenly striving for the ordinary)* This is Miss Francis, Biff, she's a buyer. They're painting her room. Go back, Miss Francis, go back . . .

THE WOMAN   But my clothes, I can't go out naked in the hall!

BIFF *slowly sits down on his suitcase as the argument continues offstage.*

THE WOMAN   Where's my stockings? You promised me stockings, Willy!

WILLY   I have no stockings here!

THE WOMAN   You had two boxes of size nine sheers for me, and I want them!

WILLY   Here, for God's sake, will you get outa here!

THE WOMAN *(enters holding a box of stockings)*   I just hope there's nobody in the hall. That's all I hope. *(To* BIFF*)* Are you football or baseball?

BIFF   Football.

THE WOMAN *(angry, humiliated)*   That's me too. G'night. *(She snatches her clothes from* WILLY, *and walks out)*

WILLY *(after a pause)*   Well, better get going. I want to get to the school first thing in the morning. Get my suits out of the closet. I'll get my valise. *(BIFF *doesn't move*)* What's the matter? *(BIFF *remains motionless, tears falling*)* She's a buyer. Buys for J. H. Simmons. She lives down the hall—they're painting. You don't imagine— *(He breaks off. After a pause)* Now listen, pal, she's just a buyer. She sees merchandise in her room and they have to keep it looking just so . . . *(Pause. Assuming command)* All right, get my suits. *(BIFF *doesn't move*)* Now stop crying and do as I say. I gave you an order. Biff, I gave you an order! Is that what you do when I give you an order? How dare you cry! *(Putting his arm around* BIFF*)* Now look, Biff, when you grow up you'll understand about these things. You mustn't —you mustn't overemphasize a thing like this. I'll see Birnbaum first thing in the morning.

BIFF   Never mind.

WILLY *(getting down beside* BIFF*)*   Never mind! He's going to give you those points. I'll see to it.

BIFF   He wouldn't listen to you.

WILLY   He certainly will listen to me. You need those points for the U. of Virginia.

BIFF   I'm not going there.

WILLY   Yeh? If I can't get him to change that mark you'll make it up in summer school. You've got all summer to—

BIFF *(his weeping breaking from him)* Dad . . .

WILLY *(infected by it)* Oh, my boy . . .

BIFF Dad . . .

WILLY She's nothing to me, Biff. I was lonely, I was terribly lonely.

BIFF You—you gave her Mama's stockings! *(His tears break through and he rises to go)*

WILLY *(grabbing for BIFF)* I gave you an order!

BIFF Don't touch me, you—liar!

WILLY Apologize for that!

BIFF You fake! You phony little fake! You fake! *(Overcome, he turns quickly and weeping fully goes out with his suitcase.* WILLY *is left on the floor on his knees)*

WILLY I gave you an order! Biff, come back here or I'll beat you! Come back here! I'll whip you!

STANLEY comes quickly in from the right and stands in front of WILLY.

WILLY *(shouts at STANLEY)* I gave you an order . . .

STANLEY Hey, lets pick it up, pick it up, Mr. Loman. *(He helps* WILLY *to his feet)* Your boys left with the chippies. They said they'll see you home.

A second waiter watches some distance away.

WILLY But we were supposed to have dinner together.

Music is heard, WILLY's *theme.*

STANLEY Can you make it?

WILLY I'll—sure, I can make it. *(Suddenly concerned about his clothes)* Do I—I look all right?

STANLEY Sure, you look all right. *(He flicks a speck off* WILLY's *lapel)*

WILLY Here—here's a dollar.

STANLEY Oh, your son paid me. It's all right.

WILLY *(putting it in* STANLEY's *hand)* No, take it. You're a good boy.

STANLEY Oh, no, you don't have to . . .

WILLY Here—here's some more, I don't need it any more. *(After a slight pause)* Tell me—is there a seed store in the neighborhood?

STANLEY Seeds? You mean like to plant?

As WILLY *turns,* STANLEY *slips the money back into his jacket pocket.*

WILLY Yes. Carrots, peas . . .

STANLEY Well, there's hardware stores on Sixth Avenue, but it may be too late now.

WILLY *(anxiously)* Oh, I'd better hurry. I've got to get some seeds. *(He starts off to the right)* I've got to get some seeds, right away. Nothing's planted. I don't have a thing in the ground.

WILLY *hurries out as the light goes down.* STANLEY *moves over to the right after him, watches him off. The other waiter has been staring at* WILLY.

STANLEY *(to the waiter)* Well, whatta you looking at?

The waiter picks up the chairs and moves off right. STANLEY *takes the table and follows him. The light fades on this area. There is a long pause, the sound of the flute coming over. The light gradually rises on the kitchen, which is empty.* HAPPY *appears at the door of the house, followed by* BIFF. HAPPY *is carrying a large bunch of long-*

stemmed roses. He enters the kitchen, looks around for LINDA. *Not seeing her, he turns to* BIFF, *who is just outside the house door, and makes a gesture with his hands, indicating "Not here, I guess." He looks into the living-room and freezes. Inside,* LINDA, *unseen, is seated,* WILLY'S *coat on her lap. She rises ominously and quietly and moves toward* HAPPY, *who backs up into the kitchen, afraid.*

HAPPY   Hey, what're you doing up? *(*LINDA *says nothing but moves toward him implacably)* Where's Pop? *(He keeps backing to the right, and now* LINDA *is in full view in the doorway to the living-room)* Is he sleeping?

LINDA   Where were you?

HAPPY *(trying to laugh it off)*   We met two girls, Mom, very fine types. Here, we brought you some flowers. *(Offering them to her)* Put them in your room, Ma.

She knocks them to the floor at BIFF'S *feet. He has now come inside and closed the door behind him. She stares at* BIFF, *silent.*

HAPPY   Now what'd you do that for? Mom, I want you to have some flowers—

LINDA *(cutting* HAPPY *off, violently to* BIFF)   Don't you care whether he lives or dies?

HAPPY *(going to the stairs)*   Come upstairs, Biff.

BIFF *(with a flare of disgust, to* HAPPY)   Go away from me! *(To* LINDA)   What do you mean, lives or dies? Nobody's dying around here, pal.

LINDA   Get out of my sight! Get out of here!

BIFF   I wanna see the boss.

LINDA   You're not going near him!

BIFF   Where is he? *(He moves into the living-room and* LINDA *follows)*

LINDA *(shouting after* BIFF)   You invite him for dinner. He looks forward to it all day—*(*BIFF *appears in his parents' bedroom, looks around, and exits)*—and then you desert him there. There's no stranger you'd do that to!

HAPPY   Why? He had a swell time with us. Listen, when I—*(*LINDA *comes back into the kitchen)*—desert him I hope I don't outlive the day!

LINDA   Get out of here!

HAPPY   Now look, Mom . . .

LINDA   Did you have to go to women tonight? You and your lousy rotten whores!

BIFF *re-enters the kitchen.*

HAPPY   Mom, all we did was follow Biff around trying to cheer him up! *(To* BIFF)   Boy, what a night you gave me!

LINDA   Get out of here, both of you, and don't come back! I don't want you tormenting him any more. Go on now, get your things together! *(To* BIFF)   You can sleep in his apartment. *(She starts to pick up the flowers and stops herself)* Pick up this stuff, I'm not your maid any more. Pick it up, you bum, you!

HAPPY *turns his back to her in refusal.* BIFF *slowly moves over and gets down on his knees, picking up the flowers.*

LINDA   You're a pair of animals! Not one, not another living soul would have had the cruelty to walk out on that man in a restaurant!

BIFF *(not looking at her)*   Is that what he said?

LINDA   He didn't have to say anything. He was so humiliated he nearly limped when he came in.

HAPPY   But, Mom, he had a great time with us—

BIFF *(cutting him off violently)*   Shut up!

Without another word, HAPPY *goes upstairs.*

LINDA   You! You didn't even go in to see if he was all right!

BIFF *(still on the floor in front of* LINDA, *the flowers in his hand; with self-loathing)*   No. Didn't. Didn't do a damned thing. How do you like that, heh? Left him babbling in a toilet.

LINDA   You louse. You . . .

BIFF   Now you hit it on the nose! *(He gets up, throws the flowers in the wastebasket)* The scum of the earth, and you're looking at him!

LINDA   Get out of here!

BIFF   I gotta talk to the boss, Mom. Where is he?

LINDA   You're not going near him. Get out of this house!

BIFF *(with absolute assurance, determination)*   No. We're gonna have an abrupt conversation, him and me.

LINDA   You're not talking to him!

Hammering is heard from outside the house, off right. BIFF *turns toward the noise.*

LINDA *(suddenly pleading)*   Will you please leave him alone?

BIFF   What's he doing out there?

LINDA   He's planting the garden!

BIFF *(quietly)*   Now? Oh, my God!

BIFF *moves outside,* LINDA *following. The light dies down on them and comes up on the center of the apron as* WILLY *walks into it. He is carrying a flashlight, a hoe, and a handful of seed packets. He raps the top of the hoe sharply to fix it firmly, and then moves to the left, measuring off the distance with his foot. He holds the flashlight to look at the seed packets, reading off the instructions. He is in the blue of night.*

WILLY   Carrots . . . quarter-inch apart. Rows . . . one-foot rows. *(He measures it off)* One foot. *(He puts down a package and measures off)* Beets. *(He puts down another package and measures again)* Lettuce. *(He reads the package, puts it down)* One foot—*(He breaks off as* BEN *appears at the right and moves slowly down to him)* What a proposition, ts, ts. Terrific, terrific. 'Cause she's suffered, Ben, the woman has suffered. You understand me? A man can't go out the way he came in, Ben, a man has got to add up to something. You can't, you can't—*(*BEN *moves toward him as though to interrupt)* You gotta consider, now. Don't answer so quick. Remember, it's a guaranteed twenty-thousand-dollar proposition. Now look, Ben, I want you to go through the ins and outs of this thing with me. I've got nobody to talk to, Ben, and the woman has suffered, you hear me?

BEN *(standing still, considering)*   What's the proposition?

WILLY   It's twenty thousand dollars on the barrelhead. Guaranteed, gilt-edged, you understand?

BEN   You don't want to make a fool of yourself. They might not honor the policy.

WILLY   How can they dare refuse? Didn't I work like a coolie to meet every premium on the nose? And now they don't pay off? Impossible!

BEN   It's called a cowardly thing, William.

WILLY   Why? Does it take more guts to stand here the rest of my life ringing up a zero?

BEN *(yielding)*   That's a point, William. *(He moves, thinking, turns)* And twenty thousand—that *is* something one can feel with the hand, it is there.

958   *Death of a Salesman*

WILLY *(now assured, with rising power)* Oh, Ben, that's the whole beauty of it! I see it like a diamond, shining in the dark, hard and rough, that I can pick up and touch in my hand. Not like—like an appointment! This would not be another damned-fool appointment, Ben, and it changes all the aspects. Because he thinks I'm nothing, see, and so he spites me. But the funeral—*(Straightening up)* Ben, that funeral will be massive! They'll come from Maine, Massachusetts, Vermont, New Hampshire! All the old-timers with the strange license plates—that boy will be thunderstruck, Ben, because he never realized—I am known! Rhode Island, New York, New Jersey—I am known, Ben, and he'll see it with his eyes once and for all. He'll see what I am, Ben! He's in for a shock, that boy!

BEN *(coming down to the edge of the garden)* He'll call you a coward.

WILLY *(suddenly fearful)* No, that would be terrible.

BEN Yes. And a damned fool.

WILLY No, no, he mustn't, I won't have that! *(He is broken and desperate)*

BEN He'll hate you, William.

The gay music of the boys is heard.

WILLY Oh, Ben, how do we get back to all the great times? Used to be so full of light, and comradeship, the sleigh-riding in winter, and the ruddiness on his cheeks. And always some kind of good news coming up, always something nice coming up ahead. And never even let me carry the valises in the house, and si-monizing, simonizing that little red car! Why, why can't I give him something and not have him hate me?

BEN Let me think about it. *(He glances at his watch)* I still have a little time. Remarkable proposition, but you've got to be sure you're not making a fool of yourself.

BEN *drifts off upstage and goes out of sight.* BIFF *comes down from the left.*

WILLY *(suddenly conscious of* BIFF, *turns and looks up at him, then begins picking up the packages of seeds in confusion)* Where the hell is that seed? *(Indignantly)* You can't see nothing out here! They boxed in the whole goddam neighborhood!

BIFF There are people all around here. Don't you realize that?

WILLY I'm busy. Don't bother me.

BIFF *(taking the hoe from* WILLY*)* I'm saying good-by to you, Pop. *(*WILLY *looks at him, silent, unable to move)* I'm not coming back any more.

WILLY You're not going to see Oliver tomorrow?

BIFF I've got no appointment, Dad.

WILLY He put his arm around you, and you've got no appointment?

BIFF Pop, get this now, will you? Everytime I've left it's been a fight that sent me out of here. Today I realized something about myself and I tried to explain it to you and I—I think I'm just not smart enough to make any sense out of it for you. To hell with whose fault it is or anything like that. *(He takes* WILLY'S *arm)* Let's just wrap it up, heh? Come on in, we'll tell Mom. *(He gently tries to pull* WILLY *to left)*

WILLY *(frozen, immobile, with guilt in his voice)* No, I don't want to see her.

BIFF Come on! *(He pulls again, and* WILLY *tries to pull away)*

WILLY *(highly nervous)* No, no, I don't want to see her.

BIFF *(tries to look into* WILLY'S *face, as if to find the answer there)* Why don't you want to see her?

WILLY *(more harshly now)* Don't bother me, will you?

BIFF   What do you mean, you don't want to see her? You don't want them calling you yellow, do you? This isn't your fault; it's me, I'm a bum. Now come inside! (WILLY *strains to get away*) Did you hear what I said to you?

WILLY *pulls away and quickly goes by himself into the house.* BIFF *follows.*

LINDA *(to* WILLY*)*   Did you plant, dear?

BIFF *(at the door, to* LINDA*)*   All right, we had it out. I'm going and I'm not writing any more.

LINDA *(going to* WILLY *in the kitchen)*   I think that's the best way, dear. 'Cause there's no use drawing it out, you'll just never get along.

WILLY *doesn't respond.*

BIFF   People ask where I am and what I'm doing, you don't know, and you don't care. That way it'll be off your mind and you can start brightening up again. All right? That clears it, doesn't it? *(*WILLY *is silent, and* BIFF *goes to him)* You gonna wish me luck, scout? *(He extends his hand)* What do you say?

LINDA   Shake his hand, Willy.

WILLY *(turning to her, seething with hurt)*   There's no necessity to mention the pen at all, y'know.

BIFF *(gently)*   I've got no appointment, Dad.

WILLY *(erupting fiercely)*   He put his arm around . . . ?

BIFF   Dad, you're never going to see what I am, so what's the use of arguing? If I strike oil I'll send you a check. Meantime forget I'm alive.

WILLY *(to* LINDA*)*   Spite, see?

BIFF   Shake hands, Dad.

WILLY   Not my hand.

BIFF   I was hoping not to go this way.

WILLY   Well, this is the way you're going. Good-by.

BIFF *looks at him a moment, then turns sharply and goes to the stairs.*

WILLY *(stops him with)*   May you rot in hell if you leave this house!

BIFF *(turning)*   Exactly what is it that you want from me?

WILLY   I want you to know, on the train, in the mountains, in the valleys, wherever you go, that you cut down your life for spite!

BIFF   No, no.

WILLY   Spite, spite, is the word of your undoing! And when you're down and out, remember what did it. When you're rotting somewhere beside the railroad tracks, remember, and don't you dare blame it on me!

BIFF   I'm not blaming it on you!

WILLY   I won't take the rap for this, you hear?

HAPPY *comes down the stairs and stands on the bottom step, watching.*

BIFF   That's just what I'm telling you!

WILLY *(sinking into a chair at the table, with full accusation)*   You're trying to put a knife in me—don't think I don't know what you're doing!

BIFF   All right, phony! Then let's lay it on the line. *(He whips the rubber tube out of his pocket and puts it on the table)*

HAPPY   You crazy—

LINDA   Biff! *(She moves to grab the hose, but* BIFF *holds it down with his hand)*

BIFF   Leave it there! Don't move it!

WILLY *(not looking at it)*   What is that?

BIFF   You know goddam will what that is.

WILLY *(caged, wanting to escape)*   I never saw that.

BIFF   You saw it. The mice didn't bring it into the cellar! What is this supposed to do, make a hero out of you? This supposed to make me sorry for you?

WILLY   Never heard of it.

BIFF   There'll be no pity for you, you hear it? No pity!

WILLY *(To* LINDA*)*   You hear the spite!

BIFF   No, you're going to hear the truth—what you are and what I am!

LINDA   Stop it!

WILLY   Spite!

HAPPY *(coming down toward* BIFF*)*   You cut it now!

BIFF *(To* HAPPY*)*   The man don't know who we are! The man is gonna know! *(To* WILLY*)* We never told the truth for ten minutes in this house!

HAPPY   We always told the truth!

BIFF *(turning on him)*   You big blow, are you the assistant buyer? You're one of the two assistants to the assistant, aren't you?

HAPPY   Well, I'm practically—

BIFF   You're practically full of it! We all are! And I'm through with it. *(To* WILLY*)* Now hear this, Willy, this is me.

WILLY   I know you!

BIFF   You know why I had no address for three months? I stole a suit in Kansas City and I was in jail. *(To* LINDA, *who is sobbing)* Stop crying. I'm through with it.

LINDA *turns away from them, her hands covering her face.*

WILLY   I suppose that's my fault!

BIFF   I stole myself out of every good job since high school!

WILLY   And whose fault is that?

BIFF   And I never got anywhere because you blew me so full of hot air I could never stand taking orders from anybody! That's whose fault it is!

WILLY   I hear that!

LINDA   Don't, Biff!

BIFF   It's goddam time you heard that! I had to be boss big shot in two weeks, and I'm through with it!

WILLY   Then hang yourself! For spite, hang yourself!

BIFF   No! Nobody's hanging himself, Willy! I ran down eleven flights with a pen in my hand today. And suddenly I stopped, you hear me? And in the middle of that office building, do you hear this? I stopped in the middle of that building and I saw—the sky. I saw the things that I love in this world. The work and the food and time to sit and smoke. And I looked at the pen and said to myself, what the hell am I grabbing this for? Why am I trying to become what I don't want to be? What am I doing in an office, making a contemptuous, begging fool of myself, when all I want is out there, waiting for me the minute I say I know who I am! Why can't I say that, Willy? *(He tries to make* WILLY *face him, but* WILLY *pulls away and moves to the left)*

WILLY *(with hatred, threateningly)*   The door of your life is wide open!

BIFF   Pop! I'm a dime a dozen, and so are you!

WILLY *(turning on him now in an uncontrolled outburst)*   I am not a dime a dozen! I am Willy Loman, and you are Biff Loman!

BIFF *starts for* WILLY, *but is blocked by* HAPPY. *In his fury,* BIFF *seems on the verge of attacking his father.*

BIFF   I am not a leader of men, Willy, and neither are you. You were never anything but a hard-working drummer who landed in the ash can like all the rest of them! I'm one dollar an hour, Willy! I tried seven states and couldn't raise it. A buck an hour! Do you gather my meaning? I'm not bringing home any prizes any more, and you're going to stop waiting for me to bring them home!

WILLY *(directly to* BIFF*)*   You vengeful, spiteful mut!

BIFF *breaks from* HAPPY. WILLY, *in fright, starts up the stairs.* BIFF *grabs him.*

BIFF *(at the peak of his fury)*   Pop, I'm nothing! I'm nothing, Pop. Can't you understand that? There's no spite in it any more. I'm just what I am, that's all.

BIFF's *fury has spent itself, and he breaks down, sobbing, holding on to* WILLY, *who dumbly fumbles for* BIFF's *face.*

WILLY *(astonished)*   What're you doing? What're you doing? *(To* LINDA*)* Why is he crying?

BIFF *(crying, broken)*   Will you let me go, for Christ's sake? Will you take that phony dream and burn it before something happens? *(Struggling to contain himself, he pulls away and moves to the stairs)* I'll go in the morning. Put him—put him to bed.

(Exhausted, BIFF *moves up the stairs to his room)*

WILLY *(after a long pause, astonished, elevated)*   Isn't that—isn't that remarkable? Biff—he likes me!

LINDA   He loves you, Willy!

HAPPY *(deeply moved)*   Always did, Pop.

WILLY   Oh, Biff! *(Staring wildly)* He cried! Cried to me. *(He is choking with his love, and now cries out his promise)* That boy—that boy is going to be magnificent!

BEN *appears in the light just outside the kitchen.*

BEN   Yes, outstanding, with twenty thousand behind him.

LINDA *(sensing the racing of his mind, fearfully, carefully)*   Now come to bed, Willy. It's all settled now.

WILLY *(finding it difficult not to rush out of the house)*   Yes, we'll sleep. Come on. Go to sleep, Hap.

BEN   And it does take a great kind of a man to crack the jungle.

In accents of dread, BEN's *idyllic music starts up.*

HAPPY *(his arm around* LINDA*)*   I'm getting married, Pop, don't forget it. I'm changing everything. I'm gonna run that department before the year is up. You'll see, Mom. *(He kisses her)*

BEN   The jungle is dark but full of diamonds, Willy.

WILLY *turns, moves, listening to* BEN.

LINDA   Be good. You're both good boys, just act that way, that's all.

HAPPY   'Night, Pop. *(He goes upstairs)*

LINDA *(to* WILLY*)* Come, dear.

BEN *(with greater force)*   One must go in to fetch a diamond out.

WILLY *(to* LINDA, *as he moves slowly along the edge of the kitchen, toward the door)* I just want to get settled down, Linda. Let me sit alone for a little.

LINDA *(almost uttering her fear)* I want you upstairs.

WILLY *(taking her in his arms)* In a few minutes, Linda. I couldn't sleep right now. Go on, you look awful tired. *(He kisses her)*

BEN Not like an appointment at all. A diamond is rough and hard to the touch.

WILLY Go on now. I'll be right up.

LINDA I think this is the only way, Willy.

WILLY Sure, it's the best thing.

BEN Best thing!

WILLY The only way. Everything is gonna be—go on, kid, get to bed. You look so tired.

LINDA Come right up.

WILLY Two minutes.

LINDA *goes into the living-room, then reappears in her bedroom.* WILLY *moves just outside the kitchen door.*

WILLY Loves me. *(Wonderingly)* Always loved me. Isn't that a remarkable thing? Ben, he'll worship me for it!

BEN *(with promise)* It's dark there, but full of diamonds.

WILLY Can you imagine that magnificence with twenty thousand dollars in his pocket?

LINDA *(calling from her room)* Willy! Come up!

WILLY *(calling into the kitchen)* Yes! Yes. Coming! It's very smart, you realize that, don't you, sweetheart? Even Ben sees it. I gotta go, baby. 'By! By! *(Going over to* BEN, *almost dancing)* Imagine? When the mail comes he'll be ahead of Bernard again!

BEN A perfect proposition all around.

WILLY Did you see how he cried to me? Oh, if I could kiss him, Ben!

BEN Time, William, time!

WILLY Oh, Ben, I always knew one way or another we were gonna make it, Biff and I!

BEN *(looking at his watch)* The boat. We'll be late. *(He moves slowly off into the darkness)*

WILLY *(elegiacally, turning to the house)* Now when you kick off, boy, I want a seventy-yard boot, and get right down the field under the ball, and when you hit, hit low and hit hard, because it's important, boy. *(He swings around and faces the audience)* There's all kinds of important people in the stands, and the first thing you know . . . *(Suddenly realizing he is alone)* Ben! Ben, where do I . . . ? *(He makes a sudden movement of search)* Ben, how do I . . . ?

LINDA *(calling)* Willy, you coming up?

WILLY *(uttering a gasp of fear, whirling about as if to quiet her)* Sh! *(He turns around as if to find his way; sounds, faces, voices, seem to be swarming in upon him and he flicks at them, crying)* Sh! Sh! *(Suddenly music, faint and high, stops him. It rises in intensity, almost to an unbearable scream. He goes up and down on his toes, and rushes off around the house)* Shhh!

LINDA Willy?

There is no answer. LINDA *waits.* BIFF *gets up off his bed. He is still in his clothes.* HAPPY *sits up.* BIFF *stands listening.*

LINDA *(with real fear)* Willy, answer me! Willy!

There is the sound of a car starting and moving away at full speed.

LINDA No!

BIFF *(rushing down the stairs)* Pop!

As the car speeds off, the music crashes down in a frenzy of sound, which becomes the soft pulsation of a single cello string. BIFF *slowly returns to his bedroom. He and* HAPPY *gravely don their jackets.* LINDA *slowly walks out of her room. The music has developed into a dead march. The leaves of day are appearing over everything.* CHARLEY *and* BERNARD, *somberly dressed, appear and knock on the kitchen door.* BIFF *and* HAPPY *slowly descend the stairs to the kitchen as* CHARLEY *and* BERNARD *enter. All stop a moment when* LINDA, *in clothes of mourning, bearing a little bunch of roses, comes through the draped doorway into the kitchen. She goes to* CHARLEY *and takes his arm. Now all move toward the audience, through the wall-line of the kitchen. At the limit of the apron,* LINDA *lays down the flowers, kneels, and sits back on her heels. All stare down at the grave.*

REQUIEM

CHARLEY It's getting dark, Linda.

LINDA *doesn't react. She stares at the grave.*

BIFF How about it, Mom? Better get some rest, heh? They'll be closing the gate soon.

LINDA *makes no move. Pause.*

HAPPY *(deeply angered)* He had no right to do that. There was no necessity for it. We would've helped him.

CHARLEY *(grunting)* Hmmm.

BIFF Come along, Mom.

LINDA Why didn't anybody come?

CHARLEY It was a very nice funeral.

LINDA But where are all the people he knew? Maybe they blame him.

CHARLEY Naa. It's a rough world, Linda. They wouldn't blame him.

LINDA I can't understand it. At this time especially. First time in thirty-five years we were just about free and clear. He only needed a little salary. He was even finished with the dentist.

CHARLEY No man only needs a little salary.

LINDA I can't understand it.

BIFF There were a lot of nice days. When he'd come home from a trip; or on Sundays, making the stoop; finishing the cellar; putting on the new porch; when he built the extra bathroom; and put up the garage. You know something, Charley, there's more of him in that front stoop than in all the sales he ever made.

CHARLEY Yeah. He was a happy man with a batch of cement.

LINDA He was so wonderful with his hands.

BIFF He had the wrong dreams. All, all, wrong.

HAPPY *(almost ready to fight* BIFF*)* Don't say that!

BIFF He never knew who he was.

CHARLEY *(stopping* HAPPY'S *movement and reply. To* BIFF*)* Nobody dast blame this man. You don't understand: Willy was a salesman. And for a salesman, there is no rock bottom to the life. He don't put a bolt to a nut, he don't tell you the law or give you medicine. He's a man way out there in the blue, riding on a smile and a shoeshine. And when they start not smiling back—that's an earthquake. And then you get yourself a couple of spots on your hat, and you're finished. Nobody dast blame this man. A salesman is got to dream, boy. It comes with the territory.

BIFF   Charley, the man didn't know who he was.

HAPPY *(infuriated)*   Don't say that!

BIFF   Why don't you come with me, Happy?

HAPPY   I'm not licked that easily. I'm staying right in this city, and I'm gonna beat this racket! *(He looks at BIFF, his chin set)* The Loman Brothers!

BIFF   I know who I am, kid.

HAPPY   All right, boy. I'm gonna show you and everybody else that Willy Loman did not die in vain. He had a good dream. It's the only dream you can have—to come out number-one man. He fought it out here, and this is where I'm gonna win it for him.

BIFF *(with a hopeless glance at HAPPY, bends toward his mother)*   Let's go, Mom.

LINDA   I'll be with you in a minute. Go on, Charley. *(He hesitates)* I want to, just for a minute. I never had a chance to say good-by.

CHARLEY *moves away, followed by* HAPPY. BIFF *remains a slight distance up and left of* LINDA. *She sits there, summoning herself. The flute begins, not far away, playing behind her speech.*

LINDA   Forgive me, dear. I can't cry. I don't know what it is, but I can't cry. I don't understand it. Why did you ever do that? Help me, Willy, I can't cry. It seems to me that you're just on another trip. I keep expecting you. Willy, dear, I can't cry. Why did you do it? I search and search and I search, and I can't understand it, Willy. I made the last payment on the house today. Today, dear. And there'll be nobody home. *(A sob rises in her throat)* We're free and clear. *(Sobbing more fully, released)* We're free. *(BIFF comes slowly toward her)* We're free . . . We're free . . .

BIFF *lifts her to her feet and moves out up right with her in his arms.* LINDA *sobs quietly.* BERNARD *and* CHARLEY *come together and follow them, followed by* HAPPY. *Only the music of the flute is left on the darkening stage as over the house the hard towers of the apartment buildings rise into sharp focus, and*

The Curtain Falls

Response Statement Assignments

1. Tragedies are traditionally about the fate of great individuals. What **text strategies** influence your interpreting this play as a tragedy?

2. What kind of social or political assumptions would probably lead you to argue that Willy Loman is not a tragic figure, not a victim of a harsh system, not someone to be pitied, but rather someone who has been immoral and inefficient and who therefore deserves his failure? Discuss your own view of Willy in relation to *your* political and social convictions.

3. The process of reading a play differs from that of reading many novels or short stories because you get so little actual analysis or third-person observation of a character. You have mainly only the character's own words and actions on which to base your evaluation. In short, you usually encounter more **gaps** in character description in a play than in a story. First, explore the different types of **strategies** you generally use to analyze characters in plays as opposed to stories. Then explore in detail the strategies you used (and the assumptions underlying them) to develop an opinion of Willy Loman.
4. Why do you think *Death of a Salesman* has been so popular a play? What in the dominant **ideology** of America over the past forty years has this play tapped into? To what extent do you personally believe this dominant ideology, and how does it affect your reading of the play?

EDWARD ALBEE (b. 1928)

The Sandbox

PLAYERS

THE YOUNG MAN, *25, a good-looking, well-built boy in a bathing suit*
MOMMY, *55, a well-dressed, imposing woman*
DADDY, *60, a small man; gray, thin*

GRANDMA, *86, a tiny, wizened woman with bright eyes*
THE MUSICIAN, *no particular age, but young would be nice*

NOTE. When, in the course of the play, MOMMY and DADDY call each other by these names, there should be no suggestion of regionalism. These names are of empty affection and point up the pre-senility and vacuity of their characters.

THE SCENE. *A bare stage, with only the following: Near the footlights, far stage-right, two simple chairs set side by side, facing the audience; near the footlights, far stage-left, a chair facing stage-right with a music stand before it; farther back, and stage-center, slightly elevated and raked, a large child's sandbox with a toy pail and shovel; the background is the sky, which alters from brightest day to deepest night.*
   At the beginning, it is brightest day; the YOUNG MAN *is alone on stage to the rear of the sandbox, and to one side. He is doing calisthenics; he does calisthenics until quite at the very end of the play. These calisthenics, employing the arms only, should suggest the beating and fluttering of wings. The* YOUNG MAN *is, after all, the Angel of Death.*

MOMMY *and* DADDY *enter from stage-left,* MOMMY *first.*

MOMMY *(motioning to* DADDY*)*   Well, here we are; this is the beach.
DADDY *(whining)*   I'm cold.
MOMMY *(dismissing him with a little laugh)*   Don't be silly; it's as warm as toast. Look at that nice young man over there: *he* doesn't think it's cold. *(Waves to the* YOUNG MAN*)* Hello.

YOUNG MAN *(with an endearing smile)* Hi!

MOMMY *(looking about)* This will do perfectly . . . don't you think so, Daddy? There's sand there . . . and the water beyond. What do you think, Daddy?

DADDY *(vaguely)* Whatever you say, Mommy.

MOMMY *(with the same little laugh)* Well, of course . . . whatever I say. Then, it's settled, is it?

DADDY *(shrugs)* She's *your* mother, not mine.

MOMMY *I* know she's my mother. What do you take me for? *(A pause)* All right, now; let's get on with it. *(She shouts into the wings, stage-left)* You! Out there! You can come in now.

The MUSICIAN *enters, seats himself in the chair, stage-left, places music on the music stand, is ready to play.* MOMMY *nods approvingly.*

MOMMY Very nice; very nice. Are you ready, Daddy? Let's go get Grandma.

DADDY Whatever you say, Mommy.

MOMMY *(leading the way out, stage-left)* Of course, whatever I say. *(To the* MUSICIAN*)* You can begin now.

The MUSICIAN *begins playing;* MOMMY *and* DADDY *exit, the* MUSICIAN, *all the while playing, nods to the* YOUNG MAN.

YOUNG MAN *(with the same endearing smile)* Hi!

After a moment, MOMMY *and* DADDY *re-enter, carrying* GRANDMA. *She is borne in by their hands under her armpits; she is quite rigid; her legs are drawn up; her feet do not touch the ground; the expression on her ancient face is that of puzzlement and fear.*

DADDY Where do we put her?

MOMMY *(the same little laugh)* Wherever I say, of course. Let me see . . . well . . . all right, over there . . . in the sandbox. *(Pause)* Well, what are you waiting for, Daddy? . . . The sandbox!

Together they carry GRANDMA *over to the sandbox and more or less dump her in.*

GRANDMA *(righting herself to a sitting position, her voice a cross between a baby's laugh and cry)* Ahhhhhh! Graaaaa!

DADDY *(dusting himself)* What do we do now?

MOMMY *(to the* MUSICIAN*)* You can stop now. *(The* MUSICIAN *stops. Back to* DADDY*)* What do you mean, what do we do now? We go over there and sit down, of course. *To the* YOUNG MAN*)* Hello there.

YOUNG MAN *(again smiling)* Hi!

MOMMY *and* DADDY *move to the chairs, stage-right, and sit down. A pause.*

GRANDMA *(same as before)* Ahhhhhh! Ah-haaaaaa! Graaaaaa!

DADDY Do you think . . . do you think she's . . . comfortable?

MOMMY *(impatiently)* How would I know?

DADDY *(pause)* What do we do now?

MOMMY *(as if remembering)* We . . . wait. We . . . sit here . . . and we wait . . . that's what we do.

DADDY *(after a pause)* Shall we talk to each other?

MOMMY *(with that little laugh; picking something off her dress)* Well, *you* can talk, if you want to . . . if you can think of anything to *say* . . . if you can think of any-thing *new.*

DADDY *(thinks)*   No . . . I suppose not.

MOMMY *(with a triumphant laugh)*   Of course not!

GRANDMA *(banging the toy shovel against the pail)*   Haaaaaa! Ah-haaaaaa!

MOMMY *(out over the audience)*   Be quiet, Grandma . . . just be quiet, and wait.

GRANDMA *throws a shovelful of sand at* MOMMY.

MOMMY *(still out over the audience)*   She's throwing sand at me! You stop that, Grandma; you stop throwing sand at Mommy! *(To* DADDY*)* She's throwing sand at me.

DADDY *looks around at* GRANDMA, *who screams at him.*

GRANDMA   GRAAAAA!

MOMMY   Don't look at her. Just . . . sit here . . . be very still . . . and wait. *(To the* MUSICIAN*)* You . . . uh . . . you go ahead and do whatever it is you do.

The MUSICIAN *plays.* MOMMY *and* DADDY *are fixed, staring out beyond the audi-ence.* GRANDMA *looks at them, looks at the* MUSICIAN, *looks at the sandbox, throws down the shovel.*

GRANDMA   Ah-haaaaaa! Graaaaaa! *(Looks for reaction; gets none. Now . . . directly to the audience)* Honestly! What a way to treat an old woman! Drag her out of the house . . . stick her in a car . . . bring her out here from the city . . . dump her in a pile of sand . . . and leave her here to set. I'm eighty-six years old! I was married when I was seventeen. To a farmer. He died when I was thirty. *(To the* MUSICIAN*)* Will you stop that, please? *(The* MUSICIAN *stops playing)* I'm a feeble old woman . . . how do you expect anybody to hear me over that peep! peep! peep! *(To herself)* There's no respect around here. *(To the* YOUNG MAN*)* There's no respect around here!

YOUNG MAN *(same smile)*   Hi!

GRANDMA *(after a pause, a mild double-take, continues, to the audience)*   My hus-band died when I was thirty *(indicates* MOMMY*)*, and I had to raise that big cow over there all by my lonesome. You can imagine what *that was like.* Lordy! *(To the* YOUNG MAN*)* Where'd they get *you?*

YOUNG MAN   Oh . . . I've been around for a while.

GRANDMA   I'll bet you have! Heh, heh, heh. Will you look at you!

YOUNG MAN *(flexing his muscles)*   Isn't that something? *(Continues his calisthen-ics)*

GRANDMA   Boy, oh boy; I'll say. Pretty good.

YOUNG MAN *(sweetly)*   I'll say.

GRANDMA   Where ya from?

YOUNG MAN   Southern California.

GRANDMA *(nodding)*   Figgers; figgers. What's your name, honey?

YOUNG MAN   I don't know . . .

GRANDMA *(to the audience)*   Bright, too!

YOUNG MAN   I mean . . . I mean, they haven't given me one yet . . . the studio . . .

GRANDMA *(giving him the once-over)*   You don't say . . . you don't say. Well . . . uh, I've got to talk some more . . . don't you go 'way.

YOUNG MAN   Oh, no.

GRANDMA *(turning her attention back to the audience)* Fine; fine. *Then, once more, back to the* YOUNG MAN*)* You're . . . you're an actor, hunh?

YOUNG MAN *(beaming)* Yes. I am.

GRANDMA *(to the audience again; shrugs)* I'm smart that way. *Anyhow,* I had to raise . . . *that* over there all by my lonesome; and what's next to her there . . . that's what she married. Rich? I tell you . . . money, money, money. They took me off the *farm* . . . which was real decent of them . . . and they moved me into the big town house with *them* . . . fixed a nice place for me under the stove . . . gave me an army blanket . . . and my own dish . . . my very own dish! So, what have I got to complain about? Nothing, of course. I'm not complaining. *(She looks up at the sky, shouts to someone off stage)* Shouldn't it be getting dark now, dear?

The lights dim; night comes on. The MUSICIAN *begins to play; it becomes deepest night. There are spots on all the players, including the* YOUNG MAN, *who is, of course, continuing his calisthenics.*

DADDY *(stirring)* It's nighttime.

MOMMY Shhhh. Be still . . . wait.

DADDY *(whining)* It's so hot.

MOMMY Shhhhhh. Be still . . . wait.

GRANDMA *(to herself)* That's better. Night. *(To the* MUSICIAN*)* Honey, do you play all through this part? *(The* MUSICIAN *nods.)* Well, keep it nice and soft; that's a good boy. *The* MUSICIAN *nods again; plays softly.)* That's nice.

There is an off-stage rumble.

DADDY *(starting)* What was that?

MOMMY *(beginning to weep)* It was nothing.

DADDY It was . . . it was . . . thunder . . . or a wave breaking . . . or something.

MOMMY *(whispering, through her tears)* It was an off-stage rumble . . . and you know what *that* means . . .

DADDY I forget . . .

MOMMY *(barely able to talk)* It means the time has come for poor Grandma . . . and I can't bear it!

DADDY *(vacantly)* I . . . suppose you've got to be brave.

GRANDMA *(mocking)* That's right, kid; be brave. You'll bear up; you'll get over it.

Another off-stage rumble . . . louder.

MOMMY Ohhhhhhhhhh . . . poor Grandma . . . poor Grandma . . .

GRANDMA *(to* MOMMY*)* I'm fine! I'm all right! It hasn't happened yet!

A violent off-stage rumble. All the lights go out, save the spot on the YOUNG MAN; *the* MUSICIAN *stops playing.*

MOMMY Ohhhhhhhhh . . . Ohhhhhhhhhh . . .

Silence.

GRANDMA Don't put the lights up yet . . . I'm not ready; I'm not quite ready. *(Silence)* All right, dear . . . I'm about done.

The lights come up again, to brightest day; the MUSICIAN *begins to play.* GRANDMA *is discovered, still in the sandbox, lying on her side, propped up on an elbow, half covered, busily shoveling sand over herself.*

GRANDMA *(muttering)* I don't know how I'm supposed to do anything with this goddam toy shovel . . .

DADDY Mommy! It's daylight!

MOMMY *(brightly)* So it is! Well! Our long night is over. We must put away our tears, take off our mourning . . . and face the future. It's our duty.

GRANDMA *(still shoveling; mimicking)* . . . take off our mourning . . . face the future . . . Lordy!

MOMMY *and* DADDY *rise, stretch.* MOMMY *waves to the* YOUNG MAN.

YOUNG MAN *(with that smile)* Hi!

GRANDMA *plays dead.* (!) MOMMY *and* DADDY *go over to look at her; she is a little more than half buried in the sand; the toy shovel is in her hands, which are crossed on her breast.*

MOMMY *(before the sandbox; shaking her head)* Lovely! It's . . . it's hard to be sad . . . she looks . . . so happy. *(With pride and conviction)* It pays to do things well. *(To the* MUSICIAN*)* All right, you can stop now, if you want to. I mean, stay around for a swim, or something, it's all right with us. *(She sighs heavily.)* Well, Daddy . . . off we go.

DADDY Brave Mommy!

MOMMY Brave Daddy!

They exit, stage-left.

GRANDMA *(after they leave; lying quite still)* It pays to do things well . . . Boy, oh boy! *(She tries to sit up)* . . . well, kids . . . *(but she finds she can't)* . . . I . . . I can't get up. I . . . I can't move . . .

The YOUNG MAN *stops his calisthenics, nods to the* MUSICIAN, *walks over to* GRANDMA, *kneels down by the sandbox.*

GRANDMA I . . . can't move . . .

YOUNG MAN Shhhhh . . . be very still . . .

GRANDMA I . . . I can't move . . .

YOUNG MAN Uh . . . ma'am; I . . . I have a line here.

GRANDMA Oh, I'm sorry, sweetie; you go right ahead.

YOUNG MAN I am . . . uh . . .

GRANDMA Take your time, dear.

YOUNG MAN *(prepares; delivers the line like a real amateur)* I am the Angel of Death. I am . . . uh . . . I am come for you.

GRANDMA What . . . wha . . . *(then, with resignation . . . ohhhh . . . ohhhh, I see.*

The YOUNG MAN *bends over, kisses* GRANDMA *gently on the forehead.*

GRANDMA *(her eyes closed, her hands folded on her breast again, the shovel between her hands, a sweet smile on her face)* Well . . . that was very nice, dear . . .

YOUNG MAN *(still kneeling)* Shhhhh . . . be still . . .

GRANDMA What I meant was . . . you did that very well, dear . . .

YOUNG MAN *(blushing)* . . . oh . . .

GRANDMA No; I mean it. You've got that . . . you've got a quality.

YOUNG MAN *(with his endearing smile)* Oh . . . thank you; thank you very much . . . ma'am.

GRANDMA *(slowly; softly—as the* YOUNG MAN *puts his hands on top of* GRANDMA'S*)*
You're . . . you're welcome . . . dear.

Tableau. The MUSICIAN *continues to play as the curtain slowly comes down.*

Response Statement Assignments

1. How do you respond to reading a play in which a young boy performs calisthenics throughout most of the play? What do the "calisthenics" remind you of? What do you think about the boy and his actions? Why do you respond as you do?
2. How do you react to Grandma's description of what her daughter and son-in-law have done for her? Do you believe her? Do you believe Mommy's concern when she says "It means the time has come for poor Grandma . . . and I can't bear it"?
3. Does all of this strike you as bizarre, as absurd, as funny, as serious—or perhaps some mixture of all of these? Does the way in which the characters speak, the actors move, and the set is focused on a sandbox surprise you?
4. What, in your own experience, does the play remind you of?
5. What **reading strategies,** in your opinion, best served to **naturalize** the play's action?
6. How do you go about interpreting the significance of any one of the characters in this play?
7. Like a number of other dramas in this anthology (for example, *Six Characters in Search of an Author*), this play calls attention to itself as *a play,* in other words, it breaks the illusion that it is a realistic event. How do you respond to this **text strategy?** Does the fact that you have other plays like this in your **literary repertoire** change your reading strategies of this play in any way?
8. Do you feel you have a greater or a lesser range of interpretive possibilities with a play like this one that does not pretend to be realistic? Explain.
9. If you have read more realistic plays, compare and contrast the strategies you use to interpret the "absurdist" characters here with realistic characters (such as Willy Loman in *Death of a Salesman* or Ruth Younger in *Raisin in the Sun*).
10. What particular aspects of twentieth-century American culture and **ideology** create conditions in which plays like *The Sandbox* can be produced? Does this play speak directly to any interests of yours?

LORRAINE HANSBERRY (1930–1965)

A Raisin in the Sun

To Mama: in gratitude for the dream

CHARACTERS

RUTH YOUNGER

TRAVIS YOUNGER

WALTER LEE YOUNGER *(Brother)*

BENEATHA YOUNGER

LENA YOUNGER *(Mama)*

JOSEPH ASAGAI

GEORGE MURCHISON

KARL LINDNER

BOBO

MOVING MEN

The action of the play is set in Chicago's Southside, sometime between World War II and the present.

ACT I
SCENE I. *Friday morning*
SCENE II. *The following morning*

ACT II
SCENE I. *Later, the same day*
SCENE II. *Friday night, a few weeks later*
SCENE III. *Saturday, moving day, one week later*

ACT III
An hour later

> What happens to a dream deferred?
> Does it dry up
> Like a raisin in the sun?
> Or fester like a sore—
>
> And then run?
> Does it stink like rotten meat?
> Or crust and sugar over—
> Like a syrupy sweet?
>
> Maybe it just sags
> Like a heavy load.
>
> *Or does it explode?*

Langston Hughes[1]

ACT I

SCENE I. *The Younger living room would be a comfortable and well-ordered room if it were not for a number of indestructible contradictions to this state of being. Its furnishings are typical and undistinguished and their primary feature now is that they*

---

[1] From "Dream Deferred." Copyright 1951 by Langston Hughes. Reprinted from *The Panther and the Lash* by Langston Hughes, by permission of Alfred A. Knopf, Inc.

have clearly had to accommodate the living of too many people for too many years—
and they are tired. Still, we can see that at some time, a time probably no longer remembered by the family (except perhaps for MAMA), the furnishings of this room
were actually selected with care and love and even hope—and brought to this apartment and arranged with taste and pride.

That was a long time ago. Now the once loved pattern of the couch upholstery has
to fight to show itself from under acres of crocheted doilies and couch covers which
have themselves finally come to be more important than the upholstery. And here a
table or a chair has been moved to disguise the worn places in the carpet; but the carpet has fought back by showing its weariness, with depressing uniformity, elsewhere
on its surface.

Weariness has, in fact, won in this room. Everything has been polished, washed,
sat on, used, scrubbed too often. All pretenses but living itself have long since vanished from the very atmosphere of this room.

Moreover, a section of this room, for it is not really a room unto itself, though the
landlord's lease would make it seem so, slopes backward to provide a small kitchen
area, where the family prepares the meals that are eaten in the living room proper,
which must also serve as dining room. The single window that has been provided for
these "two" rooms is located in this kitchen area. The sole natural light the family
may enjoy in the course of a day is only that which fights its way through this little
window.

At left, a door leads to a bedroom which is shared by MAMA and her daughter,
BENEATHA. At right, opposite, is a second room (which in the beginning of the life of
this apartment was probably a breakfast room), which serves as a bedroom for
WALTER and his wife, RUTH.

Time: Sometime between World War II and the present.

Place: Chicago's Southside.

At rise: It is morning dark in the living room. TRAVIS is asleep on the make-down
bed at center. An alarm clock sounds from within the bedroom at right, and presently
RUTH enters from that room and closes the door behind her. She crosses sleepily toward the window. As she passes her sleeping son she reaches down and shakes him a
little. At the window she raises the shade and a dusky Southside morning light comes
in feebly. She fills a pot with water and puts it on to boil. She calls to the boy, between
yawns, in a slightly muffled voice.

RUTH is about thirty. We can see that she was a pretty girl, even exceptionally so,
but now it is apparent that life has been little that she expected, and disappointment
has already begun to hang in her face. In a few years, before thirty-five even, she will
be known among her people as a "settled woman."

She crosses to her son and gives him a good, final, rousing shake.

RUTH   Come on now, boy, it's seven thirty! *(Her son sits up at last, in a stupor of
sleepiness.)* I say hurry up, Travis! You ain't the only person in the world got to use
a bathroom! *(The child, a sturdy, handsome boy of ten or eleven, drags himself out
of the bed and almost blindly takes his towels and "today's clothes" from drawers
and a closet and goes out to the bathroom, which is in an outside hall and which is
shared by another family or families on the same floor. RUTH crosses to the bedroom door at right and opens it and calls in to her husband.)* Walter Lee! . . . It's
after seven thirty! Lemme see you do some waking up in there now! *(She waits.)*
You better get up from there, man! It's after seven thirty I tell you. *(She waits*

again.) All right, you just go ahead and lay there and next thing you know Travis be finished and Mr. Johnson'll be in there and you'll be fussing and cussing round here like a mad man! And be late too! *(She waits, at the end of patience.)* Walter Lee—it's time for you to get up!

She waits another second and then starts to go into the bedroom, but is apparently satisfied that her husband has begun to get up. She stops, pulls the door to, and returns to the kitchen area. She wipes her face with a moist cloth and runs her fingers through her sleep disheveled hair in a vain effort and ties an apron around her housecoat. The bedroom door at right opens and her husband stands in the doorway in his pajamas, which are rumpled and mismated. He is a lean, intense young man in his middle thirties, inclined to quick nervous movements and erratic speech habits—and always in his voice there is a quality of indictment.

WALTER   Is he out yet?

RUTH   What you mean *out?* He ain't hardly got in there good yet.

WALTER *(wandering in, still more oriented to sleep than to a new day)*   Well, what was you doing all that yelling for if I can't even get in there yet? *(Stopping and thinking)* Check coming today?

RUTH   They *said* Saturday and this is just Friday and I hopes to God you ain't going to get up here first thing this morning and start talking to me 'bout no money—'cause I 'bout don't want to hear it.

WALTER   Something the matter with you this morning?

RUTH   No—I'm just sleepy as the devil. What kind of eggs you want?

WALTER   Not scrambled. *(*RUTH *starts to scramble eggs.)* Paper come? *(*RUTH points impatiently to the rolled up Tribune *on the table, and he gets it and spreads it out and vaguely reads the front page.)* Set off another bomb yesterday.

RUTH *(maximum indifference)*   Did they?

WALTER *(looking up)*   What's the matter with you?

RUTH   Ain't nothing the matter with me. And don't keep asking me that this morning.

WALTER   Ain't nobody bothering you. *(Reading the news of the day absently again)* Say Colonel McCormick is sick.

RUTH *(affecting tea-party interest)*   Is he now? Poor thing.

WALTER *(sighing and looking at his watch)*   Oh, me. *(He waits.)* Now what is that boy doing in that bathroom all this time? He just going to have to start getting up earlier. I can't be being late to work on account of him fooling around in there.

RUTH *(turning on him)*   Oh, no he ain't going to be getting up no earlier no such thing! It ain't his fault that he can't get to bed no earlier nights 'cause he got a bunch of crazy good-for-nothing clowns sitting up running their mouths in what is supposed to be his bedroom after ten o'clock at night. . . .

WALTER   That's what you mad about, ain't it? The things I want to talk about with my friends just couldn't be important in your mind, could they?

He rises and finds a cigarette in her handbag on the table and crosses to the little window and looks out, smoking and deeply enjoying this first one.

RUTH *(almost matter of factly, a complaint too automatic to deserve emphasis)*   Why you always got to smoke before you eat in the morning?

WALTER *(at the window)*   Just look at 'em down there. . . . Running and racing to work . . . *(He turns and faces his wife and watches her a moment at the stove, and then, suddenly)* You look young this morning, baby.

RUTH *(indifferently)* Yeah?

WALTER Just for a second—stirring them eggs. It's gone now—just for a second it was—you looked real young again. *(Then, drily)* It's gone now—you look like yourself again.

RUTH Man, if you don't shut up and leave me alone.

WALTER *(looking out to the street again)* First thing a man ought to learn in life is not to make love to no colored woman first thing in the morning. You all some evil people at eight o'clock in the morning.

TRAVIS *appears in the hall doorway, almost fully dressed and quite wide awake now, his towels and pajamas across his shoulders. He opens the door and signals for his father to make the bathroom in a hurry.*

TRAVIS *(watching the bathroom)* Daddy, come on!

WALTER *gets his bathroom utensils and flies out to the bathroom.*

RUTH Sit down and have your breakfast, Travis.

TRAVIS Mama, this is Friday. *(Gleefully)* Check coming tomorrow, huh?

RUTH You get your mind off money and eat your breakfast.

TRAVIS *(eating)* This is the morning we supposed to bring the fifty cents to school.

RUTH Well, I ain't got no fifty cents this morning.

TRAVIS Teacher say we have to.

RUTH I don't care what teacher say. I ain't got it. Eat your breakfast, Travis.

TRAVIS I *am* eating.

RUTH Hush up now and just eat!

The boy gives her an exasperated look for her lack of understanding, and eats grudgingly.

TRAVIS You think Grandmama would have it?

RUTH No! And I want you to stop asking your grandmother for money, you hear me?

TRAVIS *(outraged)* Gaaaleee! I don't ask her, she just gimme it sometimes!

RUTH Travis Willard Younger—I got too much on me this morning to be—

TRAVIS Maybe Daddy—

RUTH *Travis!*

The boy hushes abruptly. They are both quiet and tense for several seconds.

TRAVIS *(presently)* Could I maybe go carry some groceries in front of the supermarket for a little while after school then?

RUTH Just hush, I said. *(TRAVIS jabs his spoon into his cereal bowl viciously, and rests his head in anger upon his fists.)* If you through eating, you can get over there and make up your bed.

The boy obeys stiffly and crosses the room, almost mechanically, to the bed and more or less carefully folds the covering. He carries the bedding into his mother's room and returns with his books and cap.

TRAVIS *(sulking and standing apart from her unnaturally)* I'm gone.

RUTH *(looking up from the stove to inspect him automatically)* Come *here.* (He crosses to her and she studies his head.) If you don't take this comb and fix this here head, you better! (TRAVIS *puts down his books with a great sigh of oppression, and crosses to the mirror. His mother mutters under her breath about his "stub-*

bornness.") 'Bout to march out of here with that head looking just like chickens slept in it! I just don't know where you get your stubborn ways. . . . And get your jacket, too. Looks chilly out this morning.

TRAVIS *(with conspicuously brushed hair and jacket)* I'm gone.

RUTH Get carfare and milk money—*(waving one finger)*—and not a single penny for no caps, you hear me?

TRAVIS *(with sullen politeness)* Yes'm.

He turns in outrage to leave. His mother watches after him as in his frustration he approaches the door almost comically. When she speaks to him, her voice has become a very gentle tease.

RUTH *(mocking; as she thinks he would say it)* Oh, Mama makes me so mad sometimes, I don't know what to do! *(She waits and continues to his back as he stands stock-still in front of the door.)* I wouldn't kiss that woman good-bye for nothing in this world this morning! *(The boy finally turns around and rolls his eyes at her, knowing the mood has changed and he is vindicated; he does not, however, move toward her yet.)* Not for nothing in this world! *(She finally laughs aloud at him and holds out her arms to him and we see that it is a way between them, very old and practiced. He crosses to her and allows her to embrace him warmly but keeps his face fixed with masculine rigidity. She holds him back from her presently and looks at him and runs her fingers over the features of his face. With utter gentleness—)* Now—whose little old angry man are you?

TRAVIS *(the masculinity and gruffness start to fade at last)* Aw gaalee—Mama . . .

RUTH *(mimicking)* Aw—gaaaaalleeeee, Mama! *(She pushes him, with rough playfulness and finality, toward the door.)* Get on out of here or you going to be late.

TRAVIS *(in the face of love, new aggressiveness)* Mama, could I *please* go carry groceries?

RUTH Honey, it's starting to get so cold evenings.

WALTER *(coming in from the bathroom and drawing a make-believe gun from a make-believe holster and shooting at his son)* What is it he wants to do?

RUTH Go carry groceries after school at the supermarket.

WALTER Well, let him go . . .

TRAVIS *(quickly, to the ally)* I *have* to—she won't gimme the fifty cents. . . .

WALTER *(to his wife only)* Why not?

RUTH *(simply, and with flavor)* 'Cause we don't have it.

WALTER *(to RUTH only)* What you tell the boy things like that for? *(Reaching down into his pants with a rather important gesture)* Here, son—

He hands the boy the coin, but his eyes are directed to his wife's. TRAVIS *takes the money happily.*

TRAVIS Thanks, Daddy.

He starts out. RUTH *watches both of them with murder in her eyes.* WALTER *stands and stares back at her with defiance, and suddenly reaches into his pocket again on an afterthought.*

WALTER *(without even looking at his son, still staring hard at his wife)* In fact, here's another fifty cents. . . . Buy yourself some fruit today—or take a taxicab to school or something!

TRAVIS Whoopee—

He leaps up and clasps his father around the middle with his legs, and they face each other in mutual appreciation; slowly WALTER LEE *peeks around the boy to catch the violent rays from his wife's eyes and draws his head back as if shot.*

WALTER   You better get down now—and get to school, man.

TRAVIS *(at the door)*   O.K. Good-bye. *(He exits.)*

WALTER *(after him, pointing with pride)*   That's *my* boy. *(She looks at him in disgust and turns back to her work.)* You know what I was thinking 'bout in the bathroom this morning?

RUTH   No.

WALTER   How come you always try to be so pleasant!

RUTH   What is there to be pleasant 'bout!

WALTER   You want to know what I was thinking 'bout in the bathroom or not!

RUTH   I know what you thinking 'bout.

WALTER *(ignoring her)*   'Bout what me and Willy Harris was talking about last night.

RUTH *(immediately—a refrain)*   Willy Harris is a good-for-nothing loud mouth.

WALTER   Anybody who talks to me has got to be a good-for-nothing loud mouth, ain't he? And what you know about who is just a good-for-nothing loud mouth? Charlie Atkins was just a "good-for-nothing loud mouth" too, wasn't he! When he wanted me to go in the dry-cleaning business with him. And now—he's grossing a hundred thousand a year. A hundred thousand dollars a year! You still call *him* a loud mouth!

RUTH *(bitterly)*   Oh, Walter Lee. . . . *(She folds her head on her arms over the table.)*

WALTER *(rising and coming to her and standing over her)*   You tired, ain't you? Tired of everything. Me, the boy, the way we live—this beat-up hole—everything. Ain't you? *(She doesn't look up, doesn't answer.)* So tired—moaning and groaning all the time, but you wouldn't do nothing to help, would you? You couldn't be on my side that long for nothing, could you?

RUTH   Walter, please leave me alone.

WALTER   A man needs for a woman to back him up. . . .

RUTH   Walter—

WALTER   Mama would listen to you. You know she listen to you more than she do me and Bennie. She think more of you. All you have to do is just sit down with her when you drinking your coffee one morning and talking 'bout things like you do and—*(He sits down beside her and demonstrates graphically what he thinks her methods and tone should be)*—you just sip your coffee, see, and say easy like that you been thinking 'bout that deal Walter Lee is so interested in, 'bout the store and all, and sip some more coffee, like what you saying ain't really that important to you—And the next thing you know, she be listening good and asking you questions and when I come home—I can tell her the details. This ain't no fly-by-night proposition, baby. I mean we figured it out, me and Willy and Bobo.

RUTH *(with a frown)*   Bobo?

WALTER   Yeah. You see, this little liquor store we got in mind cost seventy-five thousand and we figured the initial investment on the place be 'bout thirty thousand, see. That be ten thousand each. Course, there's a couple of hundred you got to pay so's you don't spend your life just waiting for them clowns to let your license get approved—

RUTH   You mean graft?

WALTER *(frowning impatiently)* Don't call it that. See there, that just goes to show you what women understand about the world. Baby, don't *nothing* happen for you in this world 'less you pay *somebody* off!

RUTH Walter, leave me alone! *(She raises her head and stares at him vigorously— then says, more quietly)* Eat your eggs, they gonna be cold.

WALTER *(straightening up from her and looking off)* That's it. There you are. Man say to his woman: I got me a dream. His woman say: Eat your eggs. *(Sadly, but gaining in power)* Man say: I got to take hold of this here world, baby! And a woman will say: Eat your eggs and go to work. *(Passionately now)* Man say: I got to change my life, I'm choking to death, baby! And his woman say—*(in utter an-guish as he brings his fists down on his thighs)*—Your eggs is getting cold!

RUTH *(softly)* Walter, that ain't none of our money.

WALTER *(not listening at all or even looking at her)* This morning, I was lookin' in the mirror and thinking about it. . . . I'm thirty-five years old; I been married eleven years and I got a boy who sleeps in the living room—*(very, very quietly)*— and all I got to give him is stories about how rich white people live. . . .

RUTH Eat your eggs, Walter.

WALTER *Damn my eggs . . . damn all the eggs that ever was!*

RUTH Then go to work.

WALTER *(looking up at her)* See—I'm trying to talk to you 'bout myself—*(shaking his head with the repetition)*—and all you can say is eat them eggs and go to work.

RUTH *(wearily)* Honey, you never say nothing new. I listen to you every day, every night and every morning, and you never say nothing new. *(Shrugging)* So you would rather *be* Mr. Arnold than be his chauffeur. So—I would *rather* be living in Buckingham Palace.

WALTER That is just what is wrong with the colored woman in this world. . . . Don't understand about building their men up and making 'em feel like they somebody. Like they can do something.

RUTH *(drily, but to hurt)* There *are* colored men who do things.

WALTER No thanks to the colored woman.

RUTH Well, being a colored woman, I guess I can't help myself none.

She rises and gets the ironing board and sets it up and attacks a huge pile of rough-dried clothes, sprinkling them in preparation for the ironing and then rolling them into tight fat balls.

WALTER *(mumbling)* We one group of men tied to a race of women with small minds.

His sister BENEATHA enters. She is about twenty, as slim and intense as her brother. She is not as pretty as her sister-in-law, but her lean, almost intellectual face has a handsomeness of its own. She wears a bright-red flannel nightie, and her thick hair stands wildly about her head. Her speech is a mixture of many things; it is different from the rest of the family's insofar as education has permeated her sense of English —and perhaps the Midwest rather than the South has finally—at last—won out in her inflection; but not altogether, because over all of it is a soft slurring and trans-formed use of vowels which is the decided influence of the Southside. She passes through the room without looking at either RUTH or WALTER and goes to the outside door and looks, a little blindly, out to the bathroom. She sees that it has been lost to the Johnsons. She closes the door with a sleepy vengeance and crosses to the table and sits down a little defeated.

BENEATHA   I am going to start timing those people.

WALTER   You should get up earlier.

BENEATHA   *(her face in her hands. She is still fighting the urge to go back to bed)*   Really—would you suggest dawn? Where's the paper?

WALTER   *(pushing the paper across the table to her as he studies her almost clinically, as though he has never seen her before)*   You a horrible-looking chick at this hour.

BENEATHA   *(drily)*   Good morning, everybody.

WALTER   *(senselessly)*   How is school coming?

BENEATHA   *(in the same spirit)*   Lovely. Lovely. And you know, biology is the greatest. *(Looking up at him)* I dissected something that looked just like you yesterday.

WALTER   I just wondered if you've made up your mind and everything.

BENEATHA   *(gaining in sharpness and impatience)*   And what did I answer yesterday morning—and the day before that?

RUTH   *(from the ironing board, like someone disinterested and old)*   Don't be so nasty, Bennie.

BENEATHA   *(still to her brother)*   And the day before that and the day before that!

WALTER   *(defensively)*   I'm interested in you. Something wrong with that? Ain't many girls who decide—

WALTER AND BENEATHA   *(in unison)*   —"to be a doctor."

Silence.

WALTER   Have we figured out yet just exactly how much medical school is going to cost?

RUTH   Walter Lee, why don't you leave that girl alone and get out of here to work?

BENEATHA   *(exits to the bathroom and bangs to the door)*   Come on out of there, please! *(She comes back into the room)*

WALTER   *(looking at his sister intently)*   You know the check is coming tomorrow.

BENEATHA   *(turning on him with a sharpness all her own)*   That money belongs to Mama, Walter, and it's for her to decide how she wants to use it. I don't care if she wants to buy a house or a rocket ship or just nail it up somewhere and look at it. It's hers. Not ours—*hers.*

WALTER   *(bitterly)*   Now ain't that fine! You just got your mother's interest at heart, ain't you, girl? You such a nice girl—but if Mama got that money she can always take a few thousand and help you through school too—can't she?

BENEATHA   I have never asked anyone around here to do anything for me!

WALTER   No! And the line between asking and just accepting when the time comes is big and wide—ain't it!

BENEATHA   *(with fury)*   What do you want from me, Brother—that I quit school or just drop dead, which!

WALTER   I don't want nothing but for you to stop acting holy 'round here. Me and Ruth done made some sacrifices for you—why can't you do something for the family?

RUTH   Walter, don't be dragging me in it.

WALTER   You are in it—Don't you get up and go work in somebody's kitchen for the last three years to help put clothes on her back?

RUTH   Oh, Walter—that's not fair. . . .

WALTER   It ain't that nobody expects you to get on your knees and say thank you, Brother; thank you, Ruth; thank you, Mama—and thank you, Travis, for wearing the same pair of shoes for two semesters—

BENEATHA *(dropping to her knees)* Well—I *do* —all right?—thank everybody . . . and forgive me for ever wanting to be anything at all . . . forgive me, forgive me!

RUTH Please stop it! Your mama'll hear you.

WALTER Who the hell told you you had to be a doctor? If you so crazy 'bout messing 'round with sick people—then go be a nurse like other women—or just get married and be quiet. . . .

BENEATHA Well—you finally got it said. . . . It took you three years but you finally got it said. Walter, give up; leave me alone—it's Mama's money.

WALTER *He was my father, too!*

BENEATHA So what? He was mine, too—and Travis' grandfather—but the insurance money belongs to Mama. Picking on me is not going to make her give it to you to invest in any liquor stores—*(underbreath, dropping into a chair)*—and I for one say, God bless Mama for that!

WALTER *(to* RUTH*)* See—did you hear? Did you hear!

RUTH Honey, please go to work.

WALTER Nobody in this house is ever going to understand me.

BENEATHA Because you're a nut.

WALTER Who's a nut?

BENEATHA You—you are a nut. Thee is mad, boy.

WALTER *(looking at his wife and his sister from the door, very sadly)* The world's most backward race of people, and that's a fact.

BENEATHA *(turning slowly in her chair)* And then there are all those prophets who would lead us out of the wilderness—*(*WALTER *slams out of the house.)*—into the swamps!

RUTH Bennie, why you always gotta be pickin' on your brother? Can't you be a little sweeter sometimes? *(Door opens.* WALTER *walks in.)*

WALTER *(to* RUTH*)* I need some money for carfare.

RUTH *(looks at him, then warms; teasing, but tenderly)* Fifty cents? *(She goes to her bag and gets money.)* Here, take a taxi.

WALTER *exits.* MAMA *enters. She is a woman in her early sixties, full-bodied and strong. She is one of those women of a certain grace and beauty who wears it so unobtrusively that it takes a while to notice. Her dark-brown face is surrounded by the total whiteness of her hair, and, being a woman who has adjusted to many things in life and overcome many more, her face is full of strength. She has, we can see, wit and faith of a kind that keep her eyes lit and full of interest and expectancy. She is, in a word, a beautiful woman. Her bearing is perhaps most like the noble bearing of the women of the Hereros of Southwest Africa—rather as if she imagines that as she walks she still bears a basket or a vessel upon her head. Her speech, on the other hand, is as careless as her carriage is precise—she is inclined to slur everything—but her voice is perhaps not so much quiet as simply soft.*

MAMA Who that 'round here slamming doors at this hour?

She crosses through the room, goes to the window, opens it, and brings in a feeble little plant growing doggedly in a small pot on the window sill. She feels the dirt and puts it back out.

RUTH That was Walter Lee. He and Bennie was at it again.

MAMA My children and they tempers. Lord, if this little old plant don't get more sun than it's been getting it ain't never going to see spring again. *(She turns from the window.)* What's the matter with you this morning, Ruth? You looks right peaked. You aiming to iron all them things? Leave some for me. I'll get to 'em this afternoon. Bennie honey, it's too drafty for you to be sittin 'round half dressed. Where's your robe?

BENEATHA   In the cleaners.

MAMA   Well, go get mine and put it on.

BENEATHA   I'm not cold, Mama, honest.

MAMA   I know—but you so thin. . . .

BENEATHA *(irritably)*   Mama, I'm not cold.

MAMA *(seeing the make-down bed as* TRAVIS *has left it)*   Lord have mercy, look at that poor bed. Bless his heart—he tries, don't he? *(She moves to the bed* TRAVIS *has sloppily made up.)*

RUTH   No—he don't half try at all 'cause he knows you going to come along behind him and fix everything. That's just how come he don't know how to do nothing right now—you done spoiled that boy so.

MAMA   Well—he's a little boy. Ain't supposed to know 'bout housekeeping. My baby, that's what he is. What you fix for his breakfast this morning?

RUTH *(angrily)*   I feed my son, Lena!

MAMA   I ain't meddling—*(underbreath; busy-bodyish)*   I just noticed all last week he had cold cereal, and when it starts getting this chilly in the fall a child ought to have some hot grits or something when he goes out in the cold—

RUTH *(furious)*   I gave him hot oats—is that all right!

MAMA   I ain't meddling. *(Pause)* Put a lot of nice butter on it? *(*RUTH *shoots her an angry look and does not reply.)* He likes lots of butter.

RUTH *(exasperated)*   Lena—

MAMA *(to* BENEATHA. MAMA *is inclined to wander conversationally sometimes)*   What was you and your brother fussing 'bout this morning?

BENEATHA   It's not important, Mama.

She gets up and goes to look out at the bathroom, which is apparently free, and she picks up her towels and rushes out.

MAMA   What was they fighting about?

RUTH   Now you know as well as I do.

MAMA *(shaking her head)*   Brother still worrying his self sick about that money?

RUTH   You know he is.

MAMA   You had breakfast?

RUTH   Some coffee.

MAMA   Girl, you better start eating and looking after yourself better. You almost thin as Travis.

RUTH   Lena—

MAMA   Un-hunh?

RUTH   What are you going to do with it?

MAMA   Now don't you start, child. It's too early in the morning to be talking about money. It ain't Christian.

RUTH   It's just that he got his heart set on that store—

MAMA   You mean that liquor store that Willy Harris want him to invest in?

RUTH   Yes—

MAMA   We ain't no business people, Ruth. We just plain working folks.

RUTH   Ain't nobody business people till they go into business. Walter Lee say colored people ain't never going to start getting ahead till they start gambling on some different kinds of things in the world—investments and things.

MAMA What done got into you, girl? Walter Lee done finally sold you on investing.

RUTH No. Mama, something is happening between Walter and me. I don't know what it is—but he needs something—something I can't give him any more. He needs this chance, Lena.

MAMA *(frowning deeply)* But liquor, honey—

RUTH Well—like Walter say—I spec people going to always be drinking themselves some liquor.

MAMA Well—whether they drinks it or not ain't none of my business. But whether I go into business selling it to 'em *is,* and I don't want that on my ledger this late in life. *(Stopping suddenly and studying her daughter-in-law)* Ruth Younger, what's the matter with you today? You look like you could fall over right there.

RUTH I'm tired.

MAMA Then you better stay home from work today.

RUTH I can't stay home. She'd be calling up the agency and screaming at them, "My girl didn't come in today—send me somebody! My girl didn't come in!" Oh, she just have a fit. . . .

MAMA Well, let her have it. I'll just call her up and say you got the flu—

RUTH *(laughing)* Why the flu?

MAMA 'Cause it sounds respectable to 'em. Something white people get, too. They know 'bout the flu. Otherwise they think you been cut up or something when you tell 'em you sick.

RUTH I got to go in. We need the money.

MAMA Somebody would of thought my children done all but starved to death the way they talk about money here late. Child, we got a great big old check coming tomorrow.

RUTH *(sincerely, but also self-righteously)* Now that's your money. It ain't got nothing to do with me. We all feel like that—Walter and Bennie and me—even Travis.

MAMA *(thoughtfully, and suddenly very far away)* Ten thousand dollars—

RUTH Sure is wonderful.

MAMA Ten thousand dollars.

RUTH You know what you should do, Miss Lena? You should take yourself a trip somewhere. To Europe or South America or someplace—

MAMA *(throwing up her hands at the thought)* Oh, child!

RUTH I'm serious. Just pack up and leave! Go on away and enjoy yourself some. Forget about the family and have yourself a ball for once in your life—

MAMA *(dryly)* You sound like I'm just about ready to die. Who'd go with me? What I look like wandering 'round Europe by myself?

RUTH Shoot—these here rich white women do it all the time. They don't think nothing of packing up they suitcases and piling on one of them big steamships and—swoosh!—they gone, child.

MAMA Something always told me I wasn't no rich white woman.

RUTH Well—what are you going to do with it then?

MAMA I ain't rightly decided. *(Thinking. She speaks now with emphasis.)* Some of it got to be put away for Beneatha and her schoolin'—and ain't nothing going to touch that part of it. Nothing. *(She waits several seconds, trying to make up her mind about something, and looks at* RUTH *a little tentatively before going on.)*

Been thinking that we maybe could meet the notes on a little old two-story some-where, with a yard where Travis could play in the summertime, if we use part of the insurance for a down payment and everybody kind of pitch in. I could maybe take on a little day work again, few days a week—

RUTH *(studying her mother-in-law furtively and concentrating on her ironing, anxious to encourage without seeming to)* Well, Lord knows, we've put enough rent into this here rat trap to pay for four houses by now. . . .

MAMA *(looking up at the words "rat trap" and then looking around and leaning back and sighing—in a suddenly reflective mood—)* "Rat trap"—yes, that's all it is. *(Smiling)* I remember just as well the day me and Big Walter moved in here. Hadn't been married but two weeks and wasn't planning on living here no more than a year. *(She shakes her head at the dissolved dream.)* We was going to set away, little by little, don't you know, and buy a little place out in Morgan Park. We had even picked out the house. *(Chuckling a little)* Looks right dumpy today. But Lord, child, you should know all the dreams I had 'bout buying that house and fixing it up and making me a little garden in the back—*(She waits and stops smiling.)* And didn't none of it happen. *(Dropping her hands in a futile gesture)*

RUTH *(keeps her head down, ironing)* Yes, life can be a barrel of disappointments, sometimes.

MAMA Honey, Big Walter would come in here some nights back then and slump down on that couch there and just look at the rug, and look at me and look at the rug and then back at me—and I'd know he was down then . . . really down. *(After a second very long and thoughtful pause; she is seeing back to times that only she can see.)* And then, Lord, when I lost that baby—little Claude—I almost thought I was going to lose Big Walter too. Oh, that man grieved hisself! He was one man to love his children.

RUTH Ain't nothin' can tear at you like losin' your baby.

MAMA I guess that's how come that man finally worked hisself to death like he done. Like he was fighting his own war with this here world that took his baby from him.

RUTH He sure was a fine man, all right. I always liked Mr. Younger.

MAMA Crazy 'bout his children! God knows there was plenty wrong with Walter Younger—hard-headed, mean, kind of wild with women—plenty wrong with him. But he sure loved his children. Always wanted them to have something—be something. That's where Brother gets all these notions, I reckon. Big Walter used to say, he'd get right wet in the eyes sometimes, lean his head back with the water standing in his eyes and say, "Seem like God didn't see fit to give the black man nothing but dreams—but He did give us children to make them dreams seem worth while." *(She smiles.)* He could talk like that, don't you know.

RUTH Yes, he sure could. He was a good man, Mr. Younger.

MAMA Yes, a fine man—just couldn't never catch up with his dreams, that's all.

BENEATHA *comes in, brushing her hair and looking up to the ceiling, where the sound of a vacuum cleaner has started up.*

BENEATHA What could be so dirty on that woman's rugs that she has to vacuum them every single day?

RUTH I wish certain young women 'round here who I could name would take inspiration about certain rugs in a certain apartment I could also mention.

BENEATHA *(shrugging)* How much cleaning can a house need, for Christ's sakes.

MAMA *(not liking the Lord's name used thus)* Bennie!

RUTH Just listen to her—just listen!

BENEATHA Oh, God!

MAMA If you use the Lord's name just one more time—

BENEATHA *(a bit of a whine)* Oh, Mama—

RUTH Fresh—just fresh as salt, this girl!

BENEATHA *(dryly)* Well—if the salt loses its savor—

MAMA Now that will do. I just ain't going to have you 'round here reciting the scriptures in vain—you hear me?

BENEATHA How did I manage to get on everybody's wrong side by just walking into a room?

RUTH If you weren't so fresh—

BENEATHA Ruth, I'm twenty years old.

MAMA What time you be home from school today?

BENEATHA Kind of late. *(With enthusiasm)* Madeline is going to start my guitar lessons today.

MAMA *and* RUTH *look up with the same expression.*

MAMA Your *what* kind of lessons?

BENEATHA Guitar.

RUTH Oh, Father!

MAMA How come you done taken it in your mind to learn to play the guitar?

BENEATHA I just want to, that's all.

MAMA *(smiling)* Lord, child, don't you know what to do with yourself? How long it going to be before you get tired of this now—like you got tired of that little play-acting group you joined last year? *(Looking at* RUTH*)* And what was it the year before that?

RUTH The horseback-riding club for which she bought that fifty-five dollar riding habit that's been hanging in the closet ever since!

MAMA *(to* BENEATHA*)* Why you got to flit so from one thing to another, baby?

BENEATHA *(sharply)* I just want to learn to play the guitar. Is there anything wrong with that?

MAMA Ain't nobody trying to stop you. I just wonders sometimes why you has to flit so from one thing to another all the time. You ain't never done nothing with all that camera equipment you brought home—

BENEATHA I don't flit! I—I experiment with different forms of expression—

RUTH Like riding a horse?

BENEATHA —People have to express themselves one way or another.

MAMA What is it you want to express?

BENEATHA *(angrily)* Me! *(*MAMA *and* RUTH *look at each other and burst into raucous laughter.)* Don't worry—I don't expect you to understand.

MAMA *(to change the subject)* Who you going out with tomorrow night?

BENEATHA *(with displeasure)* George Murchison again.

MAMA *(pleased)* Oh—you getting a little sweet on him?

RUTH You ask me, this child ain't sweet on nobody but herself—*(Underbreath)* Express herself!

They laugh.

BENEATHA Oh—I like George all right, Mama. I mean I like him enough to go out with him and stuff, but—

RUTH *(for devilment)*   What does *and stuff* mean?

BENEATHA   Mind your own business.

MAMA   Stop picking at her now, Ruth. *(A thoughtful pause, and then a suspicious sudden look at her daughter as she turns in her chair for emphasis)* What *does* it mean?

BENEATHA *(wearily)*   Oh, I just mean I couldn't ever really be serious about George. He's—he's so shallow.

RUTH   Shallow—what do you mean he's shallow? He's *rich!*

MAMA   Hush, Ruth.

BENEATHA   I know he's rich. He knows he's rich, too.

RUTH   Well—what other qualities a man got to have to satisfy you, little girl?

BENEATHA   You wouldn't even begin to understand. Anybody who married Walter could not possibly understand.

MAMA *(outraged)*   What kind of way is that to talk about your brother?

BENEATHA   Brother is a flip—let's face it.

MAMA *(to* RUTH, *helplessly)*   What's a flip?

RUTH *(glad to add kindling)*   She's saying he's crazy.

BENEATHA   Not crazy. Brother isn't really crazy yet—he—he's an elaborate neurotic.

MAMA   Hush your mouth!

BENEATHA   As for George. Well. George looks good—he's got a beautiful car and he takes me to nice places and, as my sister-in-law says, he is probably the richest boy I will ever get to know and I even like him sometimes—but if the Youngers are sitting around waiting to see if their little Bennie is going to tie up the family with the Murchisons, they are wasting their time.

RUTH   You mean you wouldn't marry George Murchison if he asked you someday? That pretty, rich thing? Honey, I knew you was odd—

BENEATHA   No I would not marry him if all I felt for him was what I feel now. Besides, George's family wouldn't really like it.

MAMA   Why not?

BENEATHA   Oh, Mama—The Murchisons are honest-to-God-real-*live*-rich colored people, and the only people in the world who are more snobbish than rich white people are rich colored people. I thought everybody knew that. I've met Mrs. Murchison. She's a scene!

MAMA   You must not dislike people 'cause they well off, honey.

BENEATHA   Why not? It makes just as much sense as disliking people 'cause they are poor, and lots of people do that.

RUTH *(a wisdom-of-the-ages manner. To* MAMA*)*   Well, she'll get over some of this—

BENEATHA   Get over it? What are you talking about, Ruth? Listen, I'm going to be a doctor. I'm not worried about who I'm going to marry yet—if I ever get married.

MAMA AND RUTH   *If!*

MAMA   Now, Bennie—

BENEATHA   Oh, I probably will . . . but first I'm going to be a doctor, and George, for one, still thinks that's pretty funny. I couldn't be bothered with that, I am going to be a doctor and everybody around here better understand that!

MAMA *(kindly)*   'Course you going to be a doctor, honey, God willing.

BENEATHA *(drily)*   God hasn't got a thing to do with it.

MAMA   Beneatha—that just wasn't necessary.

BENEATHA   Well—neither is God. I get sick of hearing about God.

MAMA Beneatha!

BENEATHA I mean it! I'm just tired of hearing about God all the time. What has He got to do with anything? Does He pay tuition?

MAMA You 'bout to get your fresh little jaw slapped!

RUTH That's just what she needs, all right!

BENEATHA Why? Why can't I say what I want to around here, like everybody else?

MAMA It don't sound nice for a young girl to say things like that—you wasn't brought up that way. Me and your father went to trouble to get you and Brother to church every Sunday.

BENEATHA Mama, you don't understand. It's all a matter of ideas, and God is just one idea I don't accept. It's not important, I am not going out and be immoral or commit crimes because I don't believe in God. I don't even think about it. It's just that I get tired of Him getting credit for all the things the human race achieves through its own stubborn effort. There simply is no blasted God—there is only man and it is he who makes miracles!

MAMA *absorbs this speech, studies her daughter and rises slowly and crosses to* BENEATHA *and slaps her powerfully across the face. After, there is only silence and the daughter drops her eyes from her mother's face, and* MAMA *is very tall before her.*

MAMA Now—you say after me, in my mother's house there is still God. *(There is a long pause and* BENEATHA *stares at the floor wordlessly.* MAMA *repeats the phrase with precision and cool emotion.)* In my mother's house there is still God.

BENEATHA In my mother's house there is still God.

A long pause.

MAMA *(walking away from* BENEATHA, *too disturbed for triumphant posture. Stopping and turning back to her daughter)* There are some ideas we ain't going to have in this house. Not long as I am at the head of this family.

BENEATHA Yes, ma'am.

MAMA *walks out of the room.*

RUTH *(almost gently, with profound understanding)* You think you a woman, Bennie—but you still a little girl. What you did was childish—so you got treated like a child.

BENEATHA I see. *(Quietly)* I also see that everybody thinks it's all right for Mama to be a tyrant. But all the tyranny in the world will never put a God in the heavens! *(She picks up her books and goes out.)*

RUTH *(goes to* MAMA's *door)* She said she was sorry.

MAMA *(coming out, going to her plant)* They frightens me, Ruth. My children.

RUTH You got good children, Lena. They just a little off sometimes—but they're good.

MAMA No—there's something come down between me and them that don't let us understand each other and I don't know what it is. One done almost lost his mind thinking 'bout money all the time and the other done commence to talk about things I can't seem to understand in no form or fashion. What is it that's changing, Ruth?

RUTH *(soothingly, older than her years)* Now . . . you taking it all too seriously. You just got strong-willed children and it takes a strong woman like you to keep 'em in hand.

MAMA *(looking at her plant and sprinkling a little water on it)* They spirited all right, my children. Got to admit they got spirit—Bennie and Walter. Like this little old plant that ain't never had enough sunshine or nothing—and look at it. . . .

She has her back to RUTH, *who has had to stop ironing and lean against something and put the back of her hand to her forehead.*

RUTH *(trying to keep* MAMA *from noticing)* You . . . sure . . . loves that little old thing, don't you? . . .

MAMA Well, I always wanted me a garden like I used to see sometimes at the back of the houses down home. This plant is close as I ever got to having one. *(She looks out of the window as she replaces the plant.)* Lord, ain't nothing as dreary as the view from this window on a dreary day, is there? Why ain't you singing this morning, Ruth? Sing that "No Ways Tired." That song always lifts me up so—*(She turns at last to see that* RUTH *has slipped quietly into a chair, in a state of semiconsciousness.)* Ruth! Ruth honey—what's the matter with you . . . Ruth!

Curtain.

SCENE II. *It is the following morning; a Saturday morning, and house cleaning is in progress at the Youngers. Furniture has been shoved hither and yon and* MAMA *is giving the kitchen-area walls a washing down.* BENEATHA, *in dungarees, with a handkerchief tied around her face, is spraying insecticide into the cracks in the walls. As they work, the radio is on and a Southside disc-jockey program is inappropriately filling the house with a rather exotic saxophone blues.* TRAVIS, *the sole idle one, is leaning on his arms, looking out of the window.*

TRAVIS Grandmama, that stuff Bennie is using smells awful. Can I go downstairs, please?

MAMA Did you get all them chores done already? I ain't see you doing much.

TRAVIS Yes'm—finished early. Where did Mama go this morning?

MAMA *(looking at* BENEATHA*)* She had to go on a little errand.

TRAVIS Where?

MAMA To tend to her business.

TRAVIS Can I go outside then?

MAMA Oh, I guess so. You better stay right in front of the house, though . . . and keep a good lookout for the postman.

TRAVIS Yes'm. *(He starts out and decides to give his* AUNT BENEATHA *a good swat on the legs as he passes her.)* Leave them poor little old cockroaches alone, they ain't bothering you none.

He runs as she swings the spray gun at him both viciously and playfully. WALTER *enters from the bedroom and goes to the phone.*

MAMA Look out there, girl, before you be spilling some of that stuff on that child!

TRAVIS *(teasing)* That's right—look out now! *(He exits.)*

BENEATHA *(drily)* I can't imagine that it would hurt him—it has never hurt the roaches.

MAMA Well, little boys' hides ain't as tough as Southside roaches.

WALTER *(into phone)* Hello—Let me talk to Willy Harris.

MAMA You better get over there behind the bureau. I seen one marching out of there like Napoleon yesterday.

WALTER   Hello. Willy? It ain't come yet. It'll be here in a few minutes. Did the lawyer give you the papers?

BENEATHA   There's really only one way to get rid of them, Mama—

MAMA   How?

BENEATHA   Set fire to this building.

WALTER   Good. Good. I'll be right over.

BENEATHA   Where did Ruth go, Walter?

WALTER   I don't know. *(He exits abruptly.)*

BENEATHA   Mama, where did Ruth go?

MAMA *(looking at her with meaning)*   To the doctor, I think.

BENEATHA   The doctor? What's the matter? *(They exchange glances.)* You don't
think—

MAMA *(with her sense of drama)*   Now I ain't saying what I think. But I ain't never
been wrong 'bout a woman neither.

The phone rings.

BENEATHA *(at the phone)*   Hay-lo . . . *(Pause, and a moment of recognition)* Well—
when did you get back! . . . And how was it? . . . Of course I've missed you—in my
way. . . . This morning? No . . . house cleaning and all that and Mama hates it if I
let people come over when the house is like this. . . . You *have?* Well, that's different. . . . What is it— Oh, what the hell, come on over. . . . Right, see you then. *(She
hangs up.)*

MAMA *(who has listened vigorously, as is her habit)*   Who is that you inviting over
here with this house looking like this? You ain't got the pride you was born with!

BENEATHA   Asagai doesn't care how houses look, Mama—he's an intellectual.

MAMA *Who?*

BENEATHA   Asagai—Joseph Asagai. He's an African boy I met on campus. He's
been studying in Canada all summer.

MAMA   What's his name?

BENEATHA   Asagai, Joseph. A-sah-guy . . . He's from Nigeria.

MAMA   Oh, that's the little country that was founded by slaves way back. . . .

BENEATHA   No, Mama—that's Liberia.

MAMA   I don't think I never met no African before.

BENEATHA   Well, do me a favor and don't ask him a whole lot of ignorant questions about Africans. I mean, do they wear clothes and all that—

MAMA   Well, now, I guess if you think we so ignorant 'round here maybe you
shouldn't bring your friends here—

BENEATHA   It's just that people ask such crazy things. All anyone seems to know
about when it comes to Africa is Tarzan—

MAMA *(indignantly)*   Why should I know anything about Africa?

BENEATHA   Why do you give money at church for the missionary work?

MAMA   Well, that's to help save people.

BENEATHA   You mean to save them from *heathenism*—

MAMA *(innocently)*   Yes.

BENEATHA   I'm afraid they need more salvation from the British and the French.

RUTH *comes in forlornly and pulls off her coat with dejection. They both turn to look
at her.*

RUTH *(dispiritedly)*   Well, I guess from all the happy faces—everybody knows.

BENEATHA   You pregnant?

MAMA   Lord have mercy, I sure hope it's a little old girl. Travis ought to have a sister.

BENEATHA *and* RUTH *give her a hopeless look for this grandmotherly enthusiasm.*

BENEATHA   How far along are you?

RUTH   Two months.

BENEATHA   Did you mean to? I mean did you plan it or was it an accident?

MAMA   What do you know about planning or not planning?

BENEATHA   Oh, Mama.

RUTH *(wearily)*   She's twenty years old, Lena.

BENEATHA   Did you plan it, Ruth?

RUTH   Mind your own business.

BENEATHA   It is my business—where is he going to live, on the *roof? (There is silence following the remark as the three women react to the sense of it.)* Gee—I
didn't mean that, Ruth, honest. Gee. I don't feel like that at all. I—I think it is
wonderful.

RUTH *(dully)*   Wonderful.

BENEATH   Yes—really.

MAMA *(looking at* RUTH, *worried)*   Doctor say everything going to be all right?

RUTH *(far away)*   Yes—she says everything is going to be fine. . . .

MAMA *(immediately suspicious)*   "She"—What doctor you went to?

RUTH *folds over, near hysteria.*

MAMA *(worriedly hovering over* RUTH*)* Ruth honey—what's the matter with you—
you sick?

RUTH *has her fists clenched on her thighs and is fighting hard to suppress a scream
that seems to be rising in her.*

BENEATHA   What's the matter with her, Mama?

MAMA *(working her fingers in* RUTH*'s shoulder to relax her)*   She be all right.
Women gets right depressed sometimes when they get her way. *(Speaking softly,
expertly, rapidly)* Now you just relax. That's right . . . just lean back, don't think
'bout nothing at all . . . nothing at all—

RUTH   I'm all right. . . .

*The glassy-eyed look melts and then she collapses into a fit of heavy sobbing. The bell
rings.*

BENEATHA   Oh, my God—that must be Asagai.

MAMA *(to* RUTH*)*   Come on now, honey. You need to lie down and rest awhile . . .
then have some nice hot food.

They exit, RUTH*'s weight on her mother-in-law.* BENEATHA, *herself profoundly disturbed, opens the door to admit a rather dramatic-looking young man with a large
package.*

ASAGAI   Hello, Alaiyo—

BENEATHA *(holding the door open and regarding him with pleasure)*   Hello . . .
(Long pause) Well—come in. And please excuse everything. My mother was very
upset about my letting anyone come here with the place like this.

ASAGAI *(coming into the room)*   You look disturbed too. . . . Is something wrong?

BENEATHA *(still at the door, absently)* Yes . . . we've all got acute ghetto-itus. *(She smiles and comes toward him, finding a cigarette and sitting.)* So—sit down! How was Canada?

ASAGAI *(a sophisticate)* Canadian.

BENEATHA *(looking at him)* I'm very glad you are back.

ASAGAI *(looking back at her in turn)* Are you really?

BENEATHA Yes—very.

ASAGAI Why—you were quite glad when I went away. What happened?

BENEATHA You went away.

ASAGAI Ahhhhhhhh.

BENEATHA Before—you wanted to be so serious before there was time.

ASAGAI How much time must there be before one knows what one feels?

BENEATHA *(stalling this particular conversation. Her hands pressed together, in a deliberately childish gesture)* What did you bring me?

ASAGAI *(handing her the package)* Open it and see.

BENEATHA *(eagerly opening the package and drawing out some records and the colorful robes of a Nigerian woman)* Oh, Asagai! . . . You got them for me! . . . How beautiful . . . and the records too! *(She lifts out the robes and runs to the mirror with them and holds the drapery up in front of herself.)*

ASAGAI *(coming to her at the mirror)* I shall have to teach you how to drape it properly. *(He flings the material about her for the moment and stands back to look at her.)* Ah— *Oh-pay-gay-day, oh-gbah-mu-shay.* *(A Yoruba exclamation for admiration)* You wear it well . . . very well . . . mutilated hair and all.

BENEATHA *(turning suddenly)* My hair—what's wrong with my hair?

ASAGAI *(shrugging)* Were you born with it like that?

BENEATH *(reaching up to touch it)* No . . . of course not. *(She looks back to the mirror, disturbed.)*

ASAGAI *(smiling)* How then?

BENEATHA You know perfectly well how . . . as crinkly as yours . . . that's how.

ASAGAI And it is ugly to you that way?

BENEATHA *(quickly)* Oh, no—not ugly . . . *(More slowly, apologetically)* But it's so hard to manage when it's, well—raw.

ASAGAI And so to accommodate that—you mutilate it every week?

BENEATHA It's not mutilation!

ASAGAI *(laughing aloud at her seriousness)* Oh . . . please! I am only teasing you because you are so very serious about these things. *(He stands back from her and folds his arms across his chest, as he watches her pulling at her hair and frowning in the mirror.)* Do you remember the first time you met me at school? . . . *(He laughs.)* You came up to me and said—and I thought you were the most serious little thing I had ever seen—you said: *(He imitates her.)* "Mr. Asagai—I want very much to talk to you. About Africa. You see, Mr. Asagai, I am looking for my identity?" *(He laughs.)*

BENEATHA *(turning to him, not laughing)* Yes—*(Her face quizzical, profoundly disturbed.)*

ASAGAI *(still teasing and reaching out and taking her face in his hands and turning her profile to him)* Well . . . it is true that this is not so much a profile of a Hollywood queen as perhaps a queen of the Nile—*(A mock dismissal of the importance of the question)* But what does it matter? Assimilationism is so popular in your country.

BENEATHA *(wheeling, passionately, sharply)* I am not an assimilationist!

ASAGAI *(the protest hangs in the room for a moment and* ASAGAI *studies her, his laughter fading)* Such a serious one. *(There is a pause.)* So—you like the robes? You must take excellent care of them—they are from my sister's personal wardrobe.

BENEATHA *(with incredulity)* You—you sent all the way home—for me?

ASAGAI *(with charm)* For you—I would do much more. . . . Well, that is what I came for. I must go.

BENEATHA Will you call me Monday?

ASAGAI Yes . . . We have a great deal to talk about. I mean about identity and time and all that.

BENEATHA Time?

ASAGAI Yes. About how much time one needs to know what one feels.

BENEATHA You never understood that there is more than one kind of feeling which can exist between a man and a woman—or, at least, there should be.

ASAGAI *(shaking his head negatively but gently)* No. Between a man and a woman there need be only one kind of feeling. I have that for you. . . . Now even . . . right this moment. . . .

BENEATHA I know—and by itself—it won't do. I can find that anywhere.

ASAGAI For a woman it should be enough.

BENEATHA I know—because that's what it says in all the novels that men write. But it isn't. Go ahead and laugh—but I'm not interested in being someone's little episode in America or—*(with feminine vengeance)*—one of them! *(ASAGAI has burst into laughter again.)* That's funny as hell, huh!

ASAGAI It's just that every American girl I have known has said that to me. White —black—in this you are all the same. And the same speech, too!

BENEATHA *(angrily)* Yuk, yuk, yuk!

ASAGAI It's how you can be sure that the world's most liberated women are not liberated at all. You all talk about it too much!

MAMA *enters and is immediately all social charm because of the presence of a guest.*

BENEATHA Oh—Mama—this is Mr. Asagai.

MAMA How do you do?

ASAGAI *(total politeness to an elder)* How do you do, Mrs. Younger. Please forgive me for coming at such an outrageous hour on a Saturday.

MAMA Well, you are quite welcome. I just hope you understand that our house don't always look like this. *(Chatterish)* You must come again. I would love to hear all about—*(not sure of the name)*—your country. I think it's so sad the way our American Negroes don't know nothing about Africa 'cept Tarzan and all that. And all that money they pour into these churches when they ought to be helping you people over there drive out them French and Englishmen done taken away your land.

The mother flashes a slightly superior look at her daughter upon completion of the recitation.

ASAGAI *(taken aback by this sudden and acutely unrelated expression of sympathy)* Yes . . . yes. . . .

MAMA *(smiling at him suddenly and relaxing and looking him over)* How many miles is it from here to where you come from?

ASAGAI Many thousands.

MAMA *(looking at him as she would* WALTER*)* I bet you don't half look after your-self, being away from your mama either. I spec you better come 'round here from time to time and get yourself some decent home-cooked meals. . . .

ASAGAI *(moved)* Thank you. Thank you very much. *(They are all quiet, then—)* Well . . . I must go. I will call you Monday, Alaiyo.

MAMA What's that he call you?

ASAGAI Oh—"Alaiyo." I hope you don't mind. Is it what you would call a nick-name, I think. It is a Yoruba word. I am a Yoruba.

MAMA *(looking at* BENEATHA*)* I—I thought he was from—

ASAGAI *(understanding)* Nigeria is my country. Yoruba is my tribal origin—

BENEATHA You didn't tell us what Alaiyo means . . . for all I know, you might be calling me Little Idiot or something. . . .

ASAGAI Well . . . let me see . . . I do not know how just to explain it. . . . The sense of a thing can be so different when it changes languages.

BENEATHA You're evading.

ASAGAI No—really it is difficult. . . . *(Thinking)* It means . . . it means One for Whom Bread—Food—Is Not Enough. *(He looks at her.)* Is that all right?

BENEATHA *(understanding, softly)* Thank you.

MAMA *(looking from one to the other and not understanding any of it)* Well . . . that's nice. . . . You must come see us again—Mr.—

ASAGAI Ah-sah-guy . . .

MAMA Yes . . . Do come again.

ASAGAI Good-bye. *(He exits.)*

MAMA *(after him)* Lord, that's a pretty thing just went out here! *(Insinuatingly, to her daughter)* Yes, I guess I see why we done commence to get so interested in Africa 'round here. Missionaries my aunt Jenny! *(She exits.)*

BENATHA Oh, Mama! . . .

She picks up the Nigerian dress and holds it up to her in front of the mirror again. She sets the headdress on haphazardly and then notices her hair again and clutches at it and then replaces the headdress and frowns at herself. Then she starts to wriggle in front of the mirror as she thinks a Nigerian woman might. TRAVIS *enters and regards her.*

TRAVIS You cracking up?

BENEATHA Shut up.

She pulls the headdress off and looks at herself in the mirror and clutches at her hair again and squinches her eyes as if trying to imagine something. Then, suddenly, she gets her raincoat and kerchief and hurriedly prepares for going out.

MAMA *(coming back into the room)* She's resting now. Travis, baby, run next door and ask Miss Johnson to please let me have a little kitchen cleanser. This here can is empty as Jacob's kettle.

TRAVIS I just come in.

MAMA Do as you told. *(He exits and she looks at her daughter.)* Where you going?

BENEATHA *(halting at the door)* To become a queen of the Nile!

She exits in a breathless blaze of glory. RUTH *appears in the bedroom doorway.*

MAMA Who told you to get up?

RUTH   Ain't nothing wrong with me to be lying in no bed for. Where did Bennie go?

MAMA   *(drumming her fingers)*   Far as I could make out—to Egypt. *(RUTH just looks at her.)* What time is it getting to?

RUTH   Ten twenty. And the mailman going to ring that bell this morning just like he done every morning for the last umpteen years.

TRAVIS *comes in with the cleanser can.*

TRAVIS   She say to tell you that she don't have much.

MAMA   *(angrily)*   Lord, some people I could name sure is tight-fisted! *(Directing her grandson)* Mark two cans of cleanser down on the list there. If she that hard up for kitchen cleanser, I sure don't want to forget to get her none!

RUTH   Lena—maybe the woman is just short on cleanser—

MAMA   *(not listening)*   —Much baking powder as she done borrowed from me all these years, she could done gone into the baking business!

The bell sounds suddenly and sharply and all three are stunned—serious and silent —mid-speech. In spite of all the other conversations and distractions of the morning, this is what they have been waiting for, even TRAVIS, *who looks helplessly from his mother to his grandmother.* RUTH *is the first to come to life again.*

RUTH   *(to* TRAVIS*)   Get down them steps, boy!*

TRAVIS *snaps to life and flies out to get the mail.*

MAMA   *(her eyes wide, her hand to her breast)*   You mean it done really come?

RUTH   *(excitedly)*   Oh, Miss Lena!

MAMA   *(collecting herself)*   Well . . . I don't know what we all so excited about 'round here for. We known it was coming for months.

RUTH   That's a whole lot different from having it come and being able to hold it in your hands . . . a piece of paper worth ten thousand dollars. . . . *(TRAVIS bursts back into the room. He holds the envelope high above his head, like a little dancer, his face is radiant and he is breathless. He moves to his grandmother with sudden slow ceremony and puts the envelope into her hands. She accepts it, and then merely holds it and looks at it).* Come on! Open it . . . Lord have mercy, I wish Walter Lee was here!

TRAVIS   Open it, Grandmama!

MAMA   *(staring at it)*   Now you all be quiet. It's just a check.

RUTH   *Open it. . . .*

MAMA   *(still staring at it)*   Now don't act silly. . . . We ain't never been no people to act silly 'bout no money—

RUTH   *(swiftly)*   We ain't never had none before—*open it!*

MAMA *finally makes a good strong tear and pulls out the thin blue slice of paper and inspects it closely. The boy and his mother study it raptly over* MAMA*'s shoulders.*

MAMA   Travis! *(She is counting off with doubt.)*   Is that the right number of zeros.

TRAVIS   Yes'm . . . ten thousand dollars. Gaalee, Grandmama, you rich.

MAMA   *(she holds the check away from her, still looking at it. Slowly her face sobers into a mask of unhappiness)*   Ten thousand dollars. *(She hands it to* RUTH.*)* Put it away somewhere, Ruth. *(She does not look at* RUTH; *her eyes seem to be seeing something somewhere very far off.)* Ten thousand dollars they give you. Ten thousand dollars.

TRAVIS *(to his mother, sincerely)* What's the matter with Grandmama—don't she want to be rich?

RUTH *(distractedly)* You go on out and play now, baby. *(TRAVIS exits. MAMA starts wiping dishes absently, humming intently to herself. RUTH turns to her, with kind exasperation.)* You're gone and got yourself upset.

MAMA *(not looking at her)* I spec if it wasn't for you all . . . I would just put that money away or give it to the church or something.

RUTH Now what kind of talk is that. Mr. Younger would just be plain mad if he could hear you talking foolish like that.

MAMA *(stopping and staring off)* Yes . . . he sure would. *(Sighing)* We got enough to do with that money, all right. *(She halts then, and turns and looks at her daughter-in-law hard; RUTH avoids her eyes and MAMA wipes her hands with finality and starts to speak firmly to RUTH.)* Where did you go today, girl?

RUTH To the doctor.

MAMA *(impatiently)* Now, Ruth . . . you know better than that. Old Doctor Jones is strange enough in his way but there ain't nothing 'bout him makes somebody slip and call him "she"—like you done this morning.

RUTH Well, that's what happened—my tongue slipped.

MAMA You went to see that woman, didn't you?

RUTH *(defensively, giving herself away)* What woman you talkin about?

MAMA *(angrily)* That woman who—

WALTER *enters in great excitement.*

WALTER Did it come?

MAMA *(quietly)* Can't you give people a Christian greeting before you start asking about money?

WALTER *(to RUTH)* Did it come? *(RUTH unfolds the check and lays it quietly before him, watching him intently with thoughts of her own. WALTER sits down and grasps it close and counts off the zeros.)* Ten thousand dollars—*(He turns suddenly, frantically to his mother and draws some papers out of his breast pocket.)* Mama—look. Old Willy Harris put everything on paper—

MAMA Son—I think you ought to talk to your wife. . . . I'll go on out and leave you alone if you want—

WALTER I can talk to her later—Mama, look—

MAMA Son—

WALTER WILL SOMEBODY PLEASE LISTEN TO ME TODAY!

MAMA *(quietly)* I don't 'low no yellin' in this house, Walter Lee, and you know it— *(WALTER stares at them in frustration and starts to speak several times.)* And there ain't going to be no investing in no liquor stores. I don't aim to have to speak on that again.

A long pause.

WALTER Oh—so you don't aim to have to speak on that again? So *you* have decided. . . . *(Crumpling his papers)* Well, *you* tell that to my boy tonight when you put him to sleep on the living-room couch. . . . *(Turning to MAMA and speaking directly to her)* Yeah—and tell it to my wife, Mama, tomorrow when she has to go out of here to look after somebody else's kids. And tell it to *me*, Mama, every time we need a new pair of curtains and I have to watch *you* go out and work in somebody's kitchen. Yeah, you tell me then!

WALTER *starts out.*

RUTH Where you going?

WALTER I'm going out!

RUTH Where?

WALTER Just out of this house somewhere—

RUTH *(getting her coat)* I'll come too.

WALTER I don't want you to come!

RUTH I got something to talk to you about, Walter.

WALTER That's too bad.

MAMA *(still quietly)* Walter Lee—*(She waits and he finally turns and looks at her.)* Sit down.

WALTER I'm a grown man, Mama.

MAMA Ain't nobody said you wasn't grown. But you still in my house and my presence. And as long as you are—you'll talk to your wife civil. Now sit down.

RUTH *(suddenly)* Oh, let him go on out and drink himself to death! He makes me sick to my stomach! *(She flings her coat against him.)*

WALTER *(violently)* And you turn mine too, baby! *(RUTH goes into their bedroom and slams the door behind her.)* That was my greatest mistake—

MAMA *(still quietly)* Walter, what is the matter with you?

WALTER Matter with me? Ain't nothing the matter with *me!*

MAMA Yes there is. Something eating you up like a crazy man. Something more than me not giving you this money. The past few years I been watching it happen to you. You get all nervous acting and kind of wild in the eyes—*(WALTER jumps up impatiently at her words.)* I said sit there now, I'm talking to you!

WALTER Mama—I don't need no nagging at me today.

MAMA Seem like you getting to a place where you always tied up in some kind of knot about something. But if anybody ask you 'bout it you just yell at 'em and bust out the house and go out and drink somewheres. Walter Lee, people can't live with that. Ruth's a good, patient girl in her way—but you getting to be too much. Boy, don't make the mistake of driving that girl away from you.

WALTER Why—what she do for me?

MAMA She loves you.

WALTER Mama—I'm going out. I want to go off somewhere and be by myself for a while.

MAMA I'm sorry 'bout your liquor store, son. It just wasn't the thing for us to do. That's what I want to tell you about—

WALTER I got to go out, Mama—*(He rises.)*

MAMA It's dangerous, son.

WALTER What's dangerous?

MAMA When a man goes outside his home to look for peace.

WALTER *(beseechingly)* Then why can't there never be no peace in this house then?

MAMA You done found it in some other house?

WALTER No—there ain't no woman! Why do women always think there's a woman somewhere when a man gets restless. *(Coming to her)* Mama—Mama—I want so many things. . . .

MAMA Yes, son—

WALTER I want so many things that they are driving me kind of crazy. . . . Mama —look at me.

MAMA I'm looking at you. You a good-looking boy. You got a job, a nice wife, a fine boy and—

WALTER A job. *(Looks at her)* Mama, a job? I open and close car doors all day long. I drive a man around in his limousine and I say, "Yes, sir; no, sir; very good, sir; shall I take the Drive, sir?" Mama, that ain't no kind of job . . . that ain't nothing at all. *(Very quietly)* Mama, I don't know if I can make you understand.

MAMA Understand what, baby?

WALTER *(quietly)* Sometimes it's like I can see the future stretched out in front of me—just plain as day. The future, Mama. Hanging over there at the edge of my days. Just waiting for me—a big, looming blank space—full of *nothing*. Just waiting for *me*. *(Pause)* Mama—sometimes when I'm downtown and I pass them cool, quiet-looking restaurants where them white boys are sitting back and talking 'bout things . . . sitting there turning deals worth millions of dollars . . . sometimes I see guys don't look much older than me—

MAMA Son—how come you talk so much 'bout money?

WALTER *(with immense passion)* Because it is life, Mama!

MAMA *(quietly)* Oh—*(Very quietly)* So now it's life. Money is life. Once upon a time freedom used to be life—now it's money. I guess the world really do change. . . .

WALTER No—it was always money, Mama. We just didn't know about it.

MAMA No . . . something has changed. *(She looks at him.)* You something new, boy. In my time we was worried about not being lynched and getting to the North if we could and how to stay alive and still have a pinch of dignity too. . . . Now here come you and Beneatha—talking 'bout things we ain't never even thought about hardly, me and your daddy. You ain't satisfied or proud of nothing we done. I mean that you had a home; that we kept you out of trouble till you was grown; that you don't have to ride to work on the back of nobody's streetcar—You my children—but how different we done become.

WALTER You just don't understand, Mama, you just don't understand.

MAMA Son—do you know your wife is expecting another baby? (WALTER *stands, stunned, and absorbs what his mother has said.)* That's what she wanted to talk to you about. (WALTER *sinks down into a chair.)* This ain't for me to be telling—but you ought to know. *(She waits.)* I think Ruth is thinking 'bout getting rid of that child.

WALTER *(slowly understanding)* No—no—Ruth wouldn't do that.

MAMA When the world gets ugly enough—a woman will do anything for her family. *The part that's already living.*

WALTER You don't know Ruth, Mama, if you think she would do that.

RUTH *opens the bedroom door and stands there a little limp.*

RUTH *(beaten)* Yes I would too, Walter. *(Pause)* I gave her a five-dollar down payment.

There is total silence as the man stares at his wife and the mother stares at her son.

MAMA *(presently)* Well—*(Tightly)* Well—son, I'm waiting to hear you say something. . . . I'm waiting to hear how you be your father's son. Be the man he was. . . . *(Pause)* Your wife say she going to destroy your child. And I'm waiting to hear you talk like him and say we a people who give children life, not who destroys them—*(She rises.)* I'm waiting to see you stand up and look like your daddy and say we done give up one baby to poverty and that we ain't going to give up nary another one. . . . I'm waiting.

WALTER   Ruth—

MAMA   If you a son of mine, tell her! (WALTER *turns, looks at her and can say nothing. She continues, bitterly.*) You . . . you are a disgrace to your father's memory. Somebody get me my hat.

Curtain

ACT II

SCENE I. *Time: Later the same day.*

At rise: RUTH *is ironing again. She has the radio going. Presently* BENEATHA'*s bedroom door opens and* RUTH'*s mouth falls and she puts down the iron in fascination.*

RUTH   What have we got on tonight!

BENEATHA *(emerging grandly from the doorway so that we can see her thoroughly robed in the costume* ASAGAI *brought)*   You are looking at what a well-dressed Nigerian woman wears—*(She parades for* RUTH, *her hair completely hidden by the headdress; she is coquettishly fanning herself with an ornate oriental fan, mistakenly more like Butterfly than any Nigerian that ever was.)* Isn't it beautiful? *(She promenades to the radio and, with an arrogant flourish, turns off the good loud blues that is playing.)* Enough of this assimilationist junk! (RUTH *follows her with her eyes as she goes to the phonograph and puts on a record and turns and waits ceremoniously for the music to come up. Then, with a shout—)* OCOMO-GOSIAY!

RUTH *jumps. The music comes up, a lovely Nigerian melody.* BENEATHA *listens, enraptured, her eyes far away—"back to the past." She begins to dance.* RUTH *is dumbfounded.*

RUTH   What kind of dance is that?

BENEATHA   A folk dance.

RUTH *(Pearl Bailey)*   What kind of folks do that, honey?

BENEATHA   It's from Nigeria. It's a dance of welcome.

RUTH   Who you welcoming?

BENEATHA   The men back to the village.

RUTH   Where they been?

BENEATHA   How should I know—out hunting or something. Anyway, they are coming back now. . . .

RUTH   Well, that's good.

BENEATHA *(with the record)*

> *Alundi, alundi*
> *Alundi alunya*
> *Jop pu a jeepua*
> *Ang gu sooooooooooo*
>
> *Ai yai yae . . .*
> *Ayehaye—alundi . . .*

WALTER *comes in during this performance; he has obviously been drinking. He leans against the door heavily and watches his sister, at first with distaste. Then his eyes look off—"back to the past"—as he lifts both his fists to the roof, screaming.*

Lorraine Hansberry   997

WALTER YEAH ... AND ETHIOPIA STRETCH FORTH HER HANDS AGAIN!

RUTH *(drily, looking at him)* Yes—and Africa sure is claiming her own tonight. *(She gives them both up and starts ironing again.)*

WALTER *(all in a drunken, dramatic shout)* Shut up! ... I'm digging them drums ... them drums move me! ... *(He makes his weaving way to his wife's face and leans in close to her.)* In my *heart of hearts—(he thumps his chest)*—I am much warrior!

RUTH *(without even looking up)* In your heart of hearts you are much drunkard.

WALTER *(coming away from her and starting to wander around the room, shouting)* Me and Jomo ... *(Intently, in his sister's face. She has stopped dancing to watch him in this unknown mood.)* That's my man, Kenyatta. *(Shouting and thumping his chest)* FLAMING SPEAR! HOT DAMN! *(He is suddenly in possession of an imaginary spear and actively spearing enemies all over the room.)* OCOMOGOSIAY ... THE LION IS WAKING ... OWIMOWEH! *(he pulls his shirt open and leaps up on a table and gestures with his spear. The bell rings.* RUTH *goes to answer.)*

BENEATHA *(to encourage* WALTER, *thoroughly caught up with this side of him)* OCOMOGOSIAY, FLAMING SPEAR!

WALTER *(on the table, very far gone, his eyes pure glass sheets. He sees what we cannot, that he is a leader of his people, a great chief, a descendant of Chaka, and that the hour to march has come)* Listen, my black brothers—

BENEATHA OCOMOGOSIAY!

WALTER —Do you hear the waters rushing against the shores of the coastlands—

BENEATHA OCOMOGOSIAY!

WALTER —Do you hear the screeching of the cocks in yonder hills beyond where the chiefs meet in council for the coming of the mighty war—

BENEATHA OCOMOGOSIAY!

WALTER —Do you hear the beating of the wings of the birds flying low over the mountains and the low places of our land—

RUTH *opens the door.* GEORGE MURCHISON *enters.*

BENEATHA OCOMOGOSIAY!

WALTER —Do you hear the singing of the women, singing the war songs of our fathers to the babies in the great houses ... singing the sweet war songs? OH, DO YOU HEAR, MY BLACK BROTHERS!

BENEATHA *(completely gone)* We hear you, Flaming Spear—

WALTER Telling us to prepare for the greatness of the time—*(To* GEORGE*)* Black Brother! *(He extends his hand for the fraternal clasp.)*

GEORGE Black Brother, hell!

RUTH *(having had enough, and embarrassed for the family)* Beneatha, you got company—what's the matter with you? Walter Lee Younger, get down off that table and stop acting like a fool. ...

WALTER *comes down off the table suddenly and makes a quick exit to the bathroom.*

RUTH He's had a little to drink. ... I don't know what her excuse is.

GEORGE *(to* BENEATHA*)* Look honey, we're going *to* the theater—we're not going to be *in* it ... so go change, huh?

RUTH You expect this boy to go out with you looking like that?

BENEATHA *(looking at* GEORGE*)* That's up to George. If he's ashamed of his heritage—

GEORGE Oh, don't be so proud of yourself, Bennie—just because you look eccentric.

BENEATHA How can something that's natural be eccentric?

GEORGE That's what being eccentric means—being natural. Get dressed.

BENEATHA I don't like that, George.

RUTH Why must you and your brother make an argument out of everything people say?

BENEATHA Because I hate assimilationist Negroes!

RUTH Will somebody please tell me what assimila-whoever means!

GEORGE Oh, it's just a college girl's way of calling people Uncle Toms—but that isn't what it means at all.

RUTH Well, what does it mean?

BENEATHA *(cutting* GEORGE *off and staring at him as she replies to* RUTH*)* It means someone who is willing to give up his own culture and submerge himself completely in the dominant, and in this case, *oppressive* culture!

GEORGE Oh, dear, dear, dear! Here we go! A lecture on the African past! On our Great West African Heritage! In one second we will hear all about the great Ashanti empires; the great Songhay civilizations; and the great sculpture of Bénin —and then some poetry in the Bantu—and the whole monologue will end with the word *heritage! (Nastily)* Let's face it, baby, your heritage is nothing but a bunch of raggedy-assed spirituals and some grass huts!

BENEATHA *Grass huts!* (RUTH *crosses to her and forcibly pushes her toward the bedroom.)* See there . . . you are standing there in your splendid ignorance talking about people who were the first to smelt iron on the face of the earth! (RUTH *is pushing her through the door.)* The Ashanti were performing surgical operations when the English—(RUTH *pulls the door to, with* BENEATHA *on the other side, and smiles graciously at* GEORGE. BENEATHA *opens the door and shouts the end of the sentence defiantly at* GEORGE)—were still tattooing themselves with blue dragons. . . . *(She goes back inside.)*

RUTH Have a seat, George. *(They both sit.* RUTH *folds her hands rather primly on her lap, determined to demonstrate the civilization of the family.)* Warm, ain't it? I mean for September. *(Pause)* Just like they always say about Chicago weather: If it's too hot or cold for you, just wait a minute and it'll change. *(She smiles happily at this cliché of clichés.)* Everybody say it's got to do with them bombs and things they keep setting off. *(Pause)* Would you like a nice cold beer?

GEORGE No, thank you. I don't care for beer. *(He looks at his watch)* I hope she hurries up.

RUTH What time is the show?

GEORGE It's an eight-thirty curtain. That's just Chicago, though. In New York standard curtain time is eight forty. *(He is rather proud of this knowledge.)*

RUTH *(properly appreciating it)* You get to New York a lot?

GEORGE *(offhand)* Few times a year.

RUTH Oh—that's nice. I've never been to New York.

WALTER *enters. We feel he has relieved himself, but the edge of unreality is still with him.*

WALTER New York ain't got nothing Chicago ain't. Just a bunch of hustling people all squeezed up together—being "Eastern." *(He turns his face into a screw of displeasure.)*

GEORGE   Oh—you've been?

WALTER   *Plenty* of times.

RUTH *(shocked at the lie)*   Walter Lee Younger!

WALTER *(staring her down)*   Plenty! *(Pause)* What we got to drink in this house? Why don't you offer this man some refreshment? *(To* GEORGE*)* They don't know how to entertain people in this house, man.

GEORGE   Thank you—I don't really care for anything.

WALTER *(feeling his head; sobriety coming)*   Where's Mama?

RUTH   She ain't come back yet.

WALTER *(looking* MURCHISON *over from head to toe, scrutinizing his carefully casual tweed sports jacket over cashmere V-neck sweater over soft eyelet shirt and tie, and soft slacks, finished off with white buckskin shoes)* Why all you college boys wear them fairyish-looking white shoes?

RUTH   Walter Lee!

GEORGE MURCHISON *ignores the remark.*

WALTER *(to* RUTH*)*   Well, they look crazy as hell—white shoes, cold as it is.

RUTH *(crushed)*   You have to excuse him—

WALTER   No he don't! Excuse me for what? What you always excusing me for! I'll excuse myself when I needs to be excused! *(A pause)* They look as funny as them black knee socks Beneatha wears out of here all the time.

RUTH   It's the college *style*, Walter.

WALTER   Style, hell. She looks like she got burnt legs or something!

RUTH   Oh, Walter—

WALTER *(an irritable mimic)*   Oh, Walter! Oh, Walter! *(To* MURCHISON*)* How's your old man making out? I understand you all going to buy that big hotel on the Drive? *(He finds a beer in the refrigerator, wanders over to* MURCHISON, *sipping and wiping his lips with the back of his hand, and straddling a chair backwards to talk to the other man.)* Shrewd move. Your old man is all right, man. *(Tapping his head and half winking for emphasis)* I mean he knows how to operate. I mean he thinks *big,* you know what I mean, I mean for a *home,* you know? But I think he's kind of running out of ideas now. I'd like to talk to him. Listen, man, I got some plans that could turn this city upside down. I mean I think like he does. *Big.* Invest big, gamble big, hell, lose *big* if you have to, you know what I mean. It's hard to find a man on this whole Southside who understands my kind of thinking—you dig? *(He scrutinizes* MURCHISON *again, drinks his beer, squints his eyes and leans in close, confidential, man to man.)* Me and you ought to sit down and talk sometimes, man. Man, I got me some ideas. . . .

GEORGE *(with boredom)*   Yeah—sometimes we'll have to do that, Walter.

WALTER *(understanding the indifference, and offended)*   Yeah—well, when you get the time, man. I know you a busy little boy.

RUTH   Walter, please—

WALTER *(bitterly, hurt)*   I know ain't nothing in this world as busy as you colored college boys with your fraternity pins and white shoes. . . .

RUTH *(covering her face with humiliation)*   Oh, Walter Lee—

WALTER   I see you all that time—with the books tucked under your arms—going to your *(British A—a mimic)* "clahsses." And for what! What the hell you learning over there? Filling up your heads—*(counting off on his fingers)*—with the sociology and the psychology—but they teaching you how to be a man? How to take over and run the world? They teaching you how to run a rubber plantation or a steel mill? Naw—just to talk proper and read books and wear white shoes. . . .

GEORGE *(looking at him with distaste, a little above it all)* You're all wacked up with bitterness, man.

WALTER *(intently, almost quietly, between the teeth, glaring at the boy)* And you—ain't you bitter, man? Ain't you just about had it yet? Don't you see no stars gleaming that you can't reach out and grab? You happy?—You contented son-of-a-bitch—you happy? You got it made? Bitter? Man, I'm a volcano. Bitter? Here I am a giant—surrounded by ants! Ants who can't even understand what it is the giant is talking about.

RUTH *(passionately and suddenly)* Oh, Walter—ain't you with nobody!

WALTER *(violently)* No! 'Cause ain't nobody with me! Not even my own mother!

RUTH Walter, that's a terrible thing to say!

BENEATHA *enters, dressed for the evening in a cocktail dress and earrings.*

GEORGE Well—hey, you look great.

BENEATHA Let's go, George. See you all later.

RUTH Have a nice time.

GEORGE Thanks. Good night. *(To* WALTER, *sarcastically)* Good night, *Prometheus.* (Beneatha *and* GEORGE *exit.)*

WALTER *(to* RUTH) Who is Prometheus?

RUTH I don't know. Don't worry about it.

WALTER *(in fury, pointing after* GEORGE) See there—they get to a point where they can't insult you man to man—they got to go talk about something ain't nobody never heard of!

RUTH How do you know it was an insult? *(To humor him)* Maybe Prometheus is a nice fellow.

WALTER Prometheus! I bet there ain't even no such thing! I bet that simple-minded clown—

RUTH Walter—*(She stops what she is doing and looks at him.)*

WALTER *(yelling)* Don't start!

RUTH Start what?

WALTER Your nagging! Where was I? Who was I with? How much money did I spend?

RUTH *(plaintively)* Walter Lee—why don't we just try to talk about it. . . .

WALTER *(not listening)* I been talking with people who understand me. People who care about the things I got on my mind.

RUTH *(wearily)* I guess that means people like Willy Harris.

WALTER Yes, people like Willy Harris.

RUTH *(with a sudden flash of impatience)* Why don't you all just hurry up and go into the banking business and stop talking about it!

WALTER Why? You want to know why? 'Cause we all tied up in a race of people that don't know how to do nothing but moan, pray and have babies!

The line is too bitter even for him and he looks at her and sits down.

RUTH Oh, Walter . . . *(Softly)* Honey, why can't you stop fighting me?

WALTER *(without thinking)* Who's fighting you? Who even cares about you?

This line begins the retardation of his mood.

RUTH   Well—*(She waits a long time, and then with resignation starts to put away her things.)* I guess I might as well go on to bed. . . . *(More or less to herself)* I don't know where we lost it . . . but we have. . . . *(Then, to him)* —I'm sorry about this new baby, Walter. I guess maybe I better go on and do what I started . . . I guess I just didn't realize how bad things was with us . . . I guess I just didn't really realize —*(She starts out to the bedroom and stops.)* You want some hot milk?

WALTER   Hot milk?

RUTH   Yes—hot milk.

WALTER   Why hot milk?

RUTH   'Cause after all that liquor you come home with you ought to have something hot in your stomach.

WALTER   I don't want no milk.

RUTH   You want some coffee then?

WALTER   No, I don't want no coffee. I don't want nothing hot to drink. *(Almost plaintively)* Why you always trying to give me something to eat?

RUTH   *(standing and looking at him helplessly)*   What else can I give you, Walter Lee Younger?

She stands and looks at him and presently turns to go out again. He lifts his head and watches her going away from him in a new mood which began to emerge when he asked her "Who cares about you?"

WALTER   It's been rough, ain't, it baby? *(She hears and stops but does not turn around and he continues to her back.)* I guess between two people there ain't never as much understood as folks generally thinks there is. I mean like between me and you—*(She turns to face him.)* How we gets to the place where we scared to talk softness to each other. *(He waits, thinking hard himself).* Why you think it got to be like that? *(He is thoughtful, almost as a child would be.)* Ruth, what is it gets into people ought to be close?

RUTH   I don't know, honey. I think about it a lot.

WALTER   On account of you and me, you mean? The way things are with us. The way something done come down between us.

RUTH   There ain't so much between us, Walter. . . . Not when you come to me and try to talk to me. Try to be with me . . . a little even.

WALTER   *(total honesty)*   Sometimes . . . sometimes . . . I don't even know how to try.

RUTH   Walter—

WALTER   Yes?

RUTH   *(coming to him, gently and with misgiving, but coming to him)*   Honey . . . life don't have to be like this. I mean sometimes people can do things so that things are better. . . . You remember how we used to talk when Travis was born . . . about the way we were going to live . . . the kind of house . . . *(She is stroking his head.)* Well, it's all starting to slip away from us. . . .

MAMA *enters, and* WALTER *jumps up and shouts at her.*

WALTER   Mama, where have you been?

MAMA   My—them steps is longer than they used to be. Whew! *(She sits down and ignores him.)* How you feeling this evening, Ruth?

RUTH *shrugs, disturbed some at having been prematurely interrupted and watching her husband knowingly.*

WALTER Mama, where have you been all day?
MAMA *(still ignoring him and leaning on the table and changing to more comfortable shoes)* Where's Travis?
RUTH I let him go out earlier and he ain't come back yet. Boy, is he going to get it!
WALTER Mama!
MAMA *(as if she has heard him for the first time)* Yes, son?
WALTER Where did you go this afternoon?
MAMA I went downtown to tend to some business that I had to tend to.
WALTER What kind of business?
MAMA You know better than to question me like a child, Brother.
WALTER *(rising and bending over the table)* Where were you, Mama? *(Bring his fists down and shouting)* Mama, you didn't go do something with that insurance money, something crazy?

The front door opens slowly, interrupting him, and TRAVIS *peeks his head in, less than hopefully.*

TRAVIS *(to his mother)* Mama, I—
RUTH "Mama I" nothing! You're going to get, it boy! Get on in that bedroom and get yourself ready!
TRAVIS But I—
MAMA Why don't you all never let the child explain hisself.
RUTH Keep out of it now, Lena.

MAMA *clamps her lips together, and* RUTH *advances toward her son menacingly.*

RUTH A thousand times I have told you not to go off like that—
MAMA *(holding out her arms to her grandson)* Well—at least let me tell him something. I want him to be the first one to hear . . . Come here, Travis. *(The boy obeys, gladly.)* Travis—*(she takes him by the shoulder an looks into his face)*—you know that money we got in the mail this morning?
TRAVIS Yes'm—
MAMA Well—what you think your grandmama gone and done with that money?
TRAVIS I don't know, Grandmama.
MAMA *(putting her finger on his nose for emphasis)* She went out and she bought you a house! *(The explosion comes from* WALTER *at the end of the revelation and he jumps up and turns away from all of them in a fury.* MAMA *continues, to* TRAVIS*)* You glad about the house? It's going to be yours when you get to be a man.
TRAVIS Yeah—I always wanted to live in a house.
MAMA All right, gimme some sugar then—*(*TRAVIS *puts his arms around her neck as she watches her son over the boy's shoulder. Then to* TRAVIS, *after the embrace)* Now when you say your prayers tonight, you thank God and your grandfather— 'cause it was him who give you the house—in his way.
RUTH *(taking the boy from* MAMA *and pushing him toward the bedroom)* Now you get out of here and get ready for your beating.
TRAVIS Aw, Mama—

RUTH   Get on in there—*(Closing the door behind him and turning radiantly to her mother-in-law)* So you went and did it!

MAMA *(quietly, looking at her son with pain)*   Yes, I did.

RUTH *(raising both arms classically)*   Praise God! *(Looks at* WALTER *a moment, who says nothing. She crosses rapidly to her husband.)* Please honey—let me be glad . . . you be glad too. *(She has laid her hands on his shoulders, but he shakes himself free of her roughly, without turning to face her.)* Oh, Walter . . . a home . . . a home. *(She comes back to* MAMA*.)* Well—where is it? How big is it? How much it going to cost?

MAMA   Well—

RUTH   When we moving?

MAMA *(smiling at her)*   First of the month.

RUTH *(throwing back her head with jubilance)*   Praise God!

MAMA *(tentatively, still looking at her son's back turned against her and* RUTH*)* It's —it's a nice house too. . . . *(She cannot help speaking directly to him. An imploring quality in her voice, her manner, makes her almost like a girl now.)* Three bedrooms—nice big one for you and Ruth. . . . Me and Beneatha still have to share our room, but Travis have one of his own—and *(with difficulty)* I figure if the—new baby—is a boy, we could get one of them double-decker outfits. . . . And there's a yard with a little patch of dirt where I could maybe get to grow me a flowers. . . . And a nice big basement. . . .

RUTH   Walter honey, be glad—

MAMA *(still to his back, fingering things on the table)*   'Course I don't want to make it sound fancier than it is. . . . It's just a plain little old house—but it's made good and solid—and it will be *ours*. Walter Lee—it makes a difference in a man when he can walk on the floors that belong to *him*. . . .

RUTH   Where is it?

MAMA *(frightened at this telling)*   Well—well—it's out there in Clybourne Park—

RUTH'S *radiance fades abruptly, and* WALTER *finally turns slowly to face his mother with incredulity and hostility.*

RUTH   Where?

MAMA *(matter-of-factly)*   Four o six Clybourne Street, Clybourne Park.

RUTH   Clybourne Park? Mama, there ain't no colored people living in Clybourne Park.

MAMA *(almost idiotically)*   Well, I guess there's going to be some now.

WALTER *(bitterly)*   So that's the peace and comfort you went out and bought for us today!

MAMA *(raising her eyes to meet his finally)*   Son—I just tried to find the nicest place for the least amount of money for my family.

RUTH *(trying to recover from the shock)*   Well—well—'course I ain't one never been 'fraid of no crackers, mind you—but—well, wasn't there no other houses no-where?

MAMA   Them houses they put up for colored in them areas way out all seem to cost twice as much as other houses. I did the best I could.

RUTH *(struck senseless with the news, in its various degrees of goodness and trouble, she sits a moment, her fists propping her chin in thought, and then she starts to rise, bringing her fists down with vigor, the radiance spreading from cheek to cheek again)*   Well—well!—All I can say is—if this is my time in life—*my time*—to say good-bye—*(and she builds with momentum as she starts to circle the room with an exuberant, almost tearfully happy release)*—to these Goddamned cracking walls! —*(she pounds the walls)*—and these marching *roaches!*—*(she wipes at an imaginary army of marching roaches)*—and this cramped little closet which ain't now or never was no kitchen! . . . then I say it loud and good, *Hallelujah! and good-bye misery . . . . I don't never want to see your ugly face again! (She laughs joyously, having practically destroyed the apartment, and flings her arms up and lets them come down happily, slowly, reflectively, over her abdomen, aware for the first time perhaps that the life therein pulses with happiness and not despair.)* Lena?

MAMA *(moved, watching her happiness)* Yes, honey?

RUTH *(looking off)* Is there—is there a whole lot of sunlight?

MAMA *(understanding)* Yes, child, there's a whole lot of sunlight.

Long pause.

RUTH *(collecting herself and going to the door of the room* TRAVIS *is in)* Well—I guess I better see 'bout Travis. *(To* MAMA*)* Lord, I sure don't feel like whipping nobody today! *(She exits.)*

MAMA *(The mother and son are left alone now and the mother waits a long time, considering deeply, before she speaks)* Son—you—you understand what I done, don't you? *(*WALTER *is silent and sullen.)* I—I just seen my family falling apart today . . . just falling to pieces in front of my eyes. . . . We couldn't of gone on like we was today. We was going backwards 'stead of forwards—talking 'bout killing babies and wishing each other was dead . . . . When it gets like that in life—you just got to do something different, push on out and do something bigger. . . . *(She waits.)* I wish you say something, son . . . I wish you'd say how deep inside you you think I done the right thing—

WALTER *(crossing slowly to his bedroom door and finally turning there and speaking measuredly)* What you need me to say you done right for? *You* the head of this family. You run our lives like you want to. It was your money and you did what you wanted with it. So what you need for me to say it was all right for? *(Bitterly, to hurt her as deeply as he knows is possible)* So you butchered up a dream of mine —you—who always talking 'bout your children's dreams. . . .

MAMA Walter Lee—

He just closes the door behind him. MAMA *sits alone, thinking heavily.*

Curtain

SCENE II. *Time: Friday night, a few weeks later.*
At rise: Packing crates mark the intention of the family to move. BENEATHA *and* GEORGE *come in, presumably from an evening out again.*

GEORGE O.K. . . . O.K., whatever you say. . . . *(They both sit on the couch. He tries to kiss her. She moves away.)* Look, we've had a nice evening; let's not spoil it, huh? . . .

He again turns her head and tries to nuzzle in and she turns away from him, not with distaste but with momentary lack of interest; in a mood to pursue what they were talking about.

BENEATHA I'm *trying* to talk to you.

GEORGE We always talk.

BENEATHA Yes—and I love to talk.

GEORGE *(exasperated; rising)* I know it and I don't mind it sometimes . . . I want you to cut it out, see—The moody stuff, I mean. I don't like it. You're a nice-looking girl . . . all over. That's all you need, honey, forget the atmosphere. Guys aren't going to go for the atmosphere—they're going to go for what they see. Be glad for that. Drop the Garbo routine. It doesn't go with you. As for myself, I want a nice —*(groping)*—simple *(thoughtfully)*—sophisticated girl . . . not a poet—O.K.?

She rebuffs him again and he starts to leave.

BENEATHA Why are you angry?

GEORGE Because this is stupid! I don't go out with you to discuss the nature of "quiet desperation" or to hear all about your thoughts—because the world will go on thinking what it thinks regardless—

BENEATHA Then why read books? Why go to school?

GEORGE *(with artificial patience, counting on his fingers)* It's simple. You read books—to learn facts—to get grades—to pass the course—to get a degree. That's all—it has nothing to do with thoughts.

A long pause.

BENEATHA I see. *(A longer pause as she looks at him)* Good night, George.

GEORGE *looks at her a little oddly, and starts to exit. He meets* MAMA *coming in.*

GEORGE Oh—hello, Mrs. Younger.

MAMA Hello, George, how you feeling?

GEORGE Fine—fine, how are you?

MAMA Oh, a little tired. You know them steps can get you after a day's work. You all have a nice time tonight?

GEORGE Yes—a fine time. Well, good night.

MAMA Good night. *(He exits.* MAMA *closes the door behind her.)* Hello, honey. What you sitting like that for?

BENEATHA I'm just sitting.

MAMA Didn't you have a nice time?

BENEATHA No.

MAMA No? What's the matter?

BENEATHA Mama, George is a fool—honest. *(She rises.)*

MAMA *(hustling around unloading the packages she has entered with. She stops.)* Is he, baby?

BENEATHA Yes.

BENEATHA *makes up* TRAVIS' *bed as she talks.*

MAMA You sure?

BENEATHA Yes.

MAMA Well—I guess you better not waste your time with no fools.

BENEATHA *looks up at her mother, watching her put groceries in the refrigerator. Finally she gathers up her things and starts into the bedroom. At the door she stops and looks back at her mother.*

BENEATHA Mama—

MAMA Yes, baby—

BENEATHA   Thank you.

MAMA   For what?

BENEATHA   For understanding me this time.

She exits quickly and the mother stands, smiling a little, looking at the place where BENEATHA *just stood.* RUTH *enters.*

RUTH   Now don't you fool with any of this stuff, Lena—

MAMA   Oh, I just thought I'd sort a few things out.

The phone rings. RUTH *answers.*

RUTH   *(at the phone)*   Hello—Just a minute. *(Goes to the door)* Walter, it's Mrs. Arnold. *(Waits. Goes back to the phone. Tense)* Hello. Yes, this is his wife speaking . . . He's lying down now. Yes . . . well, he'll be in tomorrow. He's been very sick. Yes—I know we should have called, but we were so sure he'd be able to come in today. Yes—yes, I'm very sorry. Yes . . . Thank you very much. *(She hangs up.* WALTER *is standing in the doorway of the bedroom behind her.)* That was Mrs. Arnold.

WALTER   *(indifferently)*   Was it?

RUTH   She said if you don't come in tomorrow that they are getting a new man. . . .

WALTER   Ain't that sad—ain't that crying sad.

RUTH   She said Mr. Arnold has had to take a cab for three days. . . . Walter, you ain't been to work for three days! *(This is a revelation to her.)* Where you been, Walter Lee Younger? *(*WALTER *looks at her and starts to laugh.)* You're going to lose your job.

WALTER   That's right . . .

RUTH   Oh, Walter, and with your mother working like a dog every day—

WALTER   That's sad too—Everything is sad.

MAMA   What you been doing for these three days, son?

WALTER   Mama—you don't know all the things a man what got leisure can find to do in this city. . . . What's this—Friday night? Well—Wednesday I borrowed Willy Harris' car and I went for a drive . . . just me and myself and I drove and drove . . . Way out . . . way past South Chicago, and I parked the car and I sat and looked at the steel mills all day long. I just sat in the car and looked at them big black chimneys for hours. Then I drove back and I went to the Green Hat. *(Pause)* And Thursday—Thursday I borrowed the car again and I got in it and I pointed it the other way and I drove the other way—for hours—way, way up to Wisconsin, and I looked at the farms. I just drove and looked at the farms. Then I drove back and I went to the Green Hat. *(Pause)* And today—today I didn't get the car. Today I just walked. All over the South Side. And I looked at the Negroes and they looked at me and finally I just sat down on the curb at Thirty-ninth and South Parkway and I just sat there and watched the Negroes go by. And then I went to the Green Hat. You all sad? You all depressed? And you know where I am going right now—

RUTH *goes out quietly.*

MAMA   Oh, Big Walter, is this the harvest of our days?

WALTER   You know what I like about the Green Hat? *(He turns the radio on and a steamy, deep blues pours into the room.)* I like this little cat they got there who blows a sax. . . . He blows. He talks to me. He ain't but 'bout five feet tall and he's got a conked head and his eyes is always closed and he's all music—

MAMA *(rising and getting some papers out of her handbag)* Walter—

WALTER And there's this other guy who plays the piano . . . and they got a sound. I mean they can work on some music. . . . They got the best little combo in the world in the Green Hat. . . . You can just sit there and drink and listen to them three men play and you realize that don't nothing matter worth a damn, but just being there—

MAMA I've helped do it to you, haven't I, son? Walter, I been wrong.

WALTER Naw—you ain't never been wrong about nothing, Mama.

MAMA Listen to me, now. I say I been wrong, son. That I been doing to you what the rest of the world been doing to you. *(She stops and he looks up slowly at her and she meets his eyes pleadingly.)* Walter—what you ain't never understood is that I ain't got nothing, don't own nothing, ain't never really wanted nothing that wasn't for you. There ain't nothing as precious to me. . . . There ain't nothing worth holding on to, money, dreams, nothing else—if it means—if it means it's going to destroy my boy. *(She puts her papers in front of him and he watches her without speaking or moving.)* I paid the man thirty-five hundred dollars down on the house. That leaves sixty-five hundred dollars. Monday morning I want you to take this money and take three thousand dollars and put it in a savings account for Beneatha's medical schooling. The rest you put in a checking account—with your name on it. And from now on any penny that come out of it or that go in it is for you to look after. For you to decide. *(She drops her hands a little helplessly.)* It ain't much, but it's all I got in the world and I'm putting it in your hands. I'm telling you to be the head of this family from now on like you supposed to be.

WALTER *(stares at the money)* You trust me like that, Mama?

MAMA I ain't never stop trusting you. Like I ain't never stop loving you.

She goes out, and WALTER *sits looking at the money on the table as the music continues in its idiom, pulsing in the room. Finally, in a decisive gesture, he gets up, and, in mingled joy and desperation, picks up the money. At the same moment,* TRAVIS *enters for bed.*

TRAVIS What's the matter, Daddy? You drunk?

WALTER *(sweetly, more sweetly than we have ever known him)* No, Daddy ain't drunk. Daddy ain't going to never be drunk again. . . .

TRAVIS Well, good night, Daddy.

The father has come from behind the couch and leans over, embracing his son.

WALTER Son, I feel like talking to you tonight.

TRAVIS About what?

WALTER Oh, about a lot of things. About you and what kind of man you going to be when you grow up. . . . Son—son, what do you want to be when you grow up?

TRAVIS A bus driver.

WALTER *(laughing a little)* A what? Man, that ain't nothing to want to be!

TRAVIS Why not?

WALTER 'Cause, man—it ain't big enough—you know what I mean.

TRAVIS I don't know then. I can't make up my mind. Sometimes Mama asks me that too. And sometimes when I tell her I just want to be like you—she says she don't want me to be like that and sometimes she says she does. . . .

WALTER *(gathering him up in his arms)* You know what, Travis? In seven years you going to be seventeen years old. And things is going to be very different with us in seven years, Travis. . . . One day when you are seventeen I'll come home—home from my office downtown somewhere—

TRAVIS You don't work in no office, Daddy.

WALTER No—but after tonight. After what your daddy gonna do tonight, there's going to be offices—a whole lot of offices. . . .

TRAVIS What you gonna do tonight, Daddy?

WALTER You wouldn't understand yet, son, but your daddy's gonna make a transaction . . . a business transaction that's going to change our lives. . . . That's how come one day when you 'bout seventeen years old I'll come home and I'll be pretty tired, you know what I mean, after a day of conferences and secretaries getting things wrong the way they do . . . 'cause an executive's life is hell, man—*(The more he talks, the farther away he gets.)* And I'll pull the car up on the driveway . . . just a plain black Chrysler, I think, with white walls—no—black tires. More elegant. Rich people don't have to be flashy . . . though I'll have to get something a little sportier for Ruth—maybe a Cadillac convertible to do her shopping in. . . . And I'll come up the steps to the house and the gardner will be clipping away at the hedges and he'll say, "Good evening, Mr. Younger." And I'll say, "Hello, Jefferson, how are you this evening?" And I'll go inside and Ruth will come downstairs and meet me at the door and we'll kiss each other and she'll take my arm and we'll go up to your room to see you sitting on the floor with the catalogues of all the great schools in America around you. . . . All the great schools in the world! And—and I'll say, all right son—it's your seventeenth birthday, what is it you've decided? . . . Just tell me where you want to go to school and you'll *go*. Just tell me, what it is you want to be—and you'll *be* it. . . . Whatever you want to be—Yessir! *(He holds his arms open for* TRAVIS.*)* You just name it, son . . . *(*TRAVIS *leaps into them)* and I hand you the world!

WALTER'S *voice has risen in pitch and hysterical promise and on the last line he lifts* TRAVIS *high.*

Blackout

SCENE III. *Time: Saturday, moving day, one week later.*

Before the curtain rises, RUTH'S *voice, a strident, dramatic church alto, cuts through the silence.*

It is, in the darkness, a triumphant surge, a penetrating statement of expectation: "Oh Lord, I don't feel no ways tired! Children, oh, glory hallelujah!"

As the curtain rises we see that RUTH *is alone in the living room, finishing up the family's packing. It is moving day. She is nailing crates and tying cartons.* BENEATHA *enters, carrying a guitar case, and watches her exuberant sister-in-law.*

RUTH Hey!

BENEATHA *(putting away the case)* Hi.

RUTH *(pointing at a package)* Honey—look in that package there and see what I found on sale this morning at the South Center. *(*RUTH *gets up and moves to the package and draws out some curtains.* Lookahere—hand-turned hems!

BENEATHA How do you know the window size out there?

RUTH *(who hadn't thought of that)* Oh—Well, they bound to fit something in the whole house. Anyhow, they was too good a bargain to pass up. *(RUTH slaps her head, suddenly remembering something.)* Oh, Bennie—I meant to put a special note on that carton over there. That's your mamma's good china and she wants 'em to be very careful with it.

BENEATHA   I'll do it.

BENEATHA *finds a piece of paper and starts to draw large letters on it.*

RUTH   You know what I'm going to do soon as I get in that new house?

BENEATHA   What?

RUTH   Honey—I'm going to run me a tub of water up to here. . . . *(With her fingers practically up to her nostrils)* And I'm going to get in it—and I am going to sit . . . and sit in that hot water and the first person who knocks to tell *me* to hurry up and come out—

BENEATHA   Gets shot at sunrise.

RUTH *(laughing happily)*   You said it, sister! *(Noticing how large* BENEATHA *is absentmindedly making the note)* Honey, they ain't going to read that from no airplane.

BENEATHA *(laughing herself)* I guess I always think things have more emphasis if they are big, somehow.

RUTH *(looking up at her and smiling)*   You and your brother seem to have that as a philosophy of life. Lord, that man—done changed so 'round here. You know—you know what we did last night? Me and Walter Lee?

BENEATHA   What?

RUTH *(smiling to herself)*   We went to the movies. *(Looking at* BENEATHA *to see if she understands)* We went to the movies. You know the last time me and Walter went to the movies together?

BENEATHA   No.

RUTH   Me neither. That's how long it been. *(Smiling again)* But we went last night. The picture wasn't much good, but that didn't seem to matter. We went—and we held hands.

BENEATHA   Oh, Lord!

RUTH   We held hands—and you know what?

BENEATHA   What?

RUTH   When we come out of the show it was late and dark and all the stores and things was closed up . . . and it was kind of chilly and there wasn't many people on the streets . . . and we was still holding hands, me and Walter.

BENEATHA   You're killing me.

WALTER *enters with a large package. His happiness is deep in him; he cannot keep still with his new-found exuberance. He is singing and wiggling and snapping his fingers. He puts his package in a corner and puts a phonograph record, which he has brought in with him, on the record player. As the music comes up he dances over to* RUTH *and tries to get her to dance with him. She gives in at last to his raunchiness and in a fit of giggling allows herself to be drawn into his mood and together they deliberately burlesque an old social dance of their youth.*

BENEATHA *(regarding them a long time as they dance, then drawing in her breath for a deeply exaggerated comment which she does not particularly mean)* Talk about —olddddddddddd-fashioneddddddddd—Negroes!

WALTER *(stopping momentarily)*   What kind of Negroes?

He says this in fun. He is not angry with her today, nor with anyone. He starts to dance with his wife again.

BENEATHA   Old-fashioned.

WALTER *(as he dances with* RUTH*)*   You know, when these *New Negroes* have their convention—*(pointing at his sister)*—that is going to be the chairman of the Committee on Unending Agitation. *(He goes on dancing, then stops.)* Race, race, race! . . . Girl, I do believe you are the first person in the history of the entire human race to successfully brainwash yourself. *(*BENEATHA *breaks up and he goes on dancing. He stops again, enjoying his tease.)* Damn, even the N double A C P takes a holiday sometimes! *(*BENEATHA *and* RUTH *laugh. He dances with* RUTH *some more and starts to laugh and stops and pantomimes someone over and operating table.)* I can just see that chick someday looking down at some poor cat on an operating table before she starts to slice him, saying . . . *(pulling his sleeves back maliciously)* "By the way, what are your views on civil rights down there? . . ."*

He laughs at her again and starts to dance happily. The bell sounds.

BENEATHA   Sticks and stones may break my bones but . . . words will never hurt me!

BENEATHA *goes to the door and opens it as* WALTER *and* RUTH *go on with the clowning.* BENEATHA *is somewhat surprised to see a quiet-looking middle-aged white man in a business suit holding his hat and a briefcase in his hand and consulting a small piece of paper.*

MAN   Uh—how do you do, miss. I am looking for a Mrs.—*(he looks at the slip of paper)* Mrs. Lena Younger?

BENEATHA *(smoothing her hair with slight embarrassment)*   Oh—yes, that's my mother. Excuse me. *(She closes the door and turns to quiet the other two.)* Ruth! Brother! Somebody's here. *(Then she opens the door. The man casts a curious quick glance at all of them.)* Uh—come in please.

MAN *(coming in)*   Thank you.

BENEATHA   My mother isn't here just now. Is it business?

MAN   Yes . . . well, of a sort.

WALTER *(freely, the Man of the House)*   Have a seat. I'm Mrs. Younger's son. I look after most of her business matters.

RUTH *and* BENEATHA *exchange amused glances.*

MAN *(regarding* WALTER*, and sitting)*   Well—My name is Karl Lindner . . .

WALTER *(stretching out his hand)*   Walter Younger. This is my wife—*(*RUTH *nods politely)*—and my sister.

LINDNER   How do you do.

WALTER *(amiably, as he sits himself easily on a chair, leaning with interest forward on his knees and looking expectantly into the newcomer's face)*   What can we do for you, Mr. Lindner!

LINDNER *(some minor shuffling of the hat and briefcase on his knees)*   Well—I am a representative of the Clybourne Park Improvement Association—

WALTER *(pointing)*   Why don't you sit your things on the floor?

LINDNER   Oh—yes. Thank you. *(He slides the briefcase and hat under the chair.)* And as I was saying— I am from the Clybourne Park Improvement Association and we have had it brought to our attention at the last meeting that you people—

or at least your mother—has bought a piece of residential property at—*(he digs for the slip of paper again)*—four o six Clybourne Street. . . .

WALTER   That's right. Care for something to drink? Ruth, get Mr. Lindner a beer.

LINDNER *(upset for some reason)*   Oh—no, really. I mean thank you very much, but no thank you.

RUTH *(innocently)*   Some coffee?

LINDNER   Thank you, nothing at all.

BENEATHA *is watching the man carefully.*

LINDNER   Well, I don't know how much you folks know about our organization. *(He is a gentle man; thoughtful and somewhat labored in his manner.)* It is one of those community organizations set up to look after—oh, you know, things like block upkeep and special projects and we also have what we call our New Neighbors Orientation Committee. . . .

BENEATHA *(drily)*   Yes—and what do they do?

LINDNER *(turning a little to her and then returning the main force to WALTER)* Well —it's what you might call a sort of welcoming committee, I guess. I mean they, we, I'm the chairman of the committee—go around and see the new people who move into the neighborhood and sort of give them the lowdown on the way we do things out in Clybourne Park.

BENEATHA *(with appreciation of the two meanings, which escape RUTH and WALTER)*   Un-huh.

LINDNER   And we also have the category of what the association calls—*(he looks elsewhere)*—uh—special community problems. . . .

BENEATHA   Yes—and what are some of those?

WALTER   Girl, let the man talk.

LINDNER *(with understated relief)*   Thank you. I would like to explain this thing in my own way. I mean I want to explain to you in a certain way.

WALTER   Go ahead.

LINDNER   Yes. Well. I'm going to try to get right to the point. I'm sure we'll all appreciate that in the long run.

BENEATHA   Yes.

LINDNER   Well—

WALTER   Be still now!

LINDNER   Well—

RUTH *(still innocently)*   Would you like another chair—you don't look comfortable.

LINDNER *(more frustrated than annoyed)*   No, thank you very much. Please. Well —to get right to the point I—*(a great breath, and he is off at last)* I am sure you people must be aware of some of the incidents which have happened in various parts of the city when colored people have moved into certain areas—*(BENEATHA exhales heavily and starts tossing a piece of fruit up and down in the air.)* Well— because we have what I think is going to be a unique type of organization in American community life—not only do we deplore that kind of thing—but we are trying to do something about it. *(BENEATHA stops tossing and turns with a new and quizzical interest to the man.)* We feel—*gaining confidence in his mission because of the interest in the faces of the people he is talking to)*—we feel that most of the trouble in this world, when you come right down to it—*(he hits his knee for emphasis)*—most of the trouble exists because people just don't sit down and talk to each other.

RUTH *(nodding as she might in church, pleased with the remark)*   You can say that again, mister.

LINDNER *(more encouraged by such affirmation)*   That we don't try hard enough in this world to understand the other fellow's problem. The other guy's point of view.

RUTH   Now that's right.

BENEATHA *and* WALTER *merely watch and listen with genuine interest.*

LINDNER   Yes—that's the way we feel out in Clybourne Park. And that's why I was elected to come here this afternoon and talk to you people. Friendly like, you know, the way people should talk to each other and see if we couldn't find some way to work this thing out. As I say, the whole business is a matter of *caring* about the other fellow. Anybody can see that you are a nice family of folks, hard-working and honest I'm sure. *(BENEATHA frowns slightly, qizzically, her head tilted regarding him.)* Today everybody knows what it means to be on the outside of *something*. And of course, there is always somebody who is out to take the advantage of people who don't always understand.

WALTER   What do you mean?

LINDNER   Well—you see our community is made up of people who've worked hard as the dickens for years to build up that little community. They're not rich and fancy people; just hard-working, honest people who don't really have much but those little homes and a dream of the kind of community they want to raise their children in. Now, I don't say we are perfect and there is a lot wrong in some of the things they want. But you've got to admit that a man, right or wrong, has the right to want to have the neighborhood he lives in a certain kind of way. And at the moment the overwhelming majority of our people out there feel that people get along better, take more of a common interest in the life of the community, when they share a common background. I want you to believe me when I tell you that race prejudice simply doesn't enter into it. It is a matter of the people of Clybourne Park believing, rightly or wrongly, as I say, that for the happiness of all concerned that our Negro families are happier when they live in their *own* communities.

BENEATHA *(with a grand and bitter gesture)*   This, friends, is the Welcoming Committee!

WALTER *(dumbfounded, looking at* LINDNER*)*   Is this what you came marching all the way over here to tell us?

LINDNER   Well, now we've been having a fine conversation. I hope you'll hear me all the way through.

WALTER *(tightly)*   Go ahead, man.

LINDNER   You see—in the face of all the things I have said, we are prepared to make your family a very generous offer. . . .

BENEATHA   Thirty pieces and not a coin less!

WALTER   Yeah?

LINDNER *(putting on his glasses and drawing a form out of the briefcase)*   Our association is prepared, through the collective effort of our people, to buy the house from you at a financial gain to your family.

RUTH   Lord have mercy, ain't this the living gall!

WALTER   All right, you through?

LINDNER   Well, I want to give you the exact terms of the financial arrangement—

WALTER   We don't want to hear no exact terms of no arrangements. I want to know if you got any more to tell us 'bout getting together?

LINDNER *(taking off his glasses)*   Well—I don't suppose that you feel . . .

WALTER   Never mind how I feel—you got any more to say 'bout how people ought to sit down and talk to each other? . . . Get out of my house, man. *(He turns his back and walks to the door.)*

LINDNER *(looking around at the hostile faces and reaching and assembling his hat and briefcase)*   Well—I don't understand why you people are reacting this way. What do you think you are going to gain by moving into a neighborhood where you just aren't wanted and where some elements—well—people can get awful worked up when they feel that their whole way of life and everything they've ever worked for is threatened.

WALTER   Get out.

LINDNER *(at the door, holding a small card)*   Well—I'm sorry it went like this.

WALTER   Get out.

LINDNER *(almost sadly, regarding* WALTER*)*   You just can't force people to change their hearts, son.

He turns and puts his card on the table and exits. WALTER *pushes the door to with stinging hatred, and stands looking at it.* RUTH *just sits and* BENEATHA *just stands. They say nothing,* MAMA *and* TRAVIS *enter.*

MAMA   Well—this all the packing got done since I left out of here this morning. I testify before God that my children got all the energy of the dead. What time the moving men due?

BENEATHA   Four o'clock. You had a caller, Mama. *(She is smiling, teasingly.)*

MAMA   Sure enough—who?

BENEATHA *(her arms folded saucily)*   The Welcoming Committee.

WALTER *and* RUTH *giggle.*

MAMA *(innocently)*   Who?

BENEATHA   The Welcoming Committee. They said they're sure going to be glad to see you when you get there.

WALTER *(devilishly)*   Yeah, they said they can't hardly wait to see your face.

Laughter.

MAMA *(sensing their facetiousness)*   What's the matter with you all?

WALTER   Ain't nothing the matter with us. We just telling you 'bout the gentleman who came to see you this afternoon. From the Clybourne Park Improvement Association.

MAMA   What he want?

RUTH *(in the same mood as* BENEATHA *and* WALTER*)* To welcome you, honey.

WALTER   He said they can't hardly wait. He said the one thing they don't have, that they just *dying* to have out there is a fine family of colored people! *(To* RUTH *and* BENEATHA*)* Ain't that right!

RUTH AND BENEATHA *(mockingly)*   Yeah! He left his card in case—

They indicate the card, and MAMA *picks it up and throws it on the floor—understanding and looking off as she draws her chair up to the table on which she has put her plant and some sticks and some cord.*

MAMA   Father, give us strength. *(Knowingly—and without fun)* Did he threaten us?

BENEATHA   Oh—Mama—they don't do it like that any more. He talked Brother-hood. He said everybody ought to learn how to sit down and hate each other with good Christian fellowship.

She and WALTER *shake hands to ridicule the remark.*

MAMA *(sadly)*   Lord, protect us. . . .

RUTH   You should hear the money those folks raised to buy the house from us. All we paid and then some.

BENEATHA   What they think we going to do—eat 'em?

RUTH   No, honey, marry 'em.

MAMA *(shaking her head)*   Lord, Lord, Lord. . . .

RUTH   Well—that's the way the crackers crumble. Joke.

BENEATHA *(laughingly noticing what her mother is doing)*   Mama, what are you doing?

MAMA   Fixing my plant so it won't get hurt none on the way. . . .

BENEATHA   Mama, you going to take *that* to the new house?

MAMA   Uh-huh—

BENEATHA   That raggedy-looking old thing?

MAMA *(stopping and looking at her)*   It expresses *me.*

RUTH *(with delight, to* BENEATHA*)*   So there, Miss Thing!

WALTER *comes to* MAMA *suddenly and bends down behind her and squeezes her in his arms with all his strength. She is overwhelmed by the suddenness of it and, though delighted, her manner is like that of* RUTH *with* TRAVIS.

MAMA   Look out now, boy! You make me mess up my thing here!

WALTER *(his face lit, he slips down on his knees beside her, his arms still about her)*   Mama . . . you know what it means to climb up in the chariot?

MAMA *(gruffly, very happy)*   Get on away from me now. . . .

RUTH *(near the gift-wrapped package, trying to catch* WALTER*'s eye)*   Psst—

WALTER   What the old song say, Mama . . . .

RUTH   Walter—Now? *(She is pointing at the package.)*

WALTER *(speaking the lines, sweetly, playfully, in his mother's face)*

> I got wings . . . you got wings . . .
> All God's Children got wings . . .

MAMA   Boy—get out of my face and do some work. . . .

WALTER

> When I get to heaven gonna put on my wings.
> Gonna fly all over God's heaven . . .

BENEATHA *(teasingly, from across the room)*   Everybody talking 'bout heaven ain't going there!

WALTER *(to* RUTH, *who is carrying the box across to them)*   I don't know, you think we ought to give her that. . . . Seems to me she ain't been very appreciative around here.

MAMA *(eyeing the box, which is obviously a gift)*   What is that?

WALTER *(taking it from* RUTH *and putting it on the table in front of* MAMA*)*   Well—what you all think? Should we give it to her?

RUTH   Oh—she was pretty good today.

MAMA   I'll good you—*(She turns her eyes to the box again.)*

BENEATHA   Open it, Mama.

She stands up, looks at it, turns and looks at all of them, and then presses her hands together and does not open the package.

WALTER   *(sweetly)*   Open it, Mama. It's for you. *(MAMA looks in his eyes. It is the first present in her life without its being Christmas. Slowly she opens her package and lifts out, one by one, a brand-new sparkling set of gardening tools.* WALTER *continues, prodding)* Ruth made up the note—read it . . .

MAMA   *(picking up the card and adjusting her glasses)*   "To our own Mrs. Miniver —Love from Brother, Ruth and Beneatha." Ain't that lovely. . . .

TRAVIS   *(tugging at his father's sleeve)*   Daddy, can I give her mine now?

WALTER   All right, son. *(TRAVIS flies to get his gift.)* Travis didn't want to go in with the rest of us, Mama. He got his own. *(Somewhat amused)* We don't know what it is. . . .

TRAVIS   *(racing back in the room with a large hatbox and putting it in front of his grandmother)*   Here!

MAMA   Lord have mercy, baby. You done gone and bought your grandmother a hat?

TRAVIS   *(very proud)*   Open it!

She does and lifts out an elaborate, but very elaborate, wide gardening hat, and all the adults break up at the sight of it.

RUTH   Travis, honey, what is that?

TRAVIS   *(who thinks it is beautiful and appropriate)*   It's a gardening hat! Like the ladies always have on in the magazines when they work in their gardens.

BENEATHA   *(giggling fiercely)*   Travis—we were trying to make Mama Mrs. Miniver—not Scarlett O'Hara!

MAMA   *(indignantly)*   What's the matter with you all! This here is a beautiful hat! *(Absurdly)* I always wanted me one just like it!

She pops it on her head to prove it to her grandson, and the hat is ludicrous and considerably oversized.

RUTH   Hot dog! Go, Mama!

WALTER   *(doubled over with laughter)*   I'm sorry, Mama—but you look like you ready to go out and chop you some cotton sure enough!

They all laugh except MAMA, out of deference to TRAVIS' feelings.

MAMA   *(gathering the boy up to her)*   Bless your heart—this is the prettiest hat I ever owned—(WALTER, RUTH, *and* BENEATHA *chime in noisily, festively and insincerely congratulating* TRAVIS *on his gift.)* What are we all standing around here for? We ain't finished packin' yet. Bennie, you ain't packed one book.

The bell rings.

BENEATHA   That couldn't be the movers . . . it's not hardly two good yet—

BENEATHA *goes into her room.* MAMA *starts for door.*

WALTER   *(turning, stiffening)*   Wait—wait—I'll get it. *(He stands and looks at the door.)*

MAMA You expecting company, son?

WALTER *(just looking at the door)* Yeah—yeah. . . .

MAMA *looks at* RUTH, *and they exchange innocent and unfrightened glances.*

MAMA *(not understanding)* Well, let them in, son.

BENEATHA *(from her room)* We need some more string.

MAMA Travis—you run to the hardware and get me some string cord.

MAMA *goes out and* WALTER *turns and looks at* RUTH. TRAVIS *goes to a dish for money.*

RUTH Why don't you answer the door, man?

WALTER *(suddenly bounding across the floor to her)* 'Cause sometimes it hard to let the future begin! *(Stooping down in her face)*

> I got wings! You got wings!
> All God's children got wings!

(He crosses to the door and throws it open. Standing there is a very slight little man in a not too prosperous business suit and with haunted frightened eyes and a hat pulled down tightly, brim up, around his forehead. TRAVIS *passes between the men and exits.* WALTER *leans deep in the man's face, still in his jubilance.)*

> When I get to heaven gonna put on my wings.
> Gonna fly all over God's heaven . . .

(The little man just stares at him.)
> Heaven—

(Suddenly he stops and looks past the little man into the empty hallway.) Where's Willy, man?

BOBO He ain't with me.

WALTER *(not disturbed)* Oh—come on in. You know my wife.

BOBO *(dumbly, taking off his hat)* Yes—h'you, Miss Ruth.

RUTH *(quietly, a mood apart from her husband already, seeing* BOBO*)* Hello, Bobo.

WALTER You right on time today. . . . Right on time. That's the way! *(He slaps* BOBO *on his back.)* Sit down . . . lemme hear.

RUTH *stands stiffly and quietly in back of them, as though somehow she senses death, her eyes fixed on her husband.*

BOBO *(his frightened eyes on the floor, his hat in his hands)* Could I please get a drink of water, before I tell you about it, Walter Lee?

WALTER *does not take his eyes off the man.* RUTH *goes blindly to the tap and gets a glass of water and brings it to* BOBO.

WALTER There ain't nothing wrong, is there?

BOBO Lemme tell you—

WALTER Man— didn't nothing go wrong?

BOBO Lemme tell you—Walter Lee. *(Looking at* RUTH *and talking to her more than to* WALTER*)* You know how it was. I got to tell you how it was. I mean first I got to tell you how it was all the way . . . I mean about the money I put in, Walter Lee. . . .

WALTER *(with taut agitation now)* What about the money you put in?

BOBO   Well—it wasn't much as we told you—me and Willy—*(He stops.)* I'm sorry, Walter. I got a bad feeling about it. I got a real bad feeling about it. . . .

WALTER   Man, what you telling me about all this for? . . . Tell me what happened in Springfield. . . .

BOBO   Springfield.

RUTH *(like a dead woman)*   What was supposed to happen in Springfield?

BOBO *(to her)*   This deal that me and Walter went into with Willy—Me and Willy was going to go down to Springfield and spread some money 'round so's we wouldn't have to wait so long for the liquor license. . . . That's what we were going to do. Everybody said that was the way you had to do, you understand, Miss Ruth?

WALTER   Man—what happened down there?

BOBO *(a pitiful man, near tears)*   I'm trying to tell you, Walter.

WALTER *(screaming at him suddenly)*   THEN TELL ME, GODDAMMIT . . . WHAT'S THE MATTER WITH YOU?

BOBO   Man . . . I didn't go to no Springfield, yesterday.

WALTER *(halted, life hanging in the moment)*   Why not?

BOBO *(the long way, the hard way to tell)*   'Cause I didn't have no reasons to. . . .

WALTER   Man, what are you talking about!

BOBO   I'm talking about the fact that when I got to the train station yesterday morning—eight o'clock like we planned . . . Man—*Willy didn't never show up.*

WALTER   Why . . . where was he . . . where is he?

BOBO   That's what I'm trying to tell you . . . I don't know . . . I waited six hours . . . I called his house . . . and I waited . . . six hours . . . I waited in that train station six hours . . . *(Breaking into tears)* That was all the extra money I had in the world. . . . *(Looking up at WALTER with the tears running down his face)* Man, *Willy is gone.*

WALTER   Gone, what you mean Willy is gone? Gone where? You mean he went by himself. You mean he went off to Springfield by himself—to take care of getting the license—*(Turns and looks anxiously at RUTH)* You mean maybe he didn't want too many people in on the business down there? *(Looks to RUTH again, as before)* You know Willy got his own ways. *(Looks back to BOBO)* Maybe you was late yesterday and he just went on down there without you. Maybe—maybe—he's been callin' you at home tryin' to tell you what happened or something. Maybe—maybe—he just got sick. He's somewhere—he's got to be somewhere. We just got to find him—me and you got to find him. *(Grabs BOBO senselessly by the collar and starts to shake him)* We got to!

BOBO *(in sudden angry, frightened agony)*   What's the matter with you, Walter! *When a cat take off with your money he don't leave you no maps!*

WALTER *(turning madly, as though he is looking for WILLY in the very room)*   Willy! . . . Willy . . . don't do it. . . . Please don't do it. . . . Man, not with that money . . . Man, please, not with that money . . . Oh, God . . . Don't let it be true. . . . *(He is wandering around, crying out for WILLY and looking for him or perhaps for help from God.)* Man . . . I trusted you . . . Man, I put my life in your hands. . . . *(He starts to crumple down on the floor as RUTH just covers her face in horror. MAMA opens the door and comes into the room, with BENEATHA behind her.)* Man . . . *(He starts to pound the floor with his fists, sobbing wildly.)* That money is made out of my father's flesh. . . .

BOBO *(standing over him helplessly)*   I'm sorry, Walter. . . . *(Only WALTER's sobs reply. BOBO puts on his hat.)* I had my life staked on this deal, too. . . . *(He exits.)*

MAMA *(to* WALTER*)*   Son—*(She goes to him, bends down to him, talks to his bent head.)* Son . . . Is it gone? Son, I gave you sixty-five hundred dollars. Is it gone? All of it? Beneatha's money too?

WALTER *(lifting his head slowly)*   Mama . . . I never . . . went to the bank at all. . . .

MAMA *(not wanting to believe him)*   You mean . . . your sister's school money . . . you used that too . . . Walter? . . .

WALTER   Yessss! . . . All of it. . . . It's all gone. . . .

There is total silence. RUTH *stands with her face covered with her hands;* BENEATHA *leans forlornly against a wall, fingering a piece of red ribbon from the mother's gift.* MAMA *stops and looks at her son without recognition and then, quite without thinking about it, starts to beat him senselessly in the face.* BENEATHA *goes to them and stops it.*

BENEATHA   Mama!

MAMA *stops and looks at both of her children and rises slowly and wanders vaguely, aimlessly away from them.*

MAMA   I seen . . . him . . . night after night . . . come in . . . and look at that rug . . . and then look at me . . . the red showing in his eyes . . . the veins moving in his head. . . . I seen him grow thin and old before he was forty . . . working and working and working like somebody's old horse . . . killing himself . . . and you—you gave it all away in a day. . . .

BENEATHA   Mama—

MAMA   Oh, God . . . *(She looks up to Him.)* Look down here—and show me the strength.

BENEATHA   Mama—

MAMA *(folding over)*   Strength . . .

BENEATHA *(plaintively)*   Mama . . .

MAMA   Strength!

Curtain

ACT III

An hour later.

At curtain, there is a sullen light of gloom in the living room, gray light not unlike that which began the first scene of Act I. At left we can see WALTER within his room, alone with himself. He is stretched out on the bed, his shirt out and open, his arms under his head. He does not smoke, he does not cry out, he merely lies there, looking up at the ceiling, much as if he were alone in the world.

In the living room BENEATHA sits at the table, still surrounded by the now almost ominous packing crates. She sits looking off. We feel that this is a mood struck perhaps an hour before, and it lingers now, full of the empty sound of profound disappointment. We see on a line from her brother's bedroom the sameness of their attitudes. Presently the bell rings and BENEATHA rises without ambition or interest in answering. It is ASAGAI, smiling broadly, striding into the room with energy and happy expectation and conversation.

ASAGAI   I came over . . . I had some free time. I thought I might help with the packing. Ah, I like the look of packing crates! A household in preparation for a journey! It depresses some people . . . but for me . . . it is another feeling. Something full of the flow of life, do you understand? Movement, progress . . . It makes me think of Africa.

BENEATHA   Africa!

ASAGAI   What kind of a mood is this? Have I told you how deeply you move me?

BENEATHA   He gave away the money, Asagai. . . .

ASAGAI   Who gave away what money?

BENEATHA   The insurance money. My brother gave it away.

ASAGAI   Gave it away?

BENEATHA   He made an investment! With a man even Travis wouldn't have trusted.

ASAGAI   And it's gone?

BENEATHA   Gone!

ASAGAI   I'm very sorry. . . . And you, now?

BENEATHA   Me? . . . Me? . . . Me I'm nothing. . . . Me. When I was very small . . . we used to take our sleds out in the wintertime and the only hills we had were the ice-covered stone steps of some houses down the street. And we used to fill them in with snow and make them smooth, and slide down them all day . . . and it was very dangerous you know . . . far too steep . . . and sure enough one day a kid named Rufus came down too fast and hit the sidewalk . . . and we saw his face just split open right there in front of us. . . . And I remember standing there looking at his bloody open face thinking that was the end of Rufus. But the ambulance came and they took him to the hospital and they fixed the broken bones and they sewed it all up . . . and the next time I saw Rufus he just had a little line down the middle of his face. . . . I never got over that. . . .

WALTER *sits up, listening on the bed. Throughout this scene it is important that we feel his reaction at all times, that he visibly respond to the words of his sister and* ASAGAI.

ASAGAI   What?

BENEATHA   That was what one person could do for another, fix him up—sew up the problem, make him all right again. That was the most marvelous thing in the world. . . . I wanted to do that. I always thought it was the one concrete thing in the world that a human being could do. Fix up the sick, you know—and make them whole again. This was truly being God. . . .

ASAGAI   You wanted to be God?

BENEATHA   No—I wanted to cure. It used to be so important to me. I wanted to cure. It used to matter. I used to care. I mean about people and how their bodies hurt. . . .

ASAGAI   And you've stopped caring?

BENEATHA   Yes—I think so.

ASAGAI   Why?

WALTER *rises, goes to the door of his room and is about to open it, then stops and stands listening, leaning on the door jamb.*

BENEATHA   Because it doesn't seem deep enough, close enough to what ails mankind—I mean this thing of sewing up bodies or administering drugs. Don't you understand? It was a child's reaction to the world. I thought that doctors had the secret to all the hurts. . . . That's the way a child sees things—or an idealist.

ASAGAI   Children see things very well sometimes—and idealists even better.

BENEATHA I know that's what you think. Because you are still where I left off—you still care. This is what you see for the world, for Africa. You with the dreams of the future will patch up all Africa—you are going to cure the Great Sore of colonialism with Independence—

ASAGAI Yes!

BENEATHA Yes—and you think that one word is the penicillin of the human spirit: "Independence!" But then what?

ASAGAI That will be the problem for another time. First we must get there.

BENEATHA And where does it end?

ASAGAI End? Who even spoke of an end? To life? To living?

BENEATHA An end to misery!

ASAGAI *(smiling)* You sound like a French intellectual.

BENEATHA No! I sound like a human being who just had her future taken right out of her hands! While I was sleeping in my bed in there, things were happening in this world that directly concerned me—and nobody asked me, consulted me—they just went out and did things—and changed my life. Don't you see there isn't any real progress, Asagai, there is only one large circle that we march in, around and around, each of us with our own little picture—in front of us—our own little mirage that we think is the future.

ASAGAI That is the mistake.

BENEATHA What?

ASAGAI What you just said—about the circle. It isn't a circle—it is simply a long line—as in geometry, you know, one that reaches into infinity. And because we cannot see the end—we also cannot see how it changes. And it is very odd but those who see the changes are called "idealists"—and those who cannot, or refuse to think, they are the "realists." It is very strange, and amusing too, I think.

BENEATHA You—you are almost religious.

ASAGAI Yes . . . I think I have the religion of doing what is necessary in the world —and of worshipping man—because he is so marvelous, you see.

BENEATHA Man is foul! And the human race deserves its misery!

ASAGAI You see: *you* have become the religious one in the old sense. Already, and after such a small defeat, you are worshipping despair.

BENEATHA From now on, I worship the truth—and the truth is that people are puny, small and selfish. . . .

ASAGAI Truth? Why is it that you despairing ones always think that only you have the truth? I never thought to see *you* like that. You! Your brother made a stupid, childish mistake—and you are grateful to him. So that now you can give up the ailing human race on account of it. You talk about what good is struggle; what good is anything? Where are we all going? And why are we bothering?

BENEATHA *And you cannot answer it!* All your talk and dreams about Africa and Independence. Independence and then what? What about all the crooks and petty thieves and just plain idiots who will come into power to steal and plunder the same as before—only now they will be black and do it in the name of the new Independence—You cannot answer that.

ASAGAI *(shouting over her) I live the answer! (Pause)* In my village at home it is the exceptional man who can even read a newspaper . . . or who ever *sees* a book at all. I will go home and much of what I will have to say will seem strange to the people of my village. . . . But I will teach and work and things will happen, slowly and swiftly. At times it will seem that nothing changes at all . . . and then again . . .

the sudden dramatic events which make history leap into the future. And then quiet again. Retrogression even. Guns, murder, revolution. And I even will have moments when I wonder if the quiet was not better than all that death and hatred. But I will look about my village at the illiteracy and disease and ignorance and I will not wonder long. And perhaps . . . perhaps I will be a great man. . . . I mean perhaps I will hold on to the substance of truth and find my way always with the right course . . . and perhaps for it I will be butchered in my bed some night by the servants of the empire. . . .

BENEATHA *The martyr!*

ASAGAI . . . or perhaps I shall live to be a very old man, respected and esteemed in my new nation. . . . And perhaps I shall hold office and this is what I'm trying to tell you, Alaiyo; perhaps the things I believe now for my country will be wrong and outmoded, and I will not understand and do terrible things to have things my way or merely to keep my power. Don't you see that there will be young men and women, not British soldiers then, but my own black countrymen . . . to step out of the shadows some evening and slit my then useless throat? Don't you see they have always been there . . . that they always will be. And that such a thing as my own death will be an advance? They who might kill me even . . . actually replenish me!

BENEATHA Oh, Asagai, I know all that.

ASAGAI Good! Then stop moaning and groaning and tell me what you plan to do.

BENEATHA Do?

ASAGAI I have a bit of a suggestion.

BENEATHA What?

ASAGAI *(rather quietly for him)* That when it is all over—that you come home with me—

BENEATHA *(slapping herself on the forehead with exasperation born of misunderstanding)* Oh—Asagai—at this moment you decide to be romantic!

ASAGAI *(quickly understanding the misunderstanding)* My dear, young creature of the New World—I do not mean across the city—I mean across the ocean; home —to Africa.

BENEATHA *(slowly understanding and turning to him with murmured amazement)* To—to Nigeria?

ASAGAI Yes! . . . *(Smiling and lifting his arms playfully)* Three hundred years later the African Prince rose up out of the seas and swept the maiden back across the middle passage over which her ancestors had come—

BENEATHA *(unable to play)* Nigeria?

ASAGAI Nigeria. Home. *(Coming to her with genuine romantic flippancy)* I will show you our mountains and our stars; and give you cool drinks from gourds and teach you the old songs and the ways of our people—and, in time, we will pretend that—*(very softly)*—you have only been away for a day—

She turns her back to him, thinking. He swings her around and takes her full in his arms in a long embrace which proceeds to passion.

BENEATHA *(pulling away)* You're getting me all mixed up—

ASAGAI Why?

BENEATHA Too many things—too many things have happened today. I must sit down and think. I don't know what I feel about anything right this minute. *(She promptly sits down and props her chin on her fist.)*

ASAGAI *(charmed)* All right, I shall leave you. No—don't get up. *(Touching her, gently, sweetly)* Just sit awhile and think. . . . Never be afraid to sit awhile and think. *(He goes to door and looks at her.)* How often I have looked at you and said, "Ah—so this is what the New World hath finally wrought. . . ."

He exits. BENEATHA *sits on alone. Presently* WALTER *enters from his room and starts to rummage through things, feverishly looking for something. She looks up and turns in her seat.*

BENEATHA *(hissingly)* Yes—just look at what the New World hath wrought! . . . Just look! *(She gestures with bitter disgust.)* There he is! *Monsieur le petit bourgeois noir*—himself! There he is—Symbol of a Rising Class! Entrepreneur! Titan of the system! *(*WALTER *ignores her completely and continues frantically and destructively looking for something and hurling things to floor and tearing things out of their place in his search.* BENEATHA *ignores the eccentricity of his actions and goes on with the monologue of insult.)* Did you dream of yachts on Lake Michigan, Brother? Did you see yourself on that Great Day sitting down at the Conference Table, surrounded by all the mighty bald-headed men in America? All halted, waiting, breathless, waiting for your pronouncements on industry? Waiting for you—Chairman of the Board? *(*WALTER *finds what he is looking for—a small piece of white paper—and pushes it in his pocket and puts on his coat and rushes out without ever having looked at her. She shouts after him.)* I look at you and I see the final triumph of stupidity in the world!

The door slams and she returns to just sitting again. RUTH *comes quickly out of* MAMA*'s room.*

RUTH Who was that?

BENEATHA Your husband.

RUTH Where did he go?

BENEATHA Who knows—maybe he has an appointment at U.S. Steel.

RUTH *(anxiously, with frightened eyes)* You didn't say nothing bad to him, did you?

BENEATHA Bad? Say anything bad to him? No—I told him he was a sweet boy and full of dreams and everything is strictly peachy keen, as the ofay kids say!

MAMA *enters from her bedroom. She is lost, vague, trying to catch hold, to make some sense of her former command of the world, but it still eludes her. A sense of waste overwhelms her gait; a measure of apology rides on her shoulders. She goes to her plant, which has remained on the table, looks at it, picks it up and takes it to the window sill and sits it outside, and she stands and looks at it a long moment. Then she closes the window, straightens her body with effort and turns around to her children.*

MAMA Well—ain't it a mess in here, though? *(A false cheerfulness, a beginning of something)* I guess we all better stop moping around and get some work done. All this unpacking and everything we got to do. *(*RUTH *raises her head slowly in response to the sense of the line; and* BENEATHA *in similar manner turns very slowly to look at her mother.)* One of you all better call the moving people and tell 'em not to come.

RUTH Tell 'em not to come?

MAMA Of course, baby. Ain't no need in 'em coming all the way here and having to go back. They charges for that too. *(She sits down, fingers to her brow, thinking.)* Lord, ever since I was a little girl, I always remember people saying, "Lena—Lena Eggleston, you aims too high all the time. You needs to slow down and see life a little more like it is. Just slow down some." That's what they always used to say down home—"Lord, that Lena Eggleston is a high-minded thing. She'll get her due one day!"

RUTH   No, Lena. . . .

MAMA   Me and Big Walter just didn't never learn right.

RUTH   Lena, no! We gotta go. Bennie—tell her. . . . *(She rises and crosses to* BENEATHA *with her arms outstretched.* BENEATHA *doesn't respond.)* Tell her we can still move . . . the notes ain't but a hundred and twenty-five a month. We got four grown people in this house—we can work. . . .

MAMA   *(to herself)*   Just aimed too high all the time—

RUTH   *(turning and going to* MAMA *fast—the words pouring out with urgency and desperation)*   Lena—I'll work. . . . I'll work twenty hours a day in all the kitchens in Chicago. . . . I'll strap my baby on my back if I have to and scrub all the floors in America and wash all the sheets in America if I have to—but we got to move. . . . We got to get out of here. . . .

MAMA *reaches out absently and pats* RUTH's *hand.*

MAMA   No—I see things differently now. Been thinking 'bout some of the things we could do to fix this place up some. I seen a second-hand bureau over on Maxwell Street just the other day that could fit right there. *(She points to where the new furniture might go.* RUTH *wanders away from her.)* Would need some new handles on it and then a little varnish and then it look like something brand-new. And— we can put up them new curtains in the kitchen. . . . Why this place be looking fine. Cheer us all up so that we forget trouble ever came. . . . *(To* RUTH*)* And you could get some nice screens to put up in your room around the baby's bassinet. . . . *(She looks at both of them, pleadingly.)* Sometimes you just got to know when to give up some things . . . and hold on to what you got.

WALTER *enters from the outside, looking spent and leaning against the door, his coat hanging from him.*

MAMA   Where you been, son?

WALTER   *(breathing hard)*   Made a call.

MAMA   To who, son?

WALTER   To The Man.

MAMA   What man, baby?

WALTER   The Man, Mama. Don't you know who The Man is?

RUTH   Walter Lee?

WALTER   *The Man.*   Like the guys in the streets say—The Man. Captain Boss— Mistuh Charley . . . Old Captain Please Mr. Bossman . . .

BENEATHA   *(suddenly)*   Lindner!

WALTER   That's right! That's good. I told him to come right over.

BENEATHA   *(fiercely, understanding)*   For what? What do you want to see him for!

WALTER   *(looking at his sister)*   We going to do business with him.

MAMA   What you talking 'bout, son?

WALTER   Talking 'bout life, Mama. You all always telling me to see life like it is. Well—I laid in there on my back today . . . and I figured it out. Life just like it is.

Who gets and who don't get. *(He sits down with his coat on and laughs.)* Mama, you know it's all divided up. Life is. Sure enough. Between the takers and the "tooken." *(He laughs.)* I've figured it out finally. *(He looks around at them.)* Yeah. Some of us always getting "tooken." *(He laughs.)* People like Willy Harris, they don't never get "tooken." And you know why the rest of us do? 'Cause we all mixed up. Mixed up bad. We get to looking 'round for the right and the wrong; and we worry about it and cry about it and stay up nights trying to figure out 'bout the wrong and the right of things all the time. . . . And all the time, man, them takers is out there operating, just taking and taking. Willy Harris? Shoot—Willy Harris don't even count. He don't even count in the big scheme of things. But I'll say one thing for old Willy Harris . . . he's taught me something. He's taught me to keep my eye on what counts in this world. Yeah—*(shouting out a little)* Thanks, Willy!

RUTH   What did you call that man for, Walter Lee?

WALTER   Called him to tell him to come on over to the show. Gonna put on a show for the man. Just what he wants to see. You see, Mama, the man came here today and he told us that them people out there where you want us to move—well they so upset they willing to pay us not to move out there. *(He laughs again.)* And— and oh, Mama—you would of been proud of the way me and Ruth and Bennie acted. We told him to get out . . . Lord have mercy! We told the man to get out. Oh, we was some proud folks this afternoon, yeah. *(He lights a cigarette.)* We were still full of that old-time stuff. . . .

RUTH   *(coming toward him slowly)*   You talking 'bout taking them people's money to keep us from moving in that house?

WALTER   I ain't just talking 'bout it, baby—I'm telling you that's what's going to happen.

BENEATHA   Oh, God! Where is the bottom! Where is the real honest-to-God bottom so he can't go any farther!

WALTER   See—that's old stuff. You and that boy that was here today. You all want everybody to carry a flag and a spear and sing some marching songs, huh? You wanna spend your life looking into things and trying to find the right and the wrong part, huh? Yeah. You know what's going to happen to that boy someday— he'll find himself sitting in a dungeon, locked in forever—and the takers will have the key! Forget it, baby! There ain't no causes—there ain't nothing but taking in this world, and he who takes most is smartest—and it don't make a damn bit of difference *how*.

MAMA   You making something inside me cry, son. Some awful pain inside me.

WALTER   Don't cry, Mama. Understand. That white man is going to walk in that door able to write checks for more money than we ever had. It's important to him and I'm going to help him . . . I'm going to put on the show, Mama.

MAMA   Son—I come from five generations of people who was slaves and share-croppers—but ain't nobody in my family never let nobody pay 'em no money that was a way of telling us we wasn't fit to walk the earth. We ain't never been that poor. *(Raising her eyes and looking at him)* We ain't never been that dead inside.

BENEATHA   Well—we are dead now. All the talk about dreams and sunlight that goes on in this house. All dead.

WALTER   What's the matter with you all! I didn't make this world! It was give to me this way! Hell, yes, I want some yachts someday! Yes, I want to hang some real pearls 'round my wife's neck. Ain't she supposed to wear no pearls? Somebody tell me—tell me, who decides which women is suppose to wear pearls in this world. I tell you I am a *man*—and I think my wife should wear some pearls in this world!

This last line hangs a good while and WALTER *begins to move about the room. The word "man" has penetrated his consciousness; he mumbles it to himself repeatedly between strange agitated pauses as he moves about.*

MAMA   Baby, how you going to feel on the inside?

WALTER   Fine! . . . Going to feel fine . . . a man. . . .

MAMA   You won't have nothing left then, Walter Lee.

WALTER *(coming to her)*   I'm going to feel fine, Mama. I'm going to look that son-of-a-bitch in the eyes and say—*(he falters)*—and say, "All right, Mr. Lindner—*(he falters even more)*—that's your neighborhood out there. You got the right to keep it like you want. You got the right to have it like you want. Just write the check and—the house is yours." And, and I am going to say—*(His voice almost breaks.)* And you—you people just put the money in my hand and won't have to live next to this bunch of stinking niggers! . . . *(He straightens up and moves away from his mother, walking around the room.)* Maybe—maybe I'll just get down on my black knees. . . . *(He does so;* RUTH *and* BENNIE *and* MAMA *watch him in frozen horror.)* Captain, Mistuh, Bossman. *(He starts crying.)* A-hee-hee-hee! *(Wringing his hands in profoundly anguished imitation)* Yasssssuh! Great White Father, just gi' ussen de money, fo' God's sake, and we's ain't gwine come out deh and dirty up yo' white folks neighborhood. . . .

He breaks down completely, then gets up and goes into the bedroom.

BENEATHA   That is not a man. That is nothing but a toothless rat.

MAMA   Yes—death done come in this here house. *(She is nodding, slowly, reflectively)* Done come walking in my house. On the lips of my children. You what supposed to be my beginning again. You—what supposed to be my harvest. *(To* BENEATHA*)* You—you mourning your brother?

BENEATHA   He's no brother of mine.

MAMA   What you say?

BENEATHA   I said that that individual in that room is no brother of mine.

MAMA   That's what I thought you said. You feeling like you better than he is today? *(*BENEATHA *does not answer.)* Yes? What you tell him a minute ago? That he wasn't a man? Yes? You give him up for me? You done wrote his epitaph too—like the rest of the world? Well, who give you the privilege?

BENEATHA   Be on my side for once! You saw what he just did, Mama! You saw him—down on his knees. Wasn't it you who taught me—to despise any man who would do that. Do what he's going to do.

MAMA   Yes—I taught you that. Me and your daddy. But I thought I taught you something else too . . . I thought I taught you to love him.

BENEATHA   Love him? There is nothing left to love.

MAMA   There is always something left to love. And if you ain't learned that, you ain't learned nothing. *(Looking at her)* Have you cried for that boy today? I don't mean for yourself and for the family 'cause we lost the money. I mean for him; what he been through and what it done to him. Child, when do you think is the time to love somebody the most; when they done good and made things easy for everybody? Well then, you ain't through learning—because that ain't the time at all. It's when he's at his lowest and can't believe in hisself 'cause the world done whipped him so. When you starts measuring somebody, measure him right, child, measure him right. Make sure you done taken into account what hills and valleys he come through before he got to wherever he is.

TRAVIS *bursts into the room at the end of the speech, leaving the door open.*

TRAVIS   Grandmama—the moving men are downstairs! The truck just pulled up.
MAMA *(turning and looking at him)*   Are they, baby? They downstairs?

She sighs and sits. LINDNER *appears in the doorway. He peers in and knocks lightly, to gain attention, and comes in. All turn to look at him.*

LINDNER *(hat and briefcase in hand)*   Uh—hello . . .

RUTH *crosses mechanically to the bedroom door and opens it and lets it swing open freely and slowly as the lights come up on* WALTER *within, still in his coat, sitting at the far corner of the room. He looks up and out through the room to* LINDNER.

RUTH   He's here.

A long minute passes and WALTER *slowly gets up.*

LINDNER *(coming to the table with efficiency, putting his briefcase on the table and starting to unfold papers and unscrew fountain pens)*   Well, I certainly was glad to hear from you people. (WALTER *has begun to trek out of the room, slowly and awkwardly, rather like a small boy, passing the back of his sleeve across his mouth from time to time.)* Life can really be so much simpler than people let it be most of the time. Well—with whom do I negotiate? You, Mrs. Younger, or your son here? (MAMA *sits with her hands folded on her lap and her eyes closed as* WALTER *advances.* TRAVIS *goes close to* LINDNER *and looks at the papers curiously.)* Just some official papers, sonny.
RUTH   Travis, you go downstairs.
MAMA *(opening her eyes and looking into* WALTER's)   No. Travis, you stay right here. And you make him understand what you doing, Walter Lee. You teach him good. Like Willy Harris taught you. You show where our five generations done come to. Go ahead, son—
WALTER *(looks down into his boy's eyes.* TRAVIS *grins at him merrily and* WALTER *draws him beside him with his arm lightly around his shoulders)*   Well, Mr. Lindner. (BENEATHA *turns away.)* We called you—*(there is a profound, simple groping quality in his speech)*—because, well, me and my family—*(He looks around and shifts from one foot to the other.)* Well—we are very plain people. . . .
LINDNER   Yes—
WALTER   I mean—I have worked as a chauffeur most of my life—and my wife here, she does domestic work in people's kitchens. So does my mother. I mean—we are plain people. . . .
LINDNER   Yes, Mr. Younger—
WALTER *(really like a small boy, looking down at his shoes and then up at the man)*   And—uh—well, my father, well, he was a laborer most of his life.
LINDNER *(absolutely confused)*   Uh, yes—
WALTER *(looking down at his toes once again)*   My father almost beat a man to death once because this man called him a bad name or something, you know what I mean?
LINDNER   No, I'm afraid I don't.

WALTER (*finally straightening up*)   Well, what I mean is that we come from people who had a lot of pride. I mean—we are very proud people. And that's my sister over there and she's going to be a doctor—and we are very proud—

LINDNER   Well—I am sure that is very nice, but—

WALTER (*starting to cry and facing the man eye to eye*)   What I am telling you is that we called you over here to tell you that we are very proud and that this is— this is my son, who makes the sixth generation of our family in this country, and that we have all thought about your offer and we have decided to move into our house because my father—my father—he earned it. (*MAMA has her eyes closed and is rocking back and forth as though she were in church, with her head nodding the amen yes.*) We don't want to make no trouble for nobody or fight no causes— but we will try to be good neighbors. That's all we got to say. (*He looks the man absolutely in the eyes.*) We don't want your money. (*He turns and walks away from the man.*)

LINDNER (*looking around at all of them*)   I take it then that you have decided to occupy.

BENEATHA   That's what the man said.

LINDNER (*to MAMA in her reverie*)   Then I would like to appeal to you, Mrs. Younger. You are older and wiser and understand things better I am sure. . . .

MAMA (*rising*)   I am afraid you don't understand. My son said we are going to move and there ain't nothing left for me to say. (*Shaking her head with double meaning*) You know how these young folks is nowaways, mister. Can't do a thing with 'em. Good-bye.

LINDNER (*folding up his materials*)   Well—if you are that final about it. . . . There is nothing left for me to say. (*He finishes. He is almost ignored by the family, who are concentrating on WALTER LEE. At the door LINDNER halts and looks around.*) I sure hope you people know what you're doing. (*He shakes his head and exits.*)

RUTH (*looking around and coming to life*)   Well, for God's sake—if the moving men are here—LET'S GET THE HELL OUT OF HERE!

MAMA (*into action*)   Ain't it the truth! Look at all this here mess. Ruth, put Travis' good jacket on him. . . . Walter Lee, fix your tie and tuck your shirt in, you look just like somebody's hoodlum. Lord have mercy, where is my plant? (*She flies to get it amid the general bustling of the family, who are deliberately trying to ignore the nobility of the past moment.*) You all start on down. . . . Travis child, don't go empty-handed. . . . Ruth, where did I put that box with my skillets in it? I want to be in charge of it myself. . . . I'm going to make us the biggest dinner we ever ate tonight. . . . Beneatha, what's the matter with them stockings? Pull them things up, girl. . . .

The family starts to file out as two moving men appear and begin to carry out the heavier pieces of furniture, bumping into the family as they move about.

BENEATHA   Mama, Asagai—asked me to marry him today and go to Africa—

MAMA (*in the middle of her getting-ready activity*)   He did? You ain't old enough to marry nobody—(*Seeing the moving men lifting one of her chairs precariously*) Darling, that ain't no bale of cotton, please handle it so we can sit in it again. I had that chair twenty-five years. . . .

The movers sigh with exasperation and go on with their work.

BENEATHA (*girlishly and unreasonably trying to pursue the conversation*)   To go to Africa, Mama—be a doctor in Africa. . . .

MAMA (*distracted*) Yes, baby—

WALTER Africa! What he want you to go to Africa for?

BENEATHA To practice there. . . .

WALTER Girl, if you don't get all them silly ideas out of your head! You better marry yourself a man with some loot. . . .

BENEATHA (*angrily, precisely as if the first scene of the play*) What have you got to do with who I marry!

WALTER Plenty. Now I think George Murchison—

He and BENEATHA *go out yelling at each other vigorously;* BENEATHA *is heard saying that she would not marry* GEORGE MURCHISON *if he were Adam and she were Eve, etc. The anger is loud and real till their voices diminish.* RUTH *stands at the door and turns to* MAMA *and smiles knowingly.*

MAMA (*fixing her hat at last*) Yeah—they something all right, my children. . . .

RUTH Yeah—they're something. Let's go, Lena.

MAMA (*stalling, starting to look around at the house*) Yes—I'm coming. Ruth—

RUTH Yes?

MAMA (*quietly, woman to woman*) He finally come into his manhood today, didn't he? Kind of like a rainbow after the rain. . . .

RUTH (*biting her lip lest her own pride explode in front of* MAMA) Yes, Lena.

WALTER'*s voice calls for them raucously.*

MAMA (*waving* RUTH *out vaguely*) All right, honey—go on down. I be down directly.

RUTH *hesitates, then exits.* MAMA *stands, at last alone in the living room, her plant on the table before her as the lights start to come down. She looks around at all the walls and ceilings and suddenly, despite herself, while the children call below, a great heaving thing rises in her and she puts her fist to her mouth, takes a final desperate look, pulls her coat about her, pats her hat and goes out. The lights dim down. The door opens and she comes back in, grabs her plant, and goes out for the last time.*

Curtain

Response Statement Assignments

1. Clearly Ruth and Mama both are torn by the decision of whether or not to have the abortion. What are the reasons for your response to their final decision?

2. Think about the differences between this family structure and your own. Describe those differences as you write about your response to the abortion conflict in the play.

3. How do you respond to Mama's relationship with her son Walter, especially her disagreements? Why do you think that Mama and Ruth think alike and have the expectations that they have, while Walter's expectations are so clearly different?

4. Which of their expectations correspond to your own expectations about how your life should be and about what you will have to do in order to meet what seem like the appropriate objectives?

5. Do you feel that you and the characters in the play have expectations that stem from, among other factors, gender, race, religion, ethnicity, urban life?
6. What characteristics of this play make it a "realistic" play?
7. What differences does your own background make to your reading of this play?
8. Do you think it has "universal" appeal? Examine your own views on the issues you choose to discuss. How do you think they affect your own reading?
9. Choose *one* scene from the play and discuss how you envisage it being staged. What crucial problems of staging do you find, and how would you want to solve them to influence an audience's response?

TOM STOPPARD (b. 1937)

Rosencrantz and Guildenstern Are Dead

CHARACTERS

ROSENCRANTZ	GERTRUDE
GUILDENSTERN	POLONIUS
THE PLAYER	HORATIO
ALFRED	FORTINBRAS
TRAGEDIANS	AMBASSADOR
HAMLET	1ST SOLDIER
OPHELIA	2ND SOLDIER
CLAUDIUS	COURT AND ATTENDANTS

ACT I

Two ELIZABETHANS *passing the time in a place without any visible character.*

They are well dressed—hats, cloaks, sticks and all.

Each of them has a large leather money bag.

GUILDENSTERN*'s bag is nearly empty.*

ROSENCRANTZ*'s bag is nearly full.*

The reason being: they are betting on the toss of a coin, in the following manner: GUILDENSTERN *(hereafter* "GUIL.") *takes a coin out of his bag, spins it, letting it fall.* ROSENCRANTZ *(hereafter* "ROS.") *studies it, announces it as "heads" (as it happens) and puts it into his own bag. Then they repeat the process. They have apparently been doing this for some time.*

The run of "heads" is impossible, yet ROS. *betrays no surprise at all—he feels none. However, he is nice enough to feel a little embarrassed at taking so much money off his friend. Let that be his character note.*

GUIL *is well alive to the oddity of it. He is not worried about the money, but he is worried by the implications; aware but not going to panic about it—his character note.*

GUIL. *sits.* ROS. *stands (he does the moving, retrieving coins).*
GUIL. *spins.* ROS. *studies coin.*

ROS. Heads.

He picks it up and puts it in his bag. The process is repeated.

Heads.

Again.

Heads.

Again.

Heads.

Again.

Heads.
GUIL. *(flipping a coin)*   There is an art to the building up of suspense.
ROS. Heads.
GUIL. *(flipping another)*   Though it can be done by luck alone.
ROS. Heads.
GUIL. If that's the word I'm after.
ROS. *(raises his head at* GUIL.)   Seventy-six—love.

GUIL. *gets up but has nowhere to go. He spins another coin over his shoulder without looking at it, his attention being directed at his environment or lack of it.*

Heads.
GUIL. A weaker man might be moved to re-examine his faith, if in nothing else at least in the law of probability. *(He slips a coin over his shoulder as he goes to look upstage.)*
ROS. Heads.

GUIL., *examining the confines of the stage, flips over two more coins as he does so, one by one of course.* ROS. *announces each of them as "heads."*

GUIL. *(musing)*   The law of probability, it has been oddly asserted, is something to do with the proposition that if six monkeys *(he has surprised himself)* . . . if six monkeys were . . .
ROS. Game?
GUIL. Were they?
ROS. Are you?
GUIL. *(understanding)*   Game. *(Flips a coin.)* The law of averages, if I have got this right, means that if six monkeys were thrown up in the air for long enough they would land on their tails about as often as they would land on their——
ROS. Heads. *(He picks up the coin.)*
GUIL. Which even at first glance does not strike one as a particularly rewarding speculation, in either sense, even without the monkeys. I mean you wouldn't *bet* on it. I mean *I* would, but *you* wouldn't. . . . *(As he flips a coin.)*

ROS. Heads.

GUIL. Would you? *(Flips a coin.)*

ROS. Heads.

Repeat.

Heads. *(He looks up at* GUIL.—*embarrassed laugh.)* Getting a bit of a bore, isn't it?

GUIL. *(coldly)* A bore?

ROS. Well . . .

GUIL. What about the suspense?

ROS. *(innocently)* What suspense?

Small pause.

GUIL. It must be the law of diminishing returns. . . . I feel the spell about to be broken. *(Energizing himself somewhat. He takes out a coin, spins it high, catches it, turns it over on to the back of his other hand, studies the coin—and tosses it to* ROS. *His energy deflates and he sits.)*

Well, it was an even chance . . . if my calculations are correct.

ROS. Eighty-five in a row—beaten the record!

GUIL. Don't be absurd.

ROS. Easily!

GUIL. *(angry)* Is that *it,* then? Is that all?

ROS. What?

GUIL. A new record? Is that as far as you are prepared to go?

ROS. Well . . .

GUIL. No questions? Not even a pause?

ROS. You spun them yourself.

GUIL. Not a flicker of doubt?

ROS. *(aggrieved, aggressive)* Well, I won—didn't I?

GUIL. *(approaches him—quieter)* And if you'd lost? If they'd come down against you, eighty-five times, one after another, just like that?

ROS. *(dumbly)* Eighty-five in a row? *Tails?*

GUIL. Yes! What would you think?

ROS. *(doubtfully)* Well . . . *(Jocularly.)* Well, I'd have a good look at your coins for a start!

GUIL. *(retiring)* I'm relieved. At least we can still count on self-interest as a predictable factor. . . . I suppose it's the last to go. Your capacity for trust made me wonder if perhaps . . . you, alone . . . *(He turns on him suddenly, reaches out a hand.)* Touch.

ROS. *clasps his hand.* GUIL. *pulls him up to him.*

GUIL. *(more intensely):* We have been spinning coins together since——*(He releases him almost as violently.)* This is not the first time we have spun coins!

ROS. Oh no—we've been spinning coins for as long as I remember.

GUIL. How long is that?

ROS. I forget. Mind you—eighty-five times!

GUIL. Yes?

ROS. It'll take some beating, I imagine.

GUIL. Is *that* what you imagine? Is that it? No *fear?*

ROS. Fear?

GUIL. *(in fury—flings a coin on the ground)—*   Fear! The crack that might flood your brain with light!

ROS. Heads.... *(He puts it in his bag.)*

GUIL. *sits despondently. He takes a coin, spins it, lets it fall between his feet. He looks at it, picks it up, throws it to* ROS., *who puts it in his bag.*

GUIL. *takes another coin, spins it, catches it, turns it over on to his other hand, looks at it, and throws it to* ROS., *who puts it in his bag.*

GUIL. *takes a third coin, spins it, catches it in his right hand, turns it over onto his left wrist, lobs it in the air, catches it with his left hand, raises his left leg, throws the coin up under it, catches it and turns it over on the top of his head, where it sits.* ROS. *comes, looks at it, puts it in his bag.*

ROS. I'm afraid——

GUIL. So am I.

ROS. I'm afraid it isn't your day.

GUIL. I'm afraid it is.

Small pause.

ROS. Eighty-nine.

GUIL. It must be indicative of something, besides the redistribution of wealth. *(He muses.)* List of possible explanations. One: I'm willing it. Inside where nothing shows, I am the essence of a man spinning double-headed coins, and betting against himself in private atonement for an unremembered past. *(He spins a coin at* ROS.)

ROS. Heads.

GUIL. Two: time has stopped dead, and the single experience of one coin being spun once has been repeated ninety times.... *(He flips a coin, looks at it, tosses it to* ROS.) On the whole, doubtful. Three: divine intervention, that is to say, a good turn from above concerning him, cf. children of Israel, or retribution from above concerning me, cf. Lot's wife. Four: a spectacular vindication of the principle that each individual coin spun individually *(he spins one)* is as likely to come down heads as tails and therefore should cause no surprise each individual time it does. *(It does. He tosses it to* ROS.)

ROS. I've never known anything like it!

GUIL. And a syllogism: One, he has never known anything like it. Two, he has never known anything to write home about. Three, it is nothing to write home about.... Home ... What's the first thing you remember?

ROS. Oh, let's see.... The first thing that comes into my head, you mean?

GUIL. No—the first thing you remember.

ROS. Ah. *(Pause.)* No, it's no good, it's gone. It was a long time ago.

GUIL. *(patient but edged)*   You don't get my meaning. What is the first thing after all the things you've forgotten?

ROS. Oh I see. *(Pause.)* I've forgotten the question.

GUIL. *leaps up and paces.*

GUIL. Are you happy?

ROS. What?

GUIL. Content? At ease?

ROS. I suppose so.

GUIL. What are you going to do now?

ROS. I don't know. What do you want to do?

GUIL. I have no desires. None. *(He stops pacing dead.)* There was a messenger . . . that's right. We were sent for. *(He wheels at* ROS. *and raps out)* Syllogism the second: One, probability is a factor which operates within natural forces. Two, probability is not operating as a factor. Three, we are now within un-, sub- or supernatural forces. Discuss. *(*ROS. *is suitably startled. Acidly.)* Not too heatedly.

ROS. I'm sorry I—What's the matter with you?

GUIL. The scientific approach to the examination of phenomena is a defence against the pure emotion of fear. Keep tight hold and continue while there's time. Now—counter to the previous syllogism: tricky one, follow me carefully, it may prove a comfort. If we postulate, and we just have, that within un-, sub- or supernatural forces *the probability is* that the law of probability will not operate as a factor, then we must accept that the probability of the *first* part will not operate as a factor, in which case the law of probability *will* operate as a factor within un-, sub- or supernatural forces. And since it obviously hasn't been doing so, we can take it that we are not held within un-, sub- or supernatural forces after all; in all probability, that is. Which is a great relief to me personally. *(Small pause.)* Which is all very well, except that——*(He continues with tight hysteria, under control.)* We have been spinning coins together since I don't know when, and in all that time (if it *is* all that time) I don't suppose either of us was more than a couple of gold pieces up or down. I hope that doesn't sound surprising because its very unsurprisingness is something I am trying to keep hold of. The equanimity of your average tosser of coins depends upon a law, or rather a tendency, or let us say a probability, or at any rate a mathematically calculable chance, which ensures that he will not upset himself by losing too much nor upset his opponent by winning too often. This made for a kind of harmony and a kind of confidence. It related the fortuitous and the ordained into a reassuring union which we recognized as nature. The sun came up about as often as it went down, in the long run, and a coin showed heads about as often as it showed tails. Then a messenger arrived. We had been sent for. Nothing else happened. Ninety-two coins spun consecutively have come down heads ninety-two consecutive times . . . and for the last three minutes on the wind of a windless day I have heard the sound of drums and flute. . . .

ROS. *(cutting his fingernails)* Another curious scientific phenomenon is the fact that the fingernails grow after death, as does the beard.

GUIL. What?

ROS. *(loud)* Beard!

GUIL. But you're not dead.

ROS. *(irritated)* I didn't say they *started* to grow after death! *(Pause, calmer.)* The fingernails also grow before birth, though *not* the beard.

GUIL. *What?*

ROS. *(shouts)* Beard! What's the matter with you? *(Reflectively.)* The toenails, on the other hand, never grow at all.

GUIL. *(bemused)* The toenails never grow at all?

ROS. Do they? It's a funny thing—I cut my fingernails all the time, and every time I think to cut them, they need cutting. Now, for instance. And yet, I never, to the best of my knowledge, cut my toenails. They ought to be curled under my feet by now, but it doesn't happen. I never think about them. Perhaps I cut them absent-mindedly, when I'm thinking of something else.

GUIL. *(tensed up by this rambling)* Do you remember the first thing that happened today?

ROS. *(promptly)* I woke up, I suppose. *(Triggered.)* Oh—I've got it now—that man, a foreigner, he woke us up—

GUIL. A messenger. *(He relaxes, sits.)*

ROS. That's it—pale sky before dawn, a man standing on his saddle to bang on the shutters—shouts—What's all the row about?! Clear off!—But then he called our names. You remember that—this man woke us up.

GUIL. Yes.

ROS. We were sent for.

GUIL. Yes.

ROS. That's why we're here. *(He looks round, seems doubtful, then the explanation.)* Travelling.

GUIL. Yes.

ROS. *(dramatically)* It was urgent—a matter of extreme urgency, a royal summons, his very words: official business and no questions asked—lights in the stable-yard, saddle up and off headlong and hotfoot across the land, our guides outstripped in breakneck pursuit of our duty! Fearful lest we come too late!!

Small pause.

GUIL. Too late for what?

ROS. How do I know? We haven't got there yet.

GUIL. Then what are we doing here, I ask myself.

ROS. You might well ask.

GUIL. We better get on.

ROS. You might well think.

GUIL. We better get on.

ROS. *(actively)* Right! *(Pause.)* On where?

GUIL. Forward.

ROS. *(forward to footlights)* Ah. *(Hesitates.)* Which way do we——*(He turns round.)* Which way did we——?

GUIL. Practically starting from scratch. . . . An awakening, a man standing on his saddle to bang on the shutters, our names shouted in a certain dawn, a message, a summons . . . A new record for heads and tails. We have not been . . . picked out . . . simply to be abandoned . . . set loose to find our own way. . . . We are entitled to some direction. . . . I would have thought.

ROS. *(alert, listening)* I say——! I say——

GUIL. Yes?

ROS. I can hear—I thought I heard—music.

GUIL. *raises himself.*

GUIL. Yes?

ROS. Like a band. *(He looks around, laughs embarrassedly, expiating himself.)* It sounded like—a band. Drums.

GUIL. Yes.

ROS. *(relaxes)* It couldn't have been real.

GUIL. "The colours red, blue and green are real. The colour yellow is a mystical experience shared by everybody"—demolish.

ROS. *(at edge of stage)* It must have been thunder. Like drums . . .

By the end of the next speech, the band is faintly audible.

GUIL. A man breaking his journey between one place and another at a third place of no name, character, population or significance, sees a unicorn cross his path and disappear. That in itself is startling, but there are precedents for mystical encounters of various kinds, or to be less extreme, a choice of persuasions to put it down to fancy; until—"My God," says a second man, "I must be dreaming, I thought I saw a unicorn." At which point, a dimension is added that makes the experience as alarming as it will ever be. A third witness, you understand, adds no further dimension but only spreads it thinner, and a fourth thinner still, and the more witnesses there are the thinner it gets and the more reasonable it becomes until it is as thin as reality, the name we give to the common experience. . . . "Look, look!" recites the crowd. "A horse with an arrow in its forehead! It must have been mistaken for a deer."

ROS. *(eagerly)* I knew all along it was a band.

GUIL. *(tiredly)* He knew all along it was a band.

ROS. Here they come!

GUIL. *(at the last moment before they enter—wistfully)* I'm sorry it wasn't a unicorn. It would have been nice to have unicorns.

The TRAGEDIANS *are six in number, including a small* BOY (ALFRED). *Two pull and push a cart piled with props and belongings. There is also a* DRUMMER, *a* HORN-PLAYER *and a* FLAUTIST. *The* SPOKESMAN *("the* PLAYER*") has no instrument. He brings up the rear and is the first to notice them.*

PLAYER Halt!

The group turns and halts.

(Joyously.) An audience!

ROS. *and* GUIL. *half rise.*

Don't move!

They sink back. He regards them fondly.

Perfect! A lucky thing we came along.

ROS. For us?

PLAYER Let us hope so. But to meet two gentlemen on the road—we would not hope to meet them off it.

ROS. No?

PLAYER Well met, in fact, and just in time.

ROS. Why's that?

PLAYER Why, we grow rusty and you catch us at the very point of decadence—by this time tomorrow we might have forgotten everything we ever knew. That's a thought, isn't it? *(He laughs generously.)* We'd be back where we started—improvising.

ROS. Tumblers, are you?

PLAYER   We can give you a tumble if that's your taste, and times being what they are. . . . Otherwise, for a jingle of coin we can do you a selection of gory romances, full of fine cadence and corpses, pirated from the Italian; and it doesn't take much to make a jingle—even a single coin has music in it.

They all flourish and bow, raggedly.

Tragedians, at your command.

ROS. *and* GUIL. *have got to their feet.*

ROS.   My name is Guildenstern, and this is Rosencrantz.

GUIL. *confers briefly with him.*

(*Without embarrassment.*)   I'm sorry—*his* name's Guildenstern, and *I'm* Rosencrantz.

PLAYER   A pleasure. We've played to bigger, of course, but quality counts for something. I recognized you at once—

ROS.   And who are we?

PLAYER   —as fellow artists.

ROS.   I thought we were gentlemen.

PLAYER   For some of us it is performance, for others, patronage. They are two sides of the same coin, or, let us say, being as there are so many of us, the same side of two coins. (*Bows again.*) Don't clap too loudly—it's a very old world.

ROS.   What is your line?

PLAYER   Tragedy, sir. Deaths and disclosures, universal and particular, denouements both unexpected and inexorable, transvestite melodrama on all levels including the suggestive. We transport you into a world of intrigue and illusion . . . clowns, if you like, murderers—we can do you ghosts and battles, on the skirmish level, heroes, villains, tormented lovers—set pieces in the poetic vein; we can do you rapiers or rape or both, by all means, faithless wives and ravished virgins—*flagrante delicto* at a price, but that comes under realism for which there are special terms. Getting warm, am I?

ROS. (*doubtfully*)   Well, I don't know. . . .

PLAYER   It costs little to watch, and little more if you happen to get caught up in the action, if that's your taste and times being what they are.

ROS.   What are they?

PLAYER   Indifferent.

ROS.   Bad?

PLAYER   Wicked. Now what precisely is your pleasure? (*He turns to the* TRAGEDIANS.) Gentlemen, disport yourselves.

The TRAGEDIANS *shuffle into some kind of line.*

There! See anything you like?

ROS. (*doubtful, innocent*)   What do they do?

PLAYER   Let your imagination run riot. They are beyond surprise.

ROS.   And how much?

PLAYER   To take part?

ROS.   To watch.

PLAYER   Watch what?

ROS.   A private performance.

PLAYER   How private?

ROS.   Well, there are only two of us. Is that enough?

PLAYER   For an audience, disappointing. For voyeurs, about average.

ROS.   What's the difference?

PLAYER   Ten guilders.

ROS. *(horrified)*   Ten *guilders!*

PLAYER   I mean eight.

ROS.   Together?

PLAYER   Each. I don't think you understand—

ROS.   What are you *saying?*

PLAYER   What am I saying—seven.

ROS.   Where have you *been?*

PLAYER   Roundabout. A nest of children carries the custom of the town. Juvenile companies, they are the fashion. But they cannot match our repertoire . . . we'll stoop to anything if that's your bent. . . .

He regards ROS. *meaningfully but* ROS. *returns the stare blankly.*

ROS.   They'll grow up.

PLAYER *(giving up)*   There's one born every minute. *(To* TRAGEDIANS*)* On-ward!

The TRAGEDIANS *start to resume their burdens and their journey.* GUIL. *stirs himself at last.*

GUIL.   Where are you going?

PLAYER   Ha-alt!

They halt and turn.

   Home, sir.

GUIL.   Where from?

PLAYER   Home. We're travelling people. We take our chances where we find them.

GUIL.   It was chance, then?

PLAYER   Chance?

GUIL.   You found us.

PLAYER   Oh yes.

GUIL.   You were looking?

PLAYER   Oh no.

GUIL.   Chance, then.

PLAYER   Or fate.

GUIL.   Yours or ours?

PLAYER   It could hardly be one without the other.

GUIL.   Fate, then.

PLAYER   Oh yes. We have no control. Tonight we play to the court. Or the night after. Or to the tavern. Or not.

GUIL.   Perhaps I can use my influence.

PLAYER   At the tavern?

GUIL.   At the court, I would say I have some influence.

PLAYER   Would you say so?

GUIL.   I have influence yet.

PLAYER   Yet what?

GUIL. *seizes the* PLAYER *violently.*

GUIL.   I have influence!

The PLAYER *does not resist.* GUIL. *loosens his hold.*

(More calmly.)   You said something—about getting caught up in the action——
PLAYER *(gaily freeing himself)* I did!—I did!—You're quicker than your friend. . . . *(Confidingly.)* Now for a handful of guilders I happen to have a private and uncut performance of *The Rape of the Sabine Women*—or rather woman, or rather Alfred——*(Over his shoulder.)* Get your skirt on, Alfred——

The BOY *starts struggling into a female robe.*

. . . and for eight you can participate.

GUIL. *backs,* PLAYER *follows.*

. . . taking either part.

GUIL. *backs.*

. . . or both for ten.

GUIL. *tries to turn away,* PLAYER *holds his sleeve.*

. . . with encores——

GUIL. *smashes the* PLAYER *across the face. The* PLAYER *recoils.* GUIL. *stands trembling.*

(Resigned and quiet).   Get your skirt off, Alfred. . . .

ALFRED *struggles out of his half-on robe.*

GUIL. *(shaking with rage and fright)* It could have been—it didn't have to be *obscene.* . . . It could have been—a bird out of season, dropping bright-feathered on my shoulder. . . . It could have been a tongueless dwarf standing by the road to point the way. . . . I was *prepared.* But it's this, is it? No enigma, no dignity, nothing classical, portentous, only this—a comic pornographer and a rabble of prostitutes. . . .
PLAYER *(acknowledging the description with a sweep of his hat, bowing; sadly)* You should have caught us in better times. We were purists then. *(Straightens up.)* Onward.

The PLAYERS *make to leave.*

ROS. *(his voice has changed: he has caught on)* Excuse me!
PLAYER   Ha-alt!

They halt.

A-al-l-fred!

ALFRED *resumes the struggle. The* PLAYER *comes forward.*

ROS.   You're not—ah—exclusively players, then?
PLAYER   We're inclusively players, sir.
ROS.   So you give—exhibitions?
PLAYER   Performances, sir.
ROS.   Yes, of course. There's more money in that, is there?
PLAYER   There's more trade, sir.

ROS. Times being what they are.

PLAYER Yes.

ROS. Indifferent.

PLAYER Completely.

ROS. You know I'd no idea——

PLAYER No——

ROS. I mean, I've *heard* of—but I've never actually——

PLAYER No.

ROS. I mean, what exactly do you *do?*

PLAYER We keep to our usual stuff, more or less, only inside out. We do on stage the things that are supposed to happen off. Which is a kind of integrity, if you look on every exit being an entrance somewhere else.

ROS. *(nervy, loud)* Well, I'm not really the type of man who—no, but don't hurry off—sit down and tell us about some of the things people ask you to do——

The PLAYER *turns away.*

PLAYER On-ward!

ROS. Just a minute!

They turn and look at him without expression.

Well, all right—I wouldn't mind seeing—just an idea of the kind of—*(Bravely.)* What will you do for that? *(And tosses a single coin on the ground between them.)*

The PLAYER *spits at the coin, from where he stands.*

The TRAGEDIANS *demur, trying to get at the coin. He kicks and cuffs them back.*

On!

ALFRED *is still half in and out of his robe. The* PLAYER *cuffs him.*

(To ALFRED*)* What are you playing at?

ROS. *is shamed into fury.*

ROS. Filth! Disgusting—I'll report you to the authorities—*perverts!* I know your game all right, it's all filth!

The PLAYERS *are about to leave,* GUIL. *has remained detached.*

GUIL. *(casually)* Do you like a bet?

The TRAGEDIANS *turn and look interested. The* PLAYER *comes forward.*

PLAYER What kind of bet did you have in mind?

GUIL. *walks half the distance towards the* PLAYER, *stops with his foot over the coin.*

GUIL. Double or quits.

PLAYER Well . . . heads.

GUIL. *raises his foot. The* PLAYER *bends. The* TRAGEDIANS *crowd round. Relief and congratulations. The* PLAYER *picks up the coin.* GUIL. *throws him a second coin.*

GUIL. Again?

Some of the TRAGEDIANS *are for it, others against.*

GUIL. Evens.

The PLAYER *nods and tosses the coin.*

GUIL. Heads.

It is. He picks it up.

Again.

GUIL. *spins coin.*

PLAYER   Heads.

It is. PLAYER *picks up coin. He has two coins again. He spins one.*

GUIL. Heads.

It is. GUIL. *picks it up. Then tosses it immediately.*

PLAYER *(fractional hesitation)*   Tails.

But it's heads. GUIL. *picks it up.* PLAYER *tosses down his last coin by way of paying up, and turns away.* GUIL. *doesn't pick it up; he puts his foot on it.*

GUIL. Heads.
PLAYER   No!

Pause. The TRAGEDIANS *are against this.*

   (Apologetically.)   They don't like the odds.
GUIL. *(lifts his foot, squats; picks up the coin still squatting; looks up)*   You were right—heads. *(Spins it, slaps his hand on it, on the floor.)* Heads I win.
PLAYER   No.
GUIL. *(uncovers coin)*   Right again. *(Repeat.)* Heads I win.
PLAYER   No.
GUIL. *(uncovers coin)*   Right again. *(Repeat.)* Heads I win.
PLAYER   No!

He turns away, the TRAGEDIAN *with him.* GUIL. *stands up, comes close.*

GUIL.   Would you believe it? *(Stands back, relaxes, smiles.)* Bet me the year of my birth doubled is an odd number.
PLAYER   *Your* birth——!
GUIL.   If you don't trust me don't bet me.
PLAYER   Would you trust *me?*
GUIL.   *Bet* me then.
PLAYER   My birth?
GUIL.   Odd numbers you win.
PLAYER   You're on——

The TRAGEDIANS *have come forward, wide awake.*

GUIL.   Good. Year of your birth. Double it. Even numbers I win, odd numbers I lose.

Silence. An awful sigh as the TRAGEDIANS *realize that any number doubled is even. Then a terrible row as they object. Then a terrible silence.*

PLAYER   We have no money.

GUIL. *turns to him.*

GUIL.   Ah. Then what *have* you got?

The PLAYER *silently brings* ALFRED *forward.* GUIL. *regards* ALFRED *sadly.*

Was it for this?

PLAYER   It's the best we've got.

GUIL. *(looking up and around)*   Then the times are bad indeed.

The PLAYER *starts to speak, protestation, but* GUIL. *turns on him viciously.*

The very *air* stinks.

The PLAYER *moves back.* GUIL. *moves down to the footlights and turns.*

Come here, Alfred.

ALFRED *moves down and stands, frightened and small.*

(Gently.)   Do you lose often?

ALFRED   Yes, sir.

GUIL.   Then what could you have left to lose?

ALFRED   Nothing, sir.

Pause. GUIL. *regards him.*

GUIL.   Do you like being . . . an actor?

ALFRED   No, sir.

GUIL. *looks around, at the audience.*

GUIL.   You and I, Alfred—we could create a dramatic precedent here.

And ALFRED, *who has been near tears, starts to sniffle.*

Come, come, Alfred, this is no way to fill the theatres of Europe.

The PLAYER *has moved down, to remonstrate with* ALFRED. GUIL. *cuts him off again.*

(Viciously.)   Do you know any good plays?

PLAYER   Plays?

ROS. *(coming forward, faltering shyly)*   Exhibitions. . . .

GUIL.   I thought you said you were actors.

PLAYER *(dawning)*   Oh. Oh well, we *are.* We are. But there hasn't been much
call——

GUIL.   You lost. Well then—one of the Greeks, perhaps? You're familiar with the
tragedies of antiquity, are you? The great homicidal classics? Matri, patri, fratri,
sorrori, uxori and it goes without saying——

ROS.   Saucy——

GUIL.   —Suicidal!—hm? Maidens aspiring to godheads——

ROS.   And vice versa——

GUIL.   Your kind of thing, is it?

PLAYER   Well, no, I can't say it is, really. We're more of the blood, love and rhetoric
school.

GUIL.   Well, I'll leave the choice to you, if there is anything to choose between
them.

PLAYER   They're hardly divisible, sir—well, I can do you blood and love without
the rhetoric, and I can do you blood and rhetoric without the love, and I can do
you all three concurrent or consecutive, but I can't do you love and rhetoric without the blood. Blood is compulsory—they're all blood, you see.
GUIL.   Is that what people want?
PLAYER   It's what we do. *(Small pause. He turns away.)*

GUIL. *touches* ALFRED *on the shoulder.*

GUIL. *(wry, gentle)*   Thank you; we'll let you know.

The PLAYER *has moved upstage.* ALFRED *follows.*

PLAYER *(to* TRAGEDIANS*)*   Thirty-eight!
ROS. *(moving across, fascinated and hopeful)*   Position?
PLAYER   Sir?
ROS.   One of your—tableaux?
PLAYER   No, sir.
ROS.   Oh.
PLAYER *(to the* TRAGEDIANS, *now departing with their cart, already taking various
props off it)*   Entrances there and there *(indicating upstage).*

The PLAYER *has not moved his position for his last four lines. He does not move now.*
GUIL. *waits.*

GUIL.   Well . . . aren't you going to change into your costume?
PLAYER   I never change out of it, sir.
GUIL.   Always in character.
PLAYER   That's it.

Pause.

GUIL.   Aren't you going to—come *on?*
PLAYER   I *am* on.
GUIL.   But if you *are* on, you can't *come* on. *Can* you?
PLAYER   I *start* on.
GUIL.   But it hasn't *started.* Go on. We'll look out for you.
PLAYER   I'll give you a wave.

He does not move. His immobility is now pointed, and getting awkward. Pause. ROS.
walks up to him till they are face to face.

ROS.   Excuse me.

Pause. The PLAYER *lifts his downstage foot. It was covering* GUIL.'S *coin.* ROS. *puts
his foot on the coin. Smiles.*

Thank you.

The PLAYER *turns and goes.* ROS. *has bent for the coin.*

GUIL. *(moving out)*   Come on.
ROS.   I say—that was lucky.
GUIL. *(turning)*   What?
ROS.   It was tails.

He tosses the coin to GUIL. *who catches it. Simultaneously—a lighting change sufficient to alter the exterior mood into interior, but nothing violent.*

And OPHELIA *runs on in some alarm, holding up her skirts—followed by* HAMLET.
OPHELIA *has been sewing and she holds the garment. They are both mute.* HAMLET, *with his doublet all unbraced, no hat upon his head, his stockings fouled, ungartered and downgyved to his ankle, pale as his shirt, his knees knocking each other . . . and with a look so piteous, he takes her by the wrist and holds her hard, then he goes to the length of his arm, and with his other hand over his brow, falls to such perusal of her face as he would draw it. . . . At last, with a little shaking of his arm, and thrice his head waving up and down, he raises a sigh so piteous and profound that it does seem to shatter all his bulk and end his being. That done he lets her go, and with his head over his shoulder turned, he goes out backwards without taking his eyes off her . . . she runs off in the opposite direction.*

ROS. *and* GUIL. *have frozen.* GUIL. *unfreezes first. He jumps at* ROS.

GUIL.   Come on!

But a flourish—enter CLAUDIUS *and* GERTRUDE, *attended.*

CLAUDIUS   Welcome, dear Rosencrantz . . . *(he raises a hand at* GUIL. *while* ROS. *bows—*GUIL. *bows late and hurriedly)* . . . and Guildenstern.

He raises a hand at ROS. *while* GUIL. *bows to him—*ROS. *is still straightening up from his previous bow and halfway up he bows down again. With his head down, he twists to look at* GUIL., *who is on the way up.*

Moreover that we did much long to see you,
The need we have to use you did provoke
Our hasty sending.

ROS. *and* GUIL. *still adjusting their clothing for* CLAUDIUS*'s presence.*

Something have you heard
Of Hamlet's transformation, so call it,
Sith nor th'exterior nor the inward man
Resembles that it was. What it should be,
More than his father's death, that thus hath put him,
So much from th'understanding of himself,
I cannot dream of. I entreat you both
That, being of so young days brought up with him
And sith so neighboured to his youth and haviour
That you vouchsafe your rest here in our court
Some little time, so by your companies
To draw him on to pleasures, and to gather
So much as from occasion you may glean,
Whether aught to us unknown afflicts him thus,
That opened lies within our remedy.
GERTRUDE   Good *(fractional suspense)* gentlemen . . .

They both bow.

He hath much talked of you,
And sure I am, two men there is not living
To whom he more adheres. If it will please you

To show us so much gentry and goodwill
As to expand your time with us awhile
For the supply and profit of our hope,
Your visitation shall receive such thanks
As fits a king's remembrance.

ROS.   Both your majesties
Might, by the sovereign power you have of us,
Put your dread pleasures more into command
Than to entreaty.

GUIL.   But we both obey,
And here give up ourselves in the full bent
To lay our service freely at your feet,
To be commanded.

CLAUDIUS   Thanks, Rosencrantz *(turning to* ROS. *who is caught unprepared, while* GUIL. *bows)* and gentle Guildenstern *(turning to* GUIL. *who is bent double).*

GERTRUDE *(correcting)*   Thanks Guildenstern *(turning to* ROS., *who bows as* GUIL. *checks upward movement to bow too—both bent double, squinting at each other)* ... and gentle Rosencrantz *(turning to* GUIL., *both straightening up—*GUIL. *checks again and bows again).*

And I beseech you instantly to visit
My too much changed son. Go, some of you,
And bring these gentlemen where Hamlet is.

Two ATTENDANTS *exit backwards, indicating that* ROS. *and* GUIL. *should follow.*

GUIL.   Heaven make our presence and our practices
Pleasant and helpful to him.

GERTRUDE   Ay, amen!

ROS. *and* GUIL. *move towards a downstage wing. Before they get there,* POLONIUS *enters. They stop and bow to him. He nods and hurries upstage to* CLAUDIUS. *They turn to look at him.*

POLONIUS   The ambassadors from Norway, my good lord, are joyfully returned.

CLAUDIUS   Thou still hast been the father of good news.

POLONIUS   Have I, my lord? Assure you, my good liege,
I hold my duty as I hold my soul,
Both to my God and to my gracious King;
And I do think, or else this brain of mine
Hunts not the trail of policy so sure
As it hath used to do, that I have found
The very cause of Hamlet's lunacy. . . .

Exeunt—leaving ROS. *and* GUIL.

ROS.   I want to go home.

GUIL.   Don't let them confuse you.

ROS.   I'm out of my step here——

GUIL.   We'll soon be home and high—dry and home—I'll——

ROS.   It's all over my *depth*——

GUIL.   —I'll hie you home and——

ROS.   —out of my head——

GUIL. —dry you high and——

ROS. *(cracking, high)* —over my step over my head body!—I tell you it's all stopping to a death, it's boding to a depth, stepping to a head, it's all heading to a dead stop——

GUIL. *(the nursemaid)* There! . . . and we'll soon be home and dry . . . and *high* and dry . . . *(Rapidly.)* Has it ever happened to you that all of a sudden and for no reason at all you haven't the faintest idea how to spell the word—"wife"—or "house"—because when you write it down you just can't remember ever having seen those letters in that order before . . . ?

ROS. I remember——

GUIL. Yes?

ROS. I remember when there were no questions.

GUIL. There were always questions. To exchange one set for another is no great matter.

ROS. Answers, yes. There were answers to everything.

GUIL. You've forgotten.

ROS. *(flaring)* I haven't forgotten—how I used to remember my own name—and yours, oh *yes!* There were answers everywhere you *looked.* There was no question about it—people knew who I was and if they didn't they asked and I told them.

GUIL. You did, the trouble is, each of them is . . . plausible, without being instinctive. All your life you live so close to truth, it becomes a permanent blur in the corner of your eye, and when something nudges it into outline it is like being ambushed by a grotesque. A man standing in his saddle in the half-lit half-alive dawn banged on the shutters and called two names. He was just a hat and a cloak levitating in the grey plume of his own breath, but when he called we came. That much is certain—we came.

ROS. Well I can tell you I'm sick to death of it. I don't care one way or another, so why don't you make up your mind.

GUIL. We can't afford anything quite so arbitrary. Nor did we come all this way for a christening. All *that*—preceded us. But we are comparatively fortunate; we might have been left to sift the whole field of human nomenclature, like two blind men looting a bazaar for their own portraits. . . . At least we are presented with alternatives.

ROS. Well as from now——

GUIL. —But not choice.

ROS. You made me look ridiculous in there.

GUIL. I looked just as ridiculous as you did.

ROS. *(an anguished cry)* Consistency is all I ask!

GUIL. *(low, wry rhetoric)* Give us this day our daily mask.

ROS. *(a dying fall)* I want to go home. *(Moves.)* Which way did we come in? I've lost my sense of direction.

GUIL. The only beginning is birth and the only end is death—if you can't count on that, what can you count on?

They connect again.

ROS. We don't owe anything to anyone.

GUIL. We've been caught up. Your smallest action sets off another somewhere else, and is set off by it. Keep an eye open, an ear cocked. Tread warily, follow instructions. We'll be all right.

ROS. For how long?

GUIL. Till events have played themselves out. There's a logic at work—it's all done for you, don't worry. Enjoy it. Relax. To be taken in hand and led, like being a child again, even without the innocence, a child—it's like being given a prize, an extra slice of childhood when you least expect it, as a prize for being good, or compensation for never having had one. . . . Do I contradict myself?

ROS. I can't remember. . . . What have we got to go on?

GUIL. We have been briefed. Hamlet's transformation. What do you recollect?

ROS. Well, he's changed, hasn't he? The exterior and inward man fails to resemble

———

GUIL. Draw him on to pleasures—glean what afflicts him.

ROS. Something more than his father's death——

GUIL. He's always talking about us—there aren't two people living whom he dotes on more than us.

ROS. We cheer him up—find out what's the matter——

GUIL. Exactly, it's a matter of asking the right questions and giving away as little as we can. It's a game.

ROS. And then we can go?

GUIL. And receive such thanks as fits a king's remembrance.

ROS. I like the sound of that. What do you think he means by remembrance.

GUIL. He doesn't forget his friends.

ROS. Would you care to estimate?

GUIL. Difficult to say, really—some kings tend to be amnesiac, others I suppose—the opposite, whatever that is. . . .

ROS. Yes—but——

GUIL. Elephantine . . . ?

ROS. Not how long—how much?

GUIL. *Retentive*—he's a very retentive king, a royal retainer. . . .

ROS. What are you playing at?

GUIL. Words, words. They're all we have to go on.

Pause.

ROS. Shouldn't we be doing something—constructive?

GUIL. What did you have in mind? . . . A short, blunt human pyramid . . . ?

ROS. We could go.

GUIL. Where?

ROS. After him.

GUIL. Why? They've got us placed now—if we start moving around, we'll all be chasing each other all night.

Hiatus.

ROS. *(at footlights)* How very intriguing! *(Turns.)* I feel like a spectator—an appalling business. The only thing that makes it bearable is the irrational belief that somebody interesting will come on in a minute. . . .

GUIL. See anyone?

ROS. No. You?

GUIL. No. *(At footlights.)* What a fine persecution—to be kept intrigued without ever quite being enlightened. . . . *(Pause.)* We've had no practice.

ROS. We could play at questions.

GUIL. What good would that do?

ROS. Practice!

GUIL. Statement! One—love.

ROS. Cheating!

GUIL. How?

ROS. I hadn't started yet.

GUIL. Statement. Two—love.

ROS. Are you counting that?

GUIL. What?

ROS. Are you counting that?

GUIL. Foul! No repetitions. Three—love. First game to . . .

ROS. I'm not going to play if you're going to be like that.

GUIL. Whose serve?

ROS. Hah?

GUIL. Foul! No grunts. Love—one.

ROS. Whose go?

GUIL. Why?

ROS. Why not?

GUIL. What for?

ROS. Foul! No synonyms! One—all.

GUIL. What in God's name is going on?

ROS. Foul! No rhetoric. Two—one.

GUIL. What does it all add up to?

ROS. Can't you guess?

GUIL. Were you addressing me?

ROS. Is there anyone else?

GUIL. Who?

ROS. How would I know?

GUIL. Why do you ask?

ROS. Are you serious?

GUIL. Was that rhetoric?

ROS. No.

GUIL. Statement! Two—all. Game point.

ROS. What's the matter with you today?

GUIL. When?

ROS. What?

GUIL. Are you deaf?

ROS. Am I dead?

GUIL. Yes or no?

ROS. Is there a choice?

GUIL. Is there a God?

ROS. Foul! No *non sequiturs,* three—two, one game all.

GUIL. *(seriously)* What's your name?

ROS. What's yours?

GUIL. I asked you first.

ROS. Statement. One—love.

GUIL. What's your name when you're at home?

ROS. What's yours?

GUIL. When I'm at home?

ROS. Is it different at home?

GUIL. What home?

ROS. Haven't you got one?

GUIL. Why do you ask?

ROS. What are you driving at?

GUIL. *(with emphasis)* What's your name?!

ROS. Repetition. Two—love. Match point to me.

GUIL. *(seizing him violently)* WHO DO YOU THINK YOU ARE?

ROS. Rhetoric! Game and match! *(Pause.)* Where's it going to end?

GUIL. That's the question.

ROS. It's *all* questions.

GUIL. Do you think it matters?

ROS. Doesn't it matter to you?

GUIL. Why should it matter?

ROS. What does it matter why?

GUIL. *(teasing gently)* Doesn't it *matter* why it matters?

ROS. *(rounding on him)* What's the *matter* with you?

Pause.

GUIL. It doesn't matter.

ROS. *(voice in the wilderness)* . . . What's the game?

GUIL. What are the rules?

Enter HAMLET *behind, crossing the stage, reading a book—as he is about to disappear* GUIL. *notices him.*

GUIL. *(sharply)* Rosencrantz!

ROS. *(jumps)* What!

HAMLET *goes. Triumph dawns on them, they smile.*

GUIL. There! How was that?

ROS. Clever!

GUIL. Natural?

ROS. Instinctive.

GUIL. Got it in your head?

ROS. I take my hat off to you.

GUIL. Shake hands.

They do.

ROS. Now I'll try you—Guil—!

GUIL. —Not yet—catch me unawares.

ROS. Right.

They separate. Pause. Aside to GUIL.

  Ready?

GUIL. *(explodes)* Don't be stupid.

ROS. Sorry.

Pause.

GUIL. *(snaps)* Guildenstern!

ROS. *(jumps)* What?

He is immediately crestfallen, GUIL. *is disgusted.*

GUIL. Consistency is all I ask!
ROS. *(quietly)* Immortality is all I seek. . . .
GUIL. *(dying fall)* Give us this day our daily week. . . .

Beat.

ROS. Who was that?
GUIL. Didn't you know him?
ROS. He didn't know me.
GUIL. He didn't see you.
ROS. I didn't see him.
GUIL. We shall see. I *hardly* knew him, he's changed.
ROS. You could see that?
GUIL. Transformed.
ROS. How do you know?
GUIL. Inside and out.
ROS. I see.
GUIL. He's not himself.
ROS. He's changed.
GUIL. I could see that.

Beat.

   Glean what afflicts him.
ROS. Me?
GUIL. Him.
ROS. How?
GUIL. Question and answer. Old ways are the best ways.
ROS. He's afflicted.
GUIL. You question, I'll answer.
ROS. He's not himself, you know.
GUIL. I'm him, you see.

Beat.

ROS. Who am I then?
GUIL. You're yourself.
ROS. And he's you?
GUIL. Not a bit of it.
ROS. Are you afflicted?
GUIL. That's the idea. Are you ready?
ROS. Let's go back a bit.
GUIL. I'm afflicted.
ROS. I see.
GUIL. Glean what afflicts me.
ROS. Right.
GUIL. Question and answer.
ROS. How should I begin?
GUIL. Address me.

ROS. My dear Guildenstern!

GUIL. *(quietly)* You've forgotten—haven't you?

ROS. My dear Rosencrantz!

GUIL. *(great control)* I don't think you quite understand. What we are attempting is a hypothesis in which *I* answer for *him,* while *you* ask me questions.

ROS. Ah! Ready?

GUIL. You know what to do?

ROS. What?

GUIL. Are you stupid?

ROS. Pardon?

GUIL. Are you deaf?

ROS. Did you speak?

GUIL. *(admonishing)* Not now——

ROS. Statement.

GUIL. *(shouts)* Not now! *(Pause.)* If I had any doubts, or rather hopes, they are dispelled. What could we possibly have in common except our situation? *(They separate and sit.)* Perhaps he'll come back this way.

ROS. Should we go?

GUIL. Why?

Pause.

ROS. *(starts up. Snaps fingers)* Oh! You mean—you pretend to be *him,* and *I* ask you questions!

GUIL. *(dry)* Very good.

ROS. You had me confused.

GUIL. I could see I had.

ROS. How should I begin?

GUIL. Address me.

They stand and face each other, posing.

ROS. My honoured Lord!

GUIL. My dear Rosencrantz!

Pause.

ROS. Am I pretending to be you, then?

GUIL. Certainly not. If you like. Shall we continue?

ROS. Question and answer.

GUIL. Right.

ROS. Right. My honoured lord!

GUIL. My dear fellow!

ROS. How are you?

GUIL. Afflicted!

ROS. Really? In what way?

GUIL. Transformed.

ROS. Inside or out?

GUIL. Both.

ROS. I see. *(Pause.)* Not much new there.

GUIL. Go into details. *Delve.* Probe the background, establish the situation.

ROS. So—so your uncle is the king of Denmark?!

GUIL. And my father before him.

ROS. His father before him?

GUIL. No, my father before him.

ROS. But surely——

GUIL. You might well ask.

ROS. Let me get it straight. Your father was king. You were his only son. Your father dies. You are of age. Your uncle becomes king.

GUIL. Yes.

ROS. Unorthodox.

GUIL. Undid me.

ROS. Undeniable. Where were you?

GUIL. In Germany.

ROS. Usurpation, then.

GUIL. He slipped in.

ROS. Which reminds me.

GUIL. Well, it would.

ROS. I don't want to be personal.

GUIL. It's common knowledge.

ROS. Your mother's marriage.

GUIL. He slipped in.

Beat.

ROS. *(lugubriously)* His body was still warm.

GUIL. So was hers.

ROS. Extraordinary.

GUIL. Indecent.

ROS. Hasty.

GUIL. Suspicious.

ROS. It makes you think.

GUIL. Don't think I haven't thought of it.

ROS. And with her husband's brother.

GUIL. They were close.

ROS. She went to him——

GUIL. —Too close——

ROS. —for comfort.

GUIL. It looks bad.

ROS. It adds up.

GUIL. Incest to adultery.

ROS. Would you go so far?

GUIL. Never.

ROS. To sum up: your father, whom you love, dies, you are his heir, you come back to find that hardly was the corpse cold before his young brother popped onto his throne and into his sheets, thereby offending both legal and natural practice. Now why exactly are you behaving in this extraordinary manner?

GUIL. I can't imagine! *(Pause.)* But all that is well known, common property. Yet he sent for us. And we did come.

ROS. *(alert, ear cocked)* I say! I heard music——

GUIL. We're here.

ROS. —Like a band—I thought I heard a band.

GUIL.   Rosencrantz . . .
ROS. *(absently, still listening)*   What?

Pause, short.

GUIL. *(gently wry)*   Guildenstern . . .
ROS. *(irritated by the repetition)*   What?
GUIL.   Don't you discriminate at all?
ROS. *(turning dumbly)*   Wha'?

Pause.

GUIL.   Go and see if he's there.
ROS.   Who?
GUIL.   There.

ROS. *goes to an upstage wing, looks, returns, formally making his report.*

ROS.   Yes
GUIL.   What is he doing?

ROS. *repeats movement.*

ROS.   Talking.
GUIL.   To himself?

ROS. *starts to move.* GUIL. *cuts in impatiently.*

Is he alone?
ROS.   No.
GUIL.   Then he's not talking to himself, is he?
ROS.   Not *by* himself. . . . Coming this way, I think. *(Shiftily.)* Should we go?
GUIL.   Why? We're marked now.

HAMLET *enters, backwards, talking, followed by* POLONIUS, *upstage.* ROS. *and* GUIL.
occupy the two downstage corners looking upstage.

HAMLET   . . . for you yourself, sir, should be as old as I am if like a crab you could
    go backward.
POLONIUS *(aside)*   Though this be madness, yet there is method in it. Will you walk
    out of the air, my lord?
HAMLET   Into my grave.
POLONIUS   Indeed, that's out of the air.

HAMLET *crosses to upstage exit,* POLONIUS *asiding unintelligibly until——*

My lord, I will take my leave of you.
HAMLET   You cannot take from me anything that I will more willingly part withal
    —except my life, except my life, except my life. . . .
POLONIUS *(crossing downstage)*   Fare you well, my lord. *(To* ROS.*)* You go to seek
    Lord Hamlet? There he is.
ROS. *(to* POLONIUS*)*   God save you sir.

POLONIUS *goes.*

GUIL. *(calls upstage to* HAMLET*)*   My honoured lord!
ROS.   My most dear lord!

HAMLET *centred upstage, turns to them.*

HAMLET   My excellent good friends! How dost thou Guildenstern? *(Coming down-stage with an arm raised to* ROS., GUIL. *meanwhile bowing to no greeting.* HAMLET *corrects himself. Still to* ROS.*)* Ah Rosencrantz!

They laugh good-naturedly at the mistake. They all meet midstage, turn upstage to walk, HAMLET *in the middle, arm over each shoulder.*

HAMLET   Good lads how do you both?

Blackout.

ACT II

HAMLET, ROS. *and* GUIL. *talking, the continuation of the previous scene. Their conversation, on the move, is indecipherable at first. The first intelligible line is* HAMLET*'s, coming at the end of a short speech—see Shakespeare Act II, scene ii.*

HAMLET   S'blood, there is something in this more than natural, if philosophy could find it out.

A flourish from the TRAGEDIANS' *band.*

GUIL.   There are the players.

HAMLET   Gentlemen, you are welcome to Elsinore. Your hands, come then. *(He takes their hands.)* The appurtenance of welcome is fashion and ceremony. Let me comply with you in this garb, lest my extent to the players (which I tell you must show fairly outwards) should more appear like entertainment than yours. You are welcome. *(About to leave.)* But my uncle-father and aunt-mother are deceived.

GUIL.   In what, my dear lord?

HAMLET   I am but mad north north-west; when the wind is southerly I know a hawk from a handsaw.

POLONIUS *enters as* GUIL. *turns away.*

POLONIUS   Well be with you gentlemen.

HAMLET *(to* ROS.*)*   Mark you, Guildenstern *(uncertainly to* GUIL.*)* and you too; at each ear a hearer. That great baby you see there is not yet out of his swaddling clouts. . . . *(He takes* ROS. *upstage with him, talking together.)*

POLONIUS   My Lord! I have news to tell you.

HAMLET *(releasing* ROS. *and mimicking)*   My lord, I have news to tell you. . . . When Roscius was an actor in Rome . . .

ROS. *comes downstage to rejoin* GUIL.

POLONIUS *(as he follows* HAMLET *out)*   The actors are come hither my lord.

HAMLET   Buzz, buzz.

Exeunt HAMLET *and* POLONIUS. ROS. *and* GUIL. *ponder. Each reluctant to speak first.*

GUIL.   Hm?

ROS.   Yes?

GUIL.   What?

ROS. I thought you . . .

GUIL. No.

ROS. Ah.

Pause.

GUIL. I think we can say we made some headway.

ROS. You think so?

GUIL. I think we can say that.

ROS. I think we can say he made us look ridiculous.

GUIL. We played it close to the chest of course.

ROS. *(derisively)* "Question and answer. Old ways are the best ways"! He was scoring off us all down the line.

GUIL. He caught us on the wrong foot once or twice, perhaps, but I thought we gained some ground.

ROS. *(simply)* He murdered us.

GUIL. He might have had the edge.

ROS. *(roused)* Twenty-seven—three, and you think he might have had the edge?! He *murdered* us.

GUIL. What about our evasions?

ROS. Oh, our evasions were lovely. "Were you sent for?" he says. "My lord, we were sent for. . . ." I didn't know where to put myself.

GUIL. He had six rhetoricals——

ROS. It was question and answer, all right. Twenty-seven questions he got out in ten minutes, and answered three. I was waiting for you to *delve.* "When is he going to start *delving?*" I asked myself.

GUIL. —And two repetitions.

ROS. Hardly a leading question between us.

GUIL. We got his *symptoms,* didn't we?

ROS. Half of what he said meant something else, and the other half didn't mean anything at all.

GUIL. Thwarted ambition—a sense of grievance, that's my diagnosis.

ROS. Six rhetorical and two repetition, leaving nineteen, of which we answered fifteen. And what did we get in return? He's depressed! . . . Denmark's a prison and he'd rather live in a nutshell; some shadow-play about the nature of ambition, which never got down to cases, and finally one direct question which might have led somewhere, and led in fact to his illuminating claim to tell a hawk from a handsaw.

Pause.

GUIL. When the wind is southerly.

ROS. And the weather's clear.

GUIL. And when it isn't he can't

ROS. He's at the mercy of the elements. *(Licks his finger and holds it up—facing audience.)* Is that southerly?

They stare at audience.

GUIL. It doesn't *look* southerly. What made you think so?

ROS. I didn't *say* I think so. It could be northerly for all I know.

GUIL. I wouldn't have thought so.

ROS. Well, if you're going to be dogmatic.

GUIL. Wait a minute—we came from roughly south according to a rough map.

ROS. I see. Well, which way did we come in? *(GUIL. looks round vaguely.)* Roughly.

GUIL. *(clears his throat)* In the morning the sun would be easterly. I think we can assume that.

ROS. That it's morning?

GUIL. If it is, and the sun is over *there (his right as he faces the audience)* for instance, *that (front)* would be northerly. On the other hand, if it is not morning and the sun is over *there (his left)* . . . *that* . . . *(lamely)* would *still* be northerly. *(Picking up.)* To put it another way, if we came from down there *(front)* and it is morning, the sun would be up there *(his left)*, and if it is actually over *there (his right)* and it's still morning, we must have come from up *there (behind him)*, and if *that* is southerly *(his left)* and the sun is really over *there (front)*, then it's afternoon. However, if none of these is the case——

ROS. Why don't you go and have a look?

GUIL. Pragmatism?!—is that all you have to offer? You seem to have no conception of where we stand! You won't find the answer written down for you in the bowl of a compass—I can tell you that. *(Pause.)* Besides, you can never tell this far north—it's probably dark out there.

ROS. I merely suggest that the position of the sun, if it is out, would give you a rough idea of the time; alternatively, the clock, if it is going, would give you a rough idea of the position of the sun. I forget which you're trying to establish.

GUIL. I'm trying to establish the direction of the wind.

ROS. There isn't any wind. *Draught,* yes.

GUIL. In that case, the origin. Trace it to its source and it might give us a rough idea of the way we came in—which might give us a rough idea of south, for further reference.

ROS. It's coming up through the floor. *(He studies the floor.)* That can't be south, can it?

GUIL. That's not a direction. Lick your toe and wave it around a bit.

ROS. *considers the distance of his foot.*

ROS. No, I think you'd have to lick it for me.

Pause.

GUIL. I'm prepared to let the whole matter drop.

ROS. Or I could lick yours, of course.

GUIL. No thank you.

ROS. I'll even wave it around for you.

GUIL. *(down ROS.'s throat)* What in God's name is the matter with you?

ROS. Just being friendly.

GUIL. *(retiring)* Somebody might come in. It's what we're counting on, after all. Ultimately.

Good pause.

ROS. Perhaps they've all trampled each other to death in the rush. . . . Give them a shout. Something provocative. *Intrigue* them.

GUIL. Wheels have been set in motion, and they have their own pace, to which we are . . . condemned. Each move is dictated by the previous one—that is the meaning of order. If we start being arbitrary it'll just be a shambles: at least, let us hope so. Because if we happened, just happened to discover, or even suspect, that our spontaneity was part of their order, we'd know that we were lost. *(He sits.)* A Chinaman of the T'ang Dynasty—and, by which definition, a philosopher—dreamed he was a butterfly, and from that moment he was never quite sure that he was not a butterfly dreaming it was a Chinese philosopher. Envy him; in his two-fold security.

A good pause. ROS. *leaps up and bellows at the audience.*

ROS.   Fire!

GUIL. *jumps up.*

GUIL.   Where?

ROS.   It's all right—I'm demonstrating the misuse of free speech. To prove that it exists. *(He regards the audience, that is the direction, with contempt—and other directions, then front again.)* Not a move. They should burn to death in their shoes. *(He takes out one of his coins. Spins it. Catches it. Looks at it. Replaces it.)*

GUIL.   What was it?

ROS.   What?

GUIL.   Heads or tails?

ROS.   Oh. I didn't look.

GUIL.   Yes you did.

ROS.   Oh, did I? *(He takes out a coin, studies it.)* Quite right—it rings a bell.

GUIL.   What's the last thing you remember?

ROS.   I don't wish to be reminded of it.

GUIL.   We cross our bridges when we come to them and burn them behind us, with nothing to show for our progress except a memory of the smell of smoke, and a presumption that once our eyes watered.

ROS. *approaches him brightly, holding a coin between finger and thumb. He covers it with his other hand, draws his fists apart and holds them for* GUIL. GUIL. *considers them. Indicates the left hand,* ROS. *opens it to show it empty.*

ROS.   No.

Repeat process. GUIL. *indicates left hand again.* ROS. *shows it empty.*

Double bluff!

*Repeat process—*GUIL. *taps one hand, then the other hand, quickly.* ROS. *inadvertently shows that both are empty.* ROS. *laughs as* GUIL. *turns upstage.* ROS. *stops laughing, looks around his feet, pats his clothes, puzzled.*

POLONIUS *breaks that up by entering upstage followed by the* TRAGEDIANS *and* HAMLET.

POLONIUS *(entering)*   Come sirs.

HAMLET   Follow him, friends. We'll hear a play tomorrow. *(Aside to the* PLAYER, *who is the last of the* TRAGEDIANS*)* Dost thou hear me, old friend? Can you play *The Murder of Gonzago?*

PLAYER   Ay, my lord.

HAMLET   We'll ha't tomorrow night. You could for a need study a speech of some dozen or sixteen lines which I would set down and insert in't, could you not?

PLAYER   Ay, my lord.
HAMLET   Very well. Follow that lord, and look you mock him not.

The PLAYER *crossing downstage, notes* ROS. *and* GUIL. *Stops.* HAMLET *crossing downstage addresses them without pause.*

HAMLET   My good friends, I'll leave you till tonight. You are welcome to Elsinore.
ROS.   Good, my lord.

HAMLET *goes.*

GUIL.   So you've caught up.
PLAYER *(coldly)*   Not yet, sir.
GUIL.   Now mind your tongue, or we'll have it out and throw the rest of you away,
   like a nightingale at a Roman feast.
ROS.   Took the very words out of my mouth.
GUIL.   You'd be *lost* for words.
ROS.   You'd be tongue-tied.
GUIL.   Like a mute in a monologue.
ROS.   Like a nightingale at a Roman feast.
GUIL.   Your diction will go to pieces.
ROS.   Your lines will be cut.
GUIL.   To dumbshows.
ROS.   And dramatic pauses.
GUIL.   You'll never *find* your tongue.
ROS.   Lick your lips.
GUIL.   Taste your tears.
ROS.   Your breakfast.
GUIL.   You won't know the difference.
ROS.   There won't be any.
GUIL.   We'll take the very words out of your mouth.
ROS.   So you've caught on.
GUIL.   So you've caught up.
PLAYER *(tops)*   Not yet! *(Bitterly.)* You left us.
GUIL.   Ah! I'd forgotten—you performed a dramatic spectacle on the way. Yes, I'm
   sorry we had to miss it.
PLAYER *(bursts out)*   We can't look each other in the face! *(Pause, more in control.)*
   You don't understand the humiliation of it—to be tricked out of the single as-
   sumption which makes our existence viable—that somebody is *watching*. . . . The
   plot was two corpses gone before we caught sight of ourselves, stripped naked in
   the middle of nowhere and pouring ourselves down a bottomless well.
ROS.   Is *that* thirty-eight?
PLAYER *(lost)*   There we were—demented children mincing about in clothes that
   no one ever wore, speaking as no man ever spoke, swearing love in wigs and
   rhymed couplets, killing each other with wooden swords, hollow protestations of
   faith hurled after empty promises of vengeance—and every gesture, every pose,
   vanishing into the thin unpopulated air. We ransomed our dignity to the clouds,
   and the uncomprehending birds listened. *(He rounds on them.)* Don't you see?!
   We're *actors*—we're the opposite of people! *(They recoil nonplussed, his voice
   calms.)* Think, in your head, *now,* think of the most . . . *private* . . . *secret* . . . *intimate* thing you have done secure in the knowledge of its privacy. . . . *(He gives*

them—and the audience—a good pause. ROS. *takes on a shifty look.)* Are you thinking of it? *(He strikes with his voice and his head.)* Well, I saw you do it!

ROS. *leaps up, dissembling madly.*

ROS. You never! It's a lie! *(He catches himself with a giggle in a vacuum and sits down again.)*

PLAYER We're actors. . . . We pledged our identities, secure in the conventions of our trade, that someone would be watching. And then, gradually, no one was. We were caught, high and dry. It was not until the murderer's long soliloquy that we were able to look around; frozen as we were in profile, our eyes searched you out, first confidently, then hesitantly, then desperately as each patch of turf, each log, every exposed corner in every direction proved uninhabited, and all the while the murderous King addressed the horizon with his dreary interminable guilt. . . . Our heads began to move, wary as lizards, the corpse of unsullied Rosalinda peeped through his fingers, and the King faltered. Even then, habit and a stubborn trust that our audience spied upon us from behind the nearest bush, forced our bodies to blunder on long after they had emptied of meaning, until like runaway carts they dragged to a halt. No one come forward. No one shouted at us. The silence was unbreakable, it imposed itself upon us; it was obscene. We took off our crowns and swords and cloth of gold and moved silent on the road to Elsinore.

Silence. Then GUIL. *claps solo with slow measured irony.*

GUIL. Brilliantly re-created—if these eyes could weep! . . . Rather strong on metaphor, mind you. No criticism—only a matter of taste. And so here you are—with a vengeance. That's a figure of speech . . . isn't it? Well let's say we've made up for it, for you may have no doubt whom to thank for your performance at the court.

ROS. We are counting on you to take him out of himself. You are the pleasures which we draw him on to—*(he escapes a fractional giggle but recovers immediately)* and by that I don't mean your usual filth; you can't treat royalty like people with normal perverted desires. They know nothing of that and you know nothing of them, to your mutual survival. So give him a good clean show suitable for all the family, or you can rest assured you'll be playing the tavern tonight.

GUIL. Or the night after.

ROS. Or not.

PLAYER We already have an entry here. And always have had.

GUIL. You've played for him before?

PLAYER Yes, sir.

ROS. And what's *his* bent?

PLAYER Classical.

ROS. Saucy!

GUIL. What will you play?

PLAYER *The Murder of Gonzago.*

GUIL. Full of fine cadence and corpses.

PLAYER Pirated from the Italian. . . .

ROS. What is it about?

PLAYER It's about a King and Queen. . . .

GUIL. Escapism! What else?

PLAYER Blood——

GUIL. —Love and rhetoric.

PLAYER   Yes. *(Going.)*

GUIL.   Where are you going?

PLAYER   I can come and go as I please.

GUIL.   You're evidently a man who knows his way around.

PLAYER   I've been here before.

GUIL.   We're still finding our feet.

PLAYER   I should concentrate on not losing your heads.

GUIL.   Do you speak from knowledge?

PLAYER   Precedent.

GUIL.   You've been here before.

PLAYER   And I know which way the wind is blowing.

GUIL.   Operating on two levels, are we?! How clever! I expect it comes naturally to you, being in the business so to speak.

The PLAYER*'s grave face does not change. He makes to move off again.* GUIL. *for the second time cuts him off.*

The truth is, we value your company, for want of any other. We have been left so much to our own devices—after a while one welcomes the uncertainty of being left to other people's.

PLAYER   Uncertainty is the normal state. You're nobody special.

He makes to leave again. GUIL. *loses his cool.*

GUIL.   But for God's sake what are we supposed to *do?!*

PLAYER   Relax. Respond. That's what people do. You can't go through life questioning your situation at every turn.

GUIL.   But we don't know what's going on, or what to do with ourselves. We don't know how to *act.*

PLAYER   Act natural. You know why you're here at least.

GUIL.   We only know what we're told, and that's little enough. And for all we know it isn't even true.

PLAYER   For all anyone knows, nothing is. Everything has to be taken on trust; truth is only that which is taken to be true. It's the currency of living. There may be nothing behind it, but it doesn't make any difference so long as it is honoured. One acts on assumptions. What do you assume?

ROS.   Hamlet is not himself, outside or in. We have to glean what afflicts him.

GUIL.   He doesn't give much away.

PLAYER   Who does, nowadays?

GUIL.   He's—melancholy.

PLAYER   Melancholy?

ROS.   Mad.

PLAYER   How is he mad?

ROS.   Ah. *(To* GUIL.*)* How is he mad?

GUIL.   More morose than mad, perhaps.

PLAYER   Melancholy.

GUIL.   Moody.

ROS.   He has moods.

PLAYER   Of moroseness?

GUIL.   Madness. And yet.

ROS.   Quite.

GUIL. For instance.

ROS. He talks to himself, which might be madness.

GUIL. If he didn't talk sense, which he does.

ROS. Which suggests the opposite.

PLAYER Of what?

Small pause.

GUIL. I think I have it. A man talking sense to himself is no madder than a man talking nonsense not to himself.

ROS. Or just as mad.

GUIL. Or just as mad.

ROS. And he does both.

GUIL. So there you are.

ROS. Stark raving sane.

Pause.

PLAYER Why?

GUIL. Ah. *(To* ROS.*)* Why?

ROS. Exactly.

GUIL. Exactly what?

ROS. Exactly why.

GUIL. Exactly why *what?*

ROS. What?

GUIL. *Why?*

ROS. Why what, exactly?

GUIL. Why is he mad?!

ROS. *I* don't know!

Beat.

PLAYER The old man thinks he's in love with his daughter.

ROS. *(appalled)* Good God! We're out of our depth here.

PLAYER No, no, no—*he* hasn't got a daughter—the old man thinks he's in love with *his* daughter.

ROS. The old man is?

PLAYER Hamlet, in love with the old man's daughter, the old man thinks.

ROS. Ha! It's beginning to make sense! Unrequited passion!

The PLAYER *moves.*

GUIL. *(Fascist.)* Nobody leaves this room! *(Pause, lamely.)* Without a *very* good reason.

PLAYER Why not?

GUIL. All this strolling about is getting too arbitrary by half—I'm rapidly losing my grip. From now on reason will prevail.

PLAYER I have lines to learn.

GUIL. Pass!

The PLAYER *passes into one of the wings.* ROS. *cups his hands and shouts into the opposite one.*

ROS. Next!

But no one comes.

GUIL. What did you expect?
ROS. Something . . . someone . . . nothing.

They sit facing front.

Are you hungry?
GUIL. No, are you?
ROS. *(thinks)* No. You remember that coin?
GUIL. No.
ROS. I think I lost it.
GUIL. What coin?
ROS. I don't remember exactly.

Pause.

GUIL. Oh, that coin . . . clever.
ROS. I can't remember how I did it.
GUIL. It probably comes natural to you.
ROS. Yes, I've got a show-stopper there.
GUIL. Do it again.

Slight pause.

ROS. We can't afford it.
GUIL. Yes, one must think of the future.
ROS. It's the normal thing.
GUIL. To have one. One is, after all, having it all the time . . . now . . . and now . . .
    and now. . . .
ROS. It could go on for ever. Well, not for *ever,* I suppose. *(Pause.)* Do you ever
    think of yourself as actually *dead,* lying in a box with a lid on it?
GUIL. No.
ROS. Nor do I, really. . . . It's silly to be depressed by it. I mean one thinks of it like
    being *alive* in a box, one keeps forgetting to take into account the fact that one is
    dead . . . which should make all the difference . . . shouldn't it? I mean, you'd
    never *know* you were in a box, would you? It would be just like being *asleep* in a
    box. Not that I'd like to sleep in a box, mind you, not without any air—you'd
    wake up dead, for a start, and then where would you be? Apart from inside a box.
    That's the bit I don't like, frankly. That's why I don't think of it. . . .

GUIL. *stirs restlessly, pulling his cloak round him.*

Because you'd be helpless, wouldn't you? Stuffed in a box like that, I mean you'd
be in there for ever. Even taking into account the fact that you're dead, it isn't a
pleasant thought. *Especially* if you're dead, really . . . *ask* yourself, if I asked you
straight off—I'm going to stuff you in this box now, would you rather be alive or
dead? Naturally, you'd prefer to be alive. Life in a box is better than no life at all. I
expect. You'd have a chance at least. You could lie there thinking—well, at least
I'm not dead! In a minute someone's going to bang on this lid and tell me to come
out. *(Banging the floor with his fists.)* "Hey you, whatsyername! Come out of
there!"
GUIL. *(jumps up savagely)* You don't have to flog it to death!

Pause.

ROS. I wouldn't think about it, if I were you. You'd only get depressed. *(Pause.)* Eternity is a terrible thought. I mean, where's it going to end? *(Pause, then brightly.)* Two early Christians chanced to meet in Heaven. "Saul of Tarsus yet!" cried one. "What are *you* doing here?!" ... "Tarsus-Schmarsus," replied the other, "I'm Paul already." *(He stands up restlessly and flaps his arms.)* They don't care. We count for nothing. We could remain silent till we're green in the face, they wouldn't come.

GUIL. Blue, red.

ROS. A Christian, a Moslem and a Jew chanced to meet in a closed carriage.... "Silverstein!" cried the Jew. "Who's your friend?" ... "His name's Abdullah," replied the Moslem, "but he's no friend of mine since he became a convert." *(He leaps up again, stamps his foot and shouts into the wings.)* All right, we know you're in there! Come out talking! *(Pause.)* We have no control. None at all ... *(He paces.)* Whatever became of the moment when one first knew about death? There must have been one, a moment, in childhood when it first occurred to you that you don't go on for ever. It must have been shattering—stamped into one's memory. And yet I can't remember it. It never occurred to me at all. What does one make of that? We must be born with an intuition of mortality. Before we know the words for it, before we know that there are words, out we come, bloodied and squalling with the knowledge that for all the compasses in the world, there's only one direction, and time is its only measure. *(He reflects, getting more desperate and rapid.)* A Hindu, a Buddhist and a lion-tamer chanced to meet, in a circus on the Indo-Chinese border. *(He breaks out.)* They're taking us for granted! Well, I won't stand for it! In future, notice will be taken. *(He wheels again to face into the wings.)* Keep out, then! I forbid anyone to enter! *(No one comes. Breathing heavily.)* That's better....

Immediately, behind him a grand procession enters, principally CLAUDIUS, GERTRUDE, POLONIUS *and* OPHELIA. CLAUDIUS *takes* ROS.*'s elbow as he passes and is immediately deep in conversation: the context is Shakespeare Act III, scene i.* GUIL. *still faces front as* CLAUDIUS, ROS., *etc., pass upstage and turn.*

GUIL. Death followed by eternity ... the worst of both worlds. It *is* a terrible thought.

He turns upstage in time to take over the conversation with CLAUDIUS. GERTRUDE *and* ROS. *head downstage.*

GERTRUDE Did he receive you well?

ROS. Most like a gentleman.

GUIL. *(returning in time to take it up)* But with much forcing of his disposition.

ROS. *(a flat lie and he knows it and shows it, perhaps catching* GUIL.*'s eye)* Niggard of question, but of our demands most free in his reply.

GERTRUDE Did you assay him to any pastime?

ROS. Madam, it so fell out that certain players
We o'erraught on the way: of these we told him
And there did seem in him a kind of joy
To hear of it. They are here about the court,
And, as I think, they have already order
This night to play before him.

POLONIUS 'Tis most true

And he beseeched me to entreat your Majesties
To hear and see the matter.
CLAUDIUS   With all my heart, and it doth content me
To hear him so inclined.
Good gentlemen, give him a further edge
And drive his purpose into these delights.
ROS.   We shall, my lord.
CLAUDIUS *(leading out procession)*
Sweet Gertrude, leave us, too,
For we have closely sent for Hamlet hither,
That he, as t'were by accident, may here
Affront Ophelia. . . .

Exeunt CLAUDIUS *and* GERTRUDE.

ROS. *(peevish)*   Never a moment's peace! In and out, on and off, they're coming at
us from all sides.
GUIL.   You're never satisfied.
ROS.   Catching us on the trot. . . . Why can't *we* go by *them*?
GUIL.   What's the difference?
ROS.   I'm going.

ROS. *pulls his cloak round him.* GUIL. *ignores him. Without confidence* ROS. *heads
upstage. He looks out and comes back quickly.*

He's coming.
GUIL.   What's he doing?
ROS.   Nothing.
GUIL.   He must be doing something.
ROS.   Walking.
GUIL.   On his hands?
ROS.   No, on his feet.
GUIL.   Stark naked?
ROS.   Fully dressed.
GUIL.   Selling toffee apples?
ROS.   Not that I noticed.
GUIL.   You could be wrong?
ROS.   I don't think so.

Pause.

GUIL.   I can't for the life of me see how we're going to get into conversation.

HAMLET *enters upstage, and pauses, weighing up the pros and cons of making his
quietus.* ROS. *and* GUIL. *watch him.*

ROS.   Nevertheless, I suppose one might say that this was a chance. . . . One might
well . . . accost him. . . . Yes, it definitely looks like a chance to me. . . . Something
on the lines of a direct informal approach . . . man to man . . . straight from the
shoulder. . . . Now look here, what's it all about . . . sort of thing. Yes. Yes, this
looks like one to be grabbed with both hands, I should say . . . if I were asked. . . .
No point in looking at a gift horse till you see the whites of its eyes, etcetera. *(He
has moved towards* HAMLET *but his nerve fails. He returns.)* We're overawed,

that's our trouble. When it comes to the point we succumb to their personality.
. . .

OPHELIA *enters, with prayerbook, a religious procession of one.*

HAMLET   Nymph, in thy orisons be all my sins remembered.

At his voice she has stopped for him, he catches her up.

OPHELIA   Good my lord, how does your honour for this many a day?
HAMLET   I humbly thank you—well, well, well.

They disappear talking into the wing.

ROS.   It's like living in a public park!
GUIL.   Very impressive. Yes, I thought your direct informal approach was going to stop this thing dead in its tracks there. If I might make a suggestion—shut up and sit down. Stop being perverse.
ROS. *(near tears)*   I'm not going to stand for it!

A FEMALE FIGURE, *ostensibly the* QUEEN, *enters.* ROS. *marches up behind her, puts his hands over her eyes and says with a desperate frivolity.*

ROS.   Guess who?!
PLAYER *(having appeared in a downstage corner)*   Alfred!

ROS. *lets go, spins around. He has been holding* ALFRED, *in his robe and blond wig.* PLAYER *is in the downstage corner still.* ROS. *comes down to that exit. The* PLAYER *does not budge. He and* ROS. *stand toe to toe.*

ROS.   Excuse me.

The PLAYER *lifts his downstage foot.* ROS. *bends to put his hand on the floor. The* PLAYER *lowers his foot.* ROS. *screams and leaps away.*

PLAYER *(gravely)*   I beg your pardon.
GUIL. *(to* ROS.*)*   What did he do?
PLAYER   I put my foot down.
ROS.   My hand was on the floor!
GUIL.   You put your hand under his foot?
ROS.   I——
GUIL.   What for?
ROS.   I thought——*(Grabs* GUIL.*)* Don't leave me!

He makes a break for an exit. A TRAGEDIAN *dressed as a* KING *enters.* ROS. *recoils, breaks for the opposite wing. Two cloaked* TRAGEDIANS *enter.* ROS. *tries again but another* TRAGEDIAN *enters, and* ROS. *retires to midstage. The* PLAYER *claps his hands matter-of-factly.*

PLAYER   Right! We haven't got much time.
GUIL.   What are you doing?
PLAYER   Dress rehearsal. Now if you two wouldn't mind just moving back . . . there . . . good. . . . *To* TRAGEDIANS*)* Everyone ready? And for goodness' sake, remember what we're doing. *(To* ROS. *and* GUIL.*)* We always use the same costumes more or less, and they forget what they are supposed to be *in* you see. . . . Stop picking your nose, Alfred. When Queens have to they do it by a cerebral process passed down in the blood. . . . Good. Silence! Off we go!

PLAYER-KING   Full thirty times hath Phoebus' cart——

PLAYER *jumps up angrily.*

PLAYER   No, no, no! Dumbshow first, your confounded majesty! *(To* ROS. *and* GUIL.*)* They're a bit out of practice, but they always pick up wonderfully for the deaths—it brings out the poetry in them.

GUIL.   How nice.

PLAYER   There's nothing more unconvincing than an unconvincing death.

GUIL.   I'm sure.

PLAYER *claps his hands.*

PLAYER   Act One—moves now.

The mime. Soft music from a recorder. PLAYER-KING *and* PLAYER-QUEEN *embrace. She kneels and makes a show of protestation to him. He takes her up, declining his head upon her neck. He lies down. She, seeing him asleep, leaves him.*

GUIL.   What is the dumbshow for?

PLAYER   Well, it's a device, really—it makes the action that follows more or less comprehensible; you understand, we are tied down to a language which makes up in obscurity what it lacks in style.

The mime (continued)—enter another. He takes off the SLEEPER*'s crown, kisses it. He has brought in a small bottle of liquid. He pours the poison in the* SLEEPER*'s ear, and leaves him. The* SLEEPER *convulses heroically, dying.*

ROS.   Who was that?

PLAYER   The King's brother and uncle to the Prince.

GUIL.   Not exactly fraternal.

PLAYER   Not exactly avuncular, as time goes on.

The QUEEN *returns, makes passionate action, finding the* KING *dead. The* POISONER *comes in again, attended by two others (the two in cloaks). The* POISONER *seems to console with her. The dead body is carried away. The* POISONER *woos the* QUEEN *with gifts. She seems harsh awhile but in the end accepts his love. End of mime, at which point, the wail of a woman in torment and* OPHELIA *appears, wailing, closely followed by* HAMLET *in a hysterical state, shouting at her, circling her, both mid-stage.*

HAMLET   Go to, I'll no more on't; it hath made me mad!

She falls on her knees weeping.

I say we will have no more marriage! *(His voice drops to include the* TRAGEDIANS, *who have frozen.)* Those that are married already *(he leans close to the* PLAYER-QUEEN *and* POISONER, *speaking with quiet edge)* all but one shall live. *(He smiles briefly at them without mirth, and starts to back out, his parting shot rising again.)* The rest shall keep as they are. *(As he leaves,* OPHELIA *tottering upstage, he speaks into her ear a quick clipped sentence.)* To a nunnery, go.

He goes out. OPHELIA *falls on to her knees upstage, her sobs barely audible. A slight silence.*

PLAYER-KING   Full thirty times hath Phoebus' cart——

CLAUDIUS *enters with* POLONIUS *and goes over to* OPHELIA *and lifts her to her feet. The* TRAGEDIANS *jump back with heads inclined.*

CLAUDIUS   Love? His affections do not that way tend,
    Or what he spake, though it lacked form a little,
    Was not like madness. There's something
    In his soul o'er which his melancholy sits on
    Brood, and I do doubt the hatch and the
    Disclose will be some danger; which for to
    Prevent I have in quick determination thus set
    It down: he shall with speed to England . . .

*Which carries the three of them—*CLAUDIUS, POLONIUS, OPHELIA—*out of sight. The* PLAYER *moves, clapping his hands for attention.*

PLAYER   Gentle*men! (They look at him.)* It doesn't seem to be coming. We are not getting it at all. *(To* GUIL.*)* What did you think?
GUIL.   What was I supposed to think?
PLAYER *(to* TRAGEDIANS*)*   You're not getting across!

ROS. *had gone halfway up to* OPHELIA; *he returns.*

ROS.   That didn't look like love to me.
GUIL.   Starting from scratch again . . .
PLAYER *(to* TRAGEDIANS*)*   It was a *mess.*
ROS. *(to* GUIL.*)*   It's going to be chaos on the night.
GUIL.   Keep back—we're spectators.
PLAYER   Act Two! Positions!
GUIL.   Wasn't that the end?
PLAYER   Do you call that an ending?—with practically everyone on his feet? My goodness no—over your dead body.
GUIL.   How am I supposed to take that?
PLAYER   Lying down. *(He laughs briefly and in a second has never laughed in his life.)* There's a design at work in all art—surely you know that? Events must play themselves out to aesthetic, moral and logical conclusion.
GUIL.   And what's that, in this case?
PLAYER   It never varies—we aim at the point where everyone who is marked for death dies.
GUIL.   Marked?
PLAYER   Between "just desserts" and "tragic irony" we are given quite a lot of scope for our particular talent. Generally speaking, things have gone about as far as they can possibly go when things have got about as bad as they reasonably get. *(He switches on a smile.)*
GUIL.   Who decides?
PLAYER *(switching off his smile)   Decides?* It is *written.*

He turns away. GUIL. *grabs him and spins him back violently.*

(Unflustered)   Now if you're going to be subtle, we'll miss each other in the dark. I'm referring to oral tradition. So to speak.

GUIL. *releases him.*

We're tragedians, you see. We follow directions—there is no *choice* involved. The bad end unhappily, the good unluckily. That is what tragedy means. *(Calling)* Positions!

The TRAGEDIANS *have taken up positions for the continuation of the mime: which in this case means a love scene, sexual and passionate, between the* QUEEN *and the* POISONER/KING.

PLAYER   Go!

The lovers begin. The PLAYER *contributes a breathless commentary for* ROS. *and* GUIL.

Having murdered his brother and wooed the widow—the poisoner mounts the throne! Here we see him and his queen give rein to their unbridled passion! She little knowing that the man she holds in her arms——!

ROS.   Oh, I say—here—really! You can't do that!

PLAYER   Why not?

ROS.   Well, really—I mean, people want to be *entertained*—they don't come expecting sordid and gratuitous filth.

PLAYER   You're wrong—they do! Murder, seduction and incest—what do you want—*jokes*?

ROS.   I want a good story, with a beginning, middle and end.

PLAYER *(to* GUIL.)   And you?

GUIL.   I'd prefer art to mirror life, if it's all the same to you.

PLAYER   It's all the same to me, sir. *(To the grappling* LOVERS)   All right, no need to indulge yourselves. *(They get up. To* GUIL.)   I come on in a minute. Lucianus, nephew to the king! *(Turns his attention to the* TRAGEDIANS)   Next!

They disport themselves to accommodate the next piece of mime, which consists of the PLAYER *himself exhibiting an excitable anguish (choreographed, stylized) leading to an impassioned scene with the* QUEEN *(cf. "The Closet Scene," Shakespeare Act III, scene iv) and a very stylized reconstruction of a* POLONIUS *figure being stabbed behind the arras (the murdered* KING *to stand in for* POLONIUS) *while the* PLAYER *himself continues his breathless commentary for the benefit of* ROS. *and* GUIL.

PLAYER   Lucianus, nephew to the king . . . usurped by his uncle and shattered by his mother's incestuous marriage . . . loses his reason . . . throwing the court into turmoil and disarray as he alternates between bitter melancholy and unrestricted lunacy . . . staggering from the suicidal *(a pose)* to the homicidal *(here he kills* POLONIUS") . . . he at last confronts his mother and in a scene of provocative ambiguity—*(a somewhat oedipal embrace)* begs her to repent and recant——*(He springs up, still talking.)* The King—*(he pushes forward the* POISONER/KING) tormented by guilt—haunted by fear—decides to despatch his nephew to England —and entrusts this undertaking to two smiling accomplices—friends—courtiers—to two spies——

He has swung round to bring together the POISONER/KING *and the two cloaked* TRAGEDIANS; *the latter kneel and accept a scroll from the* KING.

—giving them a letter to present to the English court——! And so they depart—on board ship——

The two SPIES *position themselves on either side of the* PLAYER, *and the three of them sway gently in unison, the motion of a boat; and then the* PLAYER *detaches himself.*

—and they arrive——

One SPY *shades his eyes at the horizon.*

—and disembark—and present themselves before the English king——*(He wheels round)* The English king——

An exchange of headgear creates the ENGLISH KING *from the remaining player—that is, the* PLAYER *who played the original murdered king.*

But where is the Prince? Where indeed? The plot has thickened—a twist of fate and cunning has put into their hands a letter that seals their deaths!

The two SPIES *present their letter; the* ENGLISH KING *reads it and orders their deaths. They stand up as the* PLAYER *whips off their cloaks preparatory to execution.*

Traitors hoist by their own petard?—or victims of the gods?—we shall never know!

The whole mime has been fluid and continuous but now ROS. *moves forward and brings it to a pause. What brings* ROS. *forward is the fact that under their cloaks the two* SPIES *are wearing coats identical to those worn by* ROS. *and* GUIL., *whose coats are now covered by their cloaks.* ROS. *approaches "his"* SPY *doubtfully. He does not quite understand why the coats are familiar.* ROS. *stands close, touches the coat, thoughtfully. . . .*

ROS.   Well, if it isn't——! No, wait a minute, don't tell me—it's a long time since—where was it? Ah, this is taking me back to—when was it? I know you, don't I? I never forget a face—*(he looks into the* SPY*'s face)* . . . not that I know yours, that is. For a moment I thought—no, I don't know you, do I? Yes, I'm afraid you're quite wrong. You must have mistaken me for someone else.

GUIL. *meanwhile has approached the other* SPY, *brow creased in thought.*

PLAYER *(to* GUIL.)   Are you familiar with this play?
GUIL.   No.
PLAYER   A slaughterhouse—eight corpses all told. It brings out the best in us.
GUIL. *(tense, progressively rattled during the whole mime and commentary)*   You!
  —What do *you* know about *death*?
PLAYER   It's what the actors do best. They have to exploit whatever talent is given to them, and their talent is dying. They can die heroically, comically, ironically, slowly, suddenly, disgustingly, charmingly, or from a great height. My own talent is more general. I extract significance from melodrama, a significance which it does not in fact contain; but occasionally, from out of this matter, there escapes a thin beam of light that, seen at the right angle, can crack the shell of mortality.
ROS.   Is that all they can do—die?
PLAYER   No, no—they kill beautifully. In fact some of them kill even better than they die. The rest die better than they kill. They're a team.
ROS.   Which ones are which?
PLAYER   There's not much in it.
GUIL. *(fear, derision)*   Actors! The mechanics of cheap melodrama! That isn't *death*! *(More quietly.)* You scream and choke and sink to your knees, but it doesn't

bring death home to anyone—it doesn't catch them unawares and start the whisper in their skulls that says—"One day you are going to die." *(He straightens up.)* You die so many times; how can you expect them to believe in your death?

PLAYER   On the contrary, it's the only kind they do believe. They're conditioned to it. I had an actor once who was condemned to hang for stealing a sheep—or a lamb, I forget which—so I got permission to have him hanged in the middle of a play—had to change the plot a bit but I thought it would be effective, you know —and you wouldn't believe it, he just *wasn't* convincing! It was impossible to suspend one's disbelief—and what with the audience jeering and throwing peanuts, the whole thing was a *disaster*!—he did nothing but cry all the time—right out of character—just stood there and cried. . . . Never again.

In good humour he has already turned back to the mime: the two SPIES *awaiting execution at the hands of the* PLAYER, *who takes his dagger out of his belt.*

Audiences know what to expect, and that is all that they are prepared to believe in. *(To the* SPIES*)* Show!

The SPIES *die at some length, rather well.*

The light has begun to go, and it fades as they die, and as GUIL. *speaks.*

GUIL.   No, no, no . . . you've got it all wrong . . . you can't act death. The *fact* of it is nothing to do with seeing it happen—it's not gasps and blood and falling about— that isn't what makes it death. It's just a man failing to reappear, that's all—now you see him, now you don't, that's the only thing that's real: here one minute and gone the next and never coming back—an exit, unobtrusive and unannounced, a disappearance gathering weight as it goes on, until, finally, it is heavy with death.

The two SPIES *lie still, barely visible. The* PLAYER *comes forward and throws the* SPIES' *cloaks over their bodies.* ROS. *starts to clap, slowly.*

Blackout.

A second of silence, then much noise. Shouts . . . " The King rises!" . . . "Give o'er the play!" . . . and cries for "Lights, lights, lights!"
   When the light comes, after a few seconds, it comes as a sunrise.
   The stage is empty save for two cloaked figures sprawled on the ground in the approximate positions last held by the dead SPIES. *As the light grows, they are seen to be* ROS. *and* GUIL., *and to be resting quite comfortably.* ROS. *raises himself on his elbows and shades his eyes as he stares into the auditorium. Finally:*

ROS.   That must be east, then. I think we can assume that.

GUIL.   I'm assuming nothing.

ROS.   No, it's all right. That's the sun. East.

GUIL. *(looks up)*   Where?

ROS.   I watched it come up.

GUIL.   No . . . it was light all the time, you see, and you opened your eyes very, very slowly. If you'd been facing back there you'd be swearing *that* was east.

ROS. *(standing up)*   You're a mass of prejudice.

GUIL.   I've been taken in before.

ROS. *(looks out over the audience)*   Rings a bell.

GUIL.   They're waiting to see what we're going to do.

ROS.   Good old east.

GUIL.   As soon as we make a move they'll come pouring in from every side, shouting obscure instructions, confusing us with ridiculous remarks, messing us about
from here to breakfast and getting our names wrong.

ROS. *starts to protest but he has hardly opened his mouth before:*

CLAUDIUS *(off stage—with urgency)*   Ho, Guildenstern!

GUIL. *is still prone. Small pause.*

ROS. AND GUIL.   You're wanted. . . .

GUIL. *furiously leaps to his feet as* CLAUDIUS *and* GERTRUDE *enter. They are in some
desperation.*

CLAUDIUS   Friends both, go join you with some further aid: Hamlet in madness
hath Polonius slain, and from his mother's closet hath he dragged him. Go seek
him out; speak fair and bring the body into the chapel. I pray you haste in this. *(As
he and* GERTRUDE *are hurrying out.)* Come Gertrude, we'll call up our wisest
friends and let them know both what we mean to do. . . .

They've gone. ROS. *and* GUIL. *remain quite still.*

GUIL.   Well . . .
ROS.   Quite . . .
GUIL.   Well, well.
ROS.   Quite, quite. *(Nods with spurious confidence.)* Seek him out. *(Pause.)* Etce-
tera.
GUIL.   Quite.
ROS.   Well. *(Small pause.)* Well, that's a step in the right direction.
GUIL.   You didn't like him?
ROS.   Who?
GUIL.   Good God, I hope more tears are shed for *us*! . . .
ROS.   Well, it's *progress,* isn't it? Something positive. Seek him out. *(Looks round
without moving his feet.)* Where does one begin . . . ? *(Takes one step towards the
wings and halts.)*
GUIL.   Well, that's a step in the right direction.
ROS.   You think so? He could be anywhere.
GUIL.   All right—you go that way, I'll go this way.
ROS.   Right.

They walk towards opposite wings. ROS. *halts.*

No.

GUIL. *halts.*

You go this way—I'll go that way.
GUIL.   All right.

They march towards each other, cross. ROS. *halts.*

ROS.   Wait a minute.

GUIL. *halts.*

I think we should stick together. He might be violent.
GUIL.   Good point. I'll come with you.

GUIL. *marches across to* ROS. *They turn to leave.* ROS. *halts.*

ROS.   No, I'll come with *you.*
GUIL.   Right.

They turn, march across to the opposite wing. ROS. *halts.*

GUIL. *halts.*

ROS.   I'll come with *you, my* way.
GUIL.   All right.

They turn again and march across. ROS. *halts.* GUIL. *halts.*

ROS.   I've just thought. If we both go, he could come *here.* That would be stupid, wouldn't it?
GUIL.   All right—I'll stay, you go.
ROS.   Right.

GUIL. *marches to midstage.*

   I say.

GUIL. *wheels and carries on marching back towards* ROS., *who starts marching downstage. They cross.* ROS. *halts.*

   I've just thought.

GUIL. *halts.*

   We ought to stick together; he might be violent.

GUIL.   Good point.

GUIL. *marches down to join* ROS.. *They stand still for a moment in their original positions.*

   Well, at last we're getting somewhere.

Pause.

   Of course, he might not come.
ROS. *(airily)*   Oh, he'll come.
GUIL.   We'd have some explaining to do.
ROS.   He'll come. *(Airily wanders upstage.)* Don't worry—take my word for it— *(Looks out—is appalled.)* He's coming!
GUIL.   What's he doing?
ROS.   Walking.
GUIL.   Alone?
ROS.   No.
GUIL.   Not walking?
ROS.   No.
GUIL.   Who's with him?
ROS.   The old man.
GUIL.   Walking?
ROS.   No.
GUIL.   Ah. That's an opening if ever there was one. *(And is suddenly galvanized into action.)* Let him walk into the trap!

ROS. What trap?

GUIL. You stand there! Don't let him pass!

He positions ROS. *with his back to one wing, facing* HAMLET'*s entrance.*

GUIL. *positions himself next to* ROS., *a few feet away, so that they are covering one side of the stage, facing the opposite side.* GUIL. *unfastens his belt.* ROS. *does the same. They join the two belts, and hold them taut between them.* ROS.'*s trousers slide slowly down.*

HAMLET *enters opposite, slowly, dragging* POLONIUS'*s body. He enters upstage, makes a small arc and leaves by the same side, a few feet downstage.*

ROS. *and* GUIL., *holding the belts taut, stare at him in some bewilderment.*

HAMLET *leaves, dragging the body. They relax the strain on the belts.*

ROS. That was close.

GUIL. There's a limit to what two people can do.

They undo the belts: ROS. *pulls up his trousers.*

ROS. *(worriedly—he walks a few paces towards* HAMLET'*s exit)* He *was* dead.

GUIL. Of course he's dead!

ROS. *(turns to* GUIL) Properly.

GUIL. *(angrily)* Death's death, isn't it?

ROS. *falls silent. Pause.*

Perhaps he'll come back this way.

ROS. *starts to take off his belt.*

No, no, no!—if we can't learn by experience, what else have we got?

ROS. *desists.*

Pause.

ROS. Give him a shout.

GUIL. I thought we'd been into all that.

ROS. *(shouts)* Hamlet!

GUIL. Don't be absurd.

ROS. *(shouts)* Lord Hamlet!

HAMLET *enters.* ROS. *is a little dismayed.*

What have you done, my lord, with the dead body?

HAMLET Compounded it with dust, whereto 'tis kin.

ROS. Tell us where 'tis, that we may take it thence and bear it to the chapel.

HAMLET Do not believe it.

ROS. Believe what?

HAMLET That I can keep your counsel and not mine own. Besides, to be de-manded of a sponge, what replication should be made by the son of a king?

ROS. Take you me for a sponge, my lord?

HAMLET   Ay, sir, that soaks up the King's countenance, his rewards, his authorities. But such officers do the King best service in the end. He keeps them, like an ape, in the corner of his jaw, first mouthed, to be last swallowed. When he needs what you have gleaned, it is but squeezing you and, sponge, you shall be dry again.

ROS.   I understand you not, my lord.

HAMLET   I am glad of it: a knavish speech sleeps in a foolish ear.

ROS.   My lord, you must tell us where the body is and go with us to the King.

HAMLET   The body is with the King, but the King is not with the body. The King is a thing——

GUIL.   A thing, my lord——?

HAMLET   Of nothing. Bring me to him.

HAMLET *moves resolutely towards one wing. They move with him, shepherding. Just before they reach the exit,* HAMLET, *apparently seeing* CLAUDIUS *approaching from off stage, bends low in a sweeping bow.* ROS. *and* GUIL., *cued by* HAMLET, *also bow deeply—a sweeping ceremonial bow with their cloaks swept round them.* HAMLET, *however, continues the movement into an about-turn and walks off in the opposite direction.* ROS. *and* GUIL., *with their heads low, do not notice.*

No one comes on. ROS. *and* GUIL. *squint upwards and find that they are bowing to nothing.*

CLAUDIUS *enters behind them. At first words they leap up and do a double-take.*

CLAUDIUS   How now? What hath befallen?

ROS.   Where the body is bestowed, my lord, we cannot get from him.

CLAUDIUS   But where is he?

ROS. *(fractional hesitation)*   Without, my lord; guarded to know your pleasure.

CLAUDIUS *(moves):*   Bring him before us.

This hits ROS. *between the eyes but only his eyes show it. Again his hesitation is fractional. And then with great deliberation he turns to* GUIL.

ROS.   Ho! Bring in the lord.

Again there is a fractional moment in which ROS. *is smug,* GUIL. *is trapped and betrayed.* GUIL. *opens his mouth and closes it.*

The situation is saved: HAMLET, *escorted, is marched in just as* CLAUDIUS *leaves.* HAMLET *and his* ESCORT *cross the stage and go out, following* CLAUDIUS.

Lighting changes to Exterior.

ROS. *(moves to go):*   All right, then?

GUIL. *(does not move; thoughtfully)*   And yet it doesn't seem enough; to have breathed such significance. Can that be all? And why us?—anybody would have done. And we have contributed nothing.

ROS.   It was a trying episode while it lasted, but they've done with us now.

GUIL.   Done what?

ROS.   I don't pretend to have understood. Frankly, I'm not very interested. If they won't tell us, that's their affair. *(He wanders upstage towards the exit.)* For my part, I'm only glad that that's the last we've seen of him—*(And he glances off stage and turns front, his face betraying the fact that* HAMLET *is there.)*

GUIL.   I knew it wasn't the end. . . .

ROS. *(high)*   What else?!

GUIL.   We're taking him to England. What's he doing?

ROS. *goes upstage and returns.*

ROS.   Talking.

GUIL.   To himself?

ROS. *makes to go,* GUIL. *cuts him off.*

Is he alone?

ROS.   No, he's with a soldier.

GUIL.   Then he's not talking to himself, is he?

ROS.   Not *by* himself. . . . Should we go?

GUIL.   Where?

ROS.   Anywhere.

GUIL.   Why?

ROS. *puts up his head listening.*

ROS.   There it is again. *(In anguish.)* All I ask is a change of ground!

GUIL. *(coda)*   Give us this day our daily round. . . .

HAMLET *enters behind them, talking with a soldier in arms.* ROS. *and* GUIL. *don't look round.*

ROS.   They'll have us hanging about till we're dead. At least. And the weather will change. *(Looks up.)* The spring can't last for ever.

HAMLET   Good sir, whose powers are these?

SOLDIER   They are of Norway, sir.

HAMLET   How purposed, sir, I pray you?

SOLDIER   Against some part of Poland.

HAMLET   Who commands them, sir?

SOLDIER   The nephew to old Norway, Fortinbras.

ROS.   We'll be cold. The summer won't last.

GUIL.   It's autumnal.

ROS. *(examining the ground)*   No leaves.

GUIL.   Autumnal—nothing to do with leaves. It is to do with a certain brownness at the edges of the day. . . . Brown is creeping up on us, take my word for it. . . . Russets and tangerine shades of old gold flushing the very outside edge of the senses . . . deep shining ochres, burnt umber and parchments of baked earth—reflecting on itself and through itself, filtering the light. At such times, perhaps, coincidentally, the leaves might fall, somewhere, by repute. Yesterday was blue, like smoke.

ROS. *(head up, listening)*   I got it again then.

They listen—faintest sound of TRAGEDIANS' *band.*

HAMLET   I humbly thank you, sir.

SOLDIER   God by you, sir. *(Exit.)*

ROS. *gets up quickly and goes to* HAMLET.

ROS.   Will it please you go, my lord?

HAMLET   I'll be with you straight. Go you a little before.

HAMLET *turns to face upstage.* ROS. *returns down.* GUIL. *faces front, doesn't turn.*

GUIL.   Is he there?

ROS.   Yes.

GUIL.   What's he doing?

ROS. *looks over his shoulder.*

ROS.   Talking.

GUIL.   To himself?

ROS.   Yes.

Pause. ROS. *makes to leave.*

ROS.   He *said* we can go. Cross my heart.

GUIL.   I like to know where I am. Even if I don't know where I am, I like to know
   that. If we go there's no knowing.

ROS.   No knowing what?

GUIL.   If we'll ever come back.

ROS.   We don't want to come back.

GUIL.   That may very well be true, but do we want to go?

ROS.   We'll be free.

GUIL.   I don't know. It's the same sky.

ROS.   We've come this far.

He moves towards exit. GUIL. *follows him.*

And besides, anything could happen yet.

They go.

Blackout.

ACT III

Opens in pitch darkness.
Soft sea sounds.

After several seconds of nothing, a voice from the dark . . .

GUIL.   Are you there?

ROS.   Where?

GUIL. *(bitterly)*   A flying start. . . .

Pause.

ROS.   Is that you?

GUIL.   Yes.

ROS.   How do you know?

GUIL. *(explosion)*   Oh-for-God's-sake!

ROS.   We're not finished, then?

GUIL.   Well, we're here, aren't we?

ROS.   Are we? I can't see a thing.

GUIL.   You can still *think,* can't you?

ROS.   I think so.

GUIL.   You can still *talk.*

ROS.   What should I say?

GUIL.   Don't bother. You can *feel,* can't you?

ROS. Ah! There's life in me yet!

GUIL. What are you feeling?

ROS. A leg. Yes, it feels like my leg.

GUIL. How does it feel?

ROS. Dead.

GUIL. Dead?

ROS. *(panic)* I can't feel a thing!

GUIL. Give it a pinch! *(Immediately he yelps.)*

ROS. Sorry.

GUIL. Well, that's cleared that up.

Longer pause: the sound builds a little and identifies itself—the sea. Ship timbers, wind in the rigging, and then shouts of sailors calling obscure but inescapably nautical instructions from all directions, far and near: A short list:

Hard a larboard!
Let go the stays!
Reef down me hearties!
Is that you, cox'n?
Hel-llo! Is that you?
Hard a port!
Easy as she goes!
Keep her steady on the lee!
Haul away, lads!
(Snatches of sea shanty maybe.)
Fly the jib!
Tops'l up, me maties!

When the point has been well made and more so.

ROS. We're on a boat. *(Pause.)* Dark, isn't it?

GUIL. Not for night.

ROS. No, not for *night.*

GUIL. Dark for day.

Pause.

ROS. Oh yes, it's dark for *day.*

GUIL. We must have gone north, of course.

ROS. Off course?

GUIL. Land of the midnight sun, that is.

ROS. Of course.

Some sailor sounds.
A lantern is lit upstage—in fact by HAMLET.
The stage lightens disproportionately—
Enough to see:
ROS. *and* GUIL. *sitting downstage.*
Vague shapes of rigging, etc., behind.

I think it's getting light.

GUIL. Not for night.

ROS. This far north.

GUIL. Unless we're off course.

ROS. *(small pause)* Of course.

A better light—Lantern? Moon? . . . Light.
Revealing, among other things, three large man-sized casks on deck, upended, with
lids. Spaced but in line. Behind and above—a gaudy striped umbrella, on a pole
stuck into the deck, tilted so that we do not see behind it—one of those huge six-foot-
diameter jobs. Still dim upstage. ROS. *and* GUIL. *still facing front.*

ROS. Yes, it's lighter than it was. It'll be night soon. This far north. *(Dolefully.)* I
suppose we'll have to go to sleep. *(He yawns and stretches.)*

GUIL. Tired?

ROS. No . . . I don't think I'd take to it. Sleep all night, can't see a thing all day. . . .
Those eskimos must have a quiet life.

GUIL. Where?

ROS. What?

GUIL. I thought you—— *(Relapses.)* I've lost all capacity for disbelief. I'm not sure
that I could even rise to a little gentle scepticism.

Pause.

ROS. Well, shall we stretch our legs?

GUIL. I don't feel like stretching my legs.

ROS. I'll stretch them for you, if you like.

GUIL. No.

ROS. We could stretch each other's. That way we wouldn't have to go anywhere.

GUIL. *(pause)* No, somebody might come in.

ROS. In where?

GUIL. Out here.

ROS. In out here?

GUIL. On deck.

ROS. *considers the floor: slaps it.*

ROS. Nice bit of planking, that.

GUIL. Yes, I'm very fond of boats myself. I like the way they're—contained. You
don't have to worry about which way to go, or whether to go at all—the question
doesn't arise, because you're on a *boat*, aren't you? Boats are safe areas in the
game of tag . . . the players will hold their positions until the music starts. . . . I
think I'll spend most of my life on boats.

ROS. Very healthy.

ROS. *inhales with expectation, exhales with boredom.* GUIL. *stands up and looks over*
the audience.

GUIL. One is free on a boat. For a time. Relatively.

ROS. What's it like?

GUIL. Rough.

ROS. *joins him. They look out over the audience.*

RUS I think I'm going to be sick.

GUIL. *licks a finger, holds it up experimentally.*

GUIL. Other side, I think.

ROS. *goes upstage: Ideally a sort of upper deck joined to the downstage lower deck by short steps. The umbrella being on the upper deck.* ROS. *pauses by the umbrella and looks behind it.* GUIL. *meanwhile has been resuming his own theme—looking out over the audience——*

Free to move, speak, extemporise, and yet. We have not been cut loose. Our truancy is defined by one fixed star, and our drift represents merely a slight change of angle to it: we may seize the moment, toss it around while the moments pass, a short dash here, an exploration there, but we are brought round full circle to face again the single immutable fact—that we, Rosencrantz and Guildenstern, bearing a letter from one king to another, are taking Hamlet to England.

By which time, ROS. *has returned, tiptoeing with great import, teeth clenched for secrecy, gets to* GUIL., *points surreptitiously behind him—and a tight whisper:*

ROS. I say—he's there!
GUIL. *(unsurprised)* What's he doing?
ROS. Sleeping.
GUIL. It's all right for him.
ROS. What is?
GUIL. He can sleep.
ROS. It's all right for him.
GUIL. He's got us now.
ROS. He can sleep.
GUIL. It's all done for him.
ROS. He's got us.
GUIL. And we've got nothing. *(A cry.)* All I ask is our common due!
ROS. For those in peril on the sea. . . .
GUIL. Give us this day our daily cue.

Beat, pause. Sit. Long pause.

ROS. *(after shifting, looking around)* What now?
GUIL. What do you mean?
ROS. Well, nothing is happening.
GUIL. We're on a boat.
ROS. I'm aware of that.
GUIL. *(angrily)* Then what do you expect? *(Unhappily.)* We act on scraps of information . . . sifting half-remembered directions that we can hardly separate from instinct.

ROS. *puts a hand into his purse, then both hands behind his back, then holds his fists out.*

GUIL. *taps one fist.*

ROS. *opens it to show a coin.*

He gives it to GUIL.

He puts his hand back into his purse. Then both hands behind his back, then holds his fists out.

GUIL. *taps one.*

ROS. *opens it to show a coin. He gives it to* GUIL.

Repeat.

Repeat.

GUIL. *getting tense. Desperate to lose.*

Repeat.

GUIL. *taps a hand, changes his mind, taps the other, and* ROS. *inadvertently reveals that he has a coin in both fists.*

GUIL.   You had money in both hands.
ROS. *(embarrassed)*   Yes.
GUIL.   Every time?
ROS.   Yes.
GUIL.   What's the point of that?
ROS. *(pathetic)*   I wanted to make you happy.

Beat.

GUIL.   How much did he give you?
ROS.   Who?
GUIL.   The King. He gave us some money.
ROS.   How much did he give you?
GUIL.   I asked you first.
ROS.   I got the same as you.
GUIL.   He wouldn't discriminate between us.
ROS.   How much did you get?
GUIL.   The same.
ROS.   How do you know?
GUIL.   You just told me—how do *you* know?
ROS.   He wouldn't discriminate between us.
GUIL.   Even if he could.
ROS.   Which he never could.
GUIL.   He couldn't even be sure of mixing us up.
ROS.   Without mixing us up.
GUIL. *(turning on him furiously)*   Why don't you say something original! No wonder the whole thing is so stagnant! You don't take me up on anything—you just repeat it in a different order.
ROS.   I can't think of anything original. I'm only good in support.
GUIL.   I'm sick of making the running.
ROS. *(humbly)*   It must be your dominant personality. *(Almost in tears.)* Oh, what's going to become of us!

And GUIL. *comforts him, all harshness gone.*

GUIL.   Don't cry . . . it's all right . . . there . . . there, I'll see we're all right.
ROS.   But we've got nothing to go on, we're out on our own.
GUIL.   We're on our way to England—we're taking Hamlet there.
ROS.   What for?

GUIL. What for? Where have you been?

ROS. When? *(Pause.)* We won't know what to do when we get there.

GUIL. We take him to the King.

ROS. Will *he* be there?

GUIL. No—the king of England.

ROS. He's expecting us?

GUIL. No.

ROS. He won't know what we're playing at. What are we going to *say*?

GUIL. We've got a letter. You remember the letter.

ROS. Do I?

GUIL. Everything is explained in the letter. We count on that.

ROS. Is that it, then?

GUIL. What?

ROS. We take Hamlet to the English king, we hand over the letter—what then?

GUIL. There may be something in the letter to keep us going a bit.

ROS. And if not?

GUIL. Then that's it—we're finished.

ROS. At a loose end?

GUIL. Yes.

Pause.

ROS. Are there likely to be loose ends? *(Pause.)* Who is the English king?

GUIL. That depends on when we get there.

ROS. What do you think it says?

GUIL. Oh . . . greetings. Expressions of loyalty. Asking of favours, calling in of debts. Obscure promises balanced by vague threats. . . . Diplomacy. Regards to the family.

ROS. And about Hamlet?

GUIL. Oh yes.

ROS. And us—the full background?

GUIL. I should say so.

Pause.

ROS. So we've got a letter which explains everything.

GUIL. You've got it.

ROS. *takes that literally. He starts to pat his pockets, etc.*

What's the matter?

ROS. The letter.

GUIL. Have you got it?

ROS. *(rising fear)* Have I? *(Searches frantically.)* Where would I have put it?

GUIL. You can't have lost it.

ROS. I must have!

GUIL. That's odd—I thought he gave it to me.

ROS. *looks at him hopefully.*

ROS. Perhaps he did.

GUIL. But you seemed so sure it was *you* who hadn't got it.

ROS. *(high)* It *was* me who hadn't got it!

GUIL. But if he gave it to me there's no reason why you should have had it in the first place, in which case I don't see what all the fuss is about you *not* having it.

ROS. *(pause)* I admit it's confusing.

GUIL. This is all getting rather undisciplined. . . . The boat, the night, the sense of isolation and uncertainty . . . all these induce a loosening of the concentration. We must not lose control. Tighten up. Now. Either you have lost the letter or you didn't have it to lose in the first place, in which case the King never gave it to you, in which case he gave it to me, in which case I would have put it into my inside top pocket, in which case *(calmly producing the letter)* . . . it will be . . . here. *(They smile at each other.)* We mustn't drop off like that again.

Pause. ROS. *takes the letter gently from him.*

ROS. Now that we have found it, why were we looking for it?

GUIL. *(thinks)* We thought it was lost.

ROS. Something else?

GUIL. No.

Deflation.

ROS. Now we've lost the tension.

GUIL. What tension?

ROS. What was the last thing I said before we wandered off?

GUIL. When was that?

ROS. *(helplessly)* I can't remember.

GUIL. *(leaping up)* What a shambles! We're just not getting anywhere.

ROS. *(mournfully)* Not even England. I don't believe in it anyway.

GUIL. What?

ROS. England.

GUIL. Just a conspiracy of cartographers, you mean?

ROS. I mean I don't believe it! *(Calmer.)* I have no image. I try to picture us arriving, a little harbour perhaps . . . roads . . . inhabitants to point the way . . . horses on the road . . . riding for a day or a fortnight and then a palace and the English king. . . . That would be the logical kind of thing. . . . But my mind remains a blank. No. We're slipping off the map.

GUIL. Yes . . . yes. . . . *(Rallying.)* But you don't believe anything till it happens. And it *has* all happened. Hasn't it?

ROS. We drift down time, clutching at straws. But what good's a brick to a drowning man?

GUIL. Don't give up, we can't be long now.

ROS. We might as well be dead. Do you think death could possibly be a boat?

GUIL. No, no, no . . . Death is . . . not. Death isn't. You take my meaning. Death is the ultimate negative. Not-being. You can't not-be on a boat.

ROS. I've frequently not been on boats.

GUIL. No, no, no—what you've been is not on boats.

ROS. I wish I was dead. *(Considers the drop.)* I could jump over the side. That would put a spoke in their wheel.

GUIL. Unless they're counting on it.

ROS. I shall remain on board. That'll put a spoke in their wheel. *(The futility of it, fury.)* All right! We don't question, we don't doubt. We perform. But a line must be drawn somewhere, and I would like to put it on record that I have no confidence in England. Thank you. *(Thinks about this.)* And even if it's true, it'll just be another shambles.

GUIL. I don't see why.

ROS. *(furious)* He won't know what we're talking about.—What are we going to *say*?

GUIL. We say—Your majesty, we have arrived!

ROS. *(kingly)* And who are you?

GUIL. We are Rosencrantz and Guildenstern.

ROS. *(barks)* Never heard of you!

GUIL. Well, we're nobody special——

ROS. *(regal and nasty)* What's your game?

GUIL. We've got our instructions——

ROS. First I've heard of it——

GUIL. *(angry)* Let me finish—— *(Humble.)* We've come from Denmark.

ROS. What do you want?

GUIL. Nothing—we're delivering Hamlet——

ROS. Who's he?

GUIL. *(irritated)* You've heard of *him*——

ROS. Oh, I've heard of him all right and I want nothing to do with it.

GUIL. But——

ROS. You march in here without so much as a by-your-leave and expect me to take in every lunatic you try to pass off with a lot of unsubstantiated——

GUIL. We've got a letter——

ROS. *snatches it and tears it open.*

ROS. *(efficiently)* I see . . . I see . . . well, this seems to support your story such as it is—it is an exact command from the king of Denmark, for several different reasons, importing Denmark's health and England's too, that on the reading of this letter, without delay, I should have Hamlet's head cut off——!

GUIL. *snatches the letter.* ROS., *double-taking, snatches it back.* GUIL. *snatches it half back. They read it together, and separate.*

Pause.

They are well downstage looking front.

ROS. The sun's going down. It will be dark soon.

GUIL. Do you think so?

ROS. I was just making conversation. *(Pause.)* We're his *friends.*

GUIL. How do you know?

ROS. From our young days brought up with him.

GUIL. You've only got their word for it.

ROS. But that's what we depend on.

GUIL. Well, yes, and then again no. *(Airily.)* Let us keep things in proportion. Assume, if you like, that they're going to kill him. Well, he is a man, he is mortal, death comes to us all, etcetera, and consequently he would have died anyway, sooner or later. Or to look at it from the social point of view—he's just one man among many, the loss would be well within reason and convenience. And then again, what is so terrible about death? As Socrates so philosophically put it, since we don't know what death is, it is illogical to fear it. It might be . . . very nice. Certainly it is a release from the burden of life, and, for the godly, a haven and a reward. Or to look at it another way—we are little men, we don't know the ins and outs of the matter, there are wheels within wheels, etcetera—it would be presumptuous of us to interfere with the designs of fate or even of kings. All in all, I think we'd be well advised to leave well alone. Tie up the letter—there—neatly—like that.—They won't notice the broken seal, assuming you were in character.

ROS.   But what's the point?

GUIL.   Don't apply logic.

ROS.   He's done nothing to us.

GUIL.   Or justice.

ROS.   It's awful.

GUIL.   But it could have been worse. I was beginning to think it was. *(And his relief comes out in a laugh.)*

Behind them HAMLET *appears from behind the umbrella. The light has been going. Slightly.* HAMLET *is going to the lantern.*

ROS.   The position as I see it, then. We, Rosencrantz and Guildenstern, from our young days brought up with him, awakened by a man standing on his saddle, are summoned, and arrive, and are instructed to glean what afflicts him and draw him on to pleasures, such as a play, which unfortunately, as it turns out, is abandoned in some confusion owing to certain nuances outside our appreciation—which, among other causes, results in, among other effects, a high, not to say, homicidal, excitement in Hamlet, whom we, in consequence, are escorting, for his own good, to England. Good. We're on top of it now.

HAMLET *blows out the lantern. The stage goes pitch black. The black resolves itself to moonlight, by which* HAMLET *approaches the sleeping* ROS. *and* GUIL. *He extracts the letter and takes it behind his umbrella; the light of his lantern shines through the fabric,* HAMLET *emerges again with a letter, and replaces it, and retires, blowing out his lantern.*

Morning comes.

ROS. *watches it coming—from the auditorium. Behind him is a gay sight. Beneath the re-tilted umbrella, reclining in a deck-chair, wrapped in a rug, reading a book, possibly smoking, sits* HAMLET.

ROS. *watches the morning come, and brighten to high noon.*

ROS.   I'm assuming nothing. *(He stands up,* GUIL. *wakes.)* The position as I see it, then. That's west unless we're off course, in which case it's night; the King gave me the same as you, the King gave you the same as me; the King never gave me the letter, the King gave you the letter, we don't know what's in the letter; we take Hamlet to the English king, it depending on when we get there who he is, and we hand over the letter, which may or may not have something in it to keep us going, and if not, we are finished and at a loose end, if they have loose ends. We could have done worse. I don't think we missed any chances. . . . Not that we're getting much help. *(He sits down again. They lie down—prone.)* If we stopped breathing we'd vanish.

The muffled sound of a recorder. They sit up with disproportionate interest.

GUIL.   Here we go.

ROS.   Yes, but what?

They listen to the music.

GUIL. *(excitedly)*   Out of the void, finally, a sound; while on a boat (admittedly) outside the action (admittedly) the perfect and absolute silence of the wet lazy slap of water against water and the rolling creak of timber—breaks; giving rise at once to the speculation or the assumption or the hope that something is about to happen; a pipe is heard. One of the sailors has pursed his lips against a woodwind, his fingers and thumb governing, shall we say, the ventages, whereupon, giving it breath, let us say, with his mouth, it, the pipe, discourses, as the saying goes, most eloquent music. A thing like that, it could change the course of events. *(Pause.)* Go and see what it is.

ROS.   It's someone playing on a pipe.

GUIL.   Go and find him.

ROS.   And then what?

GUIL.   I don't know—request a tune.

ROS.   What for?

GUIL.   Quick—before we lose our momentum.

ROS.   Why!—something is happening. It had quite escaped my attention!

He listens: Makes a stab at an exit. Listens more carefully: Changes direction.

GUIL. *takes no notice.*

ROS. *wanders about trying to decide where the music comes from. Finally he tracks it down—unwillingly—to the middle barrel. There is no getting away from it. He turns to* GUIL. *who takes no notice.* ROS., *during this whole business, never quite breaks into articulate speech. His face and his hands indicate his incredulity. He stands gazing at the middle barrel. The pipe plays on within. He kicks the barrel. The pipe stops. He leaps back towards* GUIL. *The pipe starts up again. He approaches the barrel cautiously. He lifts the lid. The music is louder. He slams down the lid. The music is softer. He goes back towards* GUIL. *But a drum starts, muffled. He freezes. He turns. Considers the left-hand barrel. The drumming goes on within, in time to the flute. He walks back to* GUIL. *He opens his mouth to speak. Doesn't make it. A lute is heard. He spins round at the third barrel. More instruments join in. Until it is quite inescapable that inside the three barrels, distributed, playing together a familiar tune which has been heard three times before, are the* TRAGEDIANS.

They play on.

ROS. *sits beside* GUIL. *They stare ahead.*

The tune comes to an end.

Pause.

ROS.   I thought I heard a band. *(In anguish.)* Plausibility is all I presume!

GUIL. *(coda)*   Call us this day our daily tune. . . .

The lid of the middle barrel flies open and the PLAYER'*s head pops out.*

PLAYER   Aha! All in the same boat, then! *(He climbs out. He goes round banging on the barrels.)*
Everybody out!

Impossibly, the TRAGEDIANS *climb out of the barrels. With their instruments, but not their cart. A few bundles. Except* ALFRED. *The* PLAYER *is cheerful.*

(To ROS.*)*   Where are we?
ROS.   Travelling.
PLAYER   Of course, we haven't got there yet.
ROS.   Are we all right for England?
PLAYER   You look all right to me. I don't think they're very particular in England. Al-l-fred!

ALFRED *emerges from the* PLAYER'*s barrel.*

GUIL.   What are you doing here?
PLAYER   Travelling. *(To* TRAGEDIANS*)* Right—blend into the background!

The TRAGEDIANS *are in costume (from the mime): A King with crown,* ALFRED *as Queen, Poisoner and the two cloaked figures.*

They blend.

(To GUIL.*)*   Pleased to see us? *(Pause.)* You've come out of it very well, so far.
GUIL.   And you?
PLAYER   In disfavour. Our play offended the King.
GUIL.   Yes.
PLAYER   Well, he's a second husband himself. Tactless, really.
ROS.   It was quite a good play nevertheless.
PLAYER   We never really got going—it was getting quite interesting when they stopped it.

Looks up at HAMLET.

That's the way to travel. . . .
GUIL.   What were you doing in there?
PLAYER   Hiding. *(Indicating costumes.)* We had to run for it just as we were.
ROS.   Stowaways.
PLAYER   Naturally—we didn't get paid, owing to circumstances ever so slightly beyond our control, and all the money we had we lost betting on certainties. Life is a gamble, at terrible odds—if it was a bet you wouldn't take it. Did you know that any number doubled is even?
ROS.   Is it?
PLAYER   We learn something every day, to our cost. But we troupers just go on and on. Do you know what happens to old actors?
ROS.   What?
PLAYER   Nothing. They're still acting. Surprised, then?
GUIL.   What?
PLAYER   Surprised to see us?
GUIL.   I knew it wasn't the end.

PLAYER   With practically everyone on his feet. What do you make of it, so far?

GUIL.   We haven't got much to go on.

PLAYER   You speak to him?

ROS.   It's possible.

GUIL.   But it wouldn't make any difference.

ROS.   But it's possible.

GUIL.   Pointless.

ROS.   It's allowed.

GUIL.   Allowed, yes. We are not restricted. No boundaries have been defined, no inhibitions imposed. We have, for the while, secured, or blundered into, our release, for the while. Spontaneity and whim are the order of the day. Other wheels are turning but they are not our concern. We can breathe. We can relax. We can do what we like and say what we like to whomever we like, without restriction.

ROS.   Within limits, of course.

GUIL.   Certainly within limits.

HAMLET *comes down to footlights and regards the audience. The others watch but don't speak.* HAMLET *clears his throat noisily and spits into the audience. A split second later he claps his hand to his eye and wipes himself. He goes back upstage.*

ROS.   A compulsion towards philosophical introspection is his chief characteristic, if I may put it like that. It does not mean he is mad. It does not mean he isn't. Very often, it does not mean anything at all. Which may or may not be a kind of madness.

GUIL.   It really boils down to symptoms. Pregnant replies, mystic allusions, mistaken identities, arguing his father is his mother, that sort of thing; intimations of suicide, forgoing of exercise, loss of mirth, hints of claustrophobia not to say delusions of imprisonment; invocations of camels, chameleons, capons, whales, weasels, hawks, handsaws—riddles, quibbles and evasions; amnesia, paranoia, myopia; day-dreaming, hallucinations; stabbing his elders, abusing his parents, insulting his lover, and appearing hatless in public—knock-kneed, droop-stockinged and sighing like a love-sick schoolboy, which at his age is coming on a bit strong.

ROS.   And talking to himself.

GUIL.   And talking to himself.

ROS. *and* GUIL. *move apart together.*

Well, where has that got us?

ROS.   He's the Player.

GUIL.   His play offended the King——

ROS.   —offended the King——

GUIL.   —who orders his arrest——

ROS.   —orders his arrest——

GUIL.   —so he escapes to England——

ROS.   On the boat to which he meets——

GUIL.   Guildenstern and Rosencrantz taking Hamlet——

ROS.   —who also offended the King——

GUIL.   —and killed Polonius——

ROS.   —offended the King in a variety of ways——

GUIL.   —to England. *(Pause.)* That seems to be it.

ROS. *jumps up.*

ROS.   Incidents! All we get is incidents! Dear God, is it too much to expect a little sustained action?!

And on the word, the PIRATES *attack. That is to say: Noise and shouts and rushing about. "Pirates."'*

Everyone visible goes frantic. HAMLET *draws his sword and rushes downstage.* GUIL., ROS. *and* PLAYER *draw swords and rush upstage. Collision.* HAMLET *turns back up. They turn back down. Collision. By which time there is general panic right upstage. All four charge upstage with* ROS., GUIL. *and* PLAYER *shouting:*

> At last!
> To arms!
> Pirates!
> Up there!
> Down there!
> To my sword's length!
> Action!

All four reach the top, see something they don't like, waver, run for their lives downstage:

HAMLET, *in the lead, leaps into the left barrel.* PLAYER *leaps into the right barrel.* ROS. *and* GUIL. *leap into the middle barrel. All closing the lids after them.*

*The lights dim to nothing while the sound of fighting continues. The sound fades to nothing. The lights come up. The middle barrel (*ROS.'*s and* GUIL.'*s) is missing.*

The lid of the right-hand barrel is raised cautiously, the heads of ROS. *and* GUIL. *appear.*

*The lid of the other barrel (*HAMLET'*s) is raised. The head of the* PLAYER *appears.*

All catch sight of each other and slam down lids.

Pause.

Lids raised cautiously.

ROS.   *(relief)* They've gone. *(He starts to climb out.)* That was close. I've never thought quicker.

They are all three out of barrels. GUIL. *is wary and nervous.* ROS. *is light-headed. The* PLAYER *is phlegmatic. They note the missing barrel.*

ROS. *looks round.*

ROS.   Where's——?

The PLAYER *takes off his hat in mourning.*

PLAYER   Once more, alone—on our own resources.

GUIL. *(worried)*   What do you mean? Where is he?

PLAYER   Gone.

GUIL.   Gone where?

PLAYER   Yes, we were dead lucky there. If that's the word I'm after.

ROS. *(not a pick up)*   Dead?

PLAYER   Lucky.

ROS. *(he means)*   Is he dead?

PLAYER   Who knows?

GUIL. *(rattled)*   He's not coming back?

PLAYER   Hardly.

ROS.   He's dead then. He's dead as far as we're concerned.

PLAYER   Or we are as far as he is. *(He goes and sits on the floor to one side.)* Not too bad, is it?

GUIL. *(rattled)*   But he can't—we're supposed to be—we've got a *letter*—we're going to England with a letter for the King——

PLAYER   Yes, that much seems certain. I congratulate you on the unambiguity of your situation.

GUIL.   But you don't understand—it contains—we've had our instructions——the whole thing's pointless without him.

PLAYER   Pirates could happen to anyone. Just deliver the letter. They'll send ambassadors from England to explain. . . .

GUIL. *(worked up)*   Can't you see—the pirates left us home and high—dry and home—drome——*(Furiously.)* The pirates left us high and dry!

PLAYER *(comforting)*   There . . .

GUIL. *(near tears)*   Nothing will be resolved without him. . . .

PLAYER   There . . . !

GUIL.   We need Hamlet for our release!

PLAYER   There!

GUIL.   What are we supposed to do?

PLAYER   This.

He turns away, lies down if he likes. ROS. *and* GUIL. *apart.*

ROS.   Saved again.

GUIL.   Saved for what?

ROS. *sighs.*

ROS.   The sun's going down. *(Pause.)* It'll be night soon. *(Pause.)* If that's west. *(Pause.)* Unless we've——

GUIL. *(shouts)*   Shut up! I'm sick of it! Do you think conversation is going to help us now?

ROS. *(hurt, desperately ingratiating)*   I—I bet you all the money I've got the year of my birth doubled is an odd number.

GUIL. *(moan)*   No-o.

ROS.   *Your* birth!

GUIL. *smashes him down.*

GUIL. *(broken)*   We've travelled too far, and our momentum has taken over; we move idly towards eternity, without possibility of reprieve or hope of explanation.

ROS.   Be happy—if you're not even *happy* what's so good about surviving? *(He picks himself up.)* We'll be all right. I suppose we just go on.

GUIL.   Go where?

ROS.   To England.

GUIL.   England! *That's* a dead end. I never believed in it anyway.

ROS.   All we've got to do is make our report and that'll be that. Surely.

GUIL.   I don't *believe* it—a shore, a harbour, say—and we get off and we stop someone and say—Where's the King?—And he says, Oh, you follow that road there
and take the first left and—— *(Furiously.)* I don't believe any of it!

ROS.   It doesn't sound very plausible.

GUIL.   And even if we came face to face, what do we say?

ROS.   We say—We've arrived!

GUIL.   *(kingly)*   And who are you?

ROS.   We are Guildenstern and Rosencrantz.

GUIL.   Which is which?

ROS.   Well, I'm—You're——

GUIL.   What's it all about?——

ROS.   Well, we were bringing Hamlet—but then some pirates——

GUIL.   I don't begin to understand. Who are all these people, what's it got to do
with me? You turn up out of the blue with some cock and bull story——

ROS. *(with letter)*   We have a letter——

GUIL. *(snatches it, opens it)*   A letter—yes—that's true. That's something . . . a letter . . . *(Reads.)* "As England is Denmark's faithful tributary . . . as love between
them like the palm might flourish, etcetera . . . that on the knowing of this contents, without delay of any kind, should those bearers, Rosencrantz and Guildenstern, put to sudden death——"

He double-takes. ROS. *snatches the letter.* GUIL. *snatches it back.* ROS. *snatches it half
back. They read it again and look up.*

The PLAYER *gets to his feet and walks over to his barrel and kicks it and shouts into
it.*

PLAYER   They've gone! It's all over!

One by one the PLAYERS *emerge, impossibly, from the barrel, and form a casually
menacing circle round* ROS. *and* GUIL., *who are still appalled and mesmerised.*

GUIL. *(quietly)*   Where we went wrong was getting on a boat. We can move, of
course, change direction, rattle about, but our movement is contained within a
larger one that carries us along as inexorably as the wind and current. . . .

ROS.   They had it in for us, didn't they? Right from the beginning. Who'd have
thought that we were so important?

GUIL.   But why? Was it all for this? Who are we that so much should converge on
our little deaths? *(In anguish to the* PLAYER*)* Who are *we?*

PLAYER   You are Rosencrantz and Guildenstern. That's enough.

GUIL.   No—it is not enough. To be told so little—to such an end—and still, finally,
to be denied an explanation——

PLAYER   In our experience, most things end in death.

GUIL. *(fear, vengeance, scorn)*   Your experience!—*Actors!*

He snatches a dagger from the PLAYER'*s belt and holds the point at the* PLAYER'*s
throat: the* PLAYER *backs and* GUIL. *advances, speaking more quietly.*

I'm talking about death—and you've never experienced *that*. And you cannot *act* it. You die a thousand casual deaths—with none of that intensity which squeezes out life . . . and no blood runs cold anywhere. Because even as you die you know that you will come back in a different hat. But no one gets up after *death*—there is no applause—there is only silence and some second-hand clothes, and that's— *death*——

And he pushes the blade in up to a hilt. The PLAYER *stands with huge, terrible eyes, clutches at the wound as the blade withdraws: he makes small weeping sounds and falls to his knees, and then right down.*

While he is dying, GUIL., *nervous, high, almost hysterical, wheels on the* TRAGE-DIANS—

If we have a destiny, then so had he—and if this is ours, then that was his—and if there are no explanations for us, then let there be none for him——

The TRAGEDIANS *watch the* PLAYER *die: they watch with some interest. The* PLAYER *finally lies still. A short moment of silence. Then the* TRAGEDIANS *start to applaud with genuine admiration. The* PLAYER *stands up, brushing himself down.*

PLAYER *(modestly)* Oh, come, come, gentlemen—no flattery—it was merely competent——

The TRAGEDIANS *are still congratulating him. The* PLAYER *approaches* GUIL., *who stands rooted, holding the dagger.*

PLAYER   What did you think? *(Pause.)* You see, it *is* the kind they do believe in— it's what is expected.

He holds his hand out for the dagger. GUIL. *slowly puts the point of the dagger on to the* PLAYER's *hand, and pushes . . . the blade slides back into the handle. The* PLAYER *smiles, reclaims the dagger.*

For a moment you thought I'd—cheated.

ROS. *relieves his own tension with loud nervy laughter.*

ROS.   Oh, very good! *Very* good! Took me in completely—didn't he take you in completely—*(claps his hands).* Encore! Encore!

PLAYER *(activated, arms spread, the professional)*   Deaths for all ages and occa-sions! Deaths by suspension, convulsion, consumption, incision, execution, as-phyxiation and malnutrition—! Climactic carnage, by poison and by steel—! Double deaths by duel—! Show!—

ALFRED, *still in his Queen's costume, dies by poison: the* PLAYER, *with rapier, kills the "*KING*" and duels with a fourth* TRAGEDIAN, *inflicting and receiving a wound. The two remaining* TRAGEDIANS, *the two "*SPIES*" dressed in the same coats as* ROS. *and* GUIL., *are stabbed, as before. And the light is fading over the deaths which take place right upstage.*

(Dying amid the dying—tragically, romantically.) So there's an end to that—it's commonplace: light goes with life, and in the winter of your years the dark comes early. . . .

GUIL. *(tired, drained, but still an edge of impatience; over the mime)*   No . . . no . . .

not for *us,* not like that. Dying is not romantic, and death is not a game which will soon be over . . . Death is not anything . . . death is not . . . It's the absence of presence, nothing more . . . the endless time of never coming back . . . a gap you can't see, and when the wind blows through it, it makes no sound. . . .

The light has gone upstage. Only GUIL. *and* ROS. *are visible as* ROS.*'s clapping falters to silence.*

Small pause.

ROS.   That's it, then, is it?

No answer. He looks out front.

The sun's going down. Or the earth's coming up, as the fashionable theory has it.

Small pause.

Not that it makes any difference.

Pause.

What was it all about? When did it begin?

Pause. No answer.

Couldn't we just stay put? I mean no one is going to come on and drag us off. . . . They'll just have to wait. We're still young . . . fit . . . we've got years. . . .

Pause. No answer.

(A cry.) We've done nothing wrong! We didn't harm anyone. Did we?

GUIL.   I can't remember.

ROS. *pulls himself together.*

ROS.   All right, then. I don't care. I've had enough. To tell you the truth, I'm relieved.

And he disappears from view. GUIL. *does not notice.*

GUIL.   Our names shouted in a certain dawn . . . a message . . . a summons . . . There must have been a moment, at the beginning, where we could have said—no. But somehow we missed it. *(He looks round and sees he is alone.)*

Rosen.—?
Guil.—?

He gathers himself.

Well, we'll know better next time. Now you see me, now you—*(and disappears).*

Immediately the whole stage is lit up, revealing, upstage, arranged in the approximate positions last held by the dead TRAGEDIANS, *the tableau of court and corpses which is the last scene of Hamlet.*

That is: The KING, QUEEN, LAERTES *and* HAMLET *all dead.* HORATIO *holds* HAMLET. FORTINBRAS *is there.*

So are two AMBASSADORS *from England.*

AMBASSADOR   The sight is dismal;
and our affairs from England come too late.
The ears are senseless that should give us hearing
to tell him his commandment is fulfilled,
that Rosencrantz and Guildenstern are dead.
Where should we have our thanks?

HORATIO   Not from his mouth,
had it the ability of life to thank you:
He never gave commandment for their death.
But since, so jump upon this bloody question,
you from the Polack wars, and you from England,
are here arrived, give order that these bodies
high on a stage be placed to the view;
and let me speak to the yet unknowing world
how these things came about: so shall you hear
of carnal, bloody and unnatural acts,
of accidental judgments, casual slaughters,
of deaths put on by cunning and forced cause,
and, in this upshot, purposes mistook
fallen on the inventors' heads: all this can I
truly deliver.

But during the above speech, the play fades out, overtaken by dark and music.

Essay

Introducing the Essay

The Essay as "Literature"

When anyone asks the question "What is literature?" the answer seems self-evident because readers usually assume that literature is "fictional" writing—poetry, novels, stories, plays. Or perhaps literature is defined as "imaginative" writing where the situations created—although recognizable —are not *real,* that is, not to be verified by what is called reality. Nobody asks whether the characters in Updike's story "A & P" exist in real life. When you read Andrew Marvell's "To His Coy Mistress," you don't say it's a historically verifiable document; you say it's a poem. In it you recognize a work of imaginative fiction that somehow reflects upon, is parallel to, or is even a diversion from, "real" life. Readers may see literature as "representative" or "universal"; they may see it as relevant to their own experience, but they don't try to test it empirically. While literature often uses ordinary speech, it fails to provide direct instructions for acting in the world, in the way traffic signs like *Turn Right Here* or *No Way Out* do.

One definition of literature might be that literature cues readers to produce and experience a fictional or imaginative world. But such definitions rest on a firm distinction between the world of "fact" and the world of "fiction," as if these worlds constituted definable and distinct entities. In fact, such distinctions are not so simple. Even with so-called imaginative writing, the distinction between "fiction" and "fact" is a blurred one. There really is a place called Denmark, the setting of Shakespeare's *Hamlet,* just as many of the place names mentioned in Joyce Carol Oates's story "How I Contemplated My Life" are also those of real places. We can actually visit both Denmark and (a little less expensively) Detroit.

Often we find included under the heading of "literature" a number of texts that were not written as "fictional" or "imaginative," including essays such as those by Francis Bacon or Crèvecoeur as well as autobiographies, literary criticism, histories, volumes of letters, sermons, and political addresses. They are certainly not "fictional" in the conventional sense. There are other blurrings and ambiguities about the notion of what constitutes "literature." The word *novel,* for instance, used to be applied to both true events and fictional texts. Even today "literature" includes factual material like Tom Wolfe's accounts of hippies in the sixties, Jack Kerouac's *On the Road,* or the so-called non-fiction novels of Norman Mailer. The writers who contributed to the world's great sacred books, the Koran and the Bible, did not write them as "literature" although that is how they are often treated, even by many believers.

Some experts define literature by its distinctive use of language; some suggest that literature is language different from ordinary, everyday language. "I wonder, by my troth, what thou and I did, till we loved" is certainly not today considered ordinary language, but that is largely because the language of Donne's poem "The Good-Morrow" is four hundred years old and therefore sounds archaic to us. Yet a contemporary poem like E.E. Cummings's "anyone lived in a little how town" is hardly what you would overhear at a party. Although most of its words are ordinary, the way they are organized is not. But the language of a poem like Jim Daniels's "Short-Order Cook," though ordinary and organized deliberately to sound precisely like ordinary speech, does not disqualify it from being a poem.

The whole concept of "ordinary" language is itself questionable. There is no single "ordinary" language. What is ordinary for one group or class of people certainly is not for another. Nor is there any so-called ordinary language that cannot be read in a "literary" manner, even the language of road signs and public notices. As the contemporary critic Terry Eagleton explains, many apparently straightforward public notices can be read by using literary devices. For instance, the word *refuse* in "Refuse to be put in this basket" can be read as both the verb meaning "to express unwillingness" and the noun meaning "garbage." The fun of that sentence is that it is a pun: it can mean either or both simultaneously. In short, we can read such a sentence for its wordplay—and see it as we would literature—as well as for its content. Eagleton's point is that wordplay and ambiguity are often believed to be inherently "literary" uses of language. He argues, however, that whether a text is literary or not really depends on how it is read.

All language, for instance, can be read metaphorically. Conventions of reading often encourage you to read texts in particular ways (we discussed conventions of reading fairy tales on p. 50), and you probably have certain conventions very deeply embedded within your own literary repertoire. If your literary repertoire includes the assumption that fiction should always be read "realistically," you may have difficulty reading a story like Sukenick's "The Birds." Most people assume, if they come across a note attached to their refrigerator, that it is trying to give them information—"Feed the Cat" or "Buy milk," for example. They will naturally assume that it is meant to have one meaning and communicates this meaning directly, as opposed to a poem, which may have many meanings and which will not necessarily be explicit about any of them. William Carlos Williams's poem, "This Is Just to Say" (p. 541), however, blurs this distinction, but such distinctions between *literal* and *figurative* meaning, between *monovalence* and *polyvalence,* can always be blurred by strong readers who question the conventional separation of literary from non-literary texts.

In fact, there is no inherent "literary" use of language or even any inherent meaning of the word *literature.* What we mean by literature is continually changing. Some texts—even those we assume everyone would see as literature, such as Shakespeare's plays—may start their lives as "non-literature" and over the course of time become *canonized,* almost in a religious sense, as literature. Shakespeare's plays started out as very utilitarian scripts in a commercial playhouse. Nobody thought of them as serious literary texts. It was only over time that they became seen as literature. Over time, the **canon** of literature, even of so-called great literature, is continually changing: it is always being constructed, for diverse though explicable reasons, by different societies in different ways. Like every other aesthetic human product, what is thought to be a valuable text or "literature" changes over time. What we have chosen to include in this anthology as poetry, fiction, and drama constitutes, for the most part, works considered to be in the "canon." Nonetheless, we had to choose among many possible selections; we had to decide both what we considered to be literature and also what literature you might enjoy.

In this anthology, we invite you to ponder the "literary" qualities not only of many texts we have traditionally termed *literature* but also of non-literary texts using, to some extent, the same techniques. Like literary texts, the essays here are produced by the constraints and conflicts of their particular culture. We want you to generalize the information you have gained about yourself as a reader of literature and apply it to contexts and issues raised in these essays. When you read either literary or non-literary texts, your questions and interpretations often emerge from the contradictions of your own culture. You therefore do not have direct access to "the meaning" of an essay any more than to the meaning of a piece of literature. Once again you use the knowledge in your own repertoire to interact with the repertoire of the text to create your own interpretation, the product of diverse cultural forces. The cognitive processes that readers undergo when they read any text follow similar patterns. Thus as you now move from literary to non-literary texts, you will not change the mental processes by which you read and interpret.

Becoming a Strong Reader of the Essay

Nonetheless, when readers normally speak of an *essay,* or more broadly of *discursive prose,* they are generally expressing some differences found in their repertoires, in practice if not in theory, between a non-fictional essay and a fictional poem, short story, or play. If these differences are not in the texts, where are they? The differences are in fact the *uses* to which a society puts certain texts. In other words, texts are read differently because of the assumptions from both **literary and general repertoires** that readers bring to their readings of texts. You should always ask yourself these questions: For what *purpose* am I reading a given text? Am I reading it for information or for some other reason?

Readers habitually see essays as *referential,* that is, as *referring* more directly to the real, outside world than we assume literature attempts to do. Consequently many readers assume that the major purpose of reading an essay is to discover "facts" about the world. But such an assumption fails to recognize that any text, even if it purports to be factual, is still an *interpretation,* and that any reading of a text is again an act of interpretation rather than a discovery of its or the world's "true meaning." You can, for example read Crèvecoeur's "What Is an American?" to focus on its elegant use of language, its cultural presuppositions, and your own responses to the issues it raises, or you might want to assess it historically for information about how an eighteenth-century writer saw the new American republic. Reading for these different ends does not change the *text*: it changes the *purposes* for which you want to use it. You may read a scientific article, a philosophical argument, an account of a football game, or a religious or political address and in each case analyze the stylistic features—the uses of powerful metaphors and the characteristic tone. You may also want to probe the text's factual accuracy or (if you are being an especially strong reader) its unconscious assumptions.

What readers do, in short, is to take up a particular attitude toward an essay because of the assumptions they bring to it and the inferences they draw from it. When readers read for information about the world, they read *through* the language as if it were transparent, as if it gives them a kind of direct window onto the world. At this *referential* end of discourse, words are taken by readers to "refer" to or be the signs of things—mathematical equations, road signs, directions for assembling ping-pong tables. Like realistic paintings, such writing forces the reader to look *through* the medium to what it tries to represent. Consider, however, the prose of Gertrude Stein's "As a Wife Has a Cow," on page 40, or perhaps a painting by a twentieth-century abstract expressionist like Mark Rothko or Jackson Pollock. In such cases we look *at,* not through, the medium—whether in paint or in language—to analyze the effects of its techniques, its colors or metaphors, its formal and emotional dimensions. If we try to ask of a Rothko painting, "What is it a picture *of?*" it becomes clear that we don't get a very satisfactory answer. If we don't possess a knowledge of the conventions of abstract art in our repertoires, then we may not appreciate a Rothko painting. When we do acquire such knowledge, we may be able to do so.

The terms *through* and *at* come from Richard Lanham's books, *Style: An Anti-Textbook* and *Literacy and the Survival of Humanism,* in which he points out how readers continually shift between these two extremes in reading different texts. The texts don't change, but the assumptions readers bring to them (that is, the kind of reading readers give them) certainly do.

The essays collected here seem naturally to invite the reader to read *through* them, referentially, to gain information about the world. The traditional way of doing this task is for the reader to follow through the argument as carefully as possible, thereby staying close to the logical position the writer seems to require. You may choose to summarize or restate the argument in your own words, and it often seems easier to do so with a piece of discursive prose rather than with a poem or story because most readers regard essays as if they are automatically referential. Further, most readers generally believe that with such writing they should be faithful to the writer's "intention."

But even when you try to be as faithful as possible to the writer's argument and what you perceive to be the writer's intention, we want you next to think in these two additional ways:

1. Examine your *own* repertoire, especially the assumptions and beliefs that you bring to the text. How does your repertoire coincide with or differ from the repertoire of the text on central issues?
2. Probe the text for what it does *not* say about the issues it raises. In other words, look for the implied assumptions of the text, not just what it explicitly asserts. Remember that what a writer takes for granted and therefore does not make explicit is just where the text's relation to its general ideology can be found.

At this second stage of reading the essays, you are doing something you are by now familiar with: you are standing back from the argument and considering your own responses to the issues it raises. What questions do *you* have to introduce to the argument? What opposing views are you provoked to think about as a result of reading it? If you use these two steps, you are, in short, starting to develop a strong reading of your own—and to probe the ways the text articulates the conflicts of its time, either past or present.

One of the paradoxical discoveries that you may make as you look *through* the language of these essays is that you can also look *at* it. In short, even in the most referential prose, the techniques of fictional (or non-referential) language can be found. Similarly, although most readers associate metaphor, connotative language, and rhetorical figures with literary texts— texts in which they look *at* rather than *through* language—rhetorical figures as well as connotative language exist in every kind of writing. Martin Luther King, Jr.'s sermons and speeches (see p. 1220) provide many examples of figurative language. In short, characteristics generally considered specifically *literary* are inevitably found in non-fictional or discursive prose. Indeed in any kind of writing, it is in the rhetorically powerful words of the text that the conflicts lie, waiting to be uncovered.

The Pervasiveness of Metaphor: Susan Sontag's "Illness as Metaphor"

Most people generally think of *metaphor*—a verbal linking of two unlike objects to suggest a likeness or relationship between them—as a *figure of speech* used only in poetry. Metaphor, however, is a powerful force in all our language, and you will discover abundant metaphors if you search for them in almost any magazine or newspaper article. Susan Sontag's "Illness as Metaphor" (p. 1223) analyzes how metaphor pervades both our language and our ideas about cancer and tuberculosis. In her essay, Sontag analyzes metaphors for illness in two ways: first, she discusses various mental and physical characteristics that have been metaphorically attributed to people with cancer or tuberculosis; and second, she discusses how diseases have been metaphorically associated with social and political problems. Here is a brief extract from that text:

TB is thought to be relatively painless. Cancer is thought to be, invariably, excruciatingly painful. TB is thought to provide an easy death, while cancer is the spectacularly wretched one. For over a hundred years TB remained the preferred way of giving death a meaning—an edifying, refined disease. Nineteenth-century literature is stocked with descriptions of almost symptomless, unfrightened, beatific deaths from TB, particularly of young people, such as Little Eva in *Uncle Tom's Cabin* and Dombey's son Paul in *Dombey and Son* and Smike in *Nicholas Nickleby,* where Dickens described TB as the "dread disease" which "refines" death. . . .

While TB takes on qualities assigned to the lungs, which are part of the upper, spiritualized body, cancer is notorious for attacking parts of the body (colon, bladder, rectum, breast, cervix, prostate, testicles) that are embarrassing to acknowledge. Having a tumor generally arouses some feelings of shame, but in the hierarchy of the body's organs, lung cancer is felt to be less shameful than rectal cancer. And one non-tumor form of cancer now turns up in commercial fiction in the role once monopolized by TB, as the romantic disease which cuts off a young life. (The heroine of Erich Segal's *Love Story* dies of leukemia—the "white" or TB-like form of the disease, for which no mutilating surgery can be proposed—not of stomach or breast cancer.) A disease of the lungs is, metaphorically, a disease of the soul. Cancer, as a disease that can strike anywhere, is a disease of the body. Far from revealing anything spiritual, it reveals that the body is all too woefully, just the body. . . .

Nobody conceives of cancer the way TB was thought of—as a decorative, often lyrical death. Cancer is a rare and still scandalous subject for poetry; and it seems unimaginable to aestheticize the disease.

It may initially seem silly or irrational to us that people in the nine-teenth century associated tuberculosis with an increase in sexual passion or an increase in emotional and poetic sensitivity. We may find such ideas irra-tional because we live in a historical period that emphasizes physical fitness; we think that a delicate pallor is unattractive rather than appealing, that health is a sign of strength and vigor rather than of vulgarity. But metaphors, as well as more general cultural assumptions, are *conventional* rather than natural. Therefore notions about beauty, illness, and sensitivity change from one historical period to another and from one culture to another.

Sontag suggests that even though cancer is one of the major forms of illness today, as tuberculosis was in the nineteenth century, it does not share any of the positive connotations associated with tuberculosis. She argues that cancer is thought of only in negative terms because of its intrinsic dif-ference from tuberculosis: cancer cannot be helped by a change in climate or surroundings (Keats traveled to Italy to help his TB); it causes particu-larly agonizing deaths; it attacks embarrassing parts of the body. Sontag does not take into account, however, that our society does not romanticize any physical illness, that we would now no longer associate tuberculosis with increased sensitivity or sexuality. But she does recognize that, to some extent, we do romanticize mental illness today. Thus she argues that it is not just the illness itself but society's attitude toward a given disease that deter-mines the way illnesses are regarded.

In the last two paragraphs, we have analyzed Sontag's essay by trying to read *through* it to understand the argument that she develops about the metaphorical function of illnesses in our society. But we might now try to move to a second stage and attempt to situate Sontag's argument histori-cally and analyze it rhetorically, in other words, to look *at* it as well as *through* it. Clearly, in her analysis, cancer seems the worse of the two dis-eases to have, at least from a social perspective. But she neglects to mention the social stigma associated with tuberculosis among those of the poorer classes or the slow excruciating death suffered by many tuberculosis vic-tims. This omission may be because she is trying to analyze the diseases *as metaphors,* but she does, on a number of occasions, talk much more di-rectly about the reality of having cancer than about the reality of having tu-berculosis.

Now let us stand back a little from her argument. Why do you think Sontag's analysis moves in this particular direction? Do you think it is a flaw in her presentation? Some readers may think that Sontag treats cancer somewhat more seriously because she is historically removed from the tu-berculosis epidemics of the nineteenth century. Others may argue that it is because everyone thinks that the diseases of one's own time are always worse than those of other times. Perhaps it is because she has experienced cancer herself. We can therefore read this essay, just as we have read various poems and stories, *differently,* against its grain, not just for the information it tries to impart, but also for the cultural and personal attitudes it articulates. Different readers' interpretations of this essay will probably differ as much as those of any poem. Readers who read "at" rather than "through" do not stay simply within the argument the text contains; instead they contribute their own probing questions, broader concerns, and knowledge to construct their own responses.

While our society no longer romanticizes any physical illness, it does treat cancer more metaphorically than it treats nearly any other sickness except perhaps AIDS. (The metaphors currently used to describe AIDS would be a profitable topic for you to discuss as an extension of Sontag's argument.) As she points out, cancer is still regarded in our society as distasteful: cancer patients are often shunned by neighbors and friends; they may be turned down for promotions in their jobs; they themselves tend to be secretive about their disease, as if they may be somehow contagious or might have done something to avoid the illness. Not only is cancer feared in our society because it attacks invisibly, slowly, and arbitrarily, but also because of how cancer is used as a metaphor for uncontrollable political and social problems. When Watergate or the Marcos dictatorship in the Philippines is described as "a cancer" by politicians, notions of evil, subterfuge, and corruption become associated with cancer in a way that they would never be associated with a broken leg, heart trouble, or glaucoma.

No one will ever be able to pin down exactly how or why certain metaphors function in any given historical period; nonetheless, all societies have characteristic metaphors—ones that illustrate their *ideology,* that is, their values, beliefs, assumptions. The modern French critic Roland Barthes (one of whose essays is on p. 1191) has pointed to the power of what he calls "mythologies": stories and sustained metaphors that all societies have, embodying the deepest values of that society—what we have here termed its *ideology.* The "American Dream" is one such mythology, as is the American belief that we should all be strong, self-reliant, autonomous individuals. So you can at least try to become increasingly attuned to the metaphors that are used today. You may then recognize, first, that many of your opinions are based on conventional, historically conditioned assumptions and values rather than on permanent, unchanging truths; and, second, that metaphors are not obscure figures of speech used only in poetry but rather that they pervade every aspect of our language. In fact, without metaphor, our language would lose much of its evocative power. Even though Sontag's essay is closely argued, readers can see how, by careful attention to the argument, they can use her ideas to extend their insights into what they understand of themselves and their society. Consider, for instance, the usual way you would read such an essay. As you read it, you inevitably start reacting to its argument. You let it speak, as far as it can, for itself. But in one sense that is impossible: "it" is not speaking—*you* are reading it. Automatically you bring to it *your* questions, issues, and concerns, even if they are only partly formulated in your conscious mind.

What readers of the essays in this anthology should attempt to do—as we have already suggested throughout the poetry and fiction sections—is to become conscious of their **literary** and **general repertoires**. As readers read, they in fact start to construct an essay of their own in their heads (the word *essay* comes from the French *essai,* meaning attempt or trial). You therefore never just passively absorb a text. Even if you are unaware of the preconceptions you bring to your reading, your conception of an essay's argument is always filtered through your own personal experiences and previous ideas about the subject. You, in fact, interpret or rework everything you read according to your own preconceptions. We suggest that you try to become much more self-conscious about the questions and concerns you bring to an essay and about the manner in which you construct your rethinking and recreating of its argument. In short, even with a piece of discursive prose, *you* can choose the kind of reading you want to do.

You should try to apply the same kind of close scrutiny to the text itself. When you construct a reading of an essay (or any kind of text), you are probing it not just for its "intended" or surface or literal meaning, but for the meanings it betrays of its unconscious assumptions, that is, its general repertoire. You are trying to probe it in the same way you probe your own repertoire by asking such questions as the following—to answer them you may have to consult such sources as history texts or encyclopedias:

- What is the historical context from which this essay derives?
- What kinds of ideological conflicts underlie the assumptions of the essay?
- What conflicts is it not dealing with or might it be trying to suppress?

Of course, remember that you yourself will always be reading from *your* own particular vantage point in *your* historical time. When you read historical texts, ask the question that lies behind Raymond Williams's perceptive inquiry into the history of the word *individual:* What forces and movements in the past have made me what I am in the present? You too, like the texts you read, have been created by the past—by social institutions, educational organizations, prescribed ways of thinking and feeling, in short, by ideology. None of us created these things: they were here long before we were, and sometimes we seem to have very limited powers over them—until of course, through education and self-awareness, we become more knowledgeable about them. In "Illness as Metaphor," Susan Sontag makes a similar point—that readers, rather like texts, are affected by (or as is sometimes said metaphorically, "written by") many influences from their pasts. These influences are varied and often contradictory: they include such parts of our general repertoires as religion, education, politics, gender, class, race, income level, and lifestyle.

Ideology in Language: Raymond Williams's "Individual"

The literary and cultural critic Raymond Williams has written a series of short essays on what he calls "key words" to illustrate the interactions between language and society. Language is produced by the society that uses it: it is a fluid social practice that is continually changing (rewritten, we might say, by conflicting discourses). Williams's book traces the historical changes that have occurred in many of the most important words in our culture. He shows how, over long historical periods, language articulates not only changing but often conflicting cultural and social values—how, in short, language conveys the ideology and ideological struggles of a culture. A reader goes to a dictionary for what appear to be authoritative definitions of words, but what dictionaries do not show is how the same words have changed their meanings over time. In particular, those words that carry a culture's deepest values and assumptions—its ideology—are in continual flux and contradiction. Instead of there being "fixed" or definitive meanings of any word, there is a broad *range of meanings* that convey and, in a very real sense, create our culture's values. Here is Williams's discussion of one remarkably powerful "key word," one that has acquired major importance in history and one that perhaps you take for granted in your political, religious, or other discussions—the word *individual.*

RAYMOND WILLIAMS (b. 1926)

Individual

from *Keywords*

Individual originally meant indivisible. That now sounds like paradox. 'Individual' stresses a distinction from others; 'indivisible' a necessary connection. The development of the modern meaning from the original meaning is a record in language of an extraordinary social and political history.

The immediate fw *individualis,* mL, is derived from *individuus,* L, C6, a negative (*in-*) adjective from rw *dividere,* L—divide. *Individuus* was used to translate *atomos,* Gk—not cuttable, not divisible. Boethius, C6, defined the meanings of *individuus:*

> Something can be called individual in various ways: that is called individual which cannot be divided at all, such as unity or spirit (i); that which cannot be divided because of its hardness, such as steel, is called individual (ii); some-thing is called individual, the specific designation of which is not applicable to

---

The following abbreviations are used in the text.

fw: immediate forerunner of a word, in the same or another language.
rw: ultimate traceable word, from which 'root' meanings are derived.
q.v.: see entry under word noted.
C: followed by numeral, century (C19: nineteenth century).
eC: first period (third) of a century.
lC: last period (third) of a century.
Gk: Classical Greek.
L: Latin.
mL: Medieval Latin.

Quotations followed by a name and date only, or a date only, are from examples cited in OED. Other quotations are followed by specific sources.

anything of the same kind, such as Socrates (iii). *(In Porphyrium commentarium liber secundus)*

Individualis and **individual** can be found in the sense of essential indivisibility in medieval theological argument, especially in relation to the argument about the unity of the Trinity (the alternate form, *indivisible,* was also then used). Thus: 'to the . . . glorie of the hye and indyvyduall Trynyte' (1425). Sense (i) continued in more general use into C17: '*Individuall,* not to bee parted, as man and wife' (1623); ' . . . would divide the individuall Catholicke Church into severall Republicks' (Milton, 1641). Sense (ii), in physics, was generally taken over by *atom,* from C17. It is sense (iii), indicating a single distinguishable person, which has, from eC17, the most complicated history.

The transition is best marked by uses of the phrase 'in the individuall' as opposed to 'in the general'. Many of these early uses can be read back in a modern sense, for the word is still complex. Thus: 'as touching the Manners of learned men, it is a thing personal and individual' (Bacon, *Advancement of Learning,* I, iii; 1605). In the adjective the first developing sense is 'idiosyncratic' or 'singular': 'a man should be something that men are not, and individuall in somewhat beside his proper nature' (Browne, 1646). The sense is often, as here, pejorative. The word was used in the same kind of protest that Donne made against the new 'singularity' or 'individualism':

For every man alone thinks he hath got
To be a Phoenix, and that then can be
None of that kind of which he is but he.
(*First Anniversarie,* 1611).

In this form of thought, the ground of human nature is common; the 'individual' is often a vain or eccentric departure from this. But in some arguments the contrast between 'in the general' and 'in the individual' led to the crucial emergence of the new noun. It was almost there in Jackson (1641): 'Peace . . . is the very supporter of Individualls, Families, Churches, Commonwealths', though 'individualls' is here still a class. It was perhaps not till Locke (*Human Understanding,* III, vi; 1690) that the modern social sense emerged, but even then still as an adjective: 'our Idea of any individual Man'.

The decisive development of the singular noun was indeed not in social or political thought but in two special fields: logic, and, from C18, biology. Thus: 'an individual . . . in Logick . . . signifies that which cannot be divided into more of the same name or nature' (Phillips, 1658). This formal classification was set out in Chambers (1727–41): 'the usual division in logic is made into genera . . . those genera into species, and those species into individuals'. The same formal classification was then available to the new biology. Until C18 **individual** was rarely used without explicit relation to the group of which it was, so to say, the ultimate indivisible division. This is so even in what reads like a modern use in Dryden:

That individuals die, his will ordains;
The propagated species still remains.
(Dryden, *Fables Ancient and Modern,* 1700)

It is not until lC18 that a crucial shift in attitudes can be clearly seen in uses of the word: 'among the savage nations of hunters and fishers, every individual . . . is . . . employed in useful labour' (Adam Smith, *Wealth of Nations,* i, Introd., 1776). In the course of C19, alike in biology and in political thought, there was a remarkable efflorescence of the word. In evolutionary biology there was Darwin's recognition (*Origin of Species,* 1859) that 'no one supposes that all the individuals of the same species are cast in the same actual mould'. Increasingly the phrase 'an individual'—a single example of a group—was joined and overtaken by the 'individual': a fundamental order of being.

The emergence of notions of **individuality,** in the modern sense, can be related to the break-up of the medieval social, economic and religious order. In the general movement against feudalism there was a new stress on a man's personal existence over and above his place or function in a rigid hierarchical society. There was a related stress, in Protestantism, on a man's direct and individual relation to God, as opposed to this relation MEDIATED (q.v.) by the Church. But it was not until lC17 and C18 that a new mode of analysis, in logic and mathematics, postulated the individual as the substantial entity (cf. Leibniz's 'monads'), from which other categories and especially collective categories were derived. The political thought of the Enlightenment mainly followed this model. Argument began from individuals, who had an initial and primary existence, and laws and forms of society were derived from them: by submission, as in Hobbes; by contract or consent, or by the new version of natural law, in liberal thought. In classical economics, trade was described in a model which postulated separate individuals who decided, at some starting point, to enter into economic or commercial relations. In utilitarian ethics, separate individuals calculated the consequences of this or that action which they might undertake. Liberal thought based on 'the individual' as starting point was criticized from conservative positions—'the individual is foolish . . . the species is wise' (Burke)—but also, in C19, from socialist positions, as most thoroughly in Marx, who attacked the opposition of the abstract categories 'individual' and 'society' and argued that the individual is a social creation, born into relationships and DETERMINED (q.v.) by them.

The modern sense of **individual** is then a result of the development of a certain phase of scientific thought and of a phase of political and economic thought. But already from eC19 a distinction began to be made within this. It can be summed up in the development of two derived words: **individuality** and **individualism.** The latter corresponds to the main movement of liberal political and economic thought. But there is a distinction indicated by Simmel: 'the individualism of uniqueness—*Einzigheit*—as against that of singleness—*Einzlheit'.* 'Singleness'—abstract individualism—is based, Simmel argued, on the quantitative thought, centred in mathematics and physics, of C18. 'Uniqueness', by contrast, is a qualitative category, and is a concept of the Romantic movement. It is also a concept of evolutionary biology, in which the species is stressed and the individual related to it, but with the recognition of uniqueness within a kind. Many arguments about 'the individual' now confuse the distinct senses to which **individualism** and **individuality** point. **Individuality** has the longer history, and comes out of the complex of meanings in which **individual** developed, stressing both a unique person and his (indivisible) membership of a group. **Individualism** is a C19 coinage: 'a novel expression, to which a novel idea has given birth' (tr. Tocqueville, 1835): a theory not only of abstract individuals but of the primacy of individual states and interests.

Williams's essay effectively demonstrates the complex interaction that exists between language and society. The history of the word *individual,* as Williams presents it, demonstrates that its meanings have been quite contradictory. As Williams points out about *individual,* "the development of the modern meaning from the original meaning is a record in language of an extraordinary social and political history." This history traces the changes in a word that once meant an indivisible community through to "a single distinguishable person" and then to the notion of "*the* individual," assumed by our society for the past century to be "a fundamental order of being." For someone to have called you an individual in the seventeenth century would have been almost an insult—as if implying that you were strange or eccentric.

For many people today, however, and particularly for Americans, the concept of the individual as a unique being, with the capacity to overcome adversity, to speak out freely, to excel, and to stand apart from the crowd, seems an absolute, unchanging truth about the nature of human existence. Most Americans want to believe that there is something unique in each human spirit. But Williams argues that this conception of the individual is *historically determined.* It is a matter of convention, not a permanent truth. He argues, in fact, that our desire to believe in the uniqueness of each person has little to do with the persons themselves and much more to do with the time period in which we live. In other words, the dominant ideology of our culture is such that we almost cannot help valuing the worth of the individual. We come to realize, in time, that our notions about the self do not exist independently of our culture.

We may not at first be aware of how our society influences us, but our lack of awareness does not lessen the extent of that influence. This is not to suggest that we have no control over what we think and believe but only that our range of choices is to a large extent formed by our social context. One way of gaining greater flexibility within a cultural context is to try to become increasingly self-conscious about the ways in which society influences us. In relation to our concept of the word *individual,* recall that we have magazines with titles like *Self* and perfume ads that tell women (and men) that their nature will be best expressed if they wear a certain scent. Psychologists have been telling people for years that they could get over their problems if they just learned how to "express themselves."

We have thus far been reading "through" Williams's essay, trying to fill it out with specific examples from our own culture. But we can also choose to read "at" his discussion. Note, for example, that Williams implies that the meaning of "individual" changed rather gradually over time. He emphasizes the sequential changes, but he doesn't particularly investigate how the word can mean different things *in the same time period.* For example, most advertisements that encourage everyone to become more of an individual by using a particular product—whether it is serving a certain sherry to impress guests, wearing certain clothes to impress employers, reading certain magazines or newspapers to aquire status with friends—actually are setting standards for *conformity,* not individuality. Nonetheless, millions of people buy the same products in order, supposedly, to demonstrate their individuality.

Thus we should not conclude simply that the meaning of "individual" has changed over time. What has changed are the connotations that people have brought to the word—derived from ideological emphases and conflicts of the times. Recall what was said in the poetry section (p. 380) on *connotation.* There we suggested that the connotations or suggestiveness of words derives not from "subjective" whim but from the ideology of the particular age. We have frequently asked our own students to analyze the different connotations the word *individual* has today and have found a deep split between those for whom it has positive connotations of boldness, uniqueness, and interest, and those for whom it has more negative connotations of idiosyncrasy and uncooperativeness. "It depends on the context," wrote one of our students. "I like to think of myself as an individual, but if I were working on a group project or even involved in a committed relationship, too much individuality could become counterproductive." Williams's analysis of the word therefore points not just to history but to its present usage—and to the ideological conflict it embodies in our own time. The contradictions within words are also contradictions in the wider society.

After reading Williams's essay, note how you yourself use the word *individual.* Perhaps write down three or four sentences in which you use it; then try to locate them in Williams's discussion. His essay allows readers to see how a word's meanings shift, transformed by a society's broader changes and struggles. (A selection of other entries from Williams's book *Keywords* begins on page 1203.)

As you develop your own strong reading of the Williams essay, investigate other examples of how *individual, individualism,* and *individuality* are being used in everyday commonsense language—in the media, novels, even daily conversation. See if they reveal perhaps conflicting connotations and values. Such investigations might well lead to a debate with friends about values and beliefs that will reveal many of your own immediate conflicts and contradictions—and not only in the ways you use words but also in the ways you live your lives.

The Political Unconscious of a Text: Crèvecoeur's "What Is an American?"

In reading the Williams essay, we noticed how *individual* is a word in which many interpretations struggle for mastery. Recognizing that ideological conflicts are often reflected in word usage can help you become a stronger reader of texts. Learn not just to look for the dominant meanings of words but also to locate the struggles for dominance that may be going on below the surface of the text. In other words, as a strong reader, you must probe the text for the assumptions and struggles it does not articulate, looking for what the critic Fredric Jameson has called the text's *political unconscious.* To find the text's political unconscious, you must look for the signs or (to use a medical metaphor) the "symptoms" of what lies behind the ideas on the surface of the text. You can do this by focusing on the key *connotative* words and phrases that express the dominant values of the period in which the text was written. The relationship between connotation and the broader social or historical *field of meaning* is the focus of a "symptomatic" reading. To test this kind of strong reading, here is a brief extract, "What Is an American?" from Michel-Guillaume-Jean de Crèvecoeur's *Letters from an American Farmer,* published in 1782, a larger extract of which appears on page 1158.

I wish I could be acquainted with the feelings and thoughts which must agitate the heart and present themselves to the mind of an enlightened Englishman, when he first lands on this continent. . . . Here he sees the industry of his native country displayed in a new manner, and traces in their works the embryos of all the arts, sciences, and ingenuity which flourish in Europe. Here he beholds fair cities, substantial villages, extensive fields, an immense country filled with decent houses, good roads, orchards, meadows, and bridges, where a hundred years ago all was wild, woody, and uncultivated! What a train of pleasing ideas this fair spectacle must suggest; it is a prospect which must inspire a good citizen with the most heartfelt pleasure. The difficulty consists in the manner of viewing so extensive a scene. He is arrived on a new continent; a modern society offers itself to his contemplation, different from what he had hitherto seen. . . .

The Americans were once scattered all over Europe; here they are incorporated into one of the finest systems of population which has ever appeared, and which will hereafter become distinct by the power of the different climates they inhabit. The American ought therefore to love this country much better than that wherein either he or his forefathers were born. Here the rewards of his industry follow with equal steps the progress of his labour; his labour is founded on the basis of nature, *self-interest;* can it want a stronger allurement? Wives and children, who before in vain demanded of him a morsel of bread, now, fat and frolicsome, gladly help their father to clear those fields whence exuberant crops are to arise to feed and to clothe them all; without any part being claimed, either by a despotic prince, a rich abbot, or a mighty lord. Here religion demands but little of him; a small voluntary salary to the minister, and gratitude to God; can he refuse these? The American is a new man, who acts upon new principles; he must therefore entertain new ideas, and form new opinions. From involuntary idleness, servile dependence, penury, and useless labour, he has passed to toils of a very different nature, rewarded by ample subsistence.—This is an American. . . .

But how is this accomplished in that crowd of low, indigent people, who flock here every year from all parts of Europe? I will tell you; they no sooner arrive than they immediately feel the good effects of that plenty of provisions we possess; they fare on our best food, and they are kindly entertained; their talents, character, and peculiar industry are immediately inquired into; they find countrymen everywhere disseminated, let them come from whatever part of Europe. . . .

From nothing to start into being; from a servant to the rank of a master; from being the slave of some despotic prince, to become a free man, invested with lands, to which every municipal blessing is annexed! What a change indeed! It is in consequence of that change that he becomes an American. This great metamorphosis has a double effect, it extinguishes all his European prejudices, he forgets that mechanism of subordination, that servility of disposition which poverty had taught him; and sometimes he is apt to forget too much, often passing from one extreme to the other. If he is a good man, he forms schemes of future prosperity, he proposes to educate his children better than he has been educated himself; he thinks of future modes of conduct, feels an ardour to labour he never felt before. Pride steps in and leads him to everything that the laws do not forbid; he respects them; with a heart-felt gratitude he looks toward the east, toward that insular government from whose wisdom all his new felicity is derived, and under whose wings and protection he now lives.

Clearly in this and in the longer selection, Crèvecoeur is focusing on the question of what it is to be an American in the eighteenth century, and some of you might think the text suggests certain important aspects of what it is to be an American now. As you read the essay (p. 1158), compare it with the essay by Hilary Masters (p. 1115). Crèvecoeur sees, first, the essential nature of America as masculine—aggressive, forward-looking, conquering the wilderness, concerned with modernity, and (in some sense) democratic. He clearly uses significant key words that are invested with rich emotional associations such as *free,* as in "here man is free as he ought to be." *New* is repeated for emphasis in "new laws, a new mode of living, a new social system" and "What then is the American, this new man?" as well as "The American is a new man, who acts upon new principles," and elsewhere. *Freedom,* another charged word used repeatedly, remains a crucial part of America's dominant ideology. When you analyze the concept, therefore, you must probe it carefully: what does *freedom* signify in this, or any other, context? Are there ways in which its connotations are contradictory? Here it seems to be associated with "new," with a revolutionary break with older, hierarchical kinds of government, especially those based on aristocracy and monarchy. It is seemingly associated with the notion of an autonomous citizen, though generally an American man able to choose his course of action, free to move about and carve out "his" property and values from the vast wilderness that opens up before him endlessly. Then "for the first time in his life," he "counts for something . . . from nothing to start into being."

Most of the connotations of these words are very positive, but if you probe below the surface, can you find tensions and contradictions that are symptoms of problems and that will give you clues about the *political unconscious* of the text? For example, are there ways in which the freedom of certain men to carve out their property can infringe on the freedom of others? Is Crèvecoeur's essay, though ostensibly arguing for freedom for all, in some ways arguing for the privileges of certain classes? Or for a society in which men have most of the privileges? One of our students wrote in her response statement on this essay:

> Why is the author always talking about free "men"? What about the women? Why were they to be excluded from the American Dream? Perhaps at the beginning of our history women were unable to take a full part in the conquering of the frontier, but Crèvecoeur's idea of America is not, contrary to his assertion, very civilized in that it dismisses the women. By the time he is writing, it sounds as if America was becoming a more civilized and peaceful place, but it was still a very sexist place if his account is to be believed. The Women's Movement talks about the need for "*her*story" as opposed to *his*tory. Now I know what it means.

This student's response is a very compelling one, a potentially strong reading in which she has examined her own general repertoire and written about the significant differences she found between it and that of the text. But she has not simply noted the differences and left the matter there. She has linked Crèvecoeur's views to the history of the American frontier and brought her own contemporary perspective to bear as well. An awareness of sexism in language and in social attitudes generally is not part of the repertoire of this text, but it is decidedly part of the reader's, and the result is a fascinating mismatching of the repertoires of text and reader. In her response our student has located the political unconscious of the text, those issues that are not acknowledged in the essay but which she has shown are relevant to it.

Another concept in this essay that has been crucial to America is "change" or "metamorphosis." Americans have invested very heavily in continual movement forward, in changing perspectives, new frontiers, new relationships—almost as if change itself were an inherent good. Is this culture a rabidly consuming one? Do Americans abandon their pasts too eagerly to get to the new—the supposedly better model or gadget or position or person? Even in the eighteenth century, Crèvecoeur voices some reservations on these questions. While he is praising what he terms the "great metamorphosis" of America, he sounds a worrying note: sometimes we are "apt to forget too much, often passing from one extreme to another." It is at a junction like this that you can see a concept—in this case, *change*—as a site of struggle because the text itself points out potentially contradictory attitudes toward the notion of change that existed at the time of its writing. The rich, conflicting nature of a text's political unconscious begins to show itself in lines like this. If you choose to investigate our country's contradictory attitudes toward change, you might consider the history of American culture since, say, World War II. (Again, Hilary Masters' essay is an excellent commentary on this post-war period.)

Freedom, newness, change. These concepts—part of a mythology or ideology that has dominated our history—are clearly emotionally rich and often contradictory words. In a symptomatic reading, in which you try to discover the political unconscious of the text, you simply cannot take the meaning of such terms for granted. As we did with "individual" in the Williams essay, you must probe these words from your own perspective and values, and perhaps do some research on eighteenth-century America in order to be able to ask and answer significant questions: Freedom for whom? For everyone? With what limits? With what consequence for power, prosperity, a sense of community? Newness—but with what losses? Are all old things, even slightly used things, to be abandoned? What economic consequences does such an ideology have? Change; but at what cost? What psychological or social consequences does a belief in change have?

In asking such questions, you are not merely probing the central metaphors of a text; you are also asking questions about your whole culture, your history, and your own place in that culture and history. An ideological or what is sometimes called a "symptomatic" reading of a text primarily concerns the political unconscious of a text—that powerful yet hidden aspect of its language that links it to our history and to the state of our culture today. You can do this kind of analysis as freely with essays, and with discursive prose generally, as you can with texts considered to be "literature."

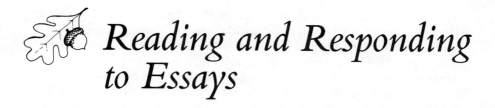

Reading and Responding to Essays

Read this essay and the discussion that follows on page 1120.

HILARY MASTERS (b. 1928)

So Long, Natty Bumppo

Now that all the rivers have been named and the woods are dying, we look into the territory behind. Comfort is to be found in this old terrain, in the shadows that obscure the facts of its crossing and in the crossing itself as the hardships and the cruel events of that passage become separated in memory from the journey's end. But this may be a false comfort. The woods are deep, and they are also a convenient dump for the embarrassments and wastes we don't wish to remember, for the obscure burial of those who didn't make it to journey's end with the rest of us.

In the last Presidential campaign, Mr. Mondale spent his time reminding his audience of the hardships and sacrifices made in the past in order to suggest the same could be done again, that the moral stamina was still within the national character to confront the budget crisis and to deal with a suicidal arms race. His review of the past events was found to be uninteresting, even boring, by a vast majority of his audience.

President Reagan spoke only of the passage done. We have come through the woods and into the sunny savannah and if there are shadows behind us, they assume the mythic shapes of folk heroes who stand tall with clean hands and clear eyes, as all heroes must. The fact that Reagan had to sort through the Democrat dustbin for three of his more important shadows—FDR, Harry Truman, and Jack Kennedy—does not prove the lack of such heroes in the Republican kit so much as it does show his understanding of the American imagination's need for the *recollections* of these leaders uncomplicated by the grime and gore that accompanied their passage through our history and which, incidentally, made them the important leaders that they were.

Ronald Reagan's appeal has always been attributed to his glamour and an actor's ability to communicate, but his canny insight into the American character, its unique attachment with the past—false or not—has always been underestimated. Not so much a creation of Hollywood, Ronald Reagan is a character imagined by Norman Rockwell, one of the more successful nostalgia-mongers in our cultural fabric. To review Rockwell's cast of characters as pictured on the old covers of the *Saturday Evening Post* is to review the roles played by President Reagan—the young baseball player doing his best, the kid getting his first medical examination, the draftee confronting the tough (but basically okay) top sergeant, the older, wiser, and indulgent brother-uncle-druggist-dad-hometown pal who listens to the problem and slips you the solution when no one is looking.

Whether Reagan thinks being President is another role to be played is unimportant because the great majority of Americans think of the office as a role to be played, and they like the way he plays it with all the allusions to a past that never existed, a metaphor for our history that omits incidents and personalities which do not fit into the Reagan-Rockwell cover.

For it seems likely a majority of voters in 1984 saw through the role Reagan was playing, but it didn't matter. They voted for him anyway. The polls following the first Mondale-Reagan debate gave Mondale a clear majority, around 56%, in terms of his knowledge of government, ability to discuss and handle the issues, and so on, but the same percentile of those interviewed said they would vote for Reagan. So, they were saying, even though we think that Reagan does not show the background and expertise for the office that Mondale does, we will still vote for him. And they did.

So Reagan must be given credit for identifying and playing to that same kind of bifocal blindness which Lionel Trilling gave to F. Scott Fitzgerald's characters—they fell for what they could see was false. "Possibly," Nick Carraway says of Gatsby, "it had occurred to him that the colossal significance of that light had now vanished forever." Yet, in the concluding lines of Fitzgerald's masterwork, Carraway defines the fatal attraction of that light across the bay. "Gatsby believed in the green light, the orgiastic future that year by year recedes before us . . . So we beat on, boats against the current, borne ceaselessly into the past."

Not just Fitzgerald, but almost every important writer in the American anthology has had to explore this region we call our past. Hawthorne was sorry it was not more complex—moonlight in the ruins—while James's characters sifted through European ruins for something to wear. Hemingway simplified our past in terms of a virgin wilderness where the waters could heal existential wounds, but Faulkner warned that such rambling in the domain without a good light can be disastrous. Dos Passos named the trespassers, the despoilers, of this elusive, forever-green region, and so on. But long ago, it was James Fenimore Cooper who posted the boundaries and empowered its first and only warden, Natty Bumppo.

It is a sorry example of Mark Twain's blind side—or maybe his perceptive envy—to see him poke fun at this tragic figure in his famous essay "Fenimore Cooper's Literary Offenses." One remembers his eager courtship of millionaires, the barons of American industry who bought up regions of our past to ravish their resources as they sentimentalized their history. Yet, in that luminous moment on the raft when Huck decides not to turn Jim back into slavery, Twain dramatizes one of the moral problems that goes with the territory and if he mistakes the direction of that territory, as Wright Morris has suggested others have, he must be revered for illuminating its major catastrophe.

But we are still going the wrong direction, taking this most-traveled path into a false wood, this psuedo past, and Ronald Reagan is only one more actor playing Natty Bumppo as he guides us around the ugly settlements and the debris of the white man's pollution. Chingachgook is no longer a wretched drunk nor even a savage whose name can be spoofed—but a sanitized tipsy Indian, an excellent model for a Norman Rockwell painting or even a Walt Disney cartoon. Here, let us remember Sitting Bull, the great Sioux Chief and foe of Custer, turned into a circus freak by Buffalo Bill's Wild West Show.

Therefore, in the fall of 1984, Reagan was performing to houses already packed with audiences prepared to give standing ovations to anyone who could play upon this yearning for a past that never existed. Particularly, Americans seem ready to turn into the territory behind, into a backlot of nostalgia, and into regions of the mind and memory that offer refuge from the awesome realities of Twentieth Century existence.

The human imagination, American edition, is at work constructing a fiction around the fears and frustrations of daily life—the pollutions of place, mind, and body that continually despoil us and the constant threat of a nuclear pollution that may ultimately destroy us. More than a flight to the suburbs, the present exodus is backward into a fraudulent history, and figures like Ronald Reagan are the guides.

Evidences of this withdrawal to "simpler" times appear across the cultural prairie. Consumers have been led toward diets of so-called *natural foods,* and though the healthful value of such foods is to be assumed, as with most food, the mystique of eating nuts and berries carries a special persuasion. Similarly, the spirit of the environmental campaign, the back-to-nature movement, may not only reflect a concern for our natural resources but also speak for a desire to turn away from the horrible environments we have made of our cities and to leave them—possibly, in smoking ruins—for the unspoiled regions of the imagination, a hike into the fantasy of roughing it like Natty Bumppo.

Moreover, small-town America has come back into its own—not the same small-town America that our poets and writers in the early part of the century described as places of hypocrisy and spiritual death but a cosmetized, back-lot hicksville complete with plastic pickle barrels and sunbonnets made in Taiwan. Popular films and novels celebrate the virtues and clean air, if not the empty heads, to be found in such environs, and many of these plots are laid in time past, a great number prior to World War II. The satisfaction of these constructions comes from the fact the old regions have been cleared of the thorny problems which truly choke our history.

Because, as an audience, we have come out all right, the feeling is urged that the problems have been dealt with. We have gone beyond the wilderness and can safely, and enjoyably, look back at the problems of racism, political persecution, or intoler-ance—consider them to be shadowy fictions only. Putting them into this retrograde regionalism has the same appeal as did President Reagan's television commercials.

For the last ten years, the PBS radio program "A Prairie Home Companion" has been installing the history of an imaginary village in northern Minnesota into the minds of its listeners. Weekly, the genial host of the program gives tours of Lake Woebegone, pointing out some of its residents, stopping in at cafes and shops and recounting its communal events. Folksey, humorous, and seemingly homespun, the narrative creates the image of a town that "time has passed by" as its creator and guide says, a place—if not a last resort—where a listener can escape the sophisticated banality of contemporary life.

"A Prairie Home Companion" is a good example of the retrograde regionalism, the false nostalgia, that appeals to Americans these days even up to the level of na-tional politics. It is a program that could only be heard during the Reagan Era. Each weekly installment is like a Norman Rockwell cover come to life—or at least scripted so by a clever and resourceful author. All the worries and problems of its residents are those that can be chuckled over. Crises occur at cake sales, and desperation is to be found in the home team's losing streak. Was it really like that? Was Sinclair Lewis wrong about Sauk City? The success of such novels as *Ladies of the Club* suggests a large readership which demands Lewis's version be re-written if it can't be proved wrong.

The Reagan-Rockwell version of our truth is also to be found in the manner in which "A Prairie Home Companion" addresses the serious problems of American life. The religious intolerance between Lutherans and Roman Catholics, a schism that is no less hateful in many communities now than it was in the 16th Century, is gently poked with fun. Town eccentrics, *singled out because they are different,* make for amusing lessons in what normal behavior should be in the town coffee shop or the drug store. Children raise the dickens but are easily chastised. Old people are in-dependent, sometimes cantankerous, but at heart good natured—and always well cared for.

Blacks and Jews never turn up at the coffee shop or during town meetings or at church. One wonders if there are any in town at all, and the absence of these people in this mythical community raises the terrifying aspect of this look into the territory behind. Wouldn't it be nice, the genial host seems to be saying, if these particular peoples, and the problems they have caused us, never existed in our town, our his-tory, at all? It's like reading *Huckleberry Finn* without that moment on the raft.

The great number of memoirs that have appeared on publishers' lists might also be seen as an indication of this turn into the past—almost anyone's past. The curios-ity to know the lives of the celebrated has always been part of the human intellect, but the current American version directs attention to ordinary histories as well. A rightful connection was made between nostalgia for simpler times and the artful ma-nipulation of that nostalgia when Garrison Keillor, the creator of "Lake Woebe-gone," read Russell Baker's prize-winning memoir, *Growing Up,* in a series of programs over the PBS network. Keillor's mellifluous voice gave full stretch to the single-suspender charm of Baker's work, and, interestingly, if a listener turned on the program halfway through, he might have thought he was hearing about the village in Minnesota rather than the North Carolina of the columnist's childhood.

American authors have made American fiction unique by their attempts to preserve the values and character of particular regions. "Do Nebraska," Henry James might well have said to a young Willa Cather as he had similarly advised Edith Wharton to look at her own region of New York society. Lately, some novelists—enough perhaps to make a trend—have chosen not a region *to do* but a past-as-region, and the area is similar to Lake Woebegone in its absence of the issues and anxieties that confound the modern conscience and make it yearn for the good old days.

William Kennedy's series of Albany novels are the best-written example of this retrograde regionalism. All four are set in the Albany, N.Y., of the 1930's, comfortably prior to World War II, the Holocaust, the atom bomb, and the more violent rips in the American social fabric. Moreover, the naturalistic style employed by Kennedy—a mixture of Farrell and Cain with a dash of Runyon—must give the readers on the Book of the Month Club list a welcome refreshment, as it is a prose innocent of the complexities, if not the challenges, of most contemporary fiction.

Kennedy's exclusive view of American life was quickly appreciated by Hollywood. His script for Francis Ford Coppola's *Cotton Club* is a spurious look backward into the Harlem of the 1930's with none of the genuine truths of racism, just a bunch of folks with natural rhythm and, being a Coppola film, the obligatory romanticising of gangsters for good measure.

The films *The Godfather,* one and two, imbued criminals with a moral code and principles that James Fenimore Cooper would have sadly recognized. By contrast, a film like *Prizzi's Honor* is almost an angry parody of the earlier series and one sees with John Huston's stern eye the real shape of these monsters. It is not a pretty part of the forest, and because it does not play to the ready-made yen we all have for the pretty part of the forest, the Huston film will probably fail at the box office.

After so many false leads into the wrong territory, the guide can no longer be trusted. It is not old Natty's fault. His signs are ignored or debased by those who serve the popular culture, such as Sylvester Stallone's recent return in *Rambo* to the immoral wilderness of Vietnam to "win" that war and purge the communal guilt. Perhaps the time has come to follow a different scout, a different course out of this retrograde regionalism. Our history offers us many guides and not all of them have been men.

Women, in one fashion or another, have often made a retreat from bad times—whether into the convents of the Middle Ages or the yellow rooms of more recent days—but not to restore a community that kept them in menial roles and punished them if they tried to do something else. For them, the good old days were few, so these disengagements were occasions for survival while they gained energy and fresh perspective for a way through hostile territory.

Contemporary American writers like Plath, Sexton, and Rich—and going on to Oates, Walker and Phillips (these only a small number to represent many)—seem to have made a similar trek while evolving a new kind of regionalism, one drawn from within themselves, from their own histories or those of women who have preceded them. In the celebration of their pasts, these authors are creating a genre that reviews the passage but keeps a clear eye on the path ahead. Their special concerns, fears, and anxieties are little changed from those that occupied their grandmothers because the conditions are pretty much the same. Slogans like "You've Come A Long Way, Baby" are a cruel parody of the actual conditions for women in the market place (the old labor leader John L. Lewis's dictum comes to mind: an equal pay-check makes for equality) and such institutions as insurance companies and the U.S. Supreme Court by their current policies continue the old inequations. The compensation Lewis and Clark paid Sacajawea for guiding them safely through the Northwest Territory was probably her "marriage" to the expedition's interpreter, Charbonneau.

So the view back into the territory from Gender Gap may be the best prospect from which American politics and culture can find another path. With no false nostalgia to distort their vision, these writers and their peers seem to be putting together a body of literature that seeks to confront the complacency of the current settlement by honestly reviewing the events of the passage and some of the people, many of them women, who didn't quite make it. If we are not out of this retrograde regionalism yet, maybe here is a base camp from which we may find our way.

So long, Natty Bumppo—hello, Sacajawea.

Response Statement Assignment

After rereading the general guidelines for writing response statements (p. 15), write a response statement on the following topic: We can define *myth* as a story that tries to explain what we are and thereby expresses the ideology of a culture. In this essay, Hilary Masters writes of America as a myth-making society, mentioning mythic heroes, mythic journeys, and especially what he perceives as a need for a nostalgic myth of history, a belief in a past that never really existed but one that gives us comfort. We prefer the myth, he argues, to the more complex reality.

With Masters' observations in mind, how do you respond to America being described in these terms? What mythic patterns do you see operating in your life as an American? Do you agree with Masters' analysis of the current political scene? What aspects of your own **general repertoire** influence your response to his argument? Write a detailed response to these questions.

Sample Student Response Statement

Here is one student's initial response statement written on this assignment:

    We Americans spend a lot of time trying to ''explain
    ourselves''--in television, in newspapers, and in essays like
    this one. What we mainly try to do is to look at the present

and try to project the future, since we are in fact a very forward-looking country. Somehow most of the past doesn't appear that relevant to our lives today, particularly when we consider how fast everything changes.

Masters wants us to look at the past more closely. In fact he thinks that we have a wrong interpretation of it and that we look back on "a past that never existed." That makes the United States sound like Russia or Orwell's <u>1984</u>. I don't believe that in a free and open society most Americans would fall "for what they could see was false." Only if you don't look forward can you be deceived by "this region we call our past," the "pseudo past" as Masters calls it.

I grew up in a small Midwest town, and I know what Masters is writing about. Just outside of town was a huge sugar beet factory, and on some days the stench was a bit like living in Pittsburgh or Cleveland. I have listened to "Prairie Home Companion" and it reminds me more of the way my father, who also grew up in the same town, talks about his childhood when it seems everyone was content and there was no unemployment. In fact, history books show that things weren't so good. Many people left the town, and there was a great deal of economic misery, even for members of my father's family. So maybe there is something to what Masters calls "the retrograde regionalism, the false nostalgia." You hear it everywhere, including popular songs like John Cougar Mellencamp's "Small Town." It's all very well for a big rock star to praise small-town living. He doesn't have to live there any more.

In summary, there seems to be a great deal to say for Masters' views of small-town America. Perhaps he is right about today's nostalgia. But how can we find out about the real past? That's a difficult question. Even more important is how we can direct ourselves to the future, where the real America is.

Discussion

This is a thoughtful response to a very provoking and brilliant essay. It also reveals how the student is caught up in the contradictions of which Masters writes. Most significant perhaps is the way he reveals himself in the ideological conflicts he is writing about and the way he genuinely tries to probe his own general repertoire for some guidance as to why he feels as he does. On the one hand, he wants to reject Masters' analysis of America's fascination for "a past that never existed": that seems unpatriotic. On the other hand, he knows from his own experience something of the limitations of small-town America. Subsequent discussion with the student revealed his grandparents used to save copies of the *Saturday Evening Post* with Norman

Rockwell covers. Likewise, it's obvious that the student is as skeptical of his father's idealizing his small-town past as he is of the rock singer John Cougar Mellencamp's false nostalgia for a place in which he doesn't have to live.

There are a number of ways of deepening this analysis, making it into a distinctively "strong" reading. The most pertinent is to direct the writer to discussions of ideology and myth. Once his attention was drawn to the similarities and differences between the text's general **ideology** and his own repertoire, he became aware of how his reading could be made even stronger. He also did some research—in particular, he brought into his reading some discussion of myth as presented in Roland Barthes' essay (p. 1191). This use of powerful theoretical arguments is a particularly good way of strengthening a response statement—not into something more "objective" but into a stronger, more persuasive reading. Thus in the rewriting, two new paragraphs replaced the original paragraph 2.

Response Statement: Revision

Roland Barthes explains that all societies have myths that carry the dominant ideological values of the culture. America seems to be a place where many myths are prevalent. Hilary Masters mentions some that he locates in our history and literature--the need for identifying folk heroes, for journeying through and conquering the terrain, and for turning our past into a rosy-colored world that helps justify what we have made it. The real past gets obscured, and we have to work hard to get at it. Sometimes, we even prefer the myth to the reality since, as Masters points out, we have ''this yearning for a past that never existed.''

In some ways, this makes America sound a bit like Russia or Orwell's 1984. As an American, I am reluctant to believe that in a free and open society like ours, most Americans would fall ''for what they could see was false.'' More likely, many people aren't aware of many things that have in fact occurred in our society. In this regard, Masters' treatment of ''this region we call the past'' is very convincing. He argues that it is too easy to accept a rosy view of the past--as a time of heroes and of conquering the landscape, and also as a time of tranquillity and harmony just like in a Norman Rockwell magazine cover. Masters argues that this is a false past, and that it is possible to get a truer picture--from, for instance, the women writers he mentions. But I wonder if they would be creating yet another myth.

The crucial thing about the development of this response statement is that by the broadening of his repertoire—the awareness that he can bring to

bear new information for interpreting some of the myths of our country—
our student moves toward producing a lively and strong reading. It is a
process that can never be completely finished—since no reading is ever final.

Additional Response Assignments

1. The author takes a distinctive view of the Reagan presidency. How do
   your own views on the subject influence your appreciation of his argument?
2. What is the point of the discussion of women writers in Masters' argument? When you encountered it, did it modify your interpretation of his
   essay?
3. Knowing this piece of writing was an essay, and therefore supposedly
   more **referential** than "literature," did you find the author's references to
   literary works useful, irritating, or convincing?
4. Literature, we have argued, is a way of reading more than a way of writing. Describe specifically some types of reading strategies that you used
   to read Masters' essay that differ from those you would use to read a
   short story. Did you concentrate more on the **argument** than the **metaphors** Masters uses? Did you agree with or respond in any other way to
   his essay? Were you reading "through" his essay (see p. 1100)?

FREDERICK DOUGLASS (1817?–1895)

Excerpts from **The Life of Frederick Douglass**

I was born in Tuckahoe, near Hillsborough, and about twelve miles from Easton, in
Talbot county, Maryland. I have no accurate knowledge of my age, never having
seen any authentic record containing it. By far the larger part of the slaves know as
little of their ages as horses know of theirs, and it is the wish of most masters within
my knowledge to keep their slaves thus ignorant. I do not remember to have ever
met a slave who could tell of his birthday. They seldom come nearer to it than
planting-time, harvest-time, cherry-time, spring-time, or fall-time. A want of information concerning my own was a source of unhappiness to me even during childhood. The white children could tell their ages. I could not tell why I ought to be
deprived of the same privilege. I was not allowed to make any inquiries of my master
concerning it. He deemed all such inquiries on the part of a slave improper and impertinent, and evidence of a restless spirit. The nearest estimate I can give makes me
now between twenty-seven and twenty-eight years of age. I come to this, from hearing my master say, some time during 1835, I was about seventeen years old.

My mother was named Harriet Bailey. She was the daughter of Isaac and Betsey
Bailey, both colored, and quite dark. My mother was of a darker complexion than
either my grandmother or grandfather.

My father was a white man. He was admitted to be such by all I ever heard speak of my parentage. The opinion was also whispered that my master was my father; but of the correctness of this opinion, I know nothing; the means of knowing was withheld from me. My mother and I were separated when I was but an infant—before I knew her as my mother. It is a common custom, in the part of Maryland from which I ran away, to part children from their mothers at a very early age. Frequently, before the child has reached its twelfth month, its mother is taken from it, and hired out on some farm a considerable distance off, and the child is placed under the care of an old woman, too old for field labor. For what this separation is done, I do not know, unless it be to hinder the development of the child's affection toward its mother, and to blunt and destroy the natural affection of the mother for the child. This is the inevitable result.

I never saw my mother, to know her as such, more than four or five times in my life; and each of these times was very short in duration, and at night. She was hired by a Mr. Stewart, who lived about twelve miles from my home. She made her journeys to see me in the night, travelling the whole distance on foot, after the performance of her day's work. She was a field hand, and a whipping is the penalty of not being in the field at sunrise, unless a slave has special permission from his or her master to the contrary—a permission which they seldom get, and one that gives to him that gives it the proud name of being a kind master. I do not recollect of ever seeing my mother by the light of day. She was with me in the night. She would lie down with me, and get me to sleep, but long before I waked she was gone. Very little communication ever took place between us. Death soon ended what little we could have while she lived, and with it her hardships and suffering. She died when I was about seven years old, on one of my master's farms, near Lee's Mill. I was not allowed to be present during her illness, at her death, or burial. She was gone long before I knew any thing about it. Never having enjoyed, to any considerable extent, her soothing presence, her tender and watchful care, I received the tidings of her death with much the same emotions I should have probably felt at the death of a stranger.

Called thus suddenly away, she left me without the slightest intimation of who my father was. The whisper that my master was my father, may or may not be true; and, true or false, it is of but little consequence to my purpose whilst the fact remains, in all its glaring odiousness, that slaveholders have ordained, and by law established, that the children of slave women shall in all cases follow the condition of their mothers; and this is done too obviously to administer to their own lusts, and make a gratification of their wicked desires profitable as well as pleasurable; for by this cunning arrangement, the slaveholder, in cases not a few, sustains to his slaves the double relation of master and father.

I know of such cases; and it is worthy of remark that such slaves invariably suffer greater hardships, and have more to contend with, than others. They are, in the first place, a constant offence to their mistress. She is ever disposed to find fault with them; they can seldom do any thing to please her; she is never better pleased than when she sees them under the lash, especially when she suspects her husband of showing to his mulatto children favors which he withholds from his black slaves. The master is frequently compelled to sell this class of his slaves, out of deference to the feelings of his white wife; and, cruel as the deed may strike any one to be, for a man to sell his own children to human flesh-mongers, it is often the dictate of humanity for him to do so; for, unless he does this, he must not only whip them himself, but must stand by and see one white son tie up his brother, of but few shades darker complexion than himself, and ply the gory lash to his naked back; and if he lisp one word of disapproval, it is set down to his parental partiality, and only makes a bad matter worse, both for himself and the slave whom he would protect and defend.

Every year brings with it multitudes of this class of slaves. It was doubtless in consequence of a knowledge of this fact, that one great statesman of the south predicted the downfall of slavery by the inevitable laws of population. Whether this prophecy is ever fulfilled or not, it is nevertheless plain that a very different-looking class of people are springing up at the south, and are now held in slavery, from those originally brought to this country from Africa; and if their increase will do no other good, it will do away the force of the argument, that God cursed Ham, and therefore American slavery is right. If the lineal descendants of Ham are alone to be scripturally enslaved, it is certain that slavery at the south must soon become unscriptural; for thousands are ushered into the world, annually, who, like myself, owe their existence to white fathers, and those fathers most frequently their own masters.

I have had two masters. My first master's name was Anthony. I do not remember his first name. He was generally called Captain Anthony—a title which, I presume, he acquired by sailing a craft on the Chesapeake Bay. He was not considered a rich slaveholder. He owned two or three farms, and about thirty slaves. His farms and slaves were under the care of an overseer. The overseer's name was Plummer. Mr. Plummer was a miserable drunkard, a profane swearer, and a savage monster. He always went armed with a cowskin and a heavy cudgel. I have known him to cut and slash the women's heads so horribly, that even master would be enraged at his cruelty, and would threaten to whip him if he did not mind himself. Master, however, was not a humane slaveholder. It required extraordinary barbarity on the part of an overseer to affect him. He was a cruel man, hardened by a long life of slaveholding. He would at times seem to take great pleasure in whipping a slave. I have often been awakened at the dawn of day by the most heart-rending shrieks of an own aunt of mine, whom he used to tie up to a joist, and whip upon her naked back till she was literally covered with blood. No words, no tears, no prayers, from his gory victim, seemed to move his iron heart from its bloody purpose. The louder she screamed, the harder he whipped; and where the blood ran fastest, there he whipped longest. He would whip her to make her scream, and whip her to make her hush; and not until overcome by fatigue, would he cease to swing the blood-clotted cowskin. I remember the first time I ever witnessed this horrible exhibition. I was quite a child, but I well remember it. I never shall forget it whilst I remember any thing. It was the first of a long series of such outrages, of which I was doomed to be a witness and a participant. It struck me with awful force. It was the blood-stained gate, the entrance to the hell of slavery, through which I was about to pass. It was a most terrible spectacle. I wish I could commit to paper the feelings with which I beheld it.

This occurrence took place very soon after I went to live with my old master, and under the following circumstances. Aunt Hester went out one night,—where or for what I do not know,—and happened to be absent when my master desired her presence. He had ordered her not to go out evenings, and warned her that she must never let him catch her in company with a young man, who was paying attention to her belonging to Colonel Lloyd. The young man's name was Ned Roberts, generally called Lloyd's Ned. Why master was so careful of her, may be safely left to conjecture. She was a woman of noble form, and of graceful proportions, having very few equals, and fewer superiors, in personal appearance, among the colored or white women of our neighborhood.

Aunt Hester had not only disobeyed his orders in going out, but had been found in company with Lloyd's Ned; which circumstance, I found, from what he said while whipping her, was the chief offence. Had he been a man of pure morals himself, he might have been thought interested in protecting the innocence of my aunt; but those who knew him will not suspect him of any such virtue. Before he commenced whipping Aunt Hester, he took her into the kitchen, and stripped her from neck to waist, leaving her neck, shoulders, and back, entirely naked. He then told her to cross her hands, calling her at the same time a d——d b——h. After crossing her hands, he tied them with a strong rope, and led her to a stool under a large hook in the joist, put in for the purpose. He made her get upon the stool, and tied her hands to the hook. She now stood fair for his infernal purpose. Her arms were stretched up at their full length, so that she stood upon the ends of her toes. He then said to her, "Now you d——d b——h, I'll learn you how to disobey my orders!" and after rolling up his sleeves, he commenced to lay on the heavy cowskin, and soon the warm, red blood (amid heart-rending shrieks from her, and horrid oaths from him) came dripping to the floor. I was so terrified and horror-stricken at the sight, that I hid myself in a closet, and dared not venture out till long after the bloody transaction was over. I expected it would be my turn next. It was all new to me. I had never seen any thing like it before. I had always lived with my grandmother on the outskirts of the plantation, where she was put to raise the children of the younger women. I had therefore been, until now, out of the way of the bloody scenes that often occurred on the plantation.

My master's family consisted of two sons, Andrew and Richard; one daughter, Lucretia, and her husband, Captain Thomas Auld. They lived in one house, upon the home plantation of Colonel Edward Lloyd. My master was Colonel Lloyd's clerk and superintendent. He was what might be called the overseer of the overseers. I spent two years of childhood on this plantation in my old master's family. It was here that I witnessed the bloody transaction recorded in the first chapter; and as I received my first impressions of slavery on this plantation, I will give some description of it, and of slavery as it there existed. The plantation is about twelve miles north of Easton, in Talbot county, and is situated on the border of Miles River. The principal products raised upon it were tobacco, corn, and wheat. These were raised in great abundance; so that, with the products of this and the other farms belonging to him, he was able to keep in almost constant employment a large sloop, in carrying them to market at Baltimore. This sloop was named Sally Lloyd, in honor of one of the colonel's daughters. My master's son-in-law, Captain Auld, was master of the vessel; she was otherwise manned by the colonel's own slaves. Their names were Peter, Isaac, Rich, and Jake. These were esteemed very highly by the other slaves, and looked upon as the privileged ones of the plantation; for it was no small affair, in the eyes of the slaves, to be allowed to see Baltimore.

Colonel Lloyd kept from three to four hundred slaves on his home plantation, and owned a large number more on the neighboring farms belonging to him. The names of the farms nearest to the home plantation were Wye Town and New Design. "Wye Town" was under the overseership of a man named Noah Willis. New Design was under the overseership of a Mr. Townsend. The overseers of these, and all the rest of the farms, numbering over twenty, received advice and direction from the managers of the home plantation. This was the great business place. It was the seat of government for the whole twenty farms. All disputes among the overseers were settled here. If a slave was convicted of any high misdemeanor, became unmanageable, or evinced a determination to run away, he was brought immediately here, severely whipped, put on board the sloop, carried to Baltimore, and sold to Austin Woolfolk, or some other slave-trader, as a warning to the slaves remaining.

Here, too, the slaves of all the other farms received their monthly allowance of food, and their yearly clothing. The men and women slaves received, as their monthly allowance of food, eight pounds of pork, or its equivalent in fish, and one bushel of corn meal. Their yearly clothing consisted of two coarse linen shirts, one pair of linen trousers, like the shirts, one jacket, one pair of trousers for winter, made of coarse negro cloth, one pair of stockings, and one pair of shoes; the whole of which could not have cost more than seven dollars. The allowance of the slave children was given to their mothers, or the old women having the care of them. The children unable to work in the field had neither shoes, stockings, jackets, nor trousers, given to them; their clothing consisted of two coarse linen shirts per year. When these failed them, they went naked until the next allowance-day. Children from seven to ten years old, of both sexes, almost naked, might be seen at all seasons of the year.

There were no beds given the slaves, unless one coarse blanket be considered such, and none but the men and women had these. This, however, is not considered a very great privation. They find less difficulty from the want of beds, than from the want of time to sleep; for when their day's work in the field is done, the most of them having their washing, mending, and cooking to do, and having few or none of the ordinary facilities for doing either of these, very many of their sleeping hours are consumed in preparing for the field the coming day; and when this is done, old and young, male and female, married and single, drop down side by side, on one common bed,—the cold, damp floor,—each covering himself or herself with their miserable blankets; and here they sleep till they are summoned to the field by the driver's horn. At the sound of this, all must rise, and be off to the field. There must be no halting; every one must be at his or her post; and woe betides them who hear not this morning summons to the field; for if they are not awakened by the sense of hearing, they are by the sense of feeling; no age nor sex finds any favor. Mr. Severe, the overseer, used to stand by the door of the quarter, armed with a large hickory stick and heavy cowskin, ready to whip any one who was so unfortunate as not to hear, or, from any other cause, was prevented from being ready to start for the field at the sound of the horn.

Mr. Severe was rightly named: he was a cruel man. I have seen him whip a woman, causing the blood to run half an hour at the time; and this, too, in the midst of her crying children, pleading for their mother's release. He seemed to take pleasure in manifesting his fiendish barbarity. Added to his cruelty, he was a profane swearer. It was enough to chill the blood and stiffen the hair of an ordinary man to hear him talk. Scarce a sentence escaped him but that was commenced or concluded by some horrid oath. The field was the place to witness his cruelty and profanity. His presence made it both the field of blood and of blasphemy. From the rising till the going down of the sun, he was cursing, raving, cutting, and slashing among the slaves of the field, in the most frightful manner. His career was short. He died very soon after I went to Colonel Lloyd's; and he died as he lived, uttering, with his dying groans, bitter curses and horrid oaths. His death was regarded by the slaves as the result of a merciful providence.

Mr. Severe's place was filled by a Mr. Hopkins. He was a very different man. He was less cruel, less profane, and made less noise, than Mr. Severe. His course was characterized by no extraordinary demonstrations of cruelty. He whipped, but seemed to take no pleasure in it. He was called by the slaves a good overseer.

The home plantation of Colonel Lloyd wore the appearance of a country village. All the mechanical operations for all the farms were performed here. The shoemaking and mending, the blacksmithing, cartwrighting, coopering, weaving, and grain-grinding, were all performed by the slaves on the home plantation. The whole place wore a business-like aspect very unlike the neighboring farms. The number of houses, too, conspired to give it advantage over the neighboring farms. It was called by the slaves the *Great House Farm.* Few privileges were esteemed higher, by the slaves of the out-farms, than that of being selected to do errands at the Great House Farm. It was associated in their minds with greatness. A representative could not be prouder of his election to a seat in the American Congress, than a slave on one of the out-farms would be of his election to do errands at the Great House Farm. They regarded it as evidence of great confidence reposed in them by their overseers; and it was on this account, as well as a constant desire to be out of the field from under the driver's lash, that they esteemed it a high privilege, one worth careful living for. He was called the smartest and most trusty fellow, who had this honor conferred upon him the most frequently. The competitors for this office sought as diligently to please their overseers, as the office-seekers in the political parties seek to please and deceive the people. The same traits of character might be seen in Colonel Lloyd's slaves, as are seen in the slaves of the political parties.

The slaves selected to go to the Great House Farm, for the monthly allowance for themselves and their fellow-slaves, were peculiarly enthusiastic. While on their way, they would make the dense old woods, for miles around, reverberate with their wild songs, revealing at once the highest joy and the deepest sadness. They would compose and sing as they went along, consulting neither time nor tune. The thought that came up, came out—if not in the word, in the sound;—and as frequently in the one as in the other. They would sometimes sing the most pathetic sentiment in the most rapturous tone, and the most rapturous sentiment in the most pathetic tone. Into all of their songs they would manage to weave something of the Great House Farm. Especially would they do this, when leaving home. They would then sing most exultingly the following words:—

> "I am going away to the Great House Farm!
> O, yea! O, yea! O!"

This they would sing, as a chorus, to words which to many would seem unmeaning jargon, but which, nevertheless, were full of meaning to themselves. I have sometimes thought that the mere hearing of those songs would do more to impress some minds with the horrible character of slavery, than the reading of whole volumes of philosophy on the subject could do.

I did not, when a slave, understand the deep meaning of those rude and apparently incoherent songs. I was myself within the circle; so that I neither saw nor heard as those without might see and hear. They told a tale of woe which was then altogether beyond my feeble comprehension; they were tones loud, long, and deep; they breathed the prayer and complaint of souls boiling over with the bitterest anguish. Every tone was a testimony against slavery, and a prayer to God for deliverance from chains. The hearing of those wild notes always depressed my spirit, and filled me with ineffable sadness. I have frequently found myself in tears while hearing them. The mere recurrence to those songs, even now, afflicts me; and while I am writing these lines, an expression of feeling has already found its way down my cheek. To those songs I trace my first glimmering conception of the dehumanizing character of slavery. I can never get rid of that conception. Those songs still follow me, to deepen my hatred of slavery, and quicken my sympathies for my brethren in bonds. If any one wishes to be impressed with the soul-killing effects of slavery, let him go to Colonel Lloyd's plantation, and, on allowance-day, place himself in the deep pine woods, and there let him, in silence, analyze the sounds that shall pass through the chambers of his soul,—and if he is not thus impressed, it will only be because "there is no flesh in his obdurate heart."

I have often been utterly astonished, since I came to the north, to find persons who could speak of the singing, among slaves, as evidence of their contentment and happiness. It is impossible to conceive of a greater mistake. Slaves sing most when they are most unhappy. The songs of the slave represent the sorrows of his heart; and he is relieved by them, only as an aching heart is relieved by its tears. At least, such is my experience. I have often sung to drown my sorrow, but seldom to express my happiness. Crying for joy, and singing for joy, were alike uncommon to me while in the jaws of slavery. The singing of a man cast away upon a desolate island might be as appropriately considered as evidence of contentment and happiness, as the singing of a slave; the songs of the one and of the other are prompted by the same emotion.

As to my own treatment while I lived on Colonel Lloyd's plantation, it was very similar to that of the other slave children. I was not old enough to work in the field, and there being little else than field work to do, I had a great deal of leisure time. The most I had to do was to drive up the cows at evening, keep the fowls out of the garden, keep the front yard clean, and run of errands for my old master's daughter, Mrs. Lucretia Auld. The most of my leisure time I spent in helping Master Daniel Lloyd in finding his birds, after he had shot them. My connection with Master Daniel was of some advantage to me. He became quite attached to me, and was a sort of protector of me. He would not allow the older boys to impose upon me, and would divide his cakes with me.

I was seldom whipped by my old master, and suffered little from any thing else than hunger and cold. I suffered much from hunger, but much more from cold. In hottest summer and coldest winter, I was kept almost naked—no shoes, no stockings, no jacket, no trousers, nothing on but a coarse tow linen shirt, reaching only to my knees. I had no bed. I must have perished with cold, but that, the coldest nights, I used to steal a bag which was used for carrying corn to the mill. I would crawl into this bag, and there sleep on the cold, damp, clay floor, with my head in and feet out. My feet have been so cracked with the frost, that the pen with which I am writing might be laid in the gashes.

We were not regularly allowanced. Our food was coarse corn meal boiled. This was called *mush*. It was put into a large wooden tray or trough, and set down upon the ground. The children were then called, like so many pigs, and like so many pigs they would come and devour the mush; some with oyster-shells, others with pieces of shingle, some with naked hands, and none with spoons. He that ate fastest got most; he that was strongest secured the best place; and few left the trough satisfied.

I was probably between seven and eight years old when I left Colonel Lloyd's plantation. I left it with joy. I shall never forget the ecstasy with which I received the intelligence that my old master (Anthony) had determined to let me go to Baltimore, to live with Mr. Hugh Auld, brother to my old master's son-in-law, Captain Thomas Auld. I received this information about three days before my departure. They were three of the happiest days I ever enjoyed. I spent the most part of all these three days in the creek, washing off the plantation scurf, and preparing myself for my departure.

The pride of appearance which this would indicate was not my own. I spent the time in washing, not so much because I wished to, but because Mrs. Lucretia had told me I must get all the dead skin off my feet and knees before I could go to Baltimore; for the people in Baltimore were very cleanly, and would laugh at me if I looked dirty. Besides, she was going to give me a pair of trousers, which I should not put on unless I got all the dirt off me. The thought of owning a pair of trousers was great indeed! It was almost a sufficient motive, not only to make me take off what would be called by pig-drovers the mange, but the skin itself. I went at it in good earnest, working for the first time with the hope of reward.

The ties that ordinarily bind children to their homes were all suspended in my case. I found no severe trial in my departure. My home was charmless; it was not home to me; on parting from it, I could not feel that I was leaving any thing which I could have enjoyed by staying. My mother was dead, my grandmother lived far off, so that I seldom saw her. I had two sisters and one brother, that lived in the same house with me; but the early separation of us from our mother had well nigh blotted the fact of our relationship from our memories. I looked for home elsewhere, and was confident of finding none which I should relish less than the one which I was leaving. If, however, I found in my new home hardship, hunger, whipping, and nakedness, I had the consolation that I should not have escaped any one of them by staying. Having already had more than a taste of them in the house of my old master, and having endured them there, I very naturally inferred my ability to endure them elsewhere, and especially at Baltimore; for I had something of the feeling about Baltimore that is expressed in the proverb, that "being hanged in England is preferable to dying a natural death in Ireland." I had the strongest desire to see Baltimore. Cousin Tom, though not fluent in speech, had inspired me with that desire by his eloquent description of the place. I could never point out any thing at the Great House, no matter how beautiful or powerful, but that he had seen something at Baltimore far exceeding, both in beauty and strength, the object which I pointed out to him. Even the Great House itself, with all its pictures, was far inferior to many buildings in Baltimore. So strong was my desire, that I thought a gratification of it would fully compensate for whatever loss of comforts I should sustain by the exchange. I left without a regret, and with the highest hopes of future happiness.

We sailed out of Miles River for Baltimore on a Saturday morning. I remember only the day of the week, for at that time I had no knowledge of the days of the month, nor the months of the year. On setting sail, I walked aft, and gave to Colonel Lloyd's plantation what I hoped would be the last look. I then placed myself in the bows of the sloop, and there spent the remainder of the day in looking ahead, interesting myself in what was in the distance rather than in things near by or behind.

In the afternoon of that day, we reached Annapolis, the capital of the State. We stopped but a few moments, so that I had no time to go on shore. It was the first large town that I had ever seen, and though it would look small compared with some of our New England factory villages, I thought it a wonderful place for its size—more imposing even than the Great House Farm!

We arrived at Baltimore early on Sunday morning, landing at Smith's Wharf, not far from Bowley's Wharf. We had on board the sloop a large flock of sheep; and after aiding in driving them to the slaughterhouse of Mr. Curtis on Louden Slater's Hill, I was conducted by Rich, one of the hands belonging on board of the sloop, to my new home in Alliciana Street, near Mr. Gardner's ship-yard, on Fells Point.

Mr. and Mrs. Auld were both at home, and met me at the door with their little son Thomas, to take care of whom I had been given. And here I saw what I had never seen before; it was a white face beaming with the most kindly emotions; it was the face of my new mistress, Sophia Auld. I wish I could describe the rapture that flashed through my soul as I beheld it. It was a new and strange sight to me, brightening up my pathway with the light of happiness. Little Thomas was told, there was his Freddy,—and I was told to take care of little Thomas; and thus I entered upon the duties of my new home with the most cheering prospect ahead.

I look upon my departure from Colonel Lloyd's plantation as one of the most interesting events of my life. It is possible, and even quite probable, that but for the mere circumstance of being removed from that plantation to Baltimore, I should have to-day, instead of being here seated by my own table, in the enjoyment of freedom and the happiness of home, writing this Narrative, been confined in the galling chains of slavery. Going to live at Baltimore laid the foundation, and opened the gateway, to all my subsequent prosperity. I have ever regarded it as the first plain manifestation of that kind providence which has ever since attended me, and marked my life with so many favors. I regarded the selection of myself as being somewhat remarkable. There were a number of slave children that might have been sent from the plantation to Baltimore. There were those younger, those older, and those of the same age. I was chosen from among them all, and was the first, last, and only choice.

I may be deemed superstitious, and even egotistical, in regarding this event as a special interposition of divine Providence in my favor. But I should be false to the earliest sentiments of my soul, if I suppressed the opinion. I prefer to be true to myself, even at the hazard of incurring the ridicule of others, rather than to be false, and incur my own abhorrence. From my earliest recollection, I date the entertainment of a deep conviction that slavery would not always be able to hold me within its foul embrace; and in the darkest hours of my career in slavery, this living word of faith and spirit of hope departed not from me, but remained like ministering angels to cheer me through the gloom. This good spirit was from God, and to him I offer thanksgiving and praise.

Response Statement Assignments

1. How do you respond to the prose style of Douglass's narrative? Do you find it sincere? Accessible? Persuasive? Moving?
2. What difference does your own background make to your response to Douglass's writing?
3. What does Douglass's narrative reveal about the general **ideology** of the country at the time when he was writing? What part of the American dream do you think he shares and what part is he excluded from?
4. Compare and contrast your **general repertoire** with Douglass's and explore some of the factors—historical, economic, racial—that make you relate to Douglass's position or that distance you from it.
5. What parts of your specifically *literary repertoire* match up with Douglass's essay?

TOM WOLFE (b. 1931)

The Pump House Gang

Our boys never hair out. The black panther has black feet. Black feet on the crumbling black panther, Pan-thuh. Mee-dah. Pam Stacy, 16 years old, a cute girl here in La Jolla, California, with a pair of orange bell-bottom hip-huggers on, sits on a step about four steps down the stairway to the beach and she can see a pair of revolting black feet without lifting her head. So she says it aloud, "The black panther."

Somebody farther down the stairs, one of the boys with the *major* hair and khaki shorts, says, "The black feet of the black panther."

"Mee-dah," says another kid. This happens to be the cry of a, well, *underground* society known as the Mac Meda Destruction Company.

"The pan-thuh."

"The poon-thuh."

All these kids, 17 of them, members of the Pump House crowd, are lollygagging around the stairs down to Windansea Beach, La Jolla, California, about 11 A.M., and they all look at the black feet, which are a woman's pair of black street shoes, out of which stick a pair of old veiny white ankles, which lead up like a senile cone to a fudge of tallowy, edematous flesh, her thighs, squeezing out of her bathing suit, with old faded yellow bruises on them, which she probably got from running eight feet to catch a bus or something. She is standing with her old work-a-hubby, who has on *san*dals: you know, a pair of navy-blue anklet socks and these sandals with big, wide, new-smelling tan straps going this way and that, *for keeps.* Man, they look like orthopedic sandals, if one can imagine that. Obviously, these people come from Tucson or Albuquerque or one of those hincty adobe towns. All these hincty, crumbling black feet come to La Jolla-by-the-sea from the adobe towns for the weekend. They even drive in cars all full of thermos bottles and mayonnaisey sandwiches and some kind of latticework wooden-back support for the old crock who drives and Venetian blinds on the back window.

"The black panther."

"Pan-thuh."

"Poon-thuh."

"Mee-dah."

Nobody says it to the two old crocks directly. God, they must be practically 50 years old. Naturally, they're carrying every piece of garbage imaginable: the folding aluminum chairs, the newspapers, the lending-library book with the clear plastic wrapper on it, the sunglasses, the sun ointment, about a vat of goo—

It is a Mexican standoff. In a Mexican standoff, both parties narrow their eyes and glare but nobody throws a punch. Of course, nobody in the Pump House crowd would ever even jostle these people or say anything right to them; they are too cool for that.

Everybody in the Pump House crowd looks over, even Tom Coleman, who is a cool person. Tom Coleman, 16 years old, got thrown out of his garage last night. He is sitting up on top of the railing, near the stairs, up over the beach, with his legs apart. Some nice long willowy girl in yellow slacks is standing on the sidewalk but leaning into him with her arms around his body, just resting. Neale Jones, 16, a boy with great lank perfect surfer's hair, is standing nearby with a Band-aid on his upper lip, where the sun has burnt it raw. Little Vicki Ballard is up on the sidewalk. Her older sister, Liz, is down the stairs by the pump house itself, a concrete block, 15 feet high, full of machinery for the La Jolla water system. Liz is wearing her great "Liz" styles, a hulking rabbit-fur vest and black-leather boots over her Levis, even though it is about 85 out here and the sun is plugged in up there like God's own dentist lamp and the Pacific is heaving in with some fair-to-middling surf. Kit Tilden is lollygagging around, and Tom Jones, Connie Carter, Roger Johnson, Sharon Sandquist, Mary Beth White, Rupert Fellows, Glenn Jackson, Dan Watson from San Diego, they are all out here, and everybody takes a look at the panthers.

The old guy, one means, you know, he must be practically 50 years old, he says to his wife, "Come on, let's go farther up," and he takes her by her fat upper arm as if to wheel her around and aim her away from here.

But she says, "No! We have just as much right to be here as they do."

"That's *not the point*—"

"Are you going to—"

"*Mrs. Roberts,*" the work-a-day hubby says, calling his own wife by her official married name, as if to say she took a vow once and his word is law, even if he is not testing it with the blonde kids here—"farther up, *Mrs. Roberts.*"

They start to walk up the sidewalk, but one kid won't move his feet, and, oh, god, her work-a-hubby breaks into a terrible shaking Jello smile as she steps over them, as if to say, Excuse me, sir, I don't mean to make trouble, please, and don't you and your colleagues rise up and jump me, screaming *Gotcha*—

Mee-dah!

But exactly! This beach *is* verboten for people practically 50 years old. This is a segregated beach. They can look down on Windansea Beach and see nothing but lean tan kids. It is posted "no swimming" (for safety reasons), meaning surfing only. In effect, it is segregated by age. From Los Angeles on down the California coast, this is an era of age segregation. People have always tended to segregate themselves by age, teenagers hanging around with teenagers, old people with old people, like the old men who sit on the benches up near the Bronx Zoo and smoke black cigars. But before, age segregation has gone on within a larger community. Sooner or later during the day everybody has melted back into the old community network that embraces practically everyone, all ages.

But in California today surfers, not to mention rock and roll kids and the hotrodders or Hair Boys, named for their fanciful pompadours—all sorts of sets of kids —they don't merely hang around together. They establish whole little societies for themselves. In some cases they live with one another for months at a time. The "Sunset Strip" on Sunset Boulevard used to be a kind of Times Square for Hollywood hot dogs of all ages, anyone who wanted to promenade in his version of the high life. Today "The Strip" is almost completely the preserve of kids from about 16 to 25. It is lined with go-go clubs. One of them, a place called It's Boss, is set up for people 16 to 25 and won't let in anybody over 25, and there are some terrible I'm-dying-a-thousand-deaths scenes when a girl comes up with her boyfriend and the guy at the door at It's Boss doesn't think she looks under 25 and tells her she will have to produce some identification proving she is young enough to come in here and live The Strip kind of life and—she's *had* it, because she can't get up the I.D. and nothing in the world is going to make a woman look stupider than to stand around trying to argue *I'm younger than I look, I'm younger than I look.* So she practically shrivels up like a Peruvian shrunken head in front of her boyfriend and he trundles her off, looking for some place you can get an old doll like this into. One of the few remaining clubs for "older people," curiously, is the Playboy Club. There are apartment houses for people 20 to 30 only, such as the Sheri Plaza in Hollywood and the E'Questre Inn in Burbank. There are whole suburban housing developments, mostly private developments, where only people over 45 or 50 can buy a house. Whole towns, meantime, have become identified as "young": Venice, Newport Beach, Balboa—or "old": Pasadena, Riverside, Coronado Island.

. . . . That is what makes it so weird when all these black pan-thuhs come around to pick up "surfing styles," like the clothing manufacturers. They don't know what any of it means. It's like archeologists discovering hieroglyphics or something, and they say, god, that's neat—Egypt!—but they don't know what the hell it is. They don't know anything about . . . *The Life.* It's great to think of a lot of old emphysematous pan-thuhs in the Garment District in New York City struggling in off the street against a gummy 15-mile-an-hour wind full of soot and coffee-brown snow and gasping in the elevator to clear their old nicotine-phlegm tubes on the way upstairs to make out the invoices on a lot of surfer stuff for 1966, the big nylon windbreakers with the wide, white horizontal competition stripes, nylon swimming trunks with competition stripes, bell-bottom slacks for girls, the big hairy sleeveless jackets, vests, the blue "tennies," meaning tennis shoes, and the . . . *look,* the Major Hair, all this long lank blonde hair, the plain face kind of tanned and bleached out at the same time, but with big eyes. It all starts in a few places, a few strategic groups, the Pump House gang being one of them, and then it moves up the beach, to places like Newport Beach and as far up as Malibu.

Well, actually there is a kind of back-and-forth thing with some of the older guys, the old heroes of surfing, like Bruce Brown, John Severson, Hobie Alter and Phil Edwards. Bruce Brown will do one of those incredible surfing movies and he is out in the surf himself filming Phil Edwards coming down a 20-footer in Hawaii, and Phil has on a pair of nylon swimming trunks, which he has had made in Hawaii, because they dry out fast—and it is like a grapevine. Everybody's got to have a pair of nylon swimming trunks, and then the manufacturers move in, and everybody's making nylon swimming trunks, boxer trunk style, and pretty soon every kid in Utica, N.Y., is buying a pair of them, with the competition stripe and the whole thing, and they never heard of Phil Edwards. So it works back and forth—but so what? Phil Edwards is part of it. He may be an old guy, he is 27 years old, but he and Bruce Brown, who is even older, 29, and John Severson, 31, and Hobie Alter, 28, never haired out to the square world even though they make thousands. Hair refers to courage. A guy who "has a lot of hair" is courageous; a guy who "hairs out" is yellow.

Bruce Brown and Severson and Alter are known as the "surfing millionaires." They are not millionaires, actually, but they must be among the top businessmen south of Los Angeles. Brown grossed something around $500,000 in 1965 and he has only about three people working for him. He goes out on a surfboard with a camera encased in a plastic shell and takes his own movies and edits them himself and goes around showing them himself and narrating them at places like the Santa Monica Civic Auditorium, where 24,000 came in eight days once, at $1.50 a person, and all he has to pay is for developing the film and hiring the hall. John Severson has the big surfing magazine, *Surfer*. Hobie Alter is the biggest surfboard manufacturer, all hand-made boards. He made 5000 boards in 1965 at $140 a board. He also designed the "Hobie" skate boards and gets 25 cents for every one sold. He grossed between $900,000 and $1 million in 1964.

God, if only everybody could grow up like these guys and know that crossing the horror dividing line, 25 years old, won't be the end of everything. One means, keep on living *The Life* and not get sucked into the ticky-tacky life with some insurance salesman sitting forward in your stuffed chair on your wall-to-wall telling you that life is like a football game and you sit there and take that stuff. The hell with that! Bruce Brown has the money and *The Life*. He has a great house on a cliff about 60 feet above the beach at Dana Point. He is married and has two children, but it is not that hubby-mommy you're-breaking-my-gourd scene. His office is only two blocks from his house and he doesn't even have to go on the streets to get there. He gets on his Triumph scrambling motorcycle and cuts straight across a couple of vacant lots and one can see him . . . *bounding* to work over the vacant lots. The Triumph hits ruts and hummocks and things and Bruce Brown bounces into the air with the motor—*thragggggh*—moaning away, and when he gets to the curbing in front of his office, he just leans back and pulls up the front wheel and hops it and gets off and walks into the office barefooted. *Barefooted;* why not? He wears the same things now that he did when he was doing nothing but surfing. He has on a faded gray sweatshirt with the sleeves cut off just above the elbows and a pair of faded corduroys. His hair is the lightest corn yellow imaginable, towheaded, practically white, from the sun. Even his eyes seem to be bleached. He has a rain-barrel old-apple-tree Tom-Sawyer little-boy roughneck look about him, like Bobby Kennedy.

Sometimes he carries on his business right there at the house. He has a dugout room built into the side of the cliff, about 15 feet down from the level of the house. It is like a big pale green box set into the side of the cliff, and inside is a kind of upholstered bench or settee you can lie down on if you want to and look out at the Pacific. The surf is crashing like a maniac on the rocks down below. He has a telephone in there. Sometimes it will ring, and Bruce Brown says hello, and the surf is crashing away down below, roaring like mad, and the guy on the other end, maybe one of the TV networks calling from New York or some movie hair-out from Los Angeles, says:

"What is all that noise? It sounds like you're sitting out in the surf."

"That's right," says Bruce Brown, "I have my desk out on the beach now. It's nice out here."

The guy on the other end doesn't know what to think. He is another Mr. Efficiency who just got back from bloating his colon up at a three-hour executive lunch somewhere and now he is Mr.-Big-Time-Let's-Get-This-Show-on-the-Road.

"On the beach?"

"Yeah. It's cooler down here. And it's good for you, but it's not so great for the desk. You know what I have now? A warped leg."

"A warped leg?"

"Yeah, and this is an $800 desk."

Those nutball California kids—and he will still be muttering that five days after Bruce Brown delivers his film, on time, and Mr. Efficiency is still going through memo thickets or heaving his way into the bar car to Darien—in the very moment that Bruce Brown and Hobie Alter are both on their motorcycles out on the vacant lot in Dana Point. Hobie Alter left his surf board plant about two in the afternoon because the wind was up and it would be good catamaranning and he wanted to go out and see how far he could tip his new catamaran without going over, and he did tip it over, about half a mile out in high swells and it was hell getting the thing right side up again. But he did, and he got back in time to go scrambling on the lot with Bruce Brown. They are out there, roaring over the ruts, bouncing up in the air, and every now and then they roar up the embankment so they can . . . fly, going up in the air about six feet off the ground as they come up off the embankment— *thraaagggggh*—all these people in the houses around there come to the door and look out. These two . . . nuts are at it again. Well, they can only fool around there for 20 minutes, because that is about how long it takes the cops to get there if anybody gets burned up enough and calls, and what efficient business magnate wants to get hauled off by the Dana Point cops for scrambling on his motorcycle in a vacant lot.

Bruce Brown has it figured out so no one in the whole rubber-bloated black pan-thuh world can trap him, though. He bought a forest in the Sierras. There is nothing on it but trees. His own wilds: no house, no nothing, just Bruce Brown's forest. Beautiful things happen up there. One day, right after he bought it, he was on the edge of his forest, where the road comes into it, and one of these big rancher king motheroos with the broad belly and the $70 lisle Safari shirt comes tooling up in a Pontiac convertible with a funnel of dust pouring out behind. He gravels it to a great flashy stop and yells:

"Hey! You!"

Of course, what he sees is some towheaded barefooted kid in a torn-off sweatshirt fooling around the edge of the road.

"Hey! You!"

"Yeah?" says Bruce Brown.

"Don't you know this is private property?"

"Yeah," says Bruce Brown.

"Well, then, why don't you get yourself off it?"

"Because it's mine, it's my private property," says Bruce Brown. "Now you get *your*self off it."

And Safari gets a few rays from that old appletree rain-barrel don't-cross-that-line look and doesn't say anything and roars off, slipping gravel, the dumb crumbling pan-thuh.

But . . . perfect! It is like, one means, you know, poetic justice for all the nights

Bruce Brown slept out on the beach at San Onofre and such places in the old surfing days and would wake up with some old crock's black feet standing beside his head and some phlegmy black rubber voice saying:

"All right, kid, don't you know this is private property?"

And he would prop his head up and out there would be the Pacific Ocean, a kind of shadowy magenta-mauve, and one thing, *that* was nobody's private property—

But how many Bruce Browns can there be? There is a built-in trouble with age segregation. Eventually one *does* reach the horror age of 25, the horror dividing line. Surfing and the surfing life have been going big since 1958, and already there are kids who—well, who aren't kids anymore, they are pushing 30, and they are stagnating on the beach. Pretty soon the California littoral will be littered with these guys, stroked out on the beach like beached white whales, and girls, too, who can't give up the mystique, the mysterioso mystique, Oh Mighty Hulking Sea, who can't *conceive* of living any other life. It is pathetic when they are edged out of groups like the Pump House gang. Already there are some guys who hang around with the older crowd around the Shack who are stagnating on the beach. Some of the older guys, like Gary Wickham, who is 24, are still in *The Life,* they still have it, but even Gary Wickham will be 25 one day and then 26 and then . . . . and then even pan-thuh age. Is one really going to be pan-thuh age one day? Watch those black feet go. And Tom Coleman still snuggles with Yellow Slacks, and Liz still roosts moodily in her rabbit fur at the bottom of the Pump House and Pam still sits on the steps contemplating the mysterioso mysteries of Pump House ascension and John and Artie still bob, tiny pink porcelain shells, way out there waiting for godsown bitchen *set,* and godsown sun is still turned on like a dentist's lamp and so far—

—the panthers scrape on up the sidewalk. They are at just about the point Leonard Anderson and Donna Blanchard got that day, December 6, 1964, when Leonard said, Pipe it, and fired two shots, one at her and one at himself. Leonard was 18 and Donna was 21—21!—god, for a girl in the Pump House gang that is almost the horror line right there. But it was all so mysterioso. Leonard was just lying down on the beach at the foot of the Pump House, near the stairs, just talking to John K. Weldon down there, and then Donna appeared at the top of the stairs and Leonard got up and went up the stairs to meet her, and they didn't say anything, they weren't *angry* over anything, they never had been, although the police said they had, they just turned and went a few feet down the sidewalk, away from the Pump House and—blam blam!—these two shots. Leonard fell dead on the sidewalk and Donna died that afternoon in Scripps Memorial Hospital. Nobody knew what to think. But one thing it seemed like—well, it seemed like Donna and Leonard thought they had lived *The Life* as far as it would go and now it was running out. All that was left to do was—but that is an *insane* idea. It can't be like that, *The Life* can't run out, people can't change all that much just because godsown chronometer runs on and the body packing starts deteriorating and the fudgy tallow shows up at the thighs where they squeeze out of the bathing suit—

Tom, boy! John, boy! Gary, boy! Neale, boy! Artie, boy! Pam, Liz, Vicki, Jackie Haddad! After all this—just a pair of bitchen black panther bunions inching down the sidewalk away from the old Pump House stairs?

Response Statement Assignments

1. How would you characterize the prose style of the essay? Pay special attention to tone, verb tense, and vocabulary.
2. Did the account of the "Pump House gang" sound unfamiliar to you?
3. As someone living more than twenty years after the essay was written, what in your **general repertoire** produced the particular reactions you had to the essay?
4. What do you think of the sixties?
5. Could you imagine any of the Pump House gang belonging to your parents' generation? Or being your parents?
6. What is distinctively *American* about the California scene as Wolfe describes it? What aspects of our country's general **ideology** are evoked in this essay? What aspects of your own repertoire evolve from this general ideology?

ADRIENNE E. HARRIS (b. 1941)

Women, Baseball, and Words
Introduction

In this essay I look at three nested problems: How does baseball as a part of mass culture reflect and produce ideology? How does language and the intricate glossing practices through which baseball is interpreted ensure it as a male preserve? Finally, how and why is baseball appropriated as male space? How are women kept out?

It was the latter problem that I stumbled upon as I began to write about baseball and ideology. I thought it would be easy. I grew up going to ball games. My father took me to the Triple A games in the International League in Toronto. We took the streetcar down Bathurst Street to the old Maple Leaf Stadium (now torn down) to see Havana, Montreal, Buffalo. I saw black players in the mid-1940s later to play in the majors: Junior Gilliam and Elston Howard as young minor leaguers, and a lot of older players on the downside of a career in the bigs. I was taught to play baseball virtually the day after my father returned from the war. There is a family picture of me, dated May 15, 1945. I am wearing a red coat with a velvet collar and I am batting left-handed and leaning into the pitch. My father took me to the Polo Grounds to see Musial play in a doubleheader against the Giants: his absolutely favorite modern player for his absolutely favorite team. I have a personally signed autograph from Ducky Medwick, from my husband's point of view a virtually crucial aspect of my dowry. My father, who took no observable interest in my formal education, had one requirement for a fully furnished mind: that I be well acquainted with the details of baseball occurring in the 30 years before my birth. The postcard of choice, then, on my first visit to the Hall of Fame was the plaque of Sunny Jim Bottomley. As a 13-year-old, I spent one summer writing and rewriting the opening paragraph of a novel to be based on the 1919 Black Sox scandal, a key line being naturally "say it ain't so, Joe."

Over the years boyfriends and husbands took me to baseball games. Once I went with a woman. We took a thermos of Bloody Marys to the then teetotal Exhibition Stadium to see the Blue Jays. Currently I live my baseball life at the edge of my husband's cohort of sports buddies; writers, journalists, academics, and fans; men now in their 40s who spend the baseball season in a litter of box scores and baseball minutiae. The season is a seamless experience of watching, attending, listening to, reading about, and talking baseball. Periodicals sent on a weekly or bi-weekly basis to our house include: *Baseball Chapel News, The Sporting News, Baseball America* (the infamously subtitled "baseball junkies" newspaper), the *Proceedings of the Society of Baseball Researchers.*

So I know quite a bit about baseball. And I like it a great deal. Recently I was asked to bring my professional expertise to an analysis of George Steinbrenner. The sportswriter making the inquiry listened politely to my considered evaluation of psychopathy and narcissism, of Steinbrenner's treatment of Gossage and Jackson as the projection of bad internal objects, paid me a consulting fee, and subsequently explained that legal counsel at the glossy mag in question thought diagnostic labels *did* constitute libel. Still I was encouraged. This spring a young male graduate student approached me about doing a thesis on baseball. "I couldn't help myself," he said with the embarrassed air of someone confessing a mild perversion. I am not sure whether his chagrin is triggered by wishing to do a scholarly treatment of baseball or having a woman chair his dissertation.

As someone writing and thinking about ideology and psyche, I thought the conjunction of baseball, me, and critical theory would be natural. This personal history turns out to be part of the problem. I get to baseball through men: fathers, lovers, husbands, buddies, students. For baseball is a social space appropriated by and for men. Women have been read out of baseball as subjective actors thoroughly. Although they have sued their way into the locker room and cajoled their way into the stands, their marginality is given and absolute.

Writing about baseball raised the problem of legitimacy from the outset. With what authority could I speak? The marginal voice is often tinged with a complex mixture of envy, incompetence, and inauthenticity. As a woman writing about baseball, I encounter the pervasive and complex relation of women to authority. To speak as a woman about baseball is to be immediately entangled with baseball's ideological function and to be at odds with it. The evidence of this confrontation is in the struggle, the rupture, the discordance between my voice and the variable, but coherent male voice of baseball.

The intractable problem of voice, the difficulty in writing about baseball, required at the outset a consideration of baseball as an ideological operation. First, therefore, I want to review those assessments of sports' ideological function which take primarily a structural Marxist perspective, make a critique of that treatment, and then situate baseball within that analysis. What I will argue is that baseball is an interesting anomaly in modern mass audience sports, that its ideological operation needs to be specified in its particularity, and that to an unusual degree for a sport, baseball is dependent on language for the production and maintenance of this operation.

It is often argued that language always operates as ideology (Bakhtin, 1981). Additionally, however, a number of crucial ideological activities operate in non-linguistic ways. A left critique of sport attends to the ways that sporting events simultaneously produce and mask ideology through the action, visual images, the theatricality. My point about baseball in this regard is two-fold. First, baseball represents a fascinating but complex and contradictory instance of this operation. Second, baseball's heavy reliance on the linguistic and speech acts which surround it are unusual in sport. It is perhaps more akin to other art or cultural forms. It is this feature of baseball as a densely *interpreted* activity that renders it so difficult and intractable to the marginal female voice.

Sports and Ideology

Sport as a metaphor for modern culture: This is the usual organizing argument in the critique of sports (Brohm, 1978; Aronowitz, 1973). It is, for example, a mirror for racism. It can reflect and represent the organization of industrial production and bureaucracy, the transformation of vivid energy into game and strategy, the co-optation of play, and the co-optation of class struggle and even national consciousness into structured competition. Jean-Marie Brohm has developed this analysis with respect to Olympic competition.

The public performance of sports and athletic events, at many levels, orchestrates a management of impulse, a disciplining of the body, a theatre for submission and masochism from which desire has been drained. Certain aspects of most modern sport are anti-pleasure, devoid of humor or playfulness. The ravages done to the body and spirit by modern work are masked by promoting assault on the body as high art, as choice. The tempo of modern work and its insistent accompaniment, the clock, are replicated in sports. The 100 yard dash, swimming relays, football, soccer, basketball, position men against time as well as against each other. From the most grueling marathon to the split-second track event, the athlete is held to the regulatory judgment of the clock, calculated to the millisecond.

The body is held in an intense and masochistic relationship to the clock and to technology. There are several elements at work here—one is the exhaustion and debilitation inherent in working to the clock. Rabinbach's treatment of the appearance of exhaustion sees fatigue as it is first manifest in neurasthenia, at the onset of industrial production (1982). Racing against the clock, fighting 'til the bell rings to signal the end of the round, playing out the period in hockey, pit man against time with the implicit threat that the body can be broken in this struggle, depleted and wrecked in a struggle with a perfectly implacable, relentless, unbeatable enemy—time.

There is also the matter of injury itself, of the escalation in certain sports of a technology that brings risk of injury: skiing, speed skating, bigger, heavier tennis racquets, high tech running shoes. All these technological advances which accompany the rationalizing of training are marketed as improvements but raise also the spectre and incidence of injury.

Sports medicine specializes in repair and reconstruction, a mechanization of the body in rebuilt knees and shoulders. Sports reporting has an almost perfect mix of the military and the mechanical; the envied and adored athlete is set for endurance, effacing spirit and humanity to become the disciplined singleminded machine/cyborg.

Eros, playfulness, desire, and youth are managed and removed from the social body through organized sport. Cary Goodman examines this process in the eradication of street games from the Lower East Side, a strategy which coopts immigrant energy and working class spirit in the early years of immigration at the turn of the century (Goodman, 1979). Assimilation was, in part, accomplished through moving the collectivity of the streets into the playgrounds. In concert with the assimilating and socializing effects of public education, organized games, parks, sports leagues were developed and arranged by bourgeois social reformers collaboratively in some cases with state institutions like the police—the Police Athletic Leagues being, in New York, the most visible example.

In the production of modern sports activity, both at the amateur and at the professional level, many transfers are effected. The body, first of all, is a site of transfer. Technology replaces play and sex. The athlete's body becomes a non-sexual machine. Jane Fonda and women working out replace the indolent sex goddess of the 1950's. Muscles in place of nipples. The teasing playfulness of Gussie Moran's lace panties in women's tennis has given way to the sinew, muscle, and computer-programmed body and diet of Martina. In the male athlete's body we celebrate force, effort, precision, strength, and often pure will. One hallmark of our species, at least in terms of evolutionary biology, is fine motor control through the human hand, the opposable thumb. This feature is increasingly unimportant in industrial life and most modern sport.

In sum then, sport is a theatrical space arranged for displays of person and body images, then made available on a mass level. These images can be the very stuff of individual fantasy and subjectivity. Sports figures as creatures of will and as bodies in relation to time and to machinery are part of the social material which is constitutive in the creation of self in the individual. Sports for both male and female provide a socially derived perception of the body characterized and identified in historically specific ways. Additionally, the glorification of "games," the taming of struggle into "fair" competition, the whole idea of "fairness" and rule-governed behavior embedded as it is in a political and social context of lawless capital development and imperialism, are all forms of mystification. Brohm evokes these ideas in an insight connecting sports and social repression, epitomized in the use of the soccer stadium in Chile as the site for mass torture and death during the coup. He makes an imaginative disjunctive connection, asking really that one permit the play of substitution. Imagine the agonies, torn muscles, effort, blood, jarred teeth, bones cracking—"normalized" on the soccer field—and contemplate a relation—suggestive, mystifying, and disorienting, in the image of the soccer stadium turned to a real theatre of death and torture.

Placing phenomena like play, gaming, competition, fair play, and idealized body (in fact a distorted and fetishized body) into the world of sports is itself an ideological operation. Placing these activities in the world of physical action, styles of play and types of bodies are "naturalized" as they are idealized.

In the development and rationalization of play, the structure of sport and the attendant image of the social body moves in conjunction with the facts and conditions of modern work. Play has become hard work, training, regimentation. Masochistic self-discipline and work to the point of pain and collapse is now the goal of even the casual jogger. Consider the presence—as an impowered imago—of the older male coach, stop-watch in hand, drilling, screaming, cursing, demanding of his exhausted ravaged players—more; Counsilman, the swimming coach at Indiana, Schembechler, football at Michigan; Lydiard, the punitive running coach in New Zealand; Bear Bryant; Woody Hayes; their tyrannies made heroic or on occasion high comic art through the medium of sports reporting. One item must be highlighted: the stop-watch. Brohm's collection of essays is titled, *The Prison of Measured Time,* and he marks the tendency in modern sports to celebrate speed, to measure performance, to encapsulate activity and energy inside schedule.

There is accuracy in this perspective but there are problems and limits; sports comes to sound like prison. This perspective on sports as co-optation and repression has at base a reactionary and behaviorist psychology. It assumes a conditioned and conditionable subject; it leaves few options in interpreting mass audience response to professional sports, or individual participation in sports beyond a paranoid theory of mindless unresistant co-optation.

It would seem preferable to treat sports as an arena of conflict, resistance, and struggle in which events and experiences are *potentially* available to a more liberatory impulse. In the race or press against the stopwatch there is desire, will, conscious action. There is the longing to break out, to transcend. It is the impossibility of full satisfaction, the fierce longing for better, fewer, higher, stronger that speaks to an ineluctable aspect of human desire and speaks against the notion of blind conditioning. The longing, the will, the fantasy is uncapturable, though strongly contested, because of this impossibility of satisfaction. That is, in fact, the revolutionary potential of human desire and why it is so fiercely attached and organized by state and capitalist formations.

Sports celebrates activity. Even the spectator's vicarious action or fantasy operates as a potential for action, and in the case of team sports, collective experience. Indeed, modern professional sports coopts collective spirit, but the capacity for assistance, the feeling for cooperative "team play" remains in the mass audience.

There is, of course, a systematic masking of economic and social realities in the sanctification of "fair play" in much modern sport. But fairness and equality are ideals which are not destroyed in sport. The utopian vision of lawful and equitable action among individuals and groups *is* mystified and degraded in the sports science, and at the same time these ideas and visions remain as potential, as dream.

The role of organized sports in class struggle lies primarily in the management of poor, working class, and immigrant urban youth. While this is demonstrable there are gaps in this sort of structural or mechanical analysis. Parks, playgrounds, and amateur sports leagues are not simply cages. Parks, for example, are rather volatile, expanding, unpredictable social spaces, a place of encounter and struggle for many social groups.

In Canada, where organized hockey leagues are a dominant force in most urban cities for boys from 5 to adulthood, the aspiration and participation of boy and parent is quite complex. As the parent of a 10-year-old on a Toronto team, I spent a winter sitting in chilly ice rinks watching a motley collection of little boys struggling towards skill and competence. In the stands, I listened to the other parents, most of them tired from boring, enervating jobs, delighted to sit sociably in the stands with other adults (single mothers primarily and a handful of often singleminded sports-obsessed fathers). These women were pleased to have company, and pleased, above all, to have their kids off the streets. Harry Edwards's critique of the image of the black athletic superstar's success and upward mobility as *fiction* promoted by the tiny percentage of successful token athletes is apt and telling. But parents and children in these organized youth leagues often come to see them as a place of socialization, sociability, a piece of cultural and social life amidst work conditions and personal circumstance too frequently lonely and alienating.

Ideology in Baseball

We need to situate baseball in this analysis quite carefully. In at least three key aspects baseball does not provide the direct social mirroring which a conventional account of sports' ideological functioning would suggest. First in relation to time and second in relation to words, baseball is a sport uniquely placed in cultural life. It is in projecting a mythical alternative to modern life that baseball claims its capacity to charm and its ideological power. Sociological or critical theory has been acute in its attention to structural formations in modern culture whose latent and manifest content as image operate on mass psyche. But in some sports and many cultural formations (and baseball is a particularly powerful example) there is interpretation inseparable from image and spectacle. Baseball is not only enacted, played, and displayed in the mass media, it is also glossed, interpreted, spoken. The claim here, taken from Giddens's social action theory and ethnomethodology, is that social life is produced as a "skilled performance" and always surrounded and made meaningful through language and interpretation (Giddens, 1979). These glossing practices are inseparable aspects of all social action and social life. An analysis of baseball must pay particular attention to the words, speech, writing, broadcast commentary, statistics, and technical symbolic displays as crucial ingredients of the impact on mass culture and mass psyche.

Finally, within baseball the body is valued, constructed, and displayed differently from the masochistic, ravaged grand guignol of so many other contemporary sports.

Baseball and Time

Baseball is centrally a place without time and without women. It provides men with absolute luxury: no stopwatch, no schedule, no women. Baseball carries within it a memory of pre-industrial America. It is less enmeshed in the economy of gambling, in the traffic and commerce of desire, more frankly symbolic, more specifically dependent on its interpretive acts, its mediations, to do its ideological work. The fit with novels, poetic discourse, and a narrative tradition is much tighter than for most other sports.

A first order interpretive production is the imaginary origins of baseball. Mythically, baseball originates in a pre-timed, pre-industrial America: America before the stopwatch and America before feminism and suffrage. In fact professional league baseball seems to have developed in two initially distinct places: gentlemen's athletic clubs and industrial teams. Historically, sports is a cultural space not unlike nightclubs, racing, cabaret, etc.: a site for the mutually fascinated connections between upper and lower classes. From these two social strata the professional league formed at the turn of the century. The industrial teams have an interesting history as they were formed primarily by management at the time when union organizing began to heat up. Teams constituted an inspired way of tapping the spirit of collectivity and loyalty siphoned into obedience to management and fan-dom, a brilliant co-optation, which was then covered and mystified by the tale of baseball's invention by the Civil War general Abner Doubleday.

Several years ago, during the baseball strike, the following apocryphal story passed among baseball writers. When Lincoln was shot and lay dying, he summoned Abner Doubleday to his bedside. "Don't let baseball die," he croaked. A sanctified American ritual, the "national" pastime is thus invented by the Civil War victor, its virgin birth occurring in a pastoral perfectly pre-industrial pre-urban upper New York State town. Baseball, a game for lads after work, for gentlemen on the village green—this is its timeless birth image, the Hall at Cooperstown its basilica, filled with relics and inspirational films and archives.

> The players below us—Mays, DiMaggio, Ruth, Snodgrass—swim and blur in memory. The ball floats over to Terry Turner and the end of this game may never come. (Angell, 1972, p. 319)

Baseball is a liturgical experience; its forms preserve historical memory and tradition unchanged and unchangeable. This has its high art rendering in the work of Roger Angell, but it is a young man's sensibility too. W. P. Kinsella, in a recent novel (1982), writes about an Iowa farmer oddly out of phase with the contemporary world of work and action, though conveniently gifted with an utterly devoted and luscious wife. The hero spends the novel building an "imaginary" ballpark in an Iowa cornfield where he replays the crucial games in the 1919 White Sox season, a futile evocation of the lost memory of desire and fulfillment before the splitting, before the schizoid moment, before the Black Sox.

Modern adaptations are dangerous and unsettling. Streamlining of technique or training is faintly suspect. The lore of baseball is held in the heads and mouths of aging scouts, oldtimers, ancient trainers. Astroturf, the DH rule, uppity black ballplayers, "head" cases like Templeton and Ivie endanger the fragile ecology of this myth. Best to remember that though Ricky Henderson stole more bases than anyone, he and Ty Cobb still had to run the same 90 feet from first to second. This is the sort of reassuring homily that helps old codgers like *New York Post* reporter Dick Young sleep at night.

Baseball is unique as a popular modern sport played without a stopwatch. That artifact, born of rationalized industrial practice, of experimental psychology and time motion studies, is now the *engine* of most popular sport. Violence, staccato stop-start, the relentlessness of these timed sports duplicates modern work. It is as though they hit an addicted troubled place in the collective psyche, as though our paced work, our classroom schedules, our recreational lives all lived off and needed the same intense hit. But not baseball. Whatever its spatial intricacy, there is no clock, or more properly no clock with a second hand—a technical innovation associated with industrialization. You might have to go home or stop listening if it got too late or it rained. One major league team preserves the fiction of a leisurely afternoon sport by not putting in lights.

Interestingly, evening baseball came to most teams just prior to the Second World War. There is a fascinating letter in the Hall of Fame from President Roosevelt to the Commissioner of baseball, urging the delicate task of maintaining baseball. It was important not to suggest that there were teams of men avoiding the war effort. At the same time, people working late shifts for the war effort needed some entertainment. Baseball carefully presented could be an antidote both to war and to work.

Baseball intersects with time in other interesting ways. It is not only outside time, it is continuous. There are two discrete hits of football each week: Sunday afternoon and Monday night (a replay). Baseball is daily and weaves through one's day continuously. There are morning box scores, later editions of the paper for West Coast games, afternoon TV, the radio chattering through the summer night air, trips to the ballpark. And these are only the first order mediations of the experience. There is all the subsequent arcana and interpretation—glossy magazines, books, baseball cards, compendia of statistics and lore, the weekly *Sporting News,* think pieces in high and low tone journalism, editorials on the relation of baseball to life, previews of the upcoming season, filler items in gossip columns. In a telling slip, a friend referred, wishfully, to the time from the last game of the World Series to the beginning of spring training as "the long weekend." When baseball is on, it is blissfully, timelessly, everywhere.

Writing about an impending football strike, Frederick Exley created a cast of angry, dispirited, economically challenged fans reacting to the disaster of no football. What will it mean? Less time logged in bars. A loss of income for the bartenders. The loss of a safe place free of women's words. The article quotes a real/imaginary male fan reflecting on a probable rise in family violence in the absence of that time-out from women that football affords. Whether this is a behavioral or sociological truth, the symbolic presentation is clear. The function of this game is the management of alienation, the sublimation of violent impulse. Let me watch this game where men violently and relentlessly hurt and touch each other, allow me freedom from women's requiring voice, and I will not strike you.

Around the baseball strike different fears emerged. It was the loss of a pure world, the intrusion of money (decoded as black and hispanic players with economic demands) and high salaries. Even worse it was the appearance of all the grit and antagonistic clang of labor, unions, arbitration, all the conditions baseball was initially designed to deny. It was a threatened loss of the past, of the known remembered world of men's childhood of a sublimated phallic time.

In summary, baseball is positioned in relation to time in a quite unique way in modern American sport. Baseball is presented in such a way (and here as we shall see later, language and interpretation are crucial) that this connection to the past, its summarizing of an innocent youthful past idealized but lost, is embodied in the action. It has, in this way, an almost ceremonial quality. This is not merely nostalgia or sentimentality. Indeed nostalgia can be almost a perversion of the rich response to baseball seen simultaneously as past and as present. Angell noted this in a perceptive and self-reflective moment in his account of watching Ron Darling pitch at Yale (Angell, 1982). Angell sits in the company of 90-year-old Hall of Fame pitcher Joe Wood. Angell is the prime practitioner of the historicized and religious presentation of baseball. He notices that he is sitting in the stands with a head full of memories and historical connections, self-consciously constituting a thick cultural experience. Joe Wood only wants to talk about the game he's actually seeing. He's interested in this 20-year-old "phenom." Angell's making tradition.

By virtue of its particular carrying of the past (primarily through its encircling interpretive practices), by its continuousness, its dailiness, and by its untimed structure, baseball stands against modern industrial practice, and the tendencies in modern social life to bureaucratize, to efface historical memory, to promote "social amnesia." If there is a cultural experience opposite to baseball, it is probably the evening TV news. The 60-second spot, the flash video, the fast take, designed to be consumed and forgotten virtually as its image fades. Baseball is about remembering.

This continuity, essentially a diachronic movement, is represented structurally within each baseball game in the cycling and repetitive narrative which begins each time with the opposition of pitcher and batter, father and son. Synchronically, baseball records repetition, leisure, variability. In its earliest conception and in most of the modern history, baseball's freedom from timing, the absence of the stopwatch, made it appear almost unrationalizable; an inning could take five minutes or an hour. Outs can be made with the precision and dispatch of the double play, or the high velocity bullet throw from the outfield to catch a runner at home; or in a quite opposite style, a ground ball can be fielded carefully, almost casually, so the throw to pick off the man at first seems made in slow motion. Freed from the clock, baseball counterposes human effort. The speed or intricacy of the pitch is set against the eye and hand of the batter. The accuracy of the fielder versus the speed of the runner. Humans are the calibraters of action here, not machines.

There are of course other untimed sports: tennis, curling, cricket. But tennis is only recently a mass spectator sport; curling is a passionately played amateur sport, for the most part tucked away in small northern industrial towns. The closest analogy to baseball can be cricket.

C. L. R. James (1984) has recently republished his cricket writing, and it suggests that for Britain and its colonies (although not perhaps with the same wide audience or class base as baseball) there are strong parallels. But for an American mass audience, as a sport of long tenure—our "national pastime"—baseball entails a unique interplay of diachronic and synchronic structure in the use of time, timelessness, and continuity.

Another James (unrelated biographically or intellectually to C. L. R.) is calling this into question. Bill James (1984) has over the past five years introduced into baseball new statistics which may delightfully increase our sense of the intricacy of the game—but which raise also the spectre of rationalized timing. He celebrates (though not of course being solely responsible for its inception) the practice of timing fastballs, clocking pitchers' and catchers' release time. Physicists have recently become interested in research on the actual movement of curve balls, initiating a debate that illustrates the conflict between abstract rationalizing and practical knowledge. Scouts, coaches, players talk of rising and falling curves, breaking balls, and sliders, and they successfully instruct young batters on the management of these pitches. The rising curve is indeed an illusion of movement, but hitting it requires not abstract rational analysis, but a pragmatic history of sensory motor learning and practice in equilibrating body, stance, eye, and reflex in action.

Baseball and Desire: The Sexual Body

Baseball has always seemed to me to be pre-genital. Phallic yes, but not genital. Baseball lies in the domain of latency with its suspended sexuality, its sublimated energy, its leisured discipline and cordiality, its space and time for language and calculation. Baseball hits young males at that developmental period where the separation and alienation from women is peaking. It captures its fans first as boys between 7 and 12 who imprint on a team, a hero, a player. Baseball's mythic heroes have a boyish quality, whatever the reality—there is the image of the childlike Babe Ruth, the polite well-mannered Robinson. The Boy's Own Annual aspect of the ideal ballplayers' attributes are seen in the hard pressing team player Munson; the proud, intense, and dignified Gibson; the rapscallion Dean brothers. Whether earnest schoolboy, hard playing youth, or errant rascal, the screen of idealized boyhood is placed over the social reality of players. In the annual *Baseball Register,* each player lists, among other things, his "hobbies" (surely an atavistic term). Rusty Staub is reported as favoring that ultimate old fashioned boy's pastime—stamp collecting.

Now it is important to acknowledge that this is both the condition within the modern game and an evocation of a lost world mourned by Roger Angell and that elderly clan of sportswriters. Real baseball is also in a transitional state. Cocaine, the modern player as conglomerate surrounded by agents, lawyers, and accountants, alcoholism, drug dependency all exist within baseball mixed in with these myths of boyishness and southern boyishness in particular. Black players bring a sexier, naughtier sting to the game, though one might see the public persona of someone like Reggie Jackson as embodying both aspects—blonde companions in Studio 54 alongside that boy's passion for cars.

It is mostly Italian players who project an image of sexuality: the Cerones and Mazzillis who turn up as pinups and models for underwear. It is Mazzilli who is reputed to have had his pants tailored to show off such a pretty ass. Tommy John and Goose Gossage, by contrast, look like the draped baggykneed, loose-through-the-crotch uniformed players of the turn of the century. There is little of the homoerotic imagery or style of football. No tiny butts, tight ends, male armour, handoffs, embraces, and ass patting. It seems a sport sexually and symbolically more innocent. It is about boyhood—of the individual and the country.

For the witness, the spectator, baseball's sensuality is auditory and visual, not genital; its pleasure is in looking and being looked at, at the color and geometry and symmetry of the field. A game of inches, but also a game with time to talk—on the field and off. None of the terse commands of the football huddle or the screamed sideline coaching of basketball—the racing time-outs and excruciatingly orchestrated game endings. Managers curse and argue, walk briskly to the mound to yank their pitcher, coaches flap and brush their signals across their chests and arms. It is not slow motion but it is leisurely. The catcher needles the batter, signs to the pitcher. There is a rhythm and pace to each pitch, and that rhythm is played and replayed through the voice of the announcer, the radio commentator. One sits in the stands, beer is yelled for, peanuts and hotdogs announced, amidst the rise and fall of voices, single cries, roars, boos. There is the punctuation of the game's sounds. There is the sound of the ball being hit. There is the visual appeal of watching the moving conjunction of ball and player, the soothing connection of ball and glove pocket. This is not genital sex pleasure exactly, but it is body pleasure, the pleasure of looking, the excitement of sounds and sights.

The ravages of the body, the crucified ruined body of the sports figure, the masochistic ritual of work to the point of pain are not idealized in baseball. Except in pitching. It is interesting that one modern modification of the game—the DH rule in the American League—seems particularly injurious to pitchers. Instead of the natural rhythm of the batting order with its lesser dangers lower in the list, the DH rule makes everything a struggle. The rotator cuff injury—as a modern phenomenon and a symbolic object within baseball—may be a manifestation of technology. The arm turns into a machine either easily worn out or replaced by a high tech medical repair job. In this development one may see the first signs of the promotion and idealization of masochism, the wrecking of the body for competition and winning. Currently within baseball, there is a contradiction. There is manager Billy Martin burning out the arms of hot young pitchers, and simultaneously there is the anachronism embodied in the wonderful Phil Niekro—a 45-year-old defeating time and batters with the intricacy of the knuckleball. The opposable thumb is again crucial in the production of sliders, forkballs, and breaking pitches.

Baseball and Words

Over the airways, in the daily press, in "think" pieces, in box scores, in glossy magazines, in the stands with a buddy, or over your shoulder to some strange guy sitting behind you, baseball is *talked* as it is played and watched. And its talk is as crucial to its meaning as any hit, any sacrifice fly, any breaking curve. Marbled through the visual jewel of baseball, against the irregular saccadic rhythms of men's movements, men talk. Unlike the tempo of hockey or basketball, where speech skates across the stream of jump cut, of continuous play, baseball displays itself more amply and more spaciously. It opens large spaces and long moments into which words and fantasy can arch and curl.

> . . . our afternoon slid by, a distraction of baseball and memory. I almost felt myself at some dreamlike doubleheader, merging the then and the now. (Angell, 1982, p. 372)

In this endless moment of congealing memory, men talk. There is infield chatter, the staccato fast funny style of an announcer, the counterpointing yells and bitter remonstrance of a fan. A sheet flaps down over the top deck, a hand-lettered love note to some player or team. Diamond Vision writes, quotes stats, blinks on up-dated scores and pitching changes all over the leagues. *In extremis,* if you need it, there is Sports Phone where a man will give you a high speed run down on every sporting event ongoing at that moment. Each modality—the box score, the format-ted computer printout on TV or the scoreboard, the sports writing for the daily paper—has its own style and syntax, its own particularized orthography or graphics or phonology. But all these dialects of baseball, these coded commentaries, are in the male register. If I could ape its written form, I could pass, but I could never speak it. Baseball speech is hip, witty, competitive, strong on laid back irony, nothing too heavyhanded or earnest. That would be "bush," a curious term, sexually loaded and contemptuous of marginality. Baseball is the only literary domain I know where "nonchalant" is used as a verb.

You need a low-keyed style, hip one-liners that will carry you past the dugout entry into the good old boys' life in the locker room. Wilfred Sheed, in an ambiva-lent review of Red Smith's collected essays, complained/envied/confessed that Smith's material could only have come from a lifetime of hard drinking, hard talk-ing bouts where you have to keep your wits going, manage your booze and your head, and keep playing in that funny jiving chatter of men talking sport.

I once sat mute, envious, and wildly appreciative, amidst a group of 40-year-olds (my cohort). They were sportswriters, writers, academics, men who had lolled back in stadium seats and talked at and with other men all their life. We sat in a tiny park in St. Petersburg, watching spring training. Down on the field, armed with press passes, these same men hung back, the bodies and posture suddenly the slack but respectful pose of the 8-year-old fan. I watched *these* men watch 18-year-olds curve, swivel, move, throw, catch, *do* baseball. Back in the stands speech returned and they amused themselves making up lists of imaginary teams—the fish team: Thon, Trout; the furniture team: Lamp, John, etc. These men offered up a flow of ironic comment as an endless anonymous line of beefy young Twins (Minnesota was play-ing the Cardinals) moved through batting practice. These men took pleasure in each others' company, in the event arrayed before them and around them in that pretty park. An afternoon of many pleasures: food appeared, beer and ribs, nachos dripped in cheese, ice cream. Someone from the *St. Louis Post-Dispatch* came over to gossip over the fate of a new Cardinal pitcher, the sun hit the water behind Al Lang park, we slathered on suntan lotion. But it was words, words, male wit and male speech that bound it together. In this company I had no voice, no substance, no way into this lyrical moment. The talk is authoritative, the commentary culled from life-times with the statistics, the lore, the received wisdom of baseball. It was boys talking to boys, it was the absolute male privilege to talk baseball.

There is the heart-stopping prose of Roger Angell:

Baseball's time is seamless and invisible, a bubble within which players move to exactly the same pace and rhythm as their predecessors. This is the way the game was played in our youth, and in our father's youth and even back then, back in the country days—there must have been the same feeling, that time could be stopped. (Angell, 1972)

There is the ironic ear of Gilbert Sorrentino:

Telling you on the phone what Joe Chooch said about what Gil Hodges said down in St. Petersburg after Tommy Agee said something to somebody about something. "So that was the final batting order, man." Your mouth open, what to say to him. Leo, Leo leave me alone. We are not friends anymore. Tell it to the marines, tell it to Pete Hamill. (Sorrentino, 1971, p. 127)

And then there is the irritating scolding voice of Dick Young. This is men's discourse.

The function of this talk is not only to make meaning, to gloss the game and themselves. These words also bind men across generations and time, building up complex layers of experience creating a thick piece of culture and ideology in which men move and operate. This is the unique contribution baseball and its discourse makes to the reproduction of social life. Phil Rizzuto, announcing a Yankee game, lives out some remnant of the baseball he actually played in the '40s. (One can go several innings with *no* word of the game in progress.) He discusses his difficulties getting to the game, his devotion to baseball: "You know, I spend more time at Yankee Stadium than I do in my own home" (precisely the wish of most of his male listeners). He sends messages and birthday greetings to cronies, squabbles and jokes with his co-announcers, and very occasionally drops a word about the game he is observing. These words, these glossing practices bring the men who listen and watch into an intricate and multilayered experience of themselves and a game played over time and outside it. It is 1948, it is 1984. The man who speaks is a 28-year-old shortstop, a 60-year-old announcer. The stats and chatter and background he offers up over the airwaves link him and his listeners to the whole genealogy of men in baseball. The man who listens to Rizzuto becomes for the moment the 8-year-old boy who fell asleep with his radio cupped to his ear, the 25-year-old warming up in the bullpen: an American male made "real" in the matrix of words and play.

Joseph Glick, a psychologist doing market research for a major league team in a southern city, reports a whole radio audience of older fans who prefer *not* to go to the park. That is, they want baseball only mediated through its talk. His speculation? For older fans, the shift into the modern game is so disquieting that they prefer to hear it, to accommodate the radio play-by-play to their own imagination, their own past, a past in which among other things all the players are *white*.

Sportswriters' entry into the locker room to the privileged talk with players requires the meshing of hip male voices. There are some subtexts, some variations in code, to be sure; the code for race is complex. There is a tough black street style which has replaced the decorous calm black voice of the Robinson era. There are generational shifts, a new pious register for the born-again Christians, and a confessional voice for the reformed drinker and dope taker. There are varying registers for ethnicity: sharp urban talk, Stengelese, assorted versions of good old boy talk. Wilfred Sheed, commenting on the charm of Red Barber in the 1940s, notes "he was famous in his day for a soft somewhat homogeneous southern voice" and goes on to complain about the contemporary shift to company shills, the voice of baseball in the pocket of management.

A woman writer or photographer moving into these domains is in a hopeless bind. Even having sued her way into the locker room, her presence transforms the camaraderie of the dugout or dressing room into sex war. Glen Waggoner, a new sportswriter who won an instant entry into the players' domain by virtue of a baseball-filled head, an ironic pen, and an East Texas accent, reports a post-game scene in Yankee Stadium where a woman writer is faced with a naked Rick Cerone. In what must be an evolutionary first, a male uses display and his dick to keep a woman away. The official male version is that it isn't happening. Waggoner gives it his deep-fried East Texas best: "Hell, Cerone was just drying off, airing them out." First day on the job and he has the style and speech just right.

Although only men can speak this discourse, not all men really claim it legitimately. You do have to be a man, but one oddly alert to and in tension over boyhood and power. A man can easily get the tone wrong, a woman always will. Emily Vermeule writing in the *New York Times Magazine* quotes a graceful Roger Angell paragraph on Luis Tiant and baseball as timeless archaeology. She then goes on to write a fulsome account of baseball as the combat of classical mythology. Flowering conceits, extravagant prose—the style is constantly wrong, and the piece set against the Angell quote illuminates precisely the impossibility of the female voice. When Angell's laconic spare style makes the allusions to classicism hip, a woman "reading" baseball through the rituals of war in Greece appears only to have missed the point.

But men get the tone wrong too. George Steinbrenner talks the heavy irrational register of "corporate-speak," the irritated boss whose verbal style is a form of shaking the players like some intricate toy he is too hamhanded to wind up. He speaks a weird mixture of sentimentality (weeping over the betrayal by sons: Dent, Tommy John, Dave) and vicious castrating scorn. Two seasons ago he dished out a punishing commentary that sent Reggie Jackson to the doctors, walking naked down some hospital hallway to have his head and vision examined, like a man at a slave auction. This is an aberrant dialect, sick and peculiar. Its antidote proved to be that purer form of fan chant—"Steinbrenner sucks," a phenomenon described with wonderful lunacy in the sports section of *The Daily Worker* as an instance of the spontaneous eruption of class solidarity between blacks and hispanics and working people allied in the struggles of labor against management.

The pure form, the standard dialect of baseball is conducted currently in a reedy, high-timbred male voice, strung somewhat ambiguously along the life span between 8 and 40. It is not an asexual voice, but one for whom the storms of sex are pushed out of view. Talk, banter, commentary, analysis, evocation, taunting, the work of baseball talk is the creation and distribution of a complex male world in which real and imaginary men feel connected. It is not merely that men speak about baseball. Rather speaking and interpreting is baseball. It is not merely that I'm not big enough to play baseball, or that I might throw like a girl (that most deadly threat to all tomboy sports participants), that I'm not tough or hip enough. It is rather that baseball both in its words and practices is coded for gender and it is coded male. Whatever its meaning as an economic unit, its evolution in current corporate life, it is a social form which requires, depends, feeds off, and is irreducibly bound up in a series of glossing practices which humorously, argumentatively, silkily make its meaning.

Baseball and Women

French feminist thought in the past decade has been particularly tuned to the question of authorship, subjectivity and the feminine text. This is not the reductionist position that women are outside language, rather that the problem of legitimacy is deeply connected to language and to women's problematic relation to speech. To examine the difficulties for women in inserting themselves into the symbolic order through an insertion into language as a speaking subject is to encounter in a central way the interconnection of gender, sexuality, and subjectivity.

There is no female subject "I" in baseball. There is no place, as Kristeva elaborates, that the writing, speaking, female "I" can easily inhabit. How to enter the symbolic space as subject? Women have no voice in baseball. Teresa Wright looks supportively at Gary Cooper in *Pride of the Yankees.* Young women packed into their jeans hang over the infield fence near the dugout waiting to be looked at and chosen. Women wait for men to be finished with sports. The problem is legitimacy, entrance as subject. If I speak I will have to change my skin, speak a false mock male self. It would be ludicrous. And if I dared speech, who could I imagine I am to the listener/reader? Men and their words are everywhere. Words through microphones, tapped over the wire services, yelled across the stadium and all woven into a field of action where only men move and play. I can be other, the "you" sent to the kitchen at the end of the inning, the "you" standing in front of those flinty mirrors at Shea, backcombing my hair.

So does this mean that there are no women in baseball? Not quite. Women can be near baseball. Women enter as the object: of desire, of comic laughter, of contempt, or irritation. Women, not to put too fine a point on it, can be pussy in baseball. Baseball Annies adore, squeal, put out for baseball. That this is both true and big business is clear from the switching of Bucky Dent and Lee Mazzilli, a trade conducted frankly in the expectation of pulling 14-year-old girls into Yankee Stadium. A year earlier, Mazzilli was traded from the Mets and the erotic graffiti in the women's bathroom took a distinctly downward turn. When he played outfield at Shea, regardless of how ludicrously, young women covered the walls of the bathroom with lacey girl handwriting: about buns and being well hung and the Italian stallion. So it is the marginal closeted world of the women's john that one must enter to uncover female desire and fantasy.

Another anecdote from spring training. Watching those "cruelly young" (an Angell phrase) men heft and swing large stiff bats, the quite sexy men I am with have mysteriously turned into prepubescent fans. Some boy's body has taken over as they cluster around the dugout. Who am I in this tableau? The girlfriend, the groupie. I try to be invisible, hang out at the edges. Suddenly a woman appears—very blond, more Candy Darling than Teresa Wright. She is wearing a white jump suit cut very low. She has a press pass, noted amidst much grumbling from the male writers. As she moves close to the players, moves to enter this male domain, she turns into object. She is examined with an eerie mixture of desire and contempt: woman as part-object. With that tradeoff she can approach the players, sit in the dugout, flip on her tape recorder, but she has paid a terrible price. She sits beside some player never as a writing, speaking commentator of baseball, only as "gash." Her presence, of course, alters the social valence for me too. I have three, possibly four choices. I can be object too, flirting, watching, not speaking but answering. I can be invisible. I could be somebody's mother, desire and desirability bleached out. Or I can turn myself inside out, be the little tomboy of my childhood.

If you don't want to enter that male talk as its prey or object, you can come in as mock boy. What is the etymology of "tomboy"? Or its sociology? It is a developmental moment, its short half-life to be engulfed by the hormonal fires of adolescence. As adults and as social scientists, we look at this time in the life of the young with considerable ambiguity. I would like to consider the "tomboy" as a last free space for girls before the rigors of adolescent socialization and the ambiguity of gendered sexuality, a permitted phallic time for women without much social retribution. Young women's athletics, always the refuge of the rebellious few and now somewhat more sanctioned, may well be one of those brief relatively free zones of body extension and pleasure where a female physical subjectivity can be potentiated. Before the clotted pleasures of adolescent romance and sexuality, with the unpredictable, objectifying male eye, sport for women is the body as use-value. It is ominous that the current fashion for an athletic body may erode this sensibility. It may be important that clinicians are now noting that a number of anorexics mask their self-starvation under an excessive preoccupation with exercise.

Nonetheless, with qualification, it may be possible to see young women's sports as a legitimation of competence, muscular effort, and body skill in a homosocial world. But however experienced inside one's skin, seen from outside, women's softball leagues, slow pitch games, basketball leagues, and track teams are often pale versions of the grim serious training regimen of male. The Babe Ruth League and junior hockey systems all promote a professionalized indentured apprentice experience for the young male. His body, even before professional status, *can* have exchange value. He is held and trained in a system of sports organized as a controlled escalator ride into adulthood: His uniform, moves, and style miniaturize the adult model. For women it is time out from the sex-appropriate adult model, but the exchange for that freedom is trivialization and marginality. You can stay a pale imitation of a boy for a while. But over time these mannerisms and styles take on, in the culture's terms, an odd pathological quality. The adult women playing a man's sport or fan to a man's teams appear silly or odd. What to make of the famous Dodger fan of the 1950s, "Hilda," howling in Ebbets Field? The tomboy has temporary license —like the people (primarily men) in Natalie Davis's account of cross-dressing and carnival in 16th-century Europe (Davis, 1975). The short-term permitted reversal informs and legitimates its opposite within the social order.

There is, I think, a hidden story of women playing baseball. The key feature of this story is marginality, a freaky androgyny. There is Joan Joyce, now a talented golf pro on the women's circuit, who was arguably the best woman softball pitcher ever. In an exhibition she struck out Ted Williams four times. The operative word here is exhibition. Her skill is displayed as sideshow, not legitimated as sports activity. The name of a team of touring women players in the 1930s: Slapsie Maxie's Curvaceous Cuties. In the Second World War, women's leagues toured the U.S. and Canada.

P. K. Wrigley's All American Girls' (sic) League played serious competent competitive baseball in the '40s. At the end of the war, like their sisters who had entered and worked competently in industry and the paid work force, they were remarginalized and disappeared from the public scene.

Obviously there are powerful and popular female athletes. There was Babe Didrikson who was, by modern standards, a stunning protean talent, an Olympian in three sports—discus, hurdles, javelin. There is a modern group of tennis star, track athletics, and most recently gymnasts with a mass following and star status. But this has not happened in baseball and indeed not in any mass audience popular team sports. Professional women's basketball leagues have foundered, women's volleyball is an amateur sport. It remains an interesting question why women team sports, women in groups, fail to inflame and enter the popular imagination.

Women own sports teams, but undergo curious transformation in so doing. Georgianne Frontiere owns a football team. She has been pictured in popular magazines, taking exercise practice with her team, lying on the field with her legs spread: an imputed relation to her team. The other famous woman owner was Joan Payson, who owned and reputedly loved the Mets. Her era coincided with the Mets' tenure of Casey Stengel. They appear in the theatre of baseball rather like Margaret Dumont and Groucho Marx, ludicrous comic figures. Payson's ownership became loveable, silly, an old woman's slightly embarrassing fancy.

There is a place for good girls in baseball. It has a literal as well as metaphoric position. The Waiting Room offers a space where decorous girls (wives, mostly) await the men after work. A baseball wife has just put out a magazine for other such wives. It is called, unironically, *The Waiting Room* and has glossy pictures of beautifully groomed women and features articles which ask gingerly how women in their 30s and 40s, coming into some possession of self and potential, deal with the player-spouse whose life work may be ending. And just recently, there has been an act of rebellion. Two baseball ex-wives record the psychic costs of marginality: infidelity, transience, loneliness, rage.

Woman, as in so much cultural space, cannot be fully subject in baseball. Siren or groupie, obedient wife, foolish fan or tomboy eunuch, woman as object in this world is marginalized, locked hopelessly in the oscillating categories of good and bad girl, an object of contempt or humor. So when I want to write, talk, think about baseball there is no "I" where I can feel comfortable. There is no "I" with the authority and right and easy style to enter the discourse, to produce and reproduce the social life of baseball. A critic? A female critique drawing the connections between ideology, superstructure, and mass culture? It sounds like somebody's mother telling the boys to stop playing and come in and be sensible. It's time to do your homework. Have your lunch. What's all this male phallic nonsense about bats and balls? Men have fled from this hectoring maternal voice whenever they have heard it. There is no way to speak with love, for that desire is transmuted into the desire to be loved or some strange pre-oedipal strategy to stay the little boy and so be with father.

As an absolute requisite of maintaining its image, its symbolic structure, and its ideological work, women are read out of baseball, excluded from its action, its images, and its discourse. It is an activity performed by men for other men to watch and speak about. Woman as speaking subject is excluded, both specifically from the practice of baseball and generally from authority in discourse. One is accustomed now to the appropriation of social space by men, which is legitimated variously. There might be violence, danger, war. There is a sanctity to male sexuality that brooks no female mixing in. But baseball is none of these things—neither overly violent, nor dangerous (except to pitchers' shoulders and catchers' thumbs) nor sexual. It is deeply inscribed as a piece of lengthy American social and cultural history. It is thus one aspect of a social and cultural apparatus that excludes women not merely from sport but from history and historical time.

References

Angell, R. (1972). *The Summer Game.* New York: Popular Library.

Angell, R. (1982). *Late Innings.* New York: Simon and Schuster.

Aronowitz, S. (1973). *False Promises.* New York: McGraw-Hill.

Bakhtin, M. (1981). *The Dialogic Imagination.* (Slavic Series No. 1.) Austin: University of Texas Press.

Brohm, J. M. (1978). *The Prisoner of Measured Time.* London: Ink Links.

Davis, N. Z. (1975). *Society and Culture in Early Modern France: Eight Essays.* Stanford, CA: Stanford University Press.

Giddens, A. (1979). *Central Problems in Social Theory.* Berkeley, CA: University of California Press.

Goodman, C. (1979). *Choosing Sides.* New York: Schocken.

James, C. L. R. (1984). *Beyond a Boundary.* New York: Pantheon.

James, W. (1984). *The Bill James Book of Baseball.* New York: Bantam.

Kinsella, W. P. (1982). *Shoeless Joe.* Boston: Houghton Mifflin.

Kristeva, J. (1980). *Desire in Language.* New York: Columbia University Press.

Rabinbach, A. (1982). The Body without fatigue: A nineteenth century utopia. In B. Dresher, D. Sabean, & A. Cherlin (eds.), *Political Symbolism in Modern Europe* (pp. 42–62). New Brunswick, NJ: Transaction Books Press.

Sorrentino, G. (1971). *Imaginative Qualities of Actual Things.* New York: Pantheon.

Response Statement Assignments

1. Do you think there is such a thing as women's language? Or men's language? In other words, are there characteristic ways we speak and write based on gender? If so, give some specific examples.

2. How might gender-specific language arise? Is it *inherently* gender-specific or culturally produced?

3. Consider Harris's argument in relation to: (a) another apparently male-dominated activity such as football. Think of the ritual associated with the Superbowl. Do women watching the game on TV share their male counterparts' knowledge, assumptions, potential identification with the players, or do they (as one of our students put it) "go out and make the

lasagna"? (b) an apparently female-dominated activity such as fashion, sewing, or child-rearing. To what extent are the particular language patterns of such activities gender-specific? Do you sense any historical developments in the sharing of these languages between men and women?

Anthology of Essays

MICHEL-GUILLAUME-JEAN DE CRÈVECOEUR (1735–1813)

What Is an American?

I wish I could be acquainted with the feelings and thoughts which must agitate the heart and present themselves to the mind of an enlightened Englishman, when he first lands on this continent. He must greatly rejoice that he lived at a time to see this fair country discovered and settled; he must necessarily feel a share of national pride, when he views the chain of settlements which embellishes these extended shores. When he says to himself, this is the work of my countrymen, who, when convulsed by factions, afflicted by a variety of miseries and wants, restless and impatient, took refuge here. They brought along with them their national genius, to which they principally owe what liberty they enjoy, and what substance they possess. Here he sees the industry of his native country displayed in a new manner, and traces in their works the embryos of all the arts, sciences, and ingenuity which flourish in Europe. Here he beholds fair cities, substantial villages, extensive fields, an immense country filled with decent houses, good roads, orchards, meadows, and bridges, where an hundred years ago all was wild, woody, and uncultivated! What a train of pleasing ideas this fair spectacle must suggest; it is a prospect which must inspire a good citizen with the most heartfelt pleasure. The difficulty consists in the manner of viewing so extensive a scene. He is arrived on a new continent; a modern society offers itself to his contemplation, different from what he had hitherto seen. It is not composed, as in Europe, of great lords who possess everything, and of a herd of people who have nothing. Here are no aristocratical families, no courts, no kings, no bishops, no ecclesiastical dominion, no invisible power giving to a few a very visible one; no great manufacturers employing thousands, no great refinements of luxury. The rich and the poor are not so far removed from each other as they are in Europe. Some few towns excepted, we are all tillers of the earth, from Nova Scotia to West Florida. We are a people of cultivators, scattered over an immense territory, communicating with each other by means of good roads and navigable rivers, united by the silken bands of mild government, all respecting the laws, without dreading their power, because they are equitable. We are all animated with the spirit of an industry which is unfettered and unrestrained, because each person works for himself. If he travels through our rural districts he views not the hostile castle, and the haughty mansion, contrasted with the clay-built hut and miserable cabin, where cattle and men help to keep each other warm, and dwell in meanness, smoke, and indigence. A pleasing uniformity of decent competence appears throughout our habitations. The meanest of our log-houses is a dry and comfortable habitation. Lawyer or merchant are the fairest titles our towns afford; that of a farmer is the only appellation of the rural inhabitants of our country. It must take some time ere he can reconcile himself to our dictionary, which is but short in words of dignity, and names of honour. There, on a Sunday, he sees a congregation of respectable farmers and their wives, all clad in neat homespun, well mounted, or riding in their own humble waggons. There is not among them an esquire, saving the unlettered magistrate. There he sees a parson as simple as his flock, a farmer who does not riot on the labour of others. We have no princes, for whom we toil, starve, and bleed: we are the most perfect society now existing in the world. Here man is free as he ought to be; nor is this pleasing equality so transitory as many others are. Many ages will not see the shores of our great lakes replenished with inland nations, nor the unknown bounds of North America entirely peopled. Who can tell how far it extends? Who can tell the millions of men whom it will feed and contain? for no European foot has as yet traveled half the extent of this mighty continent!

The next wish of this traveller will be to know whence came all these people? they are a mixture of English, Scotch, Irish, French, Dutch, Germans, and Swedes. From this promiscuous breed, that race now called Americans have arisen. The eastern provinces must indeed be excepted, as being the unmixed descendants of Englishmen. I have heard many wish that they had been more intermixed also: for my part, I am no wisher, and think it much better as it has happened. They exhibit a most conspicuous figure in this great and variegated picture; they too enter for a great share in the pleasing perspective displayed in these thirteen provinces. I know it is fashionable to reflect on them, but I respect them for what they have done; for the accuracy and wisdom with which they have settled their territory; for the decency of their manners; for their early love of letters; their ancient college, the first in this hemisphere; for their industry; which to me who am but a farmer, is the criterion of everything. There never was a people, situated as they are, who with so ungrateful a soil have done more in so short a time. Do you think that the monarchical ingredients which are more prevalent in other governments, have purged them from all foul stains? Their histories assert the contrary.

In this great American asylum, the poor of Europe have by some means met together, and in consequence of various causes; to what purpose should they ask one another what countrymen they are? Alas, two thirds of them had no country. Can a wretch who wanders about, who works and starves, whose life is a continual scene of sore affliction or pinching penury; can that man call England or any other kingdom his country? A country that had no bread for him, whose fields procured him no harvest, who met with nothing but the frowns of the rich, the severity of the laws, with jails and punishments; who owned not a single foot of the extensive surface of this planet? No! urged by a variety of motives, here they came. Every thing has tended to regenerate them; new laws, a new mode of living, a new social system; here they are become men: in Europe they were as so many useless plants, wanting vegetative mould, and refreshing showers; they withered, and were mowed down by want, hunger, and war; but now by the power of transplantation, like all other plants they have taken root and flourished! Formerly they were not numbered in any civil lists of their country, except in those of the poor; here they rank as citizens. By what invisible power has this surprising metamorphosis been performed? By that of the laws and that of their industry. The laws, the indulgent laws, protect them as they arrive, stamping on them the symbol of adoption; they receive ample rewards for their labours; these accumulated rewards procure them lands; those lands confer on them the title of freemen, and to that title every benefit is affixed which men can possibly require. This is the great operation daily performed by our laws. From whence proceed these laws? From our government. Whence the government? It is derived from the original genius and strong desire of the people ratified and confirmed by the crown. This is the great chain which links us all, this is the picture which every province exhibits, Nova Scotia excepted. There the crown has done all; either there were no people who had genius, or it was not much attended to: the consequence is, that the province is very thinly inhabited indeed; the power of the crown in conjunction with the musketos has prevented men from settling there. Yet some parts of it flourished once, and it contained a mild-harmless set of people. But for the fault of a few leaders, the whole were banished. The greatest political error the crown ever committed in America, was to cut off men from a country which wanted nothing but men!

What attachment can a poor European emigrant have for a country where he had nothing? The knowledge of the language, the love of a few kindred as poor as himself, were the only cords that tied him: his country is now that which gives him land, bread, protection, and consequence: *Ubi panis ibi patria,*[1] is the motto of all emigrants. What then is the American, this new man? He is either an European, or the descendant of an European, hence that strange mixture of blood, which you will find in no other country. I could point out to you a family whose grandfather was an Englishman, whose wife was Dutch, whose son married a French woman, and whose present four sons have now four wives of different nations. *He* is an American, who, leaving behind him all his ancient prejudices and manners, receives new ones from the new mode of life he has embraced, the new government he obeys, and the new rank he holds. He becomes an American by being received in the broad lap of our great *Alma Mater.* Here individuals of all nations are melted into a new race of men,

---

[1] Where there is bread, that is the homeland.

whose labours and posterity will one day cause great changes in the world. Americans are the western pilgrims, who are carrying along with them that great mass of arts, sciences, vigour, and industry which began long since in the east; they will finish the great circle. The Americans were once scattered all over Europe; here they are incorporated into one of the finest systems of population which has ever appeared, and which will hereafter become distinct by the power of the different climates they inhabit. The American ought therefore to love this country much better than that wherein either he or his forefathers were born. Here the rewards of his industry follow with equal steps the progress of his labour; his labour is founded on the basis of nature, *self-interest;* can it want a stronger allurement? Wives and children, who before in vain demanded of him a morsel of bread, now, fat and frolicsome, gladly help their father to clear those fields whence exuberant crops are to arise to feed and to clothe them all; without any part being claimed, either by a despotic prince, a rich abbot, or a mighty lord. Here religion demands little of him; a small voluntary salary to the minister, and gratitude to God; can he refuse these? The American is a new man, who acts upon new principles; he must therefore entertain new ideas, and form new opinions. From involuntary idleness, servile dependence, penury, and useless labour, he has passed to toils of a very different nature, rewarded by ample subsistence.—This is an American.

British America is divided into many provinces, forming a large association, scattered along a coast 1500 miles extent and about 200 wide. This society I would fain examine, at least such as it appears in the middle provinces; if it does not afford that variety of tinges and gradations which may be observed in Europe, we have colours peculiar to ourselves. For instance, it is natural to conceive that those who live near the sea, must be very different from those who live in the woods; the intermediate space will afford a separate and distinct class.

Men are like plants; the goodness and flavour of the fruit proceeds from the peculiar soil and exposition in which they grow. We are nothing but what we derive from the air we breathe, the climate we inhabit, the government we obey, the system of religion we profess, and the nature of our employment. Here you will find but few crimes; these have acquired as yet no root among us. I wish I was able to trace all my ideas; if my ignorance prevents me from describing them properly, I hope I shall be able to delineate a few of the outlines, which are all I propose.

Those who live near the sea, feed more on fish than on flesh, and often encounter that boisterous element. This renders them more bold and enterprising; this leads them to neglect the confined occupations of the land. They see and converse with a variety of people; their intercourse with mankind becomes extensive. The sea inspires them with a love of traffic, a desire of transporting produce from one place to another; and leads them to a variety of resources which supply the place of labour. Those who inhabit the middle settlements, by far the most numerous, must be very different; the simple cultivation of the earth purifies them, but the indulgences of the government, the soft remonstrances of religion, the rank of independent freeholders, must necessarily inspire them with sentiments, very little known in Europe among people of the same class. What do I say? Europe has no such class of men; the early knowledge they acquire, the early bargains they make, give them a great degree of sagacity. As freemen they will be litigious; pride and obstinacy are often the cause of law suits; the nature of our laws and governments may be another. As citizens it is easy to imagine, that they will carefully read the newspapers, enter into every political disquisition, freely blame or censure governors and others. As farmers they will be careful and anxious to get as much as they can, because what they get is their own. As northern men they will love the cheerful cup. As Christians, religion curbs them not in their opinions; the general indulgence leaves every one to think for themselves in spiritual matters; the laws inspect our actions, our thoughts are left to God. Industry, good living, selfishness, litigiousness, country politics, the pride of freemen, religious indifference, are their characteristics. If you recede still farther from the sea, you will come into more modern settlements; they exhibit the same strong lineaments, in a ruder appearance. Religion seems to have still less influence, and their manners are less improved.

Now we arrive near the great woods, near the last inhabited districts; there men seem to be placed still farther beyond the reach of government, which in some measure leaves them to themselves. How can it pervade every corner; as they were driven there by misfortunes, necessity of beginnings, desire of acquiring large tracts of land, idleness, frequent want of economy, ancient debts; the re-union of such peoples does not afford a very pleasing spectacle. When discord, want of unity and friendship; when either drunkenness or idleness prevail in such remote districts; contention, inactivity, and wretchedness must ensue. There are not the same remedies to these evils as in a long established community. The few magistrates they have, are in general little better than the rest; they are often in a perfect state of war; that of a man against man, sometimes decided by blows, sometimes by means of the law; that of man against every wild inhabitant of these venerable woods, of which they are come to dispossess them. There men appear to be no better than carnivorous animals of a superior rank, living on the flesh of wild animals when they can catch them, and when they are not able, they subsist on grain. He who would wish to see America in its proper light, and have a true idea of its feeble beginnings and barbarous rudiments, must visit our extended line of frontiers where the last settlers dwell, and where he may see the first labours of settlement, the mode of clearing the earth, in all their different appearances; where men are wholly left dependent on their native tempers, and on the spur of uncertain industry, which often fails when not sanctified by the efficacy of a few moral rules. There, remote from the power of example and check of shame, many families exhibit the most hideous parts of our society. They are a kind of forlorn hope, preceding by ten or twelve years the most respectable army of veterans which come after them. In that space, prosperity will polish some, vice and the law will drive off the rest, who uniting again with others like themselves will recede still farther; making room for more industrious people, who will finish their improvements, convert the loghouse into a convenient habitation, and rejoicing that the first heavy labours are finished, will change in a few years that hitherto barbarous country into a fine fertile, well regulated district. Such is our progress, such is the march of the Europeans toward the interior parts of this continent. In all societies there are off-casts; this impure part serves as our precursors or pioneers; my father himself was one of that class, but he came upon honest principles, and was therefore one of the few who held fast; by good conduct and temperance, he transmitted to me his fair inheritance, when not above one in fourteen of his contemporaries had the same good fortune.

Forty years ago this smiling country was thus inhabited; it is now purged, a general decency of manners prevails throughout, and such has been the fate of our best countries.

Exclusive of those general characteristics, each province has its own, founded on the government, climate, mode of husbandry, customs, and peculiarity of circumstances. Europeans submit insensibly to these great powers, and become, in the course of a few generations, not only Americans in general, but either Pennsylvanians, Virginians, or provincials under some other name. Whoever traverses the continent must easily observe those strong differences, which will grow more evident in time. The inhabitants of Canada, Massachusetts, the middle provinces, the southern ones will be as different as their climates; their only points of unity will be those of religion and language.

As I have endeavoured to show you how Europeans become Americans; it may not be disagreeable to show you likewise how the various Christian sects introduced, wear out, and how religious indifference becomes prevalent. When any considerable number of a particular sect happen to dwell contiguous to each other, they immediately erect a temple, and there worship the Divinity agreeably to their own peculiar ideas. Nobody disturbs them. If any new sect springs up in Europe it may happen that many of its professors will come and settle in America. As they bring their zeal with them, they are at liberty to make proselytes if they can, and to build a meeting and to follow the dictates of their consciences; for neither the government nor any other power interferes. If they are peaceable subjects, and are industrious, what is it to their neighbours how and in what manner they think fit to address their prayers to the Supreme Being? But if the sectaries are not settled close together, if they are mixed with other denominations, their zeal will cool for want of fuel, and will be extinguished in a little time. Then the Americans become as to religion, what they are as to country, allied to all. In them the name of Englishman, Frenchman, and European is lost, and in like manner, the strict modes of Christianity as practised in Europe are lost also. This effect will extend itself still farther hereafter, and though this may appear to you as a strange idea, yet it is a very true one. I shall be able perhaps hereafter to explain myself better; in the meanwhile, let the following example serve as my first justification.

Let us suppose you and I to be travelling; we observe that in this house, to the right, lives a Catholic, who prays to God as he has been taught, and believes in transubstantiation; he works and raises wheat, he has a large family of children, all hale and robust; his belief, his prayers offend nobody. About one mile farther on the same road, his next neighbour may be a good honest plodding German Lutheran, who addresses himself to the same God, the God of all, agreeably to the modes he has been educated in, and believes in consubstantiation; by so doing he scandalises nobody; he also works in his fields, embellishes the earth, clears swamps, etc. What has the world to do with his Lutheran principles? He persecutes nobody, and nobody persecutes him, he visits his neighbours, and his neighbours visit him. Next to him lives a seceder, the most enthusiastic of all sectaries; his zeal is hot and fiery, but separated as he is from others of the same complexion, he has no congregation of his own to resort to, where he might cabal and mingle religious pride with worldly obstinacy. He likewise raises good crops, his house is handsomely painted, his orchard is one of the fairest in the neighbourhood. How does it concern the welfare of the country, or of the province at large, what this man's religious sentiments are, or really whether he has any at all? He is a good farmer, he is a sober, peaceable, good citizen: William Penn himself would not wish for more. This is the visible character, the invisible one is only guessed at, and is nobody's business. Next again lives a Low Dutchman, who implicitly believes the rules laid down by the synod of Dort. He conceives no other idea of a clergyman than that of an hired man; if he does his work well he will pay him the stipulated sum; if not he will dismiss him, and do without his sermons, and let his church be shut up for years. But notwithstanding this coarse idea, you will find his house and farm to be the neatest in all the country; and you will judge by his waggon and fat horses, that he thinks more of the affairs of this world than of those of the next. He is sober and laborious, therefore he is all he ought to be as to the affairs of this life; as for those of the next, he must trust to the great Creator. Each of these people instruct their children as well as they can, but these instructions are feeble compared to those which are given to the youth of the poorest class in Europe. Their children will therefore grow up less zealous and more indifferent in matters of religion than their parents. The foolish vanity, or rather the fury of making Proselytes, is unknown here; they have no time, the seasons call for all their attention, and thus in a few years, this mixed neighbourhood will exhibit a strange religious medley, that will be neither pure Catholicism nor pure Calvinism. A very perceptible indifference even in the first generation, will become apparent; and it may happen that the daughter of the Catholic will marry the son of the seceder, and settle by themselves at a distance from their parents. What religious education will they give their children? A very imperfect one. If there happens to be in the neighbourhood any place of worship, we will suppose a Quaker's meeting; rather than not show their fine clothes, they will go to it, and some of them may perhaps attach themselves to that society. Others will remain in a perfect state of indifference; the children of these zealous parents will not be able to tell what their religious principles are, and their grandchildren still less. The neighbourhood of a place of worship generally leads them to it, and the action of going thither, is the strongest evidence they can give of their attachment to any sect. The Quakers are the only people who retain a fondness for their own mode of worship; for be they ever so far separated from each other, they hold a sort of communion with the society, and seldom depart from its rules, at least in this country. Thus all sects are mixed as well as all nations; thus religious indifference is imperceptibly disseminated from one end of the continent to the other; which is at present one of the strongest characteristics of the Americans. Where this will reach no one can tell, perhaps it may leave a vacuum fit to receive other systems. Persecution, religious pride, the love of contradiction, are the food of what the world commonly calls religion. These motives have ceased here; zeal in Europe is confined; here it evaporates in the great distance it has to travel; there it is a grain of powder inclosed, here it burns away in the open air, and consumes without effect.

But to return to our back-settlers. I must tell you, that there is something in the proximity of the woods, which is very singular. It is with men as it is with the plants and animals that grow and live in the forests; they are entirely different from those that live in the plains. I will candidly tell you all my thoughts but you are not to expect that I shall advance any reasons. By living in or near the woods, their actions are regulated by the wildness of the neighbourhood. The deer often come to eat their grain, the wolves to destroy their sheep, the bears to kill their hogs, the foxes to catch their poultry. This surrounding hostility immediately puts the gun into their hands; they watch these animals, they kill some; and thus by defending their property, they soon become professed hunters; this is the progress; once hunters, farewell to the plough. The chase renders them ferocious, gloomy, and unsociable; a hunter wants no neighbour, he rather hates them, because he dreads the competition. In a little time their success in the woods makes them neglect their tillage. They trust to the natural fecundity of the earth, and therefore do little; carelessness in fencing often exposes what little they sow to destruction; they are not at home to watch; in order therefore to make up the deficiency, they go oftener to the woods. That new mode of life brings along with it a new set of manners, which I cannot easily describe. These new manners being grafted on the old stock, produce a strange sort of lawless profligacy, the impressions of which are indelible. The manners of the Indian natives are respectable, compared with this European medley. Their wives and children live in sloth and inactivity; and having no proper pursuits, you may judge what education the latter receive. Their tender minds have nothing else to contemplate but the example of their parents; like them they grow up a mongrel breed, half civilised, half savage, except nature stamps on them some constitutional propensities. That rich, that voluptuous sentiment is gone that struck them so forcibly; the possession of their freeholds no longer conveys to their minds the same pleasure and pride. To all these reasons you must add, their lonely situation, and you cannot imagine what an effect on manners the great distances they live from each other has! Consider one of the last settlements in its first view: of what is it composed? Europeans who have not that sufficient share of knowledge they ought to have, in order to prosper; people who have suddenly passed from oppression, dread of government, and fear of laws, into the unlimited freedom of the woods. This sudden change must have a very great effect on most men, and on that class particularly. Eating of wild meat, whatever you may think, tends to alter their temper: though all the proof I can adduce, is, that I have seen it: and having no place of worship to resort to, what little society this might afford is denied them. The Sunday meetings, exclusive of religious benefits, were the only social bonds that might have inspired them with some degree of emulation in neatness. Is it then surprising to see men thus situated, immersed in great and heavy labours, degenerate a little? It is rather a wonder the effect is not more diffusive. The Moravians and the Quakers are the only instances in exception to what I have advanced. The first never settle singly, it is a colony of the society which emigrates; they carry with them their forms, worship, rules, and decency: the others never begin so hard, they are always able to buy improvements, in which there is a great advantage, for by that time the country is recovered from its first barbarity. Thus our bad people are those who are half cultivators and half hunters; and the worst of them are those who have degenerated altogether into the hunting state. As old ploughmen and new men of the woods, as Europeans and new made Indians, they contract the vices of both; they adopt the moroseness and ferocity of a native, without his mildness, or even his industry at home. If manners are not refined, at least they are rendered simple and inoffensive by tilling the earth; all our wants are supplied by it, our time is divided between labour and rest, and leaves none for the commission of great misdeeds. As hunters it is divided between the toil of the chase, the idleness of repose, or the indulgence of inebriation. Hunting is but a licentious idle life, and if it does not always pervert good dispositions; yet, when it is united with bad luck, it leads to want: want stimulates that propensity to rapacity and injustice, too natural to needy men, which is the fatal gradation. After this explanation of the effects which follow by living in the woods, shall we yet vainly flatter ourselves with the hope of converting the Indians? We should rather begin with converting our back-settlers; and now if I dare mention the name of religion, its sweet accents would be lost in the immensity of these woods. Men thus placed are not fit either to receive or remember its mild instructions; they want temples and ministers, but as soon as men cease to remain at home, and begin to lead an erratic life, let them be either tawny or white, they cease to be its disciples.

Thus have I faintly and imperfectly endeavoured to trace our society from the sea to our woods! yet you must not imagine that every person who moves back, acts upon the same principles, or falls into the same degeneracy. Many families carry with them all their decency of conduct, purity of morals, and respect of religion; but these are scarce, the power of example is sometimes irresistible. Even among these back-settlers, their depravity is greater or less, according to what nation or province they belong. Were I to adduce proofs of this, I might be accused of partiality. If there happens to be some rich intervals, some fertile bottoms, in those remote districts, the people will there prefer tilling the land to hunting, and will attach themselves to it; but even on these fertile spots you may plainly perceive the inhabitants to acquire a great degree of rusticity and selfishness.

It is in consequence of this straggling situation, and the astonishing power it has on manners, that the back-settlers of both the Carolinas, Virginia, and many other parts, have been long a set of lawless people; it has been even dangerous to travel among them. Government can do nothing in so extensive a country, better it should wink at these irregularities, than that it should use means inconsistent with its usual mildness. Time will efface those stains: in proportion as the great body of population approaches them they will reform, and become polished and subordinate. Whatever has been said of the four New England provinces, no such degeneracy of manners has ever tarnished their annals; their back-settlers have been kept within the bounds of decency, and government, by means of wise laws, and by the influence of religion. What a detestable idea such people must have given to the natives of the Europeans! They trade with them, the worst of people are permitted to do that which none but persons of the best characters should be employed in. They get drunk with them, and often defraud the Indians. Their avarice, removed from the eyes of their superiors, knows no bounds; and aided by the little superiority of knowledge, these traders deceive them, and even sometimes shed blood. Hence those shocking violations, those sudden devastations which have so often stained our frontiers, when hundreds of innocent people have been sacrificed for the crimes of a few. It was in consequence of such behaviour, that the Indians took the hatchet against the Virginians in 1774. Thus are our first steps trod, thus are our first trees felled, in general, by the most vicious of our people; and thus the path is opened for the arrival of a second and better class, the true American freeholders; the most respectable set of people in this part of the world; respectable for their industry, their happy independence, the great share of freedom they possess, the good regulation of their families, and for extending the trade and the dominion of our mother country.

Europe contains hardly any other distinctions but lords and tenants; this fair country alone is settled by freeholders, the possessors of the soil they cultivate, members of the government they obey, and the framers of their own laws, by means of their representatives. This is a thought which you have taught me to cherish; our difference from Europe, far from diminishing, rather adds to our usefulness and consequence as men and subjects. Had our forefathers remained there, they would only have crowded it, and perhaps prolonged those convulsions which had shook it so long. Every industrious European who transports himself here, may be compared to a sprout growing at the foot of a great tree; it enjoys and draws but a little portion of sap; wrench it from the parent roots, transplant it, and it will become a tree bearing fruit also. Colonists are therefore entitled to the consideration due to the most useful subjects; a hundred families barely existing in some parts of Scotland, will here in six years, cause an annual exportation of 10,000 bushels of wheat: 100 bushels being but a common quantity for an industrious family to sell, if they cultivate good land. It is here then that the idle may be employed, the useless become useful, and the poor become rich; but by riches I do not mean gold and silver, we have but little of those metals; I mean a better sort of wealth, cleared lands, cattle, good houses, good clothes, and an increase of people to enjoy them.

There is no wonder that this country has so many charms, and presents to Europeans so may temptations to remain in it. A traveller in Europe becomes a stranger as soon as he quits his own kingdom; but it is otherwise here. We know, properly speaking, no strangers; this is every person's country; the variety of our soils, situations, climates, governments, and produce, hath something which must please everybody. No sooner does an European arrive, no matter of what condition, than his eyes are opened upon the fair prospect; he hears his language spoke, he retraces many of his own country manners, he perpetually hears the names of families and towns with which he is acquainted; he sees happiness and prosperity in all places disseminated; he meets with hospitality, kindness, and plenty everywhere; he beholds hardly any poor, he seldom hears of punishments and executions; and he wonders at the elegance of our towns, those miracles of industry and freedom. He cannot admire enough our rural districts, our convenient roads, good taverns, and our many accommodations; he involuntarily loves a country where everything is so lovely. When in England, he was a mere Englishman; here he stands on a larger portion of the globe, not less than its fourth part, and may see the productions of the north, in iron and naval stores; the provisions of Ireland, the grain of Egypt, the indigo, the rice of China. He does not find, as in Europe, a crowded society, where every place is overstocked; he does not feel that perpetual collision of parties, that difficulty of beginning, that contention which oversets so many. There is room for everybody in America; has he any particular talent, or industry? he exerts it in order to procure a livelihood, and it succeeds. Is he a merchant? the avenues of trade are infinite; is he eminent in any respect? he will be employed and respected. Does he love a country life? pleasant farms present themselves; he may purchase what he wants, and thereby become an American farmer. Is he a labourer, sober and industrious? he need not go many miles, nor receive many informations before he will be hired, well fed at the table of his employer, and paid four or five times more than he can get in Europe. Does he want uncultivated lands? thousands of acres present themselves, which he may purchase cheap. Whatever be his talents or inclinations, if they are moderate, he may satisfy them. I do not mean that every one who comes will grow rich in a little time; no, but he may procure an easy, decent maintenance, by his industry. Instead of starving he will be fed, instead of being idle he will have employment; and these are riches enough for such men as come over here. The rich stay in Europe, it is only the middling and the poor that emigrate. Would you wish to travel in independent idleness, from north to south, you will find easy access, and the most cheerful reception at every house; society without ostentation, good cheer without pride, and every decent diversion which the country affords, with little expense. It is no wonder that the European who has lived here a few years, is desirous to remain; Europe with all its pomp, is not to be compared to this continent, for men of middle stations, or labourers.

An European, when he first arrives, seems limited in his intentions, as well as in his views; but he very suddenly alters his scale; two hundred miles formerly appeared a very great distance, it is now but a trifle; he no sooner breathes our air than he forms schemes, and embarks in designs he never would have thought of in his own country. There the plentitude of society confines many useful ideas, and often extinguishes the most laudable schemes which here ripen into maturity. Thus Europeans become Americans.

But how is this accomplished in that crowd of low, indigent people, who flock here every year from all parts of Europe? I will tell you; they no sooner arrive than they immediately feel the good effects of that plenty of provisions we possess: they fare on our best food, and they are kindly entertained; their talents, character, and peculiar industry are immediately inquired into; they find countrymen everywhere disseminated, let them come from whatever part of Europe. Let me select one as an epitome of the rest; he is hired, he goes to work, and works moderately; instead of being employed by a haughty person, he finds himself with his equal, placed at the substantial table of the farmer, or else at an inferior one as good; his wages are high, his bed is not like that bed of sorrow on which he used to lie: if he behaves with propriety, and is faithful, he is caressed, and becomes as it were a member of the family. He begins to feel the effects of a sort of resurrection; hitherto he had not lived, but simply vegetated; he now feels himself a man, because he is treated as such; the laws of his own country had overlooked him in his insignificancy; the laws of this cover him with their mantle. Judge what an alteration there must arise in the mind and thoughts of this man; he begins to forget his former servitude and dependence, his heart involuntarily swells and glows; this first swell inspires him with those new thoughts which constitute an American. What love can he entertain for a country where his existence was a burthen to him; if he is a generous good man, the love of this new adoptive parent will sink deep into his heart. He looks around, and sees many a prosperous person, who but a few years before was as poor as himself. This encourages him much, he begins to form some little scheme, the first, alas, he ever formed in his life. If he is wise he thus spends two or three years, in which time he acquires knowledge, the use of tools, the modes of working the lands, felling trees, etc. This prepares the foundation of a good name, the most useful acquisition he can make. He is encouraged, he has gained friends; he is advised and directed, he feels bold, he purchases some land; he gives all the money he has brought over, as well as what he has earned, and trusts to the God of harvests for the discharge of the rest. His good name procures him credit. He is now possessed of the deed, conveying to him and his posterity the fee simple and absolute property of two hundred acres of land, situated on such a river. What an epocha in this man's life! He is become a freeholder, from perhaps a German boor—he is now an American, a Pennsylvanian, an English subject. He is naturalised, his name is enrolled with those of the other citizens of the province. Instead of being a vagrant, he has a place of residence; he is called the inhabitant of such a county, or of such a district, and for the first time in his life counts for something; for hitherto he has been a cypher. I only repeat what I have heard many say, and no wonder their hearts should glow, and be agitated with a multitude of feelings, not easy to describe. From nothing to start into being; from a servant to the rank of a master; from being the slave of some despotic prince, to become a free man, invested with lands, to which every municipal blessing is annexed! What a change indeed! It is in consequence of that change that he becomes an American. This great metamorphosis has a double effect, it extinguishes all his European prejudices, he forgets that mechanism of subordination, that servility of disposition which poverty had taught him; and sometimes he is apt to forget too much, often passing from one extreme to the other. If he is a good man, he forms schemes of future prosperity, he proposes to educate his children better than he has been educated himself; he thinks of future modes of conduct, feels an ardour to labour he never felt before. Pride steps in and leads him to everything that the laws do not forbid: he respects them; with a heart-felt gratitude he looks toward the east, toward that insular government from whose wisdom all his new felicity is derived, and under whose wings and protection he now lives. These reflections constitute him the good man and the good subject. Ye poor Europeans, ye who sweat, and work for the great—ye, who are obliged to give so many sheaves to the church, so many to your lords, so many to your government, and have hardly any left for yourselves—ye, who are held in less estimation than favourite hunters or useless lap-dogs—ye, who only breathe the air of nature, because it cannot be withheld from you; it is here that ye can conceive the possibility of those feelings I have been describing; it is here the laws of naturalisation invite every one to partake of our great labours and felicity, to till unrented, untaxed lands! Many, corrupted beyond the power of amendment, have brought with them all their vices, and disregarding the advantages held to them, have gone on in their former career of iniquity, until they have been overtaken and punished by our laws. It is not every emigrant who succeeds; no, it is only the sober, the honest, and industrious: happy those to whom this transition has served as a powerful spur to labour, to prosperity, and to the good establishment of children, born in the days of their poverty; and who had no other portion to expect but the rags of their parents, had it not been for their happy emigration. Others again, have been led astray by this enhancing scene; their new pride, instead of leading them to the fields, has kept them in idleness; the idea of possessing lands is all that satisfies them—though surrounded with fertility, they have mouldered away their time in inactivity, misinformed husbandry, and ineffectual endeavours. How much wiser, in general, the honest Germans than almost all other Europeans; they hire themselves to some of their wealthy landsmen, and in that apprenticeship learn everything that is necessary. They attentively consider the prosperous industry of others, which imprints in their minds a strong desire of possessing the same advantages. This forcible idea never quits them, they launch forth, and by dint of sobriety, rigid parsimony, and the most persevering industry, they commonly succeed. Their astonishment at their first arrival from Germany is very great—it is to them a dream; the contrast must be powerful indeed; they observe their countrymen flourishing in every place; they travel through whole counties where not a word of English is spoken; and in the names and the language of the people, they retrace Germany. They have been an useful acquisition to this continent, and to Pennsylvania in particular; to them it owes some share of its prosperity: to their mechanical knowledge and patience it owes the finest mills in all America, the best teams of horses, and many other advantages. The recollection of their former poverty and slavery never quits them as long as they live.

The Scotch and the Irish might have lived in their own country perhaps as poor, but enjoying more civil advantages, the effects of their new situation do not strike them so forcibly, nor has it so lasting an effect. From whence the difference arises I know not, but out of twelve families of emigrants of each country, generally seven Scotch will succeed, nine German, and four Irish. The Scotch are frugal and laborious, but their wives cannot work so hard as German women, who on the contrary vie with their husbands, and often share with them the most severe toils of the field, which they understand better. They have therefore nothing to struggle against, but the common casualties of nature. The Irish do not prosper so well; they love to drink and to quarrel; they are litigious, and soon take to the gun, which is the ruin of everything; they seem beside to labour under a greater degree of ignorance in husbandry than the others; perhaps it is that their industry had less scope, and was less exercised at home. I have heard many relate, how the land was parcelled out in that kingdom; their ancient conquest has been a great detriment to them, by over-setting their landed property. The lands possessed by a few, are leased down *ad infinitum,* and the occupiers often pay five guineas an acre. The poor are worse lodged there than anywhere else in Europe; their potatoes, which are easily raised, are perhaps an inducement to laziness; their wages are too low, and their whisky too cheap.

There is no tracing observations of this kind, without making at the same time very great allowances, as there are everywhere to be found, a great many exceptions. The Irish themselves, from different parts of that kingdom, are very different. It is difficult to account for this surprising locality, one would think on so small an island an Irishman must be an Irishman; yet it is not so, they are different in their aptitude to, and in their love of labour.

The Scotch on the contrary are all industrious and saving; they want nothing more than a field to exert themselves in, and they are commonly sure of succeeding. The only difficulty they labour under is, that technical American knowledge which requires some time to obtain; it is not easy for those who seldom saw a tree, to conceive how it is to be felled, cut up, and split into rails and posts.

As I am fond of seeing and talking of prosperous families, I intend to finish this letter by relating to you the history of an honest Scotch Hebridean, who came here in 1774, which will show you in epitome what the Scotch can do, wherever they have room for the exertion of their industry. Whenever I hear of any new settlement, I pay it a visit once or twice a year, on purpose to observe the different steps each settler takes, the gradual improvements, the different tempers of each family, on which their prosperity in a great nature depends; their different modifications of industry, their ingenuity, and contrivance; for being all poor, their life requires sagacity and prudence. In the evening I love to hear them tell their stories, they furnish me with new ideas; I sit still and listen to their ancient misfortunes, observing in many of them a strong degree of gratitude to God, and the government. Many a well meant sermon have I preached to some of them. When I found laziness and inattention to prevail, who could refrain from wishing well to these new countrymen, after having undergone so many fatigues. Who could withhold good advice? What a happy change it must be, to descend from the high, sterile, bleak lands of Scotland, where everything is barren and cold, to rest on some fertile farms in these middle provinces! Such a transition must have afforded the most pleasing satisfaction.

The following dialogue passed at an out-settlement, where I lately paid a visit:

Well, friend, how do you do now; I am come fifty odd miles on purpose to see you; how do you go on with your new cutting and slashing? Very well, good Sir, we learn the use of the axe bravely, we shall make it out; we have a belly full of victuals every day, our cows run about, and come home full of milk, our hogs get fat of themselves in the woods: Oh, this is a good country! God bless the king and William Penn; we shall do very well by and by, if we keep our healths. Your loghouse looks neat and light, where did you get these shingles? One of our neighbors is a New-England man, and he showed us how to split them out of chestnut-trees. Now for a barn, but all in good time, here are fine trees to build with. Who is to frame it, sure you don't understand that work yet? A countryman of ours who has been in America these ten years, offers to wait for his money until the second crop is lodged in it. What did you give for your land? Thirty-five shillings per acre, payable in seven years. How many acres have you got? An hundred and fifty. That is enough to begin with; is not your land pretty hard to clear? Yes, Sir, hard enough, but it would be harder still if it were ready cleared, for then we should have no timber, and I love the woods much; the land is nothing without them. Have not you found out any bees yet? No, Sir; and if we had we should not know what to do with them. I will tell you by and by. You are very kind. Farewell, honest man, God prosper you; whenever you travel toward —— —, inquire for J.S. He will entertain you kindly, provided you bring him good tidings from your family and farm. In this manner I often visit them, and carefully examine their houses, their modes of ingenuity, their different ways; and make them all relate all they know, and describe all they feel. These are scenes which I believe you would willingly share with me. I well remember your philanthropic turn of mind. Is it not better to contemplate under these humble roofs, the rudiments of future wealth and population, than to behold the accumulated bundles of litigious papers in the office of a lawyer? To examine how the world is gradually settled, how the howling swamp is converted into a pleasing meadow, the rough ridge into a fine field; and to hear the cheerful whistling, the rural song, where there was no sound heard before, save the yell of the savage, the screech of the owl or the hissing of the snake? Here an European, fatigued with luxury, riches, and pleasures, may find a sweet relaxation in a series of interesting scenes, as affecting as they are new. England, which now contains so many domes, so many castles, was once like this; a place woody and marshy; its inhabitants, now the favourite nation for arts and commerce, were once painted like our neighbours. The country will flourish in its turn, and the same observations will be made which I have just delineated. Posterity will look back with avidity and pleasure, to trace, if possible, the era of this or that particular settlement.

Pray, what is the reason that the Scots are in general more religious, more faithful, more honest, and industrious than the Irish? I do not mean to insinuate national reflections, God forbid! It ill becomes any man, and much less an American; but as I know men are nothing of themselves, and that they owe all their different modifications either to government or other local circumstances, there must be some powerful causes which constitute this great national difference.

Agreeable to the account which several Scotchmen have given me of the north of Britain, of the Orkneys, and the Hebride Islands, they seem, on many accounts, to be unfit for the habitation of men; they appear to be calculated only for great sheep pastures. Who then can blame the inhabitants of these countries for transporting themselves hither? This great continent must in time absorb the poorest part of Europe; and this will happen in proportion as it becomes better known; and as war, taxation, oppression, and misery increase there. The Hebrides appear to be fit only for the residence of malefactors, and it would be much better to send felons there than either to Virginia or Maryland. What a strange compliment has our mother country paid to two of the finest provinces in America! England has entertained in that respect very mistaken ideas; what was intended as a punishment, is become the good fortune of several; many of those who have been transported as felons, are now rich, and strangers to the stings of those wants that urged them to violations of the law: they are become industrious, exemplary, and useful citizens. The English government should purchase the most northern and barren of those islands; it should send over to us the honest, primitive Hebrideans, settle them here on good lands, as a reward for their virtue and ancient poverty; and replace them with a colony of her wicked sons. The severity of the climate, the inclemency of the seasons, the sterility of the soil, the tempestuousness of the sea, would afflict and punish enough. Could there be found a spot better adapted to retaliate the injury it had received by their crimes? Some of those islands might be considered as the hell of Great Britain, where all evil spirits should be sent. Two essential ends would be answered by this simple operation. The good people, by emigration, would be rendered happier; the bad ones would be placed where they ought to be. In a few years the dread of being sent to that wintry region would have a much stronger effect than that of transportation. —This is no place of punishment; were I a poor hopeless, breadless Englishman, and not restrained by the power of shame, I should be very thankful for the passage. It is of very little importance how, and in what manner an indigent man arrives; for if he is but sober, honest, and industrious, he has nothing more to ask of heaven. Let him go to work, he will have opportunities enough to earn a comfortable support, and even the means of procuring some land; which ought to be the utmost wish of every person who has health and hands to work. I knew a man who came to this country, in the literal sense of the expression, stark naked; I think he was a Frenchman, and a sailor on board an English man-of-war. Being discontented, he had stripped himself and swam ashore; where, finding clothes and friends, he settled afterwards at Maraneck, in the county of Chester, in the province of New York: he married and left a good farm to each of his sons. I knew another person who was but twelve years old when he was taken on the frontiers of Canada, by the Indians; at his arrival at Albany he was purchased by a gentleman, who generously bound him apprentice to a tailor. He lived to the age of ninety, and left behind him a fine estate and a numerous family, all well settled; many of them I am acquainted with.—Where is then the industrious European who ought to despair?

After a foreigner from any part of Europe is arrived, and become a citizen; let him devoutly listen to the voice of our great parent, which says to him, "Welcome to my shores, distressed European; bless the hour in which thou didst see my verdant fields, my fair navigable rivers, and my green mountains!—If thou wilt work, I have bread for thee; if thou wilt be honest, sober, and industrious, I have greater rewards to confer on thee—ease and independence. I will give thee fields to feed and clothe thee; a comfortable fireside to sit by, and tell thy children by what means thou hast prospered; and a decent bed to repose on. I shall endow thee beside with the immunities of a freeman. If thou wilt carefully educate thy children, teach them gratitude to God and reverence to that government, that philanthropic government, which has collected here so many men and made them happy. I will also provide for thy progeny; and to every good man this ought to be the most holy, the most powerful, the most earnest wish he can possibly form, as well as the most consolatory prospect when he dies. Go thou and work and till; thou shalt prosper, provided thou be just, grateful, and industrious."

SIGMUND FREUD (1856–1939)

The Dream as Wish-Fulfilment

When, after passing through a narrow defile, one suddenly reaches a height beyond which the ways part and a rich prospect lies outspread in different directions, it is well to stop for a moment and consider whither one shall turn next. We are in somewhat the same position after we have mastered this first interpretation of a dream. We find ourselves standing in the light of a sudden discovery. The dream is not comparable to the irregular sounds of a musical instrument, which, instead of being played by the hand of a musician, is struck by some external force; the dream is not meaningless, not absurd, does not presuppose that one part of our store of ideas is dormant while another part begins to awake. It is a perfectly valid psychic phenomenon, actually a wish-fulfilment; it may be enrolled in the continuity of the intelligible psychic activities of the waking state; it is built up by a highly complicated intellectual activity. But at the very moment when we are about to rejoice in this discovery a host of problems besets us. If the dream, as this theory defines it, represents a fulfilled wish, what is the cause of the striking and unfamiliar manner in which this fulfilment is expressed? What transformation has occurred in our dream-thoughts before the manifest dream, as we remember it on waking, shapes itself out of them? How has this transformation taken place? Whence comes the material that is worked up into the dream? What causes many of the peculiarities which are to be observed in our dream-thoughts; for example, how is it that they are able to contradict one another? . . . Is the dream capable of teaching us something new concerning our internal psychic processes, and can its content correct opinions which we have held during the day? I suggest that for the present all these problems be laid aside, and that a single path be pursued. We have found that the dream represents a wish as fulfilled. Our next purpose should be to ascertain whether this is a general characteristic of dreams, or whether it is only the accidental content of the particular dream ("the dream about Irma's injection") with which we have begun our analysis; for even if we conclude that every dream has a meaning and psychic value, we must nevertheless allow for the possibility that this meaning may not be the same in every dream. The first dream which we have considered was the fulfilment of a wish; another may turn out to be the realization of an apprehension; a third may have a reflection as its content; a fourth may simply reproduce a reminiscence. Are there, then, dreams other than wish-dreams; or are there none but wish-dreams?

It is easy to show that the wish-fulfilment in dreams is often undisguised and easy to recognize, so that one may wonder why the language of dreams has not long since been understood. There is, for example, a dream which I can evoke as often as I please, experimentally, as it were. If, in the evening, I eat anchovies, olives, or other strongly salted foods, I am thirsty at night, and therefore I wake. The waking, however, is preceded by a dream, which has always the same content, namely, that I am drinking. I am drinking long draughts of water; it tastes as delicious as only a cool drink can taste when one's throat is parched; and then I wake, and find that I have an actual desire to drink. The cause of this dream is thirst, which I perceive when I wake. From this sensation arises the wish to drink, and the dream shows me this wish as fulfilled. It thereby serves a function, the nature of which I soon surmise. I sleep well, and am not accustomed to being waked by a bodily need. If I succeed in appeasing my thirst by means of the dream that I am drinking, I need not wake up in order to satisfy that thirst. It is thus a *dream of convenience*. The dream takes the place of action, as elsewhere in life. Unfortunately, the need of water to quench the thirst cannot be satisfied by a dream, as can my thirst for revenge upon Otto and Dr. M., but the intention is the same. Not long ago I had the same dream in a somewhat modified form. On this occasion I felt thirsty before going to bed, and emptied the glass of water which stood on the little chest beside my bed. Some hours later, during the night, my thirst returned, with the consequent discomfort. In order to obtain water, I should have had to get up and fetch the glass which stood on my wife's bed-table. I thus quite appropriately dreamt that my wife was giving me a drink from a vase; this vase was an Etruscan cinerary urn, which I had brought home from Italy, and had since given away. But the water in it tasted so salt (apparently on account of the ashes) that I was forced to wake. It may be observed how conveniently the dream is capable of arranging matters. Since the fulfilment of a wish is its only purpose, it may be perfectly egoistic. Love of comfort is really not compatible with considera-tion for others. The introduction of the cinerary urn is probably once again the ful-filment of a wish; I regret that I no longer possess this vase; it, like the glass of water at my wife's side, is inaccessible to me. The cinerary urn is appropriate also in con-nection with the sensation of an increasingly salty taste, which I know will compel me to wake.[1]

Such convenience-dreams came very frequently to me in my youth. Accustomed as I had always been to working until late at night, early waking was always a matter of difficulty. I used then to dream that I was out of bed and standing at the wash-stand. After a while I could no longer shut out the knowledge that I was not yet up; but in the meantime I had continued to sleep. The same sort of lethargy-dream was dreamed by a young colleague of mine, who appears to share my propensity for sleep. With him it assumed a particularly amusing form. The landlady with whom he was lodging in the neighbourhood of the hospital had strict orders to wake him every morning at a given hour, but she found it by no means easy to carry out his

---

[1] The facts relating to dreams of thirst were known also to Weygandt, who speaks of them as follows: "It is just this sensation of thirst which is registered most accurately of all; it always causes a representation of quenching the thirst. The manner in which the dream represents the act of quenching the thirst is manifold, and is specified in accordance with some recent recollection. A universal phenomenon noticeable here is the fact that the representation of quenching the thirst is immediately followed by disappointment in the inefficacy of the imag-ined refreshment." But he overlooks the universal character of the reaction of the dream to the stimulus. If other persons who are troubled by thirst at night awake without dreaming beforehand, this does not constitute an objection to my experiment, but characterizes them as persons who sleep less soundly. Cf. here *Isaiah xxix.* 8: "It shall even be as when an hungry man dreameth, and, behold, he eateth; but he awaketh, and his soul is empty: or as when a thirsty man dreameth, and, behold he drinketh; but he awaketh, and, behold, he is faint. . . ."

orders. One morning sleep was especially sweet to him. The woman called into his room: "Herr Pepi, get up; you've got to go to the hospital." Whereupon the sleeper dreamt of a room in the hospital, of a bed in which he was lying, and of a chart pinned over his head, which read as follows: "Pepi M., medical student, 22 years of age." He told himself in the dream: "If I am already at the hospital, I don't have to go there," turned over, and slept on. He had thus frankly admitted to himself his motive for dreaming.

Here is yet another dream of which the stimulus was active during sleep: One of my women patients, who had been obliged to undergo an unsuccessful operation on the jaw, was instructed by her physicians to wear by day and night a cooling apparatus on the affected cheek; but she was in the habit of throwing it off as soon as she had fallen asleep. One day I was asked to reprove her for doing so; she had again thrown the apparatus on the floor. The patient defended herself as follows: "This time I really couldn't help it; it was the result of a dream which I had during the night. In the dream I was in a box at the opera, and was taking a lively interest in the performance. But Herr Karl Meyer was lying in the sanatorium and complaining pitifully on account of pains in his jaw. I said to myself, 'Since I haven't the pains, I don't need the apparatus either'; that's why I threw it away." The dream of this poor sufferer reminds me of an expression which comes to our lips when we are in a disagreeable situation: "Well, I can imagine more amusing things!" The dream presents these "more amusing things!" Herr Karl Meyer, to whom the dreamer attributed her pains, was the most casual acquaintance of whom she could think.

It is quite as simple a matter to discover the wish-fulfilment in several other dreams which I have collected from healthy persons. A friend who was acquainted with my theory of dreams, and had explained it to his wife, said to me one day: "My wife asked me to tell you that she dreamt yesterday that she was having her menses. You will know what that means." Of course I know: if the young wife dreams that she is having her menses, the menses have stopped. I can well imagine that she would have liked to enjoy her freedom a little longer, before the discomforts of maternity began. It was a clever way of giving notice of her first pregnancy. Another friend writes that his wife had dreamt not long ago that she noticed milk-stains on the front of her blouse. This also is an indication of pregnancy, but not of the first one; the young mother hoped she would have more nourishment for the second child than she had for the first.

A young woman who for weeks had been cut off from all society because she was nursing a child who was suffering from an infectious disease dreamt, after the child had recovered, of a company of people in which Alphonse Daudet, Paul Bourget, Marcel Prévost and others were present; they were all very pleasant to her and amused her enormously. In her dream these different authors had the features which their portraits give them. M. Prévost, with whose portrait she is not familiar, looked like the man who had disinfected the sickroom the day before, the first outsider to enter it for a long time. Obviously the dream is to be translated thus: "It is about time now for something more entertaining than this eternal nursing."

Perhaps this collection will suffice to prove that frequently, and under the most complex conditions, dreams may be noted which can be understood only as wish-fulfilments, and which present their content without concealment. In most cases these are short and simple dreams, and they stand in pleasant contrast to the confused and overloaded dream-compositions which have almost exclusively attracted the attention of the writers on the subject. But it will repay us if we give some time to the examination of these simple dreams. The simplest dreams of all are, I suppose, to be expected in the case of children whose psychic activities are certainly less complicated than those of adults. Child psychology, in my opinion, is destined to render the same services to the psychology of adults as a study of the structure or development of the lower animals renders to the investigation of the structure of the higher orders of animals. Hitherto but few deliberate efforts have been made to make use of the psychology of the child for such a purpose.

The dreams of little children are often simple fulfilments of wishes, and for this reason are, as compared with the dreams of adults, by no means interesting. They present no problem to be solved, but they are invaluable as affording proof that the dream, in its inmost essence, is the fulfilment of a wish. I have been able to collect several examples of such dreams from the material furnished by my own children.

For two dreams, one that of a daughter of mine, at that time eight and a half years of age, and the other that of a boy of five and a quarter, I am indebted to an excursion to Hallstatt, in the summer of 1896. I must first explain that we were living that summer on a hill near Aussee, from which, when the weather was fine, we enjoyed a splendid view of the Dachstein. With a telescope we could easily distinguish the Simony hut. The children often tried to see it through the telescope—I do not know with what success. Before the excursion I had told the children that Hallstatt lay at the foot of the Dachstein. They looked forward to the outing with the greatest delight. From Hallstatt we entered the valley of Eschern, which enchanted the children with its constantly changing scenery. One of them, however, the boy of five, gradually became discontented. As often as a mountain came into view, he would ask: "Is that the Dachstein?" whereupon I had to reply: "No, only a foot-hill." After this question had been repeated several times he fell quite silent, and did not wish to accompany us up the steps leading to the waterfall. I thought he was tired. But the next morning he came to me, perfectly happy, and said: "Last night I dreamt that we went to the Simony hut." I understood him now; he had expected, when I spoke of the Dachstein, that on our excursion to Hallstatt he would climb the mountain, and would see at close quarters the hut which had been so often mentioned when the telescope was used. When he learned that he was expected to content himself with foot-hills and a waterfall he was disappointed, and became discontented. But the dream compensated him for all this. I tried to learn some details of the dream; they were scanty. "You go up steps for six hours," as he had been told.

On this excursion the girl of eight and a half had likewise cherished wishes which had to be satisfied by a dream. We had taken with us to Hallstatt our neighbour's twelve-year-old boy; quite a polished little gentleman, who, it seemed to me, had already won the little woman's sympathies. Next morning she related the following dream: "Just think, I dreamt that Emil was one of the family, that he said 'papa' and 'mamma' to you, and slept at our house, in the big room, like one of the boys. Then mamma came into the room and threw a handful of big bars of chocolate, wrapped in blue and green paper, under our beds." The girl's brothers, who evidently had not inherited an understanding of dream-interpretation, declared, just as the writers we have quoted would have done: "That dream is nonsense." The girl defended at least one part of the dream, and from the standpoint of the theory of the neuroses it is interesting to learn which part it was that she defended: "That Emil was one of the family was nonsense, but that about the bars of chocolate wasn't." It was just this latter part that was obscure to me, until my wife furnished the explanation. On the way home from the railway-station the children had stopped in front of a slot-machine, and had wanted exactly such bars of chocolate, wrapped in paper with a metallic lustre, such as the machine, in their experience, provided. But the mother thought, and rightly so, that the day had brought them enough wish-fulfilments, and therefore left this wish to be satisfied in the dream. This little scene had escaped me. That portion of the dream which had been condemned by my daughter I understood without any difficulty. I myself had heard the well-behaved little guest enjoining the children, as they were walking ahead of us, to wait until 'papa' or 'mamma' had come up. For the little girl the dream turned this temporary relationship into a permanent adoption. Her affection could not as yet conceive of any other way of enjoying her friend's company permanently than the adoption pictured in her dream, which was suggested by her brothers. Why the bars of chocolate were thrown under the bed could not, of course, be explained without questioning the child.

From a friend I have learned of a dream very much like that of my little boy. It was dreamed by a little girl of eight. Her father, accompanied by several children, had started on a walk to Dornbach, with the intention of visiting the Rohrer hut, but had turned back, as it was growing late, promising the children to take them some other time. On the way back they passed a signpost which pointed to the Hameau. The children now asked him to take them to the Hameau, but once more, and for the same reason, they had to be content with the promise that they should go there some other day. Next morning the little girl went to her father and told him, with a satisfied air: "Papa, I dreamed last night that you were with us at the Rohrer hut, and on the Hameau." Thus, in the dream her impatience had anticipated the fulfilment of the promise made by her father.

Another dream, with which the picturesque beauty of the Aussee inspired my daughter, at that time three and a quarter years of age, is equally straightforward. The little girl had crossed the lake for the first time, and the trip had passed too quickly for her. She did not want to leave the boat at the landing, and cried bitterly. The next morning she told us: "Last night I was sailing on the lake." Let us hope that the duration of this dream-voyage was more satisfactory to her.

My eldest boy, at that time eight years of age, was already dreaming of the realization of his fancies. He had ridden in a chariot with Achilles, with Diomedes as charioteer. On the previous day he had shown a lively interest in a book on the myths of Greece which had been given to his elder sister.

If it can be admitted that the talking of children in their sleep belongs to the sphere of dreams, I can relate the following as one of the earliest dreams in my collection: My youngest daughter, at that time nineteen months old, vomited one morning, and was therefore kept without food all day. During the night she was heard to call excitedly in her sleep: "Anna F(r)eud, *st'awbewy, wild st'awbewy, om'lette, pap!*" She used her name in this way in order to express the act of appropriation; the menu presumably included everything that would seem to her a desirable meal; the fact that two varieties of strawberry appeared in it was a demonstration against the sanitary regulations of the household, and was based on the circumstance, which she had by no means overlooked, that the nurse had ascribed her indisposition to an over-plentiful consumption of strawberries; so in her dream she avenged herself for this opinion which met with her disapproval.[1]

When we call childhood happy because it does not yet know sexual desire, we must not forget what a fruitful source of disappointment and renunciation, and therefore of dream-stimulation, the other great vital impulse may be for the child.[2] Here is a second example. My nephew, twenty-two months of age, had been instructed to congratulate me on my birthday, and to give me a present of a small basket of cherries, which at that time of the year were scarce, being hardly in season. He seemed to find the task a difficult one, for he repeated again and again: "Cherries in it," and could not be induced to let the little basket go out of his hands. But he knew how to indemnify himself. He had, until then, been in the habit of telling his mother every morning that he had dreamt of the "white soldier," an officer of the guard in a white cloak, whom he had once admired in the street. On the day after the sacrifice on my birthday he woke up joyfully with the announcement, which could have referred only to a dream: *"He[r] man eaten all the cherries!"*[3]

---

[1] The dream afterwards accomplished the same purpose in the case of the child's grandmother, who is older than the child by about seventy years. After she had been forced to go hungry for a day on account of the restlessness of her floating kidney, she dreamed, being apparently translated into the happy years of her girlhood, that she had been "asked out," invited to lunch and dinner, and had at each meal been served with the most delicious tidbits.

[2] A more searching investigation into the psychic life of the child teaches us, of course, that sexual motives, in infantile forms, play a very considerable part, which has been too long overlooked, in the psychic activity of the child. This permits us to doubt to some extent the happiness of the child, as imagined later by adults. Cf. *Three Contributions to the Theory of Sex.*

[3] It should be mentioned that young children often have more complex and obscure dreams, while, on the other hand, adults, in certain circumstances, often have dreams of a simple and infantile character. How rich in unsuspected content the dreams of children no more than four or five years of age may be is shown by the examples in my *Analyse der Phobie eines fünfjährigen Knaben* (*Jahrbuch von Bleuler-Freud,* vol. i, 1909), and Jung's "Experiences Concerning the Psychic Life of the Child," translated by Brill, *American Journal of Psychology,* April 1910. For analytically interpreted dreams of children, see also von Hug-Hellmuth, Putnam, Raalte, Spielrein, and Tausk; others by Banchieri, Busemann, Doglia, and especially Wigam, who emphasizes the wish-fulfilling tendency of such dreams. On the other hand, it seems that dreams of an infantile type reappear with especial frequency in adults who are transferred into the midst of unfamiliar conditions. Thus Otto Nordenskjöld, in his book, *Antarctic* (1904, vol. i, p. 336), writes as follows of the crew who spent the winter with him: "Very characteristic of the trend of our inmost thoughts were our dreams, which were never more vivid and more numerous. Even those of our comrades with whom dreaming was formerly exceptional had long stories to tell in the morning, when we exchanged our experiences in the world of phantasy. They all had reference to that outside world which was now so far removed from us, but they often fitted into our immediate circumstances. An especially characteristic dream was that in which one of our comrades believed himself back at school, where the task was assigned to him of skinning miniature seals, which were manufactured especially for purposes of instruction. Eating and drinking constituted the pivot around

What animals dream of I do not know. A proverb for which I am indebted to one of my pupils professes to tell us, for it asks the question: "What does the goose dream of?" and answers: "Of maize."[1] The whole theory that the dream is the fulfilment of a wish is contained in these two sentences.[2]

We now perceive that we should have reached our theory of the hidden meaning of dreams by the shortest route had we merely consulted the vernacular. Proverbial wisdom, it is true, often speaks contemptuously enough of dreams—it apparently seeks to justify the scientists when it says that "dreams are bubbles"; but in colloquial language the dream is predominantly the gracious fulfiller of wishes. "I should never have imagined that in my wildest dreams," we exclaim in delight if we find that the reality surpasses our expectations.

---

which most of our dreams revolved. One of us, who was especially fond of going to big dinner parties, was delighted if he could report in the morning 'that he had had a three-course dinner.' Another dreamed of tobacco, whole mountains of tobacco; yet another dreamed of a ship approaching on the open sea under full sail. Still another dream deserves to be mentioned: The postman brought the post and gave a long explanation of why it was so long delayed; he had delivered it at the wrong address, and only with great trouble was he able to get it back. To be sure, we were often occupied in our sleep with still more impossible things, but the lack of phantasy in almost all the dreams which I myself dreamed, or heard others relate, was quite striking. It would certainly have been of great psychological interest if all these dreams could have been recorded. But one can readily understand how we longed for sleep. That alone could afford us everything that we all most ardently desired." I will continue by a quotation from Du Prel (p. 231): "Mungo Park, nearly dying of thirst on one of his African expeditions, dreamed constantly of the well-watered valleys and meadows of his home. Similarly Trenck, tortured by hunger in the fortress of Magdeburg, saw himself surrounded by copious meals. And George Back, a member of Franklin's first expedition, when he was on the point of death by starvation, dreamed continually and invariably of plenteous meals."

[1] A Hungarian proverb cited by Ferenczi states more explicitly that "the pig dreams of acorns, the goose of maize." A Jewish proverb asks: "Of what does the hen dream?"—"Of millet" (*Sammlung jüd. Sprichw. u. Redensarten.*, edit. by Bernstein, 2nd ed., p. 116).

[2] I am far from wishing to assert that no previous writer has ever thought of tracing a dream to a wish. (Cf. the first passages of the next chapter.) Those interested in the subject will find that even in antiquity the physician Herophilos, who lived under the First Ptolemy, distinguished between three kinds of dreams: dreams sent by the gods; natural dreams—those which come about whenever the soul creates for itself an image of that which is beneficial to it, and will come to pass; and mixed dreams—those which originate spontaneously from the juxtaposition of images, when we see that which we desire. From the examples collected by Scherner, J. Stärcke cites a dream which was described by the author himself as a wish-fulfilment (p. 239). Scherner says: "The phantasy immediately fulfills the dreamer's wish, simply because this existed vividly in the mind." This dream belongs to the "emotional dreams." Akin to it are dreams due to "masculine and feminine erotic longing," and to "irritable moods." As will readily be seen, Scherner does not ascribe to the wish any further significance for the dream than to any other psychic condition of the waking state; least of all does he insist on the connection between the wish and the essential nature of the dream.

GEORGE ORWELL (1903–1950)
Politics and the English Language

Most people who bother with the matter at all would admit that the English language is in a bad way, but it is generally assumed that we cannot by conscious action do anything about it. Our civilization is decadent and our language—so the argument runs—must inevitably share in the general collapse. It follows that any struggle against the abuse of language is a sentimental archaism, like preferring candles to electric light or hansom cabs to aeroplanes. Underneath this lies the half-conscious belief that language is a natural growth and not an instrument which we shape for our own purposes.

Now, it is clear that the decline of a language must ultimately have political and economic causes: it is not due simply to the bad influence of this or that individual writer. But an effect can become a cause, reinforcing the original cause and producing the same effect in an intensified form, and so on indefinitely. A man may take to drink because he feels himself to be a failure, and then fail all the more completely because he drinks. It is rather the same thing that is happening to the English language. It becomes ugly and inaccurate because our thoughts are foolish, but the slovenliness of our language makes it easier for us to have foolish thoughts. The point is that the process is reversible. Modern English, especially written English, is full of bad habits which spread by imitation and which can be avoided if one is willing to take the necessary trouble. If one gets rid of these habits one can think more clearly, and to think clearly is a necessary first step towards political regeneration: so that the fight against bad English is not frivolous and is not the exclusive concern of professional writers. I will come back to this presently, and I hope that by that time the meaning of what I have said here will have become clearer. Meanwhile, here are five specimens of the English language as it is now habitually written.

These five passages have not been picked out because they are especially bad—I could have quoted far worse if I had chosen—but because they illustrate various of the mental vices from which we now suffer. They are a little below the average, but are fairly representative samples. I number them so that I can refer back to them when necessary:

1. I am not, indeed, sure whether it is not true to say that the Milton who once seemed not unlike a seventeenth-century Shelley had not become, out of an experience ever more bitter in each year, more alien [*sic*] to the founder of that Jesuit sect which nothing could induce him to tolerate.

   Professor Harold Laski (Essay in *Freedom of Expression*)

2. Above all, we cannot play ducks and drakes with a native battery of idioms which prescribes such egregious collocations of vocables as the Basic *put up with* for *tolerate* or *put at a loss* for *bewilder*.

   Professor Lancelot Hogben *(Interglossa)*

3. On the one side we have the free personality: by definition it is not neurotic, for it has neither conflict nor dream. Its desires, such as they are, are transparent, for they are just what institutional approval keeps in the forefront of consciousness; another institutional pattern would alter their number and intensity; there is little in them that is natural, irreducible, or culturally dangerous. But *on the other side,* the social bond itself is noticing but the mutual reflection of these self-secure integrities. Recall the definition of love. Is not this the very picture of a small academic? Where is there a place in this hall of mirrors for either personality or fraternity?

Essay on Psychology in Politics (New York)

4. All the "best people" from the gentlemen's clubs, and all the frantic fascist captains, united in common hatred of Socialism and bestial horror of the rising tide of the mass revolutionary movement, have turned to acts of provocation, to foul incendiarism, to medieval legends of poisoned wells, to legalize their own destruction of proletarian organizations, and rouse the agitated petty-bourgeoisie to chauvinistic fervor on behalf of the fight against the revolutionary way out of the crisis.

Communist Pamphlet

5. If a new spirit *is* to be infused into this old country, there is one thorny and contentious reform which must be tackled, and that is the humanization and galvanization of the B.B.C. Timidity here will bespeak canker and atrophy of the soul. The heart of Britain may be sound and of strong beat, for instance, but the British lion's roar at present is like that of Bottom in Shakespeare's *Midsummer Night's Dream*—as gentle as any sucking dove. A virile new Britain cannot continue indefinitely to be traduced in the eyes, or rather ears, of the world by the effete languors of Langham Place, brazenly masquerading as "standard English." When the voice of Britain is heard at nine o'clock, better far and infinitely less ludicrous to hear aitches honestly dropped than the present priggish, inflated, inhibited, school-ma'amish arch braying of blameless bashful mewing maidens!

Letter in Tribune

Each of these passages has faults of its own, but, quite apart from avoidable ugliness, two qualities are common to all of them. The first is staleness of imagery; the other is lack of precision. The writer either has a meaning and cannot express it, or he inadvertently says something else, or he is almost indifferent as to whether his words mean anything or not. This mixture of vagueness and sheer incompetence is the most marked characteristic of modern English prose, and especially of any kind of political writing. As soon as certain topics are raised, the concrete melts into the abstract and no one seems able to think of turns of speech that are not hackneyed: prose consists less and less of *words* chosen for the sake of their meaning, and more and more of *phrases* tacked together like the sections of a prefabricated henhouse. I list below, with notes and examples, various of the tricks by means of which the work of prose-construction is habitually dodged:

Dying Metaphors

A newly invented metaphor assists thought by evoking a visual image, while on the other hand a metaphor which is technically "dead" (e.g., *iron resolution*) has in effect reverted to being an ordinary word and can generally be used without loss of vividness. But in between these two classes there is a huge dump of worn-out metaphors which have lost all evocative power and are merely used because they save people the trouble of inventing phrases for themselves. Examples are: *Ring the changes on, take up the cudgels for, toe the line, ride roughshod over, stand shoulder to shoulder with, play into the hands of, no axe to grind, grist to the mill, fishing in troubled waters, on the order of the day, Achilles' heel, swan song, hotbed.* Many of these are used without knowledge of their meaning (what is a "rift," for instance?), and incompatible metaphors are frequently mixed, a sure sign that the writer is not interested in what he is saying. Some metaphors now current have been twisted out of their original meaning without those who use them even being aware of the fact. For example, *toe the line* is sometimes written *tow the line.* Another example is *the hammer and the anvil,* now always used with the implication that the anvil gets the worst of it. In real life it is always the anvil that breaks the hammer, never the other way about: a writer who stopped to think what he was saying would be aware of this, and would avoid perverting the original phrase.

Operators or Verbal False Limbs

These save the trouble of picking out appropriate verbs and nouns, and at the same time pad each sentence with extra syllables which give it an appearance of symmetry. Characteristic phrases are *render inoperative, militate against, make contact with, be subjected to, give rise to, give grounds for, have the effect of, play a leading part (role) in, make itself felt, take effect, exhibit a tendency to, serve the purpose of,* etc., etc. The keynote is the elimination of simple verbs. Instead of being a single word, such as *break, stop, spoil, mend, kill,* a verb becomes *a phrase,* made up of a noun or adjective tacked on to some general-purpose verb such as *prove, serve, form, play, render.* In addition, the passive voice is wherever possible used in preference to the active, and noun constructions are used instead of gerunds *(by examination of* instead of *by examining).* The range of verbs is further cut down by means of the *-ize* and *de-* formations, and the banal statements are given an appearance of profundity by means of the *not un-* formation. Simple conjunctions and prepositions are replaced by such phrases as *with respect to, having regard to, the fact that, by dint of, in view of, in the interests of, on the hypothesis that;* and the ends of sentences are saved from anticlimax by such resounding common-places as *greatly to be desired, cannot be left out of account, a development to be expected in the near future, deserving of serious consideration, brought to a satisfactory conclusion,* and so on and so forth.

Pretentious Diction

Words like *phenomenon, element, individual* (as noun), *objective, categorical, effective, virtual, basic, primary, promote, constitute, exhibit, exploit, utilize, eliminate, liquidate,* are used to dress up simple statements and give an air of scientific impartiality to biased judgments. Adjectives like *epoch-making, epic, historic, unforgettable, triumphant, age-old, inevitable, inexorable, veritable,* are used to dignify the sordid processes of international politics, while writing that aims at glorifying war usually takes on an archaic color, its characteristic words being: *realm, throne, chariot, mailed fist, trident, sword, shield, buckler, banner, jackboot, clarion.* Foreign words and expressions such as *cul de sac, ancien régime, deus ex machina, mutatis mutandis, status quo, gleichschaltung, weltanschauung,* are used to give an air of culture and elegance. Except for the useful abbreviations *i.e., e.g.,* and *etc.,* there is no real need for any of the hundreds of foreign phrases now current in English. Bad writers, and especially scientific, political and sociological writers, are nearly always haunted by the notion that Latin or Greek words are grander than Saxon ones, and unnecessary words like *expedite, ameliorate, predict, extraneous, deracinated, clandestine, subaqueous* and hundreds of others constantly gain ground from their Anglo-Saxon opposite numbers.[1] The jargon peculiar to Marxist writing *(hyena, hangman, cannibal, petty bourgeois, these gentry, lacquey, flunkey, mad dog, White Guard,* etc.) consists largely of words and phrases translated from Russian, German or French; but the normal way of coining a new word is to use a Latin or Greek root with the appropriate affix and, where necessary, the *-ize* formation. It is often easier to make up words of this kind *(deregionalize, impermissible, extramarital, nonfragmentary* and so forth) than to think up the English words that will cover one's meaning. The result, in general, is an increase in slovenliness and vagueness.

Meaningless Words

In certain kinds of writing, particularly in art criticism and literary criticism, it is normal to come across long passages which are almost completely lacking in meaning.[2] Words like *romantic, plastic, values, human, dead, sentimental, natural, vitality,* as used in art criticism, are strictly meaningless, in the sense that they not only do not point to any discoverable object, but are hardly ever expected to do so by the reader. When one critic writes, "The outstanding feature of Mr. X's work is its living

---

[1] An interesting illustration of this is the way in which the English flower names which were in use till very recently are being ousted by Greek ones, *snapdragon* becoming *antirrhinum, forget-me-not* becoming *myosotis,* etc. It is hard to see any practical reason for this change of fashion: it is probably due to an instinctive turning-away from the more homely word and a vague feeling that the Greek word is scientific.

[2] Example: "Comfort's catholicity of perception and image, strangely Whitmanesque in range, almost the exact opposite in aesthetic compulsion, continues to evoke that trembling atmospheric accumulative hinting at a cruel, an inexorably serene timelessness. . . . Wrey Gardiner scores by aiming at simple bull's-eyes with precision. Only they are not simple, and through this contented sadness runs more than the surface bitter-sweet of resignation." *(Poetry Quarterly.)*

quality," while another writes, "the immediately striking thing about Mr. X's work is its peculiar deadness," the reader accepts this as a simple difference of opinion. If words like *black* and *white* were involved, instead of the jargon words *dead* and *living,* he would see at once that language was being used in an improper way. Many political words are similarly abused. The word *Fascism* has now no meaning except in so far as it signifies "something not desirable." The words *democracy, socialism, freedom, patriotic, realistic, justice,* have each of them several different meanings which cannot be reconciled with one another. In the case of a word like *democracy,* not only is there no agreed definition, but the attempt to make one is resisted from all sides. It is almost universally felt that when we call a country democratic we are praising it: consequently the defenders of every kind of régime claim that it is a democracy, and fear that they might have to stop using the word if it were tied down to any one meaning. Words of this kind are often used in a consciously dishonest way. That is, the person who uses them has his own private definition, but allows his hearer to think he means something quite different. Statements like *Marshal Pétain was a true patriot, The Soviet Press is the freest in the world, The Catholic Church is opposed to persecution,* are almost always made with intent to deceive. Other words used in variable meanings, in most cases more or less dishonestly, are: *class, totalitarian, science, progressive, reactionary, bourgeois, equality.*

Now that I have made this catalogue of swindles and perversions, let me give another example of the kind of writing that they lead to. This time it must of its nature be an imaginary one. I am going to translate a passage of good English into modern English of the worst sort. Here is a well-known verse from *Ecclesiastes:*

I returned and saw under the sun, that the race is not to the swift, nor the battle to the strong, neither yet bread to the wise, nor yet riches to men of understanding, nor yet favour to men of skill; but time and chance happeneth to them all.

Here it is in modern English:

Objective consideration of contemporary phenomena compels the conclusion that success or failure in competitive activities exhibits no tendency to be commensurate with innate capacity, but that a considerable element of the unpredictable must invariably be taken into account.

This is a parody, but not a very gross one. Exhibit (3), above, for instance, contains several patches of the same kind of English. It will be seen that I have not made a full translation. The beginning and ending of the sentence follow the original meaning fairly closely, but in the middle the concrete illustrations—race, battle, bread—dissolve into the vague phrase "success or failure in competitive activities." This had to be so, because no modern writer of the kind I am discussing—no one capable of using phrases like "objective consideration of contemporary phenomena"—would ever tabulate his thoughts in that precise and detailed way. The whole tendency of modern prose is away from concreteness. Now analyze these two sentences a little more closely. The first contains forty-nine words but only sixty syllables, and all its words are those of everyday life. The second contains thirty-eight words of ninety syllables: eighteen of its words are from Latin roots, and one from Greek. The first sentence contains six vivid images, and only one phrase ("time and chance") that could be called vague. The second contains not a single fresh, arresting phrase, and in spite of its ninety syllables it gives only a shortened version of the meaning contained in the first. Yet without a doubt it is the second kind of sentence that is gaining ground in modern English. I do not want to exaggerate. This kind of writing is not yet universal, and outcrops of simplicity will occur here and there in the worst-written page. Still, if you or I were told to write a few lines on the uncertainty of human fortunes, we should probably come much nearer to my imaginary sentence than to the one from *Ecclesiastes*.

As I have tried to show, modern writing at its worst does not consist in picking out words for the sake of their meaning and inventing images in order to make the meaning clearer. It consists in gumming together long strips of words which have already been set in order by someone else, and making the results presentable by sheer humbug. The attraction of this way of writing is that it is easy. It is easier—even quicker, once you have the habit—to say *In my opinion it is not an unjustifiable assumption that* than to say *I think*. If you use ready-made phrases, you not only don't have to hunt about for words; you also don't have to bother with the rhythms of your sentences, since these phrases are generally so arranged as to be more or less euphonious. When you are composing in a hurry—when you are dictating to a stenographer, for instance, or making a public speech—it is natural to fall into a pretentious, Latinized style. Tags like *a consideration which we should do well to bear in mind* or *a conclusion to which all of us would readily assent* will save many a sentence from coming down with a bump. By using stale metaphors, similes and idioms, you save much mental effort, at the cost of leaving your meaning vague, not only for your reader but for yourself. This is the significance of mixed metaphors. The sole aim of a metaphor is to call up a visual image. When these images clash—as in *The Fascist octopus has sung its swan song, the jackboot is thrown into the melting pot*—it can be taken as certain that the writer is not seeing a mental image of the objects he is naming; in other words he is not really thinking. Look again at the examples I gave at the beginning of this essay. Professor Laski (1) uses five negatives in fifty-three words. One of these is superfluous, making nonsense of the whole passage, and in addition there is the slip *alien* for *akin,* making further nonsense, and several avoidable pieces of clumsiness which increase the general vagueness. Professor Hogben (2) plays ducks and drakes with a battery which is able to write prescriptions, and, while disapproving of the everyday phrase *put up with,* is unwilling to look *egregious* up in the dictionary and see what it means; (3), if one takes an uncharitable attitude towards it, is simply meaningless: probably one could work out its intended meaning by reading the whole of the article in which it occurs. In (4), the writer knows more or less what he wants to say, but an accumulation of stale phrases chokes him like tea leaves blocking a sink. In (5), words and meaning have almost parted company. People who write in this manner usually have a general emotional meaning—they dislike one thing and want to express solidarity with another—but they are not interested in the detail of what they are saying. A scrupulous writer, in every sentence that he writes, will ask himself at least four questions, thus: What am I trying to say? What words will express it? What image or idiom will make it clearer? Is this image fresh enough to have an effect? And he will probably ask himself two more: Could I put it more shortly? Have I said anything that is avoidably ugly? But you are not obliged to go to all this trouble. You can shirk it by simply throwing your mind open and letting the ready-made phrases come crowding in. They will construct your sentences for you—even think your thoughts for you, to a certain extent—and at need they will perform the important service of partially concealing your meaning even from yourself. It is at this point that the special connection between politics and the debasement of language becomes clear.

In our time it is broadly true that political writing is bad writing. Where it is not true, it will generally be found that the writer is some kind of rebel, expressing his private opinions and not a "party line." Orthodoxy, of whatever color, seems to demand a lifeless, imitative style. The political dialects to be found in pamphlets, leading articles, manifestos, White Papers and the speeches of undersecretaries do, of course, vary from party to party, but they are all alike in that one almost never finds in them a fresh, vivid, home-made turn of speech. When one watches some tired hack on the platform mechanically repeating the familiar phrases—*bestial atrocities, iron heel, bloodstained tyranny, free peoples of the world, stand shoulder to shoulder*—one often has a curious feeling that one is not watching a live human being but some kind of dummy: a feeling which suddenly becomes stronger at moments when the light catches the speaker's spectacles and turns them into blank discs which seem to have no eyes behind them. And this is not altogether fanciful. A speaker who uses that kind of phraseology has gone some distance towards turning himself into a machine. The appropriate noises are coming out of his larynx, but his brain is not involved as it would be if he were choosing his words for himself. If the speech he is making is one that he is accustomed to make over and over again, he may be almost unconscious of what he is saying, as one is when one utters the responses in church. And this reduced state of consciousness, if not indispensable, is at any rate favorable to political conformity.

In our time, political speech and writing are largely the defense of the indefensible. Things like the continuance of British rule in India, the Russian purges and deportations, the dropping of the atom bombs on Japan, can indeed be defended, but only by arguments which are too brutal for most people to face, and which do not square with the professed aims of political parties. Thus political language has to consist largely of euphemism, question-begging and sheer cloudy vagueness. Defenseless villages are bombarded from the air, the inhabitants driven out into the countryside, the cattle machine-gunned, the huts set on fire with incendiary bullets: this is called *pacification*. Millions of peasants are robbed of their farms and sent trudging along the roads with no more than they can carry: this is called *transfer of population* or *rectification of frontiers*. People are imprisoned for years without trial, or shot in the back of the neck or sent to die of scurvy in Arctic lumber camps: this is called *elimination of unreliable elements*. Such phraseology is needed if one wants to name things without calling up mental pictures of them. Consider for instance some comfortable English professor defending Russian totalitarianism. He cannot say outright, "I believe in killing off your opponents when you can get good results by doing so." Probably, therefore, he will say something like this:

> While freely conceding that the Soviet regime exhibits certain features which the humanitarian may be inclined to deplore, we must, I think, agree that a certain curtailment of the right to political opposition is an unavoidable concomitant of transitional periods, and that the rigors which the Russian people have been called upon to undergo have been amply justified in the sphere of concrete achievement.

The inflated style is itself a kind of euphemism. A mass of Latin words falls upon the facts like soft snow, blurring the outlines and covering up all the details. The great enemy of clear language is insincerity. When there is a gap between one's real and one's declared aims, one turns as it were instinctively to long words and exhausted idioms, like a cuttlefish squirting out ink. In our age there is no such thing as "keeping out of politics." All issues are political issues, and politics itself is a mass of lies, evasions, folly, hatred and schizophrenia. When the general atmosphere is bad, language must suffer. I should expect to find—this is a guess which I have not sufficient knowledge to verify—that the German, Russian and Italian languages have all deteriorated in the last ten to fifteen years, as a result of dictatorship.

But if thought corrupts language, language can also corrupt thought. A bad usage can spread by tradition and imitation, even among people who should and do know better. The debased language that I have been discussing is in some ways very convenient. Phrases like *a not unjustifiable assumption, leaves much to be desired, would serve no good purpose, a consideration which we should do well to bear in mind,* are a continuous temptation, a packet of aspirins always at one's elbow. Look back through this essay, and for certain you will find that I have again and again committed the very faults I am protesting against. By this morning's post I have received a pamphlet dealing with conditions in Germany. The author tells me that he "felt impelled" to write it. I open it at random, and here is almost the first sentence that I see: "[The Allies] have an opportunity not only of achieving a radical transformation of Germany's social and political structure in such a way as to avoid a nationalistic reaction in Germany itself, but at the same time of laying the foundations of a cooperative and unified Europe." You see, he "feels impelled" to write—feels, presumably, that he has something new to say—and yet his words, like cavalry horses answering the bugle, group themselves automatically into the familiar dreary pattern. This invasion of one's mind by ready-made phrases *(lay the foundations, achieve a radical transformation)* can only be prevented if one is constantly on guard against them, and every such phrase anaesthetizes a portion of one's brain.

I said earlier that the decadence of our language is probably curable. Those who deny this would argue, if they produced an argument at all, that language merely reflects existing social conditions, and that we cannot influence its development by any direct tinkering with words and constructions. So far as the general tone or spirit of a language goes, this may be true, but it is not true in detail. Silly words and expressions have often disappeared, not through any evolutionary process but owing to the conscious action of a minority. Two recent examples were *explore every avenue* and *leave no stone unturned,* which were killed by the jeers of a few journalists. There is a long list of flyblown metaphors which could similarly be got rid of if enough people would interest themselves in the job; and it should also be possible to laugh the *not un-* formation out of existence,[3] to reduce the amount of Latin and Greek in the average sentence, to drive out foreign phrases and strayed scientific words, and, in general, to make pretentiousness unfashionable. But all these are minor points. The defense of the English language implies more than this, and perhaps it is best to start by saying what it does *not* imply.

To begin with it has nothing to do with archaism, with the salvaging of obsolete words and turns of speech, or with the setting up of a "standard English" which must never be departed from. On the contrary, it is especially concerned with the scrapping of every word or idiom which has outworn its usefulness. It has nothing to do with correct grammar and syntax, which are of no importance so long as one makes one's meaning clear, or with the avoidance of Americanisms, or with having what is called a "good prose style." On the other hand it is not concerned with fake simplicity and the attempt to make written English colloquial. Nor does it even imply in every case preferring the Saxon word to the Latin one, though it does imply using the fewest and shortest words that will cover one's meaning. What is above all needed is to let the meaning choose the word, and not the other way about. In prose, the worst thing one can do with words is to surrender to them. When you think of a concrete object, you think wordlessly, and then, if you want to describe the thing you have been visualizing you probably hunt about till you find the exact words that seem to fit in. When you think of something abstract you are more inclined to use words from the start, and unless you make a conscious effort to prevent it, the existing dialect will come rushing in and do the job for you, at the expense of blurring or even changing your meaning. Probably it is better to put off using words as long as possible and get one's meaning as clear as one can through pictures or sensations. Afterwards one can choose—not simply *accept*—the phrases that will best cover the meaning, and then switch round and decide what impression one's words are likely to make on another person. This last effort of the mind cuts out all stale or mixed images, all prefabricated phrases, needless repetitions, and humbug and vagueness generally. But one can often be in doubt about the effect of a word or a phrase, and one needs rules that one can rely on when instinct fails. I think the following rules will cover most cases:

(i) Never use a metaphor, simile or other figure of speech which you are used to seeing in print.

(ii) Never use a long word where a short one will do.

(iii) If it is possible to cut a word out, always cut it out.

(iv) Never use the passive where you can use the active.

---

[3] One can cure oneself of the *not un-* formation by memorizing this sentence: *A not unblack dog was chasing a not unsmall rabbit across a not ungreen field.*

(v) Never use a foreign phrase, a scientific word or a jargon word if you can think of an everyday English equivalent.

(vi) Break any of these rules sooner than say anything outright barbarous.

These rules sound elementary, and so they are, but they demand a deep change of attitude in anyone who has grown used to writing in the style now fashionable. One could keep all of them and still write bad English, but one could not write the kind of stuff that I quoted in those five specimens at the beginning of this article.

I have not here been considering the literary use of language, but merely language as an instrument for expressing and not for concealing or preventing thought. Stuart Chase and others have come near to claiming that all abstract words are meaningless, and have used this as a pretext for advocating a kind of political quietism. Since you don't know what Fascism is, how can you struggle against Fascism? One need not swallow such absurdities as this, but one ought to recognize that the present political chaos is connected with the decay of language, and that one can probably bring about some improvement by starting at the verbal end. If you simplify your English, you are freed from the worst follies of orthodoxy. You cannot speak any of the necessary dialects, and when you make a stupid remark its stupidity will be obvious, even to yourself. Political language—and with variations this is true of all political parties, from Conservatives to Anarchists—is designed to make lies sound truthful and murder respectable, and to give an appearance of solidity to pure wind. One cannot change this all in a moment, but one can at least change one's own habits, and from time to time one can even, if one jeers loudly enough, send some worn-out and useless phrase—some *jackboot, Achilles' heel, hotbed, melting pot, acid test, veritable inferno* or other lump of verbal refuse—into the dustbin where it belongs.

ROLAND BARTHES (1915–1980)
The Photographic Message

The press photograph is a message. Considered overall this message is formed by a source of emission, a channel of transmission and a point of reception. The source of emission is the staff of the newspaper, the group of technicians certain of whom take the photo, some of whom choose, compose and treat it, while others, finally, give it a title, a caption and a commentary. The point of reception is the public which reads the paper. As for the channel of transmission, this is the newspaper itself, or, more precisely, a complex of concurrent messages with the photograph as centre and surrounds constituted by the text, the title, the caption, the lay-out and, in a more abstract but no less 'informative' way, by the very name of the paper (this name represents a knowledge that can heavily orientate the reading of the message strictly speaking: a photograph can change its meaning as it passes from the very conservative *L'Aurore* to the communist *L'Humanité*). These observations are not without their importance for it can readily be seen that in the case of the press photograph the three traditional parts of the message do not call for the same method of investigation. The emission and the reception of the message both lie within the field of a sociology: it is a matter of studying human groups, of defining motives and attitudes, and of trying to link the behaviour of these groups to the social totality of which they are a part. For the message itself, however, the method is inevitably different: whatever the origin and the destination of the message, the photograph is not simply a product or a channel but also an object endowed with a structural autonomy. Without in any way intending to divorce this object from its use, it is necessary to provide for a specific method prior to sociological analysis and which can only be the immanent analysis of the unique structure that a photograph constitutes.

Naturally, even from the perspective of a purely immanent analysis, the structure of the photograph is not an isolated structure; it is in communication with at least one other structure, namely the text—title, caption or article—accompanying every press photograph. The totality of the information is thus carried by two different structures (one of which is linguistic). These two structures are co-operative but, since their units are heterogeneous, necessarily remain separate from one another: here (in the text) the substance of the message is made up of words; there (in the photograph) of lines, surfaces, shades. Moreover, the two structures of the message each occupy their own defined spaces, these being contiguous but not 'homogenized', as they are for example in the rebus which fuses words and images in a single line of reading. Hence, although a press photograph is never without a written commentary, the analysis must first of all bear on each separate structure; it is only when the study of each structure has been exhausted that it will be possible to understand the manner in which they complement one another. Of the two structures, one is already familiar, that of language (but not, it is true, that of the 'literature' formed by the language-use of the newspaper; an enormous amount of work is still to be done in this connection), while almost nothing is known about the other, that of the photograph. What follows will be limited to the definition of the initial difficulties in providing a structural analysis of the photographic message.

The Photographic Paradox

What is the content of the photographic message? What does the photograph transmit? By definition, the scene itself, the literal reality. From the object to its image there is of course a reduction—in proportion, perspective, colour—but at no time is this reduction a *transformation* (in the mathematical sense of the term). In order to move from the reality to its photograph it is in no way necessary to divide up this reality into units and to constitute these units as signs, substantially different from the object they communicate; there is no necessity to set up a relay, that is to say a code, between the object and its image. Certainly the image is not the reality but at least it is its perfect *analogon* and it is exactly this analogical perfection which, to common sense, defines the photograph. Thus can be seen the special status of the photographic image: *it is a message without a code;* from which proposition an important corollary must immediately be drawn: the photographic message is a continuous message.

Are there other messages without a code? At first sight, yes: precisely the whole range of analogical reproductions of reality—drawings, paintings, cinema, theatre. In fact, however, each of those messages develops in an immediate and obvious way a supplementary message, in addition to the analogical content itself (scene, object, landscape), which is what is commonly called the *style* of the reproduction; second meaning, whose signifier is a certain 'treatment' of the image (result of the action of the creator) and whose signified, whether aesthetic or ideological, refers to a certain 'culture' of the society receiving the message. In short, all these 'imitative' arts comprise two messages: a *denoted* message, which is the *analogon* itself, and a *connoted* message, which is the manner in which the society to a certain extent communicates what it thinks of it. This duality of messages is evident in all reproductions other than photographic ones: there is no drawing, no matter how exact, whose very exactitude is not turned into a style (the style of 'verism'); no filmed scene whose objectivity is not finally read as the very sign of objectivity. Here again, the study of these connoted messages has still to be carried out (in particular it has to be decided whether what is called a work of art can be reduced to a system of significations); one can only anticipate that for all these imitative arts—when common—the code of the connoted system is very likely constituted either by a universal symbolic order or by a period rhetoric, in short by a stock of stereotypes (schemes, colours, graphisms, gestures, expressions, arrangements of elements).

When we come to the photograph, however, we find in principle nothing of the kind, at any rate as regards the press photograph (which is never an 'artistic' photograph). The photograph professing to be a mechanical analogue of reality, its first-order message in some sort completely fills its substance and leaves no place for the development of a second-order message. Of all the structures of information[1], the

---

[1] It is a question, of course, of 'cultural' or culturalized structures, not of operational structures. Mathematics, for example, constitutes a denoted structure without any connotation at all; should mass society seize on it, however, setting out for instance an algebraic formula in an article on Einstein, this originally purely mathematical message now takes on a very heavy connotation, since it *signifies* science.

photograph appears as the only one that is exclusively constituted and occupied by a 'denoted' message, a message which totally exhausts its mode of existence. In front of a photograph, the feeling of 'denotation', or, if one prefers, of analogical pleni-tude, is so great that the description of a photograph is literally impossible; *to de-scribe* consists precisely in joining to the denoted message a relay or second-order message derived from a code which is that of language and constituting in relation to the photographic analogue, however much care one takes to be exact, a connotation: to describe is thus not simply to be imprecise or incomplete, it is to change struc-tures, to signify something different to what is shown.[2]

This purely 'denotative' status of the photograph, the perfection and plenitude of its analogy, in short its 'objectivity', has every chance of being mythical (these are the characteristics that common sense attributes to the photograph). In actual fact there is a strong probability (and this will be a working hypothesis) that the photographic message too—at least in the press—is connoted. Connotation is not necessarily im-mediately graspable at the level of the message itself (it is, one could say, at once in-visible and active, clear and implicit) but it can already be inferred from certain phenomena which occur at the levels of the production and reception of the mes-sage: on the one hand, the press photograph is an object that has been worked on, chosen, composed, constructed, treated according to professional, aesthetic or ideo-logical norms which are so many factors of connotation; while on the other, this same photograph is not only perceived, received, it is *read,* connected more or less consciously by the public that consumes it to a traditional stock of signs. Since every sign supposes a code, it is this code (of connotation) that one should try to establish. The photographic paradox can then be seen as the co-existence of two messages, the one without a code (the photographic analogue), the other with a code (the 'art', or the treatment, or the 'writing', or the rhetoric, of the photograph); structurally, the paradox is clearly not the collusion of a denoted message and a connoted message (which is the—probably inevitable—status of all the forms of mass communica-tion), it is that here the connoted (or coded) message develops on the basis of a mes-sage *without a code.* This structural paradox coincides with an ethical paradox: when one wants to be 'neutral', 'objective', one strives to copy reality meticulously, as though the analogical were a factor of resistance against the investment of values (such at least is the definition of aesthetic 'realism'); how then can the photograph be at once 'objective' and 'invested', natural and cultural? It is through an understand-ing of the mode of imbrication of denoted and connoted messages that it may one day be possible to reply to that question. In order to undertake this work, however, it must be remembered that since the denoted message in the photograph is absolutely analogical, which is to say *continuous,* outside of any recourse to a code, there is no need to look for the signifying units of the first-order message; the connoted message on the contrary does comprise a plane of expression and a plane of content, thus necessitating a veritable decipherment. Such a decipherment would as yet be pre-

---

[2] The description of a drawing is easier, involving, finally, the description of a structure that is already connoted, fashioned with a *coded* signification in view. It is for this reason perhaps that psychological texts use a great many drawings and very few photographs.

mature, for in order to isolate the signifying units and the signified themes (or values) one would have to carry out (perhaps using tests) directed readings, artificially varying certain elements of a photograph to see if the variations of forms led to variations in meaning. What can at least be done now is to forecast the main planes of analysis of photographic connotation.

Connotation Procedures

Connotation, the imposition of second meaning on the photographic message proper, is realized at the different levels of the production of the photograph (choice, technical treatment, framing, lay-out) and represents, finally, a coding of the photographic analogue. It is thus possible to separate out various connotation procedures, bearing in mind however that these procedures are in no way units of signification such as a subsequent analysis of a semantic kind may one day manage to define; they are not strictly speaking part of the photographic structure. The procedures in question are familiar and no more will be attempted here than to translate them into structural terms. To be fully exact, the first three (trick effects, pose, objects) should be distinguished from the last three (photogenia, aestheticism, syntax), since in the former the connotation is produced by a modification of the reality itself, of, that is, the denoted message (such preparation is obviously not peculiar to the photograph). If they are nevertheless included amongst the connotation procedures, it is because they too benefit from the prestige of the denotation: the photograph allows the photographer to *conceal elusively* the preparation to which he subjects the scene to be recorded. Yet the fact still remains that there is no certainty from the point of view of a subsequent structural analysis that it will be possible to take into account the material they provide.

1. *Trick effects.* A photograph given wide circulation in the American press in 1951 is reputed to have cost Senator Millard Tydings his seat; it showed the Senator in conversation with the Communist leader Earl Browder. In fact, the photograph had been faked, created by the artificial bringing together of the two faces. The methodological interest of trick effects is that they intervene without warning in the plane of denotation; they utilize the special credibility of the photograph—this, as was seen, being simply its exceptional power of denotation—in order to pass off as merely denoted a message which is in reality heavily connoted; in no other treatment does connotation assume so completely the 'objective' mask of denotation. Naturally, signification is only possible to the extent that there is a stock of signs, the beginnings of a code. The signifier here is the conversational attitude of the two figures and it will be noted that this attitude becomes a sign only for a certain society, only given certain values. What makes the speakers' attitude the sign of a reprehensible familiarity is the tetchy anti-Communism of the American electorate; which is to say that the code of connotation is neither artificial (as in a true language) nor natural, but historical.

2. *Pose.* Consider a press photograph of President Kennedy widely distributed at the time of the 1960 election: a half-length profile shot, eyes looking upwards, hands joined together. Here it is the very pose of the subject which prepares the reading of

the signifieds of connotation: youthfulness, spirituality, purity. The photograph clearly only signifies because of the existence of a store of stereotyped attitudes which form ready-made elements of signification (eyes raised heavenwards, hands clasped). A 'historical grammar' of iconographic connotation ought thus to look for its material in painting, theatre, associations of ideas, stock metaphors, etc., that is to say, precisely in 'culture'. As has been said, pose is not a specifically photographic procedure but it is difficult not to mention it insofar as it derives its effect from the analogical principle at the basis of the photograph. The message in the present instance is not 'the pose' but 'Kennedy praying': the reader receives as a simple denotation what is in actual fact a double structure—denoted-connoted.

3. *Objects.* Special importance must be accorded to what could be called the posing of objects, where the meaning comes from the objects photographed (either because these objects have, if the photographer had the time, been artificially arranged in front of the camera or because the person responsible for lay-out chooses a photograph of this or that object). The interest lies in the fact that the objects are accepted inducers of associations of ideas (book-case = intellectual) or, in a more obscure way, are veritable symbols (the door of the gas-chamber for Chessman's execution with its reference to the funeral gates of ancient mythologies). Such objects constitute excellent elements of signification: on the one hand they are discontinuous and complete in themselves, a physical qualification for a sign, while on the other they refer to clear, familiar signifieds. They are thus the elements of a veritable lexicon, stable to a degree which allows them to be readily constituted into syntax. Here, for example, is a 'composition' of objects: a window opening on to vineyards and tiled roofs; in front of the window a photograph album, a magnifying glass, a vase of flowers. Consequently, we are in the country, south of the Loire (vines and tiles), in a bourgeois house (flowers on the table) whose owner, advanced in years (the magnifying glass), is reliving his memories (the photograph album)—François Mauriac in Malagar (photo in *Paris-Match*). The connotation somehow 'emerges' from all these signifying units which are nevertheless 'captured' as though the scene were immediate and spontaneous, that is to say, without signification. The text renders the connotation explicit, developing the theme of Mauriac's ties with the land. Objects no longer perhaps possess a *power,* but they certainly possess meanings.

4. *Photogenia.* The theory of photogenia has already been developed (by Edgar Morin in *Le Cinéma ou l'homme imaginaire*[3]) and this is not the place to take up again the subject of the general signification of that procedure; it will suffice to define photogenia in terms of informational structure. In photogenia the connoted message is the image itself, 'embellished' (which is to say in general sublimated) by techniques of lighting, exposure and printing. An inventory needs to be made of these techniques, but only insofar as each of them has a corresponding signified of connotation sufficiently constant to allow its incorporation in a cultural lexicon of technical 'effects' (as for instance the 'blurring of movement' or 'flowingness' launched by Dr. Steinert and his team to signify space-time). Such an inventory

---

[3] [Edgar Morin, *Le Cinéma ou l'homme imaginaire,* Paris 1956.]

would be an excellent opportunity for distinguishing aesthetic effects from signifying effects—unless perhaps it be recognized that in photography, contrary to the intentions of exhibition photographers, there is never *art* but always *meaning;* which precisely would at last provide an exact criterion for the opposition between good painting, even if strongly representational, and photography.

5. *Aestheticism.* For if one can talk of aestheticism in photography, it is seemingly in an ambiguous fashion: when photography turns painting, composition or visual substance treated with deliberation in its very material 'texture', it is either so as to signify itself as 'art' (which was the case with the 'pictorialism' of the beginning of the century) or to impose a generally more subtle and complex signified than would be possible with other connotation procedures. Thus Cartier-Bresson constructed Cardinal Pacelli's reception by the faithful of Lisieux like a painting by an early master. The resulting photograph, however, is in no way a painting: on the one hand, its display of aestheticism refers (damagingly) to the very idea of a painting (which is contrary to any true painting); while on the other, the composition signifies in a declared manner a certain ecstatic spirituality translated precisely in terms of an objective spectacle. One can see here the difference between photograph and painting: in a picture by a Primitive, 'spirituality' is not a signified but, as it were, the very being of the image. Certainly there may be coded elements in some paintings, rhetorical figures, period symbols, but no signifying unit refers to spirituality, which is a mode of being and not the object of a structured message.

6. *Syntax.* We have already considered a discursive reading of object-signs within a single photograph. Naturally, several photographs can come together to form a sequence (this is commonly the case in illustrated magazines); the signifier of connotation is then no longer to be found at the level of any one of the fragments of the sequence but at that—what the linguists would call the suprasegmental level—of the concatenation. Consider for example four snaps of a presidential shoot at Rambouillet: in each, the illustrious sportsman (Vincent Auriol) is pointing his rifle in some unlikely direction, to the great peril of the keepers who run away or fling themselves to the ground. The sequence (and the sequence alone) offers an effect of comedy which emerges, according to a familiar procedure, from the repetition and variation of the attitudes. It can be noted in this connection that the single photograph, contrary to the drawing, is very rarely (that is, only with much difficulty) comic; the comic requires movement, which is to say repetition (easy in film) or typification (possible in drawing), both these 'connotations' being prohibited to the photograph.

Text and Image

Such are the main connotation procedures of the photographic image (once again, it is a question of techniques, not of units). To these may invariably be added the text which accompanies the press photograph. Three remarks should be made in this context.

Firstly, the text constitutes a parasitic message designed to connote the image, to 'quicken' it with one or more second-order signifieds. In other words, and this is an important historical reversal, the image no longer *illustrates* the words; it is now the words which, structurally, are parasitic on the image. The reversal is at a cost: in the traditional modes of illustration the image functioned as an episodic return to denotation from a principal message (the text) which was experienced as connoted since, precisely, it needed an illustration; in the relationship that now holds, it is not the image which comes to elucidate or 'realize' the text, but the latter which comes to sublimate, patheticize or rationalize the image. As however this operation is carried out accessorily, the new informational totality appears to be chiefly founded on an objective (denoted) message in relation to which the text is only a kind of secondary vibration, almost without consequence. Formerly, the image illustrated the text (made it clearer); today, the text loads the image, burdening it with a culture, a moral, an imagination. Formerly, there was reduction from text to image; today, there is amplification from the one to the other. The connotation is now experienced only as the natural resonance of the fundamental denotation constituted by the photographic analogy and we are thus confronted with a typical process of naturalization of the cultural.

Secondly, the effect of connotation probably differs according to the way in which the text is presented. The closer the text to the image, the less it seems to connote it; caught as it were in the iconographic message, the verbal message seems to share in its objectivity, the connotation of language is 'innocented' through the photograph's denotation. It is true that there is never a real incorporation since the substances of the two structures (graphic and iconic) are irreducible, but there are most likely degrees of amalgamation. The caption probably has a less obvious effect of connotation than the headline or accompanying article: headline and article are palpably separate from the image, the former by its emphasis, the latter by its distance; the first because it breaks, the other because it distances the content of the image. The caption, on the contrary, by its very disposition, by its average measure of reading, appears to duplicate the image, that is, to be included in its denotation.

It is impossible however (and this will be the final remark here concerning the text) that the words 'duplicate' the image; in the movement from one structure to the other second signifieds are inevitably developed. What is the relationship of these signifieds of connotation to the image? To all appearances, it is one of making explicit, of providing a stress; the text most often simply amplifying a set of connotations already given in the photograph. Sometimes, however, the text produces (invents) an entirely new signified which is retroactively projected into the image, so much so as to appear denoted there. *'They were near to death, their faces prove it'*, reads the headline to a photograph showing Elizabeth and Philip leaving a plane— but at the moment of the photograph the two still knew nothing of the accident they had just escaped. Sometimes too, the text can even contradict the image so as to produce a compensatory connotation. An analysis by Gerbner *(The Social Anatomy of the Romance Confession Cover-girl)* demonstrated that in certain romance magazines the verbal message of the headlines, gloomy and anguished, on the cover always accompanied the image of a radiant cover-girl; here the two messages enter into a compromise, the connotation having a regulating function, preserving the irrational movement of projection-identification.

Photographic Insignificance

We saw that the code of connotation was in all likelihood neither 'natural' nor 'artificial' but historical, or, if it be preferred, 'cultural'. Its signs are gestures, attitudes, expressions, colours or effects, endowed with certain meanings by virtue of the practice of a certain society: the link between signifier and signified remains if not unmotivated, at least entirely historical. Hence it is wrong to say that modern man projects into reading photographs feelings and values which are characterial or 'eternal' (infra- or trans-historical), unless it be firmly specified that *signification* is always developed by a given society and history. Signification, in short, is the dialectical movement which resolves the contradiction between cultural and natural man.

Thanks to its code of connotation the reading of the photograph is thus always historical; it depends on the reader's 'knowledge' just as though it were a matter of real language [*langue*], intelligible only if one has learned the signs. All things considered, the photographic 'language' [*'langage'*] is not unlike certain ideographic languages which mix analogical and specifying units, the difference being that the ideogram is experienced as a sign whereas the photographic 'copy' is taken as the pure and simple denotation of reality. To find this code of connotation would thus be to isolate, inventoriate and structure all the 'historical' elements of the photograph, all the parts of the photographic surface which derive their very discontinuity from a certain knowledge on the reader's part, or, if one prefers, from the reader's cultural situation.

This task will perhaps take us a very long way indeed. Nothing tells us that the photograph contains 'neutral' parts, or at least it may be that complete insignificance in the photograph is quite exceptional. To resolve the problem we would first of all need to elucidate fully the mechanism of reading (in the physical, and no longer the semantic sense of the term), of the perception of the photograph. But on this point we know very little. How do we read a photograph? What do we perceive? In what order, according to what progression? If, as is suggested by certain hypotheses of Brune and Piaget, there is no perception without immediate categorization, then the photograph is verbalized in the very moment it is perceived; better, it is only perceived verbalized (if there is a delay in verbalization, there is disorder in perception, questioning, anguish for the subject, traumatism, following G. Cohen-Séat's hypothesis with regard to filmic perception). From this point of view the image—grasped immediately by an inner metalanguage, language itself—in actual fact has no denoted state, is immersed for its very social existence in at least an initial layer of connotation, that of the categories of language. We know that every language takes up a position with regard to things, that it connotes reality, if only in dividing it up; the connotations of the photograph would thus coincide, *grosso modo,* with the overall connotative planes of language.

In addition to 'perceptive' connotation, hypothetical but possible, one then encounters other, more particular, modes of connotation, and firstly a 'cognitive' connotation whose signifiers are picked out, localized, in certain parts of the analogon. Faced with such and such a townscape, I *know* that this is a North African country because on the left I can see a sign in Arabic script, in the center a man wearing a gandoura, and so on. Here the reading closely depends on my culture, on my knowledge of the world, and it is probable that a good press photograph (and they are all good, being selected) makes ready play with the supposed knowledge of its readers, those prints being chosen which comprise the greatest possible quantity of information of this kind in such a way as to render the reading fully satisfying. If one photographs Agadir in ruins, it is better to have a few signs of 'Arabness' at one's disposal, even though 'Arabness' has nothing to do with the disaster itself; connotation drawn from knowledge is always a reassuring force—man likes signs and likes them clear.

Perceptive connotation, cognitive connotation; there remains the problem of ideological (in the very wide sense of the term) or ethical connotation, that which introduces reasons or values into the reading of the image. This is a strong connotation requiring a highly elaborated signifier of a readily syntactical order: conjunction of people (as was seen in the discussion of trick effects), development of attitudes, constellation of objects. A son has just been born to the Shah of Iran and in a photograph we have: royalty (cot worshipped by a crowd of servants gathering round), wealth (several nursemaids), hygiene (white coat, cot covered in Plexiglass), the nevertheless human condition of kings (the baby is crying)—all the elements, that is, of the myth of princely birth as it is consumed today. In this instance the values are apolitical and their lexicon is abundant and clear. It is possible (but this is only a hypothesis) that political connotation is generally entrusted to the text insofar as political choices are always, as it were, in bad faith: for a particular photograph I can give a right-wing reading or a left-wing reading (see in this connection an IFOP survey published by *Les Temps modernes* in 1955). Denotation, or the appearance of denotation, is powerless to alter political opinions: no photograph has ever convinced or refuted anyone (but the photograph can 'confirm' insofar as political consciousness is perhaps non-existent outside the *logos*: politics is what allows *all* languages.

These few remarks sketch a kind of differential table of photographic connotations, showing, if nothing else, that connotation extends a long way. Is this to say that a pure denotation, a *this-side of language,* is impossible? If such a denotation exists, it is perhaps not at the level of what ordinary language calls the insignificant, the neutral, the objective, but, on the contrary, at the level of absolutely traumatic images. The trauma is a suspension of language, a blocking of meaning. Certainly situations which are normally traumatic can be seized in a process of photographic signification but then precisely they are indicated via a rhetorical code which distances, sublimates and pacifies them. Truly traumatic photographs are rare, for in photography the trauma is wholly dependent on the certainty that the scene 'really' happened: *the photographer had to be there* (the mythical definition of denotation). Assuming this (which, in fact, is already a connotation), the traumatic photograph (fires, shipwrecks, catastrophes, violent deaths, all captured 'from life as lived') is the photograph about which there is nothing to say; the shock-photo is by structure insignificant: no value, no knowledge, at the limit no verbal categorization can have a hold on the process instituting the signification. One could imagine a kind of law: the more direct the trauma, the more difficult is connotation; or again, the 'mythological' effect of a photograph is inversely proportional to its traumatic effect.

Why? Doubtless because photographic connotation, like very well structured signification, is an institutional activity; in relation to society overall, its function is to integrate man, to reassure him. Every code is at once arbitrary and rational; recourse to a code is thus always an opportunity for man to prove himself, to test himself through a reason and a liberty. In this sense, the analysis of codes perhaps allows an easier and surer historical definition of a society than the analysis of its signifieds, for the latter can often appear as trans-historical, belonging more to an anthropological base than to a proper history. Hegel gave a better definition of the ancient Greeks by outlining the manner in which they made nature signify than by describing the totality of their 'feelings and beliefs' on the subject. Similarly, we can perhaps do better than to take stock directly of the ideological contents of our age; by trying to reconstitute in its specific structure the code of connotation of a mode of communication as important as the press photograph we may hope to find, in their very subtlety, the forms our society uses to ensure its peace of mind and to grasp thereby the magnitude, the detours and the underlying function of that activity. The prospect is the more appealing in that, as was said at the beginning, it develops with regard to the photograph in the form of a paradox—that which makes of an inert object a language and which transforms the unculture of a 'mechanical' art into the most social of institutions.

JOHN F. KENNEDY (1919–1963)
Inaugural Address

We observe today not a victory of party but a celebration of freedom, symbolizing an end as well as a beginning, signifying renewal as well as change. For I have sworn before you and Almighty God the same solemn oath our forebears prescribed nearly a century and three-quarters ago.

The world is very different now. For man holds in his mortal hands the power to abolish all forms of human poverty and all forms of human life. And yet the same revolutionary belief for which our forebears fought is still at issue around the globe, the belief that the rights of man come not from the generosity of the state but from the hand of God.

We dare not forget today that we are the heirs of that first revolution. Let the word go forth from this time and place, to friend and foe alike, that the torch has been passed to a new generation of Americans, born in this century, tempered by war, disciplined by a hard and bitter peace, proud of our ancient heritage, and unwilling to witness or permit the slow undoing of those human rights to which this nation has always been committed, and to which we are committed today at home and around the world.

Let every nation know, whether it wishes us well or ill, that we shall pay any price, bear any burden, meet any hardship, support any friend, oppose any foe to assure the survival and the success of liberty.

This much we pledge—and more.

To those old allies whose cultural and spiritual origins we share, we pledge the loyalty of faithful friends. United, there is little we cannot do in a host of cooperative ventures. Divided, there is little we can do, for we dare not meet a powerful challenge at odds and split asunder.

To those new states whom we welcome to the ranks of the free, we pledge our word that one form of colonial control shall not have passed away merely to be replaced by a far more iron tyranny. We shall not always expect to find them supporting our view. But we shall always hope to find them strongly supporting their own freedom, and to remember that, in the past, those who foolishly sought power by riding the back of the tiger ended up inside.

To those peoples in the huts and villages of half the globe struggling to break the bonds of mass misery, we pledge our best efforts to help them help themselves, for whatever period is required, not because the Communists may be doing it, not because we seek their votes, but because it is right. If a free society cannot help the many who are poor, it cannot save the few who are rich.

To our sister republics south of our border, we offer a special pledge: to convert our good words into good deeds, in a new alliance for progress, to assist free men and free governments in casting off the chains of poverty. But this peaceful revolution of hope cannot become the prey of hostile powers. Let all our neighbors know that we shall join with them to oppose aggression or subversion anywhere in the Americas. And let every other power know that this hemisphere intends to remain the master of its own house.

To that world assembly of sovereign states, the United Nations, our last best hope in an age where the instruments of war have far outpaced the instruments of peace, we renew our pledge of support: to prevent it from becoming merely a forum for invective, to strengthen its shield of the new and the weak, and to enlarge the area in which its writ may run.

Finally, to those nations who would make themselves our adversary, we offer not a pledge but a request: that both sides begin anew the quest for peace, before the dark powers of destruction unleashed by science engulf all humanity in planned or accidental self-destruction.

We dare not tempt them with weakness. For only when our arms are sufficient beyond doubt can we be certain beyond doubt that they will never be employed.

But neither can two great and powerful groups of nations take comfort from our present course—both sides overburdened by the cost of modern weapons, both rightly alarmed by the steady spread of the deadly atom, yet both racing to alter that uncertain balance of terror that stays the hand of mankind's final war.

So let us begin anew, remembering on both sides that civility is not a sign of weakness, and sincerity is always subject to proof. Let us never negotiate out of fear, but let us never fear to negotiate.

Let both sides explore what problems unite us instead of belaboring those problems which divide us.

Let both sides, for the first time, formulate serious and precise proposals for the inspection and control of arms, and bring the absolute power to destroy other nations under the absolute control of all nations.

Let both sides seek to invoke the wonders of science instead of its terrors. Together let us explore the stars, conquer the deserts, eradicate disease, tap the ocean depths and encourage the arts and commerce.

Let both sides unite to heed in all corners of the earth the command of Isaiah to "undo the heavy burdens . . . [and] let the oppressed go free."

And if a beachhead of cooperation may push back the jungle of suspicion, let both sides join in creating a new endeavor, not a new balance of power, but a new world of law, where the strong are just and the weak secure and the peace preserved.

All this will not be finished in the first one hundred days. Nor will it be finished in the first one thousand days, nor in the life of this Administration, nor even perhaps in our lifetime on this planet. But let us begin.

In your hands, my fellow citizens, more than mine, will rest the final success or failure of our course. Since this country was founded, each generation of Americans has been summoned to give testimony to its national loyalty. The graves of young Americans who answered the call to service surround the globe.

Now the trumpet summons us again—not as a call to bear arms, though arms we need; not as a call to battle, though embattled we are; but a call to bear the burden of a long twilight struggle, year in and year out, "rejoicing in hope, patient in tribulation," a struggle against the common enemies of man: tyranny, poverty, disease and war itself.

Can we forge against these enemies a grand and global alliance, North and South, East and West, that can assure a more fruitful life for all mankind? Will you join in that historic effort?

In the long history of the world, only a few generations have been granted the role of defending freedom in its hour of maximum danger. I do not shrink from this responsibility; I welcome it. I do not believe that any of us would exchange places with any other people or any other generation. The energy, the faith, the devotion which we bring to this endeavor will light our country and all who serve it, and the glow from that fire can truly light the world.

And so, my fellow Americans, ask not what your country can do for you; ask what you can do for your country.

My fellow citizens of the world, ask not what America will do for you, but what together we can do for the freedom of man.

Finally, whether you are citizens of America or citizens of the world, ask of us here the same high standards of strength and sacrifice which we ask of you. With a good conscience our only sure reward, with history the final judge of our deeds, let us go forth to lead the land we love, asking His blessing and His help, but knowing that here on earth God's work must truly be our own.

RAYMOND WILLIAMS (b. 1926)

Keywords
(Selection)

The following abbreviations are used in the text.
 fw: immediate forerunner of a word, in the same or another language.
 rw: ultimate traceable word, from which 'root' meanings are derived.
 q.v.: see entry under word noted.
 C: followed by numeral, century (C19: nineteenth century).
 eC: first period (third) of a century.
 mC: middle period (third) of a century.
 lC: last period (third) of a century.
 c.: (before a date) approximately.
 F: French.
 Gk: Classical Greek.
 L: Latin.
 mL: Medieval Latin.
OED: *New English Dictionary on Historical Principles* (Oxford).

Quotations followed by a name and date only, or a date only, are from examples cited in OED. Other quotations are followed by specific sources.

Consumer

In modern English **consumer** and **consumption** are the predominant descriptive nouns of all kinds of use of goods and services. The predominance is significant in that it relates to a particular version of economic activity, derived from the character of a particular economic system, as the history of the word shows.

Consume has been in English since C14, from fw *consumer,* F, and the variant *consommer,* F (these variants have a complicated but eventually distinct history in French), rw *consumere,* L—to take up completely, devour, waste, spend. In almost all its early English uses, **consume** had an unfavourable sense; it meant to destroy, to use up, to waste, to exhaust. This sense is still present in 'consumed by fire' and in the popular description of pulmonary phthisis as **consumption.** Early uses of **consumer,** from C16, had the same general sense of destruction or waste.

It was from mC18 that **consumer** began to emerge in a neutral sense in descriptions of bourgeois political economy. In the new predominance of an organized market, the acts of making and of using goods and services were newly defined in the increasingly abstract pairings of *producer* and **consumer,** *production* and **consumption.** Yet the unfavourable connotations of **consume** persisted, at least until lC19, and it was really only in mC20 that the word passed from specialized use in political economy to general and popular use. The relative decline of *customer,* used from C15 to describe a buyer or purchaser, is significant here, in that *customer* had always implied some degree of regular and continuing relationship to a supplier, whereas **consumer** indicates the more abstract figure in a more abstract market.

The modern development has been primarily American but has spread very quickly. The dominance of the term has been so great that even groups of informed and discriminating purchasers and users have formed *Consumers' Associations.* The development relates primarily to the planning and attempted control of markets which is inherent in large-scale industrial capitalist (and state-capitalist) production, where, especially after the depression of lC19, manufacture was related not only to the supply of known needs (which *customer* or *user* would adequately describe) but to the planning of given kinds and quantities of production which required large investment at an early and often predictive stage. The development of modern commercial *advertising* (persuasion, or *penetration* of a market) is related to the same stage of capitalism: the creation of needs and wants and of particular ways of satisfying them, as distinct from and in addition to the notification of available supply which had been the main earlier function of *advertising* (where that kind of persuasion could be seen as *puff* and *puffery*). **Consumer** as a predominant term was the creation of such manufacturers and their agents. It implies, ironically as in the earliest senses, the using-up of what is going to be produced, though once the term was established it was given some appearance of autonomy (as in the curious phrase **consumer choice**). It is appropriate in terms of the history of the word that criticism of a wasteful and 'throw-away' society was expressed, somewhat later, by the description **consumer society.** Yet the predominance of the capitalist model ensured its widespread and often overwhelming extension to such fields as politics, education and health. In any of these fields, but also in the ordinary field of goods and services, to say *user* rather than **consumer** is still to express a relevant distinction.

Democracy

Democracy is a very old word but its meanings have always been complex. It came into English in C16, from fw *démocratie,* F, *democratia,* mL—a translation of *demokratia,* Gk, from rw *demos*—people, *kratos*—rule. It was defined by Elyot, with specific reference to the Greek instance, in 1531: 'an other publique weal was amonge the Atheniensis, where equalitie was of astate among the people . . . This manner of governaunce was called in greke *Democratia,* in latine, *Popularis potentia,* in englisshe the rule of the comminaltie.' It is at once evident from Greek uses that everything depends on the senses given to *people* and to *rule.* Ascribed and doubtful early examples range from obeying 'no master but the law' (? Solon) to 'of the people, by the people, for the people' (? Cleon). More certain examples compare 'the insolence of a despot' with 'the insolence of the unbridled commonalty' (cit. Herodotus) or define a government as democracy 'because its administration is in the hands, not of the few, but of the many'; also, 'all that is opposed to despotic power, has the name of democracy' (cit. Thucydides). Aristotle (*Politics,* IV, 4) wrote: 'a democracy is a state where the freemen and the poor, being in the majority, are invested with the power of the state'. Yet much depends here on what is meant by 'invested with power': whether it is ultimate sovereignty or, at the other extreme, practical and unshared rule. Plato made Socrates say (in *Republic,* VIII, 10) that 'democracy comes into being after the poor have conquered their opponents, slaughtering some and banishing some, while to the remainder they give an equal share of freedom and power'.

This range of uses, near the roots of the term, makes any simple derivation impossible. It can, however, be said at once that several of these uses—and especially those which indicate a form of popular class rule—are at some distance from any orthodox modern 'Western' definition of **democracy**. Indeed the emergence of that orthodox definition, which has its own uncertainties, is what needs to be traced. 'Democracy' is now often traced back to medieval precedents and given a Greek authority. But the fact is that, with only occasional exceptions, **democracy,** in the records that we have, was until C19 a strongly unfavourable term, and it is only since 1C19 and eC20 that a majority of political parties and tendencies have united in declaring their belief in it. This is the most striking historical fact.

Aquinas defined **democracy** as popular power, where the ordinary people, by force of numbers, governed—oppressed—the rich; the whole people acting like a tyrant. This strong class sense remained the predominant meaning until 1C18 and eC19, and was still active in mC19 argument. Thus: 'Democracie, when the multitude have government', Fleming (1576) (for the class sense of *multitude* see MASSES); 'democratie, where free and poore men being the greater number, are lords of the estate' (1586); 'democracy . . . nothing else than the power of the multitude', Filmer, *Patriarcha* (1680). To this definition of the *people* as the *multitude* there was added a common sense of the consequent type of *rule*: a **democracy** was a state in which all had the right to rule and did actually rule; it was even contrasted (e.g. by Spinoza) with a state in which there was rule by representatives, including elected representatives. It was in this sense that the first political constitution to use the term **democracy**—that of Rhode Island in 1641—understood it: 'popular government; that is to say it is in the power of the body of freemen orderly assembled, or a major part of them, to make or constitute just Lawes, by which they will be regulated, and to depute from among themselves such ministers as shall see them faithfully executed between man and man'.

This final clause needs to be emphasized, since a new meaning of democracy was eventually arrived at by an alteration of the practice here indicated. In the case of Rhode Island, the people or a major part of them made laws in orderly assembly; the ministers 'faithfully executed' them. This is not the same as the **representative democracy** defined by Hamilton in 1777. He was referring to the earlier sense of **democracy** when he observed that 'when the deliberative or judicial powers are vested wholly or partly in the collective body of the people, you must expect error, confusion and instability. But a representative democracy, where the right of election is well secured and regulated, and the exercise of the legislative executive and judicial authorities is vested in select persons . . . etc.' It is from this altered American use that a dominant modern sense developed. Bentham formulated a general sense of democracy as rule by the majority of the people, and then distinguished between 'direct democracy' and 'representative democracy', recommending the latter because it provided continuity and could be extended to large societies. These important practical reasons have since been both assumed and dropped, so that in mC20 an assertion of **democracy** in the Rhode Island sense, or in Bentham's *direct* sense, could be described as 'anti-democratic', since the first principle of **democracy** is taken to be rule by elected representatives. The practical arguments are of course serious, and in some circumstances decisive, but one of the two most significant changes in the meaning of **democracy** is this exclusive association with one of its derived forms, and the attempted exclusion of one of its original forms; at one period, its only form.

The second major change has to do with interpretation of *the people*. There is some significant history in the various attempts to limit 'the people' to certain qualified groups: freemen, owners of property, the wise, white men, men, and so on. Where **democracy** is defined by a process of election, such limited constitutions can be claimed to be fully **democratic**: the mode of choosing representatives is taken as more important than the proportion of 'the people' who have any part in this. The development of democracy is traced through institutions using this mode rather than through the relations between all the people and a form of government. This interpretation is orthodox in most accounts of the development of English democracy. Indeed **democracy** is said to have been 'extended' stage by stage, where what is meant is clearly the right to vote for representatives rather than the old (and until eC19 normal English) sense of *popular power*. The distinction became critical in the period of the French Revolution. Burke was expressing an orthodox view when he wrote that 'a perfect democracy' was 'the most shameless thing in the world' (*Reflections on the Revolution in France*, 1790) for **democracy** was taken to be 'uncontrolled' popular power under which, among other things, minorities (including especially the minority which held substantial property) would be suppressed or oppressed. **Democracy** was still a revolutionary or at least a radical term to mC19, and the specialized development of **representative democracy** was at least in part a conscious reaction to this, over and above the practical reasons of extent and continuity.

It is from this point in the argument that two modern meanings of **democracy** can be seen to diverge. In the socialist tradition, **democracy** continued to mean *popular power:* a state in which the interests of the majority of the people were paramount and in which these interests were practically exercised and controlled by the majority. In the liberal tradition, **democracy** meant open election of representatives and certain conditions (**democratic rights,** such as free speech) which maintained the openness of election and political argument. These two conceptions, in their extreme forms, now confront each other as enemies. If the predominant criterion is popular power in the popular interest, other criteria are often taken as secondary (as in the **People's Democracies**) and their emphasis is specialized to 'capitalist democracy' or 'bourgeois democracy'. If the predominant criteria are elections and free speech, other criteria are seen as secondary or are rejected; an attempt to exercise popular power in the popular interest, for example by a General Strike, is described as **anti-democratic,** since **democracy** has already been assured by other means; to claim economic EQUALITY (q.v.) as the essence of democracy is seen as leading to 'chaos' or to **totalitarian democracy** or *government by trade unions*. These positions, with their many minor variants, divide the modern meanings of **democracy** between them, but this is not usually seen as historical variation of the term; each position, normally, is described as 'the only true meaning', and the alternative use is seen as propaganda or hypocrisy.

Democratic (from eC19) is the normal adjective for one or other of these kinds of belief or institution. But two further senses should be noted. There is an observable use of **democratic** to describe the conditions of open argument, without necessary reference to elections or to power. Indeed, in one characteristic use freedom of speech and assembly are *the* 'democratic rights', sufficient in themselves, without reference to the institution or character of political power. This is a limiting sense derived from the liberal emphasis, which in its full form has to include election and popular sovereignty (though not popular rule) but which often opposes sustained **democratic** activity, such as challenges to an elected *leader* or his policies on other than formal or 'appropriate' occasions. There is also a derived sense from the early class reference to the 'multitude': to be **democratic,** to have **democratic** manners or feelings, is to be unconscious of class distinctions, or consciously to disregard or overcome them in everyday behaviour: acting *as if* all people were equal, and deserved equal respect, whether this is really so or not. Thus a man might be on 'plain and natural' terms with everyone he met, and might further believe in free speech and free assembly, yet, following only these senses, could for example oppose universal suffrage, let alone government directed solely to the interests of the majority. The senses have in part been extended, in part moved away, from what was formerly and is probably still the primary sense of the character of political power. Meanwhile *demagogy* and *demagogie,* fw *demagogós,* Gk, rw *demos*—people, *agogós*—leader, *agein*—lead, carried from the Greek the predominantly unfavourable sense, of 'irresponsible agitator' rather than 'popular leader', in a familiar kind of political prejudice. It was used similarly in English from C17, and cf. *agitator,* first used in the sense of 'agent' by soldiers' delegates in the Parliament of 1647–9, but given its derogatory sense mainly from C18.

No questions are more difficult than those of **democracy,** in any of its central senses. Analysis of variation will not resolve them, though it may sometimes clarify them. To the positive opposed senses of the socialist and liberal traditions we have to add, in a century which unlike any other finds nearly all political movements claiming to stand for **democracy** or **real democracy,** innumerable conscious distortions: reduction of the concepts of *election, representation* and *mandate* to deliberate formalities or merely manipulated forms; reduction of the concept of *popular power,* or government in the *popular interest,* to nominal slogans covering the rule of a bureaucracy or an oligarchy. It would sometimes be easier to believe in democracy, or to stand for it, if the C19 change had not happened and it were still an unfavourable or factional term. But that history has occurred, and the range of contemporary sense is its confused and still active record.

Family

Family has an especially significant social history. It came into English in 1C14 and eC15, from fw *familia,* L—household, from rw *famulus*—servant. The associated adjective **familiar** appears to be somewhat earlier in common use, and its range of meanings reminds us of the range of meanings which were predominant in **family** before mC17. There is the direct sense of the Latin *household,* either in the sense of a group of servants or a group of blood-relations and servants living together in one house. **Familiar** related to this, in phrases like **familiar angel, familiar devil** and the later noun **familiar,** where the sense is of being associated with or serving someone.

There is also the common C15 and C16 phrase **familiar enemy,** to indicate an enemy within one's household, 'within the gates', and thence by extension an enemy within one's own people. But the strongest early senses of **familiar** were those which are still current in modern English: on terms of friendship or intimate with someone (cf. 'don't be too familiar'); well known, well used to or habitual (cf. 'familiar in his mouth as household words', *Henry V*). These uses came from the experience of people living together in a household, in close relations with each other and well used to each other's ways. They do not, and **familiar** still does not, relate to the sense of a blood-group.

Family was then extended, from at latest C15, to describe not a household but what was significantly called a *house,* in the sense of a particular lineage or kingroup, ordinarily by descent from a common ancestor. This sense was extended to indicate a people or group of peoples, again with a sense of specific descent from an ancestor; also to a particular religious sense, itself associated with previous social meanings, as in 'the Father of our Lord Jesus Christ, of whom the whole family in heaven and earth is named' (*Ephesians* 3:14,15). **Family** in the Authorized Version of the Bible (1611) was restricted to these wide senses: either a large kin-group, often virtually equivalent to *tribe* (*Genesis* 10:5; 12:3; *Jeremiah* 1:15; 31:1; *Ezekiel* 20:32) or the kin-group of a common father: 'and then shall he (a brother) depart from thee, both he and his children with him, and shall return unto his own family, and unto the possession of his fathers shall he return' (*Leviticus* 25:41; cf. *Numbers* 36:6). The lC16 and C17 sect of the **Family of Love** or **Familists** is interesting in that it drew on the sense of a large group, but made this open and voluntary through love.

In none of the pre-mC17 senses, therefore, can we find the distinctive modern sense of a small group confined to immediate blood relations. When this sense of relations between parents and children was required in A.V. *Genesis* it was rendered by *near kin.* Yet it is clear that between C17 and C19 the sense of the small kingroup, usually living in one house, came to be dominant; so dominant indeed that in C20 there has been an invention of terms to distinguish between this and the surviving subordinate sense of a large kin-group: the distinction between **nuclear family** and **extended family.** It is very difficult to trace this evolution, which has a complicated social history. We can still read from 1631: 'his family were himself and his wife and daughters, two mayds and a man', where the sense is clearly that of *household.* This survived in rural use, with living-in farm servants who ate at the same table, until lC18 and perhaps beyond; the later distinction between **family** and *servants* was in this instance much resented. There was also a long influence from aristocratic use, in the sense of *lineage,* and this remained strong in the characteristic C18 **found a family.** Class distinction was expressed as late as C19 (and residually beyond it) in phrases like 'a person of no family', where the large kin-group is evidently in question but in the specialized sense of traceable lineage. Expressions like **the family** were still used to C20 to indicate a distinguishable upper-class group: 'the family is in residence', where the kin-group sense has clearly been separated from the household sense, since the servants are there in any case (but not 'in residence' even if 'resident').

The specialization of **family** to the small kin-group in a single house can be related to the rise of what is now called the **bourgeois family.** But this, with its senses of household and property, relates more properly, at least until C19, to the older sense. From eC19 (James Mill) we find this definition: 'the group which consists of a Father, Mother and Children is called a Family'; yet the fact that the conscious definition is necessary is in itself significant. Several 1C17 and C18 uses of **family** in a small kin-group sense often refer specifically to children: 'but duly sent his family and wife' (Pope, *Bathurst*), where the sense of household, however, may still be present. **Family-way,** common since eC18, referred first to the sense of **familiar** but then, through the specific sense of children, to pregnancy. There was thus considerable overlap, between mC17 and 1C18, of these varying senses of lineage, household, large kin-group and small kin-group.

The dominance of the sense of small kin-group was probably not established before eC19. The now predominant pressure of the word, and the definition of many kinds of feeling in relation to it, came in mC19 and later. This can be represented as the apotheosis of the **bourgeois family,** and the sense of the isolated family as a working economic unit is clearly stressed in the development of capitalism. But it has even stronger links to early capitalist production, and the C19 development represents, in one sense, a distinction between a man's *work* and his **family:** he works to support a **family;** the **family** is supported by his work. It is more probable, in fact, that the small kin-group definition, supported by the development of smaller separate houses and therefore households, relates to the new working class and lower-middle class who were defined by wage-labour: not **family** as lineage or property or as including these, and not **family** as *household* in the older established sense which included servants, but the near kin-group which can define its social relationships, in any positive sense, only in this way. **Family** or **family and friends** can represent the only immediately positive attachments in a large-scale and complex wage-earning society. And it is significant that class-feeling, the other major response to the new society, used *brother* and *sister* to express class affiliation, as in trade union membership, though there is also in this a clear religious precedent in certain related religious sects. It is significant also that this use of *brother* and *sister* came to seem artificial or comic in middle-class eyes. **Family,** there, combined the strong sense of immediate and positive blood-group relationships and the strong implicit sense of property.

It is a fascinating and difficult history, which can be only partly traced through the development of the word. But it is a history worth remembering when we hear that 'the **family,** as an institution, is breaking up' or that, in times gone by and still hopefully today, 'the **family** is the necessary foundation of all order and morality'. In these and similar contemporary uses it can be useful to remember the major historical variations, with some of their surviving complexities, and the sense, through these, of radically changing definitions of primary relationships.

Literature

Literature is a difficult word, in part because its conventional contemporary meaning appears, at first sight, so simple. There is no apparent difficulty in phrases like **English literature** or **contemporary literature**, until we find occasion to ask whether all books and writing are **literature** (and if they are not, which kinds are excluded and by what criteria) or until, to take a significant example, we come across a distinction between **literature** and *drama* on the grounds, apparently, that drama is a form primarily written for spoken performance (though often also to be read). It is not easy to understand what is at stake in these often confused distinctions until we look at the history of the word.

Literature came into English, from C14, in the sense of polite learning through reading. Its fw, *littérature*, F, *litteratura*, L, had the same general sense. The rw is *littera*, L—letter (of the alphabet). Thus a man of **literature,** or of *letters*, meant what we would now describe as a man of wide reading. Thus: 'hes nocht sufficient literatur to undirstand the scripture' (1581); 'learned in all literature and erudition, divine and humane' (Bacon, 1605). It can be seen from the Bacon example that the noun of condition—being well-read—is at times close to the objective noun—the books in which a man is well-read. But the main sense can be seen from the normal adjective, which was **literate,** from C15, rather than **literary,** which appeared first in C17 as a simple alternative to **literate** and only acquired its more general meaning in C18, though cf. Cave's Latin title *Historia Literaria,* 1688. As late as Johnson's *Life of Milton,* the earlier usage was still normal: 'he had probably more than common literature, as his son addresses him in one of his most elaborate Latin poems' (1780).

Literature, that is to say, corresponded mainly to the modern meanings of **literacy,** which, probably because the older meaning had then gone, was a new word from 1C19. It meant both an ability to read and a condition of being well-read. This can be confirmed from the negatives. **Illiterate** usually meant poorly-read or ill-educated: 'Judgis illitturate' (1586); 'my illeterate and rude stile' (1597); and as late as Chesterfield (1748): 'the word *illiterate,* in its common acceptance, means a man who is ignorant of those two languages' (Greek and Latin). Even more clearly there was the now obsolete **illiterature,** from 1C16: 'the cause . . . ignorance . . . and . . . illiterature' (1592). By contrast, from eC17, the **literati** were the highly-educated.

But the general sense of 'polite learning', firmly attached to the idea of printed books, was laying the basis for the later specialization. Colet, in C16, distinguished between literature and what he called **blotterature;** here the sense of inability to write clear letters is extended to a kind of book which was below the standards of polite learning. But the first certain signs of a general change in meaning are from C18. **Literary** was extended beyond its equivalence to **literate:** probably first in the general sense of well-read but from mC18 to refer to the practice and profession of writing: 'literary merit' (Goldsmith, 1759); 'literary reputation' (Johnson, 1773). This appears to be closely connected with the heightened self-consciousness of the profession of authorship, in the period of transition from patronage to the bookselling market. Where Johnson had used **literature** in the sense of being highly literate in his *Life of Milton,* in his *Life of Cowley* he wrote, in the newly objective sense: 'an author whose pregnancy of imagination and elegance of language have deservedly set him high in the ranks of literature'. (His *Dictionary* definition was 'learning, skill in letters'.) Yet **literature** and **literary,** in these new senses, still referred to the whole body of books and writing; or if distinction was made it was in terms of falling below the level of polite learning rather than of particular kinds of writing. A philosopher such as Hume quite naturally described his 'Love of literary Fame' as his 'ruling passion'. All works within the orbit of polite learning came to be described as **literature** and all such interests and practices as **literary**. Thus Hazlitt, in *Of Persons One Would Wish to Have Seen* (*Winterslow*, II), reports: 'Ayrton said, "I suppose the two first persons you would choose to see would be the two greatest names in English literature, Sir Isaac Newton and Mr Locke"' (c. 1825).

That now common phrase, **English literature**, is itself part of a crucial development. The idea of a *Nationallitteratur* developed in Germany from the 1770s, and the following can be recorded: *Über die neuere deutsche Litteratur* (Herder, 1767); *Les Siècles de littérature française* (1772); *Storia della letteratura italiana* (1772). **English literature** appears to have followed these, though it is implicit in Johnson. The sense of 'a nation' having 'a literature' is a crucial social and cultural, probably also political, development.

What has then to be traced is the attempted and often successful specialization of **literature** to certain kinds of writing. This is difficult just because it is incomplete; a **literary editor** or a **literary supplement** still deals generally with all kinds of books. But there has been a specialization to a sense which is sometimes emphasized (because of the remaining uncertainty) in phrases like **creative literature** and **imaginative literature** (cf. CREATIVE and IMAGINATIVE as descriptions of kinds of writing; cf. also FICTION). In relation to the past, **literature** is still a relatively general word: Carlyle and Ruskin, for example, who did not write novels or poems or plays, belong to **English literature**. But there has been a steady distinction and separation of other kinds of writing—philosophy, essays, history, and so on—which may or may not possess **literary merit** or be of **literary interest** (meaning that 'in addition to' their intrinsic interest as philosophy or history or whatever they are 'well written') but which are not now normally described as **literature**, which may be understood as well-written books but which is even more clearly understood as well-written books of an *imaginative* or *creative* kind. The teaching of English, especially in universities, is understood as the teaching of **literature**, meaning mainly poems and plays and novels; other kinds of 'serious' writing are described as *general* or *discursive*. Or there is **literary criticism**—judgment of how a (*creative* or *imaginative*) work is written—as distinct, often, from discussion of 'ideas' or 'history' or 'general subject-matter'. At the same time many, even most poems and plays and novels are not seen as **literature**; they fall below its level, in a sense related to the old distinction of *polite learning;* they are not 'substantial' or 'important' enough to be called **works of literature**. A new category of **popular literature** or the **sub-literary** has then to be instituted, to describe works which may be *fiction* but which are not *imaginative* or *creative*, which are therefore devoid of AESTHETIC (q.v.) interest, and which are not ART (q.v.).

Clearly the major shift represented by the modern complex of **literature,** *art, aesthetic, creative* and *imaginative* is a matter of social and cultural history. **Literature** itself must be seen as a late medieval and Renaissance isolation of the skills of reading and of the qualities of the book; this was much emphasized by the development of printing. But the sense of *learning* was still inherent, and there were also the active arts of *grammar* and *rhetoric*. Steadily, with the predominance of print, *writing* and *books* became virtually synonymous; hence the subsequent confusion about *drama,* which was writing for speech (but then Shakespeare is obviously **literature,** though with the *text* proving this). Then **literature** was specialized towards *imaginative writing,* within the basic assumptions of Romanticism. It is interesting to see what word did service for this before the specialization. It was, primarily, *poetry,* defined in 1586 as 'the arte of making: which word as it hath alwaies beene especially used of the best of our English Poets, to expresse the very faculty of speaking or wryting Poetically' (note the inclusion of *speaking*). Sidney wrote in 1581: 'verse being an ornament and no cause to Poetry: sith there have been many most excellent Poets, that never versified'. The specialization of *poetry* to metrical composition is evident from mC17, though this was still contested by Wordsworth: 'I here use the word "Poetry" (though against my own judgment) as opposed to the word "Prose", and synonymous with metrical composition' (1798). It is probable that this specialization of *poetry* to verse, together with the increasing importance of prose forms such as the NOVEL (q.v.), made **literature** the most available general word. It had behind it the Renaissance sense of *litterae humanae,* mainly then for secular as distinct from religious writing, and a generalizing use of *letters* had followed from this. *Belles lettres* was developed in French from mC17; it was to narrow when *literature* was eventually established. *Poetry* had been the high skills of writing and speaking in the special context of high imagination; the word could be moved in either direction. **Literature,** in its C19 sense, repeated this, though excluding speaking. But it is then problematic, not only because of the further specialization to *imaginative* and *creative* subject-matter (as distinct from *imaginative* and *creative* writing) but also because of the new importance of many forms of writing for speech (*broadcasting* as well as *drama*) which the specialization to books seemed by definition to exclude.

Significantly in recent years **literature** and **literary,** though they still have effective currency in post-C18 senses, have been increasingly challenged, on what is conventionally their own ground, by concepts of *writing* and *communication* which seek to recover the most active and general senses which the extreme specialization had seemed to exclude. Moreover, in relation to this reaction, **literary** has acquired two unfavourable senses, as belonging to the printed book or to past literature rather than to active contemporary writing and speech; or as (unreliable) evidence from books rather than 'factual inquiry'. This latter sense touches the whole difficult complex of the relations between *literature* (poetry, *fiction, imaginative* writing) and *real* or actual experience. Also, of course, *literary* has been a term of disparagement in discussion of certain other arts, notably painting and music, where the work in its own medium is seen as insufficiently autonomous, and as dependent on 'external' meanings of a 'literary' kind. This sense is also found in discussion of film. Meanwhile **literacy** and **illiteracy** have become key social concepts, in a much wider perspective than in the pre-C19 sense. **Illiteracy** was extended, from C18, to indicate general inability to read and write, and **literacy,** from 1C19, was a new word invented to express the achievement and possession of what were increasingly seen as general and necessary skills.

MICHEL FOUCAULT (1926–1984)

The Order of Things

This book first arose out of a passage in Borges, out of the laughter that shattered, as I read the passage, all the familiar landmarks of my thought—*our* thought, the thought that bears the stamp of our age and our geography—breaking up all the ordered surfaces and all the planes with which we are accustomed to tame the wild profusion of existing things, and continuing long afterwards to disturb and threaten with collapse our age-old distinction between the Same and the Other. This passage quotes a 'certain Chinese encyclopaedia' in which it is written that 'animals are divided into: (a) belonging to the Emperor, (b) embalmed, (c) tame, (d) sucking pigs, (e) sirens, (f) fabulous, (g) stray dogs, (h) included in the present classification, (i) frenzied, (j) innumerable, (k) drawn with a very fine camelhair brush, (l) *et cetera,* (m) having just broken the water pitcher, (n) that from a long way off look like flies'. In the wonderment of this taxonomy, the thing we apprehend in one great leap, the thing that, by means of the fable, is demonstrated as the exotic charm of another system of thought, is the limitation of our own, the stark impossibility of thinking *that.*

But what is it impossible to think, and what kind of impossibility are we faced with here? Each of these strange categories can be assigned a precise meaning and a demonstrable content; some of them do certainly involve fantastic entities—fabulous animals or sirens—but, precisely because it puts them into categories of their own, the Chinese encyclopaedia localizes their powers of contagion; it distinguishes carefully between the very real animals (those that are frenzied or have just broken the water pitcher) and those that reside solely in the realm of imagination. The possibility of dangerous mixtures has been exorcized, heraldry and fable have been relegated to their own exalted peaks; no inconceivable amphibious maidens, no clawed wings, no disgusting, squamous epidermis, none of those polymorphous and demoniacal faces, no creatures breathing fire. The quality of monstrosity here does not affect any real body, nor does it produce modifications of any kind in the bestiary of the imagination; it does not lurk in the depths of any strange power. It would not even be present at all in this classification had it not insinuated itself into the empty space, the interstitial blanks *separating* all these entities from one another. It is not the 'fabulous' animals that are impossible, since they are designated as such, but the narrowness of the distance separating them from (and juxtaposing them to) the stray dogs, or the animals that from a long way off look like flies. What transgresses the boundaries of all imagination, of all possible thought, is simply that alphabetical series (a, b, c, d) which links each of those categories to all the others.

Moreover, it is not simply the oddity of unusual juxtapositions that we are faced with here. We are all familiar with the disconcerting effect of the proximity of extremes, or, quite simply, with the sudden vicinity of things that have no relation to each other; the mere act of enumeration that heaps them all together has a power of enchantment all its own: 'I am no longer hungry,' Eusthenes said. 'Until the morrow, safe from my saliva all the following shall be: Aspics, Acalephs, Acanthocephalates, Amoebocytes, Ammonites, Axolotls, Amblystomas, Aphislions, Anacondas, Ascarids, Amphisbaenas, Angleworms, Amphipods, Anaerobes, Annelids, Anthozoans. . . .' But all these worms and snakes, all these creatures redolent of decay and slime are slithering, like the syllables which designate them, in Eusthenes' saliva: that is where they all have their *common locus,* like the umbrella and the sewing-machine on the operating table; startling though their propinquity may be, it is nevertheless warranted by that *and,* by that *in,* by that *on* whose solidity provides proof of the possibility of juxtaposition. It was certainly improbable that arachnids, ammonites, and annelids should one day mingle on Eusthenes' tongue, but, after all, that welcoming and voracious mouth certainly provided them with a feasible lodging, a roof under which to coexist.

The monstrous quality that runs through Borges's enumeration consists, on the contrary, in the fact that the common ground on which such meetings are possible has itself been destroyed. What is impossible is not the propinquity of the things listed, but the very site on which their propinquity would be possible. The animals '(i) frenzied, (j) innumerable, (k) drawn with a very fine camelhair brush'—where could they ever meet, except in the immaterial sound of the voice pronouncing their enumeration, or on the page transcribing it? Where else could they be juxtaposed except in the non-place of language? Yet, though language can spread them before us, it can do so only in an unthinkable space. The central category of animals 'included in the present classification', with its explicit reference to paradoxes we are familiar with, is indication enough that we shall never succeed in defining a stable relation of contained to container between each of these categories and that which includes them all: if all the animals divided up here can be placed without exception in one of the divisions of this list, then aren't all the other divisions to be found in that one division too? And then again, in what space would that single, inclusive division have *its* existence? Absurdity destroys the *and* of the enumeration by making impossible the *in* where the things enumerated would be divided up. Borges adds no figure to the atlas of the impossible; nowhere does he strike the spark of poetic confrontation; he simply dispenses with the least obvious, but most compelling, of necessities; he does away with the *site,* the mute ground upon which it is possible for entities to be juxtaposed. A vanishing trick that is masked or, rather, laughably indicated by our alphabetical order, which is to be taken as the clue (the only visible one) to the enumerations of a Chinese encyclopaedia. . . . What has been removed, in short, is the famous 'operating table'; and rendering to Roussel[1] a small part of what is still his due, I use that word 'table' in two superimposed senses: the nickel-plated, rubbery table swathed in white, glittering beneath a glass sun devouring all shadow —the table where, for an instant, perhaps forever, the umbrella encounters the sewing-machine; and also a table, a *tabula,* that enables thought to operate upon the entities of our world, to put them in order, to divide them into classes, to group them according to names that designate their similarities and their differences—the table upon which, since the beginning of time, language has intersected space.

---

[1] Raymond Roussel, the French novelist. Cf. Michel Foucault's *Raymond Roussel* (Paris, 1963). [Translator's note.]

That passage from Borges kept me laughing a long time, though not without a certain uneasiness that I found hard to shake off. Perhaps because there arose in its wake the suspicion that there is a worse kind of disorder than that of the *incongruous,* the linking together of things that are inappropriate; I mean the disorder in which fragments of a large number of possible orders glitter separately in the dimension, without law or geometry, of the *heteroclite;* and that word should be taken in its most literal, etymological sense: in such a state, things are 'laid', 'placed', 'arranged' in sites so very different from one another that it is impossible to find a place of residence for them, to define a *common locus* beneath them all. *Utopias* afford consolation: although they have no real locality there is nevertheless a fantastic, untroubled region in which they are able to unfold; they open up cities with vast avenues, superbly planted gardens, countries where life is easy, even though the road to them is chimerical. *Heterotopias* are disturbing, probably because they secretly undermine language, because they make it impossible to name this *and* that, because they shatter or tangle common names, because they destroy 'syntax' in advance, and not only the syntax with which we construct sentences but also that less apparent syntax which causes words and things (next to and also opposite one another) to 'hold together'. This is why utopias permit fables and discourse: they run with the very grain of language and are part of the fundamental dimension of the *fabula;* heterotopias (such as those to be found so often in Borges) desiccate speech, stop words in their tracks, contest the very possibility of grammar at its source; they dissolve our myths and sterilize the lyricism of our sentences.

It appears that certain aphasiacs, when shown various differently coloured skeins of wool on a table top, are consistently unable to arrange them into any coherent pattern; as though that simple rectangle were unable to serve in their case as a homogeneous and neutral space in which things could be placed so as to display at the same time the continuous order of their identities or differences as well as the semantic field of their denomination. Within this simple space in which things are normally arranged and given names, the aphasiac will create a multiplicity of tiny, fragmented regions in which nameless resemblances agglutinate things into unconnected islets; in one corner, they will place the lightest-coloured skeins, in another the red ones, somewhere else those that are softest in texture, in yet another place the longest, or those that have a tinge of purple or those that have been wound up into a ball. But no sooner have they been adumbrated than all these groupings dissolve again, for the field of identity that sustains them, however limited it may be, is still too wide not to be unstable; and so the sick mind continues to infinity, creating groups then dispersing them again, heaping up diverse similarities, destroying those that seem clearest, splitting up things that are identical, superimposing different criteria, frenziedly beginning all over again, becoming more and more disturbed, and teetering finally on the brink of anxiety.

The uneasiness that makes us laugh when we read Borges is certainly related to the profound distress of those whose language has been destroyed: loss of what is 'common' to place and name. Atopia, aphasia. Yet our text from Borges proceeds in another direction; the mythical homeland Borges assigns to that distortion of classification that prevents us from applying it, to that picture that lacks all spatial coherence, is a precise region whose name alone constitutes for the West a vast reservoir of utopias. In our dreamworld, is not China precisely this privileged *site* of *space?* In our traditional imagery, the Chinese culture is the most meticulous, the most rigidly ordered, the one most deaf to temporal events, most attached to the pure delineation of space; we think of it as a civilization of dikes and dams beneath the eternal face of the sky; we see it, spread and frozen, over the entire surface of a continent surrounded by walls. Even its writing does not reproduce the fugitive flight of the voice in horizontal lines; it erects the motionless and still-recognizeable images of things themselves in vertical columns. So much so that the Chinese encyclopaedia quoted by Borges, and the taxonomy it proposes, lead to a kind of thought without space, to words and categories that lack all life and place, but are rooted in a ceremonial space, overburdened with complex figures, with tangled paths, strange places, secret passages, and unexpected communications. There would appear to be, then, at the other extremity of the earth we inhabit, a culture entirely devoted to the ordering of space, but one that does not distribute the multiplicity of existing things into any of the categories that make it possible for us to name, speak, and think.

When we establish a considered classification, when we say that a cat and a dog resemble each other less than two greyhounds do, even if both are tame or embalmed, even if both are frenzied, even if both have just broken the water pitcher, what is the ground on which we are able to establish the validity of this classification with complete certainty? On what 'table', according to what grid of identities, similitudes, analogies, have we become accustomed to sort out so many different and similar things? What is this coherence—which, as is immediately apparent, is neither determined by an *a priori* and necessary concatenation, nor imposed on us by immediately perceptible contents? For it is not a question of linking consequences, but of grouping and isolating, of analysing, of matching and pigeon-holing concrete contents; there is nothing more tentative, nothing more empirical (superficially, at least) than the process of establishing an order among things; nothing that demands a sharper eye or a surer, better-articulated language; nothing that more insistently requires that one allow oneself to be carried along by the proliferation of qualities and forms. And yet an eye not consciously prepared might well group together certain similar figures and distinguish between others on the basis of such and such a difference: in fact, there is no similitude and no distinction, even for the wholly untrained perception, that is not the result of a precise operation and of the application of a preliminary criterion. A 'system of elements'—a definition of the segments by which the resemblances and differences can be shown, the types of variation by which those segments can be affected, and, lastly, the threshold above which there is a difference and below which there is a similitude—is indispensable for the establishment of even the simplest form of order. Order is, at one and the same time, that which is given in things as their inner law, the hidden network that determines the way they confront one another, and also that which has no existence except in the grid created by a glance, an examination, a language; and it is only in the blank spaces of this grid that order manifests itself in depth as though already there, waiting in silence for the moment of its expression.

The fundamental codes of a culture—those governing its language, its schemas of perception, its exchanges, its techniques, its values, the hierarchy of its practices—establish for every man, from the very first, the empirical orders with which he will be dealing and within which he will be at home. At the other extremity of thought, there are the scientific theories or the philosophical interpretations which explain why order exists in general, what universal law it obeys, what principle can account for it, and why this particular order has been established and not some other. But between these two regions, so distant from one another, lies a domain which, even though its role is mainly an intermediary one, is nonetheless fundamental: it is more confused, more obscure, and probably less easy to analyse. It is here that a culture, imperceptibly deviating from the empirical orders prescribed for it by its primary codes, instituting an initial separation from them, causes them to lose their original transparency, relinquishes its immediate and invisible powers, frees itself sufficiently to discover that these orders are perhaps not the only possible ones or the best ones; this culture then finds itself faced with the stark fact that there exists, below the level of its spontaneous orders, things that are in themselves capable of being ordered, that belong to a certain unspoken order; the fact, in short, that order *exists*. As though emancipating itself to some extent from its linguistic, perceptual, and practical grids, the culture superimposed on them another kind of grid which neutralized them, which by this superimposition both revealed and excluded them at the same time, so that the culture, by this very process, came face to face with order in its primary state. It is on the basis of this newly perceived order that the codes of language, perception, and practice are criticized and rendered partially invalid. It is on the basis of this order, taken as a firm foundation, that general theories as to the ordering of things, and the interpretation that such an ordering involves, will be constructed. Thus, between the already 'encoded' eye and reflexive knowledge there is a middle region which liberates order itself: it is here that it appears, according to the culture and the age in question, continuous and graduated or discontinuous and piecemeal, linked to space or constituted anew at each instant by the driving force of time, related to a series of variables or defined by separate systems of coherences, composed of resemblances which are either successive or corresponding, organized around increasing differences, etc. This middle region, then, in so far as it makes manifest the modes of being of order, can be posited as the most fundamental of all: anterior to words, perceptions, and gestures, which are then taken to be more or less exact, more or less happy, expressions of it (which is why this experience of order in its pure primary state always plays a critical role); more solid, more archaic, less dubious, always more 'true' than the theories that attempt to give those expressions explicit form, exhaustive application, or philosophical foundation. Thus, in every culture, between the use of what one might call the ordering codes and reflections upon order itself, there is the pure experience of order and of its modes of being.

The present study is an attempt to analyse that experience. I am concerned to show its developments, since the sixteenth century, in the mainstream of a culture such as ours: in what way, as one traces—against the current, as it were—language as it has been spoken, natural creatures as they have been perceived and grouped together, and exchanges as they have been practised; in what way, then, our culture has made manifest the existence of order, and how, to the modalities of that order, the exchanges owed their laws, the living beings their constants, the words their sequence and their representative value; what modalities of order have been recognized, posited, linked with space and time, in order to create the positive basis of knowledge as we find it employed in grammar and philology, in natural history and biology, in the study of wealth and political economy. Quite obviously, such an analysis does not belong to the history of ideas or of science: it is rather an inquiry whose aim is to rediscover on what basis knowledge and theory became possible; within what space of order knowledge was constituted; on the basis of what historical *a priori*, and in the element of what positivity, ideas could appear, sciences be established, experience be reflected in philosophies, rationalities be formed, only, perhaps, to dissolve and vanish soon afterwards. I am not concerned, therefore, to describe the progress of knowledge towards an objectivity in which today's science can finally be recognized; what I am attempting to bring to light is the epistemological field, the *episteme* in which knowledge, envisaged apart from all criteria having reference to its rational value or to its objective forms, grounds its positivity and thereby manifests a history which is not that of its growing perfection, but rather that of its conditions of possibility; in this account, what should appear are those configurations within the *space* of knowledge which has given rise to the diverse forms of empirical science. Such an enterprise is not so much a history, in the traditional meaning of that word, as an 'archaeology'.

Now, this archaeological inquiry has revealed two great discontinuities in the *episteme* of Western culture: the first inaugurates the Classical age (roughly half-way through the seventeenth century) and the second, at the beginning of the nineteenth century, marks the beginning of the modern age. The order on the basis of which we think today does not have the same mode of being as that of the Classical thinkers. Despite the impression we may have of an almost uninterrupted development of the European *ratio* from the Renaissance to our own day, despite our possible belief that the classifications of Linnaeus, modified to a greater or lesser degree, can still lay claim to some sort of validity, that Condillac's theory of value can be recognized to some extent in nineteenth-century marginalism, that Keynes was well aware of the affinities between his own analyses and those of Cantillon, that the language of *general grammar* (as exemplified in the authors of Port-Royal or in Bauzée) is not so very far removed from our own—all this quasi-continuity on the level of ideas and themes is doubtless only a surface appearance; on the archaeological level, we see that the system of positivities was transformed in a wholesale fashion at the end of the eighteenth and beginning of the nineteenth century. Not that reason made any progress: it was simply that the mode of being of things, and of the order that divided them up before presenting them to the understanding, was profoundly altered. If the natural history of Tournefort, Linnaeus, and Buffon can be related to anything at all other than itself, it is not to biology, to Cuvier's comparative anatomy, or to Darwin's theory of evolution, but to Bauzée's general grammar, to the analysis of money and wealth as found in the works of Law, or Véron de Fortbonnais, or Turgot. Perhaps knowledge succeeds in engendering knowledge, ideas in transforming themselves and actively modifying one another (but how?—historians have not yet enlightened us on this point); one thing, in any case, is certain: archaeology, addressing itself to the general space of knowledge, to its configurations, and to the mode of being of the things that appear in it, defines systems of simultaneity, as well as the series of mutations necessary and sufficient to circumscribe the threshold of a new positivity.

In this way, analysis has been able to show the coherence that existed, throughout the Classical age, between the theory of representation and the theories of language, of the natural orders, and of wealth and value. It is this configuration that, from the nineteenth century onward, changes entirely; the theory of representation disappears as the universal foundation of all possible orders; language as the spontaneous *tabula,* the primary grid of things, as an indispensable link between representation and things, is eclipsed in its turn; a profound historicity penetrates into the heart of things, isolates and defines them in their own coherence, imposes upon them the forms of order implied by the continuity of time; the analysis of exchange and money gives way to the study of production, that of the organism takes precedence over the search for taxonomic characteristics, and, above all, language loses its privileged position and becomes, in its turn, a historical form coherent with the density of its own past. But as things become increasingly reflexive, seeking the principle of their intelligibility only in their own development, and abandoning the space of representation, man enters in his turn, and for the first time, the field of Western knowledge. Strangely enough, man—the study of whom is supposed by the naïve to be the oldest investigation since Socrates—is probably no more than a kind of rift in the order of things, or, in any case, a configuration whose outlines are determined by the new position he has so recently taken up in the field of knowledge. Whence all the chimeras of the new humanisms, all the facile solutions of an 'anthropology' understood as a universal reflection on man, half-empirical, half-philosophical. It is comforting, however, and a source of profound relief to think that man is only a recent invention, a figure not yet two centuries old, a new wrinkle in our knowledge, and that he will disappear again as soon as that knowledge has discovered a new form.

It is evident that the present study is, in a sense, an echo of my undertaking to write a history of madness in the Classical age; it has the same articulations in time, taking the end of the Renaissance as its starting-point, then encountering, at the beginning of the nineteenth century, just as my history of madness did, the threshold of a modernity that we have not yet left behind. But whereas in the history of madness I was investigating the way in which a culture can determine in a massive, general form the difference that limits it, I am concerned here with observing how a culture experiences the propinquity of things, how it establishes the *tabula* of their relationships and the order by which they must be considered. I am concerned, in short, with a history of resemblance: on what conditions was Classical thought able to reflect relations of similarity or equivalence between things, relations that would provide a foundation and a justification for their words, their classifications, their systems of exchange? What historical *a priori* provided the starting-point from which it was possible to define the great checkerboard of distinct identities established against the confused, undefined, faceless, and, as it were, indifferent background of differences? The history of madness would be the history of the Other—of that which, for a given culture, is at once interior and foreign, therefore to be excluded (so as to exorcize the interior danger) but by being shut away (in order to reduce its otherness); whereas the history of the order imposed on things would be the history of the Same—of that which, for a given culture, is both dispersed and related, therefore to be distinguished by kinds and to be collected together into identities.

And if one considers that disease is at one and the same time disorder—the existence of a perilous otherness within the human body, at the very heart of life—and a natural phenomenon with its own constants, resemblances, and types, one can see what scope there would be for an archaeology of the medical point of view. From the limit-experience of the Other to the constituent forms of medical knowledge, and from the latter to the order of things and the conceptions of the Same, what is available to archaeological analysis is the whole of Classical knowledge, or rather the threshold that separates us from Classical thought and constitutes our modernity. It was upon this threshold that the strange figure of knowledge called man first appeared and revealed a space proper to the human sciences. In attempting to uncover the deepest strata of Western culture, I am restoring to our silent and apparently immobile soil its rifts, its instability, its flaws; and it is the same ground that is once more stirring under our feet.

MARTIN LUTHER KING, JR. (1929–1968)

"I Have a Dream"

I am happy to join with you today in what will go down in history as the greatest demonstration for freedom in the history of our nation.

Five score years ago, a great American, in whose symbolic shadow we stand today, signed the Emancipation Proclamation. This momentous decree came as a great beacon light of hope to millions of Negro slaves who had been seared in the flames of withering injustice. It came as a joyous daybreak to end the long night of their captivity.

But one hundred years later, the Negro still is not free; one hundred years later, the life of the Negro is still sadly crippled by the manacles of segregation and the chains of discrimination; one hundred years later, the Negro lives on a lonely island of poverty in the midst of a vast ocean of material prosperity; one hundred years later, the Negro is still languished in the corners of American society and finds himself in exile in his own land.

So we've come here today to dramatize a shameful condition. In a sense we've come to our nation's capital to cash a check. When the architects of our republic wrote the magnificent words of the Constitution and the Declaration of Independence, they were signing a promissory note to which every American was to fall heir.

This note was the promise that all men, yes, black men as well as white men, would be guaranteed the unalienable rights of life, liberty, and the pursuit of happiness.

It is obvious today that America has defaulted on this promissory note in so far as her citizens of color are concerned. Instead of honoring this sacred obligation, America has given the Negro people a bad check, a check which has come back marked "insufficient funds." But we refuse to believe that the bank of justice is bankrupt. We refuse to believe that there are insufficient funds in the great vaults of opportunity of this nation. And so we've come to cash this check, a check that will give us upon demand the riches of freedom and the security of justice.

We have also come to this hallowed spot to remind America of the fierce urgency of now. This is no time to engage in the luxury of cooling off or to take the tranquilizing drug of gradualism. Now is the time to make real the promises of democracy; now is the time to rise from the dark and desolate valley of segregation to the sunlit path of racial justice; now is the time to lift our nation from the quicksands of racial injustice to the solid rock of brotherhood; now is the time to make justice a reality for all of God's children. It would be fatal for the nation to overlook the urgency of the moment. This sweltering summer of the Negro's legitimate discontent will not pass until there is an invigorating autumn of freedom and equality.

Nineteen sixty-three is not an end, but a beginning. And those who hope that the Negro needed to blow off steam and will now be content, will have a rude awakening if the nation returns to business as usual. There will be neither rest nor tranquility in America until the Negro is granted his citizenship rights. The whirlwinds of revolt will continue to shake the foundations of our nation until the bright day of justice emerges.

But there is something that I must say to my people, who stand on the worn threshold which leads into the palace of justice. In the process of gaining our rightful place, we must not be guilty of wrongful deeds. Let us not seek to satisfy our thirst for freedom by drinking from the cup of bitterness and hatred. We must forever conduct our struggle on the high plain of dignity and discipline. We must not allow our creative protests to degenerate into physical violence. Again and again we must rise to the majestic heights of meeting physical force with soul force. The marvelous new militancy, which has engulfed the Negro community, must not lead us to a distrust of all white people. For many of our white brothers, as evidenced by their presence here today, have come to realize that their destiny is tied up with our destiny. And they have come to realize that their freedom is inextricably bound to our freedom. We cannot walk alone. And as we walk, we must make the pledge that we shall always march ahead. We cannot turn back.

There are those who are asking the devotees of Civil Rights, "When will you be satisfied?" We can never be satisfied as long as the Negro is the victim of the unspeakable horrors of police brutality; we can never be satisfied as long as our bodies, heavy with the fatigue of travel, cannot gain lodging in the motels of the highways and the hotels of the cities; we cannot be satisfied as long as the Negro's basic mobility is from a smaller ghetto to a larger one; we can never be satisfied as long as our children are stripped of their selfhood and robbed of their dignity by signs stating

"For Whites Only"; we cannot be satisfied as long as the Negro in Mississippi cannot vote and a Negro in New York believes he has nothing for which to vote. No! No, we are not satisfied, and we will not be satisfied until "justice rolls down like waters and righteousness like a mighty stream."

I am not unmindful that some of you have come here out of great trials and tribulations. Some of you have come fresh from narrow jail cells. Some of you have come from areas where your quest for freedom left you battered by the storms of persecution and staggered by the winds of police brutality. You have been the veterans of creative suffering. Continue to work with the faith that unearned suffering is redemptive. Go back to Mississippi. Go back to Alabama. Go back to South Carolina. Go back to Georgia. Go back to Louisiana. Go back to the slums and ghettos of our Northern cities, knowing that somehow this situation can and will be changed. Let us not wallow in the valley of despair.

I say to you today, my friends, so even though we face the difficulties of today and tomorrow, I still have a dream. It is a dream deeply rooted in the American dream. I have a dream that one day this nation will rise up and live out the true meaning of its creed, "We hold these truths to be self-evident, that all men are created equal." I have a dream that one day on the red hills of Georgia, sons of former slaves and the sons of former slave owners will be able to sit down together at the table of brotherhood. I have a dream that one day even the state of Mississippi, a state sweltering with the heat of injustice, sweltering with the heat of oppression, will be transformed into an oasis of freedom and justice. I have a dream that my four little children will one day live in a nation where they will not be judged by the color of their skin, but by the content of their character.

I HAVE A DREAM TODAY!

I have a dream that one day down in Alabama—with its vicious racists, with its Governor having his lips dripping with the words of interposition and nullification —one day right there in Alabama, little black boys and black girls will be able to join hands with little white boys and white girls as sisters and brothers.

I HAVE A DREAM TODAY!

I have a dream that one day every valley shall be exalted, and every hill and mountain shall be made low. The rough places will be plain and the crooked places will be made straight, "and the glory of the Lord shall be revealed, and all flesh shall see it together."

This is our hope. This is the faith that I go back to the South with. With this faith we will be able to hew out of the mountain of despair a stone of hope. With this faith we will be able to transform the jangling discords of our nation into a beautiful symphony of brother-hood. With this faith we will be able to work together, to pray together, to struggle together, to go to jail together, to stand up for freedom together, knowing that we will be free one day. And this will be the day. This will be the day when all of God's children will be able to sing with new meaning, "My country 'tis of thee, sweet land of liberty, of thee I sing. Land where my father died, land of the pilgrim's pride, from every mountainside, let freedom ring." And if America is to be a great nation, this must become true.

So let freedom ring from the prodigious hilltops of New Hampshire; let freedom ring from the mighty mountains of New York; let freedom ring from the heightening Alleghenies of Pennsylvania; let freedom ring from the snow-capped Rockies of Colorado; let freedom ring from the curvaceous slopes of California. But not only that. Let freedom ring from Stone Mountain of Georgia; let freedom ring from Lookout Mountain of Tennessee; let freedom ring from every hill and mole hill of Mississippi. "From every mountainside, let freedom ring."

And when this happens, and when we allow freedom to ring, when we let it ring from every village and every hamlet, from every state and every city, we will be able to speed up that day when all of God's children, black men and white men, Jews and Gentiles, Protestants and Catholics, will be able to join hands and sing in the words of the old Negro spiritual: "Free at last. Free at last. Thank God Almighty, we are free at last."

SUSAN SONTAG (b. 1933)
Illness as Metaphor

I

Two diseases have been spectacularly, and similarly, encumbered by the trappings of metaphor: tuberculosis and cancer.

The fantasies inspired by TB in the last century, by cancer now, are responses to a disease thought to be intractable and capricious—that is, a disease not understood—in an era in which medicine's central premise is that all diseases can be cured. Such a disease is, by definition, mysterious. For as long as its cause was not understood and the ministrations of doctors remained so ineffective, TB was thought to be an insidious, implacable theft of a life. Now it is cancer's turn to be the disease that doesn't knock before it enters; cancer fills the role of an illness experienced as a ruthless, secret invasion—a role it will keep until, one day, its etiology becomes as clear and its treatment as effective as those of TB have become.

Although the way in which disease mystifies is set against a backdrop of new expectations, the disease itself (once TB, cancer today) arouses thoroughly old-fashioned kinds of dread. Any disease that is treated as a mystery and acutely enough feared will be felt to be morally, if not literally, contagious. Thus, a surprisingly large number of people with cancer find themselves being shunned by relatives and friends and are the object of practices of decontamination by members of their household, as if cancer, like TB, were an infectious disease. Contact with someone afflicted with a disease regarded as a mysterious malevolency inevitably feels like a trespass; worse, like the violation of a taboo. The very names of such diseases are felt to have a magic power. In Stendhal's *Armance* (1827), the hero's mother refuses to say "tuberculosis," for fear that pronouncing the word will hasten the course of her son's malady. And Karl Menninger has observed (in *The Vital Balance*) that "the very word 'cancer' is said to kill some patients who would not have succumbed (so quickly) to the malignancy from which they suffer." This observation is offered in support of anti-intellectual pieties and a facile compassion all too triumphant in contemporary medicine and psychiatry. "Patients who consult us because of their suffering and their distress and their disability," he continues, "have every right to resent being plastered with a damning index tab." Dr. Menninger recommends that physicians generally abandon "names" and "labels" ("our function is to help these people, not to further afflict them")—which would mean, in effect, increasing secretiveness and medical paternalism. It is not naming as such that is pejorative or damning, but the name "cancer." As long as a particular disease is treated as an evil, invincible predator, not just a disease, most people with cancer will indeed be demoralized by learning what disease they have. The solution is hardly to stop telling cancer patients the truth, but to rectify the conception of the disease, to de-mythicize it.

When, not so many decades ago, learning that one had TB was tantamount to hearing a sentence of death—as today, in the popular imagination, cancer equals death—it was common to conceal the identity of their disease from tuberculars and, after they died, from their children. Even with patients informed about their disease, doctors and family were reluctant to talk freely. "Verbally I don't learn anything definite," Kafka wrote to a friend in April 1924 from the sanatorium where he died two months later, "since in discussing tuberculosis . . . everybody drops into a shy, evasive, glassy-eyed manner of speech." Conventions of concealment with cancer are even more strenuous. In France and Italy it is still the rule for doctors to communicate a cancer diagnosis to the patient's family but not the patient; doctors consider that the truth will be intolerable to all but exceptionally mature and intelligent patients. (A leading French oncologist has told me that fewer than a tenth of his patients know they have cancer.) In America—in part because of the doctors' fear of malpractice suits—there is now much more candor with patients, but the country's largest cancer hospital mails routine communications and bills to outpatients in envelopes that do not reveal the sender, on the assumption that the illness may be a secret from their families. Since getting cancer can be a scandal that jeopardizes one's love life, one's chance of promotion, even one's job, patients who know what they have tend to be extremely prudish, if not outright secretive, about their disease. And a federal law, the 1966 Freedom of Information Act, cites "treatment for cancer" in a clause exempting from disclosure matters whose disclosure "would be an unwarranted invasion of personal privacy." It is the only disease mentioned.

All this lying to and by cancer patients is a measure of how much harder it has become in advanced industrial societies to come to terms with death. As death is now an offensively meaningless event, so that disease widely considered a synonym for death is experienced as something to hide. The policy of equivocating about the nature of their disease with cancer patients reflects the conviction that dying people are best spared the news that they are dying, and that the good death is the sudden one, best of all if it happens while we're unconscious or asleep. Yet the modern denial of death does not explain the extent of the lying and the wish to be lied to; it does not touch the deepest dread. Someone who has had a coronary is at least as likely to die of another one within a few years as someone with cancer is likely to die soon from cancer. But no one thinks of concealing the truth from a cardiac patient: there is nothing shameful about a heart attack. Cancer patients are lied to, not just because the disease is (or is thought to be) a death sentence, but because it is felt to be obscene—in the original meaning of that word: ill-omened, abominable, repugnant to the senses. Cardiac disease implies a weakness, trouble, failure that is mechanical; there is no disgrace, nothing of the taboo that once surrounded peoples afflicted with TB and still surrounds those who have cancer. The metaphors attached to TB and to cancer imply living processes of a particularly resonant and horrid kind.

II

Throughout most of their history, the metaphoric uses of TB and cancer crisscross and overlap. The *Oxford English Dictionary* records "consumption" in use as a synonym for pulmonary tuberculosis as early as 1398.[1] (John of Trevisa: "Whan the blode is made thynne, soo folowyth consumpcyon and wastyng.") But the premodern understanding of cancer also invokes the notion of consumption. The OED gives as the early figurative definition of cancer: "Anything that frets, corrodes, corrupts, or consumes slowly and secretly." (Thomas Paynell in 1528: "A canker is a melancolye impostume eatynge partes of the bodye.") The earliest literal definition of cancer is a growth, lump, or protuberance, and the disease's name—from the Greek *karkínos* and the Latin *cancer,* both meaning crab—was inspired, according to Galen, by the resemblance of an external tumor's swollen veins to a crab's legs, not, as many people think, because a metastatic disease crawls or creeps like a crab. But etymology indicates that tuberculosis was also once considered a type of abnormal extrusion: the word tuberculosis—from the Latin *tūberculum,* the diminutive of *tūber,* bump, swelling—means a morbid swelling, protuberance, projection, or growth.[2] Rudolf Virchow, who founded the science of cellular pathology in the 1850s, thought of the tubercle as a tumor.

Thus, from late antiquity until quite recently, tuberculosis was—typologically—cancer. And cancer was described, like TB, as a process in which the body was consumed. The modern conceptions of the two diseases could not be set until the advent of cellular pathology. Only with the microscope was it possible to grasp the distinctiveness of cancer, as a type of cellular activity, and to understand that the disease did not always take the form of an external or even palpable tumor. (Before the mid-nineteenth century, nobody could have identified leukemia as a form of cancer.) And it was not possible definitively to separate cancer from TB until after

---

[1] Godefroy's *Dictionnaire de l'ancienne langue française* cites Bernard de Gordon's *Pratiqum* (1495): *"Tisis, c'est ung ulcere du polmon qui consume tout le corp."*

[2] The same etymology is given in the standard French dictionaries. *"La tubercule"* was introduced in the sixteenth century by Ambroise Paré from the Latin *tūberculum,* meaning *"petite bosse"* (little lump). In Diderot's *Encyclopédie,* the entry on tuberculosis (1765) cites the definition given by the English physician Richard Morton in his *Phthisiologia* (1689): *"des petits tumeurs qui paraissent sur la surface du corps."* In French, all tiny surface tumors were once called *"tubercules";* the word became limited to what we identify as TB only after Koch's discovery of the tubercle bacillus.

1882, when tuberculosis was discovered to be a bacterial infection. Such advances in medical thinking enabled the leading metaphors of the two diseases to become truly distinct and, for the most part, contrasting. The modern fantasy about the cancer could then begin to take shape—a fantasy which from the 1920s on would inherit most of the problems dramatized by the fantasies about TB, but with the two diseases and their symptoms conceived in quite different, almost opposing, ways.

●

TB is understood as a disease of one organ, the lungs, while cancer is understood as a disease that can turn up in any organ and whose outreach is the whole body.

TB is understood as a disease of extreme contrasts: white pallor and red flush, hyperactivity alternating with languidness. The spasmodic course of the disease is illustrated by what is thought of as the prototypical TB symptom, coughing. The sufferer is wracked by coughs, then sinks back, recovers breath, breathes normally; then coughs again. Cancer is a disease of growth (sometimes visible; more characteristically, inside), of abnormal, ultimately lethal growth that is measured, incessant, steady. Although there may be periods in which tumor growth is arrested (remissions), cancer produces no contrasts like the oxymorons of behavior—febrile activity, passionate resignation—thought to be typical of TB. The tubercular is pallid some of the time; the pallor of the cancer patient is unchanging.

TB makes the body transparent. The X-rays, which are the standard diagnostic tool, permit one, often for the first time, to see one's insides—to become transparent to oneself. While TB is understood to be, from early on, rich in visible symptoms (progressive emaciation, coughing, languidness, fever), and can be suddenly and dramatically revealed (the blood on the handkerchief), in cancer the main symptoms are thought to be, characteristically, invisible—until the last stage, when it is too late. The disease, often discovered by chance or through routine medical checkup, can be far advanced without exhibiting any appreciable symptoms. One has an opaque body that must be taken to a specialist to find out if it contains cancer. What the patient cannot perceive, the specialist will determine by analyzing tissues taken from the body. TB patients may see their X-rays or even possess them: the patients at the sanatorium in *The Magic Mountain* carry theirs around in their breast pockets. Cancer patients don't look at their biopsies.

TB was—still is—thought to produce spells of euphoria, increased appetite, exacerbated sexual desire. Part of the regimen for patients in *The Magic Mountain* is a second breakfast, eaten with gusto. Cancer is thought to cripple vitality, make eating an ordeal, deaden desire. Having TB was imagined to be an aphrodisiac, and to confer extraordinary powers of seduction. Cancer is considered to be de-sexualizing. But it is characteristic of TB that many of its symptoms are deceptive—liveliness that comes from enervation, rosy cheeks that look like a sign of health but come from fever—and an upsurge of vitality may be a sign of approaching death. (Such gushes of energy will generally be self-destructive, and may be destructive of others: recall the Old West legend of Doc Holliday, the tubercular gunfighter released from moral restraints by the ravages of his disease.) Cancer has only true symptoms.

TB is disintegration, febrilization, dematerialization; it is a disease of liquids—the body turning to phlegm and mucus and sputum and, finally, blood—and of air, of the need for better air. Cancer is degeneration, the body tissues turning to something hard. Alice James, writing in her journal a year before she died from cancer in 1892, speaks of "this unholy granite substance in my breast." But this lump is alive, a fetus with its own will. Novalis, in an entry written around 1798 for his encyclopedia project, defines cancers, along with gangrene, as "full-fledged *parasites*—they grow, are engendered, engender, have their structure, secrete, eat." Cancer is a demonic pregnancy. St. Jerome must have been thinking of a cancer when he wrote: "The one there with his swollen belly is pregnant with his own death" ("*Alius tumenti aqualiculo mortem parturit*"). Though the course of both diseases is emaciating, losing weight from TB is understood very differently from losing weight from cancer. In TB the person is "consumed," burned up. In cancer, the patient is "invaded" by alien cells, which multiply, causing an atrophy or blockage of bodily functions. The cancer patient "shrivels" (Alice James's word) or "shrinks" (Wilhelm Reich's word).

TB is a disease of time; it speeds up life, highlights it, spiritualizes it. In both English and French, consumption "gallops." Cancer has stages rather than gaits; it is (eventually) "terminal." Cancer works slowly, insidiously: the standard euphemism in obituaries is that someone has "died after a long illness." Every characterization of cancer describes it as slow, and so it was first used metaphorically. "The word of hem crepith as a kankir," Wyclif wrote in 1382 (translating a phrase in II Timothy 2:17); and among the earliest figurative uses of cancer are as a metaphor for "idleness" and "sloth."* Metaphorically, cancer is not so much a disease of time as a disease or pathology of space. Its principal metaphors refer to topography (cancer "spreads" or "proliferates" or is "diffused"; tumors are surgically "excised"), and its most dreaded consequence, short of death, is the mutilation or amputation of part of the body.

TB is often imagined as a disease of poverty and deprivation—of thin garments, thin bodies, unheated rooms, poor hygiene, inadequate food. The poverty may not be as literal as Mimi's garret in *La Bohème;* the tubercular Marguerite Gautier in *La Dame aux camélias* lives in luxury, but inside she is a waif. In contrast, cancer is a disease of middle-class life, a disease associated with affluence, with excess. Rich countries have the highest cancer rates, and the rising incidence of the disease is seen as resulting, in part, from a diet rich in fat and proteins and from the toxic effluvia of the industrial economy that creates affluence. The treatment of TB is identified with the stimulation of appetite, cancer treatment with nausea and the loss of appetite. The undernourished nourishing themselves—alas, to no avail. The overnourished, unable to eat.

The TB patient was thought to be helped, even cured, by change of environment. There was a notion that TB was a wet disease, a disease of humid and dank cities.

---

* As cited in the OED, which gives as an early figurative use of "canker": "that pestilent and most infectious canker, idlenesse"—T. Palfreyman, 1564. And of "cancer" (which replaced "canker" around 1700): "Sloth is a Cancer, eating up that Time Princes should cultivate for Things sublime"—Edmund Ken, 1711.

The inside of the body became damp ("moisture in the lungs" was a favored locution) and had to be dried out. Doctors advised travel to high, dry places—the mountains, the desert. But no change of surroundings is thought to help the cancer patient. The fight is all inside one's own body. It may be, is increasingly thought to be, something in the environment that has caused the cancer. But once cancer is present, it cannot be reversed or diminished by a move to a better (that is, less carcinogenic) environment.

TB is thought to be relatively painless. Cancer is thought to be, invariably, excruciatingly painful. TB is thought to provide an easy death, while cancer is the spectacularly wretched one. For over a hundred years TB remained the preferred way of giving death a meaning—an edifying, refined disease. Nineteenth-century literature is stocked with descriptions of almost symptomless, unfrightened, beatific deaths from TB, particularly of young people, such as Little Eva in *Uncle Tom's Cabin* and Dombey's son Paul in *Dombey and Son* and Smike in *Nicholas Nickleby*, where Dickens described TB as the "dread disease" which "refines" death.

> if its grosser aspect . . . in which the struggle between soul and body is so gradual, quiet, and solemn, and the result so sure, that day by day, and grain by grain, the mortal part wastes and withers away, so that the spirit grows light and sanguine with its lightening load. . . .*

Contrast these ennobling, placid TB deaths with the ignoble, agonizing cancer deaths of Eugene Gant's father in Thomas Wolfe's *Of Time and the River* and of the sister in Bergman's film *Cries and Whispers*. The dying tubercular is pictured as made more beautiful and more soulful; the person dying of cancer is portrayed as robbed of all capacities of self-transcendence, humiliated by fear and agony.

●

These are contrasts drawn from the popular mythology of both diseases. Of course, many tuberculars died in terrible pain, and some people die of cancer feeling little or no pain to the end; the poor and the rich both get TB and cancer; and not everyone who has TB coughs. But the mythology persists. It is not just because pulmonary tuberculosis is the most common form of TB that most people think of TB, in contrast to cancer, as a disease of one organ. It is because the myths about TB do not fit the brain, larynx, kidneys, long bones, and other sites where the tubercle bacillus can also settle, but do have a close fit with the traditional imagery (breath, life) associated with the lungs.

While TB takes on qualities assigned to the lungs, which are part of the upper, spiritualized body, cancer is notorious for attacking parts of the body (colon, blad-

---

* Nearly a century later, in his edition of Katherine Mansfield's posthumously published *Journal,* John Middleton Murry uses similar language to describe Mansfield on the last day of her life. "I have never seen, nor shall I ever see, any one so beautiful as she was on that day; it was as though the exquisite perfection which was always hers had taken possession of her completely. To use her own words, the last grain of 'sediment,' the last 'traces of earthly degradation,' were departed for ever. But she had lost her life to save it."

der, rectum, breast, cervix, prostate, testicles) that are embarrassing to acknowledge. Having a tumor generally arouses some feelings of shame, but in the hierarchy of the body's organs, lung cancer is felt to be less shameful than rectal cancer. And one non-tumor form of cancer now turns up in commercial fiction in the role once monopolized by TB, as the romantic disease which cuts off a young life. (The heroine of Erich Segal's *Love Story* dies of leukemia—the "white" or TB-like form of the disease, for which no mutilating surgery can be proposed—not of stomach or breast cancer.) A disease of the lungs is, metaphorically, a disease of the soul.* Cancer, as a disease that can strike anywhere, is a disease of the body. Far from revealing anything spiritual, it reveals that the body is, all too woefully, just the body.

Such fantasies flourish because TB and cancer are thought to be much more than diseases that usually are (or were) fatal. They are identified with death itself. In *Nicholas Nickleby,* Dickens apostrophized TB as the

> disease in which death and life are so strangely blended, that death takes the glow and hue of life, and life the gaunt and grisly form of death; disease which medicine never cured, wealth never warded off, or poverty could boast exemption from. . . .

And Kafka wrote to Max Brod in October 1917 that he had "come to think that tuberculosis . . . is no special disease, or not a disease that deserves a special name, but only the germ of death itself, intensified. . . ." Cancer inspires similar speculations. Georg Groddeck, whose remarkable views on cancer in *The Book of the It* (1923) anticipate those of Wilhelm Reich, wrote:

> Of all the theories put forward in connection with cancer, only one has in my opinion survived the passage of time, namely, that cancer leads through definite stages to death. I mean by that that what is not fatal is not cancer. From that you may conclude that I hold out no hope of a new method of curing cancer . . . [only] the many cases of so-called cancer. . . .

For all the progress in treating cancer, many people still subscribe to Groddeck's equation: cancer = death. But the metaphors surrounding TB and cancer reveal much about the idea of the morbid, and how it has evolved from the nineteenth century (when TB was the most common cause of death) to our time (when cancer is the most dreaded disease). The Romantics moralized death in a new way: with the TB death, which dissolved the gross body, etherealized the personality, expanded consciousness. It was equally possible, through fantasies about TB, to aestheticize death. Thoreau, who had TB, wrote in 1852: "Death and disease are often beautiful, like . . . the hectic glow of consumption." Nobody conceives of cancer the way TB

---

* The Goncourt brothers, in their novel *Madame Gervaisais* (1869), called TB "this illness of the lofty and noble parts of the human being," contrasting it with "the diseases of the crude, base organs of the body, which clog and soil the patient's mind. . . ." In Mann's early story "Tristan," the young wife has tuberculosis of the trachea: ". . . the trachea, and not the lungs, thank God! But it is a question whether, if it had been the lungs the new patient could have looked any more pure and ethereal, any remoter from the concerns of this world, than she did now as she leaned back pale and weary in her chaste white-enamelled arm-chair, beside her robust husband, and listened to the conversation."

was thought of—as a decorative, often lyrical death. Cancer is a rare and still scandalous subject for poetry; and it seems unimaginable to aestheticize the disease.

III

The most striking similarity between the myths of TB and cancer is that both are, or were, understood as diseases of passion. Fever in TB was a sign of an inward burning: the tubercular is someone "consumed" by ardor, that ardor leading to the dissolution of the body. The use of metaphors drawn from TB to describe love—the image of a "diseased" love, of a passion that "consumes"—long antedates the Romantic movement.* Starting with the Romantics, the image was inverted, and TB was conceived as a variant of the disease of love. In a heartbreaking letter of November 1, 1820 from Naples, Keats, forever separated from Fanny Brawne, wrote, "If I had any chance of recovery [from tuberculosis], this passion would kill me." As a character in *The Magic Mountain* explains: "Symptoms of disease are nothing but a disguised manifestation of the power of love; and all disease is only love transformed."

As once TB was thought to come from too much passion, afflicting the reckless and sensual, today many people believe that cancer is a disease of insufficient passion, afflicting those who are sexually repressed, inhibited, unspontaneous, incapable of expressing anger. These seemingly opposite diagnoses are actually not so different versions of the same view (and deserve, in my opinion, the same amount of credence). For both psychological accounts of a disease stress the insufficiency or the balking of vital energies. As much as TB was celebrated as a disease of passion, it was also regarded as a disease of repression. The high-minded hero of Gide's *The Immoralist* contracts TB (paralleling what Gide perceived to be his own story) because he has repressed his true sexual nature; when Michel accepts Life, he recovers. With this scenario, today, Michel would have to get cancer.

As cancer is now imagined to be the wages of repression, so TB was once explained as the ravages of frustration. What is called a liberated sexual life is believed by some people today to stave off cancer, for virtually the same reason that sex was often prescribed to tuberculars as a therapy. In *The Wings of the Dove,* Milly Theale's doctor advises a love affair as a cure for her TB; and it is when she discovers that her duplicitous suitor, Merton Densher, is secretly engaged to her friend Kate Croy that she dies. And in his letter of November 1820, Keats exclaimed: "My dear Brown, I should have had her when I was in health, and I should have remained well."

According to the mythology of TB, there is generally some passionate feeling which provokes, which expresses itself in, a bout of TB. But the passions must be thwarted, the hopes blighted. And the passion, although usually love, could be a political or moral passion. At the end of Turgenev's *On the Eve* (1860), Insarov, the young Bulgarian revolutionary-in-exile who is the hero of the novel, realizes that he

---

* As In Act II, Scene 2 of Sir George Etherege's play *The Man of Mode* (1676): "When love grows diseas'd, the best thing we can do is to put it to a violent death; I cannot endure the torture of a lingring and consumptive passion."

can't return to Bulgaria. In a hotel in Venice, he sickens with longing and frustration, gets TB, and dies.

According to the mythology of cancer, it is generally a steady repression of feeling that causes the disease. In the earlier, more optimistic form of this fantasy, the repressed feelings were sexual; now in a notable shift, the repression of violent feelings is imagined to cause cancer. The thwarted passion that killed Insarov was idealism. The passion that people think will give them cancer if they don't discharge it is rage. There are no modern Insarovs. Instead, there are cancerphobes like Norman Mailer, who recently explained that had he not stabbed his wife (and acted out "a murderous nest of feeling") he would have gotten cancer and "been dead in a few years himself." It is the same fantasy that was once attached to TB, but in rather a nastier version.

The source for much of the current fancy that associates cancer with the repression of passion is Wilhelm Reich, who defined cancer as "a disease following emotional resignation—a bio-energetic shrinking, a giving up of hope." Reich illustrated his influential theory with Freud's cancer, which he thought began when Freud, naturally passionate and "very unhappily married," yielded to resignation:

> He lived a very calm, quiet, decent family life, but there is little doubt that he was very much dissatisfied genitally. Both his resignation and his cancer were evidence of that. Freud had to give up, as a person. He had to give up his personal pleasures, his personal delights, in his middle years . . . . if my view of cancer is correct, you just give up, you resign—and, then, you shrink.

Tolstoy's "The Death of Ivan Ilyich" is often cited as a case history of the link between cancer and characterological resignation. But the same theory has been applied to TB by Groddeck, who defined TB as

> the pining to die away. The desire must die away, then, the desire for the in and out, the up and down of erotic love, which is symbolized in breathing. And with the desire the lungs die away . . . . the body dies away . . . *

As do accounts of cancer today, the typical accounts of TB in the nineteenth century all feature resignation as the cause of the disease. They also show how, as the disease advances, one *becomes* resigned—Mimi and Camille die because of their renunciation of love, beatified by resignation. Robert Louis Stevenson's autobiographical essay "Ordered South," written in 1874, describes the stages whereby the tubercular is "tenderly weaned from the passion of life," and an ostentatious resignation is characteristic of the rapid decline of tuberculars as reported at length in fiction. In *Uncle Tom's Cabin,* Little Eva dies with preternatural serenity, announcing to her father a few weeks before the end: "My strength fades away every day, and I know I must go." All we learn of Milly Theale's death in *The Wings of the Dove* is that "she turned her face to the wall." TB was represented as the prototypical passive death.

---

* The passage continues: " . . . because desire increases during the illness, because the guilt of the ever-repeated symbolic dissipation of semen in the sputum is continually growing greater, . . . because the It allows pulmonary disease to bring beauty to the eyes and cheek, alluring poisons!"

Often it was a kind of suicide. In Joyce's "The Dead," Michael Furey stands in the rain in Gretta Conroy's garden the night before she leaves for the convent school; she implores him to go home; "he said he did not want to live" and a week later he dies.

TB sufferers may be represented as passionate but are, more characteristically, deficient in vitality, in life force. (As in the contemporary updating of this fantasy, the cancer-prone are those who are not sufficiently sensual or in touch with their anger.) This is how those two famously tough-minded observers, the Goncourt brothers, explain the TB of their friend Murger (the author of *Scènes de la vie de Bohème*): he is dying "for want of vitality with which to withstand suffering." Michael Furey was "very delicate," as Gretta Conroy explains to her "stout, tallish," virile, suddenly jealous husband. TB is celebrated as the disease of born victims, of sensitive, passive people who are not quite life-loving enough to survive. (What is hinted at by the yearning but almost somnolent belles of Pre-Raphaelite art is made explicit in the emaciated, hollow-eyed, tubercular girls depicted by Edvard Munch.) And while the standard representation of a death from TB places the emphasis on the perfected sublimation of feeling, the recurrent figure of the tubercular courtesan indicates that TB was also thought to make the sufferer sexy.

Like all really successful metaphors, the metaphor of TB was rich enough to provide for two contradictory applications. It described the death of someone (like a child) thought to be too "good" to be sexual: the assertion of an angelic psychology. It was also a way of describing sexual feelings—while lifting the responsibility for libertinism, which is blamed on a state of objective, physiological decadence or deliquescence. It was both a way of describing sensuality and promoting the claims of passion and a way of describing repression and advertising the claims of sublimation, the disease inducing both a "numbness of spirit" (Robert Louis Stevenson's words) and a suffusion of higher feelings. Above all, it was a way of affirming the value of being more conscious, more complex psychologically. Health becomes banal, even vulgar . . . .

●

In the modern period, the use of disease imagery in political rhetoric implies other, less lenient assumptions. The modern idea of revolution, based on an estimate of the unremitting bleakness of the existing political situation, shattered the old, optimistic use of disease metaphors. John Adams wrote in his diary, in December 1772:

> The Prospect before me . . . is very gloomy. My Country is in deep Distress, and has very little Ground of Hope . . . . The Body of the People seem to be worn out, by struggling, and Venality, Servility and Prostitution, eat and spread like a Cancer.

Political events started commonly to be defined as being unprecedented, radical; and eventually both civil disturbances and wars come to be understood as, really, revolutions. As might be expected, it was not with the American but with the French

Revolution that disease metaphors in the modern sense came into their own—particularly in the conservative response to the French Revolution. In *Reflections on the Revolution in France* (1790), Edmund Burke contrasted older wars and civil disturbances with this one, which he considered to have a totally new character. Before, no matter what the disaster, "the organs . . . of the state, however shattered, existed." But, he addressed the French, "your present confusion, like a palsy, has attacked the fountain of life itself."

As classical theories of the polis have gone the way of the theories of the four humours, so a modern idea of politics has been complemented by a modern idea of disease. Disease equals death. Burke invoked palsy (and "the living ulcer of a corroding memory"). The emphasis was soon to be on diseases that are loathsome and fatal. Such diseases are not to be managed or treated; they are to be attacked. In Hugo's novel about the French Revolution, *Quatre-vingt-treize* (1874), the revolutionary Gauvain, condemned to the guillotine, absolves the Revolution with all its bloodshed, including his own imminent execution,

> because it is a storm. A storm always knows what it is doing . . . . Civilization was in the grip of plague; this gale comes to the rescue. Perhaps it in not selective enough. Can it act otherwise? It is entrusted with the arduous task of sweeping away disease! In face of the horrible infection, I understand the fury of the blast.

It is hardly the last time that revolutionary violence would be justified on the grounds that society has a radical, horrible illness. The melodramatics of the disease metaphor in modern political discourse assume a punitive notion: of the disease not as a punishment but as a sign of evil, something to be punished.

Modern totalitarian movements, whether of the right or of the left, have been peculiarly—and revealingly—inclined to use disease imagery. The Nazis declared that someone of mixed "racial" origin was like a syphilitic. European Jewry was repeatedly analogized to syphilis, and to a cancer that must be excised. Disease metaphors were a staple of Bolshevik polemics, and Trotsky, the most gifted of all communist polemicists, used them with the greatest profusion—particularly after his banishment from the Soviet Union in 1929. Stalinism was called a cholera, a syphilis, and a cancer.* To use only fatal diseases for imagery in politics gives the metaphor a much more pointed character. Now, to liken a political event or situation to an illness is to impute guilt, to prescribe punishment.

---

* Cf. Isaac Deutscher, *The Prophet Outcast: Trotsky, 1929–1940* (1963): " 'Certain measures,' Trotsky wrote to [Philip] Rahv [on March 21, 1938], 'are necessary for a struggle against incorrect theory, and others for fighting a cholera epidemic. Stalin is incomparably nearer to cholera than to a false theory. The struggle must be intense, truculent, merciless. An element of "fanaticism" . . . is salutary.' " And: "Trotsky spoke of the 'syphilis of Stalinism' or of the 'cancer that must be burned out of the labour movement with a hot iron' . . . . "

Notably, Solzhenitsyn's *Cancer Ward* contains virtually no uses of cancer as a metaphor —for Stalinism, or for anything else. Solzhenitsyn was not misrepresenting his novel when, hoping to get it published in the Soviet Union, he told the Board of the Union of Writers in 1967 that the title was not "some kind of symbol," as was being charged, and that "the subject is specifically and literally cancer."

This is particularly true of the use of cancer as a metaphor. It amounts to saying, first of all, that the event or situation is unqualifiedly and unredeemably wicked. It enormously ups the ante. Hitler, in his first political tract, an anti-Semitic diatribe written in September 1919, accused the Jews of producing "a racial tuberculosis among nations."[†] Tuberculosis still retained its prestige as the overdetermined, culpable illness of the nineteenth century. (Recall Hugo's comparison of monasticism with TB.) But the Nazis quickly modernized their rhetoric, and indeed the imagery of cancer was far more apt for their purposes. As was said in speeches about "the Jewish problem" throughout the 1930s, to treat a cancer, one must cut out much of the healthy tissue around it. The imagery of cancer for the Nazis prescribes "radical" treatment, in contrast to the "soft" treatment thought appropriate for TB—the difference between sanatoria (that is, exile) and surgery (that is, crematoria). (The Jews were also identified with, and became a metaphor for, city life—with Nazi rhetoric echoing all the Romantic clichés about cities as a debilitating, merely cerebral, morally contaminated, unhealthy environment.)

To describe a phenomenon as a cancer is an incitement to violence. The use of cancer in political discourse encourages fatalism and justifies "severe" measures—as well as strongly reinforcing the widespread notion that the disease is necessarily fatal. The concept of disease is never innocent. But it could be argued that the cancer metaphors are in themselves implicitly genocidal. No specific political view seems to have a monopoly on this metaphor. Trotsky called Stalinism the cancer of Marxism; in China in the last year, the Gang of Four have become, among other things, "the cancer of China." John Dean explained Watergate to Nixon: "We have a cancer within—close to the Presidency—that's growing." The standard metaphor of Arab polemics—heard by Israelis on the radio every day for the last twenty years—is that Israel is "a cancer in the heart of the Arab world" or "the cancer of the Middle East," and an officer with the Christian Lebanese rightist forces besieging the Palestine refugee camp of Tal Zaatar in August 1976 called the camp "a cancer in the Lebanese body." The cancer metaphor seems hard to resist for those who wish to register indignation. Thus, Neal Ascherson wrote in 1969 that the Slansky Affair "was—is—a huge cancer in the body of the Czechoslovak state and nation"; Simon Leys, in *Chinese Shadows,* speaks of "the Maoist cancer that is gnawing away at the face of China"; D. H. Lawrence called masturbation "the deepest and most dangerous cancer of our civilization"; and I once wrote, in the heat of despair over America's war on Vietnam, that "the white race is the cancer of human history."

But how to be morally severe in the late twentieth century? How, when there is so much to be severe about; how, when we have a sense of evil but no longer the relig-

---

[†] "[The Jew's] power is the power of money which in the form of interest effortlessly and interminably multiplies itself in his hands and forces upon nations that most dangerous of yokes. ... Everything which makes men strive for higher things, whether religion, socialism, or democracy, is for him only a means to an end, to the satisfaction of a lust for money and domination. His activities produce a racial tuberculosis among nations. ..." A late-nineteenth-century precursor of Nazi ideology, Julius Langbehn, called the Jews "only a passing pest and cholera." But in Hitler's TB image there is already something easily transferred to cancer: the idea that Jewish power "effortlessly and interminably multiplies."

ious or philosophical language to talk intelligently about evil. Trying to comprehend "radical" or "absolute" evil, we search for adequate metaphors. But the modern disease metaphors are all cheap shots. The people who have the real disease are also hardly helped by hearing their disease's name constantly being dropped as the epitome of evil. Only in the most limited sense is any historical event or problem like an illness. And the cancer metaphor is particularly crass. It is invariably an encouragement to simplify what is complex and an invitation to self-righteousness, if not to fanaticism.

It is instructive to compare the image of cancer with that of gangrene. With some of the same metaphoric properties as cancer—it starts from nothing; it spreads; it is disgusting—gangrene would seem to be laden with everything a polemicist would want. Indeed, it was used in one important moral polemic—against the French use of torture in Algeria in the 1950s; the title of the famous book exposing that torture was called *La Gangrène*. But there is a large difference between the cancer and the gangrene metaphors. First, causality is clear with gangrene. It is external (gangrene can develop from a scratch); cancer is understood as mysterious, a disease with multiple causes, internal as well as external. Second, gangrene is not as all-emcompassing a disaster. It leads often to amputation, less often to death; cancer is presumed to lead to death in most cases. Not gangrene—and not the plague (despite the notable attempts by writers as different as Artaud, Reich, and Camus to impose that as a metaphor for the dismal and the disastrous)—but cancer remains the most radical of disease metaphors. And just because it is so radical, it is particularly tendentious—a good metaphor for paranoids, for those who need to turn campaigns into crusades, for the fatalistic (cancer = death), and for those under the spell of ahistorical revolutinary optimism (the idea that only the most radical changes are desirable). As long as so much militaristic hyperbole attaches to the description and treatment of cancer, it is a particularly unapt metaphor for the peace-loving.

It is, of course, likely that the language about cancer will evolve in the coming years. It must change, decisively, when the disease is finally understood and the rate of cure becomes much higher. It is already changing, with the development of new forms of treatment. As chemotherapy is more and more supplanting radiation in the treatment of cancer patients, an effective form of treatment (already a supplementary treatment of proven use) seems likely to be found in some kind of immunotherapy. Concepts have started to shift in certain medical circles, where doctors are concentrating on the steep buildup of the body's immunological responses to cancer. As the language of treatment evolves from military metaphors of aggressive warfare to metaphors featuring the body's "natural defenses" (what is called the "immunodefensive system" can also—to break entirely with the military metaphor —be called the body's "immune competence"), cancer will be partly de-mythicized; and it may then be possible to compare something to a cancer without implying either a fatalistic diagnosis or a rousing call to fight by any means whatever a lethal, insidious enemy. Then perhaps it will be morally permissible, as it is not now, to use cancer as a metaphor.

But at that time, perhaps nobody will want any longer to compare anything awful to cancer. Since the interest of the metaphor is precisely that it refers to a disease so overlaid with mystification, so charged with the fantasy of inescapable fatality. Since our views about cancer, and the metaphors we have imposed on it, are so much a vehicle for the large insufficiencies of this culture, for our shallow attitude toward death, for our anxieties about feeling, for our reckless improvident responses to our real "problems of growth," for our inability to construct an advanced industrial society which properly regulates consumption, and for our justified fears of the increasingly violent course of history. The cancer metaphor will be made obsolete, I would predict, long before the problems it has reflected so persuasively will be resolved.

Appendix

Documenting the Research Paper

Although the major form we recommend is the response statement, you will undoubtedly be required at some time to write a research paper, in which you develop your readings fully and, where necessary, quote other readers, critics, and authorities. We suggest you set out your research paper according to the following guidelines, which are in accord with the MLA documentation system (1984 version).

Sample First Page of the Research Paper

```
Jennifer J. Even
Professor McCormick
76-242
28 April 1986

            ''Unending Dream of Commentary'':
      How Critics Engage with Doris Lessing's
            Summer Before the Dark

        As the reader drowns under the ever accumulating
flood of criticism, he is justified in asking, why is
there criticism rather than silent admiration? What
ineluctable necessity in literature makes it generate
unending oceans of commentary, wave after wave covering
the primary textual rocks, hiding them, washing them,
uncovering them again, but leaving them, after all,
just as they were?
                                    J. Hillis Miller

Criticism, according to J. Hillis Miller, is ''an
ever-renewed, ever-unsuccessful attempt to 'get it right,'
to name things by their right names'' (331). I would like to
```

add to Miller's definition that criticism is a particular
reading of the text based on the critic's literary, social
and cultural repertoire, a reading that is often viewed as
unacceptable only because the critic's repertoire differs
from the reader's. In this paper I would like first of all
to explain briefly the notion of repertoire, and secondly to
examine several critical readings of Doris Lessing's Summer
Before the Dark to illustrate how these critics often assume
the universality of their particular repertoires and thus
seem to come up with ''wrong'' interpretations in the eyes of
readers with different repertoires. Then perhaps finally I
can attempt to deal with Hillis Miller's question, Why is
there criticism?

A person's repertoire is a subset of assumptions from
the ideology which surrounds him or her--cultural, social,
literary assumptions. One's literary repertoire contains
strategies for reading a piece of discourse--traditional
strategies, with expectations of full plot development,
unity of details, and resolution and closure revolving
around the author's intended meaning; and what we may call
Hillis Millerish strategies, deconstructionist assumptions

Document Sources Fully and Accurately

Although you need not acknowledge a source for generally known information such as the dates during which William Wordsworth lived or the na-
tionality of Nathaniel Hawthorne, you must identify the exact source and
location of each statement, fact, or idea you borrow from another person or
work. There are many different ways to acknowledge sources, but one of the
simplest and most efficient is the MLA system, which requires only a brief
parenthetical reference in the text of the paper, keyed to a complete bibliographical entry in the list of works cited at the end of the essay. For most
parenthetical references, you will need to cite only the author's last name
and the number of the page from which the statement or idea was taken; if
you mention the author's name in the text of your paper, the page number

alone is sufficient. This format also allows you to include within the parentheses additional information, such as title or volume number, if it is needed for clarity. Documentation for some of the most common types of sources is discussed in the sections below.

References to Single-Volume Books

Response statements do not normally incorporate documented references to other works. In research papers, articles and single-volume books are the two types of works you are most likely to refer to. When citing them, either mention the author's name in the text and note the appropriate page number in parentheses immediately after the citation, or acknowledge both name and page number in the parenthetical reference, leaving a space between the two. If punctuation is needed, insert the mark outside the final parenthesis.

Author's name cited in the text

Terry Eagleton has argued that Literary and Cultural Studies should "look to the various sign-systems and signifying practices in our society, all the way from *Moby-Dick* to the Muppet Show" (207).

Note that the period ending the sentence occurs *after* the parenthetical reference, not before.

Author's name cited in parentheses

Literary and Cultural Studies should "look at the various sign-systems and signifying practices in our society, all the way from *Moby-Dick* to the Muppet Show" (Eagleton 207).

Corresponding bibliographic entry

Eagleton, Terry. *Literary Theory: An Introduction.* Oxford: Basil Blackwell, 1983.

If the work you are citing has two or three authors, cite all their last names in parentheses, following the conventions for spacing and punctuation noted above. If there are more than three authors, use the last name of the author listed first on the title page, plus the abbreviation et al.

Sample parenthetical references

(Dollimore and Sinfield 153)

(Barker et al. 111)

(McCormick, Waller, and Flower 65)

Corresponding bibliographic entries

Dollimore, Jonathan, and Alan Sinfield. *Political Shakespeare: New Essays in Cultural Materialism.* Manchester: Manchester UP, 1985.

McCormick, Kathleen, Gary Waller, and Linda Flower. *Reading Texts.* Lexington: Heath, 1987.

Barker, Francis, et al. *Confronting the Crisis: War, Politics and Culture in the Eighties.* Colchester: U of Essex, 1984.

References to Articles

In text, references to articles are handled in exactly the same way as references to single-volume books. The bibliographic citations, however, are somewhat different in that you don't cite a publisher, but must cite the volume in which the article appeared. Scholarly journals generally appear four to six times annually, and each year of the journal has a volume number (that is, Volume 12 for all of 1986). Each individual issue within a given year is also numbered or labeled with a month or a season (that is, Volume 12, Number 3; or Volume 12, Spring 1986).

Journals with Continuous Pagination

If the journal you are citing paginates its issues for a given year continuously (for example, Volume 12, Number 3 begins with page 467, where the previous issue left off), you need not cite the issue number, month, or season in your bibliographic entry.

Bibliographic entry for article in journal with continuous pagination

Booth, Wayne C. "Pluralism in the Classroom." *Critical Inquiry* 12 (1986): 468–79.

Journals That Page Each Issue Separately

If the journal issues for a given year are not paginated continuously (that is, issue number 3 of Volume 12 begins with page 1), they you must cite the issue number, month, or season as well as the volume number in your bibliographic entry.

Bibliographic entry for article in journal that pages each issue separately or that uses only issue numbers

Fish, Stanley, "Why No One's Afraid of Wolfgang Iser." *Diacritics* 11 (Spring 1981): 2–13.

Lyon, George Ella. "Contemporary Appalachian Poetry: Sources and Directions." *Kentucky Review* 2.2 (1981): 3–22.

References to Works in an Anthology

When referring to a work in an anthology, either cite the author's name in the text and indicate in parentheses the page number in the anthology where the source is located, or acknowledge both name and page reference parenthetically. Only in the full citation in your bibliography do you give the name of the editor of the anthology.

Author's name cited in text

One of the most widely recognized facts about James Joyce, in Lionel Trilling's view, "is his ambivalence toward Ireland, of which the hatred was as relentless as the love was unfailing" (153).

Author's name cited in parentheses

One of the most widely recognized facts about James Joyce "is his ambivalence toward Ireland, of which the hatred was as relentless as the love was unfailing" (Trilling 153).

Corresponding bibliographic entry

Trilling, Lionel. "James Joyce in His Letters." In *Joyce: A Collection of Critical Essays.* Ed. William M. Chace. Englewood Cliffs: Prentice, 1974.

References to More Than One Work by an Author

When you paraphrase or quote from more than one work by an author, give the title as well as the name of the author and the page reference so that the reader will know which work is being cited. If you mention the author's name in the text, you need not duplicate it in the parenthetical reference. Just cite the title (or a shortened version of it), skip a space, and insert the page number, as in the second example below. If you do not mention the author's name in the text, cite it first in the parenthetical reference, put a comma after it, skip a space, and insert the title. Then skip a space again and insert the page number (see the third example below).

Title cited in text

Siegfried J. Schmidt argues in his article "On Writing Histories of Literature" that the seventies "will go down in the history [of literary studies] as a period concerned with the writing of new histories of literature" (279).

Title cited in parentheses

Siegfried J. Schmidt argues that the seventies "will go down in the history [of literary studies] as a period concerned with the writing of new histories of literature" ("Histories" 279).

In the words of a major critic of the field, the seventies "will go down in the history [of literary studies] as a period concerned with the writing of new histories of literature" (Schmidt, "Histories" 279).

Corresponding entries in the list of works cited

Schmidt, Siegfried J. *Foundations for the Empirical Study of Literature.* Trans. Robert de Beaugrande. Hamburg: Buske, 1982.

_____. "On Writing Histories of Literature. Some Remarks from a Constructivist Point of View." *Poetics* 14 (1985): 279–301.

References to Works of Unknown Authorship

If you borrow information or ideas from an article or book in which the name of the author is not given, cite the title instead, either in the text of the paper or in parentheses, and include the page reference.

Title cited in the text

According to an article entitled "Sidney at Kalamazoo" in the *Sidney Newsletter,* planning is now under way for next year's Kalamazoo sessions (43).

Title cited in parentheses

Planning is now under way for next year's Kalamazoo sessions ("Sidney at Kalamazoo" 43).

Corresponding bibliographic entry

"Sidney at Kalamazoo." *Sidney Newsletter* 2.2 (1981): 27.

References to Multivolume Works

When you borrow from one volume of a multivolume work, cite the volume of your source in parentheses as an arabic number *without* the abbreviation Vol., and put a colon after it. Then skip a space and insert the page reference.

Sample references

Frazer points out that scapegoat rituals have been common throughout history, not only in primitive societies but also "among the civilized nations of Europe" (9: 47).

Scapegoat rituals have been common throughout history, not only in primitive societies but also "among the civilized nations of Europe" (Frazer 9: 47).

Corresponding bibliographic entry

Frazer, Sir James G. *The Golden Bough: A Study of Magic and Religion.* 3rd ed. 12 vols. New York: Macmillan, 1935.

References to Information Gathered from Interviews

When citing an oral source, either mention the informant's name when you introduce the quotation or paraphrase or give the name in a parenthetical reference.

Informant's name cited in text

When asked about her response, Debra Bernstein, one of our students, said that "it grew out of my belief that all contemporary fiction should be disruptive."

Informant's name cited in parentheses

When asked about her response, one of our students said that "it grew out of my belief that all contemporary fiction should be disruptive" (Bernstein).

Corresponding bibliographic entry

Bernstein, Debra. Personal interview, July 4, 1987.

References to Literary Works

When citing works of literature, observe the following guidelines for each genre.

Novels and Other Prose Works Subdivided into Chapters or Sections

Begin the parenthetical reference with the author's last name and the page number (the author's name may be omitted if it is mentioned in the text of the paper or if the authorship is evident from the context) and insert a semicolon. Then skip a space and give the number of the chapter (with the abbreviation Ch.) as well as the number of any other subdivisions.

Sample reference

At the beginning of *The Great Gatsby,* Nick Carraway characterizes himself as someone who has "a sense of the fundamental decencies" (Fitzgerald 1; Ch. 1)—a trait that he displays throughout the novel.

Corresponding bibliographic entry

Fitzgerald, F. Scott. *The Great Gatsby.* New York: Scribner's, 1925.

Poems

When quoting or paraphrasing a poem that is divided into sections, cite the number of the book, part, or canto plus the line number(s). There is no need for abbreviations such as bk. (book) or l. (line), but the first time you cite the work write out the word line or lines so that the reader will not mistake the line numbers for page references. If the poem you are citing has no subdivisions, line numbers alone are usually sufficient to identify the source—provided that the author and title are identified in the text of the paper.

Sample reference to a poem with subdivisions

One of Byron's satiric techniques is to juxtapose the comical with the serious, as in this passage from *Don Juan:*

> But I am apt to grow too metaphysical:
> "The time is out of joint,"—and so am I;
> I quite forget this poem's merely quizzical,
> And deviate from matters rather dry.
> (9: lines 321–24)

Note: If you omit the word lines, put a period after the number of the section (in this case Canto 9) and, without spacing, insert the line number(s): (9.321–324).

Sample reference to a poem without subdivisions

One of the questions that might be answered in any analysis of Jeffers's "Hurt Hawks" is whether the author's viewpoint is reflected in the narrator's statement "I'd sooner, except the penalties, kill a man than a hawk" (line 18).

Corresponding bibliographic entries

Byron, George Gordon, Lord. *Don Juan.* In *Lord Byron: Don Juan and Other Satirical Poems.* Ed. Louis Bredvold, New York: Odyssey, 1935.

Jeffers, Robinson. "Hurt Hawks." *Selected Poems.* New York: Random, 1928.

Plays

When citing a play, give the act and scene number without abbreviations, plus the line numbers if the work is in verse.

Sample reference

Shakespeare repeatedly describes Denmark in images of unnaturalness, as in Horatio's comparison of Denmark with Rome just before Caesar's murder, when "The graves stood tenantless and sheeted dead/Did squeak and gibber in the Roman streets" (I.i.115–6).

Note: Upper-case Roman numerals are traditionally used for act numbers and lower-case Roman numerals for scene numbers.

Corresponding bibliographic entry

Shakespeare, William. *Hamlet.* In *Shakespeare: Twenty-Three Plays and the Sonnets.* Ed. Thomas Parrot. Rev. ed. New York: Scribner's, 1953.

Bibliography

In preparing the bibliography (or list of Works Cited) for your research paper, arrange all the works cited alphabetically.

Works Cited

Barker, Frances, et al. *Confronting the Crisis: War, Politics, and Culture in the Eighties.* Colchester: U of Essex, 1984.

Byron, George Gordon, Lord. *Don Juan.* In *Lord Byron: Don Juan and Other Satirical Poems.* Ed. Louis Bredvold. New York: Odyssey, 1935.

Dollimore, Jonathan, and Alan Sinfield. *Shakespeare: New Essays in Cultural Materialism.* Manchester: Manchester UP, 1985.

Eagleton, Terry. *Theory: An Introduction.* Oxford: Basil Blackwell, 1983.

Fitzgerald, F. Scott. *The Great Gatsby.* New York: Scribner's, 1925.

Frazer, Sir James G. *The Golden Bough: A Study of Magic and Religion.* 3rd ed. 12 vols. New York: Macmillan, 1935.

Jeffers, Robinson. *Selected Poems.* New York: Random, 1928.

Lessing, Doris. *Summer Before the Dark.* New York: Knopf, 1973.

McCormick, Kathleen A., Gary F. Waller, and Linda Flower. *Reading Texts.* Lexington: Heath, 1987.

Miller, Hillis. "Stevens' Rock and Criticism as Cure, II." *Georgia Review* 30.2 (1976), 330–48.

Schmidt, Siegfried J. *for the Empirical Study of Literature.* Trans. Robert de Beaugrande. Hamburg: Buske, 1982.

———. "On Writing Histories of Literature: Some Remarks from a Constructivist Point of View." *Poetics* 14 (1985): 279–301.

Shakespeare, William. *Shakespeare: Twenty-Three Plays and the Sonnets.* Ed. Thomas Parrot. Rev. ed. New York: Scribner's, 1953.

"Sidney at Kalamazoo." *Sidney Newsletter* 4.3 (1982): 43.

Trilling, Lionel. "James Joyce in His Letters." In *Joyce: A Collection of Critical Essays.* Ed. William M. Chace. Englewood Cliffs: Prentice, 1974. 143–165.

Glossary
of Terms

absurd The *theater of the absurd* refers to plays written primarily in the 1950s and 1960s by dramatists such as Samuel Beckett, Eugene Ionesco, and Jean Genet. These works explore the tension between humankind's desire for purpose and the apparent purposelessness of the world. Rather than adopting realism's conventional assumption that the theater should mirror life and present a unified, coherent view of characters and situation, the theater of the absurd calls attention to the theatricality of drama and the incoherence of characters and situations, and to illusion, lack of communication, and futility. Nonetheless, these plays are frequently hilarious and uplifting in their brilliance. Ionesco's *The Gap* and Pirandello's *Six Characters in Search of an Author* are examples. The adjective *absurd* is also used to describe literary forms other than drama.

analysis With respect to discussion of literary text, a term used interchangeably with *explication.* Analysis focuses on studying textual characteristics in isolation, rather than integrating those characteristics with the overall effects of the text. Such an approach, which is associated especially with *formalism,* tends to ignore the vital place of the reader in the making of meaning; it isolates the text from the contexts in which it is written and read and tends to promote the notion that "true" or "objective" meanings somehow exist "in" texts.

argument The line of reasoning that holds a piece of writing together and that readers often reproduce in a *summary* or *interpretation.* Although readers' reproductions of a work's argument may differ widely, they will generally reflect the effect of *text strategies* used in the writing to direct the readers' attention to particular aspects of the text at the expense of others.

assumptions The prior knowledge, values, and beliefs a reader brings to his or her reading experiences. Assumptions may be conscious (for example, strategies designed to produce a specific kind of reading), or they may be unconscious (for example, preexisting ideological values that deeply influence the reader).

authorial intention Many readers assume that the author is the only person who knows what his or her text "really means." This assumption implies that (1) authors are unified beings who always know what they mean, (2) authors have the ability to imbed their intentions and meanings in a work, and (3) readers have the ability to discover these intentions when reading. The approach advocated in this anthology rejects this assumption on the grounds that it is based on a naive objectivism regarding readers, writers, and texts. Although the life of the author may be of interest and may have an intimate connection with the literary work, it is important to remember that a literary text does not "belong to" the author. Even the author's use of the first person "I" in a work does not guarantee that the work is autobiographical. Unconscious as well as conscious factors influence the writing of a text, and thus the intentions of the author are not authoritatively recoverable from the text and should not be the major concern of criticism. A work's meanings are always the product of what a reader brings to his or her reading and what the author has encoded in the text. What is thought to be the dominant meaning of a text changes from one historical period to another. Authors can be seen as the first readers of their own works, perhaps even privileged readers, but certainly not final authoritative readers.

blanks As defined by Wolfgang Iser in *The Act of Reading* (Johns Hopkins University Press, 1978), those absences or *indeterminacies* in a text that must be completed or resolved by a reader. Blanks, or gaps, can be filled in a number of ways and hence are one of the major sources of readers' different interpretations of texts. Blanks cannot be said to exist in an objective sense in any given text because various readers, depending on their *repertoires,* will "discover" different blanks in the text.

canon The tradition of literary works generally held to be the best or the greatest in the language. Although the works of some writers (for example, Shakespeare) are held to be universally canonical, the canon is continually changing to reflect the values and concerns that different ages bring to their assessment of literature.

character The fictional representation of a person. In many fictional and dramatic texts written between the eighteenth and twentieth centuries, characters are constructed so as to encourage "realistic" and coherent readings. The characters are developed to be psychologically consistent. In most earlier and a great deal of recent literature, there is less inclination to encourage "realistic" readings of characters. In non-realistic (or non-illusionist) texts—for instance, Shakespearean drama, fairy stories, and much contemporary fiction—there is no such encouragement. Characters can be read as stereotypical or inconsistent since the focus is not on creating the illusion of coherence, but on providing a set of verbal codes that the reader experiences in the continuous process of reading. As the German dramatist Berthold Brecht said, "When a character behaves by contradictions, that's only because nobody can be identically the same at two unidentical moments . . . the continuity of the ego is a myth." The notion of a unified character, therefore, belongs to a particular type of literature known as classic realism. Although classic realism is no longer the dominant literary form, the habits it spawned remain residually powerful today in the interpretation of character.

cognitive style The general ways in which a person takes in, processes, and reacts to what he or she perceives. For example, some people seem by temperament to have a much higher tolerance for ambiguity than others. They enjoy employing reading strategies that open up multiple meanings of a text and feel no compulsion to reduce responses to a single meaning. Other people seem always to seek resolution in their reading, as well as in their lives in general. Similarly, some people read more connotatively than others. These are the people who notice double entendres and discover multiple meanings in poetry and in general conversation; perhaps they themselves like to make puns. In contrast, there are those who tend always to read literally; whether they are reading a poem or a letter from a friend, it does not occur to them to "read between the lines." This book advocates that you become self-consciously analytical about your cognitive style in order to understand why you read the way you do; it also suggests that by expanding your repertoires you can develop and enrich your cognitive style so that you will be able to control it rather than letting it control you.

connotation, denotation The associations we bring to a word or phrase—emotive, social, cultural, ideological—are its connotations. Although the term is most commonly applied to poetry, all words can be read for their connotations. Words that carry cultural values—for example, love, duty, democracy, freedom—can be a particularly powerful focus of connotations. Connotations may be contradictory, as the associations we bring are produced by the wider cultural forces of our society. Connotation is conventionally contrasted with denotation, which is considered to be the "real," "true," or "literal" meaning of a word. Connotation and denotation may also apply to visual, olfactory, and other experiences, as Roland Barthes explains in the extract from *Mythologies* (see pp. 1191–1200).

consistency building A reading strategy described by Wolfgang Iser in *The Act of Reading* (Johns Hopkins University Press, 1978) whereby readers at various points in their readings seek to combine into a meaningful, consistent whole the diffuse and often inconsistent material they are reading. To build consistency is to place closure on the text, to decide temporarily what it is "about." Iser suggests that in the process of reading, readers alternately open up and close off interpretive possibilities. In the consistency-building phases of reading, readers synthesize materials, which necessarily involves excluding some of what they have read. Although this synthesis should never be seen as final, it is necessary for readers to take stock so that they can once again open up to the text as they continue their reading. See also *wandering viewpoint*.

context The surrounding situation. Both reading and writing occur in linguistic, social, cultural, and ideological contexts. The interpretation of any language unit depends on the context in which it is read. See also *cultural situatedness.*

convention Structural patterns or similarities occurring frequently in a large number of works. Such patterns become so widely used that they are taken for granted, often either becoming clichés or becoming thought of as "natural." For example, the division of a play into acts, the telling of a story from a particular unified perspective, and the division of a poem called a sonnet into fourteen lines are all conventional strategies of literary texts. These conventions encourage certain prescribed ways of reading. An awareness of the conventions of writing and reading can enable readers to read a text more self-consciously "against the grain."

couplet In English poetry, two lines of equal length, linked by rhyme: for example,
> Had we but world enough, and time,
> This coyness, lady, were no crime.
> (Andrew Marvell, "To His Coy Mistress")

criticism A generic term used to cover the act of analysis, interpretation and judgment, usually associated with close reading. The term is often qualified by an adjective describing a particular attitude toward the text under review: for example, structuralist criticism, formalist criticism, Freudian criticism.

cultural situatedness A person's (or subject's) place within a particular culture with its presuppositions, values, and *ideology,* all of which deeply influence assumptions about reading and writing. Readers and writers alike are the products of (situated in) specific cultures.

culture A complex word, the dominant meanings of which encompass the relationships between works and practices of literature, art, music, etc., and the whole way of life of the people producing them. It can point to a discriminating or elitist view of human aesthetic productions (that is, "high" culture), but it is used more broadly to refer to the totality of practices and institutions of human society.

discourses The innumerable ways, or structures, by which a society's knowledge and hence language are collected, organized, and controlled. In order to function within a particular discourse, we learn its rules, concepts, and problems and so become a member of that discourse community. Because a society is made up of many and frequently contradictory discourses, we are all subject to (or written by) many different discourses.

dominant Any society contains many contradictory values, practices, and beliefs that are also reflected in the language and literature current in that society. Those cultural practices that are more powerful than others and exert more influence are termed dominant. Because a society is continually in flux, meanings dominant in any one age may become marginalized in another, and vice versa.

explication See **analysis.**

fiction Broadly and somewhat crudely defined, a mode of writing that gives us imaginative or mental experiences that are not literally true in that they did not occur in the "real" world. Thus fiction is often opposed to fact, or what is equally crudely called "reality." Historically, certain puritanical views have often led to a distrust of fiction as deceptive or even immoral. In another sense, fiction refers to any mental activity whereby we construct models of reality or explanations for ourselves, shaping material in our minds the way a novelist or artist does in order to make sense of phenomena by imposing interpretations upon them. In its narrowest and perhaps most common sense, fiction is often identified with narrative (usually prose) compositions such as novels or short stories.

foreground (verb) To bring to explicit consciousness; to make explicit (used with *assumptions,* concerns, implications).

formalism A mode of analysis that focuses on what are considered to be objective, even scientific, descriptions of the devices (especially stylistic) of a literary text—particularly those that highlight its supposedly distinctive "literary" use of language. Formalism has much in common with *New Criticism.*

free association A kind of writing that stresses the personal relevance of the work. Rather than focusing on the interaction of the *repertoires* of text and reader, it is characterized by "subjective" experiences.

free verse A loose descriptive term for poetry that has no recognizable metrical pattern and closely resembles ordinary speech. The fact that readers must establish their own intonation, speed of reading, and stresses tends to intensify their involvement. Much modern poetry is written in free verse.

gaps See **blanks.**

genre A term used loosely to mean the "kind" or "form" of literature, vaguely analogous to the biological term "species." Standard genres include poetry, fiction, drama, and essay, but within each category sub-genres are conventionally distinguished. For example, fiction is divided into novel, romance, story, and so on. There are no fixed or absolute distinctions among genres. They are largely the product of reader assumption and expectation, and as such are useful conventions rather than real categories.

historicism An approach to criticism that focuses self-consciously on the placing of a text within a historical context—that is, the ideas, material practices, or conventions of its time. An earlier historicism held that because such criticism was based on a detailed, objective reconstruction of the past, it revealed the "true" meanings of texts. A more recent version of historicism acknowledges that history is of necessity written from the perspective of the present, and so, rather than being objective, historicism is the product of questions, preoccupations, and issues important to the historians themselves.

ideology The conscious or unconscious beliefs, habits, and social practices of a particular society. These often seem true, correct, and universal to members of that society, when in fact they are relative and specific to the society. Ideology pervades every aspect of our lives from our table manners to our politics; it is reflected in the kinds of clothes we wear just as much as in our religious and educational practices. We are most likely to become conscious of our own ideology when we visit or study a foreign culture whose lifestyles and customs are radically different from our own. Ideologies are continually in conflict within any society; at a given point, however, certain ones are always *dominant.* Ideology can be divided usefully into literary ideology (beliefs, assumptions, and ideas about literature) and general ideology (beliefs, assumptions, and ideas about all other matters, including politics, religion, and lifestyle). See also *repertoire.*

indeterminacy An ambiguity or a blank in a text that requires the reader's active involvement to supply or determine the meaning. (See *blanks.*)

interpretation Used loosely to signify any act of textual analysis, usually with a stress on meaning. The fact that perceived inconsistencies in the argument are ironed out and personal or "subjective" associations are avoided tends to give interpretations an apparent (though false) objectivity. See also *free association, response statement,* and *summary.*

intertextuality The implicit references to one text that occur in another; alternatively, the influences of one text on another. In one sense all texts are intertextual, since none is written in a vacuum, unaffected by those written previously. But the term is generally applied when influences are more specific. For example, an intertextual relationship exists between Donald Justice's poem "Counting the Mad" (see p. 1) and the nursery rhyme "This Little Piggy Went to Market," and between Tom Stoppard's *Rosencrantz and Guildenstern Are Dead* and William Shakespeare's *Hamlet.* Your reading experience of "Counting the Mad" and *Rosencrantz and Guildenstern Are Dead* will be enhanced if your repertoire includes the earlier texts.

irony Verbal irony is often used to emphasize a clash between what words say and what they "really mean." It is invoked when a person uses words that, literally interpreted, express the opposite of what he or she intends. For example, "I had a great day," stated ironically, means the day was terrible. Dramatic irony occurs when an audience has relevant information of which the character is unaware, and thus can derive from the character's words or actions meanings unintended by the character. For example, the audience sees irony in Hamlet's assertions that he will immediately avenge his father's death, as they know that his fate is to continually delay. Situational, or circumstantial, irony arises when the opposite of what one expects happens. For example, you work all night to finish a paper, only to have your disk crash an hour before you are supposed to hand it in. Nothing is inherently ironical. Irony in literature depends on the matching of repertoires—the matching of a text that can be read ironically with a reader who is attuned to irony.

literature An ambiguous term pointing to a historical, not a universal, category of writings. What one society calls literature, another may not. As printed books became more accessible from the Renaissance onward, the word came increasingly to stand for specialized "imaginative" writing, usually of a high quality. The particular texts that should be accorded the title, however, cannot easily be agreed on. Thus literature is an evaluative category, not a scientific one.

lyric A short, concentrated, songlike, and evocative poem, usually written in the first person. Originally a lyric was a song sung to the lyre.

matching of repertoires The interaction that occurs between the **repertoires** (general and literary) of the reader and those of the text when a text is read.

metaphor A word or phrase that brings different meanings together, usually either abstract and concrete or literal and figurative. Although it is sometimes argued that *all* language use is metaphorical, it is generally assumed that metaphor is the particular mark of poetry. According to Aristotle, "metaphor consists in giving the thing a name that belongs to something else," thereby forcing the reader to consider one in terms of the other. "Love is a disease," "his heart shattered," "a Calico Cat," and "her facial rash broke out" are all examples. A *mixed metaphor* occurs when the concrete example conjures up (deliberately or not) incongruous associations: for example, "he bulldozed his way through the bottleneck." For further discussion, see pages 383–385.

meter The regularities of rhythm in poetry that create, often in complex and attractive ways, expectations of pattern, regularity, and surprise. In most English poetry the rhythm is based on the stressed syllables in a line of verse. Although each reader will bring slightly different reading patterns to a poem and so there will inevitably be debate about its exact meter, a well-written poem will direct the reader to a preferred or dominant reading, usually through the interaction of meter with meaning. Meter is measured in units called feet, the principal types of which in English are as follows:

iambic, in which a stressed syllable is preceded by an unstressed syllable, as in the word *ăgaińst.*

trochee, in which a stressed syllable is followed by an unaccented syllable, as in the word *híghĕr* or *céntĕr.*

anapest, in which two unstressed syllables are followed by a stressed one, as in the word *ĭntĕrcépt* or the phrase *ăt thĕ córe.*

dactyl, in which a stressed syllable is followed by two unstressed syllables, as in the word *déspĕraŤe* or the phrase *hére tŏ ă.*

spondee, in which two syllables are accented, as in the phrase *juḿp iń* or *áll díes.* A line of poetry with two feet is called a *dimeter;* with three, a *trimeter;* with four, a *quatrameter;* with five, a *pentameter;* and with six, a *sexameter. Iambic pentameter,* with five feet each consisting of a stressed syllable preceded by an unstressed syllable, is the most common English metrical pattern. Its dominance is due to a long-established assumption that it is close to the rhythm of "natural" human speech. In any good poetry, the meter will vary according to the sense. A poem will include among its textual strategies directions to its readers on how it might best be read, and meter is one of these strategies. We judge the effectiveness of the poem not by how well it keeps to some set pattern, but by its effect in opening us up, in our readings, to the possibilities of various meanings.

mood The atmosphere—frightening, calming, oppressive—created for the reader by a text. The manner in which the characters and the setting are described contributes to the mood.

myth In one sense, ancient stories that set out a society's religious or social beliefs. The Greek myths, for example, recount the exploits of the Greek gods. In another sense, myths are narratives used by a society to try to make sense of or account for the common patterns of social life in that society. This second sense of myth is close to *ideology*: Myths may be said to be the narratives of a culture's dominant *ideology*.

naturalization The process by which readers reduce what is strange, disturbing, or out of the ordinary in a text by interpreting or assimilating it so that it fits within acceptable cognitive and cultural norms. For example, readers often try to naturalize Gregor Samsa's metamorphosis into a bug in Franz Kafka's "The Metamorphosis" by arguing that his becoming a bug is really no different from his becoming disfigured in a car accident or suffering a serious physical ailment, since in any of these instances the victim may be ostracized from his family. To develop such an interpretation in order to assimilate the strangeness of this text into more easily negotiable terms is to deny the oddness, the absurdity, the impossibility of Gregor's becoming a bug. All acts of reading involve some degree of naturalization, but it is important to recognize that naturalizing is a learned, conventional reading strategy that you can choose when and when not to employ.

New Criticism The dominant mode in American literary criticism and education between the 1930s and the 1960s, characterized by an intense focus on "close reading" of the text, to the exclusion of the effects on or contribution of the reader (termed by its theorists the "affective fallacy") and the intentions of the author (the "intentional fallacy").

open text A text that encourages its readers to take up different, even contradictory attitudes toward the issues it raises; alternatively, a text that is deliberately incomplete, either stylistically or structurally, with major *blanks* for readers to fill.

overdetermined A term used to describe an event when its causes and interpretations are multiple, interconnected, and perhaps unanalyzable, so that one single cause cannot be isolated without distortion.

paradigm A model of reality or of a field of inquiry constructed to explain, as exhaustively as is possible at the time, the phenomena that appear to be significant. A *paradigm shift* occurs when the model of reality changes.

plot The sequence in which the events of a story occur. Plots frequently follow the pattern *exposition* (background information), *rising action* (the building of tension), *climax* (resolution), *falling action* (untangling of tensions), *conclusion.* Although most readers assume that this five-part organization of action makes for realism, actually it is simply the most conventional way of telling a story; it does not in fact parallel the way events occur in real life. Experimental fiction frequently plays with readers' expectations about plot; for instance, tension may be left unresolved or a story may have little or no action.

point of view The perspective from which a story is told. A story may be told in either the first person or the third person. A *first-person observer* tells the story but is not involved in it. A *first-person participant* both tells and is involved in the story. A naive first-person storyteller, such as a child, is frequently called the *innocent eye.* Third-person perspectives are classified according to the amount of information the narrator possesses regarding the characters' inner thoughts.

Third-person omniscience implies that the narrative voice knows all the characters' thoughts. If the narrative voice comments on the story or characters, the point of view is *editorial omniscience*. If the voice has access to the thoughts of only one or a few of the characters, the point of view is *third-person limited*. Some third-person narratives have an *unreliable narrator*. If the narrative voice does not have access to any characters' thoughts and does not comment on the action of the story, but simply records the facts, the point of view is said to be *objective*. Readers should keep in mind that a point of view is a convention of storytelling, a particular type of textual strategy, not an objective fact about stories.

political unconscious According to Fredric Jameson in *The Political Unconscious* (Cornell University Press, 1980), that level of historical meaning—usually expressing historical contradictions—that underlies all reading and all texts.

reader-centered criticism The mode of criticism, in part advocated by the *Lexington Introduction to Literature,* that stresses the active role played by readers in the construction of readings of texts. Readings, however, are not merely "subjective," since readers are themselves "constructed" by ideological and other factors in their society. Reading, that is to say, is not just a matter of cognition but is deeply affected by cultural factors as well.

reading strategies The techniques used by a reader to process a text, such as creating themes, identifying with characters, looking for a consistent point of view, creating literal/figurative distinctions, filling in gaps, relating the text being read to other texts, relating the text to personal experiences, responding to certain *text strategies* (such as viewpoint, tone, meter, mood) in particular ways, reading playfully for multiple meanings, and relating "personal" responses to the text to larger aspects of the culture. Although some of your reading strategies will evolve as a response to certain text strategies that you encounter, this book suggests that, regardless of what kind of text you are reading, you adopt strategies that will "open" the text up as much as possible in terms of exposing multiple meanings and setting it in a larger cognitive and cultural context. To do this with texts that employ traditional text strategies which encourage you to create closure, it is often necessary to read "against the grain"—that is, to use reading strategies that defy the text strategies.

realism A term used loosely to describe a mode of writing that creates the illusion that "reality" is represented in language. It might more accurately be called "illusionism." Realism presupposes that the world of natural objects and events is unproblematic, clearly given, and available for objective observation and description. It assumes that literature "reflects" life or "expresses" reality rather than being a verbal construction of an interpretation of life. What literature and art "reflect," in the final sense, is not "reality" but *ideology.*

referential Referring to the real world. Referential discourse has as its dominant or preferred meaning a "literal" or "factual" set of events or circumstances.

repertoires The particular sets of beliefs, assumptions, values, ideas, and practices distilled by each text and each reader from a society's *ideology.* One's repertoires can be usefully divided into a literary and a general repertoire. The repertoire of every reader, like that of every text, is different in particular respects from all others (otherwise everyone would think and feel the same), but all are drawn from the same ideological background. See also *ideology.*

response statement An informed record of a reader's initial or predominant reaction to a text. As used in the *Lexington Introduction,* response statements require that readers analyze the assumptions underlying their responses to texts—that is, that they explore their own cognitive strategies, the strategies of the text, and also the literary and general *ideology* of both reader and text. This involves an analysis of the readers' own *repertoires* and those of the text and calls for the development of cognitive and cultural awareness. Response statements also require that readers explore the implications of their assumptions, not only for future reading experiences, but for other areas of their lives. For general guidelines on writing response statements, see pages 15–20.

rhyme The echo of sound that ties two or more lines together in a poem. Rhymes encode a pattern of repetition of identical or similarly stressed sounds, often in a very elaborate organization. Rhyme was one of the dominant devices of poetry until this century; now it tends to be used only for isolated, local effects.

satire A literary form that uses wit or humor to attack a particular object or person. Reading a work for its satirical impact involves a close match of reading strategies with textual strategies. It may also require becoming aware of the object of attack and being familiar with some of the normal standards assumed by the satire. Satire tends to become dated quickly, as the objects of attack lose their relevance. But some satires or satirical aspects of a work can be given renewed life by generalization; for example, parts of *Hamlet* can be read as satirical attacks on corrupt politicians and hypocritical civil servants in general.

scansion The convention by which the rhythms of poetry are described. In ordinary speech, the syllables of words are given different emphasis to show particular meanings: for example,
Andrew, are you coming *in* for dinner? (as opposed to staying *out*)
Andrew, are you coming in for *dinner*? (as opposed to coming in for some other purpose)
Andrew, are *you* coming in for dinner? (as opposed to Michael's coming in)
In poetry, strong and weak emphases on different syllables have traditionally been the basis for distinguishing different *meters.* Strong syllables are stressed more than weak syllables: for example,
      Ăš vírtŭoŭs mén páss, mĭĺdlў ăwáy,
      Ănd whíspĕr tó thĕir soúls tŏ gó
Although many poems, especially those written before the twentieth century, are relatively regular, some variation of emphasis is always possible; it is rare for a line to be absolutely regular in its meter. No two people will scan a poem in exactly the same way. The best guide is to read a poem in your natural voice and listen to where the emphasis falls. See *meter.*

setting The locale, including the place as well as the historical time period in which a story takes place. The setting often contributes to the *mood* of a literary work.

simile A rhetorical device that compares two phenomena using "like" or "as": for example, "O my Luve's like a red, red rose." See the discussion on metaphor, simile, and allegory (p. 383).

site of struggle Language is a site of struggle in that conflicting meanings (and, behind them, ideological positions) struggle for dominance—for the "right" to be seen as natural or "true." Texts or people, as well as individual words, can be described as sites of struggle.

soliloquy An important structural device in drama, particularly that written in the time of Shakespeare, whereby a single character, alone on the stage, addresses his or her words (usually some personal or intimate revelation) directly to the audience.

strong reading A reading or response that attempts to be very self-conscious about its assumptions and goals. Such a reading may go "against the grain" of a text for any of a number of reasons: the reader's *ideology* differs vastly from that of the literary work; the reader perceives significances in the work that could not have been part of the author's repertoire; the reader deliberately tries to read from an alternative perspective, such as a feminist or a religious perspective.

subject We often think of ourselves as individuals, with unique rights and an "essential" nature that is "ours." But we are all produced by our society's distinctive ideology, constituted by the many discourses of society. The "I" that speaks and acts in the world is subjected to these discourses, which offer the "I" various positions as a subject. The "individual" or "person," then, is not a free or fixed category, but an ensemble—as Lacan puts it, the "I" is not a point, but a process. To recognize that we are all subjects, historically and socially produced, is to recognize that we are all deeply affected by social and historical forces, that character is not a fixed but a continually changing or "decentered" entity.

summary Writing that paraphrases the argument the writer perceives "in" a work. Summary tends to be reductive and to present itself (falsely) as objective. See also *free association, interpretation, response statement,* and *strong reading.*

symbol A linguistic device that uses vivid language to compress a complex or abstract idea into a representation such that any discussion or explication of its significance inevitably leads the reader into a longer, often very elaborate process of explanation. A symbol is like an expanded *metaphor,* working by the accumulation of associations. An idea whose explanation might be lengthy, difficult to understand, or even unintelligible can be rendered vivid and powerful by a symbol. See the discussion of metaphor, simile, and allegory on pages 383–385.

symptomatic analysis A mode of analysis that probes the text not for its surface or preferred meaning, but for symptoms of the pressures and concerns that brought the text into being, of which even the writer may have been unaware. Symptomatic analysis is usually only possible in a time period different from that in which the text was originally written and thus relatively independent of the original ideological pressures.

text In one sense, the work—that is, the novel, poem, play, story, etc.; in another sense, that which is produced by the interaction of the work and the reader. Whereas the work can be seen as a finished object enclosed within the covers of a book, the text is an unstable product or process that changes from reading to reading. This distinction, articulated by Roland Barthes and other writers, is a somewhat esoteric one, but it does usually draw attention to the fact that the text is produced anew by each reader.

text strategies The formal techniques used in writing a text, including rhyme, meter, metaphor, plot, setting, character, theme, flashback, flashforward, point of view, description, dialogue, introduction, rising action, climax, falling action, and various techniques of realism. From your experience of reading, you have acquired certain *reading strategies*; when these match the text strategies, you generally feel very comfortable reading the text. When you encounter texts with whose strategies you are unfamiliar (such as Pirandello's *Six Characters in Search of an Author,* in which characters call themselves characters and do not pretend to be "real"), you may reject the text as "nonsense," but this is only because you do not have in your literary repertoire the reading strategies by which to process it. The approach to reading advocated in the *Lexington Introduction* involves expanding your repertoire of reading strategies both so that you can match the strategies of traditional and untraditional texts and so that you can choose when to read texts "against the grain" (that is, to self-consciously employ strategies that counter those of the text in order to do a *strong reading*).

theatricality The distinctive quality of being acted, or played, in a theater. Frequently avant-garde theater defies the conventions of *realism* by overtly calling attention to the fact that a play is a play, not "real life."

theme Loosely defined, what a literary work is "about," in the sense of its main idea or its message. Although many readers believe that they *find* themes in literary works, in fact they *produce* those themes by paying attention to some details and ignoring others. Themes such as appearance and reality, society's attack on individuals' rights, women as an oppressed majority, or love conquers all are so general that they can be applied to almost any text one chooses. The term is therefore not an especially precise one.

theory The philosophy of or self-conscious thought about a discipline or subject.

voice The "person" construed by a reader of a literary work (usually a poem) as being the speaker, sometimes identified with the author. Voice in this sense is a creation of the reader, who is imagining that a lyric or other kind of poem is a direct "speaking" communication. A work's voice, like a person's, is inevitably overdetermined—that is, made up of conflicting voices.

wandering viewpoint A reading strategy described by Wolfgang Iser in *The Act of Reading* (John Hopkins University Press, 1978) whereby readers maintain an openness to the text by allowing themselves to revise their ideas on what they think the text is "about." Readers are thought to move back and forth between *consistency building* (placing closure on texts) and modifying their perspective about the text as they read further and gain more information. To maintain a wandering viewpoint is to be willing to reassess what one remembers as having occurred in a text and to revise expectations of what should happen later in the text. See *consistency building*.

Acknowledgments

FICTION

Margaret Atwood. "Loulou; or The Domestic Life of the Language" from *Bluebeard's Egg* by Margaret Atwood. Reprinted by permission of The Canadian Publishers, McClelland & Stewart Limited, Toronto. Published by Houghton Mifflin Company, 1986. Reprinted by permission of the author.

Ann Beattie. "Shifting" from *Secrets and Surprises,* copyright © 1976, 1977, 1978 by Ann Beattie. Reprinted by permission of Random House, Inc.

Lynne Barrett. "Inventory" by Lynne Barrett. First published in *The Minnesota Review.* Copyright 1983 by Lynne Barrett. Reprinted by permission of the author.

John Barth. "Lost in the Funhouse," copyright © 1967 by The Atlantic Monthly Company from the book *Lost in the Funhouse.* Reprinted by permission of Doubleday & Company, Inc.

Donald Barthelme. "Porcupines at the University" from *Amateurs* by Donald Barthelme. Copyright © 1970 by Donald Barthelme. Originally appeared in *The New Yorker.* Reprinted by permission of Farrar, Straus and Giroux, Inc.

Italo Calvino. From *Italian Folktale,* copyright 1956 by Giulio Einaudi editore, s.p.a., English translation copyright © 1980 by Harcourt Brace Jovanovich, Inc. Reprinted by permission of Harcourt Brace Jovanovich, Inc.

Raymond Carver. "Cathedral" from *Cathedral,* copyright © 1981, 1982, 1983 by Raymond Carver. Reprinted by permission of Alfred A. Knopf, Inc.

Ralph Ellison. "Battle Royal" from *Invisible Man,* copyright 1948 by Ralph Ellison. Reprinted by permission of Random House, Inc.

William Faulkner. "A Rose for Emily" from *Collected Stories of William Faulkner,* copyright 1930 and renewed 1958 by William Faulkner. Reprinted by permission of Random House, Inc.

Ernest Hemingway. "Hills Like White Elephants" from *Men Without Women,* copyright 1927 Charles Scribner's Sons; copyright renewed 1955 Ernest Hemingway. Reprinted with the permission of Charles Scribner's Sons.

James Joyce. "The Dead" from *Dubliners,* copyright 1916 by B. W. Huebsch. Definitive text copyright © 1967 by the Estate of James Joyce. Reprinted by permission of Viking Penguin, Inc.

Franz Kafka. "The Metamorphosis" from *The Penal Colony* by Franz Kafka, trans. Willa and Edwin Muir. Copyright © 1948, 1976 by Schocken Books Inc. Reprinted by permission of Schocken Books Inc.

Milan Kundera. "The Hitchhiking Game" from *Laughable Loves* by Milan Kundera, translated by Suzanne Rappaport. Text copyright © 1974 by Alfred A. Knopf, Inc. Reprinted by permission of the publisher.

D. H. Lawrence. "The Rocking Horse Winner" from *The Complete Short Stories of D. H. Lawrence,* Vol. III. Copyright 1933 by The Estate of D. H. Lawrence, renewed © 1961 by Angelo Ravagli and C. Montague Weekley, Executors of the Estate of Frieda Lawrence Ravagli. Reprinted by permission of Viking Penguin, Inc.

Guy de Maupassant. "Miss Harriet" from *The Collected Novels and Stories of Guy de Maupassant,* translated by Ernest Boyd. Copyright 1923 and renewed 1951 by Alfred A. Knopf, Inc. Reprinted by permission of Alfred A. Knopf.

Alice Munro. "Lives of Girls and Women" from *Lives of Girls and Women* by Alice Munro. Copyright © 1971 by McGraw-Hill Ryerson. Reprinted by permission of Virginia Barber Agency and the author.

Toni Morrison. "SeeMotherMotherIsVeryNice" from *The Bluest Eye,* copyright © 1970 by Toni Morrison. Reprinted by permission of Henry Holt and Company, Inc.

Joyce Carol Oates. "How I Contemplated My Life from the Detroit House of Correction," from *The Wheel of Love and Other Stories.* Copyright © 1970, 1969, 1968, 1967, 1966, 1965 by Joyce Carol Oates. Reprinted by permission of the publisher, Vanguard Press, Inc.

Ann Petry. "Like a Winding Sheet" from *Miss Muriel and Other Stories,* copyright 1945, 1947, © 1958, 1965, 1971 by Ann Petry. Reprinted by permission of Houghton Mifflin Company.

Ronald Sukenick. "The Birds," copyright © 1969 by Ronald Sukenick. Reprinted by permission of International Creative Management.

Gertrude Stein. "As a Wife Has a Cow: A Love Story" from *Selected Writings of Gertrude Stein,* edited by Carl Van Vechten. Copyright 1946 by Random House, Inc. Reprinted by permission of the publisher.

John Updike. "A & P" from *Pigeon Feathers and Other Stories,* copyright © 1962 by John Updike. Reprinted by permission of Alfred A. Knopf, Inc.

Alice Walker. "Nineteen Fifty-five" from *You Can't Keep a Good Woman Down,* copyright © 1981 by Alice Walker. Reprinted by permission of Harcourt Brace Jovanovich, Inc.

A. R. Ammons. "Auto Mobile" is reprinted from *Collected Poems, 1951–1971*, by A. R. Ammons, by permission of W. W. Norton & Company, Inc. © 1972 by A. R. Ammons.

Laurie Anderson. "O Superman," reprinted by permission of Difficult Music.

John Ashbery. "And *Ut Pictura Poesis* Is Her Name," and "Crazy Weather," from *Houseboat Days* by John Ashbery. Copyright © John Ashbery, 1975, 1976, 1977. Reprinted by permission of Viking Penguin, Inc. "Decoy" from *The Double Dream of Spring.* Copyright © 1970 by John Ashbery. Reprinted by permission of Georges Borchardt, Inc. and the Author.

Margaret Atwood. "The Animals in That Country," by Margaret Atwood, Copyright Oxford University Press Canada 1968; used by permission of the publisher. "This is a Photograph of Me" from *The Circle Game* (Toronto: House of Anansi Press Ltd., 1967) and "you fit into me" from *Power Politics* (Toronto: House of Anansi Press Ltd., 1971). Reprinted by permission of the publisher.

W. H. Auden. "Lullaby," and "Musée des Beaux Arts" by W. H. Auden: *Collected Poems*, by W. H. Auden, edited by Edward Mendelson, by permission of Random House, Inc. and Faber & Faber Ltd.

John Berryman. "A Professor's Song," and "Dream Songs" 4, 14, 375 from *The Dream Songs* by John Berryman. Copyright © 1965, 1966, 1967, 1968, 1969 by John Berryman. Reprinted by permission of Farrar, Straus and Giroux, Inc.

Earle Birney. "For George Lemming" from *Ghost in the Wheels.* Used by permission of The Canadian Publishers, McClelland and Stewart Limited, Toronto.

Elizabeth Bishop. "The Fish," "Varick Street," and "Letter to N.Y." from *The Complete Poems 1927–1979* by Elizabeth Bishop. Copyright 1940, 1947, renewed 1968, 1975 by Elizabeth Bishop. Reprinted by permission of Farrar, Straus and Giroux, Inc.

Gwendolyn Brooks. "We Real Cool" by Gwendolyn Brooks. Reprinted by permission of the author.

Raymond Carver. "Prosser" from *Fires,* copyright © 1983 by Raymond Carver. Reprinted by permission of Capra Press, Santa Barbara.

Leonard Cohen. "Untitled Poem" from The *Energy of Slaves.* Copyright © Leonard Cohen. Used by permission of Machet & Machet and The Canadian Publishers, McClelland and Stewart Limited, Toronto. All rights reserved.

Gerald Costanzo. "Dinosaurs of the Hollywood Delta" by Gerald Costanzo. Reprinted by permission of Carnegie-Mellon University Press.

Robert Creeley. "I Know A Man," "If You," and "The Way" from *For Love: Poems 1950–1960.* Copyright © 1962 Robert Creeley. Reprinted with the permission of Charles Scribner's Sons.

Countee Cullen. "Yet Do I Marvel" from *On These I Stand* by Countee Cullen. Copyright 1925 by Harper & Row, Publisher, Inc.; renewed 1953 by Ida M. Cullen. Reprinted by permission of Harper & Row, Publishers, Inc.

e e cummings. "my sweet old etcetera" and "she being Brand" are reprinted from *IS 5* poems by E. E. Cummings, Copyright 1926 by Horace Liveright. Copyright renewed 1953 by E. E. Cummings. "somewhere i have never travelled, gladly beyond," reprinted from *ViVa* Poems 1959 by E. E. Cummings. Copyright © 1979, 1973 by the Trustees for the E. E. Cummings Trust. Copyright © 1979, 1973 by George James Firmage. "O sweet spontaneous," reprinted from *Tulips & Chimneys* by E. E. Cummings, Copyright © 1923, 1925 and renewed 1951, 1953 by E. E. Cummings. Copyright © 1973, 1976 by George James Firmage. Copyright © 1973, 1976 by the Trustees for the E. E. Cummings Trust. All poems reprinted by permission of Liveright Publishing Corporation.

Jim Daniels. "The Poetry Reading . . ." by Jim Daniels. Reprinted by permission of Carnegie-Mellon University Press.

Georgio Di Cicco. "The Man Called Beppino" from *The Tough Romance.* Used by permission of The Canadian Publishers, McClellan and Stewart Limited, Toronto.

Emily Dickinson. "Success is counted sweetest," "I never saw a Moor—," "I Taste a liquor never brewed," "The soul selects her own society," "I died for Beauty—but was scarce," "I heard a fly buzz when I died," "I like to see it lap the miles," "Because I could not stop for death," and "A narrow fellow in the grass," by Emily Dickinson. Reprinted by permission of the publishers and the trustees of Amherst College from *The Poems of Emily Dickinson,* edited by Thomas H. Johnson, Cambridge, Mass.: The Belknap Press of Harvard University Press, copyright 1951, © 1955, 1979, 1983 by the President and Fellows of Harvard College.

Stephen Dunn. "Day and Night Handball" by Stephen Dunn. Reprinted by permission of Carnegie-Mellon University Press.

Mike Doyle. "Growing a Beard" by Mike Doyle. Reprinted by permission of Auckland University Press and Mike Doyle.

Bob Dylan. "The Times They Are A-Changin'" by Bob Dylan. © 1963 Warner Bros. Inc. All Rights Reserved. Used By Permission. "I Shall Be Released" by Bob Dylan. Copyright © 1967, 1970 by Dwarf Music. All rights reserved. International copyright secured. Reprinted by permission.

Richard Eberhart. "The Fury of Aerial Bombardment" from *Collected Poems 1930–1976* by Richard Eberhart. Copyright © 1960, 1976 by Richard Eberhart. Reprinted by permission of Oxford University Press, Inc.

T. S. Eliot. "Rhapsody on a Windy Night," "The Love Song of J. Alfred Prufrock," and "Gerontion" from *Collected Poems 1909–1962* by T. S. Eliot, copyright 1936 by Harcourt Brace Jovanovich, Inc.; copyright © 1963, 1964 by T. S. Eliot. Reprinted by permission of Harcourt Brace Jovanovich, Inc. and Faber & Faber Ltd.

Lawrence Ferlinghetti. "In Goya's Greatest Scenes" from *A Coney Island of the Mind* by Lawrence Ferlinghetti. Copyright © 1958 by Lawrence Ferlinghetti. Reprinted by permission of New Directions Publishing Corporation.

Robert Frost. "Mending Wall," "Stopping by Woods on a Snowy Evening," "The Road Not Taken" and "Birches" from *The Poetry of Robert Frost* edited by Edward Connery Latham. Copyright 1916, 1923, 1930, 1939, © 1969 by Holt, Rinehart and Winston. Copyright 1944, 1951, © 1958 by Robert Frost. Copyright © 1967 by Lesley Frost Ballantine. Reprinted by permission of Henry Holt and Company, Inc.

Nikki Giovanni. "Nikki-Rosa" from *Black Feeling, Black Talk, Black Judgment* by Nikki Giovanni. Copyright © 1968, 1970 by Nikki Giovanni. By permission of William Morrow & Company.

Robert Hass. "Picking Blackberries with a Friend Who Has Been Reading Jacques Lacan" and "Meditation at Lagunitas" from *Praise,* copyright © 1974, 1975, 1976, 1977, 1978, 1979 by Robert Hass, published by The Ecco Press in 1979. Reprinted by permission.

Thomas Hardy. "Neutral Tones," "Channel Firing," "Ah, Are You digging on My Grave?" "The Man He Killed," and "Drummer Hodge" from *The Complete Poems of Thomas Hardy* edited by James Gibson (New York: Macmillan, 1978).

Anthony Hecht. "The Dover Bitch" from *The Hard Hours.* Copyright © 1967 Anthony Hecht. Reprinted with the permission of Atheneum Publishers, Inc.

A. E. Housman. "Loveliest of trees, the cherry now" from "A Shropshire Lad" — Authorized Edition — from *The Collected Poems of A. E. Housman.* Copyright 1939, 1940, © 1965 by Holt, Rinehart and Winston. Copyright © 1967, 1968 by Robert E. Symons. Reprinted by permission of Henry Holt and Company, Inc..

Langston Hughes. "Theme for English B" from *Montage of a Dream Deferred.* Copyright 1951 by Langston Hughes. Copyright renewed 1979 by George Houston Bass. Reprinted by permission of Harold Ober Associates Incorporated.

Ted Hughes. "Crow's First Lesson" and "Crow's Theology" from *Crow* by Ted Hughes. Copyright © 1971 by Ted Hughes. "The Thought Fox" from *New Selected Poems* by Ted Hughes. Copyright © 1957 by Ted Hughes. Reprinted by permission of Harper & Row, Publishers, Inc. and Faber and Faber Publishers.

Randall Jarrell. "A Girl in a Library" from *The Complete Poems* by Randall Jarrell. Copyright © 1951, renewed 1969 by Mrs. Randall Jarrell. Reprinted by permission of Farrar, Straus and Giroux, Inc.

Carolyn Kizer. "Afternoon Happiness" as published in *Poetry* and *YIN: New Poems* (BOA Editions). Reprinted by permission of Carolyn Kizer.

Kenneth Koch. "Mending Sump" by Kenneth Koch. Copyright © 1962 by Kenneth Koch. Reprinted by permission of Grove Press.

Robert Kroetsch. "Mile Zero" from The *Stone Hammer Poems.* Reprinted by permission of Oolichan Books.

Patrick Lane. "Passing Into Storm" from *Beware the Months of Fire.* (Toronto: House of Anansi Press, 1974). Reprinted by permission.

Philip Larkin. "The Arundel Tomb" and "The Whitsun Weddings" from *The Whitsun Weddings.* Reprinted by permission of Faber and Faber Ltd. "Church Going" from *The Less Deceived.*

Irving Layton. "The Bull Calf," "Berry Picking," and "Keine Lazarovitch 1870–1959" from *A Wild Peculiar Joy.* Used by permission of The Canadian Publishers, McClelland and Stewart Limited, Toronto and by permission of Irving Layton.

Dennis Lee. "Thursday" from *The Gods.* Used by permission of The Canadian Publishers, McClelland and Stewart Limited, Toronto.

Philip Levine. "They Feed They Lion" from *They Feed They Lion.* Copyright © 1972 Philip Levine. Reprinted with the permission of Atheneum Publishers, Inc.

Dorothy Livesay. "The Unquiet Bed" from *Collected Poems: The Two Seasons,* © Dorothy Livesay 1972. Reprinted by permission of Dorothy Livesay.

Robert Lowell. "To Speak of Woe That Is in Marriage" from *Life Studies.* Copyright © 1956, 1959 by Robert Lowell. Reprinted by permission of Farrar, Straus and Giroux, Inc.

Roger McGough. "My busconductor" and "At Lunchtime: A Story of Love" from *Modern Poets 10,* published by Penguin Books Ltd. Reprinted by permission of A. D. Peters & Co. Ltd.

Jay Meek. "The Week the Dirigible Came" by Jay Meek. Reprinted by permission of Carnegie-Mellon University Press.

Marianne Moore. "The Fish" and "Poetry" from *Collected Poems.* Copyright 1935 by Marianne Moore, renewed 1963 by Marianne Moore and T. S. Eliot. Reprinted with permission of Macmillan Publishing Company.

Howard Nemerov. "The Goose Fish" from *The Collected Poems of Howard Nemerov.* The University of Chicago Press, 1977. Reprinted by permission of the author.

John Newlove. "Crazy Riel" from *The Fat Man.* Used by permission of The Canadian Publishers, McClelland and Stewart Limited, Toronto.

Frank O'Hara. "The Day Lady Died" from *Lunch Poems.* Copyright © 1964 by Frank O'Hara. Reprinted by permission of City Lights Books. "Why I Am Not a Painter" from The Collected Poems of Frank O'Hara. Copyright © 1958 by Maureen Granville-Smith. Reprinted by permission of Alfred A. Knopf, Inc.

Michael Ondaatje. "King Kong Meets Wallace Stevens" from *There's a Trick with a Knife I'm Learning to Do: Poems 1968–83.* © Michael Ondaatje.

Kenneth Patchen. "Do the Dead Know What Time It Is?" from *Collected Poems of Kenneth Patchen.* Copyright 1939 by New Directions Publishing Corporation. Reprinted by permission of New Directions Publishing Corporation.

Marge Piercy. "Barbie Doll" from *To Be of Use.* Copyright © 1969, 1971, 1973 by Marge Piercy. Reprinted by permission of Alfred A. Knopf, Inc.

Sylvia Plath. "Morning Song," copyright © 1961 by Ted Hughes; "Tulips," Copyright © 1962 by Ted Hughes; "The Applicant," copyright © 1963 by Ted Hughes from *The Selected Poems of Sylvia Plath* edited by Ted Hughes. Reprinted by permission of Harper & Row, Publishers, Inc.

Ezra Pound. "In the Station of the Metro" and "The Seafarer" from *Personae,* Copyright 1926 by Ezra Pound. Reprinted by permission of New Directions Publishing Corporation.

Al Purdy. "Song of the Impermanent Husband." Used by permission of The Canadian Publishers, McClelland and Stewart Limited, Toronto.

Ishmael Reed. "Beware: do not read this poem" from *New Black Poetry.* Copyright © International Publishers, New York. Reprinted by permission.

Adrienne Rich. "Living in Sin" and "Aunt Jennifer's Tigers." Reprinted from *The Fact Of A Doorframe,* Poems Selected and New, 1950–1984, by Adrienne Rich, by permission of W. W. Norton & Company, Inc. Copyright © 1984 by Adrienne Rich. Copyright © 1975, 1978 by W. W. Norton & Company, Inc. Copyright © 1981 by Adrienne Rich. "A Clock in the Square," *The Change of World* by Adrienne Rich. Copyright © 1951 by Adrienne Rich, copyright renewed 1979. Reprinted by permission of the author and W. W. Norton & Company, Inc.

Kenneth Rexroth. "Proust's Madeline" from *Collected Shorter Poems.* Copyright © 1963 by Kenneth Rexroth. Reprinted by permission of New Directions Publishing Corporation.

Theodore Roethke. "Dolor" copyright 1943 by Modern Poetry Association, Inc., "My Papa's Waltz" copyright 1942 by Hearst Magazines, Inc. and "I Knew a Woman" Copyright 1954 by Theodore Roethke all from *The Collected Poems of Theodore Roethke.* Reprinted by permission of Doubleday & Co., Inc.

William Pitt Root. "Under the Umbrella of Blood" by William Pitt Root. Reprinted by permission of Ontario Review Press.

Delmore Schwartz. "The Heavy Bear Who Goes With Me" from *Selected Poems: Summer Knowledge.* Copyright 1938 by New Directions Publishing Corporation. Reprinted by permission of New Directions Publishing Corporation.

Paul Simon. "America" Copyright © 1968 Paul Simon. Used by permission.

Kendrick Smithyman. "King's College Chapel" by Kendrick Smithyman. Reprinted by permission of Aukland University Press.

Gary Snyder. "Looking at Pictures to be Put Away" from *The Back Country.* Copyright © 1968 by Gary Snyder. Reprinted by permission of New Directions Publishing Corporation.

Bruce Springsteen. "Darkness on the Edge of Town," Copyright © 1978 Bruce Springsteen. Used with permission.

Wallace Stevens. "The Emperor of Ice-Cream," "Anecdote of a Jar," and "Thirteen Ways of Looking at a Blackbird" from *The Collected Poems of Wallace Stevens.* Copyright 1923 and renewed 1951 by Wallace Stevens. Reprinted by permission of Alfred A. Knopf, Inc.

Dylan Thomas. "Fern Hill," "The Force That Through the Green Fuse Drives the Flower," and "Do Not Go Gentle into That Good Night" from *Poems of Dylan Thomas.* Copyright 1945 by Trustees for the

Copyrights of Dylan Thomas, 1939, 1952 by New Directions Publishing Corporation and David Higham Associates Ltd.

Robert Penn Warren. "Rumor Verified" from *New and Selected Poems 1923–1985.* Copyright © 1981 by Robert Penn Warren. "Small Eternity" from *Rumor Verified: Poems 1979–1980.* Copyright © 1981 by Robert Penn Warren. Both poems reprinted by permission of Random House, Inc. "You Sort Old Letters," reprinted by permission of Wm. Morris Agency on behalf of Robert Penn Warren.

Tom Wayman. "Unemployment" from *Waiting for Wayman.* Used by permission of The Canadian Publishers, McClelland & Stewart Limited, Toronto.

Richard Wilbur. "The Writer" from *The Mind Reader.* Copyright © 1971 by Richard Wilbur. Reprinted by permission of Harcourt Brace Jovanovich, Inc.

William Carlos Williams. "This Is Just to Say" and "The Red Wheelbarrow" from *Earlier Poems.* Copyright 1938 by New Directions Publishing Corporation. Reprinted by permission of New Directions Publishing Corporation.

W. B. Yeats. "A Prayer for My Daughter," from *Collected Poems.* Copyright 1924 by Macmillan Publishing Company, renewed 1952 by Bertha Georgie Yeats. "Leda and the Swan," and "Among School Children" from *Collected Poems.* Copyright 1928 by Macmillan Publishing Company, renewed 1956 by Georgie Yeats. "Crazy Jane Talks with the Bishop" from *Collected Poems.* Copyright 1933 by Macmillan Publishing Company, renewed 1961 by Bertha Georgie Yeats. "When You Are Old" from *Collected Poems.* All reprinted with permission of Macmillan Publishing Company.

DRAMA

Edward Albee. *The Sandbox* by Edward Albee. Copyright © 1960 by Edward Albee. Reprinted by permission of William Morris Agency on behalf of the author.

Lorraine Hansberry. From *A Raisin in the Sun,* by Lorraine Hansberry. Copyright © 1958 by Robert Nemiroff as an unpublished work. Copyright © 1959, 1966, 1984 by Robert Nemiroff. Reprinted by permission of Random House, Inc. "Dream Deferred" by Langston Hughes. Copyright 1951 by Langston Hughes. Reprinted from *The Panther and the Lash,* by Langston Hughes, by permission of Alfred A. Knopf, Inc.

Henrik Ibsen. *The Wild Duck* from *The Four Major Plays* by Henrik Ibsen, translated by R. Farquharson Sharp. From *Everyman's Library.* Reprinted by permission of J. M. Dent & Sons.

Eugene Ionesco. *The Gap* by Eugene Ionesco translated by Rosette Lamont. Reprinted from *The Massachusetts Review,* © 1969. The Massachusetts Review, Inc.

Arthur Miller. *Death of a Salesman,* by Arthur Miller. Copyright 1949, copyright © renewed 1977 by Arthur Miller. Reprinted by permission of Viking Penguin, Inc.

Luigi Pirandello. *Six Characters in Search of an Author* from *Naked Masks: Five Plays* by Luigi Pirandello, edited by Eric Bentley. Copyright 1922, 1952 by E. P. Dutton; renewed 1950 in the names of Stefano, Fausto and Lietta Pirandello, and 1980 by Eric Bentley. Reprinted by permission of the publisher, E. P. Dutton, a division of New American Library.

William Shakespeare. "Hamlet" from Evans: *The Riverside Shakespeare,* Copyright © 1974 Houghton Mifflin Company. Used with permission.

Sophocles. "Antigone" in *The Complete Greek Tragedies.* Reprinted by permission of the University of Chicago Press.

Tom Stoppard. *Rosencrantz and Guildenstern Are Dead,* copyright © 1967 by Tom Stoppard. Reprinted by permission of Grove Press, Inc. and Faber and Faber.

ESSAYS

Roland Barthes. "The Photographic Message" from *Image/Music/Text* by Roland Barthes. Copyright © 1977 by Roland Barthes. Reprinted by permission of Hill and Wang, a division of Farrar, Straus and Giroux, Inc.

Michel Foucault. "Preface" from *The Order of Things: An Archeology of the Human Sciences,* translated by Alan Sheridan-Smith. Copyright © 1970 by Random House, Inc. Reprinted by permission of Pantheon Books, a Division of Random House, Inc. and by permission of Methuen & Co.

Sigmund Freud. "The Dream Is the Fulfillment of a Wish" from *Basic Writings of Sigmund Freud,* translated and edited by Dr. A. A. Brill, Modern Library, 1938, New York. Copyright 1938 by Gioia B. Bernheim and Edmund Brill, copyright renewed 1965. Reprinted by permission.

Adrienne E. Harris. "Women, baseball, and words" in *PsychCritique, 1* (1), pp. 35–54, 1985. Reprinted by permission of Ablex Publishing Corporation.

Martin Luther King, Jr. "I Have a Dream." Copyright © 1963 by Martin Luther King, Jr. Reprinted by permission of Joan Daves.

Hilary Masters. "So Long, Natty Bumpo" from issue #35 of *The Ohio Review,* 1985. Reprinted by permission of *The Ohio Review.*

George Orwell. "Politics and the English Language" from *Shooting an Elephant and Other Essays.* Copyright 1946 by Sonia Brownell Orwell; renewed 1974 by Sonia Orwell. Reprinted by permission of Harcourt Brace Jovanovich, Inc. and the Estate of the late Sonia Brownell Orwell and Martin Secker and Warburg Ltd.

Susan Sontag. Excerpts from *Illness as Metaphor,* copyright © 1977, 1978 by Susan Sontag. Reprinted by permission of Farrar, Straus and Giroux, Inc.

Tom Wolfe. "The Pump House Gang" from *The Pump House Gang* by Tom Wolfe. Copyright © 1966 by the World Journal Tribune Corporation. Copyright © 1964, 1965, 1966 by New York Herald Tribune, Inc. Reprinted by permission of Farrar, Straus and Giroux, Inc.

Raymond Williams. Text from *Keywords: A Vocabulary of Culture and Society, Revised Edition.* Copyright © 1976, 1983 by Raymond Williams. Reprinted by permission of Oxford University Press, Inc. and Collins Publishers.

Index of Authors, Titles, First Lines of Poems

Names of authors appear in SMALL CAPITALS, titles of readings in *italics*, and first lines of poems in roman type. If title and first line coincide, the title alone is entered; titles supplied for untitled works appear in [*italic bracketed*]. Listed under each author are the titles of works appearing here.

Index of Concepts

absurd, theater of the, 632, 633
"against the grain," 13, 14, 52, 383, 1103
allegory, 384
ambiguities, 9, 12, 13, 400, 1098
American Dream, 74–75, 1100, 1104, 1112–1114
analysis, 87, 88
annotations, 17–18, 379
argument, 386, 389, 393, 631, 1100, 1101, 1104
assumptions, 6, 28, 38, 90, 1100, 1101, 1103
author's intentions, 378, 1101

blanks, 9

canon, 376, 1099
characters, 15, 21, 29, 60–61, 72–74, 623, 624, 627, 628, 635–637
chorus, 634
class discussion, 20–21
climax, 37
close reading, 399
cognitive processes, 1099
cognitive style, 45
connotations, 380, 381–383, 1101, 1103
conventions, 28, 29, 376, 633, 637
counterdominant, 8
courtly love, 393
critics, literary, 3
cubism, 43, 45
culture, 5, 6, 53, 387, 391, 637, 1099

dialogue, 4, 633
discourse, 1100
discursive prose, 1100–1102
dominant ideology, 6, 11
drama, introducing, 623–637

essay, introducing the, 1097–1114

fact versus fiction, 1097, 1100
fairy story, 50–52
feminist reading, 15, 51, 87, 394
fiction, introducing, 27–75, 1097–1099
figurative language, 383–385, 1099, 1101–1102
first-person point of view, 37

gaps, 9, 12, 22, 29–30, 42, 382, 390
gender-specific reading, 72–73, 394
general ideology, 5, 72
general repertoire, 5, 8, 10–12, 28, 29, 54–55, 72–75, 88, 377, 623, 1100, 1105
genre, 38–39
goals, reading, 12–13

history, 8, 11, 1106–1110

ideology, 5, 6, 54, 72, 88, 1104–1106
impact, 383
indeterminacy, 9–10, 390
individual, 29, 624, 1106–1110
inferences, 1100
interactive reading, 3
interpretation, 387, 391, 395, 1099, 1100
interpretive strategies, 45–46
intertextuality, 22
irony, 2, 39

key words, 1105–1106

language, 27, 1098, 1100, 1105
literal meaning, 1099
literary ideology, 5, 6
literary repertoire, 5, 9–10, 12–13, 28, 29–30, 52–54, 623, 1100, 1105
literature, defined, 1097, 1098–99, 1100
logic, 633, 1101

1 2 3 4 5 6 7 8 9 0